Dictionary of Literary Biography

1. *The American Renaissance in New England*, edited by Joel Myerson (1978)
2. *American Novelists Since World War II*, edited by Jeffrey Helterman and Richard Layman (1978)
3. *Antebellum Writers in New York and the South*, edited by Joel Myerson (1979)
4. *American Writers in Paris, 1920-1939*, edited by Karen Lane Rood (1980)
5. *American Poets Since World War II*, 2 parts, edited by Donald J. Greiner (1980)
6. *American Novelists Since World War II, Second Series*, edited by James E. Kibler Jr. (1980)
7. *Twentieth-Century American Dramatists*, 2 parts, edited by John MacNicholas (1981)
8. *Twentieth-Century American Science-Fiction Writers*, 2 parts, edited by David Cowart and Thomas L. Wymer (1981)
9. *American Novelists, 1910-1945*, 3 parts, edited by James J. Martine (1981)
10. *Modern British Dramatists, 1900-1945*, 2 parts, edited by Stanley Weintraub (1982)
11. *American Humorists, 1800-1950*, 2 parts, edited by Stanley Trachtenberg (1982)
12. *American Realists and Naturalists*, edited by Donald Pizer and Earl N. Harbert (1982)
13. *British Dramatists Since World War II*, 2 parts, edited by Stanley Weintraub (1982)
14. *British Novelists Since 1960*, 2 parts, edited by Jay L. Halio (1983)
15. *British Novelists, 1930-1959*, 2 parts, edited by Bernard Oldsey (1983)
16. *The Beats: Literary Bohemians in Postwar America*, 2 parts, edited by Ann Charters (1983)
17. *Twentieth-Century American Historians*, edited by Clyde N. Wilson (1983)
18. *Victorian Novelists After 1885*, edited by Ira B. Nadel and William E. Fredeman (1983)
19. *British Poets, 1880-1914*, edited by Donald E. Stanford (1983)
20. *British Poets, 1914-1945*, edited by Donald E. Stanford (1983)
21. *Victorian Novelists Before 1885*, edited by Ira B. Nadel and William E. Fredeman (1983)
22. *American Writers for Children, 1900-1960*, edited by John Cech (1983)
23. *American Newspaper Journalists, 1873-1900*, edited by Perry J. Ashley (1983)
24. *American Colonial Writers, 1606-1734*, edited by Emory Elliott (1984)
25. *American Newspaper Journalists, 1901-1925*, edited by Perry J. Ashley (1984)
26. *American Screenwriters*, edited by Robert E. Morsberger, Stephen O. Lesser, and Randall Clark (1984)
27. *Poets of Great Britain and Ireland, 1945-1960*, edited by Vincent B. Sherry Jr. (1984)
28. *Twentieth-Century American-Jewish Fiction Writers*, edited by Daniel Walden (1984)
29. *American Newspaper Journalists, 1926-1950*, edited by Perry J. Ashley (1984)
30. *American Historians, 1607-1865*, edited by Clyde N. Wilson (1984)
31. *American Colonial Writers, 1735-1781*, edited by Emory Elliott (1984)
32. *Victorian Poets Before 1850*, edited by William E. Fredeman and Ira B. Nadel (1984)
33. *Afro-American Fiction Writers After 1955*, edited by Thadious M. Davis and Trudier Harris (1984)
34. *British Novelists, 1890-1929: Traditionalists*, edited by Thomas F. Staley (1985)
35. *Victorian Poets After 1850*, edited by William E. Fredeman and Ira B. Nadel (1985)
36. *British Novelists, 1890-1929: Modernists*, edited by Thomas F. Staley (1985)
37. *American Writers of the Early Republic*, edited by Emory Elliott (1985)
38. *Afro-American Writers After 1955: Dramatists and Prose Writers*, edited by Thadious M. Davis and Trudier Harris (1985)
39. *British Novelists, 1660-1800*, 2 parts, edited by Martin C. Battestin (1985)
40. *Poets of Great Britain and Ireland Since 1960*, 2 parts, edited by Vincent B. Sherry Jr. (1985)
41. *Afro-American Poets Since 1955*, edited by Trudier Harris and Thadious M. Davis (1985)
42. *American Writers for Children Before 1900*, edited by Glenn E. Estes (1985)
43. *American Newspaper Journalists, 1690-1872*, edited by Perry J. Ashley (1986)
44. *American Screenwriters, Second Series*, edited by Randall Clark, Robert E. Morsberger, and Stephen O. Lesser (1986)
45. *American Poets, 1880-1945, First Series*, edited by Peter Quartermain (1986)
46. *American Literary Publishing Houses, 1900-1980: Trade and Paperback*, edited by Peter Dzwonkoski (1986)
47. *American Historians, 1866-1912*, edited by Clyde N. Wilson (1986)
48. *American Poets, 1880-1945, Second Series*, edited by Peter Quartermain (1986)
49. *American Literary Publishing Houses, 1638-1899*, 2 parts, edited by Peter Dzwonkoski (1986)
50. *Afro-American Writers Before the Harlem Renaissance*, edited by Trudier Harris (1986)
51. *Afro-American Writers from the Harlem Renaissance to 1940*, edited by Trudier Harris (1987)
52. *American Writers for Children Since 1960: Fiction*, edited by Glenn E. Estes (1986)
53. *Canadian Writers Since 1960, First Series*, edited by W. H. New (1986)
54. *American Poets, 1880-1945, Third Series*, 2 parts, edited by Peter Quartermain (1987)
55. *Victorian Prose Writers Before 1867*, edited by William B. Thesing (1987)
56. *German Fiction Writers, 1914-1945*, edited by James Hardin (1987)
57. *Victorian Prose Writers After 1867*, edited by William B. Thesing (1987)
58. *Jacobean and Caroline Dramatists*, edited by Fredson Bowers (1987)
59. *American Literary Critics and Scholars, 1800-1850*, edited by John W. Rathbun and Monica M. Grecu (1987)
60. *Canadian Writers Since 1960, Second Series*, edited by W. H. New (1987)
61. *American Writers for Children Since 1960: Poets, Illustrators, and Nonfiction Authors*, edited by Glenn E. Estes (1987)
62. *Elizabethan Dramatists*, edited by Fredson Bowers (1987)
63. *Modern American Critics, 1920-1955*, edited by Gregory S. Jay (1988)
64. *American Literary Critics and Scholars, 1850-1880*, edited by John W. Rathbun and Monica M. Grecu (1988)
65. *French Novelists, 1900-1930*, edited by Catharine Savage Brosman (1988)
66. *German Fiction Writers, 1885-1913*, 2 parts, edited by James Hardin (1988)
67. *Modern American Critics Since 1955*, edited by Gregory S. Jay (1988)
68. *Canadian Writers, 1920-1959, First Series*, edited by W. H. New (1988)
69. *Contemporary German Fiction Writers, First Series*, edited by Wolfgang D. Elfe and James Hardin (1988)

70 *British Mystery Writers, 1860-1919*, edited by Bernard Benstock and Thomas F. Staley (1988)

71 *American Literary Critics and Scholars, 1880-1900*, edited by John W. Rathbun and Monica M. Grecu (1988)

72 *French Novelists, 1930-1960*, edited by Catharine Savage Brosman (1988)

73 *American Magazine Journalists, 1741-1850*, edited by Sam G. Riley (1988)

74 *American Short-Story Writers Before 1880*, edited by Bobby Ellen Kimbel, with the assistance of William E. Grant (1988)

75 *Contemporary German Fiction Writers, Second Series*, edited by Wolfgang D. Elfe and James Hardin (1988)

76 *Afro-American Writers, 1940-1955*, edited by Trudier Harris (1988)

77 *British Mystery Writers, 1920-1939*, edited by Bernard Benstock and Thomas F. Staley (1988)

78 *American Short-Story Writers, 1880-1910*, edited by Bobby Ellen Kimbel, with the assistance of William E. Grant (1988)

79 *American Magazine Journalists, 1850-1900*, edited by Sam G. Riley (1988)

80 *Restoration and Eighteenth-Century Dramatists, First Series*, edited by Paula R. Backscheider (1989)

81 *Austrian Fiction Writers, 1875-1913*, edited by James Hardin and Donald G. Daviau (1989)

82 *Chicano Writers, First Series*, edited by Francisco A. Lomelí and Carl R. Shirley (1989)

83 *French Novelists Since 1960*, edited by Catharine Savage Brosman (1989)

84 *Restoration and Eighteenth-Century Dramatists, Second Series*, edited by Paula R. Backscheider (1989)

85 *Austrian Fiction Writers After 1914*, edited by James Hardin and Donald G. Daviau (1989)

86 *American Short-Story Writers, 1910-1945, First Series*, edited by Bobby Ellen Kimbel (1989)

87 *British Mystery and Thriller Writers Since 1940, First Series*, edited by Bernard Benstock and Thomas F. Staley (1989)

88 *Canadian Writers, 1920-1959, Second Series*, edited by W. H. New (1989)

89 *Restoration and Eighteenth-Century Dramatists, Third Series*, edited by Paula R. Backscheider (1989)

90 *German Writers in the Age of Goethe, 1789-1832*, edited by James Hardin and Christoph E. Schweitzer (1989)

91 *American Magazine Journalists, 1900-1960, First Series*, edited by Sam G. Riley (1990)

92 *Canadian Writers, 1890-1920*, edited by W. H. New (1990)

93 *British Romantic Poets, 1789-1832, First Series*, edited by John R. Greenfield (1990)

94 *German Writers in the Age of Goethe: Sturm und Drang to Classicism*, edited by James Hardin and Christoph E. Schweitzer (1990)

95 *Eighteenth-Century British Poets, First Series*, edited by John Sitter (1990)

96 *British Romantic Poets, 1789-1832, Second Series*, edited by John R. Greenfield (1990)

97 *German Writers from the Enlightenment to Sturm und Drang, 1720-1764*, edited by James Hardin and Christoph E. Schweitzer (1990)

98 *Modern British Essayists, First Series*, edited by Robert Beum (1990)

99 *Canadian Writers Before 1890*, edited by W. H. New (1990)

100 *Modern British Essayists, Second Series*, edited by Robert Beum (1990)

101 *British Prose Writers, 1660-1800, First Series*, edited by Donald T. Siebert (1991)

102 *American Short-Story Writers, 1910-1945, Second Series*, edited by Bobby Ellen Kimbel (1991)

103 *American Literary Biographers, First Series*, edited by Steven Serafin (1991)

104 *British Prose Writers, 1660-1800, Second Series*, edited by Donald T. Siebert (1991)

105 *American Poets Since World War II, Second Series*, edited by R. S. Gwynn (1991)

106 *British Literary Publishing Houses, 1820-1880*, edited by Patricia J. Anderson and Jonathan Rose (1991)

107 *British Romantic Prose Writers, 1789-1832, First Series*, edited by John R. Greenfield (1991)

108 *Twentieth-Century Spanish Poets, First Series*, edited by Michael L. Perna (1991)

109 *Eighteenth-Century British Poets, Second Series*, edited by John Sitter (1991)

110 *British Romantic Prose Writers, 1789-1832, Second Series*, edited by John R. Greenfield (1991)

111 *American Literary Biographers, Second Series*, edited by Steven Serafin (1991)

112 *British Literary Publishing Houses, 1881-1965*, edited by Jonathan Rose and Patricia J. Anderson (1991)

113 *Modern Latin-American Fiction Writers, First Series*, edited by William Luis (1992)

114 *Twentieth-Century Italian Poets, First Series*, edited by Giovanna Wedel De Stasio, Glauco Cambon, and Antonio Illiano (1992)

115 *Medieval Philosophers*, edited by Jeremiah Hackett (1992)

116 *British Romantic Novelists, 1789-1832*, edited by Bradford K. Mudge (1992)

117 *Twentieth-Century Caribbean and Black African Writers, First Series*, edited by Bernth Lindfors and Reinhard Sander (1992)

118 *Twentieth-Century German Dramatists, 1889-1918*, edited by Wolfgang D. Elfe and James Hardin (1992)

119 *Nineteenth-Century French Fiction Writers: Romanticism and Realism, 1800-1860*, edited by Catharine Savage Brosman (1992)

120 *American Poets Since World War II, Third Series*, edited by R. S. Gwynn (1992)

121 *Seventeenth-Century British Nondramatic Poets, First Series*, edited by M. Thomas Hester (1992)

122 *Chicano Writers, Second Series*, edited by Francisco A. Lomelí and Carl R. Shirley (1992)

123 *Nineteenth-Century French Fiction Writers: Naturalism and Beyond, 1860-1900*, edited by Catharine Savage Brosman (1992)

124 *Twentieth-Century German Dramatists, 1919-1992*, edited by Wolfgang D. Elfe and James Hardin (1992)

125 *Twentieth-Century Caribbean and Black African Writers, Second Series*, edited by Bernth Lindfors and Reinhard Sander (1993)

126 *Seventeenth-Century British Nondramatic Poets, Second Series*, edited by M. Thomas Hester (1993)

127 *American Newspaper Publishers, 1950-1990*, edited by Perry J. Ashley (1993)

128 *Twentieth-Century Italian Poets, Second Series*, edited by Giovanna Wedel De Stasio, Glauco Cambon, and Antonio Illiano (1993)

129 *Nineteenth-Century German Writers, 1841-1900*, edited by James Hardin and Siegfried Mews (1993)

130 *American Short-Story Writers Since World War II*, edited by Patrick Meanor (1993)

131 *Seventeenth-Century British Nondramatic Poets, Third Series*, edited by M. Thomas Hester (1993)

132 *Sixteenth-Century British Nondramatic Writers, First Series*, edited by David A. Richardson (1993)

133 *Nineteenth-Century German Writers to 1840*, edited by James Hardin and Siegfried Mews (1993)

134 *Twentieth-Century Spanish Poets, Second Series*, edited by Jerry Phillips Winfield (1994)

135 *British Short-Fiction Writers, 1880-1914: The Realist Tradition*, edited by William B. Thesing (1994)

136 *Sixteenth-Century British Nondramatic Writers, Second Series*, edited by David A. Richardson (1994)

137 *American Magazine Journalists, 1900-1960, Second Series*, edited by Sam G. Riley (1994)
138 *German Writers and Works of the High Middle Ages: 1170-1280*, edited by James Hardin and Will Hasty (1994)
139 *British Short-Fiction Writers, 1945-1980*, edited by Dean Baldwin (1994)
140 *American Book-Collectors and Bibliographers, First Series*, edited by Joseph Rosenblum (1994)
141 *British Children's Writers, 1880-1914*, edited by Laura M. Zaidman (1994)
142 *Eighteenth-Century British Literary Biographers*, edited by Steven Serafin (1994)
143 *American Novelists Since World War II, Third Series*, edited by James R. Giles and Wanda H. Giles (1994)
144 *Nineteenth-Century British Literary Biographers*, edited by Steven Serafin (1994)
145 *Modern Latin-American Fiction Writers, Second Series*, edited by William Luis and Ann González (1994)
146 *Old and Middle English Literature*, edited by Jeffrey Helterman and Jerome Mitchell (1994)
147 *South Slavic Writers Before World War II*, edited by Vasa D. Mihailovich (1994)
148 *German Writers and Works of the Early Middle Ages: 800-1170*, edited by Will Hasty and James Hardin (1994)
149 *Late Nineteenth- and Early Twentieth-Century British Literary Biographers*, edited by Steven Serafin (1995)
150 *Early Modern Russian Writers, Late Seventeenth and Eighteenth Centuries*, edited by Marcus C. Levitt (1995)
151 *British Prose Writers of the Early Seventeenth Century*, edited by Clayton D. Lein (1995)
152 *American Novelists Since World War II, Fourth Series*, edited by James and Wanda Giles (1995)
153 *Late-Victorian and Edwardian British Novelists, First Series*, edited by George M. Johnson (1995)
154 *The British Literary Book Trade, 1700-1820*, edited by James K. Bracken and Joel Silver (1995)
155 *Twentieth-Century British Literary Biographers*, edited by Steven Serafin (1995)
156 *British Short-Fiction Writers, 1880-1914: The Romantic Tradition*, edited by William F. Naufftus (1995)
157 *Twentieth-Century Caribbean and Black African Writers, Third Series*, edited by Bernth Lindfors and Reinhard Sander (1995)
158 *British Reform Writers, 1789-1832*, edited by Gary Kelly and Edd Applegate (1995)
159 *British Short-Fiction Writers, 1800-1880*, edited by John R. Greenfield (1996)
160 *British Children's Writers, 1914-1960*, edited by Donald R. Hettinga and Gary D. Schmidt (1996)
161 *British Children's Writers Since 1960, First Series*, edited by Caroline Hunt (1996)
162 *British Short-Fiction Writers, 1915-1945*, edited by John H. Rogers (1996)
163 *British Children's Writers, 1800-1880*, edited by Meena Khorana (1996)
164 *German Baroque Writers, 1580-1660*, edited by James Hardin (1996)
165 *American Poets Since World War II, Fourth Series*, edited by Joseph Conte (1996)
166 *British Travel Writers, 1837-1875*, edited by Barbara Brothers and Julia Gergits (1996)
167 *Sixteenth-Century British Nondramatic Writers, Third Series*, edited by David A. Richardson (1996)
168 *German Baroque Writers, 1661-1730*, edited by James Hardin (1996)
169 *American Poets Since World War II, Fifth Series*, edited by Joseph Conte (1996)
170 *The British Literary Book Trade, 1475-1700*, edited by James K. Bracken and Joel Silver (1996)
171 *Twentieth-Century American Sportswriters*, edited by Richard Orodenker (1996)
172 *Sixteenth-Century British Nondramatic Writers, Fourth Series*, edited by David A. Richardson (1996)
173 *American Novelists Since World War II, Fifth Series*, edited by James R. Giles and Wanda H. Giles (1996)
174 *British Travel Writers, 1876-1909*, edited by Barbara Brothers and Julia Gergits (1997)
175 *Native American Writers of the United States*, edited by Kenneth M. Roemer (1997)
176 *Ancient Greek Authors*, edited by Ward W. Briggs (1997)
177 *Italian Novelists Since World War II, 1945-1965*, edited by Augustus Pallotta (1997)
178 *British Fantasy and Science-Fiction Writers Before World War I*, edited by Darren Harris-Fain (1997)
179 *German Writers of the Renaissance and Reformation, 1280-1580*, edited by James Hardin and Max Reinhart (1997)
180 *Japanese Fiction Writers, 1868-1945*, edited by Van C. Gessel (1997)
181 *South Slavic Writers Since World War II*, edited by Vasa D. Mihailovich (1997)
182 *Japanese Fiction Writers Since World War II*, edited by Van C. Gessel (1997)
183 *American Travel Writers, 1776-1864*, edited by James J. Schramer and Donald Ross (1997)
184 *Nineteenth-Century British Book-Collectors and Bibliographers*, edited by William Baker and Kenneth Womack (1997)
185 *American Literary Journalists, 1945-1995, First Series*, edited by Arthur J. Kaul (1998)
186 *Nineteenth-Century American Western Writers*, edited by Robert L. Gale (1998)
187 *American Book Collectors and Bibliographers, Second Series*, edited by Joseph Rosenblum (1998)
188 *American Book and Magazine Illustrators to 1920*, edited by Steven E. Smith, Catherine A. Hastedt, and Donald H. Dyal (1998)
189 *American Travel Writers, 1850-1915*, edited by Donald Ross and James J. Schramer (1998)
190 *British Reform Writers, 1832-1914*, edited by Gary Kelly and Edd Applegate (1998)
191 *British Novelists Between the Wars*, edited by George M. Johnson (1998)
192 *French Dramatists, 1789-1914*, edited by Barbara T. Cooper (1998)
193 *American Poets Since World War II, Sixth Series*, edited by Joseph Conte (1998)
194 *British Novelists Since 1960, Second Series*, edited by Merritt Moseley (1998)
195 *British Travel Writers, 1910-1939*, edited by Barbara Brothers and Julia M. Gergits (1998)
196 *Italian Novelists Since World War II, 1965-1995*, edited by Augustus Pallotta (1998)
197 *Late-Victorian and Edwardian British Novelists, Second Series*, edited by George M. Johnson (1998)

Documentary Series

1 *Sherwood Anderson, Willa Cather, John Dos Passos, Theodore Dreiser, F. Scott Fitzgerald, Ernest Hemingway, Sinclair Lewis,* edited by Margaret A. Van Antwerp (1982)

2 *James Gould Cozzens, James T. Farrell, William Faulkner, John O'Hara, John Steinbeck, Thomas Wolfe, Richard Wright,* edited by Margaret A. Van Antwerp (1982)

3 *Saul Bellow, Jack Kerouac, Norman Mailer, Vladimir Nabokov, John Updike, Kurt Vonnegut,* edited by Mary Bruccoli (1983)

4 *Tennessee Williams,* edited by Margaret A. Van Antwerp and Sally Johns (1984)

5 *American Transcendentalists,* edited by Joel Myerson (1988)

6 *Hardboiled Mystery Writers: Raymond Chandler, Dashiell Hammett, Ross Macdonald,* edited by Matthew J. Bruccoli and Richard Layman (1989)

7 *Modern American Poets: James Dickey, Robert Frost, Marianne Moore,* edited by Karen L. Rood (1989)

8 *The Black Aesthetic Movement,* edited by Jeffrey Louis Decker (1991)

9 *American Writers of the Vietnam War: W. D. Ehrhart, Larry Heinemann, Tim O'Brien, Walter McDonald, John M. Del Vecchio,* edited by Ronald Baughman (1991)

10 *The Bloomsbury Group,* edited by Edward L. Bishop (1992)

11 *American Proletarian Culture: The Twenties and The Thirties,* edited by Jon Christian Suggs (1993)

12 *Southern Women Writers: Flannery O'Connor, Katherine Anne Porter, Eudora Welty,* edited by Mary Ann Wimsatt and Karen L. Rood (1994)

13 *The House of Scribner, 1846-1904,* edited by John Delaney (1996)

14 *Four Women Writers for Children, 1868-1918,* edited by Caroline C. Hunt (1996)

15 *American Expatriate Writers: Paris in the Twenties,* edited by Matthew J. Bruccoli and Robert W. Trogdon (1997)

16 *The House of Scribner, 1905-1930,* edited by John Delaney (1997)

17 *The House of Scribner, 1931-1984,* edited by John Delaney (1998)

Yearbooks

1980 edited by Karen L. Rood, Jean W. Ross, and Richard Ziegfeld (1981)

1981 edited by Karen L. Rood, Jean W. Ross, and Richard Ziegfeld (1982)

1982 edited by Richard Ziegfeld; associate editors: Jean W. Ross and Lynne C. Zeigler (1983)

1983 edited by Mary Bruccoli and Jean W. Ross; associate editor: Richard Ziegfeld (1984)

1984 edited by Jean W. Ross (1985)

1985 edited by Jean W. Ross (1986)

1986 edited by J. M. Brook (1987)

1987 edited by J. M. Brook (1988)

1988 edited by J. M. Brook (1989)

1989 edited by J. M. Brook (1990)

1990 edited by James W. Hipp (1991)

1991 edited by James W. Hipp (1992)

1992 edited by James W. Hipp (1993)

1993 edited by James W. Hipp, contributing editor George Garrett (1994)

1994 edited by James W. Hipp, contributing editor George Garrett (1995)

1995 edited by James W. Hipp, contributing editor George Garrett (1996)

1996 edited by Samuel W. Bruce and L. Kay Webster, contributing editor George Garrett (1997)

1997 edited by Matthew J. Bruccoli and George Garrett, with the assistance of L. Kay Webster (1998)

Concise Series

Concise Dictionary of American Literary Biography, 6 volumes (1988-1989): *The New Consciousness, 1941-1968; Colonization to the American Renaissance, 1640-1865; Realism, Naturalism, and Local Color, 1865-1917; The Twenties, 1917-1929; The Age of Maturity, 1929-1941; Broadening Views, 1968-1988.*

Concise Dictionary of British Literary Biography, 8 volumes (1991-1992): *Writers of the Middle Ages and Renaissance Before 1660; Writers of the Restoration and Eighteenth Century, 1660-1789; Writers of the Romantic Period, 1789-1832; Victorian Writers, 1832-1890; Late Victorian and Edwardian Writers, 1890-1914; Modern Writers, 1914-1945; Writers After World War II, 1945-1960; Contemporary Writers, 1960 to Present.*

Dictionary of Literary Biography® • Volume One Hundred Ninety-Seven

Late-Victorian and Edwardian British Novelists
Second Series

Dictionary of Literary Biography® • Volume One Hundred Ninety-Seven

Late-Victorian and Edwardian British Novelists
Second Series

Edited by
George M. Johnson
University College of the Cariboo

A Bruccoli Clark Layman Book
Gale Research
Detroit, Washington, D.C., London

Advisory Board for
DICTIONARY OF LITERARY BIOGRAPHY

John Baker
William Cagle
Patrick O'Connor
George Garrett
Trudier Harris

Matthew J. Bruccoli and Richard Layman, Editorial Directors
C. E. Frazer Clark Jr., Managing Editor
Karen Rood, Senior Editor

Printed in the United States of America

This publication is a creative work fully protected by all applicable copyright laws, as well as by misappropriation, trade secret, unfair competition, and other applicable laws. The authors and editors of this work have added value to the underlying factual material herein through one or more of the following: unique and original selection, coordination, expression, arrangement, and classification of the information.

All rights to this publication will be vigorously defended.

Copyright © 1999 by Gale Research
27500 Drake Road
Farmington Hills, MI 48331

All rights reserved including the right of reproduction in
whole or in part in any form.

Library of Congress Cataloging-in-Publication Data

Late-Victorian and Edwardian British Novelists. Second series / edited by
  George M. Johnson.
  p. cm.–(Dictionary of literary biography; v. 197)
"A Bruccoli Clark Layman book."
Includes bibliographical references and index.
ISBN 0-7876-1852-7 (alk. paper)
1. Novelists, English–19th century–Biography–Dictionaries. 2. Novelists, English–20th century–Biography–Dictionaries. 3. English fiction–19th century–Bio-bibliography–Dictionaries. 4. English fiction–20th century–Bio-bibliography–Dictionaries. 5. English fiction–19th century–Dictionaries. 6. English fiction–20th century–Dictionaries.
I. Johnson, George M. II. Series.
PR863.L382 1998
823'.809–dc21   98-29261
                                                             CIP

In memory of my grandparents

Roy Malcolm Knapp (1898–1976)
Margaret Winnifred Knapp (1896–1978)

Contents

Plan of the Series xiii
Introduction xv

Martin Donisthorpe Armstrong
  (1882-1974) 3
  Kenneth Womack

Elizabeth von Arnim (Countess
  Mary Annette Beauchamp Russell)
  (1866-1941) 9
  Katherine E. Ayer

J. D. Beresford (1873-1947) 15
  George M. Johnson

Phyllis Bottome (1882-1963) 30
  Marilyn Hoder-Salmon

Thomas Burke (1886-1945) 40
  Richard Bleiler

Mona Caird (1854-1932) 50
  Carolyn Christensen Nelson

Gilbert Cannan (1884-1955) 58
  Diana Farr

Mary Cholmondeley (1859-1925) 67
  Karen M. Carney

Lucy Lane Clifford (1853-1929) 71
  P. Joan Smith

Victoria Cross (Annie Sophie Cory)
  (1868-1952) 79
  Shoshana Milgram Knapp

Clemence Dane (Winifred Ashton)
  (1888-1965) 88
  Leonard R. N. Ashley

Gertrude Dix (circa 1874 - ?) 95
  Carol L. Hale

Ella Hepworth Dixon (1855 or 1857-1932) 99
  Margaret Diane Stetz

W. L. George (1882-1926) 110
  Kenneth Womack

Douglas Goldring (1887-1960) 117
  Paul W. Salmon

Sarah Grand (Frances Elizabeth
  Clarke McFall) (1854-1943) 125
  Carolyn Christensen Nelson

Cicely Hamilton (1872-1952) 132
  Sue Thomas

Mary Agnes Hamilton (1884-1962) 140
  Maria Aline Seabra Ferreira

Margaret Harkness (John Law)(1854-1923) 150
  Eileen Sypher

Frank Harris (1856-1931) 156
  George Allan Cate

Stephen Hudson (1868?-1944) 163
  George J. Johnson

Oliver Madox Hueffer (1876-1931) 171
  Michele K. Troy

Violet Hunt (1862-1942) 180
  Donald Mason

Ethel Colburn Mayne (1865-1941) 187
  Susan Winslow Waterman

Stephen McKenna (1888-1967) 202
  George J. Johnson

C. E. Montague
  (1867-1928) 212
  Eric Thompson

Arthur Morrison (1863-1945) 219
  Leonard R. N. Ashley

Barry Pain (1864-1928) 224
  Jan Peter F. van Rosevelt

George Paston (Emily Morse Symonds)
  (1860-1936) 238
  Rebecca Brittenham

Henry Handel Richardson (Ethel Florence
  Lindsay)
  (1870-1946) 244
  Laurie Clancy

Elizabeth Robins (1862-1952) 256
  Sue Thomas

Contents

Ethel Sidgwick (1877–1970) 264
Lynn M. Alexander

G. B. Stern (1890–1973) 269
Colleen Hobbs

Netta Syrett (1865–1943) 275
Jill Tedford Jones

Robert Tressell (Robert Phillipe Noonan)
(1870–1911) 285
David Smith

E. L. Voynich (1864–1960) 292
Shoshana Milgram Knapp

Israel Zangwill (1864–1926) 302
Meri-Jane Rochelson

Checklist of Further Readings.............................317
Contributors 325
Cumulative Index 329

Plan of the Series

... Almost the most prodigious asset of a country, and perhaps its most precious possession, is its native literary product — when that product is fine and noble and enduring.

Mark Twain*

The advisory board, the editors, and the publisher of the *Dictionary of Literary Biography* are joined in endorsing Mark Twain's declaration. The literature of a nation provides an inexhaustible resource of permanent worth. We intend to make literature and its creators better understood and more accessible to students and the reading public, while satisfying the standards of teachers and scholars.

To meet these requirements, *literary biography* has been construed in terms of the author's achievement. The most important thing about a writer is his writing. Accordingly, the entries in *DLB* are career biographies, tracing the development of the author's canon and the evolution of his reputation.

The purpose of *DLB* is not only to provide reliable information in a convenient format but also to place the figures in the larger perspective of literary history and to offer appraisals of their accomplishments by qualified scholars.

The publication plan for *DLB* resulted from two years of preparation. The project was proposed to Bruccoli Clark by Frederick C. Ruffner, president of the Gale Research Company, in November 1975. After specimen entries were prepared and typeset, an advisory board was formed to refine the entry format and develop the series rationale. In meetings held during 1976, the publisher, series editors, and advisory board approved the scheme for a comprehensive biographical dictionary of persons who contributed to North American literature. Editorial work on the first volume began in January 1977, and it was published in 1978. In order to make *DLB* more than a reference tool and to compile volumes that individually have claim to status as literary history, it was decided to organize volumes by topic, period, or genre. Each of these freestanding volumes provides a biographical-bibliographical guide and overview for a particular area of literature. We are convinced that this organization—as opposed to a single alphabet method—constitutes a valuable innovation in the presentation of reference material. The volume plan necessarily requires many decisions for the placement and treatment of authors who might properly be included in two or three volumes. In some instances a major figure will be included in separate volumes, but with different entries emphasizing the aspect of his career appropriate to each volume. Ernest Hemingway, for example, is represented in *American Writers in Paris, 1920-1939* by an entry focusing on his expatriate apprenticeship; he is also in *American Novelists, 1910-1945* with an entry surveying his entire career, as well as in *American Short-Story Writers, 1910-1945, Second Series* with an entry concentrating on his short stories. Each volume includes a cumulative index of the subject authors and articles. Comprehensive indexes to the entire series are planned.

Since 1981 the series has been further augmented by the *DLB Yearbooks,* which update published entries and add new entries to keep the *DLB* current with contemporary activity. There have also been *DLB Documentary Series* volumes which provide biographical and critical source materials for figures whose work is judged to have particular interest for students. One of these companion volumes is entirely devoted to Tennessee Williams.

We define literature as the *intellectual commerce of a nation:* not merely as belles lettres but as that ample and complex process by which ideas are generated, shaped, and transmitted. *DLB* entries are not limited to "creative writers" but extend to other figures who in their time and in their way influenced the mind of a people. Thus the series encompasses historians, journalists, publishers, book collectors, and screenwriters. By this means readers of *DLB* may be aided to perceive literature not as cult scripture in the keeping of intellectual high priests but firmly positioned at the center of a nation's life.

*From an unpublished section of Mark Twain's autobiography, copyright by the Mark Twain Company

Plan of the Series

  DLB includes the major writers appropriate to each volume and those standing in the ranks behind them. Scholarly and critical counsel has been sought in deciding which minor figures to include and how full their entries should be. Wherever possible, useful references are made to figures who do not warrant separate entries.

  Each *DLB* volume has an expert volume editor responsible for planning the volume, selecting the figures for inclusion, and assigning the entries. Volume editors are also responsible for preparing, where appropriate, appendices surveying the major periodicals and literary and intellectual movements for their volumes, as well as lists of further readings. Work on the series as a whole is coordinated at the Bruccoli Clark Layman editorial center in Columbia, South Carolina, where the editorial staff is responsible for accuracy and utility of the published volumes.

  One feature that distinguishes *DLB* is the illustration policy—its concern with the iconography of literature. Just as an author is influenced by his surroundings, so is the reader's understanding of the author enhanced by a knowledge of his environment. Therefore *DLB* volumes include not only drawings, paintings, and photographs of authors, often depicting them at various stages in their careers, but also illustrations of their families and places where they lived. Title pages are regularly reproduced in facsimile along with dust jackets for modern authors. The dust jackets are a special feature of *DLB* because they often document better than anything else the way in which an author's work was perceived in its own time. Specimens of the writers' manuscripts and letters are included when feasible.

  Samuel Johnson rightly decreed that "The chief glory of every people arises from its authors." The purpose of the *Dictionary of Literary Biography* is to compile literary history in the surest way available to us—by accurate and comprehensive treatment of the lives and work of those who contributed to it.

The DLB Advisory Board

Introduction

Interest in late-Victorian and Edwardian novelists has recently been generated by feminist studies such as Ann Ardis's *New Woman, New Novels: Feminism and Early Modernism* (1990); socialist analyses, notably H. Gustav Klaus's collection *The Rise of Socialist Fiction 1880–1914* (1987); and more-general studies, including Peter Keating's *The Haunted Study: A Social History of the English Novel 1875–1914* (1989) and David Trotter's *The English Novel in History 1895–1920* (1993). All of these works take into account writers who are not included in the established canon, some of them completely forgotten. *DLB 153* and *DLB 197: Late-Victorian and Edwardian British Novelists, First Series* and *Second Series,* attempt to respond to and foster that interest by providing more-detailed analyses of some of these writers. These volumes cover novelists ranging from those who began to write in the 1880s, or who had achieved acclaim by then, to those who had started to write before the end of World War I (though the entries treat the entire body of work of each writer).

While *DLB 153* treated mainly novelists who worked in the romance tradition, the present volume is primarily concerned with those who are considered realists. In his *Modernism and Romance* (1908) Rolfe A. Scott-James associated romance with an attitude of wonderment toward life; with the mysterious and the unknown, the psychical and the supernatural; and with a sense of incipient adventure. Realism, on the other hand, "takes its cue from the ordinary, unalterable course of real life." Another contemporary critic, Clayton Hamilton, rejected definitions of realism that argue that the realist shows people what they are as opposed to what they should be; is oriented to character rather than action; and describes contemporary and familiar places rather than remote settings. Instead, in his *A Manual of the Art of Fiction* (1918), he distinguished between the genres on the basis of method: the realist inductively draws on pieces of evidence around him or her, whereas the romanticist applies a deductive method, working from general truths to particular imagined situations. In his article "Bennet Wells, and the Persistence of Realism" (1994) Robert Squillace concurs that philosophical stance is more important than mimetic qualities in distinguishing romance and realism: "Realism assumes reality, that is, the existence of a phenomenal world separate and knowable by consciousness. The struggle to recognize that separation and gather that knowledge is the chief theme of the realist work. By the same token, the realist novel purports to sharpen a reader's perception of the real world exterior to it." Despite these definitions, in practice the boundaries between romanticism and realism blur, since some writers embed romance plots, blend elements of fantasy, or satirize romance conventions within realistic works.

The labels most often applied to these years—including *fin de siècle, decadent, Edwardian,* and *Early Modern*—seem inadequate and incomplete, and this period is often parceled out between the Victorian and the Modern or disparaged as transitional. This situation is reflected in the literary academy. A question raised by the critic Samuel Hynes in his 1972 study, *Edwardian Occasions,* is just as relevant today: "Every English department has its Victorianists and its Modernists, but who has ever heard of an academic Edwardianist?" For the lack of a better term, the title *Late-Victorian and Edwardian* has been adopted for these volumes.

When discussing the novel of this period, traditional literary histories, such as J. I. M. Stewart's *Eight Modern Writers* (1963), survey only a handful of its practitioners—all male—including Joseph Conrad, Thomas Hardy, H. G. Wells, Arnold Bennett, and John Galsworthy. All too frequently literary historians justify passing over or slighting the era by citing Virginia Woolf's deliberately dramatic and defensive comments about the caliber of novel writing during these years. It is ironic that Woolf's comments should have exerted such an impact, since Woolf herself began writing during the period she criticized (although she identified herself with the next generation of writers, labeled Georgians, after the accession to the throne of George V in 1910). In "Mr. Bennett and Mrs. Brown" (1923), one of several polemical essays on this topic, Woolf reduces the Edwardian camp to Bennett, Galsworthy, and Wells. She then ranges this camp against the Georgian writers, whom she limits to E. M. Forster, D. H. Lawrence, Lytton Strachey, James Joyce, and

T. S. Eliot. In her essay "Modern Fiction" in *The Common Reader* (1925) she accuses the Edwardian "culprits" of being materialists because "they are concerned not with the spirit but with the body" and "spend immense skill and immense industry making the trivial and the transitory appear the true and the enduring." Where the Victorians created vivid, memorable characters, the Edwardians fail to do so and "Life escapes" their novels as a consequence. In contrast, the younger writers, most notably Joyce, "attempt to come closer to life," even if "there was no English novelist living [in 1910] from whom they could learn their business," and they must discard most of the conventions of the novel to do so. Not often noticed about Woolf's claims is the context in which she wrote. She was responding to a specific criticism by Bennett of her inability to create memorable characters. She was also trying to define and justify her own "modernist" aesthetic. She did not, however, restrict her critique of her predecessors' fiction to their manner of presentation but also attacked the Edwardians' selection of subject matter. Edwardian fiction, though, was far more diverse and amorphous than that of the three admittedly important novelists targeted by Woolf, and this *DLB* volume will expose the limitations of her view.

The 1890s are often cast as the decade of decadence, of aesthetes and absinthe, during which a pervasive sense of ending was played out in alternating moods of skepticism, jaded witticism, and ennui. Oscar Wilde, who said "Life is such a disappointment," is held up as iconic of the malaise. The aesthetes, however, represented only a tiny and often-ridiculed fragment of this society, a society caught up in a whirlwind of activity directed at improving the plight of humanity. As Karl Beckson stresses in his *London in the 1890s: A Cultural History* (1992), there was a strong sense of renewal, of embracing the new, as captured in Havelock Ellis's *The New Spirit* (1890) at the beginning of the decade and in the various "New" movements launched during it, including New Woman, New Hedonism, New Imperialism, New Psychology, New Drama, New Journalism, New Humour, and, most pertinently, New Fiction. This time was one of ferment, of paradoxes and crosscurrents.

The era that began with the death of Queen Victoria on 22 January 1901 and the ascension to the throne of Edward VII has most frequently been depicted as a crass and superficial age, one of philistinism and extravagance, epitomized by the image of the Edwardian garden party. Certainly the rebellious new king, described privately by Henry James as "an arch-vulgarian," enjoyed his pleasures, which included lavish entertaining along with ostentatious dress, the company of pretty women, horse racing, yachting, and shooting. And there is no doubt that he was a popular king who encouraged a sense of liberation and joie de vivre among his subjects. Vita Sackville-West captures that world perceptively and treats it scathingly in her 1931 novel *The Edwardians*. She describes it as "a world where pleasure fell like a ripened peach for the outstretching of a hand." The reality, however, is that only about 1 percent of the population could afford to participate in this opulent world. This 1 percent owned 69 percent of the national capital, the highest concentration of wealth in modern British history. As for the rest, as Donald Read notes in his *Edwardian England* (1982): "Eight out of ten Edwardians were working class, and most of these passed large parts of their lives below the poverty line, first defined by Seebohm Rowntree in his famous book on *Poverty, A Study of Town Life* (1901)." The majority could not even conceive of the notion of extravagance: Paul Thompson writes in his *The Edwardians: The Remaking of British Society* (1992) that "very little that could be re-used was wasted. Children picked from street gutters, rubbish heaps and river banks. They crawled under market stalls to look for fallen food, and queued at public houses and restaurants for the day's leftovers. . . . Women, as patient, cheap workers, were especially used for refuse work." To make matters worse, this society inherited from the Victorians rigid segregation along class lines.

Recognition of such disparity helps deflate a myth that this period was a golden age of security and leisure. In part this myth was perpetuated by those who mournfully and nostalgically gazed back at it over the chasm of horror of World War I, in which 30 percent of British men aged fifteen to twenty-four were slaughtered. One of those who escaped and mythologized the prewar period was Siegfried Sassoon, who wrote that "the years of my youth were going down for ever in the weltering western gold, and the future would take me far from that sunset embered horizon." Similar views continue to be reflected in popular writing about the age; for example, Gerald Sparrow says in his *Vintage Edwardian Murder* (1971) that Edward's "reign was the last comparatively untroubled one of the golden era of the British Monarchy" and that "the Edwardians believed in their land of hope and glory, because life in many ways was glorious and certainly full of hope."

The number and severity of the crises that riddled these years, however, suggest that far from being a golden age of security and leisure, this time was one of tension and conflict; World War I was only a dramatic culmination of these conflicts.

Working-class unrest was dramatically exhibited on Bloody Sunday, 13 November 1887, when, after weeks of demonstrations marked by sporadic outbursts of looting and vandalism, police attacked marchers in Trafalgar Square who were demonstrating for free speech, injuring more than one hundred demonstrators (at least one of whom subsequently died). In the East End the dockworkers struck, achieving victory in 1889. Labor continued to gain momentum, as dramatized by severe and widespread labor disputes and strikes by coal miners, dockworkers, and transport workers between 1910 and 1912, culminating in Labour Party electoral victories in 1924 and 1929. The suffragist movement leaped ahead with the formation in 1889 of the women's Protective Provident League (later called the Women's Trade Union League) and the Women's Franchise League; in 1903 the Women's Social and Political Union was formed. By the summer of 1909 the union had become militant, with its members rioting, hunger striking, and committing criminal acts to draw attention to their fight to gain the vote and, more broadly, to combat political and moral injustice. A particularly notable incident of civil disobedience was Emily Davison's martyrdom in June 1913: she ran out onto the Derby racetrack, attempted to grab the bridle of a horse owned by King George V, and suffered a fatal skull fracture. The Boer War of 1899 to 1902, pitting the inefficient, blundering British forces against the much smaller force of the South African Boers, caused an even deeper questioning of justice, as well as of imperialism, especially since the British appeared to be motivated solely by the desire to protect gold and diamond interests. There followed the electoral sweep by the Liberal Party in 1906, after which the new government attempted to introduce radical social reforms; the attempt was blocked by the House of Lords. The failure of the Irish Home Rule bill led to the Easter Rising of 1916 in Dublin. England had declared war on Germany on 4 August 1914. Though the war was expected to last only a few months, it dragged on for more than four years and involved many other nations. It also transformed class and gender relations and the moral code.

These glimpses into the successive tensions of these years reinforce J. B. Priestley's claim in *The Edwardians* (1972) that "the Edwardian was never a golden age, but seen across the dark years afterwards it could easily be mistaken for one." Priestley locates the tension among the middle classes: "the members of the upper middle class felt that property and position were being threatened. In the lower middle class, respectability itself, often newly-won, had to be guarded. There was a feeling that religion, the family, decency, social and political stability, the country itself, were all in danger." The history of labor conflict, however, demonstrates that the working class was just as deeply embroiled. Even the wealthiest of the upper class started to feel a slight flutter of change. They stopped, for instance, building large country houses during these years.

Given the number and range of conflicts and upheavals in the late-Victorian and Edwardian years, it is not surprising that this period has been labeled transitional. Between 1890 and 1918 many aspects of British society were utterly transformed. In 1890 the average person had not heard of the motorcar, motorcycle, radiotelegraphy, airships (let alone airplanes), tanks, X rays, radium, and Bakelite (heralding the age of plastics), all of which were invented or discovered during this period. Advances in scientific theory include Ernst Haeckel's contributions to evolution theory, Max Planck's quantum theory (1900), Albert Einstein's Special Theory of Relativity (1905), and Niels Bohr's electric theory of matter (1913). Ironically, this scientific probing was perceived as undermining the Newtonian universe, and it contributed to distrust of the mechanistic view of the world. The reaction against scientific positivism took the form of a revival of romanticism and philosophical idealism. The Victorian quest for a replacement for traditional religious belief continued—as the rise in popularity of the Society for Psychical Research, Theosophy, Eastern mysticism, and comparative religion attests. Though Sigmund Freud considered himself a scientist, psychoanalysis was introduced to Great Britain by members of the Society for Psychical Research. Psychoanalysis focused attention on the irrational aspects of the human being and contributed to dissolving the rigid Victorian boundary between the sane and the insane. By 1918 it had received enormous impetus through its contribution to identifying and treating shell shock, a term invented in England during the war for what is today known as post-traumatic stress disorder. In the years prior to the war, the metaphysical psychology of Henri Bergson became enormously popular in Great Britain. His poetically written arguments altered conceptions of time and memory and were directed toward illustrating that the universe is essentially spiritual rather than material, a notion captured in his conception of the elan vital, the life force. All of these discoveries and developments contributed to a sense of rapid change and instability.

Contemporaries from C. F. G. Masterman, an Edwardian Liberal politician, to William Butler Yeats recognized and commented on the transitional nature of this period, but it was a feeling that was to persist. Edwin Muir titled his 1926 collection of essays on contemporary literature *Transition* and wrote that "in ages of transition, on the other hand, everything makes the writer more uncertain, saps his faith, only nourished from himself, and gives his work an air either of vacillation or of violence." Literary historians from G. S. Fraser (*The Modern Writer and His World*, 1964) to William Frierson (*The English Novel in Transition*, 1965) to Hynes have subsequently applied this label. More recently, however, scholars such as Keating have argued that consciousness of transition existed earlier, in the Victorian age. And John Lester, in his *Journey through Despair 1880–1914: Transformations in British Literary Culture* (1968), has suggested that if the period from 1880 to 1914 "was a transition, the transit is not yet completed. In some larger sense, that age must in fact have been a beginning."

Fiction writing during the late-Victorian and Edwardian period existed in a state in which great variety and innumerable possibilities were entertained, before lines had hardened between modernists and traditionalists and between commercial and serious novelists. The encyclopedic structure of the *Dictionary of Literary Biography* enables the diversity among these novelists to be recognized and yet also acknowledges webs of interconnectedness. The volumes on late-Victorian and Edwardian British novelists deal with so-called minor novelists, those not considered, to use traditional terminology, of the first or in some cases even of the second or third ranks. Aside from expanding one's sense of the culture of the period, these novelists play several more-important roles. Many were closely connected with the major figures and aided them in various ways, from providing material and emotional support to championing them in the press—especially if they ran afoul of the censor. If their work was not experimental, many experimented in their lives, making their biographies intrinsically fascinating: the scandalous lives of Frank Harris and Oliver Madox Hueffer come to mind. Since many of these novelists wrote best-sellers, they typically touched the lives of more of their contemporary readers than their longer-remembered and more critically acclaimed colleagues. In some instances their work has been undeservedly forgotten for such reasons as politics and gender. The triumph and pervasiveness of a modernist aesthetic and its reflection in literary criticism have contributed to relegating some of these novelists to obscurity. Some were dismissed as genre writers, not worthy of consideration in the mainstream development of the English novel. One even wonders whether the sheer size of the output of most of the writers represented here has discouraged scholars from probing their work. Perhaps most important, these novelists bring to light the eddies and undercurrents that reveal a much more complex cultural stream than appears on the surface and make generalizations about their epoch less comfortable.

The origins of the late-Victorian neorealistic impulse in British fiction are complex. Much attention has been paid to the influence of Emile Zola and his first English disciple George Moore (see, for example, George Levine's *The Realistic Imagination: English Fiction from Frankenstein to Lady Chatterley* [1981] or Ioan M. Williams's *The Realist Novel in England: A Study in Development* [1974]). The writers included here were influenced by earlier realists, including James, Stephen Crane, George Eliot, and George Meredith. But at least three other closely related origins come clearly into view through examining the writers in this volume.

The first has to do with the economic situation of many of them. Most were "Grub Street" writers, dependent on writing for their income. Many were able to pursue careers in writing because of the growing public demand for reading material, including newspapers, magazines, and novels, as more of the populace became literate and better educated. Many of the writers represented here started their careers as journalists and then turned out a novel or more a year while continuing to supplement their income with journalism. As journalists they were trained to write about what they observed, and this quality helps to account for a strong documentary impulse in their fiction that makes it particularly sensitive to societal changes. Although journalism attained a more professional status when a charter was granted to the Institute of Journalists in 1889, some journalism of the period gained a negative reputation. The New Journalism, as it was called, was often derided for pandering to the masses by focusing on trivia and treating its subject matter sensationally and irresponsibly. *A Modern Amazon* (1894), by George Paston (Emily Morse Symonds), provides a glimpse into the Fleet Street world of the 1890s; in the Edwardian period C. E. Montague, who wrote for *The Manchester Guardian,* satirized journalistic corruption in *A Hind Let Loose* (1910).

On the positive side, as Keating notes, the New Journalists expanded the subject matter of journalism to include the everyday and mundane. They often carried out personal interviews and attempted to experience the lives of their subjects. The novelists in this volume wrote for a wide range of journals from the *Westminster Gazette* (J. D. Beresford and Mona Caird) and *Woman's World* (Ella Hepworth Dixon) to the avant-garde decadent periodical *The Yellow Book* (Victoria Cross, Ella Colburn Mayne, and Netta Syrett), which first appeared in April 1894. Many of the novelists in this volume closely monitored the trends of readership out of economic necessity when they turned their hands to novel writing. Several were lucky enough to produce best-sellers, a term that had come into common use by 1889. Some, however, such as Beresford, also complained about the limitations their readership placed on their art.

Second, only a few of these writers were born into the privileged classes; many came from the middle, lower-middle, and working classes and had a strong commitment to social and political change. This commitment resulted in a strong countertrend to the aesthetic fiction of the 1890s in polemical novels concerned with social conditions and class tensions. These novels reflected the intense interest in the plight of the urban poor. Though most were written by middle-class authors, there was a spate of working-class novels, most notably Thomas Burke's tales of Asians in the Limehouse district of London, as well as works by Margaret Harkness (John Law), Arthur Morrison (notably *A Child of the Jago*, 1896), Barry Pain, Elizabeth Robins, and Israel Zangwill. Such novelists were roundly criticized for writing propaganda, which was not thought to be the proper sphere of fiction. Socialism gained political momentum in England with the consolidation in 1900 of various groups, including the trade unions, into the Independent Labour Representation Committee, the forerunner of the Labour Party, which elected its first twenty-nine members to Parliament in 1906. Many of the Edwardian generation of novelists in this volume, including Harris, W. L. George, Douglas Goldring, and Cicely Hamilton, considered themselves socialists, and one, Mary Agnes Hamilton, was even elected as a Labour member of Parliament. They, too, wrote novels advocating social change, notably George's *A Bed of Roses* (1911). The obscure writer Robert Tressell's *The Ragged-Trousered Philanthropists* (1914), an unsentimental and polemical examination of workers in the painting and decorating trade, has probably had the longest-lasting impact of the novels of social change; it has never gone out of print.

Third, a more daring realism than in mid-Victorian fiction was made possible by changes to the means of production and distribution of novels. Since the mid nineteenth century, circulating libraries such as Mudie's had encouraged publishers to produce "triple-decker," or three-volume, novels because they were too expensive for most individuals to buy; thus, would-be novel readers were forced to pay an annual fee of about a guinea to subscribe to the libraries that could afford to purchase the novels. During the 1880s and 1890s these libraries came under increasing attack from writers such as Moore because of the censorship they exerted so as not to offend their largely middle-class and female readers. Then, in 1894, Mudie's decided to reduce the amount that it would pay publishers per volume, rendering the triple-decker uneconomical and sending it on its way to extinction. Several of the novelists included in this volume started their careers writing triple-deckers, including Mary Cholmondeley and Sarah Grand (Frances Elizabeth Clarke McFall), before switching to the one-volume format. The newer publishers, such as John Lane and Elkin Matthews, Edward Arnold, and Grant Richards, quickly seized the opportunity to supply the demand for one-volume novels. Since they did not have to worry about acceptance by the circulating libraries, they could take greater risks with the subject matter of these novels.

Most of the types of realistic fiction produced in the late-Victorian and Edwardian eras came to be labeled "unpleasant fiction," and there were debates on its place in literature. One of the first of these types was New Woman fiction. Though the "Woman Question"—the controversy in print over the place of women in the Victorian social order—had been debated at least since the 1860s and had been expressed in fictional form in such novels as Olive Schreiner's *The Story of an African Farm* (1883), the New Woman novel was not formally identified until 1894. In March of that year Grand published an article titled "The New Aspect of the Woman Question" in the *North American Review,* and the novelist Ouida responded contentiously with a piece titled "The New Woman." New Woman novelists reacted against the Victorian ideal of the Angel in the House—the self-sacrificing, self-effacing, silent wife, mother, and household manager—as well as Victorian hypocrisy on issues such as prostitution. Instead, they portrayed women who questioned or even rejected the roles handed to them, or who became victims of the injustice inherent in those traditional roles. Many advocated equality in one or more of the political, educational, economic, and sexual realms. In her entry on Syrett, Jill Tedford Jones identifies the three major problems of the New Woman: an unsympathetic family, limited job opportunities, and an unhappy marriage. The label notwithstanding, these novelists were by no means a homogenous group, and several of them denied their association with the label or represented the New Woman with ambivalence in their fiction, as did Harkness. The importance of this trend is attested to in Beckson's estimate that more than one hundred of these novels were published between 1883 and 1900. More important, as revisionists such as Ardis have argued, the New Woman novelists contributed to the development of modernism. These novelists discarded the notion of an innate female nature and undermined the conception of identity as single, seamless, and coherent. Their experimentation in form included disrupting the linearity of their narratives, manipulating narrative perspective, and even writing in impressionistic and stream-of-consciousness styles.

Though New Woman protagonists were first described by women writers, such as Caird in *The Daughters of Danaus* (1894), the New Woman novel was quickly coopted and rendered less threatening by male writers, including Grant Allen on the popular level in *The Woman Who Did* (1895) and Hardy on the level of high culture in *Jude the Obscure* (1895). Although both novels attack hypocrisy associated with the institution of marriage, they retreat from the radical implications of their narratives at their denouements. Allen's protagonist bears and raises an illegitimate daughter but commits suicide and thus is "punished" for her moral transgression, and Hardy's Sue Bridesbead loses her unconventionality. New Woman novelists even served as the model for New Woman protagonists in novels by men, as Violet Hunt did in fictions by Wells and James. Despite the prevalence and influence of the New Woman novel, this body of women's writing has until recently been erased from literary history. The present volume contributes to restoring the place of the New Woman novelists by including more-detailed analyses of more of them than are to be found in any other standard reference work. The selection of New Woman novelists in this volume includes Caird, Cholmondeley, Cross, Dixon, Grand, Hunt, Harkness, Paston, Robins, Syrett, and Gertrude Dix.

While several of these writers ceased to publish New Woman novels after the turn of the century, the New Woman debate continued to attract media attention, and New Women continued to appear in novels by writers in this volume, such as Pain (*Wilhelmina*, 1906) and George (*A Bed of Roses*, 1911), as well as by better-known novelists, including Bennett (*Anna of the Five Towns*, 1902) and Wells (*Ann Veronica*, 1907). Feminism advocated more forcefully women's right to vote. Late-nineteenth-century suffragists, those of either sex who sought the vote through legal means, were overtaken by the more-militant suffragettes, many of whom were willing to break the law to achieve their ends. Older novelists, such as Hunt and Robins, became more politically active, joining suffragette organizations such as the Women's Social and Political Union and the Women Writers Suffrage League. A new generation of novelists, including Phyllis Bottome, Mary Agnes Hamilton, and G. B. Stern, graphically depicted the trials of the feminist in the modern world.

Another trend in realism in part spawned by and overlapping with the New Woman novel was the sex novel. Under the influences of naturalism, psychology, and psychiatry, novelists turned to a "scientific" examination of the frequently disastrous impact of heredity and environment on their protagonists, and, most notoriously, to portrayals of illicit or irregular sexual liaisons. According to Keating, beginning in the mid 1890s thematic treatment of these relationships occupied a central position in British fiction. A few of the novels discussed in this volume anticipate this trend, notably Harkness's *A City Girl* (1887), in which a working-class girl has sexual relations with a married middle-class man, and Grand's *Ideala* (1889) with its treatment of men's immorality. Grand moved on to discuss syphilis and cross-dressing in *The Heavenly Twins* (1893). Dix's *The Image Breakers* (1895) broached the possibly even more taboo subject of erotic love between women, though the treatment is circumspect.

Although there was a crackdown on immorality after Wilde's trial in 1895, by the turn of the century the sex novel was even more daring. As Keating points out, "it could now be assumed that there was no such thing as normal or orthodox sexuality; no single generally acceptable pattern for family life; no one kind of sexuality that was attributable to all women and all men." Some novelists explored sexuality more candidly within the romance genres and thus escaped the censor. Pain's scientific romance *An Exchange of Souls* (1911) includes a subtext of transvestism and "sexual inversion," as homosexuality was then termed, and Clemence Dane depicts an affair between two women teachers in her social romance *The Regiment of Women* (1917). Of all the novelists included here, Cross treats sexuality in the most sensationally erotic manner within extravagant romance plots. Nevertheless, one reviewer noted that she imitates the frankness of Zola, and Shoshana Milgrim Knapp in this volume finds Cross's treatment of gender and sexuality "tantalizingly radical." The term *sex-problem novel* alludes to the assumption that sex itself or the response to sexuality—for example, repression—was the problem, rather than whether an act was moral or not. Examples of the treatment of sex as "problem" include Robins's *A Dark Lantern* (1905), George's *A Bed of Roses*, dealing with prostitution, and Gilbert Cannan's *Round the Corner* (1913). Better-known practitioners of the sex-problem novel, such as Lawrence, need to be viewed in the light of this trend.

The topics of madness and degeneracy and the relation between madness and genius also became the focus of attention from realist writers as early as the 1890s. This trend occurred concurrently with more-thorough probing of psychological behavior and aberrations in it by psychologists such as William James in *Principles of Psychology* (1890), and Havelock Ellis in *The Criminal* (1890), and it is likely that psychologists and novelists exerted a mutual influence. As Keating mentions, Morrison's *A Child of the Jago* reflects the popularity of Cesare Lombroso's descriptions of identifiable criminal types. Psychotic breakdown features in Grand's *The Heavenly Twins*.

Around the turn of the century the novel of morbid psychological analysis frequently took the form of the autobiographical life-novel or bildungsroman. With its typically subjective approach and its tracing events from childhood through youth to adulthood, the life-novel lent itself to satirical expression of rebellion, especially against cruel and repressive Victorian upbringings. The best-known English examples, including Samuel Butler's *The Way of All Flesh* (begun in the 1870s but not published until 1903), Forster's *The Longest Journey* (1907), Lawrence's *Sons and Lovers* (1913), and Joyce's *A Portrait of the Artist as a Young Man* (1916) have overshadowed those discussed in this series, including Grand's *The Beth Book* (1897), Henry Handel Richardson's *The Getting of Wisdom* (1910), Beresford's *Jacob Stahl* trilogy (1911, 1912, and 1915), Syrett's *The Victorians* (1915), and Cannan's *Mendel* (1916). Many other writers, including George, Mary Agnes Hamilton, Hunt, Mayne, Robins, Stephen Hudson (Sydney Schiff), and Ethel Sidgwick, explored psychological themes and were frequently criticized for their morbidity. Several were well versed in the new depth psychologies of Freud, C. G. Jung, Alfred Adler, William McDougall, and others—notably Beresford, Syrett, and Stern. Perhaps the closest connection to the new psychology was developed by Bottome, who underwent analysis with Adler in the 1920s, published a biography of him in 1939, and conveyed her insights into the mentally ill in *Old Wine* (1925) and *Private Worlds* (1934).

Psychological distress, mental illness, and particularly shell shock figured prominently in the many novels about World War I as novelists worked through their frequently conflicting feelings about the war. The majority of writers in this volume contributed in some way to the war effort. Several of them, including Bottome and Dixon, accepted a role under C. F. G. Masterman in the British government's newly formed Ministry of Information, which had the mission of "the organization of public statements of the strength of the British case and principles in the war by well-known men of letters." Only a few enlisted—Armstrong, Goldring, and Hueffer—as most were too old for active service, though age did not stop Montague, who joined up at forty-seven and saw active service for a few months. Only one of the novelists included here, Cannan, was opposed to the war from its outset. Though several of the romance novelists included in the *First Series* volume tended to be uncritical of the war, at least in its early phases, the realists took a harsher view, especially after 1916, a year of "imaginative vacuum," as Hynes calls it in his *A War Imagined: The First World War and English Culture* (1991). Questioning and criticism of the war is reflected in novels such as *Dead Yesterday* (1917), by Mary Agnes Hamilton; *First the Blade* (1918), by Dane; and *The Fortune: A Romance of Friendship* (1917), by Goldring, who had become a conscientious objector in 1916 and ridicules the smug Whitehall attitude toward war. This trickle of antiwar novels continued through the 1920s with novels such as Goldring's *The Black Curtain* (1920), Bottome's *Old Wine*, and Montague's *Rough Justice* (1926) and became a flood from about 1929. One of the most prevalent themes in the war novels is the devastating impact of the war and war loss on the relationships of ordinary people. In Cicely Hamilton's *William—an Englishman* (1919) the protagonist never recovers from the war-related loss of his wife; Syrett's *The Wife of a Hero* (1918) warns against the dangers of sudden war marriages; and Hueffer's *Needles and Pins* (1924) addresses the issue of the war hero threatened on his return to England by the increasing power of women.

The war heightened the long-standing fascination with psychical research, as those who were grieving attempted to make contact with lost loved ones through telepathy or with the help of a medium. Accounts of these communications, such as Sir Oliver Lodge's *Raymond* (1916), were enormously popular. Psychical research had attained a degree of respectability as early as 1882 with the formation of the Society for Psychical Research by a group of highly respected, mainly Cambridge-educated intellectuals. The society's main aim was to sift the "scientific" evidence for the survival of human personality beyond death. Accordingly, it discussed all types of phenomena normally imperceptible to the five senses and introduced to the British the latest foreign developments in the field of psychiatry and abnormal psychology, including telepathy, invasion of personality, dual personality, ideé fixes, and prevision. Though the assimilation of these topics in fiction helped to temper the harshness of naturalism in British fiction and spawned the neo-Romantic revival that is discussed in the *First Series* volume, some of the novelists in this volume considered psychic phenomena within the realm of the knowable and thus treated it realistically. Morrison and Syrett published psychical stories in the 1890s while writing realistic novels. After the turn of the century Pain turned to the psychical, satirizing phony spiritualists in *Wilhelmina in London* (1906) and dealing more seriously with the topic of the transmigration of souls in *An Exchange of Souls,* a topic also taken up by Lucy Lane Clifford in *Miss Fingal* (1919). Cross anticipated the World War I trend of telepathic communication with deceased soldiers in *The Religion of Evelyn Hastings* (1905), set during the Boer War. From the 1920s onward Beresford and Syrett treated psychical themes in their fiction.

Novelists tended to move further into the realm of romance when writing futuristic and fantasy fiction, but writers' social consciousness also found expression in utopian and, more frequently, in dystopian novels. Beresford's *Goslings* (1913) is an early example; more of the writers in this volume wrote such works in the 1920s and 1930s, including Cicely Hamilton in *Theodore Savage* (1922), Stephen McKenna in *The Oldest God* (1926) and *Beyond Hell* (1926), Harris in *Pantopia* (1930), Caird in *The Great Wave* (1931), Cross in *Martha Brown* (1935), and Dane in *The Arrogant History of White Ben* (1939).

Not all of the realist fiction produced in the late-Victorian and Edwardian periods conveyed such serious aims or fell under the heading of unpleasant fiction. In the early 1890s several writers, including Pain and Zangwill, found themselves labeled as New Humourists, though, as Jan Peter van Rosevelt points out, the distinction between old and new humor is no longer clear, if it ever was. These writers treated facetiously some of the serious topics of the day, including the marriage problem, as in Zangwill's *The Bachelor Club* (1891) and *The Old Maid's Club* (1892) and Pain's mocking of the vivisection issue in *The Octave of Claudius* (1892). Dixon also employed humor for satiric ends in *My Flirtations* (1892). This strain of bemused satire continued into the new century with Hueffer, who targeted the conventions of romance in such works as *Where Truth Lies: A Study in the Improbable* (1911). Even more pleasant were the novel of manners or drawing-room dramas of Sidgwick, Martin Donisthorpe Armstrong, and Elizabeth von Arnim.

The writers treated in this volume come from Ireland (Grand, Harris, Mayne, McKenna, Tressell) and England, from the Isle of Wight (Caird) to Norwich (Paston) and Newcastle-on-Tyne (Armstrong). Others were born in the far reaches of the British Empire but gravitated to its hub, such as Arnim and Richardson, who were born in Australia; Clifford, from Barbados; and Cross, from India. A few were from relatively recent immigrant families, including Stern and Zangwill (who were also Jewish), and others migrated from foreign countries, including George from France and Robins from the United States. Also, all classes with the exception of the titled aristocracy are represented, from working class (Burke) to middle (Beresford, Cannan, and Cicely Hamilton) to upper middle (Armstrong, Caird). Biographical threads link these writers in all types of relationships, from friendship to intertextuality. One of the most long-standing friendships was that between Hunt and Goldring, and, as Sue Thomas notes in this volume, in her novel *The Open Question* (1898) Robins consciously drew on Grand's *The Heavenly Twins*.

The pattern of connections extends beyond the boundaries of this series, since many of these novelists were connected with better-known and canonized writers. Armstrong was related to William Wordsworth; Arnim was a cousin of Katherine Mansfield; Hueffer was the brother of Ford Madox Ford; Hunt was romantically involved with Ford; and Cannan married J. M. Barrie's former wife. Bottome, Clifford, Dixon, Goldring, and Robins developed friendships with major writers of the era including Wilde, James, Yeats, Lawrence, and Ezra Pound.

These interwoven biographical and textual threads constitute the discourse of the novel during these years. To pick out and place under the magnifying glass a few of these threads, such as the novels of Bennett, Galsworthy, and Wells, is to distort one's perception of the richness of the fabric. It is hoped that this volume will contribute to making clearer the variety of the novel during these years of its flourishing and will make the complexity of the relationship between the late-Victorian and Edwardian novel and its culture more apparent.

I would like to express my gratitude to Dr. John Ferns for his suggestion that I write for the *DLB* and for his encouragement throughout the project. I also would like to thank my father, George J. Johnson, for his astute comments on this introduction. I appreciated Deborah Morrison's careful proofreading of the initial versions of entries in this volume. Finally, I offer sincere thanks to all of the contributors for their fine essays, their patience, and their suggestions for illustrations.

—*George M. Johnson*

Acknowledgments

This book was produced by Bruccoli Clark Layman, Inc. Karen L. Rood is senior editor for the *Dictionary of Literary Biography* series. In-house editor is Philip B. Dematteis. He was assisted by Charles Brower and Jan Peter F. van Rosevelt.

Administrative support was provided by Ann M. Cheschi, Beverly Dill, and Tenesha S. Lee.

Bookkeeper is Neil Senol.

Copyediting supervisors are Phyllis A. Avant and Samuel W. Bruce. The copyediting staff includes Christine Copeland, Margo Dowling, Thom Harman, Jannette L. Giles, Nicole M. Nichols, and Raegan E. Quinn. Freelance copyeditors are Rebecca Mayo and Jennie Williamson.

Editorial associate is Jeff Miller.

Layout and graphics staff includes Janet E. Hill, Mark J. McEwan, and Alison Smith.

Office manager is Kathy Lawler Merlette.

Photography editors are Melissa D. Hinton, Margaret Meriwether, and Paul Talbot. Photographic copy work was performed by Joseph M. Bruccoli.

Production manager is Marie L. Parker.

SGML supervisor is Cory McNair. The SGML staff includes Linda Drake, Frank Graham, Jennifer Harwell, and Alex Snead.

Systems manager is Marie L. Parker. Software support was provided by Stephen Rahe.

Database manager is Javed Nurani. Kim Kelly performed data entry.

Typesetting supervisor is Kathleen M. Flanagan. The typesetting staff includes Pamela D. Norton, Karla Corley Price, and Patricia Flanagan Salisbury. Freelance typesetters include Deidre Murphy and Delores Plastow.

Walter W. Ross and Steven Gross did library research. They were assisted by the following librarians at the Thomas Cooper Library of the University of South Carolina: Linda Holderfield and the interlibrary-loan staff; reference-department head Virginia Weathers; reference librarians Marilee Birchfield, Stefanie Buck, Stefanie DuBose, Rebecca Feind, Karen Joseph, Donna Lehman, Charlene Loope, Anthony McKissick, Jean Rhyne, and Kwamine Simpson; circulation-department head Caroline Taylor; and acquisitions-searching supervisor David Haggard.

Dictionary of Literary Biography® • Volume One Hundred Ninety-Seven

Late-Victorian and Edwardian British Novelists
Second Series

Dictionary of Literary Biography

Martin Donisthorpe Armstrong
(2 October 1882 – 24 February 1974)

Kenneth Womack
Pennsylvania State University at Altoona

BOOKS: *Exodus, and Other Poems* (London: Lynwood, 1912);
Thirty New Poems (London: Chapman & Hall, 1918);
The Buzzards, and Other Poems (London: Secker, 1921);
The Puppet Show (Waltham St. Lawrence: Golden Cockerel, 1922; New York: Brentano's, 1923);
The Bazaar and Other Stories (London: Cape, 1924; New York: Knopf, 1924);
The Goat and Compasses (London: Cape, 1925); republished as *At the Sign of the Goat and Compasses* (New York: Harper, 1925);
Desert: A Legend (London: Cape, 1926; New York: Harper, 1926);
Lady Hester Stanhope (London: Howe, 1927; New York: Viking, 1928);
Saint Hercules, and Other Stories (London: Fleuron, 1927);
Sir Pompey and Madame Juno and Other Tales (London: Cape, 1927; Boston & New York: Houghton Mifflin, 1927);
The Stepson (London: Cape, 1927); republished as *The Water Is Wide* (New York: Harper, 1927);
Laughing, Being One of a Series of Essays Edited by J. B. Priestley and Entitled: These Diversions (London: Jarrolds, 1928; New York: Harper, 1928);
Saint Christopher's Day (London: Gollancz, 1928); republished as *All in a Day* (New York: Harper, 1929);
Portrait of the Misses Harlowe (London: Mathews & Marrot, 1928);
The Bird-Catcher, and Other Poems (London: Secker, 1929);
The Sleeping Fury (London: Gollancz, 1929; New York: Harcourt, Brace, 1929);

Martin Donisthorpe Armstrong

The Fiery Dive and Other Stories (London: Gollancz, 1929; New York: Harcourt, Brace, 1930);
Adrian Glynde (London: Gollancz, 1930); republished as *Blind Man's Mark* (New York: Harcourt, Brace, 1931);

Collected Poems (London: Secker, 1931);
The Romantic Adventures of Mr. Darby and of Sarah His Wife (London: Gollancz, 1931; New York: Harcourt, Brace, 1932);
The Paintbox (London: Black, 1931);
Lover's Leap: A Story in Three Voices (London: Gollancz, 1932; New York: Harcourt, Brace, 1933);
The Foster-Mother (London: Gollancz, 1933; New York: Harcourt, Brace, 1934);
54 Conceits: A Collection of Epigrams and Epitaphs Serious and Comic (London: Secker, 1933);
General Buntop's Miracle, and Other Stories (London: Gollancz, 1934; New York: Harcourt, Brace, 1934);
Venus over Lannery (London: Gollancz, 1936; New York: Harcourt, Brace, 1936);
A Case of Conscience and Other Tales (London: Gollancz, 1937);
Spanish Circus (London: Collins, 1937);
The Snake in the Grass (London: Gollancz, 1938);
Victorian Peep-Show (London: Joseph, 1938);
Birds of Passage (London: Friends' Peace Committee, 1938);
What Is Happiness?, by Armstrong, Gerald Bullett, Havelock Ellis, John Hilton, Storm Jameson, Eric Linklater, J. B. Priestley, V. S. Pritchett, Bertrand Russell, and Hugh Walpole (London: John Lane, 1938; New York: Kinsey, 1939);
Simplicity Jones and Other Stories (London: Collins, 1940);
The Butterfly (London: Collins, 1941);
Chichester Concert (An Ode) (Cambridge: Cambridge University Press, 1944);
Said the Cat to the Dog (London: Methuen, 1945);
Said the Dog to the Cat (London: Hodder & Stoughton, 1948);
George Burrow (London: Barker, 1950; Denver: Swallow, 1950);
Selected Stories (London: Cape, 1951).

OTHER: *Jeremy Taylor: A Selection from His Works*, compiled by Armstrong (Waltham St. Lawrence: Golden Cockerel, 1923);
Don Pedro Antonio Alarcón, *The Three-Cornered Hat*, translated by Armstrong (London: Howe, 1927; New York: Simon & Schuster, 1928);
The Major Pleasures of Life, edited by Armstrong (London: Gollancz, 1934);
The Essential Mary Webb, edited by Armstrong (London: Cape, 1949).

Martin Donisthorpe Armstrong, a writer of some renown in England for nearly three decades, published widely in a variety of forms: poetry, novels, short stories, children's fiction, literary criticism, and radio scripts. Although he devoted much of the early part of his career to poetry, playing a central role in the Georgian poetry movement in the 1920s, Armstrong turned to fiction in 1925. His dozen novels, his most substantial accomplishment as an artist, are written in the Edwardian tradition of John Galsworthy and Arnold Bennett and portray the upper-middle-class society into which Armstrong was born. These characters often reflect the class values that Armstrong espoused: respect for justice and tradition, love of the countryside, and concern for harmonious relationships between the sexes. At the same time Armstrong's novels assault the upper-class values that he deplored: snobbery, materialism, and indifference. These conflicting elements forge a kind of novel of manners in which Armstrong's characters search a troubled world for love and justice, finding neither or else succeeding only after a long and difficult struggle. Armstrong's novels provide a critique of Edwardian values through the creation of an intriguing set of characters.

Born on 2 October 1882 near Newcastle-on-Tyne into an upper-middle-class family, Armstrong experienced a delightful childhood that he later recounted in his autobiographical volume, *Victorian Peep-Show* (1938). The oldest son of Charles Armstrong, an architect, and Edith Lucy Donisthorpe Armstrong, he was related to William Wordsworth through his maternal grandmother, a cousin of the poet. Although he was always interested in literature and music, Armstrong graduated from Pembroke College, Cambridge, with a B.A. in mechanical science. He worked for two years in an architect's office before going to Italy for a year to study pre-Renaissance and Renaissance Italian art. In Florence in April 1911 he met Conrad Aiken, who was then a Harvard undergraduate. They toured Italy together, embarking on a friendship that would span nearly two decades. Although they would often reside on different continents, they would act as both editors of and agents for each other's work, with Armstrong offering Aiken's poetry to his English contacts and Aiken showing Armstrong's pieces to American editors.

Armstrong's career as a poet began with his first book, *Exodus, and Other Poems* (1912). In late 1914 he enlisted as a private in the Artists' Rifles; he obtained a commission in 1915 in the Eighth Middlesex Regiment, and in 1917 he was sent to the French front. Following the Armistice, Armstrong worked for a year in the Ministry of Pensions, resigning to pursue freelance journalism and other lit-

 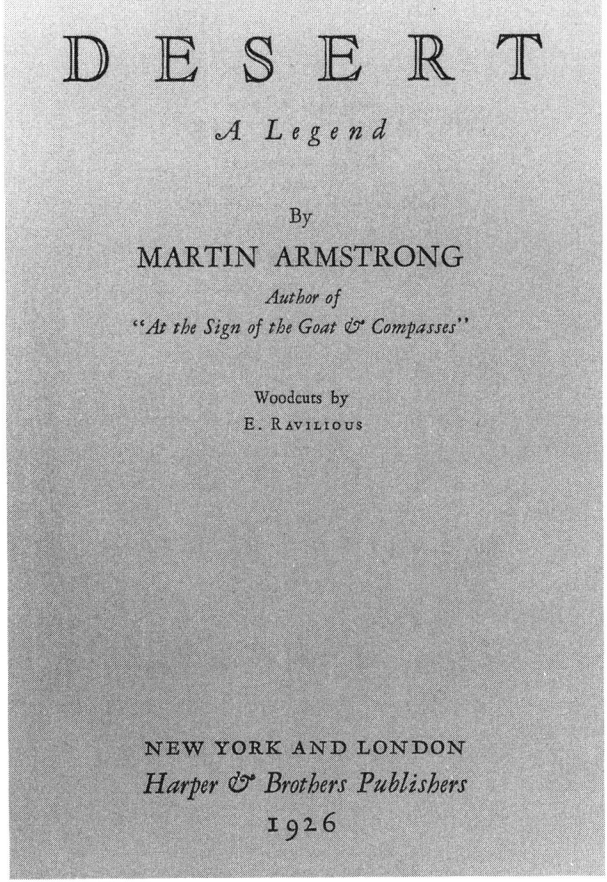

Frontispiece and title page for the U.S. edition of a 1926 novel about a hermit in ancient Egypt

erary work. During the 1920s he published often in British periodicals, including the *London Mercury, The Bookman,* and *The Spectator,* of which he was an associate editor from 1922 to 1924.

After two more volumes of poetry and two collections of stories, Armstrong published his first novel, *The Goat and Compasses* (published in the United States as *At the Sign of the Goat and Compasses*), in 1925. The Goat and Compasses is a pub in the seaside village of Crome, and the novel explores the lives of three couples who patronize it. George Prentice and Rose Jorden consummate their relationship only after Prentice migrates to Canada as a laborer and returns years later as a wealthy industrialist; in the meantime Rose endures a desolate first marriage. Rose's older sister, Bella, a barmaid at The Goat and Compasses, falls in love with a wealthy London artist, Walter Westway, who periodically visits the country to escape the rigors of city life; he initially responds to her with aloofness and snobbery. Finally, the young lovers Philip Gregory and Sally Dunk have to leave town after their affair results in the accidental death of Dan Hawney, Philip's rival for Sally's affections. Another "couple" in the novel consists of Susan Furly, an eccentric who sells magazine subscriptions door to door, and a dead sailor with whose grave she becomes obsessed and with whom she begins to imagine a romantic life. As the novel closes, Susan is committed to the Home for Feebleminded Gentlewomen.

In his next novel, *Desert: A Legend* (1926), loosely based on tales from Palladius's *Histories of the Fathers,* Armstrong shifts the setting from twentieth-century England to ancient Egypt. Malchus leaves his debauched existence and the faithless Helena behind in Alexandria to follow a religious hermit, Serapion, across the desert in search of spiritual salvation. Although reluctant at first, Serapion agrees to tutor Malchus in the monastic life of the desert and aids him in the construction of his own hermitage. There Malchus comes to terms with his earthly demons and fleshly desires. Returning to Alexandria, he arrives in Helena's chamber to discover his former paramour riddled with leprosy. The novel closes with the words: "So Malchus found his cure."

Title page for a 1927 novel about a woman's passion for her stepson

R. L. Mégroz says of Kate Patten, the heroine of Armstrong's next novel, *The Stepson* (1927; published in the United States as *The Water Is Wide*, 1927): "None of the women in Armstrong's fiction has received such careful treatment." The daughter of a widowed schoolmaster, Kate escapes her monotonous life with her unsympathetic father when she marries a wealthy elderly farmer, Ben Humphrey. Unaccustomed to her new role, Kate implores the housekeeper, Mrs. Jobson, to allow her to help with the chores: "I don't like to interfere, you see, even though I may be the mistress; but I have eyes enough to see that you do the work of six yourself. Why shouldn't I do some of your work?" After Kate discovers that her husband has kept another servant as his mistress, her stepson, David, who is about the same age as Kate, visits the farm. She develops a passion for him but soon learns that he is courting a woman from another village. In despair, Kate drowns herself in a nearby river: "The small rippling of its surface made by Kate's brief sojourn had spent itself and became as if it had never been."

While completing his fourth novel, *Saint Christopher's Day* (1928; published in the United States as *All in a Day*, 1929), Armstrong announced his engagement to Jessie McDonald Aiken, the wife of his old friend Conrad Aiken, who had left her in 1926 for another woman. Aiken felt betrayed by Armstrong, and his bitterness was only intensified when *Saint Christopher's Day* became a success. In a letter of 7 December 1928 to his friend Robert N. Linscott, Aiken wrote: "My husband in law keeps discreetly out of my way, and out of London. His book is making pots of money, and he's got himself a house in the country, which he's fixing up and furnishing for the family. I am arranging to have it bombed." Despite Aiken's last-minute overtures for a reconciliation, Armstrong married Jessie in 1930; they would have one son.

Although *Saint Christopher's Day* was a financial success for Armstrong, it remains one of his least effective prose efforts despite its many instances of rich description and detail—features that are occasionally lacking in his earlier work. As John Freeman notes, in *Saint Christopher's Day* "the passages you turn back to are not those of emotional conflict but, for example, those describing the fish department at Harrods." The reviewer for the *Times Literary Supplement* (30 September 1928) said that the work "has no wings and no vision." Armstrong attempts to capture the events of a single day—Christopher Brade's birthday—in the loveless marriage of Christopher and Rosamund Brade. As they carry out their mundane tasks—Christopher is at his office, and Rosamund is preparing for a dinner party that evening—the Brades reflect on their hatred for each other. As the novel comes to a close, Christopher cravenly escapes from his marriage by checking into a London hotel:

> Then he switched out the light, and as he got into bed Big Ben began to strike midnight. One by one, with an infinite leisure, the brazen notes followed one another into the hollow of night, now loud, now soft, as the night breeze ebbed or flowed. Christopher stretched himself luxuriously in the cold sheets. His birthday was over. The first day of his new life had already begun.

In *The Sleeping Fury* (1929) Armstrong maintains the stylistic quality of *Saint Christopher's Day* while returning to the issues of class values that permeate his early work. The novel follows Charlotte Hadlow from her childhood with her overbearing, socially ambitious mother, Lady Emily Hadlow, through her passionless marriage to the often distant yet awkwardly generous Lord Alfred Mardale.

When Charlotte tells her husband that she is in love with Maurice Wainwright, a figure from her past, and that she intends to join Wainwright on his impending voyage to Egypt, Lord Mardale's response displays the cool aloofness of his class: "It was like you to come and tell me at once; I shall always remember that." Charlotte's plans fall through, and the disgrace of a divorce is averted; but Lord Mardale is again confronted with social catastrophe when Eric Brand, the fiancé of the Mardales' daughter, Sylvia, suddenly learns that he is illegitimate. Lord Mardale's response is gentle but unyielding as he explains to Brand why the marriage cannot take place: "Don't imagine, Eric, that we have changed towards you. We haven't. But, if I were to consent to your marrying Sylvia, I should be countenancing the breaking of God's law, even though you are quite blameless. It would be contrary to my faith, Eric, and my conception of what is right, and for that reason I believe it would be bad for Sylvia." By presenting these reactions to social taboos of the Edwardian era, Armstrong underscores the institutionalized snobbery of the age.

In his 1930 novel, *Adrian Glynde* (published in the United States as *Blind Man's Mark*, 1931), Armstrong offers one of his most powerful character portraits, as well as one of his strongest indictments of class values in British society. The novel begins with Adrian, age thirteen, living with relatives in the English countryside while his socialite mother, Minnie, vacations in India. Adrian takes up the piano at his grandfather's bidding and quickly shows promise as a composer. Armstrong's descriptions of Adrian's musical development under his grandfather's tutelage are particularly effective; Mégroz notes that "few novelists write so well about music as Armstrong." The tenor of the novel changes dramatically when Adrian is removed from the idyllic countryside and plunged into the "vast, hostile strangeness" of Charminster, a boys' preparatory school. Adrian leaves Charminster to follow Ronny, an upperclassman he admired at school, to London, where he rents a room in the same boardinghouse. Around the same time, Adrian meets Lucy, who shares his love of classical music. When Ronny and Lucy begin to drift toward a romantic relationship, the confused and frustrated Adrian attempts suicide. The novel closes with the troubled young prodigy contemplating his barren future.

The condemnation of the class system in *Adrian Glynde* is surpassed in intensity only in Armstrong's 1931 masterpiece, *The Romantic Adventures of Mr. Darby and of Sarah His Wife*, the longest and most popular of his works. Although the novel has been misread as a conventional narrative—Mégroz calls it

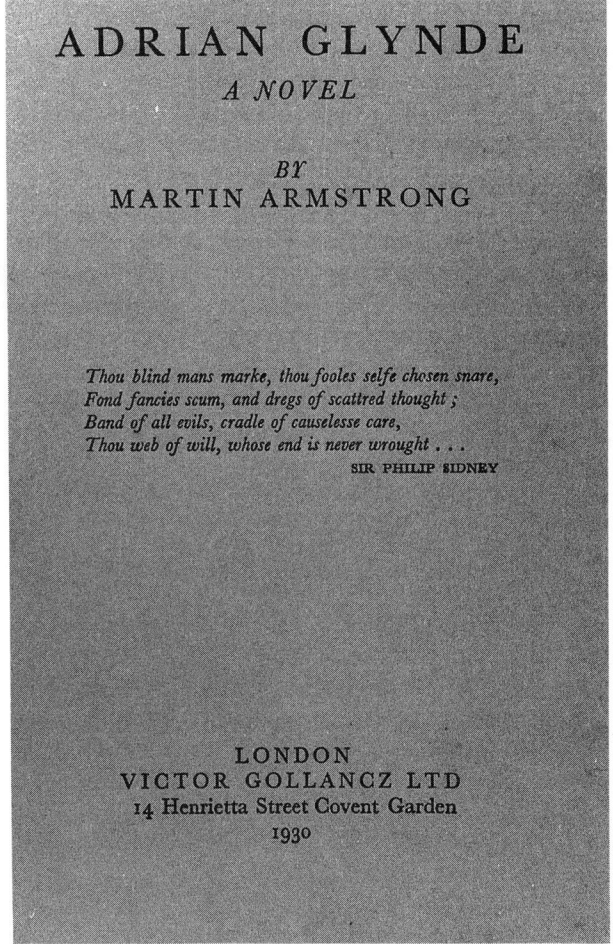

Title page for a novel about a young composer

a work of "humorous realism"—it is actually a devastating satire of the misplaced values of the upper class. In Newchester-on-Dole (based on Armstrong's boyhood home, Newcastle-on-Tyne), the routine middle-class lives of Jim and Sarah Darby are drastically altered when Jim inherits a fortune from his uncle, an Australian investor. The Darbys immediately begin to assume the trappings of the upper class. They move to London, where Jim is victimized by greedy artists and art brokers as he assembles the Darby Art Collection and Sarah involves herself in the pet charity of society women, the Hospital Co-ordination Society. At the Darbys' lavish London hotel Sarah reveals her ingrained middle-class impulses when she asks the cleaning staff to allow her to change the linens in several of the suites. She finally tells Jim that she must return to Newchester-on-Dole: "London's no place for people like us, except just for a bit of a holiday." After a disastrous expedition to Africa culminates in the tragicomic death of Jim's faithful manservant, Punnett, the Darbys divest themselves of their wealth in an effort to return to their middle-class status.

Armstrong's next novel, *Lover's Leap: A Story in Three Voices* (1932), has three first-person narrators. Philip Marling, an artist, describes his pursuit of a young pianist, Rose Bentley, at a party, at her family's country retreat, and at his studio. Interspersed throughout his narration are Rose's comments on Philip's overtures. They become engaged, but their relationship deteriorates, and they eventually part. The third voice in the narrative is that of Meriel Filmer, an actress who has escaped her husband and country life by coming to London. She attaches herself to Philip after his breakup with Rose, and she provides many of the novel's finest comic, as well as tragic, moments as she experiences the intoxicating liberation of her flight from responsibility.

The Foster-Mother (1933) explores a dysfunctional family in much the same manner as *The Stepson* and *Adrian Glynde*. In Deborah Murdle, a forlorn and desperate figure who moves from housekeeper to mistress of a country manor when she marries its owner, the former husband of her late sister, Armstrong creates one of his most complex characters. Like some of her fictional forebears in Armstrong's canon, Deborah is unable to adapt to the changes that class elevation brings. She finds her elevated status appealing but also feels burdened by the responsibilities that accompany her new role—responsibilities that are increased when she has to take charge of her late sister's two orphaned children. Deborah deceives herself into believing that she governs the manor, which is actually controlled by the servants and her husband's children by his first wife. Deborah's psyche crumbles under the pressures of her situation, and as the novel closes, she dies from a massive aneurysm while the housekeeper intentionally delays calling a doctor.

Following the publication in 1941 of the poorly received *The Butterfly,* about yet another heroine who clashes with English class norms, Armstrong abandoned the novel and turned to writing radio scripts and children's books. Two of the latter, *Said the Cat to the Dog* (1945) and its sequel, *Said the Dog to the Cat* (1948), earned him far more money than had any of his novels, volumes of poetry, or collections of short stories. In 1944 Armstrong began writing a weekly column for the BBC journal *The Listener* that ran for nearly two decades. Armstrong died on 24 February 1974.

In an unpublished 1991 letter Armstrong's nephew Michael Armstrong recalls a visit his uncle paid during the 1960s to Michael's home on the island of Jersey. Martin Armstrong good-naturedly signed several copies of his novels that Michael had collected: "I think he was flattered that I had all of his books and had read most of them." In fact, although he enjoyed considerable critical and commercial success during his career, Armstrong's presence as a literary figure has all but vanished in recent years. Nevertheless, his novels can still be appreciated as erudite, carefully constructed fictional studies of the sociology of the Edwardian era.

Bibliography:
Kenneth Womack, "Martin Donisthorpe Armstrong (1882-1974): A Primary and Secondary Bibliography," *Bulletin of Bibliography,* 51, no. 1 (1994): 69-73.

Biography:
Kenneth Womack, "Martin Donisthorpe Armstrong: A Life in Letters," *Library Chronicle of the University of Texas at Austin,* 23, no. 1 (1993): 99-117.

References:
John Freeman, "Martin Armstrong," *Bookman,* 76 (1929): 286-288;

Joseph Killorin, ed., *Selected Letters of Conrad Aiken* (New Haven: Yale University Press, 1978), p. 149;

R. L. Mégroz, "Martin Armstrong," in his *Five Novelist Poets of Today* (London: Joiner & Steele, 1933; Freeport, N.Y.: Books for Libraries Press, 1969), pp. 110-148;

Timothy Rogers, ed., *Georgian Poetry, 1911-1922: The Critical Heritage* (London: Routledge & Kegan Paul, 1977), pp. 268-280;

Kenneth Womack, "A Calendar of the Letters of Martin Donisthorpe Armstrong (1882-1974)," *Bulletin of Bibliography,* 54, no. 4 (1997): 303-316;

Womack, "Unmasking Another Villain in Conrad Aiken's Autobiographical Dream," *Biography: An Interdisciplinary Quarterly,* 19, no. 2 (1996): 137-157.

Papers:
Collections of Martin Donisthorpe Armstrong's papers are at the Harry Ransom Humanities Research Center at the University of Texas, Austin; the Center for Textual and Bibliographical Studies at Texas A&M University; and the Huntington Library, San Marino, California.

Elizabeth von Arnim
(Countess Mary Annette Beauchamp Russell)
(31 August 1866 – 9 February 1941)

Katherine E. Ayer
University of Southern California

BOOKS: *Elizabeth and Her German Garden,* anonymous (London & New York: Macmillan, 1898);

The Solitary Summer, as the author of *Elizabeth and Her German Garden* (New York & London: Macmillan, 1899);

The April Baby's Book of Tunes, with the Story of How They Came to be Written, as the author of *Elizabeth and Her German Garden* (New York & London: Macmillan, 1900);

The Benefactress, as the author of *Elizabeth and Her German Garden* (London & New York: Macmillan, 1901);

The Adventures of Elizabeth in Rügen, as the author of *Elizabeth and Her German Garden* (New York & London: Macmillan, 1904);

The Princess Priscilla's Fortnight, as the author of *Elizabeth and Her German Garden* (London: Smith, Elder, 1905; New York: Scribners, 1905);

Fräulein Schmidt and Mr. Anstruther: Being the Letters of an Independent Woman, as the author of *Elizabeth and Her German Garden* (London: Macmillan, 1907; New York: Scribners, 1907);

The Caravaners, as the author of *Elizabeth and Her German Garden* (London: Smith, Elder, 1909; New York: Doubleday, Page, 1909);

The Pastor's Wife, as the author of *Elizabeth and Her German Garden* (London: Smith, Elder, 1914; Garden City, N.Y.: Doubleday, Page, 1914);

Christine, as Alice Cholmondeley (London: Macmillan, 1917; New York: Macmillan, 1917);

Christopher and Columbus, as the author of *Elizabeth and Her German Garden* (London: Macmillan, 1919; Garden City, N.Y.: Doubleday, Page, 1919);

In the Mountains, anonymous (London: Macmillan, 1920; Garden City, N.Y.: Doubleday, Page, 1920);

Vera, as the author of *Elizabeth and Her German Garden* (London: Macmillan, 1921; Garden City, N.Y. & Toronto: Doubleday, Page, 1921);

Elizabeth von Arnim

The Enchanted April, as the author of *Elizabeth and Her German Garden* (London: Macmillan, 1922; Garden City, N.Y.: Doubleday, Page, 1923);

Love, as the author of *Elizabeth and Her German Garden* (London: Macmillan, 1925); as Elizabeth (Garden City, N.Y.: Doubleday, Page, 1925);

Introduction to Sally, as the author of *Elizabeth and Her German Garden* (London: Macmillan, 1926); as Elizabeth (Garden City, N.Y.: Doubleday, Page, 1926);

Expiation, as the author of *Elizabeth and Her German Garden* (London: Macmillan, 1929); as Elizabeth (Garden City, N.Y.: Doubleday, Doran, 1929);

Arnim's first husband, Count Henning August von Arnim-Schlagenthin, with their son, Henning Bernd, born in 1902

Father, as the author of *Elizabeth and Her German Garden* (London: Macmillan, 1931); as Elizabeth (Garden City, N.Y.: Doubleday, Doran, 1931);

The Jasmine Farm, as the author of *Elizabeth and Her German Garden* (London & Toronto: Heinemann, 1934); as Elizabeth (Garden City, N.Y.: Doubleday, Doran, 1934);

All the Dogs of My Life, as Elizabeth (London & Toronto: Heinemann, 1936; Garden City, N.Y.: Doubleday, Doran, 1936);

Mr. Skeffington, as the author of *Elizabeth and Her German Garden* (London: Heinemann, 1940); as Elizabeth (New York: Doubleday, Doran, 1940).

Collections and Editions: *One Thing in Common: A Collection of Three Novels by Elizabeth* (New York: Doubleday, Doran, 1941)—comprises *Vera, The Enchanted April,* and *Love.*

Fräulein Schmidt and Mr. Anstruther: Being the Letters of an Independent Woman, as the author of *Elizabeth and Her German Garden* (London: Virago, 1983);

Vera (London: Virago, 1983);

Elizabeth and Her German Garden, introduction by Elizabeth Jane Howard (London: Virago, 1985);

The Enchanted April, introduction by Terence de Vere White (London: Virago, 1986);

The Pastor's Wife, afterword by Lisa St. Aubin (London: Virago, 1987);

Love, introduction by Terence de Vere White (London: Virago, 1988);

The Caravaners, introduction by Kate Saunders (London: Virago, 1989);

The Adventures of Elizabeth in Rügen, introduction by Penelope Mortimer (London: Virago, 1990);

The Pastor's Wife, edited by Deborah Singmaster (London: Dent, 1998);

The Solitary Summer (London: Virago, 1993);

Mr. Skeffington (London: Virago, 1993);

Christopher and Columbus (London: Virago, 1994);

All the Dogs of My Life (London: Virago, 1995).

PLAY PRODUCTION: *Priscilla Runs Away,* London, Haymarket Theatre, 28 June 1910.

The Australian-born English novelist Elizabeth von Arnim published seventeen widely read and critically acclaimed novels between 1901 and her death in 1941. The republication since 1983 of many of her works by the feminist Virago Press and the release in 1991 of a motion-picture version of her 1922 novel *The Enchanted April* have led to a renewed interest in Arnim. In her novels female protagonists struggle to break away from oppressive family situations and restrictive social mores; the wit and sophistication with which she presents this drive for emancipation, along with her understanding of the conditions that often make such an escape both economically infeasible and psychologically improbable, inform her entire literary production.

Elizabeth von Arnim was born Mary Annette Beauchamp in Sydney on 31 August 1866, the youngest of the six children of Henry Herron Beauchamp and Elizabeth Lassetter Beauchamp. Her father, an English merchant who had made his career in Australia, returned to England with his family when "May," as she was called, was three years old. Apart from two years during which the family lived in Lausanne, Switzerland, Beauchamp grew up in London. She was educated by governesses; at girls' schools, where she took prizes in history; and at the Royal College of Music, where she studied the organ. In 1889, during a vacation in Italy with her parents, she met a widowed German count, Henning August von Arnim-Schlagenthin, who was fifteen years her senior. They were married on 21 February 1891 and settled in Berlin. In 1896 they moved to the Arnim family estate of Nassenheide in the Mark Brandenburg. They had five children: Elizabeth in 1891, Eva in 1892, Beatrix in 1893, Felicitas in 1899, and Henning Bernd in 1902. In her letters and semi-autobiographical writings Arnim's husband appears as "The Man of Wrath" and her first three children as the "April baby," the "May baby," and the "June baby," respectively.

Arnim initially began writing as a way of escaping from the burdens of managing a large household in a strange country as well as from the demands of her husband that she produce a son. Her first published work was a nonfiction account of life in Nassenheide, *Elizabeth and Her German Garden* (1898). In this first work Arnim combines an enthusiastic account of her garden and the German landscape with trenchant comments on family life and on the restrictive mores of Wilhelmine Germany. The book was an immediate popular and critical success, although it was not immune to criticism for its sentimentality. The work was translated into German, as were many of her novels.

Arnim followed *Elizabeth and Her German Garden* with *The Solitary Summer* (1899), which expands its scope to include a description of the living conditions of the poor in a nearby village and her frustrating attempts to alleviate those conditions. In these semi-autobiographical writings Arnim creates a narrative persona that, while undeniably patrician, is not clearly identifiable as either English or German and is thus endowed with a vantage point on both cultures. Since "Elizabeth" remained anonymous, her nationality and even her gender were points of debate among reviewers of the works. Arnim also completed a book of children's verse, *The April Baby's Book of Tunes, with the Story of How They Came to be Written* (1900), which was illustrated by Kate Greenaway. Despite her geographic isolation and her anonymity, Arnim began to develop a circle of literary acquaintances during this period; Hugh Walpole and E. M. Forster came to Nassenheide as tutors for Arnim's children.

The rigid social structure and Arnim's charitable activities provided material for her first novel proper, *The Benefactress* (1901). A young Englishwoman, Anna Estcourt, inherits an estate in rural northern Germany and naively attempts to establish a residence for impoverished noblewomen. The plan fails when her guests take advantage of their hostess and battle among themselves to establish social rank. Despite the well-meaning advice of her suitor, a nearby landowner, Anna alienates her guests, her employees, and the villagers. The aristocracy and the aspiring bourgeoisie are both subjected to criticism; the one truly positive figure in the novel is an elderly widowed princess who assumes a new identity as a servant rather than suffer in impoverished gentility. In this work, as in all of her novels set in Germany, Arnim creates an interlocking framework of conflicts that result from dif-

Arnim's second husband, John Francis Stanley, second Earl Russell

ferences in nationality, gender, and class. Certain stock situations produced by these conflicts recur in Arnim's later novels. For instance, the protagonist of *The Benefactress* shocks her German neighbors by treating the village pastor as an equal; Arnim depicts such behavior as normal in English society but unacceptable to the German upper classes. Similar scenes would appear in *The Caravaners* (1909) and *The Pastor's Wife* (1914).

The Adventures of Elizabeth in Rügen (1904) apparently reintroduces the first-person narrator of *Elizabeth and Her German Garden* and *The Solitary Summer*, who recounts her vacation with her maid on the Baltic island of Rügen. This narrator, however, is more clearly fictional than the one in the previous works: not only does she identify herself as German, but even at the conclusion of the novel she remains oblivious to the damage she has done by meddling in the affairs of her cousin, a suffragette married to an overbearing professor of religion. In *The Princess Priscilla's Fortnight* (1905) a German princess flees a dynastic marriage by escaping to an English country village, where her naive attempts at charity are misconstrued by the suspicious locals. The epistolary novel *Fräulein Schmidt and Mr. Anstruther: Being the Letters of an Independent Woman* (1907) comprises a series of letters from a German professor's daughter

Dust jacket for the U.S. edition of Arnim's final novel

to an English student who has jilted her; he finally asks to be allowed to come back to her, but she refuses. In researching this novel Arnim assumed the guise of an English governess, Miss Armstrong, and took a position in a professor's household in Jena. *The Caravaners* is about a German couple vacationing in England; the chauvinistic and bigoted narrator, Baron Otto von Ottringe, preoccupied with his wife's increasing independence, never notices the dislike the other vacationers develop for him. His arrogance ultimately forces the party to disband. The review of the novel in *The Spectator* (20 November 1909), while generally favorable, faulted the book for aggravating, "by its myriad pinpricks, . . . the friction between the two nations."

In 1908 financial difficulties forced Arnim and her husband to sell Nassenheide and move to England. They settled into a Georgian house, Blue Hayes, at Broadclyst, near Exeter in Devon. Henning August von Arnim-Schlagenthin died in 1910, and Arnim moved to a chalet overlooking the Rhône valley in Sierre, Switzerland. There she became acquainted with H. G. Wells, with whom she had a love affair, and reestablished contact with her cousin, the author Katherine Mansfield, who lived nearby until her death in 1923. Despite marked differences in literary style, the cousins admired each other's work.

In Arnim's 1914 novel *The Pastor's Wife* Ingeborg, the daughter of an English bishop, rashly marries a German pastor and moves with him to rural Prussia. Unable to adapt to her surroundings, to her distant and self-absorbed husband, or to her stolid and unimaginative children, she flees to Italy with an artist admirer, only to return abruptly to her husband when she realizes that the artist aims to seduce her. The novel's carefully designed structure, revolving around two misguided escapes; the representation of Ingeborg's increasing awareness of her isolation; and a use of symbolism not evident in the earlier novels make this one of Arnim's best works. In theme and in setting the novel is similar to the novel *Effi Briest* (1895), by the German realist author Theodor Fontane; since Arnim spoke and wrote fluent German and was familiar with the German literary tradition, a possible connection between the two works deserves further study. While *The Pastor's Wife* was well received, critics noted that the novel was more somber than her previous works; *The Independent* (23 November 1914) found it to be "a heavy chronicle of the bleak existence of an English girl and her uncouth German husband."

In 1916 Arnim married John Francis Stanley, second Earl Russell, the brother of the philosopher Bertrand Russell, and moved to London with him; the marriage was brief and unhappy because of Russell's unfaithfulness. Arnim's final novel set in Germany, *Christine* (1917), an epistolary work published under the pseudonym Alice Cholmondeley, is loosely based on the situation of Arnim's daughter, Felicitas, who died of pneumonia while at school in Germany in 1916. It is the most strongly anti-German of her books and, in part because of an awkward explanatory note in which the letters are presented as genuine, was not well received. Her next novel, *Christopher and Columbus* (1919), presents two half-German, half-English sisters who immigrate to America; it reflects impressions she had gained during her travels to the United States in 1916 and in 1918. Arnim and her husband were separated in 1919 but were never divorced; Arnim would be known as Countess Russell until her death. After the separation she returned to her chalet in Switzerland.

The theme of isolation and issues of national identity characterize *In the Mountains* (1920), a novel in the form of a diary that treats the experiences of three women during and immediately after World War I. Arnim's second marriage provided the material for her novel *Vera* (1921), the darkest of her

Claude Rains as Job and Bette Davis as Fanny in a scene from the 1944 movie version of Mr. Skeffington *(Warner Brothers)*

works, which explores the psychological manipulation of a hapless young woman by her emotionally domineering husband.

A vacation on the Italian Riviera in the summer of 1921 inspired Arnim's next novel, *The Enchanted April* (1922). Two mousy English wives, Mrs. Wilkins and Mrs. Arbuthnot, rent the medieval Italian castle San Salvatore for a month's vacation. To help with expenses they accept a young heiress, Louise, and an elderly dowager, Mrs. Fisher, into the party. The women are soon joined by the husbands and admirers from whom they were trying to escape. In this most cheerful of Arnim's later novels problems that would be intractable in her other works are resolved under the Italian sunshine: a stuffy husband becomes affectionate; the pompous dowager reveals an unexpected generosity of spirit; and the author of salacious historical romances and his disapproving, pious wife become reconciled. The novel's idyllic close reflects a longing for healing of the psychological scars left by World War I, which casts its shadow over the characters: Mrs. Wilkins and Mrs. Arbuthnot are initially mistaken for war widows; Caroline mourns a fallen lover; and Mrs. Fisher has retreated in her mind into an earlier age, when she was admired by Alfred Tennyson and Thomas Carlyle. The title underscores the utopian quality of the novel's resolution. Although it garnered mixed reviews, including one from Rebecca West, who opined in *The New Statesman* (2 December 1922) that Arnim had "lapsed back into the unplumbed seas of artificial femininity," *The Enchanted April* was an immediate and enduring popular success. It was a Book-of-the-Month Club choice in the United States and was adapted as a stage play in 1925 and as a motion picture in 1935.

Arnim's later novels continued to be novels of manners, focusing on power relations, often between fathers and grown daughters or between husbands and wives. Issues of class consciousness and of morality play an increasingly significant role in her later works. *Love* (1925) paints a subtle picture of a romance between an older woman and a younger man and is based on an incident in Arnim's own life. *Introduction to Sally* (1926) is a Pygmalion-like account of a husband's attempts to cultivate his working-class wife. In *Expiation* (1929) two recently widowed sisters ponder the nature of love. *Father* (1931) presents a young woman who tries to escape her domineering scholarly father. *The Jasmine Farm* (1934), the most satirical work of this period, treats a power struggle between an elderly aristocratic woman and her son's working-class mother-in-law. Arnim's autobiography, *All the Dogs of My Life* (1936), adopts a narrative device similar to that of *Elizabeth and Her German Garden:* while ostensibly discussing a pastime—here, her pet dogs—the author proffers reminiscences of her parents, her husbands, and her children.

Arnim moved to the United States in 1939 to be near her oldest daughter, who lived in Charleston, South Carolina. In her last novel, *Mr. Skeffington* (1940), the aging divorcée Fanny Skeffington, realizing that she is no longer regarded as a great beauty but as a pathetic older woman, returns to her former husband, whom she had divorced twenty-two years previously because of his philandering. Arnim presents this

Arnim at the Golden Eagle Hotel in Beaufort, South Carolina, in 1940

decision as the culmination of Fanny's development toward political awareness as well as toward self-knowledge. When she is reunited with Job Skeffington, a Jewish stockbroker who was ruined by the Great Depression and blinded during his imprisonment by the Nazis in Austria, Fanny is no longer the shallow woman who, as a minor character says, "for so many years had made the world a more beautiful place, simply by being in it." She now recognizes the importance of empathy, asking herself, "How could one endure consciousness, except by giving oneself up wholly and forever to helping, and comforting, and at last, at least, perhaps healing?" When she divorced her husband, she had felt not injury or outrage but relief that his behavior had granted her freedom. This emotional detachment is represented as a greater sin than the unfaithfulness of a husband who, in spite of his infidelities, still loved his wife. The metaphor of blindness structures the novel: preoccupied with her worries about how her former lovers view her deteriorating physical appearance, Fanny is blind to the increasingly threatening political situation. Her husband, though physically blinded, recognizes both the horrors of the emerging Third Reich and the worth of Fanny's commitment to him at the novel's close.

Mr. Skeffington met with a critical success unmatched since Arnim's earliest works. *The New York Times* (17 April 1940) recognized the political dimension of the novel: "at the last we are suddenly at grips with the special conditions of the world today." *Mr. Skeffington* represents a farewell to the Edwardian and post–World War I society that was celebrated and skewered in Arnim's previous novels. Arnim died in Charleston on 9 February 1941; three years later *Mr. Skeffington* was adapted as a motion picture, with Bette Davis and Claude Rains in the starring roles.

In 1993 the English director Mike Newell received an Academy Award nomination for his screenplay for the second motion-picture version of *The Enchanted April,* released in the United States in 1992. The movie introduced "Elizabeth" to an audience already appreciative of stories from the period, thanks to the motion-picture versions of two Forster novels, *A Room with a View* (1985) and *Howards End* (1992).

While Arnim wrote initially as a means of psychological escape, her novels increasingly brought her prestige as well as financial independence. Her works reflect a keen awareness of the contradictions and foibles of the middle and upper classes, and in this respect they stand in the tradition of the novels of John Galsworthy and Arnold Bennett. In her experimentation with narrative perspective, however, she adapts techniques more often associated with literary modernism. In her later novels dialogue assumes an increasing importance; although her works lack the subtlety of Elizabeth Bowen or Ivy Compton-Burnett, like these authors she frequently represents conversation as a means of control or treats thematically an inability or unwillingness to communicate. While she is not above resorting to formulaic plots, as in *The Princess Priscilla's Fortnight* or *Introduction to Sally,* her manipulation of point of view and her use of narrative irony largely overcome this fault. Her enthusiastic, sometimes cloyingly sentimental view of nature is balanced throughout her work by pessimism with regard to social relations; the pessimism, in turn, is offset by a witty prose style and an ironic distance from her protagonists. On the basis of these formal techniques, as well as on the grounds of her unique position between German and English literature, Arnim's work deserves further investigation.

Biographies:
Leslie De Charms, *Elizabeth of the German Garden: A Biography* (London: Heinemann, 1958);
Karen Usborne, *"Elizabeth": The Author of* Elizabeth and Her German Garden (London: Bodley Head, 1986).

Reference:
Sheila Haines, "'Angles had everywhere taken the place of curves': Elizabeth von Arnim and the German Garden," *Turn-of-the-Century Women,* 2, no. 2 (1985): 36–41.

J. D. Beresford
(7 March 1873 – 2 February 1947)

George M. Johnson
University College of the Cariboo

See also the Beresford entries in *DLB 162: British Short-Fiction Writers, 1915–1945* and *DLB 178: British Fantasy and Science-Fiction Writers Before World War I.*

BOOKS: *The Early History of Jacob Stahl* (London: Sidgwick & Jackson, 1911; Boston: Little, Brown, 1911; New York: Doran, 1911);

The Hampdenshire Wonder (London: Sidgwick & Jackson, 1911; London: Collins, 1911); republished as *The Wonder* (New York: Doran, 1917);

A Candidate for Truth (London: Sidgwick & Jackson, 1912; Boston: Little, Brown, 1912; New York: Doran, 1912);

Goslings (London: Heinemann, 1913); republished as *A World of Women* (New York: Macaulay, 1913);

The House in Demetrius Road (London: Heinemann, 1914; New York: Doran, 1914);

The Compleat Angler, A Duologue, by Beresford and Arthur Harvey-James (London: French, 1915);

H. G. Wells (London: Nisbet, 1915; New York: Holt, 1915);

The Invisible Event (London: Sidgwick & Jackson, 1915; New York: Doran, 1915);

The Mountains of the Moon (London & New York: Cassell, 1915);

Poems by Two Brothers, by Beresford and Richard Beresford (London: Macdonald, 1915);

These Lynnekers (London & New York: Cassell, 1916; New York: Doran, 1916);

Housemates (London & New York: Cassell, 1917; New York: Doran, 1917);

W. E. Ford: A Biography, by Beresford and Kenneth Richmond (London: Collins, 1917; New York: Doran, 1917);

Nineteen Impressions (London: Sidgwick & Jackson, 1918);

God's Counterpoint (London: Collins, 1918; New York: Doran, 1918);

J. D. Beresford

The Jervaise Comedy (London: Collins, 1919; New York: Macmillan, 1919);

An Imperfect Mother (London: Collins, 1920; New York: Macmillan, 1920);

Revolution: A Novel (London: Collins, 1921); republished as *Revolution: A Story of the Near Future in England* (New York & London: Putnam, 1921);

Signs and Wonders (Waltham St. Lawrence: Golden Cockerel Press, 1921; New York: Putnam, 1921);

The Prisoners of Hartling (London: Collins, 1922; New York: Macmillan, 1922);

Taken from Life, by Beresford and E. O. Hoppé (London: Collins, 1922);

The Imperturbable Duchess and Other Stories (London: Collins, 1923);

Love's Pilgrim (London: Collins, 1923; Indianapolis: Bobbs-Merrill, 1923);

Unity (London: Collins, 1924; Indianapolis: Bobbs-Merrill, 1924);

The Monkey Puzzle (London: Collins, 1925; Indianapolis: Bobbs-Merrill, 1925);

That Kind of Man (London: Collins, 1926); republished as *Almost Pagan* (Indianapolis: Bobbs-Merrill, 1926);

The Decoy (London: Collins, 1927);

The Tapestry (London: Collins, 1927; Indianapolis: Bobbs-Merrill, 1927);

The Instrument of Destiny: A Detective Story (London: Collins, 1928; Indianapolis: Bobbs-Merrill, 1928);

All or Nothing (London: Collins, 1928; Indianapolis: Bobbs-Merrill, 1928);

Writing Aloud (London: Collins, 1928);

The Meeting Place and Other Stories (London: Faber & Faber, 1929);

Real People (London: Collins, 1929);

Love's Illusion (London: Collins, 1930; New York: Dutton, 1930);

Seven, Bobsworth (London: Faber & Faber, 1930);

An Innocent Criminal (London: Collins, 1931; New York: Dutton, 1931);

The Old People (London: Collins, 1931; New York: Dutton, 1932);

The Middle Generation (London: Collins, 1932; New York: Dutton, 1933);

The Next Generation (London: Benn, 1932);

The Inheritor (London: Benn, 1933);

The Camberwell Miracle (London: Heinemann, 1933);

The Young People (London: Collins, 1933; New York: Dutton, 1934);

The Case for Faith-Healing (London: Allen & Unwin, 1934);

Peckover (London: Heinemann, 1934; New York: Dutton, 1935);

On a Huge Hill (London & Toronto: Heinemann, 1935);

Blackthorn Winter and Other Stories (London: Hutchinson, 1936);

The Faithful Lovers (London: Hutchinson, 1936; New York: Furman, 1937);

Cleo (London: Hutchinson, 1937);

Unfinished Road: A Novel (London: Hutchinson, 1938);

What I Believe, edited by R. Ellis Roberts, I Believe: A Series of Personal Statements, no. 1 (London: Heinemann, 1938);

Strange Rival (London: Hutchinson, 1939);

Snell's Folly (London: Hutchinson, 1939);

The Idea of God, edited by R. H. Ward, New Foundations, 1 (London: James Clarke, 1940);

Quiet Corner (London: Hutchinson, 1940);

"What Dreams May Come . . ." (London: Hutchinson, 1941);

A Common Enemy (London: Hutchinson, 1941);

The Benefactor (London: Hutchinson, 1943);

If This Were True— (London: Hutchinson, 1943);

The Long View (London: Hutchinson, 1943);

Men in the Same Boat, by Beresford and Esmé Wynne-Tyson (London: Hutchinson, 1943);

The Riddle of the Tower, by Beresford and Wynne-Tyson (London: Hutchinson, 1944);

The Prisoner (London: Hutchinson, 1946);

The Gift, by Beresford and Wynne-Tyson (London: Hutchinson, 1947).

PLAY PRODUCTIONS: *The Compleat Angler: A Duologue,* by Beresford and Arthur Harvey-James, Manchester, Hippodrome, 29 June 1914;

Howard and Son, by Beresford and Kenneth Richmond, London, London Coliseum, 14 August 1916.

OTHER: *The Perfect Machine,* by Beresford and Arthur Harvey-James, *English Review,* 26 (May 1918): 393–408;

"The Psychical Researcher's Tale: The Sceptical Poltergeist," in *The New Decameron,* volume 3 (Oxford: Blackwell, 1922);

"My Religion," in *My Religion: Essays by H. Walpole, R. West, J. D. Beresford, and Others* (New York: Appleton, 1926), pp. 55–61;

"Experiment in the Novel," in *Tradition and Experiment in Present-Day Literature: Addresses Delivered to the City Literary Institute by R. H Mottram, J. D. Beresford, and Others* (London: Oxford University Press, 1929), pp. 25–53;

"Human Relations," in *The Root of the Matter,* edited by H. R. L. Sheppard (London: Cassell, 1937), pp. 4–47.

SELECTED PERIODICAL PUBLICATIONS—UNCOLLECTED:

FICTION

"The Paper-Seller," *Academy* (25 January 1902): 99;

"A 'Thing Seen,'" *Academy* (31 May 1902): 563;

"A Test of Friendship," *Westminster Gazette,* 10 June 1908, p. 2;

"Miranda. VI. On Idealism," *Westminster Gazette,* 11 July, 1908, p. 2;

"Vision," *Westminster Gazette,* 15 June 1912, p. 2;

"Management," *Westminster Gazette,* 10 May 1913, p. 2;

"Pipes. A Study in British Endurance," *Westminster Gazette,* 16 February 1918, pp. 1-2;

"The Old Champion," *Manchester Guardian,* 2 October 1927, p. 20;

"The Expert," *Manchester Guardian,* 3 November 1927, p. 18;

"The Hairdresser," *Manchester Guardian,* 15 November 1927, p. 22;

"An American in Paradise," *Manchester Guardian,* 22 November 1927, p. 20;

"Master and Servant," *Manchester Guardian,* 29 November 1927, p. 20;

"Undesirable Knowledge," *Manchester Guardian,* 12 December 1927, p. 16;

"The Peasant," *Manchester Guardian,* 27 January 1928, p. 20;

"The Pricked Balloon," *Manchester Guardian,* 26 March 1928, p. 16;

"J's Education," *Manchester Guardian,* 12 April 1928, p. 16;

"The Parasite," *Manchester Guardian,* 25 June 1928, p. 18;

"Artificial Sunlight," *Manchester Guardian,* 4 July 1928, p. 30;

"Betterment," *Manchester Guardian,* 12 March 1930, p. 22;

"High Time," *Manchester Guardian,* 7 March 1934, p. 18;

"The Way Home," *Manchester Guardian,* 11 August 1936, p. 18;

"Washing-Up," *Manchester Guardian,* 9 November 1936, p. 16;

"Parachutist," by Beresford and Esmé Wynne-Tyson, *Manchester Guardian,* 23 July 1940, p. 10;

"The Parting," by Beresford and Wynne-Tyson, *Manchester Guardian,* 20 December 1940, p. 10;

"The Maginot Line," *Christian Science Monitor,* 8 May 1941, p. 22;

"The Worrit," by Beresford and Wynne-Tyson, *Manchester Guardian,* 11 June 1941, p. 4;

"Here and There," by Beresford and Wynne-Tyson, *Manchester Guardian,* 13 October 1941, p. 4;

"From a Height," *Christian Science Monitor,* 25 February 1942, p. 20;

"The Swollen-Headed Ghost," by Beresford and Wynne-Tyson, *Manchester Guardian,* 27 November 1942, p. 4;

"Waters of Lethe," by Beresford and Wynne-Tyson, *Manchester Guardian,* 4 March 1943, p. 4;

"Top of the Hill," by Beresford and Wynne-Tyson, *Manchester Guardian,* 11 June 1943, p. 4;

"This Desirable Property," by Beresford and Wynne-Tyson, *Manchester Guardian,* 8 March 1944, p. 4;

"Other Corners," by Beresford and Wynne-Tyson, *Woman's Magazine* (September 1945): 17-19.

NONFICTION

"The Reading Competition," *Punch* (4 March 1908): 1171;

"On Ghosts," *Times* (London), 2 January 1914, p. 3b;

"Mr. Maartens and the Realists," *Westminster Gazette,* 30 May 1914, p. 2;

"The 'Maltruist,'" *Westminster Gazette,* 6 January 1917, pp. 1-2;

"Average Man," *Westminster Gazette,* 26 July 1918, pp. 1-2;

"A New Form of Matter," *Harper's,* 138 (May 1919): 803-810;

"Psychoanalysis and the Novel," *London Mercury,* 2 (1919-1920): 426-434;

"The Crux of Psychical Research: Part I," *Westminster Gazette,* 6 March 1920, p. 8;

"The Crux of Psychical Research: Part II," *Westminster Gazette,* 13 March 1920, p. 8;

"More New Facts in Psychical Research," *Harper's,* 144 (March 1922): 475-482;

"The Successors of Charles Dickens," *Nation and Athenaeum,* 34 (29 December 1923): 487-488;

"Common-Sense of the Book Trade," *Nation and Athenaeum,* 35 (27 September 1924): 775-776;

"Unpleasant Fiction," *Bookman* (London), 68 (April 1925): 11;

"What Literary Men Believe in Religion," *Literary Digest,* 87 (31 October 1925): 24-25;

"Experience," *Manchester Guardian,* 30 December 1927, p. 16;

"The Work of Henry Williamson," *Bookman* (London), 73 (January 1928): 207-208;

"The Plane Trees," *Nation and Athenaeum,* 42 (4 February 1928): 682;

"New Books That Ought to Be Better Known," *Nation and Athenaeum,* 75 (December 1928): 166;

"The Mysterious in Real Life," *Bookman* (London), 77 (December 1929): 177;

"From London," *Aryan Path* (January 1930): 46-50;

"The Tendency of National Policy," *Aryan Path* (February 1930): 111-114;

"Towards a Universal Religion," *Aryan Path* (March 1930): 148-152;

"Art and Religion," *Aryan Path* (April 1930): 254-257;

"From London," *Aryan Path* (May 1930): 331-334;

"The Tendency of Recent Fiction," *Bookman* (London), 78 (May 1930): 107-108;

"On Exorcising Evil," *Aryan Path* (June 1930): 389-392;

"Science and Religion," *Aryan Path* (July 1930): 460-463;

"Looking Towards 1975," *Aryan Path* (August 1930): 495-499;

"The Colour Line," *Aryan Path* (September 1930): 566-569;

"The Soul's Dark Cottage," *Nation and Athenaeum*, 48 (4 October 1930): 13-15;

"Personal and Impersonal Methods," *Aryan Path* (October 1930): 652-656;

"The Road to Knowledge," *Saturday Review*, 150 (8 November 1930): 586-587;

"Personal and Impersonal Methods," *Aryan Path* (November 1930): 741-744;

"Utopias," *Aryan Path* (December 1930): 800-803;

"Stones for Bread," *Aryan Path* (January 1931): 47-51;

"Synthesis," *Aryan Path* (February 1931): 115-119;

"God and His Shadow," *Aryan Path* (March 1931): 207-211;

"The Discovery of the Self: An Essay in Religious Experience," *Aryan Path* (March 1931): 131-136; (April 1931): 237-243; (May 1931): 390-314;

"The Gift of Love," *Aryan Path* (June 1931): 375-379;

"The Chaos of Modern Psychology," *Aryan Path* (June 1931): 399-403;

"The Phenomena of Spiritualism," *Aryan Path* (July 1931): 460-465;

"Indian Art: Exhibition in London," *Aryan Path* (August 1931): 560-564;

"The Appearance of Dogma," *Aryan Path* (September 1931): 595-600;

"The Moral Aspect of Reincarnation," *Aryan Path* (October 1931): 679-683;

"Automatism – I. Natural Impulse and Free Will," *Aryan Path* (November 1931): 766-770;

"Automatism – II. Two Ways to Realization," *Aryan Path* (December 1931): 836-841;

"Unemployment: Past Karma and Future Hope," *Aryan Path* (January 1932): 37-40;

"God and His Shadow," *Aryan Path* (March 1932): 107-111;

"An Impractical Philosophy," *Aryan Path* (May 1932): 342-347;

"The Chaos of Modern Psychology," *Aryan Path* (June 1932): 399-403;

"The Development of Consciousness," *Aryan Path* (July 1932): 486-490;

"Old Thames," *Spectator*, 149 (23 July 1932): 105-106;

"Determination and Free Will," *Aryan Path* (August 1932): 540-544;

"Supping with the Poets," *Spectator*, 149 (27 August 1932): 256-257;

"The Evolution of Religion," *Aryan Path* (September 1932): 632-636;

"Tranquility," *Spectator* (17 September 1932): 337-338;

"John Bunyan and Women," *Spectator* (22 October 1932): 532;

"Philosophy and Mysticism," *Aryan Path* (November 1932): 766-770;

"Reflections on Bacon," *Spectator* (25 November 1932): 748-749;

"The Problem of Consciousness," *Aryan Path* (December 1932): 816-820;

"Throcking," *Spectator*, 150 (6 January 1933): 10;

"Evolution," *Aryan Path* (January 1933): 22-26;

"Nature is Alive: Human Ego is Supreme," *Aryan Path* (January 1933): 408-412;

"D. H. Lawrence: The Man of Kama-Manas," *Aryan Path* (February 1933): 93-95;

"The First Article of Belief," *Aryan Path* (March 1933): 176-179;

"The Next Step Forward," *Aryan Path* (May 1933): 294-298;

"Equality," *Aryan Path* (July 1933): 474-478;

"Old and New England," *Spectator*, 102 (25 August 1933): 246-247;

"Man and His God," *Aryan Path* (September 1933): 602-606;

"Evolution and Redemption," *Aryan Path* (October 1933): 689-692;

"The Sin of Retaliation," *Aryan Path* (December 1933): 802-805;

"A Letter from London," *Aryan Path* (February 1934): 119-122;

"Influence of Indian Thought," *Aryan Path* (April 1934): 241-245;

"The Artist and the World Today," *Bookman* (London) 86 (May 1934): 94;

"A Letter from London," *Aryan Path* (August 1934): 537-542;

"Will and Wish," *Aryan Path* (October 1934): 629-633;

"The Philosophy of A. N. Whitehead," *Aryan Path* (November 1934): 683-687;

"A Reasonable Doctrine But – !," *Aryan Path* (March 1935): 130-134;

"On Teaching," *Aryan Path* (April 1935): 235-239;

"The Faculty of Research: A Staff But Not a Sign Post," *Aryan Path* (September 1935): 547-551;

"The Heresy of Separateness," *Aryan Path* (January 1936): 25-28;

"The World is One: Western Religion and Internationalism," *Aryan Path* (February 1936): 82–86;

"The Storehouse of Memory," *Aryan Path* (June 1936): 264–268;

"The One in the Many," *Aryan Path* (September 1936): 421–425;

"New Books and Old – Reviews," *Aryan Path* (October 1936): 481;

"New Books and Old – Reviews," *Aryan Path* (November 1936): 532–533;

"The Phenomena of Jesus – I. Temptation of Jesus," *Aryan Path* (December 1936): 539–542;

"Christian Asceticism," *Aryan Path* (July 1937): 324–328;

"New Books and Old – Reviews," *Aryan Path* (September 1937): 431–432;

"The Reproof of Righteousness," *Aryan Path* (December 1937): 571–574;

"The Author's Dream," *Manchester Guardian,* 7 June 1938, p. 18;

"The Law of Love," *Aryan Path* (September 1938): 442–444;

"The Future of Religion: I. The Inevitability of a World-Religion," *Aryan Path* (November 1938): 535–538;

"The Coming of the Forerunners" (December 1938): 596–601;

"New Books and Old – Reviews," *Aryan Path* (February 1939): 114–115;

"Ways of Knowledge," *Aryan Path* (June 1939): 304–307;

"The Meeting Place of East and West," *Aryan Path* (July 1939): 355–359;

"Political Thought," *Aryan Path* (August 1939): 403;

"Indian Nationalism," *Aryan Path* (November 1939): 546–548;

"New Books and Old – Reviews," *Aryan Path* (July 1940): 368–369;

"Recent Developments in Spiritualism," *Aryan Path* (April 1942): 160–164;

"The Nature of Man," *Aryan Path* (July 1942): 317–319;

"Max Plowman," *Aryan Path* (August 1943): 367–368;

"Needed: A Living Faith," *Aryan Path* (November 1943): 512–514;

"The Federation of the World," *Aryan Path* (January 1944): 14–19;

"Moral Theology of Today," *Aryan Path* (May 1944): 220–221;

"Man and the State," *Aryan Path* (July 1944): 305–309;

"Towards Totalitarianism," *Aryan Path* (November 1944): 431–432;

"New Books and Old – Reviews," *Aryan Path* (April 1945): 147;

"Telepathy," *Aryan Path* (August 1945): 301–303;

"The Demand for Justice," *Aryan Path* (May 1946): 184–186;

"New Books and Old – Reviews," *Aryan Path* (July 1946): 275–276;

"A Statement of Belief," *Aryan Path* (October 1946): 369–373;

"Wisdom as Old as Thinking Man," *Aryan Path* (April 1947): 178–180.

Although he was once considered a leader among the younger generation of Georgian novelists, J. D. Beresford currently stands as one of the most unjustly neglected figures of the period. His first novel, *The Early History of Jacob Stahl* (1911), praised by *The New York Times* (11 June 1911) as a brilliant psychological novel, rapidly established his reputation as a solid realistic novelist. At the height of his recognition in 1924, the critic Abel Chevalley argued that of a group including D. H. Lawrence, Frank Swinnerton, and Hugh Walpole, Beresford was "the one most equally endowed with that *intelligence* and that *imagination* of life which make good writers of fiction." From the late 1920s until his death, however, financial necessity forced Beresford to churn out novels and reviews that often lacked the inspiration and quality of his earlier work. He nevertheless deserves recognition on several scores. His tireless quest for truth led him to explore an astonishing range of ideas from materialism and realism to psychical research, psychoanalysis, Eastern mysticism, and Christian Science. His adherence to the principle of the open mind kept him from limiting himself to any one of these perspectives.

Though strongly influenced by H. G. Wells, Beresford was no mere imitator; his empirical approach to the minute details of human existence was modified by his idealism, mysticism, and probing of the psyche. He was one of the first and most knowledgeable of English novelists to explore in his fiction the new dynamic psychologies of William James, F. W. H. Myers, Henri Bergson, Sigmund Freud, and Carl Jung. His *God's Counterpoint* (1918) represents an early foray into the explicitly psychoanalytic novel. In several critical essays Beresford articulated more clearly than his contemporaries the strengths and limitations of the use of the new psychology in fiction. His second novel, *The Hampdenshire Wonder* (1911), now considered a classic of fantasy literature, initiated his role as critic of English society, a role he continued both in sociological novels and in the seven subsequent futuristic and fantasy novels, all of which remain relevant. Beres-

Beresford with Walter de la Mare, whom he met in 1911 and who became his closest friend

ford's biography also deserves study, as he established friendships and exchanged ideas with Lawrence, Walter de la Mare, John Middleton Murry, and Katherine Mansfield. After Dorothy Richardson's innovative stream-of-consciousness novel *Pilgrimage* (1938) had been refused by publishers, Beresford championed his friend's cause and wrote a perceptive introduction to the work. From 1918 to 1922 he served as the main fiction reader at Collins and was thus responsible for introducing to the English public several novelists adept at psychological analysis, including F. Scott Fitzgerald, Vita Sackville-West, Storm Jameson, and Henry Williamson.

Beresford's body of work—forty-nine novels and five collections of short stories, essays, and reviews—constitutes a comprehensive and perceptive analysis of cultural change in Britain, particularly the breaking up of the old rigid social order. Despite his versatility and prolificity, an underlying idealism informs and unifies all of his work. In *Writing Aloud* (1928), a stream-of-consciousness novel manqué, he asserts that "I have but a single theme, the re-education of human beings."

John Davys Beresford was born on 7 March 1873 in Castor, Northamptonshire; he was the second child of John James Beresford, a Church of England minister, and Adelaide Elizabeth Morgan Beresford. At age three Beresford suffered a trauma that significantly altered the course of his life. His nurse neglected to change his clothes after he got wet during a carriage ride; he subsequently contracted poliomyelitis, which caused permanent lameness. Although the nurse's negligence probably had little to do with Beresford contracting the disease, which—as is now known—is caused by a virus, he and his parents blamed her. He conveys the powerful emotion associated with that event when he asserts in "Memories," an unpublished autobiography, that "The name of that nurse had a place in my youth among the outstanding criminals of the century." The illness changed the family dynamics in that his mother, estranged from her husband, who was fourteen years her senior, invested her affection in her needy second son. The father, proud of his firstborn, viewed Beresford's affliction as an embarrassment and, consequently, neglected the boy's education. Nevertheless, Beresford later claimed that his lameness helped to decide his career.

Beresford attended various schools from ages eight to sixteen— Peterborough, a public school at Oundle, a boarding school in Norfolk, and the Peterborough King's School—but he had no particular ambitions and learned nothing that fitted him for any profession. He was bullied by other students, and he remembered being called "Miss Beresford" and "being tied to an apple tree in the playground and being pelted with chestnuts." He first began writing while at school, perhaps as a way of creating a world in which he was not "defective." Beresford's education was largely informal: his mother read to him from the works of Charles Dickens and Charles Reade; later he made energetic use of the Peterborough public library to obtain Harrison Ainsworth's book; and at eighteen he discovered Samuel Richardson's *Pamela* (1741) and the works of Charles Kingsley.

At sixteen Beresford proposed becoming an engineer, but his father believed that his disability would make such a career impossible. Instead his father suggested a career in architecture, which was accepted by the lackadaisical Beresford. He articled first with the local diocesan surveyor and then at Gray's Inn in London. London opened up a new world for the sheltered youth, who was spellbound by its theaters and music halls. Though he lived briefly with his brother and then with a cousin, Beresford soon moved into a transient boardinghouse life. During this time he met G. F. Rogers, who sparked his interest in independent thinking and self-education. A physician at the London Hospital, Rogers questioned Beresford's fundamentalist faith and helped him throw off his orthodoxy "in a single evening," according to Beresford. Beresford became a convinced evolutionist, which may have caused some consternation at the rectory, where he spent the summer of 1895. Back in London in September, Beresford reluctantly began working as a draftsman for the architect Edwin T. Hall. After eight difficult and unrewarding years there, he finally realized that the career had no future. As an escape he continued to educate himself: he read the works of Samuel Laing, Charles Darwin, and other scientists and philosophers at the British Library on Saturday afternoons, as well as fiction from Mudie's lending library—notably Wells's *The Wheels of Chance* (1896). In the summer of 1901 Beresford began to write short stories. His efforts paid off when he won the prize of one guinea for the best portrait of a street character in the journal *Academy,* to which he contributed fairly regularly thereafter. A second mentor, Arthur Scaife, provided Beresford with his sociological education beginning in 1902. Beresford reached another juncture when in 1903 he read the psychical researcher Frederic W. H. Myers's *Human Personality and Its Survival of Bodily Death* (1903), which he describes in *What I Believe* (1938) as "a book of wonders that gave my mind a new twist." Myers's descriptions of the subliminal self and multiple personalities sparked Beresford's fascination with abnormal psychology and led him to adopt an idealist position.

Not only did Beresford begin writing in earnest in 1901, but he also met his future wife, Linda Lawrence, at a party. Though Beresford had been involved in a secret love affair from 1891 to 1898, his life was "singularly lacking in feminine society" at this time. Lawrence, a former actress, had been married to an actor who had deserted her, and thus various obstacles had to be overcome before the new couple finally married 28 November 1903. Lawrence's contacts in the theater inspired Beresford to write a play, which was submitted to Max Beerbohm Tree, but it was never staged. Beresford also completed a novel during this time, but it was never published. To make matters worse, Linda suffered a miscarriage several months after their honeymoon.

Beresford had escaped the slavery of office routine by becoming an agent with the New York Life Insurance Company just before his marriage. After some initial success he failed at this occupation before securing a position as editor of the bookseller W. H. Smith's first *Annual* (1906). Thereafter he wrote advertising copy for Smith and then for the bookseller S. H. Benson, eventually transforming his experiences with these firms into his novel *A Candidate for Truth* (1912).

During the Christmas season of 1905 Beresford began collaborating on plays with Arthur Harvey-James, whose stage name was Scott Craven and who had been introduced to Beresford by his wife. Harvey-James became the closest male friend of Beresford's life. At least two of their collaborations, *The Royal Heart* and *The Compleat Angler* (1914), were produced, the former playing more than two hundred times in the provinces. After Beresford lost his job with Benson, he increased his writing efforts, doing unpaid reviewing for *The Literary World,* and producing three more unpublished novels by 1907.

Beresford's marriage began to crumble under the pressures of financial distress, as well as infidelity on his wife's part, and he willingly consented to a divorce. In the midst of this personal crisis Beresford's literary fortunes finally began to change. He published a light satirical essay in *Punch* in March 1908 and was added to the review staff of the *Westminster Gazette* shortly thereafter. In the latter periodical, described by Beresford as "the most scholarly and literary of all the London evening papers," he published his first short stories, including "Miranda. VI. On Idealism" (July 1908), "A Test of Friendship" (June 1908), and "The Great Tradition" (March 1911). According to Helmut Gerber, Beresford's biographer, "All these stories favour an idealistic attitude, all have a subdued humorous tone, all have a touch of sentiment or pathos, and all use the stylistic techniques we label realistic." During 1908 Beresford also began writing *The Early History of Jacob Stahl* (1911), the first work in a trilogy that would include *A Candidate For Truth* (1912) and *The Invisible Event* (1915). These autobiographical novels trace the circuitous evolution of the introspective Jacob into awareness and the profession of novelist. Paying attention to unconscious motivation and spiritual questing, Beresford heightens realism in the manner of Wells and Arnold Bennett. Beresford's psychological orientation is suggested in the early chapters of the book, which pass over many of the events of Jacob's youth but focus on two incidents that have profound emotional consequences for the protagonist: the lameness he suffers as a result of falling from a pram while in the care of a nurse, and the loss, when he is fourteen, of his mother. Beresford also deals, though not explicitly, with Jacob's sex life, beginning in adolescence at a "moment of tensity" that is "subconsciously noted" by Jacob as he gazes at his fourteen-year-old beloved. Later Jacob marries, separates, is nearly entrapped by a sexually repressed widow, and then, in a bold move for a novel of 1915, lives with the daughter of a clergyman. Jacob's sexual desires "accumulate subconsciously," and his thoughts are often shown to have emerged from his unconscious. The spiritual dimension of these novels centers on Jacob's attraction to the ideal of self-sacrifice, brought out while he is under the influence of the charismatic preacher-cum-social worker Cecil Barker, and his eventual rejection of that ideal. In what will become a characteristic feature of Beresford's protagonists, Jacob refuses to accept dogmas, to "fall into the habit of fixed opinions," searching instead for a permanent truth that "keeps his spirit young." Whereas the first reviewers of the trilogy were unanimous in their praise of its penetrating analysis of character, "its boldness of conception and handling and its vigorous dialogue," in the words of a *New York Times* reviewer (11 June 1911), later critics do not find it as vivid and daring; however, several would agree with Abel Chevalley that it represents "a solid and durable monument," a direct descendent of Samuel Butler's *The Way of All Flesh* (1903).

Beresford's second novel published in 1911, *The Hampdenshire Wonder,* falls into the genre of speculative fiction. Ironically, it has outlasted his realistic fiction, having been frequently reprinted, and was broadcast on BBC radio as recently as 1982. The tale explores the development and the treatment by society of "The Wonder," an "abnormal" child genius named Victor Stott, whose stupendous intellect enables him to make sense of the phenomena of life from his own observation before he devours the accumulated knowledge of civilization—most of which he rejects. The Wonder agitates most of those who come into contact with him, including the journalist narrator. When the Wonder is discovered drowned in a pond, the implication is that the most narrow-minded of those his path crossed—the rector, Crashaw—is responsible for his death. The novel, influenced by Bergson's *Essai sur les données immediates de la conscience* (1889; translated as *Time and Free Will,* 1910) and *L'Évolution Creatrice* (1907; translated as *Creative Evolution,* 1911), was the first to consider seriously the consequences for an individual who reaches a higher evolutionary stage than his contemporaries. It earned the praise of George Bernard Shaw and has achieved the status of a cult classic. These early successes drew Beresford from the fringe into neo-Georgian literary circles though he was never as well connected as Virginia Woolf or Bertrand Russell. Beresford and Walpole reviewed each other's novels and developed a cautious friendship that would later be hampered by differences in aim and literary method. In contrast, Beresford had admired Wells's literary method as early as 1903 and finally met him at the Savile Club in 1913. Though the young writer sympathized with Wells's social ideals, he did not admire Wells's materialism and opposition to all forms of religion. Nevertheless, he wrote the first appreciative monograph devoted to Wells in 1915, portrayed the older author as A. B. Ellis in his novel *The Invisible Event* (1915), and maintained his friendship with Wells and Wells's wife, Jane, while in France in the 1920s. Beresford found he had more in common with Mansfield and de la Mare, whom he came to know in 1911, when all three were reviewers for the *Westminster Gazette*. Beresford and Mansfield became interested in Theosophy through A. R. Orage, editor of *The New Age,* and the two would attend classes on the theosophical teachings of Boris Ouspensky together in 1922. De la Mare became Beresford's closest friend after Harvey-James was killed in World War I in 1917. The two men influenced one another; for example, Beresford wrote *Signs and Wonders* (1921), a volume of whimsical short stories in the manner of de la Mare, to whom he dedicated the book.

In 1912 Beresford began a relationship with Beatrice "Trissie" Roskams. He attempted to change her conventional opinions and persuaded her to join him in Penzance, North Cornwall, at his retreat although it went against her beliefs. They lived together until they were married in May 1913. The first of their four children, Tristram, was born in 1914. The couple lived mainly in rural Cornwall until late in 1916, when they moved to London for the birth of their second son, Aden.

Visitors to the Penzance retreat included Walpole, Mansfield, Middleton Murry, Richardson, and Lawrence. Beresford had gotten to know Richardson, the most frequent visitor, when she was working as a part-time secretary to a dentist in Wimpole Street, and he had quickly developed a rapport with her. He acted as her literary adviser, reading the manuscript for her *Pilgrimage* and contributing an appreciative foreword. With Lawrence, whom he had met in the winter of 1915–1916, Beresford played the role of father figure. Though Beresford liked Lawrence, he claimed that Lawrence's "obsession with sex bored me," and he saw Lawrence as a "young soul" in theosophical terms. He lent Lawrence and Lawrence's wife, Freda, his Cornish house at Portcothan that winter, and in 1919 he helped Lawrence obtain a grant from the Royal Literary Fund.

During the second decade of the twentieth century Beresford also became friends with Naomi Royde-Smith, who taught him about the misuse of English; May Sinclair, whom he initially worshipped as a "High-priestess" of literature; and Ken-

Beresford with his second wife, Beatrice "Trissie" Roskans, outside their home in Cornwall

neth Richmond, a writer on education with whom he shared an interest in the Society for Psychical Research and collaborated on a biography of the medium W. E. Ford (1917). Another friend, M. David Eder–one of the first supporters of Sigmund Freud in Britain, introduced Beresford to psychoanalysis in 1912. Though initially attracted to Freud, whom he read from the perspective of psychical research, Beresford later rejected the Freudian preoccupation with sex and moved closer to C. J. Jung's position, as did Eder. The eleven novels that Beresford published between 1915 and 1924, when he left England for France, show not so much the influence of his fellow authors as his assimilation of ideas that interested him. Most of these novels continue in the vein of psychological and social realism tapped by *Jacob Stahl*. One of the exceptions is *Goslings* (1913; published as *A World of Women* in the United States), a futuristic fantasy along the lines of *The Hampdenshire Wonder*. Jasper Thrale, one of Beresford's many unconventional protagonists, attempts to warn the British of an approaching plague from Russia that threatens to annihilate the male population. Convention-bound families such as the Goslings refuse to accept the situation until forced to do so, and large-scale panic ensues. Individuals with foresight emerge and begin the task of reconstruction on socialist principles. Targets of this effective satire include the "religion of respectability" and various selfish interests, such as those that cause distortions in media reporting. The novel also represents an early sympathetic study of an all-female society.

More typical of Beresford's technique of psychological realism of the period is *The House in Demetrius Road* (1914). It focuses on Martin Bond's relations with Robin Greg, his employer, at the house called Garroch, which, with its mysterious atmosphere, nearly serves as a character. Bond's poor impression of his prospective employer almost causes him to turn down the job of helping Greg write a book on socialism, but his attraction to Margaret Hamilton, Greg's sister-in-law, and his revulsion at Greg's treatment of her persuade him to accept. Initially he does not understand the "double personality" of the house until he discovers a drunken Greg on the stairs one night and then realizes that Greg's drinking is the source of the tension. Bond aids Margaret in persuading Greg to take a cure for his alcoholism, at the end of which Greg announces his engagement to Margaret. Crestfallen but not defeated, Bond increases his intimacy with Margaret, who is determined to sacrifice herself to keep Greg from destroying himself. When the perceptive Greg realizes the nature of the relationship between Bond and Margaret, he dismisses Bond and tells him to take Margaret along. By this time Greg is drinking again, and the novel closes unsentimentally. Frank Swinnerton found this fiction, whose sales were destroyed by the outbreak of war, to be Beresford's "most vigorous novel" of the period, and biographer Helmut Gerber praised its construction. *The Mountains of the Moon* (1915) expands on the socialist theme introduced in *The House in Demetrius Road*. It features the practical idealist Arthur Grey, author of "The Mountains of the Moon: An Essay in Sociology," who struggles with his conscience about accepting an aristocratic title. Eventually he accepts the title because of a love interest and a desire to use his wealth to finance an educational project, the latter reason a characteristic scenario in Beresford's novels.

In *These Lynnekers* (1916) Beresford turns to the autobiographical family novel. It has a special interest from a biographer's viewpoint because of Beresford's remark that in it he came nearest to a description of the Beresford family although he claimed that "the central character is far from being autobiographical." The novel traces the development of Dickie, a younger Lynneker son who is determined to break through his family's "web" of religious orthodoxy and tradition, which threatens to arrest his development before it is complete. Dickie's self-education includes study of the intricacies of higher mathematics, Butler's *Erewhon* (1872), and Herbert Spencer's *Principles of Ethics* (1893). In striving to obtain the knowledge necessary to refute this orthodoxy, Dickie comes to inhibit thoughts about sexuality "almost automatically." Like other Beresford heroes, Dickie has an overly close relationship with his mother that resembles an erotic relationship, but he does not find release for his repressed thoughts until they are triggered by the lewd remarks of the novelist A. B. Ellis (based on Wells) as the two watch the beautiful Sibyl Groome. Not surprisingly, Sibyl becomes the object of Dickie's attraction, "the incarnation of some primitive response to all the desire of his life." Nor is Dickie's spiritual nature neglected by Beresford. The protagonist occasionally experiences flashes of vision, and on one such occasion he reaches his personal solution that no stage in his life or in the progress of humanity

must be judged as an absolute.... Behind all progress and all life was this permanent spirit of endurance, of resistance, of power: endurance to maintain the truth of independence to all material pains and changes; resistance to demonstrate the transience of the image; power to prove that while the symbol may be changed, the spirit shall endure inalterable to find ever new forms of expression.

These Lynnekers subtly conveys Beresford's considerable psychological insight, especially in its use of the concept of sublimation. This insight is applied to a larger canvas in *Housemates* (1917). *Housemates* is also a more intimate account of the mental odyssey of the protagonist, facilitated by its first-person viewpoint. The theme of Wilfrid Hornby's growth into independent thinking is quickly made explicit using the metaphor of a chick hatching out of its shell. Wilfrid confides that "the history of my hatching, so far as I can trace it, is written in my consciousness. I admit that I am quite unable to explain the impulse to germination." Indulged and protected by his parents and governess in his youth, Wilfrid emerges from his shell only after he breaks his engagement to a woman who typifies the conventional world and moves to a slightly disreputable boardinghouse, where he begins his practice of architecture. Incidents that take place there force Wilfrid to overcome his ambivalence and fear of humanity and to assert his independence. One cathartic moment occurs on a Saturday night as the landlord attempts to evict one of the boarders, Rose Whiting, for prostitution. She strips off her clothes while screaming that the landlord can turn her out naked. Though a relatively weak and fragile creature, in "the recklessness of her passion" she dominates and intimidates the brute opposing her. Wilfrid admires her for this and because "she was at that moment, a single and powerful personality." His success is measured by his eventual marriage to another boarder, a woman who is appropriate for him. In its representation of the struggle to overcome dividedness and achieve individuation and in its concern with sexuality, the mystical, and mental illness, *Housemates* includes many of the elements that were to preoccupy Beresford in his later writing.

In contrast, Beresford's next novel, *God's Counterpoint* (1918), stands out in his canon for several reasons. According to Beresford, it was the first English novel that was thoroughly informed by Freudian psychoanalysis, and it sold a substantial six thousand copies. It was also the only one of his novels that he acknowledged to have been influenced by psychoanalysis, and it suffers from clinical obtrusiveness more than any other of Beresford's novels. The novel traces the atypical conditions that lead to the enlightenment of Philip Maning and emphasizes the sexual and psychological over the intellectual aspects, which had been stressed in *Jacob Stahl* and *Housemates*. Philip's punitive father is the dominant influence in his early years. The protagonist internalizes his father's repressive "Don'ts" to the extent that he develops an inferiority complex. He also comes to associate sexuality with shame so that in his marriage he treats his wife as an unattainable ideal. He is seduced by and departs with her French cousin though he finally returns and reconciles with his wife. Beresford's enthusiasm for applying Freudian insights and scientific objectivity unfortunately works to preclude the reader from getting close enough to the protagonist to feel either his agony or his joy. This problem is compounded by the fact that the priggish, fastidious Philip is not a particularly likeable character.

The Jervaise Comedy (1919) seems to be a flawed version of *The Mountains of the Moon* in that it closes with an overly didactic lecture on socialism. *An Imperfect Mother* (1920) more nearly achieves integration of the ideas informing it, in this case Freudian ones, though the total effect is marred by a "Retrospect" that unnecessarily underlines the psychogenesis of the protagonist's "slight departure from the normal." The main focus of the novel is the resolution in adulthood of the conflict arising from an overly close bond between mother and son, which presumably originated in an oedipal complex. Despite that bond the son, Stephen Kirkwood, is not as fastidious as Philip Maning, and Beresford more explicitly describes Stephen's sexual impulses. Symbolic incidents involving building blocks and a ride in a crane as a demonstration of prowess might seem obvious to modern readers inured to Freud, but even perceptive contemporary critics, including Mansfield and Woolf, did not mention this symbolism in their reviews though Woolf complained that the book read like "an essay in morbid psychology."

Revolution (1921) recalls *Goslings* in its futuristic vision and deserves recognition as an early foray into the thesis novel. Paul Leaming emerges from shell-shocked withdrawal with a newfound mystical "gift of sensibility" just as a general labor strike threatens. Despite his father's conservatism, Paul remains neutral and unprejudiced even after the visionary and idealistic union leader, Isaac Perry, is assassinated. In the aftermath Paul acts as mediator to prevent further violence and to focus society on cooperating in essentials such as food production. Even his father's murder does not change his pacifist conviction, and Paul feels only compassion for the killer. Following the return of a reactionary government, Paul's first convert, the daughter of one of the decadent aristocrats Beresford criticizes in the novel, persuades him to return to London to preach a new spirit of hope. The work's main strength lies in its recognition of the need for cooperation among people, but it ends on a rather naive note of optimism about achieving this goal. Woolf criticized the novel's portrayal of a fictional revolution and its weak characterizations though she admired its "intellectual efficiency."

Title page for the U.S. edition of a 1925 novel about malicious town gossips

In *The Prisoners of Hartling* (1922) Beresford presents another study of the family unit, in this instance one held in bondage by anticipation of wealth and power from a distant relative's will. In *Love's Pilgrim* (1923) he returns to the psychology of the individual, treating themes similar to those in his earlier psychoanalytic novels but this time overcoming his apparent enthusiasm for scientific objectivity by assimilating the ideas more smoothly and avoiding the clinical retrospect that had encumbered *An Imperfect Mother*. The protagonist, Foster Innes, is similar to

Stephen Kirkwood in that his bond with his unfulfilled mother is overly close, to Philip Maning in that he is repressed and fastidious about sexuality, to Wilfrid Hornby in that he narrates his own story, and to Jacob Stahl in that he is a self-conscious cripple. Though Beresford continues to explore Freudian insights about the mother fixation, he draws more centrally on the imaginative implications of the inferiority complex (as developed by Jung and Alfred Adler) and also brings his interests in psychical research, idealism, and mysticism more fully into play. Foster's mother overprotects him because of his disability, and his love for women remains subconsciously divided until he experiences a moment of illumination. His beloved, Clare, carries out a kind of analysis on him, but it arises naturally out of the dramatic situation. Eventually Foster develops a selfless love for her, more fulfilling than his love for his mother.

By the early 1920s Beresford was well established, with fifteen critically successful novels and many short stories placed in prestigious periodicals including *The English Review* and *The Seven Arts*. Since 1918 he had been literary adviser for Collins, a position that he held at £350 per year until 1923 and that brought him closer to the center of the literary world. In this role Beresford launched several aspiring writers including Sackville-West, Jameson, and Williamson and brought writers more advanced in their careers into the fold, including Fitzgerald, Eleanor Farjeon, Michael Arlen, Lucas Malet (Mrs. St. Leger Harrison), Rose Macauley, and Alistair Crowley. Some of these, notably Farjeon and Williamson, came to be numbered among Beresford's closest friends. The job also placed him in a good position to comment on trends in the novel, which he did in such noteworthy articles as "Psychoanalysis and the Novel" (1919–1920), "The Successors of Charles Dickens" (1923), and "The Experimental Novel" (1929).

At the peak of his critical success Beresford experienced a severe spiritual crisis that was partly touched off by the antagonism of his family to his theosophical studies under Ouspensky and exacerbated by exhaustion and the warping of his literary judgment from having had for five years to deal with approximately forty manuscripts a week for Collins. In the autumn of 1923 he decided to take his family to France, a move made possible through the sale of a novel, *Unity* (1924), to a woman's magazine for £500. The novel is unremarkable except that it deals with the overcoming of spiritual dividedness, a theme that would occupy Beresford in many subsequent works. During their four-year sojourn in France the family moved many times, but Beresford was consistently charmed by the French and exhilarated by the climate. The novels of this period typically focus on characters' awakenings, the development of their mystical sensibilities, and their discovery of the principle of the open mind. Their unique qualities and experiences bring these characters into conflict with the herd mind and its fixed habits. *The Monkey Puzzle* (1925), *That Kind of Man* (1926), *The Tapestry* (1927), *All or Nothing* (1928), and *Real People* (1929) all fall into this category, with *The Monkey Puzzle* and *The Tapestry* being the most substantial and most carefully crafted. *The Monkey Puzzle*, which provides a vivid portrayal of the maliciousness of town gossips, was reprinted several times and translated into French. *The Tapestry* intricately weaves the central image of the title throughout as a commentary on the protagonist's quest to attain the mystic's life, and it avoids sentimentality at the denouement. An exception to these novels is *The Decoy* (1927), the first of several formulaic mystery stories, which does not succeed because of an implausible premise and a sentimental ending. *An Instrument of Destiny* (1928), another of these mysteries, fares better as Beresford brings to the crime novel his characteristic psychological insight and his fascination with the divided self. Its plot is clever, and Beresford shows restraint in dealing with clues.

Near the end of the Beresfords' stay in France, Trissie, at forty-six, gave birth to Elisabeth, who would become a popular children's writer. When the family returned to England in the summer of 1927, the rift between Beresford and his conventional wife had widened, and his financial situation had become precarious, necessitating an increased production. His novel *Real People* represents the worst effects of this economic pressure.

In his novels of the 1930s Beresford continued several of his preoccupations, notably with idealist and mystical protagonists who overcome their dividedness, and he returned to the more conventional family novel. Not surprisingly, some of these fictions are repetitive, while in others he manifests a tendency toward sermonizing as story, plot, and even character give way to theme and philosophy. *Love's Illusion* (1930) recalls *Jacob Stahl* in its shattering of the protagonist's illusion of romantic love and the ideal woman. *The Faithful Lovers* (1936) descends to the overly sentimental but was also one of Beresford's most popular works, judging by advertisements claiming that more than thirty-five thousand copies had been printed. More satirical essay than novel, *Seven, Bobsworth* (1930) uses the growth of "Garden City" (based on Letchworth) to show the smothering of individualist residents by those who are bound by convention.

J. D. and Trissie Beresford with their children: Tristram, Alden, Elisabeth, and Marcus

The Next Generation (1932), *Peckover* (1934), and *Cleo* (1937) resemble *Unity* in their concentration on divided individuals who achieve harmony through a mystical approach to life. The best and most psychological of these is *Peckover,* in which the division is caused by amnesia resulting from unbearable tensions in a marriage. The trilogy *Three Generations,* comprising *The Old People* (1931), *The Middle Generation* (1932), and *The Young People* (1933), follows incompatible temperaments within a family before focusing on one of the sons. Owen Hillington slowly achieves independence from the prejudices of his family background and grows toward ideals such as selfless love, which he attempts to practice with his own wife and children. Though this trilogy adds nothing new to the Beresford canon, the third volume provides some glimpses into both disturbing and refreshing changes in the postwar world, such as the appearance of the so-called fast set.

The Inheritor (1933), *The Camberwell Miracle* (1933), *On A Huge Hill* (1935), and *Unfinished Road* (1938) introduce protagonists who know their mystical way from the outset and several of whom practice faith healing, a subject about which Beresford wrote a nonfictional account in *The Case for Faith-Healing* (1934). These novels are more sermonlike, but *The Camberwell Miracle* successfully engages the reader through well-developed dramatic tension.

In 1939 Beresford moved into a new and vital stage of his career when he began collaborating with Esmé Wynne-Tyson, whom he had met eighteen months earlier in Brighton. Wynne-Tyson, a novelist and journalist who was a childhood friend of Noel Coward and had been an actress, described Beresford when she met him as being "ground down" by a routine of writing for profit and by tensions within his family arising from his unorthodox spiritual beliefs.

Through discussions with Wynne-Tyson, Beresford overcame periodic bouts of neuralgia, became a vegetarian, and generally became more spiritually integrated. As his affinity with Wynne-Tyson increased, they determined to communicate "the truth to all who may desire to know." To find the peace necessary to embark on such collaboration, Beresford moved out of his household and into a service flat in May 1939. In four months the pair completed their first novel, *Strange Rival* (1939), which was published under Beresford's name. Thereafter Wynne-Tyson, who had separated from her husband in 1930, and Beresford maintained a platonic relationship while living in a series of hotels and vegetarian guest houses, mainly in the West Country.

Their collaborations convey strong philosophical and spiritual didactic messages and did not appeal to a broad audience. The most imaginative and worthy of study are philosophical fantasies and utopian novels that advocate social renewal based on cooperative principles. *Strange Rival* recounts in fictional form Beresford's spiritual journey and his encounter with Wynne-Tyson. Trevor Lovelace, the character resembling Beresford, overcomes his disillusionment with life under Amanda Westley's influence, but he realizes that he has a "strange rival" in what she refers to as the "Divine Mind." He learns to sacrifice the selfish impulse in his love for her so that the two can be united in the book's sentimental denouement. The collaboration continued with *Snell's Folly* (1939), which takes an ironic view of misplaced philanthropy as a facile solution to the illness of society. As Helmut Gerber has noted, its strength lies in its gallery of Dickensian characters. *Quiet Corner* (1940), a philosophical fantasy, follows Timothy Gadshill's escape from his life as a stockbroker and his entry into Halycon Place, a haven where people can live out their consciences; Timothy does so by developing as an artist. The novel includes striking portraits of the residents, who have adopted such values as vegetarianism and open-mindedness about religion.

In *"What Dreams May Come . . ."* (1941), a visionary utopian novel, David Shillingford, a dreamer born into unhappy circumstances, undergoes a mental odyssey to the land of Oion after suffering a near hit by a bomb during a London air raid. Humanity has evolved in this land of the mind, where thoughts are conveyed telepathically, and the body is relatively insignificant. David returns to convey his vision of harmony, but, as is typical of Beresford's Christlike protagonists in the novels of this period, he is misunderstood and incarcerated. As the novel closes, he reunites with a soul mate from Oion. De la Mare provided inspiration for and advice on this novel, which anticipates such psychotic-episode novels as Doris Lessing's 1971 work, *Briefing For A Descent Into Hell*.

A Common Enemy (1941), in the vein of Wells's scientific romances, traces the evolution of English society on new cooperative grounds after a cosmic catastrophe brings the war to a halt. A benevolent oligarchy emerges under the guidance of the protagonist, and at the close European unity becomes a probability. Three of the four novels Beresford wrote in 1943, with varying amounts of help from Wynne-Tyson—*The Benefactor, Men in the Same Boat,* and *The Long View*—emphasize the role of personal responsibility in bringing about transformation. The fourth, *If This Were True–* (1943), shows the spiritual evolution of Lewis Arkwright, raised in complete ignorance of religion, into a mystic and faith healer. Unfortunately the novel reads like a tract and does not fully engage the reader until the dramatic tension rises near the close. In contrast, *The Riddle of the Tower* (1944) has been critically acclaimed as the most imaginatively powerful of Beresford's late fantasies. The plot recalls *"What Dreams May Come . . ."* in that the protagonist, Arthur Begbie, loses consciousness during an air raid and experiences a panoramic vision of the future of mankind. Begbie's vision, however, is one of human beings reduced to automatons motivated by fear. On his return to consciousness a mystic suggests that this future need not be fulfilled if enough individuals turn their attention to the highest ideals. In a long review in the *Daily Herald* (25 October 1944) John Betjeman called the novel "a great feat of the imagination," and Gerber places it in a league with George Orwell's *Nineteen Eighty-Four* (1949).

Beresford's final two efforts, *The Prisoner* (1946), a labored fictional autobiography, and *The Gift* (1947), another novel about the martyrdom of a Christlike figure, add nothing new to the author's extensive repertoire. As he finished the latter novel, his collaborator noticed that his energy had begun to flag. Nevertheless he embarked on a factual autobiography titled "Memories," which was not quite completed and was never published because of his wife's opposition, before he died on 2 February 1947.

In his unfinished autobiography Beresford acknowledges that he was not a born writer but that his long candidacy for truth compelled him to put his discoveries into words. He valued subject matter over manner, and he claims that he had "always been inclined to put Life before Art; and if Art cannot, however cryptically, tell me something about being by becoming a magic casement opening onto fiery realms of the imagination, I count it only as a diversion of the academic mind." Although most of Beresford's novels were carefully and meticulously written, his emphasis on subject matter contributed to his critical neglect as the wave of modernism swept over Western culture. The reader gets only a glimpse of his potential as an experimenter in the stream-of-consciousness style of his *Writing Aloud* (1928), with its revelations about the creative process. His choice to illustrate in fiction his fundamental principles, such as the fundamentally spiritual rather than material nature of the universe, practically guaranteed that he would never be a popular writer even though he could write competently in popular forms such as the detective novel and could turn out stories acceptable to mainstream magazines. Typically, and most passionately, Beresford wrote about individuals who awaken from the slumber of normality and become outsiders who are either ignored or persecuted by society. Nevertheless, the great variety of forms and subgenres in which he worked has perhaps also contributed to his neglect, as has the uneven quality of his novels composed hurriedly for financial considerations. Though Beresford deserves a place in literary history for his early and perceptive novels of psychological and psychoanalytic realism and for his innovative early short stories, it is his futuristic fantasies that might more readily find a new, if small, audience. With their warnings of potential disaster blended with a positive vision of human potential, in light of current interest in cooperative models of society and a sustainable economy the works seem as relevant today as when they were first published.

Bibliography:
Helmut E. Gerber, "J. D. Beresford: A Bibliography," *Bulletin of Bibliography,* 21 (January–April 1956): 201–204.

Biography:
Helmut E. Gerber, "J. D. Beresford: A Study of His Works and Philosophy," dissertation, University of Pennsylvania, 1952.

References:
A. St. John Adcock, "John Davys Beresford," in his *Gods of Modern Grub Street* (London: Sampson Low, Marston, 1923; New York: Stokes, 1923), pp. 33–39;

Abel Chevalley, "J. D. Beresford," in his *The Modern English Novel* (New York: Knopf, 1973), pp. 228–235;

William C. Frierson, "J. D. Beresford," in his *The English Novel in Transition 1885–1940* (Norman: University of Oklahoma Press/New York: Cooper Square, 1965), pp. 195–197;

Helmut E. Gerber, "J. D. Beresford: The Freudian Element," *Literature and Psychology,* 6 (1956): 78–86;

Gerald Gould, *The English Novel of To-Day* (London: Castle, 1924), pp. 17–18, 28–29, 50–53;

R. Hoops, *Der Einfluss der Psychoanalyse auf die Englische Literatur* (Heidelburg: Winter, 1934), pp. 93–105;

Edward A. Hungerford, "Mrs. Woolf, Freud, and J. D. Beresford," *Literature and Psychology,* 3 (August 1955): 49–51;

George M. Johnson, *J. D. Beresford* (New York: Twayne, 1998);

R. Brimley Johnson, "J. D. Beresford," in his *Some Contemporary Novelists (Men)* (Freeport, N.Y.: Books for Libraries Press, 1970), pp. 97–119;

Annie Russell Marble, *A Study of the Modern Novel, British and American, since 1900* (New York: Appleton, 1930), pp. 164–166;

Brian Stableford, "J. D. Beresford 1873–1947," in *Supernatural Fiction Writers: Fantasy and Horror,* volume 1, edited by E. F. Bleiler (New York: Scribners, 1985), pp. 457–461;

Frank Swinnerton, "Oliver Onions and J. D. Beresford," in his *The Georgian Literary Scene 1910–1935* (New York: Farrar, Straus, 1935), pp. 238–241;

Swinnerton, *Swinnerton: An Autobiography* (Garden City, N.Y.: Doubleday, 1936), pp. 290–292;

R. H. Ward, "J. D. Beresford: Artist in Living," *Aryan Path,* 18 (May 1947): 212–214;

W. J. West, *The Quest for Graham Greene* (London: Weidenfeld & Nicolson, 1997), pp. xiv–xv, 8, 10–12, 18, 112, 116, 134, 136, 138–139.

Papers:
Jon Wynne-Tyson possesses the main collection of J. D. Beresford's typescripts, diaries, and other papers. The collections of the National Library of Wales, the British Library, the University of Reading, and the New York Public Library include some of Beresford's correspondence.

Phyllis Bottome
(31 May 1882 – 22 August 1963)

Marilyn Hoder-Salmon
Florida International University

BOOKS: *Life, the Interpreter* (New York & London: Longmans, Green, 1902);
The Master Hope (London: Hurst & Blackett, 1904);
Raw Material: Some Characters and Episodes among Working Lads (London: Murray, 1906);
The Imperfect Gift (London: Murray, 1907; New York: Dutton, 1907);
Crooked Answers, by Bottome and Hope de Lisle Brock (London: Murray, 1911);
The Common Chord (London: Secker, 1913); republished as *Broken Music* (London: Hutchinson, 1914; Boston & New York: Houghton Mifflin, 1914);
The Captive (London: Chapman & Hall, 1915);
Secretly Armed (London: Chapman & Hall, 1916); republished as *The Dark Tower* (New York: Century, 1916);
The Derelict, and Also The Liqueur Glass, Mademoiselle l'Anglaise, The Awkward Turn, The Syren's Isle, Iron Stone, The Pace, Brother Leo (New York: Century, 1917); republished as *The Derelict and Other Stories* (London: Collins, 1923);
A Certain Star (London: Hodder & Stoughton, 1917); republished as *The Second Fiddle* (New York: Century, 1917);
Helen of Troy and Rose (New York: Century, 1918);
A Servant of Reality (London: Hodder & Stoughton, 1919; New York: Century, 1919);
The Crystal Heart (New York: Century, 1921);
The Kingfisher (London: Collins, 1922; New York: Doran, 1922);
The Victim and the Worm (New York: Doran, 1923);
The Perfect Wife (New York: Doran, 1924);
The Depths of Prosperity, by Bottome and Dorothy Thompson (London: Collins, 1924; New York: Doran, 1925);
Liqueur Glass: Georgian Stories (New York & London: Putnam, 1924);
Old Wine (New York: Doran, 1924; London: Collins, 1926);
The Belated Reckoning (New York: Doran, 1926; London: Collins, 1927); republished as *Belated Reckoning: Three Stories* (London: Faber & Faber, 1955);
Wild Grapes (London: Collins, 1927); republished as *The Messenger of the Gods* (New York: Doran, 1927);
Strange Fruit: Stories (London: Collins, 1928; Boston & New York: Houghton Mifflin, 1928);
Windlestraws (London: Collins, 1929; Boston & New York: Houghton Mifflin, 1929);
Tatter'd Loving (London: Collins, 1929; Boston & New York: Houghton Mifflin, 1930);

Phyllis Bottome

Wind in His Fists (London: Collins, 1931); republished as *The Devil's Due* (Boston & New York: Houghton Mifflin, 1931; London: Faber & Faber, 1948);
The Advances of Harriet (London: John Lane, 1933; Boston & New York: Houghton Mifflin, 1933);
Stella Benson (San Francisco: Grabhorn Press, 1934);
Private Worlds (London: John Lane, 1934; Boston & New York: Houghton Mifflin, 1934);
Innocence and Experience (Boston & New York: Houghton Mifflin, 1934; London: Bodley Head, 1935);
Level Crossing (London: Bodley Head, 1936; New York: Stokes, 1936);
The Mortal Storm (London: Faber & Faber, 1937; Boston: Little, Brown, 1938);
Alfred Adler, Apostle of Freedom (London: Faber & Faber, 1939); republished as *Alfred Adler: A Biography* (New York: Putnam, 1939); republished as *Alfred Adler: A Portrait from Life* (New York: Vanguard, 1957);
Murder in the Bud (London: Faber & Faber, 1939); republished as *Danger Signal* (Boston: Little, Brown, 1939);
Masks and Faces (London: Faber & Faber, 1940; Boston: Little, Brown, 1940);
The Heart of a Child (London: Faber & Faber, 1940; New York: Putnam, 1940);
Formidable to Tyrants (London: Faber & Faber, 1941); republished as *Mansion House of Liberty* (Boston: Little, Brown, 1941);
London Pride (London: Faber & Faber, 1941; Boston: Little, Brown, 1941);
Survival (New York: Sun Dial, 1941); republished as *Within the Cup* (London: Faber & Faber, 1943; Boston: Little, Brown, 1943);
Austria's Contribution towards Our New Order (London: Austrian Youth Association, 1944);
Austria, a Beautiful Country (London: Austrian Youth Association, 1944);
From the Life (London: Faber & Faber, 1944; Freeport, N.Y.: Books for Libraries Press, 1971);
The Life Line (London: Faber & Faber, 1946; Boston: Little, Brown, 1946);
Individual Countries (London: Allen & Unwin, 1946);
Search for a Soul: Fragment of an Autobiography (London: Faber & Faber, 1947; New York: Reynal & Hitchcock, 1948);
Under the Skin (London: Faber & Faber, 1950; New York: Harcourt, Brace, 1950);
Fortune's Finger (London: Faber & Faber, 1950);
The Challenge (London: Faber & Faber, 1952; New York: Harcourt, Brace, 1953);
Man and Beast (London: Faber & Faber, 1953; New York: Harcourt, Brace, 1954);
Against Whom? (London: Faber & Faber, 1954); republished as *The Secret Stair* (New York: Harcourt, Brace, 1954);
Not in Our Stars (London: Faber & Faber, 1955);
Eldorado Jane (London: Faber & Faber, 1956); republished as *Jane* (New York: Vanguard, 1956);
Walls of Glass (London: Faber & Faber, 1958; New York: Vanguard, 1958);
The Goal (London: Faber & Faber, 1962; New York: Vanguard, 1962);
Best Stories of Phyllis Bottome, edited by Daphne du Maurier (London: Faber & Faber, 1963).

Editions: *Old Wine,* introduction by Phyllis Lassner and Marilyn Hoder-Salmon (Evanston, Ill.: Northwestern University Press, 1998);
The Mortal Storm, introduction by Lassner and Hoder-Salmon (Evanston, Ill.: Northwestern University Press, 1998).

OTHER: *The Rat,* adapted by Bottome from the play by Ivor Novello and Constance Collier (London: Allan, 1926; New York: Doran, 1927);
Our New Order—or Hitler's?: A Selection of Speeches by Winston Churchill, the Archbishop of Canterbury, Anthony Eden, Franklin Delano Roosevelt, edited by Bottome (Harmondsworth & New York: Penguin, 1943).

SELECTED PERIODICAL PUBLICATIONS—UNCOLLECTED: "I Accuse," *New Republic,* 97 (28 December 1938): 232–233;
"Women after Two Wars," *Independent Woman,* 23 (February 1944): 40, 52.

Phyllis Bottome's long life of romantically tinged adventure, travel, accomplishment, and success is unrivaled by the female protagonists of her considerable body of fiction, even though many of those characters are modeled after the independence-minded New Woman of the first half of the twentieth century. Bottome was certainly one of the more prolific writers of any era, publishing between 1902 and 1962 thirty-three novels, twelve collections of short stories and novellas, three volumes of autobiography, travel books, and collections of essays on such topics as feminism, psychology, war, and memoirs of celebrated friends. Bottome's life and writing intersect to form an historical and literary record of an exceptional personality who cared deeply about humanity and modern ideas in the period that encompasses the world wars.

During her lifetime Bottome's novels were popular and critical successes. She traveled widely and counted as mentors and friends many of the

Bottome around the time she wrote Life, the Interpreter *(1902)*

creative elite, political leaders, and important families of Britain, Western and Central Europe, and America. Her subsequent descent into obscurity can be understood in the context of the neglect visited on many women writers as well as the tendency to focus critical interest solely on work of "genius." With all but two of her books out of print as of 1998 (and those two not her best work), and with scholarly attention only recently beginning to be paid to her, Bottome has been all but forgotten. Although correspondence by Bottome is to be found in the collections of well-known literary friends, including Ezra Pound, Upton Sinclair, and Dorothy Thompson, and publishers' records, there is no collection of Bottome's own papers. Fortunately, her three volumes of autobiography illuminate the way Bottome's life served as the focus and background for her fiction, particularly her rendering of major social themes of the world wars and the years between them.

A contemporary reviewer, Clarice Lorenz Aiken, wrote in *The Bookman* (October 1932) that Bottome's fiction has "subtlety, brilliant force, exquisite grace and impeccable taste and calm astuteness." A less enthusiastic assessment appeared in her obituary in *The Times* (London) on 23 August 1963, saying that while her books "fall short of high or serious distinction, the best are intelligent and accomplished and make sound reading." Bottome's fiction fits perfectly current discussions of literary "worth." According to Jane Tompkins, a text's aesthetic merit and historical relevance have equal value; certain works "express and shape the historical moment that produced them" and should be valued for that reason. In Bottome's case the "historical moment" well exceeds the ordinary, and her best novels are worthy of "high or serious distinction."

Bottome was born on 31 May 1882 (1884 is generally given as her birth year, but the baptismal record confirms 1882) in Rochester, Kent, to a British mother of an aristocratic family, Margaret Leatham Bottome, and an American clergyman father, William MacDonald Bottome. She had two older sisters, Wilmett and Mary, and a younger brother, George. Bottome's life to age eighteen in an eccentric, peripatetic, loving, and, in her words, "mercurial family" is recorded in her *Search for a Soul: A Fragment of an Autobiography* (1947). Her depiction of a Victorian child's life has a natural immediacy and novelistic narrative flow that is both riveting and to be expected of an author who claimed to have a "prodigious memory."

The combination of Bottome's father's inability to secure a permanent post in England and her mother's illnesses resulted in frequent moves, often to towns mired in poverty and industrial pollution—"smoke-invested slum[s]," as she calls them. Her father was unfailingly cheerful and loyal, but though he was a talented minister, he was also irresponsible and saw himself as a failure. His professional situation was made even more difficult by Margaret Bottome's unwillingness to play the role of a clergyman's wife. She withdrew from social intercourse, complaining of a series of vague illnesses, and the principal responsibility for the management of the family fell to Bottome's sister Wilmett. Although the Leatham family was well-to-do, and Bottome's mother had her own income, she was unaccountably parsimonious, which added to the family's stress.

One of Bottome's most telling childhood recollections concerns her encounter with a group of boys who hounded and jeered her while she was alone on a family errand. Decades later she described the incident as a "hideous storm of terror" that foreshadowed her lifelong dislike of patriarchal privilege: "Fear of your brother man, when you know yourself to be his equal, and yet realize that you have no power to prove it, is the sourest potion to which Fate can treat you."

William Bottome's American relatives urged him to resettle the family in his native country, and in 1890 they moved in with his parents and brothers in Yonkers, New York. This close-knit family of kindly uncles, a grandfather, and a dynamic grandmother, Margaret MacDonald Bottome, a popular author and lecturer on religious topics, were all strong influences in Phyllis Bottome's development. Margaret Bottome founded the King's Daughters Society and wrote a column, "Heart to Heart Talks," for the *Ladies Home Journal* for more than a quarter of a century. An affectionate memoir of her grandmother appears in Bottome's *From the Life* (1944), a book about noted figures in her circle.

When her father became pastor of Grace Church in Jamaica, Long Island, Phyllis was sent to a Catholic boarding school in Manhattan. Her parents believed that girls should receive the same education as boys; family disruptions, however, kept Bottome's formal schooling to a minimum. Her mother's health continued to decline, and as she remained homesick for England, doctors advised the family to return there. Even though Bottome's discouraged father predicted the "end of his career," they sailed home in 1896 and settled in Bournemouth. There Bottome began to take on responsibilities in her father's parishes such as organizing "improvement" clubs for boys, through which she gained firsthand knowledge of life in some of England's poorest communities.

Deterred by illness from pursuing a career in acting, Bottome wrote her first novel at age seventeen. (She was later to say that she became a novelist when she was four or five, being "an imaginative young girl with observant eyes.") She put the novel aside to nurse Wilmett, who had tuberculosis and ultimately died of the disease. Two years after putting the work aside Bottome sent the manuscript to a literary agent, and Andrew Lang of Longmans, Green and Company promptly accepted it for publication.

Life, the Interpreter (1902), while unexceptional, is well written and engrossing. More significantly, it covers many of the themes that recur throughout Bottome's works. First among her concerns are young women who reject class distinctions and put marriage aside to live independently, especially to serve downtrodden women and children. In opposition to such heroines Bottome almost vituperatively portrays society women who, deprived of any useful purpose, become manipulative and foolish and are driven to excesses by the only occupations open to them—particularly "husband hunting." Muriel Dallerton, Bottome's New Woman, explains to her guardian that "a girl nowadays isn't satisfied simply in being domestic." A male doctor of her acquaintance casually diagnoses Muriel's interest in improving life for the poor as "a case of hysteria." He is contrasted with the almost saintly Dr. Cynthia Grant, Muriel's friend and partner in the slums. Both women are pursued by ardent suitors but prefer to continue helping poor women and children. In the end Muriel and Cynthia accept men who share their ideals. Dr. Grant is the first of many women physician protagonists and minor characters in Bottome's fiction.

After the novel was published, Bottome's illness worsened, and she herself was diagnosed with tuberculosis. With the financial assistance of well-to-do friends she and her closest friend, Hope de Lisle Brock, journeyed during the next few years to Switzerland, France, and Italy for their health. She later wrote of this period, "economic pressures, ill-health, and sorrow had long been our companions." In 1904 she became engaged to Alban Ernan Forbes Dennis, of an aristocratic Scottish family, who was also recovering from tuberculosis. Later, however, Bottome grew discouraged about her health and broke the engagement.

From 1904 through the 1920s Bottome wrote a series of novels that were first serialized in American magazines such as the *Century;* she also wrote dozens of short stories, some of which she reworked as novels. These works can generally be categorized as social romances, and many of them are marred by improbable episodes and convoluted plots. Bottome frequently pairs two women, as she had in *Life, the Interpreter*. In *The Master Hope* (1904), her second novel, Daphne Fordington and Katherine Linton are nurses. Katherine's suitor is puzzled by her insistence on working. She acknowledges that nursing is "hard work . . . and if you happen to be a woman, very little pay" but explains that work is necessary for a woman's dignity. After some frivolous interventions by idle society women the plot is resolved conventionally, with Daphne and Katherine agreeing to marry their suitors.

Raw Material: Some Characters and Episodes among Working Lads (1905) is the first novel in which Bottome concentrates on poverty and the conditions that foster abuse in lower-class family life. The plot is a barely fictionalized account drawn from her work assisting her father in his parish duties: "These secret tragedies of the poor and the outcast beat in on my child's mind with a persistent ferocity," she recalled in *Search for a Soul. Raw Material* and her other works in this genre unflinchingly portray class oppression, alcoholism, and the abuse of

Bottome's husband, Capt. Alban Ernan Forbes Dennis, shortly after their marriage in 1917

women and children. The lives of children who were forced to work in factories, on barges, and in other sordid occupations inspired Bottome's deepest compassion. She had equal empathy for victims of the sex trade; in *Search for a Soul* she writes about the "holocaust of girls and women secretly set aside for this purpose [prostitution] by a policy of poverty and starvation."

Bottome traveled widely and lived in seven countries over the course of her life; as a consequence almost all of her novels involve travel or are set in foreign places. *The Imperfect Gift* (1907)—Bottome's first commercial success—and *The Captive* (1915) are typical. In *The Imperfect Gift* a British widow, ignoring family recriminations, moves to Italy with her two daughters. There they have a series of romantic entanglements, and the daughters pursue careers. In *The Captive* a free-spirited working-class woman, Maisie Brent, aspires to be an artist and studies in Rome. She is contrasted with the upper-class Rosamund Beaumont, who is a "captive" because although she makes the attempt with Maisie's prodding, she fails to escape the narrow customs of her class.

After the death of her father in 1913 the family pressures on Bottome increased. In *The Challenge* (1952), the second of her autobiographies, she would write that unmarried daughters in the early twentieth century were burdened with "the persistent weight of the older lives we could not help and yet had to support." She contrasted that burden with the improved status of unmarried daughters in the 1950s: "the most releasing of social changes" is that they are "given the rights of wage earners; and need not become domestic slaves."

Bottome made many literary friends during the period just before World War I, including Pound, Alice Meynell, H. D. (Hilda Doolittle), Richard Aldington, and May Sinclair. She recalled in *The Challenge* that while she and de Brock were "strong feminists," it was overhearing Meynell in an impassioned conversation about suffrage that led them to expand their concerns from "higher education and the opening of all careers to women" to include political gains.

In 1914 Bottome and Forbes Dennis met again in London. Forbes Dennis had been commissioned a captain in the British army, and when World War I started, he was sent to the front lines in France. In 1917 he and Bottome were married, Bottome having purchased her wedding gown during the "first serious air-raid London experienced." Forbes Dennis returned to the front, and Bottome moved to France to wait for him. When she learned that he had been sent to a London hospital for treatment of serious wounds, she returned to England. After his recovery Forbes Dennis volunteered for the front again. While he was away, Bottome kept occupied as a writer for the Ministry of Information and as a relief worker for Belgian refugees. After the war Forbes Dennis joined the diplomatic service, and in 1920 he was sent to Vienna as passport control officer for Austria, Hungary, and Yugoslavia. In Vienna, Bottome worked with the British physician Hilda Clarke, director of the Friends' Mission, and the Viennese social worker Valerie Adler in organizing the distribution of food and medical supplies. She also continued to write fiction.

The Crystal Heart (1921) is Bottome's first truly autobiographical novel. Joy and Rosemary Featherstone are the daughters of loving but self-absorbed parents. When Rosemary becomes terminally ill, Joy sacrifices her own happiness by taking on the responsibility for her sister's care. Joy's ignorance of sexuality also harms her by leading her to rebuff the man she loves. The novel's resolution is forced and melodramatic, with Joy descending into insanity and death. One can assume that Joy's chaotic overreaction is a symbolic expression of Bottome's own resentments.

The Kingfisher (1922) is about the ills of poverty. It opens with a scene of domestic violence as Jim Barton strikes back at his abusive father and accidentally kills him. The novel centers on his reclamation through education and the support of others. Jim becomes a union organizer and wins the love of Viola Egerton, an upper-class woman who defies her mother's plans for her. In the ordeal of rejecting her "proper fiancée" Viola finds her strength for the first time. Her father explains to the horrified jilted suitor, "she isn't quite herself"; Viola, overhearing the conversation, knows that she has, instead, become herself: "For the first time in her life, that which was herself, had risen up in her and acted."

In 1923 Bottome's tuberculosis returned. Her doctors advised a long sojourn in the mountains, and Forbes Dennis left his position to accompany her to Mösern, Switzerland. During the rest of the 1920s and the 1930s they lived in various places in Austria, Switzerland, and Germany.

Although many of Bottome's heroines are, in addition to being career women, excellent hostesses and cooks, domesticity is almost never described. The one exception is *The Perfect Wife* (1924), in which Anne, a traditional housewife prepared to sacrifice everything for her husband's happiness, is cast aside for Nina, a career girl.

The Depths of Prosperity (1924), co-authored by Thompson, is Bottome's first novel set in America. A ruthless New York socialite, Mrs. Irvine St. Clair, conspires to marry off her daughter, Hilary, to a degenerate Englishman. She is jealous of the girl's youth and wants her out of the way. The convoluted storyline encompasses domestic abuse, greedy and evil physicians, a murder plot, and a happy ending. It is perhaps Bottome's angriest portrayal of the depth to which a woman who lives solely to win male admiration can sink.

Old Wine (1924) empathetically portrays the social shambles of postwar Austria. Fallen aristocrats, American and British relief workers, greedy manipulators, "traditional" women, and independent professional women (including an American journalist modeled after Thompson) meet and mingle in the chaos of Vienna in the early 1920s. With its variegated cast of characters and dramatic setting, *Old Wine* is the novel that established Bottome's reputation.

After Bottome's recovery Forbes Dennis founded a language school for British and American boys in the Innsbruck region in 1924. The curriculum, which was based on preparing the boys to work for international peace, used modern learning techniques. The school lasted for four years. Bottome stayed in touch with many of its graduates, some of whom went on to distinguished careers. Their interest in education brought the couple in contact with the psychiatrist Alfred Adler; both of them studied under Adler and underwent analysis with him.

In *The Belated Reckoning* (1926) Ellen McDermott, an Englishwoman, and her American sister-in-law Angelina McDermott are traveling in Italy. They decide to rescue an American bride they believe is being abused by her new husband. Angelina exclaims, "No one who has done for women's suffrage in Western California what I have done is going to sit still and see a fellow-countrywoman wronged by a man that looks like a bilious lizard." Angelina becomes ill, and it is left to the reserved Ellen to carry out the daring rescue. The relieved bride sails back to America alone, and Ellen finds love with a vacationing Bostonian.

The contrast between conventional and inadequate parents and their imaginative and sensitive children is treated in *Wild Grapes* (1927), a bildungsroman set in America. Eight-year-old Imogen—"When she smiled there was a fierceness in her face," which is framed by wild hair the "colour of wet sand when the tide goes down"—is misunderstood by her parents and punished with unjust harshness. A kindly doctor warns them to stop treating their daughter in this way, and to offer Imogen an avenue of escape he introduces the child to literature. She wins the first prize, a silver spoon, for a class poetry recitation and trades it for the second prize: a book. Imogen's parents scorn her, believing that she has been tricked into giving up the spoon. But the child is resilient and strong: "Deep, deep down in Imogen was a longing for power; again and again she had felt this instinct rising." As she matures, Imogen feels stifled in her Maine hometown; eager for experience, she begins an affair with Maurice, a summer visitor. Her poem about their first kiss offends Maurice because it concentrates on Imogen's emotions. When Maurice rejects his responsibility for her pregnancy, she deliberately capsizes their sailboat. Maurice, encumbered by his boots, drowns as Imogen swims to shore. The second half of the novel takes place in New York, where Imogen realizes her potential as a poet.

After the Innsbruck school closed, Bottome and her husband moved to Munich with the idea of

Title page for the U.S. edition of a 1934 novel about a mental hospital

opening a new school, but the decline in political stability as the Nazi Party gained power kept them from fulfilling their plans.

Tatter'd Loving (1929)—the title is taken from a phrase in one of William Shakespeare's sonnets (1609)—is a serious study of family life. Vera obtains a divorce and marries Edward, her true love, but is forced to leave her daughter, Ariadne, behind. Mother and daughter are reunited when Ariadne is grown. Vera explains to Ariadne, a New Woman, why she stayed so long in a deeply unhappy marriage: "I had no money and no training. In those days women rarely earned their own living, certainly, not women who had been brought up in a sheltered useless seclusion out of which they'd been suddenly dipped into the world, and married off at eighteen." Generational differences eventually cause a breech, and the two women part once more. In *Good Housekeeping* (February 1931) Emily Newell Blair said that *Tatter'd Loving* had a "sparkling style, situations handled with adroitness, suspense piled on suspense, characters delineated so that they throbbed with life, yet revealed to their innermost core."

Level Crossing (1936) is one of Bottome's most intriguing romances. A rich American, Jim Lane, travels to Scotland, where he meets Deidre. Married and settled in America, the couple are awaiting the birth of their child when Deidre is kidnapped by ransom-seeking gangsters. The kidnapping is described from Deidre's point of view; there are no scenes of the distraught family or the police investigation. Nelly, the girlfriend of one of the kidnappers, helps Deidre to escape, after which Deidre refuses to assist the police in locating the criminals. Deidre's behavior is inexplicable to her husband: "The bond that had held Deidre and Nelly together in the same sisterhood was unimaginable to him." In linking two women of different economic and social statuses Bottome illustrates the commonality between women as pawns of male domination.

During her lifetime Bottome became widely known for two novels, *Private Worlds* (1934) and *The Mortal Storm* (1937). Both went through many editions in Britain and America and were made into popular Hollywood movies. While Bottome's claim that *Private Worlds* was the first novel about mental illness is inaccurate—Rebecca West's *The Return of the Soldier* (1918) had preceded it—the work is unique in its treatment of the states of mind of both the patients and the physicians at a mental hospital. The novel brought Bottome invitations to lecture in America.

The title of *Private Worlds* is a reference both to the disordered minds of the mentally ill and to "the determined isolation and reserve" of psychiatrists. Dr. Charles Drummond, the new superintendent of a mental hospital, tells Dr. Jane Everett, a respected member of the staff: "The medical profession is not, one finds, particularly suitable for women." Jane responds, restraining her anger: "'Do you not think,' after a pause, 'that people should be judged by their work as individuals, rather than by their sex?'" Later, Jane explains why men are angry at women: "It was a man-made world, and now we're asking to go shares in the working of it." Bottome threads many diverse elements into the plot, including marital infidelity, a spoiled society woman, and a murder. By the novel's end all the human entanglements are satisfactorily resolved.

In 1935 the producer Walter Wanger and the director Gregory La Cava made *Private Worlds* into a motion picture starring Charles Boyer and Claudette Colbert (Colbert was nominated for an Academy Award for her portrayal of Jane Everett). In Britain some scenes were censored as "not a fit subject for entertainment." The novel was also broadcast as a radio series by United Artists and adapted as a play. Bottome believed that her work increased public compassion for the mentally ill and contributed to the improvement of treatment facilities.

In 1935 Bottome and her husband returned to Vienna to continue their work with the Adlerian group. Forbes Dennis also studied piano to qualify for a license to teach music. When they returned to England to settle in 1936, Bottome undertook a campaign to inform the British public about the Nazi menace; her concern was met with apathy. Borrowing the title from Emile Zola, she wrote a statement, "I Accuse," castigating British political and religious leaders for ignoring the rise of fascism. Even liberal-minded weeklies and private printers refused to handle the piece, which was finally published in America in the magazine *New Republic* in 1938.

Bottome turned her zeal to fiction. In *The Mortal Storm* a German medical student, Freya Roth, resolutely continues her studies as the Nazi menace rises around her. The novel's opening scene demonstrates that Freya is a New Woman: having decided to spend her allowance on a microscope rather than the party clothes for which the funds were intended, she tells her mother: "I am definitely not going to marry–if I do at all–for ages and ages: There's my profession!" Her two older half brothers join the Nazi Party. Her father, a renowned Jewish physician (her mother is a Christian), is the chief interpreter of Nazi philosophy in the narrative. He warns Freya to keep quiet about winning a university grant: "Since they believe in force rather than persuasion, and women have less force than men, the Nazi regime must be, to that extent, antifeminine... half the human race that produces and trains the other half, will be once more degraded!" Freya becomes involved with Hans, a Communist, who tells her: "Believe me or not–to vote for this Herr Hitler, with his great voice that shakes the heart, is to bring darkness and horror into the world." After Hans is shot to death by the Nazis while attempting to ski across the mountains to the frontier, his comrades help Freya escape to America. *The Mortal Storm* became an immediate best-seller, particularly in America, where more than fifty thousand copies were sold the first year. It is generally considered her best novel.

Forbes Dennis arranged a lecture tour for Adler in England and Scotland, and he and Bottome were accompanying the psychiatrist when Adler suddenly became ill and died in Aberdeen on 28 May 1937. Bottome was writing a biography of Adler, and after an interval she and Forbes Dennis returned to Austria to interview Adler's colleagues and friends. They remained there for ten months, leaving three days before Adolf Hitler entered Vienna on 11 March 1938. Bottome's biography, *Alfred Adler, Apostle of Freedom* (1939), was a best-seller and would remain in print into the 1950s. In 1939 Bottome and her husband traveled to America, where they remained for almost a year lecturing, managing Bottome's literary business affairs, and visiting old friends such as Thompson, Sinclair, Gertrude Atherton, and President Franklin Delano Roosevelt and his family. When the bombing of London began, they hurried back to England to do what they could to help deal with the aftermath of the attacks. Just before leaving they were able to view the movie version of *The Mortal Storm,* which premiered 20 June 1940; it starred Margaret Sullavan as Freya, Frank Morgan as her father, and James Stewart as Martin (Hans).

In 1941 Bottome published *Formidable to Tyrants,* a collection of essays about the quiet fortitude of the British people and the women who served in the Ambulance Corps and the Women's Royal Naval Service; it was published in the United States the same year as *Mansion House of Liberty.* She also wrote a short novel, *London Pride* (1941), which is told from the perspective of a seven-year-old working-class child, Ben Barton. Ben prevails under adversity as a symbol of family solidarity and survival in London under siege.

In her 1946 novel *The Life Line* Bottome revisits Nazi Austria. The novel's themes, familiar to Bottome's readers—the threat of fascism, the treatment of mental illness, and the barriers faced by independent women—are meshed in an engrossing story. Mark Chalmers, a Briton vacationing in the Innsbruck region, is recruited as a spy by a friend in the Foreign Office. He becomes embroiled in the anti-Nazi movement, which brings him into contact with Dr. Ida Eichhorn, the director of a small mental hospital and a leader in the underground. At first Mark finds Ida unattractive: "Her figure was wiry and without curves; she had no allure; no poise. A mind of her own—and what a place to put it in! Mark thought discouragingly." Nevertheless, the two become lovers. When they realize that they will probably be separated for the duration, they decide to marry before parting as a symbol of their determination and hope for the future.

As her next novel, *Under the Skin* (1950), opens, Lucy Armstrong, a young British war widow, arrives on an unnamed island in the West Indies to become headmistress of Everslade, a school for island girls. The school's doctor, Philip Calgory, is of mixed white and West Indian parentage. Initially

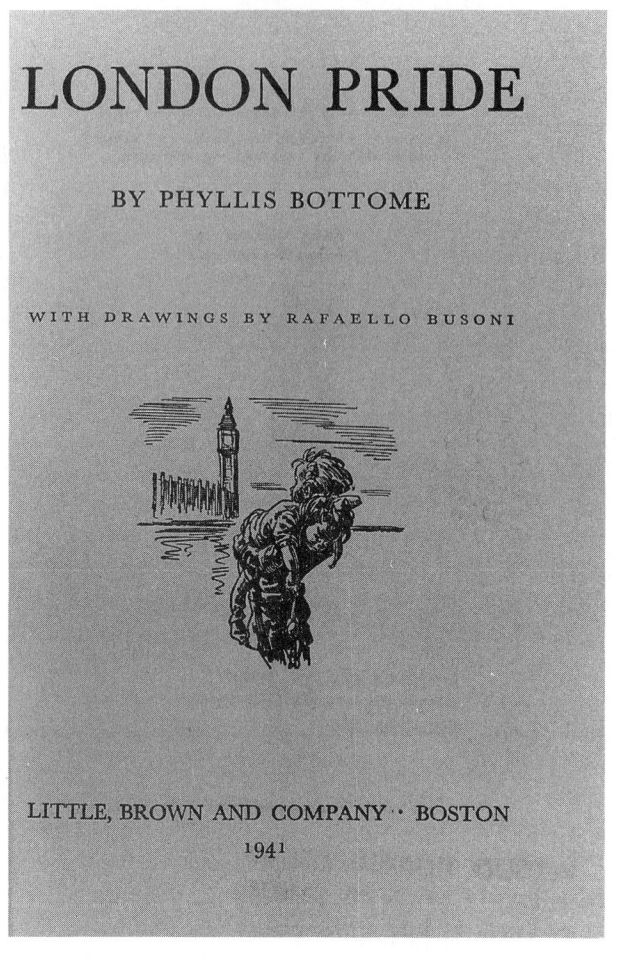

Title page for the U.S. edition of a novel about wartime London as seen through the eyes of a seven-year-old boy

wary of each other, Lucy and Philip gradually become friends, fall in love, and marry. Well traveled in the Caribbean, Bottome had studied Jamaica's history; her familiarity with the region's problems of racism, poverty, and illiteracy gives *Under the Skin* authenticity, and her treatment of interracial love is advanced for the time.

In an essay in her collection *Not in Our Stars* (1955) Bottome touches on an issue that is still being debated–the meshing of motherhood and career: "it would be equally hard to demand that a woman–who is at least 90 per cent human being to 10 per cent female–should give up a career or suppress a gift.... Perhaps the community should step in here, in order to help her solve this problem." She advocates "labor saving contrivances" in the home, nursery schools, and a new profession of trained domestic workers. She also suggests that fathers have "equal validity" with mothers in children's development. She points out that literature, "with few though notable exceptions, has always been in the hands of men" and how many aphorisms have been written against women. Bottome concludes: "Women fly; they swim; they ski; they drive cars; they shoot; they face danger as well as men"; they have, therefore, earned equality.

In her essay "Women after Two Wars," published in 1944 in *Independent Woman,* an American magazine, Bottome decries the folly of discarding women's expertise in peacetime. When a country is in the "throes of a great struggle," women are given men's jobs, in which they develop new skills and strength of character. In the peace that follows they are forced to give up their public roles, but "Fuller use of women's capacities can only be good for our nation." If mothers, however, wished to remain at home, Bottome makes the (for the time) radical suggestion that "homemaking be dignified into a profession and paid for accordingly."

Bottome published the second and third volumes of her autobiography, *The Challenge* and *The Goal,* in 1952 and 1962, respectively. *The Challenge* is particularly interesting for its evocation of Alpine resorts and the culture of illness in the early twentieth century while *The Goal* deals with Bottome's wartime experiences and literary successes. While both books are full of lively details about her adventuresome life, they lack the artistry of *Search for a Soul*, which stands with *Private Worlds* and *The Mortal Storm* as her most accomplished works. Her friend Daphne du Maurier edited *Best Stories of Phyllis Bottome*, which appeared in 1963. Bottome died in Hampstead, England, on 22 August of that year. Her husband died in 1972.

Although Bottome wrote during the era of modernist prose and knew many of the innovative authors of the period, and although her themes were often radical, her style remained traditional. Perhaps her most serious flaw as a writer was a sometimes uncontrolled imagination that led her to add bizarre subplots that detract from her narratives. But even her least successful work is of interest to the social and literary historian, and her best has engrossing description, witty narration, and characters who brim with vitality—particularly heroic and confident women and children who engage class, custom, and totalitarianism in their struggle for justice. Bottome took her craft seriously. That she continued to write through serious illnesses, family problems, relocations, two world wars, humanitarian work, and other distractions shows a strong and disciplined will, a trait not generally acknowledged in women of her era. Bottome was a witness to the upheavals and advances of a good part of the twentieth century, and she wove them into her stories; also, her voice was passionately raised against social injustice. For those reasons her work deserves to be known.

References:

Barbara Brothers, "British Women Write the Story of the Nazis: A Conspiracy of Silence," in *Forgotten Radicals: British Women Writers, 1889-1939*, edited by Angela Ingram and Daphne Patai (Chapel Hill & London: University of North Carolina Press, 1993), pp. 248-263;

Phyllis Lassner, *British Women Writers of World War II: Battlegrounds of Their Own* (New York: St. Martin's Press, 1998), pp. 216-232.

Papers:

Although there seems to be no archive of Phyllis Bottome's papers, correspondence to and from her, as well as manuscript excerpts, are in collections of the papers of other writers. In the United States these collections include the correspondence of Upton Sinclair at the Lilly Library, Indiana University; the Dorothy Thompson Collection at the Syracuse University Library; the Authors' Syndicate papers, the PEN Archives, and the papers of Compton Mackenzie and other writers at the Harry Ransom Humanities Research Library of the University of Texas at Austin; the papers of Ezra Pound at the Beinecke Rare Book and Manuscript Library, Yale University; and the papers of the British literary agent James B. Pinker at Northwestern University Library. In Britain, Bottome's correspondence with Basil Liddell Hart is at the Centre for Military Archives, London University; her correspondence with Max Beerbohm is at Merton College Library, Oxford; and her correspondence with Daphne du Maurier is at the University of Warwick Modern Records Centre, Coventry.

Thomas Burke
(1886 – 22 September 1945)

Richard Bleiler
The University of Connecticut

BOOKS: *Verses* (London: Privately printed, 1910);

Pavements and Pastures: A Book of Songs (London: Privately printed, 1912);

Nights in Town: A London Autobiography (London: Allen & Unwin, 1915); republished as *Nights in London* (New York: Holt, 1916);

Limehouse Nights: Tales of Chinatown (London: Richards, 1916); republished as *Limehouse Nights* (New York: McBride, 1917);

London Lamps: A Book of Songs (London: Richards, 1917; New York: McBride, 1919);

Twinkletoes: A Tale of Chinatown (London: Richards, 1917); republished as *Twinkletoes: A Tale of Limehouse* (New York: McBride, 1918);

Out and about: A Note-Book of London in War-Time (London: Allen & Unwin, 1919); republished as *Out and about London* (New York: Holt, 1919);

The Song Book of Quong Lee of Limehouse (London: Allen & Unwin, 1920; New York: Henry Holt, 1920);

The Outer Circle: Rambles in Remote London (London: Allen & Unwin, 1921; New York: Doran, 1921);

Whispering Windows: Tales of the Waterside (London: Richards, 1921); republished as *More Limehouse Nights* (New York: Doran, 1921);

The London Spy: A Book of Town Travels (London: Butterworth, 1922; New York: Doran, 1922);

The Wind and the Rain: A Book of Confessions (New York: Doran, 1924; London: Butterworth, 1924);

East of Mansion House (New York: Doran, 1926; London: Cassell, 1928);

The Sun in Splendour (New York: Doran, 1926; London: Constable, 1927);

Essays of To-day and Yesterday (London: Harrap, 1928);

The Bloomsbury Wonder (London: Mandrake, 1929);

The Flower of Life (London: Constable, 1929); republished as *The Flower of Life: A Christmas Fable* (Garden City, N.Y.: Doubleday, Doran, 1930);

The English Inn (London & New York: Longmans, Green, 1930; revised edition, London: Jenkins, 1947);

The Pleasantries of Old Quong (London: Constable, 1931); republished as *A Tea-Shop in Limehouse* (Boston: Little, Brown, 1931);

The Maid's Head, Norwich (London: True Temperance Association, 1931);

Go, Lovely Rose (Brooklyn, N.Y.: Sesphra Library, 1931);

The Anchor, at Bankside (London: True Temperance Association, 1932);

City of Encounters: A London Divertissement (London: Constable, 1932; Boston: Little, Brown, 1932);

The Real East End (London: Constable, 1932);

The Beauty of England (London: Harrap, 1933; New York: McBride, 1934);

London in My Time (London: Rich & Cowan, 1934; New York: Loring & Mussey, 1935);

Billy and Beryl in Chinatown (London: Harrap, 1935);

Night-Pieces: Eighteen Tales (London: Constable, 1935; New York: Appleton-Century, 1936);

Billy and Beryl in Old London (London: Harrap, 1936);

Billy and Beryl in Soho (London: Harrap, 1936);

Murder at Elstree; or, Mr. Thurtell and His Gig (London: Longmans, Green, 1936; New York: Longmans, Green, 1936);

Vagabond Minstrel: The Adventures of Thomas Dermody (London: Longmans, Green, 1936; New York: Longmans, Green, 1936);

Will Someone Lead Me to a Pub? Being a Note upon Certain of the Taverns, Old and New, of London; Presenting Something of Their Story, Their Company, and Their Quiddity (London: Routledge, 1936);

Dinner is Served!; or, Eating Round the World in London; Being a Brief Glance, for the Benefit of Visitors, at the Many Ways and Means of Dining in London; from the Fashionable Restaurants of Great Reputation, Through the Various Grill Rooms, and the Assorted Nationalities of Soho, to the Old Chop Houses and the More Dainty Snack Bars. With Some Observations upon the Gastronomical Customs of Past and

Thomas Burke

Present; Brief Sketches of Each Kind of Restaurant, and a Note of Any Special Dishes Peculiar to This or That Restaurant (London: Routledge, 1937);

The Winsome Wench: The Story of a London Inn, 1825–1900 (London: Routledge, 1938);

Abduction: A Story of Limehouse (London: Jenkins, 1939);

Living in Bloomsbury (London: Allen & Unwin, 1939);

The Streets of London Through the Centuries (London: Batsford, 1940; New York: Scribners, 1940);

The First Noel (London: Wakeham, 1940);

English Night-Life from the Norman Curfew to Present Blackout (London: Batsford, 1941; New York: Scribners, 1946);

Victorian Grotesque (London: Jenkins, 1941);

Travel in England, from Pilgrim and Pack-Horse to Light Car and Plane (London: Batsford, 1942; New York: Scribners, 1946);

English Inns (London: Collins, 1943);

Dark Nights (London: Jenkins, 1944);

The English and Their Country (London: Longmans, Green, 1945; New York: Longmans, Green, 1945);

The English Townsman as He Was and as He Is (London: Batsford, 1946; New York: Scribners, 1947);

Son of London (London: Jenkins, 1946);

The Best Stories of Thomas Burke, selected, with a foreword, by John Gawsworth (London: Phoenix House, 1950).

OTHER: *The Small People: A Little Book of Verse about Children for Their Elders,* edited by Burke (London: Chapman & Hall, 1910);

An Artist's Day Book: A Treasury of Good Counsel from the Great Masters in the Arts for Their Disciples, edited by Burke (London: Herbert & Daniel, 1911); selections republished as *Truth and Beauty* (London: Cape, 1921; Boston: Humphries, 1937); selections republished as *Life and Art* (London: Cape, 1921; Boston: Humphries, 1937);

The Contented Mind: An Anthology of Optimism, edited by Burke (London: Truslove & Hanson, 1913; New York: Stokes, n.d.);

The Charm of the West Country: An Anthology, compiled and edited by Burke (Bristol: Arrowsmith; London: Simpkin, Marshall, Hamilton, Dent, 1913);

Children in Verse: Fifty Songs of Playful Childhood, collected and edited by Burke (London: Duckworth, 1913; Boston: Little, Brown, 1914);

Kiddie Land, edited by Burke and Margaret G. Hays (London: Dean & Son, 1913);

Twinkletoes: A Tale of Chinatown

By Thomas Burke

London
Grant Richards Limited
St Martin's Street
mdcccxvii

Title page for a sentimental novel about the tragic life and early death of a dancer

The Charm of England, edited by Burke (London: Truslove & Hanson, 1914);

Bernard G. Baker, *The German Army from Within, by a British Officer Who Has Served in It,* edited by Burke (London: Hodder & Stoughton, 1914);

The Book of the Inn: Being Two Hundred Pictures of the English Inn from the Earliest Times to the Coming of the Railway Hotel, edited by Burke (London: Constable, 1927; New York: Doran, 1927);

The Ecstasies of Thomas de Quincey, edited by Burke (London: Harrap, 1928; Garden City, N.Y.: Doubleday, Doran, 1929).

Although he wrote more than forty books and was praised by critics as diverse as H. G. Wells, David Garnett, and Nikolaus Pevsner, Thomas Burke is today virtually forgotten. This neglect is not entirely undeserved, for Burke was highly uneven as a writer. He was frequently repetitive and wrote too much that is sentimental, melodramatic, and sensationalistic. Nevertheless, Burke was capable of telling an intelligent, original, insightful story, and it is unfortunate that the book for which he received the most publicity—the short-story collection *Limehouse Nights: Tales of Chinatown* (1916)—does not represent his best work, the majority of which has never been reprinted. Furthermore, Burke deserves recognition as one of the first English writers to portray Asians as individuals rather than as stereotypes, and he was often surprisingly sympathetic toward women's sexuality; he is perhaps the first writer of note to have stories in which the primary characters are (quite matter-of-factly) lesbians.

Like many writers of his generation, Burke fictionalized his life, and later volumes of his autobiography include data that cheerfully contradict material presented earlier. In *The Wind and the Rain: A Book of Confessions* (1924), for example, Burke claims that his first serious love occurred when as a twenty-year-old office boy he became enamored of Gracie Scott, a fourteen-year-old starved for affection and life. He took it upon himself to educate her, teaching her to appreciate literature and attending a concert with her before the relationship ended disastrously with Gracie's termagant aunt knocking him down and hauling the girl off into the night. Burke may indeed have had a relationship with a fourteen-year-old, but it could not have happened as he said, for at age twenty he had long since quit his position as office boy and had been employed in a literary agency for nearly two years. This misleading of readers is superficially playful, but it has the unfortunate side effect of rendering Burke an evasive, shadowy personality.

It is reasonably certain that Burke was born to humble circumstances in East London in 1886 (one source states, probably erroneously, 1887). Both parents died while he was young, and he was raised by his uncle Frank, a former innkeeper who worked as a gardener; sympathetic innkeepers were to play significant roles in Burke's fiction. Despite a variety of acquaintances, the young Burke was apparently acutely lonely. His only close friendship appears to have been with Quong Lee, an equally lonely Chinese immigrant who ran a small shop in London's Limehouse district. According to Burke, the two were unable to converse but took pleasure in each other's companionship. It is possible, however, that Quong Lee was a fictional composite of the Chinese who Burke saw in the Limehouse district or was inspired by such literary creations as Ernest Bramah's itinerant storyteller, Kai Lung, who first appeared in *The Wallet of Kai Lung* (1900).

When Burke was about nine years old, he was sent to the Hardcress Home for Orphans in the

West Country. Although he initially disliked its orderliness and drills, he formed friendships, received a trade education, and eventually came to love the structured existence it provided. Describing his release at age thirteen, Burke wrote: "I had gone into the school as into a cold isolation, as I have described from the distorted angle of a morbid child. I came out of it as from a spot which I should remember for ever as a cluster of friends and counsellors who had made me fit for the world without reward other than the work itself."

After leaving school Burke took a series of menial jobs, including that of office boy, a dead-end position he resented but endured for several years. He became a habitué of the London music halls, concerts, and opera houses, accumulating experiences and studying characters about whom he would later write. Furthermore, assisted initially by a friendly librarian, Burke discovered literature. He read voraciously and omnivorously, starving himself to buy books, eventually being transformed by what he read:

> soon my mind became a lumber-room. Philosophy, poetry, romance, truth and lies jostled one another and fought. I read every new book in the light of its predecessor. I made no attempt to range or relate them, but accepted them all, changing my ideas of life to the tune of each new author. I went about London aflame with loves and hates; hate of the city, of the office, of the jargon of commerce, of dull people, and love of London and poetry and the world of intellect and fancy, where people Did Things; and Oh, my God! How I despised, in the mad pride of intellectuality, the tattered folk I had to work among.

Burke would later claim to remember virtually everything he read, and evidence of wide reading and iconoclastic scholarship does appear throughout his writing.

Burke was fifteen when he sold his first short pieces to the boy's humor paper *Ally Sloper's Half-Holiday*. He contacted the agency of Frank Cazenove and G. H. Perris when he was eighteen and was offered a position, which he accepted. While at Cazenove and Perris, Burke associated with several successful authors, at least one of whom may have used him as a model; in *City of Encounters: A London Divertissement* (1932) he writes that "Miss Ethel Mayne . . . in a short story about a literary agency, one of a volume of stories, *Blind Eyes*, gave a sketch of a youth for whom, I am pretty sure, I was the model." As Mayne published neither a book nor a short story with that title, it appears that Burke either mis-remembered the author and title or, again, fictionalized his life. Furthermore, despite the agency's apparently congenial work environment, Burke remained acutely aware of his poverty, and he recoiled in horror and ultimately disobeyed his employers when they asked him to escort the novelist Sheila Kaye-Smith to a luncheon: "I was then morbidly shy and inarticulate, and the mere prospect of walking in my shabby clothes with a clever young girl, who would certainly be well dressed, all through Covent Garden to Portugal Street, was truly terrible to me."

Burke's first book was *Verses* (1910), a small collection of poetry published in an edition of twenty-five copies; it was perhaps written to impress a woman with whom he was in love. (In *City of Encounters* Burke claims that he was twenty when the book appeared, and that he had it printed out of vanity.) He had well-received short stories published in *The English Review* and, starting with *The Small People: A Little Book of Verse about Children for Their Elders* (1910), he began to compile and edit popular anthologies. *An Artist's Day Book: A Treasury of Good Counsel from the Great Masters in the Arts for Their Disciples* (1911), *The Charm of the West Country* (1913), *Children in Verse: Fifty Songs of Playful Childhood* (1913), *Kiddie Land* (1913), *The Contented Mind: An Anthology of Optimism* (1913), and *The Charm of England* (1914) garnered generally favorable reviews.

From 1914 to 1918 Burke worked at the American branch of the Ministry of Information, presumably as a writer, and in 1918 he married Winifred Wells, who wrote under the pen name Clare Cameron. Neither of these experiences is mentioned in Burke's volumes of autobiography.

Nights in Town: A London Autobiography (1915), a collection of essays, was Burke's first major publication. It is a paean to London and its inhabitants, for with the possible exception of Charles Dickens no author has loved London as deeply or written about it as frequently as Burke. He says early in the volume:

> As a born Londoner, I cannot remember a time when London was not part of me and I a part of London. Things that happen to London happen to me. Changes in London are changes in me, and changes in my affairs and circumstances have again and again changed the entire face of London. Whatever the mood or the occasion, London is behind it. I can never say that I am happy or downcast. London and I are happy, London and I are having a good time, or are lost in the deeps . . . . And always it is London by lamplight which I vision when I think of her, for it was the London of lamplight that first called to me, as a child.

Nights in Town is frequently delightful reading, and one of its charms is that Burke is forthright in expressing his dislikes:

[Kensington] holds all the most disagreeable things—everything that is flat, brackish, unprofitable, and self-proud. I have a grim fancy that, years ago, some genius of humour, tired of administering aperients to the intellectually costive, must have amused himself by wandering round London and collecting all that he could find most alkaloid. Then, gathering his treasures together, he dumped the whole lot down, and gave its resting-place the jangling name of Kensington.

Nor was Burke averse to mentioning the urban horrors around London: cocaine addicts, prostitutes, the homeless, and petty criminals twist through the essays, much as they do through Burke's fiction.

Limehouse Nights, Burke's first work of fiction, was published to substantial controversy. Gilbert Vivian Seldes noted in *The Dial* (19 July 1917) that the pieces in the book were "strange and terrible stories . . . about things we are none of us too anxious to name, and which Mr. Burke makes tolerable only by the flooding beauty of his telling and the human kindness of his spirit," and other reviewers concurred. In the September 1917 *Bookman* (New York) Milton Bronner said that *Limehouse Nights* "is one of the most frankly and brutally realistic books that has appeared in our tongue in a long time"; the anonymous reviewer for *Current Opinion* (November 1917) echoed this sentiment, writing that Burke "possesses the power . . . of relating the worst facts on earth in some of the very best of short stories." What the reviewers objected to—and what English circulating libraries banned—was a collection of short stories about the inhabitants of London's Chinatown. The majority were inspired by Stephen Crane's brutal realism and subject matter, but they also echo the bitter ironies of Ambrose Bierce and operate from Robert Louis Stevenson's conceit of London as Baghdad, a city in which anything and everything could and did happen.

Although the subject matter disturbed contemporary reviewers, they were unanimous in praising Burke's prose style, which is unabashedly poetic. "The Chink and the Child," for example, begins by hinting at fairy tales:

> It is a tale of love and lovers that they tell in the low-lit causeway that slinks from West India Dock Road to the dark waste of waters beyond. In Pennyfields, too, you may hear it; and I do not doubt that it is told in far-away Tai-Ping, in Singapore, in Tokio, in Shanghai, and those other gay-lamped haunts of wonder wither the wandering people of Limehouse go and whence they return so casually.

The story that follows, however, is a horrific tale of child abuse, murder, and suicide. Lonely Cheng Huan falls in love with Lucy Burrows, the abused twelve-year-old daughter of the brutal boxer Battling Burrows. Huan finds Lucy in a brothel, takes her home with him, and chastely adores her, but Burrows retrieves her and beats her to death. Cheng finds Lucy's body and commits suicide, but he leaves behind a poisonous snake that kills Burrows. Burke's poetic style is thus completely and ironically at odds with his subject matter, but the contrast intensifies the story's impact. "The Chink and the Child" proved enormously popular with readers; with suitable changes, it was filmed in 1919 and again in 1936 as *Broken Blossoms;* the earlier version (also called *The Yellow Man and the Girl*) was directed by D. W. Griffith and starred Lillian Gish and Richard Barthelmess.

Child abuse and themes of betrayal and revenge appear in the majority of the stories in *Limehouse Nights*. For example, Greaser Flanagan in "The Paw" wants his wife to return to him but is too cowardly to confront her or her Chinese lover. He thereupon beats his eleven-year-old daughter, telling her each time that the Chinese lover is responsible for her plight and ought to be killed. The confused and battered girl eventually does kill somebody—her mother. In the few *Limehouse Nights* stories in which love motivates the action, it is often a misplaced and destructive passion. Only in "The Father of Yoto," the lightest story in the collection, are events resolved positively: Tai Ling loves Marigold Vassiloff, and when she tells him that she is pregnant with his child, he is delighted; but he soon learns that Marigold has told two other men the same thing. After some tension the absurdity of the situation strikes the rivals, and at the story's conclusion Tai Ling and Marigold are happily married and have several children.

The longest story in *Limehouse Nights* is "Gina of the Chinatown," about an energetic dancer beloved by everyone who dies giving birth to an illegitimate child. The story is mawkish and sentimental, but it served as the core of Burke's first novel, *Twinkletoes: A Tale of Chinatown* (1917). Monica Minasi, nicknamed Twinkletoes because of her energetic dancing, is bright, innocent, and beloved by almost all; but the shrewish wife of Twinkletoes's father's friend Chuck Lightfoot believes that her husband is too fond of the girl. Soon after Twinkletoes's sixteenth birthday her comfortable world collapses when she learns that her idolized father is a forger sought by the police. Despondent at the news, she gets drunk and goes home with a man. After she leaves the next day, the enraged Chuck kills the man. Later he reveals to Twinkletoes what he has done, as well as why her once poor but honest father had become a forger: because they loved her. As

Chuck turns himself in for the murder, the despairing Twinkletoes throws herself into the river. Mrs. Lightfoot, who had set the police on the trail of the forger father, remains free, lonely, bitter, and drinking. *Twinkletoes* is weakly sentimental, especially when contrasted with the brutal conviction of the stories in *Limehouse Nights,* and contemporary critics had few kind words to say about it. A motion picture adaptation, directed by Charles Brabin, was released in 1926.

Although the stories in *Limehouse Nights* frequently feature Chinese men and white women as main characters, there are no stories about Chinese women. Several of the stories in Burke's second collection of short fiction, *Whispering Windows: Tales of the Waterside* (1921; published in the United States as *More Limehouse Nights,* 1921), feature Chinese women as protagonists. In "Big Boy Blue" San Lee's father, Ah Fat, wants the policeman, Boy Blue, to stop investigating him. He has San Lee serve Boy Blue poisoned tea; she drinks the tea, sacrificing herself to incriminate her father, only to discover that Ah Fat poisoned both cups. In "The Scarlet Shoes" Wing Dee falls in love with beautiful San-li-po, whose drunken father, Lee Yip, makes money renting her bed to indigent seamen, leaving her without a place to sleep. Wing Dee gives San-li-po some red shoes and contrives to keep the sailors away, but when Lee Yip discovers what is going on he throws his daughter to her death in the river. The fantastic enters the story when the shoes return to summon Wing Dee to his death.

Describing his work in Grant Overton's *When Winter Comes to Main Street* (1922), Burke said that "the stories in *Whispering Windows* deal with human creatures, thieves, drunkards, prostitutes, each of whom is striving for happiness in his or her way, and missing it, as most of us do." The predominant themes in the stories are revenge and love gone awry, often ironically treated. Sexuality and twisted emotions also motivate many of the stories. "The Cane" describes a repressed schoolmaster who does not like caning students but does so nevertheless. He is especially bothered by the attitude of Dolly Latham, who seems to enjoy being caned; one afternoon he "punished her in private, ferociously, and talked with her"—then drowns himself.

East of Mansion House (1926), Burke's next collection of fiction, is generally weak, but several stories stand out, including "The Pash," about a lesbian affair between the young Amy Rainbird and the middle-aged Miriam Englefield that is happy until Amy becomes enamored of a boy. The most pow-

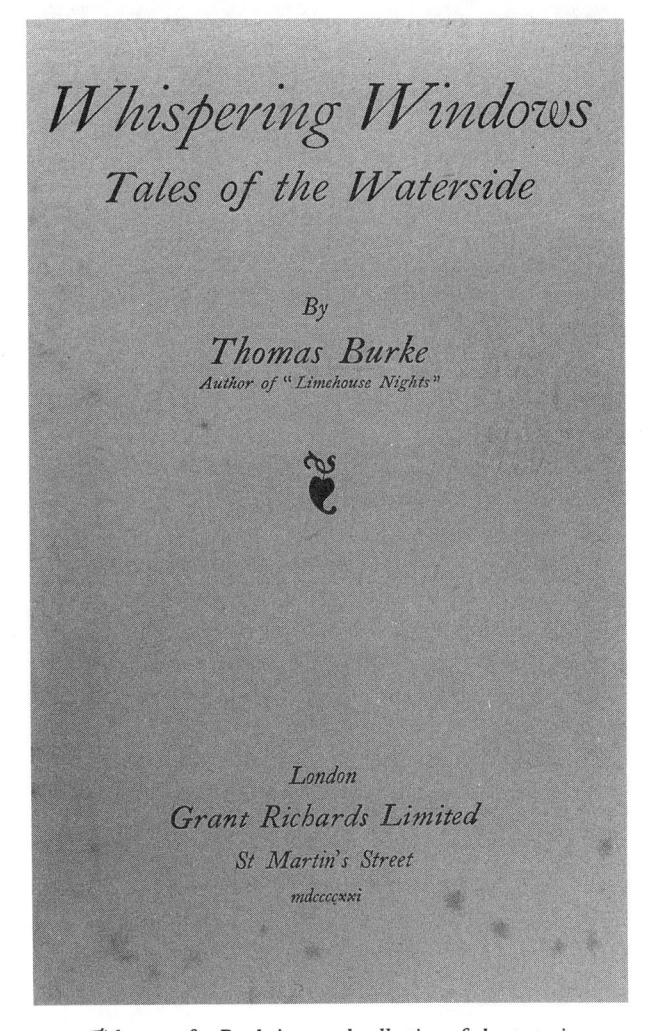

Title page for Burke's second collection of short stories

erful and timeless story is "Dow," in which, after years of fighting English prejudice, Matthew Mark Mohammed Dow becomes financially successful and believes that he is accepted by the English. When he asks Ben Christmas for the hand of his daughter, Mary, and Ben responds that Mary cannot marry a "nigger," the shock sends Dow into a lethal rage. The police are planning to shoot Dow when he is stopped by Mary's little brother, who has befriended him. The innocence of a new generation appears to triumph over prejudice and rage—but then the child calls Dow a "nigger."

The Sun in Splendour (1926), Burke's second novel, is vastly superior to *Twinkletoes,* combining elements of Edwardian naturalism and the traditional bildungsroman. Musically talented Christopher Scollard's father, David, is the music-loving publican of an inn, "The Sun in Splendour." Chris-

Title page for an historical novel about the short life of an Irish poet

topher's unhappy older brother, Eric, wants more from life than hard work and meager rewards, and Connie Giltspur hungers for love, music, and beauty. Eric runs off to work with Arthur Negretti, a casual thief; both perish in a car chase following a failed burglary. Connie runs away after being mistreated by her sadistic, food-obsessed aunt and is taken in by Ivy, a kindly prostitute. Some years later Ivy is killed protecting Connie from rape by a vicious pimp. Connie gets a job in a theater and meets Christopher, now twenty, though at the conclusion it is Christopher's friend Philip Perrinchief who courts her.

Despite some melodramatic elements, *The Sun in Splendour* is a serious discussion of the nature of art and creation. Christopher wants to write "serious" music, but as Perrinchief argues at length, nobody has two talents, and Christopher should do what he is good at, which is by no means the same as doing what he wants to do. After one of his popular compositions—dashed off on a bet—proves enormously profitable, Christopher finally recognizes that he is good at composing music everybody likes. He resigns himself to success as a composer of popular music and helps his father retire.

Burke's next two books were short novels; both are among his better works. *The Bloomsbury Wonder* (1929) begins innocuously with an anonymous first-person narrator (whose initials are T. B.) discussing Stephen Trink, a familiar figure in Bloomsbury but one who is oddly difficult to remember or describe. Regarded as a genial but shy eccentric, Trink is a writer of "metallic studies for all sorts of hole-and-corner Reviews" who is closest to the shopkeeper Horace Roake and his family. One day all of the Roakes—except one of the sons, who sensed some horror and fled—are found brutally murdered. No killers are found. The narrator eventually receives a letter from Trink, who vanished not long after the deaths and who is, of course, the murderer. Trink's description of his motivations raises the story from the horrific commonplace to the fantastic. He presents the theory that evil exists: like a germ, it is ubiquitous, unavoidable, and impossible to block. Trink claims that he became possessed by this force, that it led him to murder, and that he is now at peace and can work toward redemption. *The Bloomsbury Wonder* is an unconventional and thought-provoking crime story.

The Flower of Life (1929) begins with elderly Jane Cameron's entry into the workhouse in which she will certainly die. The narrative then describes significant passages in her life from age ten, when she was taught to work hard and loathe the idea of receiving charity. She remains honest, serious, faithful, and sober, never acting impetuously or compromising her morals. Nevertheless, she is wrongfully blamed for a theft and discharged from her job; her husband leaves her; her daughter is promiscuous and dies giving birth to an illegitimate child. Having been "good" for her entire life, Jane reaches old age alone and impoverished; she has failed, and, having failed, she accepts surrender as her lot and enters the workhouse. Though she lacks any extraordinary characteristics, her very ordinariness renders her gradual fall all the more tragic.

Burke's next work of fiction was another collection of short stories, *The Pleasantries of Old Quong* (1931). Quong Lee, an elderly Chinese shopkeeper in the Limehouse district, had first appeared in *Whispering Windows,* and the majority of the stories in *The Pleasantries of Old Quong* are narrated by him. The majority of Quong's tales are ironic, bemused observations on the darker passions of the human soul. In "The Ministering Angel" Constance Strood suffers in an unhappy marriage for twelve years. After her husband is sentenced to two years in prison, she sends him letters of such beauty that he repents and reforms. On his release he returns to her, only to discover that she has been waiting to kill him.

Many of the stories in *The Pleasantries of Old Quong* feature unsuccessful artists. "We Are the Music Makers" reuses to ironic intent the theme of *The Sun in Splendour:* Winkeldonck wants only to succeed as a popular music-hall composer, but his songs invariably appear at the wrong time; he is such a consistent failure that he emerges as a top concert pianist.

The most notable tale in *The Pleasantries of Old Quong,* and Burke's most famous story, is "The Hands of Mr. Ottermole," in which a serial killer prowls London's Mallon End, strangling residents and vanishing without a trace. Memories of Jack the Ripper survive, and tensions are high when a bright, inquisitive journalist accompanies Police Sergeant Ottermole on his rounds and eventually asks, "Now, as man to man, tell me, Sergeant Ottermole, just *why* did you kill all those inoffensive people?" Ottermole's initial answer is as disarmingly simple as it is horrific: "Well, to tell you the truth, Mr. Newspaper Man, I don't know. I really don't know. In fact, I've been worried about it myself." He continues:

"We get our ideas from lord-knows-where–from people who were dead hundreds of years before we were born. Mayn't we get our bodies in the same way? Our faces–our legs–our heads–they aren't completely ours. We don't make 'em. They come to us. And couldn't ideas come into our bodies like ideas come into our minds? Eh? Can't ideas live in nerve and muscle as well as in brain? Couldn't it be that parts of our bodies aren't really us, and couldn't ideas come into those parts all of a sudden, like ideas come into–into" he shot his arms out, showing the great white-gloved hands and hairy wrists; shot them out so swiftly to the journalist's throat that his eyes never saw them–"into *my hands!*"

"The Hands of Mr. Ottermole" was anthologized, adapted for radio and television, and in 1949 was voted the best crime story of all time by "Ellery Queen" (the writing team of Frederic Dannay and Manfred B. Lee) and eleven other critics.

Only a few of the stories in Burke's next collection, *Night-Pieces* (1935), are realistic. "Murder under the Crooked Spire" recounts the historical murder of George Collis in 1845, and "Jack Wapping" scathingly describes a day in the life of a typical English factory worker. Both are among Burke's better

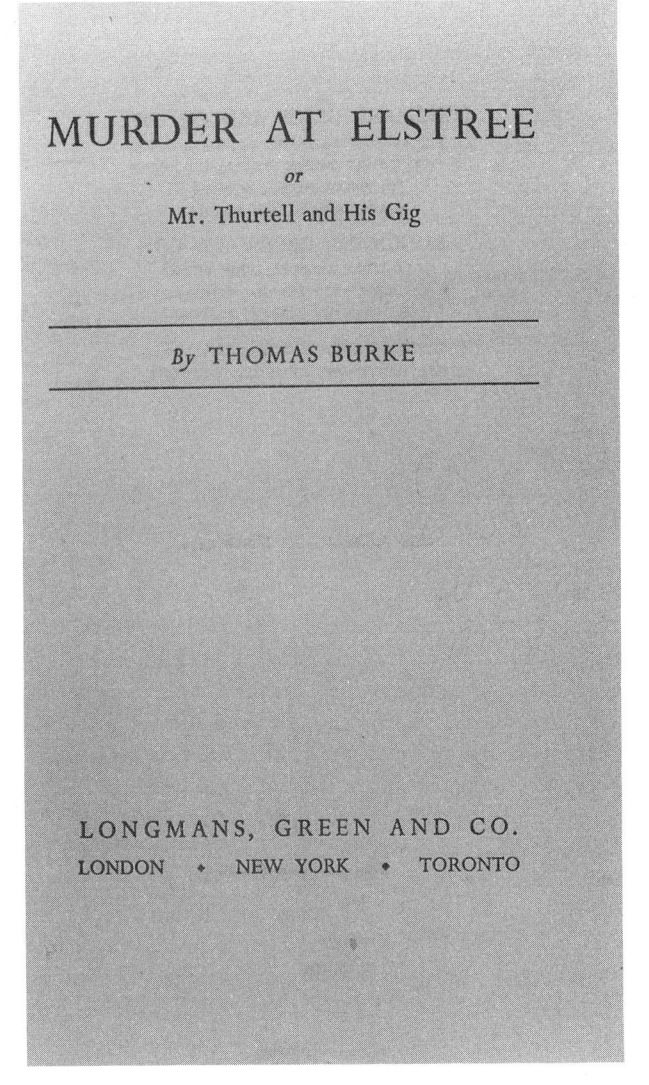

MURDER AT ELSTREE
or
Mr. Thurtell and His Gig

By THOMAS BURKE

LONGMANS, GREEN AND CO.
LONDON • NEW YORK • TORONTO

Title page for an historical novel about the 1823 murder of the confidence man William Weave by the gambler John Thurtell

work, and *Night-Pieces* is perhaps Burke's strongest collection of short stories.

The majority of the stories in *Night-Pieces* involve the fantastic emerging into mundane situations; at times this emergence is relatively benign, but in "The Black Courtyard" a murderer is haunted by the place where he committed the crime, eventually returns to reenact it, and is arrested. The creepiest story in the collection is "The Hollow Man," in which a London innkeeper is visited by the reanimated corpse of the partner he had murdered in the African jungle fifteen years before.

Burke's next three novels are historical fictions that reveal him at the height of his narrative powers. *Vagabond Minstrel: The Adventure of Thomas Dermody* (1936) is about the highly precocious Irish poet who lived from 1775 to 1802. Determined to succeed in Dublin, twelve-year-old Dermody leaves his little hometown of Ennis. Despite his great intellectual gifts, Dermody has never learned to compromise, is blind to the impression he makes on others, and has never realized that his true talents lie not in poetry but in prose. Because he resents receiving charity from those whom he considers his intellectual inferiors, he is arrogant and rude to those in a position to help him. Worst of all, he is irresponsible with money, drinks too much, and prefers to carouse with the irresponsible lower classes. Finally even the friends who know of his great gifts have had enough of him, and Dermody dies alone in a hut in the countryside. *Vagabond Minstrel* shares its bildungsroman theme with *The Sun in Splendour,* but it is an inversion of that book: as Burke interpreted it, Dermody had no Philip Perrinchief and was unable to succeed while doing something he did not want to do. The historical Dermody was less sympathetic but equally self-destructive; he is said to have declared, "I am vicious because I like it."

Murder at Elstree; or, Mr. Thurtell and His Gig (1936) is based on the murder of William Weare by John Thurtell in 1823. After earning a reputation as a crooked gambler in Norwich, Thurtell travels to London, where Weare fleeces him. Vowing revenge, Thurtell lures Weare to Elstree and murders him. Thurtell is rapidly arrested and hanged before a large crowd. George Borrow, who was among the few who liked Thurtell, appears in the novel, as does Pierce Egan, but they are faint as characters, and what makes the short novel exceptional is Burke's use of thieves' cant and early-nineteenth-century slang.

The Winsome Wench: The Story of a London Inn, 1825–1900 (1938) begins in 1825, when the English coaching trade was approaching its heyday. The Winsome Wench, a great Elizabethan inn, is run by the Woden family, who built it some two hundred years earlier. Jack Woden, frustrated that his father, Will, does not allow him any responsibilities, takes to gambling; but after gamblers kill Will to hasten Jack's inheritance, Jack renounces the cards and becomes an innkeeper. Although the coaching trade reaches new heights and permits the inn to expand, the railroads eventually put the coaches out of business and almost destroy the inn. Jack survives by leasing his grounds to the railroads, and the Winsome Wench thrives again. Jack's son Harry is uninterested in innkeeping until after he marries; then Jack's vision and Harry's management raise the Winsome Wench to new heights of success. In rapid succession, however, Harry loses his wife in childbirth and his father in a hunting accident, and he ceases to care. The inn thus enters a long decline that continues with Jack's ineffectual other son, Lucian, who is more interested in books and alcohol than business. Crooked businessmen conspire to run the inn down even further, then buy it and restore it; but after the disgusted Lucian sells the building, he drunkenly decides to set fire to the place, and he and the great old inn go up in flames. The novel is reminiscent of Thomas Mann's monumental *Buddenbrooks* (1901): it is successful as history, and it evokes the personalities and procedures of a generally forgotten profession. It is, nevertheless, a sad book.

Burke's last three books of fiction reveal a substantial decline in his narrative ability. *Abduction: A Story of Limehouse* (1939) is apparently an attempt at writing a thriller in the Edgar Wallace style: somebody is kidnapping attractive red-haired women, keeping them for ten days, then releasing them slightly scarred but otherwise intact. Scotland Yard investigates, as do Bendall, crime reporter for the *Morning Messenger,* and Hugo Floom, an elderly scholar and aesthete who figures occasionally in Burke's tales of Limehouse. There is a glorious opera singer named Barbara Malachreest, an occultist named Saul Deeming (obviously modeled after Aleister Crowley), a pub crawl around a London few know, and a completely unconvincing and anticlimactic conclusion.

The protagonist of *Victorian Grotesque* (1941) is Jimmy Rando, a comic in the music halls of late-Victorian London. An amiable but weak man, Jimmy is pushed around and insulted by his domineering wife, Hannah, and by their neighbor, the vicious young singer and dancer Birdie Bright. When Jimmy learns that Hannah has been serving as a receiver of stolen goods, he buries the loot in the garden, but Birdie sees him. She blackmails him, making arch comments about gardening and hinting about going to the police, until he begins paying her to remain silent. When Hannah learns about the blackmail, she kidnaps Birdie, but the two women are killed in a cab accident. Jimmy's career takes off, but he is haunted by guilt over the deaths, abused by Birdie's drunken slattern of a mother, blackmailed by the thief who worked for Hannah, and pursued by Birdie's suspicious boyfriend; his only escape is death. The story is capably written, but it is too pathetic to be enjoyable.

Although it includes a slightly rewritten version of *The Bloomsbury Wonder, Dark Nights* (1944), the last collection of Burke's stories published during his lifetime, consists of largely forgettable material. Nevertheless, two stories are superior. "Sweet and Low" is an amusing piece of erotic silliness; narrated by Old Quong, it concerns Dumspike, a wastrel living off the charity of his aunt. She wants him to get a job and is giving him much less money than before. Dumspike meets an attractive lower-class woman who, despite his denials, believes that he is an artist and accompanies him to his rooms. Just as she appears totally naked before the young man, the aunt arrives; Dumspike averts disaster only by then and there embracing the career of artist and declaring that the woman is his model. "Sonata in Scarlet" is darker. Hugo Floom hears wonderful music and meets its composer, only to be shocked that the man is deservedly hated and feared by all around him. The composer will not part with his music and is eventually arrested for murder and hanged. When Floom returns for the music, he discovers that it has been destroyed by the composer's girlfriend. Like *The Sun in Splendour* and *Vagabond Minstrel*, "Sonata in Scarlet" examines the nature of artistic creation.

Burke died on 22 September 1945. Like many other writers active between the world wars, he has been forgotten. Stories of addicts, lesbians, premarital sex, child abuse, and racial hatreds no longer shock; stories of Victorian music halls and artists are, at best, period pieces. Nevertheless, although he wrote too much that is mawkish and mediocre, Burke's successful works remain vital, capable of evoking love and horror while memorializing a bygone London. A thorough biography of Burke remains to be written, but the best summation of his personality and achievements can be found in Gawsworth's foreword to *The Best Stories of Thomas Burke* (1950):

"He had set himself to portray the human flotsam his omnivident eyes had noted on his walks through unfrequented by-ways; and to imagine bravely, frankly from his encounters was his necessity."

Bibliographies:

John Gawsworth, *Ten Contemporaries: Notes toward Their Definitive Bibliography,* second series (London: Joiner & Steele, 1933);

Fred B. Millet, ed., *Contemporary British Literature: A Critical Survey and 232 Author-Bibliographies,* revised edition (New York: Harcourt, Brace, 1935), pp. 160–161.

References:

St. John Adcock, *The Glory that Was Grub Street: Impressions of Contemporary Authors* (London: Sampson Low, Marston, 1926), pp. 13–22;

Arthur Nicholas Athanason, "Thomas Burke," in *Twentieth-Century Crime and Mystery Writers,* third edition, edited by Lesley Henderson, (Chicago & London: St. James Press, 1991), pp. 150–152;

Milton Bronner, "Burke of Limehouse," *Bookman* (London), 46 (September 1917): 15–17;

Grant Overton, *Cargoes for Crusoes* (New York: Doran, 1924), pp. 280–282;

Overton, *When Winter Comes to Main Street* (New York: Doran, 1922), pp. 187–195;

Gilbert Vivian Seldes, "Rediscovery and Romance," *Dial,* 63 (19 July 1917): 65–67.

Mona Caird
(24 May 1854 – 4 February 1932)

Carolyn Christensen Nelson
West Virginia University

BOOKS: *Whom Nature Leadeth,* as G. Noel Hatton, 3 volumes (London: Longmans, 1883);
One That Wins: The Story of a Holiday in Italy, as the author of "Whom Nature Leadeth" (New York: Harper, 1887);
The Wing of Azrael (3 volumes, London: Trübner, 1889; 1 volume, New York: Lovell, 1889);
A Romance of the Moors (Bristol: Arrowsmith's Bristol Library, 1891; New York: Holt, 1891);
The Daughters of Danaus (London: Bliss, Sands & Foster, 1894);
Some Truths about Vivisection (London: Victoria Street Society, 1894?);
A Sentimental View of Vivisection (London: Reeves, 1895);
Beyond the Pale: An Appeal on Behalf of the Victims of Vivisection (London: Reeves, 1897);
The Morality of Marriage, and Other Essays on the Status and Destiny of Woman (London: Redway, 1897);
The Pathway of the Gods (London: Skeffington, 1898);
The Inquisition of Science (London: National Anti-Vivisection Society, 1903);
The Logicians: An Episode in Dialogue (London: Reeves, 1905);
Romantic Cities of Provence (London: Unwin, 1906);
Personal Rights: A Presidential Address Delivered to the Forty-first Annual Meeting of the Personal Rights Association (London: Personal Rights Association, 1913);
The Stones of Sacrifice (London: Simpkin, Marshall, Hamilton, Kent, 1915);
The Great Wave (London: Wishart, 1931).
Edition: *The Daughters of Danaus,* afterword by Margaret Morganroth Gullette (New York: Feminist Press at the City University of New York, 1989).

SELECTED PERIODICAL PUBLICATIONS–UNCOLLECTED: "Defence of the So-Called Wild Woman," *Nineteenth Century,* 31 (May 1892): 811-829;
"Evolution of Compassion," *Westminster Review,* 145 (June 1896): 635-643;

Mona Caird

"Duel of the Sexes," *Fortnightly Review,* 84 (July 1905): 109-122;
"Punishment for Crimes against Women and Children," *Westminster Review,* 169 (May 1908): 550-553;
"Militant Tactics and Woman's Suffrage," *Westminster Review,* 170 (November 1908): 525-530;
"The Lot of Women," *Westminster Review,* 174 (July 1910): 52-59;
"Greater Community," *Fortnightly Review,* 110 (November 1918): 742-755.

Mona Caird was one of the most controversial of the New Woman writers, those whose fiction in the final decade of the nineteenth century challenged traditional thinking about women, depicting the restricted lives they led and the legal and social injustices from which they suffered. Caird, who used both her essays and her novels to promote her ideas, was largely responsible for beginning the great marriage debate that raged throughout the 1890s in fiction and journals. In her article "Marriage," published in the *Westminster Review* in August 1888, Caird boldly declared that respectable marriage is "the most hypocritical form of woman-purchase" and concluded that "the present form of marriage—exactly in proportion to its conformity with orthodox ideas—is a vexatious failure." Her controversial ideas provoked a tremendous response, including expressions of outrage.

While Caird was attacked by critics who said she was part of the so-called Anti-Marriage League (an epithet coined by the novelist Margaret Oliphant), Caird's essays and novels demonstrate that her opposition was not to marriage itself but to marriage as it existed in her time. Caird's controversial views on marriage, the cause of her fame and her notoriety, were only part of her much wider and more general concern, shown in all her writing, about the mistreatment of the powerless by those in authority, a practice Caird depicted as a form of modern sacrifice. In all of her fiction Caird repudiates such sacrifice and demonstrates her concern for those who are sacrificed: women, the poor, and animals.

Alice Mona Alison was born on 24 May 1854 on the Isle of Wight to Ann Jane Hector Alison and John Alison, an inventor and a landed proprietor. On 19 December 1877 she married James Alexander Henryson-Caird in London. Henryson-Caird, eight years her senior, was from a prominent family that owned a great deal of property and a mansion at Cassencary, on the southwest coast of Scotland. Caird's fondness for Scotland, particularly its scenic mountains and coast, is evident from her novels, many of which are set, at least partially, in that country. In her novels Scotland is often tied to a more primitive, superstitious, and mystical past. Caird's castle there also figures in some of her novels, including *The Wing of Azrael* (1889).

After her marriage Caird moved back and forth between London and Cassencary. Her obituary in the Glasgow *Herald* speaks of her as gracious and dignified, entertaining friends at Cassencary as a "most delightful hostess." In London she had many friends, particularly Elizabeth Sharp, also a writer, and Sharp's husband, William, a poet. She knew many other people of the literary and artistic world, such as Walter Pater, Olive Schreiner, Emma Brooke, and Dante Gabriel Rossetti.

On 22 March 1884 Caird's only child, Alister James, was born. While Caird's publications are filled with discussions on the question of marriage and the restrictions motherhood places on women's lives, her own marriage was, to all outward appearances, a happy one. Caird wrote nothing that is obviously personal about her marriage or her experience as a mother. Since she had her own career as a writer and many of her own friends with whom she traveled, it would appear that her husband gave Caird the liberty she believed that all women should have to pursue their vocations.

In 1883, under the pseudonym of G. Noel Hatton, Caird published *Whom Nature Leadeth,* her first novel. Although the melodrama of the subplot seriously weakens the work, the principal narrative develops many of the themes of Caird's later novels, including her advocacy of a woman's right to pursue work outside the domestic sphere and her rejection of self-sacrifice for the supposed benefit of others. It also anticipates Caird's much more successful novel, *The Daughters of Danaus* (1894), in that both have creative women as protagonists—here an artist and in the later novel a musician.

Whom Nature Leadeth has many intelligent and appealing women characters, as well as some conventionally unpleasant ones. The protagonist, Leonore Ravenhill, believes that excellence as an artist is antithetical to the life women are expected to lead. She fears that when she marries—marriage being "the only natural, wholesome life, as she was so often told by women"—she "must bid farewell to all hopes of genuine success" as an artist. Her prediction proves true when, as a married woman with children, she finds all of her energies dissipated in the trivial duties of a woman's life. Her husband is oblivious to her frustrations, but her friend Austin Bradley, who serves as Caird's spokesperson in the novel, warns against sacrificing oneself for the needs of others. He advises Leonore, "Go back to your studio, neglect your social duties." The novel ends with Leonore's feeling trapped in her marriage but believing in her ability to effect some change in the world and to improve people's lives through her own struggle. In Austin's prediction that "the twentieth century will be the woman's century," Caird expresses her own optimism, which reappears in subsequent novels, that conditions for women will improve.

Whom Nature Leadeth attracted little attention and went unnoticed by critics, as did Caird's next book, *One That Wins: The Story of a Holiday in Italy,* published as "by the author of 'Whom Nature Leadeth'" in 1887. Not until "Marriage," an essay that placed her in the forefront of the late-nine-

THE

Wing of Azrael.

BY

MONA CAIRD

Yesterday, this Day's madness did prepare
To-morrow's Silence, Triumph or Despair.

LONDON:
TRÜBNER & CO., LUDGATE HILL.
1889.
[*All rights reserved.*]

Title page for a pessimistic novel about marriage

teenth-century feminist movement, did Caird become a well-known and controversial figure. Her initial article was followed by a series of essays on marriage published in a variety of journals, including the *North American Review, Westminster Review, Fortnightly Review,* and *Nineteenth Century.* In her marriage essays Caird argued that present-day marriage is nothing more than a "form of woman-purchase" and that women are forced into mercenary marriages because they are given no satisfactory way to earn their own living. To resist marriage only puts a woman into the crowd of "worn-out, underpaid workers." Respectability, according to Caird, "draws its life-blood from the degradation of womanhood in marriage and prostitution." Predictably, such ideas stirred up a great deal of wrath. The solution to the marriage problem, according to Caird, lay in the economic independence of women, which could only be achieved by girls having an education similar to that of boys and women having employment opportunities equal to those of men. Under such conditions women would no longer feel driven to sell themselves in marriage to escape a life of poverty.

When Caird published her essays on marriage in a book, *The Morality of Marriage, and Other Essays on the Status and Destiny of Women* (1897), she developed many of these same ideas at length, but she also introduced another theme that much of her subsequent fiction illustrates: the reprehensibility of sacrifice of one group's interests for the benefit of another's. In *The Morality of Marriage* Caird asks why society subordinates the interests of women to the supposed greater interest of society: "Why this one-sided sacrifice, this artificial selection of victims for the good—or supposed good—of humanity?" For Caird, women are chosen to be the victims, to have their lives constricted, all choice taken away, their very sentiments prescribed, ostensibly for the "greater good"; but, Caird argues, this practice is a remnant of ancient human sacrifice from which no one really benefits.

The year following the publication of "Marriage," her most pessimistic novel on the marriage question, Caird published *The Wing of Azrael* (1889), which fictionalizes the problems concerning marriage she had written about in her essays. The interests of her protagonist, Viola Sedley, are sacrificed to those of her family, particularly her brothers. Viola is deprived of an education so that her brothers can go to college and have every social advantage. After her brothers and father accumulate huge debts, Viola is urged to marry for money to save the family from financial ruin. When she resists, her father berates her: "What's the good of a woman but to marry and look after her husband and children? What else can you do?" Viola offers to earn her own living, but her father mocks her: she has no education, and there are no occupations for women. Viola, realizing that her family, particularly her mother, will be destitute, capitulates, marrying Philip Dendraith, a cruel man whom she does not love. Her mother tells her that marriage gives her the opportunity to save Philip's soul, making the man's moral regeneration the responsibility of his wife.

When Philip's abusive and controlling behavior proves that he is a worse husband than even Viola had imagined, she begins to see Harry Lancaster, who had urged her not to marry Philip. Philip learns of her relationship with Harry and confronts her. Viola, finally, after months of remaining silent before Philip, asserts her independence, saying, "I am no longer yours—body and soul. I belong partly to myself at last. Half my soul, if not the whole, is liberated." Philip threatens to have her declared mad and locked up and hires a woman who has taken care of mental patients to watch her. In despair, Viola agrees to run off with Harry to France, but her husband learns of her plans. In an instant of blinding passion she stabs him to death. Harry arrives, but Viola, refusing to implicate him in the murder, runs off toward the sea, seemingly to commit suicide.

The Wing of Azrael portrays everything that is wrong with the marriage system. Viola has few choices, and any resistance only compounds her unhappiness. Her interests are continually sacrificed to those of others—her family or her husband. Caird's argument is that women marry from economic necessity, and thus marriages are generally miserable. Viola is not the only woman in the story who is forced into an undesirable marriage. Harry's sister Adrienne is also pressured by her mother to marry for money. Sibella Lincoln, the only female character who defies public opinion and leaves an unpleasant marriage, is shunned by other women as immoral. Sibella's experience reveals that women collude in the very system that restricts their lives, often turning against other women.

Caird's novel provides no satisfactory solution for women; it depicts no happy marriages and no alternatives to marriage. The *New York Times* review of the novel (8 July 1889) treated it briefly and flippantly, saying "that it requires great patience to get through with this interminable romance, and when done with, it is labor wasted." Certainly the novel is gloomy and often predictable, more melodrama than good fiction. It is best read as an early example of Caird's marriage novels, whose tone progressively changed over the next forty years.

A Romance of the Moors (1891), set in Yorkshire, pleads for a relationship between the sexes that is not based on the woman's servile dependence on the man. The work's happy ending comes not through marriage but through Bessie Saunders's refusal to marry Dick Coverdale to save her besmirched reputation. Bessie heeds the advice of a New Woman, Margaret Ellwood, who tells her to give Dick the freedom he needs to leave home and learn about the world. Margaret warns Bessie against her dependent devotion to Dick. He is too intelligent to desire an obedient, dutiful wife—he needs an independent woman.

This novel, like *The Pathway of the Gods* (1898) and Caird's essays on marriage, illustrates Caird's belief that happy relationships between men and women can result only when they relate to one another as independent, intelligent, and equal partners without feeling the necessity to marry. When Bessie rejects him, Dick is freed from the demands of his family to marry and resolves to leave home, unwilling to sacrifice himself to his family's interests. Caird here, as in all her work, rejects as disastrous all relationships based on sacrifice in which one person gives up freedom to satisfy another's needs.

Caird continued throughout her life to move back and forth between fiction and polemical essay to develop her ideas. Around the turn of the century, as president of the Independent Anti-Vivisection League, Caird published several pamphlets on vivisection, a practice she vehemently opposed, including *A Sentimental View of Vivisection* (1895), *Beyond the Pale: An Appeal on Behalf of the Victims of Vivisection* (1897), and *The Inquisition of Science* (1903). Her views, sympathetic to the rights of animals, were typical of those held by many feminists in the late nineteenth century. Almost all of her novels include discussions by the characters on the subject of animal rights; a character is certain to be a villain if he mistreats animals. In *The Wing of Azrael* Philip Dendraith beats his horse and kicks his cat—indications of his cruel nature that make him repulsive to Viola.

Many details of Caird's life during this time are not known. She made several trips to the Continent, going to the Carpathian Alps with Elizabeth Sharp in 1889 and to Rome in 1890–1891. A note on Caird in the *Review of Reviews* in July 1893 says that her health broke down some time after she launched the controversy on marriage in 1888 in the *Daily Telegraph*. The article explains that Caird subsequently went to the Continent for a cure and had regained her health. The writer, unable to resist criticizing Caird in the usual vein, concludes that "she is the priestess of revolt, and sympathizes with revolters everywhere."

In 1894 Caird published *The Daughters of Danaus,* considered by most critics her finest novel. It integrates her ideas on women with an intriguing plot and an outspoken heroine, Hadria Fullerton, Caird's first New Woman protagonist. While the novel deals with the marriage question, the issue is put in the context of the artistic woman who struggles to develop her talent in spite of the obstacles raised by her family and marriage. *The Daughters of Danaus* and *Whom Nature Leadeth* are among the first English novels whose center of consciousness is a woman artist. In contrast to the male *Künstlerroman* (novel about the development of an artist), however, both of Caird's novels reveal the constant claims on a woman that prevent the development of her talent. They are novels about talent unrealized.

The question that the novel develops as its subtext is "Are we the makers of our circumstances?" The novel begins with the Fullerton chil-

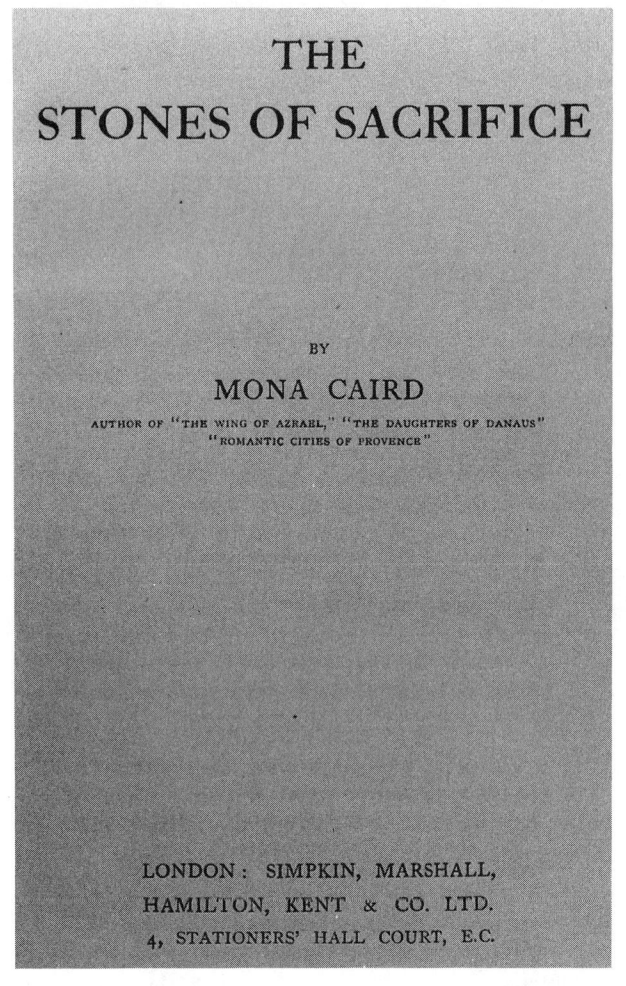

Title page for a 1915 novel that condemns the mistreatment of women and animals

dren debating American writer Ralph Waldo Emerson's ideas, specifically whether the individual is able to conquer circumstances. Hadria believes that women cannot. The conditions of a girl's life are stifling, and, Hadria insists, if Emerson had been a girl he would have known that conditions do count—hideously—in one's life: "The odds are against a girl bringing her power to maturity." Despite that acknowledgment by Hadria, for most of the novel she tries to develop her talent as a musician in the face of opposition, only to succumb finally to the same claims of family that had prevented the development of the artistic talent of many women before her.

In *The Daughters of Danaus* Caird condemns the practice of limiting women's development by relegating them to a separate sphere from men. According to Victorian gender ideology the woman's sphere was supposed to be the home, where she was responsible for domestic duties and moral leadership. Hadria challenges that idea, believing, as did Caird, that the sphere to which women had been assigned was so narrow that it created lives that were twisted, stunted, and wretched. Society's belief in separate gender spheres also justified its denial to women of educational and employment opportunities.

After marriage and giving birth to two sons, Hadria goes to Paris to study music. But the experience is short lived. The forces that drive her back home, causing her to abandon her musical training, are those that Caird believes have doomed all women of talent: social expectations and family claims. With a great sense of guilt and of duty Hadria returns to her family, realizing that the obstacles are too great for her to become an accomplished musician. The novel's discussion of the woman's sphere is linked to the question of woman's work—what it is and whether it is antithetical to a happy marriage. To explore that idea Caird presents two other women. A well-known author, Valeria Du Prel, who has never married, warns Hadria against rejecting marriage for a single life as she has done. She long believed that her work would satisfy her, and she would only accept a perfect comradeship; but as she grows older, she is terrified of solitude and loneliness. Although she is an outspoken supporter of Hadria and of women's rights and has a successful life as a writer, she says that her work does not satisfy the heart. In the contrasting choices made by Hadria and Valeria, neither of whom finds her life satisfactory, Caird demonstrates that none of the options available to women at the present time ensure happiness. Hadria tells Valeria: "It is my impression that in my life, as in the lives of most women, all roads lead to Rome. Whether one does this or that, one finds oneself in pretty much the same position at the end. It doesn't answer to rebel against the recognized condition of things, and it doesn't answer to submit." Hadria's sister Algitha, a minor character, is the only woman who combines a happy marriage with fulfilling work as she ministers to the poor in London. She is the successful New Woman who claims the right to do as she wishes with her life. Algitha and her husband share socialist ideals, believing that they can create a better world. In this novel, in contrast to Caird's later ones, socialism is presented favorably.

The novel's end finds Hadria despondent over her inability to achieve her artistic goals. She believes that her failure will hinder the progress of other women, who will not expect to fulfill their aspirations since she has failed. But she expects conditions for women to change. She believes that women are living in a transitional time when they can imagine other possibilities for their lives while realizing that conditions preclude their present attainment. Hadria dreams that women of the future will walk over a great abyss filled with the bodies of women, such as herself, who went before and failed.

The daughters of Danaus, to whom the title refers, are, in Greek mythology, fifty women who are forced to marry against their wills; on their wedding night forty-nine kill their husbands. As a punishment, in the afterlife they are forced to draw water continually in sieves from a river. To Caird this story is a metaphor for the destiny of women; marriage, about which there was little choice; and the work of women, which keeps them endlessly busy in useless and futile endeavors. Hadria says of such work: "Women will go on patiently drawing water in sieves, and pretend they are usefully employed because it tires them!"

The Daughters of Danaus does not end in marriage, as do so many Victorian novels that use the marriage plot; marriage comes early in the work so that Caird can explore it in several women's lives. *The Daughters of Danaus* stands as a pivotal novel in Caird's career. Her heroine, although facing an uncertain future, remains alive to continue her struggle.

The Pathway of the Gods is far less complex than *The Daughters of Danaus*. Julian Ford, an artist, left England fourteen years earlier, having rejected all attempts by his father to make him lead a conventional life. He travels about Europe, supported by his selling of sketches. In Rome he falls in with a group of artists who believe that the good life lies in the pursuit of beauty. Anna Carrington, a childhood friend whom Julian meets in Rome, has also escaped from a family that disapproves of her unconventional life. While Anna chafes at the demands made on her, she believes women need to sacrifice themselves for others—a belief Caird represents, paradoxically, as egotistic. Egotism can be masked as self-sacrifice, as is evident when Anna and Julian fall in love and she becomes possessive of him: she thinks that if she sacrifices everything for him, she has a right to control him. Anna realizes that though she has rid herself of the traditional woman's life at home, she nevertheless cannot shake off the old fetters entirely. She says, "We luckless beings of the transition period have to suffer the penalty of being out of line with the old conditions, before the new conditions have been formed with which we could have harmonised." Some women are destroyed in the change from the old to the new roles.

The Pathway of the Gods makes clear that the problems with relationships between men and women were as much the result of the distorted personalities women were forced to develop as they were of men's behavior. This novel presents a more hopeful view of possibilities for women; several New Women in it, particularly Clutha Lawrenson, represent what women are capable of being. Its end is visionary, as are the conclusions of all Caird's final novels. It predicts a better world freed from the violence and cruelty to which Rome has been witness.

Evidence of Caird's travels is seen in the novel's detailed descriptions of Rome. *The Pathway of the Gods* was followed by *Romantic Cities of Provence* (1906), written a few years after a tour of the south of France that Caird said was taken for reasons of health and rest. *Romantic Cities of Provence* combines travel descriptions with stories from history, such as that of Petrarch and Laura, relating to places Caird visited.

Caird's twentieth-century essays about the condition of women moved beyond calls for legal reforms, demanding woman suffrage that would give them legislative power. In "The Lot of Women," published in the *Westminster Review* in July 1910, she writes: "But it is not piecemeal modification of bad laws that is wanted; it is a voice in the making of the laws themselves.... Even if the present law could be made entirely just, that would not remove the burden of the subject position or its final consequences." Many of the New Woman writers of the late nineteenth century, such as Caird and Sarah Grand, who had been outspoken in their criticism of the social conditions for women in the 1890s, now focused on a political agenda whose primary goal was obtaining the vote for women. Caird actively supported the cause of the suffragists but never became part of its more militant group.

The Stones of Sacrifice (1915), Caird's next novel, presents a more hopeful view for women reflecting the more favorable conditions for women that had been realized by that time. The stones of the title are actual stones that form an altar dating back to Druid times on which victims were offered up to God. Sacrifice, an ancient and deep-seated idea, according to Professor Owen, a character in the novel, continues to be practiced in the present time in various forms. Caird attacks these varieties of contemporary sacrifice, all of which are justified by society as being for some higher purpose but actually serve the interests of a select group. Claudia Temple, one of the central characters, denounces her brother, Stephen, for spending all the family money on selfish pursuits while his sisters go without. To pay Stephen's expenses, his sisters must be married off to men with money. Harriet Kirk-

Title page for a novel about the destructive potential of science

patrick leaves home and lives an independent life, but her sister Mary feels obligated to stay at home and help their mother. The boredom of her life leads her to overdose on laudanum and die. Graine Galbraith, believing that "self-sacrifice is by far the easiest career for a woman," gives up her fiancé because her parents need her. Self-sacrifice for such women has a certain nobility in that it is a type of renunciation. Caird's antivivisectionism becomes part of her general denunciation of the sacrifice of the weak by the strong for a supposedly higher purpose. Gilbert Thorne defends humanity's right to torture animals for its own purposes. Alpin Dalrymple, the sensitive "New Man," calls vivisection "vicarious sacrifice," justified by men for the "god of science" but simply part of the same primitive savagery found in earlier times under more primitive gods.

In *The Stones of Sacrifice* Caird also questions the idea of an essential woman's nature. Caird believed that it cannot be known whether there is such an inherent nature since women are given only one choice, marriage and motherhood; all other avenues of experience are closed to them. Caird's ambivalence toward childbearing results from her belief that the maternal instinct is used by society to hold women in subjection: women who leave their husbands lose their children. The marriage of Alpin and Claudia is an ideal one. In their apartment each retains a private room, and they have different friends. But this marriage is the only successful one portrayed in the novel. Most marriages end in unhappiness and boredom, several in misery and despair.

While *The Daughters of Danaus* presented a favorable view of socialism, *The Stones of Sacrifice* depicts it negatively. The socialists in this novel support vivisection just as they believe in sacrificing the individual to the all-powerful state. For Caird all forms of sacrifice result from the desire of the strong to control the weak and to benefit from their sacrifice. Its practice is self-serving and destructive; no assertion of its fulfilling a higher purpose or greater good—society's or scientists' needs—is any more justified than were the pagan sacrifices to angry gods of long ago. The novel ends with Alpin again at the stones of sacrifice but this time receiving a mystical vision of hope and peace and comfort. This conclusion implies that a better world is to come.

Caird's final novel, *The Great Wave* (1931), continues to expose the abuses of power in family life, the treatment of animals, and the economic system. But it is Caird's most optimistic novel. She demonstrates that attempts to dominate the individual can be resisted successfuly. Grierson Elliot defies his family's constant attempts to manipulate him. He leads an independent life and has a happy marriage to a New Woman who is intelligent, outspoken, and cheerful.

The sense of doom that hovers over the novel arises from the fear of power used on a much larger scale, employed by stronger nations to destroy weaker ones. The work is set in the years just prior to the outbreak of World War I and is about the abuse of power that leads to all wars and to science's increasing ability to create the means of terrible destruction. The specter of domination that Caird always feared moves from a personal level onto the far more terrifying one of European conflict. *The Great Wave* is prophetic in that Grierson's scientific discoveries suggest the future development of the atomic bomb.

Grierson is from a family in Scotland that has a long tradition of military service. He resists his father's attempts to make him join the military, breaks from the family altogether, and goes to London to live with Dr. Windle, a relative who is a physics professor. Grierson becomes a scientist, believing that he can free people from lives of drudgery by discovering how to extract energy from ordinary matter.

Most of the scientists in the novel use Charles Darwin's theories as justification for improving the race through the destruction of weak individuals. Grierson feels almost alone in his desire to use science to help the poor and downtrodden. The general good, he believes, should not be advanced at the expense of the less fortunate. He discovers a source of power that has tremendous potential for humanity, but he realizes that in the wrong hands his discovery could have horrible consequences; therefore, he shares his knowledge only with those few who do not hold a "sacrificial idea."

Suggestive of the impending world war, a duel between the British Grierson and a German, Waldheim, is conducted throughout much of the novel. Waldheim is determined to get Grierson's scientific notes to fulfill his dream of a "Germany triumphant with England and the other nations at her feet." In a final physical struggle over Grierson's notebook Nora, Grierson's wife, throws it into the fire to prevent any future misuse of the information. Grierson's defeat of Waldheim prefigures the coming defeat of Germany in a war in which the two men will fight on opposing sides.

In the novel's epilogue, set after the war, a traumatized Grierson realizes the possibility that science, in its progress, will eventually provide the means for "mutual extermination." He could have been the one to provide that means had his wife not destroyed his own notes. Returning to his laboratory at the novel's end, he hopes that through science he can find ways to improve life. People need not be destroyed by the "great wave," nature's blind law, which Grierson imagines is hanging over them. Such a fate must be opposed by human will and sympathy, while science must be used for universal benefit.

The Great Wave makes a plea for human kindness to prevail on the familial, social, and international levels. Possibly the experience of her son, who had joined the army and fought in World War I, had drawn Caird's interest to international issues. Her final novel demonstrates through the marriage of Grierson and Nora that men and women can live fulfilling lives in an equal partnership. Caird's desire to make the public aware of its responsibility to the powerless and her warning of the possible misuse of science make her final novel her most visionary.

Caird died on 4 February 1932 at her home in St. John's Wood, London. One of the most outspoken of the New Woman writers of the 1890s, she is known today primarily for her essays on marriage and for her finest novel, *The Daughters of Danaus,* the only one that has recently been republished (1989). In the gradual development of Caird's heroines can be traced the changes in women's social and political position from the late nineteenth century to the 1930s, changes that Caird, along with Sarah Grand and many other New Woman writers, helped to bring about through their radical fiction with its outspoken heroines. In her essays Mona Caird demanded a better world for women, and in her fiction she demonstrated the necessity for it.

References:

Ann L. Ardis, *New Women, New Novels: Feminism and Early Modernism* (New Brunswick, N.J.: Rutgers University Press, 1990), pp. 68-72, 102-103;

Gail Cunningham, *The New Woman and the Victorian Novel* (New York: Harper & Row, 1978), pp. 69-73;

"Mrs. Mona Caird in a New Character," *Review of Reviews,* 8 (July 1893): 97;

Carolyn Christensen Nelson, *British Women Fiction Writers of the 1890s* (New York: Twayne, 1996), pp. 29-44;

Lyn Pykett, *The "Improper" Feminine: The Woman's Sensation Novel and the New Woman Writing* (London & New York: Routledge, 1992), pp. 143-148;

David Rubinstein, *Before the Suffragettes: Women's Emancipation in the 1890s* (New York: St. Martin's Press, 1986), pp. 38-39.

Gilbert Cannan
(25 June 1884 - 30 June 1955)

Diana Farr

BOOKS: *Peter Homunculus* (London: Heinemann, 1909; New York: Duffield, 1909);

Devious Ways (London: Heinemann, 1910; New York: Duffield, 1910);

Little Brother (London: Heinemann, 1912);

The Joy of the Theatre (London: Batsford, 1913; New York: Dutton, 1913);

Round the Corner: Being the Life and Death of Francis Christopher Folyat, Bachelor of Divinity, and Father of a Large Family (London: Secker, 1913; New York: Appleton, 1913);

Four Plays by Gilbert Cannan: James and John–Miles Dixon–Mary's Wedding–A Short Way with Authors (London: Sidgwick & Jackson, 1913);

Old Mole: Being the Surprising Adventures in England of Herbert Jocelyn Beenham, m.a., Sometime Sixth-form Master at Thrigsby Grammar School in the County of Lancaster (London: Secker, 1914; New York: Appleton, 1914);

Love (London: Batsford, 1914; New York: Dutton, 1914);

Satire (London: Secker, 1914; New York: Doran, 1914);

Young Earnest: The Romance of a Bad Start in Life (London: Secker, 1915; New York: Appleton, 1915);

Adventurous Love and Other Verses (London: Methuen, 1915);

Samuel Butler: A Critical Study (London: Secker, 1915);

Windmills: A Book of Fables (London: Secker, 1915; New York: Huebsch, 1920);

Mendel: A Story of Youth (London: Unwin, 1916; New York: Doran, 1916);

Three Pretty Men (London: Methuen 1916); republished as *Three Sons and a Mother* (New York: Doran, 1916);

Everybody's Husband (London: Secker, 1917; New York: Huebsch, 1917);

Freedom (London: Headley, 1917; New York: Stokes, 1918);

The Stucco House: A Novel (London: Unwin, 1917; New York: Doran, 1918);

Gilbert Cannan in his twenties

Noel: An Epic in Three Cantos, 3 volumes (London: Richards, 1917–1918); revised as *Noel: An Epic in Seven Cantos,* 1 volume (London: Secker, 1922);

Mummery: A Tale of Three Idealists (London: Collins, 1918; New York: Doran, 1919);

Pink Roses (London: Unwin, 1919; New York: Doran, 1919);

The Anatomy of Society (London: Chapman & Hall, 1919; New York: Dutton, 1919);

Time and Eternity: A Tale of Three Exiles (London: Chapman & Hall, 1919; New York: Doran, 1920);

James and John: A Play in One Act (Boston: Phillips, 1920);

Miles Dixon: A Play in Two Acts (Boston: Phillips, 1920);

Mary's Wedding: A Play in One Act (Boston: Phillips, 1920);

A Short Way with Authors: A Burlesque in One Act (Boston: Phillips, 1920);

Pugs and Peacocks (London: Hutchinson, 1921);

Sembal (London: Hutchinson, 1922; New York: Seltzer, 1924);

Annette and Bennett (London: Hutchinson, 1922; New York: Seltzer, 1923);

Love Is Less than God: The Book of the Soul (New York: Sunwise Turn, 1923);

Seven Plays (London: Secker, 1923)—comprises *Everybody's Husband, The Fat King and the Lean, In the Park, Someone to Whisper To, The Same Story, Pierrot in Hospital,* and *The Polite Art of Conversation;*

Letters from a Distance (London: Secker, 1923; New York: Seltzer, 1924);

The House of Prophecy (London: Butterworth, 1924; New York: Seltzer, 1924).

PLAY PRODUCTIONS: *Dull Monotony,* London, Stage Society, 1909;

Miles Dixon, Manchester, Gaiety Theatre, 21 November 1910;

James and John, London, Haymarket Theatre, 27 March 1911;

The Perfect Widow, Manchester, Gaiety Theatre, 18 March 1912;

Mary's Wedding, London, Coronet Theatre, 6 May 1912;

The Arbour of Refuge, London, Little Theatre, 4 February 1913;

Three, adapted from D. St. Cyr's version of Robert Bracco's *Lui, Lei, Lui,* London, Little Theatre, 4 February 1913; produced again as *Countess Coquette,* Croydon, Hippodrome Theatre, 16 August 1915;

A Short Way with Authors, London, Cosmopolis, 26 May 1913;

The Right to Kill, adapted by Cannan and Frances Keyser, London, His Majesty's Theatre, 4 May 1915;

Everybody's Husband, Birmingham, Repertory Theatre, 14 April 1917;

In the Park, London, Mary Ward Settlement, 15 October 1924.

TRANSLATIONS: *Heinrich Heine's Memoirs, from His Works, Letters, and Conversations,* edited by Gustav Karpeles (New York: John Lane, 1910);

Romain Rolland, *Jean-Christophe: Dawn Morning, Youth, Revolt* (New York: Holt, 1910); republished in two volumes as *John Christopher: Dawn and Morning* (London: Heinemann, 1910) and *John Christopher: Storm and Stress* (London: Heinemann, 1911);

Rolland, *John Christopher in Paris* (London: Heinemann, 1911); republished as *Jean-Christophe in Paris: The Marketplace, Antoinette, The House* (New York: Holt, 1911);

Rolland, *Jean Christopher—Journey's End* (London: Heinemann, 1913); republished as *Jean-Christophe: Journey's End. Love and Friendship, The Burning Bush, The New Dawn* (New York: Holt, 1913);

Julien Benda, *The Yoke of Pity (L'Ordination)* (New York: Holt, 1913);

Tatiana Alexinsky, *With the Russian Wounded* (London: Unwin, 1916);

Anton Chekhov, *The House with the Mezzanine, and Other Stories,* translated by Cannan and Samuel Solomovitch Koteliansky (New York: Scribners, 1917);

Chekhov, *My Life, and Other Stories,* translated by Cannan and Koteliansky (London: Daniel, 1920);

Mikhail Artsybahsev, *The Savage,* translated by Cannan and Mme. A. Strindberg (New York: Boni & Liveright, 1924);

Valéry Larbaud, *A. O. Barnabooth: His Diary* (London: Dent, 1924).

In a career that lasted only fifteen years before being cut short by madness, Gilbert Cannan wrote twenty-seven books, at least fourteen plays, and many articles, short stories, and columns of dramatic criticism. He also translated from German, French, and, in collaboration, Russian. Overwork was both his escape from an innate loneliness and, eventually, the final blow to his sanity.

Gilbert Eric Cannan was born in Manchester on 25 June 1884 to Henry Cannan, a shipping clerk, and Violet Wright Cannan. His grandfather James Cannan, a bank clerk and drama critic for *The Manchester City News,* was an early influence. James Cannan's wife, Agnes, was the daughter of John Storrs Smith, author of a book on Mirabeau and two volumes of poetry, as well as cofounder with James Cannan, Edwin Waugh, and Francis Epinasse of a literary coterie known as the Shandean Club. A puritanical churchgoer, Agnes Cannan disapproved of the theater and was embittered by her husband's failure to support her in the manner she expected. She withdrew gradually from the world, modeling herself on Queen Victoria, under whose portrait she sat day after day while growing increasingly fat. When staying with these grandparents it was Gilbert Cannan's lot to carry notes between them as they were no longer on speak-

Cannan's parents, Henry and Violet Wright Cannan

ing terms. As Cannan wrote in his unfinished and unpublished memoirs, "I do not know how much time I spent in that house, but my life was caught up in it to an extent which I did not realise until many years later."

At an early age Cannan became estranged from his family; he particularly felt overshadowed by his brilliant older brother, Angus. His mother was affectionate but had little time for him while his father's low opinion of him was sometimes expressed in tactless verse that was permanently etched in the boy's mind.

Passive, inclined to fantasy, and unable to communicate easily with boys his own age, Cannan began to show symptoms of the mental instability that would lead to a major breakdown in 1917 and eventually to insanity. When he was thirteen, it was decided—largely on the suggestion of his great-aunt Mary Cannan, a governess, linguist, and translator—that he should be adopted by his cousin, the economist Edwin Cannan, in Oxford.

Cannan received his early education at a state school, from which—to his parents' surprise—he followed Angus with a scholarship to Manchester Grammar School. There he showed a talent for modern languages, but it was Angus's plays that were performed at the school and reviewed in the local press. Gilbert Cannan, as his great-aunt realized, would blossom only when he escaped from his elder brother's dominance.

An essay on Friedrich Schiller won Cannan an exhibition (scholarship) to King's College, Cambridge, to study modern and medieval languages. At Cambridge he skipped lectures but read voraciously in German, French, and English; literature, drama, and philosophy were his main interests. He left in 1904 with a "pass" degree, which suggests that he suffered a breakdown in health. After a recuperative cruise to South Africa he went to London to read for the bar. The aloof air that he had worn as a protective shell at Cambridge was abandoned in London, and the "ox eyes," large head, and tadpolelike body that had been mocked by his father had matured into handsomeness. Cannan soon gained a foothold in theatrical and literary circles. Among those he met in his first years in London were James M. and Mary Barrie, George Bernard Shaw, George Meredith, Henry James, Ford Madox Ford, H. G. Wells, Ellen Terry, Joseph Conrad, and the publishers' reader and literary adviser Edward Garnett.

After being called to the bar Cannan abandoned law for writing, encouraged by a commission to translate into English Romain Rolland's ten-volume novel

Cannan (right) with his brother, Angus, and sister, Margaret

Jean-Christophe (1905–1912), the first four volumes of which had appeared in 1905–1906. His translation appeared as *John Christopher: Dawn and Morning* (1910), *John Christopher: Storm and Stress* (1911), *John Christopher in Paris* (1911), and *Jean Christopher–Journey's End* (1913). In the foreword to the final volume of the American edition (1910–1913) Cannan wrote: "I was twenty-three when I began translating *Jean Christophe,* I was twenty-seven when I finished it, so that my growing years were fortunately for me illuminated by the closest possible contact with a masterpiece with the result that in 1910 I began to write and indeed to live as though I were living in 1920. Romain Rolland was probably doing that in 1900."

As secretary of the Society for the Abolition of Censorship, which had been formed after Lord Chamberlain refused to grant a licence for Harley Granville Barker's play *Waste* (1907), Cannan came to know the Barries well; before long he accepted Mary Barrie's offer to serve as the couple's typist. Cannan, who was engaging in an unconsummated affair with the sculptor Kathleen Bruce, was soon flattered to find himself pursued by three beautiful women: Barker's wife, Lillah McCarthy; Sylvia Llewelyn Davies; and Mary Barrie. He exploited the dramatic possibilities of this situation in his first novel, *Peter Homunculus* (1909).

Bruce eventually rejected Cannan to marry the explorer Robert Falcon Scott. When the Barries dined with Cannan in his rooms at the Temple, Mary Barrie saw her chance to seduce him. His quarters needed redecorating, so she suggested that he stay at the Barries' Black Lake Cottage near Farnham, Surrey, while the work was being done. Cannan, Mary, and some women friends traveled there, and during their stay Cannan began entering Mary's bedroom via a ladder in the garden. The lovers did little to cover their tracks, and after Mary criticized the gardener, who once removed the ladder in the early hours of the morning, the man went to James Barrie with news of the adultery. When Mary refused to end the affair, calling Cannan "the only man in the world for me," Barrie filed for divorce. (An advocate of free love, Cannan believed that Barrie should have been glad that Mary had found a lover who could give her the sexual pleasure that he denied her.) The hearing was held in November 1909. In a letter to Bruce, Cannan wrote, "There is nothing to be done but to throw my

Cannan's cousin, the economist Edwin Cannan, who adopted Cannan when the boy was thirteen

work against [Barrie's], I am 25, he is 48 or 49. I have that to the good. I am happy and full of life; he is wretched and rotten to the bone, a poor sick beast with a poor sick soul."

Mary and Cannan, who had become drama critic for *The Star,* were married on 11 April 1910 and moved into Black Lake Cottage. Also in 1910 Cannan's play *Miles Dixon* was produced at the Gaiety Theatre in Manchester to good reviews–the *Manchester Guardian* critic compared Cannan with John Millington Synge–and his second novel, *Devious Ways,* and his translation of Heinrich Heine's memoirs were published. In March 1911 his short play *James and John,* about his father's strange bachelor brothers, was staged at the Haymarket Theatre in London, and St. John Hankin wrote that "Shaw, Barker and Galsworthy all believe Cannan is going to wipe them out." But such praise did little to lessen the Cannans' growing financial problems. In the spring of 1911 Mary was forced to sell her lease on Black Lake Cottage, and the couple returned to London.

But their love of the countryside soon drew the Cannans away from London again. After a short stay at a cottage at Bellingdon they took a long lease on the Mill House, Cholesbury, Buckinghamshire, a converted windmill with adjacent cottage. There Cannan entertained many of the notable figures of the day, including Garnett, Lady Ottoline Morrell, Bertrand Russell, Mark Gertler, D. H. Lawrence, Catherine Carswell, John Drinkwater, Samuel Solomovitch Koteliansky, and Dora Carrington. Cannan's popularity was at its height, but his well-disguised inferiority complex led him to surround himself with people who were younger and less established than he. Young hopefuls such as Rupert Brooke sought his opinion, and their affection and esteem provided the constant reassurance he craved.

Gertler wrote to Carrington from "a very pleasant bedroom" in the Mill House:

> But what I enjoy most is the company of Gilbert Cannan and the talks with him. He is a *true man.* There are not many like him. I like him truly. In the evenings we sit in the dimly lit Mill, where he plays Beethoven to me and then we talk and talk. Last night he read some of his poems to me. They sounded to me very good. I feel about him as if he was my greatest friend. He tells me I can use his cottage as if it were my own! I am doing no work here at all.

In 1912 Cannan published the slightly pretentious novel *Little Brother,* which is now only of interest to those who wish to understand Cannan's relationship with his adoptive father, Edwin Cannan. The work has an element of wish fulfillment as Mordaunt (based on Angus Cannan), a lecturer, reads a manuscript by Stephen (Gilbert Cannan) and falls under the influence of the brother he had despised: "It has unsettled me," he says. "It has set me wondering about things which are better not thought of: it has interfered with my world; it has haunted me, obtruded itself upon my conversation with my male friends. Nothing has happened to me since I read it, but I have found myself wondering what my brother would have thought of it. My tastes have adapted themselves to his; I have found myself laughing at things which I had hitherto always regarded with respect. A spirit of jocularity has crept into my lectures and I have shocked more that one of my pupils from Newnham and Girton." Mordaunt remembers Stephen as a boy: "He always had a white face and strange heavy eyes and the sight of it used sometimes to drive me into a frenzy, and then I would lunge out with my fists." The writing of *Little Brother,* which includes a rather cruel portrait of Edwin Cannan, was therapeutic for Cannan; but the structure is unnecessarily complicated, and Stephen rarely engages the reader's sympathy.

In 1913, the heady, largely happy year before World War I, the Cannans' Mill House parties became a legend. Charades, impromptu plays, and good food and wine broke down inhibitions and strengthened friendships. "I can't tell you with what pain I remember those days at Cholesbury," Lawrence wrote to Mary Cannan in 1918,

—the yellow leaves—and the wet nights when you came to us, and Gilbert and the dogs—and I had got pork chops—and our cottage was hot and full of the smell of sage and onions.... There was *something* in those still days before the war, which was beautiful and generous ... when we were happy with one another, really—even if we said spiteful things afterwards. I was happy, anyway.

Round the Corner: Being the Life and Death of Francis Christopher Folyat, Bachelor of Divinity, and Father of a Large Family (1913) chronicles the life of the perverse Parson Folyat, based on Cannan's grandfather Francis Arbuthnot Wright, who traded his beautiful parish of Topsham, Devon, for the poor district of St. Paul's, Salford, and broke his promise not to change the form of service there. Compassionate, ironic, and enlivened by its author's intuitive understanding of a certain type of female mind, *Round the Corner* consolidated Cannan's place as an avant-garde writer. Folyat's struggle to impose High Anglican rites on parishioners accustomed to Low Church rituals is graphically described. Cannan's sympathies are always with the lovable parson, who moves to Salford so that he can better serve God among the poor—and marry off his four daughters. Although Cannan perhaps idealizes Folyat's daughter Annette, based on his own mother, his description of her love affair with the weak-minded Bennett, based on Cannan's father, appears to be true in all but one or two minor respects. Furthermore, contemporary reports in Salford newspapers confirm that the tragic events that drive Folyat into retirement actually happened to Wright. Folyat's youngest son falls to his death while scampering across the vicarage roof, and Folyat's grief is cruelly exacerbated by the antipapist thugs who desecrate the boy's grave; the suicide of Folyat's second son, Frederic, an unhappily married lawyer about to be tried for misappropriation and embezzlement, is the final blow:

> For three weeks [Folyat] went on mechanically with his work, going blindly though the ritual, which he had fought so hard to establish, but always when he came to the Benediction and commended the congregation to the Peace of God, he knew, he could not get away with the knowledge that there was no peace in his own heart, and he rebuked himself and called himself Hypocrite.... the teaching of the gospel should, if it had any purpose, lead to a noble life, a superb preparation for eternity. But whither had it led himself? To the smallest of small lives, to the ruin of two of his children, fallen into the very snares against which they had been warned with all the threats of eternal punishment and Hell fire at the command of an appointed minister of the Christian religion.

Cannan's grandfather James Cannan appears in the novel as James Lawrie. When Lawrie meets Folyat, his son's future father-in-law—at this time Bennett is engaged to Annette's older sister, Gertrude—he reads four verses of his own poetry to the parson. Bennett himself wants to be a parson, and Folyat calls on Lawrie with the news: "Old Lawrie received it in blank astonishment. 'Well, well,' he said, 'Wants to be a parson, does he? Is it the clothes he's after? He was always a great one for dressing up.'" Later he says,

> You wish me to say will I or will I not let my son, Bennett go for a parson. Have you a mind for irony? There's irony in this. In the first place I have no money. In the second I cannot say "Yes" or "No" to that or any other thing in this house. You must see the boy's mother. I'll send you with a note. What are you staring at man? Have you never seen a prisoner before?

The *Times Literary Supplement* reviewer found *Round the Corner* disappointing and the characters unattractive: "while you cannot read it without admiration for its cleverness and literary skill, the general effect is one of squalor ... there is a claim to set forth a serious criticism of life as it is. To which the only comment is that life, seen wholly, is not like this, for all the vivid presentiment that seeks to persuade us that these stereoscopic figures are human beings." But *The Morning Post* reviewer said that the novel "must be read," and *The Nation* declared that "Mr. Cannan is so uncompromising, so whole-hearted, so sure of his psychological analysis that his picture gives true aesthetic pleasure." Other readers were shocked by Cannan's cynicism, his attacks on matrimony, and his religious bigotry. Agnostic comments by Folyat's son Serge, who is based on Wright's oldest son, Henry, added to the alarm of the large circulating libraries, which banned the novel. Filson Young commented in the *Saturday Review* that *Round the Corner* was one of the best novels that had been written in the past few years: "Having read it carefully and with profound appreciation, I can only come to the conclusion that it was banned because it was good." *Round the Corner* established Cannan as a serious novelist.

A pacifist with socialist leanings, Cannan joined the National Council Against Conscription and campaigned against British involvement in World War I. A letter to Morrell, dated 15 October 1915, sums up his views: "We have to accept the horror and take it down in our souls and when that is done then only can we turn upon it and demand in how ever a small voice that it shall cease. The war should not cease because it is horrible but because it is futile and it is foolish blasphemy. Let the wicked blaspheme, but not the innocent."

Cannan's best books do not include characters based on himself. Of these, *Mendel Story of*

The sculptor Kathleen Bruce, with whom Cannan had an unconsummated love affair

Youth (1916) is the best known, largely because it gives an accurate portrait of Gertler, to whom Cannan felt particularly close during the early Cholesbury days. Uninhibited, passionate, and naive, Gertler responded to Cannan's friendship with flattering admiration. Cannan, always sympathetic to the impoverished, let him use the Mill House garage as a studio, and although Mary complained that Gertler ate too much, he stayed for days on end, monopolizing Cannan's attention in the evenings by telling the story of his life. Gertler continued his life story on long walks with Cannan, and Cannan committed it to memory. The result was *Mendel*, a colorful novel told largely in Gertler's words.

Mendel opens with Golda Kühler and her three sons and two daughters getting off an immigrants' boat in London after a horrific sea journey to wait for Golda's husband, Jacob, whom they have not seen for two years. Seven-year-old Mendel (Gertler), the youngest of the children, earns much-needed money for the family by performing a dance for the passersby. At last Jacob arrives and takes the family to a small, unfurnished room; they are delighted because "in Austria they had the corner of a room and the three other corners were occupied by the carpenter, the stableman, and the potter. In the centre of the room stood the common water bucket and the common refuse tub."

Mendel charts a poor boy's struggle to escape a financially stunted Jewish life to become a successful painter in the Gentile world. Jacob despises Christians "as he despised luxury, pleasure, comfort, not actively nor with any hatred. He simply did not need them and he asked nothing of life. Passions seized him and he followed them." With some dramatic licence the novel describes the conflict Mendel feels between loyalty to his loving mother and the morally unprincipled life of an art student. Handicapped by class barriers, Mendel is delighted when he is taken under the wing of Mitchell (based on C. R. W. Nevinson). But Mendel drops Mitchell for the less well-placed, illegitimate Logan (John Currie), who is dogmatic, brilliant, and unstable. Cannan, who was as obsessive about his writing as Gertler was about his art, describes convincingly the tyranny and transient joys of the creative force and the depressions that were to contribute to Gertler's suicide in 1939.

After Logan kills his lover and shoots himself, Morrison (Carrington), with whom Mendel is beginning an emotionally exhausting on-and-off affair, and her friend Clowes (Dorothy Brett) ask Mendel to stay with them in the country. There he tries to explain to them something of his difficulties:

> Jews are wonderful people. They know that what matters is the impulse of the soul. It matters so much to them that they have forgotten everything else. And those who are not Jews think of everything else and forget the soul. But I know when I swing from happiness to unhappiness, from good to bad, from light to dark, then a force comes into my soul and it can move up to art and beyond art into that place where it can be free.... Don't please misunderstand me, in love I can no more be free than I can in misery.

Although Gertler's widow declared that when she read the book she could hear Gertler speaking, this speech seems to owe more to Cannan. Nevertheless much of the novel—especially some of the descriptions, sentiments, and dialogue—is written as Gertler spoke, and many of the people depicted in it felt betrayed by Gertler. William Rothenstein, an early benefactor who is not always treated kindly in the novel, was furious, and Gertler's brothers and sisters resented their marriages and affairs becoming public knowledge. Carrington wrote to him, "How angry I am over Gilbert's book. Everywhere this confounded gossip and servant-like curiosity. It's ugly and so damned vulgar." Gertler wrote to Rothenstein, "Gilbert Cannan's version is, I assure you, entirely false and I am not responsible for it. PLEASE UNDERSTAND THIS. Nor would I ever be responsible for such an agglomeration of cheap trash as is contained in this awful novel." But Gertler, although dismayed by the book, remained Cannan's friend.

Reviews of the novel were mixed. "We have always felt an artist's temperament must be an uncomfortable possession, but never has the belief been so irresistibly forced on us as after reading Gilbert Cannan's odd, brilliant study of a Jewish artist," wrote the critic for *Outlook*. The reviewer for the *Times Literary Supplement* was disappointed that there was no "governing purpose in *Mendel*, a life of episode rather than development" and complained that there was too much talk of sex but found the novel "almost continuously entertaining" and considered Morrison the most vivid personality in it. *Mendel* remains the most sought-after of Cannan's books, partly because of its value to art historians.

The Cannans entertained Belgian refugees and were sympathetic to those, like Lawrence, who had German spouses. Cannan's love of German literature and music and his interest in German philosophy, fostered in his youth by his great-aunt Mary, combined to increase his hatred of the war. In August 1916 he was exempted from active service because of a heart murmur. But the carnage of the war, financial and marital problems, and overwork had brought Cannan to a breaking point. When Mary's maid asked him to have sex with her so that she could have a baby, he complied, and she became pregnant. In the autumn of 1916, in a state of confusion, Cannan fled to shabby rooms at 31 Hallam Street in London's West End. There, lonely and poor, he suffered from delusions but continued to write and translate. A love affair with Gwen Wilson, a nineteen-year-old South African, postponed his descent into madness but led to his legal separation from Mary in 1918. After Cannan recovered from a major breakdown, he and Wilson rented a studio at 7B Elm Park Gardens, St. John's Wood. They supplemented Cannan's inadequate earnings by taking in a lodger, Henry Mond, from a wealthy Jewish family. This ménage à trois became a topic of discussion in literary London. In early 1920 Cannan went on a lecture tour to North America, where he met Alfred Stieglitz, Amy Lowell, and Georgia O'Keeffe and tried to raise money for Lawrence. Meanwhile, back in London, Wilson married Mond, dealing a mortal blow to Cannan's precarious sanity. Cannan is said to have attacked a fellow passenger on an ocean liner after hearing the news.

In old age Wilson declared that she married Mond so that she could support Cannan, the one great love of her life. But Cannan did not return to their home. In the autumn of 1921 he traveled to Paris and

Mary Barrie, the wife of the playwright James M. Barrie, who left her husband to marry Cannan

then to Port Said to begin a trip across Africa, with a commission from the *New York Freeman* to send regular dispatches en route. These were published as a book, *Letters from a Distance* (1923). The first, written from Paris on 1 November, begins, "I am wandering, dear Eusebius, in the hope of discovering an answer to the question, 'What on earth are we all up to?'" Wilson met him in South Africa, where she had the love poems he continued to write her bound in leather. He finished *Pugs and Peacocks* (1921), a lively ironic novel, and worked on *Annette and Bennett* (1922), the sequel to *Round the Corner*. In October 1921 Cannan wrote from Beira, Mozambique, that he was leaving something of himself in Africa: "my lodge in the wilderness, my garden and God knows what myth of the strange *inkoos* who cared nothing for money or drink or gold; and made friends with horses and dogs, and had no women and yet, using horrible language upon occasions, could not possibly be a missionary." *Letters from a Distance* was well received, and Cannan's novels were selling well in Scandinavia and France but less well in England. And his agent was holding onto his royalties without fulfilling his promise to send Cannan's widowed mother five pounds a month.

The three novels that Cannan described as of "the new time"–*Pugs and Peacocks, Sembal* (1922), and *The House of Prophecy* (1924)–are now period pieces that are mainly of interest to those researching the last years of World War I and its aftermath. They include a memorable portrait of Bertrand Russell as well as echoes of Morrell and others involved in the peace movement. These novels become increasingly anti-Semitic. In his last novel the likeable heroine, Matty, based on Wilson, goes off with Sembal, to the dismay of the Irishman Penrose Kennedy, based on Cannan himself.

Unable to bear London, Cannan continued to travel in Europe and the United States after his return from Africa. His disillusionment with the world order led him to write an open letter in *The New York Herald Tribune* to President Warren G. Harding in which he suggested that Abraham Lincoln's birthday should be celebrated by the release of all political prisoners and that the Treaty of Versailles should be replaced by a European Pact "drawn up by lawyers with the qualities of General Smuts."

Back in London in August 1923, Cannan destroyed many of his papers and books and set fire to his furniture, then claimed that the act was perpetrated by Mond. He had become a danger to himself and others, and his relatives had him certified as insane. On 15 April 1924 he was committed to the Priory Hospital, Roehampton; he had been working on a fourth book in the novels of the new time series, "The Soaring Bird." In 1952 he was moved to the Holloway Sanatorium, Virginia Water. He died of cancer there on 30 June 1955.

All of Cannan's novels, apart from *Peter Homunculus,* are critical of the Establishment, contemporary politics, the Church, marriage, and scheming women. He had a fine nose for hypocrisy and cant, and at his best he is profound. While frequently pessimistic, his novels are sharpened by an ironic wit. The postwar novels, however, lack the depth and structure of *Round the Corner* and sometimes reveal a confused mind trying to make sense of a world gone mad. His obituaries spoke of "a promise unfulfilled" and indications of a "genius that never developed." Future biographers of personages of the period may find useful material in his novels; therein, perhaps, lies the greatest value of his work, along with its re-creation of the flavor of the times through which he lived.

Biography:
Diana Farr, *Gilbert Cannan: A Georgian Prodigy* (London: Chatto & Windus, 1978).

References:
Mary Ansell, *Dogs and Men* (London: Duckworth, 1924);

Ansell, *Happy Houses* (London: Cassell, 1912);

May Wedderburn Cannan, *Grey Ghosts and Voices* (Kineton: Roundwood, 1976);

Dora Carrington, *Carrington: Letters and Extracts from Her Diaries,* edited by David Garnett (London: Cape, 1970);

Janet Dunbar, *J. M. Barrie: The Man behind the Image* (London: Collins, 1970);

Mark Gertler, *Selected Letters,* edited by Noel Carrington (London: Hart-Davis, 1965);

D. H. Lawrence, *The Collected Letters of D. H. Lawrence,* 2 volumes, edited by Harry T. Moore (London: Heinemann, 1962);

Frieda Lawrence, *The Memoirs and Correspondence,* edited by E. W. Tedlock (London: Heinemann, 1961);

Lawrence, *"Not I, but the Wind . . ."* (London: Heinemann, 1935);

Lady Ottoline Morrell, *The Early Memoirs of Lady Ottoline Morrell,* edited by Robert Gathorne-Hardy (London: Faber & Faber, 1963);

Morrell, *Ottoline at Garsington: Memoirs of Lady Ottoline Morrell, 1915–1918,* edited by Gathorne-Hardy (London: Faber, 1974);

John Middleton Murry, *Between Two Worlds: An Autobiography* (London: Cape, 1935);

Frank Swinnerton, *Background with Chorus: A Footnote to Changes in English Literary Fashion between 1901 and 1917* (London: Hutchinson, 1956);

Swinnerton, *Figures in the Foreground: Literary Reminiscences 1917–1940* (London: Hutchinson, 1963);

Swinnerton, *The Georgian Literary Scene: A Panorama* (London: Heinemann, 1935);

Alec Waugh, *My Brother Evelyn, and Other Profiles* (London: Cassell, 1967);

John Woodeson, *Mark Gertler: Biography of a Painter, 1891–1939* (London: Sidgwick & Jackson, 1972).

Papers:
Repositories of Gilbert Cannan's papers include the Galsworthy Papers and Diaries at the Birmingham University Library; the Koteliansky Manuscripts at the British Library; the Cannan Family Papers, the Gertler Family Papers, and the Kathleen Bruce Scott Papers and Diaries at Cambridge University Library; The Harry Ransom Humanities Research Center, University of Texas at Austin; and the Beinecke Rare Book and Manuscript Library, Yale University.

Mary Cholmondeley
(8 June 1859 - 15 July 1925)

Karen M. Carney
John Carroll University

BOOKS: *The Danvers Jewels,* as Pax (London: Bentley, 1887; New York: Harper, 1890);
Sir Charles Danvers, as "the author of *The Danvers Jewels,*" 2 volumes (London: Bentley, 1889); republished as *The Danvers Jewels and Sir Charles Danvers* (New York & London: Harper, 1899);
Diana Tempest (3 volumes, London: Bentley, 1893; 1 volume, New York: Appleton, 1893);
A Devotee: An Episode in the Life of a Butterfly (London & New York: Edward Arnold, 1897);
Red Pottage (London: Edward Arnold, 1899; New York: Harper, 1899);
Moth and Rust (London: John Murray, 1902); republished as *Moth and Rust and Other Stories* (New York: Dodd, Mead, 1902);
Prisoners—Fast Bound in Misery and Iron (London: Hutchinson, 1906; New York: Dodd, Mead, 1906);
The Lowest Rung (London: John Murray, 1908); republished as *The Hand on the Latch* (New York: Dodd, Mead, 1909);
Notwithstanding (London: John Murray, 1913); republished as *After All* (New York: Appleton, 1913);
Under One Roof: A Family Record (London: John Murray, 1918);
The Romance of His Life, and Other Romances (London: John Murray, 1921; New York: Dodd, Mead, 1921).
Edition: *Red Pottage,* introduction by Elaine Showalter (London: Virago, 1985).

In the fall of 1899 the title of Mary Cholmondeley's latest novel was on everyone's lips. "Have you read Pottage?" readers punningly asked one another, referring to Cholmondeley's best-selling *Red Pottage.* There were few who had not read it; two months after its release the book was already in its third edition, having sold more than eighteen thousand copies in England alone. *Red Pottage* made Cholmondeley's reputation, and it remains a powerful illustration of English provincial life and of the limited opportunities available to unmarried women in the late nineteenth century.

The third child and eldest daughter of Richard Hugh and Emily Beaumont Cholmondeley's eight children, Mary Cholmondeley was born in Hodnet, Shropshire, on 8 June 1859. Although in *Under One Roof: A Family Record,* her 1918 family memoir, Cholmondeley's childhood appears happy and full of country pleasures, it also had its darker side: to Percy Lubbock, who published a memoir of her in 1928, she described her younger self as "a half-savage, forlorn, uneducated creature, maimed by illness, unable to live or die, baffled at every turn." Early on she was forced to

Title page for Cholmondeley's first novel; it is inscribed by the author to her sister Essex Benson (University of Queensland)

assume management of the household and parish duties when her mother, a neurasthenic, took permanently to her bed. Cholmondeley's father, the rector of Hodnet, was affectionate and childlike. "He had the elasticity of a child, and a child's sweetness, and optimism and truthfulness, and belief in others," Cholmondeley recalled. "He had also the lack of foresight of a child, and a child's incapacity of mental grasp." After her mother's death Cholmondeley continued to live at home, caring for her father until he died in 1910.

Cholmondeley found liberation from her family responsibilities through literature. In 1877, always the pragmatist, she reflected in her journal, "What a pleasure and interest it would be to me in life to write books. I must strike out a line of some kind, and if I do not marry (for at best that is hardly likely, as I possess neither beauty nor charms) I should want some definite occupation, besides the home duties."

The following year she published her first story in *The Graphic*. In 1886 her friend Rhoda Broughton, a successful novelist, brought one of Cholmondeley's manuscripts to the notice of the publisher George Bentley. It was *The Danvers Jewels* (1887), a detective story that closely resembles Wilkie Collins's *The Moonstone* (1868). The narrator, Colonel Middleton, brings a set of rare but apparently cursed Indian jewels to the soon-to-be-married Danvers heir and thereby sets into motion a plot full of theft, murder, and intrigue. But Cholmondeley's story is also a sly and funny parody of the popular detective genre: Colonel Middleton is no amateur sleuth but a hopeless bungler who accuses the innocent, befriends the villainous, and says, in all seriousness, "When jewels are stolen, one naturally suspects some one has taken them."

When Bentley praised *The Danvers Jewels* as a "bright and humorous story" and offered to publish it as soon as he could, Cholmondeley commented in her diary, "Bright and humorous, is it? I look back with a sort of grim smile at the darkness and depression out of which this brightness and humour came." Writing was never easy for Cholmondeley; she reported "plodding wearily from chapter to chapter . . . only anxious to write my five pages a day."

Nevertheless, *The Danvers Jewels* proved so successful a story that Cholmondeley followed it up with a sequel, *Sir Charles Danvers* (1889). The reviewer for the *Athenaeum* (9 November 1989) noted that the author's "somewhat dangerous experiment—at this early period of her career—in continuing some of the threads of her first story has been entirely justified in its execution." Once again, Cholmondeley's epigrammatic wit and powers of characterization served her well and camouflaged the occasional shortcomings in the plot: "Lady Deyncourt, a beauty in her youth, a beauty in middle life, a beauty in her old age, had seen and known all the marked men of the last two generations, and had reminiscences to tell which increased in point and flavour, like old wine, the longer they were kept."

The lighthearted comedy of *The Danvers Jewels* and *Sir Charles Danvers* gave way to a more serious tone with Cholmondeley's third novel, *Diana Tempest* (1893). Her first signed work, it proved a modest success with readers and critics. The eponymous heroine, independent and proud, struggles with her love for her cousin, heir to the Tempest fortune, only to discover that her unscrupulous father has plotted to have him killed. The *Athenaeum* (18 November 1893) described the book as "an excellent drawing-room novel, full of humour, touched with real pathos, regulated by conventionality of the best order, written with finished taste and skill."

Diana Tempest was Cholmondeley's only three-volume novel; by the time she published her next book, *A Devotee: An Episode in the Life of a Butterfly*, in

Cholmondeley in 1906

1897 the Victorian "three-decker" was becoming a thing of the past. The change apparently suited Cholmondeley, who frequently experienced difficulty sustaining a long narrative. While *A Devotee* is a much slighter work than Cholmondeley's other novels, Vineta Colby cites its importance as "a trial run for the more ambitious *Red Pottage*." *A Devotee* introduces several characters who appear in the later novel, including the narrow-minded Gresleys and the bumbling Doll Loftus.

In *Red Pottage* these characters are joined by the two women whose friendship is at the heart of the novel, Rachel West and Hester Gresley. Both women struggle to define themselves in the face of social snobbery and hypocrisy. Hester, the writer, overcomes her own physical frailty to produce her magnum opus, *Husks,* which her self-righteous brother destroys; Rachel, the independent New Woman, falls in love with a man who keeps from her the terrible secret of a ruinous prior affair.

Although most reviewers greeted *Red Pottage* with high praise—it was "brilliant," "a masterpiece," comparable to the work of Charlotte Brontë, Jane Austen, and George Eliot—there were also those who branded it as scandalous. Others mistook her satiric portrayal of the Reverend Mr. Gresley—representative only of the "man with a closed mind," according to Cholmondeley—as a wholesale indictment of the English clergy. The Anglican *Guardian* (11 April 1900) saw the book as "a libel on the High Church clergy generally" and as a "perverse misinterpretation of the principles and methods of the High Church party."

Cholmondeley, the daughter of a clergyman, was horrified. In a wry and witty essay for the *Pall Mall Magazine,* "The Skeleton in the Novelist's Cupboard" (later republished as the preface to *The Lowest Rung,* 1908), Cholmondeley cited several instances in which readers had accused her of taking her fictional subjects from life. She gently chided, "It is perhaps impossible for those who do not write fiction to form any conception how easily an erroneous idea gains credence that some one has been 'put in a book'; or if the idea has once been entertained, how impossible it is to eradicate it." The costs of writing fiction, she noted, were often higher than the rewards: "A great deal of the delight [an author] may derive from a successful novel may be dimmed by the realisation that he has unwittingly pained a stranger, or worse still, an acquaintance, or immeasurably worst of all—an old friend." These are hardly the proud musings of a successful novelist.

Occasional bitterness on Cholmondeley's part was perhaps justified. Having sold the copyright to *Red Pottage,* Cholmondeley received little money for it despite its great success. Moreover, her newfound literary celebrity was itself a source of concern. "I have not written a word since January," she noted in her journal in August 1900. "But what a pity—just this year of all years to have written nothing when so much has been happening, when I am positively and actually that monster 'a celebrity,' which I may not be next year."

Indeed, Cholmondeley's later works never matched the achievement of *Red Pottage*. Her sixth book, *Moth and Rust* (1902), which includes two short stories and the title novella, was particularly disappointing. In *Red Pottage* Cholmondeley elicited sympathy and understanding for her characters even as she exposed their weaknesses; in *Moth and Rust* her tone is frequently patronizing and moralistic. The story of Janet Black, whose loyalty to a dying friend implicates her in a scandal that costs her her lover, *Moth and Rust* was generally neglected by critics and readers alike.

Cholmondeley's next novel, *Prisoners—Fast Bound in Misery and Iron* (1906), was slightly more successful. The "prisoners" of the book's title are Fay, unhappily married to an Italian duke many years her senior, and Michael, who confesses to a murder he did not commit to save Fay's reputation. While the plot again strains credulity, the book is redeemed by its portrayal of Magdalen Bellairs, a middle-aged spinster who serves as the novel's moral center: "Just as some people have the power of making something new out of refuse—paper out of rags—so Magdalen seemed to have the power of cherishing and transforming the weaker, meaner elements of the characters with which she came in contact."

More characters like Magdalen appear in *The Lowest Rung* (1908) a collection of four stories. Each centers around a strong, independent, mature female character; for instance, in the title story a middle-aged woman writer befriends a rough homeless woman who teaches her that "no artist must look at one side of life only." The reviewer for *Outlook* (1 May 1909) praised Cholmondeley's ability to elicit both sympathy and pity for her characters, arousing alternately in her readers "smiles and sober thought."

In her last full-length novel, *Notwithstanding* (1913), Cholmondeley's powers of characterization are once again her saving grace. As her friend and biographer Lubbock noted, "she spun her moralities too fine, she dropped too easily to melodrama . . . but in her power of creating a character— the paramount arm of a novelist—she shewed the measure and nature of her imagination." Much of the action of *Notwithstanding* takes place in Cholmondeley's native Midlands, where Cholmondeley and her sister Di owned a cottage. In the preface to her last book, *The Romance of His Life, and Other Romances* (1921), Cholmondeley wryly notes that to their neighbors the middle-aged sisters were "a sight to which they are as well accustomed as to the village pump, the stocks at the Church gate, or any other samples of 'still life.'" It was a far cry from the notoriety Cholmondeley had known in the days when everyone had "read Pottage."

Cholmondeley died in the summer of 1925, soon after her sixty-sixth birthday. By the time of her death her fame as a writer had been eclipsed by that of her niece, the novelist Stella Benson, and the book that had prompted comparisons to Brontë, Austen, and Eliot was only dimly remembered. Colby suggests that Cholmondeley had been "caught between worlds": "A late Victorian, she lived into the twentieth century but was never really of it." Recently, however, feminist critics such as Elaine Showalter and Ann Ardis have reclaimed Cholmondeley as one of the most innovative and radical of New Woman novelists. According to Ardis the strength of Cholmondeley and of her contemporaries Olive Schreiner, Ella Hepworth Dixon, and Mona Caird was their ability to "imagine worlds quite different from the bourgeois patriarchy in which unmarried women are deemed odd and superfluous 'side character[s].'" Certainly Cholmondeley, unmarried and forty-one when *Red Pottage* was published, resisted such easy dismissal herself. As one of her contemporaries noted, "it is unnecessary to proclaim the cleverness of the woman who wrote *Red Pottage*; whatever the hackneyed and abused word denotes, the quality was easily recognisable in that book."

Bibliography:

Jane Crisp, *Mary Cholmondeley, 1859–1925: A Bibliography* (St. Lucia, Australia: Department of English, University of Queensland, 1981).

Biography:

Percy Lubbock, *Mary Cholmondeley: A Sketch From Memory* (London: Jonathan Cape, 1928).

References:

Ann Ardis, *New Women, New Novels: Feminism and Early Modernism* (New Brunswick & London: Rutgers University Press, 1990), pp. 128–133;

Vineta Colby, "'Devoted Amateur': Mary Cholmondeley and *Red Pottage*," *Essays in Criticism*, 20 (1970): 213–228;

"The Motive Hunting Reader and the Theory of Malicious Origins." *Bookman*, 28 (1908): 312–317.

Lucy Lane Clifford
(1853 – 21 April 1929)

P. Joan Smith
McMaster University

See also the Clifford entries in *DLB 135: British Short-Fiction Writers, 1880-1914: The Realist Tradition* and *DLB 141: British Children's Writers, 1880-1914.*

BOOKS: *Children Busy, Children Glad, Children Naughty, Children Sad,* as L. C. (London: Wells, Gardner, 1881; New York: Nelson, 1881);

Anyhow Stories, Moral and Otherwise (London: Macmillan, 1882); republished as *Anyhow Stories for Children* (London: Macmillan, 1885); revised and enlarged (London: Duckworth, 1899);

The Dingy House at Kensington, anonymous (New York: Munro, 1882);

Marie May; or, Changed Aims, anonymous (London: Warne, 1884); as Clifford (London & New York: Warne, 1893);

Under Mother's Wing, as L. C. (London: Wells, Gardner, Darton, 1885; New York: Young, 1885);

Mrs. Keith's Crime: A Record, anonymous, 2 volumes (London: Bentley, 1885); republished as *Mrs. Keith's Crime: A Novel* (New York: Harper, 1885); revised edition, as Clifford (London: Eveleigh Nash & Grayson, 1925);

Very Short Stories and Verses for Children, anonymous (London: Scott, 1886);

Love-Letters of a Worldly Woman (London: Arnold, 1891; New York: Harper, 1892; enlarged edition, London: Constable, 1913);

The Last Touches and Other Stories (London: Black, 1892; New York & London: Macmillan, 1892);

Aunt Anne (New York: Harper, 1892; London: Bentley, 1892);

A Wild Proxy (London: Hutchinson, 1893); republished as *A Wild Proxy: A Tragic Comedy of Today* (New York: Cassell, 1893);

A Grey Romance, by Mrs. W. K. Clifford. And Stories by H. D. Traill, W. E. Hodgson, Etc. (London: W. H. Allen, 1894);

A Flash of Summer: A Novel (New York: Appleton, 1894); republished as *A Flash of Summer: The Story of a Simple Woman's Life* (London: Methuen, 1895);

Lucy Lane Clifford

"Dear Mr. Ghost": A Christmas Story (London: Dean, 1895);

Mere Stories (London: Black, 1896); republished as *The Dominant Note, and Other Stories* (New York: Dodd Mead, 1897);

A Woman Alone (New York & London: Macmillan, 1898); enlarged as *A Woman Alone: Three Stories* (London: Methuen, 1901);

The Likeness of the Night: A Modern Play in Four Acts (London: Black, 1900; New York: Macmillan, 1900);

A Long Duel: A Serious Comedy in Four Acts (London & New York: John Lane, 1901);

Woodside Farm (London: Duckworth, 1902); republished as *Margaret Vincent: A Novel* (New York & London: Harper, 1902);

The Getting Well of Dorothy (London: Methuen, 1904; New York: Dutton, 1917);

The Way Out (London: Daily Mail, 1904);

A Honeymoon Tragedy: A Comedy in One Act (London & New York: French, 1904);

The Modern Way–Eight Examples (London: Chapman & Hall, 1906);

The Shepherd's Purse (Cambridge: Macmillan & Bowes, 1906);

Proposals to Kathleen (New York: Barnes, 1908);

Plays: Hamilton's Second Marriage; Thomas and the Princess; The Modern Way (London: Duckworth, 1909; New York: Kennerley, 1910);

Sir George's Objection (London & New York: Nelson, 1910; enlarged, Leipzig: Tauchnitz, 1925);

A Woman Alone: In Three Acts (London: Duckworth, 1915; New York: Scribners, 1915);

The House in Marylebone: A Chronicle (London: Duckworth, 1917);

Mr. Webster, and Others (London: Collins, 1918);

Miss Fingal (Edinburgh & London: Blackwood, 1919; New York: Scribners, 1919);

Eve's Lover, and Other Stories (New York: Scribners, 1924);

The Searchlight: A Play in One Act (London & New York: French, 1925).

SELECTED PERIODICAL PUBLICATIONS–UNCOLLECTED: *A Supreme Moment. A Play in One Act, Nineteenth Century,* 46 (July 1899): 153–172;

"A Remembrance of George Eliot," *Nineteenth Century,* 74 (July-December 1913): 109–118.

The novels of Lucy Lane Clifford, who published almost exclusively under the name "Mrs. W. K. Clifford," had an avid contemporary following, both in Britain and the United States. A respected member of the late-Victorian London literary establishment, she has received little attention over the years, and she is generally only remembered in connection with her philosopher husband or for her friendships with writers such as George Eliot and Henry James.

Sophia Lucy Lane was born in 1853 in Barbados, West Indies; she was the daughter of John Lane, a planter and colonial administrator, whose father, Brandford Lane, had been speaker of the House of Assembly. She grew up under the care of her maternal grandmother, who lived in the countryside around Eltham, England, and during her childhood she began to write stories. While an art student in London she met William Kingdon Clifford, the Cambridge mathematician and philosopher, whom she married on 7 April 1875. Lucy Clifford was thus drawn into the company of such Victorian luminaries as Charles Darwin, Leslie Stephen, Herbert Spencer, James Russell Lowell, and Henry and William James. She also joined her husband at George Eliot's Sunday afternoon gatherings at the Priory, which opened up a wealth of literary connections. The couple traveled widely in their four years of marriage prior to the thirty-four-year-old W. K. Clifford's death in Madeira from pulmonary tuberculosis on 3 March 1879.

Clifford was left alone with two small daughters, Ethel and Amelia, to support (Ethel, as Lady Dilke, was to become a poet and novelist). She was encouraged to pursue a literary career by her friends–notably by Eliot, who was widowed around the same time. Eliot helped Clifford supplement her Civil List pension by giving her introductions–initially to *The Standard*–that started her writing professionally. (In an essay written for *The Nineteenth Century* [July 1913], Clifford recalls Eliot's comforting presence at that time: "to feel your hand in hers was to be sensible of all the troubled ways in your life peacefully subsiding.") Clifford spent the rest of her life writing and encouraging others from her home in St. John's Wood, counting prominent literary figures among her closest friends, particularly Henry James, whose devotion to her deepened with the years.

Influenced, perhaps, by James, Clifford's perceptive imagination led her to view humanity with precision and unbiased sympathy. She was praised in her day for her high idealism, for the dedication, optimism and sheer love of life that underlaid her work. But her novels are especially powerful in some of their darker moments; her identification with her lone female characters, searching for integrity in a society that would deny it, surfaces in her realistic renderings of their most painful situations. Her twelve novels all concern the interplay of realism and romance in affairs of the heart and are written primarily from a feminine perspective that challenges the status quo and elegantly pleads for an evolving social consciousness.

Following two collections of short stories for children Clifford's first novel, *The Dingy House at Kensington* (1882), was published anonymously in New York. An expanded version of a story published prior to her marriage, the novel is traditional, rife with Victorian literary conventions: an omniscient narrator tells of Henry Dawson, a miserly lawyer, who runs such a miserable household that his son, ironically the apple of his eye, dies of malnutrition. The bereft mother follows her son to the grave, leaving Polly, the simple, pretty daughter, alone with her father and a devoted but colorless admirer.

Into the picture steps Richard Blandford, heir to a fortune, who eschews high society and falls for Polly; but before their love can blossom Polly has to endure a wicked stepmother, her father's ignominious death, and a case of mistaken identity. The sentimentality is conventional: love conquers all, and it reaches beyond death, uniting spiritual and temporal realms. The novel was ignored by reviewers. Clifford appears to be feeling her way with this novel, her introduction to the form; the Shakespearean epigraph, however, anticipates a theme that is to recur in her fiction: "Men at some time are masters of their fates! / The fault, dear Brutus, is not in our stars, / But in ourselves." Clifford's fictional characters will always strive over the liabilities of social or natural conditioning.

In 1884 Clifford was in Italy working on her second novel, *Mrs. Keith's Crime: A Record* (1885), which was published anonymously in two volumes amid a storm of controversy. Maggie Keith is a genteel, impoverished widow whose daughter, Molly, is diagnosed with consumption. The same year Molly's older brother, Jack, dies of scarlet fever. With financial help they leave for Málaga, where a whirl of social and romantic comings and goings provides a backdrop for the action. One by one the other characters withdraw as Molly sickens. At this time Maggie learns that she, too, has consumption and that she will die before Molly. When the doctor decides to separate mother and child, Maggie chooses to kill Molly to save her from dying alone and motherless. After each takes a lethal dose, they die in each other's arms. In her final moments, although expecting to be reunited at death with her departed loved ones, Maggie feels only a tremendous sense of separation and loneliness.

Maggie's experience is narrated in the first person and in the present tense. The primal emotion thus exposed, along with Maggie's final assertive action to end her daughter's suffering, was highly provocative to the reading public. (In the preface to the sixth edition [1925], her authorship revealed, Clifford defended the book by claiming identification with Maggie and her action.) The novel is experimental, not only for its previously unheard-of topic of euthanasia, but also for its stylistic innovation. In the final pages the novel is written in a style that resembles what would later be termed stream of consciousness. Maggie muses: "I am going to . . . kill Molly. . . . I hear my father's step again; he is coming along the green lanes to meet me. How sorry he will be when he knows . . . he stops, and looks over the hedges . . . it is all the same still, just as it used to be; even the gate is broken still . . . he does not know

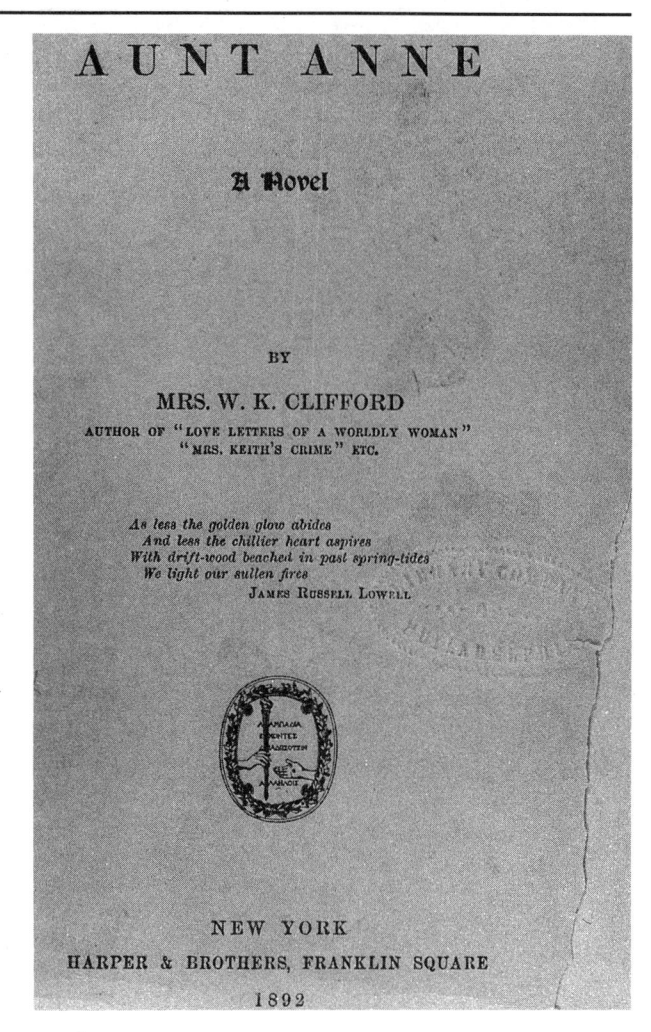

Title page for the U.S. edition of a novel about an elderly woman who falls prey to a confidence man

that it is too soon." The novel was extremely well reviewed, successfully dramatized, appeared serially in the French periodical *Le Temps,* and was industriously "pirated" by American publishers.

In the 1880s and 1890s Clifford befriended many writers. A lively correspondence with Lowell, who was at that time the American ambassador, over a period of five years reveals his fondness for Clifford. Referring ostensibly to books, he wrote on 14 December 1884: "One should be secret about one's loves and not betray the confidence they have put in one." In early 1890 Clifford introduced Rudyard Kipling to editors and publishers who would be crucial to his career. A family intimate, he sent playful hand-illustrated letters, with nonsensical language and notions, to Clifford's daughters, signing them "Ruddy." Also in the 1890s Clifford helped James, discouraged by the failure of his plays, by persuading the *Illustrated London News* to serialize his novel *The Other House* (1896).

In 1891 Clifford's third novel, *Love-Letters of a Worldly Woman,* was published in book form. It had originally been published anonymously in the *Fortnightly Review* (for a time, authorship was attributed to Oscar Wilde). This entertaining epistolary novel is divided into three parts, each composed of the correspondence between a different pair of lovers. The first, nameless, couple exchange views on life and love. She is a passionate idealist and he is a dull conformist. She minces no words in her rejection of him as the archetypal stuffy Englishman: "Yes, Good-bye dear Englishman, only our own land could have produced you . . . but for warmth and sunshine one goes to other lands than ours."

The second section centers around an original modern woman, Madge Brook (the novel's "worldly woman"), who suffers the pangs of unrequited love for the unprincipled Mark Cuthbertson. She overcomes her obsession, acknowledging that she will never experience an equal passion for another man, and accepts Sir Noel Frank's urbane proposal of marriage. Knowing that her passion for Mark is buried yet still exists, she settles for the prospect of a childless life in which she will be free to enjoy the families of her friends, with the intellectual stimulation of hosting her husband's political dinners and her own salon, and she proclaims herself satisfied.

The final correspondence recounts the drawn-out dying of romance between another generic couple. He is complacent and she is accommodating to the point of politely accepting his desire to break off the engagement. A year later he wants her back; they attempt to rekindle the romance, but she has matured enough to reject him: "[I went] on and on while you stood still. I am going farther and shall never return, but you will be in the world behind me."

It is worth noting that Clifford leaves the women who are unable to compromise their sentiments unnamed, while she gives the flexible "worldly woman" a name and identity. The theme of the modern woman's response to romance was to dominate much of Clifford's work.

The first edition of the novel sold out immediately in Great Britain, and in the United States it was pirated by several publishers (as British copyright had no authority there) and was sold at street corners in New York. A review of a new edition in the October 1913 *Bookman* (London) commented on its "almost ruthless frankness," adding that Clifford is "passionately on the side of her sex, and small blame to her if she have chosen unfavourable specimens of men."

Clifford traveled to America in the 1890s, where she was distressed to find that much of her work had been republished without authorization. During that decade she wrote four more novels. *Aunt Anne* (1892) returns to a traditional omniscient narrator in a study of illusory love, of a clash between romance and realism, of old versus new worldviews; its originality lies in the character of the aged Aunt Anne, whose self-possession and nobility of spirit enable her to rise above the liabilities of her impecunious and victimized position. A destitute relative who emerges from obscurity to dominate the conventional suburban lives of Walter and Florence Hibbett and their family, Aunt Anne is an infuriating yet endearing blend of unscrupulous narcissism and unimpeachable gentility. The reader sympathizes with her, as do Walter and Florence, as she falls prey to a seedy confidence man, Wimple, who marries her bigamously to claim a legacy he believes she will inherit. When she discovers his duplicity, Aunt Anne tells herself "that there [is] one thing at which she must clutch a little longer—her self-control and dignity." Singlehandedly she manipulates Wimple into the hands of the police. Her romance dashed, she collapses and dies, nobly presiding over her own deathbed scene.

Reception of the novel was mixed. *The Dial* (16 November 1892) saw Aunt Anne as "an old lady of amicable character, who is hopelessly unpractical in the conduct of her life, and whose vagaries suggest a mind that has nearly, if not quite, lost the balance it may once have had." *The Spectator* (6 August 1892), went so far as to compare Clifford with Jane Austen, calling Aunt Anne "an old woman who is not a type but an individual, a curious, delicate, real being, . . . at once the most original and most true creation which we have met with for a long time." The feminist scholar P. K. Isner suggests that Clifford deliberately manipulates the Victorian stereotype of the old maid to depict a character who "resists societal labelling and in her knowledge of her self" is "not an imitation female" but a "real woman."

Clifford termed her next novel, *A Wild Proxy* (1893), a personal favorite. Subtitled *A Tragic Comedy of Today* in the American edition, the novel has a bizarre plot centering on the disquieting events surrounding the marriage of the innocent Helen Lambert to the unexciting but utterly reliable Laurence Halstead. Halstead's friend Frank Merreday, an adventurer, arrives, falls in love with Helen, and contrives to spirit her away after the wedding. Despite her scruples, Helen is affected by Frank's charisma. At the novel's end Frank goes to an early grave, and Laurence and Helen are restored to one another, al-

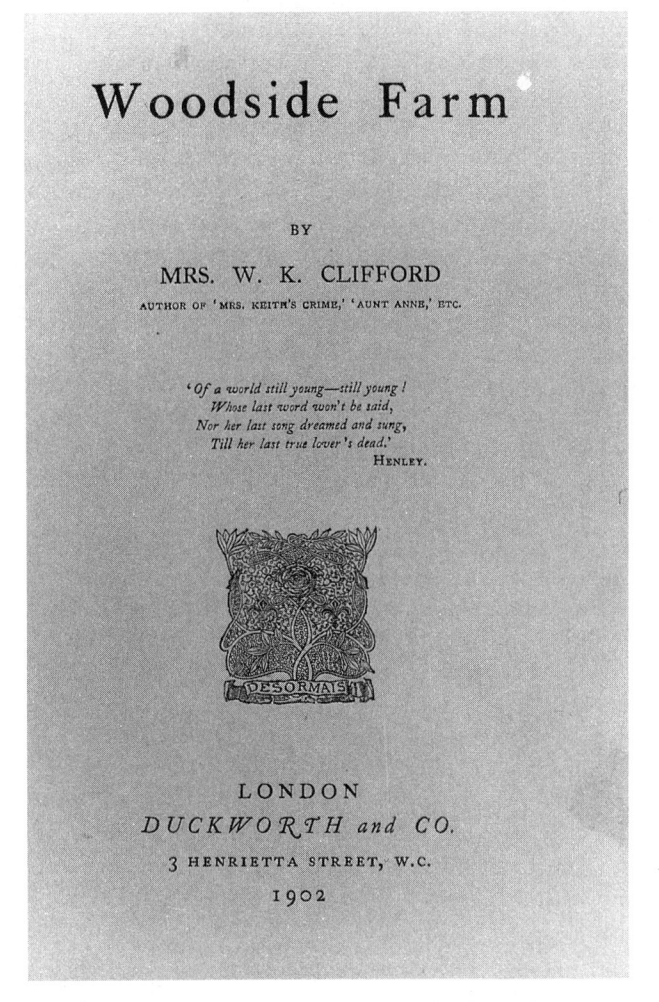

Title page for a didactic novel about a levelheaded young woman and her unconventional parents

though Laurence sadly suspects that Helen is still under Frank's spell.

Despite Clifford's own affection for the novel, reviews were unfavorable. *The Bookman* (18 June 1883), ignoring the comic intent, dismissed the work as immature and "too wild to rouse any feeling but impatience with Merreday, the Rochester-cum-Byron . . . who wishing to act the demon only plays the fool," adding that, "the worst of it is that Mrs. Clifford keeps serious in his presence."

A Grey Romance, a collection of short stories that included the title piece by Clifford and works by H. D. Traill, W. E. Hodgson, and others was published in 1894. That same year *A Flash of Summer,* a novel that had originally been serialized in the *Illustrated London News,* was published in book form. The story begins in the English countryside around Eltham, where Clifford had spent her childhood. Katherine Morris, the ward of a reluctant guardian, is forced into an abusive marriage to the odious Mr. Belcher. She escapes by ship to Genoa, becoming part of the expatriate community on board. In Italy she meets and falls in love with the exemplary Jim Alford, on leave from India, who wishes to marry her. When she confesses her story, the couple pledge their undying love but agree to do the honorable thing and return to their former lives. Soon after her arrival in England she learns that Jim died of a fever before he could return to India. Belcher locks her in the compartment of the railway carriage that is taking them home, but she escapes and drowns herself in the river alongside the tracks. In contrast to Maggie in *Mrs. Keith's Crime,* who found no unity with her loved ones at death, "as the waters met above [Katherine's] head it seemed as though her lover's arms closed round her forever."

In the preface to the 1895 edition Clifford asserted that the novel was unconnected to the "recent controversial discussion [of] marriage problems and questions" on the grounds that the plot had been conceived long before; the realism of the dialogue, however, suggests otherwise. The emotional devastation wrought in Katherine by Jim Alford's death highlights the intensity of a woman's need for emotional support in an abusive marital situation. *The New York Times* (26 April 1896) called the novel "a plea for divorce," noting its melancholy strain, "that minor key which is the predominant tone . . . in everything Mrs. Clifford writes."

Clifford's next novel, *A Woman Alone* (1898), portrays a masterful, intelligent woman in its heroine, Blanche Bowden. The magnetic center of an elite group of intellectuals, she reigns over her salon despite the growing resentment of her unambitious husband, Richard, who finally leaves for the Continent to get away from it all. When they meet in Paris two years later to discuss their differences, she falsely declares that she does not love him. Two years later, lonely and bored, her charisma faded, she learns that Richard has written the political book that is the talk of the town. Hearing that he has returned to London, sick and alone, she admits that she cannot bear life without him and begs for reconciliation. Richard's death prevents their reunion, although a dramatized version of the story (1915) provides it in a touching final scene.

A minor character, Countess Augusta, appears to summarize the novel's theme when she says to Blanche: "no woman [has] a wonderful head who [does] not pay for it sometime with her heart." Reviewing the dramatized version, *The Nation* (7 October 1915) said: "The moral enforced is that in the long run nature is likely to prove more potent than theories or argument."

Clifford was at the peak of her profession, her home continuing to provide an environment where literary talent was nurtured and vital connections made. On 24 January 1900 his domestic problems prompted James to write: "it would be so infinitely nicer to be sitting by your fire and tasting your charity—and your Benedictine!" She turned her hand to playwriting, publishing *The Likeness of the Night* in 1900, and *A Long Duel* in 1901. In the autumn of that year, following her return from six weeks in Vienna, James encouraged her to a fresh literary endeavor. A letter, dated 13 December 1901, exhorts her to reach beyond farcical comedy: "the thing is the Drama of Life!—objective and ironic . . . and brandish your spear!"

Clifford may well have taken James's advice to focus on "the Drama of Life" in her eighth novel, *Woodside Farm* (1902), which first appeared in serial form as *Margaret Vincent,* the title under which it was published in America. Traditional in form, the novel sets out to separate real values from sham; sifting true religion, true nobility, true womanhood and true love from their false, socially constructed counterparts. Margaret Vincent was born and bred in the Surrey countryside with the nonsectarian and courageously honest values of her agnostic yet deeply spiritual father and the down-to-earth simplicity of her traditional mother. Her parents' marriage was unconventional, her father, an aristocrat, preferring the natural gentility of her low-born mother over the tawdry representatives of his own class. The plot follows Margaret through her painful love affair with Tom Carringford, an appealing young man-about-town. Despite the jealous assaults from Hannah, her bigoted stepsister, and a socialite mother with her eye on Tom as a prospective son-in-law, Margaret's levelheaded wisdom and true love win the day and the couple are happily married.

The tone of the novel is noticeably didactic, particularly in the conversations concerning the integrity of agnosticism versus the hypocrisy of belief. (Mrs. Vincent tells Hannah: "It's the leading of a good life, the telling of the truth and the thinking well of others that make religion and will gain heaven—that's my belief.") Its seriousness possibly detracted from the novel's contemporary appeal. Reviewers at the time focused on the romance between Margaret's parents, which crossed social boundaries between aristocrat and countrywoman. In a June 1902 review *The Bookman* (London) said that "the story of the younger people is dull and commonplace and seems to be invented for the purpose of mollifying the outraged conventionalities."

Proposals to Kathleen (1908) was published in response to the tremendous success of *Love-Letters of a Worldly Woman.* Clifford wrote in the preface that the character of Madge from the earlier novel had been so well received in America that "perhaps some welcome may be given to the newcomer. . . . Kathleen of this book must certainly have been elder sister to the Madge of that one."

In part epistolary, the novel has a first-person narrator—a twenty-eight-year-old woman who on the eve of her wedding is reconsidering her feelings for her husband-to-be. She has been accumulating marriage proposals since she was sixteen and is reviewing a bundle of them and philosophizing on her past and present situations. She is going to marry Herbert, she says, because he is clever, fairly well off, well connected, and well placed, and she likes him—but she is not in love with him. Though she considers herself at a perfect age for marriage, she is apprehensive of the impending loss of freedom and wonders "what the reality will do in ten, in twenty years' time." She looks forward to the peace and acceptance of an unemotional worldly marriage, secure in the knowledge that she will be "part and parcel of the world's machinery and helping to carry it on." She is confident that Herbert will challenge her intellectually.

Kathleen intends to substitute realism for romance. This thoroughly modern marriage will divert her romantic needs and affections: her passion to intellect, her excitement to companionship, her desire to selfless service. But the possibility of boredom remains. She plans to "rout up [her] prig should she find her merry side again" and thinks that he shall "make merry also," but the reader may wonder if this is wishful thinking. The death of romance may lead to a wasteland; at the end of the evening the old letters are tossed into the fire. *The New York Times* (9 May 1908) saw the novel as "the clever portrayal of the heart of a woman whose idea is to become entirely worldly, although she has not yet reached that state," and on 13 June 1908 it referred to the novel's "piquant relish not to be found elsewhere."

In *Sir George's Objection* (1910) romance returns, for in this traditional novel love triumphs over genetic theory, nurture over nature, openness over hypocrisy. The novel opens in Cannero, Italy, where the widowed Helen Roberts lives in seclusion with her daughter Kitty protecting them both from a scandalous past. Kitty falls in love with the son of Sir George Kerriston, who demands a flawless pedigree in a prospective daughter-in-law. Tension mounts as Helen's attempts to repress the facts of her husband's ignominious death are foiled. All comes right in the end, and true love not only wins the day, but also reveals the hypocrisy that masquerades as virtue in the social order.

In 1913 Douglas Sladen described Clifford as "an admirable example of the modern woman, breezy, wholesome, warm-hearted, clear-visioned, lucid in expression, interested in all questions of the day, and withal one of our best novelists." That same year Clifford joined in honoring James on his seventieth birthday. At his death three years later James left her a hundred pounds in his will.

The following year *The House in Marylebone* (1917) was published. In a retrospective review in the January 1920 issue of *The Bookman* (London) Wilfrid L. Randell called the novel his second favorite because it focuses on an aspect of London life that was rarely touched on: "A group of independent business girls, not too well off, forms what one of them calls, 'a little republic' in Marylebone 'diggings,' and their joys and loves and sorrows make the book. It is naturally told as though related from one armchair to another in the fire-light." The *Times Literary Supplement* (26 July 1917) dismissed the novel as slight, adding that "there was not room in [the book] for a single finished portrait." *Punch* (8 August 1917) considered the novel dated: "Young women still live in houses in the Marylebone Road . . . but their vocations and their citizenship have both . . . grown out of all knowledge. So that charming writer, Mrs. Clifford, must forgive me if I could find only an historical interest, and no robust one at that, in her amicable retrospect."

Clifford wrote to the novelist Mary Elizabeth Braddon in 1911, urging her against overexposure and predicting that in the future Braddon's literary reputation would "be sifted down, probably, to a dozen or so [novels] and live by those." Clifford's own twelfth novel, *Miss Fingal* (1919), was to be her last. Possibly her best novel, it was her favorite among her works. It tells of the awakening of Aline Fingal, a single woman approaching her prime, who has never moved beyond her apartment-dwelling existence. She inherits a fortune, which triggers the process that leads her to emotional and spiritual fulfilment. Along with a house in town, she gains possession of a country cottage previously owned by a young couple, Linda and Dick Alliston, who have been through a traumatic divorce. On meeting Linda and her children Aline is powerfully and unaccountably drawn to the young mother, only to learn that Linda is dying. Aline is badly injured in a railway accident and hovers between life and death for weeks; on her recovery she hears that Linda has died. From then on, as if possessed by Linda's loving personality, Aline craves the motherless children, who respond positively to her—as does their estranged father, Dick. As World War I is declared she accepts the role of surrogate mother and Dick's profession of love. Though Dick is killed in action, Aline is serene in her new life.

Clifford brings a mystical dimension into this novel, which transcends the contradictions that have arisen in her previous attempts to reconcile the modern, intelligent woman with the social demands of loving relationship. Aline remains single, mature and fulfilled in her self-defined role; defying boredom, she exists to serve others rather than herself, with passionate love for her adopted children and "eyes wide open to the beauty of the world."

The novel was received with some controversy. Several critics agreed with the *Saturday Review* (10 May 1919) that the story was one of Clifford's best, particularly in its powerful handling of the "transmigration of the mother's soul into the body of the childless woman who adored the children." But *The Nation* (2 August 1919) said that "this book is in any deep and serious sense unimportant." Referring to an alleged claim that the book gave "a new clew to a baffling mystery of existence," the reviewer questioned: "Can irresponsible speech go beyond that? What all the philosophers and poets, the sages and scientists have striven for in vain—that, we are to believe, is within the grasp of a novelist of the third rank. The curious thing is that Mrs. Clifford believes it to be within her grasp."

Clifford published *Eve's Lover, and Other Stories,* her final collection of short stories, in 1924. The following year *The Searchlight,* a play that had originally appeared in *The Nineteenth Century* in 1903, was published in book form, as was a Tauchnitz edition of *Sir George's Objection,* for which she wrote a new prologue. She continued to correspond with many literary figures, including Thomas Hardy, Sir James Frazer, and Virginia Woolf, until her death on 21 April 1929. Her obituary in *The Times* (London) on 22 April was more concerned with Clifford's marital and literary connections than with her writing, making only a passing reference to the strength of the fictional characters who "live in the reader's mind long after the details of the story have been forgotten."

Economic considerations may account, in part, for the alternation between traditional and experimental novels that marked Clifford's career; but this rhythm also reveals her open-mindedness. In her search for heroines with the strength and integrity to overcome the obstacles that surrounded them, she remained sympathetic to the needs and vulnerabilities of their womanly natures. Her compromising, flexible intelligence never lost sight of the absolute nature and demands of romantic love, nor the toll its denial or avoidance might take in the lives of her heroines. After her death she was remembered largely for her personal qualities and social connections; her readership diminished, and her works attracted no critical attention. Most of her novels remain unknown, but they warrant further consideration. Their importance lies in the immediacy of Clifford's feminine perspective and in the insights provided by her engagement with a realism that could not deny romance.

References:

Marysa De Moor, "Women Authors and Their Selves: Autobiography in the Work of Charlotte Yonge, Rhoda Broughton, Mary Cholmondeley and Lucy Clifford," *Cahiers Victoriens et Edouardiens: Revue du Centre d'Études et de Recherches Victoriennes et Edouardiennes de l'Université Paul Valery, Montpelier,* 39 (April 1994): 51–63;

Mary Angela Dickens, "A Chat with Mrs. W. K. Clifford," *Windsor,* 40 (March 1920): 483–485;

Leon Edel, "Aunt Lucy," in *Henry James, The Master 1901–1916* (London: Rupert Hart-Davies, 1972), pp. 106–109;

Edel, ed., *Henry James: Selected Letters,* 4 volumes (Cambridge & London: Harvard University Press, 1974–1984);

P. K. Isner, "The Imitation Female: Views of the Grotesque and the Feminine Character in the Works of Lucy Lane Clifford," thesis, University of North Carolina at Chapel Hill, 1992;

Charles Eliot Norton, ed., *Letters of James Russell Lowell,* 3 volumes (Boston & New York: Houghton Mifflin, 1893);

Wilfrid L. Randell, "Mrs. W. K. Clifford," *Bookman* (London), 57 (January 1920): 136–138;

Douglas Sladen, *Twenty Years of My Life* (New York: Dutton, 1913), p. 127.

Papers:

Lucy Lane Clifford's letters are to be found in many locations throughout the United Kingdom, notably in the British Library Department of Manuscripts; University College Library, London; and the Brotherton Library, Leeds.

Victoria Cross
(Annie Sophie Cory)
(1 October 1868 – 2 August 1952)

Shoshana Milgram Knapp
Virginia Polytechnic Institute and State University

See also the Cross entry in *DLB 135: British Short-Fiction Writers, 1880-1914: The Realist Tradition.*

BOOKS: *The Woman Who Didn't* (London: John Lane / Boston: Roberts, 1895); republished as *A Woman Who Did Not* (Boston: Roberts, 1895);

Paula: A Sketch from Life (London: Scott, 1896; New York: Munro, 1898);

A Girl of the Klondike (London: Scott, 1899; New York: Macaulay, n.d.);

Anna Lombard (London: Long, 1901; New York: Kensington, 1902);

Six Chapters of a Man's Life (London: Scott, 1903; New York: Kennerley, 1908);

To-morrow? (London: Scott, 1904; New York: Macaulay, 1904);

The Religion of Evelyn Hastings (London: Scott, 1905; New York: Kennerley, 1908);

Life of My Heart (London: Scott, 1905; New York: Macaulay, 1915);

Six Women (London: Laurie, 1906; New York: Kennerley, 1906);

Life's Shop Window (London: Laurie, 1907; New York: Kennerley, 1907);

Five Nights (London: Long, 1908; New York: Kennerley, 1908);

The Eternal Fires (London: Laurie, 1910; New York: Kennerley, 1910);

The Love of Kusuma: An Eastern Love Story, as Bal Krishna (London: Laurie, 1910);

Self and the Other (London: Laurie, 1911; New York: Hewitt, 1911);

The Life Sentence (London: Long, 1912; New York: Macaulay, 1914);

The Night of Temptation (London: Laurie, 1912; New York: Macaulay, 1914);

The Greater Law (London: Long, 1914); republished as *Hilda against the World* (New York: Macaulay, 1914);

Daughters of Heaven (London: Laurie, 1920; New York: Brentano's, 1920);

Victoria Cross

Over Life's Edge (London: Laurie, 1921; New York: Brentano's, 1921);

The Beating Heart (London: Daniel, 1924; New York: Brentano's, 1924);

Electric Love (London: Laurie, 1929; New York: Macaulay, 1929);

The Unconscious Sinner (London: Laurie, 1930; New York: Macaulay, 1930); republished as *The Innocent Sinner* (London: Pearson, 1931);

A Husband's Holiday (London: Laurie, 1932);

The Girl in the Studio: The Story of Her Strange, New Way of Loving (London: Laurie, 1934); republished as *The Girl in the Studio* (New York: Macaulay, 1934);

Martha Brown, M.P.: A Girl of To-morrow (London: Laurie, 1935);

Jim (London: Laurie, 1937).

OTHER: "Theodora: A Fragment," in *Daughters of Decadence: Women Writers of the Fin de Siècle*, edited by Elaine Showalter (London: Virago, 1993), pp. 6–37.

The forty-year career of the writer known as Victoria Cross comprises twenty-three novels and three collections of short stories. Her notorious books—with their exotic settings, erotic events, and exuberantly imaginative invention—were read and reviewed around the world, from Singapore to Switzerland. She was known, according to Sewell Stokes, as a "veritable Noel Coward of the early Nineties." Oscar Wilde even tried to play literary matchmaker: "If one could only marry Thomas Hardy to Victoria Cross," he remarked, "he might have gained some inkling of real passion with which to animate his little keepsake pictures of starched ladies." She published most of her novels in the early years of the twentieth century, and the titles were familiar enough to be used as points of reference by other writers. In Katherine Mansfield's story "The Tiredness of Rosabel" (1908) a young woman on a bus begins to daydream of romance when she sees another passenger carrying a copy of Cross's *Anna Lombard* (1901). James Joyce mentions *The Woman Who Didn't* (1895), her first novel, in a list of books in the Circe chapter of *Ulysses* (1922). Although her treatment of sexuality was condemned, particularly in the 1890s, as absurd, overwrought, and sordid, she was admired for her extravagant plot premises, her candid evocation of spiritual and physical passion, and the visual color and emotional intensity of her descriptions of natural settings. Her basic story, transposed to a variety of settings, recounts the struggle of true passion, justified by a moral code characterized sometimes as Christian and sometimes as pagan, to overcome internal and external obstacles.

Her productivity and popularity declined in the 1920s and 1930s, and, with the exception of a single short story, she has not been reprinted since that time. Although she continued writing until 1937, she was already seen as old-fashioned by the mid 1920s, when Sewell Stokes interviewed her on the Riviera. Her daring and outrageousness, however, were undiminished. Although her final novels were published only in Britain, *Martha Brown, M.P.* (1935) and *Jim* (1937) are as flamboyant, and as willing to stretch the sublime to the point of the ridiculous, as any of her earlier works.

Biographical information on Cross is sparse, owing to her reclusiveness and the variety of countries in which she lived. Even her given name has been difficult to determine. Almost all of the standard sources give it as Vivian Cory, but according to official records and family members it was Annie Sophie Cory. To complicate matters further, she is listed on some publishing contracts and on the copyright pages of several books as Vivian (or Vivien) Cory Griffin or V. C. Griffin.

Cory was born on 1 October 1868 in Rawalpindi in the Punjab, India (today Pakistan), the youngest of the three daughters of Arthur and Elizabeth Fanny (also known as Fanny Elizabeth) Griffin Cory. Her father was a major in the Bengal Staff Corps; later he would be a colonel in the Army of Karachi, joint editor of the *Civil and Military Gazette* in Lahore, and founder and first editor of the *Sind Gazette* in Karachi. In 1865 he had published an epic poem in what he termed "a modification of the Spenserian stanza," *The Re-Conquest: A Love Story*. Both parents eventually returned to England.

Cory and her sisters were educated primarily in England but spent considerable time traveling in Europe and living in India. The eldest sister, Isabel Edith, helped her father with the *Sind Gazette* and edited it for eight years after his death in 1903. Adela, nicknamed "Violet," wrote exotic love lyrics under the pseudonym Laurence Hope; among them were *The Garden of Kama* (1901), *Stars of the Desert* (1903), and *Indian Love* (1905). Although she produced only a small body of work, her poems achieved acclaim; Cross mentioned with pride her sisterly connection with Laurence Hope and quoted her in *Jim*, her last novel.

Annie Cory is recorded as having passed the London University matriculation examination in the second division in June 1888; in 1890 she passed the intermediate arts examination. Since her name is not among the list of graduates from the university, it appears that she did not receive a degree. Her later claim that she had a "B.A. in Greek, Latin, Math, Foreign Languages, Anglo-Saxon, and English Composition," therefore, seems to be false.

Cross isolated herself from other writers and did not develop a network of intellectual or artistic colleagues. Although she began her career with the publishing firm of John Lane and *The Yellow Book*, she is absent from the reminiscences of such figures as Netta Syrett, Evelyn Sharp, Frederic Whyte, Grant Richards, Maurice Baring, W. Graham Robertson, Ernest Rhys, Vincent O'Sullivan, and Richard Le Gallienne. She was apparently shy and demure in social situations, but in business dealings she was confident, bold, and unyielding. Her nephew Malcolm Nicolson (the son of her sister Adela) described her as a "hard and calculating" businesswoman who would get into fierce arguments with bookshop owners if her books were not properly displayed. Her letters also provide telling glimpses of her penchant for self-promotion. When Eric Pinker tried to purchase the motion picture rights to *Life's Shop Window* (1907) in 1924, she insisted that her own scenario be "used and not deviated from," that "the money payment must be cash down on signing the agreement," and that "wherever and whenever the Film picture is shown or advertised my name is to appear with it as author." She boasted, moreover, that the 1915 movie version of *Five Nights* (1908), which she claimed to have "prepared" and "practically produced," earned a profit of £11,000 in the first six months alone. "So I think I can justly claim to know what the public wants in films as well as books."

Her first attempt to show that she knew what the public wanted was "Theodora: A Fragment," published in the fourth issue of *The Yellow Book* in January 1895. This description of a man's passion for a woman who is androgynous in her attire, speech, and sexual aggressiveness was attacked by Janet Hogarth in Fortnightly Review (1 April 1895) for its "sex mania" and "confused and morbid imaginings," and Blanche Crackanthorpe in *Nineteenth Century* (April 1895) targeted "Theodora" as a mediocre entry in the "charnel-house school" of literature. On the other hand, the reviewer for *Woman* called it a "penetrating study of the beginning of a passion," and according to Ada Leverson's biographer, Julie Speedie, Leverson, who affectionately parodied "Theodora" in *Punch* (2 February 1895) as "'Toolaloora: A Fragment,' by Charing Cross," privately characterized it as "brilliant." The mixed response is appropriate to the pseudonym Cory seems to have selected as a complicated joke, implying that she deserved the Victoria Cross, a medal awarded for military heroism, for her valor in defying mores of the day and that she expected to make Queen Victoria "cross" through her frankness.

The Woman Who Didn't, Cross's first novel, was published by John Lane in the Bodley Head Keynotes series, named for George Egerton's 1893 volume of sexually and psychologically candid stories. The title page and cover design were by Aubrey Beardsley. Cross was thus introduced in the double contexts of the Decadents and the New Woman novelists who were concerned with the rights of

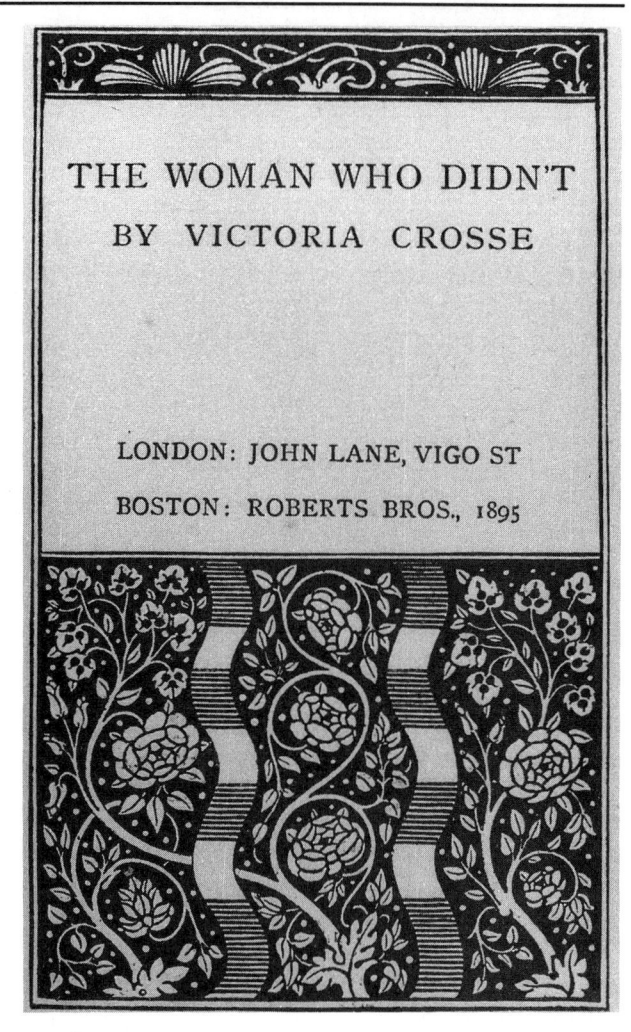

THE WOMAN WHO DIDN'T
BY VICTORIA CROSSE

LONDON: JOHN LANE, VIGO ST
BOSTON: ROBERTS BROS., 1895

Title page for the author's first novel, in which the charmless narrator unsuccessfully attempts to seduce a married woman

women and the wrongs committed by men. Her novel was misleadingly marketed (and perhaps retitled) by John Lane as a rejoinder to Grant Allen's *The Woman Who Did,* which had appeared earlier that year in the same series. Allen's novel, condemned as hideous and repulsive, deals with a woman's decision to live with a lover in free union; Cross's *The Woman Who Didn't* has as its subject not the legitimacy of marriage itself but allegiance to a preexisting commitment.

In *The Woman Who Didn't* Eurydice, a married woman, declines the affections of Evelyn, a distinctly charmless man who has spent time in the East. Although one might expect Evelyn, as the narrator, to emphasize his own good qualities, he does not appear to be a tempting romantic partner for any woman, married or single. He seizes on every hint that she tolerates his presence as if she had declared undying love; his unwarranted self-confidence and prolonged self-deception are ludicrous.

Eurydice explains that she views marriage as a symbol of self-respect, whatever the merits or defects of her husband; she enjoys Evelyn's company but is not tempted to betray what she regards as her own integrity. Physically graceful and musically gifted, Eurydice combines conventionally feminine attractions with fortitude, serenity, and principled endurance—qualities Evelyn describes, with mixed emotions, as "rather of the heroic order." From a woman he perceives as in part unwomanly, he learns to be more of a man.

The reviews of *The Woman Who Didn't* typically ignored Eurydice's distinctive qualities and displaced her from the center of attention. The reviewer for the *Speaker*, while praising the novel for "wonderful vividness and felicity of phrase," "biting irony, restrained passion and a style that is both forcible and polished," commended the "subtle study of feminine nature" without addressing the combination of strength and surrender that motivates Eurydice's conduct. The reviewer in the *Critic* (25 July 1895) dismissed it as "weird," "quaint," and thoroughly inadequate as a response to Grant Allen. *The Saturday Review* (21 September 1895) commented: "The man is almost incredibly coarse and tawdry; and the book is instinct with vulgarity from cover to cover." *Literary World* (5 October 1895) remarked on "the slightly coarse flippancy" of the narrator and expressed some surprise at the ease with which Eurydice resists temptation. In general, despite the novel's title, critical attention focused primarily on Evelyn.

In her next two novels Cross presented heroines who remain unconventional yet less markedly androgynous. The title character of *Paula: A Sketch from Life* (1896) thinks independently and charts a career as a playwright; Katrine in *A Girl of the Klondike* (1899) lives alone and relishes the freedom to drink, gamble, and protect the helpless with her six-shooter. Although the courage and ambition of these heroines make them unusual, this unusualness is not identified as the reason their romantic partners love them, nor are they explicitly described as masculine in physique, speech, or demeanor. Their strength is devoted to rescuing their lovers through self-sacrifice: Paula donates her blood for a transfusion to save her lover's life, and Katrine steps in front of a bullet aimed at her lover. The reviews were mixed. The *Morning Leader* considered *Paula* "so full of glow and charm, so aflame with the enthusiasm of art and love, that there can be little else for the reader when he has finished the volume save a feeling of warm gratitude for a daring and successful plunge into some of the depths of a passionate woman's heart." The *Athenaeum* (17 October 1896), however, judged *Paula* "as unalluring as it is unwholesome," "untidy," "wasteful," "giddy," "ghastly," and "horribly second-rate in speech and tone and manner" and called Paula herself "an exponent of the new selfishness, plus the new self-consciousness." *A Girl of the Klondike*, according to the *Academy and Literature* (11 February 1899), "contains plenty of climate, gold, dust, and gore"; the review proceeds to quote from the climactic moment in which Katrine gives her life for the man she loves. The consensus—fascinated disapproval, disapproving fascination—was expressed by *The Saturday Review*, commenting on Paula: "The book carries one along with it, and fascinates one almost against one's better judgment." With her next novel Cross tested her readers by breaking more taboos than in all of her earlier works put together.

Anna Lombard (1901) became Cross's first major success. Anna, an Indian general's daughter educated in England, secretly marries Gaida Khan, a Pathan servant, although she is also devoted to Gerald Ethridge, an intelligent, enlightened assistant commissioner. Anna thus not only experiences passion for a man of a different race and class but simultaneously loves another man she deems more worthy of her esteem and affection. After Gaida dies of cholera, Anna learns that she is pregnant by him, and Gerald immediately marries her. The baby, a son, reminds Anna of her physical desire for Gaida; she believes that as long as the child lives she will not be able to forget her lover, which will make it impossible for her to love her husband. She smothers the child, spends a year in solitary penance, and then joins Gerald in a true (and presumably lasting) marriage. In a preface to later editions of the novel Cross wrote: "I endeavoured to draw in Gerald Ethridge a character whose actions should be in accordance with the principles laid down by Christ."

Given the interracial romance, the complex multiple infidelities, Anna's incestuous passion for her son, and the infanticide, the preface did not protect the novel from accusations of immorality. William Alden in *The New York Times* (1 June 1901), for example, saw *Anna Lombard* as "brazen" and "nauseating," the sort of book "which no man should read immediately before dinner unless he wishes to lose his appetite." *Academy and Literature* (4 May 1901) noted that Anna seemed to think of herself as a man and found her "hysterically sexual." The reviewer for the *Athenaeum* resented being asked to admire a "horrible" woman whose "ill-regulated sexuality is disgusting." William T. Stead, however, featured *Anna Lombard* as a "Book of the Month" in his *Review of Reviews*, with an extended summary and a critique of what he deemed a "remarkable novel," powerful in its intensity and insightful in its perspective on "the ethics of sex." Other reviewers described Anna as "a striking character in the portrait galleries of fiction" (*Daily News*) and "a pure woman—good, sincere, clean, fit to be admired and beloved" (*Vanity Fair*). *Anna Lombard* ultimately sold more than six million copies and went through more than forty editions; its shocking elements did not preclude its popularity.

In 1902 Cross's mother's younger brother, Heneage Mackenzie Griffin, who had become wealthy through silver mining and real estate in Colorado, left the United States. He would live with or near Cross for most of the rest of his life and would name her as the chief heir to his large fortune.

Encouraged by the success of *Anna Lombard,* Cross returned to "Theodora." In *Six Chapters of a Man's Life* (1903) she frames the former fragment, providing a prehistory for the story, which had begun in medias res, and going beyond the lovers' union. She also assigns a clear moral/religious message. She intended the novel, she says in the preface, as a "lasting protest against all egoism, all love of love for the sake of pleasure to the lover."

The novel explores further the issue of sexual identity and develops hints implied in the fragment. Theodora, a free-thinking heiress, explains her philosophy—a pagan adherence to pleasure and beauty and an indifference to creeds and systems that she sees as arbitrary—to Cecil Ray, an Egyptologist, who is in basic agreement with her. In the fragment Cecil had considered Theodora's Eastern outfit "not at all complete without the trousers" and had expressed a wish for a "chum," a "companion," a "fellow" to go with him to Egypt. In the novel Theodora adopts full male dress, burns her hair, and, passing as a man, joins Cecil on his journey. He finds their relationship more stimulating and satisfying than any romance he has had or any marriage he has imagined, yet he is jealous of Theodora's interactions with both men and women. The final crisis, which contrasts Cecil's indecision and inconsistency with Theodora's resolution and power, is ignited by an erotic dance by a white-skinned seventeen-year-old Levantine boy. Aroused, Cecil kisses Theodora, which brings her to the attention of their Egyptian host. He and a group of armed men bar the door and tell Cecil and Theodora that if Theodora submits to their desires for a week, the two will be allowed to live. Theodora sacrifices conventional "virtue" to save their lives, but when she returns a week later, her face covered with sores, Cecil is "stricken with loathing." The novel ends with her suicide. Cross implies that Cecil was unable to expe-

Dust jacket for the author's final novel, published in 1937

rience, much less to communicate, an appropriate response to a woman who wanted to be his equal in a relationship unfettered by the conventional emphases on a woman's beauty and honor.

Although the novel provoked protest, reviewers commended the writer's "vivid imagination" (*Liverpool Mercury*), intense drama (*Daily News*), "uncommon literary ability" (*Aberdeen Free Press*), and cleverness (*Scotsman, Birmingham Post*). In his *Review of Reviews* Stead called Cross "a woman of genius" and the novel "a difficult book to forget." He interpreted it, however, as "a vision of lost souls mutually tempting and tempted, with no redeeming gleam from a higher and purer world" and "a study of lost souls making their damnation sure." Although *Six Chapters of a Man's Life* did not achieve the sales of *Anna Lombard,* it was evidently less disturbing to the reading public than "Theodora" had been in 1895.

Cross published three books in the next two years. In *To-morrow?* (1904), a gloomy cautionary tale about the dangerous combination of procrastination and professionalism, a writer and a painter postpone their marriage when they encounter personal and professional obstacles. Instead of celebrating their mutual love, Cross illustrates the possible consequences of self-denial. The ambition of the writer, who is suggestively named Victor, is a "fierce, instinctive impulse," a "driving necessity," and ultimately has fatal consequences; by the time he is ready to marry Lucia, she is dead. Alden in *The New York Times* (23 July 1904) saw the novel as a "tragic story of unrecognized genius"; the *Review of Reviews* noted that it was as "bold and vigorous as its predecessors." "For intensity and energy," said the reviewer for the *Pall Mall Gazette* (23 July 1904), "*To-morrow?* certainly stands high among the fiction of the year."

The Religion of Evelyn Hastings (1905), in which the heroine communes telepathically with her husband, who lies wounded on the African veldt, inspired the *Review of Reviews* to label Cross "a quick change artist." This novel, the review continued, "a romance which is based upon a miracle," is "absolutely unlike any of the others which have made her famous, yet it is in its way quite as remarkable and as original as any excepting her *chef d'oeuvre,* 'Anna Lombard.'" The *Athenaeum* (25 February 1905), while criticizing Cross for residual "repulsive realism" and "a certain grossness," expressed an amused tolerance for her nondoctrinal theories of religion. *Life of My Heart,* also published in 1905, recalls the initial premise of *Anna Lombard:* Frances, the daughter of an Indian general, is passionately in love with Hamakhan, a young Pathan. Hamakhan demands her submission to him; yet he is kinder and more sympathetic than Gaida in *Anna Lombard.* Although the resolution is tragic, Cross presents an interracial romance as difficult but not doomed.

In 1905 Cross began to negotiate with the publisher T. Werner Laurie, who would bring out the English editions of most of the rest of her books. Their first project was *Six Women* (1906), a collection of previously unpublished short stories dealing with romantic longing (generally frustrated and predominately interracial). In all of their contracts Laurie promised to make "no alteration of any nature whatsoever in the text of the author's work, nor shall anything be added to nor omitted from it." *Six Women* also marked Cross's first dealing with Mitchell Kennerley as her American publisher. He would publish a dozen of her volumes, including reprints of earlier works such as *The Woman Who Didn't* and *Anna Lombard.*

Within the next few years Cross wrote two novels that rivaled *Anna Lombard* in popularity and gave full rein to the evocation of sexual passion, permitting characters to violate legal restrictions and social conventions without guilt. In *Life's Shop Window,* published in 1907, Lydia marries Bernard, a kind, honorable Arizona rancher; leaves him for Pelham, a cultured Englishman of independent means; considers leaving Pelham for Ivan, a half-Russian, half-English explorer-writer she meets in Turkey; and ultimately returns to Pelham. One cannot, after all, continue to exchange one's purchases from life's shop window.

Reviewers continued to attack her sexual candor while acknowledging her power. The *Times Literary Supplement* (18 January 1907) said: "Victoria Cross has considerable gifts as a novelist—both descriptive and emotional; but she suffers from this fatal limitation, that for her life means love-making. . . ." The *Review of Reviews,* however, praised it as "very powerful" and reported that the "whole round world becomes but the setting of the more perfect marvel, a human soul in a woman's body." *The New York Times* (9 February 1907) commented: "Another book by the author whose identity, for good reason, has been successfully concealed under the pseudonym 'Victoria Cross' carries to lengths which will amaze readers whom it does not disgust that author's habitual audacity in imitating the 'frankness' of [Emile] Zola. . . . Queen Victoria would not have liked 'Victoria Cross' but it well may be that the royal critic would have called her a 'powerful,' though very naughty, writer." The *Cleveland Town Topics* asserted that "Victoria Cross writes the most beautiful English in print." The *Japan Gazette* predicted: "Nothing will ever dim her fame or stop the sale of her books." "She writes," said the *Singapore Free Press,* "as our descendants in the next century will write when our civilisation will have advanced to the point she has already reached."

Cross herself thought that this novel, read as a whole, would refute accusations of immorality. She tried to use it to prove that she was, as she claimed, a high-minded writer. "I am sending you an autographed copy of *Life's Shop Window,*" she wrote on 20 July 1909 to a Mr. Harris, "and I should be so glad if you will read it through carefully from beginning to end and form your own opinion on it. People who are jealous of me always hurl at my writings the reproach that they are immoral. From my point of view I have never written a single immoral line in my life. I am immensely proud of my books and would read them aloud to a jury of Bishops with the greatest pleasure any time."

In *Five Nights,* published in 1908, Cross situates Trevor, a painter, in a romantic dilemma similar to that of Anna Lombard: he feels a "frenzy of hungered, starving love" for Suzee, a young Eskimo woman, yet he shares an "exquisite mental companionship" with his cousin Viola, a professional singer. Cross contrasts independent Viola (who sends Trevor away without explanation when she discovers she is pregnant) with clinging Suzee (who tries to become pregnant in order to keep Trevor). The response to this novel, following closely on *Life's Shop Window*, was the usual mixture of enthusiasm, fascination, and remonstrance.

Lee Morrison wrote a stage version of *Five Nights* that was performed in the British provinces but not in London. The 1915 film version of the novel produced considerable controversy and led to a demand for stronger centralized censorship of films. Although the British Board of Film Censors passed the film, and it was freely shown in Liverpool, Cardiff, and Bristol, it was considered indecent by authorities in such cities as London, Preston, Bath, Walsall, and Brighton.

In 1910 Cross published two novels that were simpler in structure but more extravagant in plot premises than *Life's Shop Window* and *Five Nights*. The heroine of *The Eternal Fires*, an orphaned schoolgirl engaged to the headmaster's son, dreams that she is the bride of Apollo and that she will become immortal if she bears the god's child and settles it securely in life; she awakens pregnant, and—after writing a volume of poems, giving birth to her son, working as an artist's model, and marrying a millionaire—she apparently succeeds when a fire breaks out on her yacht and her soul ascends to the gods. *Reedy's Mirror* (26 May 1910) found the plot "mystical, melodramatic, and absurd in treatment," tainted by salacity, and, on the whole, "putrescently prurient." This was the last of her novels to be published by Kennerley.

The Love of Kusuma is a purported translation from "Hindustani" by "Bal Krishna," with an introduction by Cross, but it is a typical Cross novel of romantic adventure and longing. The romance of Kusuma and Mohan triumphs over the obstacle of Kusuma's arranged marriage with a wealthy and unscrupulous suitor. In her introduction Cross discusses the uncompromising directness of the Eastern idea of love and the work's vivid descriptions of the Indian setting. Bal Krishna's "genius," she says, "will carry the writer forward and place him triumphantly in the front rank of our novelists."

In *Self and the Other* (1911) the romance of an Indian nurse and a British civil servant ends in tragedy, but Cross outlines the possibility of a relationship based on "a kindred Mind," a Platonic "admiration for the mind and soul of another," and unreserved devotion. The *Times Literary Supplement* (12 January 1911) noted approvingly that "love, which with this writer is generally a kind of delirium, assumes a more genuine form."

After portraying the union of matched spirits, Cross turned to mismatches. The title of *The Life Sentence* (1912) refers to several difficult—and preposterous—marriages. Flora, at sixteen, is married to Bruce, a man forty years her senior, with a heart condition; they live together amicably and chastely for many years. She then meets Rhys, who is separated from his wife, who refuses to divorce him. Bruce dies on the night Flora runs off with Rhys, and Flora faces another kind of life sentence: a guilty conscience. Also published in 1912, *The Night of Temptation* (which Cross had originally titled "The Enchanted Garden") is, in part, yet another version of *Anna Lombard,* a copy of which the heroine brings along with her to the Egyptian desert for moral guidance. Regina, an independent young painter, is dismayed to see her lover Everest, a traveler and free-thinker, attracted by his superficial cousin Sibyl. Even though she is pregnant, Regina risks her life to rescue Sibyl from a lioness instead of yielding to the temptation of letting the animal devour her rival. Cross contrasts Regina's moral and physical courage with Sibyl's manipulative seduction. The *Times Literary Supplement* considered it a "love story quite as foolish as it is unwholesome."

In *The Greater Law* (1914), retitled *Hilda against the World* for the American edition the same year, Cross invents the disease of "amentia"—a lack of "moral sense," ignorance of sexuality, and extreme suggestibility—to provide the plot premise for one of her most bizarre novels. Hilda, a well-educated and idealistic young woman, loves Roland, an older man who informs her—after they have gone off together to Florence—that he is yoked to a mad wife. When Hilda becomes pregnant, she is married off to Clive, a victim of amentia. Hilda eventually cures and comes to love Clive, and she rejects Roland as a coward and a bully.

The reviewer for *The Saturday Review* (17 October 1914) not only condemned the novel's immorality and ridiculed its story line but also attacked Cross as an exemplar of the bad times in the arts: "To deal with this book upon its merits as a novel of the day would be out of reason. It is not literature. It is not even reputable journalism. But it is an immensely popular commodity; and its appearance in thousands upon the market is not to be overlooked.... It is the easy, fluid perfunctoriness of the whole thing, its vulgarity of idea, its utter lack of style, dignity, reality, and sense of real value, that makes a book like this a power for mischief."

After 1914 Cross's pace slowed. Her sister Isabel had died in 1912, and her mother died in 1916. She returned to publication in 1920 with *Daughters of Heaven,* a volume of short stories dedicated to her mother. The following year she published *Over Life's Edge* (1921), a novel about a successful writer suggestively named "Violet Cresswell" who retreats to a desert island in grief over her mother's death. The heroine experiences good luck—the man she left behind shows up, and his wife is conveniently dead—as well as bad: on discovering that the man she has rescued from a shipwreck is a cheerfully unrepentant medical researcher who has experimented on animals, she has her companion kill him. *The New York Times* (4 June 1922) praised the "finely wrought descriptions of the sea in various moods" and judged the book "a rather colorful, dramatic, and occasionally surprising narrative by a past mistress in the art of light fiction."

Cross's next work to appear was another collection of short fiction, *The Beating Heart* (1924), in which several stories deal with a subtheme of *Over Life's Edge,* her concern for animal welfare and support of the antivivisection movement. She was less prolific and less popular although she offered to do all she could to promote her books. Laurie frequently requested extensions of his leases on her books, having on hand thousands of unsold copies. Four years went by before the appearance of *Electric Love* (1929), a novel set in the Hungarian military, with more romantic complications than usual: Lena, the brave, unconventional daughter of a general, is loved by Bela, a kind lieutenant; she prefers Rinyi, a dashing captain (complete with mad wife). Rinyi kills the husband of one of his previous lovers and is infected with syphilis by a female fellow prisoner. Lena's sexual experiences include prostituting herself to obtain a singing contract and marrying Bela to save Rinyi from execution. Apparently trying to shock a jaded audience, Cross juxtaposes her heroine's actions with what is described as a "fierce natural chastity." Further aiming for shock, she went so far as to suggest a "cruel bloodthirsty picture" for the cover to increase sales.

The spine of Cross's next novel, *The Unconscious Sinner* (1930), promised a "drama of sex vitality with a most unusual and amazing situation." This claim was not an exaggeration. Rosa, engaged to a charming millionaire explorer, spurns the advances of a married, middle-aged man but conceives a child by him unconsciously when she sleepwalks to his room. Later she stabs the married man—as before, while sleepwalking—and delivers a stillborn child; she is eventually cleared and is able to marry her millionaire. The outrageous premise was somewhat successful as a bid for attention from a vanishing audience; there was some interest in the novel but also some nervousness about the description of unconscious sexual activity. When Laurie negotiated with C. Arthur Pearson for cheap reprints of this and other titles, she agreed to change the title to *The Innocent Sinner* (1931).

Cross's last four novels appeared under Laurie's imprint in the 1930s, but her popularity had clearly crested; three of the novels were published only in England. The sedate heroine of *A Husband's Holiday* (1932) disguises herself as a sultry adventuress to attract her own husband. *The Girl in the Studio: The Story of Her Strange, New Way of Loving* (1934) portrays its heroine as living independently as an artist, arousing the affections of assorted possessive men, and deflecting their attentions until one proves himself worthy of her exclusive love by not demanding it.

Cross's last two works of fiction return to the themes of her earlier work. The androgynous woman, the treasured unique figure of her early fiction, becomes the rule. Her heroines do not merely adopt a man's costume (as did Theodora) or experience a man's sexual dilemma (as did Anna Lombard) but live as men-women in a world that matches them. *Martha Brown, M.P.: A Girl of To-morrow* (1935), a utopian fantasy set in a thirtieth-century England in which women are the dominant sex, further develops the notion that masculinity is attractive in a woman; the heroine, who is responsible for major reforms in politics, education, and the arts, flies her own plane from lover to lover. Yet the picture is not entirely benign. Women have assumed male garb, mannerisms, and privileges—they dress in pants, smoke pipes, tower over their clinging spouses, and run the world—without any noticeable improvement in the ability of men and women to understand each other or to get along. The dichotomies remain: Martha Brown is the mother of two pretty boys and two sturdy girls. Of the men depicted, many are servants, and Martha's husband, who is bored in the suburbs with his four children, wants a career of his own.

Although Martha has helped to establish schools in which children are trained in truthfulness, kindness, and sympathy, she is chillingly oblivious to the well-being of those close to her. She refers to an inconvenient lover as an "insect." She is unable to do more than smile smugly at the admiration and affection lavished on her by lovers, friends, and colleagues. She is indifferent to her children: "She did not care for her children and she always felt constrained and awkward with them." The ending is troubling in its ambivalence. Shortly before agreeing to serve as prime minister, Martha meets an American, Bruce Campbell Campbell (tall, strong, vigorous, and unperfumed), and goes with him when he returns to the United States, where men have remained dominant. She joins him over the dead body of the husband who could not bear to lose her. Martha appears to flee her own strength, and she perceives her departure as a kind of death.

In *Jim,* published in 1937, a writer tries to forget his grief over his abandonment by his lover by pursuing the "Unknown," a mysterious woman whose lovely face he glimpses in a distant mountain cabin; when he climbs to reach her, he discovers that she is a Harpy. He spends his last moments gazing at her beautiful face as she eats his heart. The novel seems to express pessimism about relations between men and women and about literature as well. Jim is the victim not only of the Harpy but also of literary taste: one of his stories was rejected for being too good.

Cross's uncle and companion, Griffin, died in 1939. During the 1940s Cross became friendly with Leonard Bradford, American consul in Marseilles, and transferred more than £100,000 of her money to him. Perhaps he hinted at or offered romance; it was rumored in the family that "V. C." was planning to marry an American.

Cross died on 2 August 1952 at the Clinica Capitanio in Milan, leaving her entire remaining fortune—more than £100,000, in addition to farm property in Northamptonshire and Shropshire—to Paolo Tosi, a Milan diamond dealer "in consideration of the debt of gratitude I owe him." She was buried, following her instructions next to Griffin at L'Anzo d'Intelvi. The administrator of her estate sued Bradford, alleging that the diplomat had taken advantage of Cross's emotional vulnerability and her dislike of Britain and British taxes by promising to save her assets from confiscation by the socialist British government if she would turn them over to him. Bradford claimed that the money was a gift, in gratitude to him for raising her spirits when her grief over Griffin's death nearly drove her to commit suicide (as both of her sisters had done).

Cross apparently saw her work as worthy of the highest comparisons: a bookshelf in *Hilda against the World* includes, side by side, the works of John Milton and Victoria Cross. Although she is unlikely to achieve the status to which she aspired, her plots remain intriguing, her style unabashedly colorful, her treatment of gender and sexuality tantalizingly radical in its implications.

References:

Ann L. Ardis, *New Women, New Novels: Feminism and Early Modernism* (New Brunswick, N.J.: Rutgers University Press, 1990), pp. 52, 68, 85, 103, 142, 189-190;

Nicola Beauman, *A Very Great Profession: The Woman's Novel, 1914-1939* (London: Virago, 1983), pp. 187-188, 191, 194;

Lesley Blanch, "Laurence Hope–A Shadow in the Sunlight," in her *Under a Lilac-Bleeding Star* (London: John Murray, 1963), pp. 184-208;

Wendell V. Harris, *British Short Fiction in the Nineteenth Century: A Literary and Bibliographic Guide* (Detroit: Wayne State University Press, 1979), pp. 114, 127;

Janet E. Hogarth, "Literary Degenerates," *Fortnightly Review,* new series 57 (1895): 586-592;

Shoshana Milgram Knapp, "Real Passion and the Reverence for Life: Sexuality and Antivivisection in the Fiction of Victoria Cross," in *Rediscovering Forgotten Radicals: British Women Writers, 1889-1939,* edited by Angela Ingram and Daphne Patai (Chapel Hill: University of North Carolina Press, 1993), pp. 156-171;

Knapp, "Revolutionary Androgyny in the Fiction of Victoria Cross," in *Seeing Double: Revisioning Edwardian and Modernist Literature,* edited by Carola M. Kaplan and Anne B. Simpson (New York: St. Martin's Press, 1996), pp. 3-19;

Knapp, "Stead among the Feminists: From Victoria Cross Onwards," *News-Stead,* 2 (1993): 15-25;

Edward S. Lauterbach and W. Eugene David, *The Transitional Age: British Literature 1880-1920* (Troy, N.Y.: Whitston, 1973), p. 81;

J. Lewis May, *John Lane and the Nineties* (London: Bodley Head, 1936);

Katherine Lyon Mix, *A Study in Yellow: The Yellow Book and Its Contributors* (Lawrence: University of Kansas Press, 1960), pp. 253-254;

Carolyn Christensen Nelson, *British Women Writers of the 1890's* (New York: Twayne, 1996), pp. 2, 81, 92-94;

Daphne Patai, "When Women Rule: Defamiliarization and Sex-Role Reversal," *Extrapolation,* 23 (Spring 1982): 56-69;

Julie Speedie, *Wonderful Sphinx: The Biography of Ada Leverson* (London: Virago, 1993), p. 73;

Sewell Stokes, "How I Won My Victoria Cross," in his *Pilloried!* (London: Richards, 1928), pp. 71-83.

Papers:

Many of Victoria Cross's publishing contracts and letters to publishers are in the library of the University of Reading. Her correspondence with the Society of Authors is at the British Library. A few additional letters are in the Berg Collection of the New York Public Library, the Harry Ransom Humanities Research Center at the University of Texas at Austin, and Virginia Polytechnic Institute and State University.

Clemence Dane
(Winifred Ashton)
(21 February 1888 - 23 March 1965)

Leonard R. N. Ashley
Brooklyn College of The City University of New York

See also the Dane entry in *DLB 10: Modern British Dramatists, 1900-1945.*

BOOKS: *Regiment of Women* (London: Heinemann, 1917; New York: Macmillan, 1917);

First the Blade: A Comedy of Growth (New York: Macmillan, 1918; London: Heinemann, 1918);

Legend (London: Heinemann, 1919; New York: Macmillan, 1920);

A Bill of Divorcement: A Play in Three Acts (London: Heinemann, 1921; New York: Macmillan, 1921);

Will Shakespeare: An Invention in Four Acts (London: Heinemann, 1921; New York: Macmillan, 1922);

Shivering Shocks; or, The Hiding Place: A Play for Boys (London & New York: S. French, 1923);

The Way Things Happen: A Story in Three Acts (London: Heinemann, 1923; New York: Macmillan, 1924);

Granite: A Tragedy (London: Heinemann, 1926; New York: Macmillan, 1926);

Wandering Stars, Together with The Lover (London: Heinemann, 1924; New York: Macmillan, 1924);

Naboth's Vineyard: A Stage Piece (London: Heinemann, 1925; New York: Macmillan, 1925);

The Women's Side (London: Jenkins, 1926; New York: Doran, 1927);

A Traveller Returns: A Play in One Act (London & New York: French, 1927);

The Babyons: A Family Chronicle (London: Heinemann, 1927); republished as *The Babyons, Chronicle of a Family,* 4 volumes (Garden City, N.Y.: Doubleday, Doran, 1928)—comprises *Third Person Singular, Midsummer Men, Creeping Jenny,* and *Lady Babylon;* republished in one volume (Garden City, N.Y.: Doubleday, Doran, 1928);

Photograph by E. O. Hoppé

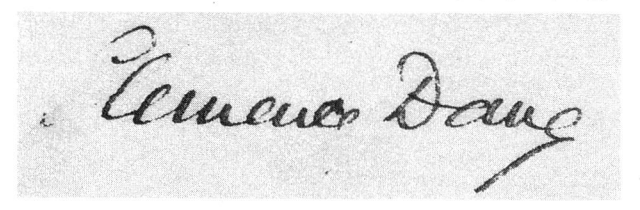

The Dearly Beloved of Benjamin Cobb (London: Benn, 1927);

Mariners (London: Heinemann, 1927; New York: Macmillan, 1927);

Mr. Fox: A Play for Boys (London & New York: French, 1927);

Adam's Opera: The Text of a Play, libretto by Dane, music by Richard Addinsell (London: Heinemann, 1928; Garden City, N.Y.: Doubleday, Doran, 1929);

Enter Sir John, by Dane and Helen Simpson (New York: Cosmopolitan, 1928; London: Hodder & Stoughton, 1929);

The King Waits: A Tale (Garden City, N.Y.: Doubleday, Doran, 1928; London: Heinemann, 1929);

Tradition and Hugh Walpole (London: Heinemann, 1929; Garden City, N.Y.: Doubleday, Doran, 1929);

Printer's Devil, by Dane and Simpson (London: Hodder & Stoughton, 1930); republished as *Author Unknown* (New York: Cosmopolitan, 1930);

Broome Stages (London: Heinemann, 1931; Garden City, N.Y.: Doubleday, Doran, 1931);

Recapture: A Clemence Dane Omnibus (London: Heinemann, 1932)—comprises *The Writer's Partner, Regiment of Women, The Lover, A Bill of Divorcement, Legend, Will Shakespeare, The Dearly Beloved of Benjamin Cobb, Adam's Opera, Creeping Jenny, Granite,* and *The King Waits;*

Re-Enter Sir John, by Dane and Simpson (London: Hodder & Stoughton, 1932; New York: Farrar & Rinehart, 1932);

Wild Decembers: A Play in Three Acts (London: Heinemann, 1932; Garden City, N.Y.: Doubleday, Doran, 1932);

Come of Age: The Text of a Play in Music and Words, music by Addinsell (Garden City, N.Y.: Doubleday, Doran, 1934; London: Heinemann, 1938);

Moonlight Is Silver: A Play in Three Acts (London: Heinemann, 1934);

Claude Houghton: Appreciation, by Dane and Hugh Walpole (London: Heinemann, 1935);

Fate Cries Out: Nine Tales (London: Heinemann, 1935; Garden City, N.Y.: Doubleday, Doran, 1935);

"The Amateur Gentleman": Synopsis of the Film by Clemence Dane from the Novel by Jeffrey Farnol (London: Criterion Film Productions, 1936);

The Moon Is Feminine (London: Heinemann, 1938; Garden City, N.Y.: Doubleday, Doran, 1938);

The Arrogant History of White Ben (Garden City, N.Y.: Doubleday, Doran, 1939; London & Toronto: Heinemann, 1939);

Cousin Muriel: A Play (London & Toronto: Heinemann, 1940);

England's Darling: A Play in One Act, music by Addinsell (London: Heinemann, 1940);

Trafalgar Day, 1940 (London: Heinemann, 1940; Garden City, N.Y.: Doubleday, Doran, 1941);

Christmas in War-Time (Garden City, N.Y.: Doubleday, Doran, 1941);

The Golden Reign of Queen Elizabeth (London: Heinemann, 1941);

The Saviours: Seven Plays on One Theme, music by Addinsell (London: Heinemann, 1942; Garden City, N.Y.: Doubleday, Doran, 1942)—comprises *Merlin, The Hope of Britain, England's Darling, The May King, The Light of Britain, Remember Nelson,* and *The Unknown Soldier;*

The Lion and the Unicorn: A Play in Three Acts (London & Toronto: Heinemann, 1943);

He Brings Great News: A Story (London & Toronto: Heinemann, 1944; New York: Random House, 1945);

Call Home the Heart: A Play (London: Heinemann, 1947);

The Flower Girls (London: M. Joseph, 1954; New York: Norton, 1955);

Eighty in the Shade: A Play in Three Acts (London: Heinemann, 1959);

Approaches to Drama (London: Oxford University Press, 1961);

Collected Plays, volume 1 (London: Heinemann, 1961)—comprises *Scandal at Coventry, Granite, A Bill of Divorcement, Wild Decembers,* and *Till Time Shall End;*

The Godson: A Fantasy (London: M. Joseph, 1964; New York: Norton, 1964);

London Has a Garden (London: M. Joseph, 1964; New York: Norton, 1964);

The Scoop and Behind the Screen, by Dane, Agatha Christie, Dorothy L. Sayers, Walpole, E. C. Bentley, and Anthony Berkeley (London: Gollancz, 1983; New York: Harper & Row, 1983).

Edition: *Regiment of Women,* introduction by Alison Hennegan (London: Virago, 1995).

PLAY PRODUCTIONS: *A Bill of Divorcement,* London, St. Martin's Theatre, 14 March 1921;

The Terror, Liverpool, Liverpool Playhouse, 10 September 1921;

Will Shakespeare: An Invention in Four Acts, London, Shaftesbury Theatre, 17 November 1921;

The Way Things Happen, adapted by Dane from her novel *Legend,* New York, Lyceum Theatre, 28 January 1923;

Granite, London, Ambassadors' Theatre, 15 June 1926;

Mariners, New York, Plymouth Theatre, 28 March 1927;

Adam's Opera, London, Old Vic Theatre, 3 December 1928;

Gooseberry Fool, London, Players' Theatre, 1 November 1929;

Wild Decembers, London, Apollo Theatre, 26 May 1932;

Moonlight Is Silver, London, Queen's Theatre, 19 September 1934;

Come of Age, music by Addinsell, New York, Maxine Elliott's Theatre, 1 December 1934;

The Happy Hypocrite, adapted by Dane from the story by Sir Max Beerbohm, London, His Majesty's Theatre, 8 April 1936;

L'Aiglon, adapted by Dane from the play by Edmond Rostand, music by Addinsell, London, 1938;

Cousin Muriel, London, Globe Theatre, 7 March 1940;

The Golden Reign of Queen Elizabeth, London, 1941;

Cathedral Steps, London, St. Paul's Cathedral, 29 September 1942;

Alice's Adventures in Wonderland and Through the Looking-Glass, adapted by Dane from the works of Lewis Carroll, music by Addinsell, London, 1943;

Call Home the Heart, London, St. James's Theatre, 10 April 1947;

Eighty in the Shade, London, Globe Theatre, 8 January 1959.

TELEVISION SCRIPT: *Till Time Shall End,* BBC-TV, 1958.

RADIO SCRIPTS: *The Scoop,* serial, by Dane and others, BBC, 1931;

The Saviours, play series, BBC, 1940–1941;

Henry VIII, adapted by Dane from the play by William Shakespeare, BBC, 1954;

Don Carlos, adapted by Dane from the play by J. C. F. von Schiller, BBC, 1955;

Scandal at Coventry, broadcast, BBC, 1958.

MOTION PICTURES: *The Tunnel* (also released as *Transatlantic Tunnel*), additional dialogue by Dane, screenplay by Kurt Siodmak and L. DuGarde Peach, Gaumont-British Picture Corporation, 1935;

Anna Karenina (also released as *Love*), scenario by Dane, screenplay by Dane and Salka Viertel, M-G-M, 1935;

The Amateur Gentleman, screenplay by Dane and Edward Knoblock, United Artists, 1936;

Farewell Again (also released as *Troopship*), screenplay by Dane, Ian Hay, Patrick Kirwin, and Wolfgang Wilhelm, London Films, 1937;

Fire Over England, screenplay by Dane and Sergei Nolbandov, London Films, 1937;

St. Martin's Lane (also released as *Sidewalks of London*), screenplay by Dane, Bartlett Cormack, Charles Laughton, Erich Pommer, and Tim Whelan, May Flower Films, 1938;

Salute John Citizen, screenplay by Dane and Elizabeth Baron, 1942;

Perfect Strangers (released in the United States as *Vacation from Marriage*), screenplay by Dane and Anthony Pellisier, M-G-M, 1945;

Bonnie Prince Charlie, screenplay by Dane, London Films, 1948;

Bride of Vengeance, screenplay by Dane, Cyril Hume, and Michael Hogan, Paramount, 1949;

The Angel with the Trumpet, screenplay by Dane, Karl Hartl, and Frank Tassie, London Films, 1950.

OTHER: *100 Enchanted Tales,* compiled, with a foreword, by Dane (London: M. Joseph, 1937);

Friedrich Hebbel, *Herod and Mariamne,* adaptation by Dane (Garden City, N.Y.: Doubleday, Doran, 1938);

Edmond Rostand, *L'Aiglon,* adapted by Dane, music by Richard Addinsell (London: Heinemann, 1938);

The Shelter Book: A Gathering of Tales, Poems, Essays, Notes, and Notions . . . for Use in Shelters, Tubes, Basements and Cellars in War-time, edited by Dane (London & New York: Longmans, Green, 1940);

The Nelson Touch: An Anthology of Lord Nelson's Letters, compiled by Dane (London & Toronto: Heinemann, 1942);

Lewis Carroll, *Alice's Adventures in Wonderland and Through the Looking-Glass,* dramatic adaptation by Dane, music by Addinsell (London: French, 1948).

The career of Winifred Ashton, who published under the pseudonym Clemence Dane—taken from the church of St. Clements Dane, in The Strand—extended over nearly half a century. She long entertained the public with a variety of fiction, plays, screenplays, and other writing but never seemed to outshine popular women novelists such as Daphne du Maurier and Dorothy Sayers. Critics were always hoping that she would create something as sensational as her first novel but more profound, that she would, as the drama historian Allardyce Nicoll put it, transcend the "appeal to broadly popular audiences" and "gradually develop a taste for caviare." *Regiment of Women* got her off to a fast start in fiction. Plays such as *A Bill of Divorcement* (1921) and *Granite* (1926) had good runs. Her short stories and nonfiction writing were respectfully received. Moreover, she took to the new media and reached millions with her radio and television scripts and motion-picture screenwriting: she and Anthony Pellisier shared an Oscar for their screenplay for *Vacation from Marriage* (1945).

Ashton was born on 21 February 1888 in Greenwich to Arthur Charles Ashton, a commission

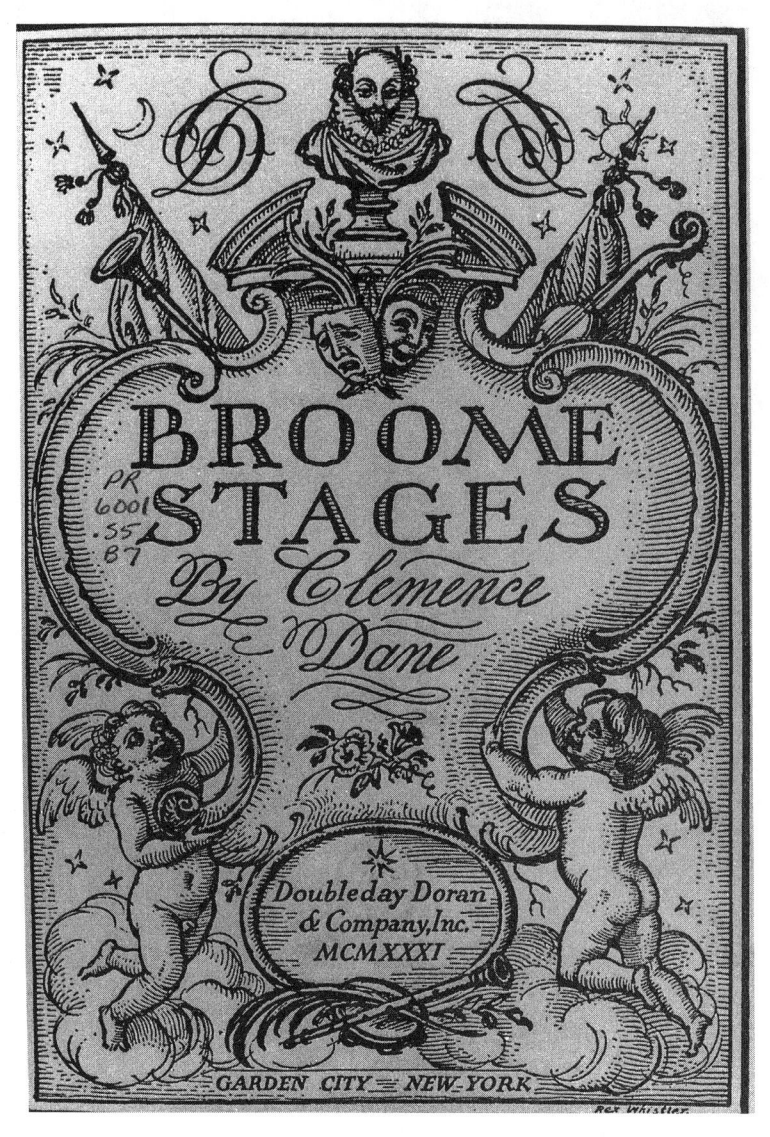

Title page for the U.S. edition of a novel about seven generations of a theatrical family

merchant, and Florence Bentley Ashton. She shocked her bourgeois family when she decided to study art. She had real talent for portraiture—her bust of the actor-manager, dramatist, and composer Ivor Novello is in the lobby of The Theatre Royal, Drury Lane—and she liked the bohemian way of life of painters and sculptors. She studied at the Slade School of Art in London from 1904 to 1906 and in Dresden in 1906-1907. She taught languages abroad until she went on the stage in 1913 under the name Diana Portis in *Eliza Comes to Stay,* a comedy by Henry Vernon Esmond. After World War I, however, she found herself teaching in a girls' school.

The hothouse atmosphere of the school is captured in Dane's first novel, *Regiment of Women.* Though she drops the word *monstrous* from the quotation from John Knox that forms her title, the novel was shocking for its time because it involves a close relationship—almost an affair—between two women teachers: Claire Hartill and Alwynne Durand. There is sentiment and shock, including a death, and some prefiguring of Muriel Spark's treatment of the relationships between teachers and their pet pupils in *The Prime of Miss Jean Brodie* (1961). Dane's novel is an emotional argument for coeducation and a melodramatic warning against the dangers of corruption in the confined spaces of a single-sex school (a topic that several novelists had already exploited in regard to boys' schools). The reviewer for the *Times Literary Supplement* (25 January 1917) found *Regiment of Women* remarkable for a first novel and said that it

Dane's bust of the actor-manager, dramatist, and songwriter Ivor Novello (David Ivor Davies) at the Theatre Royal, Drury Lane, in London

showed "wisdom: a shrewd penetration into human minds and the circumstances that mould or fix them, combined with an admirable 'allroundness' of outlook upon human life."

In her next novel, *First the Blade: A Comedy of Growth* (1918), Dane draws less from life–which may explain why the characters have less life in them. Justin Cloud and Laura Valentine drift together and then drift apart, joined by familiarity and at last separated by war. The way the war broke up relationships of all kinds is a powerful and worthy theme in writing of that time, but the reader may feel that Laura is well rid of the "hero" of this slight fiction. The story's message seems less deeply felt by the author than that of *Regiment of Women*. Worse, the same sort of message is infinitely better communicated by H. G. Wells's *Joan and Peter: The Story of an Education* (1918). The plot of *First the Blade* is nearly as unfortunate as the characters: *The Boston Transcript* (31 July 1918) was generous in describing it as "leisurely," and the author's ingenuity was recruited to spin it out to "inordinate length," according to *The New York Times* (19 May 1918).

Dane's next novel, *Legend* (1919), is a much more powerful work. It is a theatrical story given color by gossips, an invented tale that takes full advantage of the atmosphere, if not actual events, that Dane encountered backstage in her brief acting career. The stage setting suits the dramatic–indeed melodramatic–way in which the character of a dead woman is raked over the coals by her so-called friends. The reader sees the London theater world from the rough side of the curtain, and the effect is impressive. Dane adapted *Legend* for the stage as *The Way Things Happen;* a 1935 production starred Katherine Cornell.

The Dearly Beloved of Benjamin Cobb (1927) is a pedestrian novel. Much better is *The Babyons* (1927), which follows a Devonshire family over the course of four centuries and includes a family curse, ghosts, gypsies, madness, melancholy, mystery, and plenty of costumes and scenery. The book was first sold as four boxed volumes–*Third Person Singular, Midsummer Men, Creeping Jenny,* and *Lady Babyon* (in which the title character finally lays the ghosts to rest)–and published in a single volume later that same year.

Sayers and Agatha Christie were two of the many women writers of detective stories the public adored in the postwar period, and Dane decided to try to join them. She teamed up with an Australian-born writer with some detective-story experience, Helen Simpson (who would later name her daughter Clemence). The first Dane-Simpson collaboration was *Enter Sir John* (1928), a well-crafted murder mystery involving an actress accused of killing another actress; the sleuth who proves her innocence, through clever work with a script, is the actor-manager Sir John. The follow-up was *Re-Enter Sir John* (1932), and though Will Cuppy in *Books* (9 August 1932) pointed out that "the main motive" was weak, Isaac Anderson, writing in *The New York Times* (14 August 1932), spoke for most readers when he said that the pair had "scored another hit." Dane and Simpson also wrote *Printer's Devil* (1930; published in the United States as *Author Unknown,* 1930). This flawed story features the literary sleuth Marmion Poole and a solution that is finally revealed after what is meant to be suspense but comes across as pointless delay. *The New York Times* (30 March 1930) kindly said that the actual mystery was "baffling but brief."

The generally economical style of Dane's detective-story collaborations is not to be found in a picaresque saga with a theater background that she wrote on her own. *Broome Stages* (1931) follows the romantic adventures of seven generations of a theatrical family, from the eighteenth century to modern times. The dynasty whose saga *Broome Stages* recounts descends from a strolling player, Richard Broome, born in 1715, who spends his childhood

Dane at her easel (photograph by Cole Lesley)

making brooms until a witch changes the course of his life and he falls in with a troupe of players. In time he becomes the grandfather of a duchess. In the modern world rewards are somewhat different, but the reader can still expect success from the latest of the Broomes: "He was a Broome, and he was going to carry on as the Broomes have always carried on, in the direction he wants to go, although the whole of theatrical England had decided to turn round and go the other way." The stereotypical individuality, not to say eccentricity, that the British public expects from "theatricals" is, in *Broome Stages,* excused by the success the actors achieve as they become as snobbish as their betters and clamber out of the lower classes into the upper ones. Hierarchies are not, however, threatened: clearly, not many families can become dynasties in any profession, and these cherished exceptions prove the rule. *Broome Stages* uses British history more as scenery than as subject, theatrical backdrop rather than factual background. H. C. Harwood said in *The Saturday Review* that the author handled the horde of characters well, but "'Broome Stages' bored me. The individuals are too much alike in their bright promise, brittle charm, curt amours, and early decay. The family is too remote not only from the life of England but from the changes of the stage."

The Moon Is Feminine (1938) was also successful, perhaps because of the popular interest at the time in its setting: Brighton in the early nineteenth century. Lady Molly; her green-eyed lover, Henry Cope, a boy from the sea; and a seal are involved in a tragic fantasy with a slight but deftly handled plot that was dismissed by Harold Brighouse in the *Manchester Guardian* (26 April 1938) as "obscure."

The Arrogant History of White Ben (1939) is an allegory–White Ben is a scarecrow–of Britain in 1950. By 1950, Dane predicts, England will be a dystopia, the war that was looming as she wrote producing "no victors, only the vanquished." Graham Greene found the portentous satire of *The Arrogant History of White Ben* "curiously empty . . . rather overdressed for its subject–so many irrelevant dawns and sunsets, and jewels five lines long."

Despite the skepticism about the war she expressed in *The Arrogant History of White Ben*, when World War II began Dane demonstrated her patriotism by editing *The Shelter Book: A Gathering of Tales, Poems, Essays, Notes, and Notions . . . for Use in Shelters, Tubes, Basements and Cellars in War-time* (1940), as well as *The Nelson Touch* (1942), an edition of the British naval hero Horatio Nelson's letters; publishing two books of patriotic verse, *Trafalgar Day, 1940* (1940) and *Christmas in War-Time* (1941); and writing equally patriotic plays and novels, such as *The Golden Reign of Queen Elizabeth* (1941), *The Saviours: Seven Plays on One Theme* (1942), and *He Brings Great News* (1944).

After the war Dane mostly wrote for the stage and the motion-picture industry. She had one more successful novel, *The Flower Girls* (1954). Like *Broome Stages*, *The Flower Girls* is a lengthy saga of life on the stage. *The Flower Girls* is one of those huge novels that people regret leaving after a long read. It tells of how the First Family of the British Stage descended from Job Florister and his wife, Rosina de Maria Grosse. Their children were Julius; Paxton; the "Flower Girls," Lily, Mary, and Myrtle; and Ernest, and the novel is populated by their offspring, some legitimate and others not, in a bewildering tangle. If the novel centers on anyone in this crowd, it is Jacey P. Florister, the only child of Ernest Florister and Isobel Pinken, born in 1919. His mother ran out on his father, and Jacey wound up with her in Los Angeles. Born English, he becomes a naturalized American so that the First Family is transatlantic. Jacey manages The Flower Theatre in London's West End and also has American theatrical connections. "London-New York-New York-London" becomes the "rhythm" of his life. He is more successful in the United States because his stage Englishman act goes over better there.

It was Dane's experience as an actress and her abiding love of everything theatrical—there is a striking theatricality in her artworks, such as the bust of Novello or her painting of Noel Coward—that made the detective stories with a backstage background, *Broome Stages* and *The Flower Girls*, successful. When she did not have this extra inspiration, Dane tended to turn out work.

Dane was made a dame commander of the British Empire near the end of her busy public life. She lived in a period more congenial to her unabashedly melodramatic plays and usually romantic novels than the literary market of today tends to be, and she now occupies a small but permanent niche with her plays *A Bill of Divorcement* and (in the unpopular field of modern verse drama) *Will Shakespeare* (1921). Although her novels are largely forgotten today, her first, *Regiment of Women,* has been rediscovered by feminist scholars and was republished in 1995 as part of Virago's Lesbian Landmarks Series.

Bibliography:
Fred B. Millet, ed., *Contemporary British Literature: A Critical Survey and 232 Author-Bibliographies,* revised edition (New York: Harcourt, Brace, 1935), pp. 190–191.

References:
Leonard R. N. Ashley, "Clemence Dane," in *An Encyclopedia of British Women Writers,* edited by Paul Schlueter and June Schlueter (New York & London: Garland, 1983), pp. 134–137;

Gabriele Griffin, "Clemence Dane," in *British Women Writers: A Critical Reference Guide,* edited by Janet Todd (New York: Continuum, 1989), pp. 174–175;

David Waldron Smithers, *Therefore, Imagine–: The Works of Clemence Dane* (Turnbridge Wells: Dragonfly, 1988).

Gertrude Dix
(Circa 1874 – ?)

Carol L. Hale
University of Wisconsin–Eau Claire

BOOKS: *The Girl from the Farm* (London: Lane / Boston: Roberts, 1895);
The Image Breakers (London: Heinemann, 1900; New York: Stokes, 1900).

SELECTED PERIODICAL PUBLICATIONS—UNCOLLECTED: "Hard Labour in the Hospitals," *Westminster Review,* 140 (December 1893): 627-634;
"Manzanita (From England to California)," *Sunset,* 26 (March 1911): 324.

Critical focus on the novelists of the New Woman movement has brought Gertrude Dix to scholarly attention for reconsideration. This new interest has been hindered, however, by the scarcity of information not only about the details of her life but also about its most basic facts. All who have recently written about Dix cite Samson Bryher's record (circa 1931) of Bristol's socialist movement from 1888 to 1900 that mentions Dix as one of "Two others worthy of special mention"; Bryher identifies her simply as "Miss Gertrude Dix (the authoress of *The Image Breakers,* and *The Girl from the Farm*)." Although Bryher's history is primarily devoted to male socialists, he also provides detailed entries on and photographs of women; one may assume, then, that his sparse account of Dix indicates no general dismissal of female participation. Researchers have assumed this sole citation to be the only extant information about Dix.

An 1893 article in the *Westminster Review* by a Gertrude Dix discusses the conditions nurses face in hospitals, as well as in the economic system in general. Several features of the article suggest that the novelist Dix could have been the author. The writer clearly speaks from a position of working-class solidarity; her language at times suggests a socialist analysis—in a reference to "the present system of cut-throat capitalism," for example, or to Walter Besant, demonstrating her awareness of contemporary literary discourse around class issues. Indeed one passage in the article expresses a view similar to the one that informs *The Girl from the Farm* (1895): "philanthropy creates with one hand the evil which with the other it seeks to relieve." The tone of another observation—a sardonic suggestion that as a "womanly woman" a nurse "should take delight in self-sacrifice"—is a cutting critique of that feminine icon, the Angel in the House. Of potential biographical significance is the fact that the author of the article clearly speaks not only from research but also from personal experience. She need not have been regularly employed as a nurse to have gained this firsthand experience, however: she describes the case of "Special or lady-probationers" in the "large general hospitals" who "pay the expenses of their board and lodging, and are engaged for shorter periods" than the other probationary nurses. And she does not wholly identify with the nurses; at one point she makes reference to "their," as opposed to "our," lives. Furthermore she remarks that "Only one who has actually lived among nurses, as one of them, can perhaps realise. . . ," suggesting that her nursing experience was deliberately sought out better to inform the article. Part of the writer's motivation may also be indicated in the observation that "It is tacitly felt that the nurse is better occupied in the pursuit of her duties than in rushing into print." Perhaps further research will confirm whether Dix the novelist was also Dix the journalist and sometime nurse.

That Dix did write for periodicals is borne out in an entry in *Who Was Who in Literature 1906-1934* (1979), which, in addition to naming her as author of the two novels, refers to several magazines (though *Westminster Review* is not among them) to which she contributed. The entry includes neither birth nor death dates, but it does add a parenthetical "Mrs. Nicol" after her name and gives her place of residence as Weimar, California. Unfortunately the sources of information for the *Who Was Who* volume are not indicated. Two pieces of supporting evidence, however, link Dix to the United States. First, Lyle H. Wright's *American Fiction 1876-1900* indexes *The Girl from the Farm,* which is certainly surprising

Title page for a novel about the intertwined lives of an unnamed farm girl and an independent New Woman

on first glance; however, the introductory notes to this volume explain that "foreign-born" authors are included if they had an American co-author—which she did not—or if they "considered the United States as their permanent home." Second, the March 1911 issue of the San Francisco periodical *Sunset* includes a poem by a Gertrude Dix: "Manzanita (From England to California)." The movement in the poem is not only from England to California but also from bleak to vibrant images and from a solitary "I" to a companionate "we." Further research in state government documents may provide at least birth and death dates for Dix and perhaps information about a marriage.

The Girl from the Farm, set in the fictional town of Allington, has as its main characters the unnamed title figure; twenty-five-year-old Hilary Marchant; Katharine Marchant, his twenty-three-year-old sister; their parents, Cuthbert Marchant, dean of Allington, and Ellen Marchant; and Mary Field, Katharine's friend in London. The action begins in March and concludes the following February. Hilary's chance meeting with and attraction to the girl from the farm opens the novel, but the narrative shifts quickly to focus on Katharine. A Cambridge graduate and a vibrant, energetic young woman, she intends to find teaching and journalistic work in London, where she plans to live with her friend Mary Field, who has organized the Woman's Literary and Scientific Association. But when Mr. Marchant is diagnosed with an ocular deterioration that will soon result in blindness, Katharine postpones these plans in order to help him finish the book he has been researching for years. The girl from the farm comes to the Marchant household as a servant, and Hilary seduces her. When he loses interest in her, she returns to the farm. Meanwhile it has become clear that the dean wants to keep Katharine at his side even beyond the completion of his work; Katharine is frustrated and thrown into despair by this turn of events. After some time the girl from the farm returns to Allington, pregnant with Hilary's child. The lives of the girl and of Katharine become entwined, bringing the conflict between Katharine and her parents to its climax. Katharine decides to care for the girl, whom her brother and parents have abandoned; as the novel closes she and the girl are taking the train "to London—and Mary."

An epigraph from the philosopher Georg Wilhelm Friedrich Hegel forecasts the novel's conflicts:

> Two opposed Rights come forth: the one breaks itself to pieces against the other: in this way both alike suffer loss; while both alike are justified, the one towards the other: not as if this were right; that other wrong. On the one side is the religious claim, the unconscious moral habit: the other principle over against it is the equally religious claim—the claim of the consciousness of the reason, creating a world out of itself, the claim to eat of the tree of the knowledge of good and evil.

With the action taking place primarily in the deanery and on its grounds, the novel's setting aptly symbolizes the patriarchal claims that, in Katharine's case, weigh particularly heavily. Furthermore, Katharine's father illustrates in himself the opposition of Hegel's "two opposed Rights": many years earlier he had turned from a work in which he had sought to reconcile religion and science, replacing this doubt-inspiring research with "On the Role Played by Accent in Latin Verse." Marchant's deteriorating eyesight may be understood as figuring his self-imposed intellectual blindness, chosen when he realized the impossibility of the reconciliation between faith and reason he had hoped to effect. Katharine "console[s] herself with the thought that her imprisonment was but for a while, and that at no very distant day she would be able to employ herself in some work more relevant to life than the compilation of a philological treatise for a few professors to wrangle over." The pettiness of the dialogue implied by "wrangling" contrasts with the far more dramatic debate (and schism) that would have accompanied Marchant's originally contemplated work; Katharine's virtual imprisonment in the deanery serves as a foil to the women's penitentiary to which her mother devotes her time.

The novel explores the ways in which women's roles are assigned to them by their gender and by their class. This exploration is set within the conflict over the question of the work most appropriate for Katharine and, by implication, conflict over how she should find meaning in life. This leads inevitably to a dispute over the varieties of knowledge and experience suitable to women—always moderated by their place within class structures. Through Mrs. Marchant's philanthropic work with the women's prison, the novel explores the confinement of women at the hands of other women and the control that the ruling class exerts over philanthropy—how it will be handled and who shall receive it. To her mother's disappointment Katharine shows no interest in philanthropy; there are oblique hints that her plans with Mary Field have something to do with class issues, and though they are not specifically socialists, their sympathies seem to run in that direction. Dix's exploration of Katharine Marchant's dilemma—she is caught between the claims of religion and those of reason, with the struggle manifesting itself in many ways at once—is both poignant and incisive. It reflects not only the New Woman's choices but every woman's choices—even a century later.

Almost nothing is known about the contemporary response to the novel. The publisher, John Lane, brought the work out as volume 14 in its Keynote Series, which displays a certain sympathy with the New Woman movement; in addition to Dix's book the series includes Grant Allen's *The Woman Who Did* (1895). The reviewer for *The Athenaeum* described the novel as "one of those wearisome books that deal with the modern daughter of emancipated views," by which the reviewer was "entirely" unmoved. Sales figures for the novel are unavailable. Critics have focused on Dix's second novel, *The Image Breakers* (1900), rather than *The Girl from the Farm;* yet the first novel not only provides an introduction to its successor but also

Title page for a novel about the experiences of two women: a working-class artist and a socialist writer

stands equally worthy of attention in the category of New Woman fiction.

The main characters in *The Image Breakers* include Leslie Ardent, a working-class artist with socialist sympathies; Rosalind Dangerfield, a socialist writer; Rosalind's husband, Herbert, a mill owner; Justin Ferrar, editor of an anarchist paper; and John Redgold, a socialist who has pragmatically decided to pursue Labour Party agendas. The action occurs over a period of four years, opening and closing in summer. The friendship of Leslie and Rosalind links their two stories, which otherwise constitute nearly separate plots. The narrative opens on a scene of great tenderness and devotion between the two women that is at once innocent and sensual. Rosalind is committed to socialism and disenchanted with her marriage; in his younger days her husband leaned toward socialism, but as a mill owner he is in the capitalist camp. Writing and submitting socialist articles as "R. Dangerfield," Rosalind makes contact with Ferrar; she ultimately leaves her husband to live in an anarchist community with Ferrar. Leslie, who supports herself by doing commercial illustrations while she pursues her art, meets John Redgold, and they become lovers. The evolution of these two romantic relationships, including the conflicts they raise between and within the two women, make up the narrative. These relationships necessarily involve the characters' varying views of alternative politics and values; indeed the extent to which these worlds overlap—and the extent to which the characters do or do not recognize this—plays a vital role in the conflicts. In the end Rosalind loses interest in Ferrar, who has proven emotionally unworthy and disloyal; Leslie, who had with great reluctance refused Redgold's proposal of marriage, is reunited with him after a separation.

Disparity between the ideal and the real, both in relationships and in political movements, informs the work. Illustrating this disparity are the questions of whether a woman might find her most fulfilling relationship with another woman or with a man and with a man as a comrade or a lover, of whether biological procreation or intellectual creation might constitute her most fulfilling work, and what the dynamic between relationship and work might be.

Sales figures for *The Image Breakers* are not available, and reviewers seem to have ignored the novel. The work has received scholarly attention primarily for its presentation of the New Woman but also for its strong intimation of erotic love between the two protagonists—though this element appears early in the novel and remains undeveloped. Focusing on the fate of Rosalind Dangerfield, in particular on her poor treatment by a male leader of the socialist movement, Ann Ardis suggests in "'The Journey from Fantasy to Politics'" (1993) that the novel "exposes the class and gender biases" that have prevented the socialist revolution from occurring. Ardis identifies the "cultural icon of 'the good woman'" as the broken image of the title, and certainly Rosalind's choices support this interpretation. By the end of the novel, although Rosalind retains her sympathy for the working class, she longs to retreat to the "peace" of a religious order. Rosalind's desire for a cloistered life suggests a retreat to the Law of the Father.

The work includes more than a single image breaker, however: Leslie's choices are also bound up in the novel's symbolism. For example, as the novel opens the narrator describes Leslie lying asleep in terms that evoke the sculpted image on a tomb: white, pure, and still. Midway through the novel Redgold dreams of having married Leslie and of Leslie, in anger, breaking a beautiful white statue. When he investigates the fragments, he finds a suggestion of Leslie's face among the pieces on the floor. At the novel's end Leslie, gazing at her face in a cottage mirror, notes that the mirror's frame—a snake—stands for Eternity; next to her face there appears "the man also": Redgold. The mirrored gaze of the couple conveys not a static image but the fluidity of reflection, shifting between individual and mutual perspectives. Redgold's dream as a point of departure suggests that Dix portrays Rosalind and Leslie as the image breakers, who shatter roles that others—especially men—insist on for them. What Dix is trying to portray in the dynamic that links the demise of the white statue, the new relationship between Redgold and Leslie figured in the mirror, and Rosalind's ultimate solitude, invites consideration.

In addition to creating versions of the New Woman in her two novels, Dix sets those portrayals in the context of class conflict and explores questions of political justice both in the larger society and within individual relationships. In so doing she helped create and nurture a new vision of what a woman's narrative might be. For this reason her fiction remains of great interest.

References:

Ann Ardis, "'The Journey from Fantasy to Politics': The Representation of Socialism and Feminism in *Gloriana* and *The Image-Breakers*," in *Rediscovering Forgotten Radicals: British Women Writers 1889–1939,* edited by Angela Ingram and Daphne Patai (Chapel Hill: University of North Carolina Press, 1993), pp. 43–56;

Ardis, *New Women, New Novels: Feminism and Early Modernism* (New Brunswick, N.J.: Rutgers University Press, 1990), pp. 124, 127–128, 134–135, 138–139, 155, 159–160, 166, 170–171, 175;

Samson Bryher, *An Account of the Labour and Socialist Movement in Bristol: Part II (To End of XIXth Century)* (Bristol: Labour Weekly, circa 1931);

Lyle H. Wright, *American Fiction 1876–1900: A Contribution toward a Bibliography* (San Marino, Cal.: Huntington Library, 1966).

Ella Hepworth Dixon
(1855 or 1857 – 12 January 1932)

Margaret Diane Stetz
Georgetown University

BOOKS: *My Flirtations,* as Margaret Wynman (London: Chatto & Windus, 1892; Philadelphia: Lippincott, 1893);

The Story of a Modern Woman (London: Heinemann, 1894; New York: Cassell, 1894; Leipzig: Tauchnitz, 1895);

One Doubtful Hour and Other Side-lights on the Feminine Temperament (London: Richards, 1904; Leipzig: Tauchnitz, 1904);

"As I Knew Them": Sketches of People I Have Met on the Way (London: Hutchinson, 1930).

Edition: *The Story of a Modern Woman,* introduction by Kate Flint (London: Merlin, 1990).

SELECTED PERIODICAL PUBLICATIONS—UNCOLLECTED: "Murder—or Mercy? A Story of To-day," *Woman's World,* 1 (1888): 466–469;

"On Cloaks," *Woman's World,* 2 (1889): 509–513;

"Women on Horseback," *Woman's World,* 2 (1889): 227–233;

"A Garden in the South," *Woman's World,* 3 (1890): 247–250;

"A Literary Lover," *Woman's World,* 3 (1890): 638–641;

"London in Khaki," *New York Independent,* 26 July 1900, pp. 1794–1796.

PLAY PRODUCTION: *The Toyshop of the Heart,* London, The Playhouse, 26 November 1908.

Photograph by Hoppé, London

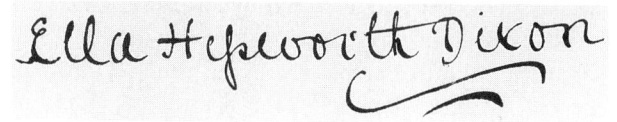

The New Woman writers at the end of the nineteenth century are often assumed to have been outside of the English social order that they criticized, as was the case, for example, with politically radical South Africans such as Olive Schreiner or sexually adventurous Americans such as Gertrude Atherton. If not foreign born, then they are still thought to have belonged by birth or by choice to those who distanced themselves from bourgeois British preoccupations, as was true of E. Nesbit, a founder of Fabian Socialism and a partner in an open marriage. But novelists such as Florence Henniker, who produced the brilliantly bitter tale of marital hypocrisy *Second Fiddle* (1912), and Ella Hepworth Dixon, author of *My Flirtations* (1892) and *The Story of a Modern Woman* (1894), serve as reminders that some of the harshest censure of the English social system came from insiders who were appalled by the exploitation of women on which that system depended. Dixon differed from Henniker, however, in that she primarily used humor to expose these abuses and to free female readers from the voices urging them to submit to their fate as mere possessions and ornaments. She was also unique in fighting oppression on two fronts simultaneously. Her targets were both the conservative ranks of gentlemen with professions, who moved in the sexist spheres of business and politics, and the equally misogynist counterestablishment of male bohemians and aesthetes who made the practice of art another occasion for mistreating women. For Dixon a writing career was a means of achieving financial independence and personal autonomy, but the writing of realist fiction, in particular, became a vehicle for unveiling and denouncing social relations between the sexes in the dual worlds that she inhabited.

Dixon was born into a London milieu that was at once respectably middle class and defiantly artistic in either 1855 or 1857, according to conflicting sources. To her Irish mother, Marian MacMahon Dixon, she attributed her early consciousness of women's issues, and she spoke admiringly in her 1930 memoir, *"As I Knew Them,"* of the feminist atmosphere that her mother created while raising six children and maintaining a lively salon for visiting writers and painters in their Regent's Park house. From her father, too, she received a childhood grounding in the importance of taking women seriously as professionals, for William Hepworth Dixon, in his capacity as editor of *The Athenaeum,* employed and befriended many female essayists. It was her father's editorship of that mainstream intellectual periodical from 1853 to 1869 that raised him from the ranks of an ordinary journalist from Manchester to the position of a literary lion whose society was worth cultivating and thus eased his daughter's entry into both the drawing rooms of prosperous capitalists and the studios of the struggling avant-garde. After her father's death, which coincided with the beginning of her own career, she used this privileged inheritance to advance herself in the literary world even as, in *The Story of a Modern Woman,* she criticized the patriarchal biases that made such maneuvers necessary.

Thanks to her progressive family, Dixon received both a lady's education and one that was more intellectually and socially unconventional. Like Mary Erle in *The Story of a Modern Woman,* she contracted typhoid fever while studying with a private tutor in Heidelberg, where she was sent to learn German language and philosophy, as well as how to play the piano. She also attended the London School of Music and, more daringly for a young woman of her class, studied painting in Paris, working in the ateliers of two French artists. Her experiences in Paris provided the background for her story "The Sweet o' the Year," published in *The Yellow Book* for April 1896. Such early exposure to Continental travel gave her a dislike for English provincialism that manifested itself in the searing satirical portrait of the residents of "Northaw," a suburb of "Mudchester," in *My Flirtations*. She also acquired a taste for adventure. Her 1897 entry for *Who's Who* lists the physically active sports of cycling and boating as her chief recreations, along with travel to challenging destinations, including Russia, Algeria, Morocco, and Canada. These explorative instincts proved professionally useful in her pursuit of a livelihood through journalism, the career that supported Dixon both during and after her brief period in the 1890s as a novelist.

Over the decades her reviews, sketches, essays, and short stories appeared in newspapers and magazines that catered to diverse audiences of all political stripes, including *The World, The Times* (London), *The Daily Mail, The Sketch, The Illustrated London News, The St. James's Gazette, The Westminster Gazette,* and *The Manchester Guardian*. In *My Flirtations* she offers a caricature, at once affectionate and painfully anti-Semitic, of a late-Victorian newspaper magnate—a composite sketch that reflects her social and business acquaintance with the Levy-Lawson family, founders and proprietors of *The Daily Telegraph,* one of the papers for which she worked. She briefly experienced the profession of authorship from the other side, as it were, when from March 1895 through September 1896 she shouldered the editorship of a magazine of her own, *The Englishwoman,* intended for a female readership. Its target audience was not, however, the politically conscious and reform-minded New Women, with whom the public identified Dixon. Rather, its articles reached out to the conventional interests of ladies, and the inaugural issue presented features with titles such as "Society's Doings," "To Those about to Furnish," "A Day's Shopping," and "Housekeeping: The Everyday Dinner." Yet even here Dixon found ways of introducing the avant-garde among the staid; the March 1895 debut of the magazine also included short stories by Violet Hunt and Robert Hichens, a profile of the French aesthete Pierre Loti, and book reviews of such eyebrow-raising texts as George Gissing's novel *In the Year of Jubilee* and George Egerton's 1894 volume of feminist stories, *Discords*. Such careful planting of radical authors and ideas among the columns of household advice was intended to domesticate the Decadents, Naturalists, and New Women and to create a bond between them and the middle-class female audience at the same time their artistic and social projects were being demonized elsewhere in the popular press. Her efforts as an editor were appreciated by the critic H. D. Traill, who reviewed the second number of *The Englishwoman* in *The Graphic* (4 May 1895), speaking favorably of the evident "energy and intelligence in the conduct of it."

Perhaps Dixon's most memorable experience with the world of late-Victorian magazine publishing was her association from 1888 to 1890 with *Woman's World,* edited by Oscar Wilde just before his plays swept him to unprecedented fame on the West End stage. Her contributions to Wilde's venture ranged from lightweight nonfiction features such as articles on horseback riding and on cloaks to remarkable short stories such as "A Literary Lover." This last was a sophisticated tragicomedy that predicted in content as well as style the longer works of fiction soon to follow. It took as its subject a woman's growing outrage at a male novelist who has posed as a suitor to gather material for his work. Dixon not only objected to such appropriations of women by male artists but also turned the tables on the appropriators, including her own editor at *Woman's World.* In *My Flirtations* she skewers Wilde's social conduct through the portrait of the malicious and fickle Valentine Redmond, who treats women as decorative objects—goods to be inspected, ranked according to their aesthetic value, held up briefly for admiration among his group of sycophantic "boys," and discarded like any other novelty. In the story "'The World's Slow Stain,'" collected in *One Doubtful Hour and Other Side-lights on the Feminine Temperament* (1904), she decries the intellectually vampirish qualities of the dramatist Gilbert Vincent, another Wilde surrogate, who maintains an ambiguous personal hold upon a New Woman novelist in order to make "an exhaustive study" of her for his own profit and pleasure. In *The Story of a Modern Woman* she also criticizes Wilde's behavior as an editor toward female authors. The "well-dressed, supercilious-looking young man of thirty" who edits *The Fan,* a monthly for ladies, rudely forces Mary Erle to wait in the anteroom of his office while he remains closeted with a male social acquaintance: "The business, it would seem, on which they were engaged was of a somewhat hilarious nature, for frequent guffaws of laughter reached her, and there was an unmistakable odour of cigarettes. Ten minutes, fifteen minutes, twenty minutes went slowly by." When he finally deigns to speak with her about contributing to the magazine, it is in a tone of the utmost condescension that alters immediately once he learns that she is a member of the class to which he aspires and an intimate of the aristocrats whose favor he seeks.

From the short story "A Literary Lover" that Dixon produced for Wilde's magazine in 1890 it was an easy transition to move to fiction writing on a larger scale. *My Flirtations* first appeared as a serial publication in *The Lady's Pictorial* with illustrations by J. Bernard Partridge before its publication in book form. Perhaps because its satirical portraits so often suggested living (and easily identifiable) originals, Dixon chose to issue it under a pseudonym, hitting on the playful one of Margaret Wynman for her story of a young woman who proves only too popular as an object of conquest for a series of vain, foolish, and grasping men who are drawn as much by her position as the daughter of a member of the Royal Academy as by her personal attractions. In the March 1896 issue of *The Englishwoman,* published during Dixon's term of editorship, an anonymous tale called "The Feeble Fib," possibly her own unsigned work, appeared. Certainly, its account of a first-time author's experience in the literary marketplace of the early 1890s parallels closely Dixon's fate after she turned novelist:

> "When you have finished your book, Brandon," she advised, "send it to Irvine and Irvine. They will publish it in their 'Nom-de-plume' series. You will have an eccentric, idiotic poster all to yourself in the new art style, and the puzzle of the hour will be: 'What is the writer's name?' Is it a he or a she? Then, when the papers have criticized your book, praised it, slashed it and discussed it for all it is worth, your real name will be discovered; interviewers will regard you as a special prize; your photo will be attempted in the evening newspapers, and you will be famous."

Actual critical response to *My Flirtations* ran along just such shallow and predictable lines. Not unexpectedly, *The Athenaeum* spoke glowingly of the novel as a "bright and amusing satire on various types of modern young men, and of their vagaries under the influence of a young lady not indisposed to flirt." On the other hand, the Boston-based *Literary World* reacted with strong disapproval—both artistic and, it seems, moral—to the American publication of the book, likening the volume to a society belle in her frivolous evening dress: "*My Flirtations,* by Margaret Wynman, is appropriately bound in changeable shotted silk, which gives it every advantage of original and fascinating appearance while it is fresh, but frays out at a careless touch and will not wear well at all."

Though its methods of argument were indeed those of comedy and its debut came in the modest venue of a women's magazine, Dixon's episodic novel attempts far more than simple entertainment. It is situated squarely in the midst of two important literary controversies that spilled over into the sphere of actual life. The first of these was the debate, associated with journalism and fiction by New Women, over the role of marriage as a social and economic necessity, especially for women of the middle classes. The second was the sometimes angry conversation that had sprung up between male practitioners of aestheticism and their female counterparts, who were also advocates of art-for-art's-sake but who chafed under the exploitation of women involved in the act of masculine "appreciation." On both of these subjects Dixon took a hard line in *My Flirtations,* positioning the novel in support of those who defined courtship and marriage as institutions that served only men's interests and those who looked at the woman-worshiping ways of the aesthetes as male narcissism in disguise.

Early reviewers seemed disposed to conflate the author of the novel with its adolescent comic narrator, speaking of the book as though it had been written both by, as well as about, a "young lady not indisposed to flirt." In fact, when *My Flirtations* was published in 1892, Dixon was already in her mid to late thirties, and she had long ago removed herself from the marriage market. This distance enabled her to see clearly the enterprise of courtship as a business—one in which middle-class women who had received no training in commercial principles were at a grave disadvantage compared to their shrewder male counterparts. Far from always reflecting the naive view of the narrator, Dixon's own perspective on the marriage industry was often closer to that of the narrator's older sister, Christina, a tart-tongued bystander with radical tendencies. Christina experiments with socialism and vegetarianism and finds the unconsciously risible behavior of the narrator's suitors "really diverting to behold." As Dixon suggests repeatedly in her novel, laughter was one of the few weapons that women possessed in a situation in which men came far better armed and determined to conquer.

Female laughter might ward off, as nothing else could, pursuit by such conceited, selfish wife-hunters as Mr. Hanbury Price, the stingy and small-minded product of an "eminently respectable suburb," a man "so suspicious . . . that he even suspected himself." To compensate for his fear that "he might not yet get the desired return for his money," he shortchanges everyone, including the narrator, whom he plies with discount chocolates from the Civil Service Stores and hopes to acquire on the cheap:

> It grieves me to think what we must have cost Mr. Hanbury Price in hansoms, for our house, as he more than once explained, is inconveniently situated for omnibuses. Whether he really imagined himself to be in love I have never been able to decide, but he was obviously haunted by dreadful forebodings as to the expense of a young lady with my tastes and proclivities. He used to lecture me about taking care of my gowns, and suggested that I was recklessly extravagant in the matter of feather boas and shoes.

"All this," the reader is told, "contributed to Christina's joy," for she is a satirist who loves to point out the absurdities of the well-to-do Mr. Price as he "struggles between economy and the tender passion."

So, too, laughter proves the chief defense against other predatory gentlemen such as Elisha Van Schuyler, an American who all but makes love to the narrator before announcing that he has a fiancée in Buffalo and who, even after his marriage, is "always to be found straying about at the very end of the tether" of wedlock. It also helps to fend off Anthony Lambert, the "eldest son of Norfolk People" and a lieutenant in the Blankshire Regiment: "He had, in a supreme degree, the magnetism which comes of perfect health, good spirits, and complete self-satisfaction," which permits him to amuse himself irresponsibly with the narrator and several other women, married and unmarried, at the same time. As the narrator says, "Everybody at home liked Tony, except, I think, Christina, who said she couldn't understand his slang, and that he made a draught in the drawing-room." It is no wonder that the narrator says of her sister, "Christina can be, on occasion, almost brutally cynical; but then she is clever, and when I want to get out of a scrape I go to her."

Sororal laughter circulates throughout the novel, offering the sole protection against the social imperative to marry that increasingly closes in on the female protagonists. As in other New Woman texts from the same period, such as "Virgin Soil" in Egerton's *Discords,* the mother serves as chief agent of this social pressure, informing her daughter "that she married my father at seventeen, and settled down after that" and reining in all attempts to learn more about the male-controlled world beyond the drawing room by announcing "that she had 'no patience with such philandering.'" Under such circumstances laughter alone cannot serve as a permanent refuge for middle-class women, who have been raised and equipped to follow no profession but a domestic one.

In the final chapter of *My Flirtations* the novel's tone darkens as the still immature narrator is drawn inexorably into a loveless union with John Ford, "the well-known stockbroker," a "slightly rotund" forty-six-year-old for whom talking "was somewhat hard work": "'Nice little frock,' he said at last. 'Like to see little girls in white. Ought always to dress in white.' And this was the first and last occasion on which Mr. John Ford has ever paid me a compliment." Soon the narrator has, indeed, dressed in those bridal raiments of "shimmering white and silver" that she calls, with mixed emotion, "Symbols of the Eternal Feminine" and that suggest, through Dixon's carefully managed description of them, both angels' wings and grave clothes. This death-dealing marriage comes about through the narrator's ill-fated entanglement in the world of masculine business, for which she is both intellectually and financially unprepared, and turns on John Ford's willingness to rescue her from a debt contracted in ignorance. At the end the narrator goes to her doom in a spirit of good-humored resignation yet confesses to a mood that is far from the imagined romantic ideal promulgated in the 1890s by so many conventional tales from *The Lady's Pictorial*: "Mother—dear mother!—looks at me solicitously, and follows me about the house with a biscuit and a glass of port wine. . . . It reminds me of once, long ago, when I was ill. And to be sure I am tired, very tired." She seems, indeed, worn out not only by the prenuptial struggle to cope with "nervous interviews . . . with attorneys" over "perfectly incomprehensible documents" that make "one feel for all the world as if one were signing a death-warrant" but also by the long and futile process of attempting to resist domesticity that is recorded throughout the novel.

It is the genius of Dixon's early exercise in fiction writing to see the coils of respectability as neither more nor less fatal to women than the bohemian alternative offered by late-Victorian male aesthetes. In real life such leaders of new art movements as Walter Pater, George Moore, Henry James, Edmund Gosse, and Max Beerbohm were fixtures of Dixon's own social circle, thanks, in part, to her close acquaintance with Sir Claude Phillips, who became art critic for *The Daily Telegraph* and keeper of the Wallace Collection. But the unpleasant process of being subjected to the evaluative gaze of male artist figures had begun in the author's childhood, starting with visits to the Dixons' drawing room by the Pre-Raphaelites, who paved the way for the aesthetes; as Dixon records in *"As I Knew Them,"* "It was Sir John Everett Millais who, looking at my bright red hair, told me I should always wear a touch of orange."

Dixon's criticism was, therefore, that of a sympathetic observer upon and sometime participant in the movement to make the creation and enjoyment of beauty the only measure of success. In *My Flirtations* her own aesthetic leanings shaped, in particular, her horrified and rather snobbish denunciation of Philistines who inhabited "brand-new, red-brick mansion[s]" decorated by "paint[ing] . . . everything within reach with sprawling red roses or startling white daisies" and who entertained curates with "lemonade" and "shandy-gaff" at "the inevitable picnic" held "in a damp field, where there was an unmistakable odour of manure." Yet these bourgeois types pose no greater danger to the narrator than the many male aesthetes who populate the novel, men who are out to annex her to their collections of rare *objets* and artifacts or to reduce her to inspiration for their own projects.

First among these admirers, for whom the narrator exists principally as a picture to be studied and discussed, is Gilbert Mandell, a disciple of Walter Pater, Richard Wagner, and Edgar Degas: "He said I was 'suggestive'—whatever that meant—and that my mind was 'receptive.' . . . [He] had charming rooms in St. James's, where he gave frequent tea-

Dixon around the time she began to write

parties, which were sparsely attended by a handful of modish women, interlarded with thin, youngish-old men, who spent their lives criticising the critics." He is followed eventually by Julian Clancy, formerly in the diplomatic service and now "author of novels of modern society," who is "given to rave about the exquisite effects one saw in a London fog" and whose true passion is not the narrator but the parties that he throws in his house, which is "hung with old brocade, and as dainty as the boudoir of some eighteenth-century beauty." Later the narrator encounters a Continental variation on the type, Rene Levasseur, a "painter, one of new school of *vibristes.*" Before informing her quite incorrectly that she, like all women, entertains a "hopeless attachment" to him, he subjects her to modeling for one of his plein air fancies: "He did me in a scarlet gown, with a scarlet parasol, in full sunlight, against the blue Mediterranean, and I remember he painted my face in scarlet and purple zigzags. Even my worst enemy has never accused me of vanity, but I must say I was annoyed."

Most sinister among these aesthetes is Claud Carson, the poet—a composite figure owing much in his manners and affectations to an encounter that Dixon had with Richard Le Gallienne, who, according to *"As I Knew Them,"* wrote a poem during a country-house weekend and proclaimed her the subject of it. Carson's specialty is seducing women, or stopping just short of doing so, in order to turn them into material for new lyrics in his continuing series of verse called *Roses of Passion,* a volume posing as art-for-art's-sake that is really nothing more than a boastful and self-congratulatory record of his conquests. In the guise of a suitor he insinuates himself into the narrator's drawing room and threatens to dedicate to her his compromising erotic poems. But the narrator and her sister, Christina, out for a ride in their carriage, happen to catch sight of him in the shabby neighborhood where he keeps under wraps his working-class wife (or mistress) and their child. The Philistine-hating aesthete proves, in the end, an upholder of conventional double standards where gender is concerned, and aestheticism is revealed as a mere cover for exploiting women of all classes, whether as material or as providers of sexual or social diversion. In *My Flirtations* Dixon raises her voice in protest against the misogynist practices of the painters and writers who styled themselves the enemies of bourgeois sexual norms and the idolators of women.

In her stories composed during the latter half of the 1890s Dixon turned again and again to this concern about the victimization of women at the hands of the men who profess to adore them—regardless of whether the supposed worshipers are those of the respectable or of the artistic worlds. Ten of these stories were collected in 1904 for the volume *One Doubtful Hour and Other Side-lights on the Feminine Temperament,* published by Grant Richards, who was making a name for himself by bringing out the works of New Women, Socialists, Decadents, and other turn-of-the-century radicals. As in *My Flirtations,* many of the selections for *One Doubtful Hour* combine feminist arguments with comic techniques. Among the best of the satirical tales is "The Disenchantment of Diana," which ends happily with the escape of a young woman from the clutches of an "illustrious poet" many years her senior, who has composed a "sonnet-sequence about a certain 'Lily-maid with wide, calm eyes'" and then insisted on her marrying him.

As in the far more somber *The Story of a Modern Woman,* however, Dixon also composed some of her later sketches in a bleaker key. The most despairing is the title story, "One Doubtful Hour." Effie Lauder, who recognizes all too clearly "that it was humiliating for a woman past thirty not to have a penny of her own" but who has received only the commercially useless education of a lady, has been to India and back in search of a husband. Still unmarried on her return to Westsea, the town she left behind two years earlier, she pins her last hopes on the man with whom she flirted on the voyage home. Meanwhile, she attends a ball at the Westsea Assembly Rooms and, passed over for dances by men in search of younger partners, she sits alone, filled with disgust at the familiar futility of the scene she observes:

> How well she knew it all! How often she had been carried off triumphantly by some temporary admirer who had prosecuted a vague suit in those same passages, on the same meagre cane chairs! A young woman passed her, looking up with frankly inviting eyes at the middle-aged man on whose arm she hung a little.... It was the old, old tragi-comedy; the degrading, unceasing pursuit of the possible husband.

Onto this unhappy stage comes the man who had been so attentive on the boat from India:

> The woman, made desperate with disappointment, snatched at this straw of happiness like one who is drowning. With worn, cheap smiles and inviting eyes, she essayed to make herself desirable. She felt giddy and faint with hunger as they swung round in the waltz.... Already, with her quick feminine imagination, she saw him forming part of her favourite picture; he was reading the newspaper in a cosy, lamp-lit room, while she did fancy-work by the fire....

> She was wrapped in a sort of dream... Well, all her anxieties, her worries, her frustrated hopes, would soon be at an end. This night, indeed, was going to be the one night of her life.

But the man, who had been drawn to these feminine wiles on shipboard, where the presence of an eager woman was a welcome diversion, now views Effie with "repulsion" as having "the air of a lean and hungry huntress." Reading on his face the disgust that seals her doom, she flees from the ball to the shelter of her bedroom:

> She looked round the little room, with its damp-stained walls and shabby furniture, seeing a vista of drab years in which she would be only half alive. The little bed, too, in which she would wake up, morning after morning, year after year.... What if—what if—she went to sleep—and simply did not wake in the morning?

A year before the publication of Edith Wharton's *The House of Mirth,* Dixon's Effie Lauder anticipates the choice made by Wharton's protagonist and also aligns her fate with that of earlier New Woman heroines such as Grant Allen's Herminia Barton (*The Woman Who Did,* 1895) who flee the "littleness" of their gendered circumstances and prospects by dying. But "One Doubtful Hour" is unique among these in its pessimism, for the story concludes not with this suicide but with a birth in the lodgings upstairs from the room where Effie's body rests: "'Ask the doctor to be good enough to step up again for a moment,' urged a shrill feminine voice on the stair—a voice which added, as if in reply to some question, 'Yes, it's a girl—a very fine little girl.'" The cycle continues, and "the old tragicomedy" begins again with a new protagonist, predestined for the exploitative and degrading labor of husband-hunting and, presumably, for early death. Meanwhile, the individual woman, a mere substitutable cog in the great social mechanism, lies unmourned and all but forgotten amid the joyous commotion that greets her replacement.

Like Christina of *My Flirtations,* who responds with enthusiasm to many radical contemporary "isms," Dixon herself fell under the spell of French Naturalism not long after the writing of her first novel, and its hold on her literary imagination proved to be a lasting one. But the keenest expressions of her conversion to Naturalist doctrine appear in her second novel, *The Story of a Modern Woman,* which explicitly links its protest against the unjust limitations of women's roles within the social order to the more fundamental injustice of the Darwinian natural order. It did so, moreover, two years before the publication of Thomas Hardy's *Jude the Obscure* (1896), a novel that its author later claimed to have provided the first fictional portrait of the New Woman.

The narrative of *The Story of a Modern Woman* both begins and ends in Highgate Cemetery (the actual site of the grave of William Hepworth Dixon), where the protagonist's celebrated father is buried—a location that offers poignant contrasts between the cessation of individual consciousness and the untroubled continuation of the reproductive cycle. Even as Professor Erle is being eulogized at the novel's opening, the natural world signals its indifference to young Mary Erle's loss of her chief emotional and economic support:

> "Nature," continued the orator, in his measured, lecture-room tones, "Nature, who works in inexorable ways, has taken to herself a life full of arduous toil, of epoch-making achievement, of immeasurable possibilities, but to what end, and for what purpose, is not given to us, who stand to-day with full hearts and yearning eye around his last resting-place, to know."

> The sun was warm overhead, the scent of the pink may was strong in the nostrils; a joyous twittering in an adjacent bush told of mating birds, of new life in the nests, of Nature rioting in an insolent triumph.

Still more distressing, though, is the prospect this site affords simultaneously of England's urban center, which operates according to the competitive and ruthless principles of social Darwinism, the late-Victorian economic philosophy with which Dixon also demonstrates her acquaintance throughout the novel:

> Out yonder, at their feet, the dun-colour of the buildings lost in the murkiness of the horizon line, London was spread out. Here and there a dome, a spire loomed out of the dim bluish-grey panorama. A warm haze hung over the great city; here and there a faint fringe of tree-tops told of a placid park; now and again the shrill whistle of an engine, blown northward by the wind, spoke of the bustle of journeys, of the turmoil of railway-stations, of partings, of arrivals, of the change and travail of human life, of the strangers who come, of the failures who must go.

Confronting this spectacle, the protagonist makes a courageous but, as it will turn out, quite hopeless declaration to her adolescent brother:

> "Jim," said the girl suddenly, taking the boy by the arm, "there's London! We're going to make it listen to us, you and I. We're not going to be afraid of it—just because it's big, and brutal, and strong."

With no comfort to be found either in the retreat to a rhetorically feminized Nature or in the embrace of a rhetorically masculinized image of the city, Mary Erle must battle her way through the world. This effort Dixon announces through the almost comical understatement of one of the novel's chapter titles, "Mary Tries to Live Her Life," but the odds against such efforts succeeding are enormous. In her introduction to the 1990 edition of *The Story of a Modern Woman* Kate Flint speaks admiringly of Mary as a "survivor"; yet in the context of the novel's Darwinian atmosphere, where the ultimate measure of fitness as a survivor is one's ability to compete and to reproduce, Mary's childless and unmarried state at the end of the narrative predicts her rapid extinction from the records of human history.

Compounding the difficulties for Mary Erle, in a way not true for her brother, Jim, are the workings of gender roles within the late-Victorian social system. Women and men suffer within a hostile and mechanistic universe, but women of all classes suffer more, thanks to the oppressive social laws that men use to control them. For Dixon the intolerable situation of the middle-class woman in particular is summed up in the demand not merely for submission and compliance but for cheerfulness in the face of masculine tyranny and cruelty. Throughout the text a sense of outrage radiates, moving outward from the protagonist's consciousness into the omniscient narrator's commentary and finally to the reader's own response. The process is illustrated in a scene that describes the aftermath of an insulting announcement by Mary's fiancé of his wish not to see her often:

> It was almost as if he had struck her. There was a sort of ball in her throat. Her cheeks had got hot; there was colour enough in them now, and her hands shook as she poured out the tea which the maid-of-all-work had brought in. But she must not look as if she cared. A woman—especially in her own house—should always smile. It was on that acquiescent feminine smile that the whole fabric of civilization rested. And for the next half-hour, as Vincent Hemming discoursed of the unusual opportunities he had enjoyed in Calcutta, in Sydney, and in Ottawa of studying the different systems of government which obtained in various parts of the British Empire, Mary was a model hostess.

Is Mary a New Woman? was a question raised by contemporary reviewers, writing at a moment when fictional protagonists who espoused feminist positions were in the spotlight, thanks to creators such as Egerton and Sarah Grand. Many, however, agreed with the pronouncement of the critic for the *The Athenaeum* (16 June 1894) that Dixon's "heroine has little in common with the self-assertive, heartless, sexless thing whom various writers have recently brought into fashion." Certainly, the character is required by the text to articulate views no more controversial than her insistence that "'I can't, I won't, deliberately injure another woman.... All we modern women mean to help each other now.'" At the end of the novel she remains in emotional thrall to Vincent Hemming, the undeserving former fiancé who throws her over for a more lucrative marriage even after he attempts to persuade her to run away and live with him as his mistress. As the narrator says early in the narrative, "It is to be feared that Mary, with all her somewhat worldly training, was, as far as her affections were concerned, astonishingly naive. She was only a girl after all." And even at the novel's conclusion she appears to be only a "modern woman" rather than a "New" one, still more influenced and acted upon than she might be, seemingly incapable of analyzing the political dimensions of her personal experience, and disinclined to work with others to effect change. The final image of her is as a solitary figure poised above the "blurred" urban prospect of London's "great sea of dwellings," buffeted by the harshness of both the social and the natural worlds: "Henceforward she was to stand alone, to fight the dreary battle of life unaided." (This tableau prefigures, and perhaps inspires, the ambiguous image that concludes D. H. Lawrence's *Sons and Lovers* in 1913.) Mary Erle does not hear the confident sound of a call to become the voice of Womanhood that the character Mary Desmond hears under similar circumstances at the close of Egerton's *The Wheel of God* (1898).

Critics have debated whether *The Story of a Modern Woman,* with its apolitical protagonist, should be considered a New Woman novel. As outlined by Ann Ardis in *New Women, New Novels* (1990), one of the defining characteristics of New Woman writers is the explicitness with which they "challenged the naturalness of sex, gender, and class distinctions." On matters of class, in particular, Dixon's text proves contradictory at best and retrogressive at worst. The author's elitist sympathies color the representations of the middle and, especially, the lower middle classes in highly negative ways. Her greatest scorn is reserved for those members of the lower classes who show any desire to climb—who refuse to accept what Ardis would call the "naturalness" of their place. Such is the treatment of Violet Higgins, the nouveau-riche young woman from a provincial Northern family who becomes the bride of Mary's fiancé: "Mary gave one swift, comprehensive glance at . . . [her], taking in her under-bred face, with its beady eyes and fretful mouth, her over-trimmed clothes and her uneasy attitude." So, too, the female students—"young women of the lower middle class; daughters of retail shopkeepers . . . [with] hair [that] left, like their speech, something to be desired"—who study drawing alongside Mary at the "Central London School of Art" must be held at a social distance from the better-born and more morally correct protagonist: "[Mary] dreaded the confidences of the young ladies, some of whom had prosperous flirtations, carried on in neighbouring pastry-cooks shops." That the reader is expected to share in this snobbish perspective becomes painfully clear from the narrator's description of the difference between the satirically presented Miss Simpkins, a "strapping young woman with a large vague face, which somehow suggested a muffin . . . who carried a small edition of [John Ruskin's] *Modern Painters* about in a leather hand-bag, together with . . . some ham sandwiches," and the idealized protagonist: "Mary Erle, with her neat hair and her well made black dress, looked like a little princess as she sat . . . among the outer ring of easels." Notions of female solidarity, it seems, cannot overcome what the text presents as the inherent superiority in both conduct and appearance of women of Mary's class.

Similarly, the meteoric ascent of the painter Perry Jackson represents, on the one hand, the triumph of Darwinian principles of adaptation and appropriation as he rises from origins in "an upholsterer's shop in the Hampstead Road" to take over the magnificent Kensington house and studio of an artist whose career has faltered—a house that he lays at Mary's feet when he proposes to her. But no success can disguise what Dixon shows to be the immutable and ineradicable "look of a grown-up London street-boy" that reveals him as unworthy of the new place he inhabits as well as unworthy of aspiring to Mary's hand. At the moment when he makes his hopeless romantic appeal, Mary remains acutely conscious of his recurring "difficulty with his aspirates" and of the impossibility of taking seriously an offer of marriage from "a little man with a shock head . . . whose parents, moreover, sold cheap dining-room suites." Such assumptions about the permanence of class markings, as impressed from birth on the characters' speech and bodies, are never examined critically but are always endorsed by the novel.

The sole members of a class beneath Mary's to receive any sympathy are women at the very bottom of the social order, too far "fallen," in all senses of the word, to pose any threat of advance-

Binding for Dixon's first novel

ment within the London hierarchy. Even they, however, are confined to the margins of the narrative, appearing mainly as the occasional subjects of conversation between the protagonist and her closest friend, the aristocratic Alison Ives (a character that may have been inspired by one of Dixon's older sisters, Edith, who died at the age of twenty-two). Evelina, for example, is an unmarried mother whom Alison employs as a servant with the intention of rescuing her: "'She isn't much more than a child, you know, and she has such a good heart,'" Alison explains patronizingly. "'I think she likes to talk to me: she tells me her little story.'" Only in the case of a nameless figure, identified by the number of the hospital bed that she occupies in the consumptive ward of a charity hospital, does this comfortably distant relationship between women of privilege and those whom they rescue turn into something closer and more serious. Alison learns that the "gentleman" responsible for the ruin of "Number Twenty-Seven" is the doctor now courting Alison herself, and she contracts a fever that leads rapidly to her death. As she dies, she passes on to Mary her philosophy of mutual aid among women:

> "Promise me that you will never, never do anything to hurt another woman.... I don't suppose for an instant you ever would. But there come times in our lives when we can do a great deal of good, or an incalculable amount of harm. If women only used their power in the right way! If we were only united we could lead the world."

Hers is, however, a philosophy notable for the absence of any challenge to the "naturalness" of "sex, gender, and class distinctions." What it promotes, instead of such radicalism, is an unthreatening insistence upon individual female self-restraint over self-indulgence and a most traditional Victorian emphasis on the importance of nurturing as the middle-class woman's true power. It is clear, moreover, that the vision of a united female population achieving strength is still a class-based one in which only women such as herself and Mary, who have the economic luxury of abjuring self-interested choices, will be prepared to lead the world.

Also missing from Alison Ives's version of feminist doctrine is the critique of masculine social and political practices that had characterized New Woman arguments and antagonized male reviewers of New Woman novels. Yet such a critique is present in *The Story of a Modern Woman* after all. It makes itself felt not in the rhetoric employed by either of the two major female figures, who remain merely "modern" women to the end, but in the third-person narrative. Dixon uses her text to produce a New Woman reader—a reader who is more radical than her protagonists and who sees more clearly than they the systematic injustices, as well as the casual selfishness, of the men whom Mary and Alison continue to idealize and to mourn.

Often Dixon accomplishes this radicalization merely by withholding explicit judgments and inviting the reader to supply them or by narrating scenes beyond the point where her protagonist is present. In the climactic chapter called "The Temptation," for instance, Mary's former suitor, now unhappily joined to his "under-bred" but rich wife, attempts to persuade his old love to elope with him. Throughout his speech the reader grows increasingly incensed at the tone of his appeal, which combines condescension and egotism in equal measure. "'Mary,'" he begins in addressing this woman of thirty-three, "'my little girl!'":

> "Come to me, let us begin a new life, a *real* life, dear. You are above the prejudices of our false civilisation, you are capable of being a true woman, of giving up something for the man you love.... We would work together. You would inspire me to noble things.... Other women—great women—have been strong enough, single-hearted enough, to do as much for the men they loved."

After rejecting him in order to do no injury to his wife and daughter, Mary does not congratulate herself on a lucky escape but instead suffers the hellish torments of longing, doubt, and regret:

> The woman within her cried aloud in the darkness. What had she done that she was always to be sacrificed? Why was she to miss the best that life has to offer?
>
> She lay there a long time, miserable, stricken, helpless.

In this dark night of the soul she even contemplates killing herself, although she overcomes the impulse.

Unknown to Mary, however, her former lover, Vincent Hemming, has had a rather different sort of evening. Dixon permits the reader to follow him out Mary's door and into the London streets, where his resolve to end his unsatisfactory marriage by fleeing to France gradually dissipates in the face of concerns about propriety, as well as other, more material distractions:

> It was too late now to catch the evening mail, for he had no clothes, and he thought, with a grim smile, that a man couldn't cross the Channel, even if he had been defrauded of his dearest hopes, in a frock coat and a tall hat.... He thought he would go to a restaurant and have some dinner....
> And afterwards he had an indistinct impression of a meal at which, in his wretchedness, he went on ordering pints of champagne, of the corridor of a music-hall, of rustling gowns, of scarlet smiles, and of some one, very young and rather pretty, who leant upon his arm. It must have been a kind of dream, a sort of madness, he thought afterwards, when he had returned, a day or two later, to the decorous solemnity of his home in Queen's Gate.

Dixon allows that casual phrase, "a day or two later"—a brilliantly damning detail—to speak for itself. The reader sees, though Mary does not, just how quickly this devoted lover has exercised his privilege as a man and moreover as an amoral, Darwinian creature to replace one woman with a younger, fitter substitute. While Mary expresses the anguish of loss throughout the subsequent scene, the reader experiences a different set of reflections and emotions, including outrage and anger at the injustice of a gender system that leaves unpunished, even encourages, such moral negligence on the part of "gentlemen."

To the end of the novel Mary remains in an unfortunate political limbo as a modern woman who is awakened just enough to recognize "'the torture of women's lives—the helplessness, the impotence, the emptiness!'" She is unable, however, to fix the blame or to seek the remedy. Through her story Dixon brings the audience to a point of greater understanding from which direct action in the social community beyond the text becomes possible. Armed with the recognition that the exploitation of women by men is the central fact on which "the whole fabric of civilization rested," the audience can begin to dismantle that foundation. Thus, a reader of the 1890s who may have entered this text as a troubled modern woman in search of a story about social relations that would mirror her own would have left it a New Woman, ready to create a world in which a different and better sort of narrative about gender could be written.

With the waning of popular interest in New Woman novels after the start of the next century Dixon turned away from fiction that promoted these feminist causes so dear to her heart. In the last three decades of her life she became more and more a working journalist. A professional pen-for-hire, she supplied everything from art and book reviews for newspapers to pro-British propaganda for the Ministry of Information during World War I. Her creative energies expended themselves largely in occasional play writing. In *"As I Knew Them"* she speaks of an unfinished theatrical piece on which she collaborated with her friend H. G. Wells some time around 1905. In 1908 her one-act play *The Toyshop of the Heart* enjoyed a single performance at a charity matinee. In *The Saturday Review* her longtime acquaintance Max Beerbohm described its comical portrait of an "adventuress" in pursuit of a young man of good family as "very amusingly drawn." But the piece seems not to have been revived, and no record of further efforts for the theater exists.

Ella Hepworth Dixon's importance, then, rests primarily on her two novels of the 1890s. With characteristic modesty she used the occasion of her published memoirs in 1930 to disclaim her significance as a creator of fiction and portrayed herself instead as a humble denizen of the world of newspaper and magazine offices whose main distinction was her wide network of social acquaintance among late-Victorian and Edwardian artists, writers, and politicians. She was, nevertheless, a pioneer in the representation of middle-class and upper-middle-class women's lives under patriarchy, a subject to which she brought all the resources of a talent both for pathos and for comedy. Though *The Story of a Modern Woman* alone among her works is available in print—and that in an edition for sale only in Great Britain—Dixon has much to offer a late-twentieth-century audience. For those women readers, in particular, who are still struggling to replace the "acquiescent feminine smile" demanded by culture with a sly feminist grin, she remains a model and a guide.

References:

Ann L. Ardis, *New Women, New Novels: Feminism and Early Modernism* (New Brunswick, N.J. & London: Rutgers University Press, 1990), pp. 101, 106–113, 117, 133–134, 160–161, 166, 170–171, 175;

Max Beerbohm, "A Comedy of the Suburbs," in his *Last Theatres. 1904–1910* (London: Hart-Davis, 1970), pp. 410–412;

"The Feeble Fib," *Englishwoman,* 13 (March 1896): 9–17;

Kate Flint, *The Woman Reader, 1837–1914* (Oxford: Clarendon Press, 1993), pp. 201–202, 309–310, 315;

Margaret Diane Stetz, "New Grub Street and the Woman Writer of the 1890s," in *Transforming Genres: New Approaches to British Fiction of the 1890s,* edited by Nikki Lee Manos and Meri-Jane Rochelson (New York: St. Martin's Press, 1994), pp. 21–45;

Stetz, "Turning Points: Ella Hepworth Dixon," *Turn-of-the-Century Women,* 2 (Winter 1984), 2–11;

H. D. Traill, "The World of Letters," *Graphic,* 327 (4 May 1895): 531.

W. L. George
(20 March 1882 – 30 January 1926)

Kenneth Womack
Pennsylvania State University at Altoona

BOOKS: *Engines of Social Progress* (London: A. & C. Black, 1907);

France in the Twentieth Century (London: Rivers, 1908; New York: Lane, 1909);

Labour and Housing at Port Sunlight (London: Rivers, 1909);

A Bed of Roses (London: Palmer, 1911; New York: Brentano, 1911);

The City of Light: A Novel of Modern Paris (London: Constable, 1912; New York: Brentano, 1912);

Israel Kalisch (London: Constable, 1913); republished as *Until the Daybreak* (New York: Dodd, Mead, 1913);

Woman and To-morrow (London: Jenkins, 1913; New York: Appleton, 1913);

Dramatic Actualities (London: Sidgwick & Jackson, 1914);

The Making of an Englishman (London: Constable, 1914; New York: Dodd, Mead, 1914); republished as *The Little Beloved* (Boston: Little, Brown, 1916);

The Second Blooming (London: Unwin, 1914; Boston: Little, Brown, 1915);

Anatole France (London: Nisbet, 1915; New York: Holt, 1915);

Olga Nazimov, and Other Stories, by George and Helen George (London: Mills & Boon, 1915);

The Intelligence of Woman (Boston: Little, Brown, 1916; London: Jenkins, 1917);

The Strangers' Wedding: The Comedy of a Romantic (London: Unwin, 1916; Boston: Little, Brown, 1916);

A Novelist on Novels (London: Collins, 1918); republished as *Literary Chapters* (Boston: Little, Brown, 1918);

Blind Alley (London: Unwin, 1919; Boston: Little, Brown, 1919);

Eddies of the Day (London & New York: Cassell, 1919);

Caliban (London: Methuen, 1920; New York: Harper, 1920);

W. L. George

The Confessions of Ursula Trent (London: Chapman & Hall, 1921); republished as *Ursula Trent* (New York: Harper, 1921);

Hail Columbia! Random Impressions of a Conservative English Radical (New York & London: Putnam, 1921); republished as *Hail Columbia!* (London: Chapman & Hall, 1923);

A London Mosaic, with pictures by Philippe Forbes-Robertson (London: Collins, 1921; New York: Stokes, 1921);

Her Unwelcome Husband (New York: Harper, 1922);

The Stiff Lip (London: Chapman & Hall, 1922); republished as *One of the Guilty* (London: Chapman & Hall, 1923; New York: Harper, 1923);

The Triumph of Gallio (London: Chapman & Hall, 1924; New York: Harper, 1924);

How to Invest Your Money (London: A. & C. Black, 1924);

The Story of Woman (London: Chapman & Hall, 1925; New York: Harper, 1925);

Children of the Morning (London: Chapman & Hall, 1926; New York & London: Putnam, 1927);

Gifts of Sheba (London: Chapman & Hall, 1926; New York: Putnam, 1926);

Historic Lovers (London: Hutchinson, 1926);

The Ordeal of Monica Mary (London: Hutchinson, 1927);

The Selected Short Stories (London: Chapman & Hall, 1927).

OTHER: *The Gilt on the Gingerbread: A Human Document,* foreword by George (London: Williams & Norgate, 1925);

Edgar Saltus, *Purple and Fine Women,* introduction by George (Chicago: Pascal Covici, 1925);

Guido Bruno, ed., *Frank Harris: In Memoriam; Fragments from His New York Days,* by George, Walter Kingsley, George Bernard Shaw, and Frank Harris (New York: Privately printed, 1933).

Despite his death at forty-three, W. L. George completed twenty-eight books—novels, short-story collections, and volumes of nonfiction—during his short literary career, with four more published posthumously. His concern for the place and treatment of women is evident throughout much of his prodigious fictional and nonfictional output. During his lifetime George's novels won him a sizable readership, particularly in America, which he toured in 1920 to great acclaim. In addition to his commercial success George enjoyed a favorable response from critics, owing largely to his overt and enduring interest in examining the "Woman Question" that defined the sexual and social politics of much of the late-Victorian and Edwardian period. For this reason the critics of George's day often numbered him among the ranks of such socially progressive writers as George Bernard Shaw and George Gissing. In his later work George was, however, unable to fulfill the promise of his important first novel, *A Bed of Roses* (1911), and he produced only a handful of volumes during the balance of his lifetime that merit critical attention today. Nevertheless, the expansive and thoroughly modern social and political arguments embedded in George's works offer a true measure both of his historical value and of his contributions to the literature of his era.

Born in Paris on 20 March 1882, Walter Lionel George lived with his British parents in France until 1905, when he traveled to England for the first time, having only learned English three years previously. Before leaving France he studied chemistry, engineering, and law and served in the French army. During his early years in England he worked in an office, later embarking on a successful career as a journalist and publishing three social and economic nonfiction works: *Engines of Social Progress* (1907), *France in the Twentieth Century* (1908), and *Labour and Housing at Port Sunlight* (1909). In 1908 he married Helen Porter, and by 1911 he had worked as a special correspondent for several London newspapers, traveling for them to France, Belgium, and Spain. The commercial success of *A Bed of Roses* allowed him to retire from journalism and devote all of his energies to his creative work.

Throughout his life George remained committed to Marxism; during the British railway strike of 1919 he advocated implementing a communist political structure to resolve the strike. In *A Novelist on Novels* (1918) he offers a glimpse of the socialist ideology that frequently drives his narratives and reveals his intention to use his fiction as a means for promoting and reinvigorating the social discourse of his era. George argues that "if literature be at all a living force it must evolve as much as man, and more if it is to lead him; it must establish a correspondence between itself and the uneasy souls for which it exists.... While the older novelists were static, we have to be kinetic." George remained convinced that only the arts—"the future of genius"—possessed the power to create real social change: "They will not vanish, for mankind needs always to express itself, its aspiration, its content, its discontent; those three can be expressed only in the arts."

George's political ideology is most evident in his first novel. By having his female protagonist confront the overarching social and political constraints that govern her life, in *A Bed of Roses* he at once challenges and dismisses the repressive treatment of women in the novels of the Victorian era. In his novels, particularly in *A Bed of Roses,* he offers a portrait of the New Woman of the early twentieth century, at the same time attacking the myths of femininity propagated by Victorian literature and creating a fictive world in which women make significant life decisions and live deliberately in the face of their troubled economic and social positions. George's narratives extol the promise of the new century as a radically evolving

Title page for the U.S. edition of a portrait of a New Woman of the early twentieth century

world free of the sexual politics that had controlled and constructed women's lives.

As *A Bed of Roses* begins, Victoria Fulton returns to England from India following the death of her alcoholic husband, prepared for the freedom and possibilities that life in London appears to offer: "A pleasurable feeling of excitement ran through Victoria's body, for she was going to discover London, to have adventures." But a persistent loneliness marks Victoria's life in England. Whether dining alone in restaurants, working as a waitress, or making her first naive attempts at forging romantic relationships, she remains troubled by an oppressive lack of choices. After nearly six months in London she collapses in frustration. Unskilled and socially alienated, Victoria exclaims to her brother, Edward: "I've tried everything I could think of, agencies, societies, papers, everything. I can't get a post. I must do something. I've got to take what I can get. I know it now; we women are just raw material. The world uses as much of us as it needs and throws the rest on the scrap heap." After suffering through traumatic experiences in her search for financial security and personal fulfillment she succumbs to the advice of her friend Anthony Farwell and becomes a prostitute: "You are a woman," he tells her, "your body is your fortune, your only fortune, so translate it into gold.... Let your touch be soft as velvet, your grip as hard as steel. Shrink from nothing, rise to treachery, let the worldly nadir be your zenith."

In her 1989 dissertation, "Female Emancipation at the Turn of the Century," Patricia Ann Moore notes that in *A Bed of Roses* "George deals with prostitution, not as a crime committed by women against society, but as a means of survival when all other struggles for life have been exhausted." George makes explicit his argument equating prostitution with other forms of female enslavement through his depiction of Victoria's friendship with Betty, a frail working-class woman who longs for a husband. Betty believes that marriage offers the only means of escaping poverty and despair, a concept that perplexes Victoria. "You seem to think marriage is the only way out for women," Victoria tells Betty. "Well, isn't it?" Betty replies. "What else is there?" Victoria later argues that marriage and prostitution share essentially the same social and economic constructs: "So long as a woman is economically dependent on a man she's a slave, a plaything. Legally or illegally joined it's exactly the same thing." Victoria views marriage as a "monetary contract," the larger symbol of a "society of men, crushing, grinding down women, sweating their labour, starving their brains, urging them on to the surrender of what makes a woman worth while."

Victoria discovers personal freedom only when she has fully embraced her new economic role in the "society of men." When Farwell wonders whether Victoria suffers unnecessarily in her quest to gain her independence, she replies: "I can't pay too high a price for what I think I'll get. I don't mean these jewels or these clothes, that's only my professional uniform. When I've served my time I shall get that for which no woman can pay too much: I shall be economically independent, free." As the novel comes to a close, Victoria realizes her dream of financial and personal independence. Leaving London, she rents a country house and assumes her new place within the more prosperous and affluent ranks of society—a social standing that, as both a widow and an unskilled laborer, she would surely not have attained through more "honest" vocations. Through her earnings as a prostitute Victoria purchases the trappings of social respectability, and, as George demonstrates in the novel's conclusion, society now recognizes and values her.

The London publisher Alston Rivers appeared ready to bring out the novel in 1910. As George remembered in *A Novelist on Novels,* however, "some horrid internal convulsion must have suddenly occurred in the firm; they must have lost their nerve; or perhaps my corrupting influence was gradual and progressive; at any rate, they suddenly sent the book to their legal advisor, who wired back that it would almost certainly be prosecuted." After sending the novel to a succession of publishers George finally placed it with Frank Palmer, who published it after George edited some seventy pages from the manuscript. Despite George's removal of those passages, which were, as he put it later, "so true to life that I realised they must cause offence," several British and American libraries banned the novel because of its frank treatment of prostitution.

The subject matter of *A Bed of Roses,* as well as a series of rave critical reviews, probably account for the commercial success of the work. The 30 March 1911 issue of the *Times Literary Supplement,* for example, praised *A Bed of Roses* as "a novel of undeniable insight and considerable literary skill by a writer who is interested in social problems" but went on to caution that it "is certainly not for readers whose experience of the baser side of life in London is small." The review concluded that *A Bed of Roses* offered a depiction of a female protagonist "welcoming without a pang a course of life (described in very definite outline and colour) which provides at the cost of her character relief from poverty and a growing provision against future want." The novelist and critic Sheila Kaye-Smith praised the novel, citing George as "a specialist on Woman, and especially on Woman as opposed to morals." Kaye-Smith also noted that George's principal value as an artist committed to social change stemmed from his interest in "Woman chiefly because she is part of Society, and under modern changes and complications in many ways the most interesting and difficult part."

George's next novel, *The City of Light: A Novel of Modern Paris* (1912), enjoyed a level of commercial success similar to that of his first. George's readers clearly longed, however, for the sensational qualities that had propelled *A Bed of Roses* into the public consciousness. According to Kaye-Smith, "The public was pleased, and there is no doubt that from a literary point of view *The City of Light* is infinitely superior to *A Bed of Roses.* But it did not contain the same provoking qualities, and Mr. George's name was still linked with the former in the public mind."

While *The City of Light* lacks the provocative sociological qualities of George's first novel, it features a deep and moving character study of a protagonist confronted with his mixed heritage, a subject that closely parallels George's own experience as the son of British citizens who was raised as a Frenchman. Henri Duvernoy comes of age in France, troubled by the conflicting social views of his affluent parents, particularly his mother, who are obsessed with what they perceive as Henri's immaturity and his inability to manage the considerable income that he stands to inherit. Henri him-

Title page for a novel about a young man's struggle to break free from his mother's domination

Title page for a novel about a bored wife's extramarital affair

self is worried about his youthful inexperience: "Like most young Frenchmen of his age he had little to learn of sex and everything to learn of love; his adventures, when he recalled them at all, were unworthy of the name, so brutish and material were they.... For a Frenchman he was backward, as shyness and vague fears had forbidden him to do more than glance from the corners of his eyes at the beauties who languish in open cabs in the minor alleys of the Bois de Boulogne."

Henri's life changes forever when he encounters the beautiful Suzanne. She awakens his latent sense of self, and their relationship creates a rift between him and his parents because of Suzanne's lower-class status. Convinced that Suzanne only intends to marry her son for his money, Henri's mother continually blocks the couple's plans to marry. As the novel comes to a close, nearly three years after he proposed to Suzanne, Henri finally confronts his mother and seizes the remaining threads of his wounded, troubled self. Once free of his mother's seemingly inexorable bonds, Henri discovers the social gospel that drives much of George's fiction: "Fighting's the only duty: fighting against oppression and fighting against wrong."

In his third novel, *Israel Kalisch* (1913), set in Poland, George offers a portrait of the international political scene. The relatively poor sales of the novel forced George to recognize the public's interest in the provocative qualities of his first novel, qualities that *Israel Kalisch* lacked. That same year he published a nonfiction work, *Woman and To-morrow,* which examines feminist issues, and the following year saw the publication of *Dramatic Actualities* (1914), a critical literary study.

Although much of George's literary reputation rests on *A Bed of Roses,* his two 1914 novels, *The Making of an Englishman* and *The Second Blooming,* are perhaps the most fully realized of his fictional efforts, both in their development of character and in their treatment of social issues. In *The Making of an Englishman,* the most autobiographical of his novels, a Frenchman, Lucien Cadoresse, migrates to England, where he attempts to adapt himself to British life and culture. Much of the novel's narrative focuses on the relationship between Lucien—a self-portrait—and his landlady's daughters, Maud and Edith, who represent contrasting English female types. Maud, the eldest, flirts with Lucien, although she ultimately refuses his advances unless he proposes to her. His relationship with Edith evolves naturally as the two become acquainted intellectually. The novel culminates in Lucien's marriage to Edith and his application for British citizenship—the final, symbolic proof of his acceptance of the English way of life. More significantly, the work offers a portrait of a man who travels to London to seek his fortune and in the process arrives at a deeper understanding of the female intellect. As the novel concludes, Lucien gazes at Edith and realizes the change that has taken place in his attitude toward women: "the blue eyes that held mine were the same, filled with wonder, some fear, some delight perhaps, as I had so often seen them, and, dark in the pallor of her face, they suddenly reassured me, told me that here was the everlasting woman before me that defied the impermanence of the flesh."

In *The Second Blooming* George raises the controversial topic of extramarital relationships. Grace Kinnersley is the wife of Edward Kinnersley, a successful barrister. After some years in an uneventful marriage—and after the initial fervor of their romance passes—Grace chooses to engage in an affair, the "second blooming" of the title. George contrasts Grace with her sisters Mary and Clara: the former is a happily married mother and emblem of contentment, the latter a New Woman suffragist and progressive feminist. Grace's affair initially reinvigorates her, and she continues to evolve intellectually even when the romance fades:

> She was filled with a splendid realization that it had all been so fine.... She had loved and she had piled up memories which would inflame her life, irradiate the future. It was as if she had turned her back upon a light so brilliant that still it shone upon her and still lighted her path as she plodded on away from it.

After the publication of *The Second Blooming*, Kaye-Smith says, George's "fate was sealed," for he had finally returned to the controversial themes that his audience wanted. He felt compelled to mine the same narrative vein for the balance of his career: "Editors demanded from him articles on feminist subjects, on the war as it affected women, and, later, on every problem connected with women.... He made efforts to escape but his jailers were inexorable—he *should* write about women, and if by any chance he did not his work should be judged a failure."

During World War I, George worked in the Ministry of Munitions, although he continued to write and publish. His wife died in 1914 after a lengthy illness. The following year George published a well-received collection of short stories, *Olga Nazimov, and Other Stories* (1915), some of which he had cowritten with his wife. He also published a biographical study, *Anatole France* (1915), and perhaps his most significant nonfiction work, *The Intelligence of Woman* (1916).

In *The Intelligence of Woman* George examines the nature of the feminine intellect and the paradox of the improved social status of the New Woman: "while man accords woman an improved social position, he continues to describe her as illogical, petty, jealous, vain, untruthful, disloyal to her own sex; quite as frequently he charges her with being over-loyal to her own sex; there is no pleasing him." In addition to attempting to redefine the place of women in an evolving society, George predicts that the nuclear family will eventually disintegrate in favor of a more progressive, enlightened brand of association: "we can have no more slave daughters and slave wives, nor shall we chain together people who spy out one another's loves and crush one another's youth.... There is a time to come ... when the family, humanized, will be human."

In 1916 George married Helen Agnes Madden, with whom he would have two sons. His career proceeded with the publication of *The Strangers' Wedding: The Comedy of a Romantic* (1916) and *Blind Alley* (1919). In *Eddies of the Day* (1919) and *Caliban* (1920) he departed the feminist themes that had brought him fame, opting to work in the journalistic mode that marked his first publishing efforts. In 1920 he embarked on an extensive lecture tour of the United States. During his trek across the country he enjoyed the praise of many American literary critics—among them Donald Lawder, who hailed the author as one of the emerging forces of British literary realism—while devoting much of his energy to examining the sociological nuances of American life, from the conditions of New York City jails to the squalor of the cattle yards and meat-packing houses of Chicago. George's visit to America ended tragically with the sudden death of his second wife during their visit to Houston, Texas.

George's next novel, *The Confessions of Ursula Trent*, appeared in 1921, and that same year he married Kathleen Geipel, a novelist. In *The Confessions of Ursula Trent* George again endeavors to analyze the female temperament, although in this instance he writes the novel from the vantage point of the narrative's female protagonist. As Kaye-Smith remarks, "George invariably writes better as a man sympathetically observing women than, as it were, from inside a woman's skin." While the novel succeeds in its illustrations of women as slaves of a larger social machine, it fails in the paucity of its characterization—an ineffectual quality that lingers throughout much of George's later fictional efforts. Indeed, by the early 1920s his novels appeared to be mere attempts at replicating the more original and significant sociological arguments of *A Bed of Roses* and *The Second Blooming*, illustrating Kaye-Smith's observation that his later work "represents his maximum surrender to the popular demand."

In 1921 George published two journalistic efforts, *Hail Columbia! Random Impressions of a Conservative English Radical*, a study commemorating his tour of America, and *A London Mosaic*, on the architecture and social geography of London. In the early 1920s he published three more novels, *Her Unwelcome Husband* (1922), *The Stiff Lip* (1922), and *The Triumph of Gallio* (1924). Each received generally poor notices—particularly *The Triumph of Gallio*, a novel that George intended as a sort of self-portrait of a stoic and realist. Many critics criticized it as an arrogant display of self-absorption. Their derisive response left George embittered. His next volume, *How to Invest Your Money* (1924), is a straightforward book of financial advice. In 1925 he published *The Story of Woman*, a journalistic study in which he attempts to put into historical perspective the role of the New Woman in post-Victorian culture.

In 1925 George fell victim to a creeping paralysis of the central nervous system, which gradually rendered him unable to move and, in his final days, to speak. With the aid of his wife and private secretary he completed work on his novel *Gifts of Sheba* (1926). Four more works were to be published posthumously: a collection of short biographical sketches, *Historic Lovers* (1926), and the novels *Children of the Morning* (1926), *The Ordeal of Monica Mary* (1927), and *The Selected Short Stories* (1927). George succumbed to his illness on 30 January 1926.

W. L. George's novels and sociological studies represent his determined effort to represent the evolution of the New Woman and promote social change. Although his attempts to satisfy the desires of his audience may have contributed to the blurring of his remarkable social vision in his later, ineffectual efforts, the bold and controversial narratives of his best novels—particularly *A Bed of Roses*, *The Making of an Englishman*, and *The Second Blooming*—constitute important contributions to the literature of his day.

References:

Frank Harris, "W. L. George," in his *Contemporary Portraits (Third Series)* (New York: Harris, 1920), pp. 143–147;

C. Lewis Hind, "W. L. George," in his *More Authors and I* (New York: Dodd, Mead, 1922), pp. 118–123;

Sheila Kaye-Smith, "W. L. George," *Fortnightly Review*, 712 (1 April 1926): 521–527;

Donald Lawder, "W. L. George on American Literature," *Bookman*, 52 (November 1920): 193–197;

Patricia Ann Moore, "Female Emancipation at the Turn of the Century," dissertation, University of Denver, 1989;

Roderick Random, "A London Letter," *Saturday Review of Literature* (U.S.) (13 March 1926): 633;

Frank Swinnerton, "W. L. George," in his *A London Bookman* (London: Secker, 1928), pp. 46–47.

Douglas Goldring
(7 January 1887 – 9 April 1960)

Paul W. Salmon
University of Guelph

BOOKS: *A Country Boy and Other Poems* (London: Adelphi, 1910);

Ways of Escape: A Book of Adventure, (London: Melrose, 1911; New York: Duffield, 1912);

Streets: A Book of London Verses (London: M. Goschen, 1912); republished as *Streets, and Other Verses* (London: Selwyn & Blount, 1920; New York: Seltzer, 1921);

The Permanent Uncle (London: Constable, 1912; New York: Dutton, 1912);

Dream Cities: Notes of an Autumn Tour in Italy and Dalmatia (London & Leipzig: Unwin, 1913);

The Loire: The Record of a Pilgrimage from Gerbier de Joncs to St. Nazaire (London: Constable, 1913); republished as *Along France's River of Romance, the Loire; The Chateau Country—Its Personality, Its Architecture, Its People and Its Associations* (New York: McBride, Nast, 1913);

The Adventuress and Other Stories (London: M. Goschen, 1913);

It's an Ill Wind (London: Allen & Unwin, 1915);

In the Town: A Book of London Verses (London: Selwyn & Blount, 1916);

On the Road: A Book of Travel Songs (London: Selwyn & Blount, 1916);

Margot's Progress (London: Nash, 1916; New York: Seltzer, 1920);

The Fortune: A Romance of Friendship (Dublin & London: Maunsel, 1917; New York: Scott & Seltzer, 1917; enlarged and revised edition, London: Harmsworth, 1931);

Polly (London: Nash, 1917);

Dublin: Explorations and Reflections, as "An Englishman" (Dublin & London: Maunsel, 1917);

A Stranger in Ireland, "An Englishman, author of 'Dublin: Explorations and Reflections'" (Dublin: Talbot Press / London: Unwin, 1918);

The Fight for Freedom: A Play in Four Acts (London: Daniel, 1919);

Nooks and Corners of Sussex and Hampshire (London: Nash, 1920);

The Black Curtain (London: Chapman & Hall, 1920);

Douglas Goldring in 1929 (photograph by Phillips)

The Solvent, by Goldring and Hubert Nepean (London: Daniel, 1920);

Reputations: Essays in Criticism (London: Chapman & Hall, 1920; New York: Seltzer, 1920);

James Elroy Flecker: An Appreciation, with Some Biographical Notes (London: Chapman & Hall, 1922; New York: Seltzer, 1923);

Nobody Knows (London: Chapman & Hall, 1923; Boston: Small, Maynard, 1923);

Miss Linn (London: Chapman & Hall, 1924);

Gone Abroad: A Story of Travel, Chiefly in Italy and the Balearic Isles (London: Chapman & Hall, 1925; Boston & New York: Houghton Mifflin, 1925);

Cuckoo: A Comedy of Adjustments (London: Chapman & Hall, 1925; New York: McBride, 1926);

Northern Lights and Southern Shade (London: Chapman & Hall, 1926; Boston: Houghton Mifflin, 1926);

The Merchant of Souls (London: Jarrolds, 1926);

The Façade (London: Jarrolds, 1927; New York: McBride, 1928);

The French Riviera and the Valley of the Rhône from Avignon to Marseilles (London: Harrap, 1928; New York: Farrar & Rinehart, 1932);

People and Places (Boston & New York: Houghton Mifflin, 1929)—comprises chapters from *Gone Abroad* and *Northern Lights and Southern Shade*;

Sardinia: The Island of the Nuraghi (London: Harrap, 1930; New York: Morrow, 1931);

Impacts: The Trip to the States and Other Adventures of Travel (London: Eyre & Spottiswoode, 1931);

The Coast of Illusion (London: John Lane, 1932);

Pacifists in Peace and War (London: Wishart, 1932);

Liberty and Licensing (London: Harmsworth, 1932);

To Portugal (London: Rich & Cowan, 1934);

Royal London, edited by F. A. Mercer (London: The Studio / New York: Studio Publications, 1935);

Odd Man Out: The Autobiography of a "Propaganda Novelist" (London: Chapman & Hall, 1935);

Pot Luck in England (London: Chapman & Hall, 1936);

A Tour in Northumbria (London: Allen & Unwin, 1938);

Facing The Odds (London: Cassell, 1940);

South Lodge: Reminiscences of Violet Hunt, Ford Madox Ford and the English Review Circle (London: Constable, 1943; Folcroft, Pa.: Folcroft Library Editions, 1977);

The Nineteen Twenties: A General Survey and Some Personal Memories (London: Nicholson & Watson, 1945; Folcroft, Pa.: Folcroft Library Editions, 1975);

Journeys in the Sun: Memories of Happy Days in France, Italy and the Balearic Islands (London: Macdonald, 1946);

Marching With the Times, 1931–1946 (London & Brussels: Nicholson & Watson, 1947);

The Last Pre-Raphaelite: A Record of the Life and Writings of Ford Madox Ford (London: Macdonald, 1948); republished as *Trained For Genius: The Life and Writings of Ford Madox Ford* (New York: Dutton, 1949);

Life Interests (London: Macdonald, 1948);

Home Ground: A Journey Through the Heart of England (London: Macdonald, 1949);

Foreign Parts: An Autumn Tour in France (London: Macdonald, 1950);

Regency Portrait Painter: The Life of Sir Thomas Lawrence, P.R.A. (London: Macdonald, 1951);

Three Romantic Countries: Reminiscences of Travel in Dalmatia, Ireland, and Portugal (London: Macdonald, 1951);

The South of France: The Lower Rhône Valley and the Mediterranean Seaboard from Martigues to Mentou (London: Macdonald, 1952);

Privileged Persons (London: Richards, 1955).

In the present age of literary specialization Douglas Goldring's intellectual range and diversity of interests is striking. The author of more than fifty books, he was a biographer, travel writer, poet, novelist, short-story writer, historian, critic, dramatist, and autobiographer. In addition, he had a keen interest in architecture, painting, travel, politics, and fine wines. In *South Lodge: Reminiscences of Violet Hunt, Ford Madox Ford and the English Review Circle* (1943) Goldring recalls his indignation at being called a mere journalist by Joseph Conrad at a time when the twenty-one-year-old Goldring thought of himself solely as a poet. Despite his literary works being praised by such contemporaries as Ford Madox Ford, Ezra Pound, James Elroy Flecker, D. H. Lawrence, and Romain Rolland, neither his novels nor his poems have enjoyed sustained critical interest. The fact that the strong autobiographical impulse in his writing is combined with a sense of history and of place makes his work a fascinating chronicle of his times, both in terms of the specific personalities mentioned—Ford, Lawrence, Flecker, Conrad, Pound, Violet Hunt, and Norman Douglas—and of Goldring's description of the tumultuous transition from the Edwardian to the post–World War I era.

Goldring was born on 7 January 1887 in Greenwich, England, the youngest of five children. Both grandfathers were lawyers, and his father was an architect. His childhood was troubled, as a remark in his *The Nineteen Twenties: A General Survey and Some Personal Memories* (1945) makes clear:

> Fond though I was of my father and mother, loyal though I am to the ties of blood and tradition, devoted as I have never ceased to be to the land of my birth, it would be dishonest of me to pretend that the home into which I was born was either happy or congenial. As soon as I possibly could I escaped from it and stood on my own feet.

The tension between Goldring and his mother seems to have been particularly acute. In *Life Interests* (1948) he refers to her as a "fanatical Anglo-Catholic," and in *Odd Man Out: The Autobiography of a "Propaganda Novelist"* (1935) he recounts a painful, drawn-out psychological battle with her and describes his eventual "escape from the intellectual captivity of my priest-ridden home."

Goldring was educated at Felsted School in Dunnow, Essex, a venerable Church of England boarding school that had been founded in 1564, and Magdalen College School, a prepatory school for Oxford. He acquired at these institutions the typical British public-school education of which he was to be acidly critical in later years. In 1905 he received his first earnings as a writer for some verses accepted by *The Academy*.

Goldring matriculated at Oxford in 1906. There his interest in poetry deepened, and poets such as Ernest Dowson, Charles-Pierre Baudelaire, Paul Verlaine, A. C. Swinburne, Arthur Symons, Francis Thompson, and A. E. Housman became his principal sources of inspiration. During his first term he met the novelist and playwright W. Somerset Maugham, who took a kindly interest in Goldring's early attempts at writing poetry and introduced him to modern French poetry.

After a year at Oxford, Goldring was forced by financial problems to quit school and take a full-time job at the popular magazine *Country Life*. By the early summer of 1908, while still working at *Country Life*, Goldring became Ford's subeditor for the short-lived but significant *The English Review*. Goldring's association with the magazine lasted only a year, but he was greatly impressed by Ford. He was later to call Ford his "principal formative influence—intellectually speaking." Goldring saw Ford as someone whose dedication to literature was never compromised by the tangled circumstances of his life. Through Ford, Goldring met many of the literary luminaries of the time, once even interviewing George Bernard Shaw for *The English Review*.

In March 1910 Goldring founded and edited *The Tramp*, an illustrated literary/travel magazine that he envisioned as a periodical that would combine the literary strengths of *The English Review* and the rural mystique of *Country Life*. The first number of *The Tramp* included contributions by novelists Hunt and Arnold Bennett, and the magazine became famous for the caliber of its contents; subsequent contributors included Ford, Rose Macaulay, Jack London, John Drinkwater, Edward Thomas, W. H. Davies, Francis Brett Young, Wyndham Lewis (some of whose "Wild Body" stories appeared in the journal from June to December 1910), and Constance Garnett (who translated several short stories by Anton Chekov, who then was virtually unknown to English readers). Goldring was

Goldring's friend, the poet James Elroy Flecker

plagued by financial difficulties, and after a year-long struggle the magazine ceased publication.

That year marked the beginning of Goldring's close association, both personal and professional, with another contributor to *The Tramp*, the poet Flecker, an association that would last until Flecker's death in 1915. Several poems by Flecker appeared originally in *The Tramp*. In 1910 Goldring published at his Adelphi Press Flecker's *Thirty-Six Poems*, as well as a volume of his own juvenilia, *A Country Boy and Other Poems*. As the title of the latter work suggests, it was strongly influenced by Housman's *A Shropshire Lad* (1896), to which Goldring had first been exposed at Felsted School.

Ways of Escape: A Book of Adventure (1911) was a first for Goldring on several levels: it was his first book of prose, his first travel book, and his first book on France. France exerted a strong influence on Goldring throughout his career, as can be seen in several of his works, including travel books such as the critically praised *The Loire: The Record of a Pilgrimage from Gerbier de Joncs to St. Nazaire* (1913) and

The French Riviera and the Valley of the Rhône from Avignon to Marseilles (1928), and in the prevalence of French locales in such novels as *The Façade* (1927) and *The Coast of Illusion* (1932).

Reviewers of *Ways of Escape* and *The Loire* praised Goldring for his ability to create scenic vignettes that resonate with authenticity. Of *Ways of Escape*, a reviewer in the Christmas 1911 issue of the British edition of *The Bookman* said that "Goldring's book is essentially personal. He takes you to a few, but not all, of the recognized sights of Arles, or Liege, or Paris, but he heeds humanity more than sights." Throughout his career critics tended to regard Goldring's work as most successful when he focused on the personal and when he exercised his narrative skills to evoke a vignette or weave an anecdote concerning his personal experiences on the road.

The tendency of critics to praise those aspects of his travel writing that reflect his narrative skills also suggests the interrelation in his work between fiction and nonfiction, for example in travel writing imbued with story and in fiction and poetry that reveal a strong sense of physical setting. A case in point is *Streets: A Book of London Verses* (1912). This work consists of a series of poems, each of which takes inspiration from a specific London street or neighborhood, and the poems reflect both London's diversity and the range of moods it can provoke in a sensitive observer. Ironically, despite Goldring's contact with key modernists such as Ford and Pound, his poetry is technically traditional. Much the same method is followed in *On the Road: A Book of Travel Songs* (1916), which comprises pieces taking their inspiration from provincial or foreign towns.

As a result of Goldring's fledgling undertakings as a publisher he was entrusted in 1912 with the task of resuscitating an ailing publishing firm that he renamed Max Goschen. As literary editor for the firm from 1912 to 1914 Goldring published his own *Streets* and the collection *The Adventuress and Other Stories* (1913), as well as Flecker's *The Golden Journey to Samarkand* (1913) and *The King of Alsander* (1914) and Ford's *Collected Poems* (1913).

Goldring's knowledge of the more pragmatic sides of publishing meant that his advice was often solicited by other literary artists. In 1914 Wyndham Lewis enlisted Goldring to act in an advisory capacity in the inception of the notorious journal *Blast*, and Goldring was able to secure the services of a printer who was willing to carry out Lewis's innovative and eccentric concepts of layout design. In 1915 Goldring founded the publishing firm of Selwyn and Blount, which was soon taken over by other owners, and was to retain a lifelong fondness for the publishing side of literary endeavor.

Goldring enlisted in the British Army in August 1914, soon after the outbreak of World War I. He was given a commission in October, but soon afterward he became seriously ill with acute rheumatism, and later that month he was invalided out of the army. This curtailment of his military service was a bitter disappointment to him at the time; but by 1916, when he was fit again, he had become a conscientious objector.

Goldring was radically politicized by the war; in *South Lodge* he remarks: "Like many others I had developed a political consciousness in the cataclysm of war, which cut me completely adrift from my inherited background, as well as from the champagne and oysters of my pre-war dancing days." Throughout his subsequent writings the notion of the war as the catalyst of social upheaval runs as an almost perpetual undercurrent and frequently erupts to the surface in the form of direct commentary. As he notes elsewhere in *South Lodge:* "London, right up to August, 1914, remained 'Edwardian.' It only became 'Georgian' during the Armistice years which followed victory. The period between 1907 and 1914 witnessed the last wild orgie [*sic*] in which the dying Victorian world indulged before its downfall."

Goldring spent the last years of the war in Ireland, in an exile necessitated by the unpopularity of his political position. It was, however, an important time for Goldring, both personally and professionally. On 27 November 1917 he married Beatrix (Betty) Duncan of Dublin. In *The Nineteen Twenties* Goldring fondly recalls having been captivated not only by the artistic and musical Betty but also by the stimulating atmosphere of her entire household. Goldring's mother-in-law, Ellie Duncan, was a lifelong friend of the Irish poet William Butler Yeats, and the social circle into which Goldring found himself drawn also included the novelist George Moore and many other luminaries of Dublin intellectual life. The Goldring's had two sons, Hugh and Patrick. Hugh was to die of wounds received during World War II.

While in Ireland, Goldring published two books under the pseudonym "An Englishman"—*Dublin: Explorations and Reflections* (1917) and *A Stranger in Ireland* (1918). For the author these books were honest attempts "on the one hand to tell Southern Ireland that numbers of English people had the deepest sympathy with them in their struggle for 'self-determination,' and on the other hand to give English readers an unprejudiced picture of the Irish scene."

Goldring's wartime politicization is apparent in *The Fortune: A Romance of Friendship* (1917), which marks a decisive shift away from the relative frivolity of novels of manners such as *The Permanent Uncle* (1912) and *Margot's Progress* (1916). A strongly polemical work, *The Fortune* deals with the progressive influence that James Murdoch, an Anglo-Irishman, has on Harold Firbank, the son of a stuffy, middle-class English family. At the outbreak of World War I, James is a socialist and pacifist, while Harold and his wife, like the majority of the British people, hold more traditionally patriotic views. The latter part of the book shows how James wins Harold and his wife over to his beliefs.

The novel has strongly autobiographical elements, particularly with respect to the close affinities between Goldring and Harold. The descriptions of Harold's stultifying home life in the novel's opening chapters are reminiscent of Goldring's accounts of his own childhood. Like Goldring, Harold sees Oxford as a means of escape, but because of financial concerns he is forced to leave Oxford without a degree. Harold's life further echoes Goldring's when he marries a woman from Ireland and becomes a close observer of the tense Irish situation in the years prior to World War I. The first part of the novel ends with the success of a play written by Harold titled *The Fortune*.

A fundamental flaw in the novel is its unconvincing characterization of James Murdoch. Although he is clearly intended to be the novel's moral center, and his pacificism and prolabor sympathies are implicitly endorsed, he does not seem to know anyone from the working class that he so ardently champions and, with his liking for the arts and the finer material things, he comes across as more aristocrat than proletarian. Despite his avowed pacifism, James is ultimately more fascist than pacifist in his behavior, jealously controlling Harold's life and at one point slapping a woman whose political views strike him as juvenile.

The novel is weighed down by lengthy expositions of various ideological positions. As a reviewer noted in *The New York Times* (9 November 1919), "The mixing of art and propaganda is a somewhat delicate operation, requiring a peculiar talent. Mr. Douglas Goldring has talent and a great deal of it, but not that particular kind." In a short review in the January 1918 *Egoist* T. S. Eliot pronounced the first half of *The Fortune* "boring" but nonetheless deemed the work "unquestionably a brilliant novel." Many years later, in his preface to Goldring's *Life Interests*, Alec Waugh claimed that the work "was the first English novel . . . to ridicule the smug Whitehall attitude to the war, to attack the criminal complaisance of those who were doing well out of the war and who advertised and boosted the war as a personal and social panacea for every human ailment. *The Fortune* said, in 1917 when it was difficult and unpopular to say them, most of the things that it was easy and fashionable to say in 1927."

Goldring in 1935 (photograph by Helena Thornhill)

After World War I, Goldring found himself in precarious financial circumstances. In January 1919 he and his wife returned to London, where they sublet Yeats's London flat for six months. He was engaged to do secretarial work for the politician Joseph King, who had lost his parliamentary seat in the "coupon election" of December 1918 and who had just joined the Labour Party. For thirty years Goldring was to remain on terms of affection and intimacy with King. Another friend who came to his aid at this time was Pound. Before the war Pound had accepted some poems from Goldring that had appeared in the former's *Catholic Anthology* (1915). In 1919 Pound sold several poems and articles by Goldring to American periodicals with which Pound had connections.

After an initial period of loneliness and dislocation Goldring was drawn back into London intellectual circles through a series of literary parties Harold Monro gave in his rooms over the Poetry Bookshop on Devonshire Street. At the first of these Goldring met Waugh, who had recently burst into the ranks of best-selling novelists with *The Loom of Youth* (1917). On the strength of Waugh's appreciation of *The Fortune* his father's firm, Chapman and Hall, became Goldring's publisher. Goldring had first made Monro's acquaintance in 1913 but became even more closely acquainted with him in the 1920s. In prewar days Goldring had contributed verses to Monro's *Poetry and Drama* magazine. In the *Monthly Chapbook* (the postwar successor to *Poetry and Drama*), Monro first published Goldring's antiwar poem "Triumphal Ode," which satirized Victory Day, as well as several of the essays that were subsequently included in Goldring's *Reputations: Essays in Criticism* (1920).

For Goldring 1919 was a year of intensive literary and political activity; he describes it in *The Nineteen Twenties* as "the fullest and most crowded twelve months I had up to then experienced, or have ever experienced since." His play *The Fight for Freedom,* which he had written in Ireland, was published that year. In the preface he pleads for the development in Britain of a "People's Theatre" modeled on the populist theaters in Russia, Germany, Austria, and Holland.

Through King's influence Goldring became a paid worker for the Fight the Famine Council and spent some weeks in the summer of 1919 investigating conditions in Germany on the council's behalf. He also met with Dr. Hugo Seckel, who had cotranslated *The Fortune* in collaboration with Hermynia Zur Muhlen, the translator of *The Fight for Freedom.* While he was in Frankfurt, Muhlen's translation of *The Fight for Freedom* appeared in a Berlin Communist journal, *Die Weissen Blatte.*

In that same year Goldring joined the London 1917 Club. The club had been founded to celebrate the outbreak of the Russian Revolution and as a place in which to talk freely without fear of the Defence of the Realm Act. The club included among its members writers such as Aldous Huxley, Osbert Sitwell, Siegfried Sassoon, E. M. Forster, Rose Macaulay, and Virginia and Leonard Woolf. Also at this time Goldring came under the influence of the noted social reformer and opponent of colonialism, E. D. Morel.

In 1919 Goldring and several colleagues began the People's Theatre Society, principally to facilitate a London production of Lawrence's play *The Widowing of Mrs. Holroyd.* Goldring's plans for this play did not materialize, but the creation of the society and the publication by Goldring of an essay, "The Later Work of D. H. Lawrence," which Lawrence admired, brought the two writers closer together. Goldring had first met Lawrence in 1909 through Ford. Just after World War I, Goldring had sent a typescript of Lawrence's *Women in Love* (1920) to the American publisher Thomas Seltzer, which led to Seltzer's publication of twenty works by Lawrence between 1920 and 1925. In 1919 Goldring was able to persuade the publisher C. W. Daniel to begin publishing under Goldring's general editorship a new series of revolutionary plays called Plays For a People's Theatre. Both Goldring's *The Fight for Freedom* and Lawrence's *Touch and Go* (1920) were published in this series.

Goldring was also able to find the time in 1919 to write the antiwar novel *The Black Curtain,* which he dedicated to Lawrence and which was published by Chapman and Hall in 1920. The novel opens in 1913 on the eve of World War I and follows Philip Kane, a foreign correspondent for a London newspaper, as he becomes increasingly radicalized through his friendship with a Russian communist, Ivan Smirnoff, and then through his love affair with Anne Drummond, a member of the Worker's Peace Federation, whom he later marries. Anne is imprisoned, while pregnant, on trumped-up charges of treason; although she is soon released, her mistreatment at the hands of officials leads to her death and that of the baby. A grieving Philip vows to keep the spirit of Anne's radicalism alive, and the novel ends with the hint that Vladimir Lenin is the new messiah who will liberate the workers of the world from imperialist tyranny.

Although *The Black Curtain,* like many of Goldring's novels, has a contrived plot that is primarily a framework to allow the author to advance his political convictions, it does evoke the almost hysterical revelry in London society just prior to the outbreak of the war. Goldring's examination of how the British government used the war as a pretext for betraying the public trust, colluding with war profiteers, and manipulating the press for its own ends was considered "subversive" by contemporaries and remains trenchant today.

Reputations also reflects the influence of the war on Goldring's critical stance. One of the volume's most characteristic essays, "An Outburst on Gissing," is, as its title suggests, strident and angry in tone and, as a review in *The Bookman* (London; July 1920) noted, "as much a denunciation of late Victorianism as a criticism of the novelist." Goldring believed that because of critical hostility toward *Reputations* he was frozen out of all decently paid reviewing for several years and that his career was seriously damaged by an unofficial boycott by several major newspapers that prevented his works from being reviewed.

For Goldring, as for so many writers, the 1920s were a period of wandering and self-imposed exile, a period that embraced both exuberant freedom and aimlessness. In 1920, during a Christmas visit to Ireland, Goldring witnessed the strong-arm tactics of the British Black and Tans. Soon afterward he conducted a party of tourists to Florence, Rome, and Naples, a trip that provided him with an opportunity to renew his friendship with Norman Douglas. Throughout the early 1920s he also made frequent trips to Paris and the Mediterranean. In 1922 his marriage ended in divorce.

The combination of "lost generation" aimlessness and social consciousness that characterize Goldring's perspective during this period can be found in both his travel writing and his fiction. A trilogy of novels that he wrote during the decade—*Nobody Knows* (1923), *Cuckoo: A Comedy of Adjustments* (1925) and *The Façade* (1927)—"reflected the tribulations, experiments and futilities of the ordinary hard-up 'intellectuals' of the period, the less successful writers, painters, and 'idealists' who had to earn their livings," he said in *Odd Man Out*. *Nobody Knows* centers on a journalist, Gilbert Vayle, adrift and unemployed in postwar London. As the novel opens, Gilbert's marriage to Chloe is quickly disintegrating, and the implacable howls of their three-year-old baby boy become a piercing reminder of their depressing circumstances. Gilbert cannot find work because of the unpopular views he has expressed in his antiwar novels and because of his pro-Irish criticism of British military action in Ireland. Although less directly autobiographical than either *The Fortune* or *The Black Curtain*, *Nobody Knows* reflects the marital strife and grim financial circumstances that characterized Goldring's return to London after the war, and Gilbert's political views closely parallel the author's.

Unlike Goldring's earlier political novels, *Nobody Knows* makes the analysis of social behavior more prominent than the political propaganda. As the title suggests, the world of this novel is one of social and moral instability, where the traditional foundations of knowledge and values have crumbled and "nobody knows" what to believe. It is a world characterized by frenzied escapist experimentation with sexual promiscuity, abuse of alcohol and drugs, and restless global wanderings. The novel chronicles Gilbert's increasing dissatisfaction with a world without fixed values and his realization that, despite its faults, marriage is an institution that possesses a fixity that he feels his life requires. Goldring tries to evaluate the phenomenon of female emancipation in the 1920s, but the novel suffers from a stereotyping of female characters—there is an implicit assumption that any woman dedicated to political ideas must be both sexually repressed and unable to come to terms with her true feminine emotional nature. Despite Goldring's avowed socialism, this is another novel that demonstrates that his hopes for the future were not centered on the masses but on the idea of a spiritual aristocracy that would lead and function as role models for the working class.

In 1925 Goldring was appointed lecturer in English at the University College of Commerce in Gothenburg, Sweden. Two works published at this time reflect the influence of his travels at this time. The novel *Cuckoo: A Comedy of Adjustments* presents the amorous adventures among the English artistic set in the Italian Riviera. A travel book, *Northern Lights and Southern Shade* testifies to Goldring's overriding sympathy for southern Europe, a sympathy that, in this book at least, leads Goldring to give rather short shrift to Sweden and the Swedish people. A review in the September 1926 issue of *The Bookman* praised Goldring once again as the kind of traveler who is "the picker-up of unconsidered trifles on the way, whose writings delight us because they represent the antithesis of the conventional guide-book."

Goldring gave up his academic appointment when he married Malin Nordstrom on 24 April 1927; the two honeymooned in Paris in September. In November, Goldring accepted an invitation from the Boston publisher of his travel books to visit the United States for the purpose of writing a book about the country. He had not been in New York more than three weeks when he received a cable from his wife that her sister and brother-in-law had died in tragic circumstances and that she was returning to Paris from Cannes to look after her mother. Goldring was fortunate that his friend Ford was on hand; as Arthur Mizener writes in his biography of Ford: "Ford took care of everything. He cabled Stella [his wife] to watch over Mrs. Goldring in Paris, packed for the stricken Goldring, and saw him into the boat."

When Goldring returned to Europe, he and his wife settled in Nice. During their stay on the Riviera Malin practiced as a masseuse. Between 1927 and 1932 Goldring was general editor for The Kitbag Travel Books series, published in London by the firm of George Harrap.

The Goldrings moved to London in March 1930. That year he published *Sardinia: The Island of the Nuraghi,* about a trip he had taken in December 1928. The book was acclaimed for Goldring's evocative impressions of people and places. But one passage is a disturbing historical curiosity: Goldring's enthusiastic description of a model village called "Mussolini" where the Fascist regime has made immense improvements in drainage and water reclamation. The passage is a reminder of how the darker implications of Fascist ideology only gradually revealed themselves to intellectuals in the 1930s, even to those with avowed socialist convictions such as Goldring.

Other works by Goldring in this decade include *The Coast of Illusion* (1932), a novel set on the Côte D'Azur; *To Portugal* (1934), a travel book that was criticized for the absence of the kind of personal impressions that were deemed to be his trademark; and *Odd Man Out,* described by a reviewer in the *London Mercury* as a "first-rate autobiography." In 1937 he founded the Georgian Group, a branch of the Society for the Protection of Ancient Buildings.

In the 1940s Goldring wrote three of his most noteworthy books. In *The Nineteen Twenties* he offers an account of the period that is shaped by his controversial but highly fascinating socialist perspective. *South Lodge* and *The Last Pre-Raphaelite: A Record of the Life and Writings of Ford Madox Ford* (1948) both have their origin in Goldring's intimate knowledge of Ford and his circle during the *English Review* years. Goldring had first met Violet Hunt in the summer of 1907 and was her friend from 1908 until her death in January 1942. According to Hunt's biographer, Barbara Belford, Goldring inherited Hunt's library.

The Last Pre-Raphaelite is the first biography of Ford, and while this biased account has been superseded by more-balanced and more-meticulous biographies, subsequent biographers remain indebted both to Goldring's eyewitness accounts of events and people and to some of Goldring's interpretations of motivation and behavior. In many ways this book and *South Lodge* are representative of both the weaknesses and strengths of Goldring's art: his writing is dated both by its amateur psychoanalysis and by its sexism.

Goldring died on 9 April 1960 in relative obscurity. His works, particularly the biographical and autobiographical volumes, deserve reconsideration, for they constitute an insightful record of several decades of British social history. Goldring held firm socialist convictions without being narrowly doctrinaire, and he was considerably ahead of his time in his understanding of the manner in which cultural institutions such as the media preserve the ideological status quo. Although sometimes clumsily polemical, his novels remain valuable for such political observations. Goldring also had the ability to write about people he knew in a way that imparts to the reader a vivid sense of personality and also conveys a sense that Goldring's own life was made richer for the contact with the individuals in question. In addition he was capable of insightful self-analysis. He was well aware that his friendship with many of the literary giants of his era did not guarantee immortality for himself. As he says in *South Lodge,* with charming self-deprecation: "If only copiousness of output staked a claim to immortality, some learned Dr. Smellfungus of the future could surely be relied upon to dust me a niche!"

References:

Barbara Belford, *Violet: The Story of the Irrepressible Violet Hunt and Her Circle of Lovers and Friends— Ford Madox Ford, H. G. Wells, Somerset Maugham, and Henry James* (New York: Simon & Schuster, 1990);

Joan Hardwick, *An Immodest Violet: The Life of Violet Hunt* (London: Deutsch, 1990), pp. 67–68, 97–98, 184–187;

Arthur Mizener, *The Saddest Story: A Biography of Ford Madox Ford* (New York: World, 1971).

Sarah Grand
(Frances Elizabeth Clarke McFall)
(10 June 1854 – 12 May 1943)

Carolyn Christensen Nelson
West Virginia University

BOOKS: *Two Dear Little Feet,* as Frances Elizabeth McFall (London: Jarrods, 1873);

Ideala: A Study from Life, anonymous (Warrington: Privately printed, 1888; London: Bentley, 1889; New York: Appleton, 1893);

A Domestic Experiment, anonymous (Edinburgh & London: Blackwood, 1891);

The Heavenly Twins (Warrington: Privately printed, 1892; 3 volumes, London: Heinemann, 1893; 1 volume, New York: Cassell, 1893); excerpt republished as *The Tenor and the Boy* (London: Heinemann, 1899);

Singularly Deluded, anonymous (Edinburgh: Blackwood, 1893; New York: Appleton, 1893);

Our Manifold Nature: Stories from Life (London: Heinemann, 1894; New York: Appleton, 1894);

The Beth Book (London: Heinemann, 1897; New York: Appleton, 1897);

The Modern Man and Maid (London: Marshall, 1898);

The Human Quest: Being Some Thoughts in Contribution to the Subject of the Art of Human Happiness (London: Heinemann, 1900);

Babs the Impossible (New York & London: Harper, 1900; London: Hutchinson, 1901);

Emotional Moments (London: Hurst & Blackett, 1908);

Adnam's Orchard (London: Heinemann, 1912; New York: Appleton, 1913);

The Winged Victory (London: Heinemann, 1916; New York: Appleton, 1916);

Variety (London: Heinemann, 1922).

Editions: *Our Manifold Nature: Stories from Life* (Freeport, N.Y.: Books for Libraries Press, 1969);

The Beth Book: Being a Study of the Life of Elizabeth Caldwell Maclure, a Woman of Genius, introduction by Elaine Showalter (London: Virago, 1980; New York: Dial, 1981);

The Heavenly Twins, introduction by Carol A. Senf (Ann Arbor: University of Michigan Press, 1992).

SELECTED PERIODICAL PUBLICATIONS–

Sarah Grand in 1900

UNCOLLECTED: "The Morals and Manners of Appearance," *Humanitarian,* 3 (August 1893): 87–94;

"The New Aspect of the Woman Question," *North American Review,* 158 (March 1894): 270–276;

"The Man of the Moment," *North American Review,* 158 (May 1894): 620–627;

"The Modern Girl," *North American Review,* 158 (June 1894): 706–714;

"The New Woman and the Old," *Lady's Realm,* 4 (August 1898): 466-470;

"The Modern Young Man," *Temple Magazine,* 2 (September 1898): 883-886;

"The Case of the Modern Spinster," *Pall Mall Magazine,* 51 (January 1913): 52-56;

"The Case of the Modern Married Woman," *Pall Mall Magazine,* 51 (February 1913): 203-209.

Sarah Grand was a feminist writer whose novels were highly popular in the 1890s. The 1893 edition of *The Heavenly Twins* (first published in a private edition the previous year) sold twenty thousand copies in England in its first week and was a best-seller in the United States. Grand was one of the New Woman writers, novelists of the 1890s whose heroines questioned, challenged, and often rejected the traditional roles handed them by society. The novel became their platform for protest and their agent for change. These novelists, who dealt with matters of sexuality with a new openness, were best known for their attacks on traditional marriage, which they believed institutionalized female oppression and validated the double standard of sexual morality. Their heroines demanded new freedoms, including the right to pursue an education or a sexual partner of their own choosing. Although Grand is credited with coining the term *New Woman,* she was not the most radical of the New Woman writers. While she challenged many of the conventions that oppressed women in marriage and peopled her novels with villainous male characters, she believed women's ultimate happiness lay in marriage, but a marriage contracted on quite a different basis than was presently possible.

Grand was born Frances Elizabeth Bellenden Clarke in Donaghadee, County Down, Ireland, on 10 June 1854, the fourth of five children of Margaret Bell Sherwood Clarke and Edward John Bellenden Clarke. Her father was a naval officer and her mother the daughter of a Yorkshire squire. The family moved to Yorkshire on the death of her father, when she was seven. She was educated at home with her sister, and from fourteen to sixteen she attended the Royal Naval School at Twickenham and a finishing school in Kensington. Soon after she was brought home from the latter school, probably for financial reasons, she married an army surgeon, David Chambers McFall, to escape her unhappy home life. The thirty-nine-year-old McFall was a widower with two sons. *The Beth Book* (1897), a semi-autobiographical novel that covers its heroine's early years, closely approximates the events in Grand's life in many details, including Beth's marriage at a young age to a doctor, Daniel McClure, who turns out to be a thoroughly unpleasant man.

On 7 October 1871 the McFalls had a son, David Archibald (Archie). From 1873 to 1879, the family traveled widely as David Chambers McFall was stationed in Singapore, Ceylon, China, Japan, Norwich, Malta, Normandy, and the Isle of Wight. In 1881 they moved to Warrington, Lancashire, where David Chambers McFall retired from military service. Grand used some of the experiences of these years in her fiction: part of *The Heavenly Twins* is set in Malta among military men and their wives, and Norwich was the inspiration for the fictional cathedral town of Morningquest, the setting of her three most important novels.

Grand began writing early in her marriage. In 1873 she published *Two Dear Little Feet,* an earnest tale on the evils of wearing tight shoes that is more lecture than story, but it combined two interests that would become evident in her later fiction: physiology (an interest she probably gained from her physician husband) and a desire for rational dress. Few of her other stories were accepted, and those few were often in such publications as *Aunt Judy's Magazine for Young People.* In 1879 she began working on *Ideala: A Study from Life* and *The Tenor and the Boy,* a story that was later incorporated into *The Heavenly Twins* and also published separately (1899). After both were repeatedly rejected by publishers, she paid to have *Ideala* published in 1888 without her name. Richard Bentley republished it the following year.

Ideala is Grand's first important work, and it introduces characters and themes that *The Heavenly Twins* and *The Beth Book* would continue to develop. The novel lacks drama and develops mainly through long conversations on women's issues between Ideala and others, particularly a brother and sister, Lord Dawne and Claudia. These conversations are related secondhand by the narrator, Lord Dawne, a shadowy and ineffectual figure. The novel raises important questions about marriage, the position of women in society, and the immorality of men. Ideala, whose husband is abusive and promiscuous, first debates whether she should leave him and then whether she should live with a sympathetic man, Lorrimer, with whom she falls in love. Ideala compares marriage to slavery in that all of a girl's society and family conspire to force her into marriage. She declares: "A woman is made to swear to love a man who will probably prove unlovable, to honor a man who is as likely as not to be undeserving of honor, and to obey a man who may be incapable of judging what is best either for himself or her . . . if men were all they ought to be, wouldn't we obey them gladly? To be able to do so is all we ask."

This was the rallying cry Grand repeated over and over in her fiction and essays: men must raise themselves morally to be worthy of women's love. Ideala finally leaves her husband, is persuaded by her friends to reject Lorrimer, goes alone to China, and returns having found her vocation: she will devote her life to uniting women to improve the world. She states: "Women have never yet united to use their influence steadily and all together against that of which they disapprove." Ideala intends to help women do just that: she will become the figure of the future woman, pure and dedicated to improving the world for women. She becomes part of a group seeking this new order that appears again in *The Heavenly Twins* and *The Beth Book*. Although *Ideala* is short on action and long on moralizing, it was successful and was reprinted three times in 1889. The reviewer for *The Spectator* (12 January 1889), while calling the manner of narration defective, gave the novel "high praise" and said that "Ideala stands to us in the light of a real living character." Grand used Ideala's unhappy marriage to present her objections to the conditions under which women married and to the immoral and unworthy men that they had forced upon them.

The success of *Ideala* gave Grand the financial security she needed to leave her husband; she also abandoned her son. Her marriage ended in 1890, and if, as seems probable, the unpleasant husbands of the heroines in *Ideala, The Heavenly Twins,* and *The Beth Book,* who are often doctors or military men or both, are all modeled on David Chambers McFall, it can only be concluded that Grand's marriage was most unhappy. These husbands are intruding, demanding, ill-mannered, promiscuous, and sometimes even violent to their wives. The husband in *The Beth Book* is the director of a lock hospital, one that confined prostitutes with venereal disease; Grand's husband worked in such a hospital for several years.

The Contagious Diseases Acts, which allowed for the seizing of women thought to be prostitutes and testing them for venereal diseases, were a particular target of Victorian feminists since they implied that women, rather than being victims of male promiscuity, were responsible for the spread of disease. Grand supported Josephine Butler's attempts to repeal the Contagious Diseases Acts. For Grand and other crusaders for women's rights venereal disease became a physical symbol of men's immorality and the plight of innocent women. While women were kept in ignorance about sexually transmitted diseases and were required to bring purity to marriage, they were often infected by men living by a far different sexual standard. Grand introduced this

The army surgeon David Chambers McFall, whom Grand married when she was sixteen (by permission of Gordon McFall)

attack on male immorality and syphilis as a symbol of that immorality in her next important novel, *The Heavenly Twins*.

Grand spent the next several years primarily in London, with periodic trips to such places as Ramsgate and Paris for rests. The Blackwood firm published *A Domestic Experiment* (1891) and *Singularly Deluded* (1893), neither of which was successful, but was unwilling to risk the controversies that might ensue from *The Heavenly Twins,* with its treatment of such shocking new ideas in fiction as syphilis and cross-dressing and its polemically strident tone. As she had done with *Ideala,* Grand had *The Heavenly Twins* privately printed (1892). Finally, William Heinemann agreed to publish the book, which appeared on 7 August 1893. The pseudonym Sarah Grand first appeared on this novel and became the name by which Frances McFall was subsequently known. Her choice of a name has been seen as a feminist statement in that she rejected her husband's name, refused to assume a male pseudonym, and

Title page for a novel that deals with such topics as cross-dressing and syphilis (Special Collections, Thomas Cooper Library, University of South Carolina)

proclaimed herself in an unabashed manner as "Grand."

The Heavenly Twins was a great success and one of the best-sellers of the decade. Heinemann reprinted it six times in the first year, and Cassell and Company published it in America, where it sold five times as many copies as in England that year. It was the most popular of Grand's novels; many of her later works are credited to "Sarah Grand, author of *The Heavenly Twins*." The novel is flawed artistically, however. It lacks a unified narrative voice and a unified plot—some subplots are only marginally related to the whole. It is wordy and digressive, attempting too much. But its faults are compensated for by its expansive treatment of the three women whose intertwined lives are chronicled. Their different fates allow Grand to attack many of the wrongs committed against women, from the double moral standard to the disparity in education of boys and girls.

Angelica and Diavolo, the twins of the title, are energetic and delightful children. But in spite of Angelica's greater intellectual promise, it is her brother who will receive an education outside the home and have a career. Angelica, who knows that marriage is her destiny, decides to have it on her own terms and proposes to a kindly man who is a friend of the family and old enough to be her father. In her unconventional proposal she says, "Marry me, *and let me do as I like*." The marriage is happy but hardly based on passion. Angelica addresses her husband as "Daddy," and he allows her the freedom she had requested. In the episode titled "The Tenor and the Boy" Grand raises daring questions on gender roles and sexuality by using the device of cross-dressing. Angelica goes out at night in her brother's clothes to experience life as a man and spends a great deal of time with a tenor at the cathedral who thinks she is a boy. The relationship, while remaining platonic, has overtones of homosexuality and certainly of love outside the bonds of marriage.

Edith Beale, the most traditional of the heroines, follows her parents' advice on whom to marry and contracts syphilis from her husband, who has a disreputable past. She gives birth to a deformed syphilitic child, goes mad, and dies. Edith was the daughter of a bishop, and the innocence she brings to marriage is what leads to her destruction. She had trusted her father's advice and her husband's goodness. Before she dies she attacks her father, her husband, and the doctor who treats her as those "who represent the arrangement of society which has made it possible for me and my child to be sacrificed in this way." Edith's fate is the means by which Grand exposes a system that denies women education and knowledge and thus allows men to exploit and destroy them.

Evadne is the most interesting and realistic of the three heroines. Although she is self-educated and intelligent, she holds conventional views until her wedding day, when she learns that her husband, Major Colquhoun, has a dissolute past, of which her father has known all along. She decides to leave him immediately, but at her parents' urging she agrees to stay with him for appearance's sake with the understanding that the marriage will never be consummated. Believing that standards of purity apply equally to men and women, she will not join herself to a man who has shown an utter disregard for women. When her aunt urges her to forgive him, take him back, and improve him, she replies: "You think I should act as women have been always advised to act in such cases, that I should sacrifice myself to save that man's soul. I take a different view of it. I see that the world is not a bit the better for centuries of self-sacrifice on the woman's part and therefore I think it is time we tried a more effectual plan. And I propose now to sacrifice the man instead of the woman." Evadne's husband eventually dies, and she has a happier second marriage to a doctor, with whom she has children, but she has been permanently scarred. Years of repressing her personality and her sexuality have made her hysterical and suicidal, and she has to lead a reclusive life. The novel's ending does, however, provide a degree of happiness for Evadne and Angelica.

Grand's novels were generally criticized by reviewers for their faulty construction, their inconsistent characters, and the author's intrusive voice. *The Nation* (16 November 1893), in its review of *The Heavenly Twins* and *Ideala,* mentioned such problems but also praised the novels for their originality, calling them "large-purposed books, dealing with the greatest problems of life." The reviewer went on, however, to criticize "the moralizing that well-nigh swamps the moral" in *The Heavenly Twins*. That novel was further criticized for its "tangle of themes and counter-themes," "its lack of unity," and the inconsistent characterization of Evadne. *Ideala* was said to be a "slighter but more perfect work." But the reviewer pointed out that "both books are noticeable far beyond the ordinary. Their author stands in some peril as a reformer, of trying to cure all maladies with one medicine."

The review of *The Heavenly Twins* in *The Athenaeum* (18 March 1893) also criticized the novel's "chaotic and haphazard arrangement" and its "plethora of material which might with advantage have been distributed over several novels." Grand's twins, however, were declared to be "among the most delightful and amusing children in fiction," and in Evadne, Grand was judged to have created a realistic woman, not a cold abstraction. *The Spectator* (25 March 1893) complained about Grand's polemics, which "have gone far to spoil her novels," and about her penchant for raising issues that could not be discussed in a journal with a "mixed clientele." Generally the reviewers recognized Grand as a reformer who addressed significant issues, even if her novels were not always equal to the task.

Grand became active in the Rational Dress Society, for which she became a popular lecturer. She also wrote articles and stories that addressed many of the same issues her novels had raised: marriage, divorce, and the different standards of morality for men and women. Some of her stories were published as *Our Manifold Nature: Stories from Life* (1894).

Caricature of Grand skewering a "Mere Man" in Harper's Weekly *(2 November 1901)*

The term *New Woman* first appears in her essay "The New Aspect of the Woman Question" in the *North American Review* (March 1894) as a description of a woman who has "been sitting apart in silent contemplation all these years, thinking and thinking, until at last she solved the problem and proclaimed for herself what was wrong with Home-is-the-woman's-Sphere, and prescribed the remedy." In the same article Grand attacks men for the ways they have deprived women of a proper education, then jeered at them for their lack of knowledge and degraded them in marriage. She suggests that man "undergo a moral reeducation" so that women can enjoy "the sacred duties of wife and mother." In the May 1894 issue of the *North American Review* she again attacks man's immoral behavior, his lack of virtue and self-denial, and declares that "the new woman came to correct him."

The Beth Book is the last of the three novels that feature the circle of strong women who first appeared in *Ideala*. *The Beth Book* is essentially a bildungsroman, and in its detailed treatment of Beth's early life, modeled after Grand's, one sees the way girls' interests are sacrificed to boys'. After Beth's father dies, her mother uses every bit of money the family has so

Grand in her eighties

that Beth's brothers can have an education and cut a fine figure among their friends, while Beth wears ragged clothes and suffers from malnutrition. To escape this life Beth marries a much older man who abuses and is unfaithful to her. Beth begins to write in a hidden room she sets up in the house. Eventually she leaves her husband and continues to write, but by the end of the novel she has become an orator. She joins Ideala and Angelica in a new order of women working to effect change. While she had to work at her writing, her ability to move women to action through oratory is a "natural gift."

The Spectator (13 November 1897) called *The Beth Book* an "impassioned and polemical pamphlet on the marriage question" and a continuation of "the sex-crusade" begun in *The Heavenly Twins*. *The Athenaeum* (27 November 1897) was quite critical, declaring the book too heavy-handed; Grand was accused of nagging instead of telling a story. The review was particularly critical of her characterizations, arguing that she succeeds only "in producing some pretty loathsome men" who are "simply ridiculous puppets" and in making Beth appear stupid. The absence of realistic male figures in her novels has been noted by Gillian Kersley in her biography of Grand, *Darling Madame: Sarah Grand and Devoted Friend* (1983): "Frances hit back at her husband, father and brothers by emasculating the few good men in her novels, and vilifying the rest. This method proved safe and successful for her, but reduced her heroes to cardboard cut-outs, always too good or too bad to be true."

Babs the Impossible (1900) has a high-spirited heroine who is much like Angelica of *The Heavenly Twins*. This novel has more complex and appealing male characters and little of the moralizing of her earlier works. Babs does not marry and she directs her own life, and her problems are of her own making. *The Athenaeum* (20 April 1901) called the novel Grand's best, finding in it a unity that her previous works had lacked. The reviewer declared Babs "absolutely real."

In 1901 Grand went to the United States, lecturing all around the country for four months. She met Samuel Clemens (Mark Twain), who had thoroughly annotated his copy of *The Heavenly Twins*. Returning to England, she continued to speak on a variety of women's issues. She joined the Women Writers' Suffrage League, an auxiliary of the National Union of Women's Suffrage Societies, and became president of the Tunbridge Wells branch of the latter organization.

Adnam's Orchard (1912) and *The Winged Victory* (1916), which deal with the land question and home industries, were to be part of a new trilogy, but the third book was never written. While these novels have a kinder view of men and are far less polemical than Grand's earlier work, they were not as popular and received little critical attention. Kersley says that "the characters show a mixture of bad and good, but the protagonists haven't the strength, conviction or purpose of Beth or Evadne."

During World War I Grand served as president of the Tunbridge Wells branch of the National Council of Women. In 1920 she moved to Bath. In 1922 she was selected to serve as "mayoress" of the city; the mayor, Cedric Chivers, a widower, needed someone to help him in his civic responsibilities. She served for six years, attending dinners and giving out awards. Her reputation as a novelist had faded; most of her novels had gone out of print; and few in Bath knew of her earlier celebrity.

In 1925 Grand met Gladys Singers-Biggs, who became her devotee; Singers-Biggs's diaries provide a great deal of information on the later years of Grand's life and are excerpted in Kersley's biography. Singers-Biggs's slavish dependency mark her as a woman quite unlike the ones Grand portrayed admiringly in her fiction. While Grand seemed to be flattered by Singers-Biggs's attention, she nevertheless kept the woman at a distance. Grand spent the last year of her life in Calne, Wiltshire, where she went for safety during World War II. She died on 12 May 1943.

Grand outlived her reputation by several decades. Her death came fifty years after the publication of *The Heavenly Twins* had thrust her into the public eye as a rather scandalous writer on women's issues. Many of the conditions affecting women that Grand had attacked had been righted. Time and progress had changed women's lives and moved the debate out of the novel and into the political realm. Issues formerly considered scandalous could be openly addressed as part of the public discourse. By the time of Grand's death many could barely remember who she was. It took the modern feminist movement and a renewed interest in women writers and women's issues of the past to bring her back to literary attention. Elaine Showalter's inclusion of Grand in *A Literature of Their Own: British Women Novelists from Brontë to Lessing* (1977) sparked a renewed interest in her writings and led to the only biography of Grand, Kersley's *Darling Madame*. Republication of *The Beth Book* and *The Heavenly Twins* followed in 1980 and 1992, respectively.

Sarah Grand treated matters of sexuality and problems confronting women with a new frankness. Victorian writers before her had revealed the obstacles women faced in their attempts to move beyond the confines of their social roles, to get an education, and to lead fulfilling lives. But most of them showed women defeated and destroyed. Grand's lively, intelligent, and energetic heroines do not want to be like men. They are men's moral superiors and demand that men rise to their standards of purity. Grand was unusual for her time in that she created heroines who defy the system, make demands, and yet often achieve a degree of happiness and fulfillment. These qualities of her heroines, the New Women whom she so aptly named, make her fiction memorable.

Bibliography:

Joan Huddleston, *Sarah Grand: A Bibliography* (Queensland: University of Queensland Press, 1979).

Biography:

Gillian Kersley, *Darling Madame: Sarah Grand and Devoted Friend* (London: Virago, 1983).

References:

Marilyn Bonnell, "The Legacy of Sarah Grand's *The Heavenly Twins*," *English Literature in Transition 1880–1920,* 36, no. 4 (1993): 467–478;

A. R. Cunningham, "The 'New Woman Fiction' of the 1890's," *Victorian Studies,* 17 (December 1973): 177–186;

Carolyn Christensen Nelson, *British Women Fiction Writers of the 1890s* (New York: Twayne, 1996), pp. 8–20;

Lyn Pykett, *The "Improper" Feminine: The Woman's Sensation Novel and the New Woman Writing* (London & New York: Routledge, 1992), pp. 152–159, 174–176, 183–186;

Elaine Showalter, *A Literature of Their Own: British Women Novelists from Brontë to Lessing* (Princeton, N.J.: Princeton University Press, 1977), pp. 204–210.

Papers:

The unpublished journals of Gladys Singers-Biggs, much of which pertains to Sarah Grand's life, are in the Public Reference Library, Bath.

Cicely Hamilton

(15 June 1872 - 6 December 1952)

Sue Thomas
La Trobe University

See also the Hamilton entry in *DLB 10: Modern British Dramatists, 1900-1945.*

BOOKS: *Diana of Dobson's* (New York: Century, 1908);

Marriage as a Trade (London: Chapman & Hall, 1909; New York: Moffatt, Yard, 1909);

Beware! A Warning–to Suffragists, illustrated by M. Lowndes (London: Artists Suffrage League, circa 1909);

A Matter of Sport (London: Suffrage Atelier, circa 1909);

How the Vote Was Won, by Hamilton and Christopher St. John (Christabel Marshall) (London: Woman's Press, 1909; Chicago: Dramatic Publishing, circa 1910);

A Pageant of Great Women (London: Suffrage Shop, 1910);

Just to Get Married (London: Chapman & Hall, 1911);

Jack and Jill and a Friend (London: S. French, 1911; New York: S. French, 1914);

The Pot and the Kettle, by Hamilton and St. John (London: Edith Craig, circa 1913);

Just to Get Married: A Comedy in Three Acts (New York & London: S. French, 1914);

A Matter of Money (London: Chapman & Hall, 1916);

Senlis (London: Collins, 1917);

William–an Englishman (London: Skeffington, 1919; New York: Stokes, 1920);

Theodore Savage: A Story of the Past or the Future (London: Parsons, 1922); revised as *Lest Ye Die: A Story from the Past or of the Future* (London: Cape, 1928; New York: Scribners, 1928);

The Child in Flanders: A Nativity Play in a Prologue, Five Tableaux, and an Epilogue, music by Theodore Flint (London: S. French / New York: S. French, 1922);

Diana of Dobson's: A Romantic Comedy in Four Acts (London: S. French / New York: S. French, 1925);

The Old Adam: A Fantastic Comedy, British Drama League Library of Modern British Drama, no.

Cicely Hamilton

13 (Oxford: Blackwell, 1926; New York: Brentano's, 1927);

The Old Vic, by Hamilton and Lilian Baylis (London: Cape, 1926; New York: Doran, 1926);

Modern Germanies as Seen by an Englishwoman (London & Toronto: Dent, 1931; enlarged, 1933);

Full Stop (London & Toronto: Dent, 1931);

Modern Italy as Seen by an Englishwoman (London & Toronto: Dent, 1932);

Little Arthur's History of the Twentieth Century (London: Dent, 1933);

Modern France as Seen by an Englishwoman (London & Toronto: Dent, 1933);

Modern Russia as Seen by an Englishwoman (London & Toronto: Dent, 1934; New York: Dutton, 1934);

Modern Austria as Seen by an Englishwoman (London: Dent, 1935);
Life Errant (London: Dent, 1935);
Modern Ireland as Seen by an Englishwoman (London: Dent, 1936; New York: Dutton, 1936);
Modern Scotland as Seen by an Englishwoman (London: Dent, 1937; New York: Dutton, 1937);
Modern England as Seen by an Englishwoman (London: Dent, 1938; New York: Dutton, circa 1938);
Modern Sweden as Seen by an Englishwoman (London: Dent, 1939; New York: Dutton, 1939);
Lament for Democracy (London: Dent, 1940);
The Englishwoman, British Life and Thought, no. 9 (London & New York: Published for the British Council by Longmans, Green, 1940);
Nina Boyle (London: Marie Lawson for the Nina Boyle Committee, circa 1944);
Mr. Pompous and the Pussy-cat: A Play for Children in Three Acts (London: S. French, 1948);
Holland To-day (London: Dent, 1950).

Editions: *Marriage as a Trade,* introduction by Jan Lewis (London: Women's Press, 1981);
How the Vote was Won, in *How the Vote Was Won, and Other Suffragette Plays,* edited by Candida Lacey, introduction by Dale Spender (London & New York: Methuen, 1985);
Diana of Dobson's, in *New Woman Plays,* edited, with an introduction, by Linda Fitzsimmons and Viv Gardner (London: Methuen, 1991).

PLAY PRODUCTIONS: *The Sixth Commandment,* Brighton Pier, 11 May 1906;
The Sergeant of Hussars, London, Bijou Theatre, 23 June 1907;
Mrs. Vance, London, Victoria Hall, 27 October 1907;
Diana of Dobson's, London, Kingsway Theatre, 12 February 1908; New York, Savoy Theatre, 5 September 1909;
How the Vote Was Won, by Hamilton and Christopher St. John, London, Royalty Theatre, 13 April 1909;
Anti-Suffrage Waxworks, London, Women's Social and Political Union Women's Exhibition, Prince's Skating Rink, 1909;
The Pot and the Kettle, London, Scala Theatre, 12 November 1909;
A Pageant of Great Women, London, Scala Theatre, 12 November 1909;
Just to Get Married: A Comedy in Three Acts, London, Little Theatre, 8 November 1910;
The Home Coming, London, Aldwych Theatre, 18 November 1910;
The Cutting of the Knot, Glasgow, Royalty Theatre, 13 March 1911; produced again as *A Matter of Money,* London, Little Theatre, 9 February 1913;
Jack and Jill and a Friend, London, Kingsway Theatre, 8 May 1911; produced again as *Jack and Jill,* Glasgow, Pavilion, 15 April 1912;
The Constant Husband, London, Palladium Theatre, 19 February 1912;
Lady Noggs, adapted from Edgar Jepson's stories, London, Comedy Theatre, 15 February 1913;
Phyl, Brighton, West Pier, 10 March 1913; Manchester, Gaiety Theatre, 13 May 1918;
The Lady Killer, London, Little Theatre, 3 April 1914;
The Child in Flanders, Abbeville, 25 December 1917;
Mrs. Armstrong's Admirer, London, Excelsior Hall, 21 January 1920;
The Brave and the Fair, London, Excelsior Hall, 16 February 1920;
The Human Factor, Birmingham, Repertory Theatre, 8 November 1924; produced again as *The Old Adam,* London, Kingsway Theatre, 17 November 1925;
The Beggar Prince, London, Embassy Theatre, 26 December 1929;
Caravan, adapted from Carl Zuckmayer's *Katherina Knie,* London, Queen's Theatre, 7 April 1932.

OTHER: Ethel Smyth, *The March of the Women,* words by Hamilton, music by Smyth (London: J. Curwen / Germantown, Pa.: Curwen, 1911);
"The Beggar Prince," in *The Beggar Prince and Four Other Modern Plays* (Glasgow: Collins, 1936).

SELECTED PERIODICAL PUBLICATIONS—UNCOLLECTED: "How the Vote Was Won," *Women's Franchise,* 20 (14 November 1907): 227–228;
"The Sins We Do Not Speak Of," *Time and Tide,* 9 (2 November 1928): 1035;
"Mrs. Vance," *Englishwoman,* 1 (February 1909): 62–71;
"Phyl," *Women's Suffrage the Common Cause of Humanity,* 5 (21 November 1913): 570–571, 594–596; (28 November 1913): 618–619; (5 December 1913): 644–645; (12 December 1913): 671–673; (19 December 1913): 694–695; (26 December): 710–711; (2 January 1914): 728–729; (16 January 1914): 768–769; (23 January 1914): 788–789; (30 January 1914): 808–809; – (6 February 1914): 830–831.

Cicely Hamilton's work as a woman suffrage playwright and polemicist between 1908 and 1914 and her involvements with the Women Writers'

Frontispiece for American edition of Hamilton's Diana of Dobson's *(1908)*

Suffrage League, Actresses' Franchise League, and Edith Craig's Pioneer Players have been the principal objects of scholarly interest in her. Since 1979 Hamilton's plays *Diana of Dobson's* (1908), *How the Vote Was Won* (1909), and *A Pageant of Great Women* (1909); her feminist tract *Marriage as a Trade* (1909); and her illustrated satirical poem *Beware! A Warning—to Suffragists* (circa 1909) have been reprinted, either alone or in anthologies, but her novels have been neglected. The selectivity of critical interest in Hamilton has obscured her achievements in fiction and has only partially recontextualized her writing historically.

Born in London on 15 June 1872, Cicely Mary Hammill was the eldest child of Denzill and Maud Hammill. Her father was a captain in the Gordon Highlanders who rose to the rank of major general before moving on to a diplomatic career. At his death in 1891 he was vice consul at Bonny in West Africa. In her autobiography *Life Errant* (1935) Hamilton, who changed her last name when she became an actress, mentions an early "parting" from her mother, although its nature is not explained. She and her siblings were boarded out to a Clapham family and later raised by aunts in Bournemouth. Hamilton was educated at boarding schools in Malvern and Bad Homburg. In 1890 she became a pupil teacher at a Midlands school. Around 1892 she went on the stage, supplementing her income by doing translations, writing journalism, and, under various undisclosed pseudonyms, submitting stories to popular magazines. She toured in provincial "fit-up" theater (where all properties, including the proscenium arch, were carried by the company from place to place) and in Edmund Tearle's company. She settled in London in about 1903, hoping to establish herself there as an actor and playwright. Before 1914 she performed in commercial theater, the avant-garde productions of the Play Actors and Pioneer Players companies, and Actresses' Franchise League plays and gave vocal recitals. Her most acclaimed role was Mrs. Knox in Bernard Shaw's *Fanny's First Play* at the Little Theatre, London, in 1911.

In 1907 Hamilton became active in the woman's suffrage movement. Hamilton and Bessie Hatton founded the Women Writers' Suffrage League in 1908, and Hamilton became a founding member of the Actresses' Franchise League later that year. She was also a member of the Women's Freedom League, which broke away from the Women's Social and Political Union in 1907, and later of the Women's Tax Resistance League. She was on the founding editorial board of the suffragist periodical *Englishwoman,* begun in 1909. For the cause she wrote plays, articles, satirical future fantasies, poems, and the lyrics to Ethel Smyth's suffragist anthem, *The March of the Women* (1911); spoke at woman's suffrage meetings and at homes; and participated in public debates on suffrage issues.

In *Life Errant* Hamilton says that her personal revolt was "feminist rather than suffragist; what I rebelled at chiefly was the dependence implied in the idea of 'destined' marriage, 'destined' motherhood—the identification of success with marriage, of failure with spinsterhood, the artificial concentration of the hopes of girlhood on sexual attraction and maternity." In "How the Vote Was Won" (1907), a satirical fantasy of the future that was adapted for the stage by Hamilton and Christopher St. John (pseudonym of Christabel Marshall) in 1909, female suffrage is achieved by working women going on strike and demanding the support of male relatives. In *Marriage as a Trade* (1909) Hamilton addresses the economic and social pressures that coerce women into marriage and consent to oppression. She articulates a feminist aesthetic founded on "freedom of thought and expression, wide liberty of outlook and unhampered liberty of communication" and incompatible with the "deliberate stunting and repression" of women's intellects, the "repression of individuality and the inducement of artificiality." These aspects of socialization, she argues, produce in women artists a dependency on plots about women "existing for love and maternity" and on attempts "to render life or beauty as man desires that a woman should see and render it."

Hamilton was a dedicated spinster. She enjoyed rich and enduring female friendships, which Lis Whitelaw uses as the basis of her circumstantial argument in *The Life and Rebellious Times of Cicely Hamilton: Actress, Writer, Suffragist* (1990) that Hamilton was a lesbian. In "The Sins We Do Not Speak Of" (1928), however, Hamilton, who was deeply religious, condemns lesbianism and male homosexuality in formulaic biblical language as abominations, although she criticizes some of the social persecution of gay people.

Diana of Dobson's, her first full-length play, was her most enduring. Not published until 1925, it had two successful runs at London's Kingsway Theatre beginning in February of 1908 and then toured nearly continuously in the provinces for twenty years. In an interview given shortly before the play opened Hamilton disingenuously claimed:

> Although I take a great interest in the social and industrial questions of the day, in so far as they affect women generally, I had no serious object in writing "Diana of Dobson's." Of course, I am hoping that the story may prove interesting to the general public, who do not know as a rule about the lives of shop-girls, and the want of consideration with which some of them are treated by their employers . . . My idea in writing "Diana of Dobson's" was partly to contrast two temperaments as the outcome of totally opposite surroundings.

Hamilton had accepted a lump sum of £100 as payment for the play rather than royalties, which would have totaled much more. Perhaps spurred by this misjudgment and encouraged by the example of Elizabeth Robins's lucrative revision of her play *Votes for Women* (1907) as the novel *The Convert* (1907), Hamilton novelized *Diana of Dobson's* for the American market. It was published in 1908, a year before a disastrous production was staged in New York.

The three novels Hamilton published before 1918–*Diana of Dobson's, Just to Get Married* (1911), and *A Matter of Money* (1916)—were all novelizations of her full-length plays. Her early novelizations tend to add sections explanatory of emotional turmoil and to fill out details of gesture, voice, and movement that would be provided in stage performance by the actors. A reviewer of the novel version of *Diana of Dobson's* in *The New York Times* (11 July 1908) praised her use of dialogue rather than "actual descriptions" to achieve a "clear, unlabored delineation of character."

The romantic endings of the dramatic versions of *Diana of Dobson's* and *Just to Get Married: A Comedy in Three Acts* (1914) have been read by such critics as Jane Eldridge Miller, Harriet Blodgett, and Sheila Stowell as what Miller calls "theatrical compromises" for a popular audience that "became ideological contradictions" in Hamilton's feminism. Such a reading of Hamilton's work overlooks important dimensions of her attitudes to and representations of class formation and consumption and is based implicitly on the expectation that her heroines, Diana Massingberd and Georgina Vicary, should meet the ideological demands of late-twentieth-century feminists.

The opening scene of *Diana of Dobson's* sets up generic expectations: it focuses on the regimented lives and drudgery of the shop assistants in the live-in female dormitory of Dobson's drapery emporium. It is informed by the then-current middle-class interest in the sociological detail of lower-class labor and living conditions. The worlds of the workers and the homeless of the final scene are pointedly contrasted with the romance of middle-class "slumming" expeditions among the poor. The escape fantasies of the assistants focus on marriage and violating the 127 rules of the emporium. Virtuously rebellious Diana Massingberd, the uneducated daughter of a country doctor who became impoverished after her father's death, receives a legacy of £300 that she resolves to spend in a short orgy of upper-middle-class feminine consumption. In the 8 February 1908 issue of *The Pall Mall Gazette* Lena Ashwell, who played Diana in the first production of the play, interpreted Diana's "state of revolt" as a product of a bohemian nature; in the novel Hamilton attributes Diana's rebelliousness to her Irish ethnicity and déclassé middle-class origins.

Diana's posing as an upper-middle-class heiress at a Swiss holiday resort results in marriage proposals from both a former employer, the drapery magnate (and Jewish stereotype) Sir Jabez Grinlay, and the spendthrift "Captain the Honourable" Victor Bretherton. Diana's disgust at the living conditions of Sir Jabez's employees leads to a debate between the two, with Diana taking the side of labor and Sir Jabez that of capital. After Diana is compelled to reveal her disguise to Bretherton, to whom she is attracted, she challenges him to earn his living without the help of family and friends. His pride

Hamilton (far right, facing camera) at a 1910 suffragist demonstration. On her right are feminist Edith Craig and Christopher St. John (Christabel Marshall), Hamilton's sometime collaborator.

stung, he proceeds to attempt to do so in London. The pair, unemployed, destitute, and homeless (although Bretherton does have the power to end his plight, since he has an independent annual income of £600), meet again by chance on the Embankment. They agree to marry and live on Bretherton's income. This compact represents for Bretherton a practical settling for constrained consumption, for Diana a modest realization of her feminine fantasy self. As the reviewer of the novel noted in *The New York Times,* echoing reviews of the London production of the play, "[T]he old problem of capital vs. labor is met squarely—and left unsolved."

In the novel version of *Just to Get Married* (1914) the unskilled and uneducated Georgina Vicary, brought up by her uncle and aunt, Sir Theodore and Lady Catherine Grayle, resists her apparent "destiny" of romantic courtship and upper-middle-class marriage. Her aunt carefully grooms her to catch the eye of the eligible bachelor Adam Lankester, who has earned his living for many years in Canada but has returned to an inheritance. Georgina's white skin, suggestive of "pure" Englishness and a veneer of innocence of designs on marriage, is contrasted with his bronzed skin, which implies colonial labor and the wealth that makes him a suitable marriage partner. He fits the stereotype of the good-hearted, rough, gullible, laconic colonial male, and he idolizes Georgina's appearance of genteel delicacy. Marriage offers Georgina a chance to escape from her agonizing low self-esteem and to make her family happy. Georgina and Adam become engaged, but, pushed into greater honesty by guilt and embarrassment at Adam's devotion, she jilts him. Leaving home to seek shelter with a spinster friend, Frances Melliship, who makes a meager living as a commercial artist, Georgina walks to the railway station during a storm, symbolic of her tempestuous feelings and desire for Adam. Meeting Adam at the station, she asks him to marry her, and he accepts. Her muddy clothes symbolize her moral compromise. The alternatives for Georgina—a life with Frances financed by a small allowance from her uncle or a return home—are, respectively, unpalatable and humiliating. Her memories of an earlier stay with Frances are full of disgust at the squalor of Frances's living conditions and of the poor and dull food.

The conclusion of *Just to Get Married* attracted a mixed response: some reviewers of the 1910 stage version saw it as evidence of Hamilton's failure to sustain her nerve in wittily criticizing the institutions of courtship and marriage, while others, such as the reviewer for *The Sketch* (16 November 1910), who questioned Georgina's motives, found it "cruel, cynical, and legitimate." In the novel Georgina's upper-middle-class snobbery is more explicitly made the reason for her rejecting Frances's offer of accommodation. Blodgett reads this rejection as an unfortunate confirmation of a widespread antifeminist "lack of faith in female potential for real growth and sustained endeavor."

Hamilton's growing confidence in handling complex characterization is also apparent in the novella "Phyl," serialized in the suffrage journal *Common Cause* in 1913–1914. Phyllis Chester is a governess confronted by the typical problems of class ambiguity and sexual vulnerability inherent in that role, a situation common in nineteenth-century British literature. Phyl rebels against her situation. Her rebelliousness is motivated by her resentment of the angelically submissive and devitalized office-worker sister Cathy who has raised her, her anger at the class condescension of the family she works for, and her desire for upper-middle-class hedonism. Her employer, Mrs. Ponsonby, unfairly suspects her of flirting with Jack Ashburton Folliott, on whom she has matrimonial designs for her daughter, and fires her. In a "passionate outburst against the dullness of her lot" Phyl accepts Jack's proposal that she become his mistress; she enjoys his "liking and protection." They fall in love as each helps the other to realize fantasies of escape. When Jack's fortune is almost all embezzled by his solicitor, he proposes marriage as part of a plan to immigrate to Australia, and Phyl accepts because of the pleasure and relief it will bring Cathy. The novella is remarkably free from moralizing about adultery and provides insight into the role of rescue fantasies in heterosexual romance in the period.

At one level Hamilton's novel *A Matter of Money* concerns the topical question of the economics of divorce; on another level, as a review of the play version in *Votes for Women* (14 February 1913) noted, it examines "the suffering involved where human passions clash with expediency and with codes of morality." The novel awkwardly mixes melodrama and psychological exploration of the complexities of marital and adulterous relationships. Married but estranged from her wealthy husband, Herbert, on whom she is financially dependent, Lucia Coventry has an affair with a struggling doctor, Godfrey Channing. Driven to despair by the social and economic implications if she were to divorce Herbert and Godfrey were to divorce his wife, Ada, as well as by Godfrey's division between what Hamilton calls "the striving personalities of primitive, irresponsible human lover and ordered professional citizen"—he still has feelings for his wife and their invalid daughter—Lucia commits suicide by walking in front of a train.

The ravages of World War I had a profound effect on Hamilton's imagination and her politics and brought about decisive changes in her career. She worked as a clerk with the National Union of Women's Suffrage Societies' Scottish Women's Hospital Unit at Royaumont from November 1914 until May 1917, when she joined Lena Ashwell's Concerts at the Front company based in Abbeville. She and Gertrude Jennings founded a repertory company there. In 1918–1919 she played with Concerts at the Front around Winchester and in 1919 in the occupied Rhineland.

Hamilton was particularly perturbed by the spectacle of fleeing refugees, interpreting the creation of such groups as a new military strategy: "the use of the enemy civilian population as an auxiliary destructive force." Her novel *Theodore Savage: A Story of the Past or the Future* (1922) presents an apocalyptic vision of civilization destroyed by a combination of war technology and this strategy. Theodore Savage, a middle-class bureaucrat, is so caught up in his acquisitive desire for collectibles, including the "delicate" upper-middle-class Phillida Rathbone as his wife, that the international tensions and politics that lead to war are not immediate and real to him.

In the foreword to *Lest Ye Die: A Story from the Past or of the Future* (1928), her revision of *Theodore Savage*, Hamilton elaborates her central theses: that the combination of scientific knowledge applied to warfare and human combativeness is a threat to civilization and that the biblical story of the Fall may express a human reaction to a previous historical cycle of destruction of civilization by science. Hamilton interprets the temptation as masculine desine for mastery over nature. Hamilton's graphic vision of apocalypse entails a destruction of domestic order brought about by displacement of population, a reversion to savage foraging for food and shelter, the loss of visible class distinctions, and the slow remaking of family and community on barbaric and reactionary lines. Despite his utter contempt for Ada, a Cockney woman, Theodore takes her as his partner to satiate his sexual needs. Ada, a stereotypical product of her working-class environment and commodity capitalism, becomes the epitome of feminine regressiveness. Hamilton's revision of *Theodore Savage* as *Lest Ye Die* consists of a new prologue and a reworking of the first five chapters that updates the war technology and alters the courtship plot involving Theodore and Phillida (making her his object of desire rather than his fiancée).

Reviewers who accepted the novel's first thesis proclaimed its significance, and Hamilton's vision of anarchy and barbarism haunted the imaginations of some readers for decades. "I hope that all speakers for pacifist societies, for the League of Nations Union and for those women's organizations which put 'Peace' on their programmes, will read, mark and learn almost by heart this terrible, enthralling and supremely important book," wrote Vera Brittain in her review of *Lest Ye Die* in *Time and Tide* (20 July 1928).

William—an Englishman (1919), conceptualized before the war as a futuristic fantasy mocking the rhetoric of sex war and class war used by suffragettes and socialists, respectively, opens as an acid satire on the narrow focus of militant suffragettes and socialists. William Tully, a socialist, and Griselda Watkins, a suffragette who has been briefly imprisoned for her activism, had not "entertained the idea of a European War. . . . Rumors of war they had always regarded as foolish and malicious inventions set afloat in the interest of Capitalism and Conservatism with the object of diverting attention from Social Reform or the settlement of the Woman question."

The novel develops after its opening satirical chapters into a study of William's conversion from socialism to nationalism with the onset of World War I. Hamilton had by this time begun to interpret history in terms of cycles of action and reaction. She traces two of these cycles in *William*. William and Griselda are honeymooning in the Belgian Ardennes when the German army invades. His conversion is brought about by what the couple witnesses there and what they suffer at the hands of German soldiers. Griselda is raped, run over by a German motorcycle, and dies from her injuries; William is pressed into doing physical labor for the Germans and is humiliated by them. Hamilton uses religious symbolism to imply that Griselda's death is a truer martyrdom than the "martyrdom" that had been conferred on her by the suffragettes for her prison experience.

The rhetoric of socialism cannot help William make sense of his experience, so he falls back on the biblical rhetoric of "hell and the mouth of hell" familiar from childhood. He begins to read more widely to acquire some historical framework in which to place the war. His romance with his new vision of England, which helps him overcome feelings of "impotent misery," starts to pall when he is initially rejected as a volunteer, is numbed by the bureaucratic routine of his life as a military clerk, and as the memory of Griselda becomes less poignant, assuaging "his fury for instant and personal revenge." He is killed unheroically by injuries sustained during an air raid.

William—an Englishman was awarded the Femina-Vie Heureuse Prize, and of Hamilton's fiction only this novel has attracted sustained comment. Echoing the sentiments of respectful early reviewers, Nicola Beauman says that *William—an Englishman* is a "deeply profound comment on the impact of war on two 'ordinary' people . . . it has a moral which almost transcends patriotism which is that everyone matters in his own way." Jane Marcus reviles the novel as "a shameless example of the ideological repression of both socialism and feminism that was one of the major social achievements of World War I" and that resulted in the "slaughter of a whole generation in the name of democracy." Claire M. Tylee develops a psychoanalytic reading in which William and Griselda are aspects of Hamilton's divided self, the "shameful, feminine side of herself had to die off . . . if she were to survive" and the "aggression which Hamilton felt at the wound to her sense of her own worth, when the 'You' in the message 'Your Country Needs You' did not mean women" is "deflected onto the archetypally male threat, the Hun."

After the war Hamilton earned her principal income from writing through journalism; she tried to reestablish herself as a playwright, but her subject matter, war, did not meet with commercial acceptance. Her journalism ranges widely, but she had a special interest in League of Nations politics; international disputes in Europe; the rise of militarism, Nazism, Fascism, and totalitarianism; the limitations of democracy; and the dangers of war technology. In *Life Errant* she represents the "man's preserve of politics" as outside the domain of "normality" as it was socially constituted for women—but it was a preserve she entered with gusto.

Hamilton became a libertarian feminist with conservative leanings who persistently defined the individual and "civilization" against the "barbarities" and emotionalism of the collective and the popular mind. She was active in the Six Point Group, which campaigned for specific reforms based on equal rights for women; the Open Door Council, which fought against protective legislation limiting women's work; and the New Generation League, which she promoted birth control, and was on the editorial board of the independent feminist weekly *Time and Tide*.

During the 1930s Hamilton began a series of descriptive travel books about European countries that were widely acclaimed, especially for her efforts at fair-mindedness. Her thematically thin novel *Full Stop* (1931) concerns prime ministerial aspirant John Royle, who learns that he has only a short time to live. This scenario seems to have been concocted to dramatize the human desire for affirmation of a spiritual afterlife and to allow Hamilton to denounce politicking. The satirical spirit of Hamilton's futuristic fantasy *Little Arthur's History of the Twentieth Century* (1933) was well received. What the reviewer in the *Times Literary Supplement* (23 November 1933) called her "light but venomed lance" is directed at such targets as increasing government regulation, war technology, international diplomacy, and irresponsible democracy.

In 1937 Hamilton was awarded a Civil List pension for her services to literature. She continued to write travel books, political commentary, a history of Englishwomen (1940), and reviews. During World War II she worked for the Royaumont Canteen and the Chelsea Fire Service. She became actively involved with the British League for European Freedom in 1945, an organization that lobbied for Western democracies to oppose Soviet aggression and human rights violations in Eastern Europe, and edited its weekly press bulletin from 1946 until shortly before her death on 6 December 1952.

Cicely Hamilton was regarded by her contemporaries as a skillful and witty writer of topical plays and novels of ideas marked by deft characterization and bereft of didacticism. Her fiction engaged with and challenged contemporary debates about and understandings of women and the moralities of heterosexual romance, marriage, and the dangers of war technology and new military strategies. Once largely forgotten, since the late 1970s Hamilton's writing has gained increased scholarly attention and recognition as part of an important female tradition in theater, premodernism, and writing about World War I.

Bibliography:
Sue Thomas, "Cicely Hamilton on Theatre: A Preliminary Bibliography," *Theatre Notebook: A Journal of the History and Technique of British Theatre,* 49 (1995): 99–107.

Biography:
Lis Whitelaw, *The Life and Rebellious Times of Cicely Hamilton: Actress, Writer, Suffragist* (London: Women's Press, 1990).

References:
Nicola Beauman, *A Very Great Profession: The Women's Novel 1914–39* (London: Virago, 1983), pp. 131–132;

Harriet Blodgett, "Cicely Hamilton, independent feminist," *Frontiers,* 11, nos. 2–3 (1990): 99–104;

Jane Marcus, "Corpus/Corps/Corpse: Writing the Body in/at War," in *Arms and the Woman: War, Gender, and Literary Representation,* edited by Helen M. Cooper, Adrienne Auslander Munich, and Susan Merrill Squier (Chapel Hill: University of North Carolina Press, 1989), pp. 124–167;

Jane Eldridge Miller, *Rebel Women: Feminism, Modernism and the Edwardian Novel* (London: Virago, 1994), pp. 131–132;

Sheila Stowell, *A Stage of Their Own: Feminist Playwrights of the Suffrage Era* (Manchester: Manchester University Press, 1992), pp. 71–99;

Sue Thomas, "Cicely Hamilton," in *British Playwrights, 1880–1956: A Research and Production Sourcebook,* edited by William Demastes and Katherine E. Kelly (Westport, Conn.: Greenwood, 1996), pp. 189–199;

Claire M. Tylee, *The Great War and Women's Consciousness: Images of Militarism and Womanhood in Women's Writings, 1914–64* (London: Macmillan, 1990), pp. 133–141.

Mary Agnes Hamilton
(1884 - 1962)

Maria Aline Seabra Ferreira
University of Aveiro (Portugal)

BOOKS: *The Story of Abraham Lincoln* (London: Jack, 1906; New York: Dutton, 1906);

A Junior History of Rome to the Death of Caesar (Oxford: Clarendon Press, 1910);

Greek Saints and Their Festivals (Edinburgh & London: Blackwood, 1910);

Less Than the Dust (London: Heinemann, 1912; Boston: Houghton Mifflin, 1912);

Greek Legends (Oxford: Clarendon Press, 1912);

Outlines of Greek and Roman History (Oxford: Clarendon Press, 1913); London & New York: Milford, 1918);

Yes (London: Heinemann, 1914);

Dead Yesterday (London: Duckworth, 1916; New York: Doran, 1916);

Full Circle (London: Collins, 1919);

The Last Fortnight (London: Collins, 1920);

The Principles of Socialism with Notes for Lecturers and Class Leaders (London: Independent Labour Party Information Committee, 1921);

Ancient Rome: The Lives of Great Men (Oxford: Clarendon Press), 1922;

Follow My Leader (London: Cape, 1922);

The Man of To-Morrow: J. Ramsay MacDonald, as Iconoclast (London: Parsons, 1923); republished as *J. Ramsay MacDonald, the Man of Tomorrow* (New York: Seltzer, 1924); revised and adapted as *J. Ramsay MacDonald* (London: Cape, 1929; New York: Cape & Smith, 1929);

An Outline of Ancient History to A.D. 180, by Hamilton and A. W. F. Blunt (Oxford: Clarendon Press / New York: Oxford University Press, 1924);

Fit to Govern!, as Iconoclast (London: Parsons, 1924);

England's Labour Rulers, as Iconoclast (New York: Seltzer, 1924);

Margaret Bondfield (London: Parsons, 1924; New York: Seltzer, 1925);

J. Ramsay MacDonald (1923-25), as Iconoclast (London: Parsons, 1925; New York: Seltzer, 1925);

Mary MacArthur: A Biographical Sketch (London: Parsons, 1925; New York: Seltzer, 1925);

Mary Agnes Hamilton (photograph by C. Harris)

Thomas Carlyle (London: Parsons, 1926; New York: Holt, 1926);

Greece (Oxford: Clarendon Press, 1926);

Folly's Handbook (London: Cape, 1927; New York: Harcourt, Brace, 1927);

Special Providence: A Tale of 1917 (London: Allen & Unwin, 1930); republished as *Three against Fate* (Boston & New York: Houghton Mifflin, 1930);

Murder in the House of Commons (London: Hamilton, 1931; Boston & New York: Houghton Mifflin, 1932);

In America To-day (London: Hamilton, 1932);

Rome: A Short History (Oxford: Clarendon Press, 1932);

Sidney and Beatrice Webb: A Study in Contemporary Biography (London: Sampson Low, Marston, 1933; Boston & New York: Houghton Mifflin, 1933);

John Stuart Mill (London: Hamilton, 1933);

Life Sentence (London: Hamilton, 1935); republished as *Sentenced to Life* (Boston & New York: Houghton Mifflin, 1935);

Newnham: An Informal Biography (London: Faber & Faber, 1936);

Arthur Henderson: A Biography (London & Toronto: Heinemann, 1938);

The Labour Party To-Day: What It Is and How It Works (London: Labour Book Service, 1939);

Women at Work: A Brief Introduction to Trade Unionism for Women (London: Routledge, 1941);

British Trade Unions (London: Oxford University Press, 1943);

Remembering My Good Friends (London: Cape, 1944);

British Democracy in War Time (London: Ministry of Information, 1945);

The Place of the United States of America in World Affairs, Montague Burton International Relations Lecture (Nottingham: University College, 1947);

Up-Hill All the Way: A Third Cheer for Democracy (London: Cape, 1953).

OTHER: *In the League and Out,* by Hamilton, Norman Thomas, and Raymond Leslie Buell [121st New York luncheon discussion, 4 January 1930] (New York: Foreign Policy Association, 1930);

England Seeks a Way Out, by Hamilton and William A. Orton [123rd New York luncheon discussion, 9 January 1932] (New York: Foreign Policy Association, 1932);

"Confessions of an M.P.," *Harper's Monthly Magazine,* European edition (April 1932);

The Boat Train, edited by Hamilton (London: Allen & Unwin, 1934);

Arthur Moeller van den Bruck, *Germany's Third Empire,* edited and translated by E. O. Lorimer, introduction by Hamilton (London: Allen & Unwin, 1934);

"Changes in Social Life," in *Our Freedom and Its Results,* edited by Ray Strachey (London: Hogarth Press, 1936), pp. 231–285.

TRANSLATIONS: Gustav Frenssen, *Holyland* (London: Constable, 1906; Boston: Estes, 1906);

Yves Guyot, *The Comedy of Protection* (London: Hodder & Stoughton, 1906);

M. S. Nordau, *The Interpretation of History* (London: Rebman, 1910);

Margarete Kurlbaum-Siebert, *Mary, Queen of Scots* (London: Cape, 1928; New York: Harcourt, Brace, 1929);

W. Dibelius, *England* (London: Cape, 1930; New York & London: Harper, 1930).

Mary Agnes Hamilton was a novelist, essayist, memoirist, member of Parliament for the British Labour Party, and journalist. She made an important contribution to the history of the Labour Party through her nonfiction writing, and her novels, which focused primarily on World War I and the disruption it brought to civilian life, vividly portray the war years and their aftermath. The eldest of the six children of Robert Adamson, a professor of logic at Manchester, Aberdeen, and Glasgow Universities, and Daisy Duncan, a former teacher, "Molly" Hamilton was born in 1884 in Manchester. As she recalls in her memoir *Remembering My Good Friends* (1944), hers was a wonderful childhood. She was educated first by her father and then attended the Aberdeen Girls' High School and the Glasgow High School for girls. In 1902 she went as a Mathilda Blind scholar to Newnham College, Cambridge, where she took first-class honors in classics, history, and economics. She particularly enjoyed Goldsworthy Lowes Dickinson's lectures and those of Henry Jackson on Greek philosophy. In *Remembering My Good Friends* she nostalgically evokes those times:

> Cambridge was to mean to me a great deal. But, at first, it was disappointing. Or rather Newnham was. I came from too much.... long before I left it I loved it and was deeply grateful to it. But I realized Cambridge, with its beauty, its wealth of grand and exciting people, the rich adventures of the mind it opened out, before I did any proper justice to my own college, and my good fortune in being there.

Her father's sudden death while she was still at college left his family in poor financial circumstances, but Hamilton was able to complete her degree thanks to her scholarship. During her time at Cambridge she developed her taste for politics. In *Up-Hill All the Way: A Third Cheer for Democracy* (1953) (the title an obvious reference to E. M. Forster's *Two Cheers for Democracy,* 1951), she discusses at length her reading and the progress of her thought during those years. She mentions her first contact with Karl Marx's *Das Kapital* (1867–1894), her infatuation with what Russia represented, and her gradual disillusionment with that country's socialist experiment. Her future political career appears to have started in the earnest political discussions and mock parlia-

Title page for the author's first novel, a romance set in England and Canada that she later found embarrassing

mentary sessions of those days. As Hamilton explains in *Remembering My Good Friends:*

> If we left religion alone and sex to wait for the revelations of possible matrimony, we made up for this by an intense concern with politics. Our premier society was Political—organized like a parliament, meeting once a week in the big hall, with Government and opposition; the parties (then only Liberal and Conservative) in annual turn occupying the front bench and presenting bills.

After finishing her studies at Cambridge she spent a year in Germany followed by a year as assistant lecturer in history at the University of Cardiff. She next went to London, where she became assistant to Sir Philip Gibbs on *The Review of Reviews,* assuming its editorship during his absence. In the meantime she wrote articles on literature, economics, and history for various periodicals and lectured on "The Reform of the Poor Law." In 1905 she married economist C. J. Hamilton, secretary of the Royal Economic Society; theirs was a brief, unhappy, childless union.

Before her immersion in Labour politics, the history of Greece and Rome was Hamilton's special field of interest, and she spent three years, from 1907 to 1909, in Italy and Greece doing research, which formed the basis for several works of classical history, including *Greek Saints and Their Festivals* (1910).

For the next two decades Hamilton earned her living primarily as a journalist. Virginia Woolf, whom she first met during a weekend at Lady Ottoline Morrell's home at Garsington in 1918, describes Hamilton in a diary entry dated 29 July 1918: "She is a working brain worker. Hasn't a penny of her own; & has the anxious hard working brain of a professional, earning her living all the time." Hamilton, however, was also writing books: biographies, novels, and historical studies. Her first published work was a life of Abraham Lincoln (1906). In *Up-Hill All the Way* she explains that she has "since very early years, had a passion for writing." Indeed she wrote prolifically, spanning various genres from novels and biographies to books on politics, classical culture, history, journalism, and translations.

In addition to Woolf, Hamilton was acquainted with other literary figures of the day, including Henry James, her "literary idol," as she describes him in *Remembering My Good Friends.* She met him in London in 1917 at her friend Agnes Conway's house. Conway and her mother's American sister ran a hostel for Belgian war casualties, and James came for tea to meet a group of men who, having recovered, were about to rejoin their units. Hamilton recalls that she "came away cleansed and uplifted." She also attended meetings at 44 Bedford Square, one of the principal meeting places for the Bloomsbury Group, where she met Bertrand Russell, Lady Ottoline Morrell, Lytton Strachey, J. M. Keynes, Adrian Stephen, Leonard and Virginia Woolf, Vanessa Bell, Clive Bell, Aldous and Julian Huxley, Gerald Shove, and Desmond MacCarthy among others. According to Hamilton, "the dominating mind was Bertie Russell's." Hamilton was also a founding member of the 1917 Club, named after the February Revolution in Russia. The club, whose main function was to provide a meeting place for those with an interest in peace and democracy, attracted a large membership of intellectuals and radical politicians to its premises in Gerrard Street, Soho.

Hamilton knew Virginia and Leonard Woolf well, visiting them "fairly often . . . both at Hogarth House and at Rodmell, near Lewes." She greatly admired Virginia Woolf, calling her "that lovely and richly gifted creature." Hamilton reports a conversation she had with Woolf on a hot August Sunday afternoon at Rodmell that throws light on both writers' aims and techniques: "She asked, What makes you write? I said that, with me, it was an intense interest in people and an itch to understand what made them go; she looked puzzled, shook her head. People, she said, did not much interest her; what did was the feel of life as it passed—that was what she wanted to render." Woolf, for her part, included Hamilton among her friends. In her diary entry for 22 January 1919 she reflects: "How many friends have I got? There's Lytton, Desmond, Saxon; they belong to the Cambridge stage of life.... I must insert too the set that runs parallel but does not mix, distinguished by their social & political character, headed perhaps by Margaret & including people like Goldie, Mrs. Hamilton, & intermittent figures such as Matthaei, Hobson, the Webbs—."

Hamilton had three younger sisters, Una, Sarah, and Margot. Una and Sarah were craft workers and painters, and Margot was a writer, publishing a book of poems, *A Year of War,* in 1917. Woolf voiced her opinion about Hamilton's sisters on at least two occasions in her diary. In her entry for 15 March 1919, for example, she reports that she had tea with Hamilton ("Molly that is: I had to correct myself half a dozen times") in London the day before:

> Mrs. Hamilton made me feel a little professional, for she had her table strewn with manuscripts, a book open on the desk, & she began by asking me about my novel.... She has 2 or 3 sisters, all artistic according to her, though the designs for stained glass that I saw didn't seem to me to prove it; & one is a poet, who surrounds herself with sketches of projected books on every conceivable subject, & has written a long poem which she wants us to consider publishing. "She is a poet—certainly a poet," she said, which roused my suspicions.

Hamilton's profound engagement with people and their problems, which often hinge directly on social and political issues, put her writing at odds with Woolf's more ethereal, inner-directed characterizations. Consequently it is hardly surprising that Woolf deprecated Hamilton's work in her diaries: "The truth is that Molly Hamilton with all her ability to think like a man, & her strong and serviceable mind, & her independent self-respecting life is not a writer." Despite her low opinion of Hamilton's literary skill, Woolf was always quick to praise her friend's determination and penchant for hard work: "Her courage impresses me; & the sense she gives of a machine working at high pressure all day long—the ordinary able machine of the professional working woman."

Hamilton's first novel, *Less Than the Dust* (1912), went out of print soon after it was published. Hamilton was thankful that the novel disappeared from public view, for she considered it the work of a young, inexperienced writer, with all the attendant faults. A romantic story, it relates the poignant sacrifice of a female protagonist, Delia, who is in love with her sister Pansy's husband, Adam, but marries Adam's half brother Tony to prevent Pansy's marriage from breaking up. Pansy, often left alone because of her husband's demanding work, seeks excitement during a trip to Canada and finds it in the attentions of Tony. The two decide to run away together but are thwarted by Delia, who convinces Tony that they should marry. Shortly thereafter, however, Tony discovers that he may have a child from a previous relationship, and he feels bound by duty to the child's mother. By this time Delia has grown fond of Tony, although in her heart she remains linked to Adam through her cherished memories of their deep, unuttered intellectual rapport. She realizes that her sacrifice has not been in vain, however, when she witnesses Pansy and Adam's renewed love and happiness. Although the creation of an apprentice writer, the character of Delia has psychological depth and definition, and the novel provides an extended critique of men's and women's roles in society as too stratified and in need of reassessment and change. The narrative also explores the clichés associated with the New World and particularly with Canada in a parodic, satirical vein.

Hamilton's second novel, *Yes* (1914), is permeated with soul-searching discussions about the importance of marriage, especially for a woman. James Hannah, a young artist, believes that "marriage can't mean freedom for a woman." The Traquair sisters, Joan, Chloe, and Susan, engage in animated discussions with their friends about art and the role of women artists, as well as about women's independence, their ambitions, and their aspirations. The novel concentrates on Joan's doubts about herself as an artist and her discovery of love in the figure of Sebastian Mackay, as well as on the pain brought about by a series of lovers' misunderstandings. A climactic trip to Paris proves crucial to Joan's development as an artist and as a woman.

Dead Yesterday (1916), like most of Hamilton's subsequent novels, has as its main thematic concern World War I and its devastating effects on those caught up in it. In *Remembering My Good Friends* she reflects on the destructive consequences the war had on her life at that time, a life filled with promise for

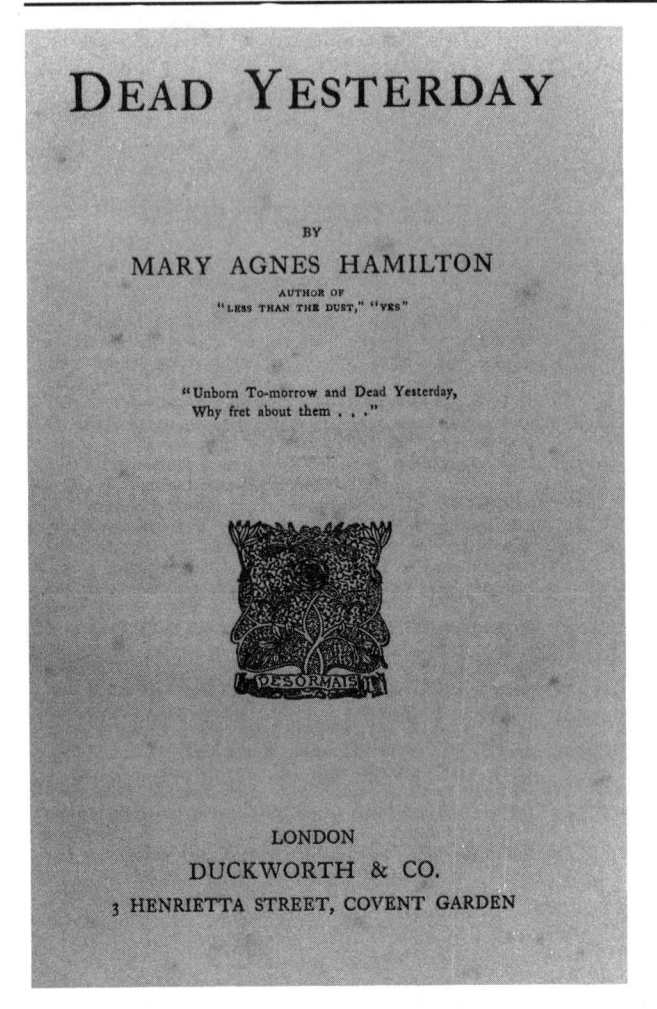

Title page for a 1916 novel depicting the impact of World War I on a group of young British intellectuals

the future and dreams to be fulfilled: "Quite literally, 1914 shattered all this. War was a shock under which we reeled. Its impact destroyed our foundations; left us staring at a world alien, hostile, terrifying, in which we did not know our way about."

Dead Yesterday caused something of a sensation with its portrayal of the predicament of the British intellectual at the outbreak of the war in August 1914 and after. While the female characters voice their profound repulsion and opposition toward the war, the men show almost a fascination for it. In *Remembering My Good Friends* Hamilton elaborates on how the characters, drawn from her own set of friends, were totally unprepared for the war and the destruction of their world:

> I there drew, faithfully, a group of youngish persons, very much like those comprising the set in which I lived, who, in July 1914, were almost completely unaware of what was coming to them; and in August, when it did come, dumbfounded. I was to be told, in 1917 and after, that they are incredible; I find it hard, now, not to endorse that view. But they were actually as I described them—earnest, politically minded, but invincibly ignorant and unprepared.

The action of *Dead Yesterday* revolves around the characters of Aurelia Leonard, a pacifist, International Socialist, and antiliberal writer (in many ways a spokeswoman for Hamilton), her daughter Daphne, and Nigel Strode, a liberal newspaper journalist, with whom Daphne falls in love. Sharon Ouditt, in her *Fighting Forces, Writing Women: Identity and Ideology in the First World War* (1994), stresses the fact that Hamilton

> was a friend of Irene Cooper Willis, the thesis of whose *England's Holy War* (1928) is traceable in Aurelia's disdain for the British Liberal press. Aurelia propounds some of the major arguments of the UDC (of which Hamilton was a member)—that a representative democracy should be established, that all diplomacy should be under parliamentary control and that international understanding should be along democratic lines.

Hamilton's political engagement (for example as a member of the Union of Democratic Control [UDC], a pacifist political organization) is apparent throughout the novel, which conducts a forceful debate between freedom and passion on the one hand and controlled organization on the other.

Aurelia Leonard's committed pacifist struggle comes through clearly in the interview she gives Nigel Strode toward the beginning of the novel. In words reminiscent of those used by suffragist and internationalist Catherine Marshall and Helena M. Swanwick, author of *Women and War* (1915), Aurelia is deeply critical of the government's militaristic effort and particularly of the role of the press in fomenting war hysteria. As she tells Nigel Strode: "How can we get the money [for social reform]—in any country in Europe—if we have to go on pouring millions into armies and navies?" She forcefully stresses that peace is "long endurance, Labour, sacrifice, conquest of the unwilling soil, just as self-control is conquest of the unwilling self. And there's no short road to it. You have to want peace passionately, with all the hardest feeling and thinking you've got." Strode, for his part, sports a contempt for reason that "was part of the fundamental creed of the younger generation, and to that generation Nigel essentially belonged. They claimed to know things more immediately. Hence they went about incessantly in search of the personal experience, above all the personal thrill, that could alone give them such knowledge." Rational thought and controlled organization, Aurelia's sphere of action, seem gradually to lose their effectiveness as "war news supplied a daily false stimulus to dull imagination: the passion of hatred gave an energy to sterile emotions," a dynamic that gives Nigel much greater control over the whole war process by means of his journalistic activities.

When Daphne and Nigel become engaged in May 1914, romantic passion makes Daphne blind to the war effort, although she knows she should be contributing, adding to her guilt: "The difficulty with me is, you know, that I'm not really, deep down, half as wretched about [the war] as I ought to be. I've got you—and that means so much that I can't take it in, that all the rest of the world has gone." Trying to escape her feelings of frustration, she follows her mother's example and devotes her time to workrooms for girls in the East End, where she witnesses firsthand the suffering of the mothers, wives, and children of dead combatants and realizes the necessity of putting an end to the horrific cataclysm of the war. Through her exposure to the harsh reality of the workrooms Daphne is confronted with the pitfalls of romantic love, which she sees as meaningless in the present situation, as well as with what she believes to be Nigel's lack of feeling, and she is finally led to break their engagement. She reflects: "As I see it, the war has come because so many people are like Nigel. . . . He can't feel, you see, and of course he wants to feel; and so must grope after things and seize them before he knows what they are. . . . He got hold of me [and] I wouldn't let go, because I loved him, and love seemed a short cut to everything." Nigel's contribution to the war propaganda is thus vehemently rejected by Daphne and Aurelia, who realize that an unbounded enthusiasm for freedom is the most effective weapon against the governmental and the press control over the progress of the war.

At the end of the novel Aurelia's country home, aptly called Wending End, becomes the refuge for a small community of women, consisting of Aurelia, Daphne, Jane, the widow of Daphne's friend lost in battle, and her baby, Leonora, born prematurely. In *Fighting Forces, Writing Women,* Ouditt examines the role of the mother figure in novels by Hamilton, Rose Macaulay, and Vera Brittain, a role that she finds "forceful . . . both symbolically and narratorially." About the ending of *Dead Yesterday* she comments that it is "earnest and radical in its refusal of heterosexual love and its positioning of maternity as something exclusive of and more powerful than patriarchy, rather than subservient to it." She continues, however, "this minor women's peace party takes place within an image of seclusion and retreat. While on the one hand this reinforces its alterity and gives the impression of strength through female bonding, it also creates a symbol of profound isolation." Their pacifist stance is thus powerfully contrasted with Nigel's active participation in promoting the war and its militaristic accoutrements through insidious propaganda in the press.

Dead Yesterday can also be said to illustrate in many ways the dilemma that Margaret Kamester and Jo Vellacott point to in their introduction to *Militarism Versus Feminism: Writings on Women and War* (1987): "Although it was not always couched in these terms, the argument was really about whether women would prove themselves responsible citizens by accepting the male-defined support roles in peace and war, agreeing to bear and nurture the warriors; or whether they would insist on taking their supposed predisposition to nurturing and conciliation into the decision-making sphere, and have the preservation of life become an important consideration in international relations."

Throughout the 1920s Hamilton contributed frequent reviews to the periodical *Time and Tide*. It provided women with an independent forum for their ideas, helping to raise their political consciousness and to make effective use of their recently acquired right to vote. During this time she wrote for *The Economist* as well. She also wrote three more novels, *Full Circle* (1919), *The Last Fortnight* (1920), and *Follow My Leader* (1922), in which the heroines are deeply involved in working for the socialist party.

In *The Last Fortnight,* a semi-autobiographical novel in which Hamilton draws on her marriage experiences, Pauline, a young poet married to Dick Cordery, has a turbulent relationship with her mother-in-law. Living with her in the same house, the couple is a constant reminder to Mrs. Cordery of the loss of a romantic relationship with her husband. To her Pauline embodies not only youth and the endless possibilities of life; she is also the woman who stands between her and her son, thus depriving her of what she considers to be her rightful share of attention. Mrs. Cordery is profoundly jealous of Pauline's active life, her writing, and her involvement with socialist work, which are sharp reminders of her own untapped resources. "The thought of her own wasted capacities rose in her like a tide, sweeping everything else away. There was no one in the world to whom she was really important. There never had been any one who would have thought the world well lost for her sake."

Pauline's relationship with Dick, for its part, is not free from tensions. Her husband disapproves of her political activity, which consumes much of her time. She feels deeply torn between her wish for purposeful activity and the traditional codes of behavior a wife was expected to follow, staying at home

Title page for a semi-autobiographical 1920 novel about a woman torn between her creative and political impulses and the demands of her husband and his mother

and devoting her life to her husband, as the following passage of dialogue illustrates:

> "If you attended to your job and gave us a better dinner it would be much more to the point."
> "And what is my job?" said Pauline, almost as though she were hopeful that Dick would throw light on a position that baffled her.
> "I am your job," said Dick.

In the end Pauline cannot take the pressure of her husband's expectations and the constant strain of her relationship with her mother-in-law, and she commits suicide. She leaves a note that explains "I'm only in people's way."

Follow My Leader, a novel that chronicles the conflict between capitalism and socialism, is again informed by Hamilton's interest and involvement with politics, as well as her ongoing concerns with the roles of women in the traditional man's world outside of the domestic sphere. The protagonist, Jane, is the daughter of a conservative politician who is struggling to find her own way: "But then, what were her views? She only knew that they were not those of any of the people who had spoken; not even of her father." Like most of Hamilton's heroines, Jane has a mind of her own, although she needs to clarify her positions through confrontation with different political agendas. She embodies Hamilton's critique of the prevailing literary conventions of the time, which specified that women be depicted as shallow and without any interests outside the traditionally "feminine": "Women in novels . . . never have any minds; not what I call operative minds; not minds that matter."

Jane's political consciousness is raised through her relationship with Sandy Colquhoun, a socialist leader who sacrifices everything, including his personal life, for the sake of the party. Jane takes to heart Sandy's lectures about socialism and his fervent addresses to the workers, urging them to keep up the fight for their rights. She follows Sandy to Glasgow, where she is plunged into the middle of a workers' strike, and she witnesses firsthand the difficulties and persecution he has to face. Although she desperately asserts "I belong to myself," when confronted with a difficult choice she is torn between her father's conservatism and Sandy's socialism. While campaigning for her father's election, she cannot forget Sandy and his principles. Even though she canvasses votes for the opposition, she manages to keep Sandy's love and respect.

In the same year that *Follow My Leader* appeared, Hamilton published another work that again emphasizes and expands upon her deep commitment to socialist work and issues: *The Principles of Socialism* (1921), in which she sets out a brief outline of socialist principles from earliest times to the present. Over the next several years she published biographies of important figures in progressive politics, including a greatly admired chronicle of the life of Labour politician J. Ramsay MacDonald, *The Man of To-morrow* (1923), which she published under the pseudonym Iconoclast, and a biography of Margaret Bondfield that appeared the next year. In *Margaret Bondfield* Hamilton draws a respectful portrait of the activist, who was a staunch defender of women's rights and an enthusiastic member of the People's Suffrage Federation, the Women's Trade Union League, and the Labour Party, becoming the first woman to serve in British government when Labour came to power in 1924. In *Fit to Govern!* (1924), a book intended to acquaint readers with the members of the first Labour government, Hamilton—again writing as Iconoclast—makes explicit her identification with Bondfield, who "has won every honour and opportunity by sheer merit, sheer hard work." In *Margaret Bondfield* Hamilton discusses the position of the woman worker, arguing that "the fundamental weakness of the woman worker was her economic position," and reflects on the potential role of trade unions in furthering women's economic goals. She states that "Margaret Bondfield and Mary Macarthur fought for women primarily because they were Socialists: their emancipation was indispensable if society was to become conscious and the State an organ of the community instead of a superimposed machine." In *Mary MacArthur: A Biographical Sketch* (1925), which has an introduction by Bondfield, Hamilton traces MacArthur's importance and role within the Labour Party and union movement and describes how she became the secretary of the Women's Trade Union League on Bondfield's recommendation. Hamilton published other biographies throughout her writing career, most notably *Arthur Henderson* (1938), which is sometimes referred to as the best of her many books.

Hamilton ran for Parliament in 1924 as a Labour candidate but did not win. Between 1929 and 1931 she served as the representative for Blackburn until the general defeat of the Labour Party. Although she was a member of Parliament for fewer than three years, her time as a Labour M.P. left a profound impression on her. In "Confessions of an M.P.," written in 1932, Hamilton reflects at length on her time in the House of Commons as fruitful, if sometimes frustrating:

> I was conscious at the time, and am conscious in retrospect, of many and serious drawbacks to the queer existence that has to be lived by the British Member of Parliament. But when I interrogate myself with the searching candor demanded of the maker of "confessions"–if those confessions are to be worth anything–I find a keen and vivid infusion of regret in my thoughts of Westminster. I wish I was still there. I want to get back. I am not, fundamentally, disillusioned about politics. I did not find politicians more disappointing than any other equally miscellaneous group of human beings. I still believe firmly in democracy, as against any other conceivable alternative.

One of the aspects that Hamilton singles out from her time in Westminster is the feeling of comradeship among the members which she calls her "main parliamentary discovery, the main treasure-trove I have brought away with me from my three years as an M.P.":

> Never and nowhere before did I so clearly understand what is meant by association. Comradeship–that is what Westminster now stands for in my mind–a comradeship so warm and real that in recollection it offsets the pains and penalties, the disillusionments and disappointments of a political period singularly rich in such, and makes me feel that it was eminently worth while to have been an M.P. and is eminently desirable to be an M.P. again.

Hamilton took her parliamentary service seriously, traveling to Geneva as a junior member of the British delegation to the assemblies of 1929 and 1930, an experience that provided her with "an inside knowledge of our foreign policy and of the foreign Office which was immensely valuable." She also served on the Balfour Committee on Trade and Industry from 1924 to 1929 and the Royal Commission on the Civil Service from 1929 to 1931. In 1930 she was elected as a member of the consultative committee of the Labour Party and in 1931 was further elevated to the party's executive committee, in which capacity she addressed the House from the front bench at a time when "the males outnumbered the females in the population as six hundred to fifteen." Her involvement in politics gave her the opportunity to put into practice those convictions she had long held. As she explains in "Confessions of an M.P.": "I went into politics simply because I had certain beliefs and opinions and to be a parliamentary candidate appeared to be the best way of furthering them."

After the 1931 Labour Party defeat she never returned to parliamentary life but continued with public service, as a governor of the BBC from 1933 to 1937 and an alderman of the London County Council between 1937 and 1940. She entered the civil service in 1940, becoming head of the United States section of the Ministry of Information. Her several trips to the United States had earlier resulted in her book *In America To-day* (1932) and a lecture delivered at the University College of Nottingham in 1947, which was published that same year as *The Place of the United States of America in World Affairs*. In 1949 her career as a public servant culminated in her being made a commander of the British Empire.

In 1930 her novel *Special Providence: A Tale of 1917* (published in the United States as *Three against Fate*) came out. The date in the title places the action squarely within the context of World War I. As one of the characters, Jean Claviger, says: "The war. They had to think about the war: to fit it in. It was the key. Somehow." War is the background as well as the shaping force against which all the events are set, distorting all human relationships within the novel. In the middle of the night Jean's friend Roberta Daisy is awakened by guns, which she at first mistakes for thunder, but soon the awful reality sweeps over her. While Jean's husband, Harold, is fighting in France, she gets better acquainted with Stephen Henshaw, a feminist she knew at Cambridge, and a romantic attachment develops between them. After his return Harold Claviger is accused of killing Stephen, but in the end he is acquitted of Stephen's murder. Roberta desperately awaits the verdict of the court, wondering during those tense days whether she loved Stephen or not. The war rules everything, thwarting some relationships and causing others to grow. As well as a poignant study of frustrated relationships, the novel is also a powerful diatribe against the war and its disruptive effects on people's lives.

Life Sentence (1935; published in the United States as *Sentenced to Life*) is also set against the backdrop of war. A young couple, Rosny and Jerry, feels helpless against the imminent threat of war and deeply revolted by the seeming inability of the foreign secretary, Naseby, to avert it. They plot to murder Naseby during a public meeting and then commit suicide. Jerry shoots Naseby but wounds him only superficially. He does not implicate Rosny as his accomplice and is sentenced to a year in prison. The novel chronicles in great detail their heartrending doubts and waverings about the best means to prevent what they perceive as a global cataclysm. George Parfitt, in his *Fiction of the First World War* (1988), asserts that war novels by women "have more to say about unease over the war than most male novels," an insight that seems perfectly appropriate for Hamilton's novels dealing with that period, permeated as they are with an obsessive concern and profound anxiety about the consequences of the war.

In 1936 her book on Newnham College came out. In *Newnham: An Informal Biography* she nostalgically remembers the fundamental influence her time there had on her future development as a politically active socialist. She traces the history of the college and its pioneering importance as a place of higher education for women. She states that Newnham

> does not today look, outside or inside, like any kind of revolutionary symbol. Cambridge and the world outside take it very much for granted. So, too, they take for granted the existence and the contribution of women with disciplined and active minds, effective arms and legs, and multifarious interests seriously and independently pursued. That a woman is, like a man, a human being, is assumed, by women as by men, to be obvious.

> Three quarters of a century ago, however, could such a result have been foreseen, it would by most women as by most men, have been regarded as a fantastic nightmare, whose outline ran counter to the profound decrees of Nature and the apparent intentions of Providence.... Newnham today stands for a change in opinion an idea that, quietly as it was initiated, worked out as a revolution.

She also expands at length on the situation of women in Victorian times and stresses the importance and support of John Stuart Mill, who, according to her, gave women

> a sense that they did matter: they were not condemned unheard and unregarded. Nor was this all he did for their cause. The vital importance of his advocacy, and the feature that gave it so powerful an effect, was that he set the issue in the light in which, for the educated mind of his generation, it had the strongest and clearest appeal. He made the cause of women part and parcel of the approach to democracy.

Hamilton expresses great admiration for Mill, who "made female enfranchisement a main plank in his political programme. Democracy in his view was unreal so long as this unjustifiable discrimination remained." She reflects on the changes in the position of women in society from Mill's time to her own, lamenting the injustices and inequalities that still beset women's lot and mentions those who helped improve it, such as Florence Nightingale, Harriet Martineau, Mary Sommerville, Elizabeth Garrett, Sophia Jex-Blake, Josephine Butler, Emily Davies, and Anne Jemima Clough.

Hamilton goes on to trace the start of schools and colleges for female students, and she places a great emphasis on the service rendered to Newnham by Henry Sidgwick and his wife, Eleanor Mildred Sidgwick. She also devotes a chapter to the First principal of Newnham, Miss Clough; elaborates on the long fight by women to acquire their rights; and finishes by reflecting on the influence the war has had in changing women's situation: "Irony, and cruel irony, there still is in the reflection that what reasoned argument and proved achievement could not win for women was given as by-product of the catastrophe of a world-war. It may be that here is no more, in effect, than the acceleration of a process anyhow inevitable, but the acceleration is striking."

Three years earlier Hamilton had devoted a whole book to Mill's importance as a forerunner of socialism and a staunch defender of women's rights (*John Stuart Mill*, 1933). In that work she argues that "everything he cared for and stood for would, now, make him a Socialist, not only in sympathy but in programme." As far as the situation of women is concerned, Hamilton states that "he was the wisest and most constant counsellor and friend of the first organised society for women's suffrage–the London National Women's Suffrage Society, founded in 1867. Six years earlier he had written his book, *The Subjection of Women*–a tribute to his wife, and so he always said, largely her work." He spared no "efforts to secure political freedom for women. He cared greatly for the education of girls.... He was a steady advocate of higher education for women and subscribed towards the establishment of scholarships for them at Cambridge."

Hamilton's pronounced political and social interests found expression in a variety of books dealing with these and other related themes. In *Sidney and Beatrice Webb: A Study in Contemporary Biography* (1933) she describes the Webbs' life and work, discussing at length their relevance for the socialist cause and the union movement and the seminal importance of their book, *History of Trade Unionism*. In her book *British Trade Unions* (1943) Hamilton traces the history of trade unionism from its beginnings to that date, examining in particular the role of women in the trade unions, and calls the Webbs' book a classic.

In *Women at Work: A Brief Introduction to Trade Unionism for Women* (1941) Hamilton had already investigated and reflected at length on the importance of unions for women. She states that the book "is concerned to relate the argument for Trade Unionism to the needs of women who work, whether in their homes or outside them." *The Labour Party To-day: What It Is and How It Works* (1939) sets out to "give a picture of the practical organisation, national and local, of the Party," about which she had written in *Fit to Govern!*: "In all our political history there is nothing more remarkable than the rise of the Labour Party." It also focuses on and rejoices in the important role women play in the party. Hamilton writes: "Equality had been complete from the beginning. The basis set up in 1900 took this for granted. Women were among the pioneers and leaders in the Socialist societies: the names of Enid Stacey and Katherine St. John Conway (Mrs. Bruce Glasier) live on the bed-roll of the I.L.P.; Margaret Bondfield, Mary Macarthur, Susan Lawrence, Ellen Wilkinson followed them in the leadership of Party Councils." She emphasizes that "Labour as a political Party was the first to make the full emancipation, political, social and economic, of women part and parcel of its fighting programme." As far as the fight for woman suffrage was concerned, Hamilton explains that by 1912, the party had entered into "a working alliance . . . with the non-militant National union of Women's Suffrage Societies of which John Stuart Mill was the patron saint—led by Dame Millicent Fawcett. Votes for women was then placed high among the items in Labour's immediate programme."

Hamilton's fictional work, a blend of pacifist and political writing, finds its place alongside that of other writers such as Rose Macaulay and Vera Brittain, while her nonfiction constitutes an important contribution to the understanding of Labour Party history and the political and social climate of the time. In her heroines' disenchantment with romantic love, Hamilton traces their quarrel with a patriarchal establishment imbued with imperialist values, their disagreement with the prevalent war mentality, and their gradual effort to find a niche in the workplace. As Ouditt maintains,

> the war in these texts is not seen as a stabilising force in which women can attain their true angelic potential and lead the race to greater heights of perfection. It is instead represented as a personal crisis that disrupts the conventional view of middle-class "reality" and forces women to question their part in maintaining the conservative stronghold that ensures their dependence on a masculine partner.

Hamilton's novels are indeed a locus of reflection on the collision between romance and war, on women's roles in a political arena dominated by men, and on women's yearning for equality in all spheres of action. As Parfitt points out, referring to novels about the war, "these novels come into their own, . . . not when viewed purely aesthetically . . . but when read as products of, and contributions to history, in the broad and proper sense of that word," a commentary that seems to fit Hamilton's fiction perfectly. Whatever their artistic failings in the eyes of such readers as Woolf, Hamilton's novels offer thoughtful psychological portraits of people in the throes of anguish caused by the war or wrestling with heartrending romantic and political choices. Although her books are out of print, it is hoped that a few of her novels will be reclaimed and reprinted by feminist publishing houses.

References:

Margaret Kamester and Jo Vellacott, eds., *Militarism versus Feminism: Writings on Women and War* (London: Virago, 1987);

Sharon Ouditt, *Fighting Forces, Writing Women: Identity and Ideology in the First World War* (London & New York: Routledge, 1994);

George Parfitt, *Fiction of the First World War: A Study* (London: Faber & Faber, 1988);

Dale Spender, *Time and Tide Wait for No Man* (London: Pandora, 1984);

Virginia Woolf, *The Diary of Virginia Woolf,* 4 volumes, edited by Quentin Bell and Anne Olivier Bell (Harmondsworth: Penguin, 1983–1987).

Margaret Harkness
(John Law)
(28 February 1854 - 10 December 1923)

Eileen Sypher
George Mason University

BOOKS: *Assyrian Life and History,* By-paths of Bible Knowledge, no. 2 (London: Religious Tract Society, 1883);

Egyptian Life and History According to the Monuments, By-paths of Bible Knowledge, no. 6 (London: Religious Tract Society, 1884);

A City Girl: A Realistic Story, as John Law (London: Vizetelly, 1887; London & New York: Garland, 1984);

Tempted London: Young Men, as Law (London: Hodder & Stoughton, 1888);

Out of Work, as Law (London: Swan Sonnenschein, 1888);

Toilers in London: or Inquiries Concerning Female Labour in the Metropolis, as Law (London: Hodder & Stoughton, 1889);

Captain Lobe: A Story of the Salvation Army, as Law (London: Hodder & Stoughton, 1889); republished as *In Darkest London: A New and Popular Edition of Captain Lobe, A Story of the Salvation Army,* Bellamy Libary, no. 8 (London: Reeves, 1891); republished as *Captain Lobe* (London: Hodder & Stoughton, 1915);

A Manchester Shirtmaker: A Realistic Story of To-day, as Law (London: Authors' Cooperative Publishing, 1890);

Imperial Credit, as Law (Adelaide: Vardon & Pritchard, 1899);

George Eastmont: Wanderer, as Law (London: Burns & Oates, 1905);

Glimpses of Hidden India, as Law (Calcutta: Thacker, Spink, 1909); revised as *Indian Snapshots: A Bird's-eye View of India from the Days of the Saib Company to the Present Time* (Calcutta & Simla: Thacker, Spink, 1912);

Modern Hyderabad (Deccan), as Law (Calcutta: Thacker, Spink, 1914);

The Horoscope, as Law (Calcutta & Simla: Thacker, Spink / London: Thacker, 1915);

A Curate's Promise: A Story of Three Weeks, September 14 - October 5, 1917, as Law (London: Hodder & Stoughton, 1921).

Edition: *Out of Work,* introduction by Bernadette Kirwan (London: Merlin / Chicago: Dee, 1990).

SELECTED PERIODICAL PUBLICATIONS—UNCOLLECTED: "Women as Civil Servants," *Nineteenth Century,* 10 (September 1881): 369-381;

"Railway Labour," *Nineteenth Century,* 12 (November 1882): 721-732;

"Girl Labour in the City," *Justice* (3 March 1888): 4-5;

"Salvationists and Socialists," *Justice* (24 March 1888): 2;

"'Salvation' and Socialism," as "One Who Knows 'John Law,'" *Pall Mall Gazette* (29 October 1890): 2;

"A Year of My Life," as John Law, *New Review,* 5 (October 1891): 375-384;

"Roses and Crucifix," as Law, *Woman's Herald* (5 December 1891 - 27 February 1892);

"The Children of the Unemployed," as Law, *New Review,* 8 (January 1893): 228-236;

"A Week on a Labour Settlement," as Law, *Fortnightly Review,* new series 56 (August 1894): 206-213.

In the late 1880s and 1890s many British writers turned to London's East End slums—a late-nineteenth-century metonym for social inequality, as Manchester had been in the midcentury. The East End became the uncharted frontier for many individuals motivated by various philanthropic and revolutionary aims: university graduates, missionaries, statisticians, political organizers, and several independent-minded upper- and middle-class women. Among the latter were the socialist writer Beatrice Webb; Eleanor Marx, the daughter of Karl Marx; and the novelist Margaret Harkness, who wrote under the name John Law. A second cousin of Potter and a friend of Eleanor Marx, Olive Schreiner, and other socialists, Harkness for many years was an overlooked member of this group, although she had achieved some popularity in her own time. Werner G. Urlaub, in his 1977 study of late-Victorian social-problem novels, says that her novels were more widely distributed than most of the other social novels of the 1890s. In subsequent years, however, Harkness's seven known novels and six nonfiction books went out of print and were largely forgotten. Since the late 1970s critics have taken a renewed interest in Harkness as a radical woman writer, and her books have begun to be reprinted.

The second of five children, Margaret Elise Harkness was born on 28 February 1854 at Upton-on-Severn, Worcestershire, into a sheltered, religious, and conservative upper-class household. Her father, Robert Harkness, an Anglican priest, was from a family of Irish origins, while her mother, Jane Waugh Law Harkness, was distantly related to the English aristocracy. Although Margaret believed the family to be financially strapped, at his death in 1886 her father left a good-sized estate. At twenty-one Harkness was sent to a finishing school at Bournemouth, where she met her second cousin, Beatrice Potter; Harkness later introduced Potter to Sidney Webb, whom she married. Potter's letters provide a portrait of Harkness in her early youth as restless and given to depression and in her twenties and thirties as ambitious and hysterical—but this portrait of Harkness as a neurotic is supplied by Potter, and no confirmation has been found. In any case, it is not surprising that the cousins became estranged in later life.

Not wanting to marry and needing an occupation, Harkness, with the approval of her family, left for London in 1877 to train as a nurse. Unhappy with this career, however, she decided in early 1881 to turn to journalism and writing novels. She wrote several journalistic pieces and, presumably out of financial desperation (she made only £150 in her first year), wrote two short volumes for the By-paths of Bible Knowledge series. Much more in line with her later works, in 1882 she wrote a short article, "Railway Labour," about deplorable working conditions. From this point on Harkness appears to have been able to eke out a living as a freelance writer.

In the late 1880s Harkness, who had become friendly with Schreiner, Eleanor Marx, Annie Besant, and Friedrich Engels, started exploring the East End, and her politics became more radical. In a pamphlet written some years later, *Imperial Credit* (1899), she explains her motives for going there: "after that saddest event of my life [her father's death in 1886] I determined to do something to lessen the miseries of those who to-day have neither land nor money." As John Goode notes, it is uncertain whether she was motivated by a form of Christian radicalism (several of her pieces were published by Christian presses) or by humanistic liberalism. The precise nature of Harkness's activities in the slums during the first few years is also unknown. She apparently did not work for the Salvation Army (at least, they have no record of her), although her fiction shows sympathy with its social programs. Whatever it was, her work took her to the worst districts.

According to Yvonne Kapp, Harkness was one of the people who introduced Eleanor Marx to the horrors of East End life. Harkness became involved in radical politics, belonging for a short time to the Social Democratic Federation before denouncing it as a "dead body" in a letter to the editor of *The Star* (25 September 1889). For a time she was part of the circle around Engels and Eleanor Marx but later broke with them. Harkness campaigned for Keir Hardie, the Scottish Labour leader, in the 1887–1888 parliamentary elections and in 1889 helped mediate in the London Dock Strike.

Probably it was the need to make money that prompted Harkness to turn to novel writing during this period. Schreiner, in a 22 March 1887 letter to Havelock Ellis, says: "Maggie has no money and she came thinking I would support her." Shortly after the visit to Schreiner, Harkness began writing novels under the pseudonym John Law, which she would use to the end of her life. She might have chosen the name because Law was her mother's maiden name, signaling her developing feminism, although it might have been chosen for John Law of Lauriston, a seventeenth-century French eccentric whose economic theories are seen by some as foreshadowing modern state socialism. During the 1880s and 1890s, her socialist period, Harkness wrote her first five novels, the ones for which she is now remembered.

Readers may find Harkness's novels difficult not because they are demanding literature but because they seem so transparent. Strangely touching, haunting portraits of the lives of the poor and those exiles from the West End who have befriended them, the works seem to be open windows in the East End. But they are more complicated than they first appear, simultaneously opening up and "packaging" the slums, revealing what is frightful in them and making them safely fictional for a middle-class reader.

Her novels are not, by traditional literary standards, "successful" on the whole; that is, they do not fully confront or attempt to answer the problems they pose. At times the novels reveal competing aims. On the one hand, Harkness seems to want to represent and applaud the underrepresented working class as surrounded and sometimes moved by radical and protofeminist ideas. On the other hand, seemingly intimidated by her middle-class readers, Harkness sometimes seems to defer to and to perpetuate a conservative, patronizing, paternalistic perspective on both the working class and women's independence.

It is, however, important to put Harkness's novels into their historical context. Although by the mid 1890s the British urban working class had become an acceptable subject in novels written by and for the middle class, it was still a marginal topic. The working-class fiction of this era, the best-known examples of which are the stories of Besant, Arthur Morrison, Rudyard Kipling, and W. Somerset Maugham, is slim. This fiction usually appears in short-story form, as if the novel format was too weighty for such representations, and is not particularly rich or complex. While it is possible to attribute this situation to individual lack of "genius" or "skill," a more plausible explanation is that the social conditions that supported writers were uncongenial. Public outcry in the late 1880s and early 1890s over the French Naturalist writer Emile Zola's sexual frankness and his focus on a potentially revolutionary working class led to literary debates that resulted in the repression of British fictional portraits of the working class.

Harkness's historical moment was also a treacherous one for a woman writer, as narrow conventions about the appropriate female voice hemmed her in. Although women were more accepted as writers, publishers expected them to uphold traditional values. Considering the position of the female writer who wanted not only to write about nontraditional, independent, even outcast women, but who also wanted to write about the slums and socialist politics, that Harkness's works were published at all is remarkable.

Common to all of Harkness's five social novels is a desire to tell the story of the working class, to represent the inadequately or unfairly represented. Harkness seems to conceive of her readers as blinded by stereotypes from knowledge of a victimized and restless working class, and she sets out to dismantle these stereotypes. Harkness's implied reader is not working class but middle class, and her purpose is not merely to edify her readers but also to warn them to take corrective action; like other novelists and chroniclers of her era, Harkness is impelled by a sense of urgency. As an East End doctor in *Captain Lobe: A Story of the Salvation Army* (1889) says, "if things go on like this we must have a revolution."

The stereotypes of the working class that Harkness dismantles and her portrait of independent women and socialists shift slightly in the course of the five novels. The first, *A City Girl* (1887), attacks the stereotype that the sexuality of poor women in the East End is either matter-of-fact or evil—a daring subject in 1887, although Harkness avoids frank sexual details. The novel depicts a girl whose consciousness is formed by her restricted social conditions. Nellie has steady work as a finisher of trousers for a "sweater," a middleman who farms out unfinished factory-made clothing. Supporting an alcoholic mother and a brutish brother, Nellie dreams of becoming a "lady" (Harkness hints that her real father was a gentleman). She falls in love with a married gentleman from the West End, Arthur Grant, whom she meets while attending a Radical meeting with her fiancé, George. Arthur and Nellie have an affair, and Nellie becomes pregnant. Harkness breaks this news to the reader carefully: Nellie has fitful dreams, and one day she trudges through a snowstorm to Arthur's West End house just to gaze at him through a window. Stunned at the expression she sees on his face as he looks on his and his wife's baby, she murmurs, "he never looked at me like that; never" and turns back. Only after Harkness has won the reader's sympathy for Nellie's loneliness does she finally reveal that Nellie is pregnant by having the harsh "sweater" call her immoral. The novel then sets out to show that Nellie, ostracized by family, employer, priest, and former fiancé, has the strength, with help from the Salvation Army, to try to bring up her baby alone, without telling Arthur. Arthur, one of the many politically progressive middle-class and aristocratic figures found in Harkness's novels, is treated not as a villain but only as ignorant and self-indulgent—a contrast to the typical contemporary feminist attacks on male sexuality. Nellie is clearly as much to "blame" in Harkness's story as is Arthur. Near the novel's end, when Arthur encounters Nellie carrying their now-dead baby and discovers that it is his, he also discovers his ignorance of Nellie's feelings, suffers remorse, and wants to make amends. He is counseled by the Salvation Army captain to do no more than provide money for the child's burial. George, having been enlightened by the captain about the injustice of his own sexual double standard, asks Nellie to marry him, and they go off together to take jobs in the country. Though Harkness follows convention in the end by killing off the illegitimate child, her allowing the independent Nellie to live, albeit married and "forgiven," provides a protofeminist ending to the plot. Engels, in one of his well-known letters on literary realism, wrote to Harkness to praise her first novel for exhibiting the "courage of the true artist" but went on to criticize *A City Girl* as "not quite realistic enough" because it portrays the East End working class as "a passive mass"—although he does acknowledge that the working class in the East End is the most passive in the world.

In her next novel Harkness sensitively handles the issue of the under- and unemployed as she starkly reveals that the "Age of Competition" means unemployment and death for some. Goode argues that in this novel Harkness has reacted to Engels's criticism by clearly showing the effects of unemployment and not allowing any individual rescues. In *Out of Work* (1888) a country carpenter, Jos Coney, recently moved to London, is forced to become a "casual," or temporary dockworker, the lowliest of the unskilled occupations. In an especially powerful part of the novel Jos hears several speeches by socialists and is arrested in the Bloody Sunday demonstration of 13 November 1887. Jos's unsuccessful attempts to find steady work among thousands of unemployed, whose voices echo his own, structure the novel. In this way the plot seeks to undermine the stereotype that is expressed by Jos's middle-class fiancée's mother: that the workers' "idle habits" are responsible for their being unemployed. The novel thereby transcends, in Goode's view, classical realism as it moves beyond focusing on an individual character. Eventually the fiancée, Polly, breaks off the engagement, and Jos returns to the countryside of which he has often dreamed—only to die of starvation. Polly is punished for her failure to comprehend Jos's poverty: she is married off to an "upright" Methodist whom she detests.

Harkness's third novel, *Captain Lobe,* the book for which she is perhaps best known, first appeared in serial form in *The British Weekly.* In this novel Harkness shifts her focus from inadequately or unfairly represented East End protagonists to the Salvation Army, stereotyped most forcefully by George Bernard Shaw in *Major Barbara* (1905). Although Harkness never seems to have sympathized with the Salvation Army's religious orientation, in a letter to the editor published in *Justice* (24 March 1888) she argued that the Social Democratic Federation and the Salvation Army "ought to work more together than they do at present, for they have many points of common interest." *Captain Lobe* depicts Salvation Army workers touring the slums, offering the reader both a sympathetic glimpse of the organization's practical work (in contrast to the socialists' rhetoric) and a panorama of deteriorating social conditions that surpasses George Gissing's novel *Nether World* (1889) in the stark detail with which it represents East End life. Women commit suicide because they have too many children; people scavenge shoes for fuel; and factory daughters struggle to keep their families alive. The novel particularly shows the strength of women Salvation Army workers, "slum saviours," who enter districts where "respectable" church people and even the police will not go. Other strong women who pass through the novel include a socialist "labor-mistress" bent on educating herself and an unnamed upper-class political activist. These

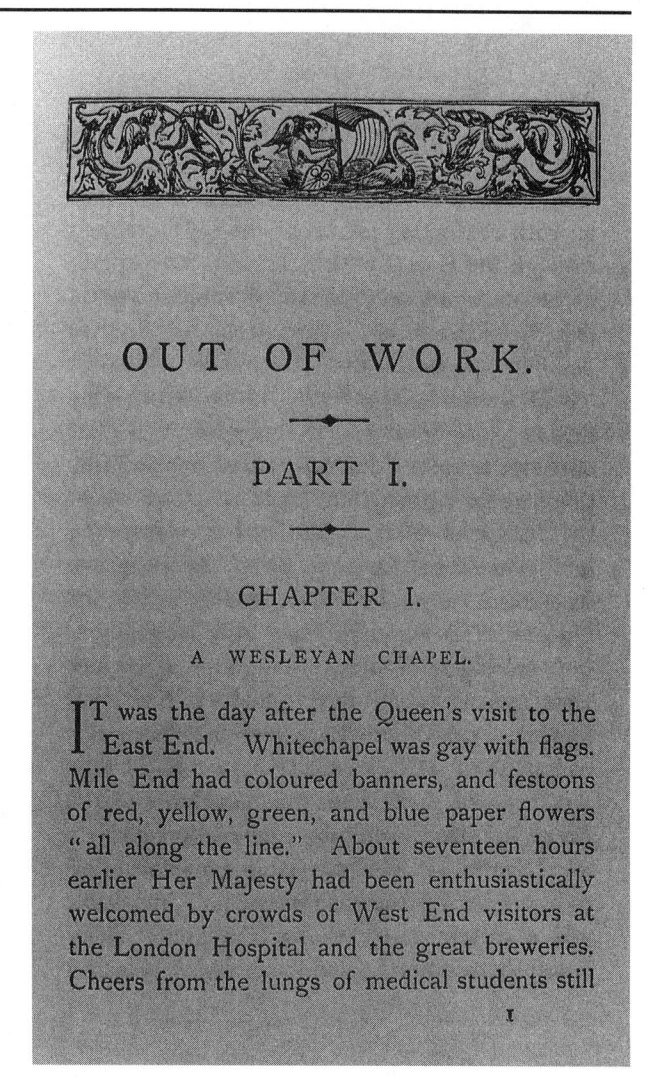

> OUT OF WORK.
>
> PART I.
>
> CHAPTER I.
>
> A WESLEYAN CHAPEL.
>
> IT was the day after the Queen's visit to the East End. Whitechapel was gay with flags. Mile End had coloured banners, and festoons of red, yellow, green, and blue paper flowers "all along the line." About seventeen hours earlier Her Majesty had been enthusiastically welcomed by crowds of West End visitors at the London Hospital and the great breweries. Cheers from the lungs of medical students still

Opening page of Margaret Harkness's 1888 novel about an impoverished temporary dockworker in London

women occasionally form female subcultures, as strong women support weaker ones.

With *A Manchester Shirtmaker: A Realistic Story of To-day* (1890) Harkness, probably as a consequence of a visit to Manchester, turns briefly from the London East End to the Manchester slums, though there is little to distinguish one locale from the other. A recently widowed and impoverished seamstress, Mary Dillon, sells her sewing machine to buy food for her baby. Finally, recognizing that it is starving, she overdoses it with opium she has stolen. In this novel Harkness confronts the stereotype that mothers who murder children are merely depraved by depicting such actions as the result of poverty and thus as something that other mothers could understand. Incarcerated in a psychiatric hospital, Mary is distraught over what she has done, and she kills herself at the very moment that a socialist doctor is making dour predictions about the future.

In 1891 Harkness, recovering from a serious illness, went on a world tour, including travels to Australia, New Zealand, and the United States, returning to England from time to time. Little is known of her activities until she published her partly autobiographical novel, *George Eastmont: Wanderer* (1905). The dedication page claims that the novel is based on Harkness's experiences during the London Dock Strike of 1889. In *George Eastmont* Harkness explores a different kind of stereotype, one also promoted by Shaw and Gissing: the eccentric aristocrat turned man of the people—even as she explores more openly than in her earlier novels another path to socialism. Harkness, unlike Shaw, treats the convert seriously, applauding his commitment. Eastmont may be at least partially based on H. H. Champion; Harkness and Champion had met while Harkness was involved in the Social Democrat Federation and later worked together mediating the strike. She admired his vision of socialism, and the two may have been involved sexually.

Eastmont, who has given up his upper-class family and his military commission to work among the poor as a socialist, unhappily marries a working-class woman and then finds that he cannot wholeheartedly support the dock strike because of its violence. True socialism, Eastmont believes, will not evolve through existing political groups. Though Harkness's earlier novels suggest that political groups are inept and fractured, this novel shows them supporting a detestable violence. Eastmont charts a different path to socialism, one that combines paternalism (he fashions himself into a "saviour of the masses") with a strategy of collectivizing the land. Eastmont helps to resolve the strike by asking for the intercession of Cardinal Lorrain—a thin veil for Henry Cardinal Manning, to whom the novel is dedicated and with whom Harkness was associated in her attempts to resolve the strike. Isolated, Eastmont wanders to Australia to join a settlement farm. After inheriting his grandfather's fortune he returns to England at the novel's close with the idea of starting an Owenite farming community on his lands, where he hopes he can learn about workers and help to train them in communal living so that they will be ready when socialism comes.

Harkness's novels reveal her radical sympathies—she attempts to show the truth about working-class life and generally favorably depicts socialist and protofeminist political ideas. But at the same time, Harkness was writing for a middle-class audience, and this putative readership limited her novels. One influence of this readership is Harkness's sensationalizing the story of the working class with melodramatic plots and conventional heroines that engage the middle-class reader's sympathy and interest in a working-class subject but still keep this subject at a distance. Furthermore, Harkness's narrator often aligns herself with her conservative reader by being remote and even condescending toward her characters. Harkness objectifies her characters by reducing them to types—the dockworker, the East End mother, the labor mistress—though her novels try to dismantle conventional stereotypes of the working class, they perpetuate others. While Engels, who celebrated the type character as the cornerstone of realist fiction, may have influenced Harkness here, her use of the type also signals her need to distance, even diminish a character. For example, in *Out of Work* Harkness's typically intrusive narrator describes Jos's brains: they are "of the same calibre as the brains of other young carpenters who had not the intellectual capacity of an educated man." She describes the labor mistress in *Captain Lobe* as a quaint specimen of a "socialist" who knows a string of words without their definitions, who "lives far away from the British Museum Reading Room, where she might graze among a herd of likeminded ladies." Typification here is a form of condescension: the narrator cannot see complexity in these characters. They are at this moment pitiful objects for her.

More important, perhaps, Harkness's desire to please a middle-class reader affects her vision of socialism in her novels. The transition to socialism will be a comfortable, paternalistic one: a few wise men will bring it about. Both *Captain Lobe* and *George Eastmont* make the case that leadership of the ignorant "masses" is necessary. For example, in *Captain Lobe* the narrator says: "He could not see that the people take pleasure in their filthy existence, he could not understand the satisfaction they get by fuddling their brains in public-houses and by coarse love-making" and "they feel as masses, not as individuals. . . . They have no confidence in themselves, any power of forming their own opinions." In *George Eastmont* disgust for the masses and disappointment in their stupidity is even more pronounced. While sometimes this disgust is political, often it is aesthetic. *George Eastmont* opens with scenes of Eastmont's disgust at his working-class wife's personal habits: her table manners and her clothes. When the workers lift him high on their shoulders after a demonstration, he feels that they are "scum."

It is no accident that Eastmont is the archsocialist hero of all these novels. As a male and an aristocrat he does not pose a threat for a middle-class reader. Eastmont need not struggle or engage in any mass activity; his position comfortably enables him to make his own contribution to socialism—which will be a long time in coming. The message to the middle class is that it need do nothing to advance socialism. The novel ends just when the difficulties could begin: just as he sets up his scheme.

Finally, perhaps in deference to the sensibilities of her middle-class readers, Harkness never really develops her characters, who are radical and independent women, potentially "New Women" who emerge in other fiction of this period. So, for example, Harkness's more potentially striking women—the mysterious socialist lady and the socialist labor mistress in *Captain Lobe,* and Miss Cameron, the unmarried Fabian in love with Eastmont—are fleeting characters, never allowed center stage, and are shown as lonely, colorless, even a bit silly. Such women might otherwise alienate the middle-class reader accustomed to young, pretty, apolitical Victorian heroines.

After *George Eastmont* Harkness's political interests changed. In *Imperial Credit* she says that she is saying "good-bye to the Labour Movement," that her "little bit of work is done," and that she has "other work to do." She gives as the reason for this change her having been "got at, abused and misunderstood by the people who call themselves socialists" because "birth, sex, and temperament have prevented me from coming forward openly among those who are fighting in the labor ranks." Even much earlier, however, Harkness had expressed anger at the socialists' divisiveness and their failure to help the poor in any real way. In subsequent writings based on her residence in India and Ceylon between 1906 and World War I her earlier concerns with the working class, socialism, and her latent feminism seem to drop away. In 1907 and 1914 she wrote two pieces about her travels in India, celebrating the humanity of parts of the country still untouched by British cultural influences. She also wrote a novel set in Ceylon, *The Horoscope* (1915), which is about the tensions between Buddhism and an imperialist British Christianity.

Following her mother's death in 1916, Harkness spent time in London before returning to France. Her last known publication was a novel, *A Curate's Promise: A Story of Three Weeks, September 14 – October 5, 1917* (1921), which concerns a curate's decision to join the Salvation Army, rather than the army, as a chaplain. Harkness did not live to inherit a trust fund bequeathed to her by her sister-in-law (she was apparently estranged from both her brothers in later life). She died in Florence on 10 December 1923.

Harkness's novels are important because they offer the student of turn-of-the-century England a different perspective than that found in the writing of better-known authors such as Gissing, Shaw, Besant, and George Moore. Not only are her novels among the few of the period to record the impact of socialist ideas on the working class, but they also provide a portrait of women both in the socialist movement and in slum life. Furthermore, though sharing some of the condescension these other writers show toward the working class, Harkness's novels reveal a "lived experience" within the slums—not as bitter outcast as Gissing does, but as an impassioned slum worker.

Margaret Harkness's novels might be characterized as radical in their attempt to open up the slums to her middle-class reader, slums seething with political disruption and the breakup of traditional gender roles. Yet the novels adopt traditional plotting and conventional characterization, particularly of women, and invoke traditional patterns of male paternalism and female domesticity. The novels generate sympathy and pity, respect and condescension toward the poor. They simultaneously represent and marginalize New Women. The novels enact, in short, some of the understandable difficulties of a middle-class turn-of-the-century woman writer who journeyed into the "other" world of the slums.

References:

Gerd Bjorhovde, *Rebellious Structures: Women Writers and the Crisis of the Novel 1880–1900* (Oslo: Norwegian University Press, 1987);

John Goode, "Margaret Harkness and the Socialist Novel," in *The Rise of Socialist Fiction 1880–1914,* edited by H. Gustav Klaus (Sussex: Harvester, 1987), pp. 47–65;

Yvonne Kapp, *Eleanor Marx* (New York: Pantheon, 1976);

"Margaret Harkness," in *The Dictionary of Labour Biography,* edited by Joyce M. Bellamy and John Saville, volume 8 (Clifton, N.J.: Kelley, 1988), pp. 103–113;

Karl Marx and Frederick Engels, *Literature and Art* (Bombay, 1956), pp. 35–38;

Deborah Nord, *The Apprenticeship of Beatrice Webb* (Amherst: University of Massachusetts Press, 1985);

Eileen Sypher, "Margaret Harkness," *Turn-of-the-Century Women,* 1 (Winter 1984): 12–26;

Sypher, "Margaret Harkness: Representing Politics in the Slums," in *Wisps of Violence: Producing Public and Private Politics in the Turn-of-the-Century British Novel* (London: Verso, 1993), pp. 105–121;

Werner G. Urlaub, *Der Spätviktorianische Sozialroman von 1880 bis 1890* (Bonn: Bouvier Verlag Herbert Grundmann, 1977).

Papers:

There is no significant collection of Margaret Harkness's papers. Twenty-one letters written between 1875 and 1887 by Harkness to Beatrice Potter are in the Passfield Collection at the British Library of Political and Economic Science, London, and a few letters from 1917 are in the Dorset Central Records Office in Dorchester.

Frank Harris
(14 February 1856 - 26 August 1931)

George Allan Cate
University of Maryland

See also the Harris entry in *DLB 156: British Short-Fiction Writers, 1880-1914: The Romantic Tradition.*

BOOKS: *Elder Conklin and Other Stories* (London: Heinemann, 1895 [i.e. 1894]; New York & London: Macmillan, 1894);

How to Beat the Boer, A Conversation in Hades (London: Heinemann, 1900);

Montes the Matador and Other Stories (London: Richards, 1900; New York: Kennerley, 1910);

The Bomb: A Novel (London: Long, 1908; New York: Kennerley, 1909); with new foreword and afterword by Harris (New York: Published by the author, 1920);

The Man Shakespeare and His Tragic Life Story (London: Palmer, 1909; New York: Kennerley, 1909); revised edition (London: Palmer, 1911);

Shakespeare and His Love: A Play in Four Acts and an Epilogue (London: Palmer, 1910);

The Women of Shakespeare (London: Methuen, 1911; New York: Kennerley, 1911);

Unpath'd Waters (London: John Lane / Toronto: Bell & Cockburn, 1913; New York: Kennerley, 1913);

Great Days: A Novel (London: John Lane / Toronto: Bell & Cockburn, 1914 [i.e. 1913]; New York: Kennerley, 1914);

The Yellow Ticket and Other Stories (London: Richards, 1914); revised as *The Veils of Isis and Other Stories* (New York: Doran, 1915);

Contemporary Portraits [First Series] (London: Methuen, 1915; New York: Kennerley, 1915);

England or Germany? (New York: Wilmarth, 1915);

Love in Youth: A Novel (New York: Doran, 1916);

Oscar Wilde: His Life and Confessions (2 volumes, New York: Published by the author, 1916; enlarged, 1918; enlarged edition, 1 volume, New York: Covici, Friede, 1930); republished as *Oscar Wilde* (London: Constable, 1938);

Contemporary Portraits: Second Series (New York: Published by the author, 1919);

The Wisdom of Frank Harris, from His Writings in Pearson's Magazine, selected by Guido Bruno (New York: Pearson's, 1919);

A Mad Love: The Strange Story of a Musician (New York: Published by the author, 1920);

Contemporary Portraits: Third Series (New York: Published by the author, 1920);

Has Life Any Meaning? Affirmative: Frank Harris . . . Negative: Percy Ward . . . Sunday, April 11th, 1920, Kimball Hall, Chicago (Chicago: Rationalist Education Society, [1920]);

My Life and Loves, 4 volumes (Paris: Privately printed, 1922-1927); enlarged edition, edited by John F. Gallagher (New York: Grove, 1963; London: W. H. Allen, 1964); revised and abridged as *My Life: Frank Harris. His Life and Adventures* (London: Richards, 1947); republished as *Frank Harris: My Life and Adventures* (London: Elek, 1958);

Contemporary Portraits: Fourth Series (New York: Brentano's, 1923; London: Richards, 1924);

Undream'd of Shores (New York: Brentano's, 1924; London: Richards, 1924);

New Preface to "The Life and Confessions of Oscar Wilde," by Harris and Lord Alfred Douglas (London: Fortune Press, 1925);

My Life (New York: Frank Harris, 1925);

Joan La Romée (Nice: Imprimerie Niçoise, 1926; New York: Frank Harris, 1926; London: Fortune Press, 1926);

Latest Contemporary Portraits (New York: Macaulay, 1927);

My Reminiscences as a Cowboy (New York: Charles Boni, 1930); revised and abridged as *On the Trail: My Reminiscences as a Cowboy* (London: John Lane, 1930);

Confessional: A Volume of Intimate Portraits, Sketches & Studies (New York: Panurge, 1930);

Pantopia: A Novel (New York: Panurge, 1930);

Bernard Shaw, an Unauthorised Biography Based on First-hand Information, with a Postscript by Mr. Shaw (London: Gollancz, 1931; New York: Simon & Schuster, 1931);

Mr. and Mrs. Daventry: A Play in Four Acts, Based on the Scenario by Oscar Wilde, edited, with an introduction, by H. Montgomery Hyde (London: Richards, 1956);

The Short Stories of Frank Harris: A Selection, edited by Elmer Gertz (Carbondale & Edwardsville: Southern Illinois University Press, 1975; London & Amsterdam: Feffer & Simons, 1975).

Edition: *The Bomb: A Novel,* introduction by John Dos Passos (Chicago & London: University of Chicago Press, 1963).

OTHER: Oscar Wilde, *Poems in Prose and Private Letters,* preface by Harris (New York: Privately printed, 1919).

Most of those who recognize Frank Harris's name today know him as the author of the sexually abundant and explicit four-volume autobiography *My Life and Loves* (1922–1927). Some may also know him as one of the personalities of the 1890s: a man equal in contemporary reckoning to W. E. Henley or Robert Louis Stevenson and equal in conversation even to the renowned Oscar Wilde, who was his good friend, as was George Bernard Shaw. As editor of the *Fortnightly Review* and then the *Saturday Review* throughout the fin de siècle, Harris brought good judgment to his journals and made many a writer's reputation.

Short and stocky with swarthy skin, a handlebar moustache, straight black hair slicked back and parted in the middle, large ears, a wide nose, and a booming bass voice that was rarely still, he seemed a great anomaly to the educated Englishman. He was a man who, as Vincent O'Sullivan puts it, "had the look of an American bar-tender or boxer's manager," yet knew a half-dozen languages fluently, was widely read, had a sharp intelligence that was both theoretical and practical, was seen as the best socialist speaker in Hyde Park and one of the best lecturers in London, was so appealing to women that he had many mistresses and married a wealthy society widow. A journalist, businessman, and editor, he also became renowned as a liar, a scoundrel, and a cad; yet there were many also who thought him wise and good. This is the Frank Harris of legend.

There is, however, another side to the legendary Frank Harris, less known but important—the literary Frank Harris. During the early 1890s he began to think of himself as primarily a writer; and from 1895 on he was constantly working on and producing books. He wrote books about Wilde, Shaw, and William Shakespeare; he wrote short pen-portraits of his contemporaries; he wrote reminiscences, essays, plays, four novels, and six volumes of short stories and was still working when he died in 1931.

James Thomas Harris was of Welsh stock, though he was born in Galway, Ireland, on 14 February 1856. His father, Thomas Vernon Harris, had risen through the ranks of Her Majesty's Coast Guard from cabin boy to command of a revenue cutter that operated off the coast of Ireland. A stern and severely strict parent with rigid Nonconformist beliefs, he taught his son duty and religion through fear and corporal punishment. Harris's mother, Anne Thomas Harris, was from Pembrokeshire and was the daughter of a Baptist preacher. She had a sweet temperament and was a comforting mother to her five children (Frank was the fourth) before dying of tuberculosis in 1860. Harris was then sent to a succession of different schools in England, finally ending up in Ruabon Grammar School in Wales. Small, bright, defensively egocentric, unhappy, and rebellious, at the age of fifteen he ran away from school, using some prize money he had won to book steerage passage to America.

From 1871 to 1872 Harris worked as a bootblack, construction worker, and hotel clerk in New York and Chicago and as a freightman and butcher in Colorado and Kansas. Joining his two older brothers in Lawrence, Kansas, in 1872, he became a

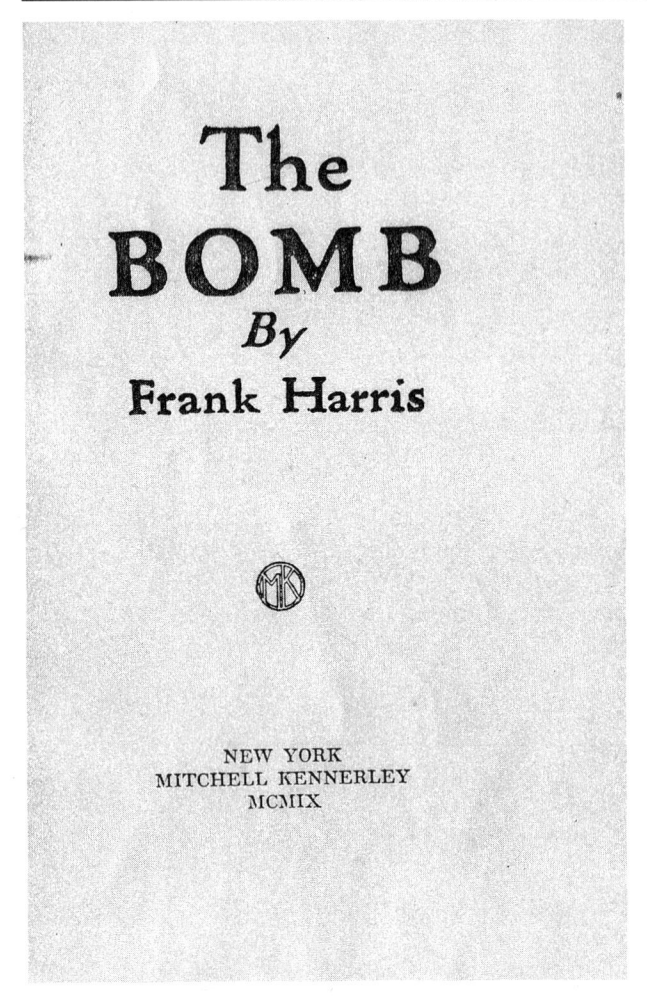

Title page for a novel based on events surrounding the 1886 Chicago Haymarket Square bombing (Bruccoli Collection of Mitchell Kennerley, Thomas Cooper Library, University of South Carolina)

businessman, read law, and was admitted to the Kansas bar in 1875. He attended lectures at the University of Kansas and came under the spell of Byron Smith, a brilliant young teacher of classics who had also absorbed the writings of Karl Marx. Smith became a lifelong inspiration to Harris, who took the name Frank to mark the beginning of his new life of resolute culture, intellectual quest, and outspoken honesty. Following Smith's lead, he went to study at the Sorbonne in Paris in 1876. He then taught French at a school in Brighton; married a Brighton woman, Florence Adams, in 1878; and studied literature, philology, and philosophy in Heidelberg, Göttingen, and Munich.

When his wife died in 1879 Harris used money he had inherited from her to travel in Italy, Greece, Austria, Russia, and Ireland. When the money ran out, he went to London and worked as a reviewer and reporter before landing a job as editor of a minor daily paper, *The Evening News,* in 1883. To the amazement of London he was, in 1886, appointed editor of the *Fortnightly Review,* one of the most distinguished and important journals in England. From that time until the end of the century he enjoyed his greatest success and influence. He married a wealthy widow, Emily Clayton, in 1887; took a fine house in Park Lane; and entertained lavishly, becoming (he claimed) friends with every famous and powerful person in England, including the Prince of Wales, and acquiring a reputation as an excellent conversationalist and an endlessly interesting, eccentric dinner guest.

In 1894, after being fired by the owners of the *Fortnightly,* Harris purchased *The Saturday Review.* During the next few years he made it into a first-rate literary and intellectual production that featured a brilliant staff of young writers and artists such as Shaw, H. G. Wells, and Max Beerbohm. Steadfast in his dedication to left-wing politics and ideas, Harris was sympathetic to anyone who was oppressed by society and its bourgeois precepts; and he remained faithful to his friendship with Wilde during Wilde's last, horrible years of trial, prison, and destitution, helping not only with money but also with his frequent supporting presence.

Harris's first published work of fiction, *Elder Conklin and Other Stories* (1895), comprises seven short stories set in the American West and based partly on Harris's experiences in Kansas and Colorado and partly on the mythic West of popular culture that was then being fabricated for the reading public. Some critics compared Harris's stories favorably to the stories of Bret Harte; others saw him more broadly as a unique writer who was also part of the tradition of American Realism in the later nineteenth century. Keeping his eye on the vicarious yearnings of his readers, in all of the stories Harris has a newcomer arrive in some Western town; there he is forced to confront both the mores of his new surroundings and, often, himself. In most cases this newcomer, while somewhat superior in culture and intellect, is shown to be the inferior of the townspeople in common sense, practical intelligence, decent behavior, courage, and humor. All of this is presented in a carefully controlled tone of good-natured irony, without moral judgments, and yet without the sacrifice of close, telling detail.

Never really at home amid British social distinctions and late-Victorian taboos, Harris, with his restless, truculent temperament, began to overextend himself financially and to shock too many people with his blunt remarks and indiscreet behavior. He was legally separated from his second wife soon after 1894. By 1898 his personal and financial decline was beginning. He sold *The Saturday Review;* began a lifelong relationship with an Irish woman, Nellie O'Hara, twenty years his junior, and went to South Africa and then to the Riviera, where he speculated disastrously in gambling casinos, hotels, and other real estate. By the turn of the century he was alternating his residence between England and France and was concentrating more than ever on his career as a writer. His play, *Mr. and Mrs. Daventry,* written at the instigation of Wilde, had a successful run in London throughout 1899, and his next few books earned him some literary esteem; but his overall decline continued.

The title story of Harris's next book of fiction—*Montes the Matador and Other Stories* (1900)—has often been praised as his best work. It was written as early as 1891, when its anxious author sent the manuscript to George Meredith, who praised it and ranked it better than the work of Prosper Mérimée, author of *Carmen* (1846). Indeed, Harris had intentionally tried to outperform Mérimée by writing the best "bull-ring story" yet. His intention is manifest in the plot of the story, which, echoing that of *Carmen,* deals with a famous matador who is deceived in love by a woman who secretly sleeps with his best friend—another, far less skillful, matador. In revenge Montes arranges for the friend to be killed in the bullring, then retires from the ring himself, brokenhearted and still not quite comprehending his own tragic nature. The last story in the collection "Sonia," was inspired by the assassination of the Russian czar Alexander II in 1881. Harris admired Sophia Perovskaia, a Russian woman who took part in the murder, and he modeled his fictional Sonia on her. Sonia has high ideals that are contrasted with the mechanical, tepid views of Lascelles, the Englishman who loves her but can never understand her self-sacrificing altruism.

Harris's sympathy with victims of injustice and leaders of social action, shown so vividly in "Sonia," comes through even more emphatically in his first and best-known novel, *The Bomb* (1909). This work was inspired by another actual event—the bombing in Haymarket Square in Chicago on 4 May 1886, for which four anarchist leaders, including Louis Lingg, were executed, although none of them threw the bomb. Harris, who spent many months in Chicago and New York researching the story, saw Lingg's trial as an example of the oppression of the working class by the owning class. To narrate the story Harris creates a fictionalized version of the real-life Rudolph Schnaubelt, a young man the government claimed was the actual thrower of the bomb and who was arrested briefly, then disappeared into legend. Schnaubelt is an immigrant

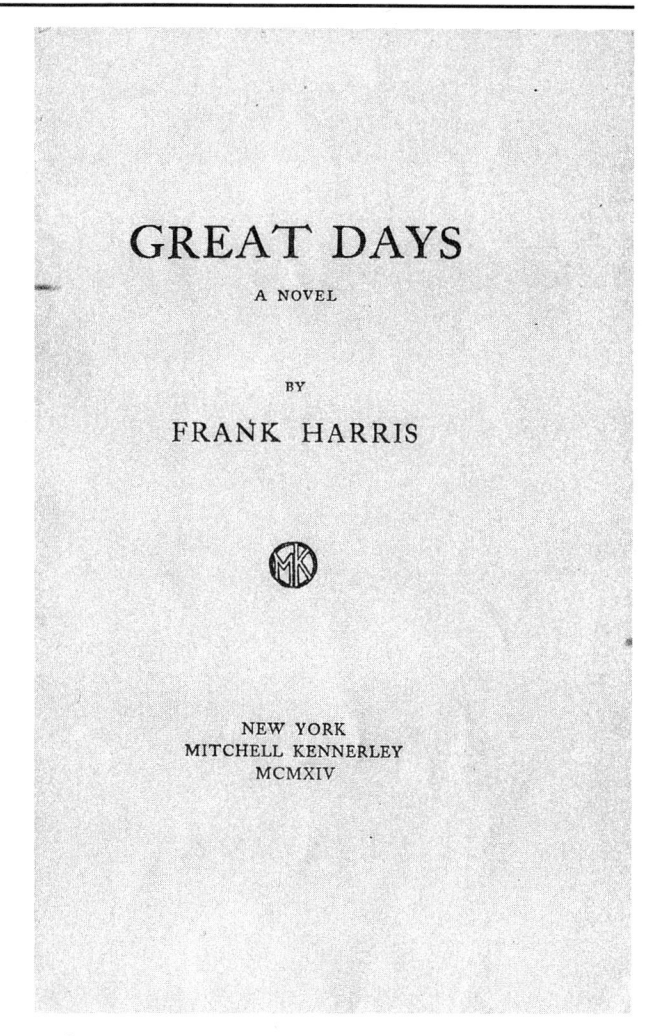

Title page for an historical novel set in the time of the French Revolution (Bruccoli Collection of Mitchell Kennerley, Thomas Cooper Library, University of South Carolina)

from Germany, and Harris's description of the many hardships he undergoes as a workman in New York and Chicago paint a vividly realistic picture of stultifying squalor imposed from above. When, after his ordeals, Schnaubelt finally meets Lingg in person, the reader can feel his response to Lingg's electric personality—a response that leads to fervent discipleship. Throughout the rest of the novel Lingg is presented as a nearly Christlike figure, and the workers as innocent victims of police brutality, political corruption, journalistic opportunism, judicial bigotry, selfish capitalism, and mass hysteria. Harris incorporates many passages verbatim from contemporary newspapers and journals to drive home his point and to blur the line between fact and fiction.

In 1914 Harris was imprisoned briefly for contempt of court in connection with a libel suit. On his release he left England forever, moving first to the

Harris at tea in the south of France (Collection of Arthur Leonard)

United States. In 1916 he purchased *Pearson's Magazine* in New York City and created a relatively avant-garde intellectual reputation for the journal.

Harris's *Great Days* (1914), set in the time of the French Revolution, is an ambitious combination of the bildungsroman and the historical novel in the manner of Frederick Marryat. Jack Morgan's gruff father is an innkeeper in the English Channel town of Hurstpoint and a smuggler whose fast boats bring in goods from France. When war is declared between England and France, Jack becomes a privateer sailing the Channel; his experiences develop him from boy to man. He gains bigger and bigger ships and successes in battle until he is captured and imprisoned in France, where he learns about the nature of the revolution and is introduced to sex. On his return to England he gains a king's commission, the hand of the aristocratic Margaret Barron, and the respect and understanding of his father, whose relationship with Jack is a major structural thread in the novel. The thematic core of the book is Jack's sympathy for the starving and downtrodden French populace. Critics have been mixed in their response to the book, ranging from Elmer Gertz, who called it "superb" in his introduction to *The Short Stories of Frank Harris* (1975), to Hesketh Pearson, who dismissed it in *Extraordinary People* (1965) as "a flat uninteresting story, written largely to display the author's nautical knowledge."

Harris's third novel, *Love in Youth* (1916) is a slight and scattered work. Unlike any other Harris production, it is frivolous and lighthearted, a romp of a story of love among the idle rich that obviously derived from Harris's own experiences. The Rhodes scholar Martin Bancroft loses his money gambling in Monte Carlo, then rents himself and his car to the Foxwells, a family of American tourists on their way to Paris. The family includes, of course, a pretty girl who falls in love with Martin and marries him after many complications and obstacles. But the plot matters little, for the trip from Monte Carlo to Paris gives Harris the opportunity to discuss many subjects, and to describe so many sights that *The New York Times* called the work "half a guide book and half a novel." Although technically a failure as a novel, it was enjoyed by critics and readers because of Harris's charming style.

A Mad Love: The Strange Story of a Musician (1920), set in Vienna in the 1890s, is about the musician and musicologist Hagedorn, whose desire to perform and create nearly die under the load of his loathing for himself and his fellow mortals. Driven to a point near madness, he is gradually brought back to physical and mental health through his marriage to Marie, a dancer. Just when the couple has everything—love, creativity, money, genius, and happiness—Hagedorn misinterprets a kiss he sees his wife give to another man. He recoils in despair, leaves Vienna, divorces his wife, abandons his music, and collapses back into his old psychoses. Not even the reappearance of his wife, with evidence that she has always been faithful, can save him, and his vitality is lost forever.

After selling his interest in *Pearson's Magazine* in 1922 Harris moved with Nellie to the south of France, settling in Nice. He spent much of his remaining life trying to make money through writing, publishing privately the scandalous *My Life and Loves* between 1922 and 1927. Harris believed that the key to successful sales was sensationalism, and, in this "autobiography" he embellishes fact with fiction and mixes fiction with fact to such a degree that even he may finally not have been able to tell the difference. But entertainment and frank outspokenness were guaranteed. Indeed, Harris's insistence on speaking openly about sex in *My Life and Loves* destroyed his career. Although it was widely translated and sold, it was banned in most countries, and Harris received few or no royalties on the illegal sales. His name became a dirty joke; his other books dropped in sales; and he was persecuted by government censors.

In 1927, after the death of his second wife, Harris finally married his longtime lover O'Hara. His last work of fiction was the utopian novel *Pantopia* (1930). Like many such works, it begins with a man shipwrecked on an unknown island that boasts the usual assortment of friendly, happy people; glorious architecture; fruitful land; and pure water. There is no war or crime, and science is put to use for the good of the whole community. The political system has an aristocracy of merit at the top, with democracy prevailing at the lower levels of society. All of the women on the island are beautiful and intelligent, and Harris is careful to show, in the best modern way, that they possess cravings for sexual excitement that are at least as strong as those of men. Reason governs the islanders' behavior, but religion is included in temples devoted to Piety, Beauty, Love, and other human virtues. At the top of a hill there is a large marble figure of a woman with arms extended aloft and eyes closed, representing both human aspiration and its blindness—a symbolic vision of the fate of humankind, which is always "straining upwards in the dark." The book is too discursive and disjointed to be effective as a novel, but it offers a summary view of the final thoughts and feelings of its author.

Harris spent his last three years in poor health and reduced circumstances in Nice, where he died on 26 August 1931. "Frank Harris," wrote John Dos Passos in 1963, was "a natural storyteller," and "tall tales so permeated his private life that his biographers were hard put to disentangle any facts at all from the web of fiction he spun about himself.... He wrote some good short stories. He might have developed into a first-rate novelist if he hadn't been such a damn liar." Many of the most important people of Harris's life—his father, Professor Smith, and his wife Nellie, particularly—are reflected repeatedly in his fiction, often so altered that their real-life characters are hard to determine. Still, Harris took his fiction writing seriously. In his early work he followed models such as Harte and Ambrose Bierce and worked within the framework of American regional realism; but in his later work he showed his allegiance to the French realists such as Guy de Maupassant and Honoré de Balzac. He was also capable of writing allegorical and symbolic stories, inspired by Leo Tolstoy and Nathaniel Hawthorne; and he experimented with frame narratives in the manner of Joseph Conrad, whom he championed. But his chief merits, according to critical consensus, are his excellent and realistic psychological observation, his surprisingly sophisticated use of tone and objectivity, and his undeniable skill in the telling of a story. His works are frequently concerned with the social forces that dominate or inhibit the individual, especially the artist.

Letters:

Moore versus Harris: An Intimate Correspondence between George Moore and Frank Harris (Detroit: Privately printed, 1921);

Autobiographical Letters of John Galsworthy: A Correspondence with Frank Harris, Hitherto Unpublished (New York: English Book Shop, 1933);

Frank Harris to Arnold Bennett: Fifty-Eight Letters, 1908–1910 (Merion Station, Pa.: Privately printed for the American Autograph Shop, 1936);

Stanley Weintraub, ed., *The Playwright and the Pirate: Bernard Shaw and Frank Harris, A Correspondence* (University Park: Pennsylvania State University Press, 1982).

Biographies:

Kate Stephens, Gerit Smith, and Mary Caldwell Smith, eds., *The Lies and Libels of Frank Harris, with Arguments by Kate Stephens* (New York: Antigone, 1929);

Elmer Gertz and A. I. Tobin, *Frank Harris: A Study in Black and White* (Chicago: Mendelsohn, 1931);

Samuel Roth, *The Private Life of Frank Harris* (New York: Faro, 1931);

Hugh Kingsmill, *Frank Harris, A Biography* (New York: Farrar & Rinehart, 1932);

E. Merrill Root, *Frank Harris* (New York: Odyssey, 1947);

Vincent Brome, *Frank Harris: The Life and Adventures of a Scoundrel* (London: Cassell, 1959; New York: Yoseloff, 1960);

Linda Morgan Bain, *Evergreen Adventurer: the Real Frank Harris* (London: Research Publishing, [1975]);

Phillippa Pullar, *Frank Harris* (London: Hamilton, 1975).

References:

Enid Bagnold, *Letters to Frank Harris and Other Friends,* edited by R. P. Lister (Andoversford, U.K.: Whittington, 1980);

Van Wyck Brooks, *The Confident Years 1885–1915* (London: J. M. Dent, 1952), pp. 155–160;

Vincent O'Sullivan, *Opinions* (London: Unicorn Press, 1959), pp. 102–118;

Robert Brainard Pearsall, *Frank Harris* (New York: Twayne, 1970);

Hesketh Pearson, *Extraordinary People* (New York & Evanston: Harper & Row, 1965), pp. 175–236;

Pearson, *Modern Men and Mummers* (London: Allen & Unwin, 1921), pp. 102–132;

Frank Scully, *Rogues' Gallery* (Hollywood: Murray & Gee, 1943), pp. 210–238;

Robert H. Sherard, *Bernard Shaw, Frank Harris, and Oscar Wilde, with a Preface by Lord Alfred Douglas and an Additional Chapter by Hugh Kingsmill* (London: Laurie, 1937);

Sherard, *Oscar Wilde Twice Defended from Andre Gide's Wicked Lies and Frank Harris's Cruel Libels* (Chicago: Argus Book Shop, 1934);

Alexander Trocchi, *What Frank Harris Did Not Say... Being the Tumultuous, Apocryphal Fifth Volume of* My Life and Loves, *as Embellished by Alexander Trocchi, With an Apologetic Preface by Maurice Girodias* (New York: Olympia, 1968).

Papers:

Frank Harris's letters and papers are scattered. The most important and extensive collections of letters and typescripts are at the New York Public Library; the Harry Ransom Humanities Research Center at the University of Texas at Austin; and the Elmer Gertz Collection of the Library of Congress.

Stephen Hudson

(12 December 1868? – 29 October 1944)

George J. Johnson
Waterdown, Ontario, Canada

BOOKS: *Concessions,* as Sydney Schiff (London & New York: John Lane, 1913);
War-Time Silhouettes (London: Allen & Unwin, 1916);
Richard Kurt (London: Secker, 1919; New York: Knopf, 1920);
Elinor Colhouse (London: Secker, 1921; New York: Knopf, 1922);
Prince Hempseed (London: Secker, 1923; New York: Knopf, 1923);
Tony (London: Constable, 1924; New York: Knopf, 1924);
Myrtle (London: Constable, 1925; New York: Knopf, 1925);
Richard, Myrtle, and I (London: Constable, 1926; New York: Knopf, 1926; revised edition, edited by Violet Schiff, Philadelphia: University of Pennsylvania Press, 1962);
Céleste, and Other Sketches (London: Blackamore, 1930);
A True Story; in Three Parts, and a Postscript (London: Constable, 1930; New York: Knopf, 1930; revised edition, London: Falcon, 1948);
The Other Side (London: Cresset, 1937).
Edition: *A True Story* (London: Dent, 1965; New York: Dutton, 1965).

OTHER: Hermann Hesse, *In Sight of Chaos,* translated by Hudson (Zurich: Seldwyla, 1923);
C. K. Scott-Moncrieff, ed., *Marcel Proust: An English Tribute,* contribution by Hudson (London: Chatto & Windus, 1923), pp. 5–11;
Marcel Proust, *Time Regained,* translated by Hudson (London: Chatto & Windus, 1931);
"Apology and Extenuation," in *Ten Contemporaries: Notes toward Their Definitive Bibliography,* by John Gawsworth (London: Benn, 1932).

Best known as the replacement translator of Marcel Proust's work following the death of C. K. Scott-Moncrieff, Sydney Schiff, who published most of his work under the name Stephen Hudson, is rarely mentioned in lists of prominent writers. In a

Stephen Hudson

review in the *New Statesman and Nation* (21 May 1949), however, Walter Allen claimed that Hudson "added something to the English novel, and no account of our fiction during the past thirty years would be complete without reference to him." His biographer, Theophilus E. M. Boll, asserts that "Stephen Hudson is second to none in the honesty and lucid art with which he has given reality to his novels of insight into individuation." To this comment Boll adds the praise of many contemporary authors and critics, including Edwin Muir, Katherine Mansfield, Thomas Mann, Aldous Huxley, Humbert Wolfe, Richard Aldington, W. Somerset Maugham, and Louis Kronenberger.

Until 1962, when Hudson's widow, Violet Schiff, published an edited version of his *Richard, Myrtle, and I* (1926), virtually nothing was known about the man born as Sydney Schiff. Violet Schiff allowed Boll to compile a biographical note from information provided by her and other family members; it prefaced the edited novel. Boll suggests that Hudson's reticence to reveal the details of his life was probably related to his penchant for including autobiographical elements in his novels and to his shyness "over his parents' marital complexities." His obituary in *The Times* (London) on 13 November 1944 further claimed that "his increasing deafness contributed to his desire for seclusion."

Sydney Schiff's father was Alfred George Schiff, the son of an expatriate German Jew who married into a prominent Austrian family in Trieste and became a successful banker. Alfred Schiff followed his father's pattern: refined and multilingual, he became a member of the London Stock Exchange six years after his arrival in England in 1860. He married Caroline Mary Ann Eliza Scates Cavell; when she met Schiff, she was the wife of John Scott Cavell and the mother of a one-year-old daughter, Louise. Although no birth record was unearthed by Boll, Schiff was told that he had been born in London as Sydney Alfred Schiff on 12 December 1868; his parents were married on 14 August 1869, following a scandal and Caroline's divorce. Only years later did Schiff, his brother, Ernest, and sisters Edith, Rose, and Marie learn from a maid that Louise was their half sister; they were told that their mother was a widow when she and their father were married.

Under Caroline Schiff, whom Boll calls "a *grande dame,* a woman of decisive presence, and bold will," Sydney Schiff had an active and cultured childhood of Sunday "open houses" and horseback riding, the latter of which he particularly enjoyed. While their mother hoped that her sons would follow her family's tradition and enter military service, their father wanted them to join the family firm. Schiff and his brother enjoyed their freedom too much to accede to either parent's wishes. Alfred Schiff was a strong disciplinarian but lacked the ability to understand or manage his sons; he finally put all of his hopes in Sydney rather than the younger and more unmanageable Ernest.

Schiff's education involved a succession of tutors, followed by G. T. Worsley's preparatory school at age twelve and Wellington College for a year at age thirteen. In September 1886 he was accepted for admission to Oxford University but refused to enter (a decision he regretted for many years) because of his father's insistence that he prepare for a specific career.

As an alternative to further schooling Schiff relocated to Alberta, Canada, in 1887 to work on the ranch of his father's friend Sir John Pepys Lister-Kaye. He liked working with horses and enjoyed the company of Sir John and his American wife, but when they returned to England and left him in charge, he soon became bored. He traveled to Cincinnati, Ohio, to work for his uncle, Charles Schiff, president of the Cincinnati Holding Company, which controlled five interlocking railway companies worth more than $54 million; but he was unhappy there, as well. He then acted on his uncle's advice to travel throughout the United States until Sir John returned. Schiff's loneliness, sense of failure, and awareness of his father's dissatisfaction with him were compounded by news from England that his beloved mother was suffering from a congenital heart condition that necessitated abandoning her strenuous social life and moving away to the milder climate of Nice for much of the year.

In Louisville, Kentucky, Schiff became infatuated with Marion Fulton Canine, the daughter of a prominent local dentist. The couple eloped and were married in Sault Ste. Marie, Ontario, on 29 August 1889. The underage Schiff claimed to be twenty-five.

Despite their shock at news of the marriage, the Schiffs welcomed the bride and groom on their arrival in England in 1890. Because Marion was not pleased to find that the family was not as wealthy as she had been led to believe or with Sydney's need to work for his father, she behaved badly. Antagonized by her new daughter-in-law, Caroline Schiff suffered several heart attacks; as a consequence Alfred provided funds for the couple to travel in the United States and Europe. Thereafter Sydney only occasionally saw his mother, always without Marion.

In 1896 Caroline Schiff died, and Alfred Schiff provided a villa and furnishings for the couple in Como, Italy. Nevertheless, the marriage floundered. According to Boll, Marion needed "admirers and affairs" to give her "the illusion of worth," and Schiff, brooding on his purposelessness and lack of direction, had an affair with an Italian girl. In 1908 Schiff's father's death provided him with an inheritance, but he became more conscious of his trifling existence, a situation exacerbated when Marion ridiculed his attempts to write; consequently, after giving her half his fortune, Schiff left Marion and went on a six-month tour of Europe.

At the opera in London in 1909 Schiff's sister Edith introduced him to Violet Zillah Beddington, the sister of a friend; Schiff fell instantly in love with

Beddington, who was six years younger than he. In 1910 Marion sued for divorce, which was granted a year later; despite her remarriage to the wealthy Gen. Sadleir Jackson, Marion sued Sydney for maintenance. The Jacksons later separated, and the general died, but Schiff still provided Marion with half his income until her death.

On 10 May 1911 Schiff and Beddington were married. The marriage brought Schiff into a large family strongly devoted to the arts. Violet stimulated his reading, introducing him to Proust in 1916, and, as Boll puts it, encouraged the "fruition of his literary genius." Her household also provided Schiff with his nom de plume: he adopted the surname of the Beddingtons' secretary, a Miss Hudson, to conceal the identities of those he described in his largely autobiographical novels. Violet also assisted in creating a hospitable environment for an array of artists, writers (including Proust and James Joyce), and musicians who visited frequently; Boll claims that Sydney and Violet "never lost a friend except by death."

Hudson's autobiographical novels trace the progress of an aspiring writer through the chaotic, capricious circumstances that threaten to destroy him to the salvation of self-discovery, aided by confidence and love. Influenced as a young man by Edward Bulwer-Lytton, Charles Dickens, and William Makepeace Thackeray (especially Bulwer-Lytton), Schiff imitated their romantic rhetoric and nonrealistic characters at first; later, as a result of Violet's influence, he came to esteem Joyce, Henry James, Sigmund Freud, and C. G. Jung and to venerate Proust, who taught him what Boll calls "the discipline of art for mind and emotions' sake." This influence led Hudson to emphasize the basic motives of his characters rather than the disguised manifestations that they exhibit; eliminating much of the detailed description in his writing, Hudson focused instead on his characters' human passions.

Concessions (1913) was Schiff's first novel and the only one published under his real name. It was dedicated to Violet, although later both husband and wife repudiated the novel. Its style imitated the romantic Bulwer-Lytton, and the male characters are idealized; yet the story is well planned. More significantly, according to Boll, the novel "has biographical value as the statement of the problem that Violet Beddington faced in helping Sydney Schiff." Three characters represent aspects of Schiff's personality: John Cooper-Saunderson, a former member of the British diplomatic service who resigned to remain in Italy and care for his young American wife, Gracie Frowde; the brilliant, egotistical painter, Douglas Mackenzie, whose complete devotion

Violet Schiff, Hudson's second wife, the model for the character of Myrtle Vendramin in several of his novels

to his work renders him unable to give of himself to others but who is totally dependent on a woman for his physical and psychological well-being; and the gentleman landowner Peter Blake, who hears the singing of Zillah Lopez, Mackenzie's wife, and falls in love with her sight unseen.

Zillah and Mackenzie's marriage is unsatisfying for her and seems to inhibit Mackenzie's painting; consequently, she leaves him for Peter, who cherishes her, thus displaying a disposition Hudson wished Violet to show toward him. Another female character who sacrifices herself for love is Peter's Spanish mother, Madame Cadajos, a widowed concert pianist: she becomes Mackenzie's mistress, providing him with the nurturing he needs to continue painting and freeing Zillah to marry Peter. She realizes, however, that she will receive no affection in return. A brief review of *Concessions* in the *Times Literary Supplement* called "the somewhat intricate plot of the novel . . . interesting, though a little too long."

Schiff had begun his second novel, *Richard Kurt,* in 1911 in Eastbourne but had put it aside while he wrote *Concessions* and a collection of short stories, *War-Time Silhouettes* (1916), the first work

Title page for the U.S. edition of the first of a series of quasi-autobiographical novels about an aspiring author

published under Schiff's pen name. During this time Violet read and recommended to him Proust's *Du côté de chez Swann* (1913; translated as *Swann's Way*, 1922), which so influenced Hudson's literary technique that *Richard Kurt* was dedicated to the French novelist. If one may infer autobiographical details from Hudson's novels, there are strong suggestions (notably in *Richard, Myrtle, and I*) that the World War I years (1914 to 1918) were a period of mental stagnation compounded by an unsuccessful attempt at farming in the country.

Completed in London, *Richard Kurt* was published in 1919. Opening with the funeral of Richard's mother, whom he worshiped, the plotless novel traces the relationship of the immature Richard and his beautiful, elegant wife of six years, Elinor, whose sneering contempt for his ambition to write demeans him and contributes to his inertia. Richard is discontented with the materialistic life into which Elinor has led him, which is typified by his father's gift, the Villa Aquafonti on Lake Como, which he and Elinor have lavishly decorated. A Vassar graduate, Mary Mackintyre, helps him understand the extent of his wife's tyranny, but she refuses to aid him in his attempt to be himself; an Italian girl, Virginia Peraldi, seems to provide Richard with the passion he desires, but her pretense of sleep during their intimate moments disgusts Richard because of its dishonesty. Finally Richard leaves and accompanies his father back to England. The father's materialism has created a gulf between the two that was bridged only when Richard won a fortune gambling at Monte Carlo eight years earlier. Realizing that his father is dying, Richard feels compassion for him for the first time in years. The *Times Literary Supplement* selected this scene and the characterization of Virginia as the only two aspects to commend in a novel that was otherwise "weak, trivial, negligible." Other critics derided its length, aimlessness, and spineless central character but commended Hudson's powers of observation, his sureness of touch in construction, and his descriptive talent.

In 1919 Hudson also edited the first issue of a London quarterly, the short-lived *Art and Letters*, while at the same time encouraging experimental young artists. His next novel, *Elinor Colhouse* (1921), describes events six years prior to those in *Richard Kurt*. Bored by his Uncle Theo's railway business, Richard travels across America and becomes infatuated with Elinor, who seduces and marries the weak-willed young man. While the story obviously recounts events in Hudson's life, he fictionalized most of the names and settings, moving his uncle's railroad business from Cincinnati to Cliftonburg and his wife's hometown from Louisville to Manitou, Michigan. The novel was commended for Hudson's powers of observation, subtle treatment of theme, and vigorous characterizations; the noted critic J. W. Krutch in *The Nation* observed "within its self-imposed limitations it is almost perfect." On the other hand, in *The New Statesman* the novelist Rebecca West found it "a thoroughly competent survey of the situation . . . [but] not a work of art."

In 1923 Hudson published *In Sight of Chaos*, a translation from the German of two essays by Hermann Hesse on Fyodor Dostoyevsky, and *Prince Hempseed*, a novel named after Richard's favorite German story and dedicated to Proust, who had died the previous year. The novel marks Hudson's first use of a first-person narrator. Set in the period preceding *Elinor Colhouse*, the novel is framed by scenes of travel, opening with the passive Richard's earliest childhood memory of being transported by pram and closing with his unwilling journey by steamer to New York at age eighteen. The novel explores the causes of Richard's weak will. In his quest for self-knowledge he struggles to understand his indifferent mother's preoccupation with her social life and her string of admirers and his demanding father's attempts to make him a productive member of a materialist society. The hypocrisy of his teachers, the snobbishness of his schoolmates, and his inept encounters with girls all heighten his sense of spiritual isolation; his naiveté is reflected in the random presentation of events and stylistic simplicity of the work. *The New York Times* criticized the novel for "gossipy discursiveness" and "shadowy" characterizations but admired the theme. *Punch* complimented Hudson for altering his literary style to match Richard's changing age but was "not so sure about the development of Richard himself."

Hudson's next novel, *Tony* (1924), is written in the form of a deathbed memoir addressed to Richard by his younger brother, Tony, who, annoyed at being left out of the series, debunks Richard's sentimental account of the events from his first trip to America in 1887 to 1919. Tony makes explicit what was implied in *Prince Hempseed,* that "Richard is an innocent who would like to control his own feelings." A cynical, clever, sensual rogue, Tony is congenial with Elinor, even encouraging her cruelty to Richard, but finds little fault with the humane and perceptive Myrtle Vendramin, who becomes Richard's second wife. The only other evidence of Tony's humanity occurs following the death of his beloved son, Cyril, in battle: Tony cries as Richard comforts him. Cyril's portrait mediates Tony's solitary communion with his dead son, from which even his mistress, Trixie, is excluded. When Tony finds a maid, Delia, entranced by the portrait, a passionate encounter ensues; later, in a rage, Delia's miner father gives Tony a beating that ultimately proves fatal.

Again Hudson used his own life experiences: his brother Ernest lost a son, Alfred, in World War I and died himself four days after receiving a beating like the one described in the novel; Myrtle Vendramin is modeled on Violet Beddington. In a lengthy review Edwin Muir claimed, "It is a triumph for Mr. Hudson to have given significance and beauty to a theme so apparently sordid, setting everything down with the modesty and cleanness of art." Other reviewers criticized the novel's ineffective narration; dreary, empty characters; and superficial, monotonous story.

In contrast to *Tony, Myrtle* (1925) is a love story of the renewal of Richard's life through the influence of the strong and nurturing Myrtle Vendramin. The story is narrated in sections by nine people who have loved Myrtle, commencing in "Nanny" with her nurse, who tells of the protected

Title page for the U.S. edition of the novel that describes the earlier life of Richard Kurt

childhood of this favored seventh child of the Vendramin family. "Jane Grey," told by her mother's companion, explores the family's musical background and explains Myrtle's role in consoling her father after the death of his eldest son, Philip; Jane is patterned after the Beddington family secretary, Miss Hudson. In "Sylvia" Myrtle's older sister details her tragic first marriage and praises Myrtle's understanding; it follows closely the life of Violet's sister Evelyn. The next six sections are narrated by men who have loved Myrtle. Adrian, a wealthy businessman, cannot understand Myrtle's preference for older and poorer men. Marcel, a young French poet, contrasts his intensity with Myrtle's calm firmness. An older composer, Sir Michael Halloran (based on Sir Arthur Sullivan), a close family friend, shares the Vendramins' love of music and proposes marriage to Myrtle. Basil Moriarity, an attractive, penniless bachelor, enjoys Myrtle's companionship and repartee. Paul Block (based on Henri Bernstein), a French playwright, unsuccessfully attempts to seduce Myrtle through a battle of wits but remains her friend. Richard Kurt recounts the steps by which Myrtle aids him in recovering from his abject, guilt-ridden marriage to Elinor. Muir praised Hudson for his "admirable" use of monologue and the "complete internal realism" of the characters; most other critics were also positive, with *The New York World* calling *Myrtle* "one of the most exquisite novels issued by an American publisher in 1925."

Richard, Myrtle, and I is a sequel to *Concessions* in that it reveals allegorically how Myrtle provided her third gift to Richard, that of creative willpower. The story traces Elinor's divorce action and the early years of Richard's marriage to Myrtle. At a psychological level the novel introduces a conflict between the ordinary and creative personalities of a writer. The narrator of the novel, the "I" of the title, is pure intellect, a particle of the "life-force" that is attempting to direct a creative artist—in this case, Richard. This aggressive persona composes a sonnet; drives Richard to overcome past inhibitions; criticizes his moral weakness and selfishness; and philosophizes about the relationships among "history, life, and literary art." It comes into conflict with other aspects of Richard's personality: his tendency to sentimentalize himself and friends whose associations impair his creativity and his desire to dwell in the past as opposed to looking ahead. A third conflict involves Richard's question to Myrtle: "I think love is more important than Art, don't you darling?" Myrtle's failure to respond dramatizes Richard's internal conflict over whether or not love is enough to make life completely satisfying. Richard comes to understand that through Myrtle these conflicts can be resolved: Myrtle's love and creative will are fulfilled through his own creativity, and Myrtle's disciplined intellect provides the organization and direction he needs to check his tendency to sentimentalize. Myrtle and "I" recognize Richard's need to deal with his haunted past before he can forge ahead. Together they become a "triune consortium."

Hudson hoped that *Richard, Myrtle, and I* would "free me for what I have still to do, to enable me to express myself with greater freedom than I have been able to do up to the present, and to speak out of my consciousness of *now*." Reviews were generally quite positive: Louis Kronenberger said, "Substance, texture, form, style—every standard by which a writer can be judged—are in Hudson's case unique things, difficult to grasp except with the whole mind and artistic consciousness." A reviewer for *The New York Times* claimed that Hudson "is one of the most brilliantly lucid novelists of ideas." Negative comments focused on the novel's lack of appeal to the common reader.

In 1930 Hudson published *Céleste, and Other Sketches,* a collection of six pieces that had originally been published in small American magazines between 1920 and 1925. In the same year *A True Story; in Three Parts, and a Postscript* appeared, bringing together, as he explains in the preface, four earlier books that "in effect constituted studies for [*A True Story*] . . . reconstituted and reknit . . . in their final form." Hudson arranges the novels in the chronological order of Richard Kurt's life: *Prince Hempseed,* which traces Richard's childhood and adolescence; *Elinor Colhouse,* which describes his meeting Elinor and their marriage; and *Richard Kurt,* which depicts the conflict and mutual indifference of their life together. The ninth memoir from *Myrtle,* in which Richard meets Myrtle and leaves Elinor, is used as a postscript. The first two novels are unaltered, whereas *Richard Kurt* is considerably reduced to remove superfluities and retain essentials: chapters 2 through 5, which recount Richard's European wanderings, are omitted to focus on the affair with Virginia at Lake Como; judgmental references to Elinor's abortion were removed from chapter 8, at Violet's suggestion, because "they made [Richard] out to be the moral prig he had ceased being"; and other sections were revised to clarify meaning. *Richard, Myrtle, and I, Tony,* and most of *Myrtle* were not used. The exclusion of these parts allows *A True Story* to focus on the character of Richard, but the overall effect of the work, according to Boll, is to "halt the forward direction of Stephen Hudson's creativity by restoring the ascendancy of the painful past."

Reviewers were generally supportive of the novel. *The Christian Science Monitor* praised "the exquisite accuracy of its atmosphere, the cleanness and lucidity of its prose, the acidity of its family portraiture"; Margaret Wallace claimed in the *New York Evening Post* (12 April 1930) that "The spiritual odyssey of Richard Kurt is a simple and straightforward narrative, powerfully and bitingly sincere." V. S. Pritchett, however, complained in *The Spectator* (29 March 1930) that "Mr Hudson has written an admonitory pamphlet on the young man's life and family, rather than a story." In an essay for John Gawsworth's *Ten Contemporaries* (1930) Hudson said that *A True Story* "represents the best I have so far been able to accomplish."

Following the death of his friend Scott-Moncrieff, Hudson translated the last part of Proust's monumental *A la recherche du temps perdu* (1913–1927; translated as *Remembrance of Things Past,* 1922–1931) as *Time Regained* (1931). In 1941 he wrote to Gawsworth that the translation was "the only work of mine I know to be worth preserving because it is the interpretation of a masterpiece every word of which was and is precious to me."

On 3 August 1934 Hudson and Violet moved to their last home, Abinger Manor on Abinger Common, near Dorking, Surrey. In 1937 Hudson published *The Other Side* and further revised *Richard Kurt* by removing what he felt were nonessentials, including the character of Mary Mackintyre, and by clarifying other passages through rewriting.

The Other Side bridges the time between *Prince Hempseed* and *Elinor Colhouse,* following nineteen-year-old Richard from his first exposure to New York City to his soulless business experience working for his Uncle Theo's railway conglomerate in Cliftonburg, Ohio. Spurning his father's demand that he pursue a moneymaking career, Richard attempts self-discovery through "feeling" or "getting inside people who feel." He suffers a heartbreaking rejection by his mother and turns to the New Orleans promoter Proctor Johnson and his mistress Cora Marshall as parental substitutes. Likewise, a brief affair with a prostitute, Pearl, turns out to be more maternal than sexual. The American experience ends abruptly. Uncle Theo returns Richard to England to avoid scandal following Richard's revelation that, out of compassion, he abetted the escape of the homesick company treasurer, Leopold Taube, who was inveigled into an embezzlement scheme by a friend but repaid the money he stole from the company. The novel in effect explains why Richard was so vulnerable to the machinations of Elinor Colhouse: his relationship with Pearl left him susceptible to any who offered to alleviate his frustrated search for love.

In an unpublished letter to Hudson, Maugham praised the novel's "extraordinary freshness and youthfulness . . . its remarkable recapture of the spirit of adolescence." In *The Sunday Referee* (14 February 1937) Humbert Wolfe called it "a book whose continuous opening up of trains of thought in readers made no instant and ephemeral assault to capture wide attention, but would become the intimate of the thoughtful many when time had allowed acquaintanceship to ripen into friendship."

Exactly ten years after Hudson moved into Abinger Manor, on 3 August 1944, at eight o'clock in the morning a German bomb destroyed the manor, as well as a nearby church and cottage: Vio-

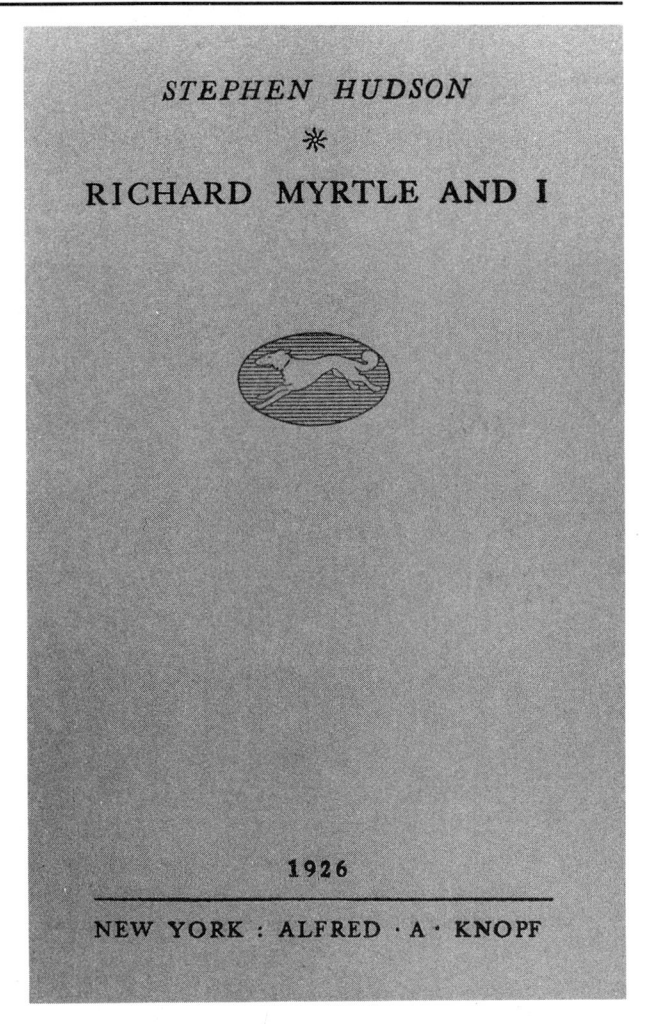

Title page for the continuation of the Richard Kurt series, focusing on the relationship between Richard and his wife Myrtle

let suffered a shattered vertebra from a bomb fragment. Although he was not injured, the incident may have had an adverse effect on Hudson's health. He died from a heart ailment a few months later, on 29 October at the Sackville Court Hotel in Hove.

Publication of Hudson's work did not cease with his death: in 1948 the last revision of *A True Story* was published, dedicated to Violet. In it *Prince Hempseed, The Other Side, Elinor Colhouse,* and the ninth part of *Myrtle* are unchanged from the 1930 edition, while the further shortened version of *Richard Kurt* was included. An epilogue found by Violet among Hudson's papers was also added: it is a paean to Violet and her influence on his development as a novelist. On its republication in 1965 this edition was prefaced by a 1930 letter from Edith Sitwell, in which she claims: "The whole panorama of Richard Kurt's life will be regarded as one of the most important works of our time. There is so much variation, that all the world seems enclosed, and this although the structure is never broken for a moment. I mean the structure on which all this great variation is built."

In 1932 Hudson had inscribed a copy of *Richard, Myrtle, and I* to Gawsworth: "I wish I were going to rewrite this book; instead I must write my name in it because you want me to." Violet Schiff took the responsibility of fulfilling this desire by revising the novel for a new edition published in 1962. She had collaborated closely with Hudson on editing and revising the original edition; for the 1962 version she clarified the relationship between Richard and "I" and removed excessive explanations and many minor characters. She also trimmed extraneous dialogue and removed many references to familial opposition and Richard's attitudes and beliefs. Finally, she added new scenes to clarify the interrelationship of the three titular personages and of Richard's relationship with Virginia. Boll says that "Comparing the two versions of *Richard, Myrtle, and I* leads one to appreciate the love and the genius for her task.... She has sacrificed many separately worthwhile details to give the utmost unity and dramatic fulfillment to a story that is unique in the history of the English novel."

In each successive novel Hudson moved closer to fulfilling Proust's maxim that art is a perpetual sacrifice of feeling for truth: in Boll's words, he "stripped the emotional camouflages that covered the pure realities of the experiences of Richard Kurt" to reveal the motives that spurred him and others to activity, sometimes years later. This emphasis on Richard's idiosyncrasies and their inexorable effect on his destiny produces the drama in Hudson's novels.

Hudson's literary vision thus led him to neglect contemporary popular demands for a strong narrative and realistic characters for a style that challenged readers' decoding powers; consequently, as Allen pointed out in 1949, "his novels were highly praised when they first appeared, but they were never popular, and they have been out of print for some years." Nevertheless, Boll felt confident, as he concluded his "Critical Essay," that readers would tire of the modern emphasis on "masses and the massing of society" and "will again recognize the discrete element that gives quality to the life of the many," as depicted by Hudson's "theme of the precarious progress of the pilgrim who would be an artist." He also suggested that Hudson's style would lead to his rediscovery: "A portent of such a rediscovery is Frank O'Connor's nostalgic reference to him in *The New York Times* of January 15, 1961. When he visits secondhand bookstores, he writes, 'My eye strays over the shelves, searching for something by the English novelist Stephen Hudson and wondering if his bare, lucid and precise prose was really as good as I once thought it.'"

Letters:

Aldous Huxley, Exhumations: Correspondance inédite avec Sydney Schiff, 1925–1937, edited by Clémentine Robert (Paris: Didier, 1976).

Bibliography:

Fred B. Millet, ed., *Contemporary British Literature: A Critical Survey and 232 Author-Bibliographies,* revised edition (New York: Harcourt, Brace, 1935), pp. 282–283.

Biography:

Theophilus E. M. Boll, "Biographical Note," in *Richard, Myrtle, and I,* by Stephen Hudson, edited by Violet Schiff (Philadelphia: University of Pennsylvania Press, 1962), pp. 9–40.

References:

Theophilus E. M. Boll, "Critical Essay," in *Richard, Myrtle, and I,* by Stephen Hudson, edited by Violet Schiff (Philadelphia: University of Pennsylvania Press), pp. 41–89;

Victor Cassidy, "Letters of Wyndham Lewis to Sydney and Violet Schiff," *Enemy News: Journal of the W. L. Society,* 21 (Summer 1985): 9–31;

Enid J. Marantz, "L'Action de Proust sur ses Traducteurs et Adaptateurs Anglais: Scott Moncrieff, Stephen Hudson, Harold Pinter," *Bulletin de la Societe du Amis de Marcel Proust et du Amis de Combray,* 31 (1981): 331–338;

Edwin Muir, "Stephen Hudson," in his *Transition: Essays on Contemporary Literature* (New York: Viking, 1926), pp. 85–97;

George D. Painter, "Proust's Letters to Sydney and Violet Schiff," *British Museum Quarterly,* 32, nos. 3–4 (1968): 68–74;

Sumanyu Satpathy, "The Schiffs and T. S. Eliot, an Aspect of a Literary Friendship," *Punjab University Research Bulletin,* 23 (April 1992): 11–19;

Nelly Stephane, "Lettres à Stephen Hudson, Aldous Huxley, et Thomas Mann," *Review Litterarie Mensuelle,* 69 (January–February 1991): 117–124.

Oliver Madox Hueffer
(9 January 1876 - 21 June 1931)

Michele K. Troy
Loyola University of Chicago

BOOKS: *Love's Disguises: A Book of Little Plays (Being Four of a Sequence and One Other)* (Hackbridge: Sign of the Rose, 1900);
In Arcady and Out: Short Stories (London: R. Brimley Johnson, 1901);
The Artistic Temperament, as Jane Wardle (London: Alston Rivers, 1907; New York: McClure, Phillips, 1907);
The Lord of Latimer Street: A Novel, as Wardle (London: Alston Rivers, 1907);
The Book of Witches (London: Nash, 1908; New York: McBride, 1909);
Margery Pigeon: A Novel, as Wardle (London: Arnold, 1909);
The Pasque-Flower: A Novel, as Wardle (London: Arnold, 1909);
The Little Gray Man: A Novel, as Wardle (London: Arnold, 1910);
Where Truth Lies: A Study in the Improbable (London: Stanley Paul, 1911);
The Spinola Rubens: An Appreciation, by Hueffer, Wallace Lowe Crowdy, and Henri Frantz (Edinburgh: Schultze, 1911);
A Vagabond in New York (New York & London: John Lane, 1913);
Hunt the Slipper: A Novel (London: Stanley Paul, 1913; New York: John Lane, 1914);
Little Pitchers (London: Stanley Paul, 1919);
Needles and Pins (London: Unwin, 1924);
French France (London: Benn, 1929; New York: Appleton, 1929);
"Cousins German" (London: Benn, 1930);
Some of the English: A Study towards a Study (London: Benn, 1930; New York: Appleton, 1930);
By Whose Authority? (London: Benn, 1931);
The Right Honourable: Being Three Days from the Life of Elbert, Second Baron Thornton Heath (London: Benn, 1931).
Edition: *The Book of Witches* (Wakefield: E. P., 1973).

PLAY PRODUCTION: *The Lord of Latimer Street: A Play in Four Acts,* London, Terry's Theatre, 26 February 1908.

Oliver Madox Hueffer in the uniform of the East Surrey Regiment

SELECTED PERIODICAL PUBLICATIONS–UNCOLLECTED: "The Next Religion," *National Review,* 56 (November 1910): 283–292;
"Lighter Side of War Described by One Who Got to the Front," *New York Times,* 3 January 1915, section 4, p. 7;
"Jack London: A Personal Sketch," *New Statesman,* 2 (December 1916): 207; reprinted in *Living Age,* 292 (13 January 1917): 124–126;
"British Delusions Concerning Americans," *National Review,* 74 (February 1920): 804–805;
"More British Delusions Concerning Americans," *National Review,* 75 (July 1920): 674–681;
"The Old Guard in Canada," *National Review,* 81 (May 1923): 438–442.

Oliver Madox Hueffer has achieved footnote fame in literary history as the younger brother of the modernist editor and writer Ford Madox Ford. Often described as an exaggerated version of Ford, Hueffer had an erratic career and became involved in financial and sexual exploits resembling those that haunted his more famous brother—to the point where certain characters and plot details in Hueffer's novels could be loosely based on the life of either brother. Best known during his lifetime as a novelist and war correspondent, Hueffer wrote many newspaper and journal articles; had several plays produced; and published four books of nonfiction, one volume of short stories, and twelve novels, five of them under the pseudonym Jane Wardle. Preoccupied with adventure rather than with the quest for literary immortality that drove his brother, Hueffer led a life that recalls the picaresque plots of some of his fiction. While he has not achieved the fame of his brother, Hueffer's literary production is worth examining because it adapts popular romance and adventure genres to satirize important social and cultural changes before and after World War I. The entertaining, often melodramatic, quality of his tales belies an ironic treatment of social concerns that many critics failed to note in his work.

Oliver Franz Hueffer, who later adopted the middle name Madox, was born in London on 9 January 1876 into a family that was prominent in literary and artistic circles. His father, Francis Hueffer, who held a doctorate in philology from Göttingen University, had immigrated to England from Germany in 1869. A prominent editor and critic, he was assistant editor of the well-respected journal *The Academy,* editor of the *New Quarterly Magazine,* and, for the last ten years of his life, music critic for *The Times* of London. Hueffer's mother, Catherine Madox Brown Hueffer, was the daughter of the Pre-Raphaelite painter Ford Madox Brown and a recognized painter in her own right. His uncle, through the marriage of his mother's sister, Lucy, was the art critic and editor William Rossetti, the brother of the Pre-Raphaelite painter Dante Gabriel Rossetti and the poet Christina Rossetti. In 1889 Hueffer and his brother moved into their grandfather Brown's home when their father's sudden death left the family in dire financial straits; their sister, Juliet, went to live with William and Lucy Rossetti.

The brothers shared the same family circumstances and received similar educations at the unconventional Praetorius boarding school and the classically oriented University College of London. Oliver flourished in this environment, while Ford often found it oppressive. This discrepancy is partly explained by Ford's bitter feeling that Hueffer was the family favorite. Describing his brother in his autobiography *It Was the Nightingale* (1933) as "a gifted and in many ways extraordinary fellow," Ford claims that Oliver was "the sparkling jewel of the family," while Ford was "its ugly duckling." Ford tells, for instance, how he was forced to give his toys to Oliver when Oliver had broken his own and how his mother made him share with Oliver some of the additional allowance his father gave him as the firstborn son. He further observes that while Grandfather Brown considered all of his grandchildren geniuses, he reserved a particular fondness for Oliver, whom he deemed a "mad" genius. While Ford remained frustrated by such comparisons, Oliver seemed to delight in them, capitalizing on his physical likeness to his brother. In a 25 May 1915 letter, for instance, Ezra Pound depicts Hueffer as "quite capable of taking advantage of the fact that he is occasionally taken for Ford" and insists that "if 'Oliver' has robbed a bank, or borrowed money or committed a rape it may be as well to . . . [deny] that Ford was there." Max Saunders even infers in his biography of Ford (1996) that the latter may have changed his name from Ford Hermann Hueffer to Ford Madox Ford partly to prevent the siblings from being confused with each other.

Hueffer seems to have been a warm-hearted, irresponsible rogue whose foibles inspired others to protect rather than to excoriate him. He was absentminded, on one occasion leaving home in his slippers to play soccer, and he often relied on his luck to the inconvenience of others. Lacking money to return to London on the train, he once walked for thirty miles, slogging through wet meadowlands, sleeping in a ditch, and charming strangers into helping him; he ended up so sick that his family had to care for him. By 1893 he was already depending on his family to rescue him from financial trouble, covering his debts by pawning his grandfather's watch, chain, and spectacles and by cutting into the yearly stipend that Catherine Hueffer had promised Ford. Hueffer's financial speculations also affected the family of his wife, Zoe Pyne, a violinist whom he married on 2 March 1897. Pyne had to give violin lessons to help support them; Hueffer also mishandled her family's trust funds. Others consistently excused such capers because Hueffer was, in Ford's words, "too good natured or obstinate" to stave off catastrophe.

Ford observes in his autobiography that to get out of financial trouble Hueffer ran "through the careers of Man About Town, Army Officer, Actor, Stockbroker, Painter, Author and under the auspices of one of his fiancées, that of Valise Manufacturer." In 1894, according to the diary of a family friend, Olive Garnett, Hueffer decided "that having tried most things and failed, it now [remained] to become an actor." While his love of theatricality in his life did not translate into skill on the stage, it did facilitate a short playwriting career. In 1899 he attempted to become a tobacco wholesaler, using money he had inherited from an uncle who was a planter in the United States, but the venture failed. In 1900 he published a volume of five plays under the title *Love's Disguise: A Book of Little Plays*. In 1901 he journeyed to the United States, returning with little money but with hopes of writing up experiences for profit. During the summer of 1902 he asked Ford to assist him in developing a journalistic career. Although he described his brother in an undated letter to H. G. Wells (written between May and August 1902) as someone who had "failed in every blessed thing that can be failed in," Ford used his contacts to help Hueffer. Hueffer's journalism became a mainstay of his income: in late 1903 he was hired by the *Manchester Guardian* to write a daily "miscellany" column, "shorts," special articles, drama criticism, personals, and a London letter.

Among his friends, Hueffer was highly regarded as a storyteller; Ford claims in his autobiography that "when it came to . . . back-chat he was the most amazing performer that I have ever heard." Translating this skill from oral to written form, Hueffer wrote fiction in a mode of comic realism that loosely resembles that of Charles Dickens and uses irony to make social commentary. Fascinated by the outcast, he often places his protagonists at or beyond the edges of "acceptable" British society. Artists, vagabonds, burglars, and pirates, as well as working-class characters such as barmaids, plumbers, and factory workers, have prominent roles in his works. Such characters allow Hueffer to play on middle- and upper-class readers' ostensible knowledge of "types" rejected by British conventionality. Preoccupied with plots involving mistaken identity—perhaps because of his penchant for impersonating his brother—Hueffer weighs appearance against reality, dissecting the criteria societies invoke to define individuals as legitimate or illegitimate. In his fiction and nonfiction Hueffer returns, in particular, to the question of how class and national stereotypes function in times of social change. Because his humor often derives from speculating on the accuracy of such stereotypes, it sometimes lapses into impropriety—as when he represents the "dirty" Italian immigrant or the "avaricious" Jew. He privileges humor over realism in most situations, even those involving serious themes such as marital infidelity, divorce, and wartime propaganda. Finally, his novels reveal his fascination with narratives of romance and adventure, while, at the same time, they caricature the ease with which readers succumb to such narratives.

The Artistic Temperament (1907), the first of the five novels Hueffer wrote under the Jane Wardle pseudonym, derides the artist figure via the painter protagonist, Stephen, who is perpetually late for appointments, careless with money, and subject to his passions, and repeatedly invokes his "temperament" as an excuse when these behaviors inconvenience others. Engaged to the daughter of a respectable banker, he falls in love with Delia, the wife of an old school friend. When Delia casts herself as the heroine who throws off predictability to enter the domain of "Art," Stephen plays the hero, construing his dalliances as further proof of his inherent artistic ability. The novel resolves several complicated blackmail subplots when Stephen marries his fiancée, fathers three children, and is elected president of the Royal Academy. While one can read the novel as straight melodrama appealing to female readers' supposed hunger for romance, it also exploits the irony of Stephen, the self-styled rebel artist who

Hueffer circa 1895

Hueffer's elder brother, the writer Ford Madox Ford, around 1910

completely incorporates himself into the system. Through this irony the novel comments on the Edwardian fear of the growing materialism of British society that E. M. Forster also made his subject—a fear that Hueffer emphasizes by describing the rapidly burgeoning suburbs, the middle class's desire to obtain symbols of prestige, and the commercialization of art. Although reviewers for the British periodicals *Academy* (23 March 1907) and *Outlook* (6 April 1907) found the novel trite and irresponsible, it was generally well received. *The New York Times* (3 August 1907) praised the work for its "insight, humor, comprehension, sympathy," while the *Nation* (8 August 1907) credited the author with a "mastery . . . of the satirical art." The book sold well and was into its third printing by 1911.

Hueffer's next two pseudonymous novels deal with the theme of mistaken identity in two different social contexts. In *The Lord of Latimer Street* (1907), which was one of his greatest popular successes, a titled landlord tries to win his female cousin's approval by engaging in the philanthropic activities that are her passion. Living incognito in the slums, he gains sympathy for the plight of the poor families who generate his wealth and becomes humbled by the difficulty of playing the charitable savior. The expected romance plot develops when a working-class woman falls in love with him but renounces her love because of the societal obstacles to mixed-class marriages. Hueffer adapted the novel as a play, which was produced in 1908. *Margery Pigeon* (1909) reverses the plot of *The Lord of Latimer Street*. The title character answers an advertisement specifically addressed to barmaids, which results in her posing as the long-lost affluent Australian niece of Lady Pomphrey. Lady Pomphrey plans for Margery to lure her sister's ineffectual son into marriage, after which she will get revenge on the sister by revealing Margery's working-class origins. Margery inadvertently thwarts her aristocratic benefactress's plans for revenge when she instead marries Lady Pomphrey's estranged son. These variations on the standard masked-identity plot reveal Hueffer's awareness of changing class structures in England. *Margery Pigeon,* in particular, comments on the aristocracy's increasing inability to define itself as distinct from other up-and-coming social classes. While critics noted Hueffer's tendency toward exaggeration in certain passages, they recommended both works. The *Athenaeum* (21 December 1909) asserted that *The Lord of Latimer Street* "is life indeed" in its realistic descriptions of poverty, while the London *Bookman* (May 1909) singled out *Margery Pigeon* as "both good reading and good literature," especially for its "lifelike" characters.

The Pasque-Flower (1909) mimics *The Artistic Temperament* in its depiction of a protagonist who must decide between two women, adding a comic treasure hunt as a frame for his dilemma. In his final pseudonymous novel, *The Little Gray Man* (1910), Hueffer moves away from love plots to produce a comic allegory in which an impecunious but self-satisfied protagonist, Carfax, must choose whether to side with Virtue, as represented by a young, upstanding salesman (the "little gray man"), or with Vice, in the person of a devious elderly man. While the novel can be interpreted as a sarcastic commentary on the pressures that an increasingly materialistic society places on individuals, reviewers generally found the plot tedious and the book lacking in merit except for its development of the title character.

While writing as Jane Wardle, Hueffer remained dependent on his journalistic output for

Frontispiece and title page for the fictionalized account of Hueffer's experiences in New York

his income. He published sketches of his American travels in *Truth* and covered the Mexican Revolution for the *Daily Express* beginning in 1910. In May 1910 he and four other journalists were arrested by Mexican secret police. Hueffer was released when he produced his British passport, but—perhaps in a deliberate attempt to garner publicity—rumors reached the press that he had been executed as a spy. In 1911 his affair with an actress resulted in a scandal that ended her marriage.

In *Where Truth Lies: A Study in the Improbable* (1911) Hueffer parodies many well-thumbed romance plots of the day, weaving them together into a rampant comedy of a clerk, Mr. Truscott, who is mistakenly kidnapped and rescued by Dolly, a master storyteller who so closely conforms her actions to trite adventure plots that she refuses to marry Truscott until he misrepresents himself as a notorious burglar. Exploiting narrative irony more outrageously than Hueffer's other works, the novel leads the duo through subplots involving murder and a forgery ring only to reveal that the intrigues they feared were fictions of their own making. Through such irony the novel gently mocks the desperate craving of "modern" individuals for romance. As the London *Bookman* (April 1911) said: "Truth does indeed lie deep in this triumph of casual exaggeration."

Hunt the Slipper (1913), a more finely tuned caper novel in the vein of the works of Wilkie Collins, has multiple narrators. The initial one, the elderly Sir Edward Fanhope, regrets the newfangled contraptions, such as motorcars, that have

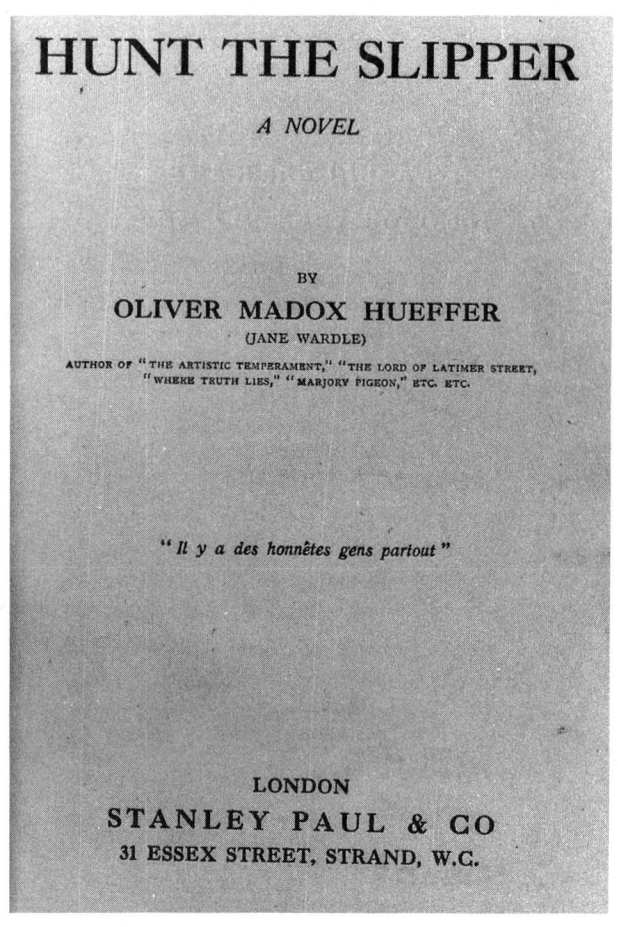

Title page for the 1913 novel in which an elderly British aristocrat journeys to America in search of the granddaughter he has never seen

corrupted an older, quieter, way of life. When he discovers the existence of a heretofore unknown granddaughter, he embarks with trepidation on a trip to the "heathen" United States to find her. There he encounters characters from various walks of life who take over the narration of his story: a former manservant masquerading as a nobleman, a British working-class woman forced into prostitution, an American stage actress whose husband has faked suicide and disappeared, and a young British nobleman of dwindling finances who is seeking his brother, the actress's missing husband, and who resolves the myriad plot complications. *Hunt the Slipper* reinforces a central theme of Hueffer's autobiographical *A Vagabond in New York,* published the same year: featuring protagonists who interact with individuals of classes and nationalities other than their own, both books argue that class and national stereotypes should not replace the more profound understanding that firsthand experience can provide. While Hueffer never promotes a full breakdown of class or national boundaries, he continues this humanistic stance and emphasizes the importance of personal experience in two of his best-known works, the nonfiction studies of national character *French France* (1929) and *Some of the English: A Study towards a Study* (1930).

Returning from Mexico shortly after the outbreak of World War I, Hueffer enlisted in the East Surrey Regiment in the fall of 1915. Wounded twice, once severely, he would nevertheless say in the preface to his novel *"Cousins German"* (1930) that "the years of the war were among the happiest, and not perhaps the least useful of his life." His next three novels, *Little Pitchers* (1919), *Needles and Pins* (1924), and *"Cousins German,"* echo this theme, employing a more muted humor than his earlier fiction as they examine the effects of war on British social customs and depict competing factions' attempts to define "truth" and moral codes in postwar England.

Little Pitchers, an often uneven experiment with narrative voice, is narrated by Dinah, the eldest child of the warmhearted but impractical Henry. Overwhelmed by the pressures of his failing business and by his fear that he will not be able to provide for his family, Henry enlists for wartime service, leaving his family and business responsibilities in the hands of his first cousin, Nancy. Henry narrowly escapes death at the front, returning to marry Nancy and run the thriving business she has established during his absence. The novel censures those who stand in the way of the happy couple, including the church leaders and politicians who condemn the married cousins for defiling "the purity of the British Home," and the press, which creates an artificially heightened patriotism that blinds the public to two corrupt officials in their midst.

By 1923 Hueffer was living in Paris with the journalist and novelist Muriel Harris, who was also employed by the *Manchester Guardian.* Hueffer had known Harris as early as 1908, when she helped him with his *The Book of Witches.* While Harris continued to use her own name professionally, she represented herself in newspaper interviews as Hueffer's wife and told a friend that they were married in the United States because "circumstances" prevented them from marrying in England. It is not clear whether Hueffer was ever legally divorced from Pyne.

The disdain for restrictive moral codes that Hueffer expresses in *Little Pitchers* recurs in *Needles and Pins.* After his wartime service Peter feels suffocated by the middle-class domesticity of his wife, Lucy, and the self-serving charity of the wealthy Mrs. Arbuthnot, who arranged his marriage and career. He meets the fiery Rachel, and the two plot to obtain their respective divorces by concocting evidence to suggest that they were having a love affair. Several private detectives, a trip to Paris, the rescue of a beguiling war orphan, and an illness later, Peter realizes that he has felt "smothered in a cloud of petticoats since the war." He escapes with the help of an artist friend, who arranges work for him in Mexico. Through this implausible resolution to a contorted plot, Hueffer offers a simplistic picture of the consequences of changing gender roles in postwar England. The novel suggests that former servicemen returned only to be diminished by the growing power of women and that such shifting gender roles make it necessary to contest the conventional view that divorce is immoral. In short, Hueffer's conservative understanding of gender roles paradoxically leads him to adapt a radical attitude toward divorce: the novel audaciously concludes that it is better for both Peter and his wife for him to remake his life in Mexico, where he can have a clear role as "a man among men."

"Cousins German" draws heavily on Hueffer's experiences in Mexico and in World War I. Anthony is a world-weary thirty-five year old who has traded English propriety for an adventurous life mining jewels and fighting in the Mexican Revolution. The onset of World War I leads him to return to England to pay off his dead father's debts. There he falls in love with Elizabeth, the sister of a friend, but she marries the distinguished Captain Lampard. Joining the army to try to forget his unrequited love for Elizabeth, Anthony inadvertently discovers that his rival is a key German spy. When he confronts Lampard, the spy decides to die heroically in battle rather than reveal to his wife that he betrayed England. Hueffer resists the temptation to have Anthony return from the battlefield to the arms of Elizabeth: he, too, is killed in the war, and Elizabeth and her son are left with the belief that Lampard died bravely. While Hueffer depicts the excitement of combat, he also shows the fear and disorientation experienced by the soldiers; in so doing he indirectly critiques the government and press for generating wartime propaganda to heighten unquestioning patriotism and to increase profits. In addition, by depicting Lampard, who represents the epitome of Englishness, as a German trained from birth to infiltrate the British military, Hueffer again raises the question of the validity of national stereotypes. The novel includes Hueffer's bleakest finale to date, intimating that postwar England maintains its composure at the expense of difficult and unacknowledged truths. The *Times Literary*

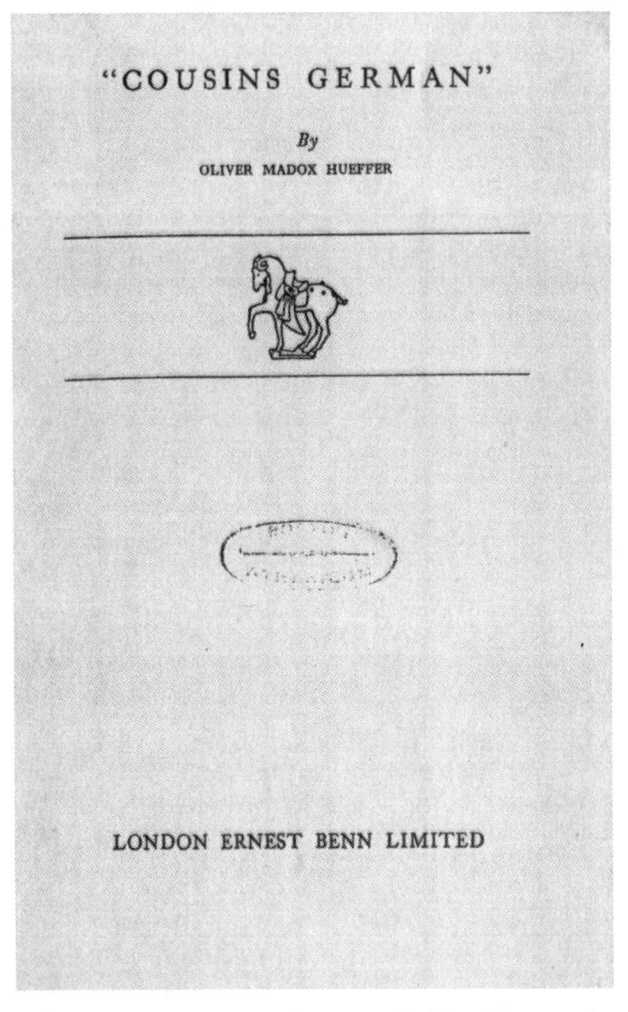

Title page for the 1930 novel about an English adventurer who fights in the Mexican Revolution and later becomes involved in espionage in World War I

Supplement (13 November 1930) called *"Cousins German"* an "exciting story set in exciting circumstances" with "admirable" character portraits and an "ingenious plot."

Hueffer's final novels represent his most sophisticated adaptation of the comic mode while at the same time they scrutinize how "truth" is defined by existing power structures. *By Whose Authority?* (1931) is set in late-seventeenth-century New York. The narrator, Sir Ralph Gardiner, travels to the colonies, where Americans of "quality" introduce him to the "right" people and warn him against those of disreputable ilk such as Capt. William Kidd, who is employed by the king to capture pirates but is rumored to be a pirate himself. In a picaresque twist of fortune Sir Ralph falls in love with Kidd's daughter, Margaret; is drawn into three years of implausible adventures on land and sea; and returns to defend Kidd from those who want to hang him as a pirate. The corrupt justice system, however, ignores Sir Ralph's firsthand testimony to protect the interests of prominent investors who are implicated in Kidd's schemes, and in the final pages of the novel the traditional comic ending of the lovers joined in marriage is overshadowed by Kidd's execution. Through the first-person narrator, who finds Margaret and Kidd more humane than the elite who slander them, the novel critiques high society's standards for assessing individual worth. Hueffer's use of irony complicates an otherwise plot-driven novel as the narrator adamantly supports Kidd's innocence in the face of strong evidence to the contrary. Through this irony, the novel suggests that the justice system's failure resides not merely in the accuracy of its verdicts but also in the honesty of its motivations: even if Kidd is guilty, the judges and politicians are worse criminals than he for closing their eyes to the available evidence so that they can cater to upper-class interests. The *Times Literary Supplement* (30 April 1931), not commenting on the irony, called the work "an excellent and high-spirited *pastiche* of Defoe" that is "true to its period both in style and episode."

The Right Honorable: Being Three Days from the Life of Elbert, Second Baron Thornton Heath (1931) is a well-controlled farce about a plumber whose father gained a peerage late in his life. The embarrassed Bert hides his title from his girlfriend, who has renamed herself Leninia to reflect her devotion to the Liberty Party—a spoof of the Communist Party dreamed up by two Jewish confidence men to swindle the unsuspecting members out of their dues. But titles are useful commodities in a capitalistic world, as Bert discovers when Abraham Lincoln, public-relations agent for a Hollywood movie icon, begs him to participate in a publicity stunt that will promote the star's popularity in Britain. Through intricate subplots in which Bert becomes the pawn of the celebrity system, the novel parodies the culture of cinematic publicity and suggests that it heightens the conformity that democracy already encouraged. The novel thus satirizes both the publicity system's reliance on, and the public's susceptibility to, stereotypical images that stand in for more nuanced realities. It also serves as the fictional counterpart to *Some of the English* for its comic rendering of what Hueffer, in the latter work, calls the "peaceful revolution." It was "only in England," he says there, that the lower class "peacefully and gently . . . possessed itself, not only of a higher standard of living as expressed in gramophones or motor bicycles, but, for good or ill, of actual place and power."

Commenting in her diary (23 March 1893) on Hueffer's early devil-may-care reputation, Garnett concluded: "No one understands him, no one knows whether he will be hanged, or become a great person." By the final decade of his life Hueffer had mediated these extremes, having become, as his brother, Ford, put it in a letter to Edgar Jepson (20 January 1923), "enormously fat & prosperous," and successful enough to connect Ford with wealthy individuals who wanted him to edit the *Transatlantic Review*. Yet the obituaries that followed Hueffer's death of a seizure on 21 June 1931 indicate that he never quite became "a great person" in his own right. *The New York Times* (23 June 1931) identified him as a writer but immediately thereafter as "Brother of Ford Madox Ford and Grandson of F. M. Brown, Artist." Today Hueffer no longer has a reputation apart from his relationship to Ford, which is paradoxical given Ford's claim in his autobiography that the press "compared his books to my own, always preferring his lightness of touch to my 'Teutonic' stolidity." Suggesting that their sibling rivalry extended to their writing, Ford observes,

Sometimes he would deliberately take one of my own subjects—to show that he was more brilliant than I. And, in England, he would always be more successful. I wonder no English publisher has thought of resuscitating his work. It had great qualities of fancy.

If Ford, here and elsewhere, portrays himself as a writer who merits more fame and praise than he received, Hueffer strikes an equally rehearsed pose at the other extreme. In the preface to *A Vagabond in New York* he foreswears any desire to be recognized as one of "those Kings of English Literature who . . . make Royal Progresses across the Atlantic and back for Literary Purposes." Instead, with hyperbolic modesty, he paints himself as "the shabby Vagabond" whose "Gutter Gleanings" cannot approximate the work of the "Great Man" for whom crowds cheer. "At least let it be remembered in his favour," Hueffer requests, "that if his point of view be petty and sordid, and with no wish or claim to be Literary, it is at least sincere."

To an extent, one can take Hueffer at his word: he gloried, after all, in parodic and farcical adaptations of often hackneyed plots. As a review of *Needles and Pins* in *Punch* (30 April 1924) concludes, "muddles and miseries, and the characters and circumstances that make for them—these are his strongest suit." Hueffer's attitudes toward social change are sometimes less enlightened than he might believe them to be, and his writing is sometimes undistinguished. Furthermore, his melodramatic plots are often resolved in quite predictable ways; yet in many instances even the most seemingly straightforward resolution holds in tension various interpretations of the "truth." Most of Hueffer's oeuvre illustrates his comment in the preface to *"Cousins German"* that representations of "truth" are generally either incomplete or misleading because "the truth cannot be told by those who know it to be true . . . that a half, or quarter, or millionth part of the truth is, in its very inadequacy, a denial of that truth." While one might easily remember Hueffer as he figured himself in *A Vagabond in New York,* as having a "vision . . . from Below, not from Above," his works are more than the amusing yarns of a prankster. Instead, like the jester, he uses targeted mockery to comment on important shifts in early-twentieth-century culture and on the coping mechanisms people used to combat their ambivalent attitudes toward such transitions. As a reader of Hueffer's work, one finds oneself making the same kinds of concessions that his family and friends made for him. Charmed by his vivid humanity and entertained by his use of an observant humor to evaluate significant social trends, one is less inclined to quibble over the occasional thinly written phrase or contrived plot.

References:

Ford Madox Ford, *It Was the Nightingale* (Philadelphia: Lippincott, 1933; London: Heinemann, 1934);

Ford, *The Letters of Ford Madox Ford,* edited by Richard M. Ludwig (Princeton: Princeton University Press, 1965);

Olive Garnett, *Olive & Stepniak: The Bloomsbury Diary of Olive Garnett, 1893-1895,* edited by Barry Johnson (London: Bartletts, 1993), pp. 148, 151-152, 167, 170, 199-203;

Garnett, *Tea and Anarchy!: The Bloomsbury Diary of Olive Garnett, 1890-1893,* edited by Johnson (London: Bartletts, 1989), pp. 79-80, 165, 202-203, 210;

Arthur Mizener, *The Saddest Story: A Biography of Ford Madox Ford* (London: Bodley Head, 1971), pp. 3-5, 12-13, 24-25, 34-35, 77, 85, 324-327, 333;

Max Saunders, *Ford Madox Ford: A Dual Life* (Oxford: Oxford University Press, 1996);

Juliet Soskice, *Chapters from Childhood: Reminiscences of an Artist's Granddaughter* (Tuxedo Park, N.Y.: Turtle Point Press, 1994), pp. 65-68.

Papers:

The John Rylands Library at the University of Manchester has significant holdings of Oliver Madox Hueffer's correspondence with the *Manchester Guardian*. The Hueffer family papers in the Soskice and Lady Stow Hill collections in the House of Lords Records Office, London, contain correspondence from and about Hueffer. The Olin Library at Cornell University and the Albert A. Berg Collection of the New York Public Library hold limited collections of correspondence from Hueffer.

Violet Hunt
(28 September 1862 - 16 January 1942)

Donald Mason
McMaster University

See also the Hunt entry in *DLB 162: British Short-Fiction Writers, 1915-1945.*

BOOKS: *The Maiden's Progress* (London: Osgood, McIlvaine, 1894; New York: Harper, 1894);
A Hard Woman (London: Chapman & Hall, 1895; New York: Appleton, 1895);
The Way of Marriage (London: Chapman & Hall, 1896);
Unkist, Unkind! (London: Chapman & Hall, 1897);
The Human Interest (London: Methuen, 1899; Chicago & New York: Stone, 1899);
Affairs of the Heart (London: Freemantle, 1900);
The Celebrity at Home (London: Chapman & Hall, 1904);
Sooner or Later (London: Chapman & Hall, 1904);
The Cat (London: Black, 1905); republished as *The Life Story of a Cat* (London: Black, 1910);
The Workaday Woman (London: Laurie, 1906);
White Rose of Weary Leaf (London: Heinemann, 1908; New York: Brentano's, 1908);
The Wife of Altamont (London: Heinemann, 1910; New York: Brentano's, 1910);
Tales of the Uneasy (London: Heinemann, 1911);
The Doll (London: Stanley Paul, 1911);
The Governess, by Hunt and Mrs. Alfred Hunt (London: Chatto & Windus, 1912);
The Celebrity's Daughter (London: Stanley Paul, 1913; New York: Brentano's, 1914);
The Desirable Alien at Home in Germany, by Hunt and Hueffer (London: Chatto & Windus, 1913);
The House of Many Mirrors (London: Stanley Paul, 1915; New York: Brentano's, 1915);
Zeppelin Nights: A London Entertainment, by Hunt and Ford Madox Hueffer (London & New York: Lane, 1916 [i.e., 1915]);
Their Lives (London: Stanley Paul, 1916; New York: Brentano's, 1916);
The Last Ditch (London: Stanley Paul, 1918);
Their Hearts (London: Stanley Paul, 1921);
The Tiger Skin (London: Heinemann, 1924);
More Tales of the Uneasy (London: Heinemann, 1925);

Violet Hunt

The Flurried Years (London: Hurst & Blackett, 1926); republished as *I Have This to Say: The Story of My Flurried Years* (New York: Boni & Liveright, 1926);
The Wife of Rossetti: Her Life and Death (London: John Lane, 1932; New York: Dutton, 1932);
The Return of the Good Soldier: Ford Madox Ford and Violet Hunt's 1917 Diary, edited by Robert Secor and Marie Secor (Victoria, B.C.: English Literary Studies, 1983).

OTHER: *The Great Poets Birthday Album,* preface and various entries by Hunt (London: Eyre & Spottiswoode, 1892);

Dialogues of the Day, four dialogues contributed by Hunt (London: Chapman & Hall, 1894);
"The Benefit of the Doubt," "Lost and Found," and "As You Were!," in *Stories and Play Stories* (London: Chapman & Hall, 1897);
Giovanni Casanova, *The Memoirs of Jacques Casanova de Seingalt,* translated by Hunt and Agnes Farley with an introduction by Hunt (London: Chapman & Hall, 1902);
Berthe Tosti, *The Heart of Ruby,* translated by Hunt (London: Chapman & Hall, 1903);
Golden String: A Day Book for Busy Men and Women, edited by Hunt and Susan, Countess of Malmesbury (London: Murray, 1912);
Margaret Hunt, *Thornicroft's Model,* preface attributed to Hunt (London: Chatto & Windus, 1912).

Violet Hunt began *The Flurried Years* (1926), her autobiography for the years 1908–1915, by suggesting, "Life is a succession of affairs, but there is always one affair for which the years, from birth, are a preparation, a hardening, a tempering, and a more or less serious erosion, possibly, of the sword of the fighter. And there comes, sooner or later, according to the sets and the entries and exits of the other actors, one's own supreme moment. One is on. And that entry, being but human, one may so easily muff. That moment, some will say, I did muff." For Hunt, life was certainly a succession of affairs, of events, dramas, battles, and bad judgments; but Hunt was also a writer of considerable note, and her work is perhaps most significant in the late twentieth century for the strength of her views on women and women's roles. She insightfully conveys her confusion and anger over the socially constructed limits placed on women and their effect on relations between the sexes.

Isobel Violet Hunt was born in Durham, England, on 28 September 1862, the eldest daughter of Margaret Hunt, a popular three-decker novelist, and Alfred Hunt, a landscape painter. Hunt's father, though never directly associated with the Pre-Raphaelite Brotherhood—which in any case had been dissolved by 1854—nevertheless shared with the various Pre-Raphaelites, as well as those later associated with the movement, a common instinct for subject detail and intense coloration, and his friendships with John Ruskin, Ford Madox Brown, and Holman Hunt (no relation), and later with Dante Gabriel Rossetti, John Millais, and Edward Burne-Jones grew in importance after the family moved to London in 1866 and had a formative and lasting effect on the young Violet.

Indeed, in later years, Hunt came to see herself as a daughter of the Pre-Raphaelites, having been brought up, as she relates in *The Wife of Rossetti: Her Life and Death* (1932), "in and out of their houses" from an early age. Ruskin, the fatherlike defender of the movement, was godfather to Violet's younger sister Venetia, or Venice as she was called (after Ruskin's *The Stones of Venice,* 1851–1853). When Violet was thirteen years old, her mother arranged for her marriage to the ailing Ruskin, then fifty-six, but this arrangement came to nothing.

In addition to expanding Alfred Hunt's artistic friendships and horizons, living in London also allowed Margaret Hunt to cultivate important literary friendships, particularly with Robert Browning, Andrew Lang, and, later, Oscar Wilde (who, Violet claimed, made a proposal of marriage to her in or around the year 1880). Tor Villa, the Hunt household in Camden Hill, became something of a social gathering spot for various artists and writers, and the social aspect of the literary world became an enduring part of Violet Hunt's life. Later, South Lodge, the house that Violet shared with her mother in Campden Hill after the death of her father in 1896, became an important literary landmark. It was frequented over the years by an almost comically diverse group of writers, including Henry James, H. G. Wells, Somerset Maugham, May Sinclair, Ford Madox Hueffer (who later changed his name to Ford Madox Ford), Ezra Pound, Margaret Radclyffe Hall, D. H. Lawrence, Rebecca West, and Wyndham Lewis. Indeed, Hunt is too often remembered for her literary relations, particularly with her famous male contemporaries, rather than as a writer herself.

Sharp, incisive, and quick-witted, Hunt's early work is written mainly in dialogue form, at which she was extremely proficient. It was only later, perhaps most effectively in her *Tales of the Uneasy* (1911), that she began to develop her descriptive abilities to their full potential. Also important at this early stage in Hunt's career was her emergence on the literary scene as a "New Woman" of the 1890s. Hunt was confident, career-minded, unconventional, and seemingly in control of herself, of her sexuality, and of her livelihood, and her early novels, particularly *The Maiden's Progress* (1894) and *A Hard Woman* (1895), strongly reflect Hunt's developing ideas about many aspects of women's lives: work, men, marriage, abuse, and the world of intellectual ideas. Hunt was already beginning to question—as she would throughout her life—how to view herself in

Hunt's parents, the painter Alfred Hunt and the novelist Margaret Hunt

relation to the often troubled and troublesome roles allotted to the woman by convention—wife, lover, mother, cook—and how she, in particular, could develop herself in relation to these roles.

In *The Human Interest* (1899), perhaps the most engaging and accomplished of her early works, Hunt began to develop the core of discontent that marked her career as a novelist. Yet, despite the disillusionment and the frustration that Phoebe Elles, the main character of the novel, endures, *The Human Interest* is not an angry book. Rather, satire and irony interplay as Phoebe, the runaway wife of an abusive husband, takes up with Edmund Rivers, a landscape painter, who proves as unsatisfactory and ineffectual a companion as her husband, Mortimer, had been in marriage. In time Phoebe begins to discover the depths of her discontent, but she is unable to devise an effective remedy to the situation. Early in the novel Phoebe remarks, "It was not this me that was glad to marry Mortimer, as he so politely put it. . . . It was another me, who had not read Ibsen. . . . Books alter one—reading alters one—life alters one, after all!" In the final scene, even Henrik Ibsen fails to provide a suitable exit, as Phoebe's attempted suicide suddenly becomes a mockery of failed potions, false sentiments, and inverted clichés. Phoebe Elles cannot, in the end, command the tragic admiration—or even the attention—granted to Hedda Gabler. Instead, Phoebe is awakened from her false death to the gentle titter of supposed friends. Hunt's emerging antiromantic strain, evident in her later writings, is here gently ironic, as the conventional romantic remedy to an ill-used life suddenly becomes the subject for comic derision. As Phoebe's friend Egidia suggests, "It is very hard to seek the sublime always and achieve—the ridiculous."

Hunt's personal life by this point was neither quite ridiculous nor sublime, though there were elements of both in her conduct throughout the years. Her choice of male companions was almost uniformly bad: from the thirteen-year-old who suggested to her mother that she would like to marry the aging Ruskin to the eighteen-year-old who fell sway to the undoubtable charms of Oscar Wilde, Hunt involved herself over the years with some of the most unlikely lovers that fate could throw her way. In 1884, following Wilde's engagement to Constance Lloyd the previous year, Hunt began to pursue relations with George Boughton, a popular portrait and landscape painter and friend of the family, who was married and almost thirty years her senior. Her long affair with Boughton, which lasted off and on until 1889, was followed by another long, sporadic affair, which lasted until 1899 with another married man, Oswald Crawfurd, again some thirty years her senior.

For some fifteen years, then, between the ages of twenty-two and thirty-seven, Hunt was constantly courting scandal. She describes Amy, her protagonist in *White Rose of Weary Leaf* (1908), as "a constitutionally rolling stone." Hunt gave Amy her own characteristic deep distrust of conventional relationships and troubled ambivalence concerning the traditional roles of wife and mother. In her unconventional relationships and in her writing Hunt searched for (but did not find) a way to redefine the conventional female/male gender roles and the ways that those roles relate. For Hunt it is the woman as adventurer, the woman who takes chances and is strong, independent, courageous, and in control, who is of central interest. As Hunt writes of Amy, "The maiden knew that men must work and women may, if they like, weep, and remember the palmy days of courtship!" To remember "the palmy days of courtship" was clearly not enough for Amy, much less for Violet Hunt.

Crawfurd was important to Hunt's career in several ways. As an editor at the publishing house of Chapman and Hall, he was well placed to further and to promote Hunt's writing, which he did throughout the 1890s. Although it would be wrong to overemphasize his usefulness to Hunt at this early point in her career—her work, in any case, was always saleable—Crawfurd's support certainly helped her to establish herself among the promising authors of the period. He also, however, gave her syphilis, which was a constant source of pain and humiliation throughout her life and no doubt hastened her mental decay in the years leading up to her death in 1942. Their long relationship was apparently damaged, demanding, and often cruel. (Hunt's diaries for the period have yet to be published.) It served to substantiate Hunt's growing understanding of the complex ways in which relationships tend to erode and to destroy the individual's (and particularly the woman's) sense of worth.

If Hunt's choice of male companions was often questionable—and unquestionably damaging to herself in some instances—her female friendships, though less numerous and less newsworthy, were nevertheless generally more positive and supportive. In the early years of the new century Hunt joined the ranks of the Women's Social and Political Union, led by Emmeline and Christabel Pankhurst. She took an active role in fund-raising, and in 1908 she was arrested for collecting money in support of Self-Denial Week outside the train station on Kensington High Street. Both Hunt and May Sinclair, the novelist and Hunt's companion in collecting for "the Cause," as both women would refer to the women's movement, found the experience of standing on the High Street more difficult than they had anticipated. As Hunt wrote in *The Flurried Years,*

> Much has been said of our heroism in "standing outside to beg," and I fancy she [Sinclair] felt as I did—as if we had suddenly been stripped naked, with a cross-sensation of being drowned in a tank and gasping for breath. We had asked all our friends and editors and readers to come and cheer us up as we stood there pilloried, and they backed us up splendidly. Mr. John Galsworthy sauntered along and tipped us immeasurably and gallantly, and Mr. Laurence Housman and Mr. Ford Madox Hueffer—everyone in fact, who wished the movement well.

Sinclair, in addition to introducing Hunt to the meetings of the Women's Freedom League and the Women's Suffrage League about this time, was also a valued literary associate and clear-sighted critic of Hunt's work. Writing in her 1922 *English Review* article on "The Novels of Violet Hunt," Sinclair provided a fair estimate of Hunt's value as a writer of fiction: "If you care for nothing but beauty, beauty of subject, beauty of form and pattern, beauty of technique, you will not care for the novels of Violet Hunt. But to the lover of austere truth telling, who would rather see things as they sometimes are than as they are not and cannot be, who prefer a natural ugliness to artificial and sentimental beauty, they will appeal by their sincerity, their unhesitating courage, their incorruptible reality." As Hunt's career progressed she seemed less drawn to an ideal, to beautiful sentiments or situations, and more inclined to severity, to characters who were either psychologically or physically damaged in some way, to situations more cruel than merely mischievous.

In *White Rose of Weary Leaf* (1908) Hunt achieved what was generally perceived to have been her greatest critical and popular success, although to the modern reader some of the *Tales of the Uneasy* (1911 and 1925) may well appear more strikingly original—more tightly constructed, more complex, and troubled in theme and tone.

Oswald Crawfurd, editor at Chapman and Hall, who helped establish Hunt as an author but also, in the course of their long and abusive affair, infected her with syphilis

Nevertheless, *White Rose of Weary Leaf* constitutes an important retelling of the conventional governess tale, and Amy resembles in the evolving complexity of her person and position a type of latter-day Jane Eyre. As Amy states it, "I like to be exceptional!"–and like Charlotte Brontë's character, Amy learns to look at the world with a certain wry detachment, gaining authority within the domestic realm while distinctly perceiving the limits that define her authority and the barriers that bar her way. Like Lady Macbeth she attempts to unsex herself, stating while still quite young that she is "oldish, a weary, cynical, anaemic woman, quite out of court" for romance. Romance, however, does come her way–if only briefly and disastrously–but only after Amy has fought her way unaided to a position of real (though still tenuous and limited) stability and respect.

Here, in particular, lies the crux of the problem for Amy, as for other of Hunt's women characters: how to manage a relationship so that the woman need not sacrifice her sense of self and her identity–her name, income, profession, values, place, authority, desires–to a man. Significantly, Amy's affair with Jeremy Dand, the married master of the household in which Amy is housekeeper, begins only after she has been removed from her position in the house by Dand's contrivance. Momentarily bereft of her authority–within the Dand household Amy had been the dominant controlling force, however much she remained officially the servant–Amy is suddenly prey to Dand's advances. Once she regains her control by concluding the affair and returning to her old position in the house, Amy is quick to complete the unsexing process, stating: "I have done this, exterminated all the woman in me!" Finally, in a reversal of conventional character roles, Dand at last becomes hysterical, while Amy remains fundamentally impervious and alone: the organizer, the manager to the last, in control of herself and her situation, however dire her situation becomes. As Hunt's narrator relates, "She had honestly tried and had as nearly as possible succeeded, in abolishing her own feminine personality. . . ." Amy perceives that a woman is generally excluded from authority by her gender and, more peculiarly and particularly, by her very sexuality—by the act of entering into intimate relations with the male—by the gender construction of wife, mother, or mistress that society ascribes to the active heterosexual female. For Amy, then, sexuality represents a loss of control, a decentering of self, and self-control has been the central, almost the sole stabilizing force in her life.

About this time, as Hunt's reputation as a popular novelist began to reach its peak, she was about to embark on that "one affair for which the years, from birth, are a preparation." Significantly, though seemingly self-confident, Hunt seemed destined to place herself in subordinate relationships to ill-chosen males who almost universally worked to undermine the inner strength and determination that ironically, made her so attractive. Ford Madox Hueffer was in 1908 a struggling though widely published writer of varied attainments. He was about to launch *The English Review,* the most important literary journal of the period, the first issue of which was to appear in December of that year. Hunt's relationship with Hueffer, with whom she lived between 1910 and 1917, was characterized by a series of intense emotional reversals. Hueffer, who was almost childishly egotistical, depressive, deluded, and chronically short of money, became the central focus of Hunt's "flurried years." In 1907 Hueffer was unhappily married, living apart from his wife, Elsie, in what were to be the "offices" of *The English Review*—which Hunt described in *The Flurried Years* as "a maisonette over a poulterer's and fishmonger's combined," the first floor office consisting of a single large room "full of corners and queernesses." Hunt had recently had affairs with Somerset Maugham and H. G. Wells and had become firm friends with Arnold Bennett and Henry James. She was, in her own words, "a woman at a loose end of life, with a visiting list of notabilities as long as your arm and some experience of literature, and especially of the genus review!"

Hueffer's wife was unwilling to grant him a divorce, and in 1910 he and Hunt moved to Germany so that Hueffer could acquire naturalized German citizenship and take advantage of German divorce laws. The naturalization process was more complex than either supposed, however, and they decided instead to return to England and claim that they had married. The ruse was unsuccessful, and a well-publicized libel suit ensued in 1912, in which Hunt's name figured prominently and scandalously. The years after the lawsuit were extremely painful for Hunt as the errant Hueffer's affections became more and more a matter of economic support—or as Hunt relates in her 1917 diary, as Hueffer became more and more "an expensive luxury."

Throughout this time, though, Hunt was writing some of her best fiction. *Their Lives* (1916) draws firmly on the world of her childhood, the lives of her parents, and Hunt's early romance with Oscar Wilde. *The Last Ditch* (1918), an epistolary novel of considerable ingenuity, details the lives of three women, two sisters and their mother, set against the backdrop of World War I and contrasting the women's attitudes to the situation as it affects them—the one daughter in America and the other and her mother in England. *Their Hearts* (1921) returns to the autobiographical world of *Their Lives*. According to Joan Hardwick, the two novels combine to dramatize "the plight of the women of Violet's generation and to explain and perhaps justify the manner in which her own life had developed."

Ironically, though Hunt has often been viewed primarily as an autobiographical novelist, perhaps her best work is contained in her *Tales of the Uneasy* (1911)—one of which, *The Tiger Skin,* was published separately as a novella in 1924. Written somewhat in the manner of a story by Henry James, *The Tiger Skin* tells of Adelaide Favarger's grotesque fascination with the subject of eugenics—the movement to manipulate and to control the genetic makeup of a society. Hunt's treatment of her subject is curiously and intriguingly detached: Adelaide hates "anything of a misbegotten or deformed nature" and ends up killing her daughter through systematic neglect and physical abuse, but Hunt refrains from offering any overt moral condemnation of the character, leaving it to the authorities within the story to pass judgment. Despite her heinous acts, Adelaide, as with all of Hunt's strong women characters, commands a certain respect, particularly in contrast to her husband, who, though broadly characterized as a humanist, lacks the moral courage to oppose his wife. A contemporary review in *The Athenaeum* praised the story as a

> grim study in morbid psychology which displays the author's remarkable gifts to the utmost. It is virtually a picture, painted with signal power and restraint, of a woman's unnatural cruelty towards her child; and so brilliant is the handling that we are led almost without reluctance through the phases of the horrible history. . . . Miss Hunt has gained greatly in craftsmanship during the last few years: her style is excellent, her

grip of her subjects sure, and her insight exceptionally clear and sane.

However sane Hunt's treatment of her subject may or may not be, in *The Tiger Skin* she offers a chilling and lasting portrayal of the depths of a particular woman's need to dominate and control.

Here, especially, lies the basis for Hunt's continuing significance and the current revival of interest in her life and work: though certainly an important early feminist in terms of her thought and conviction and, at her best, a writer of considerable power and insight, Hunt was still fundamentally isolated within a world of more powerful males. Not afraid to question the basis for the development of a woman's strength and independence, she struggled to live life on her own terms in a world that was essentially unsympathetic. In *The Wife of Rossetti* (1932), her ironically titled biography of Elizabeth Siddall, Hunt found a subject that was directly tied to and illustrative of her own concerns as a novelist: Siddall, the gifted and troubled wife of the gifted and troubled Dante Gabriel Rossetti, was defined by her beauty and trapped in a relationship in which she was infinitely more important as an artist's model than as an actual woman. As Hunt relates at the outset of her study, "The truth about Rossetti has been told, more or less: the truth about the woman he married, never."

"You *are* Society," Henry James once said to Hunt, but in this James was only partially revealing. Hunt became the model New Woman for many contemporary portraits by her fellow writers, inspiring characters by both James and H. G. Wells, and she also perfected the role of the literary socialite to an unusually high degree. But Violet Hunt was most importantly a woman writer who continually sought to redefine the role of the conventional literary heroine—and who courageously determined to question rather than to answer, to confront rather than to deny.

Biographies:

Barbara Belford, *Violet* (New York: Simon & Schuster, 1990);

Joan Hardwick, *An Immodest Violet* (London: Deutsch, 1990).

References:

Jane E. Miller, "The Edward Naumburg, Jr. Collection of Violet Hunt," *Princeton University Library Chronicle,* 51, no. 2 (Winter 1990): 210–218;

Robert Secor, "Henry James and Violet Hunt, the 'Improper Person of Babylon,'" *Journal of Modern Literature,* 13, no. 1 (March 1986): 3–36;

Joseph Wiesenfarth, "Violet Hunt Rewrites Jane Austen: *Pride and Prejudice* (1813) and *Their Lives* (1916)," *Persuasions: Journal of the Jane Austen Society of North America,* 11 (December 1989): 61–65.

Papers:

Major collections of Violet Hunt's papers and diaries are held by Cornell University and by Pennsylvania State University. A further collection of her diaries is in private hands.

Ethel Colburn Mayne
(7 January 1865 – 30 April 1941)

Susan Winslow Waterman
Rutgers University

BOOKS: *The Clearer Vision* (London: Unwin, 1898);

Jessie Vandeleur (London: George Allen, 1902);

The Fourth Ship (London: Chapman & Hall, 1908);

Enchanters of Men (London: Methuen, 1909; Philadelphia: Jacobs, 1909);

Things That No One Tells (London: Chapman & Hall, 1910);

The Romance of Monaco and Its Rulers (London: Hutchinson, 1910; New York: John Lane, 1910);

Byron, 2 volumes (London: Methuen, 1912; New York: Scribners, 1912; revised edition, 1 volume, London: Methuen, 1924; New York: Scribners, 1924);

Gold Lace: A Study of Girlhood (London: Chapman & Hall, 1913);

Browning's Heroines (London: Chatto & Windus, 1913; New York: Pott, 1914);

One of Our Grandmothers (London: Chapman & Hall, 1916);

Come In (London: Chapman & Hall, 1917);

Blindman (London: Chapman & Hall, 1919);

Nine of Hearts (London: Constable, 1923);

Inner Circle (London: Constable, 1925; New York: Harcourt, Brace, 1925);

The Life and Letters of Anne Isabella, Lady Noel Byron: From Unpublished Papers in the Possession of the Late Ralph, Earl of Lovelace (London: Constable, 1929; New York: Scribners, 1929);

A Regency Chapter: Lady Bessborough and Her Friendships (London & New York: Macmillan, 1939).

TRANSLATIONS: Anonymous, *The Confessions of a Princess* (London: John Long, 1906; New York: Doscher, 1908);

Anonymous, *The Diary of a Lost One*, edited by Margarete Boehme (London: Sisley's, 1907; New York: Hudson, 1908);

Jules Lair, *Louise de la Vallière and the Early Life of Louis XIV* (London: Hutchinson, 1908; New York: Putnam, 1908);

Raoul Pugno, *The Lessons of Raoul Pugno* (London: Boosey, 1911);

Edouard Maynial, *Casanova and His Time* (London: Chapman & Hall, 1911);

Alexandrine von Hedemann, *My Friendship with Prince Hohenlohe*, edited by Denise Petit (London: Nash, 1912; New York & London: Putnam, 1912);

Boehme, *The Department Store* (New York & London: Appleton, 1912);

Fyodor Dostoyevsky, *Letters of Fyodor Michailovitch Dostoevsky to His Family and Friends,* from the German translation of Alexander Eliasberg (London: Chatto & Windus, 1914; New York: Macmillan, 1914);

Marcelle Tinayre, *Madame de Pompadour* (New York & London: Putnam, 1925);

Emil Ludwig, *Kaiser Wilhelm II* (London & New York: Putnam, 1926); republished as *Wilhelm Hohenzollern: The Last of the Kaisers* (New York: Putnam, 1927);

Ludwig, *Goethe: The History of a Man, 1749-1832*, 2 volumes (London & New York: Putnam, 1928);

Carl Spitteler, *Selected Poems of Carl Spitteler*, translated by Mayne and James F. Muirhead (London: Putnam, 1928; New York: Macmillan, 1928);

Johannes Haller, *Philip Eulenburg, the Kaiser's Friend*, 2 volumes (London: Secker, 1930; New York: Knopf, 1930);

Arnold Hoellriegel, *The Forest Ship: A Book of the Amazon* (London & New York: Putnam, 1930; New York: Viking, 1931);

Ludwig, *Three Titans* (London & New York: Putnam, 1930);

Charles du Bos, *Byron and the Need of Fatality* (London & New York: Putnam, 1932).

OTHER: "The Spell of Proust," in *Marcel Proust, An English Tribute*, edited by C. K. Scott Moncrieff (London: Chatto & Windus, 1923; New York: Seltzer, 1923), pp. 90-95;

Edward John Trelawney, *The Adventures of a Younger Son*, introductory essay by Mayne (London: Oxford, 1925);

"The Lower Road," in *Atalanta's Garland: Being the Book of the Edinburgh University Women's Union, 1926* (Edinburgh: Constable, 1926), pp. 33-51;

Thomas James Wise, *A Byron Library: A Catalogue of Printed Books, Manuscripts and Autograph Letters by George Gordon Noel, Baron Byron*, introductory essay by Mayne (London: Privately published, 1928);

Emil Ludwig, *Gifts of Life: A Retrospect*, revised and edited by Mayne (London & New York: Putnam, 1931);

Rosie Graefenberg, *Prelude to the Past: The Autobiography of a Woman*, edited by Mayne (New York: Morrow, 1934);

"The Man of the House," in *The Faber Book of Modern Stories*, edited by Elizabeth Bowen (London: Faber & Faber, 1937), pp. 315-330;

"Stripes," in *An Anthology of Modern Short Stories*, edited by J. W. Marriott (London: Nelson, 1938), pp. 65-75;

"A Pen-and-Ink Effect," as Frances E. Huntley, in *Femmes de Siècle: Stories from the '90s. Women Writing at the End of Two Centuries*, edited, with an introduction, by Joan Smith (London: Chatto & Windus, 1992), pp. 216-221.

SELECTED PERIODICAL PUBLICATIONS–UNCOLLECTED:
POETRY
"The Tribute," *Golden Hind*, 2 (October 1923): 42.
FICTION
"Her Story and His," as Frances E. Huntley, *Chapman's Magazine*, 2 (November 1895): 286-292;

"His Glittering Hour," as Frances E. Huntley, *Chapman's Magazine*, 3 (April 1896): 439-448;

"Your New Hat," *Pall Mall Magazine*, 43 (January 1909): 72-77;

"The Colonel," *Pall Mall Magazine*, 49 (May 1912): 679-685;

"The Difference," *Transatlantic Review*, 1 (May 1924): 318-320;

"Humour," *Golden Hind*, 2 (July 1924): 19-20;

"Ugliness," *New Statesman*, 27 September 1930, pp. 761-762;

"A Bit of Her," *Life and Letters*, 11 (March 1935): 692-696.
NONFICTION
"Henry James (As seen from the 'Yellow Book')," *Little Review*, 5 (August 1918): 1-4;

[Tribute to Joseph Conrad], *Transatlantic Review*, 2 (September 1924): 345-347.

Amid the bold and heady novelties of the burgeoning modernist movement in literature at the turn of the century, it was easy enough to overlook the work of Ethel Colburn Mayne, a writer known more for the "delicacy and restraint" and "psychological subtlety" of her style than for audacious innovations in form or content. Though then frequently compared with Henry James and Katherine Mansfield–Mayne too specialized in the short story–Mayne's often enigmatic and "elliptical" fiction did not win her a wide audience, and her readership has long since disappeared along with her work. Yet Mayne's writing is nonetheless important for exemplifying a distinct tradition grounded in the "Yellow Book School" of the 1890s and for giving voice to some of its fullest expression over a period of nearly half a century. Named after *The Yellow Book*, the most notorious periodical of the 1890s, the school was paid tribute by Ford Madox Ford in his 1921 memoir *Thus to Revisit* for "concern[ing] itself with 'form,' with the expression of fine shades, with continental models and exact language." Mayne first published a story in *The Yellow Book* in 1895 and briefly worked for the magazine the following year. Literary editor Henry Harland, welcomed her to join the all-consuming quest for "*le mot juste*," and his indelible influence inspired her to continue this pursuit long after his death in 1905, adapting and refining the search according to her own singular vision and reinventing it in the modern context of her favorite site of investigation: the unexplored regions of the human psyche. In addition Mayne wrote several biographical and literary studies over the course of her lifetime, including two groundbreaking biographies of George Gordon, Lord Byron and Annabella Milbanke, Lady Byron that won the respect of such colleagues as Sir Edward Marsh, André Maurois, W. L. Courtney, Desmond MacCarthy, and Leonard Woolf. Whether biographical or fictional, her subjects benefitted from her penetrating insight and the "grace, humanity, and wit" with which she was noted for treating her subjects.

Mayne began her multifaceted literary career in Ireland, where she spent the first half of her life. The eldest child of Charles Edward Bolton Mayne and Charlotte Henrietta (Emily) Sweetman, Ethelind Frances Colburn Mayne was born in Johnstown, a small village in the northwest corner of County Kilkenny, on 7 January 1865 (not "187?," as early twentieth-century biographical dictionaries were no doubt deliberately misled to record). Since her father was a member of the Royal Irish Constabulary, the family was subject to a somewhat nomadic existence, moving next to Kinsale, County Cork, where her brother, Edward, and her sister, Violet, were born. Ultimately, Mayne's father became a resident magistrate, and they settled in the city of Cork, in the easternmost district of Blackrock, along the River Lee. She received her education in Irish private schools, learning French and German and demonstrating a facility for history. She was a voracious reader in all three languages and developed an early but enduring passion for the poetry of Heinrich Heine, which she undertook to translate for her own enjoyment. A few of her translations were published in *The Academy* (2 February 1901), but when she later tried to interest publishers in a collection, the proposal met with no success.

Little more is known of Mayne's life prior to the mid 1890s, except that she had begun to write stories and to follow avidly the frenzy of literary activity going on in London, where new periodicals were beginning to proliferate. Thus in 1894 she did not miss the highly publicized debut of *The Yellow Book*, to be edited by Henry Harland and Aubrey Beardsley and published by The Bodley Head, the firm headed by John Lane and Elkin Mathews. Nor did she disregard its open solicitation of work from unknown writers, and in 1895 she received the astonishing but welcome news that Harland had accepted one of her stories. In "Reminiscences of Henry Harland," an unpublished memoir written many years later, Mayne described this cataclysmic event: "Almost before I had realised my own temerity in thinking to begin my literary life at such an altitude, there came a letter in [Harland's] exquisite script, not only accepting the story but praising it in words which even now it thrills me to recall." The story, "A Pen-and-Ink Effect," was published in the July 1895 volume under the name "Frances E. Huntley," a pseudonym she later heartily regretted adopting and abandoned with the publication of her first volume of stories, *The Clearer Vision,* in 1898.

The story's stylistic structure—it is essentially the internal monologue of a man writing a letter to a young woman, followed by that of the woman herself—offers an early illustration of Mayne's interest in investigating human psychology via minutely narrated introspection and in examining the differences between men's and women's perceptions. The story is also useful in contrasting her confident handling of this approach with a less successful early effort, "Her Story and His," which was published in the November 1895 issue of *Chapman's Magazine*. This story shares not only the same basic structure as "A Pen-and-Ink Effect," but also the device of the letter to precipitate the turning point. Where Mayne used irony and economy to great effect in her *Yellow Book* story, however, the *Chapman's* piece suffers from sentimentality and an excess of explanation, as if its author did not trust her characters to reveal themselves in their own fashions—including through inference and omission. In "A Pen-and-Ink Effect" the reader is held in suspense, then surprised and amused by the ending, whereas in "Her Story and His" the introspection becomes overwrought, leaving the reader overwhelmed. Fortunately, Mayne soon learned the nuanced art of ambiguity.

In 1896 Mayne met two people who had a lasting impact on her life. The first was Harland. In her memoir Mayne described the events following her receipt of Harland's first letter: "From that day a correspondence, invited by him, began and continued until in December he wrote offering me what he called the 'derisory' post of his sub-editor; Miss Ella D'Arcy, who had hitherto acted in that capacity, having left England for a stay in France." She continued, "I need not enlarge on how little derisory it seemed to a girl who had lived her life until then in Ireland, and was entirely unknown to the literary world. Nor need I say with what ardour the invitation was accepted."

Mayne left Cork for London on New Year's Day 1896. D'Arcy, whose friends had nicknamed her "Goblin Ella" for her habit of disappearing without warning (and showing up again equally unexpectedly), had left London several weeks earlier. When she returned in March, D'arcy was less than pleased to find Mayne ensconced in her post, and,

Page from an unpublished memoir describing Mayne's first contact with Henry Harland, editor of The Yellow Book *(Collection of Mark Samuels Lasner)* according to Mayne, "banished" her replacement from the *Yellow Book* office. Harland, who confessed himself to be "like a cat" because "I make for the door when there's any trouble," responded to the conflict by fleeing to France before the April issue had been printed. D'Arcy seized the opportunity to avenge herself by removing Mayne's story "The Only Way" from its contents and deleting the name of "Frances Huntley" from Harland's "Yellow Dwarf" piece praising selected *Yellow Book* writers. When he learned what D'Arcy had done too late to correct it, a "furious" Harland fired her by postcard from Paris (a threat she knew better than to take seriously) and wrote a letter to Mayne apologizing for the "many little stabs" that had been inflicted on her. Yet, as Mayne reported sadly in her memoir, "That was all. I never heard from him, or saw him, again." When he did not come back to rectify the situation, Mayne had no choice but to return to Ireland. Still, she refused to blame her mentor: "I think it was meant kindly; he wanted me to forget him. . . . One might be ironical about this; but nobody could long be angry or resentful with him—if at all. . . . as to forgetting him, no one who ever knew him has done that."

The other pivotal person Mayne encountered during her brief and tumultuous time in London was Violet Hunt, whom she met at an Authors' Club tea soon after her arrival. Though opposite temperamentally—Hunt was gregarious and relished risqué adventures, and Mayne was shy and more reserved—they grew to be intimate friends, enjoying the kind of closeness that permitted frank expressions of disagreement as well as ongoing exchanges of support. When Mayne's first volume of stories was published Hunt wrote a glowing review for *The Daily Telegraph* and sent a copy of the book to Henry James, recommending it enthusiastically. Later, Mayne acted as intermediary in the protracted aftermath of Hunt's ten-year affair with Ford Madox Ford, and, when Hunt's mind began to deteriorate as a result of the syphilis she had contracted in the 1890s, Mayne solicited forbearance from their mutual friends. Together they became founding members of PEN (the International Association of Poets, Playwrights, Editors, Essayists, and Novelists) in 1921, and both served for years on the Femina Vie Heureuse prize committee. Following Mayne's move to London with her sister in 1905, they lived around the corner from each other for the better part of twenty-two years. Though Hunt had several lovers, neither woman ever married. It was said by some that Mayne's one "grand passion" was Byron. Not greatly gifted with beauty, she devoted herself wholly to her writing and to her sister, who was in poor health.

Front binding for Mayne's critically acclaimed second novel

Mayne returned to Cork in June 1896 deeply and irrevocably influenced by her brief apprenticeship with Harland. She continued writing and submitting stories to other literary journals, though without any particular success. Meanwhile, she was also working on her first novel, based on her experiences of the literary and social life enjoyed by a member of the *Yellow Book* coterie. In November 1897 she submitted "The Gate of Life" to T. Fisher Unwin, a firm with a reputation for publishing first novels by unknown writers. Ironically, the book was rejected on the grounds that it lacked verisimilitude. In his report, Unwin's chief reader, Edward Garnett, chided the author for her apparent excess of imagination: "There are no such circles as Miss Mayne describes—*none*. The art-talk—the Oscar Wildeian posing people—all are *idealized,* imagined by a clever girl." Although he granted that "her analysis of a woman's feelings is very good," it was his considered opinion that "the sketches of social celebrities, artists, famous critics etc. etc., all the *art atmosphere,*

& art *gossip* is—well humbug." Seemingly oblivious to Mayne's association with *The Yellow Book* (although his father, Richard, had also been a contributor), Garnett merely repeated the classic editor's advice, here likely to be somewhat galling to the author: "In the future she must place her heroine in a social milieu she herself has lived in, & *knows*. She must write of the people she knows, & *then* she may do good work."

Without the manuscript itself it is impossible to know how much of "The Gate of Life" remains in Mayne's first published novel, *Jessie Vandeleur* (1902)—or, indeed, if any of the original work survives in *Jessie Vandeleur* at all. The version ultimately published by George Allen also features a London social milieu peopled by avant-garde artists and writers, and some of the dialogue might be construed as "art talk," exchanged by characters who could aptly be described as "Oscar Wildeian posing people." In her choice of setting at least, Mayne heeded Garnett's injunction to situate her heroine in a milieu with which she was familiar, for the eponymous Jessie leaves a small town in Ireland for the Campden Hill district of London, where Violet Hunt lived.

Mayne may have developed the one part of her work Garnett had praised: "her analysis of a woman's feelings, . . . the *attitude* of the woman (the heroine) towards the men." Enabled by an inheritance to escape the stifling confines of tiny Widdicombe for the exciting scope of cosmopolitan London, Jessie chafes anew at the fetters implicit in her three-year engagement to Hugo Grantley, a sensitive aspiring writer employed as personal assistant to Lord Ruttledge. When Lord Ruttledge receives a diplomatic appointment to a West African country, thereby conveniently removing Hugo from the scene, Jessie exploits the freedom to pursue her literary idol, the "notorious" novelist "Deyncourt." Uncertain of securing his affections with her beauty alone ("Deyncourt worships brains"), she steals the manuscript of the unfinished novel that Hugo left in her trust, supplies an ending and has it published as her own work. Although Hugo obligingly dies in ignorance of her actions, his sister confronts Jessie, who is then forced to confess to Deyncourt. So gratified is he at this proof of her love, however, that he reciprocates her feelings, and there the novel ends.

Despite the reader's ample access to Jessie's thoughts and feelings, the character remains an enigma—not one of the mysterious sort, but merely an increasingly perplexing one who becomes by the end altogether detestable. Affecting a tone of exaggerated understatement, a *Daily News* reviewer dryly noted (9 December 1902), "The author obviously has an ambition to depict a heroine who is not a doll." The result, he warned, "is not very pleasing." In fact, Jessie comes across rather as an antiheroine; she is endowed with a budding feminist dissatisfaction with woman's lot—particularly the constricting expectations entailed by her engagement—and is made to embody the opposite of all that was considered "womanly" according to Victorian stereotypes. Where women were supposed to be self-abnegating and submissive, Jessie is narcissistic and demanding; where compassion was thought to inhere in women, she is gratuitously and remorselessly cruel. Fulfilling the negative image of woman with damning thoroughness, Jessie is also vain, manipulative, and heartless to a degree straining credulity. Yet Mayne insists on Jessie's humanity by making the reader privy to her every doubt and qualm, robbing her of the claim to evilness that might have earned her a measure of literary immortality. As the reviewer for *The Times Literary Supplement* (5 December 1902) suggested, "A still more splendid insolence might have carried her through to greatness." Instead, he regretted to declare, "Miss Mayne has failed to make her rebel great."

An equal amount of criticism was aimed at Mayne's peculiar style. Like Harland, a self-avowed disciple of "the Master," during her career she was compared to Henry James more often than to any other single author, but the so-called Jamesian obliquity noted in her own elliptical style was almost always faulted as being too cryptic for the average reader—or reviewer. Writing in 1898 about her manuscript for her first collection of short stories, *The Clearer Vision*, Edward Garnett was among the first of many critics to observe that Mayne had "modelled her own style on Henry James," but he was also not the last to complain, "she has gone too far in that direction, at times—& her stories are in consequence too difficult to catch hold of." *The Daily News* reviewer claimed that in *Jessie Vandeleur*, "Every paragraph is a series of jerks and parentheses, which produce bewildering obscurity." Betraying his discomfort with innovative combinations of language (such as characterized the pioneering yet popular short stories of George Egerton, for example), the reviewer dismissed Mayne's style as "not even intended for a parody of Henry James." He cited as evidence a passage in which some lines from Robert Browning are woven into the narrative, recalled by Hugo when he kisses Jessie and finds her aloof: "Always the same, always the cobweb, infrangible barrier—would nothing break it down? He might kiss her; she acquiesced: the cool, sweet cheek had touched his lips—yet nothing was changed; she was away from him, 'like the thistle-ball, no bar, on-

Frontispiece and title page for a critical study of women in the poetry of Robert Browning

ward whenever light winds blow ... The old trick!'" The quotation from Browning's "Two in the Compagna" was irresistibly apt, sharing and thus echoing the metaphor of the cobweb and the central image of a kiss on a woman's cheek. Mayne merely manipulated the syntax to convey the lover's frustration, expressed inwardly and therefore less articulate than speech.

During a visit to London in early 1903, Mayne was introduced by Frederic Whyte to C. F. Cazenove, a managing partner of the Literary Agency of London, who became her agent for the next ten years. Beset by doubts that her work would ever find an appreciative public following the poor sales of *Jessie Vandeleur* (for which she also blamed George Allen's incompetence), Mayne's confidence as a writer was restored by Cazenove's unflagging encouragement. Though she reminded him from time to time that she was likely to be his most unprofitable client, she nevertheless kept him busy, writing frequently from Cork to suggest possible outlets for her stories or foreign books warranting translation, soliciting his opinion of her recent work or requesting progress reports of his efforts on her behalf, and, invariably, asking for any job that might bring in some money quickly. In summer 1903, prompted by Cazenove, Mayne started her next novel, basing it on the figure of the "outsider." But she soon abandoned it, complaining that it was depressing her and making her ill. Like many of her contemporaries, notably the more successful Egerton—and, before her, Henry James—she diverted her energies in 1904 to the potentially lucrative market of the theater, collaborating with Mrs. Frances Harrod (sister of the noted actor Johnston Forbes Robertson) on an adaptation of the latter's short story "The Taming of the Brute." She then wrote another play, but both Cazenove and Hunt agreed that it lacked dramatic force and would make a better novel. Unchastened, that fall she wrote a one-act "curtain-raiser" that she named "The Bungalow," reporting to Cazenove that it contained all the elements certain of success: an exotic location (India), a love story, a ghost, and murder. "The Bungalow" was shown to Frank Curzon, Lewis Waller, Mrs. Patrick Campbell, and George Alexander but failed to find a producer. Though disappointed, Mayne accepted its rejection with equanimity and pragmatically turned it into a story, eventually included in *Things That No One Tells* (1910).

In May 1905, almost a decade after her brief sojourn at Marloes Road, Mayne and her sister moved to London and rented a flat in South Kensington, less than a mile from the former *Yellow Book* office. Her new surroundings seemed conducive to her work, for that fall she reported progress on the novel she had titled "Miss." Warning Cazenove that it promised to be a lengthy affair and needing a source of income, she broached the possibility of undertaking some translation work, and in December she was delighted to get her first book-length translation job. Unlike the scholarly historical monographs she translated later in her career, this work was a "sensational" book by an anonymous German author, published as *The Confessions of a Princess* (1906) by the firm of John Long. Mayne insisted that her name not appear on the title page, explaining that it was not the sort of book with which she wanted the public to associate her name. This omission repeated in 1907, when Sisley's published her translation of *The Diary of a Lost One,* another anonymous volume of scandalous revelations, edited by Margaret Boehme. Both books became immediate best-sellers, but Mayne received only a flat fee of less than fifty pounds for each.

She finished "Miss" toward the end of 1906, but the manuscript did not enjoy a favorable reception by Unwin, the first firm to which it was submitted. Nor did it meet with the approval of George Allen (to whom Mayne was contractually obligated to offer it) or even, to Mayne's chagrin, of Methuen, for whom she was then writing another book on commission (*Enchanters of Men,* 1909). It was not until early in 1908 that Arthur Waugh at Chapman and Hall announced that his firm was quite taken with her novel, and *The Fourth Ship* (1908), as it had been retitled, finally appeared that May. As often happens with originally unwanted works that later become popular, Mayne's novel achieved a degree of critical acclaim. The reviewer for *The Academy* (27 June 1908) proclaimed it "the finest and most finished work of fiction he has read for many years," and *The Daily Telegraph* (8 May 1908) suggested that, for the reader "to whom character, observation, literary sincerity, and true feeling are of more value than many adventures ... 'The Fourth Ship' will ... prove a sheer delight."

In this work Mayne tried a different approach than she had used in *Jessie Vandeleur,* substituting instead the equally challenging problem of building her book around a woman who had "no intellectual existence" at all. Jessie Vandeleur's antithesis, the shy, unimaginative, acquiescent Josephine St. Lawrence was conceived of as a type of outsider, that is, in terms of missing out on all the usual "bounties" of life: love, marriage, children. Mayne intended to evoke the reader's sympathy through pity for her protagonist, but she complicated that response by devising a contrasting character who was also pitiable, another woman destined always to be an outsider, in this case because of her uncommon talent and consequent dissatisfaction with the limited lifestyle imposed on women. Millicent North is a brilliant pianist who, in 1850s Ireland, is uncomfortably ahead of her time and vainly in search of some means by which to realize her ambitions. While Millie's aspirations are blighted by circumstance—she is persuaded to marry rather than attempt to pursue her quixotic plan of becoming a music teacher—Josie's more modest hopes, never fully articulated even to herself, are thwarted by Millie, who settles for the suitor Josie would have been only too glad to accept.

The work is divided into three equal parts, the first devoted to Josie, the second to Millie, and the third to Millie's three daughters, Rosamund, Daisy, and Christabel. The last section is named for Christabel, the youngest of the three, as if to emphasize the contrast between the two generations of women, a contrast that is most pronounced between the old-fashioned and narrow-minded spinster Josephine and the modern tomboy Christabel, who speaks slang, plays hockey, and has every promise of becoming one of the "New Women" her mother had so keenly desired to be.

The thwarting of that desire underlies one of the most striking and unusual aspects of *The Fourth Ship:* Mayne's portrayal of Millie as a mother. Although alerted in the middle section to the character's "histrionic" tendencies and reluctance to take on such conventional roles as wife and mother, the reader is not fully prepared for the revelation in "Christabel" that Millie has practiced emotional blackmail on her two elder daughters ever since they were children, winning their confidences when they were in distress and then using that information later to criticize or embarrass them. An integral part of her campaigns—which continue into the present of the novel—consists of writing letters, not only to her daughter's friends telling them what she thinks of them or forbidding them to visit again, but also to Rosamund and Daisy detailing her opinions of them in even plainer terms. The husband and father of the family somehow remains oblivious to the discord, and life always returns to normal after a short interval. The reduction of Millie's behavior to a simple Jekyll-and-Hyde analogy is prevented by Rosamund's insight when, resolving to put an end

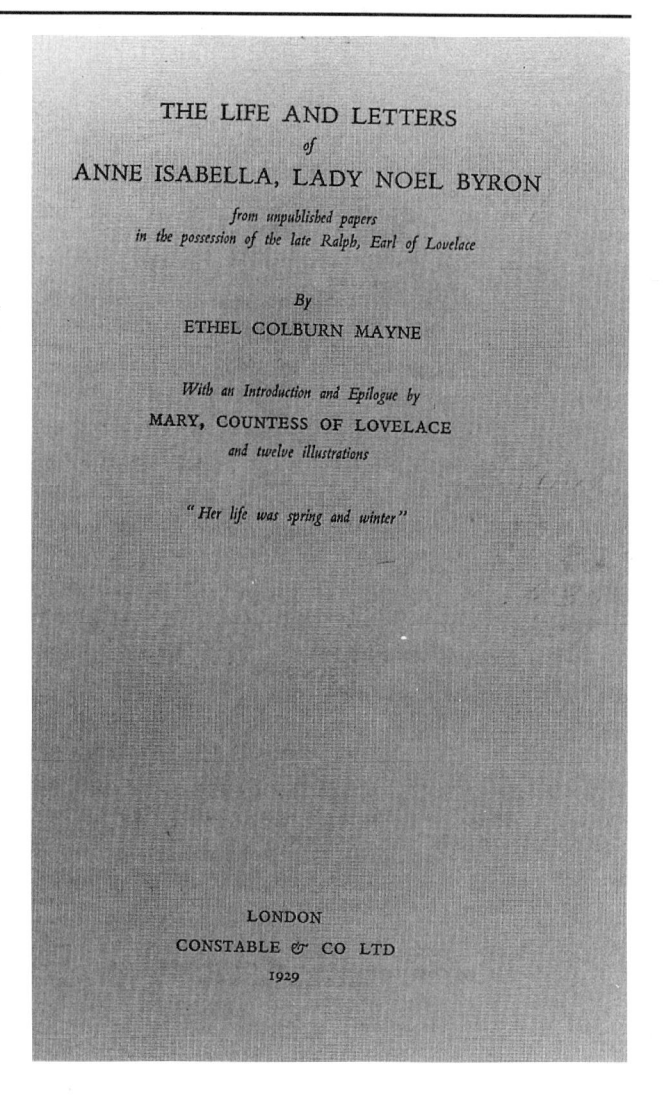

Frontispiece and title page for an important biography of Lady Byron, which drew on previously unpublished family papers

to the intolerable unpleasantness, she finally confronts her mother and refuses to play the part of dutiful victim any longer. She perceives that her mother's anger is really self-hatred born of frustration with her lot and resentment that opportunities subsequently made available to younger women were so unjustly denied to her. Rosamund persuades Millie to see her daughters' lives not as mocking hers but instead as positive testimonies to her example. Rosamund conveys the message that women must stick together to support each other, to combat more effectively the odds society has stacked against them. This resolution made the work the most upbeat of any of those in which Mayne addressed the dark underside of motherhood, from the sacrificial burning of the protagonist's "story-children" in "Herb of Grace" (*The Clearer Vision*) to a mother's jealous banishment of her daughter's beloved pet in "The Peacocks" (*Nine of Hearts*, 1923).

Over the next five years Mayne was busier than ever before. Shortly after *The Fourth Ship* appeared, she was approached about her next novel by the publisher Edward Arnold, head of a relatively young firm looking for promising new writers. (Mary Cholmondeley, author of *Red Pottage* [1899], was one of his authors.) Then Hutchinson, impressed with her translation of Jules Lair's *Louise de la Vallière and the Early Life of Louis XIV* (1908), suggested that she write an historical study of the rulers of Monaco. Also that summer, Methuen commissioned her to write a biography of Byron, an event that had the greatest significance for Mayne's career. The following summer, Methuen published her biographical study of famous women, *Enchanters of Men*, to highly complimentary reviews, and in

1910 Chapman and Hall agreed to publish Mayne's second collection of stories, *Things That No One Tells*. To Mayne's delight the book was so well received when it appeared in May that it went into a second printing that October. Writing Cazenove with the news, she eagerly asked him to calculate how much money she could expect it to bring in.

The Byron biography took Mayne four years to research and write, and the completed manuscript was dispatched to Methuen in March 1912. It was a lengthy work (ultimately published in two volumes), and there were alterations at the last minute because of the unexpected availability of private papers and portraits owned by Lady Lovelace, the widow of Byron's grandson. The book finally appeared that October, immediately winning nearly universal praise. *The Athenaeum* (2 November 1912) reported, "Miss Mayne has found a happy use for the critical, analytical, and synthetical gifts which she clearly possesses," and *The Spectator* (23 November 1912) announced its approval, "We should unhesitatingly call it the best of modern works on the subject." *The Spectator* reviewer did not claim that the book was entirely without fault, however, adding the following (by now familiar) criticism: "Sometimes the writing is very tall, so tall as to be almost unintelligible." Nevertheless, as Mayne had predicted to her agent, it was the sort of work that could "make" a reputation if done well, and indeed it has proved to be, more than any of her other books, the single work for which she is best remembered.

It was also the book that precipitated a falling-out between Mayne and Cazenove over the matter of the agent's fee. The cost of the alterations had reduced Mayne's net advance noticeably, but Cazenove deducted the 10 percent for his agency from the full amount specified in Mayne's contract with Methuen. Although she subsequently acknowledged that Cazenove was legally correct in his actions, she said that he could have shown more generosity of spirit—a comment that eloquently reveals how badly she needed the money, since the difference in question was little more than a pound. The break, agreed to when tempers were at their highest, was soon sincerely regretted, for both realized that their decade-long friendship was more important than money. Yet pride on both sides prevented reversing the decision, and their professional relationship ended—albeit on a more cordial note—shortly after the beginning of 1913. Four years after Cazenove's death Mayne turned the incident into a self-recriminating short story called "A Dab at Human Nature" (*Blindman*, 1919), in which the author's vanity is responsible for bringing about the dispute and estrangement, which in turn prompt the agent's death from depression and pneumonia.

In November 1912 Chatto and Windus proposed to Mayne that she write a critical study of the women in Robert Browning's poetry, a topic about which she was both knowledgeable and enthusiastic. She signed a contract—her first without Cazenove's representation—the following January and promptly set to work on *Browning's Heroines* (1913). As she explained in the preface, "Browning, I think, is 'coming back,' as stars come back. There has been a period of obscuration. Seventeen years ago, when *The Yellow Book* and the *National Observer* were contending for *les jeunes*, Browning was, in the more 'precious' côterie, king of modern poets. I can remember the editor of that golden Quarterly reading, declaiming, quoting, almost breathing, Browning! . . . A hundred Browning verses sing themselves around my memories of the flat in Cromwell Road." The book was published in November to highly laudatory notices. *The Saturday Review* (29 November 1913) hailed it as "the most excellent book of commentary upon Browning . . . since Mr. G. K. Chesterton wrote upon this poet the best book of his life." More than one reviewer, however, noted a "feminist" slant, with predictable ambivalence, if not outright disapproval. Even *The Saturday Review* critic went on to scold, "The author of this book is a feminist, and she does not hesitate to claim that Browning, also, was a feminist. If we have a fault to find with this book, it is just this introduction of a foolish label, equally unjust to the author herself and to her subject." But Mayne offered no apologies; instead, applauding the poet's enlightened vision, she wrote in her introduction, "Browning's power of embodying in rhythm the full beauty of girlhood is unequalled by any other English poet. . . . His girls are as brave as the young knights of other poets; and in this appreciation of a dauntless gesture in women we see one of the reasons why he may be called the first 'feminist' poet since Shakespeare."

Feminist sympathies were on her mind for more than one reason while she was writing *Browning's Heroines*. That July she completed her third novel, *Gold Lace: A Study of Girlhood* (1913), the protagonist of which was identified by many critics as feminist. In 1908, after the publication of *The Fourth Ship*, Mayne had confessed to a correspondent curious to know if she had started another novel yet, "I always feel that once the latest is finished, I *shall never write another!!* Yet," she admitted, "in my mind is a sort of notion for one all the same—I can hardly say 'a plot,' for plots refuse to come to me. It is always a *character* which lures me on to write about it."

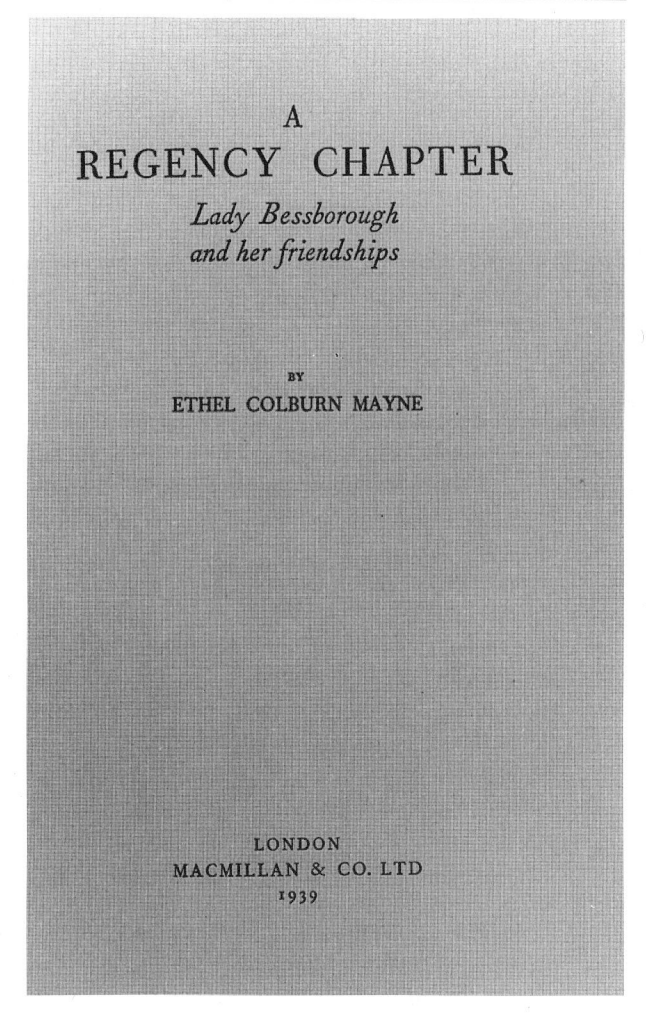

Frontispiece and title page for a chronicle of the romance between Granville George Leveson-Gower, Lord Granville, and Henrietta Frances Spencer Ponsonby, Lady Bessborough

In the case of *Gold Lace* that compelling character must have been Rhoda Henry, a cool, self-possessed young Englishwoman more candid and outspoken than Josie, less conflicted emotionally than Millie, and considerably more sympathetic than Jessie, though a parallel to the latter was drawn by those who saw Rhoda's spirited assertiveness as akin to Jessie's "liberated" narcissism. Had the two been judged by their literary tastes alone, perhaps a case could have been made for some affinity, for Jessie's library included a lengthy litany of "the modern of the moderns"—Pierre Loti, George Meredith, Henry James, Paul Verlaine, Gabriele D'Annunzio, Anatole France, Frederick Wedmore, William Butler Yeats, Arthur Symons, and George Moore—and Rhoda is introduced to the reader as "a Shavian (though deploring the later experiments in dialogue).... She had views on the Art of Fiction also, which caused her to reject the proferred bundle of Books of the Moment at the library," though she was not above indulging in the occasional popular novel. When her engagement to a young man from her father's firm does not work out—she explains to her parents that she found she did not care for him enough to marry him, a realization, she points out, that only the engagement could have made possible—Rhoda's parents send her off to Ireland to visit friends. Her father feels that she is in need of a "setdown," but although in a sense she gets one, at the same time she aims to raise the sights of the young women there by instilling in them some of her own "London pride."

The title of the novel sets up a key symbolic opposition of the plot. Despite its seemingly obvious allusion to feminine furbelows, "gold lace" in fact refers to the uniforms of the servicemen whose presence dominates the social life in the Irish towns of Rainville and Lisnaquin, homes to a naval station and military garrison, respectively. The "girlhood" being examined is for the most part that of the local young women, apparently content to be no more than the perpetual playthings of the servicemen, who move on to their next post without a backward glance. This state of affairs comes in for sharp critique when Rhoda arrives. Indignant at this insensitive treatment of her gender, and at the residents' acquiescent acceptance of it, Rhoda refuses to play the game and is initially thought cold and arrogant, but eventually she is able to make herself understood, as well as doing a little consciousness-raising along the way.

The reviewer for *The Nation* (1 November 1913) admitted himself at a loss to understand much of the dialogue between the young women in the second half of the book, but blamed his failure, typically, on Mayne's style: "No doubt a great deal of acute observation and insight into feminine ethics is interwoven into the texture of these latter chapters, but the conversation is far too complex to be true to life, and suggests overmuch Mr. Henry James's method." It seems likely, however, that critics' uneasiness with Mayne's apparent transplantation of "James's method" derived in large part from her divergent choice of subject matter. Though Rhoda is never explicitly referred to in the text as a New Woman or a feminist, she makes it her project to encourage enough self-respect in the local young women to refuse further complicity in their own exploitation—hardly a typical Jamesian scenario. Nor does any hint of James arise when, voicing her realization that "women need one another"—often, though not always, "against" men—Rhoda concludes, "We never *return* to slavery. Gold lace will have to adapt itself. Things are changing."

The unfortunate fact that things did not change soon enough to benefit some women is the story told in Mayne's next novel, *One of Our Grandmothers* (1916). In it Mayne returned to the character of Millicent North, one of the "outsiders" who had so intrigued her during the writing of *The Fourth Ship*. Millie was, in effect, before her time, and *The Fourth Ship* describes her anger, frustration, and resentment at having been denied opportunities that later became accessible to the next generation of women. *One of Our Grandmothers* acts as a prequel to the earlier novel in detailing Millie's life before her flight to Druff, providing some background, both physical and psychological, for her unusual behavior and giving the reader greater insight into her peculiarly troubled situation.

The novel opens in England just after the death of Millie's mother. Her father, pleased to discover he can live comfortably in Ireland on his deceased wife's income, decides that they should move to Killarney. Not altogether an insensitive parent, he is nevertheless unable to appreciate the potential of Millie's musical ability and unsupportive of her artistic aspirations. When she is jilted by her first love and the sanctuary of her home is invaded by a hostile, ill-bred stepmother, Millie can no longer bear life in Killarney, and she escapes to her Aunt Annette's in Druff. There she meets the new constable, Philip Maryon, who shares her passion for Alfred Tennyson and soon falls in love with her. Millie realizes she does not love him, however, or at least does not feel what she had felt for the man who deserted her, so she refuses Maryon's proposal of marriage. But her plan to move to England and support herself as a piano teacher is unexpectedly blocked, and, faced with the intolerable prospect of living at home in Killarney, Millie consents to wed Maryon.

Where *The Fourth Ship* was "painted with a broad brush," spanning generations, *One of Our Grandmothers* is minutely, even painfully, introspective, inviting the reader to share in Millie's confusion as the gifted but naive misfit tries desperately to understand her conflicting moods and emotions and to reconcile them with her circumstances. Reviewers concurred that the plot was slight but the character portraits vivid and convincing, lingering in the memory long after the story had ended. W. L. Courtney described the book in *The Daily Telegraph* (31 May 1916) as "full of delicacy and charm" and its heroine as "an admirable piece of portraiture," though he noted that Mayne's style, "follwing the model either of George Meredith or Henry James, . . . is inclined to be a little precious." In his review for *The Daily News* (10 May 1916) R. Ellis Roberts called Mayne "unrelenting in telling the truth about her heroine," adding that "Vision is sight made serene by sympathy and experience. And vision is preeminently Miss Mayne's gift."

That "vision" was not to be seen again in novel form. *One of Our Grandmothers* was Mayne's last novel to appear in print, though she did subsequently write one more, "Sentence of Life," which was never published. This may seem a brief novel-writing career, but Mayne did not consider herself primarily a novelist, and in fact was more widely regarded as a short-story writer. Since, by her own account, it was character and not plot that impelled her to write fiction, she could just as easily explore her characters' intricate psychological makeups and behaviors within the accommodating parameters of the short story—and, many of its adherents would argue, to better advantage there than in the more diffused form of the novel. Thus, in the nine-year period following *One of Our Grandmothers* Mayne produced four collections of short stories—*Come In*

(1917), *Blindman* (1919), *Nine of Hearts* (1923), and *Inner Circle* (1925)—each of which included many works that could aptly be described as character studies, particularly studies of feminine psychology.

Though her subject matter frequently featured romantic relationships, more often than not her stories portrayed the myriad ways in which love could be blighted, such as by loss of interest ("The One Way"), a third party ("Silver Paper," "India-rubber"), age differences ("The Kingfisher"), a sister's well-timed intervention ("Desert surges"), mental instability ("The Shirt of Nessus"), the male ego ("Lovells Meeting"), or death ("Franklin's Problem"). Mayne also probed the psychological mysteries of relationships, whether romantic, familial, or of another sort altogether, including the enigmatic dynamics between a newly married husband and wife ("Honoria Byron," "The Happy Day"), the extremes of feeling possible between mother and daughter ("The Separate Room," "Light"), and the bond manifested between four spinsters and the family feline ("The Man of the House"). She even explored the region of the supernatural, where psychology intersects with the occult, in such stories as "The Turret Room," "Black Magic," and "The Angry Place."

A noteworthy aspect of Mayne's stories is the fact that only one of them could be described as funny, despite the frequent presence of a wry or ironical tone, occasionally bordering on a subtle, understated bemusement. That is not to say, of course, that her work lacks a sense of humor. But the only story in which she achieves a comical effect, by using exaggeration to characterize her narrator as hopelessly self-deluded, is "Lucille," which appeared in *The Yellow Book* in January 1896, virtually at the beginning of her career. Mayne once told her agent she did not think she had a sense of humor and that she felt most fictional humor failed to "come off," boring readers instead of amusing them. Since "Lucille" could not by even the severest critic be accounted a failure in that regard, it is puzzling, and disappointing, that Mayne did not again attempt a similar approach. She did, however, turn the subject into a story called "Humour," published in *The Golden Hind* (July 1924), in which the narrator announces at the outset she has "no sense of humour" but arrives, by the ending, at a different understanding of herself than she had before.

In his review of *Come In* for *The Bookman* (February 1918) Frank Swinnerton expertly captured the essence of Mayne's method:

> One might be misled by the allusiveness of these tales, by the demand they make upon one's attention and visualising power, into the belief that they were speculative. They are not. They are all finely and surely seen, and rendered with such deliberateness, that the mind, grasping at psychological difficulties, imagines the truth that lies behind.... Miss Colburn Mayne is no conjurer. If she demands your attention it is because she is presenting conceptions absolutely clear to herself in a way that can only be appreciated by those who care for implications. It is as though one were Miss Mayne's partner, playing to her hand: the more successful the partnership (for Miss Mayne never plays false), the greater the pleasure in her refined and perceptive work.... She dexterously and wonderfully makes us see the things that happened and come to our own conclusions. That is her quite special talent, that there is not a sentence but has its implication and reverberation.

After 1925 Mayne's fictional impulses waned, possibly under the burden of added family responsibilities; in 1923 she had written to the poet Richard Church that she currently had two invalids to care for—most likely her father, as well as her sister—and confessed that "everything is gone from me except the needful energy for getting through the day." Her father died in 1927, and Mayne was awarded a Civil List pension of £85 later that year. She turned to translations as her primary source of income, undertaking an average of one full-length work each year. At the same time, until its publication in 1929, she immersed herself in the research and writing of a biography of Lady Byron, for which Lady Lovelace again gave her unrestricted access to private family papers as well as her own full cooperation.

The crowning achievement of Mayne's lifelong inquiry into the feminine psyche, *The Life and Letters of Anne Isabella, Lady Noel Byron* (1929) also achieved a not fully anticipated degree of notoriety for using previously unpublished autograph documents by Lady Byron to confirm publicly her knowledge of Byron's long-rumored incest with his half sister Augusta Leigh, as well as the cruel and abusive treatment that prompted Lady Byron finally to seek a legal separation. Mayne was roundly praised for the sensitivity and tact with which she handled the delicate subject matter and for her fairness toward and insight into the human beings embroiled in such a deplorable drama. Leonard Woolf, writing in *The Nation & Athenaeum* (6 July 1929), called it "one of the most fascinating and important biographies which have appeared for a long time," adding that "The great merit of the book is that it not only gives us the facts, but also a sympathetic and intelligent presentment of Lady Byron's character." For Mayne, this approach had always been her primary goal. In a 1933 letter to Lady Ottoline Morrell she stated simply: "[T]hat is one's aim in biography—to reveal the character through the facts." And in *The New York Times Book Review* (25 August 1929), Herbert Gorman reaffirmed "how vividly [Mayne] has set forth the character of Annabella Milbanke, Lady Byron," noting that she had managed to do so "without recourse to the many tricks of the New Biography. There is no fictionalization here, no attempt to achieve dramatic moments, no overlarding of the manuscript with 'color,' and 'period detail.' It is all straightforward but blessed by a keen feminine intuition that was exactly the thing needed to reconstruct in its complexity and completeness the figure of Byron's wife." Called by Rebecca West (*The Bookman*, November 1929) the "most popular book of the London summer season," the biography went into a second printing a month after its June debut.

In her remaining years Mayne translated four major scholarly works, began a biography of Caroline Lamb commissioned by Constable and Knopf (abandoned when Victor Gollancz published one before she had completed hers), and published at least two stories in periodicals. In 1935 the Imagist poet Hilda Doolittle wrote to Mayne soliciting a contribution on behalf of *Life and Letters,* which had recently undergone a change of editors. Mayne promised to see if she had anything available, reassuring her correspondent that she remembered her with the succinct observation, "you are not a person one forgets."

In 1939 Mayne published her last book, a biographical study of the famous love affair between Granville George Leveson-Gower, Lord Granville and Henrietta Frances Spencer Ponsonby, Lady Bessborough, which was brought out by Macmillan under the watered-down title *A Regency Chapter: Lady Bessborough and Her Friendships*. Its favorable reception gave Mayne the confidence to offer Macmillan, in early 1940, her novel "Sentence of Life," as well as a "slender volume" of her short stories. Responding with prescient pessimism to Mr. Lovat Dickson's encouragement to send him the manuscripts, she reflected, "With things as they are now, I have little or no hope of your finding them a practical proposition." She was alluding to the beginning of World War II, which she knew from her experience of the last war would make potentially marginal ventures like hers financially unfeasible. "And I fear, too," she added, "that modern 'ideals' in fiction have put me quite on the shelf when I write what I really care most about writing." Macmillan may well have agreed with either of her points, for both works were regretfully declined.

On 30 September 1940, not long after the beginning of the London Blitz, the house in Twickenham where Mayne and her widowed sister were living was bombed, hospitalizing Violet for two weeks and Mayne for six. When they had sufficiently recovered, they moved their diminished household to Torquay, in South Devon, where many years earlier they had enjoyed the ocean air and open countryside on vacations with their father. Here they were also near their two brothers, both retired military officers living in the area. Their stay, however, turned out to be brief. As *The Richmond and Twickenham Times* later reported (10 May 1941), it is likely that Mayne and her sister never completely recovered from the bombing of their home, for they both died within weeks of each other the following April, Mayne on 30 April. A letter Mayne had written to Violet Hunt almost a year earlier reveals the sad irony behind this ending to her life: in it she explains that, because of the air raids, she would not return to London to visit Hunt for the duration of the war. With grim honesty she explained, "It is true that one can only die once, as you say; but one may not wish to die that way. *I* certainly don't, and will do all I can to avoid it." With a prophetic tone of finality, she concluded, "Till the clouds lift, no more."

After Mayne's death, which was followed by Hunt's in 1942, Norah Hoult, whom Hunt had befriended in the late 1930s, published a novel closely based on Hunt's last years. Titled *There Were No Windows* (1944), the thinly fictionalized account includes a chapter featuring a luncheon visit by Mayne (who in the book is named "Edith Barlow") that provides a poignant, perceptive, and wonderfully detailed portrait of her toward the end of her life. For instance, in the following internal monologue, Hoult recounts Barlow's feelings about the air raids, clearly drawing on information that is confirmed in the letter to Hunt quoted above.

> If only the bombs would . . . refrain from making their entrance into that final sleep an ill-conditioned, inelegant affair. That was her sister's chief trouble, for her sister was nervous of the raids, lacking her own sense of fatalism. It was due to her sister that they had already sorted out their things, had indeed done some packing, so that if havoc descended they would be ready to move to that address in Bournemouth where they had had such a pleasant summer holiday before the war.

Hoult also offers observations, again presented as Barlow's thoughts, that Mayne would never have articulated aloud but that are nevertheless almost certainly true, insofar as they are verified by such available evidence as extant letters and photographs:

The war had finally put finis to her literary work: the added strain with the care of an invalid sister was too much even for her stoical will. But she didn't complain, she got along and she got about; she could see and hear; her intelligence still functioned admirably. As for her appearance that, she knew, was, in the main, an improvement on the plain, gawky and sallow girl she had once been. Then no one took any notice of her; now people looked at her respectfully, registering something like "an English gentlewoman of the old school." Men were gallant to her; . . . then they had never taken any notice of her; and it had been her own instinct to shun their attention.

The instinct to shun attention and disdain for self-promotion may have played a key role in Mayne's undeserved obscurity today. Whereas Hunt's once-flamboyant behavior and assiduously detailed diaries have guaranteed her a certain degree of remembrance by posterity (as demonstrated in part by two full-length biographies to date), Mayne never cultivated her reputation, nor did her personality or behavior lend itself to making strong impressions. For example, in his memoir *Background with Chorus* (1956), Frank Swinnerton, who was Mayne's chief contact at Chatto and Windus in 1913 and 1914 and who had sung her praises in 1917, described her as "the discreet friend of Violet Hunt, . . . a well-bred, grey-haired woman who gave literary tea-parties in Kensington."

By a mere accident of birth Mayne straddled two distinct eras in literary history, making her in some respects an outsider to both: the one passionately dedicated to pioneering innovations in the short story, keenly attentive to word and phrase but rooted in French naturalism and strenuously challenging (though not too often violating) the public's sensibilities; the other characterized by its intense fascination with human relationships and the multidimensional life of the mind but also by its more fearless flouting of propriety and convention and its shift of attention to the novel, attracted by the potential for experimentation promised by that form. Her achievement lies in effectively bridging the two, incorporating elements of both into a distinctive hybrid of "exact language" and psychological investigation that has eluded categorization and thus contemporary critical attention but that nevertheless has as valid a claim to inclusion in the "genealogies of modernism" as many of the authors whose names have since become canonical.

Today, most of her works are out of print and hard to find—fiction and nonfiction alike—even in larger university libraries. Happily, however, many of her short stories have survived in anthologies dating from the 1920s and 1930s; and more recently, her debut story, "A Pen-and-Ink Effect," found its way into the anthology *Femmes de Siècle. Stories from the '90s: Women Writing at the End of Two Centuries* (1992), an encouraging sign possibly auguring a reawakening of interest in Mayne's work. While it may have been true in 1940 that "modern 'ideals' in fiction" had put her "quite on the shelf" when she wrote what she "care[d] most about writing," literary history has proven those "ideals" just as ephemeral as the ones that they replaced. Like Browning and the stars, it may now be Mayne's turn to "come back," and time for her "period of obscuration" to come to an end.

References:

Ella D'Arcy, *Some Letters to John Lane,* edited by Alan Anderson (Edinburgh: Tragara Press, 1990), pp. 23–27;

Ford Madox Ford, *Thus to Revisit: Some Reminiscences* (London: Chapman & Hall, 1921), pp. 34–40;

Norah Hoult, *There Were No Windows* (London: Heinemann, 1944), pp. 59–76, 96–97, 99–100;

Katherine Lyon Mix, *A Study in Yellow: The Yellow Book and Its Contributors* (Lawrence: University of Kansas, 1960), pp. 252–253, 287;

Margaret D. Stetz and Mark Samuels Lasner, *The Yellow Book: A Centenary Exhibition* (Cambridge: Houghton Library, 1994);

Frank Swinnerton, *Background with Chorus: A Footnote to Changes in English Literary Fashion between 1901 and 1917* (London: Hutchinson, 1956), pp. 153, 171;

Rebecca West, *Ending in Earnest: A Literary Log* (Garden City, N.Y.: Doubleday, 1931), pp. 161–179.

Papers:

Substantial collections of Ethel Colburn Mayne's correspondence are held by the Harry Ransom Humanities Research Center at the University of Texas at Austin, the University of Reading Library, the Lilly Library at Indiana University, and the University of North Carolina Library in its A. P. Watt and Dent archives. Additional correspondence can be found in the British Library, the Bodleian Library, Oxford; the Alexander Library, Rutgers University; the Olin Library, Cornell University; and the Berg Collection at the New York Public Library.

Stephen McKenna
(27 February 1888 – 26 September 1967)

George J. Johnson
Waterdown, Ontario, Canada

BOOKS: *The Reluctant Lover* (London: Jenkins, 1912; Philadelphia: Winston, 1913);

Sheila Intervenes (London: Jenkins, 1914 [i.e., 1913]; New York: Doran, 1920);

The Sixth Sense: A Novel (London: Chapman & Hall, 1915; New York: Doran, 1920);

Sonia: Between Two Worlds (London: Methuen, 1917; New York: Doran, 1917);

Ninety-Six Hours' Leave (London: Methuen, 1917; New York: Doran, 1917);

Midas and Son (London: Methuen, 1919; New York: Doran, 1919);

Sonia Married: A Novel (London: Hutchinson, 1919; New York: Doran, 1919);

Lady Lilith, a Novel: Being the First Part of The Sensationalists (London: Hutchinson, 1920; New York: Doran, 1920);

The Education of Eric Lane, a Novel: Being the Second Part of The Sensationalists (London: Hutchinson, 1921; New York: Doran, 1921);

The Secret Victory, a Novel: Being the Third Part of The Sensationalists (London: Hutchinson, 1921; New York: Doran, 1922);

While I Remember (London: Butterworth, 1921; New York: Doran, 1921);

The Confessions of a Well-meaning Woman (London: Cassell, 1922; New York: Doran, 1922);

Soliloquy (London: Hutchinson, 1922; New York: Doran, 1923);

Tex: A Chapter in the Life of Alexander Teixeira de Mattos (London: Butterworth, 1922; New York: Dodd, Mead, 1922);

By Intervention of Providence (London: Chapman & Hall, 1923; Boston: Little, Brown, 1923);

The Commandment of Moses (London: Hutchinson, 1923; New York: Doran, 1923);

Vindication: A Novel (London: Hutchinson, 1923; Boston: Little, Brown, 1924);

Tales of Intrigue and Revenge (London: Hutchinson, 1924; Boston: Little, Brown, 1925);

To-morrow and To-morrow: a Novel (London: Butterworth, 1924; Boston: Little, Brown, 1924);

Stephen McKenna

An Affair of Honour (London: Butterworth, 1925; Boston: Little, Brown, 1925);

The Oldest God: A Novel (London: Butterworth, 1926; Boston: Little, Brown, 1926);

Saviours of Society: Being the First Part of The Realists (London: Butterworth, 1926; Boston: Little, Brown, 1926);

The Secretary of State: Being the Second Part of The Realists (London: Butterworth, 1927; Boston: Little, Brown, 1927);

Due Reckoning: Being the Third and Final Part of The Realists (London: Butterworth, 1927; Boston: Little, Brown, 1928);

The Unburied Dead (London: Butterworth, 1928); republished as *Divided Allegiance* (New York: Dodd, Mead, 1928);

The Shadow of Guy Denver (London: Butterworth, 1928; New York: Dodd, Mead, 1929);

The Datchley Inheritance (London & Melbourne: Ward, Lock, 1929; New York: Dodd, Mead, 1929);

Happy Ending: A Novel (London: Cassell, 1929); republished as *Between the Lines* (New York: Dodd, Mead, 1929);

The Redemption of Morley Darville (London: Cassell, 1930; New York: Dodd, Mead, 1930);

The Cast-iron Duke (London: Cassell, 1930; New York: Dodd, Mead, 1931);

Dermotts Rampant: A Novel (London: Chapman & Hall, 1931; New York: Dodd, Mead, 1931);

Beyond Hell (London: Chapman & Hall, 1931; New York: Dodd, Mead, 1932);

Pandora's Box, and Other Stories (London & Melbourne: Ward, Locke, 1932);

The Way of the Phoenix (London: Chapman & Hall, 1932; New York: Dodd, Mead, 1932);

Superstition (London: Hutchinson, 1932; Boston: Houghton Mifflin, 1933);

Magic Quest (London: Hutchinson, 1933);

Namesakes (London: Hutchinson, 1933);

The Undiscovered Country (London: Hutchinson, 1934);

Portrait of His Excellency (London: Hutchinson, 1934);

Sole Death (London: Hutchinson, 1935);

While of Sound Mind (London: Hutchinson, 1936);

Lady Cynthia Clandon's Husband (London: Hutchinson, 1936);

Last Confession (London: Hutchinson, 1937);

The Home That Jill Broke (London: Hutchinson, 1937);

Breasted Amazon (London: Hutchinson, 1938);

A Life for a Life (London: Hutchinson, 1939);

Mean Sensual Man (London & New York: Hutchinson, 1943);

Reginald McKenna, 1863–1943: A Memoir (London: Eyre & Spottiswoode, 1948);

Not Necessarily for Publication (London & New York: Hutchinson, 1949);

Pearl Wedding (London & New York: Hutchinson, 1951);

Life's Eventime (London: Hutchinson, 1954);

That Dumb Loving (London: Hutchinson, 1957);

A Place in the Sun (London: Hutchinson, 1962).

OTHER: Louis Marie Anne Couperus, *Old People and Things That Pass,* preface by McKenna (London: Butterworth, 1919).

A naturally reticent gentleman of the old school, Stephen McKenna revealed little about himself even in his first autobiography, *While I Remember* (1921), which focuses mainly on his surroundings. Yet in his fifty-year career, which at its peak saw the issue of two novels a year, McKenna published forty-seven novels, six nonfiction works, and numerous stories and articles; this output seems more remarkable when one notes that, of these, only one novel was published between 1939 and 1948. He also wrote four plays that remain unpublished. McKenna's Irish background and his portrayals of upper-class English society lead to comparisons with Oscar Wilde, but Wilde, unlike McKenna, was Irish born and bred, was an outsider to that society, and portrayed it with romantic imagination and humor.

Born in Beckenham, Kent, on 27 February 1888 to Leopold and Ellen (Gethen) McKenna, Stephen McKenna descended from a Protestant family whose royal Catholic forefathers had inhabited County Monaghan since the beginning of Irish history. Leopold was the older brother of Reginald, a capable chancellor of the exchequer under Herbert Asquith, a connection that, along with family wealth, gave Stephen access to the corridors of power in England. McKenna depicted this milieu more seriously and accurately than Wilde: his characters talk like titled people, and his drawing rooms exude the opulence of the aristocracy; yet he was also capable of exposing the vanity of wealth through irony and satire.

"An Irish boy brought up in England and sent to a Tory stronghold by a father who had reared him on the pure milk of late Victorian radicalism," as he described himself in *While I Remember,* McKenna attended the prestigious Westminster School, London, obtaining his B.A. from Christ College, Oxford, in 1909 and his M.A. in 1913 while a director at a company in London from 1910 to 1914. Since his frail health incapacitated him for war service, he volunteered to assist by teaching at Westminster for a year (1914–1915), apparently a rather unpleasant experience, as indicated by remarks he directs to his former pupils in his autobiography: "My incompetence was incurable. I should be well pleased to think that your memories of me are a hundredth part as unkindly as mine are of you. Does it comfort you to know that my awe of you continued for three terms?"

During this period McKenna published three novels, the first two of which, *The Reluctant Lover* (1912) and *Sheila Intervenes* (1913), were described as "artificial comedies" because of the light narrative treatment, "smart epigrams," and superficial subject matter. In *The Reluctant Lover* the twenty-something Cyril Fitzroy, a selfish member of a posturing family, rises above this background to save the life of his sixteen-year-old ward, Violet Darlington, by performing a lifesaving operation to relieve her diphtheria; consequently, she falls in love with him. The circumstances are complicated by Cyril's prior secret engagement to self-reliant Myrna Woodbridge, who has resisted the advances of Rodney Trelawney and seemingly won Cyril over; yet Cyril marries the dependent Violet. An anonymous reviewer for *Punch* (27 November 1912) criticized McKenna's concern for "the superficial witticisms and railleries of his puppets ... [rather than] with serious ideas"; but, S. P. B. Mais, in *Books and Their Writers* (1920), claimed that "There are few more readable books on the market: there is a rattling good plot, unexpected *denouement,* human characters, adorable heroines, quite a number of them."

Spirited, mischievous Sheila Farling of the second novel "intervenes" in the life of Irishman Denys Playfair, directing him into a political career and promoting a relationship between him and her bored, mother-dominated cousin, Daphne Grayling. A serious accident to Daphne's former fiancé rekindles her obligation to him; but when Denys's strenuous political activities cause him to collapse in Sheila's presence, she drops her feigned unconcern and divulges her love for him. Some critics decried the novel's slight plot and weak motivation; the critic in *The Boston Transcript* (24 March 1920) thought that publication of *Sheila Intervenes* in the United States in 1920 was a mistaken attempt to benefit from the success of McKenna's more accomplished subsequent novels. Other critics, however, commended its delightful characters, easy dialogue, and skillful handling of the main romance.

With the previous two novels, as Almay Adcock reports in his *Gods of Modern Grub Street* (1923), McKenna "was learning to use his tools; feeling his way. In *The Sixth Sense* [1915] he was beginning to find it." While also criticized in the United States in 1921 because it, too, was an earlier novel containing dull passages, *The Sixth Sense* had reached its eighth British edition in 1920. Generally reviews were positive, noting, as did a critic in *The New York Times* (20 March 1921), its "bright and shining" language, real and frank story, and clever commingling of romance and politics.

Named after Lambert Aintree's extrasensory power to read the thoughts of loved ones and foretell events involving them, *The Sixth Sense* is a fantasy tracing the activities of this somewhat effeminate author known as "Seraph," who eschews fame in favor of fellowship and fidelity. Seraph finds that this "sixth sense," which empowers him with greater awareness, creates problems for him in the struggle for the female franchise in England, where some of his upper-class women friends are held hostage by extremist suffragists, among whom are other friends. Caught in the middle, Aintree is rescued from his dilemma by yet other friends.

That year, 1915, also marks the beginning of McKenna's career as a full-time writer, as a member of the British War Trade Intelligence Department, where he performed important war work for three and one-half years, and as one of the youngest committee members for the Reform Club, the leading Liberal club in London. The last two activities reflect his interest in British social and political life, as does the subtitle of his next novel, a portrayal of these spheres from the late 1890s to the early part of World War I.

About *Sonia: Between Two Worlds* (1917) Adcock proclaimed that McKenna's fourth novel "is one of the notable things in fiction that came out of the war." This comment was verified by other critics, for example the reviewer for *The Dial* (27 September 1917), who commended the novel's convincing picture of the prewar upper class and its "sense of the traits in British character which make it survive." The public obviously agreed since the book reached twelve editions before the end of the year and was the second-most-popular book of 1917.

Despite its title the emphasis of the novel is on the narrator, George Oakley, and his friends Lord Loring and "the most charming and glowingly human hero" David O'Rane, charting their schooldays at Melton in the decadent late 1890s and a growing altruistic concern for social reform and international harmony in the years leading to World War I. Set against this background is the romance of David and the attractive but tempestuous Sonia Dainton. McKenna claimed that *Sonia* "may have something of historical value in portraying a group of men and women who were at the same time my personal friends and representative of those Governing Classes in politics, journalism, commerce and society." In the same year McKenna traveled to Canada and the United States as part of the Balfour Mission, and he published a second novel, *Ninety-Six Hours' Leave.*

Ninety-Six Hours' Leave, according to Mais, is "a book that couldn't have taken more than ninety-six hours to write." It was accepted by most critics as pure fun, a surprise after *Sonia* but successful in its own way. A group of three army officers and a sailor, on leave in London, pass off one of their own, Kit Markham, as the Italian Count Christoforo of Catania in order to circumvent the dress code of the Hotel Semiramis. The hoax is complicated by Kit's involvement with a young lady and two German spies' interest in the "Count." McKenna also adapted the novel for the stage.

McKenna left government service in 1918, and the next year he published two novels, *Midas and Son* and *Sonia Married.* Transposing the Greek myth to

England in 1913–1914, *Midas and Son* traces the enervating effect on decent, intelligent, energetic, and idealistic Deryk Lancing of an inheritance left by his father, the self-made millionaire Sir Aylmer Lancing. The social milieu is the same as that in *Sonia*, with some characters from that novel recurring. Deryk's personal life is complicated by a romantic relationship with childhood friend Idina Penrose; the well-meaning attempts of his friend, the rebel aristocrat Yolande Stornaway, to help him find a sense of purpose; and a liaison with the notorious Mrs. Lucille Welmar. As a result Deryk experiences a spiritual paralysis, and he feels powerless to avert his inexorable surrender to suicidal impulses on the eve of World War I. While Mais sarcastically accuses McKenna of regarding "the problem of Midas as a good joke," others approved of the workmanship, characterization, and truthful and consistent handling of theme.

McKenna called *Sonia Married* not a sequel but an epilogue to *Sonia: Between Two Worlds*. Set in 1916, the novel follows the breakdown of Sonia's marriage to David O'Rane. David, although blinded in the war, has remained idealistic, as opposed to the more self-centered Sonia, who turns to another man, Vincent Grayle. When the affair also fails, Sonia finds herself pregnant and homeless. Determined to accept the child as his own, David rescues the ill Sonia despite her anger at her situation. Ultimately, though, the child's birth has a salutary effect on Sonia's character. These events are set against the background of politics, war, and the radical changes being wrought in Britain. *Sonia Married* suffered by comparison to its predecessor: it was judged overlong, depressing, melodramatic, and incomprehensible to those who had not read *Sonia*; however, it was also praised for its real characters, able writing, and finished style. The novel also appeared in serial form in *Metropolitan* magazine from September 1919 to March 1920.

In the next two years McKenna published a series known collectively as *The Sensationalists*, "three brilliant studies of modern London in the form of successive novels," according to Grant Overton in *Authors of the Day* (1924). McKenna's overall title for the series refers to those "sensation-mongers" bent on startling the world through the "extravagance of their behaviour, speech, dress, and thought and in the other sense of the word, sensationalism, to live on the excitement of new experiences." Many of the characters in the trilogy also play minor roles in McKenna's previous three novels.

The first part of the trilogy, *Lady Lilith* (1920), is named after Adam's first wife in the Talmud, who is associated with the absence of death and of knowledge of good and evil in Eden prior to the Fall. A young novelist, Valentine Arden, applies the name to Lady Barbara Neave, heroine of this novel and a major character in the next two. Daughter of a viceroy of India, Barbara is a vain, heartless thrill-seeker who treats people badly yet is able to enthrall them, especially her constant critic and would-be lover, Jack Waring. Her behavior is set against the stories of six young Oxford graduates, including her cousin and David O'Rane. After rejecting Jack, Barbara appears panic-stricken, her superstitious nature affected by the realization of the harm of which she is capable. Generally well received, the novel was praised for its picture of English society before and during the war, for the ease and wit of the writing, and most especially for Barbara's spellbinding effect on the reader; however, Katherine Mansfield in *The Athenaeum* (5 November 1920) saw it as "a snob's banquet," and V. G., writing in *The Freeman* (22 December 1920), saw Barbara as "'Sonia,' only more so."

From 31 December 1920 to 19 March 1921 McKenna journeyed along the coast of South America. McKenna used the leisurely ocean travel to write fiction. The second installment of *The Sensationalists*, *The Education of Eric Lane* (1921), portrays Barbara's ensnaring and then "educating" an aspiring playwright, Eric Lane, who is also a friend of Jack Waring. Once Barbara captures Eric, however, she no longer wants him. Meanwhile, Waring returns home after being wounded during war service, and he seems to desire a reconciliation with Barbara. Comments were less favorable for this novel: reviewers found its theme jaded; however, the story, style, and characterization were praised by others.

The third volume of the trilogy, *The Secret Victory* (1921), also published in *Sovereign Magazine* (1921), was more heavily criticized for bad organization, obscure revelation of "the secret," and repetitious, exaggerated characters. Eric Lane returns to London from abroad, recovered from the machinations of Lady Barbara. He becomes involved with the pregnant Ivy Maitland and eventually is prepared to marry her to rescue her from the unscrupulous, self-centered egotist John Gaymer. John wins Ivy from Eric, whose "victory" appears to be over himself in allowing Ivy free choice and encouraging Gaymer's reform.

Also published in 1921 was McKenna's autobiography, *While I Remember*, which is more revealing of the period than of the author. He gives a better sense of himself, in fact, in the biography *Tex: A Chapter in the Life of Alexander Teixeira de Mattos* (1922), a memorial to a translator friend of six years, in which McKenna reveals that "behind the polite mask and settled air of restraint" he is "often irresponsibly outspoken, always sympathetic, warmhearted and with a very genius for friendship." This latter quality was displayed to those friends who visited him in his Lon-

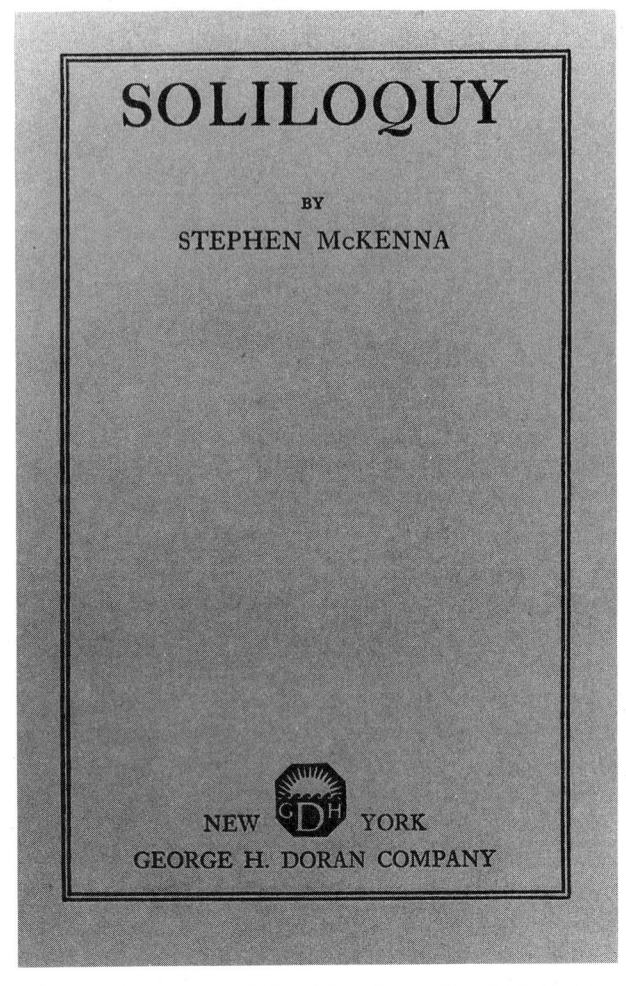

Title page for the 1923 U.S. edition of a novel in which the dying protagonist, Marion Shelby, reflects on her past wickedness

don residence at Lincoln's Inn at the end of his morning's work or at parties following the opera. At his country residence, Honeys in Berkshire, he pursued his interests in gardening, walking, and horse racing. Despite the vigor of his writing, McKenna was not a robust person, and he spent his winters traveling.

McKenna returned to England from such a trip, to the West Indies and British Guiana, in time for the appearance of *The Confessions of a Well-meaning Woman*. A monologue by Lady Ann Spenworth to a "friend of proved discretion," the story follows her intrigues as she attempts to manipulate people and circumstances to her and her son Will's benefit, not always successfully. In the telling she reveals herself as ignoble, haughty, and avaricious; yet her blind devotion to her ne'er-do-well son humanizes her. Critics were generally favorable, noting the novel's deft satire, vivacious prose, and character portrayal; dissidents complained about Lady Ann's excessive clichés and her manipulations.

Again using the first-person approach in *Soliloquy* (1922), McKenna reveals the dying thoughts of mean, sensual Marion Shelley, "the successful hostess of the last of the London salons" as she is described by the critic in *Punch* (11 October 1922), as she reflects on the malicious surroundings she has endured first while growing up on the outskirts of the scholastic communities of Oxford and Cambridge and then in literary Chelsea as a married woman. Subsequently widowed, she travels within the political circles of London, attempting the seduction of the son of the only man she had ever loved, who had nothing else to offer but himself.

Returning from another of his annual journeys in 1923, McKenna used his unpublished diary of the trip as a resource to develop a full-length travel book, *By Intervention of Providence*. That same year he published two more novels. The key to the first, *The Commandment of Moses* (1923), is the seventh injunction handed to Moses, which forbids adultery: nineteen-year-old Joan Prendergast is in love with a married officer, with whom she has had sexual relations. He is killed at Vimy Ridge, and when the guilt-ridden Joan falls in love with another man, she feels unworthy of him and worries that she must confess. Opinion was divided among the critics: some sided with *The New York Times* reviewer (1 June 1924), who called the novel a string of manufactured incidents with "tired and listless" characters, whereas others praised McKenna's insight into human nature and found Joan a charming creation. McKenna reworked the novel into a three-act unpublished play.

Vindication (1923) follows Gloria Britton, daughter of a Spanish opera singer and a penniless English rake, who seeks wealth and position to alleviate her poverty. Consequently, she must reject her true love, Norman Cartwright, the heir to Newbridge, in favor of the debauched but wealthy banker's son Freddie Kendaile. In their home, Nelby, the Kendailes become neighbors of Cartwright and his new bride; the novel follows the ensuing emotional entanglements of these two families. McKenna's analysis of the forces affecting human behavior linked him to John Galsworthy and George Eliot, according to S. C. Halbrook in *The Literary Review* (19 January 1924).

McKenna took another trip to the West Indies from 5 January to 5 March 1924, which he chronicled in another unpublished diary; on 30 January he reports that he had written fifty-two thousand words since leaving England, an average of two thousand words a day. In the islands McKenna led an active social life among the ruling British class; frequently he was the guest of an island's governor.

That year he compiled another collection of previously published short stories, *Tales of Intrigue and Re-*

venge, as well as the novel *To-morrow and To-morrow,* its title taken from a soliloquy by the weary and dispirited Macbeth near the end of Shakespeare's play. A sociological study of the period from the 1918 Armistice to the hunger strike of 1923, the novel is narrated by George Oakley, who also narrated *Sonia: Between Two Worlds. To-morrow and To-morrow* closes this cycle of novels by updating the reader on the fate of Barbara Neave, now Oakley's wife. This time she is the recipient of heartbreak, along with her husband, because of Eric Lane. The situation appears to be resolved, however, by the death of David O'Rane at the hands of strikers. Most complaints about the novel centered on the pessimistic history presented, the endless dialogue about it, and the shadowy characters; as a period study reviewers found it praiseworthy.

Only one novel appeared in 1925. *An Affair of Honour* is a light romantic comedy involving an attempt by a group of Oxford undergraduates to bolster their host's newspaper circulation by having two of their number fight a "duel" over Queen Elizabeth's character; the police suddenly arrive and take a more serious view of the event, but the paper is saved. While the pleasant, amusing narration and solid construction pleased some critics, others found it slow moving until near the end.

Pan is the focus of McKenna's second fantasy, *The Oldest God* (1926). Following World War I a wealthy American, Mrs. Reid, rents Nateby castle and invites a group of friends who had stayed there a decade before. The table talk during dinner focuses on Satan, Pan, and Christ. Six of the ten guests pledge support for Pan and sing a jocular invocation. Soon thereafter a late arrival appears bringing a guest, introduced as Mr. Strange. As narrated by Kingsbury, a diplomat, who is unmoved by Mr. Strange, the six "believers" revert to pagan behavior, eschewing the restraints of propriety. Isabel Patterson in *The Bookman* (March 1926) derided the novel as "an unhumorous, disjointed farce," and others criticized its excessive length, weak style, and lack of solid characters and story; however, D. L. Mann in *The Boston Transcript* (23 January 1926) suggested that it could turn out to be "the most challenging book of the year." Still others praised its action, theme, mingling of satire and fantasy, and construction.

Saviours of Society (1926), the first volume of a trilogy of sociopolitical novels collectively titled *The Realists.* Dominated by the self-made but selfish and ruthless Ambrose Sheridan, the novel follows his leadership of a commission investigating trade and communication within the British Empire with the goal of alleviating unemployment and "saving" England. The novel ends as he returns to confront both political and personal crises, embodied in Lord Orpington, the resigning secretary of state, and in Auriol Otway, an independent, intelligent, and idealistic young woman to whom Sheridan had proposed marriage following his divorce from Laura, his wife of twenty years. Finally, in a dramatic display of self-denial Laura affirms Sheridan's assertion that he will sacrifice his career and future if Auriol will not marry him. The portrayal of the female characters was praised by Stephen Graham in *The Saturday Review of Literature* (27 November 1926), who claimed however that "Only the politicians in the book are a little unconvincing."

The sequel to *Saviours of Society, The Secretary of State* (1927) follows the next stage of Sheridan's political career as he faces the entrenched conservative powers led by Sir John Ferrers. In his personal life Auriol, now his wife, still worships him, but she realizes that she never loved him, a situation complicated by the return from South America of a rejected suitor, Max Hendry, as well as by Auriol's discovery of two facts that would have forestalled her marriage. As Sheridan's star wanes, former wife Laura prepares to assist him, as do Auriol and Max, all willing to sacrifice their own happiness to further Sheridan's career.

In *Due Reckoning* (1927), the final part of *The Realists,* Auriol's adoration dissipates when she learns the whole truth about the defeated Sheridan. Her desire to pursue love with Max is balanced by the comfort provided by Laura for Sheridan. The reviewer in *The Times* (London; 14 July 1927) continued that paper's condemnation of all three books for being "false in [their] main conceptions, whether of character or of English political life." Louis Kronenberger in *The Saturday Review of Literature* (6 August 1927), however, praised the "strongly individualized" characters of Max and Ambrose in the second book.

The Unburied Dead (1928), published in the United States as *Divided Allegiance,* is narrated by a British-educated American, Arthur Western, whose allegiances are indeed divided by his dual heritage. The British title, according to McKenna's preface to the novel, refers to those opposed to "the changing economic order." Arthur tells of his school friends, their families, and particularly his loves: the clever social climber Doris, whom Arthur worships despite her societal transgressions; and the passive Anita, whose father, Lord Ashdown, embodies the disintegrating aristocracy. Eventually Anita frees herself from a detestable forced marriage to unite with Arthur. While praised for its natural dialogue and attractive hero, the novel was condemned by the critic for *The Saturday Review of Literature* (3 November 1928) for its conventional plot, "dead characters," and pompous theme.

Published in the same year, *The Shadow of Guy Denver* fared better at the hands of the critics, who lauded its original conception, artistic construction, and especially the revelation of the heroine's character and the development of Guy Denver, who is absent for most of the novel yet provides its motivating force. Denver is away in the colonies as his wife, Cressida, and London barrister Clifford Ottley collaborate on writing a play that charts their own love. As Cressida's less admirable qualities are revealed, Guy grows in stature, so that when he returns suddenly to London, Clifford discovers a long-sought friend.

In 1929 McKenna published two novels, *The Datchley Inheritance* and *Happy Ending* (published in the United States as *Between the Lines*). The first recounts the efforts of each of the nine Datchley grandchildren to win grandfather John's four-million-pound inheritance by being the first to marry, and the consequences for the winner. The American title of the second novel reflects the attitudes of the smart set, whose reluctance to tell the truth is due to their fear of appearing unfashionable. Beautiful, thirty-five-year-old Lola Morchard is married to Sir Harrison Morchard, a much older man with different predilections. She embarks on a six-month liaison with one of her set, Piers Shotton. The happy ending sees Piers marrying another woman, June Campion.

Neither novel was favorably reviewed. The critic for *The New Statesman and Nation* (23 February 1929) found that *The Datchley Inheritance* had too long a story, "painfully strained morality," and a shaky framework holding the separate stories together while W. E. H. in *The Boston Transcript* (25 September 1929) found *Between the Lines* "very cynical and distasteful," with an unconvincing plot.

In early 1930 McKenna's yearly travels took him to the south of France; later in the year he published two more novels to mixed reviews. *The Redemption of Morley Darville*, a comedy, appeared less interesting compared to McKenna's serious books but was complimented on its "background and incidentals," as well as its subtle irony, by the critic for *Books* (26 October 1930). W. R. Brooks in *Outlook* (7 January 1931) considered *The Cast-iron Duke* "readable and entertaining" because of its character study of the titular duke and its "extraordinary number of picturesque observances . . . maintained by great English families. . . ."

In the first novel Morley Darville, a bitter young intellectual and the author of solid but not popular books, scorns his more successful fellow writers; his "redemption" occurs when Allerdyce, one such writer, befriends him, and in the process Morley meets and falls in love with the aristocratic Penelope, who envies Morley's lifestyle, which ironically becomes like Allerdyce's. In *The Cast-iron Duke* the Welsh duke of Leonminster functions as a feudal autocrat whose dominance is heightened by the puppetlike tutor Camelford; his rule is finally successfully challenged by his willful and clever granddaughter, Moyra.

In 1931 McKenna published the unsuccessful sociological novel *Dermotts Rampant* and the more successful *Beyond Hell*, his third fantasy. The title of the first derives from the heraldic term for the beast standing on its hind legs, waiting to spring; here it describes metaphorically the Irish immigrant Dermotts, originally forced to relocate by the 1840s famine. Their loves, political careers, and social involvement are portrayed against the consequences of Victorian industrialism and decaying aristocracy in the period from the Boer War to 1921. Its theme, as enunciated by the critic for *The New Statesman and Nation*, shows that "the innovator of one generation becomes the conservative of the next." Critics found *Dermotts Rampant* lacking in action, its characters unreal, and its family history vague, but it was praised in *The New York Times* (9 August 1931) for its "fine writing" and in the 12 March 1931 edition of *The Times* for its "vigorous and amusing conception."

Beyond Hell looks ahead to the establishment of an international penal colony on Sunday Island in 1940 following the abolition of capital punishment. While assessing this experiment, the narrator, Professor Hedley Dixon, witnesses an uprising of prisoners against Loftus Hale, the idealistic sociologist and tyrant in charge of this radical attempt at human reclamation. Commingled with these events is a renewed love affair between Dixon's adoptive daughter and secretary, Clare Frensham, and a convicted murderer, Dr. Anthony Druid; and a religious conversion attempted by a "freelance" Jesuit fanatic, Father Milligan. While some critics found the mixture unconvincing, the reviewer for *The New York Times* (12 March 1931) claimed that it was done "smoothly enough and cleverly enough to make an interesting and for the most part convincing narrative."

In 1932 McKenna published a collection of short fiction, *Pandora's Box, and Other Stories,* and two novels, *The Way of the Phoenix* and his fourth fantasy, *Superstition. The Way of the Phoenix* is a sequel to *Dermotts Rampant,* following the Dermott family to 1931 and focusing primarily on the rekindled love affair between Tony Dermott and Lady Rhoda Fletcher. McKenna was praised for his portrayal of postwar disintegration, his characterization (which was compared favorably with the portrayals found in Galsworthy's Forsyte Saga), and his creation of suspense, but he was condemned for the tractlike nature of the novel, its subordinated romance, and for his coldness and detachment. Some critics detected a similar remoteness in the narrator of *Superstition,* Dr. Cameron, and were also concerned about the novel's length; but its story was hailed as "ingeniously dramatic and tantalizing conclusive" and its theme well conceived by Lisle Bell in *Books* (5 March 1933). The novel revolves around a curse placed on Harry Chiseldon by a dying, jilted lover which causes Harry to fear for the safety of anyone he loves, including Dr. Cameron's daughter; as she nears death from a mysterious disease, she suddenly and inexplicably recovers.

After 1933 most of McKenna's novels were published only in England and given only brief reviews there. Both of the novels published in 1933 involve artists: the hero of *Magic Quest,* a middle-aged London painter, is torn between the attentions of attractive young Roberta, who literally crashes into his life, and his predatory family. The protagonist worries that he is too old for Roberta, and she worries about her effect on his work. The family exploits these doubts to try and drive a wedge between them. Ultimately the couple finds happiness together. *Namesakes* follows the daily routine of popular novelist Willoughby Gaveston through the eyes of his young, somewhat neglected wife, Angela, who starts to notice a certain duplicity in her husband. The ensuing marital problems and Willoughby's personal fall are both resolved. While the critic for *Punch* (25 October 1933) found Willoughby "a brilliant study of a certain type of writer," Angela was seen as "a bundle of qualities."

Each of McKenna's 1934 novels focuses on the examination of a person's past: *The Undiscovered Country* includes the preoperative, anesthetic-induced reflections of Marcia, "wife of the fifth Earl of Bedlington": on her possible obituary; on her Victorian upbringing; on her marriage of convenience, as well as those of her three sisters; and on a liaison with her first love. Her unhappy past prompts her to allow her own children freedom of choice in marriage; when her children's unions also fail, she attempts unsuccessfully to intervene. While Marcia is an unpleasant person, the reviewer for *Punch* (11 April 1934) averred that "when she recovers consciousness, one wants to know more about her and everybody else in the book, and that is a good enough test for a story." In *Portrait of His Excellency* Leslie Vivian reflects on the real man behind the title and position of his late friend, Richard Croyle, third Viscount and first Earl Alster, governor-general of Australia. The analysis of the complex life of this soldier, politician, and public servant reveals an unstained and interesting character handled skillfully by McKenna.

McKenna's single novel of 1935, *Sole Death,* refers in its title to that circumstance of fate "when a man's loss comes to him from his gain." Set in the England of the late 1940s, the story focuses on Ida, the second wife of the lusty George, Duke of Luton, who is eyeing another woman, Bettina, to add to the twenty mistresses he has had. Motivated by love, pity for George's fading prowess, and a desire to preserve his respectability, Ida tries to keep George by providing him with an heir. She seduces their friend Colin for the purpose, a stratagem that works until George discredits himself with Bettina and Ida realizes that she had been infatuated with George but really loves Colin. The story and social setting were both praised, but the *Punch* critic claimed that "essential values are a little smudged and the lovers rather too slight and fickle to trouble the heart of the reader very deeply" (13 February 1935).

The first of two long novels published in 1936, *While of Sound Mind* is narrated by a friend who rediscovers diplomat and dilettante Mark Finchley after he has left his previous life, including a marriage, to be "reborn" as Alan Steel, social reformer and prime mover in the women's peace movement. The novel was commended as thought provoking but criticized for its lack of vitality, the result of having a phlegmatic businessman for a narrator, and for the "amoral" ending, in the judgment of the *Punch* reviewer (11 March 1936), "a pretence marriage as the background for such a Peace crusade."

The second novel, *Lady Cynthia Clandon's Husband,* describes the dilemma of Cynthia, the attractive but penniless daughter of the late Lord Ormesby, who rejects her expected suitor, "Blinker," for her lover Martin Brede, only to realize his worthlessness. Next, wealthy but common Michael Weyburn earns her love, but he nearly loses his wealth; Cynthia's character is redeemed in that she stays with Weyburn throughout this period of hardship. The critic for *The Times* (10 October 1936) commended the characters, introduced "not for their own sakes, but to serve the purpose of Lady Cynthia's education in the meaning of life."

Both of McKenna's novels of 1937 deal with forms of marital infidelity. In *Last Confession* nineteen-year-old Camilla Coniston, the naive daughter of a clergyman, is pregnant from an affair with the unhappily married Basil, Lord Mountjoy, her chief at BH2, a branch of wartime British intelligence. Mountjoy is suddenly killed in France; luckily for Camilla, a quick wartime marriage to another suitor, journalist Gerald Fawskey, and the birth of a daughter seven months later during a zeppelin raid allow her to keep her secret. Dramatic tension in the novel results from Camilla's

Frontispiece and title page for a biography of McKenna's uncle, a member of Parliament, First Lord of the Admiralty, Home Secretary, Chancellor of the Exchequer, and banker

fear of divine retribution, and McKenna was commended by a reviewer in *The Times* (London; 5 June 1937) for his ability "to keep the reader's attention until a satisfying conclusion is reached," as the title suggests.

Infidelity is more complex in *The Home That Jill Broke*. Jill's mother, Delia, has commissioned her brother Jack to investigate Jill's apparent ten-day Paris holiday with married Curtis McLane. Jill's excuse for her dalliance is a lost passport, and she offers as partial justification that her husband, Ronnie, traveled to South America to sell horses with their owner, Mrs. Lancett. At stake is the appointment of Jill's father as ambassador to the United States. In deciding how best to approach the scandal, Jack considers factors such as the mixture within Jill of Delia's family's Birmingham blood and the aristocratic Grafton-Elyot blood of her husband, Delia's early neglect of her children, and Ronnie's love for Delia until he has finally "worried the plot to conclusion," in the estimation of the critic for *The Times* (London; 11 November 1937).

Drawing its title from the mythical Amazons who burned off their right breasts to facilitate the use of the bow, *Breasted Amazon* (1938) depicts the adventures of a promiscuous twenty-six-year-old novelist, Lorna Galloway, who uses her personal amorous experiences as the basis for the popular exploits of her heroine, Rosemary Deacon. In gathering material for her fifth novel, which promises to be her greatest success yet, Lorna has an affair with the equally lusty forty-six-year-old Sir Miles Carrington. The book remains unpublished, as the reviewer for *The Times* (London; 15 October 1938) assesses, because "the Amazon Lorna, having omitted the traditional mutilation, . . . [finds] that for her the discord of love and art could not be resolved without sacrificing one for the other."

At the outbreak of World War II, McKenna, then fifty-one years old, reentered government service as secretary of the Enemy Exports Committee, Ministry of Economic Warfare, a post he occupied until 1940. He also published *A Life for a Life* (1939), a fictional account of the twenty-three-year life of Sandy Loring, Scottish marquis and earl of Great Britain from infancy because of his birth just prior to the death of his titled father in World War I. His mother's death after the Armistice leaves Sandy with his sagacious uncle George Oakleigh for a guardian, who educates him in the best schools along with his adopted brother, the son of a Scottish farmer. Both sons become communists while at Melton, a conservative school, although Sandy is more lover than revolutionary. The novel reflects on the enigmatic nature of life and the defects of the education received by Sandy's generation between the two wars. The reviewer for *The Times* (London; 7 October 1939) judged that *A Life for a Life* "ranks very high in the long list of Mr. McKenna's novels."

Four years passed before McKenna's next novel, *Mean Sensual Man* (1943), appeared. Accused by the reviewer for *The Times Literary Supplement* (14 August 1943) of being "long, loosely knit and rather hurried," filled with "light and undemanding talk" and barren political discussions, the novel depicts a powerful, influential, and wealthy editor, "Lucky" Jim Lydford, whose life is unfulfilled, especially after the departure of his married lover, Vivienne Rainham. A younger lover, Edna, provides him with a child early in the war but disappears during the Blitz. Vivienne returns to Jim following the devastation of her family's steelworks. *Mean Sensual Man* was the last work McKenna published until a biography of his uncle Reginald McKenna appeared in 1948. Five additional novels were published between 1949 and 1957, but none of them were reviewed by any of the leading papers.

McKenna's last novel, *A Place in the Sun* (1962), received a brief review in *The Times* (London; 16 February 1962) describing the plot as "leisurely" and reflective of the "older ways of fiction" in its "neat and studied contrivances." The story describes the callous attempts of a capable and charming woman, having failed in marriage and a liaison to find wealth and happiness as the aide of a wealthy elderly bachelor. At first the bachelor's unselfishness and gallantry, combined with his hidden literary achievements, seem to affect positively the woman's outlook. Unfortunately her past reasserts itself, destroying this happiness and forcing her into a new direction.

McKenna was working on the rest of his autobiography at the time of his death on 26 September 1967. In its announcement of his death *The Times* (London; 27 September 1967) declared that the "aura of aristocracy and high politics that surrounds . . . [his novels] . . . may seem a little faded at the present day, but for readers of his own generation it shone attractively enough." McKenna's readers regarded him as a master storyteller and valued his clever characters (especially his young women), competent plots, and witty dialogue. For present-day readers the novels seem to lack depth, possibly because of the shallowness of the lives portrayed, and the dialogue contained within seems stiff and affected. Although the milieu of Oxford, Mayfair, Westminster, and country houses in which most of the novels are set is totally unconnected to the experiences of most contemporary readers, for that same reason the novels should be valued for the insights into the social and political history of a different culture.

References:

Almay St. John Adcock, *Gods of Modern Grub Street* (London: Sampson Low, Marston, 1923), pp. 173–179;

S. P. B. Mais, *Books and Their Writers* (London: Grant Richards, 1920), pp. 45–50;

Grant Overton, *Authors of the Day: Studies in Contemporary Literature* (New York: Doran, 1924), pp. 380–390.

Papers:

A miscellaneous collection of Stephen McKenna's papers can be found in the archives of the Scott Library, York University, Ontario. The collection includes eleven individually bound and titled diaries typed by McKenna during his winter holidays between 1921 and 1934; typed copies of four plays written prior to 1929, all dated 19 March 1929 and signed by McKenna; a photo album; "Newspaper Cuttings," a book containing articles and short stories by McKenna from the 1920s; and a collection of pages, with illustrations, from periodicals in which six novels were published between 1919 and 1928.

C. E. Montague
(1 January 1867 - 28 May 1928)

Eric Thompson
Université du Québec à Chicoutimi

BOOKS: *A Hind Let Loose* (London: Methuen, 1910; Garden City, N.Y.: Doubleday, Page, 1924);

The Literary Play, Essays and Studies series, no. 2 (Oxford: English Association, 1910);

Dramatic Values (London: Methuen, 1911; New York: Macmillan, 1911); revised edition, London: Methuen, 1925; Garden City, N.Y.: Doubleday, Page, 1925);

The Morning's War (London: Methuen, 1913; New York: Holt, 1913);

Disenchantment (London: Chatto & Windus, 1922; New York: Brentano's, 1922);

Fiery Particles (London: Chatto & Windus, 1923; Garden City, N.Y.: Doubleday, Page, 1923);

The Right Place: A Book of Pleasures (London: Chatto & Windus, 1924; Garden City, N.Y.: Doubleday, Page, 1924);

Rough Justice: A Novel (London: Chatto & Windus, 1926; Garden City, N.Y.: Doubleday, Page, 1926);

Right Off the Map: A Novel (London: Chatto & Windus, 1927; Garden City, N.Y.: Doubleday, Page, 1927);

Action, and Other Stories (London: Chatto & Windus, 1928; Garden City, N.Y.: Doubleday, Doran, 1929);

A Writer's Notes on His Trade (London: Chatto & Windus, 1930; Garden City, N.Y.: Doubleday, Doran, 1930).

OTHER: *The Manchester Stage, 1880-1900,* essays by Montague, W. T. Arnold, Oliver Elton, and A. N. Monkhouse (Westminster: Constable, 1900);

W. T. Arnold, *Studies of Roman Imperialism,* edited by Edward Fiddes, with a memoir of Arnold by Montague and M. A. Ward, Historical Series, no. 4 (Manchester: Manchester University Press, 1906); memoir republished as *William Thomas Arnold, Journalist and Historian* (Manchester: Manchester University Press, 1907);

The Western Front, volume 2, text by Montague, drawings by Muirhead Bone (London: Published by authority of the War Office from the offices of *Country Life,* 1917); republished as *The Front Line* (New York: Hodder & Stoughton, 1917);

British Artists at the Front, 4 volumes, introductions by Montague, Campbell Dodgson, Robert Ross, and John Salis (London: Published from the offices of *Country Life* and George Newnes, 1918);

Notes from Calais Base, and Pictures of its Many Activities (London: Unwin, 1918);

Essays of Today and Yesterday (London: Harrap, 1926);

"Inexpert Approaches to Religion," in *C. E. Montague: A Memoir* by Oliver Elton (London: Chatto & Windus, 1929), pp. 291-319.

C. E. Montague

C. E. Montague is remembered not as a novelist but as a celebrated member of the staff of *The Manchester Guardian* before World War I. David Ayerst wrote that Montague was "first in the estimation of his colleagues and first in the glamour that his reputation with young men and women brought the paper throughout the first half of this century." Indeed, the reputation of *The Manchester Guardian* as a major exponent of liberal-left political opinion owed much to the views of its distinguished "leader-writer" (editorialist). But Montague also enjoyed a moderately successful career as a novelist, essayist, and short-story writer during his lifetime and deserves to be remembered as a minor writer who made some significant contributions to the literature of World War I.

Born at Ealing on 1 January 1867, Charles Edward Montague was one of four sons of Francis Montague and Rosa McCabe Montague, both of Irish extraction. He grew up in a close-knit family at Twickenham, near the Thames, and began his education at the City of London School. In 1885 he won a scholarship to Oxford, where he proved to be a decent, if not outstanding, student of the great Benjamin Jowett in classics. Always athletic, he played rugby and rowed for his college eights' team. His prowess as a swimmer was shown when he rescued a student from drowning, for which he won the bronze medal of the Royal Humane Society in 1889. The next year, after his graduation from Oxford, he began his thirty-five-year career with *The Manchester Guardian*. Montague's attachment to the newspaper was cemented by close relationships with two of its distinguished editors, W. T. Arnold and C. P. Scott. In 1898 he married Scott's daughter Madeline, and together they raised seven children.

The Manchester Guardian, as one of the staunchest supporters of Liberalism in England, opposed many Conservative government policies of the 1890s and early 1900s. Montague was kept busy formulating and articulating the paper's views on political issues ranging from the Boer War, to Irish Home Rule, to voting rights for women. However, he was not a strong partisan of party politics, preferring to indulge his literary and theatrical interests as a reviewer and promoter of the Manchester arts community. During these years he also became adept at mountaineering, bicycling, and cartography.

All of these interests are revealed in his books. His first nonperiodical publication was in 1900, when some of his essays were included in *The Manchester Stage, 1880–1900,* a collection of articles previously published in *The Manchester Guardian*. He also contributed to a memoir of his mentor, W. T. Arnold. Next came his study *The Literary Play* (1910) and his collection of newspaper theater criticism, *Dramatic Values* (1911). What these works reveal most strongly is Montague's love of William Shakespeare, a packed writing style (dense, trenchant, literary, and highly allusive), and a sly wit. He thereby well exemplified the scholar-journalist tradition of his newspaper in these writings.

A new phase in Montague's life began with the appearance of his first novel in 1910. *A Hind Let Loose* is a comic tale that displays something of the parodic comedy of William Makepeace Thackeray and the sophisticated touch of George Meredith. Although noticed, it did not sell particularly well and was dismissed facetiously by Arnold Bennett as not a book for the "intelligent masses" but rather one for the "secretly-arrogant few." Montague himself was already chagrined by what he had wrought. In a letter to his friend and colleague Allan Monkhouse he said the book was "only a sort of overgrown skit, or narrative farce, about various kinds of rotten journalism." In fact, as this statement suggests, the novel had started out as a play in 1900 for an amateur production. Perhaps Montague was embarrassed by the novel because the plot cut too close to the bone as a caricature of the *Guardian* staff. One character, the naive journalist Dick, is certainly a reflection on the younger Montague's self-conscious prose style:

> But Dick had fads. One was for a kind of writing; not the right kind; not saying what he had to say, and that's an end of it, but a plaguy, itchy fussing over some phrase, planing it down or bevelling it off, inlaying it with picked words of queer far-fetched aptness, making it clang with whole pomps of proper names, that boomed into their places, like drums and cymbals in symphonies, or twinkle and tingle, shot with ironies, or rise and fall like a voice that means more by the tune than the words. . . .

The "Hind" of the title is Fay, a well-drawn portrait of a clever and devious journalist, whose secretive editorial-writing scam for two rival newspapers creates havoc in the community. Montague's gibe at the press was good-humored if mordant satire, but the book is not easy reading because of its compact style.

Three years later he published his second novel, *The Morning's War* (1913). Once again Montague drew on personal, and family, experience. Set in Switzerland and Ireland, the story concerns two lovers whose relationship is upset by the discovery of the apostasy of the man's father, who in order to marry broke with his Catholic faith and training for the priesthood. The hero feels unworthy of his fiancée, but eventually her love helps him overcome these feelings. Montague wrote to his friend Oliver

Editors and staff of The Manchester Guardian *in 1921: Montague is in the back row, second from left. On his right is E. T. Scott; on his left are J. J. O'Neill, W. P. Crozier, and J. Bone. Seated, from left, are J. R. Scott, C. P. Scott (Montague's father-in-law), and L. T. Hobhouse.*

Elton, explaining his theme: "My line is . . . to show that with a particular couple of decent moderns it [the Church of Rome] and its powers come to precious little when up against a natural affection." The fictional father's experience may parallel that of Montague's father. The theme of the power of human love is also stated for the first time in his fiction, and it owes a great deal to the warmth of his own homelife. Finally, Montague's knowledge of alpine climbing is used effectively in the plot and setting. But the novel's content did not interest one critic, Dixon Scott, who directed his remarks instead at the book's style. Calling it a "literary novel," he referred to its rhythmic qualities in which "a dancing of dactyls, and tripping of trochees, and ruthless absence of iambs" were distinguishing characteristics of, to him, meticulously planned sentences. It is a useful reminder that Montague's formal education coincided with the heyday of the Aesthetic Movement. Along with his devotion to correct grammar and semantics, his concern for the subtleties of sound and movement in writing is one of the reasons why Frank Swinnerton, his Georgian contemporary, spoke of him as "a brilliant writer rather than a creative writer."

The outbreak of World War I was probably the key moment in Montague's life. Hitherto he had led a fairly placid existence; now he chose to enlist as a private soldier. Certainly he was patriotic, but he was hardly under any illusions about the origins of the war or the hardship he was placing on his family. Still, he took a leave of absence from the *Guardian,* dyed his prematurely white hair, lied about his age (he was forty-seven), and joined up. He was later to write in *The Western Front* (1917) that war was something most men would feel "first to be avoided by every honourable means and then to be won by every honourable means." During training Montague suffered severe facial burns in a bomb-throwing exercise on the Salisbury Plain, and this injury delayed his posting to the front. He finally arrived there in November 1915 but a few months later was hospitalized again for trench fever and sent home.

If Montague's initial experience of soldiering was brief, he still had time to absorb the conditions of frontline life. He kept a diary and wrote numerous letters to his wife, brother, and friends. In one letter he describes the "universal, ubiquitous muckiness of the whole front" and the omnipresence of rats, comments verified in dozens of similar letters by others. His respite in England must have been blissful, but his furlough from the war was short-lived. Commissioned a second lieutenant in the Intelligence Branch, he returned to France and new war duties in the winter of 1917. Among these were the production of a semihistorical account of the war from the British perspective. Beginning in December 1916 and continuing in ten monthly parts during 1917, he wrote descriptions of frontline places and events for *Country Life* magazine, the whole enterprise being under the authority and sponsorship of the War Office. This project was followed by a book, *The Western Front,* for which Montague wrote introductions to drawings by the war artist, Muirhead Bone. He wrote similar commentaries on reproductions of paintings by other war artists—C. R. W. Nevinson, Paul Nash, Sir John Lavery, and Eric Kennington—for a successor volume, *British Artists at the Front* (1918). In 1918 Montague wrote the text for another War Office publication, *Notes from Calais Base, and Pictures of its Many Activities* describing British army activities at one of its main English Channel ports.

Another of his duties in this period was to act as a "conducting officer," a euphemism for the person responsible for shepherding visiting generals and famous guests around the lines. Among his regular "guests" were the five officially designated war correspondents (or their replacements) who reported the war for the British and Empire press. This activity led to his appointment as assistant press censor at the front, a position for which he was ideally suited by experience and temperament. He appears to have been trusted and admired by the reporters with whom he worked. Montague tried to maintain a high level of professionalism while serving in a job that was often attacked later as merely that of a propagandist.

His friend Oliver Elton later said that Montague exhibited great dignity despite trying circumstances at this time. Always a reserved personality, the war sobered him further and made him more introspective. But witnesses described how excited he became during bombardments and told of their alarm when he took risks to get nearer to the action. For his work during the latter years of the war Montague was thrice mentioned in dispatches for gallantry and devotion to duty, and he received the Order of the British Empire after the war. All the while, it seems, he was silently nurturing the moods that dominate his postwar publications.

Perhaps his most important book is *Disenchantment* (1922), published when the restraints of wartime censorship had lifted. That year was to prove legendary in the history of literary modernism as T. S. Eliot's poem *The Waste Land* and James Joyce's novel *Ulysses* were both published. Montague's nonfictional, iconoclastic memoir of war is not out of place in that company. It explores several themes—life in the Regular army, satire of the general headquarters of the British army under Douglas Haig, vices of the public-school system (which sometimes allowed incompetent graduates to acquire commissions), the nature of English class feeling, and the realities of various offensive and defensive operations. Not all of these are governed by the same mood. Montague can be scathing in denunciation or bitter and resentful. The general tone is prosecutorial and seldom lighthearted; Montague writes for his own and for a younger generation of private soldiers, for whom a slow disillusionment smoldered throughout the war and after.

Much of the "disenchantment" of the title comes from the feeling that smarter political and military leadership could have ended the war sooner. Always Montague's sympathies are with the plight of the ordinary soldier, echoing the example of Henri Barbusse's *Le Feu* (1916), perhaps the most influential of the literary responses to World War I. Of course the irony that a former army censor should describe scenes and situations he had once sought to suppress from the letters of soldiers and reporters is abundantly clear. Still, whether in his private or in his official writing capacity, in peace or in war, there is no evidence that Montague tried to disguise the truth of his own feelings about the conflict.

Disenchantment was given generally favorable reviews because of its authoritative quality. But its renown was soon drowned in a flood of argumentative books by politicians and generals seeking to justify their actions. The zenith of war-book publication was reached in 1929 when a spate of brilliant novels and memoirs appeared which were, unanswerably, antiwar in tone.

Montague's contribution to the literature of World War I also includes two volumes of short stories and two novels, all published in the 1920s. Together they reveal how he was haunted by the war. *Fiery Particles* (1923), for instance, comprises nine stories, all of which concern the European war or the Irish Civil War concurrent with it. Two of these,

Title page for the first American edition of the author's 1922 memoir of World War I

"Honours Easy" and "My Friend the Swan," relate to Colin March, a character who shows up again in Montague's novel *Rough Justice* (1926). Colin, an Oxford graduate, uses his brains and connections to avoid the hardships of trench warfare while accumulating a chest full of medals for his light duties at the front. In many of the stories Montague skillfully depicts the dialects of soldiers from London and Lancaster for comic and realistic effects. One critic, Alfred C. Ward, regarded the author as among the best of contemporary short-story writers and devoted a chapter to him in a 1924 study. In 1928 Montague published a second collection, *Action, and Other Stories*. Of the thirteen pieces nine concern the war. The title work tells of how a former soldier saves the lives of two climbers while vacationing in Switzerland and rediscovers his own desire to live.

Montague was seriously ill with influenza in the winter of 1924. Since returning to *The Manchester Guardian* after his army discharge he had taken up his old duties on the paper, but he was not appointed editor when his father-in-law retired. Montague accepted this decision gracefully but decided to resign in 1925. He then bought a home at Burford, near Oxford in the Cotswolds, where he lived for the remainder of his life. He was well remembered in Manchester, however, and the University of Manchester awarded him an honorary Doctor of Letters in November 1926.

Montague's most important novel, *Rough Justice*, was published in that year as well. A family story, it is similar to John Galsworthy's Forsyte Saga trilogy (1906–1921) as a portrait of the prewar and wartime generations. The novel opens with the focus on Thomas Garth, a descendent of an old Catholic family and a junior member of the Conservative government of 1903. His son, Auberon, grows up with Molly, Thomas's ward in a Thames-side country home in Surrey, not far from London. A third youngster, Victor Nevin, is slightly older than these two and is their hero and mentor. These children are explicitly portrayed, in Elton's words, as "*patterns* of the breed that is to save old England." They are joined, too, by working men of London and Lancashire—destined to become rankers in the British army during the war—as "our strength and our hope . . . England's artesian wells of vitality [reaching] down to inexhaustible central waters of eagerness and will to live." For his part Garth is a troubled member of the Edwardian ruling class, which is unprepared for the demands of modern life; but at least he has a conscience and the will to adapt, unlike some of his contemporaries. A widower, he does his best to make Auberon and Molly worthy of their heritage, in contrast to the March family, who cynically exploit democracy for their own purposes.

The story begins to focus on the younger generation when Auberon follows Victor to Oxford while Molly pursues her studies at Cambridge. Victor is the stylish young hero of his generation while Auberon remains a dull conformist to the dismay of his father. Montague's chapters on Oxford undergraduate life are among the best of their kind in English fiction, foreshadowing those in Evelyn Waugh's *Brideshead Revisited* (1945). Yet soon the idyll is over; by late summer of 1914 the certainty of war faces England. On the last afternoon of peace, shades of its glorious past are felt in Montague's lovely description:

> The old England, too, the one that was still feudal at heart, had come to her death-bed at last. Only six or seven hours now and all her ancient belfries, from Winchester up to Durham and Carlisle, would be tolling their twelve strokes apiece for her passing. She died hard, the glorious old jade. A little wicked in her time, and now wizened, she lay handsome to-night, with the

C. E. Montague (portrait in the Collection of Andrew Montague)

fine bones showing well through the skin that was turning to wax. At any rate for what was left of that lustrous Tuesday in August, people would stay in the classes to which it had pleased God or some other authority to call them; cows would stand still to be milked; ale would be good at twopence a glass; and all the young men whom you liked would remain alive, with two arms to them each, and two legs, to employ in such tranquil pursuits as lawn-tennis in sunny gardens over the shining waters of the Thames, if it were their blest portion–or else to stretch them on hot turf among roses, as Victor and Auberon did at this moment, utterly at peace, as it still seemed, with all men and the gods, in spite of the current talk about war.

Victor, newly married to Molly, decides to enlist immediately, but Auberon delays, trying to resolve in his conscience the choice between a priestly vocation and serving his country as a soldier. Montague's own view can be heard in the thoughts of Thomas Garth as he reflects on what the conflict will be like: "Our jolly little sporting wars were over. This would be scientific killing, on the grand scale–a herding of millions of the young of Europe into model abattoirs, like the pigs at the Chicago factories."

His decision made, Auberon relishes his training as a soldier. In "rude health," he thrives on route marches and living outdoors, but when his unit is shipped to the front, he must adjust to a harsher existence. Yet for the imaginative Victor, modern war is immensely disappointing:

> This sordid, brutalising life was no honest substitute for that glamorous life of the thrilled imagination, the passionate heart and the unjaded body–the true life of war, the real historic thing, known and attested by all generations, the splendour and gloom of old battles in the Peninsula and of Marlborough's Low Country campaigns and of the fatal night falling on thronged and surrounded Sedan. In these stinking cellars and out on these blasted heaths there was only the letter of glorious war without its spirit, only the dry bones of gallant enterprise, not its breath and complexion.

Thus far *Rough Justice* is a readable chronicle of the opening year of the war, but now the plot becomes melodramatic. Victor, at first apparently dead or missing in action after a bombardment, is eventually found, convicted of desertion, and executed by firing squad. Years later Molly finally learns about her husband's cowardice and is reunited with the stolid, but honorable, Auberon as the story ends. In a kind of coda a friend of the family says of the Garths:

> "They're England, really, these Garths," says Wynnant. "The few that there are of this sort, with no wit to speak

of, and no measly fears or desires—loving like spaniels and taking their coats everlastingly off to the first thing that has to be done—it's only they that keep on putting off from day to day the crumbling away of the whole British outfit. They've won the war and scored nothing by it but losses, and now they'll just get down to work, same as ever, next job to hand, and go on preserving us gratis."

Rough Justice was well received by the critics. A few reviews were critical of its didacticism, but most praised its perceptive account of the effect of war on certain types of Englishmen. Montague's highly emblematic use of character to serve his patriotic theme in the novel contrasts with the negativism of *Disenchantment*. In the earlier nonfictional book he was ridding himself of years of pent-up bitterness about the war, whereas in *Rough Justice* he was using fiction to explore the complexity of war and discovering a positive value to all the pain he and his country had endured. In Montague's eyes it is the humble people who triumph in war, and it is they who will build a greater democracy in peacetime—despite the greed of shirkers and profiteers.

Yet this idealism is not echoed in his final novel, *Right Off the Map* (1927), an allegory about a short, inglorious war between two wholly fictitious countries, Ria and Porto—the former dominated by a British-style oligarchy, the latter being Germanic in its leadership. Apparently Montague had not yet rid himself of his bitterness over the war. In the novel Burnage, the chief Rian journalist, finds it all too easy to use his rhetoric to start a war with Porto, but soon the poor state of equipment supplied by the bootmaker, Bute, and the lack of a solid strategic plan lead the country to disaster when the Portan army turns a counterattack into total victory. The mercenary, Major Willan, who might have averted the reverse becomes the scapegoat. Throughout the story Montague casts satiric jabs at irresponsible journalism, such as: "Great, after all, is the power of the Press, if not for men's good, at least for their enfeeblement." On the whole the novel received good reviews, but it was not regarded as major fiction.

According to Elton, Montague had begun work on a new novel early in 1928 which was "to cover some twenty years before the Great War," but the work was never finished. During the last decade of his life he occasionally wrote essays on a variety of subjects, and these were collected in *The Right Place: A Book of Pleasures* (1924) and in the posthumously published *A Writer's Notes on His Trade* (1930). The first of these Montague regarded as "the happiest of my books" and represents him in a serene mood as he writes about his travels in England and on the Continent. He observes that a telescope, compass, and map are valuable as they "combine to extend your power of apprehending what you see," thereby helping you to appreciate nature's contours and details, and leaving your mind "fresher and more full of spring." He describes his hiking trips in different countries, always conscious of the history and geography of the lands he explores. His fondest moments come as he writes of the byways of England while arguing that citified Englishmen may be cleansed in mind and body as they explore the rural world. The second of these volumes includes occasional pieces on aspects of writing, such as the nature of the English language and the use of dialect in writing, which shed light on Montague's own lifelong practice of his "trade."

Montague died of pneumonia 28 May 1928, after contracting a chill while visiting Manchester. His novels were greeted with respect in his lifetime, but they were quickly forgotten after his death. He should be remembered as an earnest stylist who wrote with integrity about subjects he knew well: the newspaper game, the war in the trenches, and sports such as hiking and climbing. On the whole *Disenchantment* stands as his best memorial, for it is one of the most honest assessments of World War I from a soldier's point of view.

Bibliography:
Fred B. Millet, ed., *Contemporary British Literature: A Critical Survey and 232 Author Bibliographies*, revised edition (New York: Harcourt, Brace, 1935), pp. 370–371.

Biography:
Oliver Elton, *C. E. Montague: A Memoir* (London: Chatto & Windus, 1929).

References:
David Ayerst, *The Manchester "Guardian": Biography of a Newspaper* (Ithaca, N.Y.: Cornell University Press, 1971), pp. 248–249;

Arnold Bennett, *Books and Persons: Being Comments on a Past Epoch, 1908–1911* (New York: Doran, 1917), pp. 201–203;

Dominic Hibberd, *The First World War* (London: Macmillan, 1990), pp. 174–176, 192;

Dixon Scott, *Men of Letters* (Toronto: Hodder & Stoughton, 1917), pp. 221–228;

Frank Swinnerton, *The Georgian Scene: A Literary Panorama* (New York: Farrar & Rinehart, 1934), pp. 218, 240–244;

Alfred C. Ward, *Aspects of the Modern Short Story: English and American* (London: University of London Press, 1924), pp. 255–269.

Arthur Morrison

(1 November 1863 - 4 December 1945)

Leonard R. N. Ashley
Brooklyn College of The City University of New York

See also the Morrison entries in *DLB 70: British Mystery Writers, 1860-1919* and *DLB 135: British Short-Fiction Writers, 1880-1914: The Realist Tradition*.

BOOKS: *The Shadows around Us: Authentic Tales of the Supernatural* (London: Simpkin & Marshall, 1891);

Tales of Mean Streets (London: Methuen, 1894; Boston: Little, Brown, 1895);

Martin Hewitt, Investigator (London: Ward, Lock & Bowden, 1894; New York: Harper, 1894);

Zig-Zags at the Zoo (London: Newnes, 1895);

Chronicles of Martin Hewitt: Being the Second Series of the Adventures of Martin Hewitt, Investigator (London & New York: Ward, Lock & Bowden, 1895; New York: Appleton, 1896);

Adventures of Martin Hewitt (London & New York: Ward, Lock, 1896);

A Child of the Jago (London: Methuen, 1896; Chicago: Stone, 1896);

The Dorrington Deed-Box (London: Ward, Lock, 1896);

To London Town (London: Methuen, 1899; Chicago & New York: Stone, 1899);

Cunning Murrell (London: Methuen, 1900; New York: Doubleday, Page, 1900);

The Hole in the Wall (London: Methuen, 1902; New York: McClure, Phillips, 1902);

The Red Triangle: Being Some Further Chronicles of Martin Hewitt, Investigator (London: Nash, 1903; Boston: Page, 1903);

The Green Eye of Goona: Stories of a Case of Tokay (London: Nash, 1904); republished as *The Green Diamond* (Boston: Page, 1904);

Divers Vanities (London: Methuen, 1905);

That Brute Simmons: A Play in One Act, by Morrison and Herbert C. Sargent (New York & London: French, 1906);

The Dumb Cake: A Play in One Act, by Morrison and Richard Pryce (London: Lacy, 1907);

Green Ginger (London: Hutchinson, 1909; New York: Stokes, 1909);

Arthur Morrison

Exhibition of Japanese Prints: Illustrated Catalogue, with Notes and an Introduction (London: Fine Art Society, 1909);

Exhibition of Japanese Screens Painted by the Old Masters (London: Yamanka, 1910);

The Painters of Japan, 2 volumes (London & Edinburgh: T. C. & E. C. Jack, 1911; New York: Stokes, 1911);

Fiddle O'Dreams (London: Hutchinson, 1933).

Collection: *Short Stories of Today and Yesterday* (London: Harrap, 1929).

PLAY PRODUCTIONS: *That Brute Simmons: A Play in One Act,* by Morrison and Herbert C. Sargent, London, 1904;

The Dumb Cake: A Play in One Act, by Morrison and Richard Pryce, London, 1907;

A Stroke of Business, by Morrison and Howard Newte, London, 1907.

Arthur Morrison is best known for his detective stories and his tales of the mean streets of the crowded and desperate slums of the East End of London. His work in both genres was highly regarded; yet he largely retired from writing fiction by 1910 and died in obscurity in 1945. Many people at that time were surprised to discover that he had not died decades earlier.

Morrison was born on 1 November 1863 to Richard Morrison and Jane Cooper Morrison. Although he later asserted that he was born in Kent and that his father was an engineer, he was, in fact, born in the East End, and his father was an engine fitter. The family may have lived in Kent at some point in Morrison's childhood, and an engine fitter may be described as an engineer, but Morrison clearly was trying to separate himself from his humble beginnings. The slums he wrote about were as fearful and sad as he portrays them, and in leaving them behind in his own life he became one of too few survivors of terrible childhoods under terrible conditions. Reading his slum tales today the reader may think that he is being melodramatic, but to a greater extent than most people can now imagine, as the slums have largely been cleared, Morrison's tales were as straightforward as the photographs of New York slums made by Jacob Riis.

As a person Morrison remains something of an enigma, and little is known of his private life. In 1892 he married a Dover woman, Elizabeth Adelaide Thatcher. Their son, Guy, was born the following year; their only child, he served in World War I, surviving the conflict but dying in 1921 of "maladies consequent on war service." Morrison himself seems to have been both a sturdy and sensitive fellow in his youth and to have combined boxing and writing, perhaps under the influence of one of the working-men's institutes that sprang up in that century, such as the Young Men's Christian Association and mechanics' institute libraries. In about 1886 Morrison became a clerk in one of these institutions, The People's Palace, a charitable foundation in Mile End, in the heart of the East End slums. This foundation was one of the reform ideas of Walter Besant, author of *Children of Gibeon* (1886), a novel that deplored the evils of want in the teeming warrens of the East End and stimulated interest in some sort of outreach or settlement house for "intellectual improvement and rational amusement."

It is possible that through his clerk's job Morrison got to know or know of Besant, who was already a successful author. In any case, it is certain that Morrison started out to be a writer in the late 1880s and found employment on *The National Observer* and other periodicals. His first book was a collection of his short stories, *The Shadows around Us: Authentic Tales of the Supernatural* (1891). Such tales were eagerly sought by certain periodicals and avidly read by a public that had inherited the taste for the Victorian "penny dreadfuls" and occult sensationalism that had made money for prolific writers such as Thomas Preskett Prest.

Morrison's first success was the sketch "The Street," set in the East End, which appeared in *Macmillan's Magazine* in 1891. It caught the eye of the poet, playwright, and journalist William Ernest Henley. Henley was the editor of *The Scots Observer,* which was just then becoming *The National Observer* and seeking new material and new writers. In Morrison's work Henley saw the possibility of combining the literary with the sociological and capturing the public's enthusiasm for reading about the hard lives of the poor. Morrison eventually became the leader of a loosely knit school of such writers, which included Israel Zangwill, Barry Pain, Edwin Pugh, and W. Pett Ridge. Also, while writing for Henley's *National Observer* Morrison associated with Rudyard Kipling and James M. Barrie.

Morrison's first important book was *Tales of Mean Streets* (1894), a collection of stories most of which had first appeared in *The National Observer*. Set in the East End, the stories depict the grim slum life with both realism and affection. Morrison may have known too much about Cockney life to be sentimental about it, but there was little about Morrison's writing that was cold. Not for him was the stenographer's approach of Henry Mayhew's *London Labour and the London Poor* (1851–1862). He steered clear, however, of political argument of the sort that one sees in William Edward Tirebuck's *Miss Grace of All Souls* (1845). He knew his subject well, but he did not feel passionately about it or at least did not make his text a pretext for a plan of social reform like the socialist novelist John Law (Margaret Harkness), whom Friedrich Engels thanked for teaching him much about the underclass. Engels praised her for "truth of detail, the truthful reproduction of typical characters under typical circumstances." Morrison proved that one could have truth and detail without polemic and obvious engagé involvement.

Arthur Conan Doyle's fictional detective, Sherlock Holmes, achieved immense popularity in the pages of *The Strand* in the early 1890s. When

Sidney Paget's depiction of Morrison's fictional detective (frontispiece for Martin Hewitt, Investigator, *1894)*

Conan Doyle grew bored with writing his Holmes stories, Morrison was able to take advantage of the absence of the "Great Detective" to win readers to nineteen "Martin Hewitt" tales, beginning with "The Lenton Croft Robberies" in March 1894. The role of a Dr. Watson is taken in these tales by Brett, a journalist and a neighbor of Morrison's detective, the unassuming Mr. Hewitt. Morrison's detective stories appeared in *The Strand* and *Windsor Magazine* and were collected in several popular volumes: *Martin Hewitt, Investigator* (1894); *Chronicles of Martin Hewitt: Being the Second Series of the Adventures of Martin Hewitt, Investigator* (1895); *Adventures of Martin Hewitt* (1896); and *The Red Triangle: Being Some Further Chronicles of Martin Hewitt, Investigator* (1903). The best Martin Hewitt stories may be those in *The Red Triangle,* in which Hewitt tackles his own Professor Moriarity, the fiendishly clever hypnotist Mayes. The devious criminal and the shrewd detective understand each other, and a sharp eye can detect the beginnings of a moral ambiguity or at least complexity of character that would come to be a principal feature of some later detective fiction of distinction.

Morrison was, as William Coleman Frierson says in his *The English Novel in Transition 1885–1940* (1942), one of the English followers of Emile Zola in that he dealt in types rather than the fanciful eccentrics of the sort that Charles Dickens created. Morrison describes sociological conditions and the psychological results of them, "the genial manifestations of his characters' animality." Frierson argues that Morrison, like such writers as Kipling and W. Somerset Maugham, depicts "his poor folk as full of bravado, humor, the zest for life, and animal warmth," noting that although the reader is shown "hate, slothfulness, greed, and depravity" it is done without moralizing, and Morrison "preaches no sermon."

Morrison's best novels are concerned with the Jago, his name for the London slums. He spent much time there with a missionary, the Reverend A.

Osborne Jay, who contacted him after the publication of Morrison's *Tales of Mean Streets*. Two years after the publication of *Tales of Mean Streets* brought him some attention, Morrison published *A Child of the Jago* (1896). In this novel a young thief in Bethnal Green is seen to be trapped in the hopeless world of slum violence and degradation. "It's a world," writes V. S. Pritchett in his *The Living Novel* (1964), "of sullen days in backrooms with the baby lying half dead on the bed and the hungry women gaping listlessly at the empty cupboards, while the men go out in search of loot and drink and come back with their eyes blackened and their belts ready to flay the undeserving family." With this novel Morrison added to the literature in which such writers as Elizabeth Gaskell presented the stench of Victorian slums. Morrison maintained a more aloof attitude than most writers on social conditions. He was content to lay out the evidence and to let the reader, who vicariously experienced the life described, be judge and jury. *A Child of the Jago* was and remains a significant book. What Kipling called "the savage wars of peace" in Victoria's time were not all fought abroad in defense of imperial ambitions; some were fought in the streets of London as the desperate tried to get by from day to day.

The stories in *The Dorrington Deed-Box* (1896) are probably the best of Morrison's detective fiction. James Rigby, fearing that he is the next victim of a vendetta against his family—his father was murdered years before by an organized crime group—has entrusted the deed box with his important papers to Horace Dorrington, a private investigator, so he can pretend to be Rigby and deal with the criminals while Rigby stays in hiding. To his horror Rigby discovers that Dorrington has tricked him and intends to steal his properties using the papers in the box. Rigby tracks down Dorrington's past, and the five stories following the brilliant and unnerving "Narrative of Mr. James Rigby" detail other cases of the unscrupulous Dorrington's tireless and amoral quest for money and mastery. Modern detective fiction that features private eyes on both sides of the law can largely be traced back to Morrison's stories here.

Morrison followed with *To London Town* (1899), now forgotten but popular in its day. *Cunning Murrell* (1900) is a romantic evocation of village life in remote Essex during the earlier part of the nineteenth century, far removed from London miseries. Having begun his career with a collection of stories of the supernatural (*The Shadows around Us*), Morrison ended the decade and the century with a popular treatment of witchcraft based on the real story of James Murrell, an herb doctor and spell caster. Despite a competent and suspenseful plot, the novel was not a complete success; as an historical novelist Morrison was only run-of-the-mill.

Morrison returned to London as a setting in what some consider to be his masterpiece, *The Hole in the Wall* (1902). Morrison captures something of Dickens's way of re-creating the tribulations and terrors of childhood, mixing the real with the fantastic. Stephen Kemp goes to live with his grandfather, who keeps a public house by the Thames in Wapping, and finds out that the old man has come into the possession of a wallet, containing the huge sum of £800, that has been taken from a murdered shipowner. The plot is full of twists and turns and surprises in the style of French dramatists such as Eugene Scribe, who make an object the engine of the action. The various attempts to get the wallet and its contents produce an exciting, taut tale. The atmosphere is grim, the narration hypnotizing, and the style more direct than that of Dickens if not as memorable. Morrison gives a picture of London that is more journalistic than Dickens's; it is the London of the Industrial Revolution, and in the city's darker corners Morrison finds the kind of "spasmodic violence" that Henry James found in the work of another journalist-novelist somewhat like Morrison, Jack London. Like London, Morrison describes the abyss.

Romance creeps into the 1904 novel, *The Green Eye of Goona* (published in the United States as *The Green Diamond,* 1904). The plot revolves around Harvey Crook, an import/export merchant, who is trying to track down a gem stolen from a rajah, imported in a bottle of wine, and inadvertently sold. Each bottle in the case of wine has to be traced. As the story ends the diamond has not been recovered, leaving the way open for a sequel; but there was none.

After 1909 Morrison published only one new volume of fiction, *Fiddle O'Dreams* (1933). He retired as a journalist in 1913. Moving to High Beech, Essex, he devoted himself to his interest in oriental art. He wrote about Chinese and Japanese paintings and donated his superb collection of Japanese prints to the British Museum. During World War I he served as Chief Inspector of Special Constabulary in Epping Forest (Essex), reportedly telephoning in the first warning of the first great Zeppelin raid on London of May 1915. After World War I Morrison and his family moved back to London, settling in Cavendish Square. In 1924 Morrison was named a member of the Royal Society of Literature, becoming a member of its governing council in 1935. He moved in 1930 to High Barn, Chalmont Saint Peter, in Buckinghamshire, where he remained until his death on 4 December 1945. After he died his wife carried out his request to burn his manuscripts and personal papers.

Arthur Morrison contributed significantly to the short story in the popular fields of the supernatural and detective fiction, and he will always hold an important place in the history of the realistic novel. In his novels of mean streets he managed to make interesting what his better-known contemporary James would have regarded as a mere backdrop to the drama. Morrison made scenery significant—and he did not have to go to exotic climes. He just went to the East End. He did for London and social realism what Gaskell did for Manchester: he made it "a prophetic city" peopled with "some of those who," as Gaskell says of her own work, "elbowed me daily in the busy streets of the town." Both Gaskell and Morrison knew firsthand the streets thronged with the poor who are always with us, and Morrison's accomplishment as a chronicler of "the Jago" deserves to be remembered.

Bibliography:

Robert Calder, "Arthur Morrison: A Commentary with an Annotated Bibliography of Articles about Him," *English Literature in Transition*, 28 (1985): 276-297.

Biography:

Peter Keating, "Biographical Study," in *A Child of the Jago*, by Arthur Morrison (London: MacGibbon & Kee, 1969), pp. 11- 36.

References:

Richard Benvenuto, "The Criminal and the Community: Defining Tragic Structure in *A Child of the Jago*," *English Literature in Transition*, 31, no. 2 (1988): 152-161;

E. F. Bleiler, Introduction to *Best Martin Hewitt Detective Stories*, by Morrison (New York: Dover, 1976);

Vincent Brome, "Arthur Morrison," in his *Four Realist Novelists: Arthur Morrison, Edwin Pugh, Richard Whiteing, William Pett Ridge* (Norman: University of Oklahoma Press, 1965), pp. 7-20;

William Coleman Frierson, *The English Novel in Transition, 1885-1940* (Norman: University of Oklahoma Press, 1942), pp. 88-93;

Hugh Greene, Introduction to *The Rivals of Sherlock Holmes*, edited by Greene (New York: Pantheon, 1970);

Howard Haycraft, *Murder for Pleasure* (New York: Biblo & Tannen, 1968), pp. 64-65, 303;

Peter Keating, *The Working Classes in Victorian Fiction* (London: Routledge & Kegan Paul, 1971);

John L. Kijinski, "Ethnography in the East End: Native Customs and Colonial Solutions in *A Child of the Jago*," *English Literature in Transition*, 374 (1994): 490-501;

Michael Krzak, "Arthur Morrison's East End of London," in *Victorian Writers and the City*, edited by Jean-Paul Hulin and Pierre Coustillas (Villaneuve-d'Ascq: Publications de L'Université de Lille III, 1979), pp. 145-180;

Krzak, Preface to *Tales of Mean Streets*, by Morrison (Woodbridge: Boydell, 1983), pp. 7-17;

Anita Miller, Introduction to *A Child of the Jago*, by Morrison (Chicago: Academy, 1995);

V. S. Pritchett, "An East End Novelist," in his *The Living Novel and Later Appreciations* (New York: Random House, 1964), pp. 206-212;

H. D. Traill, "The New Fiction," in his *The New Fiction and Other Essays on Literary Subjects* (London: Hurst & Blackett, 1897), pp. 8-26.

Barry Pain

(28 September 1864 – 5 May 1928)

Jan Peter F. van Rosevelt
University of South Carolina

See also the Pain entry in *DLB 135: British Short-Fiction Writers, 1880–1914: The Realist Tradition.*

BOOKS: *In a Canadian Canoe, The Nine Muses Minus One, and Other Stories* (London: Henry, 1891);
Playthings and Parodies (London: Cassell, 1892; New York: Cassell, 1892);
Stories and Interludes (London: Henry, 1892; New York: Harper, 1892);
Graeme and Cyril (London: Hodder & Stoughton, 1893); republished as *"Two": A Story of English Schoolboy Life* (New York: Cassell, 1893);
The Kindness of the Celestial, and Other Stories (London: Henry, 1894);
The Octave of Claudius (London & New York: Harper, 1897);
The Romantic History of Robin Hood (London & New York: Harper, 1898);
Wilmay, and Other Stories of Women (London & New York: Harper, 1898);
Eliza (London: Bousfeld, 1900; Boston: Estes, 1904);
De Omnibus, by the Conductor (London: Unwin, 1901; New York: Dutton, 1914);
Another Englishwoman's Love-Letters (London: Unwin, 1901; New York: Putnam, 1901);
Nothing Serious (London: Black & White, 1901);
Stories in the Dark (London: Richards, 1901);
The One Before (London: Richards, 1902; New York: Scribners, 1902);
Eliza's Husband (London: Chatto & Windus, 1903);
Little Entertainments (London: Unwin, 1903);
Curiosities (London: Fisher, 1904);
Deals (London: Hodder & Stoughton, 1904);
Lindley Kays (London: Methuen, 1904);
Three Fantasies (London: Methuen, 1904);
The Memoirs of Constantine Dix (London: Unwin, 1905);
Robinson Crusoe's Return (London: Hodder & Stoughton, 1906; New York: Arno, 1976); revised as *The Return and Supperizing Reception of Robinson Crusoe of York, Parrot Tamer* (London: Laurie, 1921);

Barry Pain

Wilhelmina in London (London: Long, 1906);
The Diary of a Baby: Being a Free Record of the Unconscious Thought of Rosalys Ysolde Smith, Aged One Year (London: Nash, 1907);
First Lessons in Story-Writing (London: Literary Correspondence College, 1907);
The Shadow of the Unseen, by Pain and James Blyth (London: Chapman & Hall, 1907);
The Luck of Norman Dale, by Pain and Blyth (London: Nash, 1908);
The Gifted Family (London: Methuen, 1909);
Proofs before Pulping (London: Mills & Boon, 1909);

The Exiles of Faloo (London: Methuen, 1910);
Eliza Getting On (London & New York: Cassell, 1911);
An Exchange of Souls (London: Nash, 1911);
Here and Hereafter (London: Methuen, 1911);
Stories in Grey (London: Laurie, 1911; New York: Stokes, 1911);
Exit Eliza (London & New York: Cassell, 1912);
The New Gulliver, and Other Stories (London: Laurie, 1912);
Stories without Tears (London: Mills & Boon, 1912; New York: Stokes, 1914);
Eliza's Son (London: Cassell, 1913);
Mrs. Murphy (London: Laurie, 1913);
Futurist Fifteen: An Old Moore or Less Accurate Forecast of Certain Events in the Year 1915 (London: Laurie, 1914);
One Kind and Another (London: Secker, 1914; New York: Stokes, 1915);
Edwards: The Confessions of a Jobbing Gardener (London: Laurie, 1915);
Me and Harris (London: Laurie, 1916);
The Short Story (London: Secker, 1916; New York: Doran, 1916);
Confessions of Alphonse (London: Laurie, 1917);
Innocent Amusements (London: Laurie, 1918);
The Problem Club (London: Collins, 1919);
The Death of Maurice (London: Skeffington, 1920);
Marge Askinforit (London: Laurie, 1920; New York: Duffield, 1921);
Going Home: Being the Fantastic Romance of the Girl with Angel Eyes and the Man Who Had Wings (London: Laurie, 1921);
If Summer Don't (London: Laurie, 1922); republished as *If Winter Don't* (New York: Stokes, 1922);
Tamplin's Tales of His Family (London: Laurie, 1924);
This Charming Green Hat-Fair (Myickle Baalamb) (London: Laurie, 1925; New York: Adelphi, 1926);
Barry Pain: Essays of Today and Yesterday (London: Harrap, 1926);
Dumphry (London & Melbourne: Ward, Lock, 1927);
The Later Years (London: Chapman & Hall, 1927);
Forbidden Love and Other Stories (Girard, Kan.: Haldeman-Julius, 1927);
Barry Pain: Stories of To-day and Yesterday (London: Harrap, 1928);
Barry Pain, edited by E. V. Knox (London: Methuen, 1934).

Collections: *Collected Tales* (London: Secker, 1916; New York: Stokes, 1916);
Stories Barry Told Me, collected by Eva Pain (London: Longmans, Green, 1927; New York: Longmans, Green, 1928);
More Stories, introductions by John Head Bowden (London: Laurie, 1930);
Humorous Stories, introduction by Alfred Noyes (London: Laurie, 1930; Freeport, N.Y.: Books for Libraries Press, 1971);
The Eliza Books (London: Laurie, 1931);
The Eliza Stories, edited by Terry Jones (London: Pavilion, 1984; New York: Beaufort, 1984);
Stories in the Dark: Tales of Terror by Jerome K. Jerome, Robert Barr and Barry Pain, edited by Hugh Lamb (Wellingborough: Equation, 1989).

OTHER: "Pantomine Sketch," in *Grien on Rougemont; or, The Story of a Modern Robinson Crusoe,* by Henri Louis Grin (London: Lloyd, 1898).

SELECTED PERIODICAL PUBLICATIONS–
UNCOLLECTED:
FICTION
"Storicules–I. The Suicide Advertisement," *Punch,* 101 (19 August 1891): 97;
"Storicules–II. The Back-View," *Punch,* 101 (5 September 1891): 120;
"Storicules–III. The Dear Old Lady," *Punch,* 101 (12 September 1891): 132;
"Storicules–IV. A Reviewer's Confession," *Punch,* 101 (19 September 1891): 135–136;
"Storicules–V. A Born Aristocrat," *Punch,* 101 (26 September 1891): 149;
"Detected Culprits," *Cornhill,* new series 17 (September 1891): 268-276; republished in *Living Age,* 191 (24 October 1891): 204–208;
"Storicules–VI. Budwell's Revenge," *Punch,* 101 (10 October 1891): 228;
"The Portrait Painter," *Art Journal,* 54 (1892): 201–204;
"Alicia," *Bookman* (London), 2 (July–August 1892): 111–112, 146–147;
"Una at Desford," *Idler,* 2 (December 1892): 518-528;
"Cynthia's Love Affair," *English Illustrated Magazine,* 11 (February 1893): 323–329;
"Pathos of the Commonplace," *English Illustrated Magazine,* 11 (October 1893): 19–26;
"A Parochial Matter," *Black & White,* 6 (9 December 1893): 742–743;
"Blindfold," *Black & White,* 7 (17 February 1894): 208–209;
"In the Boudoir," *Black & White,* 7 (June 1894): 704;
"Faithful Fortnight," *English Illustrated Magazine,* 11 (September 1894): 1159–1164;
"Complete Recovery," *English Illustrated Magazine,* (13 December 1895): 191–195;
"The Church Militant," *Idler,* 9 (April 1896): 328-383;

"Lord Ornington," *Idler,* 10 (September 1896): 146–153;

"History of Clare Tollison," *English Illustrated Magazine,* 16 (January 1897): 233–240;

"Cheevers and the Love of Beauty," *English Illustrated Magazine,* 20 (February 1898): 325–332;

"The Artistic Success," *Idler,* 17 (April 1900): 306–309;

"Language of the Dead," *Current Literature,* 30 (January 1901): 99–100;

"Lovers on an Island," *Cosmopolitan,* 34 (December 1902): 151–157;

"Interzoos," *Strand,* 25 (June 1903): 677–682;

"A Liar and an Elephant," *Strand,* 26 (September 1903): 302–304;

"Quaint Questions," *Strand,* 45 (January 1913): 116–117; (February 1913): 221–223;

"The Journal of Aura Lovel," *Strand,* 46 (December 1913): 642–655;

"Help!," *Strand,* 48 (December 1914): 621–631;

"Celia and the Ghost," *Strand,* 52 (December 1916): 658–664;

"The Official Mind," *Strand,* 57 (April 1919): 283–286;

"The Tale of Twenty Errors," *Strand,* 60 (December 1920): 566, 573–577;

"A New Comedy of Errors," *Strand,* 61 (January 1921): 86–90; (May 1921): 412;

"A Tale with Tangles in It," *Strand,* 62 (November 1921): 452–456; (December 1921): 590;

"Bobbed Hair and Sausages," *Strand,* 69 (February 1925): 193–196;

"A New Line in Crosswords," *Strand,* 69 (March 1925): 316–318; (April 1925): 410.

NONFICTION

"The Humour of Mark Twain," *Bookman* (London), 38 (June 1910): 107–111;

"The Importance of the Reader," *Living Age,* 296 (9 March 1918): 629–631.

POETRY

"The Robin," *Punch,* 101 (7 December 1889): 269;

"Aenigmata," *Living Age,* 190 (11 July 1891): 66;

"Dream of the Dead World," *Blackwood's,* 179 (February 1906): 204–208.

Barry Pain was a prolific writer whose career spanned nearly forty years, from the late-Victorian 1880s to the Jazz Age of the 1920s. He was an accomplished essayist, parodist, novelist, short-story writer, and poet. Although best remembered now for his humorous and supernatural short stories, he wrote in several other genres, including science fiction, fantasy, mystery, adventure, and romance.

During his lifetime Pain never really established himself as a writer of serious fiction. The notice of his death in the *London Mercury* (June 1928) regretfully comments that "he never quite fulfilled his early promise, or did his gifts full justice" because "the diversity of those gifts" prevented him from pursuing a career that would have gained "the sort of reputation that has come to men of far less capacity." Pain's versatility as a writer may have worked against him, the *Mercury* goes on to note: "the sense of not knowing what sort of fare would be presented between the covers of his latest book" may have made "his lighter work more ephemeral than it need have been."

Barry Eric Odell Pain was born on 28 September 1864 in Cambridge to John Odell Pain, a well-to-do linen draper, and Maria Pain. Educated at the Sedburgh School in Yorkshire from 1879 to 1883, he matriculated at Corpus Christi College, Cambridge, in 1883 and was awarded a scholarship the following year. His college career was undistinguished: although he graduated from Cambridge in 1886 with a B.A. in the classical tripos, he did so with third-class honors. Pain later claimed that he "took his football more seriously than his scribbling," but he had contributed to the Sedburgh School magazine and to university publications.

From 1886 to 1890 Pain was an army "crammer" (tutor) in Guilford. He maintained his ties to Cambridge, editing *The Cambridge Fortnightly,* an undergraduate magazine founded in 1888, and began writing for *Granta,* the Cambridge-based literary magazine, soon after its inception in 1889. In October of that year his short story "The Hundred Gates" was accepted by *The Cornhill Magazine.* A gentle satire of the use of stock characters in contemporary novels, the story established Pain as a writer. Soon he received invitations from James Payn, editor of *The Cornhill,* and F. C. Burnard, editor of *Punch,* to become a regular contributor to their magazines. Accepting both of their invitations, he moved to London on New Year's Day 1890. There he soon found additional work writing for other popular periodicals, including *The Speaker,* the *National Observer, The Daily Chronicle,* and *Black & White.*

Pain's first book, *In a Canadian Canoe, The Nine Muses Minus One, and Other Stories* (1891), made up largely from his contributions to *Granta,* is an uneven work. The main piece begins as a meditation on the joys of boating on the rivers near Cambridge, slightly reminiscent of Jerome K. Jerome's *Three Men in a Boat* (1889), but it deteriorates into philosophical maunderings and self-conscious cleverness. It was fairly popular, however, going through three editions in the first year and a fourth in 1892. *Stories and Interludes* (1892), which also consists mainly of pieces from *Granta,* alternates short stories with poetry. *Playthings and Parodies* (1892) is a collection of pieces that originally appeared

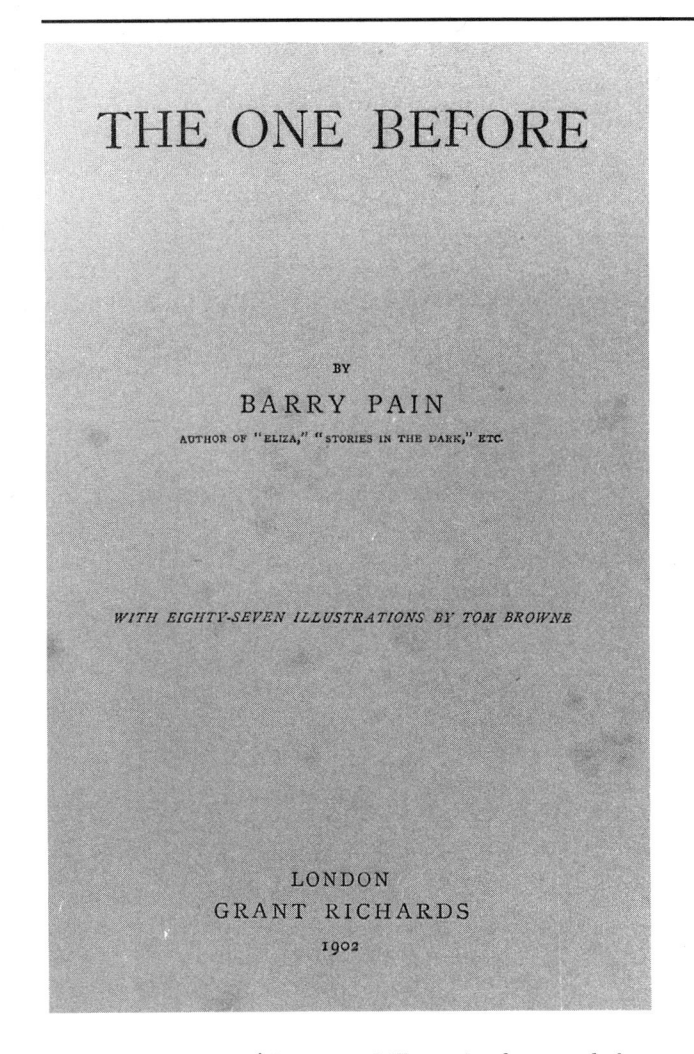

Title page and illustration for a novel about a magic ring that changes the wearer's personality

in *The Cornhill,* including the short story "The Hundred Gates."

Early in his career Pain became involved in the "New Humour" controversy. Jerome writes in his autobiography, *My Life and Times* (1926): "It was to Barry Pain that the reproach 'new humorist' was first applied. It began with a sketch of his in the 'Granta'—a simple little thing entitled 'The Love Story of a Sardine.'" Besides Pain, the so-called New Humorists included Jerome, W. W. Jacobs, William Pett Ridge, and Israel Zangwill. It is now unclear what the "New Humour" was; as J. B. Priestley remarks in his *English Humour* (1929): "There had been, it seems, a revolution in jesting, but what this revolution effected, what was thrown down and what was set up, is now something of a mystery." Pain himself dismissed the controversy, remarking in *The Idler* (June 1894): "The distinction between the old and the new humour is ridiculous and perfectly arbitrary."

In 1892 Pain married Amelia Nina Anna Lehmann, a writer who would produce several collections of plays for amateur theatricals and the novel *Saint Eva* (1897). She was the daughter of the painter Rudolf Lehmann and granddaughter of the Edinburgh publisher Robert Chambers. Her elder sister, Liza, was an accomplished singer, as their mother had been. She was also the first cousin of the barrister and journalist Rudolph Chambers Lehmann, the first editor of *Granta,* who was also on the editorial staff of *Punch.* His father, Frederick Lehmann, had been an intimate of the Brownings and had known Charles Dickens, Edward Bulwer-Lytton, and Wilkie Collins. The American writer Bret Harte and Mrs. Oscar Wilde were among the wedding guests. Pain was thus marrying into a family that was both "artistic" and "literary." At least one critic, John Clute, argues that this upward mobility marred Pain's work because it produced in him attitudes of "ambient nostalgia" and an "insecure refusal to admit that the world is unstable."

Pain's father died in 1893, leaving Pain a comfortable inheritance that enabled him and his wife to settle in Pinner. Pain would live near London for the rest of his life, and much of his fiction is set in London or its suburbs. The Pains had two daughters.

Pain's first novel, *Graeme and Cyril* (1893), was originally titled "Two" when it appeared in the boys' magazine *Chums;* it was published in the United States under the title *"Two": A Story of Schoolboy Life* (1893). It is a traditional schoolboy novel in most respects, following the careers of Graeme Kenriston and Cyril Verner from their boyhood friendship near the village of Sunningham to young adulthood as senior boys at Deptford School. Graeme succeeds, while Cyril, the more clever of the two, proves to be morally weak: on the verge of being expelled for frequenting a bookmaker, he runs away and falls into a cave, breaking his neck. The novel is largely a paean to the virtues of public-school education and defends the traditional English suspicion of cleverness as a quality that is inferior to "good sportsmanship." A Dickensian subplot revolves around Henry Burton, a Cockney boy. He first appears as an antagonist of the two friends, filled with class hatred by his father, a drunkard and thief. Through the intervention of a newly wealthy uncle from New Zealand who is determined to "make a gentleman" of him, he is sent to the same school as Graeme and Cyril. Realizing that one cannot "become" a gentleman, Henry decides that he will succeed as an artist. This is a recurrent theme in Pain's writing, perhaps reflecting his own experience: class boundaries are surmountable only by gifted individuals, such as painters and writers. The use of two main protagonists who can be seen as representing antithetical halves of a whole is another device that Pain was to repeat in many of his novels.

In 1897 Pain took over the editorship of *To-Day* from Jerome; he would continue in that post until 1905, when *To-Day* was absorbed by *London Opinion*. His second novel, *The Octave of Claudius* (1897), was originally serialized in *The Ludgate Magazine* from September 1896 to August 1897. A novel of suspense, it marks Pain's first major attempt at a serious subject. Claudius Sandell is an aspiring writer who has been disowned by his wealthy family; as the novel opens, he is near starvation. The ironically named Dr. Lamb rescues Claudius from the streets and takes the young man into his household. After Claudius recovers, the doctor makes a proposal: he will give Claudius £8,000, with the condition that after eight days (the "octave" of the title) Claudius will become a subject for Lamb's physiological research, which entails vivisection. Having lost his will to live, Claudius agrees, and much of the novel describes his adventures as a wealthy, if doomed, young man. Ironically, now that he has given up, everything goes right for Claudius: he makes a small fortune in the stock market, has a novel accepted for publication, wins the heart of a beautiful girl, and is reconciled with his father. He escapes having to fulfill his part of the bargain when the evil Dr. Lamb perishes in a fire set by the wife he has driven mad by his brutal treatment. Parts of the novel are dark and serious—the portrait of Dr. Lamb as a monomaniacal, fiendish scientist, and his physical and psychological mistreatment of his wife, for example—but much of *The Octave of Claudius* is relatively lighthearted. Although the novel was generally well received, reviewers objected both to the implausibility of the idea that anyone would agree to be vivisected, even for £8,000, and to an inconsistency of tone: *The Spectator* (25 September 1897) complained of a "certain forced facetiousness." Although Pain makes some points about scientific obsession and the rationale that the end justifies the means, he undercuts both his serious purpose and the suspense with comic puns and humorous passages. The novel was adapted as a motion picture, *A Blind Bargain,* starring Lon Chaney in the dual role of Dr. Lamb and "the Ape Man," in 1922.

The following year Pain published a short-story collection, *Wilmay, and Other Stories of Women* (1898), and a novel, *The Romantic History of Robin Hood* (1898), which is itself a loosely knit collection of short stories. A strong market for children's adventure novels existed at the end of the century, following the success of such works as Robert Louis Stevenson's *Treasure Island* (1883). Although the subject matter and illustrations in the first edition of Pain's novel would seem to indicate such a market, the novel includes characterizations and situations that are adult in orientation. For the most part, the book presents the familiar characters and episodes of the Robin Hood legend as collected and popularized by Joseph Ritson in 1795 and shaped by many writers in the nineteenth century, most notably by Sir Walter Scott in his novel *Ivanhoe* (1819). The sheriff of Nottingham is Robin's nemesis, and Little John, Will Scarlett, and the rest help Robin outwit his foe through deception, an archery contest, and so on. The critic John Adlard dismisses the novel as "hack work," and at first glance it does seem to be a rehashing of the familiar story; a closer reading, however, reveals that Pain has substantially reworked this material. His Robin Hood is not the merry woodland outlaw of popular myth but a dark figure who is periodically "overtaken by a dark mood, a distemper, as it were of mind and body," a man driven to the wilderness by "besieging thoughts." The novel is largely devoid of women, and when they do appear they possess a dangerous, destructive sexuality. Maid Marian only appears in chapter 8, where she is described as a femme fatale: "Because her body had this curve or that, and her arms were white and rounded, and her eyelashes were long, and her mouth small and scarlet—just because of such trifles she could make men stronger than her obey her." Marian has caused Robin to do something for which he has been outlawed, although his crime is not specified. Robin is thus a Byronic Romantic hero, whose nameless crime has separated him both from his beloved and from humanity. Pain follows the traditional account of Robin's demise: he is treacherously bled to death by the prioress of Kirklees under the pretext of medical treatment. But in Pain's version the prioress is Mary, the daughter of the sheriff of Nottingham, and her motive for murdering Robin seems to be revenge for his spurning of her sexual advances years earlier.

In 1900 the Pains moved to Hogarth House, Bushey, near Amelia's parents. That year Pain wrote a series of features for *Pearsons's Monthly*, "Nature's Next Moves," which burlesque contemporary speculative fiction. These slight parodies of the many imitators of H. G. Wells mark his first real venture into science fiction; later he would return to the genre with more-serious works.

Eliza (1900) was compiled from stories that had appeared in *To-Day*. Pain had trouble interesting publishers in *Eliza*, perhaps because of the similarity of the material to George and Weedon Grossmith's *The Diary of a Nobody* (1892). After the novel was accepted and published, however, it proved to be extremely popular, going through twelve editions by 1904. The never-named narrator of *Eliza* is a pompous, self-centered, lower-middle-class clerk, whose clever and resilient wife, Eliza, continuously punctures his self-deluded attempts to put on airs. Clute disparages *Eliza* for "mock[ing] working-class mores"; Pain, however, is poking fun not at a class but at an individual. As Alfred Noyes notes in his introduction to Pain's *Humorous Stories* (1930): "The humour of Barry Pain was that of a keen observer of all the tricks of the human mind, and especially those by which the human mind succeeds in deceiving itself."

The narrator of *Eliza* is precariously situated in the middle class, and much of the humor comes from his failure to see himself as one step above the working class; instead, he views himself as a member of the gentry. In the chapter "The Cards" he has visiting cards printed, over Eliza's objections that they have not paid the coal bill. In "The Public Scandal" he rails about the vulgarity of a neighbor drying laundry in her front garden, only to be brought short when told that the woman is washing *his* clothes. He is continually worried about appearances and is a snob who fawns over anyone with a title or claim to social distinction. What makes the narrator sympathetic, however, is that he is also genuinely kindhearted: in "The Pagrams" he surreptitiously lends money he cannot afford to a young couple with a new baby.

Pain capitalized on the success of *Eliza* with several sequels: *Eliza's Husband* (1903), *Eliza Getting On* (1911), *Exit Eliza* (1912), and *Eliza's Son* (1913). In *Eliza's Son* the narrator is the son—like his father, he is never named—who combines the worst qualities of his father with faults of his own: avarice and cold-bloodedness. The reviewer for *The Bookman* of London (June 1913) remarked: "His unpleasantness is unquestionable; he is a prig, a snob, and a money-grubber; and the curious thing is that, even with all these characteristics, he supplies material for laughter."

As had been the case with *Eliza*, portions of *De Omnibus, by the Conductor* (1901) first appeared in *To-Day*. The book, which sold more than eighteen thousand copies, is a series of humorous vignettes of London street life as recounted by the Cockney conductor of a horse-drawn omnibus. In 1901 Pain also published *Another Englishwoman's Love-Letters*, a parody of Laurence Housman's anonymous epistolary novel *An Englishwoman's Loveletters* (1901). Housman's novel, which purported to include the actual letters of a woman who had died, was extremely popular, selling more than thirty thousand copies in three years and going into five editions by 1920. It prompted several imitations and parodies that were inspired as much by the book's ornate binding as by the sentimentality of the text. In the introduction to his parody Pain remarks of Housman's novel: "the perusal gives one rather the feeling that one has been eating caramels to excess in a moonlit churchyard." He targets the sentimentality of Housman's novel in particular and the excesses of romantic novels in general. That same year Pain published *Nothing Serious*, a collection of humorous stories, and *Stories in the Dark*, a volume that Clute calls his "single most important collection of supernatural tales."

Pain uses a supernatural theme to humorous effect in his novel *The One Before* (1902), which revolves around a magic ring that imbues each wearer with the personality of the previous wearer. For example, when the meek Mary Bayley puts on the ring after a lion tamer has worn it, she gets the upper hand over her bullying husband and insolent servants. The stock characters and situations are similar to those in the novels of P. G. Wodehouse.

All of the stories in *Deals* (1904) have something to do with business, usually with "sharp dealing." Pain was the son of a prosperous tradesman, and many of his writings feature detailed explanations of business practices. As Pain remarks in his *First Lessons in Story-Writing* (1907), "There is probably no knowledge of any kind for which a novelist cannot find a use. The

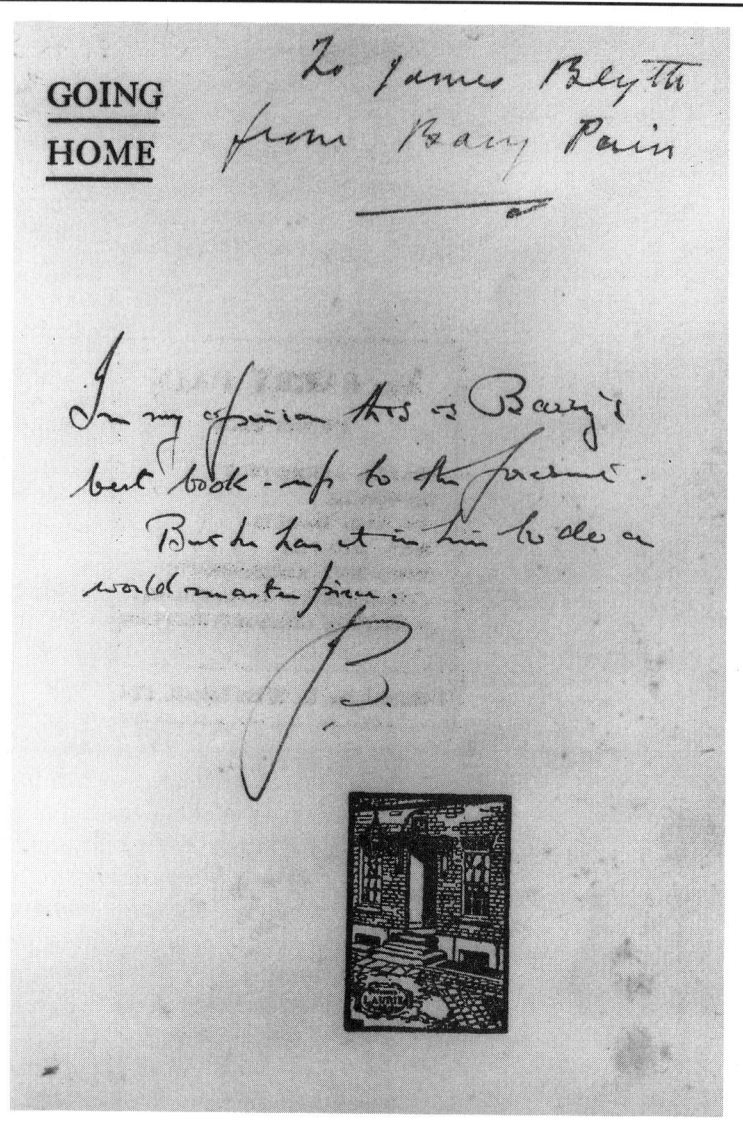

Half-title for the first edition of Pain's 1921 novel, inscribed by him to James Blyth, his sometime collaborator, with holograph remarks by Blyth (courtesy of the Lilly Library, Indiana University, Bloomington, Indiana)

real story-writer, for instance, will never be bored by men who talk their own shop; on the contrary, he will encourage them to talk their own shop. A man is not really the less interesting because he knows thoroughly what he is talking about."

In 1905 Pain published *The Memoirs of Constantine Dix;* the eponymous antihero, a burglar and sort of amateur social worker, is obviously derived from E. W. Hornung's popular "Raffles" series, which had debuted with *The Amateur Cracksman* in 1899. A. J. Raffles, a gentleman who resorts to crime but has his own code of honor, spawned several imitations besides Pain's Dix, including John Kendrick Bangs's "Raffles Holmes," purportedly the son of Sherlock Holmes and grandson of A. J. Raffles, who first appeared in *R. Holmes & Co.* (1906), and Michael Arlen's "Cavalier of the Streets," who made his first appearance in *The Strand* in 1920.

Robinson Crusoe's Return (1906), a humorous novel, has echoes not only of the obvious source, Daniel Defoe's *Robinson Crusoe* (1719), but also of Washington Irving's "Rip van Winkle" (1820). In Pain's novel Crusoe returns to contemporary England after spending centuries on his desert island, where he has discovered the secret of "eternal middle age." He has a series of misadventures, beginning with his theft of a bather's clothes as he comes ashore near Brighton. Pursued, he sneaks aboard a train. Falling in with a confidence man in London, he inadvertently becomes involved in a scheme to defraud a bank. Robbed, abandoned, and generally bewildered by modern England, Crusoe retreats to the beach, where he is reunited with his parrot and his raft. He pushes off, hoping to find the peace and monotony of his desert island once again. Pain extensively revised the novel as *The Return and Suppering Reception of Robinson Crusoe of York, Parrot Tamer* (1921). As the reviewer of the revised edition remarked in the London *Bookman* (December 1921): "What a subject for the satirist! But the reader must not look for anything so serious as satire in this little volume. It is just a riot of nonsense, thrown off in the author's most irresponsible mood."

Wilhelmina in London (1906) is the first-person narrative of eighteen-year-old Wilhelmina Castel. When her father, a dreamer and hack writer who has frittered away all his money on get-rich-quick schemes, dies, the orphaned Wilhelmina takes stock of her situation: "I had quite clearly made up my mind that there was no work in the world that I should be ashamed to do, if I could do it, but that I would not take up anything which could not possibly lead to anything. Now, nearly every feminine occupation recommended to the distressed but untrained gentlewoman is a *cul-de-sac* and when you get over the wall at the end of the *cul-de-sac* you are in the workhouse." Wilhelmina leaves her country village and goes to London, where she has a series of adventures, including a brush with phony spiritualists and an attempt at amateur detection. Finally she persuades the Pegasus Motor Company to let her learn to repair automobiles, and she becomes a successful automobile salesperson. Her career comes to a halt when the owner of the company proposes marriage. She refuses him, but they agree that it would not be seemly for her to continue working for him. Wilhelmina ruefully reflects: "So these external personal qualities which had brought me fortune before, now cut off . . . the profitable employment which I had found for myself by sheer hard work and common sense. I sometimes thought at this time that if there were no men in the world women would get on a good deal better." The work includes elements of the New Woman novel in its sympathetic depiction of Wilhelmina's attempts to succeed in a "man's world," but Pain negates this quality with a tacked-on conclusion: Wilhelmina is reconciled with her estranged grandfather, and hence with the patriarchy, and the novel ends with a happily married Wilhelmina devoting herself to caring for her husband and two children. *The Diary of a Baby: Being a Free Record of the Unconscious Thought of Rosalys Ysolde Smith, Aged One Year* (1907) is a comic fantasy about the household of an absent-minded painter and his wife, as seen through the eyes of their preternaturally intelligent infant.

In *First Lessons in Story-Writing*, written for the Literary Correspondence College, Pain reveals his technique. He advises the beginner to "Work always from character to plot, and never from plot to character. . . . Concentrate yourself upon making a real person in your mind." He remarks that "To work from character to plot is not only the more artistic way, and therefore more satisfying to the writer, but with practice it becomes the easier way." This demotion of plot to secondary status may account for the lack of structure commonly noted by critics in Pain's novels. Arnold Bennett comments that Pain "never, I think, wrote a satisfactory long book; and even his short books are usually divided into episodes each of which might well stand alone."

The Shadow of the Unseen (1907) and *The Luck of Norman Dale* (1908) are products of Pain's collaboration with James Blyth, another prolific writer of popular fiction. *The Shadow of the Unseen* is a Gothic romance with elements of the supernatural. Linda Merle inherits a house in the remote fen country. A witch, Judith Jennis, plots to destroy her in revenge for the death of her ancestor, who was killed for witchcraft by Linda's ancestor. Lawrence Hebblethwaite, the local squire, kills the giant black ram that is Judith's familiar spirit and rescues Linda from the enchantment under which Judith has placed her. After Judith is killed when her witchcraft backfires, Linda marries the much older Lawrence. The description of the country and the local people is well done, as is the rendering of dialect; but although an atmosphere of supernatural menace is evoked, the ending is anticlimactic.

The Luck of Norman Dale is a novel of suspense but is otherwise similar to Pain's other collaboration with Blyth in its elaborately described provincial setting and its extensive use of dialect. The novel is largely set in the fictional fishing village of Trawlhaven in "Daneshire," with some of the action taking place in London. The complex plot hinges on the relationship of Norman Dale and James Hardy, who fight as schoolboys for an unrevealed reason and remain enemies throughout life. The first part of the novel, set in Trawlhaven, introduces several subplots and minor characters such as the villainous drunken locksmith Bob Balls. Pain and Blyth attempt to sustain suspense through extensive use of flashbacks and delayed revelation. Gradually the reader learns that Dale is living a dual existence: he is Norman Dale in London and Benham, owner of the Benham Fishing Fleet, in Trawlhaven. After Dale was expelled from Oxford his father bankrolled his entry into the herring trade, conditional on his keeping the family name out of it. Later it is revealed that the herring business is a front for a smuggling operation. Dale is never found out, and at the novel's conclusion he is happily married and retired, while his enemies Hardy and Balls are dead; his "luck" has won out. As in *Graeme and Cyril*, Pain has paired two antithetical figures in the clever and amoral

Cover for a 1922 parody of A. S. M. Hutchinson's 1921 novel If Winter Comes *(Collection of Jan Peter F. van Rosevelt)*

Dale and the seemingly stolid and honest Hardy. In *The Luck of Norman Dale,* however, it is the amoral Dale who is victorious, while Hardy turns out to be a weak, cruel man who is only stopped from murdering Dale when he is killed through an unlikely set of coincidences—the "luck" of Norman Dale again. Although the novel is rich in information on herring fishing and smuggling, the plotting and characterization are generally poorly done.

In 1908 the Pains moved to St. John's Wood. Pain's next novel, *The Gifted Family* (1909), is a slight domestic comedy. The members of the upwardly mobile Prendergast family are almost uniformly "gifted," that is, lucky: father and son succeed in business, and the three daughters all marry well. Pain pokes fun at such topics as middle-class aspirations, manufacturers, and the medical profession (one of the daughters marries a doctor), but the satire is mild. The reviewer in the London *Bookman* (April 1909) summed it up: "this is a thoroughly cheerful story, sparkling with optimism and good nature."

The Exiles of Faloo (1910) is a departure for Pain. Most of his novels are set in England, usually in London or its suburbs, but *The Exiles of Faloo* is set in the South Pacific. The novel focuses on the attempt by the European members of the Exiles Club to maintain their control over the fictional island of Faloo in the face of a restive native population led by the capable and shrewd Westernized native king, "John Smith." The Exiles Club is a travesty of a London gentleman's club, and the mostly British members—including Sir John Sweetling, the Reverend Cyril Mast, and Lord Charles Basingstroke—have all fled to Faloo to escape the reach of the law. The one member who is not a fugitive from justice, Dr. Soames Pryce, left England after it was discovered that he had covered up the poisoning of a cruel husband by his sexually abused wife.

The catalyst for the downfall of this enclave is the arrival of the millionaire Wilberforce Lechworthy and his niece, Hilda, who are on a fact-finding trip evaluating the effects of missionaries in the South Pacific. Lechworthy, a Christian socialist manufacturer of leather goods, seems to be modeled on the industrialist Robert Owen. Lechworthy and King Smith enter into a plan to wrest control of the island's trade from the Exiles Club and sway British public opinion into guaranteeing Faloo's independence. The plan is forestalled by a rebellion of natives who are fed up with the king's gradualist approach and are especially angered by the Exiles' sexual predations. The rebellion is put down by the king, but not until the Exiles Club has been burned down and all of its members slaughtered except Dr. Pryce, who heroically defends Lechworthy and his niece from a mob bent on murder and rape. Lechworthy leaves after telling Smith that there is no hope of swaying British public opinion to secure Faloo's protection from exploitation. Although he and Smith understand that the cause of the uprising was the exploitation perpetrated by the Exiles Club, Lechworthy tells the king that to the public "Your people would seem . . . cruel and bloodthirsty; your government of them would seem unstable and impotent; they would wish to perpetuate neither." He advises the king to "Go back to the simplicity of your fathers, and trust to the obscurity of your kingdom, and here the race may recover."

In *The Exiles of Faloo* Pain seems to have drawn on Joseph Conrad's Malay Archipelago stories, such as *Almayer's Folly* (1895), in his depiction of the intersection of European and non-European cultures. The scene in which the Exiles Club is overrun is reminiscent of the battle scenes in *Lord Jim* (1900), and Conrad's savagely ironic depiction of Belgian colonialism in *Heart of Darkness* (1902) seems to have shaped Pain's description of the workings of the Exiles Club. Although Pain's message is generally anti-imperial and anticolonial, like Conrad's, it is tinged with an implicit racism. Pain, who never traveled outside of Europe and America, seems also to have drawn on Stevenson's writings on the Pacific, such as *Island Nights' Entertainments* (1893) or *In the South Seas* (1896) for his descriptive passages. Stevenson was highly critical of European intervention in the Pacific in the novella *The Beach of Falesá* (1893), which may have provided Pain with the name for his island.

Another Stevenson novel, *The Strange Case of Dr. Jekyll and Mr. Hyde* (1886), may have inspired Pain's *An Exchange of Souls* (1911). In this science-fiction novel Pain returns to the theme of scientific obsession he had introduced in *The Octave of Claudius*. The stolidly English narrator, Compton, meets the strange Dr. Daniel Myas in Paris. Back in England, he learns from his friend Dr. Habaden that Myas is "making a special investigation of the moment of death." Habaden calls Myas a "scientific vulture" and hints at "rum-funny experiments" Myas has conducted on the Continent. Later Myas comes to London and takes rooms above a shop run by Mrs. Lade and her daughter Alice. He tells Compton that he is attempting to prove the existence of the soul with the connivance of a surgeon, Vulsame, and is tutoring Alice Lade so that she can help him with his experiments. They are engaged, though he tells the disapproving Compton that this arrangement is only meant to forestall gossip; he does not intend actually to marry Alice. Summoned to Myas's residence by a telegram signed "Lade," Compton meets Vulsame, who tells him that Myas has apparently been killed by anesthetic when a mechanical device delivered too great a dose. Another device, of unknown purpose, was found smashed in the room with the body. Vulsame suspects that Alice murdered Myas, as she claims that she was not in the shed where the body was found, while he had overheard her there the night before. Compton pays Vulsame to keep quiet, because he is sure that Alice loved Myas and could not have murdered him. Later he receives a letter from Myas and learns that Myas had been attempting to exchange souls with Alice. The experiment had gone wrong, and he had awakened to find himself in her body but his body dead. Panicked, and dazed by the transference, he had destroyed critical machinery. He asks Compton to help him find and recover Alice's soul.

Compton reluctantly goes to meet Myas; he reflects that he has seen female impersonators in music halls, "a thing that always disgusts me. The more cleverly that it is done, the more loathsome it is." When he meets Myas/Alice he finds it difficult to shake hands: "Through the veil I could distinguish dimly the face of Alice Lade, but through her eyes the eyes of Daniel Myas looked out. That was, perhaps, the supreme touch of terror—the eyes of a man looking from the woman's face." Later, Myas/Alice is killed in a train crash while disguised as a man. In the end Compton, close to death, encounters the separate spirits of Myas and Alice. Pain seems to have intended to relay a cautionary message about the dangers of scientific hubris, but the novel also brings up questions of sexual identity. It could be read as a veiled account of Edwardian transvestitism and homosexuality, although it is unlikely that Pain consciously intended this reading.

Many of the tales in *Stories in Grey* (1911) touch on the supernatural; for example, in "Rose Rose," one

Dust jacket for Pain's last novel, about a middle-aged man's romance with a much younger woman (courtesy of the Lilly Library, Indiana University, Bloomington, Indiana)

of Pain's best-known short stories, a model comes to finish sitting for a painting–after she has been killed in a traffic accident, as the painter later learns to his horror. The first story in the volume, "The Autobiography of an Idea," is less macabre. Its contrast of two authors, the impoverished Albert Weeks and the independently wealthy Hon. Charles Turnour Wylmot, seems to be a humorous redaction of George Gissing's grim portrait of the literary world in his *New Grub Street* (1891).

The New Gulliver, and Other Stories (1912) includes sentimental pieces such as "When I Was King," about a poacher who is prevented from committing murder by the innocent love of a sick girl. The novella "The New Gulliver" is a dystopian political satire, a response to such utopian novels as William Morris's *News from Nowhere* (1890). The narrator, Lemuel Gulliver Jr., shipwrecked on a mysterious island, Ultima Thule, meets a strange being who identifies himself as MZ04. MZ04 appears to be human but walks on all fours and is bald and toothless. MZ04 tells Gulliver that Ultima Thule is "the one spot of earth that has emerged from barbarism" but also that "it has no geographical relation" to the world that Gulliver knows. The implication is that Gulliver has traveled to the future. Gulliver learns that MZ04 is a member of the "First Class," a race of humans who have evolved into an extremely long-lived species that avoids all risk and emotion. They rule over a "Second Class" of slaves, who are unevolved humans. After a social revolution, when "the equality of all men was claimed and the community of property," a secret society arose. This society, "The Crypt," was made up of engineers and professionals, the minority "who could acquire knowledge and could use knowledge." Since this minority had control over all machinery, heating, and electricity, as well as knowledge of the secrets of matter transmission and death rays, they soon triumphed and set up the rigid oligarchy that still exists. Gulliver escapes from the island after a sexual interlude with a beautiful member of the Second Class. On his return to England he is thought to be mentally ill and is institutionalized. Pain's political satire is sweeping and prescient: he critiques the utopian socialist thinking that would lead many to support the Russian Revolution in 1917 and later, and his description of the dictatorship of the First Class, sanctioned by "scientific" methods, presages the Fascist and National Socialist ideologies that arose in the 1920s and 1930s. His own political beliefs are impossible to determine from the novella, however, except for an apparent belief in individualism and an obvious mistrust of social revolution and scientific elites.

Mrs. Murphy (1913) is the first-person narrative of a London charwoman who recounts her experiences in a cheerfully cynical, philosophical vein. Pain's portrait of Mrs. Murphy is sympathetic, but as Noyes notes in his introduction to Pain's *Humorous Stories*, "he is not sentimentalizing about charwomen. She takes her loot home under her skirt in a way that would satisfy no modern humanitarian novelist."

Pain toured the United States in the autumn of 1914 but returned to England at the outbreak of World War I. Overage for military service, he enlisted in the anti-aircraft section of the Royal Naval Volunteer Reserve in April 1915. He attained the rank of chief petty officer and was posted to the searchlight station on Parliament Hill but was forced to resign because of severe eyestrain. He continued writing at nearly his usual pace during the war, which makes no appearance in *Edwards: The Confessions of a Jobbing Gardener* (1915), a series of loosely connected reflections on women, the dangers of teetotalism, and the best ways of swindling one's employers. Despite the subtitle's use of the word *confessions*, Edwards is not apologetic about shirking work, overcharging customers, and filching tools and supplies. He regards such things as his prerogatives and is resentful when his employers attempt to trample on his rights by expecting him to show up for work sober or do the job properly. Such attempts are not frequent, however, since, as Edwards remarks, "Them as has a bit of garden in London expects mighty little, and if they think they're not getting it, you can always put it down to the cats, or the climate, or neglect on the part of the men what worked there before you."

In *Me and Harris* (1916) the narrator is never named. Like the narrator of the *Eliza* books, he is a self-important idiot who only occasionally suspects his own foolishness. The war is mentioned throughout this work, which begins, "As regards this here war, I'm not doing anything out of the way myself, nor is my friend Harris—the reason being that we're both over the age and nowise called upon." He admits that there are the Special Constables, "for them that likes it," but says that "to spend all that time on your feet is a positive danger to your health," and "Besides, we can't all be out in the trenches. The nation's ordinary work has got to be done, ain't it? Me and Harris is doing it." How are they contributing to the war effort? "Harris breeds them Pekinese dogs. I'm living on a annuity what I bought with the money my poor wife left when she was called to her rest. Everybody's got to be doing something." Later the narrator complains that the war has caused the newspapers to be filled with place-names that are unpronounceable to Englishmen, and he advocates giving English place-names to Continental cities to make things easier for people like him.

In 1917 Pain became a member of the London Appeals Tribunal, which adjudicated claims to exemption from military service. In *Confessions of Alphonse* (1917) the title character/narrator is a Swiss-French waiter at the Restaurant Merveilleux in London. Although Pain uses Alphonse to make some shrewd observations on English character and customs, much of the humor relies on Alphonse's imprecise command of English idiom, with comments such as "You cannot make the omelette without some black sheep."

The Problem Club (1919) is a collection of "puzzle stories" that purports to be a "discreet but authorised account of some part of the proceedings" of a club of twelve gentlemen who meet once a month to be given a problem that they must solve before the next meeting. Although the problems are not really mysteries but tasks that the members must accomplish, Pain generally follows the guidelines promulgated by Monsignor Ronald Knox and the Detection Club for the "puzzle" mysteries that were to become popular in the 1920s and 1930s.

After his wife died in 1920 Pain moved to Watford. He spent much time at his club, the Arts, and in the company of friends in London. C. Lewis Hind reports in his *More Authors and I* (1922) that "whenever I see this large-limbed, bearded, kindly man, he has cronies with him, who listen with appreciative delight, to his ready humour."

The Death of Maurice (1920) is a mystery novel; but if in *The Problem Club* Pain seems to follow the Knoxian precepts of logic and fair play with the reader, in *The Death of Maurice* he tramples on all of the conventions of the classic detective story. Maurice Carteret is killed in his garden by a shotgun blast, and the narrator, his solicitor and friend William Garth, tries to solve the mystery. Knowing that Maurice was in love with Diana, the daughter of the local squire, Garth rules out suicide; he himself is a suspect, however, since he has inherited Maurice's house. The plot is convoluted, with red herrings, false suspects, sudden twists, and supernatural occurrences. In the end, Garth discovers that Maurice's cook had set a trap to frighten off poachers; the gun had discharged accidentally, striking Maurice. He muses that "Maurice was dead, and in the house that he had made beautiful for his love and for himself there was a grizzled and lonely man whom no woman could ever love. And why? Because Maurice's cook in a laudable desire to make good strawberry jam for him had tied up a gun with a bit of rotten bast. It was absurd, of course. There was no poetry in it. There was not even a story in it." Coming at the end of a nearly three-hundred-page novel, this last remark may be read either as self-reflexive irony or as an inadvertent confession of failure.

Writers on Pain frequently mention the advice that the poet and critic W. E. Henley gave him in 1891, that he should concentrate on "serious work" and to "do no humorous work," but they generally overlook the caveat Henley added: "with the exception of parody." *Marge Askinforit* (1920), Pain's parody of Margot Asquith's reminiscences, which were serialized in the *Sunday Times* of London and later published in the two-volume *An Autobiography* (1920), was extremely popular, going into five editions in 1920 alone. Although Pain is careful to say in his introduction that "Nobody in the parody is intended to be a representation or even a misrepresentation, of any real person living or dead," the novel effectively skewers many of the literary and political memoirs of the period, particularly in its absurd anecdotes of "Inmemorison," who is recognizable as Alfred Tennyson.

Not a parody, *Going Home: Being the Fantastic Romance of the Girl with Angel Eyes and the Man Who Had Wings* (1921) is similar to some of the fantasies of Arlen and the American writer Thorne Smith. It includes some mild social satire but is generally light and breezy; Hind calls the novel "a typical example of the mature Barry Pain—a mixture of realism and fantasy, blended very skilfully."

The novel opens with the trial of George Overman "for conduct likely to produce a social revolution." He has ruthlessly become "sole proprietor of every fashionable restaurant in London," creating in these establishments a "Lucullan luxury, calculated to infuriate everybody who for financial or moral reasons was unable to partake of it." Watching this splendidly absurd trial is Dora Muse, who is writing a "Book of Experiences" based on her observations of life. A typical entry is her report on her servant Jane's confession to having "cuddled" with the milkman: it is "an accurate record of direct observation. Her deductions made, were, however, open to criticism. The entire entry was classified in the index under: 'Milkmen, exceptional opportunities of.'" Overman sees her at the trial, has her traced by private detectives, and calls on her. He tells her that he is not in love with her but wants to see her as often as possible, since "The strayed angel in your eyes looks at me and calls me to better things." Dora asks her artist friend Kate Mason if there is anything strange about her eyes; Kate replies, "If it didn't sound so damned silly to say so, I should say it was a kind of look you'd expect to find in an angel." Dora reflects that she has "had strange feelings at times, explicable perhaps on some 'strayed angel' theory," a longing "to return, to go back again, like a child that is homesick." Overman calls again, and in conversation he tells Dora about an "abnormal" boy he had rescued from a Belgian carnival. The boy, who is called "Eagle," has wings. Dora is excited and demands to be taken to see the boy. The two become lovers and fly away together, looking for the lost home that both remember. The novel has a certain amount of charm, with many amusing passages and nice touches of absurdity. The plot is fairly predictable, however, and the characters are generally flat. In a note written on the title page of a presentation copy of *Going Home* in the Lilly Library at Indiana University, Blyth, Pain's friend and erstwhile collaborator, noted: "In my opinion this is Barry's best book up to the present"; he may have been thinking of the novel's clumsy allegory when he added the reservation: "But he has it in him to do a world masterpiece."

Pain's next parodic target, Arthur Stuart-Menteith Hutchinson's *If Winter Comes* (1921), was an astonishingly successful sentimental romance set during World War I; now deservedly forgotten, it went through at least thirty-five printings in three years. Pain's *If Summer Don't* (1922)—published in the United States as *If Winter Don't* (1922)—is a competent mocking of the melodramatic plot and wooden characters of Hutchinson's work.

This Charming Green Hat-Fair (Myickle Baalamb) (1925), Pain's parodic take on the writings of the popular Arlen ("Myickle Baalamb"), is a complicated pastiche, deftly mixing in elements of Arlen's short-story collections *Mayfair* (1925) and *These Charming People* (1923), as well as his best-selling novel *The Green Hat* (1924). The result is a farrago of nonsense, but Pain demonstrates a keen ear for the excesses of Arlen's ornate style and heightens them into absurdity. As with much of Pain's parodic work, the real brilliance of this book may not be appreciated by modern readers, who will generally be unfamiliar with the target of the parody. As Pain remarks in "The Humour of Mark Twain" in the London *Bookman* (June 1910): "Nothing dates quite so much as humour." He points out that satire and parody are particularly susceptible to change, as "The marksman may be shooting admirably, but as the target has been removed we do not notice it."

Though neglected both by contemporary reviewers and later critics, *The Later Years* (1927), Pain's last novel, may be his most serious and artistically successful work. When the novel opens, the twenty-six-year-old Patricia Verdon and the fifty-year-old Carteret Rome are friends, though Carteret admits to having romantic feelings for Patricia. She is leading a bohemian existence, living with her sister, Katherine, as she searches for a suitable career; Carteret, a widower, is retired. Patricia becomes involved with an actor, Eric Chisholm, who tells her that he is separated from his wife but that she refuses to give him a divorce. She finds out that he is really a bachelor and uses this story to avoid commitment. Meanwhile, Carteret, reacting to an offhand remark of Patricia's that he is only interested in women for what they can give him but is never really in love with them, ends his comfortable but loveless relationship with his longtime mistress, May Arden. Patricia confesses to Carteret that she is pregnant by Chisholm, who has disappeared. He invites her to stay with him until she gives birth. They marry to avoid scandal, with the understanding that it will be a marriage in name only. After an automobile accident Patricia miscarries. While recovering, she tells Carteret that they no longer have to keep up the pretense and can now divorce; he tells her that he truly loves her, and she admits that she loves him. The story line is unremarkable, even melodramatic at times, especially in its denouement; the dialogue is generally competently done, though it sometimes sounds artificial. But the novel succeeds because of the deft and sympathetic depiction of the main characters. Clute argues that Pain never developed as an artist, that "he wrote in 1928 as he wrote before the turn of the century"; but *The Later Years* is clearly a novel of the 1920s, comparable in subject matter and style with works by much younger authors such as F. Scott Fitzgerald, and represents a major accomplishment for the elderly, ailing Pain.

Pain died in Watford, after a lengthy illness, on 5 May 1928. He had kept working despite his illness and bouts of depression. With the exception of the *Eliza* stories and a few of his supernatural tales, his enormous body of work is now largely forgotten. To some extent, as Terry Jones remarks in the introduction to his edition of *The Eliza Stories* (1984), this situation may be a paradoxical result of Pain's popularity among his contemporaries: "the distaste which men of letters felt for the railway bookstall damaged Barry Pain's credibility in the eyes of . . . intellectuals," and "when the railway bookstalls no longer carried his popular works . . . there was thus nothing left to sustain his memory."

References:

John Adlard, "Pain, Barry Eric Odell," in *Encyclopedia of British Humorists: Geoffrey Chaucer to John Cleese*, volume 2, edited by Steven H. Gale (New York & London: Garland, 1996), pp. 829–832;

Arnold Bennett, *The Evening Standard Years,* edited by Andrew Mylett (London: Chatto & Windus, 1974), p. 344;

John Clute, "Barry Pain," in *Supernatural Fiction Writers,* volume 1, edited by E. F. Bleiler (New York: Scribners, 1985), pp. 443–448;

"Gossip of Authors and Books," *Current Literature,* 10 (July 1892): 433–437;

C. Lewis Hind, "Barry Pain," in his *More Authors and I* (London: John Lane, 1922), pp. 260–265;

Jerome K. Jerome, *My Life and Times* (New York & London: Harper, 1926), p. 160;

Arthur H. Lawrence, "The Humour of Women: Mr. Barry Pain, His Work and His Views," *The Young Woman,* 6 (1897–1898): 129–132;

Richard Le Gallienne, "Mr. Barry Pain," *Harper's Weekly,* 36 (28 May 1892): 515;

"Literary Intelligence," *London Mercury,* 18 (June 1928): 123;

Mrs. Roscoe Mullins, "Mr. Barry Pain at Home," *Sylvia's Journal,* new series 2 (February 1894): 153–157;

Alfred Noyes, "Barry Pain," *Bookman* (London), 73 (December 1927): 166–167;

J. B. Priestley, *English Humour* (London & New York: Longmans, 1929), p. 115.

Papers:

There is no major archive of Barry Pain materials. Some correspondence and a few manuscripts are held by King's College, Cambridge. A smaller collection of correspondence is at the Brotherton Library, Leeds. Individual letters are at the University of London Library; the Royal Literary Fund, London; the *Punch* Library, London; and the King's School, Canterbury.

George Paston
(Emily Morse Symonds)
(1860 - 12 September 1936)

Rebecca Brittenham
Rutgers University

See also the Paston entry in *DLB 149: Late Nineteenth- and Early Twentieth-Century British Literary Biographers.*

BOOKS: *Little Memoirs of the Nineteenth Century* (London: Privately printed, 1893; New York: Dutton, 1902);

A Modern Amazon (London: Osgood & McIlvaine, 1894);

A Bread and Butter Miss: A Sketch in Outline (London: Osgood & McIlvaine, 1895; New York: Harper, 1895);

A Study in Prejudices (London: Hutchinson, 1895; New York: Appleton, 1895);

The Career of Candida (London: Chapman & Hall, 1896; New York: Appleton, 1897);

A Fair Deceiver (London & New York: Harper, 1898);

A Writer of Books (London: Chapman & Hall, 1898; New York: Appleton, 1899);

Little Memoirs of the Eighteenth Century (London: Richards, 1901; New York: Dutton, 1901);

Side-lights on the Georgian Period (London: Methuen, 1902; New York: Dutton, 1903);

George Romney (London: Methuen, 1903);

Old Coloured Books (London: Methuen, 1905);

Social Caricature in the Eighteenth Century (London: Methuen, 1905);

B. R. Haydon and His Friends (London: Nisbet, 1905; New York: Dutton, 1905);

Lady Mary Wortley Montagu and Her Times (London: Methuen, 1907; London & New York: Putnam, 1907);

Mr. Pope, His Life and Times, 2 volumes (London: Hutchinson, 1909);

Feed the Brute (New York: S. French, 1909; London: Lacy's Acting Edition, 1909);

Tilda's New Hat (London: Lacy's Acting Edition, 1909; New York & London: S. French, 1909);

The Parents' Progress (New York & London: S. French, 1910);

The Naked Truth: A Farcical Comedy in Three Acts, by Paston and William Babington Maxwell (New York: S. French, 1910; London: S. French, 1921);

Stuffing (London & New York: S. French, 1912);

Double or Quits: A Comedy in One Act (London: S. French, 1919);

Clothes and the Woman: A Comedy in Three Acts (New York & London: S. French, 1922);

Nobody's Daughter: A Play in Four Acts (London: "The Stage" Play Publishing Bureau, 1924);

Stars: A Comedy (London & New York: S. French, 1925);

At John Murray's: Records of a Literary Circle, 1843-1892 (London: John Murray, 1932);

"To Lord Byron": Feminine Profiles Based upon Unpublished Letters, 1807-1842, by Paston and Peter Quennell (London: John Murray, 1939; New York: Scribners, 1939).

OTHER: *Mrs. Delany (Mary Granville): A Memoir, 1700-1788,* compiled by Paston (London: Richards, 1900).

SELECTED PERIODICAL PUBLICATIONS—UNCOLLECTED:

FICTION

"A Thorn in the Flesh," anonymous, *Cornhill Magazine,* 68 (December 1893): 623-636;

"Lady Journalist," *English Illustrated Magazine,* 12, no. 4 (January 1895): 65-73.

NONFICTION

"Cousins German," anonymous, *Cornhill Magazine,* 64 (September 1891): 295-300;

"A Very Important Place," anonymous, *Temple Bar,* 96 (October 1892): 255-263;

"Pagans at Play," anonymous, *Cornhill Magazine,* 69 (April 1894): 418-423;

"The Humours of Heraldry," anonymous, *Cornhill Magazine,* 70 (October 1894): 375-382;

"The Old Criticism," anonymous, *Cornhill Magazine,* 71 (February 1895): 151-157;

"Punch's Prototypes," anonymous, *Cornhill Magazine,* 71 (March 1895): 305–313;

"The Advance of Advertisement," anonymous, *Cornhill Magazine,* 72 (November 1895): 505–513;

"Portrait-painting in Words," *Cornhill Magazine,* 76 (August 1897): 207–216;

"Mrs. Samuel Pepys," anonymous, *Temple Bar,* 117 (September 1899): 91–100;

"Capture of Capetown," *Longman's Magazine,* 36 (October 1900): 526–538;

"Lady from the Mountains: Mrs. Grant of Laggan," anonymous, *Longman's Magazine,* 37 (November 1900): 32–46;

"A Censor of Modern Womanhood," *Fortnightly,* 76 (1902): 505–519;

"An Apostle of Melodrama," *Fortnightly,* 100 (November 1913): 962–975.

Emily Morse Symonds, who published nearly all of her work under the pseudonym George Paston, achieved literary recognition not only as a novelist but also as a dramatist and literary biographer. Her extensive body of work demonstrates the productive overlapping of these three interests. Her early novels reveal her to be a determined lobbyist for women's rights who explored the psychic and cultural pressures on women's marriage and career choices and the consequences of those choices. Her plays continue that exploration within particularized dramatic situations but also with a larger cast of characters and on a broader canvas of class representations. At the same time, Paston's biographical work added to her historical understanding of the position of women by tracing the idealized models of behavior, educational practices, and marital institutions that had shaped the experiences of women in previous centuries. These varied interests and achievements make Paston's work a complex and rewarding field of study. Her novels, in particular, are self-consciously revealing of the ways in which Victorian literary modes were being transmuted to serve the needs of New Woman plots and politics.

Emily Morse Symonds was born in 1860 in Norwich, where her father, the Reverend Henry Symonds, advanced from the position of curate of St. Mary-in-the-Marsh to become the precentor of the Norwich Cathedral. When her father died around 1896, she and her mother, Emily Evans Morse Symonds, moved to South Kensington, where they lived on an income that allowed them to travel, entertain, and support the initial years of Paston's writing career. A description in his journal (11 October 1896) by the novelist Arnold Bennett attests to the serenity of their household:

At South Kensington, literature, quietude, the restraint of an eighteenth-century demeanor—and sincere artistic purpose too. Miss Symonds is a frank worshipper of the eighteenth century. Her mother, an ample little lady, with a quick cheerful laugh and a most pleasant manner, is ready to enjoy anything. She recalled the pleasure with which, at 19, she read *Monte Cristo,* and joyfully accepted my offer to lend her the *Vicomte de Bragelonne* so that she might renew the "Dumas sensations."

Although Symonds was a second cousin of the well-known historian John Addington Symonds, the author of *Renaissance in Italy* (1875–1880), she was never associated with his literary circle. Bennett recalled, "I ventured to mention that I have never learnt to be enthusiastic about the work of her celebrated cousin, John Addington Symonds. To my astonishment, both she and her mother confessed that they had read very little of it, and did not care for it." Although John Addington Symonds lived abroad for portions of his adult life, the lack of connection is somewhat surprising since his letters from the 1850s and 1860s cordially mention his Uncle Henry and Aunt Emily. His only mention of their daughter in September 1891 suggests that another branch of the family had been "lying" in order to avoid having to invite Emily Morse Symonds for a visit.

It is possible that Symonds chose a male pseudonym (thus becoming one of "the many women writers who have succumbed to the mysterious attraction of the name 'George,'" as a reviewer in the December 1898 *Academy* put it) partly to gain an unqualified entrance into her profession and perhaps also to distinguish herself from her famous cousin. Like George Eliot and other worthy precursors, she retained the pseudonym long after the fact of her sex was publicly known and acknowledged.

Paston's first major piece, which she had privately printed in 1893, was *Little Memoirs of the Nineteenth Century,* a collection of biographical essays on various nineteenth-century personages. These portraits, based largely on each subject's memoirs and letters, include strong, unorthodox women such as Lady Morgan (Sydney Owenson), a governess, novelist, and travel writer, and the world traveler and mystic Lady Hester Stanhope, as well as the painter Benjamin Robert Haydon, "Prince Pücker-Muskau in England." The collection received little attention until it was republished in 1902, after Paston had established her reputation as a literary biographer. Paston's portraits of women such as Owenson and Stanhope, who challenged or flouted conventional mores, may well have provided her with material for her subsequent novels, as well as with the ability to craft fictional characterizations that recognize the social and historical pressures of her age.

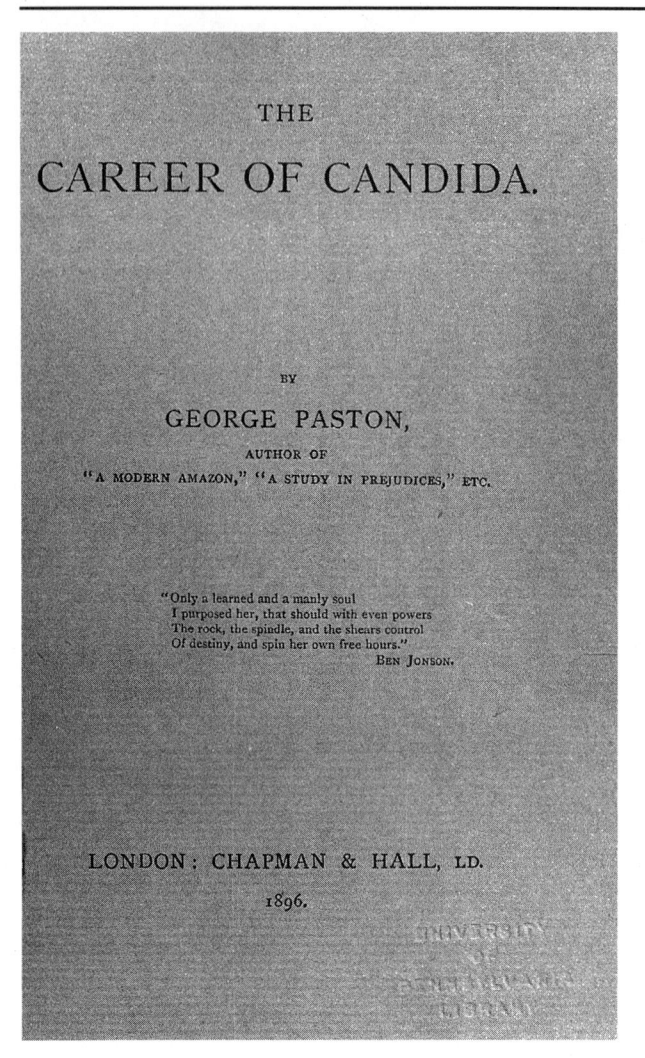

Title page for a novel about a female gymnastics instructor who sacrifices her own happiness to care for her unfaithful and alcoholic husband

After this early effort in the genre of literary biography Paston turned to fiction, producing six novels between 1894 and 1899. Each focuses on the development of a complex, individualistic female character who struggles with proscribed social roles and expectations, especially those related to marriage. In particular, these works call attention to contemporary revisions of the Victorian marriage plot. Thus, for example, in *A Modern Amazon* (1894) Regina Haughton painfully attempts to reconcile her identity as a free individual and a journalist with the expectations of marriage by changing the terms of her marriage contract. *A Bread and Butter Miss: A Sketch in Outline* (1895), about a girl's education into the cruel power plays of social and sexual relations, provides a richly comic portrait of a nineteenth-century character operating within an eighteenth-century plot device. *A Study in Prejudices* (1895) depicts the annihilation of a creative and energetic would-be artist through her marriage to an overbearingly conventional and suspicious husband.

A Bread and Butter Miss is particularly revealing of Paston's affection for the eighteenth century in its play on the conventions of the gothic. An innocent country girl is invited to join a high-society house party by a seemingly kindly acquaintance. Once there, she is gradually made to realize that her place in the network of seamy flirtations is to provide the object of dalliance for a lecherous older man, freeing his wife to carry on her own affair. Instead of succumbing to these entrapments Theodora Western responds to them with a liberating and unwavering forthrightness—like Catherine Moreland, the heroine of Jane Austen's *Northanger Abbey* (1818), reborn into New Womanhood. When her would-be seducer attempts to trick her into spending a night with him by missing the train, she foils his efforts by arranging seats in a luggage train. When the rascal offers to "take all the blame of this contretemps upon myself," Theodora replies, "I think you could hardly do less."

Reviews of these early novels were mixed. *A Modern Amazon* and *A Bread and Butter Miss* were treated as well-written but lightweight fiction. *The Athenaeum* (5 May 1894) commented that *A Modern Amazon* "will amuse more than it will engross. It does not plumb the depths of its strongest situations, but in most of them it gets well below the surface." *The Academy* said that it had "some wit and a general readableness." *A Study in Prejudices* was taken more seriously, with particular attention paid to the character of Miles Dormer, the husband. As *The Athenaeum* (19 October 1895) reviewer's suggestion that "it is open to question whether Mr. Paston entirely realizes what a poor figure Miles Dormer cuts alike in his courtship and married life" makes clear, however, readers were underestimating the ironic depth of Paston's vision. Read in the context of her biographical studies, Paston's portraits both of Miles Dormer and of his wife, Cecily, seem carefully calculated to epitomize an historical accumulation of traditional attitudes toward women, as well as to show the consequences of those attitudes in the modern world. Thus, when Miles discovers his wife's mildly flirtatious past, his disillusionment is proportionate only to a lost ideal of domestic womanhood; yet Cecily fully accepts his condemnation of her character: "I always knew that you would be disappointed in me when you found me out. Please make up your mind, once and for all, that I am a very unsatisfactory person, but that with your help I may be more worthy of your trust and affection some day."

Where Cecily's responses are scripted by traditional mores—to the point that she dies in martyrdom with her remorseful husband at her bedside—each of

Paston's successive protagonists learns to challenge, if not entirely refute, those expectations. In *The Career of Candida* (1896) the heroine is given a boy's education by her unusual father and, when offered her choice of the careers available to women, trains to become a gymnastics instructor. When Candida's unhappy marriage to an unfaithful alcoholic becomes unbearable, she is able to leave her husband and support herself and her child by returning to her career; and when the ailing husband reappears, the narrator offers a clear indictment of Candida's acceptance of marital self-sacrifice:

> And Candida walked home through the darkening streets, her eyes shining because the future lay dim before her, her step buoyant because the yoke was upon her neck again, her mind at ease because she had just assumed a grave responsibility, and her heart satisfied because she had flung all hopes of happiness away.

Since Paston lists her own recreations in the *Who's Who* of 1908 as "reading, bicycling, gymnastics," this fictional portrait of a career woman who is stronger and healthier than most men may reflect Paston's determination to cultivate physical strength and a career over marriage. Bennett commented in his journal (11 October 1896) that "Miss Symonds, on the whole the most advanced and intellectually fearless woman I have met, stuck to the old formula that a woman should marry a man 10 years her senior" because "a woman matures earlier than a man and that at 40 a woman is middle-aged, while the man . . . etc. The old reasons, which I combated, with cases in point to support my view." The disjunction between happiness and marriage that is reinforced in most of Paston's novels, however, may explain why she never married.

Although the institution of marriage was being challenged in much of the New Woman literature and some of the suffrage material of the period, Paston's views on marriage were by no means widely accepted. Some of the negative reviewers seem to object most strongly to this feminist subtext. The 5 May 1894 review of *A Modern Amazon* in *The Athenaeum* describes Regina Haughton as "just a little Ibsenite, a little 'Woman's Rights,' a little emancipationist, but as selfish in disposition and as *farouche* in manner as the most unlovely of her type." The July 1895 *Bookman* (London) review of *A Study in Prejudices,* which is generally more favorable, begins, "*A Study in Prejudices* has undoubtedly been written to catch the taste of the hour, and for this reason, that it truckles to the rough-shod fashion of trampling on the sanctities of the married life, one is inclined to condemn it without hearing."

By 1897 Paston's novelistic career was well underway, and, in contrast to the situation of her protagonists, her work was supported by a lively and loving home life. Bennett's description in his journal (11 October 1897) of the writer and her mother suggests the ideal nature of their relationship and lifestyle.

> As I listened to this mother and daughter recounting their deeds and wanderings since I last saw them, I was struck by their faculty for extracting from life pleasure and amusement. They read everything that appears, travel during several months in the year, gamble soberly when gambling is to be had, and generally make it a duty to go through life with as much pleasantness and change as will not fatigue them. Both are witty, and neither is afraid of criticizing her friends, or of getting fun out of idols. The daughter writes clever novels, and exhibits a good-humoured, railing tolerance for all "missions" including her own.
> They live alone, and love to throw a dart at "men." They are cultured and latitudinarian. They are never shocked, or very seldom, and then instead of showing it, they faintly sneer at the objectionable thing. Backed by a certain income, they know they can hold their own in any way against anybody, and the thought gives them a fine sense of security. No struggle for them! They are among the conquerors, for they have brains and wit, as well as money, and they are philosophers enough to know how to live, calmly, reticently, yet gaily, and sometimes with abandon. They have attained wisdom, in that they accept the world as it is, endeavour to improve it according to their talents, eschew impossible ideals and look after themselves.

In *A Fair Deceiver* (1898) Paston shifts attention from the institution of marriage to focus on character studies of two sisters who have fundamentally contrasting approaches to life. The younger sister, Lesbia, is a beautiful and flirtatious sensualist; the older, Magda, is determinedly pursuing an intellectual life. When Lesbia casually wins the affections of a visiting historian, Anthony, with whom Magda has fallen in love, the novel plays out the course of this misplaced but passionate attraction in ways that reveal the powerful differences between the sisters. Just as Paston makes clear that the common ground and mutual affection of Magda and Anthony would provide a stronger basis for marriage, she also provides a complex portrait of Lesbia's vibrant, nonintellectual, and nonmonogamous sensuality. While this portrayal of a woman's desire outside of marriage is unusual for its time, Lesbia finally suffers a painful and untimely death—thus allowing for a traditional, although slightly ambiguous, closure.

By contrast, Paston's final novel, *A Writer of Books* (1898), represents the culmination of her successful manipulation of the marriage plot. The novel follows the apprenticeship of a young writer from her

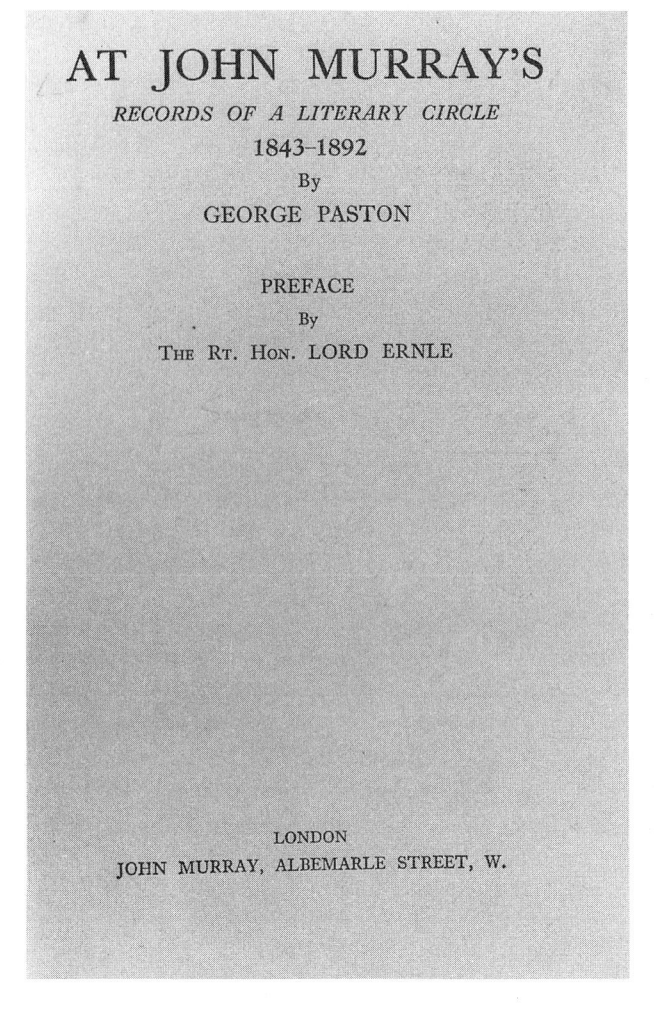

Frontispiece and title page for the last work the author completed before her death, a history of the influential British publishing house

early efforts at journalistic writing and ill-received fiction through her attempts to remain in an unsuitable marriage. In a triumphant final chapter Cosima Chudleigh leaves her unfaithful husband, rejects the opportunity to flee to a faithful lover, and sits down to write her great novel:

> Love may once have been a woman's whole existence, but that was when a skein of embroidery silk was the only other string to her bow. In the life of the modern woman, blessed with an almost inexhaustible supply of strings, love is no less episodical than in the life of a man. It may be eagerly longed for, it may be tenderly cherished, but it has been deposed for ever from its proud position of "lord of all."

Reviews of *The Career of Candida* and *A Writer of Books* were positive, although critics continued to object to the novel being used for didactic purposes. *The Spectator* (15 October 1898), for instance, commented favorably on the stylistic grace and character development in the novel but criticized Paston's views on marriage: "The Pictures of the Feminine side of New Grub Street are admirably done, and the ease and excellence of the style are so remarkable as to make one regret that this brilliant writer cannot find it in her heart or her conscience to take a happier view of the possibilities of married life."

A Writer of Books and the recognition implied there about the rewards of a career in the modern age seem to have provided Paston with a satisfactory finale to her own novelistic work. Just when she was gaining notice and respect as a novelist, she moved on to write plays and literary biographies. In December 1898, as Paston was writing the last of her novels, *The Academy* summarized "George Paston's" career as a promising young novelist while unmasking the author as a woman. The review praises her "wit" and "agile intellectuality" and discusses the merits and drawbacks of her reputation as "a writer with a purpose":

> Had she lived early in the century she would have written essays. What does interest "George Paston" is the question of "women's rights"—the inequality of women with men before the law and before social custom. The existing condition of affairs, whether right or wrong, arouses—not her indignation, for she is too serene to be actively indignant, but—a certain calm, mordant bitterness of spirit, a bitterness which is coldly resentful against men, and which despises women while it pities them.

Whatever her feelings about the limits of fiction and its reception, Paston went on to write essays and to test the capacity of biographical and dramatic forms to critique the social conditions of her own and previous centuries.

Paston's first full-length biographical study, *Mrs. Delany (Mary Granville): A Memoir, 1700–1788* (1900), was actually an abridged edition of an eighteenth-century autobiography by Granville, interspersed with correspondence that Paston had collected and some additional commentary. This technique was to become the basis for all of her biographical studies, including her longer works on Richard Benjamin Haydon (1905) and Alexander Pope (1909); in each case she relied heavily on the subject's letters and those of his or her contemporaries, as well as diary entries, memoirs, and newspaper and periodical accounts. When she collated these archival materials, adding her own commentary and general information about the period, the effect was to historicize the subject in the context of contemporary mores and estimations, highlighting their rhetorical masks and deflating their pretensions.

In compiling these biographical portraits Paston seems to have become acutely aware of the strata of class distinctions that were excluded or obscured in her earlier work. Thus, for example, in "The Ideal Woman," in *Side-lights on the Georgian Period* (1902), a polemical and cautionary account of eighteenth-century educational practices and social pressures, she notes: "It is probably needless to explain that the word 'woman' is here used to indicate the female of the upper class, since it is with the conditions of her life alone that the masculine idealist ever troubles himself." Paston attempted to remedy this deficiency in her own work by including the letters of Elizabeth Girling, the "daughter of a yeoman farmer," in the collection, just as she included James Lackington, "bootmaker and bookseller," as a representative of the "trading or labouring classes of the period" in *Little Memoirs of the Eighteenth Century* (1901).

After the publication of *Mr. Pope, His Life and Times* in 1909 Paston focused exclusively on drama; the next fifteen years brought the publication of eight plays, most of them comedies or farces. The interest in representing a broader class stratum that she exhibited in her biographical work seems to have influenced her dramatics as well. For instance, *Feed the Brute* (1909) centers with caustic humor on a hungry working-class husband who is soothed into humanity by the domestic blandishments and good cooking of his wife. *Tilda's New Hat* (1909) plays out a working-class love triangle in which Tilda, the strong central character, deliberately jeopardizes the interest of her latest beau by loaning her new and attractive hat to his former love, her own best friend. *Clothes and the Woman* (1922) continues this theme in a middle-class setting. Its protagonist, the writer Robina Fleming, discovers the power of appearance in transforming her relationships with men. Although Paston remained best known for her literary biographies, her dramatic career was also a success. *Nobody's Daughter,* a feminist drama that was first published in 1924—although it was performed as early as 1910—ran for 185 performances. Her other plays were moderately successful, as well, although she is still listed in the *Who's Who* volumes of the period as a novelist. In 1923 her mother presumably died, because that year she moved to 7 Pelham Place, where she lived alone until her own death on 12 September 1936. Her last completed work was *At John Murray's: Records of a Literary Circle, 1843–1892* (1932). Peter Quennel completed *"To Lord Byron": Feminine Profiles Based upon Unpublished Letters, 1807–1942* (1939), which Paston left unfinished at her death.

Like many of the eighteenth- and nineteenth-century characters that Paston resurrected for her two *Little Memoirs,* she was once well known and prolific and has now "fallen, whether deservedly or not, into neglect, if not oblivion." There is no biography of life and no bibliography or modern criticism of her work. Her longer biographical studies were consulted well into the twentieth century and probably outlasted other contemporary biographies as useful resources because of the wealth of primary materials that Paston collected. Her novels are rewarding both as fiction and as documentary accounts of a fascinating period in literary history.

Reference:

The Journals of Arnold Bennett, 1896–1928, 3 volumes, edited by Newman Flower (London: Cassell, 1932–1933).

Henry Handel Richardson
(Ethel Florence Lindesay)
(3 January 1870 – 20 March 1946)

Laurie Clancy
La Trobe University

BOOKS: *Maurice Guest* (London: Heinemann, 1908; New York: Reynolds, 1908);

The Getting of Wisdom (London: Heinemann, 1910; New York: Duffield, 1910; revised edition, London: Heinemann, 1931; New York: Norton, 1931);

The Fortunes of Richard Mahony: Australia Felix (London: Heinemann, 1917; New York: Holt, 1917);

The Way Home: Being the Second Part of the Chronicle of the Fortunes of Richard Mahony (London: Heinemann, 1925; New York: Norton, 1930);

Ultima Thule: Being the Third Part of the Chronicle of the Fortunes of Richard Mahony (London: Heinemann, 1929; New York: Norton, 1929);

Two Studies (London: Simpkin, Marshall/Ulysses Press, 1931);

The Bath: An Aquarelle (Sydney: Stephenson, 1933);

The End of a Childhood, and Other Stories (London: Heinemann, 1934; New York: Norton, 1934);

The Young Cosima (London: Heinemann, 1939; New York: Norton, 1939);

Myself When Young (London & Melbourne: Heinemann, 1948; New York: Norton, 1948);

The Adventures of Cuffy Mahony and Other Stories (Sydney: Angus & Robertson, 1979);

The End of a Childhood: The Complete Stories of Henry Handel Richardson (Pymble, New South Wales: Angus & Robertson, 1992).

Collection: *Henry Handel Richardson: The Getting of Wisdom: Stories, Selected Prose and Correspondence,* edited by Susan Lever and Catherine Pratt (St. Lucia, Queensland & Portland, Ore.: University of Queensland Press, 1997).

TRANSLATION: Jens Peter Jacobsen, *Siren Voices: Niels Lyhne* (London: Heinemann, 1896).

SELECTED PERIODICAL PUBLICATION—UNCOLLECTED: "Some Notes on My Books," *Southerly,* 23, no. 1 (1963): 8–19.

Henry Handel Richardson

Born in East Melbourne, Victoria, Australia, Ethel Florence Lindesay, the writer known as Henry Handel Richardson, left her native country at the age of seventeen, returning only for one brief visit to refresh her memory while working on her Richard Mahony chronicle. She is, however, probably better known in Australia than in England, where she lived, worked, and published her writings for most of her life. Although readers have admired her sensitive and closely autobiographical account of growing up in Melbourne, *The Getting of Wisdom* (1910), her poignant stories about youth and adolescence, and two other novels, her reputation largely rests on her masterpiece, *The Fortunes of Richard Mahony*, published in three separate volumes from 1917 to 1929 before finally being brought together in 1929. This trilogy is a grimly exhaustive documentation of the life of a medical practitioner on the gold fields of Ballarat, Victoria, and later in Melbourne and of the young wife who loyally supports him until his ultimate madness and death despite her failure to understand his complex and destructive personality.

Ethel Lindesay was born on 3 January 1870, the elder of two daughters of Walter Lindesay Richardson and Mary Bailey Richardson, on whom she closely modeled the protagonists of *The Fortunes of Richard Mahony*. Of Irish Protestant descent, Walter Richardson, whose father died shortly after his birth, was brought up by his mother and inherited much of her religious intensity. After graduating from the University of Edinburgh as a doctor, Richardson became dissatisfied with the opportunities around him, and in 1852, attracted by widespread reports of gold discoveries in Australia, he migrated to Victoria, where he worked for a time as a digger on the Ballarat goldfields and then as a storekeeper before reverting to the practice of medicine. In 1855 he married Mary Bailey, ten years his junior, a poorly educated but practical and loving woman who had emigrated from England in 1853. Much of Richardson's writing, she frankly confessed, is based on personal or keenly observed experience, and *The Fortunes of Richard Mahony* follows closely the events of her parents' lives, especially as recounted in letters Walter wrote to his wife, which came into Richardson's possession. Sometimes the names of the characters are changed only slightly from those of their real-life counterparts.

By the time Ethel was born in 1870 her parents had suffered through years of hardship to become relatively wealthy, more through Richardson's investments than his medical work. He passed his inherent sense of restlessness and self-doubt on to his daughter "Ettie," as she was known, who grew up in an atmosphere of uncertainty and confusion. A sudden collapse in the value of Walter's investments meant that the financial affluence he had enjoyed for a while disappeared. He was forced to return hurriedly from a European trip and again take up his medical practice in the colony. Although her sister, Ada (born a year later and known as Lil or Lillie), adapted cheerfully enough, there was continual tension between the precocious Ettie and her fiery mother. The situation with the family became worse when Walter Richardson's new practice at Hawthorn failed, and he was forced to move to the country, in Chiltern. After a bright start his practice there began to fail as well, and the oppressive summer heat caused a deep decline in his health. Ettie suffered from the constant quarreling between her parents and began walking in her sleep.

By the time Walter Richardson was forced to leave Chilton and commence a new practice in Queenscliff his health was failing fast, and he was probably in the first stages of what was then called general paralysis of the insane. Ettie and Lil, however, enjoyed Queenscliff and the relative freedom it gave them, and in her autobiographical *Myself When Young* (1948), she wrote of a romantic attachment she had with a boy four and one-half years her elder, but in characteristically unromantic terms: "I had no objection to being liked, but found the sitting hand-in-hand that went with sweethearting dull work, endurable only for the sake of the presents it brought me, in the shape of rare shells and pretty bits of seaweed." As Richardson's health declined further and his erratic behavior made him a laughingstock in the community, his wife was forced to take the position of postmistress in the small country town of Koroit in southwest Victoria while her husband was committed to a government asylum, with what would only much later be diagnosed as the tertiary stage of syphilis. He was allowed to return home in February 1879 and, as expected, died a few months later, a totally broken man at only fifty-three. It was this tragic story that Henry Handel Richardson would make the basis of her greatest novel and that would thus liberate her from her long-held feelings of shame and guilt toward her father.

In barren and isolated Koroit, Ettie had been forced back on her own resources. She had begun to write almost incessantly and to read every book she could lay her hands on, as well as practicing on her piano. Her biographer Axel Clark has spoken of Walter's declining years as "Ettie's formative years of insecurity, embarrassment and terror," but he also notes that, unlike her submissive sister, the young girl was full of independence and self-pride.

When Mary Richardson was promoted to postmistress of the much larger town of Maldon, the family moved yet again. The author has given a glowing account of this period in her life, when her mother was finally at rest in "the knowledge that her children were their happy selves again, enjoying life as they were meant to." She writes frankly of a passionate infatuation she conceived for the new vicar, a handsome, charismatic man named Jack Stretch, and of the difficulty she had in overcoming it, to the point that he was still on her mind when she left Australia six years later. When the fourteen-year-old girl learned of his imminent marriage from a friend, Richardson says, "The words were like a fresh dagger-thrust to my bleeding heart." Only many years later did Richardson discover from a chance comment that Stretch had been exceptionally fond of her: "Its effect was to bring my age-old defences of time and oblivion toppling down." Richardson traces the origins of *Maurice Guest* (1908) to her experience of this unconsummated affair.

At the age of thirteen Ettie became a boarder at the Presbyterian Ladies' College in Melbourne, and her years there gave her the material for her second novel, *The Getting of Wisdom*. She wrote in *Myself When Young* that the novel included "a very fair account of my doing at school and of those I came into contact with," though, she conceded, "seen through the eyes of a very young girl and judged accordingly." Like much of her life and fiction, it is largely an account of successive humiliations though Richardson spoke of it, oddly, as a "merry" little book, written simultaneously with *Maurice Guest* as a means of relieving herself from the distress of writing that novel. The sense of humiliation and a deep vein of pessimism runs through most, if not all, of Richardson's fiction, and even her accounts of her childhood in her autobiography have been shown to be colored with undue darkness.

Like her fictional counterpart, Laura Rambotham, she was mocked for her appalling French accent, her impoverished background, and her general assertiveness, a mask for concealing a deeply sensitive nature. She overcame these handicaps, however, with her natural intelligence. While she never became popular, she benefited from the school's often excellent teaching and showed particular promise as a pianist. Richardson sums up her experiences with characteristic wryness and maturity in *Myself When Young*: "I cannot remember ever being really happy at school. None the less I should have been sorry to miss a day of the four to five years I spent there."

At the same time, like her fictional counterpart in *The Getting of Wisdom,* she developed an intense passion for her roommate, Constance Cochran, a beautiful young woman several years older than Ettie. Richardson's account in her autobiography is as discreet as that in the novel; but after careful investigation of the circumstances Axel Clark concludes cautiously of Richardson that "in adult life she showed a strong, sympathetic interest in homosexual relations, and formed attachments with women that appear to have been essentially homosexual in character." He cites *The Getting of Wisdom* and the group of stories to which she gave the collective title "Growing Pains" as evidence that "her adolescent feelings about sexual and social intercourse between men and women included a strong element of embarrassed revulsion, and were tinged by a dislike of men." Yet, Dorothy Green in her *Henry Handel Richardson and Her Fiction* (1986) indignantly denies any such suggestion.

Ettie's relationship with Connie impeded her scholarly efforts, but she still managed to matriculate quite honorably at the end of 1886. In particular she won a long-coveted Senior Pianoforte Scholarship and had her composition, a setting of Alfred Tennyson's "The Sea-Fairies," performed at a college concert to widespread acclaim. She also became an excellent tennis player, retaining her love of the game throughout her life.

The family moved to Melbourne in January 1887, with Mary Richardson having been appointed postmistress in the inner suburb of Richmond. Life continued to be miserable in many respects for the young girl, who fought with her mother and bitterly rejected the attempts by Connie to maintain their friendship. Mary eventually resigned from her position, and with the sale of the Hawthorn house at a good profit the family was in a position to travel abroad. They sailed in August 1888, intending to stay away for a year; in reality the departure was a final one, especially for Mary Richardson, who never saw Australia again.

From England, which Mary enjoyed but Ettie compared constantly and unfavorably to her native country, the family moved to Leipzig early in 1889. Ettie was accepted as a student by a former pupil of Franz Liszt, Johannes Weidenbach, who became the model for Schwarz in *Maurice Guest*. Richardson always claimed that her eventual failure as a pianist was owing to her lifelong dislike of being stared at, but there is evidence that more than shyness was involved and that her comparative modesty about her musical talents was justified. Richardson also engaged in some composing, for which she received little encouragement. She later commented ruefully that she still thought her musical talents had been undervalued.

Leipzig was important to Ettie for another reason, however. There she met a tall, shy Scottish student of German literature named John George Robertson. Under his influence she developed a love and knowledge of a wide range of European literature, which began to distract her from her musical studies. Ettie and George, as he was known, became engaged in 1891, much to the dismay of her mother, who saw the collapse of her dream of a world-famous daughter. In her autobiography Richardson pays generous tribute to Robertson's learning and kindness and employs the word "comradeship" to describe a relationship that was clearly both intense and enduring.

Ettie left the Conservatorium in 1892 without completing her studies, for reasons which are not quite clear. She herself gave different accounts of the event, but it seems probable that it was connected with the realization that she would never achieve greatness as a musician. The Richardsons returned to England in the same year, George staying behind to complete his doctorate. In her autobiography Richardson glosses over the next three years, but they appear to have been deeply unhappy after the intellectual excitement and the glamor of Leipzig. Despite his first-class honors doctorate, George had great difficulty in obtaining a university position, being invariably passed over for native Germans, and the two lovers stayed in contact only by correspondence.

What saved her was the beginning of her career as a writer. From magazine articles she graduated to an English translation of *Niels Lyhne* (1880), a remarkably influential novel in its time by the Danish poet Jens Peter Jacobsen. She had read the German translation, which stirred her as few books had done before or since. Her translation was published by Heinemann in 1896. Both she and her fiancé struggled to make a living by writing, but the problem of when and how they would ever marry was solved by a gift of £300 from Richardson's mother. The wedding took place in Dublin, in the home of a friend of Mary Richardson's, at the end of 1895, and the couple returned to Munich, where Richardson's family had gone to facilitate sister Lil's growing career as a violinist.

Richardson's autobiography ends its account of her life here, and for the later years one must rely on Richardson's companion Olga Roncoroni. George Robertson had intended to give his own account of the couple's life together, but he died unexpectedly in 1933 after a brief illness. Richardson never recovered from this tragedy. She had hoped that he would supply whatever details of her life were demanded but with his death felt obliged to break her own strict rules of privacy and set down the bare facts of her early life.

To their relief, work came in for Robertson as regularly as his wife had predicted, and they were able to make a satisfactory, if precarious, living together in Munich until Robertson was appointed a lecturer at the University of Strasbourg, which gave him a secure income. Richardson worked on a commissioned translation of Bjornstjerne Bjornson's novel *Fiskerjenten* (1868; The Fisher Lass) and began working on her own fiction as well, a short novel that would eventually turn into *Maurice Guest*. Almost simultaneously news came from her sister, Lil, that their mother was gravely ill; although skeptical, Ettie left her husband for the first time to travel to Munich, where she discovered that Mary was on the point of death.

The agonizing death of her mother had a profound effect on Richardson, which she later recorded in the excellent, bitter short story "Death," first published in *The English Review* in 1911 but later revised and retitled "Mary Christina" for the collection *Two Studies* (1931). Death was a subject she returned to repeatedly, and it prompted some of her most powerful writing. Reminiscent in some ways of Leo Tolstoy's "The Death of Ivan Ilych," "Mary Christina" displays Richardson's characteristic skepticism though Roncoroni claimed that in later life Richardson's views on death had greatly changed: "she had arrived at the conviction that death was but the gateway to a fuller, richer life, in which so much that we do not and cannot understand while in this world would be explained and justified: suffering, frustration, apparent failure." The ending sounds a familiar note in Richardson's work: " . . . not again would she choose to be of life. Now, she asked for rest—only rest. Not immortality: no fresh existence, to be enduring and fought out in some new shadow-land, among unquiet spirits."

At the time of her mother's death she had published only a series of articles, and later in 1897 there appeared in her diary the first glimmerings of *Maurice Guest,* although it was not published until eleven years later. Roncoroni, in her memoir of Richardson, cites George Robertson's diaries:

> Possibly the first suggestion of such creative writing had come to her from her husband, namely that she should utilise her own Leipzig experiences to form a novel of a musician who failed to make good. Progress was exceedingly slow and tentative at first; but from now on the word "novel" or "work" or a pet name for her new venture, "Tinkling Cymbals," appears frequently in the diary.

Toward the end of 1898 she suffered a serious illness, the beginning of acute bronchitis, and was sent to Bordighera, Italy, to recuperate, while Robertson stayed in Strasbourg to give his lectures. A long holiday at Badenweiler in the Black Forest helped Richardson to recover, but the illness recurred intermittently throughout her life. Her sister, Lil, married a Munich eye specialist in 1900, and in the same year George engaged himself in writing his *History of German Literature,* which laid the foundation for his highly successful career as a scholar of German literature.

A slow and painstaking craftswoman, Richardson worked assiduously on her novel through 1901, as her diary entries testify. In 1903 George accepted an offer of the chair of German literature at the University of London. Richardson, however, did not immediately join him, remaining in Munich to await the birth of her sister's son in December before arriving in London in January 1904. This move represented the end of seven happy years in Strasbourg, during which, despite her illnesses, Richardson had composed many songs as well as working on articles and her novel. Her husband later said that "it was perhaps the happiest period of our lives" and that "Henry never reconciled herself to life in England" although he seems to have adapted much more easily. Lacking social con-

Richardson's father, Walter Lindesay Richardson, M.D.

tact in England, Richardson was in effect forced to devote herself to her novel, which finally appeared in 1908.

Richardson's eponymous hero is the first example in her work of a type she returned to with Richard Mahony: a man of slight talent who is not content to accept his own mediocrity and yearns destructively for a way of life more ambitious and idealistic than that to which he is by nature fitted. As Robertson said in his essay "The Art of Henry Handel Richardson" (written in 1928–1929 but first published in *Myself When Young*), "the moral of *Maurice Guest* is that, for young people who, without abundant talent, endeavour to acquire the art, it spells destruction." As a young man, Maurice rejects the banal life in his provincial English village that his parents have set out for him and travels to Leipzig to try to become a musician. There he falls in love at first sight with Louise Defrayer, a beautiful woman in her late twenties who is infatuated with the ruthless genius Eugen Schilsky. When Schilsky abandons her cruelly, Maurice's tender and selfless devotion at last pays off, and Louise becomes his mistress. They go for an idyllic "honeymoon" in the country, and for a while all is well until inevitably Louise begins to tire of the kindhearted, loving, but rather boring Maurice, and they quarrel constantly and bitterly. At the end Schilsky returns to Leipzig, and Louise immediately leaves Maurice, who shoots himself. The novel closes with a brief glimpse of Schilsky and Louise two years later: they are married, and Schilsky is well on the way to a brilliant career as a composer.

The ending confirms the suggestion that behind the novel is Richardson's reading of Friedrich Nieztsche, particularly his notion of the *Übermensch*. All is forgiven to the artist who is genuinely a genius and to whom conventional ethical standards do not apply. Much the same concept informs Richardson's final novel, *The Young Cosima* (1939). Although both the setting and the material seem in many respects deeply romantic, Richardson has divested herself of the elements of playfulness and fantasy that characterized her as a child and writes in a tone of grim, objective authority. The privileged perspective of the novel belongs to Madeleine Wade, the sensible, totally self-controlled young woman who would have married Maurice but fails to attract him.

This central theme of the novel is announced during an exchange between Madeleine and a brilliant musician named Heinz Kraft. Madeleine wants to intervene in Maurice and Louise's affair and save Maurice from himself, but Kraft comments sardonically: "The artist has as much to do with morality, as, let us say, your musical festivals have to do with art. And if his genius isn't strong enough to float him, he goes under, *und damit basta!* The better for art. There are bunglers enough." Richardson characteristically does not commit herself to one side or another, but one senses that although she is on the side of those who dare, she is merciless towards those who exceed their natural grasp. At the start of the novel Maurice writes to his parents, "Something stronger than myself drove me to it, and if I am to succeed anywhere, it will be here. And I mean to succeed, if human will can do it." Long before the end of the novel this proud note has disappeared completely, and by the end Maurice is much as Louise describes him: "a mean-souled, despicable dummy of a man!"

Maurice Guest is a stolidly written but impressive novel. Richardson has performed the task she has set for herself–"that unceasing work of selection and rejection, which it is the story-teller's duty to perform for his readers"–although in an article called "Some Notes on My Books" (first published in 1940) she later went on to suggest that the process of selection and rejection had not been rigorous enough: "I consider *The Getting of Wisdom* one of the most firmly-knit of my books. In its greater compactness of form and expression, it also shows a marked improvement on the *longeurs,* the youthful desire to leave nothing unsaid, that characterized *Maurice Guest.*" Its critical reception in England was mixed, but it was noticed admiringly by writers as diverse as John Masefield, Somerset Maugham, and Hugh Walpole and was warmly received in the United States in 1908 and in Germany when it was translated in 1912. Referring to its influence on other writers, Robertson went so far as to say that "it was, in fact, one of the best pillaged books of the first decade of the century."

Literary recognition, in fact, came late to Richardson insofar as came at all—most notably with the eventual publication of her trilogy in one volume. Even in 1977, when Virago republished *The Getting of Wisdom,* Dorothy Green noted that some London critics still referred to her as "Mr. Richardson." The masculine pseudonym, chosen because of its connection to the Irish side of her heritage, with which she identified closely; the extreme privacy of her habits; and the greater reputation of her husband all militated against the fame that some part of her nevertheless craved. But the pseudonym was also a source of considerable private satisfaction, as she revealed in "Some Notes on My Books": "I was bent on keeping my identity a secret. There had been much talk in the press of that day about the ease with which a woman's work could be distinguished from a man's; and I wanted to try out the truth of the assertion." Richardson had the last laugh: reviewers of her first two novels mostly spoke of her as masculine, and when *The Getting of Wisdom* appeared, "I was congratulated, as a man, on my extraordinary insight into a little girl's mind."

The Getting of Wisdom works in a much more familiar genre than the first novel. It is a novel of growth and discovery, frequently involving the humiliating experiences of adolescence, the brutality of the educational system, and finally the emergence of the protagonist into at least an embryonic artist. Although Robertson called it "perhaps Henry Handel Richardson's most personal and least objective book, the one into which she has put most of herself," this is true only in the literal sense that it is the one most closely based on personal experience. In its firmly ironical tone with which the narrator describes the central figure it is similar to all her other work. The romancer and fantasist that she was as a teenager disappeared once she sat down to work.

Like many Australian novels and autobiographies, *The Getting of Wisdom* is about growing up in a world in which the protagonist has no place. Laura Rambotham is sent by her impoverished but socially ambitious mother to "The Ladies' College" in Melbourne in order to acquire the culture and sophistication she could never learn in the country. A spirited and imaginative girl, Laura can never hope to fit into the stifling atmosphere of the school. She is poor and of "low" birth whereas most of the fifty-five girls are either rich or upperclass or both, and she spends much of her time in terror that her origins will be revealed.

Perhaps more important, the mode and values of education that the school attempts to instill in its pupils, as well as the staff's obsession with the acquisition of information purely by rote, are anathema to her. No assumptions are questioned, no speculation permitted. Although Laura does not possess the musical talent and creativity that Richardson exhibited at school, Laura is shown to be highly creative in temperament. In the opening scene of the novel she is depicted as "Wondrous Fair," telling a fairy story to her siblings. Her piano playing, vigorous and bold although inexperienced, is given some attention, and there are also glimpses of her literary ability in the chapter devoted to the literary society to which she belongs, though for Laura true creativity does not lie in demonstrable accomplishments but rather in an inherent disposition. Laura is most creative when she speculates on the color of certain words, to the amusement of her schoolmates, or when she insists that she has visual images of what England is like and that these are more important than the mere mechanical listing of the dates of monarchs' reigns.

Crass materialism is the butt of much of Richardson's harsh satire. "What on earth's the matter?" one of the girls asks Laura. "Dreaming? Then depend on it you've eaten something that disagreed with you." Although the authority of the Bible is constantly deferred to, this too is ironic, given the uses to which the Holy Word is put throughout the novel by the girls—as a source of coded messages, as a cover for furtive conversations, and as a sex-education manual. Although the ending is ambiguous, there is at least the suggestion that like Richardson, Laura is strong-minded enough to throw off the blighting effects of her education and go on to accomplish something important in the arts.

In 1912 Richardson made a brief return to Australia for the only time in her life in order to refresh her memories and gather material for the trilogy she must already have begun to plan. She retraced the actual country her parents traversed on the way to Ballarat, carefully observing and memorizing the landscapes, revisiting the Presbyterian Ladies College (where she claims she was refused admittance), and constantly taking notes, the book still forming in her mind.

Completed in 1915, *The Fortunes of Richard Mahony* appeared in 1917 with an additional subtitle that seems to have been intended as the generic title of the

Richardson; her mother, Mary Bailey Richardson; and her younger sister, Ada Lilian

series: *Australia Felix*. The second volume was published in 1925 as *The Way Home: Being the Second Part of the Chronicle of the Fortunes of Richard Mahony*. It was with the third volume, *Ultima Thule* (1929), that Richardson's genius was finally recognized. She was awarded the Australian Literature Society's Gold Medal in 1929 and was unsuccessfully nominated for the Nobel Prize for literature in 1932.

Describing the genesis of the trilogy, Richardson says that where most Australian novels had been tales of adventure and success, she wanted to write about the other side of life: "What of the failures, to whose lot neither fortunes nor stirring adventures fell? The misfits, who were physically and mentally incapable of adapting themselves to this strange and new world?" Knowing for the first time exactly what she had in mind, Richardson assembled the materials she needed—family letters and vague childhood memories but also (with the assiduous aid of her bibliophile husband) "histories, volumes of travel, pictures, maps"— and set to work. "The book," she recalled in *Myself When Young*, "almost wrote itself, poured forth so effortlessly and at such speed that, as with *Maurice*, I have never been able to reread it."

Laying the completed manuscript aside in 1912, she traveled to Australia for her research trip, returned to England to revise the manuscript, and by 1915 it was ready for press. William Heinemann, however, citing the distraction of the war, delayed publication until 1917. The history of the publication of the trilogy is a sad one of constant setbacks and difficulties, and there seems little doubt that this fate affected its critical reception for a long time. Although *Australia Felix* received generally good notices, it was soon forgotten in both England and the United States. Of its initial reception in her native country Richardson commented: "Opinions ranged from 'a dull but honest volume' to 'might have been written by a retired grocer.'"

Despite ill health and the convulsions of the war, Richardson ploughed slowly on with her writing, finishing *The Way Home,* which Heinemann published somewhat reluctantly to a cool reception from the critics: Richardson's most ardent supporter, William Heinemann, had died in 1921. With dismay Richardson realized that the story of Richard Mahony was still not over, and a third volume was necessary. She labored over the conclusion to the story with a deep sense of failure and pessimism: "William Heinemann once remarked that, if a writer still failed of success with his third book, his case might be considered hopeless," she wrote. "And here was I, with four books to my name, and as far from making good as ever."

When *Ultima Thule* was finished in 1928, Richardson discovered, more to her surprise than anger, that Heinemann was unwilling to publish the novel. It eventually appeared in January 1929 in a tiny edition of one thousand copies subsidized by George Robertson. To the author's amazement the novel was an instant critical and even popular success. New impressions were published monthly; *Australia Felix* and *The Way Home* were hurried back into print; and for the first time the true magnitude of the whole achievement could be fully grasped. Most satisfying of all, Heinemann went to Richardson and begged to be allowed to reassume control of her work. Overcoming her irate husband's objections, she finally allowed them to do so.

The Fortunes of Richard Mahony works, unevenly and with varying emphasis at different times, on three levels. On the simplest of these it is a comparative study of two cultures, those of England and Australia, with its protagonist unhappily crossing back and forth between the two, at home in neither. It is also the study of a particular, potentially tragic, individual, possessed of a human wish for fulfillment and understanding but temperamentally incapable of either. Most important, in the tradition of the great Russian novels that Richardson admired, it is a novel that, for all its apparent materialism of both subject matter and method, is at heart preoccupied with the most fundamental philosophical and metaphysical questions. Why are we born? Why is there death and suffering? What awaits us after death? From the brutal drowning of a puppy in Venice to John Turnham's cruel, inexplicably painful death at the height of his success, the novel implacably confronts the central mysteries and enigmas in life and attempts to resolve them.

The first volume, titled with obvious irony *Australia Felix,* opens with a poem that begins "In a shaft on the Gravel Pits, a man had been buried alive," a prefiguring of Mahony's eventual fate. Our first glimpse of Mahony on the gold fields of Ballarat is of a man patently at odds with himself and everyone around him. Politically conservative, fiercely monarchist, and intensely conscious of class, he could not be more distinct from his fellows. By the end of the novel he has married Mary, a young Irish girl, and returned to his medical practice after giving up on the diggings. Under the combined effects of emotional distress and the harsh Australian climate he collapses and recovers only partially before resolving to return to England, to the silent disapproval of Mary. The novel stresses Mahony's restlessness and dissatisfaction as well as the intensity of his spiritual and intellectual yearnings. His interests and knowledge, from spiritualism to lepidopterology, signify his impressive intellect.

In *The Way Home* Mahony finds himself predictably no happier than he was in Australia, and the contrasts between the two countries are both pointed and strikingly deliberate. The sense of space and openness in Australia is contrasted against the almost artificially patterned and domesticated fields of England. When Mary first sees the beauty of England's fields, she struggles for an analogy and finally comes up with the somewhat incongruous one of the Melbourne Botanic Gardens. Richardson says of Mahony, "But he understood what she was trying to say. If the landscape before them was lovely as a garden, it had also something of a garden's limitations. There was an air of arrangedness about it; it might have been laid out according to plan, and on pleasing, but rather finikin lines; it was all exquisite, but a trifle overdressed." Australia may be almost unbearably hot and dry, but England is dark, claustrophobic, and rainy. Later, when the Mahonys return to England a second time, Mary, whose feelings about the country are far less equivocal than her husband's, is glad that this time they are going back in comfort but regrets that nothing can be done about the rain.

As for the inhabitants, the novel is again evenhanded. The vulgarity, materialism, and effusive social manners of Australia are weighed against the snobbishness, cringing servility, and sheer malice the Mahonys encounter in England. With the exception of Mary's mother there is not a single likable person in the two English sections of the novel. Richardson says bluntly of Mahony, "Long residence in a land where every honest man was the equal of his neighbour had unfitted him for the genuflexions of the English middle-classes before the footstools of the great." This section of the novel ends with a violent attack on English society and customs:

> they had come back to find an England that had not budged by an inch; where people's outlook, habits, opinions were just what they had always been—inelastic, uninspired. Worse, these islanders seemed to preen themselves on their very rigidity, their narrow-mindedness, their ignorance of any life or country but their own; waving aside with an elegant flutter of the hand, everything of which they themselves had no cognisance.

So Mahony again takes to the sea, where he always feels at home and Mary, significantly, always feels ill. When he returns to Australia, this misanthropic, prickly man is moved by the welcome he receives.

His investments having prospered, Mahony retires prematurely and begins in earnest his studies of "life's ultimate goal, and the moral mysteries of the soul of man." It is here that the question of the stature of Mahony as a tragic protagonist arises. It would seem that to a certain extent Richard and Mary are intended to represent, in Jungian terms, the male animus and the female anima. Mahony is questing and intellectual, acting from what he perceives to be reason; Mary is content with stability and is nonintellectual, acting essentially on intuition. When Mahony says at one point that Mary does not really believe in God, she is horrified by the suggestion, although there is a sense in which it is true.

Richardson's presentation of Mary is sometimes criticized for the limitations and even banality of her common sense and the cloying domesticity with which she is preoccupied. But in many respects Richardson's real failure is in her portrayal of Mahony himself. The translation from external to internal is imperfect. The reader can never be quite convinced of Mahony's personal significance or of the passion or intensity of his quest for meaning. As a result the contest between him and Mary becomes unequal. She seems simply right most of the time in her judgments, from her distrust of her husband's speculative ventures to her skepticism at his dabbling in spiritualism, and it is

Richardson and her husband, John George Robertson, in 1896

never clear what lifts Mahony above the level of the ordinary people he affects to despise. Paradoxically, in *The Fortunes of Richard Mahony,* Mahony cannot really achieve the reader's sympathy until he is so far gone physically and mentally that he has become merely pitiable. It is only in his increasing degradation and misery that he becomes a tragic figure.

This change occurs in the third volume of the trilogy, *Ultima Thule*–the title is derived from the name of the Mahonys' house in *The Way Home* but also connotes the farthest point, the extreme limit of travel, geographically and figuratively. Even as the couple makes the belated, delightful discovery that Mary is able to have children after all, the symptoms of Mahony's failing health have begun to show more markedly. *The Way Home* ends with the news that they have been defrauded of their fortune, and Mahony is forced to hurry back to Australia. In *Ultima Thule* he is a ruined, forty-nine-year-old man, estranged from the landscape where he is fated to remain until the ironic relief of madness and death.

As he wanders from place to place practicing medicine in Hawthorn, Barambogie, Shortlands, a madhouse in Collingwood, and finally Gymgurra, he is battered remorselessly by the rigors of the climate. Richardson remains sympathetic but detached, frequently resorting to the point of view of the Mahonys' young son, Cuffy, in order to offer impersonal judgments. The boy is often an observer and unwitting critic of his parents' many marital quarrels, but he is also portrayed as the victim and object, as well as their innocent provoker, of marital discord. One of the elements that makes the novel so uncompromising is Richardson's refusal to offer anything morally uplifting in Mahony's fate. With a child's sometimes cruel honesty, Cuffy is simply relieved when his father dies, no matter how guilty he feels about it, and it is easy to read into this the author's own response to the death of her father.

As Mahony loses whatever stature he had and reverts mentally to childhood, so the treatment of him becomes profoundly moving. *Ultima Thule* is punctuated by a series of brilliant set pieces in which, without sacrificing accuracy of observation, Richardson finds images that convey the man's psychic and physical collapse–his beating of his horse, his dream trial, his attempts at suicide and his ambiguous vision after its failure, his war with Mary, and finally the onset of madness, which is manifested in his fear of eyes and culminates with his attempt to burn down the family house. In a strange irony Mary grows stronger under this adversity, although her limitations become more pronounced. Her class consciousness and snobbishness are more apparent, and the gentleness and sensitivity she had shown earlier disappears under the strain of having to fight for her family's welfare. The struggle even affects her physical appearance: "in the hard-faced unscrupulous woman with which, at the end of the time, her glass presented her, she hardly recognized herself."

The limitations of the naturalistic mode are transcended in this volume, with its encyclopedic view of man struggling in what Mahony refers to as "the web called living." The novel is marked by an almost ceremonial series of domestic rites—deaths, departures, and homecomings—which culminates in a magnificent scene in which Mahony returns from the asylum by boat.

The Fortunes of Richard Mahony is a great novel, though not perhaps a novel about a great man. In its massively symphonic structure, in the relentless exhaustiveness of its portrayal of both a family and a society, and in the centrality of the concerns it seizes upon and the questions it asks, it is extraordinarily compelling and represents the peak of Richardson's achievement as a writer.

In their recollections of her, Richardson's contemporaries often spoke of an almost reclusive figure living in the upper story of her London house and dedicated solely to writing; but until the death of her husband from cancer in 1933 she seems to have been more active than that. She enjoyed regular walks, concerts, and visits to the cinema and was also fond of motor trips, for which purpose she acquired a handsome Armstrong-Siddeley.

In 1921 Richardson made the acquaintance of twenty-six-year-old Olga Roncoroni, an organist at a movie theater the Robertsons frequented. A deep friendship developed between the two women, and Roncoroni eventually came to stay with Richardson and her husband. After George's death she remained with Richardson as a companion, though often in ill health herself. The decade of the 1920s was a difficult time for Richardson, who recalled about the writing of *The Way Home:* "I became caught up and entangled in a private matter of such urgency that, for three out of the four years the writing took me, the book was a secondary consideration. On looking back, I sometimes wonder how it ever got itself written at all." The "private matter" (about which Richardson always remained reticent) involved tending to Roncoroni's health, which included accompanying her five times a week to the clinic where she was receiving Freudian analysis. Dorothy Green writes of Roncoroni, "She was pretty, vivacious, highly intelligent, wrote manuals about her work and was above all a competent musician. Her sense of fun appealed to Ethel's lighter side, and although life in the novelist's household was not easy, she agreed to a death-bed request by Robertson 'to look after Henry' when he had gone."

Roncoroni fulfilled her promise to Robertson by giving up her job and devoting herself solely to Richardson's affairs. She continued to serve the author faithfully, in fact, even after Richardson's death, arranging for the publication of *Myself When Young* as well as a book of personal impressions and memories to which admirers of Richardson are much indebted.

The success of *Ultima Thule* and subsequent publication of the trilogy in one volume had made Richardson a more attractive prospect to publishers. She consequently returned to the series of sketches about childhood and adolescence to which she gave the collective title "Growing Pains," including them as a section of *The End of a Childhood, and Other Stories* (1934), and wrote a new story, "Succedaneum." Jacob Schwartz, the owner of Ulysses Press, asked permission to reprint "Death," which, though it was first published twenty years before, he had never forgotten. Richardson revised it, retitled it "Mary Christina" ("for when I came to read it again, it seemed to me to be more about dying than death"), and together with "Life and Death of Peterle Luthy" it appeared as *Two Studies,* to favorable reviews.

In the meantime Richardson had conceived the idea of an historical novel on the period in Cosima Wagner's life during which she first became involved with the great composer and left her husband, Hans von Bülow. A Heinemann publisher, Arnold Gyde, has taken credit for suggesting the idea, but it is probable that it was in Richardson's mind as far back as Leipzig, when she studied music under the influence of Cosima's father, Franz Liszt.

While she struggled with this project, bringing to it her usual arduous research, she consented to the release of a collection of short stories, *The End of a Childhood,* which she subsequently described as a mixed bag that she regretted publishing. She had originally intended to carry the story of the Mahonys on to the second and even third generation but found the task beyond her physical powers. She did, however, write two stories about Cuffy Mahony that continue in the grim tradition of the novels. Most of Richardson's short fiction, which includes some of the most frequently anthologized stories in Australian literature, has been gathered in two collections, *The Adventures of Cuffy Mahony and Other Stories* (1979) and *The End of a Childhood: The Complete Stories of Henry Handel Richardson* (1992).

As Richardson claimed, the stories include much of her best work. Their main themes concern adolescence and death. In "The Adventures of Cuffy Mahony" Cuffy experiences the death of his mother, Mary, and separation from his sister, which is what the children feared most. It closes on a surprisingly resilient note, however, with Cuffy's distress already subsiding: "But after a time, as tears will, they ran dry; and then, very gradually, other and pleasanter thoughts insinuated themselves."

Though the sketches of girlhood collected as "Growing Pains" vary in quality and ambition, together they form a moving and delicate study of the pains and humiliations of growing up. Often a shameful event is the central experience in the stories. While the first stories deal with young adolescents, later stories move steadily closer to the treatment of sexual dilemmas, often involving a young girl and an older female companion. The implicit note of sexual protest begins to emerge more overtly in "And Women Must Weep," about a girl who is passed over as a partner at a dance, and again in "Two Hanged Women": "Oh, these men, who walked around and chose just who they fancied and left who they didn't . . . how she hated them! It wasn't fair . . . it wasn't fair." Richardson's treatments of the subject of death—especially "The Professor's Experiment"—are equally impressive.

Her husband's death from cancer in 1933 came as a shattering blow to Richardson, and she tried for long after to maintain contact with him through spiritualism. He was an invaluable source of support to her, always placing her work first while establishing a considerable reputation of his own as a German scholar. Roncoroni wrote:

> He was her sheet-anchor; there was nothing he did not do to make her life as easy as possible and keep her happy; indeed, this was his sole object in working as he did—to make enough money to be able to send her away on voyages and holidays abroad in order that she could renew her energy when she had written herself to a standstill. To him she turned for advice and comfort; and, though he never influenced her literary work in any way, his was the one opinion on this that she really valued.

Richardson's private papers, from which Roncoroni quotes, reveal the steadfastness and intensity of the couple's love for one another.

In 1934 Richardson moved with Roncoroni to Fairlight, near Hastings, and she refused to relocate when war broke out even though they were directly in the flight path of German bombers. Edna Purdie, who succeeded Robertson in the German chair at the University of London and who became Richardson's literary executor, paid regular visits to her until World War II. Her memories of this time, recorded in *Henry Handel Richardson: Some Personal Impressions* (1957), convey something of the sense of "an indomitable will confined in an increasingly delicate frame."

The Young Cosima was finally completed and published in 1939. It is Richardson's weakest novel, the only failure among her works. Cosima sets her sights on her father's most gifted pupil, Hans von Bülow, and they marry. Like Maurice Guest, Hans has the courage to reject his conventional legal career and give up all for his music, but Cosima realizes that he remains under the control of his domineering mother and his closest friend, Wagner, "the Master," whom Cosima finds physically repulsive. Yet Cosima breaks from von Bülow and declares her love for Wagner, who accepts it almost as a right even though he had not even noticed her previously. At the end of the novel Cosima decides to acknowledge publicly her illicit relationship with the composer: "For she had heard what she believed to be a 'call'; had found her life-work. And whether she went towards it in joy or in pain was not hers to decide."

The whole emphasis of Cosima's thinking is on sacrifice, and for Wagner she gives up in the end virtually everything she possesses: her two children with von Bülow, her nationality, her religion, and her public reputation. The novel seems to endorse the suggestion that artistic creativity is a male quality and that service and self-sacrifice are female ones. Thus, seemingly without irony the narrator says of Cosima as she assists Hans early in the novel, "In short, she began to have ideas of her own for the construction of a symphony, without, alas! the manly ability to supply a note of the music."

Although Richardson was frequently accused by critics of lacking imagination and relying too much on fact, it seems that she found herself hamstrung by the constrictions of historical accuracy when writing *The Young Cosima*. She did, though, receive great satisfaction from one critical notice in which the reviewer expressed shock that brilliant German intellectuals had been made to speak like Australian bushrangers: in fact much of the dialogue was literally translated from the letters of the actual figures about whom she wrote.

During the late 1930s Richardson and her companion continued to enjoy traveling, but the outbreak of war at the end of the decade, and the subsequent period of food rationing, exacerbated a decline in Richardson's health. Although she began a new novel—tentatively titled "Nick and Sanny"—in 1939, it was clearly destined never to be finished. She was constantly ill; shortages of coal meant that winter became something of an ordeal, and money problems developed. Most frightening of all, she began to have trouble with her sight. Under the stress of the bombing and the knowledge that imminent death was quite possible, Richardson wrote, "It may be that this war will make so clean a break with the immediate past that I and my work will never be heard of again. But it may also be that the British mind will have better learnt to face realities, and that my hard, unsentimental books will come into their own."

By September 1942 she had given up all hope of continuing to work on her fiction and began her autobiography. The manuscript of "Nick and Sanny" and a long story she had also begun were parceled up with the instructions that if she did not live to complete them they should be destroyed. From the spring of 1943 onward Richardson suffered a continual series of illnesses as the air raids increased and living conditions became more and more uncomfortable. Roncoroni's graphic account of the last years of her life make painful reading. That Richardson could even write her "Reminiscences," as she called them, was a remarkable feat, as was Roncoroni's unfailing care for Richardson while seriously ill herself. An operation in 1944 revealed that Richardson had incurable cancer of the colon, but she lived on for more than a year, as active as possible under the necessary physical constraints. Her last diary entry reads poignantly, "At table again . . . But no brains." She died on 20 March 1946. She was cremated at Golders Green five days later, and her ashes were scattered off Hastings with those of her husband.

Richardson's reputation as a novelist will always remain greatest in Australia, where she is seen as inferior perhaps only to Patrick White, but outside her native country it is more problematic. This situation has arisen partly because of the stubbornly old-fashioned naturalistic mode in which she wrote and partly because her best novel is set far from any metropolitan center. But she is continually being rediscovered, with surprise and delight, by both critics and novelists, most recently Karen McLeod and Doris Lessing.

Letters:
"Letters of Henry Handel Richardson to Nettie Palmer," edited by Karl-Johan Rossing, in *Essays and Studies in English Language and Literature,* volume 14 (Uppsala, Sweden: Lundequistska, 1953).

Bibliographies:
Gay Howells, *Henry Handel Richardson 1870–1946* (Canberra: National Library of Australia, 1970);

Henry Handel Richardson: A Guide to Her Papers in the National Library of Australia (Canberra: Manuscript Section, National Library of Australia, 1975).

Biographies:
Edna Purdie and Olga Roncoroni, eds., *Henry Handel Richardson: Some Personal Impressions* (Sydney: Angus & Robertson, 1957);

Axel Clark, *Henry Handel Richardson: Fiction in the Making* (Brookvale, N.S.W.: Simon & Schuster Australia, 1990).

References:
Vincent Buckley, *Henry Handel Richardson* (Melbourne: Lansdowne, 1961; Folcroft, Penn.: Folcroft Library Editions, 1973);

Dennis Douglas, *Henry Handel Richardson's 'Maurice Guest'* (Melbourne: Arnold, 1978);

Leonie J. Gibson, *Henry Handel Richardson and Some of Her Sources* (Melbourne: Melbourne University Press, 1954);

Dorothy Green, *Henry Handel Richardson and Her Fiction* (Sydney: Allen & Unwin, 1986);

Eva Jarring Carones, *The Portrayal of Women in the Fiction of Henry Handel Richardson* (Lund: C. W. K. Gleerup, 1983);

Karen McLeod, *Henry Handel Richardson: A Critical Study* (Cambridge & New York: Cambridge University Press, 1985);

J. R. Nichols, *Art and Irony: The Tragic Vision of Henry Handel Richardson* (Washington, D.C.: University Press of America, 1982);

Nettie Palmer, *Henry Handel Richardson: A Study* (Sydney: Angus & Robertson, 1950).

Elizabeth Robins
(6 August 1862 – 8 May 1952)

Sue Thomas
La Trobe University

BOOKS: *Alan's Wife: A Dramatic Study in Three Acts,* anonymous, by Robins and Florence Bell (London: Henry, 1893);

George Mandeville's Husband, as C. E. Raimond (London: Heinemann, 1894; New York: Appleton, 1894);

The New Moon, as C. E. Raimond (London: Heinemann, 1895; New York: Appleton, 1895);

Below the Salt, as Raimond (London: Heinemann, 1896); revised as *The Fatal Gift of Beauty and Other Stories* (Chicago: Stone, 1896);

The Open Question: A Tale of Two Temperaments, as Raimond (London: Heinemann, 1898); as Elizabeth Robins (New York & London: Harper, 1899);

The Magnetic North (London: Heinemann, 1904; New York: Stokes, 1904);

A Dark Lantern: A Story with a Prologue (London: Heinemann, 1905; New York: Macmillan, 1905);

The Convert (London: Methuen, 1905; New York: Macmillan, 1907);

Votes for Women: A Play in Three Acts (Chicago: Dramatic Publishing, 1907; London: Mills & Boon, 1909);

Under the Southern Cross (New York: Stokes, 1907);

"Come and Find Me!" (London: Heinemann, 1908; New York: Century, 1908);

The Mills of the Gods (New York: Moffat, Yard, 1908); enlarged as *The Mills of the Gods, and Other Stories* (London: Butterworth, 1920);

The Florentine Frame (London: John Murray, 1909; New York: Moffat, Yard, 1909);

Why? (London: Women Writers' Suffrage League, 1910);

Under His Roof (London: Woods, 1912);

"Where Are You Going To . . . ?" (London: Heinemann, 1913); republished as *My Little Sister* (New York: Dodd, Mead, 1913);

Way Stations (New York: Dodd, Mead, 1913; London: Hodder & Stoughton, 1913);

Camilla (New York: Dodd, Mead, 1918; London: Hodder & Stoughton, 1918);

Elizabeth Robins

The Messenger (London: Hodder & Stoughton, 1919; New York: Century, 1919);

Time Is Whispering (London: Hutchinson, 1923; New York & London: Harper, 1923);

Ancilla's Share: An Indictment of Sex Antagonism, anonymous (London: Hutchinson, 1924); as Robins (Westport, Conn.: Hyperion, 1976);

The Secret That Was Kept: A Study in Fear (London: Hutchinson, 1926; New York & London: Harper, 1926);

Prudence and Peter, a Story for Children about Cooking Out-of-doors and Indoors, by Robins and Octavia

Wilberforce (London: Benn, 1928); republished as *Prudence and Peter and Their Adventures with Pots and Pans* (New York: Morrow, 1928);

Ibsen and the Actress (London: Hogarth, 1928; New York: Haskell House, 1973);

Both Sides of the Curtain (London: Heinemann, 1940);

Raymond and I (London: Hogarth, 1956; New York: Macmillan, 1956);

The Alaska-Klondike Diary of Elizabeth Robins, 1900, edited by Victoria Joan Moessner and Joanne E. Gates (Fairbanks: University of Alaska Press, 1998).

Edition: *The Convert,* introduction by Jane Marcus (London: Women's Press, 1980; Old Westbury, N.Y.: Feminist Press, 1980).

OTHER: Björnsterne Björnson, *Magnhild and Dust,* anonymous translation by Robins, in *The Novels of Björnsterne Björnsen,* edited by Edmund Gosse (London: Heinemann, 1897);

Evelyn Sharp, *Rebel Women,* introduction by Robins (London: United Suffragists, 1915);

Henry James, *Theatre and Friendship: Some Henry James Letters, with a Commentary by Elizabeth Robins,* edited by Robins (London: Cape, 1932; New York: Putnam, 1932).

PLAY PRODUCTIONS: *Alan's Wife,* by Robins and Florence Bell, London, Terry's Theatre, 28 April 1893;

Votes for Women, London, Court Theatre, 9 May 1907.

In Elizabeth Robins's own day she was best known as a dramatic interpreter of Henrik Ibsen heroines and as the author of *The Magnetic North* (1904). A pivotal moment in the decline of her reputation as a writer was the reception of *The Mills of the Gods and Other Stories* (1920) by female modernists Virginia Woolf and Katherine Mansfield. Both found the stories aesthetically old-fashioned. "The war withered a generation before its time," wrote Woolf in her review of *The Mills of the Gods and Other Stories* in the *Times Literary Supplement* (17 June 1920). Woolf, Mansfield, and Rebecca West thought that Robins's artistry, shaped by late-nineteenth-century and Edwardian generic tastes and forms and the tenor of a sexually conservative pre–World War I feminism, needed to be transcended. Since the late 1970s feminist critics and historians have celebrated Robins's theatrical innovations as performer, actress-manager, and playwright, as well as the documentary scope of *The Convert* (1905) and have offered revisionary analyses of several of the feminist groups to which she belonged. Robins's fiction and its reception played key roles in the development, contestation and historical fortunes of New Woman and first-wave British feminist fictional aesthetics.

Born on 6 August 1862 in Louisville, Kentucky, Elizabeth Robins was the eldest child of the well-to-do first cousins Hannah Maria Crow Robins, a former opera singer, and Charles Ephraim Robins, a banker. Charles Robins lost his wife's fortune in business ventures in Louisville and New York. When Elizabeth was ten, her mother, who had borne seven children in eleven years, two of whom died in infancy, and who had to cope with Charles Robins's inconsolable grief at the death of his son from his first marriage, began to suffer from severe depression. Her mental health from 1873 until her death in 1901 was precarious, and she was institutionalized in 1885. Elizabeth and her siblings were sent to live with their grandmother Jane Hussey Robins in Zanesville, Ohio, while their father attempted to support the family through his mining and farming interests. Elizabeth attended the Putnam Female Seminary. During this period an intense relationship developed between Elizabeth and her youngest brother Raymond, but the failing health of their grandmother led to the splitting up of the family when Raymond was five. Charles Robins, an advocate of Owenite socialism and scientific farming, wanted Elizabeth to become a doctor, but she wanted to be an actress. Her mother borrowed money from her doctor so that Elizabeth could have acting lessons.

Making her stage debut in 1878, Robins worked in the United States in O'Neill's Monte Cristo Traveling Company (the theater company of James O'Neill, Eugene O'Neill's father), the Boston Museum Stock Company, the touring company of H. M. Pitt, and the Edwin Booth-Lawrence Barrett troupe. She married George Richmond Parks, an actor, in 1885; he committed suicide in June 1887. They had no children, and Robins never remarried. She resolved in 1888 to pursue her acting career in England. Legendary performances in plays by Henrik Ibsen—as Hedda Tesman in *Hedda Gabler* in 1891 and Hilda Wangel in *The Master Builder* in 1893—and her efforts, at first with Marion Lea, to establish an actress-manager system, placed her at the forefront of the so-called Ibsen campaign. Reflecting on the meaning of Ibsen in a 1928 article in *Time and Tide,* Robins wrote: "Ibsen not only transformed dramatic art, he was an instrument used by the *Zeitgeist* to enfranchise the spirit of women." Her interest in Ibsen brought her the close friendships of Henry James and William Archer, and Archer became her literary mentor. Her chafing at the treatment of ac-

U.S. Binding for the first U.S. edition of Robins's 1905 novel about a woman's nervous breakdown and her subsequent sexual and poetic awakening

tresses within the actor-manager system and the notoriety gained as an Ibsen actress made it difficult for her to secure steady work in the theater; she translated and wrote to earn a living and, during the 1890s, to support family members. She retired from the stage in November 1902.

In 1893 Robins and Florence Bell anonymously adapted for the stage Elin Ameen's "Befraid," a story of female sexual passion and infanticide, as *Alan's Wife: A Dramatic Study in Three Acts*. Anonymous and pseudonymous publication provided a screen for Robins. As Joanne Gates explains in her biography of Robins, "She did not want her fiction labelled 'Ibsenish'; she feared that her reputation as actress might diminish; she continued to regard her writing as an apprenticeship."

The publisher William Heinemann, who proposed to Robins more than once, urged on her the commercial example of Sarah Grand's *The Heavenly Twins* (1893). Robins's first novel, *George Mandeville's Husband* (1894), written under the pseudonym C. E. Raimond, is a satire of the novelist and would-be playwright Lois Wilbraham, who writes under the pseudonym "George Mandeville" and embraces as her mission "the cause of Progress . . . the banner of Woman's Emancipation." Most contemporary critics found the satire excessive; Arnold Bennett (writing as "Barbara" in the 8 August 1894 *Woman*), for instance, described Lois as "much-mauled." Feminist critic Elaine Showalter reads the representation of Lois as part of Robins's difficult female affiliation complex with George Eliot. The satire of Lois's artistic and social pretensions provides the sensational interest in the narrative; the characters of dominated husband Ralph and daughter Rosina are developed in a largely sentimental register. The sensationalism and sentimentality tended to catch the attention of critics, obscuring Robins's carefully detailed study of the pathology of a mismatched marriage. Ralph, a painter of "sentimental commonplaces," wanted a delicate muse figure for a wife. As his wife's artistic ambitions grow, his are given less scope. He despises female artists and what he sees as his wife's vulgarities, bringing up their daughter, whom his wife neglects, as an embodiment of his spiritualized, conventional feminine ideal; his wife's sense of his contempt, her disappointment in her husband, and her need to win everyday power struggles feed her ambitions and vanities. The debilitating effects of their family life are made apparent in the declining health of all three. Robins's difficulties in controlling tonal shifts destabilize her subtle ironization of the perspective of Ralph, an ironization brought out sharply in the pathos of Rosina's deathbed wish to earn a living by her only skills—plain sewing and darning.

Robins's biographers, Gates and Jane Marcus, interpret *The New Moon* (1895) as a projection of her passionate but conflicting feelings for Archer. Robins's diary entry of 29 December 1924 on Archer's death implies that he, too, read the novel, with its epigraph "At digte, det er at holde/Dommedag over sig selv" (To write is to hold judgment over oneself), as an autobiographical projection. The novel's narrator is the maimed, conscience-stricken Dr. Geoffrey Monroe. Monroe, a rationalist, is contemptuous of his wife, Milly's, "enervating" superstitious beliefs, her voracious appetite for light fiction, and her invalidism. Dorothy Lance, in contrast, is making a study of scientific literature on nerves and heredity (her mother died insane) and casts over him a "spell of superb health." The novel traces the conflict of loyalty and desire in Monroe and his grief when Dorothy is melodramatically burned to death in a fire (symbolic of their unconsummated passion) after he chooses to rescue first the physically weak Milly. Mrs. De Mattos, reviewing *The New Moon* in the 25 May 1895 issue of *The Athenaeum,* found Monroe's "complex nature, his moments and movements of irresolution and doubt . . . at times vividly Ibsenish," but the novel was not as well received as *George Mandeville's Husband* had been.

Perhaps trying to capitalize on the spate of 1890s fiction representing working-class life and accents, Robins produced *Below the Salt* (1896), a collection of short stories. The reviewer in *The Academy* (28 November 1895) gives some sense of what the stories achieved: "There is no trace of that satisfaction with superficial observation—the meaningless record of daily tasks and uneducated speech—which commonly condemns stories of servant-life. They are matter-of-fact, it is true, altogether without the triumphant exaggeration with which [William Makepeace] Thackeray wrote of servants, or the triumphant idealisation of [Benjamin] Disraeli. But if they are not triumphant, they are sure: they go far into character."

The Open Question: A Tale of Two Temperaments (1898) was Robins's first popular success. A saga of three generations of the Gano family, its ambitious scope was commended by Bennett in his review for *The Academy* (26 November 1898). The central symbol is the "Fort," the midwestern house of the displaced conservative Southern matriarch Sarah Gano, in which forces of family continuity, inheritance, disintegration, and historical change are localized. Robins drew on her grandmother and aspects of her own childhood in Zanesville in creating the characters and milieu of Sarah Gano and her granddaughter Val. The fine characterization of Sarah Gano, the ironies of her Boston visit, and the humor of her interaction with the spirited, rebellious Val earned the novel extraordinary praise. The narrative draws on motifs from Grand's *The Heavenly Twins:* a contrast in the development of male and female characters and a disease that impinges on questions of marriage. In *The Open Question* the contrasted characters are the cousins Ethan and Val Gano, the disease is consumption, and the marriage question is consanguineous romance. Faced with these problems, the cousins enter into a suicide pact. The sensational element in their romance overshadows a well-detailed contrast of stifled creativity. Val's ambitions to be a singer are quashed by the prejudices of Sarah and Val's father, John, and her creative talents are channeled into writing surreptitious intimate letters to Ethan and playing the muse of Liberty to his depressive temperament. Ethan's poetic talents are imitative, developed in decadent Paris; his lack of originality reduces him eventually to quoting and writing out the words of others.

The suicide plot, predictably, proved controversial; reviewers found it morbid and thought that it spoiled an otherwise remarkable novel. W. L. Courtney, for instance, in his *The Feminine Note in Fiction* (1904) claimed that the novel had its origin in "a nightmare begotten of a perusal of Nietzsche's philosophy." In a congratulatory letter dated 13 February 1899 George Bernard Shaw—an old personal enemy—warned Robins against her naturalistic fatalism and her "talent for sensationalism," urging her to give greater scope to her "divine" sense of

Robins in 1870

humor. Robins's authorship of *The Open Question* was soon revealed by her brother Raymond and announced by the *Daily Chronicle*.

Obsessed with remaking the family fortune, Raymond had left a California law practice in 1897 to mine for gold in Alaska after accusing Elizabeth of reneging on a childhood promise that they would live together. Raymond's passion for his sister is summed up in his giving of his most treasured photograph of her to his future wife, the Women's Trade Union League campaigner Margaret Dreier, as a token of his new devotion in 1905. After securing journalism commissions from W. T. Stead, Robins traveled to Alaska in 1900 to rescue Raymond from the influence of Jesuits and a loveless engagement; she developed typhoid fever and underwent a rest cure. Raymond's experiences in gold rush Alaska, aspects of Robins's journey to Nome, and her rest cure were shortly to be turned to fictional ends.

The Magnetic North, a story of male bonding, adventure, endurance, and hardship in the Yukon, is a thinly fictionalized account of some of her brother's experiences and those of his companions, based on the diaries of Raymond and Albert Schulte and Robins's talks with Raymond. Reviewers found the minutely detailed narrative for the most part documentary and full of surprising insight into the masculine psychology of partners on a long trail, the Col. George Warren and the Boy. The Boy, who dreams of living with his sister in an orange grove, is modeled on Raymond, while Warren is patterned after Schulte. Weaknesses in the novel were identified in *The Saturday Review* (26 March 1904) as "sentimental concessions" in scenes involving Kaviak, an Inuit foundling, and Maudie, a brassy dance-hall woman with a heart of gold. The representations of the Inuit characters, seen often from the Boy's perspective, seldom reach beyond stereotypes.

Robins wanted to publish *A Dark Lantern: A Story with a Prologue* (1905) anonymously, fearing that it would be read as an autobiography with her doctor Sir Vaughn Harley being seen as Garth Vincent, the "black-magic" man, who inspires Katherine Dereham's sexual and poetic awakening. The details of Katherine's rest cure are based on Robins's notes on her own experience in recovering from typhoid fever. The realism of this part of the narrative is counterpointed generically by the aristocratic Katherine's two romances in which she is sexually attracted first to royal hereditary and then to self-made masculine power, wealth, and prestige. The young, naive Katherine falls in love with Prince Anton of Breitenlohe-Waldenstein, who is only willing to offer a woman of Katherine's class a morganatic marriage from which she recoils. Her nerves frayed by the relationship and a hectic aristocratic lifestyle, she consults Vincent, who is renowned for his brutal methods, but who has, Katherine intuits, sensitive hands. The signs of his lower class are eroticised, often in Continental and oriental allusions. Her passion for him leads her to propose a sexual relationship; they marry after she becomes pregnant. Through incidents such as her taming of his dog, Young Turk, and his breaking down the locked door of her bedroom and begging her never to lock him out again, it is implied that she tames his misogynist manners and will work to settle his frenzied class anxieties about their marriage. The final scene seems to allude to Charlotte Perkins Gilman's *The Yellow Wallpaper* (1892), pointing out a contrast in outcomes of the rest cure. Both in his medical and farming practices Garth is a sanitizing and improving agent of science. Robins implies that his rise will help sweep away the rottenness of old aristocratic standards. Contemporary critics questioned the novel's moral—simplified as "women love brutes"—and the plausibility of Garth having a successful practice.

In a 6 November 1906 article in *The Times* (London) Robins identified herself as having been "until recently an ignorant opponent of woman suffrage very much upon the grounds advanced so complacently by those ladies who tell you they have all they want and so feel at liberty to condemn the less fortunate—or less self-centred?" She was converted to the cause by the militant campaign and the oratory of members of the Women's Social and Political Union. She was a member of the board of the WSPU from 1907 to 1912 and the first president of the Women Writers's Suffrage League, and she helped organize the Actresses's Franchise League. She made speeches and wrote pamphlets, letters to newspapers, and articles, many of which were collected in *Way Stations* (1913). After limited woman suffrage was granted in 1918, Robins's activism was channeled into feminist journalism, the Association of Social and Moral Hygiene, the Women's Institute movement, the independent journal *Time and Tide*, the Six Point Group, support for hospitals for women and children, and the conversion of her Sussex property, Backsettown, into a rest home for exhausted working women.

The Convert, an expanded fictionalization of the successful play *Votes for Women* (1907), conflates documentary realism; Gothic romance in the secret of the wealthy woman with a past, Vida Levering; and renovated melodrama in the confrontation of the wronged woman and her former lover, Geoffrey Stonor. Stonor is by no means a simple villain and is now the "coming man" in Conservative politics, engaged to the ingenue Jean Dunbarton. The stagy confrontation leads to Vida's securing his (ambiguous) support for woman suffrage. The charting of Vida's conversion to the militant suffrage cause, in its early stages securely rooted in Labour politics, and her cross-class dressing to explore the living conditions of working-class and homeless women is documentary, based on detailed notes of WSPU rallies made by Robins, even down to interjections, and Mary Higgs's "Three Nights in Women's Lodging Houses" (1905). Some of the WSPU speakers are based on recognizable political figures: Ernestine Blunt is Mary Gawthorpe, Lothian Scott is Keir Hardie, and Mrs. Chisholm is Emmeline Pankhurst. Vida's suppressed anger at her former lover, who pressured her to have an abortion so that he could retain his patrimony, finds an oblique voice on the suffrage platform as she connects her suffering with that of other women. She exchanges a life she loathes—of organizing charity concerts and amusing men at social functions—for public speaking, open defiance of the conservative gendered mores of her class, and securing sanitary lodging houses for homeless women. London is represented as a city of two nations, the rich and the poor. The heckling of WSPU speakers by working-class audiences is paralleled by the more genteel, yet still biting, mockery of suffragists by the rich at dinner parties and country weekends.

Picking up the pun in Ernestine Blunt's name, a writer for *The Times* (London) suggested in a 17 October 1907 review that Robins's earnestness was evidence of the blunting of the "finer spirits" among suffrage advocates. The use of fiction as tract or propaganda was questioned by many contemporary literary reviewers. Opinion on the rally scenes was extremely divided. For H. B. Marriott Watson, in his review in *The Athenaeum* (9 November 1907), they were a "long welter of talk," and *The Times* (London) review of 17 October 1907 called them "boring" interruptions of the plot, but they were judged "strong" in a 16 November 1907 review in *The New York Times* and termed the "most interesting portion of the book" in *The New Age* (14 November 1907). Recent feminist critics such as Showalter, Marcus, and Wendy Mulford have praised the dramatic realism of the representation of WSPU activity. Susan M. Squier argues that Robins's representation of London challenges H. G. Wells's vision of the coming City of the World in his *In the Days of the Comet* (1906), providing an optimistic feminist version of the modernist city grounded in liberated female speech and the collective work of women.

In *"Come and Find Me!"* (1908) Robins again returned to Alaskan themes with two masculine romance plots—the romance of gold and of exploration—and, as Gates writes, a narrative of "female faith, perseverance and women's bonding." Critics complained that the novel was overlong and overloaded with characters, points of view, detail, and wealth of material. The documentary aspect of Robins's writing—here Hildegarde Mar's journey to Nome during a gold rush—again divided critical opinion, which ranged from dismissal as "animated journalism" in *The Saturday Review* (29 February 1908) to praise as "particularly vivid" by James Moffat in his 1 April 1908 review in *The Bookman* (London) and "admirable pieces of description" in a 27 February 1908 review in *The Times* (London).

The Florentine Frame (1909) has intertwined romantic rivalry and female ambition plots; the second was overlooked by contemporary reviewers in favor of the more sensational mother-daughter struggle for the affections of Chester Keith. As Isabella Roscoe becomes caught up in playing the patron, mentor, and muse of Keith, identified by Professor Fanshawe as the savior of American theater, her own literary ambitions, treated contemptuously by both men, are stifled in a process symbolized through Keith's gradual usurpation of her study. The most engaged reviewer, the suffrage campaigner Emmeline Pethick-Lawrence writing in *Votes for Women* (26 November 1909), read the novel as a study of the psychology of defeat of a privileged woman by a need for romance symbolized in the emptiness of the delicately wrought frame of the title.

In 1905 Robins had begun collecting material on prostitution and the "white slave traffic," material that would inform the sensational and spare *"Where Are You Going To . . . ?"* (1913), published as *My Little Sister* in the United States. Robins claimed the story was based on fact and that she verified the details with a police judge and police inspectors. The unnamed narrator is one of two sisters raised in apparently idyllic country seclusion by an ailing widow who is fanatical about protecting them from the contaminating influence of the outside world and the working class. Robins implies that the mother had previously been attacked in her home by an intruder. Conscious of her failing health, the mother resolves, after the narrator confesses her ambition to be a doctor, that the narrator and her sister, Bettina, should visit their estranged wealthy Aunt Josephine for the London season. The dressmaker who comes into their home to outfit them is an agent for a white slave trafficker. On their arrival in London the sisters are taken not to Aunt Josephine's but to a brothel. The narrator is helped to escape by a sympathetic patron. The novel's sentimental conclusion challenges readers to agitate for the abolition of the white slave traffic: the narrator imagines Bettina's face "leaning down out of Heaven" to comfort her that "not in vain her innocence had borne the burden of sin." The implicit criticism of the mother's overprotectiveness and conservatism in the early part of the novel is overwhelmed by outrage at the abduction and the seeming complacency of the police.

The novel deeply divided critics. The feminist Mrs. Ayrton Zangwill, writing in the 17 January 1913 issue of *The Suffragette,* stressed its documentary quality and defended it against criticism that it was "frightfully sensational." Other feminists applauded its untypically realistic class focus for removing the customary cloaking of the middle class in what the reviewer for *Votes for Women* (17 January 1913) called a "romantic vision of chivalry and protection." S. Miles Franklin acclaimed it as "art for life's sake" in her March 1913 review in *Life & Labor.* In contrast, the reviewer for *The Nation* (3 April 1913) found Robins shrill and hysterical: "She does distress and harrow her readers–if that is worthwhile." The review in the 3 April 1913 issue of *The New Age* was more curt: "What a pack of fools and humbugs women are!"

Robins's subsequent fiction marks a creative decline. In *Camilla* (1918) Robins's eponymous heroine is an American divorcée whose memory of her first philandering husband leads her to retreat from a second engagement to a British man. Here Robins is dealing fictionally with a dilemma similar to the one she faced in her own intense relationships with Archer in the 1890s and John Masefield in 1909–1910. Camilla's sexual conservatism and silences represent potentially sustaining points of pastoral stillness and passivity in a changing and licentious world. The clash of American and British manners provides some feeble humor. *The Messenger* (1919), a flagrantly sensational World War I spy novel, features a female German spy, Greta von Schwarzenberg, and an awkwardly managed allegorical dimension in which the idealistic American girl, Nan Ellis, is torn between pacifism and support for the war effort. In *Time Is Whispering* (1923) the autumnal romance of Judith Lathom and the misogynist Sir Henry Ellerton is marked by motifs of reconciliation: reconciliation of genders through mutual service to a more humane understanding and management of the Empire and reconciliation of genders and generations through service to love and effective management of the English countryside.

Since her visits between 1905 and 1908 to Chinsegut, the Florida property she and Raymond purchased, Robins had wanted to deal sympathetically with racial problems of the American South. It was to prove a subject she was ill equipped to address. In the introduction to her tract *Ancilla's Share: An Indictment of Sex Antagonism* (1924) Robins argued that educating colonial and "colored" troops in militarist methods would ultimately threaten white supremacy. She urged that white races "can still instruct, administer and reap reward by divine right of a high order of intelligence applied through good-will." In *The Secret That Was Kept: A Study in Fear* (1926) the major racial problems addressed are fear of African American male sexuality and management of pilfering and idle African American employees. The African American characters are stereotypes. The inheritors of the Southern property are Terence Byrne, a writer who sees potential character studies in the "evolution and devolution of races" manifested in the "educated negro and the cracker," and June Purdey, whose mind is a "neglected field" and whose power of sexual refusal is a sign of civilization that may master men with tawdry sexual pasts. The moral of the appallingly melodramatic plot involving June and her first husband,

Jim, is that white people have more to fear from their own kind—such as a jealous embezzler husband who fakes his death and his blackmailing illegitimate son by a daughter of the working-class white family cook—than from African Americans.

After 1926 Robins published *Prudence and Peter, a Story for Children about Cooking Out-of-doors and Indoors* (1928), a cookbook for children written with Octavia Wilberforce, a younger friend, and worked on many unpublished projects, among them her "Rocky Mountain Journal," in which she used records kept by her father to develop a thinly veiled autobiographical bildungsroman of a girl determined to be an actress. For many years publishers had pressed her for an autobiography. She produced *Ibsen and the Actress* (1928), based on a lecture given during the Ibsen centenary celebrations; *Theater and Friendship: Some Henry James Letters, with a Commentary* (1932), which also commemorates her dearest friend, Lady Florence Bell, who had died in 1930; and *Both Sides of the Curtain* (1940), which concentrates on her efforts to establish herself in London between 1888 and 1890. The typescript of an unpublished second volume, "Whither and How," is in the Fales Library of New York University. After the temporary disappearance of Raymond in 1932 she wrote a memoir, "Raymond and I and Our Magnetic North," based on her 1900 Alaska diary. By then an influential temperance leader and political figure, Raymond refused permission for its publication during his lifetime; it appeared as *Raymond and I* in 1956. The diary itself, edited by Victoria Joan Moessner and Joanne E. Gates, was not published until 1998.

Robins died in Brighton on 8 May 1952, having outlived many of her contemporaries and much of her fame. In Robins's fiction the voices of female artists are characteristically stifled by patriarchal conservatism. Robins's own voice, which often speaks in her fiction in "lowbrow" and now devalued generic accents, has been stifled by the highbrow modernist aesthetic that has shaped twentieth-century canon formation. Shaw's unheeded warning about her tendency toward sensationalism was accurate as even in her own day it obscured her more substantial creative achievements, and Robins's critical reputation has only been gradually reestablished since the 1970s.

Bibliography:
Sue Thomas, *Elizabeth Robins 1862–1952: A Bibliography,* Victorian Fiction Research Guides, no. 22 (St. Lucia: Department of English, University of Queensland, 1994).

Biographies:
Jane Marcus, "Elizabeth Robins," dissertation, Northwestern University, 1973;

Joanne Elizabeth Gates, *Elizabeth Robins, 1862–1952: Actress, Novelist, Feminist* (Tuscaloosa: University of Alabama Press, 1994);

Angela V. John, *Elizabeth Robins: Staging a Life, 1862–1952* (London & New York: Routledge, 1995).

References:
Mary Gay Gibson Cima, "Elizabeth Robins: Ibsen Actress Manageress," dissertation, Cornell University, 1978;

W. L. Courtney, *The Feminine Note in Fiction* (London: Chapman & Hall, 1904), p. 183;

Joanne Gates, "Elizabeth Robins: From *A Dark Lantern* to *The Convert*—A Study of Her Fictional Style and Feminist Viewpoint," *Massachusetts Studies in English,* 6, nos. 3/4 (1978): 25–40;

Wendy Mulford, "Socialist-Feminist Criticism: A Case Study, Woman Suffrage and Literature, 1906–14," in *Re-reading English,* edited by Peter Widdowson (London: Methuen, 1982), pp. 179–192;

Elaine Showalter, *A Literature of Their Own: British Women Novelists from Brontë to Lessing* (London: Virago, 1978), pp. 108–110, 220–225;

Susan M. Squier, "The Modern City and the Construction of Female Desire: Wells's *In the Days of the Comet* and Robins's *The Convert,*" *Tulsa Studies in Women's Literature,* 8 (Spring 1989): 63–75.

Papers:
Elizabeth Robins materials are held in more than forty repositories. The major collection (284 boxes) is in the Fales Library, New York University. Other significant collections are in the Harry Ransom Humanities Research Center, University of Texas at Austin; the Henry W. and Albert A. Berg Collection, New York Public Library; Smathers Library, University of Florida, Gainesville; and Washington State University, Pullman.

Ethel Sidgwick
(20 December 1877 – 29 April 1970)

Lynn M. Alexander
University of Tennessee at Martin

BOOKS: *Promise* (London: Sidgwick & Jackson, 1910; Boston: Small, Maynard, 1910);

Le Gentleman: An Idyll of the Quarter (London: Sidgwick & Jackson, 1911; Boston: Small, Maynard, 1911);

Herself (London: Sidgwick & Jackson, 1912; Boston: Small, Maynard, 1912);

Four Plays for Children: The Rose and the Ring, The Goody-Witch, The Goosegirl, Boots and the North Wind (London: Sidgwick & Jackson, 1913; Boston: Small, Maynard, 1913);

Succession: A Comedy of the Generations (London: Sidgwick & Jackson, 1913; Boston: Small, Maynard, 1913);

A Lady of Leisure (London & Toronto: Sidgwick & Jackson, 1914; Boston: Small, Maynard, 1914);

Duke Jones, a Sequel to A Lady of Leisure (London: Sidgwick & Jackson, 1914; Boston: Small, Maynard, 1914);

The Accolade (London & Toronto: Sidgwick & Jackson, 1915; Boston: Small, Maynard, 1916);

Hatchways (London: Sidgwick & Jackson, 1916; Boston: Small, Maynard, 1916);

Jamesie (London: Sidgwick & Jackson, 1918; Boston: Small, Maynard, 1918);

Madam (London: Sidgwick & Jackson, 1921; Boston: Small, Maynard, 1921);

Two Plays for Schools: The Three Golden Hairs, The Robber Bridegroom (London: Sidgwick & Jackson, 1922); republished as *The Three Golden Hairs (More Plays for Children)* (Boston: Small, Maynard, 1922);

Restoration: The Fairy-Tale of a Farm (London: Sidgwick & Jackson, 1923; Boston: Small, Maynard, 1923);

Laura: A Cautionary Story (London: Sidgwick & Jackson, 1924; Boston: Small, Maynard, 1924);

Fairy-Tale Plays: The Elves and the Shoemaker, Ricquet and the Tuft (London: Sidgwick & Jackson, 1926);

When I Grow Rich (London & New York: Harper, 1927);

Ethel Sidgwick

The Bells of Shoreditch (London: Sidgwick & Jackson, 1928);

Dorothy's Wedding: A Tale of Two Villages (London: Sidgwick & Jackson, 1931); republished as *A Tale of Two Villages* (London & New York: Harper, 1931);

Mrs. Henry Sidgwick: A Memoir by Her Niece, Ethel Sidgwick (London: Sidgwick & Jackson, 1938).

TRANSLATION: Guy de La Batut and Georges Friedmann, *A History of the French People*, translated by Sidgwick and Kathleen E. Innes (London: Methuen, 1923).

Ethel Sidgwick is a novelist frequently compared to Henry James. Her early novels received

*Sidgwick's aunt, Eleanor Mildred Sidgwick, principal of
Newnham College, in 1891*

high praise, and she was viewed as a writer of great potential, but her later novels were seen as passé because of their focus on drawing rooms and country estates.

Sidgwick was born in Rugby on 20 December 1877 to Arthur Sidgwick, a schoolmaster at Rugby School and Charlotte S. Sidgwick. She was educated at Oxford High School; she also studied literature and music privately. She never married, taught in girls' schools in England and France, and lived in Oxford during the last part of her life. She was the niece of Henry Sidgwick, a leading philosopher of ethics and one of the founders of the Society for Psychical Research, and his wife, Eleanor Mildred Sidgwick, principal of Newnham College, Cambridge, from 1892 to 1910. Ethel Sidgwick's final book was a memoir of her aunt, published in 1938. She died on 29 April 1970.

Sidgwick's first novel, *Promise* (1910), charts the first fourteen years of an Anglo-French musical prodigy, Antoine Edgell. The novel attempts to interpret the artistic temperament, but it is also a study of the different figures that influence the boy's character. The child appears strange to his widowed father and freakish to his schoolmasters; it is only his talented grandfather who grasps Antoine's mixed desires for artistic release and for a normal childhood.

One of the most marked features of Sidgwick's works is her sense of character, and *Promise* is a series of portraits of various people who are connected through their relationships with Antoine, reacting to him and to each other. One of the strongest is Antoine's mother, Henriette, who dominates the first quarter of the novel before her death. In her character one sees both the temperament of genius and its beauty, but most important, one sees the cost of a lack of discipline.

Sidgwick again contrasts the French and English temperaments in her second novel, *Le Gentleman: An Idyll of the Quarter* (1911). While this novel has a stronger plot than *Promise,* the story is still slight, particularly in comparison to the characters that carry it. Its protagonist, a young Scotsman, is in Paris to rest after overworking himself at his studies and to keep an eye on his fiancée, an English art student. Initially he presents the stereotypical British prejudices against the French and of the Scots against frivolity. But as he whiles away his time in Paris, he meets a young Frenchwoman with whom he falls in love. At the close of the novel they confess their love but decide that they must honor earlier commitments—he to his fiancée, she to her family. Sidgwick's desire to present characters who are morally superior to those around them undercuts the sympathy the reader has come to feel for the couple: neither the fiancée nor the family have shown themselves worthy of this kind of consideration. To the modern reader it is an unnecessary martyrdom that alienates rather than attracts.

Harriet Clench, the title character of Sidgwick's third novel, *Herself* (1912), is a mixture of Irish and American as probably only the British could imagine: watchful, prudent, spirited, impulsive, vivacious, resourceful, and humorous. The story is in many ways a bildungsroman; yet it is marred by a lack of either plot or epiphany. Although Harriet is a fascinating character who is eminently attractive, by the end of the novel she is slightly older and a bit more experienced but no wiser either about herself or the world. While this work, like Sidgwick's others, shows remarkable insight into human nature, the reader is left dissatisfied. Perhaps the reviewer for *The New York Times* (15 September 1912) summed it up best in warning about Sidgwick and her literary foremothers: "But the final word about them must be that they lack the big spaces of life, wherein blows the eternal winds that go round and round the earth. They are, somehow, detached from the universal experience; they lack the gripping sense of universal kinship."

Perhaps for this reason, for her fourth novel, *Succession: A Comedy of the Generations* (1913), Sidgwick returns to more-familiar territory: the young virtuoso Antoine Edgell and the artistic worlds of France and England. Although the focus is once again on Antoine, who is now a little older and beginning to make a name for himself in the music world, Sidgwick is also fascinated with the idea of the succession of genius through generations and the effect it can have on all those within the family who do not share in the gift. If the theme of *Promise* is that genius cannot be suppressed, in *Succession* it is that an artist often becomes an object to those around him. It becomes clear early in the novel that the family, especially the grandfather, Lemaure, sees Antoine's first and foremost duty to be the continuation of the musical prestige handed down from Lemaure through Henriette to Antoine. Consequently, they often use him mercilessly as a means to the end of preserving the family name.

Once again Sidgwick's strength is in her characterization more than in her plotting. There are several well-drawn characters, including Margot the housemaid, the kindly conductor Reuss, and Antoine's older brother. But it is the character of Antoine that receives the bulk of Sidgwick's concentration as he struggles with the conflict between his need for artistic expression and his need to be a part of his family and society. Although some critics complained, with justification, about the length and the repetitious nature of Antoine's successes, nervous sufferings, and illnesses, they are part of the life of a musical prodigy. As a psychological exploration of a maturing musical genius, Sidgwick's work is quite impressive.

With *A Lady of Leisure* (1914) Sidgwick moves to the setting that marks the remainder of her novels, the country house. Set partly in London and partly in a country rectory, the story is marked by the subtle interplay of thought and emotion. The "lady" of the title is Violet Ashwin, an eighteen-year-old who has "trained on the Riviera." As is emphasized from the beginning, Violet is unique; she is exquisitely feminine yet perfectly in control of herself and of every situation, no matter how difficult. As in Sidgwick's other novels, family relationships are the primary concerns: Violet tries to please but occasionally rebels against her physician father and her cold, not quite credible mother. Perhaps Violet's true strength and the weaknesses of her family are best shown when Marjory, the younger daughter, becomes infatuated with "a handsome animal," and social scandal and tragedy seem inevitable. Although Sidgwick has used foil characters before, in this novel she is more successful than in the past. Alice Eccles is not only an excellent foil to Violet but also a strong character in her own right. In fact her pride and her willingness to rebuff Violet when that wealthy young woman takes a position beside her at Lennoxes, the dressmaking establishment where they both work, paint a character that may seem more real than the perfect Miss Ashwin.

Perhaps because of the positive reviews *A Lady of Leisure* received (*The New York Times* [27 September 1914] acclaimed it as "a book whose fine polish, whose careful finish, make it a novel of distinction"), Sidgwick produced *Duke Jones, a Sequel to A Lady of Leisure* (1914). The novel begins with the honeymoon of Marjory Ashwin and Marmaduke (Duke) Jones, and in her depiction of the development of the newly married pair, Sidgwick shows much subtle perception. Duke Jones appears to be an "oatmeal coloured," rather insignificant man. Other characters describe him as "a funny little man," "the man in the street," and a "harmless little beggar." Yet Jones's seemingly colorless personality comes to dominate the complex and vivid personalities Sidgwick assembles opposite him. As one critic put it, he "illustrates the dynamic force of pure goodness, simple, unselfish, always ready to help."

Other characters from *A Lady of Leisure* include Marjory's mother, an aging beauty so desirous of the feminine power she feels slipping away that she is jealous of her own daughter and attempts to undermine Violet's position in society and in her family. More than in the previous novel, *Duke Jones* is inhabited by a host of carefully elaborated, fully enunciated characters, and the novel consequently suffers from a certain lack of emphasis. One character seems as important as another, and the overall effect is to render all of the characters indistinct. Nevertheless the novel is entertaining, and one cannot help but appreciate Sidgwick's ability to bring characters to life through dialogue, action, and reaction.

Violet Ashwin is again a central character in Sidgwick's next work, *The Accolade* (1915), but as a catalyst, not as the primary focus. The protagonist of the novel is Johnny Ingestre, who is the heir to a large estate, but whom no one would call estimable. Having spurned tradition and his irate father to have a fling at acting, Johnny becomes a prodigal at twenty-two. As part of his attempt to please his father he becomes engaged "to an eligible young woman with the proper antecedents, with whom he was in love." Johnny's choice turns out to be an attempt to appease his father rather than a soul mate. Ursula is the female character least suited to Johnny's personality in the entire novel: she is conventional, narrow, tepidly jealous, coldly disapproving of Johnny, and possesses the unfailing ability to put him in the wrong while playing the role of long-suffering martyr.

Johnny's inability to remain "settled" and his tendency to flirt come as no surprise to his friends or to the reader. In their responses to Johnny's attraction to a young family friend, Helena Faulkland, Ursula appears at her worst and Johnny at his best; for despite his seeming devil-may-care attitude, Johnny chivalrously resists temptation and protects Helena both from her attraction to him and from the whispers of society spurred on by his wife. At this point Johnny receives his accolade, the "something not ourselves that makes for righteousness."

The Accolade is the strongest of the three novels involving the Ashwins. While Sidgwick continues to provide an abundance of developed characters, the novel maintains its focus on the central conflict. Although her character development may be more restricted than in the past, it is still accomplished chiefly through nuance. There is no intrusive narrative voice; instead, the characters' own speech and their interactions determine how the reader sees and responds to them.

Sidgwick's eighth novel, *Hatchways* (1916), combines her two favorite themes, the meeting of French and English sensibilities and English country life. Gabriel du Frettay, a young French aviator, is making his first visit to England—ostensibly for his health but really on government business. Du Frettay is curious about English people—he desires "to see a Duke, if you please, and a Bishop, and a Baconian, and a boxing professional"—and their customs; his experiences, impressions, and point of view make up the majority of the text. The title of the novel comes from a small country estate near where du Frettay is visiting, the home of Ernestine Redgate. Nearby is the estate of the duchess of

THE ACCOLADE

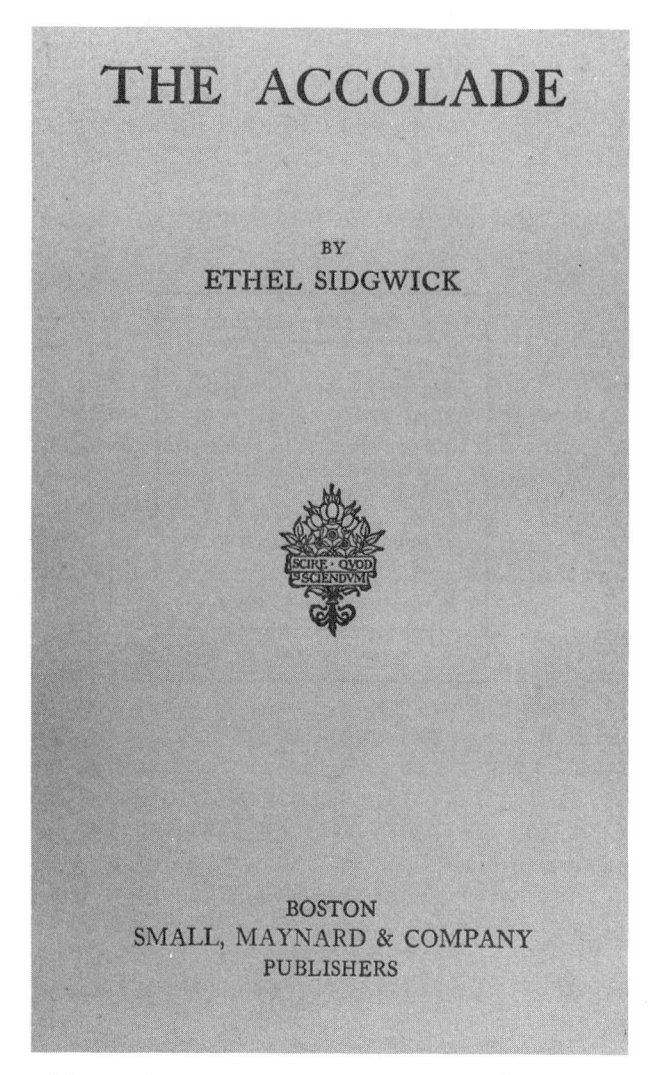

BY
ETHEL SIDGWICK

BOSTON
SMALL, MAYNARD & COMPANY
PUBLISHERS

Title page for the 1916 U.S. edition of Sidgwick's novel about a self-centered and shallow young man who develops a sense of honor

Wickford and her sons, the present duke and Iveagh ("Wick" to his friends). Soon du Frettay, an unusually insightful person, becomes aware of the hidden dramas of the two households: the duchess's plans for her sons, Iveagh's romance, and his friends' fears concerning it.

The strength of the novel is the portrayal of Ernestine. Indescribable to her friends, one of whom sums her up as "just Ernestine," she is distinguished by her charm and sense of individuality. Ernestine teaches du Frettay "what England could be": "Fresh earth, soft shadows, and gray skies. Rare sunshine, the more loved when coming.... Heroes and hero-worship. Fixed hearts, clear eyes and open arms."

The story of Ernestine's niece, Bess Ryeborn, and Iveagh, who marry at the end of *Hatchways,* continues in *Jamesie* (1918). They are the parents of the title character, who is seven years old in June 1914. The novel pictures the life of this family and their circle of friends through letters and brief notes, all informal and intimate, over a period of two years. As is common with epistolary novels, early references to people and events whose significance is not yet clear is confusing and sometimes frustrating. As the story proceeds and the reader begins to straighten out the various relationships, Sidgwick's artistry and keen insight into human nature become clear.

The group of correspondents is diverse and striking. Members, friends, or servants of two aristocratic absentee Irish families, they range from militant suffragists to ultraconservatives. World War I is always in the background, affecting the life of every character, several of whom die in the war. Jamesie is frequently represented by brief messages that capture the hearts of his correspondents with their artlessness and charm. At the close of the novel Jamesie is killed when the boat in which he is riding in the English Channel is torpedoed.

Jamesie was the last of Sidgwick's novels to receive much notice. The remainder are "drawing-room" stories, a genre that had gone out of fashion. Further, her indirect style—conversational, gradually revealing intricate relations and reactions—became even more oblique, so that the reviewer for *The New York Times* (25 August 1918) commented that one needed to read her stories twice: "through the greater part of his first perusal the reader has the sensation of being lost in a maze, or endeavoring to fit together the jumbled parts of a picture puzzle, or trying to work out the meaning of a code message without the key."

Nevertheless, Sidgwick's early works are strong presentations of character, both English and French. She is a writer of considerable merit, the majority of whose work is worthy of attention. R. Brimley Johnson's summary of Sidgwick's work in *Some Contemporary Novelists (Women)* (1920) is typical:

> Our appreciation depends on a quick intellect, familiarity with art atmosphere and book-language, a love of the fine shades. In structure and style she is not realistic; she frankly composes; yet, in her own way, lays bare the soul. She is modern: because she does not concern herself with single emotions, whole characters, a crude clash of black and white.... Nor does the narrative make up one centralised plot. It grows out of the immense complexities and interchange which super-civilisation imposes on human-nature.

Sidgwick represents the interest in the internal character that motivated the Modernist movement, and she applies her interest to the English and French, much the way James does, by putting one nationality in the setting of the other and letting the reader learn with the visitor. Her works are novels of character, not of action. And while toward the end of her career she wrote novels of an England that had disappeared and was no longer considered of interest, her early works should be of interest—particularly to scholars interested in women writers and in the Modernist movement in England.

Reference:

R. Brimley Johnson, *Some Contemporary Novelists (Women)* (London: Parsons, 1920), pp. 105–106.

G. B. Stern
(17 June 1890 – 20 September 1973)

Colleen Hobbs
Rutgers University

BOOKS: *Pantomime* (London: Hutchinson, 1914);
See-Saw (London: Hutchinson, 1914);
Twos and Threes (London: Nisbet, 1916);
Grand Chain (London: Nisbet, 1917);
A Marrying Man (London: Nisbet, 1918);
Children of No Man's Land (London: Duckworth, 1919); republished as *Debatable Ground* (New York: Knopf, 1921);
Larry Munro (London: Chapman & Hall, 1920); republished as *The China Shop* (New York: Knopf, 1921);
The Room (London: Chapman & Hall, 1922; New York: Knopf, 1922);
The Back Seat (London: Chapman & Hall, 1923; New York: Knopf, 1923);
Smoke Rings (London: Chapman & Hall, 1923; New York: Knopf, 1924);
Tents of Israel (London: Chapman & Hall, 1924); republished as *The Matriarch, a Chronicle* (New York: Knopf, 1925);
Thunderstorm (London: Chapman & Hall, 1925; New York: Knopf, 1925);
A Deputy Was King (London: Chapman & Hall, 1926; New York: Knopf, 1926);
The Happy Meddler, by Stern and Geoffrey Holdsworth (London: Ward, Lock, 1926);
Bouquet (London: Chapman & Hall, 1927; New York: Knopf, 1927);
The Dark Gentleman (London: Chapman & Hall, 1927; New York: Knopf, 1927);
Jack a'Manory (London: Chapman & Hall, 1927);
Debonair: The Story of Persephone (London: Chapman & Hall, 1928; New York: Knopf, 1928);
The Matriarch: A Play in a Prologue and Three Acts (London: Vernon, 1929; New York: S. French, 1931);
Petruchio (London: Chapman & Hall, 1929); republished as *Modesta* (New York: Knopf, 1929);
The Slower Judas (New York: Knopf, 1929);
Mosaic (London: Chapman & Hall, 1930; New York: Knopf, 1930);
The Man Who Pays the Piper (London: Heinemann, 1931);

G. B. Stern (photograph by Beck and MacGregor)

The Shortest Night (London: Heinemann, 1931; New York: Knopf, 1931);
The Rakonitz Chronicles (London: Chapman & Hall, 1932);
Little Red Horses (London: Heinemann, 1932); republished as *The Rueful Mating* (New York: Knopf, 1932);
Long Lost Father: A Comedy (London: Benn, 1932; New York: Knopf, 1933);
The Augs, an Exaggeration (London: Heinemann, 1933); republished as *Summer's Play, an Exaggeration* (New York: Knopf, 1934);
Pelican Walking (London: Heinemann, 1934);
Shining and Free, a Day in the Life of the Matriarch (London: Heinemann, 1935; New York: Knopf, 1935);

The Matriarch Chronicles (New York: Knopf, 1936);

Monogram (London: Chapman & Hall, 1936; New York: Macmillan, 1936);

Oleander River (London: Cassell, 1937; New York: Macmillan, 1937);

The Ugly Dachshund (London: Cassell, 1938; New York: Macmillan, 1938);

Long Story Short (London: Cassell, 1939);

The Woman in the Hall (London: Cassell, 1939; New York: Macmillan, 1939);

A Lion in the Garden (London: Cassell, 1940; New York: Macmillan, 1940);

Another Part of the Forest (London: Cassell, 1941; New York: Macmillan, 1941);

The Young Matriarch (London: Cassell, 1942; New York: Macmillan, 1942);

Dogs in an Omnibus (London: Cassell, 1942);

Talking of Jane Austen, by Stern and Sheila Kaye-Smith (London: Cassell, 1943); republished as *Speaking of Jane Austen* (New York & London: Harper, 1944);

Trumpet Voluntary (London: Cassell, 1944; New York: Macmillan, 1944);

The Reasonable Shores (London: Cassell, 1946; New York: Macmillan, 1946);

No Son of Mine (London: Cassell, 1948; New York: Macmillan, 1948);

Benefits Forgot (London: Cassell, 1949; New York: Macmillan, 1949);

A Duck to Water (London: Cassell, 1949; New York: Macmillan, 1949);

More about Jane Austen, by Stern and Kaye-Smith (New York: Harper, 1949); republished as *More Talk of Jane Austen* (London: Cassell, 1950);

Gala Night at "The Willows," by Stern and Rupert Croft-Cooke (London: Deane, 1950);

Ten Days of Christmas (London: Collins, 1950; New York: Harper, 1950);

The Donkey Shoe (London: Collins, 1952; New York: Macmillan, 1952);

Robert Louis Stevenson (London & New York: Published for the British Council by Longmans, Green, 1952);

A Name to Conjure With (London: Collins, 1953; New York: Macmillan, 1953);

Raffle for a Bedspread (London: Methuen, 1953);

All in Good Time (New York & London: Sheed & Ward, 1954);

He Wrote Treasure Island: The Story of Robert Louis Stevenson (London: Heinemann, 1954); republished as *Robert Louis Stevenson, the Man Who Wrote Treasure Island* (New York: Macmillan, 1954);

Johnny Forsaken (London: Collins, 1954; New York: Macmillan, 1954);

For All We Know (London: Collins, 1955; New York: Macmillan, 1956);

The Way It Worked Out (London & New York: Sheed & Ward, 1956);

And Did He Stop and Speak to You? (London: Coram, 1957; Chicago: Regnery, 1958);

Seventy Times Seven (London: Collins, 1957; New York: Macmillan, 1957);

The Patience of a Saint (London: Coram, 1958);

Unless I Marry (London: Collins, 1959; New York: Macmillan, 1959);

One Is Only Human (Chicago: Regnery, 1960);

Bernadette (Edinburgh: Thomas Nelson, 1960);

Credit Title (Edinburgh: Thomas Nelson, 1961);

The Personality of Jesus (Garden City, N.Y.: Doubleday, 1961);

Dolphin Cottage (London: Collins, 1962);

Promise Not to Tell (London: Collins, 1964).

Editions: *The Matriarch,* introduction by Julia Neuberger (New York: Penguin Virago, 1988);

A Deputy Was King, introduction by Neuberger (New York: Penguin Virago, 1988).

MOTION PICTURES: *Little Women,* screenplay by Stern, RKO, 1933;

The Woman in the Hall, screenplay by Stern and J. Arthur Rank-Wessex, Eagle-Lion, 1947.

PLAY PRODUCTIONS: *For One Night Only,* London, Little Theatre, 29 May 1911;

For Husbands Only, by Stern and Mrs. D. C. F. Harding, London, Ambassadors Theatre, 4 June 1920;

The Matriarch, London, Royalty Theatre, 8 May 1929; New York, Longacre Theater, 18 March 1930;

Debonair, by Stern and Frank Vosper, London, Lyric Theatre, 23 April 1930;

The Man Who Pays the Piper, London, St. Martin's Theatre, 10 February 1931;

Five Farthings, London, Haymarket Theatre, 10 February 1931;

Middleman, Suffern, New York, County Theatre, 8 September 1936.

OTHER: "A Love Affair," in *Aces: A Collection of Short Stories* (New York: Knickerbocker, 1924; London: Putnam, 1924);

"A Man and His Mother," in *Georgian Stories 1926* (London: Chapman & Hall, 1926);

"Toes Unmasked," in *Georgian Stories 1927* (London: Chapman & Hall, 1927);

"The Woman," in *Consequences: A Complete Story in the Manner of the Old Parlour Game* (Berkshire: Golden Cockrell, 1932);

RLS, an Omnibus, selected, with an introductory essay, by Stern (London: Cassell, 1950);

Selected Poems of Robert Louis Stevenson, edited, with an introduction, by Stern (London: Grey Walls, 1950);

Tales and Essays of Robert Louis Stevenson, edited, with an introduction, by Stern (London: Falcon, 1950);

Jane Austen, *Mansfield Park,* introduction by Stern (London: Heron, 1970);

Jane Austen, *Emma,* introduction by Stern (London: Heron, 1973).

SELECTED PERIODICAL PUBLICATIONS–UNCOLLECTED: "The Heroines of Sheila Kaye-Smith," *Yale Review,* 15 (1925): 204–208;

"Onward and Upward with the Arts: Elsie Reread," *New Yorker,* 11 (14 March 1936): 52–55;

"Somerset Maugham Comes of Age," *John O'London's Weekly,* 63 (22 January 1954): 1–4.

The prolific G. B. Stern charmed audiences in America and Great Britain with her energy, her subtle wit, and her ability to create fascinating fictional families. In her long and varied career as a novelist, journalist, and screenwriter she was known at various times as an authority on French wines (*Bouquet,* 1927), Jane Austen, and Robert Louis Stevenson. Her creation of the Matriarch series of novels, which documents five generations of the engaging Rakonitz clan, however, secured her popularity. Stern's critics argued that her skills at characterization, which combined humor with serious drama, could become formulaic, or as *The Times* (London) noted in her obituary, "too studiously light and amusing." Yet her admirers were drawn by those same qualities. A *New York Herald Tribune* review of 13 October 1957 by Caroline Turnstall looks back over Stern's career to reflect that "Fashions change; the Atomic Age comes into its own; but G. B. Stern remains delightfully the same." Stern's ability to delight through her compelling storytelling skills and wry humor ensured her a long, successful career.

Stern's parents, Elizabeth and Albert, were second-generation Jewish immigrants to London. Although they christened their daughter Gladys Bertha, she early changed her middle name to Bronwyn because she liked the sound. The Sterns lost their fortune in the Vaal River diamond crash when Stern was fourteen, and they left England. Stern lived in hotels as she attended German and Swiss girls' schools. Recalling the experience in her autobiography, *Monogram* (1936), she said that "like most females of my class and generation, I only feel half-educated; less than that, quarter-educated." In addition to the finishing school training she called "a lick and high polish," Stern attended the Academy of Dramatic Art in London. She was introduced by her friend Noel Coward to the New Zealand native Geoffrey Lisle Holdsworth, whom she married in 1919. The marriage ended in divorce. Stern then traveled to the United States to work as a screenwriter in Hollywood; while there, she conducted a lecture tour of the country. She lived in London through much of the Nazi blitzkrieg and lost all her belongings—except a favorite walking stick—to a German incendiary bomb. In addition to a steady stream of fiction and autobiography, she produced several scripts while under contract to the movie director Sir Alexander Korda, and she was heard frequently on BBC radio. Stern converted from Judaism to the Catholic faith in 1947, and her later nonfiction, *All In Good Time* (1954) and *The Way It Worked Out* (1956), deals with that decision. She died on 20 September 1973 in Wallingford, Berkshire.

Stern's literary career began when *Novel Magazine* published a poem on Pierrot in 1908. She subsequently produced short stories that appeared in popular magazines such as *The Illustrated London News* and *John O'London's Weekly*. *Smoke Rings* (1923), a collection of these early stories, illustrates Stern's interest in placing well-known literary figures in modern situations: included in the volume are "A Modern Elaine," "Ulysses Up-to-Date," and "The New Whittington." Stern's early novels continue this exploration of contemporary issues, which is carried out in sophisticated, ultramodern dialogue. For example, the characters in *Twos and Threes* (1916) easily critique George Bernard Shaw's socialism and Friedrich Nietzsche's theory of the *Übermensch* (Superman). A review of *The China Shop* (1921; first published as *Larry Munro,* 1920) claims for Stern "a position among the ablest of the post Wellsian realists." Indeed, *Children of No Man's Land* (1919), her portrayal of destructive nationalism during World War I, is dedicated to H. G. Wells. Critics found this depiction of British-German-Jewish tensions and ambiguous patriotism to be "almost terribly real."

These early efforts were critical and popular successes, but they were eclipsed by a series of novels depicting a modern Jewish family that populates the capitals of Europe from London to St. Petersburg. First published as *Tents of Israel* (1924), Stern's *The Matriarch, a Chronicle* draws heavily on her own cosmopolitan Jewish relatives. The protagonist, Anastasia Rakonitz, is based on her domineering great-aunt and, for that reason, Stern never enjoyed the Matriarch tales as much as her readers did. Anastasia rules her extended family through overt bullying, covert manipulation, and sheer strength of will. The result is an exasperating, outrageous, and thoroughly entertaining character. Anastasia's strength is needed as the Rakonitzes cope first with financial reverse and then with modernization and assimilation to Gentile practices. The weakened, aging matriarch triumphs by instilling a sense of family heritage in her granddaughter Toni, who inherits her drive and spirit. Stern takes a special delight in showcasing female competence and vigor in the newest generation of Rakonitz women. Her depiction not only illustrates the successful, sexually liberated New Woman of the 1920s but also critiques traditional gender roles as stultifying and dangerous for both men and women.

The popularity of *The Matriarch* led to its adaptation for the stage and an extended 1929 run at the Royalty Theatre. Critics complained that the extensive cast of relatives that captivated readers somewhat overwhelmed a theater audience with no knowledge of Stern's complex genealogy. They extended unqualified praise, however, to Mrs. Patrick Campbell, the legendary Victorian actress who performed the title role. The extensive family connections embedded in *The Matriarch* offered Stern many opportunities to explore and expand her canon of Rakonitz chronicles, and the project extended through four volumes and twenty-eight years. *A Deputy Was King* (1926) continues Toni's story as she marries outside her faith. *Shining and Free, a Day in the Life of the Matriarch* (1935) focuses on the eve of Anastasia's eighty-eighth birthday, using her memories to move further backward in the family line and examine her own grandmother, Babette. In the final installment, *The Young Matriarch* (1942), Toni's daughter Babette, named for that distant first matriarch, brings the tradition of female strength and authority to a new generation. Stern's treatment of the dynasty gives a rich sense of the Rakonitzes' cultural life as the family spreads across Europe, with each branch reflecting the characteristics of its own country. The combination of language and custom further complicates an already fascinating group of characters, but Stern's blend of humor and sensitivity to modern dilemmas makes the series attractive and compelling.

Stern was interested in the new theory of psychoanalysis and deftly incorporated it into her work. For example, the opening pages of *Monogram* contain Stern's sketches of her initials—a neat, artistic effort labeled "Conscious Drawing," and a less tidy, more revealing illustration labeled "Subconscious Drawing." A 1936 article in *The New Yorker*, "Onward and Upward with the Arts: Elsie Reread," shows both Stern's eclectic taste and her imaginative application of Freudian analysis. She confesses her addiction to the Elsie Dinsmore series of Victorian children's books and explains her fascination with tales in which she sees "savage, neurotic realism" in a seemingly loving domestic environment. In Mr. Dinsmore's jealous harassment of Elsie's suitors, Stern sees the evidence of a repressed attraction to his daughter; in marrying a man twenty years her senior, Elsie is "collaborating with her unconscious" to provide herself with another father figure. Stern skillfully reads the subverted violence in a series of sentimental children's tales and, with characteristic humor, finds that "our scornful tots have yet to realize that What-Grandma-Read-When-She-Was-A-Little-Girl makes the case histories at the back of Havelock Ellis look like white muslin polka dots on a light blue sash." Her interest in repression and the subconscious is developed at length in *Ten Days of Christmas* (1950), a novel in which characters apply psychoanalytic theory to conflicts at a holiday house party.

A great admiration for Austen and Stevenson led Stern to produce several volumes of critical work on these authors. In *Talking of Jane Austen* (1943), an exuberant discussion with novelist Sheila Kaye-Smith, Stern writes of the author's power to entertain, even during the Battle of Britain: "You can forget a war when reading Jane Austen for the first time, the second time, the hundredth time; you can forget strain and sorrow and perplexity and injustice and fear." Stern's and Kaye-Smith's discussion disavows any pretensions to scholarship, although it does consider serious thematic issues such as women's education and the effect of war on Austen's writing. More characteristic, however, is the extensive—and difficult—quiz offered to test readers' proficiency in Austen trivia. The first question reads: "What kind of apricot did Dr. Grant discuss with Mrs. Norris, and what was the price of it?" (The answer, known only to true Janeites, is kindly included in the text: Moor Park, seven shillings.)

Stern repeatedly declared *No Son of Mine* (1948) her favorite book. The novel, which is grounded in extensive biographical research, follows a young man with a striking physical resemblance to Stevenson. To determine his true parentage the young man investigates Stevenson and, in the process, provides readers with a thorough examination of the author's life. Critics noted that the factual component of *No Son of Mine* was sufficient for a straightforward biography. Stern did write two biographical treatments of Stevenson; her introduction to *RLS, an Omnibus* (1950), however, indicates that, with her background as a novelist, she found the nonfictional approach too limiting. "With no discourtesy towards that school of biographers who take such infinite pains to keep their heads, may one not perhaps ask what is so right about detachment? What so reprehensible about any generous surrender to a magical personality?"

Stern's resistance to detachment reveals why *No Son of Mine,* a mixture of fact and fiction, would be her favorite work. It also may explain the form she chose for her five autobiographical pieces, which adhere to no particular genre but, in a stream-of-consciousness fashion, combine literary criticism and cultural analysis with personal memoir. The reviewer for *The New York Times,* Lamberton Becker, wrote on 1 June 1941 that her second installment, *Another Part of the Forest* (1941), "would be like no other [autobiography] had she not already written *Monogram.*" Of the biographical information Stern includes, Becker finds that "You learn something of the facts of her life, but not much that 'Who's Who' would print." Stern's eclectic approach defies literary categorization and ensures that readers must abandon any expectation of a linear narration. For example, *Monogram* combines descriptions of air raids at Rebecca West's house with a feminist reading of the Peter Pan story. Of J. M. Barrie's tale, she finds that "we cannot afford to let this legend stand, this legend that we do really exult in mothering our fathers and husbands and grown-up sons; that we find in it our deepest satisfaction." *Benefits Forgot* (1949) includes a touching description of the return to a house abandoned during World War II, in addition to conversations with former prime minister David Lloyd George and a critique of her friend Laurence Olivier's movie *Henry V* (1944). It is entirely characteristic of Stern's style that she tempers serious postwar analysis with levity: during the war, she says, Eleanor Roosevelt sent her four pairs of silk stockings in gratitude for her literary contributions.

The last two installments of Stern's memoirs, *All in Good Time* and *The Way It Worked Out,* take a serious turn as she discusses her conversion to Catholicism. Here the author details her bouts of physical illness and crippling depression. As the child of nonpracticing Jews, she says she had no knowledge of her own religious heritage but only a feeling of exclusion from the mainstream practice. *All in Good Time* expresses her regret that "I had no religion at all beyond a vague, troubled wish for

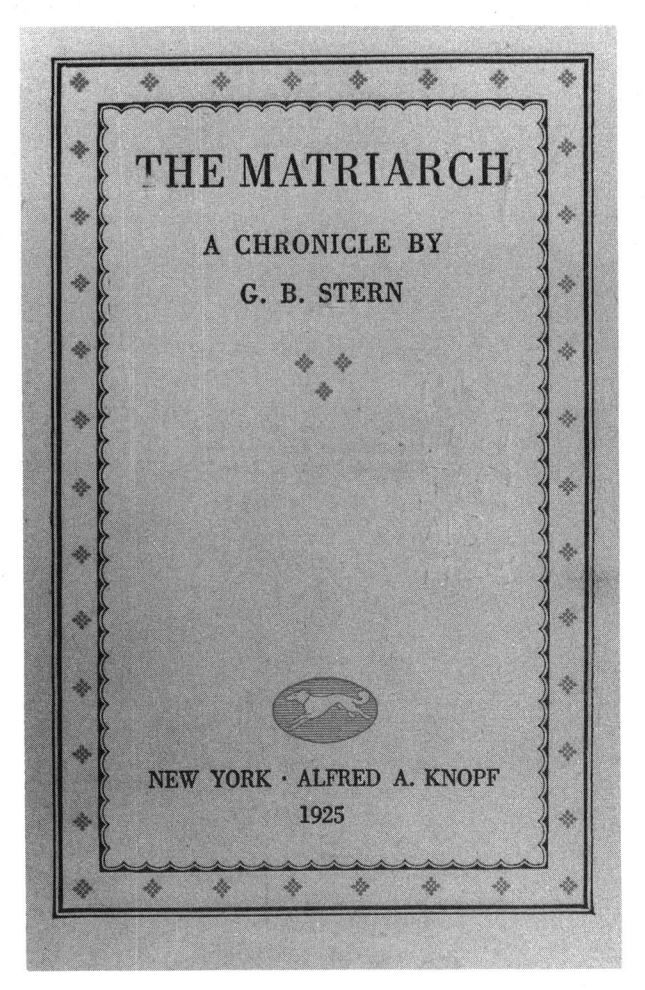

U.S. edition of the work, first published in Britain as Tents of Israel, *that initiated a series of novels chronicling a cosmopolitan Jewish family*

Christianity—'like other people.'" Her memoirs do not address the Holocaust directly, but the timing of her conversion, 1947, indicates that the murder of her Jewish relatives may have led to her crisis of faith. *The Way It Worked Out* describes her response to receiving a letter that mentions a "Matriarch" character, the Parisian relative Tante (Aunt) Berthe. She responds by recalling that "the originals of Berthe and her dear only sister Letti and Letti's son Etienne with his wife and children were all dragged away from their home in Nice during the Nazi occupation of the Midi and were never heard of again." Stern's method of listing the victims (Berthe *and* Letti *and* Etienne) emphasizes the war's toll on her family and in its stark statement of facts (they "were never heard of again") indicates why her charming stories of European Jewry ceased in 1941. Reviewers have argued that Stern's later work failed to live up to the early promise of her Matriarch series. *Johnny Forsaken* (1954), which includes an aging Czelovar cousin of the Rakonitz family, builds its plot around characters involved in an amateur theatrical society. The technique of free association that was praised in Stern's memoirs was, however, not as well received in her fiction. Toward the end of her career Stern also turned to religious topics not intended for a popular audience in works such as *Bernadette* (1960) and *The Personality of Jesus* (1961). Critics who see a falling off in Stern's later works may not have taken into account the emotional breakdown she experienced during the war, a crisis that her levity and charm camouflaged. In true unyielding "matriarchal" fashion, *Benefits Forgot* says that "I have kept myself–and others–since I was twenty, by a precarious and uncertain profession, a one-man job which also must mean certain moments of penniless, blank despair; I have heard on the telephone that my home and everything in it has been consumed by an incendiary bomb.... what with one thing and another, too personal to state in black and white, I have had enough to say now, with a sincere appeal to the future, '*Anything* for a quiet life!'" Her later work, however, reveals the cost of such an indomitable facade. *All in Good Time* describes the events leading to her conversion: "dismal–dreary–desolate–dejected–despairing.... To pull myself together, I first had to take myself apart." In reconstructing her psyche Stern may have realigned the artistic strengths and weaknesses that produced her early successes. In any case, the author whose reputation was built on the depiction of forceful Jewish women must have been altered by a wartime reality that her matriarchs could never have imagined.

Stern's fiction provides a fascinating illustration of prewar, pan-European Jewry. In addition, the implicit feminism of her Matriarch series, with its historical treatment of women's issues, invites contemporary readers who appreciate strong female characters. Renewed interest in Stern's work is indicated by the titles reissued through the Virago Modern Classics series. *The Matriarch* and *A Deputy Was King* are available in new editions with useful critical introductions, and *Monogram* is forthcoming.

Reference:

Margaret Lawrence, *School of Femininity* (New York: Stokes, 1936), pp. 198–203.

Papers:

The major collection of G. B. Stern materials is at Boston University and includes correspondence, galleys, and business records. The BBC Written Archives Centre, Reading, holds correspondence conducted with the BBC staff from 1941 to 1962. Small collections of letters are owned by Merton College, Oxford; the Bodleian Library, Oxford; University College, London; the University of Birmingham; and the Royal Society of Literature, London.

Netta Syrett

(17 March 1865 – 15 December 1943)

Jill Tedford Jones
Southwestern Oklahoma State University

See also the Syrett entry in *DLB 135: British Short-Fiction Writers, 1880-1914: The Realist Tradition.*

BOOKS: *Nobody's Fault,* Keynotes Series, no. 20 (London: John Lane, 1896; Boston: Roberts, 1896);

The Tree of Life (London & New York: John Lane, 1897);

The Garden of Delight: Fairy Tales (London: Hurst & Blackett, 1898);

Rosanne (London: Hurst & Blackett, 1902);

The Magic City and Other Fairy Tales (London: Lawrence & Bullen, 1903);

Six Fairy Plays for Children (London & New York: John Lane, 1903);

The Day's Journey (London: Chapman & Hall, 1905; Chicago: McClurg, 1906);

Women and Circumstance (London: Chapman & Hall, 1906);

The Child of Promise (London: Chapman & Hall, 1907);

Anne Page (London: Chatto & Windus, 1908; New York: John Lane, 1909);

A Castle of Dreams (London: Chatto & Windus, 1909; Chicago: McClurg, 1909);

The Castle of Four Towers (London: Duckworth, 1909);

The Vanishing Princess (London: Nutt, 1910);

The Story of Saint Catherine of Siena (London & Oxford: Mowbray, 1910; Milwaukee: Morehouse, 1910);

Olivia L. Carew (London: Chatto & Windus, 1910);

The Old Miracle Plays of England (London & Oxford: Mowbray, 1911; Milwaukee: Young Churchman, 1911);

Drender's Daughter (New York: John Lane, 1911; London: Chatto & Windus, 1911);

The Endless Journey and Other Stories (London: Chatto & Windus, 1912);

Three Women (London: Chatto & Windus, 1912);

Stories from Medieval Romance (Oxford: Clarendon, 1913);

Barbara of the Thorn (London: Chatto & Windus, 1913);

The Jam Queen (London: Methuen, 1914);

Netta Syrett

The Victorians: The Development of a Modern Woman (London: Unwin, 1915); republished as *Rose Cottingham* (New York: Putnam, 1915);

Rose Cottingham Married (London: Unwin, 1916);

Troublers of the Peace (London: Chatto & Windus, 1917);

Godmother's Garden (London: Blackie, 1918);

Robin Goodfellow and Other Fairy Plays for Children (London & New York: John Lane, 1918);

The Wife of a Hero (London: Skeffington, 1918);

The God of Chance (London: Skeffington, 1920);

One of Three (London: Hurst & Blackett, 1921);

Toby and the Odd Beasts, Royal Road Library, no. 3 (London: Thornton Butterworth, 1921; New York: Stokes, 1922);

Rachel and the Seven Wonders, Royal Road Library, no. 4 (London: Thornton Butterworth, 1921; New York: Stokes, 1922);

Two Domestics: A Play for Women in One Act (London & New York: French, 1922);

Magic London, Royal Road Library, no. 8 (London: Thornton Butterworth, 1922; revised edition, London: Thornton Butterworth, 1933);

The Fairy Doll and Other Plays for Children (New York: Dodd, Mead, 1922; London: John Lane, 1922);

Tinkelly Winkle (London: John Lane, 1923; New York, 1923);

The Path to the Sun (London: Hutchinson, 1923);

Lady Jem (London: Hutchinson, 1923); republished as *Cupid and Mr. Pepys: A Romance of the Days of the Great Diarist* (New York: Stokes, 1923);

Two Elizabeths (London: "The Stage" Play Publishing Bureau, 1924);

The House in Garden Square (London: Hutchinson, 1924);

As the Stars Come Out (London: Hutchinson, 1925);

The Mystery of Jenifer (London: Hutchinson, 1926);

Julian Carroll (London: Hutchinson, 1928);

The Shuttles of Eternity (London: Bles, 1928);

Portrait of a Rebel (London: Bles, 1929; New York: Dodd, Mead, 1930);

Strange Marriage (London: Bles, 1930; New York: Dodd, Mead, 1931);

Sketches of European History (London: John Murray, 1931);

The Manor House (London: Bles, 1932); republished as *Moon out of the Sky* (New York: Dodd, Mead, 1932);

Who Was Florriemay?, New Ninepenny Novels, no. 23 (London: Benn, 1932);

Aunt Elizabeth (London: Bles, 1933);

The House That Was (London: Rich & Cowan, 1933);

Girls of the Sixth Form, Juvenile Series (London: Mellifont Press, 1934);

Judgment Withheld (London: Bles, 1934);

Linda (London: Bles, 1935);

Angel Unawares (London: Bles, 1936);

The Farm on the Downs (London: Bles, 1936);

Fulfilment (London: Bles, 1938);

". . . As Dreams Are Made On" (London: Bles, 1939);

The Sheltering Tree (London: Bles, 1939);

Gemini (London: Bles, 1940).

PLAY PRODUCTION: *The Finding of Nancy,* London, Saint James's Theatre, 8 May 1902.

OTHER: "A School Year," in *The Little Blue Books for Children,* edited by E. V. Lucas (London: Methuen, 1902);

The Dream Garden, edited by Syrett (London: Bailie, 1905).

SELECTED PERIODICAL PUBLICATIONS–UNCOLLECTED: "That Dance at the Robson's," *Longman's,* 15 (April 1890): 630-649;

"Sylvia," *Macmillan's,* 64 (June 1891): 134-146;

"A Birthday," *Longman's,* 19 (1892): 512-527;

"Thy Heart's Desire," *Yellow Book,* 2 (July 1894): 228-255;

"A Correspondence," *Yellow Book,* 7 (October 1895): 150-173;

"Fairy-Gold," *Temple Bar,* 109 (October 1896): 218-241;

"Her Wedding Day," *Quarto,* 1 (1896): 67-84;

"Far Above Rubies," *Yellow Book,* 12 (January 1897): 250-272;

"Chiffon," *Pall Mall,* 22 (1900): 70-76;

"A Revelation in Arcadia," *Harper's Monthly,* 105 (August 1902): 327-334;

"An Idealist," *Harper's Monthly,* 106 (May 1903): 923-928;

"Poor Little Mrs. Villier's," *Venture,* 1 (1903): 53-73;

"On the Right Choice of Books for Children," *Academy* (5 December 1903): 641;

"A Common Occurrence," *Harper's Monthly,* 108 (February 1904): 345-357;

"The Disenchanted Squirrel: A Strictly Grown-Up Story," *Longman's,* 43 (1904): 82-88;

"The Last Journey," *Venture,* 2 (1905): 42-52;

"Madame de Meline," *Acorn,* 1 (October 1905): 91-111;

"The Fascination of the Dolls' House," *Temple Bar,* 133 (February 1906): 109-116;

"The Song That No One Knows," *Acorn,* no. 2 (1906): 235-258.

As a young woman Netta Syrett was a member of the coterie around the periodical *The Yellow Book* and was an active participant in the vibrant and colorful movement surrounding The Bodley Head publishing house. Her work was praised by such notables as W. Somerset Maugham, John Lane, Max Beerbohm, and Arthur Waugh. Syrett's writings between 1890 and 1900 help define the literary milieu of the fin de siecle, and like many others of the *Yellow Book* circle, she went on to develop her art in the new century. After 1900, however, she was no longer a part of any particular literary group or avant-garde movement.

She was a busy woman, turning out novels almost yearly, working with children's theater, entertaining friends, and contributing short pieces to newspapers on such topics as education and Italian customs. She never married. She prided herself on having many male friends, but once they married she made it a policy to end the friendship. Although not militant, she was involved in the Equal Rights for Women Campaign. During her career she published thirty-eight novels, eighteen short stories, four plays, and twenty children's books. She wrote on such varied and topical subjects as socialism, the woman question and its concomitant marriage question, the labor movement, educational reform, aestheticism, psychic phenomena, and psychoanalysis. Her novels were not on the best-seller lists, but she held an audience of intelligent, educated readers up until her last novel was published in 1940.

Born Janet Syrett on 17 March 1865 in Landsgate, Kent, Syrett had four sisters and one brother. Her father, Ernest Syrett, a silk merchant with liberal attitudes about education, provided a financially secure home for his family. At eleven she left home to board at Myra Lodge and attend North London Collegiate School for Girls, which set a high standard of secondary education. She then attended Cambridge Training College to prepare for a teaching career; she completed three years' course work in one year to receive her full teaching certificate. Later she would depict life at the college, as well as the potentially dull and lonely life of a teacher, in her novel *The God of Chance* (1920). She taught English for two years at a school in Swansea and then went to London to live with her four sisters and to teach at the London Polytechnic School for Girls. Katherine Lyon Mix describes the sisters' housing arrangement: "With a freedom unusual for the nineties the five Syrett girls lived in a flat of their own in Ashley Gardens, one keeping house while Kate attended Bedford College, Mabel and Nell studied art (both had pictures in *The Yellow Book*), and Netta taught in the Polytechnic School for Girls." Her family remained important to her throughout her life. She and her sisters enjoyed entertaining and gave parties at their flat to which they invited literary and artistic notables. Peter Thorp, her brother-in-law, mentions meeting Ezra Pound at one of her "literary routs." Later, Syrett enjoyed visits with Peter and her sister Nellie at their Sussex cottage, and for a few years she shared a flat with them in London. Nellie was an accomplished illustrator, trained at the Slade; she illustrated Netta's children's book *The Garden of Delight: Fairy Tales* (1898) and Netta's collection of essays and illustrations for children, *The Dream Garden* (1905). Fiona McLeod, Hilaire Belloc, Alfred Noyes, Evelyn Sharp, and Glyn Philpot contributed to the beautifully printed edition.

Other children's books and plays by Syrett include *The Magic City and Other Fairy Tales* (1903); *Six Fairy Plays for Children* (1903); *The Castle of Four Towers* (1909); *The Vanishing Princess* (1910); *Godmother's Garden* (1918), which had a popular sequel *Tinkelly Winkle* in 1923; and *Robin Goodfellow and Other Fairy Plays for Children* (1918). In her children's writing Syrett incorporates stories from classical myth and Irish, Welsh, and Scottish folklore. A favorite plot involves the appearance of a beautiful fairy princess to children who delight in the wonders she shows them and who, while with the princess, remember all previous meetings but forget the existence of the fairy world when returned to their real lives.

At the Polytechnic School, Syrett became friends with Mabel Beardsley, a fellow teacher who introduced Syrett to her brother Aubrey; through him Syrett met Henry and Aline Harland and soon was a regular guest in their home. Her friendship with the Harlands led to new interests, opportunities, and friendships. Through her association with *The Yellow Book* she became friendly with Evelyn Sharp, Ella D'Arcy, and Julie Norregard Le Gallienne, Richard Le Gallienne's wife. Syrett also developed a friendship with Constance Smedley, who records an abortive attempt to form a literary group to be called The Society of the Golden Key. The members would promote sympathetic but stern criticism of one another's works. Smedley says, "Sincerity was the chief need (so I seriously felt) of the writer who was to be critic too, and I had a great admiration for Violet Hunt, Netta Syrett, and Ella D'Arcy as being entirely sincere and unsentimental." These friendships deriving from her *Yellow Book* experience were important to her personally, but the effect of her association with John Lane and The Bodley Head on her career was even more significant.

Syrett's realistic novels written during the late Victorian and Edwardian periods provide insights into the attitudes, concerns, and movements of this transitional era in English literature. In particular, the social position, rights, needs, and development of women constitute a major theme in her fiction. All of Syrett's female protagonists ultimately rebel against authority—parental, academic, or marital. Some rebel at an early age and make life difficult for family and teachers for years. Others conform to expectations and only as adults assert themselves as individuals who defy tradition and societal pressures. Their drive for individuality and desire for self-realization characterize them as New Women.

Lane published her first novel, *Nobody's Fault* (1896), in his Keynotes Series (with cover and title page design by Aubrey Beardsley). Mix points out that to be included in this series "was to be of Lane's elite." In *Nobody's Fault* Bridget Ruan is sent to Eastchester High School, where she is distinguished by two characteristics—she is the daughter of a tavern keeper and thus of a lower class than the other girls, and she is a nonconformist. She refuses to pay attention to the fastidious demands of the headmistress and is forever receiving demerits for failure to be tidy and neat as all young girls were expected to be. Her wit and warm nature endear her to the other girls even though they know she is not a gentleman's daughter, but the education beyond her social class presents problems when she returns home to Rilchester. She does not fit into the circle of shop owners to which her parents belong. Her mother wants her to marry a bank clerk or shop owner's son, but Bridget remains aloof and antagonizes her parents' friends with her superior airs.

Bridget's anomalous social position demonstrates the contemporary erosion of boundaries between classes. Although not born to the station, she has the education, the dignity, and the sensitivity of a lady. Her mother is the wife of a tradesman and aspires to be accepted by her bourgeois neighbors and to conform to conventional middle-class values, whereas her maternal grandmother was a fisher girl who raised her daughter in a wood shanty by the sea. Within three generations the family has risen three class levels, reflecting the rapidity of social change in England. The mobility possible in this transitional period creates difficulties for Bridget. She breaks away from home, only to be miserable in her lonely lodging in London. She yearns for broader experiences and to become a writer, but she faces the obstacles so many other women had found before her: her gender, low social position, and lack of money. She eventually publishes a novel, but only after an unhappy marriage to a man who is unfaithful and who disdains her writing. She leaves her husband and runs away with the man she loves, knowing that she must bear the disapproval of society. Three major problems faced by the New Woman are catalogued here: an unsympathetic family, limited job opportunities, and an unhappy marriage. In asserting the importance of her own desires in each of these situations, Bridget brings suffering to herself and to others. Her decision to give up her lover and return home to help her mother shows strength on her part but provides a disappointing end to the novel.

In *The Tree of Life* (1897) Christine Willowfield represses her spirited, creative nature and constantly tries to please her domineering, scolding father by demonstrating that she is not the "average woman." A noted lecturer on socialism and social theory in general, Professor Willowfield is a misanthropic ogre who generally ignores his daughter and exists in an abstract, purely intellectual world. He believes "the average woman is unreasonable, and usually incapable of moral action unsupported by some outside authority." In his lectures he may speak of women as equal to men, but his true opinion is revealed in a comment to Farborough, the equally unimaginative pedant whom Christine marries: "The treatment of woman as a reasonable being is the great mistake of the age." Growing up under the guidance of a man with such opinions, Christine has much to overcome.

When Christine marries Farborough and becomes a skilled lecturer herself, she seems doomed to a life of dullness. Motherhood, however, changes her; her emotional nature emerges in her love for her child. The years of repression culminate in Syrett's most violent scene. While Christine is away on a lecturing engagement that her husband has coerced her to keep, her child becomes ill, and her husband does not send for her for fear she will miss her lecture. When she returns and discovers the child's death and her husband's inaction, she pulls a gun out of his desk and tries to shoot him. The incident is quickly hushed up, but by her action Christine is freed of the hold her father and husband have over her. She leaves her husband and turns to Kennedy, a warm, loving man she hopes will teach her to love. *The Tree of Life* is a highly dramatic, rather exaggerated story, but its central theme is the pain a repressive environment can inflict on a sensitive woman.

Literary and dramatic success ended Syrett's teaching career. She continued to publish stories in such British and American magazines as *The Yellow Book, Temple Bar, Harper's Monthly Magazine, The Venture, Longman's,* and *Pall Mall Magazine.*

In her depictions of modern women Syrett shows that often the first problem to be overcome is a restrictive home environment. Rebellion and an assertion of independence are painful necessities. One variation on this pattern is her novel *Rosanne* (1902), in which the protagonist has the unusual problem of too much freedom. Rosanne is a vivacious young woman who does not have to face parental restrictions; her decadent artist father and morally loose mother provide a different standard against which to rebel. In the end she avoids ruining the marriage of the man she loves and accepts her own pain instead of bringing it on others.

In *The Day's Journey* (1905) marriage, not the heroine's childhood, is the central problem. Cecily Merivale, possessed of innate good taste and an appreciation of beautiful things, grows up amid pleasant surroundings and is dearly loved by her widowed father, a doctor who entertains "men well known in the world of science, of letters, and of art." Her problems come after her marriage. Her writer husband, Robert, persuades her to leave London, where she was part of a lively social circle, and move to a secluded Elizabethan farmhouse. Robert soon has an affair with a young woman, Philippa Burton, who follows the whims of modern movements. Philippa is a New Woman: described by Cecily and her friend as a "floppy" type, Philippa dresses in a Bohemian fashion and fascinates enough monied people to make her lifestyle possible. Robert is attracted to her, and she justifies her response to him, citing the progressive doctrine of free love. She is a "typewriter," and Robert eventually hires her as his secretary.

Philippa is not a completely unsympathetic character. Syrett makes clear that she is the "adventuress" she is because of circumstances. Philippa says, "Do you know what life means for a woman who has no money? Do you know what it means to be turned out into the world when your parents die, without influence, without proper training for any work, just to sink or swim as you can?" She uses Richard but eventually, through Cecily's agency, marries a man who can provide the security she craves. The awkward marital situation is intensified for Cecily when her husband encourages Dick Mayne, an old love of Cecily's, to visit them regularly. The novel deals with marriage problems in a frank, straightforward way. Cecily is hurt by her husband's infidelity, but his treatment of her leads to her writing. She becomes a successful novelist, superior in reputation to him. Robert is a fool, but once he learns to see himself clearly and to appreciate Cecily, he promises to become a good husband. Cecily gives up Dick's love to return to Robert. Syrett demonstrates both that a successful marriage is not a simple matter and how the changing roles of women create problems in male-female relationships.

The eponymous protagonist of *Anne Page* (1908) faces boredom and lack of stimulation as a child but develops into an assured, lovely woman in command of her own life. Her mother dies when Anne is two, and her "morose, irritable" father makes life so unpleasant that her brother Hugh runs away from home. Anne writes in her journal, "It is a good thing to be a boy, and be able to run away. I can't, because girls can't be sailors, and there's nowhere to run to." Her drab existence is unrelieved by any excitement, and she suffers from the lack of love. When she is twenty-seven her father becomes ill, and she spends three years constantly attending him. When he dies she faces the necessity of supporting herself. She has no training, but an invalid aunt hears of her situation and hires her as a companion. For more interminable

Title page for the author's first novel, in which a young woman struggles to become a writer

years she nurses the aunt. Her quiet, monotonous existence is relieved only by her delight in the library and the garden. But on her one holiday excursion, when she goes to the coast to visit her brother and his new wife, she becomes keenly aware of the rift between literature and actual life. She returns home emotionally "torn and bleeding" and fights loneliness and despair.

The irony is that Anne's socially impoverished background has created an incomparable woman. When three young artists visit in the village and discover Anne, all three pay her adoring attentions, and she falls in love with one of them, Rene Dampierre. Anne's strength asserts itself when her aunt dies and she unexpectedly inherits the family estate, Fairholme Court. Deciding to take the chance at love that life has belatedly offered her, she goes to Paris with Rene and has three wonderful years with her younger lover. Rene becomes a successful artist, and she charms the intellectual, artistic coterie of which he is a part. She has resolved, however, that if his interest in her ever wanes, she will exit. When he does become interested in another woman, Anne quietly leaves and travels all over Europe. Rene dies at the height of his acclaim in Paris, and Anne returns to Fairholme Court, where the villagers revere her wisdom and beauty. Not knowing that she is a woman with "a past," they possessively view her as their "sweet Anne." She spends her final years with wonderful memories and among loving friends.

Consistently in Syrett's fiction those who theorize remain inferior to those who live—action and spirit characterize Syrett's ideal New Women. They are intelligent; they have experienced the pains and joys of life; and they act on high moral principles, independent of mere social theories.

Although Syrett had earlier incorporated folklore and fairy tales into her children's writing, *A Castle of Dreams,* published in 1909, was her first adult novel to rely heavily on folklore. In most of her works Syrett mentions fairies and folktales only in connection with the mental life of imaginative children and as a source of delight and escape from harsh reality. In *A Castle of Dreams,* however, she uses folklore as a primary element in recounting the experience of a young woman. Bridgit O'Shaughnessy lives in a feudal castle in County Connemara, Ireland, neglected by her absentee landlord father, who gambles away what money he does not spend on luxuries for himself. Syrett captures the fears of a child who, tucked away in a medieval castle with only servants for company, believes that she is a changeling. A mad old neighborhood woman, Eileen O'Mara, has convinced her that she is a fairy child, telling Bridgit that the real daughter of Lord and Lady O'Shaughnessy was stolen by fairies and that Brigit was substituted. The child finds it not only "very interesting" to be a fairy child but also "horribly frightening." She is freed from her terrors by the intervention of George Henry Cathcart, a scholar who "had acquired amongst the learned, even in comparative youth, a certain reputation as a philologist and antiquary." Attracted by the rich folklore and mysterious myths of Ireland, he has come to Connemara, and his advent is Bridgit's salvation. Bridgit has had no opportunity for schooling or conversation with people of her class. Cathcart offers instruction and love to the child; she offers him valuable data about Irish folklore and myths. Cathcart, escaping the pain of a broken marriage and an unfaithful wife, finds solace in giving Bridgit lessons. She becomes a scholar and an expert on folklore herself.

From Bridgit's belief in fairies as a child to her serious study of the subject as a young woman, the romantic trappings of fairyland pervade this novel. The main plot involves Lord O'Shaughnessy's return to the castle when Bridgit is twenty-two. When he discovers that his daughter has grown into a lovely woman, he decides to marry her off to his nouveau riche friend Charles Robinson to cover his debts. In London rumor has it that Lord O'Shaughnessy's daughter is kept in Fomor Castle and never seen in society because she is mad. Crushed by the discovery that people think her insane, Bridgit seeks revenge. She plays the role of the charming, gracious hostess to the obnoxious upstarts her father brings to the castle, but she tantalizes them with elusive, suggestive remarks; sings Gaelic songs in her lovely, evocative soprano voice; and gives the impression that she is, indeed, mentally unbalanced. Having commissioned a village child to provide faraway ghostly harp music, she stages eerie scenes and uses her flair for drama to keep two silly women in hysterics. Charlie Robinson, the man her father wishes her to marry, is a ludicrous fool who is an easy dupe for Bridgit.

Syrett consistently uses fairies and other creatures of fantasy to evoke the mystery and wonder of life. She disdained those with no imagination who tackled the problems of modern society with intense seriousness; she exalted those who possessed a sense of humor and an appreciation for beauty and mystery. Her works incorporating supernatural elements, both the occult stories and those featuring fairy lore, stretched her readers' imaginations and enabled them to see beyond contemporary social, political, and economic problems of the period and to perceive a broader context. Like many others in her age, she sought assurance of existence beyond the tangible, commonsense, and mundane world, and she provided two alternatives. Her fiction depicting psychic phenomena offered one answer to the existing mechanistic, scientific view of the world. Her fiction depicting fairies and magical creatures offered another—the imagination.

In *Olivia L. Carew* (1910) Olivia is the product of a New England village characterized by puritanical intensity and seriousness. She possesses what the reviewer in *The New York Times Book Review* (7 May 1910) called "the soul of a prig." Raised by her widowed, schoolmistress mother, Olivia inherits her "instinct for scrupulous nicety" and her reverence for learning. Learning, however, is valued not for its own sake but for "some mysterious superior height to which it raised the recipient." Intellect was a "fund of information acquired from textbooks to be used in the successful passing of examinations." Olivia's self-confidence, earnestness of purpose, and capacity for hard work have enabled her to succeed in school. Preparing for examinations and receiving achievement certificates have been the focus of her life. She consents to marry the attractive, wealthy young architect Richard Carew not because she loves him or because of his income or social position but because marriage to him would give her more leisure to continue her studying than teaching would.

Olivia has excelled in the educational system as it existed at the turn of the century. She is arrogant and closed-minded and represses the sexual and emotional side of her nature. She delights in lectures on Ralph Waldo Emerson and ancient history but has no appreciation for fiction or paintings. Only after her coldness and narrow-mindedness have estranged Richard and led him to other women does she perceive herself as the fool she is. This late awakening reveals itself in a dramatic way: she plans to commit suicide but is rescued at the last moment by Richard, who takes her back. Repentant, she is now eager to be a proper wife to him.

In most of Syrett's novels one of the major problems that women confront is limited experience, even ignorance. Once a woman can learn more about herself and the world and can determine for herself what she wants to do with her life, happiness becomes, if not assured, at least possible. Inextricably linked with the woman's lot is the question of marriage. Syrett does not view marriage as an evil; like many of her contemporaries, she recognizes that marriage is not a solution to women's problems. Conversely, it is often the beginning of serious problems. Broken marriages abound in Syrett's novels. In *Nobody's Fault* Bridget and her husband separate, and she almost elopes with another man. In *The Tree of Life* Christine Willowfield marries a replica of her father and winds up attempting to shoot him; in the end she does leave him to go to a man who loves her.

Nancy Drender in *Drender's Daughter* (1911) faces a conflict similar to Bridgit's in *A Castle of Dreams*. She is taken from the home of her parents, humble laborers on a large estate, and raised by the lord of the manor, Leonard Chetwynd. Chetwynd is an innovative social thinker who plans an experimental socialist village on his property. His is one of several socialist schemes depicted in Syrett's novels. For example, in an earlier effort, *The Child of Promise* (1907), she chronicled the rebellion of a girl raised in a socialist community. In neither novel does Syrett blatantly condemn socialist ideas; rather she condemns stupidity and the lack of common sense demonstrated by people such as Chetwynd who live in an arid intellectual realm and have no real feeling for the people they purport to want to serve. In *Drender's Daughter* Chetwynd plans to rear Nancy as an ideal wife. His mother, a Girton graduate, has raised him according to advanced notions of child rearing, and he suffers keen disillusionment when both his socialist theories and his theories on marriage fail. His ill-conceived alliance with the opinionated and spirited Nancy ends unhappily. Ultimately, Nancy discovers that the humble Drender is not her real father. An aristocratic artist had had an affair with her mother before her marriage to Drender; thus, Chetwynd did not get his "peasant" stock after all. Nancy's independent nature and her resolve to run away with her lover distinguish her from the prototypical Victorian wife Chetwynd desires, who would see marriage as her primary goal and raison d'être. Chetwynd's assumptions regarding Nancy's training presuppose his superiority and her acquiescence to learning certain domestic and social skills—she should be able to manage the house, and she should have some knowledge of French, art, and music, but not Greek or Latin. She is not to think but to accept unquestioningly her role as wife. Nancy, by nature, can accept no such assumptions. Chetwynd conveniently elopes with his secretary (somehow he finds this action consistent with his theories) and thus enables Nancy to divorce him and marry the man she loves.

In *Three Women* (1912) Phyllida and Katherine are two nice women who run a curio shop; Rosamund is an immoral woman married to the man Phyllida loves. Their interactions and love entanglements form the plot of the novel.

Although she dealt with supernatural elements in such early short stories as "Sylvia" (*Macmillan's*, 1891) and "Fairy-Gold" (*Temple Bar*, 1896), not until 1913 did Syrett treat psychic experiences in a novel. *Barbara of the Thorn* (1913) includes an amazing amalgam of plots. One is contemporary: Barbara Thorne, an innocent girl, inherits some money and travels to Rome, where she has a series of psychic visions that almost drive her to a nervous breakdown. The breakdown is averted with the help of friends who are interested in psychic phenomena. Barbara's visions introduce a story out of Italy's violent and dramatic fifteenth century. Slowly the reader learns of a murder and traces the effects of a curse on the Della Spina family, of which Barbara is a descendant. The story of Barbara's father and his love for a woman named Margaret Fraser is another subplot. The chronicle of intrigues, murders, and dream visions holds interest, but Syrett fails in her execution on two points: her heroine lacks verisimilitude, and Syrett relies heavily on coincidence to resolve the action.

The Victorian ideal of girlhood and womanhood forms the backdrop for *The Victorians: The Development of a Modern Woman* (1915). Rose Cottingham grows up in the repressive, stifling household of her

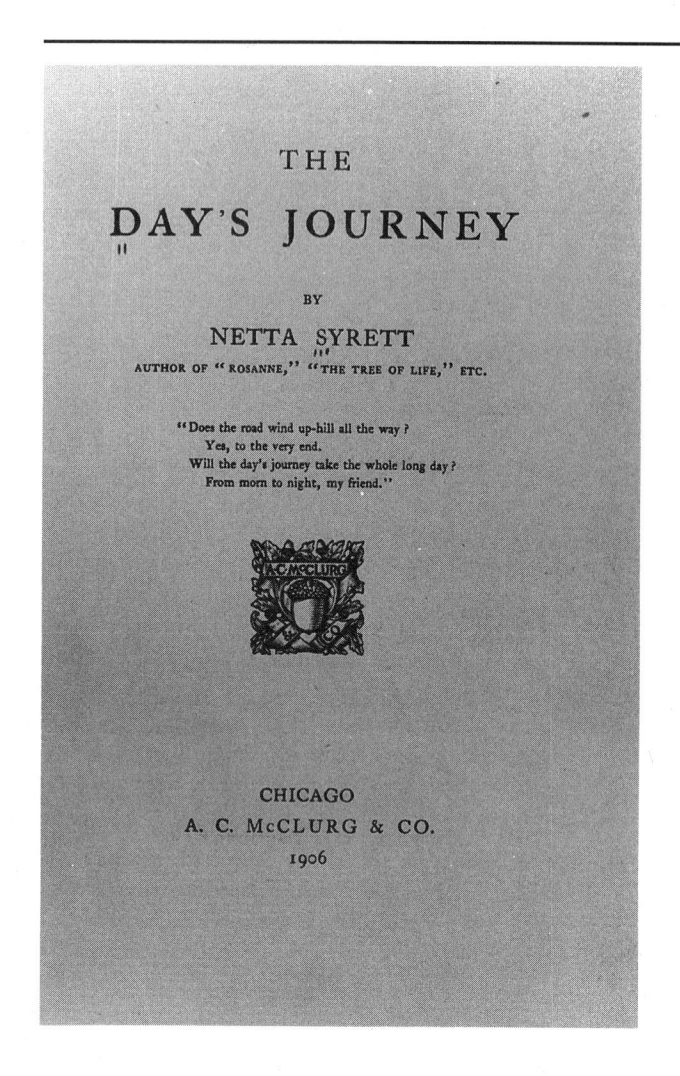

Frontispiece and title page for a novel that deals frankly with a marriage troubled by infidelity

iron-willed grandmother Mrs. Lester, who provides for Rose but does not love her. Rose is a child of extreme moods—she is either elated or depressed. During her elated moments her fecund imagination conjures fantastic schemes and creates delightful fairy tales; in her depressions she broods darkly on the seemingly endless boredom of life and fears madness. She chafes under the strictures of her weary, domineering grandmother, and because of Mrs. Lester's harangues she develops a keen sense of her own inferiority. She is not pretty like her ladylike, submissive younger sister, Lucie. She cannot sew or draw as a model young lady should. Rather, she is disruptive and hard to manage—a plague to the silly governess Miss Piddock and to her grandmother.

Sent to a "progressive" school for girls at twelve, Rose continues to suffer from a repressive environment. The Queen Victoria–like Miss Quayle finds Rose recalcitrant and unmanageable and views her ineptitude in arithmetic as simple perversity (trouble with arithmetic seems to plague all of Syrett's heroines). Rose's experiences closely parallel Syrett's girlhood experiences at Myra Lodge and North London Collegiate School for Girls. Most shockingly, in *The Victorians* Syrett goes so far as to intimate that a girl has sexual desires and fears. In her portrayal of a girl's sexual awakening Syrett is as frank and realistic as she can bring herself to be. At eighteen Rose struggles with her physical drives and puzzles over her feelings, reading French novels and giving up her studies. Syrett's realistic presentation of Rose's confusion and pain is mirrored in Rose's frankness in the novel she eventually writes. The critics praise Rose for realistically depicting her heroine's development. But Rose knows that in actuality she has not revealed all: "The young girl she had drawn, though up to a certain point true to life, was true to that point and no further. There were omissions, suppressions; there were reticences which her creator neither dared nor wished to overpass."

In writing about a girl growing up to write a "realistic" novel about a girl growing up, Syrett creates a circularity that seems particularly modern. With its foundation in autobiography and emphasis on childhood, *The Victorians* is a female bildungsroman. Like Maugham's Philip Carey in *Of Human Bondage* (1915) and James Joyce's Stephen Dedalus in *A Portrait of the Artist as a Young Man* (1916), Syrett's Rose is an individual who confronts difficulties, experiences love and passion, and grapples with the meaning of life. In her novel, however, the protagonist is a girl. Although *The Victorians* is not the earliest novel to present the development of a girl into a writer–it was preceded by Sarah Grand's *The Beth Book* (1897) and Henry Handel Richardson's *The Getting of Wisdom* (1910)–it is a rare early example. The reviewer in *The New York Times Book Review* (13 February 1916) commented: "We have recently had more than one able study of the mental, moral, and physical development of a boy from childhood to young manhood, but unless memory errs the evolution of a girl from child to young woman has been infrequently described–certainly there have been very few which end with the love story yet to come."

Rose's story is continued in *Rose Cottingham Married* (1916). *The Victorians* ends with Rose's success as a writer. *Rose Cottingham Married* picks up at that point and tells of Rose's infatuation with socialism. She meets, falls in love with, and marries a dynamic young workingman, John Dering, who is one of the more accomplished spokesmen for the movement. Having been raised in an aristocratic setting, Rose has to learn to cook and to keep house. She sinks into depression as a result of the manual labor and lack of leisure. John is so involved in his Labour Party and socialist work that he cannot perceive her deprivation or needs. At one point "a flash of intuition revealed to her that in his view, women ministered to the material needs of men, naturally, inevitably." Early in her marriage Rose has to admit that in the class she has entered "women were negligible qualities whenever serious discussions were on foot." Her husband holds the workingman's attitude toward his wife–he loves her, but he never considers her an intellectual equal. Her efforts to do what is expected of her as a wife are painful in light of the opportunities she once had.

The novel realistically describes the precarious early years of John and Rose's marriage. At one point Rose almost deserts her husband for her old friend Geoffrey Winter, who has been in love with her for years. But John makes Rose's domestic life easier by hiring help and thus enables her to return to writing. He eventually allows Rose to use her connections to further his career; in fact, John's abject dependence on Rose at the end of the book contrasts unpleasantly with the striking, independent figure in the early years. The ending of *Rose Cottingham Married* is disappointing, but the account of the struggling marriage is skillfully presented.

In *Troublers of the Peace* (1917) Syrett clarifies other changes in English life between 1890 and 1920 by juxtaposing two generations of women. The primary theme in this novel is the mother-daughter relationship. Isabel Wickham, after years of neglecting her daughter, Joan, tries to get to know Joan better and finds the abyss that has grown between them over the years difficult to bridge. Isabel epitomizes femininity and values decorum and traditional manners. Joan favors Cubist art and Otto Hirsch fabrics and wears "a garment like an overall cut short, quite plain and squared at the neck, from which it hung loose . . . the tunic being spotted all over with a design of big green and yellow rings." She furnishes her new apartment "futuristically": chairs and tables of white wood are painted with stripes and dots of vivid color. Joan is a "transition" woman. She holds on to values of the past while espousing the lifestyle of one of the most "modern" cults. Her friends include a militant suffragette who goes on a hunger strike after being arrested for bombing activities and winds up in an insane asylum, and an artist who lives in a studio with walls "decorated by means of zigzag lines of violent coloured paint shooting in all directions."

In depicting the clash between the generations, Syrett's attitude is clear. She prefers traditionally feminine women. She shows the middle-aged woman's disdain for the bad manners and ugly clothes assumed by the young, but she recognizes the vitality of youth. Although the younger generation may think that there are certain subjects or certain types that did not exist when their parents were young and that their parents thus cannot understand, she shows that an open-minded person, old or young, can appreciate the values both have to offer. The rift between the young and the old would widen after World War I, but in this 1917 novel Syrett holds that people simply have different perspectives. Some have more and broader experience than others (a difference that does not necessarily depend on age), but all share desires and dreams that are simply human.

Women's issues figure largely in Syrett's novels; the 1918 novel *The Wife of a Hero* deals with the dangers of sudden war marriages. A brainless, handsome young man weds an intelligent woman in a burst of passion, but they find the marriage untenable. The conflict intensifies when the wife becomes attracted to another man. Such problems with relationships also figure largely in Syrett's short fiction–at least fourteen of her stories portray women's problems, limitations, and passions.

After 1920 Syrett published twenty-one novels, two plays, one book of reminiscences, and eight children's books. Most of the novels with psychic themes come after 1920: *The House in Garden Square* (1924), *The Shuttles of Eternity* (1928), *Who Was Florriemay?* (1932), *The House That Was* (1933), *Angel Unawares* (1936), *The Farm on the Downs* (1936), *... As Dreams Are Made On* (1939), and *Gemini* (1940). In each novel characters transcend current time and either see scenes from the distant past or envision a future event. In all of the novels the person becomes highly distraught and fears incipient madness, but Syrett makes clear that the characters are not mad–their experiences are real.

Syrett's success as a novelist resulted from a combination of imaginative powers and technical skill. She took topical concerns and spun entertaining tales around them. Her decadent fops, reforming socialists, and rebellious young women are creatures of a past age. By capturing mannerisms, fads, slang, and popular movements in her fiction, she furnishes a rich resource for students of the period. Her novels provide a window on the mental, moral, and social climate of her day. But most important, her characters are human beings with universal frustrations, desires, and problems. The story of an individual fighting to find his or her way in life in conflict with social conventions and family pressures is as timely today as it was in 1896 when Syrett chronicled Bridget Ruan's problems in *Nobody's Fault*. Admittedly, Syrett's novels are repetitive. She has her favorite plotlines, characters, and situations, and she uses them again and again. Sometimes her plots suffer from excessive coincidence, or she passes over too many years too quickly. Instead of subtly making a point, she often hammers it home repeatedly. But she often wrote well.

Syrett died in a London nursing home on 15 December 1943. Her obituary in *The Times* (London) comments: "Her work always bore the stamp of a woman of education and intelligence." Her works merit study not only because of the insights they provide into a specific historical milieu but also because of their general readability and literary merit. Syrett realized the temporal nature of literature, and fiction in particular. Concluding her book of reminiscences, *The Sheltering Tree* (1939), she wrote:

> In a few years, or even less, everything I have written will be dead as the dodo. Already my novels are being swamped by those of the beginners in the art of fiction, who in their turn are destined to be superseded by children now in the nursery.
>
> But what does it matter? The interest and excitement of writing–with any luck, will sustain these newcomers for their lifetime, and no sensible person should ask of our transitory existence more than this. For it is much to have a difficult art to follow, and to do the best one can with words.

Her works are evidence of the interest and excitement her craft held for her. Her best novels–*The Victorians, A Castle of Dreams,* and *The Farm on the Downs* among them–stand the test of time.

Bibliography:
Jill T. Owens, "Netta Syrett: A Chronological, Annotated Bibliography of Her Works, 1890–1940," *Bulletin of Bibliography*, 45 (March 1988): 8–14.

References:
Karl Beckson, *Henry Harland: His Life and Work* (London: The Eighteen Nineties Society, 1978);

A. Brisau, "*The Yellow Book* and Its Place in the Eighteen-Nineties," *Studia Germanica Gandensia*, 8 (1966): 140–162;

Katherine Lyon Mix, *A Study in Yellow: The Yellow Book and Its Contributors* (Lawrence: University of Kansas Press, 1960);

Jill T. Owens, "The Merging of the Real and the Supernatural in the Fiction of Netta Syrett," *Publications of the Mississippi Philological Association* (1985): 18–24;

Owens, "Netta Syrett's 'Uncle': A Biographical Note on the Nineties," *University of Mississippi Studies in English*, new series 4 (1983): 191–192;

Owens, "W. Somerset Maugham and Netta Syrett: Two Perspectives on the Years 1885–1915," *Publications of the Mississippi Philological Association* (1983): 15–25;

Anne Constance Armfield (Smedley), *Crusaders: The Reminiscences of Constance Smedley* (London: Duckworth, 1929);

Arthur Waugh, "London Letter," *Critic*, 30 (2 January 1897): 11;

Harold Williams, *Modern English Writings: Being a Study of Imaginative Literature 1890–1914* (London: Sidgwick & Jackson, 1918), p. 467.

Papers:
Netta Syrett's papers are at the Bodleian Library, Oxford; the Merton College Library, Oxford; and the National Library of Scotland, Edinburgh.

Robert Tressell
(Robert Phillipe Noonan)
(1870 - 3 February 1911)

David Smith
University of Adelaide

BOOK: *The Ragged Trousered Philanthropists,* edited by Jessie Pope (London: Richards, 1914; New York: Stokes, 1914; abridged edition, London: Richards, 1918); enlarged edition, edited by F. C. Ball (London: Lawrence & Wishart, 1955; New York: Monthly Review Press, 1962).

Robert Tressell's literary significance rests entirely on one work, *The Ragged Trousered Philanthropists,* which was first published posthumously in a shortened edition in 1914. While it has not yet found a secure place in any academic literary canon, *The Ragged Trousered Philanthropists,* whether in its abridged or complete form—published in 1955—continues to be read, reprinted, and discussed. Centered on working-class life in the southern English town of Hastings at the turn of the twentieth century, it is a work whose comedy and realism, tinged with the fantastic, place it squarely in the tradition of Charles Dickens. In other respects, however—particularly in its working-class subject matter and its stated aims—it is quite distinctive. While earlier novelists had certainly written about the lives of working-class men and women, one of the aspects that makes Tressell's novel unique is the relationship he establishes between his workmen and their work. The brief horrifying glimpses of sweatshops and factories of Dickens, Charles Kingsley, Benjamin Disraeli, and even Margaret Harkness are replaced in Tressell's novel by a totally unsentimental concept of work as an integral part of human life. Moreover, this picture is presented in a work that is avowedly didactic, designed, according to the preface, "to show the conditions resulting from poverty and unemployment: to expose the futility of the measures taken to deal with them and to indicate what I believe to be the only real remedy, namely—Socialism." That such a work has survived is a tribute to its literary and nonliterary qualities.

Robert Tressell

Robert Tressell was born Robert Phillipe Noonan in Dublin in 1870. Despite the assiduous research of his main biographer, F. C. Ball, and the "resurrection" of his daughter, Kathleen, in the 1960s, the precise date of his birth and even his parentage have not been confirmed beyond doubt. It is probable that he was the illegitimate son of Mary Noonan and Samuel Croker, an inspector in the Royal Irish Constabulary and a magistrate. While the family stories of a Sir Samuel Croker have never been supported by evidence, it is reasonably certain that Tressell's early life, along with that of his seven or eight older brothers and sisters, was more middle class than working class. This world was to be soon undermined, for while Tressell was still young Croker died, and for reasons that remain obscure the family's financial resources were considerably diminished. According to Tressell, his education from the age of seven was somewhat intermittent.

Little is known about Tressell's life until the late 1880s, when he immigrated to South Africa. There he took up the trade of decorating and sign painting, which is a central part of the work experience of *The Ragged Trousered Philanthropists*. He was paid well enough to marry and have a child, Kathleen, in 1892. The marriage did not last—whether it ended by separation, divorce, or death is unclear—and Tressell found himself with sole responsibility for his daughter. Meanwhile, the tubercular condition that contributed to his own early death, evoked movingly in the novel in the sufferings of Owen, resurfaced and seems to have been exacerbated, according to his daughter in an unpublished letter of July 1969, by "the chill of the open veldt." His health was taxed even more seriously by the conditions that confronted him when he relocated to England in 1902.

Tressell left South Africa after the outbreak of the Boer War, accompanied by his daughter and one of his sisters. Staying at first in London, they soon moved to the coastal town of Hastings, where Tressell sought work in the building trades as a painter and decorator. With the English economy in a slump, Tressell's standard of living declined disastrously. As Carol Lee Hale comments in the introduction to her 1994 dissertation, a critical edition of *The Ragged Trousered Philanthropists*, "By this time in his life, Tressell was no stranger to marginalization; an illegitimate child, the youngest son in that 'second' family, a single parent, an Irishman in England, he found himself, as a member of the English working class, introduced to new experiences in disenfranchisement."

There is little doubt that this sense of marginalization—coupled with his growing commitment to socialism—fed into the emotional intensity of the book Tressell began writing. Over a period of about four years beginning in 1906 Tressell worked at a makeshift desk while Kathleen studied at the only table. Attempting to ignore daily evidence that he was dying, he wrote out in longhand a manuscript that eventually totaled some 250,000 words. He signed the work with a pen name taken from the painter's trestles mentioned several times in the novel and gave it the subtitle "Being the story of twelve months in Hell, told by one of the damned." In 1910 Tressell sent the manuscript to three publishers, only to receive three rejections.

With his health deteriorating and the economy no better, Tressell decided that his only hope for a decent existence lay in immigration to Canada. In August 1910 he left the manuscript in the care of his daughter and traveled to Liverpool to earn money for their passage. Within a few months, however, he was in the Royal Liverpool Infirmary; on 3 February 1911 he died, officially of cardiac arrest. He was buried as a pauper—a fate he eerily presages in the funeral of Jack Linden in *The Ragged Trousered Philanthropists*—in a grave designated in official documents only as Plot T.11.

The story, fortunately for literature, does not end there. Kathleen kept her one inheritance carefully preserved in a box that Tressell had designed for it, and within a few months she was working in London as a nurse-governess. By chance she mentioned the manuscript to her mistress, who in turn mentioned it to Jessie Pope, a freelance writer. Pope asked to read it, was by turns moved and exasperated, and passed it on to Grant Richards, the publisher. "The book," Richards wrote later in his *Author Hunting by an Old Literary Sportsman: Memories of Years Spent Mainly in Publishing, 1897–1925* (1934), "was damnably subversive, but it was extraordinarily real, and rather than let it go I was quite willing to drop a few score pounds on it." Thinking it was too long and repetitive, however, he asked Pope to shorten its seventeen hundred-odd pages to a more manageable length. Almost a year later, on 23 April 1914, *The Ragged Trousered Philanthropists*, by "Robert Tressall" [sic], was published.

The novel is fundamentally a work of propaganda. The world of *The Ragged Trousered Philanthropists* is a world born of the desperate passion of Tressell, who believed that his life and those of his fellow workmen and their children were wasting away under the capitalist system; what was far worse, these workmen were prepared to defend capitalism to their dying breath. Tressell shows the enslaving effects of this system on a representative group of house painters in Mugsborough (Hastings) from about 1907 to 1908, as well as the position of prominence it had assumed in their minds. With a mocking laughter that at times has a note of hysteria he scorns their misplaced philanthropy and flays the world of Sweaters and Didlums they so unthinkingly worship. At the same time he shows in their actions and in the many harangues of his socialist hero, Owen, some hope for the future: the possibilities of a better, socialist world. Yet in spite of its purely polemical intentions—or even, one could argue, in part because of them—the novel triumphantly survives. Long after the amelioration of most of the specific abuses it attacks, it may be read as a moving human document and is still capable, one feels, of making converts.

Certainly this survival is not owing to any originality of political thought on Tressell's part. Indeed, it might well be argued that part of his appeal lies in his unsectarian willingness to borrow from various strands of socialist ideology. His socialism is an eclectic, at times surprising, but always interesting combination of ideas of the time. In the outline of the socialist commonwealth, for example, given by the middle-class Barrington toward the end of the book, he borrows fairly heavily from Edward Bellamy's classic American utopia, *Looking Backward* (1882). Elsewhere his arguments often echo those in such contemporary tracts as Robert Blatchford's *Britain for the British* (1902) and *Not Guilty* (1906), H. G. Wells's *New Worlds for Old* (1908), and various Fabian publications of the time. Readers may also detect the influence of William Morris in Tressell's stress on the necessity of work being creatively satisfying: indeed, Owen's lecture on the "Oblong" is virtually a direct dramatization of the arguments presented by Morris in his 1884 lecture "Useful Work Versus Useless Toil." Finally, Tressell demonstrates sympathy with the ideas of Karl Marx in his emphasis on the importance of workers' class consciousness, in his reference to the roles of the state and religion, and in his conception of "the Great Money Trick," which seems to be a simplified version of Marx's theory of surplus value.

The juxtaposition of these names should be sufficient to indicate the impossibility of placing Tressell in any ideological niche. At the same time, however, he does have a definite set of beliefs: he is not preaching a vague socialism of sweetness and light.

Nor is there any sweetness or light in his representation of the social hell inhabited by the "philanthropists," a term Tressell uses with bitter irony to condemn their acceptance of their inferior status and their mindless support of their oppressors. The novel derives intensity from its graphic, meticulously detailed accounts of the uncertainty and meanness of their existence and their pathetic attempts to retain some signs of respectability. The accumulation of detail, characteristic of novels of the period, at times reads like a series of lifeless inventories, but more often than not the novel's documentary quality strengthens Tressell's passion. One thinks, for example, of the way in which the Lindens' prized clock is used in much the same way as

Tressell and his daughter, Kathleen, in Cape Town, South Africa, in 1896

James Joyce incorporated motifs in his works—Owen first notices the clock when he visits the Lindens; later, Mary Linden reluctantly sells it to Didlum when she is near starvation, and it finally turns up in a corner of a room in Sweater's home, "the Cave," ironically complementing Owen's decorations. Tressell underscores the point that the philanthropists' few belongings occupy an integral, almost active part in their lives, far more than do the static possessions of Edwardian middle-class gentlemen.

Most effective is Tressell's treatment of and attitude toward the philanthropists themselves. Although he certainly can be sentimental (for example, the scenes between Owen's son Frankie and his mother or the maudlin role of Barrington in the final chapter), he never treats his workmen with sentimentality. Nor does he show the slightest trace of that paternalism tinged with fear that Wells, Arthur Morrison, and Richard Whiteing display toward the proletariat. His ultimate attitude is that of an acute sense of the working class as human beings who matter and are a vital part of society and not as comic or tragic "characters"—which had been the usual treatment of the English workman up to this point in fiction. It is this attitude that guarantees the reader's indignation, sympathy, involvement in their lives, and, ultimately, appreciation (although not necessarily acceptance) of Tressell's social philosophy.

Tressell's unrelenting observation of the philanthropists' weaknesses at times leads him to be quite remorseless. Throughout the book he scrupulously records their worst characteristics: their sycophancy, their toadying, their occasional viciousness behind each other's backs, and the lack of concern that some of them show when one of their number gets into trouble at work. At many points in the novel this ignorant passivity, which Owen feels is condemning more generations to misery, arouses him to explosions of rage and contempt:

> *They were the enemy*. Those who not only quietly submitted like so many cattle to the existing state of things, but defended it and opposed and ridiculed any suggestion to alter it.
> *They were the real oppressors*—the men who spoke of themselves as "The likes of us," who, having lived in poverty and degradation all their lives considered that what had been good enough for them was good enough for the children they had been the cause of bringing into existence....
> No wonder the rich despised them and looked upon them as dirt. They *were* despicable. They *were* dirt. They admitted it and gloried in it.

Existing simultaneously with this scorn, however—indeed, the reason for it—is another feeling altogether: a feeling of concern, of respect for the philanthropists as human beings and for their value in society. Whether they are boasting emptily of the revenge they will have on their bosses or shouting down Owen's attempts to enlighten them, the workmen remain constantly, intensely alive. One worker offers a mock-elaborate introduction of Owen: "Genelmen, with your kind permission, as soon as the Professor 'as finished 'is dinner 'e will deliver 'is well-known lecture, entitled, 'Money the Principal Cause of being 'ard up'"; another offers philosophical tidbits: "It don't seem right that after living in misery and poverty all our bloody lives, workin' and slavin' all the hours that Gord A'mighty sends, that we're to be bloody well set fire to and burned in 'ell for all eternity!" These characters are full of an exuberant vitality that belies their supposed inferiority. But Tressell's feelings in this respect are shown most clearly in his portrayal of the relationship between the philanthropists and their work.

It is a relationship of a scale and depth rare in English fiction up to this point and certainly rare in any treatment of the proletariat. Tressell most assuredly does not laud work per se—his painters are no less driven than the inhabitants of a nineteenth-century sweatshop, and their hatred and resentment of the manner and conditions in which they work is no less strong—but he does present their function with respect and not just as an item for social reform. He is able, for example, to show that Jack Linden's pretensions to being a free workman are mockingly absurd; a few pages later, however, when Linden is sacked after being caught smoking, he quietly and unhurriedly gathers together his tools, his toolbag, and his work clothes and walks away from the house, his dignity intact. A similar concern is shown in the long and careful descriptions of the work the philanthropists do, in Owen's immersion in his decoration of the front room of the Cave, and preeminently in the attempts that some of them make to defeat the soul-destroying system. Newman, for example, has a family dependent on him and knows that he can be sacked at any moment, but "somehow or other he could not scamp the work to the extent that he was ordered to: and so, almost by stealth, he was in the habit of doing it—not properly—but as well as he dared."

The measure of respect accorded the philanthropists—and much of the novel is in fact devoted to the philanthropists at work—is also present in the portrayal of their lives outside work. Because Tressell believes that their everyday lives are important, he makes no attempt to sensationalize his depictions of the domestic sphere. Instead, he counters his scorn for what he thinks is their imbecilic worship of the system by indicating something of their dignity and inherent potential despite their degrading environment. Thus, Easton is eventually reconciled with his wife, Ruth, and Philpot, who avers that "There ain't no use in the likes of us trubblin our 'eds or quarrellin about politics," is shown throughout the book quietly and unobtrusively helping his fellows, culminating in his elaborate scheme to help Mary Linden without the aid appearing as charity.

Much of the dramatic tension in the novel derives from Tressell's conception of the workmen—the mingling of scorn and hatred for their misguided philanthropy with a concern for them and their potential—from the disparity between what is and what might be. But the vision in the novel of what might be—an important element in the success of the book as propaganda—is not expressed in any impossible utopian terms, as it had been, for example, in Mor-

Tressell's hand-lettered title page for the manuscript of his novel (Congress House, London)

ris's industry-free vision of the future, *News from Nowhere* (1890). Rather, Tressell expresses a belief in progress through his portrayals of the workmen's actions, of Owen's attitudes, and of his moments of explosive rage—particularly in his passionate confrontation with his corrupt employer, Rushton, toward the end of the book—and in the glimpses of the future socialist commonwealth; these glimpses are punctuated, it is important to note, by the ribald and disbelieving cries of the workmen. Their jeers stress that the world is always with them, as does the specter of death in the novel: Philpot is killed by a ladder; Linden dies in a workhouse; and Owen's blood-flecked phlegm constantly reminds him of his condition. The world stays with the workmen even when they leave Mugsborough for their annual vacation and find themselves traveling through an idyllic countryside full of rich fields and fruit. For a moment they seem to be in some future Cockaigne, but soon the confining world closes in once more: "From time to time the men in the brakes made half-hearted attempts at singing, but it never came to much, because most of them were too hungry and miserable."

At times the tension that sustains the novel nearly breaks down, particularly toward the middle of the book when the long period of unemployment in the building trade gives rise to some of Tressell's most monotonous denunciations. In the final chapter, however, the character of Barrington is brought to the fore and seriously undermines the novel's effectiveness. As Tressell's daughter suggests in an unpublished letter of October 1977, the prosperous, middle-class Barrington might be seen as an instance of Tressell "clinging to his early identity." He is one of the few characters not properly absorbed into *The Ragged Trousered Philanthropists:* he is mentioned on page 5 and is a silent observer of several scenes throughout the novel before appearing in his full glory at the "beano," offering his own conception of socialism. His ultimate, incongruous role is that of a rich deus ex machina, giving presents to the children, money and hope to Owen, and the promise to return again with a socialist van. The section, with its almost dreamlike sense of fulfillment, satisfies everything but the reader's intellect.

If Barrington can be seen as an aspect of Tressell's identity, he is also surely, as Wim Neetens comments, evidence of Tressell's succumbing to "the pull of canonical tradition," the tug of fictional convention. Barrington is in many respects a variant of a stock character of Victorian fiction, the member of the middle or upper classes living charitably among the poor. Further, the presents and money associated with his departure may be seen, along with Owen's final denunciation of his employer, as part of the emotional release that was considered so integral to the closure of the Victorian novel. Structurally, then, *The Ragged Trousered Philanthropists* looks back in many ways to the late-Victorian realist novel, as Tressell partakes of the novel tradition generally: his humor, for example, is part of a tradition that includes Wells, Henry Fielding, Jonathan Swift, George Bernard Shaw, and, preeminently, Dickens. There is another important element in the novel that is rather more innovative, however, that takes the novel tradition and makes of it something new. The tension between what is and what might be is mirrored in a formal tension created by Tressell looking back to the traditional novel and, at the same time, reworking those traditions in important ways.

The character of Owen illustrates this aspect of the novel. He might on first introduction seem to be the classic realist hero, the character around whom events will revolve and whose development will be shown in the course of the novel. In some ways he does satisfy this expected function, and, indeed, the novel ends with his vision of a future socialist commonwealth. But in other ways the narrative departs radically from this pattern, constantly weaving in fragments of other characters' stories. Consequently, the novel offers no real closure to Owen's experiences. Furthermore, Owen is cast in various roles in the course of the work, ranging from working-class hero and articulate propagandist, indistinguishable rhetorically from the narrator, to unexceptional workman. For long stretches he seems to vanish from the text even though the narrator affirms that he is present. There is, further, a sense in which the novel is a bildungsroman that traces the development not only of Owen but also of a dozen or so other working-class characters who could be said to represent various aspects of the worker's life: Bert as the innocent and vulnerable adolescent, Easton as the young husband, Linden as the old and dying cast-off, and so on.

If there is an innovative discontinuity or fragmentation in terms of characterization, a lack of sustaining emphasis on one individual, so is there discontinuity in terms of plot. Again the reader's expectations about plot are to some extent—or appear to be—satisfied: the novel offers Owen's domestic life, the decline and demise of Linden, and the seduction plot involving Ruth Easton, all typical narrative devices of Victorian melodrama. But the novel is just as much or more concerned with other matters. Time after time plot continuity is interrupted by extracts from newspapers, songs, magic-lantern slides, lectures, drawings and diagrams, and even angry, frustrated intrusions from the narrator. Indeed, for all its similarity to the nineteenth-century realist novel in terms of plot or character, ultimately *The Ragged Trousered Philanthropists* operates under a different set of priorities. When, for example, the slump displaces the workers from their jobs, the narrative shifts away from interest in their personal lives to a more general analysis of the "System," the voice of the narrator taking over as propagandist.

These sorts of authorial intrusions illustrate another important quality of the novel that distinguishes it from other didactic works of fiction: "the extent to which it recognises its own status as propaganda and offers itself for *use* as much as contemplation," as Peter Miles persuasively defines it. The act of propaganda is foregrounded by the title, which implicitly questions, inverts, and takes over for its own use the orthodox notions of philanthropy and charity; the title is, as Mary Eagleton and David Pierce comment, interpretative rather than descriptive. And not only is the activity of propaganda constantly enacted within the text, as in Owen's and Barrington's speeches, in Nora's tuition of Frankie, and in short conversations and episodes throughout the narrative, but the ways in which this book might be used are explicitly raised for the reader's consideration. For example, Owen possesses "a little library of Socialist books and pamphlets which he lent to those he hoped to influence," to which other characters refer, generally disparagingly. Owen's socialist library is, however, shown to be responsible for the conversion of at least one man, Harlow, who credits his newfound socialist loyalties to "listenin' to several lectures by Professor Owen . . . and reading [his] books and pamphlets." Even more tellingly, perhaps, at one point Frankie says that his father's favorite books are *England for the English* and *Happy Britain,* clearly a disarming reference to Blatchford's popular and influential tracts *Britain for the British* (1902) and *Merrie England* (1894).

Blatchford's tracts, as important as they were to contemporary readers, died with his time; Tressell's work, on the other hand, has been continually read and reprinted since the first shortened edition in 1914. With the publication in 1955 of the complete edition, which ends not on the depressing note of Owen contemplating suicide but rather with his vision of a future socialist commonwealth, the novel attracted a new generation of readers. Indeed, if one considers the various editions together—a more extensively abridged edition was brought out in 1918—this avowedly didactic work has gone through more than fifty reprintings in a variety of languages; it has also been dramatized several times and produced for television. It has even been said to have won the 1945 elections for the British Labour Party. While this claim may appear somewhat improbable, it is certainly the case that important writers ranging from Alan Sillitoe to George Orwell have attested to its significance in their lives.

But, perhaps most tellingly, there is evidence that whatever other success the novel has achieved, it seems to have worked on the level envisaged for it in its self-referential passages. For not only does one find testimony to the influence of the novel in dozens of working-class autobiographies, but one also finds many references to its manner of dissemination. A 1955 reviewer in *The Daily Worker*, for example, declared that among the troops in Burma it was "handed around and read and reread until it literally fell to pieces," while others have talked of scenes from it—particularly the "Great Money Trick"—being enacted on building sites and workshop floors. As Miles observes, this passionate, bitter, and witty book has "been lent and given, recommended, dramatized, excerpted, learned by heart, quoted, taught, discussed, performed, watched, photographed, and, most strikingly, imitated." If the private life of Robert Tressell remains for the most part shrouded in obscurity, then his "public" life—which, as Ball has commented, really only began after his death—remains a continuing affair.

Biographies:
F. C. Ball, *Tressell of Mugsborough* (London: Lawrence & Wishart, 1951);
Ball, *One of the Damned: The Life and Times of Robert Tressell, Author of* The Ragged Trousered Philanthropists (London: Weidenfeld & Nicolson, 1973).

References:
Jack Beeching, "*The Ragged Trousered Philanthropists*," *Our Time*, 7 (May 1948): 196-199;

Beeching, "The Uncensoring of *The Ragged Trousered Philanthropists*," *Marxist Quarterly*, 2 (October 1955): 217-229;
Mary Eagleton and David Pierce, "Robert Tressell," in their *Attitudes to Class in the English Novel from Walter Scott to David Storey* (London: Thames & Hudson, 1979), pp. 79-83;
Carol Lee Hale, "A Critical Edition of Robert Tressell's *The Ragged Trousered Philanthropists*," dissertation, Michigan State University, 1994;
Brian Mayne, "*The Ragged Trousered Philanthropists*: An Appraisal of an Edwardian Novel of Social Protest," *Twentieth-Century Literature*, 13 (July 1967): 73-83;
Peter Miles, "The Painter's Bible and the British Workman: Robert Tressell's Literary Activism," in *The British Working-Class Novel in the Twentieth Century*, edited by Jeremy Hawthorn (London: Arnold, 1984), pp. 1-17;
Jack Mitchell, "Early Harvest: Three Anti-Capitalist Novels Published in 1914," in *The Socialist Novel in Britain: Towards the Recovery of a Tradition*, edited by H. Gustav Klaus (Sussex: Harvester, 1982), pp. 67-88;
Mitchell, *Robert Tressell and the Ragged Trousered Philanthropists* (London: Lawrence & Wishart, 1969);
Wim Neetens, "Politics, Poetics, and the Popular Text: *The Ragged Trousered Philanthropists*," *Literature and History*, 14 (Spring 1988): 81-90;
Ronald Paul, "Tressell in International Perspective," in *The Rise of Socialist Fiction 1880-1914*, edited by Klaus (Sussex: Harvester, 1987), pp. 231-251;
Grant Richards, *Author Hunting by an Old Literary Sportsman: Memories of Years Spent Mainly in Publishing, 1897-1925* (London: Hamilton, 1934), p. 280;
David Smith, "The Philanthropists of Mugsborough," in his *Socialist Propaganda in the Twentieth-Century British Novel* (London: Macmillan, 1978), pp. 27-38;
Alan Swingewood, "Robert Tressell: The Working Classes as Prisoners of the System," in his *The Myth of Mass Culture* (London: Macmillan, 1977), pp. 50-58;
Frank Swinnerton, *The Adventures of a Manuscript, Being the Story of "The Ragged Trousered Philanthropists"* (London: Richards, 1956);
Raymond Williams, "The Ragged-Arsed Philanthropists," in his *Writing in Society* (London: Verso, 1983), pp. 239-256.

E. L. Voynich

(11 May 1864 - 27 July 1960)

Shoshana Milgram Knapp
Virginia Polytechnic Institute and State University

BOOKS: *The Gadfly* (New York: Holt, 1897; London: Heinemann, 1897);
Jack Raymond (London: Heinemann, 1901; New York: Mershon, 1901; Philadelphia: Lippincott, 1901);
Olive Latham (London: Heinemann, 1904; Philadelphia: Lippincott, 1904);
An Interrupted Friendship (London: Hutchinson, 1910; New York: Macmillan, 1910);
Put off Thy Shoes (New York: Macmillan, 1945; London: Heinemann, 1945).

TRANSLATIONS: V. M. Garshin, *Stories from Garshin* (London: Unwin, 1893);
Sergei Stepniak and Felix Volkhovsky, *Nihilism as It Is* (London: Unwin, 1894);
The Humour of Russia (London: Scott, 1895; New York: Scribner, 1895);
Mikhail Lermontov, *Six Lyrics from the Ruthenian of Taras Shevchenko also The Song of the Merchant Kalashnikov from the Russian of Mikhail Lermontov,* with a biographical sketch by Voynich (London: Elkin Mathews, 1911);
Frédéric Chopin, *Chopin's Letters,* edited by Henryk Opienski, with a preface and editorial notes by Voynich (New York: Knopf, 1931; London: Harmondsworth, 1932).

E. L. Voynich achieved instant and enduring renown with her first novel, a melodramatic philosophical adventure set during the Italian Risorgimento of the nineteenth century. The hero of *The Gadfly* (1897) survives political betrayal, romantic disappointment, emotional disillusionment, and physical torture. His identity disguised, the Gadfly redoubles his political efforts, transforms his cynicism into a weapon, and ultimately forces his former spiritual advisor—a priest who is also his unacknowledged father—to face the truth about himself and the corrupt Roman Catholic Church. He fights for the freedom of Italy, the love of his former sweetheart, and the soul of his father. With its suspenseful plot structure and its passion for honor and justice, *The Gadfly* is a combination of Nathaniel Hawthone's *The Scarlet Letter* (1850) and Baroness Emma Orczy's *The Scarlet Pimpernel* (1905).

E. L. Voynich

Admired by Jack London, D. H. Lawrence, and Rebecca West; adapted to the stage in 1898 by George Bernard Shaw; and acclaimed by Bertrand Russell as "the most exciting novel I have read in the English language," *The Gadfly* went through eight printings in its first four years, achieving popularity both in English and in translation.

More copies of the work have been sold in Russia than of nearly any other novel written in English. It has been published there in more than one hundred editions and has been assigned as required reading in schools. Adapted for three operas and two films, one with a scenario by the formalist critic Viktor Shklovsky and the other with a score by Dmitry Shostakovich, *The Gadfly* has remained an official classic; the Russians rank Voynich with Charles Dickens and Mark Twain. When a Russian editor discovered in 1955 that Voynich was still alive, the Soviet newspaper *Pravda* published a front-page story with the headline "Voynich Lives in New York!" In 1956 Adlai Stevenson visited the Soviet Union to arrange for the payment of long-overdue royalties for millions of copies.

The rest of Voynich's career failed to live up to her dramatic early success. Her four other novels—two of which deal with characters from *The Gadfly*—address similar political and psychological themes but with reduced intensity and insight. Voynich also published several translations and composed choral music.

Ethel Lilian Boole was born in County Cork, Ireland, on 11 May 1864, the last of the five daughters of the eminent mathematician George Boole, who died six months after her birth. Her mother was Mary Everest Boole, a writer on a variety of scientific topics. Her uncle was George Everest, the explorer who gave his name to Mount Everest.

At age eight, after contracting erysipelas, Boole went to live for two years in Lancashire with the family of her uncle Charles Boole, who beat his own children and treated his young niece cruelly. On her return home she had a nervous breakdown. At fifteen she read a book about Giuseppe Mazzini, the Italian republican, and was captivated by his image; she dressed in black until her marriage in honor of his idealism and in mourning for a world that was not yet free.

When she was eighteen Boole went to Berlin for three years to study at the Hochschule der Musik. There she read *Underground Russia* (1885), and on her return to London she asked her friend Charlotte Wilson to recommend someone to teach her Russian and provide contacts so that she could visit Russia. Wilson suggested the author of *Underground Russia,* Sergei Kravchinsky, known as Stepniak, who had assassinated the chief of the czarist secret police. Boole learned Russian from Stepniak and became deeply involved in revolutionary politics. She spent two years in Russia between 1887 and 1889, working as a tutor, governess, and music teacher. Her experiences increased her sympathy for the suffering of political prisoners and exiles.

Back in London, Boole helped Stepniak organize the Society of Friends of Russian Freedom, which published a monthly magazine, *Free Russia.* Through her association with Stepniak she met not only literary celebrities such as Shaw, Friedrich Engels, Oscar Wilde, William Morris, and Eleanor Marx but also her future husband, Mikhail Babdank-Woynicz, a Polish nationalist of aristocratic background who had been arrested for his membership in a proletarian political party, spent two years in custody in Warsaw, and exiled to Siberia, from where he had escaped to England. He anglicized his name to Wilfrid Michael Voynich and became a British citizen, and he and Boole were married in 1892. Wifrid Voynich became an internationally known dealer in antiquarian books and made frequent book-hunting trips to Europe, often with his wife; it is possible that his business was, at first, designed to conceal the smuggling of anticzarist books.

During the early years of their marriage they were in close contact with Stepniak, who encouraged Ethel Voynich to read and translate Russian literature. Under the name E. L. Voynich she published in 1893 a translation of the stories of V. M. Garshin, with an introduction by Stepniak. George Cotterell in *The Academy* (23 December 1893) noted the "spirit of absolute, unrelieved tragedy," the "calm, simple, tragic" mood of battleground narrative. In 1894 Voynich's translation of Stepniak's pamphlets appeared, with Felix Volkhovsky's "Claims of the Russian Liberals," as *Nihilism as It Is*. The Voyniches, working with Stepniak, printed and sent to Russia a variety of controversial works: the writings of the Decembrist revolutionaries, books by Aleksandr Herzen and Georgy Plekhanov, and Russian translations of works by Karl Marx and Engels. In 1894 Ethel Voynich traveled to Russia to smuggle in some of these illegal publications herself.

Her next book was also a translation, *The Humour of Russia* (1895), a selection of excerpts and stories including Fyodor Dostoyevski's "Crocodile," Nikolai Gogol's "Marriage" and "Diary of a Madman," Glyeb Uspenski's "Steam Chicken," Aleksandr Ostrovsky's "Incompatibility of Temper," Mikhail Gorbunov's "La Traviata," and "The Story of a Kopeck" by Stepniak, who also wrote an introduction to the volume. A. A. Sykes in *Proceedings of the Anglo-Russian Literary Society* (1895) commended Voynich's "excellently rendered extracts," while W. R. Murfill in *The Critic* (March 1896) found the volume "readable and enjoyable in a high measure." Reviewers for *The Academy* (25 May 1895) and *The Bookman* (London; May 1895) complimented the selection of pieces, and the latter also praised the "excellent idiomatic English."

In 1893 Voynich began the novel that became *The Gadfly*. She planned to treat the Giusseppe Mazzini movement in Italy in the 1830s and 1840s and visited Italy to obtain background information, but she did not travel alone. Although the full story did not become public until the 1960s, and some details remain obscure, Voynich traveled to Florence, Pisa, and Elba in the company of Sigmund Rosen-

Title page for Voynich's best known work: the story of Arthur Burton, an Anglo-Italian who becomes a hero in the Young Italy movement of the 1830s, fighting against the oppression of Italy by Austria and the Roman Catholic Church

blum, who later changed his name to Sidney Reilly and became famous as the "Ace of Spies," an enigmatic international agent who plotted to assassinate Vladimir Ilyich Lenin and is thought to have died at the hands of the Soviet secret police around 1925. According to Reilly's biographer Robin Bruce Lockhart, Reilly claimed to have had a brief romance with Voynich, who drew the character of the Gadfly from his shrouded origins (Reilly, too, was the product of an affair between his mother and a family friend) and his years of suffering in Brazilian plantations and jungles. Given Reilly's propensity for inventing stories about himself, it is possible that some of the adventures he reported as his own were based on Voynich's novels, rather than vice versa. It is, however, likely that the Gadfly—with his mysterious antecedents, cynical temperament, and sa-tirical manner—is in part a portrait of the romantic and risk-taking Reilly. Soviet readers and scholars, who tended to see the Gadfly as part of the Russian revolutionary tradition, were reluctant to recognize an anti-Communist as the model for a hero they claimed as their own.

The Gadfly begins with the sheltered youth of Arthur Burton. He is devoted to his mother, an Italian widow who dies when he is sixteen; his guardian and mentor, the priest Montanelli, who is also secretly his biological father; and his sweetheart, Gemma, his partner in amateur political activities. Gemma, like the young Ethel Boole, is a passionate British idealist who always dresses in black. The idyll ends when Arthur is tricked into betraying his political secrets to a priest who is also a spy; at the same time he discovers his true parentage, and he loses all trust in Montanelli and the Catholic Church. Feigning suicide, Arthur sails for South America; as Felice Rivarez, he is mutilated, lamed, and disgraced. Years later he returns to Italy as the Gadfly to serve as satirist for the Young Italy movement against Austrian tyranny. Montanelli, now a cardinal, is forced to condemn him to death but tries secretly to rescue him. The Gadfly reveals his identity but refuses to be saved unless Montanelli admits that he and his church are frauds. Montanelli refuses to join the Gadfly and his revolutionary struggle, while the Gadfly refuses to accept mercy from his hypocritical father. After writing a gentle love letter to Gemma, the Gadfly dies, cheerfully mocking the incompetent firing squad. Montanelli, too, dies after declaiming his guilt and God's.

Written half a century after the events it depicts, *The Gadfly* demands a philosophical rebirth independent of the particular events of Italy's conflict with Austria. When Montanelli questions Arthur's motivation, pointing out that Arthur is "not even an Italian," Arthur replies: "That makes no difference; I am myself. I have *seen* this thing, and I belong to it." The issues, while connected to a political situation of the 1830s, appeal to a sense of justice and a belief in progress extending beyond specific goals or national allegiances. The dullness, lifelessness, and changelessness that oppress his soul in his dismal home after his mother's death are transferred in Arthur's mind to the Austrian Empire and thus inspire his allegiance to the political cause he makes his own.

Religion is shown in the novel to be an element of the dying world that must be superseded in the new world. Voynich's novel has been taken as an attack on the Catholic Church, portrayed not merely as hypocritical but as the enemy of human life, and by extension as an attack on all religion. Although Voynich subsequently taught in a Catholic school, which would not have hired an avowed atheist, her novel makes clear that Montanelli's belief that God requires earthly misery for the sake of heavenly reward motivates his abandonment of his son and his own consequent madness. In a parallel explicitly and repeatedly drawn, Montanelli has sacrificed his son for a "greater good," and the Gadfly condemns the system of beliefs based on God's sacrifice of his son Jesus Christ. The novel's epigraph–"What have we to do with thee, Thou Jesus of Nazareth?"–comes from the Gospel episode of the Gergesene Demoniacs and connotes a rejection of Christ. The Gadfly condemns God the Father through his attack on the sacrifice of Christ, describing Montanelli as following in God's deadly footsteps. The Gadfly criticizes, too, the worship of the Son. He wonders why Christians revere the sufferings of Christ while ignoring the suffering of those around them and condemns Montanelli as a typical Christian in his evasion of personal responsibility:

> We atheists ... understand that if a man has a thing to bear, he must bear it as best he can: and if he sinks under it–why, so much the worse for him. But a Christian comes whining to his God, or his saints; or, if they won't help him, to his enemies–he can always find a back to shift his burdens to.

The Gadfly posits an absolute choice between his world and Montanelli's. Montanelli is not to be allowed to save the Gadfly's life without embracing the Gadfly's principles and thereby saving his own soul. Yet Voynich subtly implies that the Gadfly, too, is in need of salvation, even though he is a fully heroic protagonist: fearless, resolute, intelligent, disciplined, and capable of great endurance. The Gadfly targets "the mental disease called religion" as "the morbid desire to set up a fetich and adore it, to fall down and worship something." Gemma, by contrast, wants to preserve "the sense of the sacredness of human life": "to force the government's hand is not an end in itself, but only a means to an end, and ... what we really need to reform is the relation between man and man." If Gemma is right, then the Gadfly, too, needs to learn, to recover in his dealings with Gemma and Montanelli the possibilities of warmth and spontaneity he had in his youth. He needs not only to destroy but also to live. To fight the Church and what it represents, to deliver Italy from its oppressors and what they represent, he needs to be both Arthur and the Gadfly, at once possessing and surpassing his own past.

This hero, for readers on the cusp of the modern world, bridges the dichotomy between the man of sensibility and the man of action. Opposites are linked; the father and son who love each other are responsible for each other's death. The Gadfly was captured only because he stopped short of shooting Montanelli; the cardinal, at the celebration of mass, repudiates his creed for reasons that derive from his conversation with his son. Conflating Jesus Christ with his own son, he asks his people to justify the sacrifice of his son's life: "It were better that you all should rot in your vices, in the bottomless filth of damnation, and that he should live. What is the worth of your plague-spotted souls, that such a price should be paid for them?" He would not leave the Church to join the Gadfly in life, but the two are joined in death. The Gadfly's anticlerical message is spoken from the altar. The loving opponents have shaped each other.

Voynich completed her novel after returning from Italy in the fall of 1895 and began seeking a publisher. In December 1895 Stepniak was killed in a railroad accident, and the Voyniches curtailed their association with the Russian revolutionary movement.

Fearing possible objection to the novel's anticlerical content, the British publisher William Heinemann arranged to have *The Gadfly* published in the United States by Henry Holt in June 1897. When the response was predominantly positive, Heinemann published a British edition in September to large sales. In 1898 Shaw wrote a dramatization of *The Gadfly* to protect Voynich's dramatic rights by preventing anyone else from writing a play with that title. "A shocking travesty," Shaw called his play, "sufficient to secure the copyright but quite unworthy of its original."

The novel was well received in spite of its shocking subject matter–the attacks on the Church, the Gadfly's mutilated body, and his shameful careers, including servant, brothel aide, and carnival freak. William Morton Payne in *The Dial* (1 July 1897) acclaimed *The Gadfly* as "one of the strongest of the year, vivid in conception and dramatic in execution, filled with intense human feeling, and worked up to a tremendously impressive climax." Praising the "power" of "Mr. Voynich" (who was apparently assumed to be not only the creator but also the model for the Gadfly), the reviewer for *The Critic* (7 August 1897) described *The Gadfly* as an "historical novel, permeated with a deep religious interest, in which from first to last the story is dominant and absorbing." According to *The New York Times Book Review* (26 June 1897), the novel "shows a wonderfully strong hand, and descriptive powers which are rare." The reviewer for *The Bookman* (London) of February 1899, while put off by descriptions

Sidney Reilly, Russian-born British spy and adventurer, who may have been Voynich's lover and was probably the model for Arthur Burton, the hero of The Gadfly

of "too much torture, mental and physical," admired the writer's "talent and its uncompromising vigour," along with the characterization of the protagonist:

> What is wholly real and admirable is the personality of the bitter, biting, mocking, suffering Gadfly, untameable, unrelenting and always "game"–a living man, who will force the most unwilling reader's sympathy along the painful track of his career, as he won that of the men and women he worked with, so agonisingly and with such splendid loyalty.

Reviewers frequently warned their readers about the controversial subject matter, while refraining from either condoning or condemning the Gadfly's excoriation of the Church. Payne, for example, observed:

> The book is extremely outspoken at times, and will probably give to many of its readers the same sort of offence that is given, let us say, by such a poem as Mr. Swinburne's "Before a Crucifix." The note of revolt is certainly very insistent and very shrill. Those who have a sense of the stern realities that underlie even the most traditionally sacred conventions of life will be able to enter into the spirit of this book and share the mood of its author; those who have not that sense will probably read it with suspicion and shudder at its denouement.

In Russia, where the relative abstractness of the revolutionary setting made it seem applicable to any crusade for a better world, the success of *The Gadfly* endured a variety of political environments, and the Gadfly became a hero to generations of young people. It was translated as *Ovod,* published first in installments (January–June 1898) in the socialist-learning journal *Mir bozhii* and in book form in 1900. Ten years later there was another translation and a third two years later; each translation went through multiple editions, and the later editions were priced to make the book affordable to a large public.

Commentators on the novel stressed its specific historical context, alluded to in the subtitles that appeared in early editions: *A Novel of Italian Life in the 30s* and *A Novel of Revolutionary Life in the Nineteenth Century*. From the time of its first appearance in Russia, however, the novel was put to revolutionary purposes. In St. Petersburg in the late 1890s the Socialist Workers movement prepared bound volumes of the issues of *Mir Bozhii* containing the installments and distributed them to a school for workers. Eventually, however, the czar's censors caught on. The 1905 edition of the novel was confiscated, and the censors rejected dramatic versions of the play, titled "Zhertva svobody" (Sacrifice of Freedom) and "Iz bor'by za svobodu Italli" (From the Struggle for Italy's Freedom). The novel was thenceforth interpreted as an echo of the idealist Decembrist movement of 1825 and as a call to arms against the czar.

Jack Raymond (1901), Voynich's second novel, tells a contemporary story set in England. It illustrates the power of emotional and intellectual sympathy to heal a spirit wounded by cruelty and shocked by loss. Raised by his uncle, a sadistic minister, Jack triumphs over a variety of tortures–including severe beatings and unfounded accusations of "perversion" (homosexuality)–largely because of his inner resources and the friendship of a schoolmate's mother, the widow of a Polish political activist who had died in Siberia. The character of the vicar appears to be based on Voynich's uncle, Charles Boole. The character of Helen Mirski is based partly on Praskovia Karaulova, a political prisoner's wife who had befriended Voynich in Russia.

Jack is sensitive but stubborn, independent in thought and action. As a child he undergoes the vicar's daily floggings but does not conclude that life is perpetual suffering. As a youth he steals a knife, trades it for a bird (which he sets free), and when circumstantially linked by the knife to charges of homosexuality, experiences unjust accusations without assuming that injustice is inescapable. When he is sent away to a new school, he protects a smaller boy, Theo, a musical genius, and is befriended by Theo's mother, Helen Mirski, whose kindness and understanding nurture them both.

Theo is talented and ambitious but morally deficient. Jack becomes a promising medical student and a decent young man. He keeps vigil with Helen, who is dying of cancer, as Theo continues to play concerts in Berlin, Paris, and Vienna. When Theo impregnates Jack's sister, Jack forgives them and supports the sister and her child. Having been an abused child himself, Jack views the care of Theo, even as an adult, as a sacred trust from Helen, and he is loyal. *Jack Raymond,* like *The Gadfly,* is preoccupied with physical and psychological pain but concludes with at least a spiritual victory.

The New York Times Book Review (1 June 1901), while commending *Jack Raymond* as "an unusually clever novel, in spite of its faults," attacked the work for "themes which, when touched upon by a woman, are disgusting." The unspecified themes, presumably homosexuality and sadism, make *Jack Raymond* "not a book to be read before dinner by people of squeamish stomachs." Similarly, the reviewer for *The Academy* (11 May 1901) praised the "cleverness and crude power" of the novel but found the theme "astonishingly unpleasant" and made "little observation of genius, freshness, or importance."

Olive Latham (1904), like *Jack Raymond,* is a story of suffering and salvation. An even-tempered, wealthy young Englishwoman rejects a life of luxury and a marriage-minded clergyman to work as a hospital nurse and social reformer. In London she becomes involved with Vladimir Damarov, a Russian nihilist who had been a sculptor before he was converted to anarchism by his friend Karol Slavinski, a doctor, former prisoner, and survivor of spinal paralysis. Olive accuses Slavinski of ruining Damarov's life by robbing him of his true vocation, leaving the former sculptor with nothing but "hopeless faithfulness to a lost cause." When Damarov is imprisoned, she seeks him in vain, appealing to heartless officials and finally discovering his headstone in a desolate cemetery. Her ordeal, like that of Helen Mirski in *Jack Raymond,* is drawn from Voynich's memories of her Russian friend Karaulova. The persecution of Damarov and Slavinski appears to be based on her husband's experiences as a political prisoner in Siberia.

Verging on mental collapse, Olive recovers through the love of Slavinski, who awakens her emotionally by appealing to both her vulnerability and her strength. They work, as did Voynich, on an émigré newspaper in England. When Slavinski is wounded at the Polish frontier, Olive nurses him as she had nursed Damarov and as she herself was healed by Slavinski. Like the Gadfly and Jack Raymond, Olive suffers intensely but prevails.

Reviewers commented on the novel's painful realism. The *Proceedings of the Anglo-Russian Literary Society* (1904) praised the "dramatic" situations, the "original" conception, and the authentic knowledge of Russia. *The New York Times Book Review* (4 June 1904), which found the novel absorbing, vivid, "powerful and doubtless true," commented that "there is such an insistence on the cruelty of life that the most sympathetic reader must sometimes be repelled." According to *The Bookman* (London) of August 1904, *Olive Latham* is "a very remarkable book" written with "haunting poignancy and power," an "intensely human story" providing "illuminating glimpses of the bestiality and squalor of Russian peasant life, of the degeneracy of the better classes, of the horrors of the Russian prison system." Although the plot structure, like that of *Jack Raymond,* was criticized for lacking focus, *Olive Latham* was seen as more emotionally powerful than the earlier novel and as less marred by its subject matter.

An Interrupted Friendship (1910) deals with events in South America during the time of *The Gadfly,* years at which the original novel only hints. After Arthur Burton leaves Italy, his innocent trust shattered, he takes on the name Felice Rivarez and works as a plantation laborer and circus clown until, posing as a Portuguese cook, he joins a British jungle expedition and ultimately saves the lives of several officers. The protagonist is not the future Gadfly but Rene, one of the men whose lives he saves. The younger son of a French marquis, Rene has joined a dangerous scientific expedition to earn the money to cure his sister Marguerite's hip disease. Rene loves Rivarez for his courage and dignity. The friendship ends suddenly when Marguerite, attempting to offer Rivarez an affection he cannot return or even understand, Marguerite inadvertently leads him to think that Rene has revealed the secrets of his past. An operation restores Marguerite's mobility, but she is crippled again after being run over by a pushcart. The novel is deeply ambivalent about Rivarez and about the efficacy of struggle, labor, and courage. Years after the events, Rene tells his son that it is his privilege to have known "one of the rare spirits that go through the world like stars, radiating light," but it is "a dangerous thing to love them too much." *The Gadfly* may or may not constitute an autobiographical revelation of a lover's secrets; but *An Interrupted Friendship,* which asserts that a man once betrayed is forever suspicious and never forgiving, may have autobiographical overtones, as well. For all the main characters the outcome is fundamentally bleak.

Binding for the U.S. edition of Voynich's 1910 novel that describes Arthur Burton's years in exile in South America before his return to Italy

Some reviewers regarded *An Interrupted Friendship* positively and treated the new novel in its relation to *The Gadfly*. The *American Library Association Booklist* (10 April 1910), for example, judged *An Interrupted Friendship* to be "a story of commanding interest, pleasanter than the earlier one but not so strong and having the same morbid taint." The reviewer for *The Athenaeum* (19 March 1910) noted the novel's "anti-deistic animus," "intense bitterness," "dramatic energy," and "excellent" characterizations: "The artistic achievement of the book is the sour humour which shows up the diabolical effect of heroic self-denial and loving acts upon the lives of the chief characters." Payne, in *The Dial* (1 April 1910), found the novel "a true work of art," "intensely vivid from first to last, and grimly tragic," with characters at the mercy of an "implacable and savage fate." The reviewer for *The Nation* (16 June 1910) considered the novel "morbid," obsessive, and mysterious, with a "haunting force." The reviewer for *The Bookman* (London) of April 1910, apparently unaware of *The Gadfly*, noted that "one guesses vaguely that something in early life permanently destroyed his faith in man and in woman" but praised the novel for "the way in which one single indomitable soul in a sickly, painwracked body can by the force of unflinching endurance and patient example effect the regeneration of a whole company of men and save an expedition from failure." The writer for *The Independent* (19 May 1910), similarly unaware of Rivarez's background, commented on a "tragedy in his past, with which the author whets one's curiosity but which she never quite reveals" and found fascinating the psychological study of Rivarez's "isolated barricade of stoical suffering, from which he peeps with sardonic eyes at God, man and the devil." The reviewer for *The New York Times Book Review* (26 March 1910) considered the novel "unequal and disappointing," particularly in its resolution, and commented that much of it must seem "incomprehensible" to readers unfamiliar with *The Gadfly*.

In 1911 Voynich published a volume of translated verse: *Six Lyrics from the Ruthenian of Taras Shevchenko also The Song of the Merchant Kalashnikov from the Russian of Mikhail Lermontov*. In the following years she began to compose music, playing on the piano what her friends called "musical fragments."

In 1914, shortly before the outbreak of World War I, Voynich's husband had begun to transfer his main base of operations to New York, although he continued to visit his offices in London, Paris, and Florence. In 1916 Voynich, still in England, began what later became *Epitaph in Ballad Form,* a cantata based on a poem by François Villon and dedicated to the memory of Roger David Casement, an Irish revolutionary who was executed for trying to recruit an Irish Brigade from German prisoners of war. Evgenia Taratuta views this cantata as evidence of Voynich's continuing sympathy with the politically oppressed, as is the oratorio *Babylon,* which she began at about the same time. The Bolshevik Revolution, Voynich told Taratuta, inspired her to compose an oratorio based on chapter 18 of the Revelation of Saint John the Divine. In 1920 Voynich joined her husband permanently in New York and dedicated herself to composing orchestral and choral music.

Voynich continued to live in New York after the death of her husband in 1930, sharing an apartment at 450 West Twenty-fourth Street with Anne Nill, who had been her husband's assistant and served as hers for the next thirty years. In 1931 Voynich's translation of Fréderic Chopin's letters, for which she also provided a preface and editorial notes, was published. It was the most complete edition of the composer's letters to appear in English and therefore, as Alexander Nazaroff noted in *The New York Times Book Review* (20 September 1931), was of "obvious documentary and human value"; the volume was "well translated," and while the notes were "precise, authoritative, and clear," there were too few of them for the modern reader. For Voynich the translating of Chopin's letters bore an obvious connection to her second career as a composer, and Chopin's Polish nationality was a link to her husband and to the Polish characters of *Jack Raymond* and *Olive Latham*.

From 1933 to 1943 Voynich taught music at Manhattanville College of the Sacred Heart. After her retirement she told Nill, who had just returned from a three-week research trip to Washington, D.C., that she had been having all-night conversations with Beatrice, the Gadfly's ancestor, who would not let her sleep. Nill insisted that she write Beatrice's story. The result was *Put off Thy Shoes* (1945). A lengthy, multigenerational chronicle set in the eighteenth century, the novel focuses on the Gadfly's British grandparents and great-grandparents; it represents Voynich's endeavor, as she explains in the foreword, to make plausible the apparent contradictions in the Gadfly's nature, which were "truly inherent in the essential soul-stuff of the man as I conceived of him." Beatrice Rivers Telford, who marries a Warwickshire squire to escape the forcible advances of her stepfather, undergoes what Cuthbert Wright for *The New York Times Book Review* (17 May 1945) termed a "moral readjustment . . . brought about by motherhood, suffering, sacrifice, and the gradual, almost imperceptible replacement of hidden hatred by an all-embracing love." A reader of Jonathan Swift, she initially sees all men as "Yahoos" and the universe as empty of love and ideals: "clearly, whoever made the world liked it that way, just a bigger Yahoo." Outwardly a loving wife and mother, she is emotionally repressed. She develops warmth and sympathy through the adoption of a Cornish orphan, the death of her favorite son, and the near loss of two additional children. Through her association with the poor in Cornwall she sees and tries to bridge the gap between classes. As she lays her hand on the heads of a young couple—they are parents of the Gadfly's mother—she realizes the sanctifying power of love. Quoting Exodus 3:5, she thinks: "Put off thy shoes, for the place whereon thou standest is holy ground."

The reviews were enthusiastic. According to the critic for *The New Yorker* (26 May 1945), *Put off Thy Shoes* was potentially another *Gone with the Wind* (1936), combining "a substantial amount of literary skill with an equally substantial amount of insight into human character." Similarly visualizing the

Dust jacket for Voynich's last novel, which chronicles the eighteenth-century forbears of Arthur Burton

novel as a potential hit movie, Grace Frant in *The Saturday Review of Literature* (26 May 1945) suggested Greer Garson for the role of Beatrice Telford and commended the novel's suspense, plot structure, and character studies. *The American Library Association Booklist* (1 June 1945) described *Put off Thy Shoes* as "old fashioned in style, but readable." Edith Roberts in The *Chicago Sun Book Week* (10 June 1945) similarly praised the novel as being "in the grand tradition," a "study in character of intense vigor and skill."

In the late 1940s Voynich completed her oratorio *Babylon,* begun more than a decade earlier; she dedicated it to the memory of her husband. She also completed *Epitaph in Ballad Form*.

The success of *Put off Thy Shoes* revived interest in The Gadfly in England and the United States. Voynich's Russian readers had idolized that work all along, but *Put off Thy Shoes* was not translated into Russian for another ten years. Voynich's circumstances were unknown to her Russian readers, and she was unaware of her novel's influence in that country. In 1955 a group of Soviet journalists visit-

Voynich, circa 1945 (photograph by Gábor Éder)

ing the United States interviewed her at her apartment. They told her that *The Gadfly* had been a Russian cultural treasure for many years. She had not known of any Russian editions of her work after 1913. Taratuta, whose article about Voynich in a popular magazine had led to the discovery that she was alive, corresponded with the writer frequently and at length and wrote many articles and books about her, searching in government archives for letters to and from Voynich. In her remaining years the novelist received daily fan mail, visits from the Bolshoi Ballet and other cultural luminaries, official birthday greetings from the Soviet delegation to the United Nations, and royalty checks.

Voynich's novels, especially *The Gadfly*, had become even more popular in Russia after the Bolshevik Revolution, with editions brought out by publishers with official standing, among them Revolutionary Thought, the Petrograd Council of Workers, the Red Army Deputies, and the State Publishing House. Postrevolutionary reviewers regarded the Italian background as secondary and the antireligious tone and revolutionary ardor as primary. To read *The Gadfly* as an historical novel was regarded as foolish. Voynich was considered a classic Russian writer, included in the *Bolshaia Sovetskaia Entsiklopedia,* the *Literaturnaia Entsiklopedia,* and the biographical reference work *Deiateli Revolutsionnogo dvizheniia v Rossii*–although she was not included in the *Encyclopaedia Britannica* or, except in the 1944 edition, the *Encyclopedia Americana*. After 1917 the novel was brought to the stage in at least seven versions and was adapted as an opera three times and as a movie twice. The second movie, produced in Technicolor, won an award at the Cannes Film Festival.

The plays, operas, and films assured the Gadfly's place in the popular imagination, and the novel became a common literary allusion. The nickname of the heroine of Pavel Bliakhin's *Krasnye Diavoliata* (Little Red Devils, 1927) is the Gadfly. Nikolay Ostrovsky attributed his personal spiritual survival to the inspiration of the novel, and his hero Pavel Korchagin in *Kak zakalialas stal* (How the Steel Was Tempered, 1932, 1934) admires the Gadfly as a model and ideal. For Russian children reading the novel in school–in English in high school or in translation as a standard "outside reading" in seventh grade–*The Gadfly* is, according to Anne Fremantle, "*The Three Musketeers* and *The Last of the Mohicans* rolled into one." Soon after the Soviets' discovery that Voynich was still alive, *Put off Thy Shoes* was translated into Russian, and new editions of her earlier novels became available. Voynich died at her home on 27 July 1960.

Voynich's reputation in Russia has continued to depend largely on *The Gadfly*. Her hero remains an inspiration and a point of cultural reference. Cosmonauts Valentina Tereshkova and Yuri Gagarin cited the Gadfly as a personal model. In a 1958 story by A. Sharov, "Puteshevtsvie prodoilzhaetsia" (The Journey Continues), the heroine is obsessed by the novel. Critical studies–notably those by Taratuta and T. A. Shumakova–have combined biographical and bibliographical facts with enthusiastic admiration. Russian critics do not acknowledge publicly that Reilly was Voynich's lover and the probable model for the Gadfly; they emphasize instead her activities in Russia, her associations with Stepniak and Kropotkin, and her reading of Russian literature. Although *The Gadfly* was most popular between 1917 and 1929 (after the Bolshevik Revolution) and from 1955 to 1965 (after the discovery that Voynich was alive), the novel has never been out of print; a dramatic version has never been off the boards; and Voynich has never been forgotten. The novel's worldwide readership has continued, with new editions appearing in recent years in German, Spanish, and Chinese.

The Gadfly remains in print in English, as well, and continues to find new readers who recognize its considerable achievement. Although the chief goal of the characters appears to be the emancipation of Italy, and the chief target of the novel appears to be the Church, larger issues are at stake. The hero's revolutionary ardor is based not on sentimentality, anger, or a particular political program but on the hunger for freedom, the demand for truth, and the protection of human beings from the violation of their rights. *The Gadfly* presents the birth pangs of a new world—not the world of the 1830s but the turn-of-the-century world when the novel was published. Arnold Kettle, while characterizing Voynich as aesthetically inferior to Joseph Conrad and George Eliot, admires her vigorous presentation of revolutionary ardor. In the late nineteenth century he writes,

> it was no longer possible to be honest enough to be a great writer without being in some sense a revolutionary. To achieve a necessary sense of the vigour and potentiality of life, to bring a full humanity and vitality to literature, it was necessary to go outside the contracting or decaying bourgeois framework. And of the two developing revolutionary movements striking at bourgeois society at its most vulnerable points, the growing socialist movement of the working class and the anti-imperialist socialist movements of such countries as Poland and Italy, the latter movements were the most likely to strike the imagination and hold the loyalty of middle-class writers.

Voynich's work embodies the basic modernist program—criticism of the nineteenth-century social order and perspective—while retaining the narrative energy of the nineteenth-century novel. Although *The Gadfly* is not antirepresentational or aesthetically modernist in the manner of such writers as James Joyce or Gerturde Stein, it displays powerfully a sense of an uncompromising break with the recent past.

As Harvey Breit observed in *The New York Times* (31 March 1957), when the West became aware of the continuing popularity of *The Gadfly* in Russia and China, the power of the novel derives in part from the iridescent vitality of the characters, who, while loyal to their ideals, are more than animated symbols. The Gadfly, "according to Breit, is the very novel the 'thaw' critics have been calling for: it is not ideological, it is not wooden, it is not formula, the protagonists are not made up of dialectical materialist hearts and economic determinist brains. 'The Gadfly' is a novel about human beings in conflict with themselves and each other, as well as with institutions—and yet shows the 'revolutionary' novelist how the 'job' should be done."

Letters:

Izbrannye Proizvedenia v Dvukh Tomakh, volume 1, *Ovod, Olivia Letam: Pis'ma,* edited by Evgenia Taratuta (Moscow: Khudozhestvennaia literatura, 1958).

Bibliography:

T. A. Shumakova, *Etel' Lilian Voinich: Bio-biobliograficheskii ukazatel* (Moscow: Vsesoiuznoi knizhnoi palaty, 1958).

Biography:

Evgenia Taratuta, *Etel' Lilian Voinich: sud'ba pisatelia i sud'ba knigi,* revised edition (Moscow: Khudozhestvennaia literatura, 1964).

References:

Lewis Bernhardt, "*The Gadfly* in Russia," *Princeton University Library Chronicle,* 28 (Autumn 1960): 1–19;

W. L. Courtney, "Mrs. Voynich," in his *The Feminine Note in Fiction* (London: Chapman & Hall, 1904), pp. 159–177;

Anne Fremantle, "Return of the Gadfly," *Commonweal,* 74 (12 May 1961): 167–171;

Fremantle, "The Russian Best-Seller," *History Today,* 25 (September 1975): 629–637;

James G. Kennedy, "Voynich, Bennett, and Tressell: Two Alternatives for Realism in the Transition Age," *English Literature in Transition,* 13, no. 4 (1970): 254–286;

Arnold Kettle, "E. L. Voynich: A Forgotten English Novelist," *Essays in Criticism,* 7 (April 1957): 163–174;

Robin Bruce Lockhart, *Ace of Spies* (New York: Stein & Day, 1967), pp. 22–28;

Evgenia Taratuta, *Istoria Dvukh Knig: "Podpol'naia Rossia" S. M. Stepniaka-kravchinskogo i "Ovod" Etel' Lilian Voinich* (Moscow: Khudozhestvennaia literature, 1987);

Taratuta, *Po Sledam "Ovod"* (Moscow: Khudozhestvennaia literatura, 1972).

Israel Zangwill
(21 January 1864 – 1 August 1926)

Meri-Jane Rochelson
Florida International University

See also the Zangwill entries in *DLB 10: Modern British Dramatists, 1900–1945* and *DLB 135: British Short-Fiction Writers, 1880–1914: The Realist Tradition.*

BOOKS: *Motso Kleis, or the Green Chinee,* as Shloumi Yoshki ben Shlemeal (London: Privately printed, 1882);

The Premier and the Painter: A Fantastic Romance, by Zangwill and Louis Cowen as J. Freeman Bell (London: Blackett, 1888; Chicago & New York: Rand McNally, 1896);

"A Doll's House" Repaired, by Zangwill and Eleanor Marx Aveling (London: Privately printed, 1891);

The Bachelors' Club (London: Henry, 1891; New York: Brentano's, 1891);

The Big Bow Mystery (London: Henry, 1892; Chicago & New York: Rand McNally, 1895);

The Old Maids' Club (London: Heinemann, 1892; New York: Tait, 1892);

Children of the Ghetto: A Study of a Peculiar People, 2 volumes (Philadelphia: Jewish Publication Society of America, 1892); republished as *Children of the Ghetto: Being Pictures of a Peculiar People,* 3 volumes (London: Heinemann, 1892);

The Great Demonstration: A Farce in One Act, by Zangwill and Cowen (London: Capper & Newton, 1892);

Ghetto Tragedies (London: McClure/Simpkin, Marshall, 1893);

Merely Mary Ann (London, Paris & New York: Tuck, 1893);

The King of Schnorrers: Grotesques and Fantasies (London: Heinemann, 1894; New York & London: Macmillan, 1894);

Joseph the Dreamer: A Tale (London: Heinemann, 1895);

The Master (London: Heinemann, 1895; New York: Harper, 1895);

Without Prejudice (London: Unwin, 1896; New York: Century, 1896);

The Celibates' Club, Being the United Stories of The Bachelors' Club and the Old Maids' Club (London: Heinemann, 1898; New York & London: Macmillan, 1898);

Israel Zangwill in 1895

Dreamers of the Ghetto (London: Heinemann, 1898; New York: Harper, 1898);

The People's Saviour (New York & London: Harper, 1898);

"Six Persons": A Play in One Act (London & New York: S. French, 1898);

They That Walk in Darkness: Ghetto Tragedies (London: Heinemann, 1899; New York & London: Macmillan, 1899);

The Mantle of Elijah (New York & London: Harper, 1900; London: Heinemann, 1900);

Blind Children (London: Heinemann, 1903; New York: Funk & Wagnalls, 1903);

The Grey Wig: Stories and Novelettes (London: Heinemann, 1903; New York & London: Macmillan, 1903);

Merely Mary Ann: A Comedy in Four Acts (New York & London: Macmillan, 1903; London: Heinemann, 1904; revised edition, London & New York: S. French, 1921);

The Serio-Comic Governess (New York & London: Macmillan, 1904);

Ghetto Comedies (London: Heinemann, 1907; New York: Macmillan, 1907);

One and One Are Two . . . Being a Verbatim Report of the Speech Delivered at Exeter Hall, on Feb. 9th, at the Demonstration of Women's Suffrage Societies (London: Women's Social & Political Union, 1907);

Talked Out! . . . Being a Verbatim Report of the Speech at Exeter Hall, March 8th, 1907 (London: Women's Social & Political Union, 1907);

The Melting Pot: Drama in Four Acts (New York: Macmillan, 1909; London: Heinemann, 1909; revised edition, New York: Macmillan, 1914; London: Heinemann, 1914);

Votes for Women. The Lords and the Ladies . . . Speech Delivered at the Albert Hall, Dec. 11th, 1909 (London: Women's Freedom League, 1909);

Italian Fantasies (London: Heinemann, 1910; New York: Macmillan, 1910);

The Sword and the Spirit (London: Women's Press, 1910);

The War God: A Tragedy in Five Acts (London: Heinemann, 1911; New York: Macmillan, 1912);

The Next Religion: A Play in Three Acts (London: Heinemann, 1912; New York: Macmillan, 1912);

Plaster Saints: A High Comedy in Three Movements (London: Heinemann, 1914; New York: Macmillan, 1915);

The War for the World (London: Heinemann, 1916; New York: Macmillan, 1916; revised edition, 1917);

Chosen Peoples: The Hebraic Ideal Versus the Teutonic (London: Allen & Unwin, 1918; New York: Macmillan, 1919);

Hands Off Russia: Speech by Mr. Israel Zangwill at the Albert Hall, February 8th, 1919 (London: Workers Socialist Federation, 1919);

Jinny the Carrier (London: Heinemann, 1919); republished as *Jinny the Carrier: A Folk-Comedy of Rural England* (New York: Macmillan, 1919);

The Voice of Jerusalem (London: Heinemann, 1920; New York: Macmillan, 1921);

The Cockpit: Romantic Drama in Three Acts (London: Heinemann, 1921; New York: Macmillan, 1921);

The Forcing House, or The Cockpit Continued: Tragicomedy in Four Acts (London: Heinemann, 1922; New York: Macmillan, 1923);

Watchman, What of the Night? (New York: American Jewish Congress, 1923);

Too Much Money, A Farcical Comedy in Three Acts (London: Heinemann, 1924; New York: Macmillan, 1925);

We Moderns: A Post-War Comedy in Three Movements (allegro, andante, adagio) (London: Heinemann, 1925; New York: Macmillan, 1926).

Collections and Editions: *Works of Israel Zangwill* (New York: American Jewish Book Company, 1921);

The Works of Israel Zangwill: Edition de Luxe, 14 volumes (London: Globe, 1925);

Israel Zangwill Said, edited by Rabbi S. L. Zlotnick (Vancouver: Congregation Shara Tsedeck, 1935);

Speeches, Articles and Letters of Israel Zangwill, edited by Maurice Simon, foreword by Edith Ayrton Zangwill (London: Soncino Press, 1937);

Children of the Ghetto, introduction by V. D. Lippman (Leicester: Leicester University Press, 1977);

Children of the Ghetto, introduction by Meri-Jane Rochelson (Detroit: Wayne State University Press, 1998).

PLAY PRODUCTIONS: *The Great Demonstration,* by Zangwill and Louis Cowen, London, Royalty Theatre, 17 September 1892;

Aladdin at Sea, Camborne, 25 January 1893;

The Lady Journalist, London, Steinway Hall, 4 July 1893;

Six Persons, London, Theatre Royal, 22 December 1893;

Threepenny Bits, Chatham, Opera House, 25 April 1895;

Children of the Ghetto, New York, Herald Square Theatre, 11 December 1899;

The Moment of Death, New York, Wallack's Theatre, 23 October 1900;

The Revolted Daughter, London, Comedy Theatre, 22 March 1901;

Merely Mary Ann, New York, Garden Theatre, 28 December 1903;

The Serio-Comic Governess, New York, New Lyceum Theatre, 13 September 1904;

Nurse Marjorie, London, Criterion Theatre, 14 September 1906;

The Melting Pot, New York, Comedy Theatre, 6 September 1909;

The War God, London, His Majesty's Theatre, 8 November 1911;

The Next Religion, London, London Pavilion, 18 April 1912;
Plaster Saints, London, Comedy Theatre, 23 May 1914;
The Moment Before, Plymouth, Palace Theatre, 18 September 1916;
Too Much Money, Glasgow, Theatre Royal, 18 February 1918;
We Moderns, New York, Gaiety Theatre, 11 March 1923;
The King of Schnorrers, London, Scala, 1 November 1925;
The Forcing House; or, The Cockpit Continued, London, Little Theatre, 9 February 1926.

OTHER: Edward A. Morton, *Man or Beast: Studies in Unnatural History,* introduction by Zangwill (Bristol: Arrowsmith, 1893);
"My First Book," in *My First Book,* edited by Jerome K. Jerome (London: Chatto & Windus, 1897);
Mary Antin, *From Plotzk to Boston,* foreword by Zangwill (Boston: Clarke, 1899);
Anita Bartle, *"This Is My Birthday,"* introduction by Zangwill (London: Grant Richards, 1902);
Report on the Work of the Commission Sent out by the Jewish Territorial Organization to Examine the Territory Proposed for the Purpose of a Jewish Settlement in Cyrenaica, preface by Zangwill (London: ITO, 1909);
Report on the Work of the Commission Sent out by the Jewish Territorial Organization under the Auspices of the Portuguese Government to Examine the Territory Proposed for the Purpose of a Jewish Settlement in Angola, introduction by Zangwill (London: ITO, 1913);
The Jewish Pogroms in Ukraine, Authoritative Statements on the Question of Responsibility for Recent Outbreaks Against the Jews in Ukraine, by Zangwill, Julian Batchinsky, Arnold Margolin, and Mark Vishnitzer (Washington, D.C.: Friends of Ukraine, 1919);
Hannah Trager, *Pioneers in Palestine,* foreword by Zangwill (London: Routledge, 1923);
Selected Religious Poems of Solomon Ibn Gabirol, edited by Israel Davidson, translated by Zangwill (Philadelphia: The Jewish Publication Society of America, 1923);
Isidor Singer, *A Religion of Truth, Justice, and Peace,* epilogue by Zangwill (New York: Amos Society, 1924);
Amelia D. Defries, *The Interpreter Geddes,* introduction by Zangwill (London: Routledge, 1927);
The Service of the Synagogue, translated by Zangwill, Nina Salaman, and Elsie Davis, 3 volumes (New York: Hebrew Publishing, 1917);
Samuel Roth, *Now and Forever: A Conversation with Mr. Israel Zangwill on the Jew and the Future,* preface by Zangwill (New York: McBride, 1925).

SELECTED PERIODICAL PUBLICATIONS–
UNCOLLECTED:
FICTION
"Professor Grimmer," *Society,* 5 (16 November 1881): 10–12; (23 November 1881): 8, 10–11; (30 November 1881): 8, 10–11;
"Under Sentence of Marriage," as J. Freeman Bell, *Myer's Calendar and Diary* (1888–1889): 54–79.
NONFICTION
"English Judaism: A Criticism and a Classification," *Jewish Quarterly Review,* 1 (1889): 376–407;
"Growth of Respectability," *Jewish Chronicle,* Special Jubilee Number, 13 November 1891, pp. 19–20;
"That Telephone," as Z., *To-Day,* 1 (23 December 1893): 13;
"The Tree of Knowledge," *New Review,* 10 (1894): 675–690;
"The Drama as a Fine Art," *Werner's Magazine,* (November 1898): 159–166;
"Fiction as the Highest Form of Truth," *Bookman* (New York), 9 (April 1899): 100–101;
"Zionism and Territorialism," *Fortnightly Review,* 87 (1910): 645–655; *Living Age,* 265 (1910): 663–671.

Israel Zangwill's novels exemplify the multiplicity of his concerns and the diversity of his career as a journalist, playwright, and writer of fiction as well as an activist on behalf of pacifism, feminism, and Jewish nationalism. Zangwill was born on 21 January 1864 in London to Jewish immigrants Moses and Ellen Marks Zangwill, from Latvia and Poland, respectively. Like many Jewish immigrants in Britain at that time, Moses Zangwill earned his living as an old-clothes peddler, traveling through the countryside. The family later moved to Bristol, where Zangwill received his early education. After the Zangwills settled in London, Israel became a pupil teacher at the Jews' Free School and attended London University, where he studied at night and in 1884 received a degree with honors in French, English, and mental and moral science.

By June 1888 Zangwill had resigned his teaching position, either because of his opposition to the free school's policy of corporal punishment or, as his biographer Joseph Udelson argues, as a result of conflict with school authorities over Zangwill and Louis Cowen's publication in that year of *The Premier and the Painter: A Fantastic Romance,* under the pseudonym J. Freeman Bell–a name that hints at their connection to the Jews' Free School in Bell Lane. Zangwill later stated that he had written most of the novel himself. In the novel Arnold Floppington, a dreamy, intellectual, and ineffectual Conservative prime minister, changes places with Jack Dawe, a Radical sign painter and man of action who is an exact double for the government leader. Plot turns involve romantic mix-ups as well as the surprise that results when the "prime minister" shows decisiveness and a determination toward reform. Zangwill uses the novel to satirize political activists of all stripes as well as journalists who are so confident that they have the story right when in fact their knowledge is fragmentary at best. Indeed, amid the novel's playfulness can be found a distinctly self-conscious narration as well as a critique of the representational epistemology that underlies realist fiction. In the concluding narrative of a reporter and the subsequent discoveries of an Oxford professor, Zangwill presents alternative accounts of what has transpired, indicating that "from that time to this no one has ever doubted the traditional version of the great events," and by this point it is not entirely clear what the "traditional version" is. Some of Zangwill's narrative choices, however, cause confusion even as they inspire reflection. For example, all the switches of identity are made offstage, and details of diction or characterization are the only cues that identities have been transposed. The demands on the novel's first readers were apparently so great that Zangwill indicated the place of each change in the narrative in his preface to the third edition.

The Premier and the Painter includes vivid representations of life in the working-class East End and a fascinating episode in which Dawe is held captive by a group of men who appear to be Irish nationalists but in fact are opposed to Home Rule. Ultimately the politics become serious, and the premier—in fact, Jack Dawe—is assassinated. The ensuing re-creations of a coroner's inquest proceedings and correspondence in the press contribute to the narrative self-consciousness and critique of realism. The assassination itself is disconcerting in a novel otherwise insistently comic. Yet, as Elsie Bonita Adams points out in her 1970 study of Zangwill, the novel "presents a pessimistic view of human nature: the well-intentioned, kindhearted Floppington is unsuited for a world which is too corrupt for him to cope with; and the aggressive, ruthless, worldly-wise Dawe, eminently suited to rule, can never, except by a subterfuge, achieve ruling power." Whereas in Mark Twain's *The Prince and the Pauper* (1881) the prince becomes a better ruler as a result of his experience, "Floppy is still ineffectual when he returns to power." As Zangwill's narrator puts it:

> For some time he was great on philanthropy and the Slums Question. But he had no practical suggestions to offer beyond the conversion of the masses to their nominal religion. And gradually his enthusiasm waned, his magic eloquence flashed out at intervals fewer and farther between, and he settled down again into the study of musty Coleridgean metaphysics.

The earliest critics all deplored the length of the novel; even the laudatory Harry S. Lewis in *The Jewish Standard* (22 March 1889) said that, with its more than five hundred tightly packed pages, it was "undeniably far too long for the ordinary novel reader." The review in the 21 April 1888 issue of *The Athenaeum* was mixed: "In some ways it is original enough to be a law unto itself, and withal as attractive in its whimsical, wrong-headed way as at times it is tantalizing, bewildering, even tedious." William Morton Payne, in a 1 July 1896 review in *The Dial,* found it guilty of inordinate length, "prolixity, confusion, bad taste, and feebleness of wit" but praised its "brilliant passages and episodes, a plot of extraordinary ingenuity, and bits of characterization that would not have been unworthy of Dickens." Even George Saintsbury, who in a withering review in *The Academy* (14 April 1888) referred to the possible "toxic effects of such a book," admitted that "The author is really, in his way, clever; and he evidently has a fluent pen and a ready fancy—such as it is." Most reviewers hoped for more disciplined if equally inventive work in the future from this new writer. Despite disappointing sales at first, *The Premier and the Painter* went into several editions, British and American, by the end of the 1890s as Zangwill achieved greater recognition. By the third edition his own name was on the title page.

Around 1889 Zangwill became the editor of a comic magazine, *Puck,* later renamed *Ariel, or the London Puck,* which he continued to edit and write for during the next two years. There he worked with the illustrator George Hutchinson, who was to provide illustrations for much of Zangwill's subsequent short fiction and whom Lilian Falk has identified as an inspiration for his novel *The Master* (1895). In 1891 and 1892, respectively, Zangwill published two popularly successful collections of comic fiction, *The Bachelors' Club* and *The Old Maids' Club*. The books detail the ways in which the clubs' members each succumb to matrimony; they incorporate contemporary satire with romantic comedy and verbal gymnastics in a way that aligns them clearly with the New Humour school of Jerome K. Jerome and Barry Pain.

The Big Bow Mystery, a detective novella, was initially serialized in the London daily newspaper *The Star* from 22 August to 4 September 1891 and was published in book form in 1892. The plot concerns the murder of Arthur Constant, a young man of patrician origins who has devoted himself to the workers'

Caricature of Zangwill from Punch, *referring to his work with the Jewish Territorial Organization*

cause. His throat is slit as he sleeps in his bedroom in an East End rooming house. There is no sign of forced entry into the locked room, nor of any possible means of exit for a murderer. A retired detective in the neighborhood quickly takes up the case–in competition with his longtime rival, officially in charge–and suspicion soon lights on Tom Mortlake, Constant's friend and fellow activist who occupies an adjoining room. *The Big Bow Mystery* is considered one of the earliest and best examples of the sealed-room mystery in English. When it was republished in Zangwill's collection *The Grey Wig* (1903), a reviewer in *The Athenaeum* (28 March 1903) wrote that while the author seemed to be attempting to show "how such things should be written.... Paradoxes, puns, and grotesque absurdity are intermingled with the usual sordid details so inextricably that the whole thing misses the point of satire and becomes merely a badly-told example of what the author most despises." The reviewer may be referring to a red herring in the form of an aestheticist poet or to Zangwill's re-creation of a coroner's inquest report and letters to the editor that would have looked perfectly at home in other columns of *The Star* and that today contribute to the work's interest as an artifact of 1890s culture. The conclusion of *The Big Bow Mystery,* in which the murderer's surprising identity is revealed, is one of Zangwill's most effective endings. Adams calls it a "better-than-average example of its genre" because of its many ironies while Frederick L. De Naples finds Zangwill's Grodman to be one of several sinister reinterpretations of the Holmesian "great detective."

In 1892 Zangwill became a regular contributor to *The Idler* and published stories in a variety of periodicals. The major event of that year for Zangwill, however, was the publication of *Children of the Ghetto: A Study of a Peculiar People,* the novel that solidified his reputation both as an outstanding writer of fiction and as the spokesperson for English Jewry. It remains the work on which Zangwill's reputation most solidly rests. William Heinemann published the British edition of *Children of the Ghetto* and from that time on was Zangwill's primary British publisher. The appearance of the Heinemann edition in September annoyed Judge Mayer Sulzberger, director of the Jewish Publication Society of America (JPSA), which had commissioned the novel from Zangwill and had intended to publish it in December. But the book was a great success on both sides of the Atlantic. The JPSA's commission had come about as the result of an article, "English Judaism, a Criticism and a Classification," that Zangwill had written in 1889 for the new *Jewish Quarterly Review*. The article established Zangwill as an astute observer of contemporary Anglo-Jewry, fitting him well for the authorship of what Sulzberger envisioned as a "Jewish *Robert Elsmere*"—a work that would repeat the extraordinary success of Mrs. Humphry Ward's 1888 novel of spiritual searching and doubt among young Christians.

For turn-of-the-century "anglicized" English Jews the struggle concerned how to reconcile Judaism with life in the modern world. In *Children of the Ghetto* Zangwill's characters deal in various ways with assimilation, intermarriage, and rebellion against Jewish law and tradition; in the latter half of the novel a small group of articulate protagonists—Esther Ansell, Joseph Strelitski, and Raphael Leon—debate and begin to carry out alternative modes of being modern Jews. The major plot threads concern two East End families, the impoverished Ansells, whose widowed father is a peddler, and the somewhat more well-to-do Jacobses, whose household is headed by the revered scholar Reb Shemuel. Zangwill examines Esther Ansell's growth from an intelligent and intellectually curious girl who surreptitiously reads the New Testament and questions the requirements of Jewish life without daring to violate them. In the second half of the novel, which takes place ten years after the first, the reader finds that she has been rescued from poverty by wealthy West End Jewish patrons and has become the controversial though pseudonymous author of a novel highly critical of West End Jewish life.

Recent critics, most notably Bernard Winehouse and Maurice Wohlgelernter, have seen in the young Esther a projection of Zangwill; the older, more melancholy Esther bears a significant resemblance to Amy Levy, the author of the 1888 novel *Reuben Sachs*, a book similar to Esther's *Mordecai Josephs*. Esther forms a romantic attachment to Raphael Leon, the Oxford-educated editor of *The Flag of Judah;* the paper is clearly based on *The Jewish Standard,* and one can assume that Zangwill's depictions of its often absurdly chaotic office are founded on experience. Raphael takes on the mentorship of Esther. Observing her struggles between abandoning Judaism and desiring to return to older ways (indeed, at one point she goes back to the ghetto to live), Raphael calls Esther's life "an allegory of Judaism, the offspring of a great and tragic past with the germs of a rich blossoming, yet wasting with an inward canker." At the end of the novel the two plan to marry, implying that Esther will share his vision of a renewed and revitalized orthodox Judaism. Yet in the final scene, although she plans to return to England and Raphael, Esther is on a boat to America accompanied by Strelitski, the now disillusioned rabbi who seeks a universal religion based on Judaic values. In future years Zangwill would increasingly endorse the universalist option, and his 1909 play *The Melting Pot* reflects his confidence that America would be its best hope.

Hannah Jacobs's story is more typically novelistic, even melodramatic, in its representation of generational conflict over adherence to Jewish law. Hannah wishes to marry a young Jewish man who has left religious observance. The barrier to their marriage, however, is not his religious laxity but the fact that, regardless of practice, he is a descendant of Judaism's priesthood and thereby barred from marrying a divorced woman. Hannah, who had jokingly participated in a mock marriage ceremony that turned out technically to be binding, was released by means of a religious divorce. The two plan to elope, but at the last moment Hannah finds that she cannot abandon the traditions of her heritage. When Zangwill turned *Children of the Ghetto* into a play in 1899, Hannah's story formed the central plot, and it ended at this dramatic point. But in the novel's second half Zangwill explores the day-to-day ramifications of Hannah's decision and allows Reb Shemuel to express his regret at having contributed to her unhappiness.

For the most part the novel was praised on both sides of the Atlantic and, as Winehouse explains, became "the first Anglo-Jewish best-seller." The novel's first readers were less interested in its philosophical debates than its detailed depiction of the Anglo-Jewish community. Especially fascinating was the view it gave into the world of immigrant Jews in London's East End, a world that had grown considerably since 1880 and that was virtually unknown even to many in the already established British Jewish community. Most reviewers, whether familiar with the Anglo-Jewish community or not, centered their praise of the novel on its realism, and on this ground critics in *The Speaker* (22 October 1892) and the 22 November 1892 issue of *The Times* (London) called *Children of the Ghetto* "a remarkable book." *The Manchester Guardian* (18 October 1892) pronounced it "the best Jewish novel ever written" and praised both the novel's depiction of Jewish life and its intellectual content, saying that "the critic of thought will learn from Raphael Leon an ideal Judaism which [George Eliot's] Daniel Deronda did not understand." The reviewer for *The Spectator* (26 November 1892) reflected the tone of much of the negative criticism by terming the novel "much better in parts than as a whole" and calling for a glossary of Yiddish terms—a request that annoyed Zangwill, but one with which he ultimately complied.

Opinion was divided on the second half of the novel, "Grandchildren of the Ghetto." Many reviewers in the secular press agreed with the critic for *The*

STATION: ANGMERING.
TELEGRAMS: ZANGWILL, EAST-PRESTON.

FAR END.
EAST PRESTON.
SUSSEX.

12th June, 1923.

Lewis Levy, Esq.,
　　Underwood Street School,
　　　　London, E. 1.

Dear Sir,

　　Honoured as I am by your calling one of your Houses by my name, I am afraid I do not quite understand what County Council B. Schools are: and this, combined with my ignorance of the ages of the boys, makes it very difficult for me to address them.

　　I can only say that your boys appear much more fortunate in their chances of education than was the lot of the East End boys of my generation. Some of us, nevertheless, managed to acquire both education and reputation. The more shame to your pupils if they do not profit by their superior opportunities.

　　One secret in study is never to pass over anything without really understanding it. It is no good learning a thing by heart - say a geometrical proposition - if the words convey no vivid meaning to one. I know boys think some subjects are dry; but in truth there is nothing that is not palpitating with interest if only one gets hold of it properly. Let your boys remember that though things may seem dried up in books, they are all parts of the real living world around us, and we must try to translate books back into life just as a dried leaf pressed in a book must be imagined as once part of a growing tree or plant.

　　With best wishes to your House,

　　　　　　　　　　　　Faithfully yours,

　　　　　　　　　　　　Israel Zangwill

Letter from Zangwill to an East End educator (Courtesy of Thomas Cooper Library, University of South Carolina)

Graphic (19 November 1892) that in the second part "the realist becomes transformed into the controversialist and satirist, and the change is by no means for the better." As might have been expected, the satire of materialistic Jews offended some readers, and as the reviewer in the 12 December 1892 issue of *The New York Times* pointed out, Zangwill was "preparing for his [own] 'slating'" in the characters' discussions of Esther's novel, *Mordecai Josephs*. Considerable debate filled the pages of *The American Hebrew*, where Cyrus Sulzberger expressed outrage at Zangwill's airing of communal dirty linen, and Edward N. Calisch noted in his *The Jew in English Literature, as Author and Subject* (1909) that Zangwill's book "caused a commotion among some of the more super-sensitive members of the community." There is little evidence, however, of similar controversy in England, where Abrahams, in his *Jewish Chronicle* review, took exception to ways in which ghetto and West End Jews were depicted but admitted that "Perhaps . . . Mr. Zangwill's insight and observation are truer than ours even in the parts of his book that we do not quite like." Even the American journal *Menorah* (January 1893) went so far as to say that "Material ambition . . . supplies the comedy part of the book."

More-recent critics of *Children of the Ghetto* focus less on its picturesque representations and more on its reflection of ambivalence and unease in modern Jewish culture. Linda Gertner Zatlin remarks that Zangwill portrays Judaism "without the ghetto walls but within the light of contemporary skepticism," and Joseph H. Udelson notes that "If there is any genuine consistency at all in any of the characters . . ., it is certainly Esther Ansell's persistent ambivalence." Wohlgelernter's emphasis on Esther's resemblance to Zangwill suggests that the novel is a product of the author's "violent contraries" although ultimately Wohlgelernter minimizes Zangwill's conflicted attitudes toward the Jewish future. Meri-Jane Rochelson examines ambivalence in Zangwill's treatment of Yiddish in the novel and the significance of his focus on female protagonists, doubly marginalized by gender as well as ethnicity. Bryan Cheyette discusses *Children of the Ghetto* in the context of a larger consideration of writers who sought the universal but wrote the particular, "in a society which both promoted and denied racial difference." He argues that despite the praise of early Jewish reviewers, Zangwill is part of "the apologist tradition of Anglo-Jewish fiction" because he focused on the seriousness of Esther's decision-making and suggested that the spiritual values he located in the ghetto were ultimately limited in force.

In 1893 Zangwill began writing a column, "Without Prejudice," for *Pall Mall Magazine* and soon thereafter began a column called "Men, Women, and Books" for *The Critic* (New York). During this period he published two short novels, one of which was to bring him immediate financial gain, the other, enduring renown. The first, *Merely Mary Ann* (1893)—which, with a revised happy ending became Zangwill's most successful play (1903)—recounts the story of Lancelot, a young composer who struggles against both his attraction to the serving maid of the rooming house where he lives and the temptation to prostitute his talents by writing popular rather than serious music. He succumbs to both temptations, but when Mary Ann becomes an heiress at the end of the story, honor prevents him from marrying her. The ending, with Mary Ann leaving Lancelot, returning his gifts, and giving him her canary as a memento, incorporates typical Zangwillian irony as it punishes the snobbish and short-sighted suitor. Unlike Zangwill's later stories, especially those with Jewish themes, the irony is not bitter as Lancelot accepts his fate and proceeds to care for the canary. The irony that the author directs at himself, however, as Lancelot debates "popular" versus "artistic" composition, adds bite to this short novel for readers familiar with Zangwill's diverse career.

Merely Mary Ann was a popular success, although reviews were mixed. Some critics, such as the reviewer in the 29 April 1893 issue of *The Saturday Review*, objected to what now seem fairly conventional adaptations of modernist technique: the opening of the story in the midst of the action and the relative open-endedness of the conclusion. This critic also scorned the subject matter as "a tale of a commonplace little drudge in a cheap London lodging-house." In a review titled "A Shilling Soother" a critic for the *Daily Chronicle* (29 March 1893) was "old-fashioned enough" to share the dislike of the novel's conclusion but found the story as a whole "decidedly good." *The Daily Chronicle*, *The Saturday Review*, and *The Speaker* (1 April 1893) all commented on the cover of the volume, which *The Saturday Review* compared to "the lid of a French plum-box."

In August 1893 *The King of Schnorrers* began to appear serially in *The Idler*, running in six parts until January 1894. It became the best known and most enduring of Zangwill's works and was republished many times throughout the twentieth century. The 1979 musical *Petticoat Lane*, by Susan Birkenhead and Judd Woldin, is loosely based on Zangwill's novella, and a dramatic version in French was performed at the 1995 summer arts festival in Avignon. Set in eighteenth-century London, *The King of Schnorrers* recounts the adventures of Manasseh Bueno Barzillai Azevedo da Costa, a Sephardic Jew who uses his wit and Talmudic learning to make himself king of the Jewish beggars. Zangwill tweaks long-standing intercommunal rivalries between the Ashkenazic (German and East European) and Sephardic (Spanish and Portuguese) Jews—the Sephardic traditionally claiming a more culturally elite ancestry—as he draws on Jewish folklore and traditional humor to show how class distinctions are meaningless when the clever individual can place himself above the wealthy.

The King of Schnorrers was published in book form along with several short stories in 1894 in London and New York. The book received generally favorable reviews, with Manasseh defined by *The Athenaeum* (10 March 1894) as "a stupendous hero." *The Outlook* (3 March 1894) concurred, saying that there is "no more delightful personage in fiction." The critic for *The Saturday Review* (31 March 1894) proclaimed, "If there be other Schnorrers, subjects to this king, and in any degree sharers in his renown, life in the modern Ghetto is invested with a zest which we had never suspected. Mr. Zangwill has created . . . a new figure in fiction, and a new type of humour."

The King of Schnorrers was republished in 1954 to mixed responses from a new generation of critics. Wolf Mankowitz in *The Spectator* (July–December 1954) found the characters to "have a two-dimensional quality," and Milton Hindus wrote in "Does Zangwill Still Live?" in *Commentary* (March 1954) that "it seems a good deal more humorous in intention than in fact." In response to such aspersions, Charles Angoff declared in the 31 March 1954 issue of the American Jewish Congress publication *Congress Weekly* that he "persist[ed] in thinking that *The King of Schnorrers* is a fine work of both humor and satire." After another republication in 1965 Harold Fisch, reviewing the work in the magazine *Judaism* (Winter 1966), noted the absence of sentimentality in the novel and added poignantly, "Zangwill's humorous tales still have their appeal even in an age when Jewish sadness has taken away so much of Jewish laughter." His enthusiasm is seconded by Adams, Wohlgelernter, and Udelson, the last of whom refers to *The King of Schnorrers* as "Zangwill at his wittiest."

Between May and November 1894 Zangwill's novel of bohemian life, *The Master,* was being serialized in *Harper's* in the United States and in Jerome's *To-Day* in England. Published in book form in 1895, *The Master* established Zangwill as a writer of serious fiction beyond the Jewish context. Matthew Strang travels to London from rural Nova Scotia to study art and finds fame and temptation as a painter. He marries a rich woman with whom he is incompatible, and then, during a long estrangement from her in Nova Scotia, nearly enters into an affair with an attractive and sophisticated British soul mate, Mrs. Eleanor Wyndwood. An unexpected meeting in Paris with his first love, a Nova Scotian woman named Ruth Hailey, convinces him to return to his home, his family, and the sturdy values of his early religious faith. After this return Matt is able to begin "his true life-work" as a realist artist.

Many of even the most favorable reviews of *The Master* criticized its prolixity. "Art is long," wrote a reviewer in the 6 July 1895 issue of *The Critic*—a journal that at the same time was publishing Zangwill's literary reviews—" . . . and time is fleeting, but that is the very reason why one of the best devices for making art long is to shorten it." H. G. Wells, in an unsigned critique for *The Saturday Review* (18 May 1895), said that "Mr. Zangwill has made a big book of what might have been a great one"; he urged the author to stop writing for a year while he studied such stylists as Charles Dickens and Rudyard Kipling. The reviewer for *The Spectator* (13 July 1895) liked the work for the most part and recognized it as belonging to the currently fashionable genre of the novel of artistic temperament yet still found the depictions of artistic "studio-chatter" and Nova Scotia life "excessive." *The Bookman* (London) of July 1895 found fault with Zangwill's realism, claiming that the descriptions of Nova Scotia were taken from other books and that the dialect was an unconvincing pastiche. Nova Scotian linguist Lilian Falk, however, has recently disputed these long-held assumptions, pointing out that Zangwill's depictions of landscape and representation of speech are scrupulously accurate. In addition to finding sources in the works of several North American authors, Falk cites the likely influence of Hutchinson, Zangwill's illustrator in *Ariel* and *The King of Schnorrers,* whose life parallels Matt Strang's in several respects. Hutchinson grew up in rural Nova Scotia and visited there as late as 1889, shortly before beginning his association with the author.

The Master had strong supporters, however, both at the time of its publication and in the early decades of the twentieth century. Douglas Sladen's review in the 11 May 1895 issue of *Queen* places the narrative's length and density in a justifiably positive light: "'The Master' is a novel of the discursive kind, to which the masterpieces of fiction, for the most part, belong. It is like life itself—a complex mass of experiences." The *Daily News* (26 April 1895) called *The Master* a "prose epic . . . a powerful and fascinating book, and one in which the author has struck a deeper note than he has yet drawn from his studies of life." In 1918 Williams expressed the view held by many critics that Zangwill "reache[d] the top of his performance" with *The Master*. That assessment has not been maintained, but the novel is due for a reevaluation. Its story holds the reader's interest, and the love plot in particular is developed in a mature and serious way. Matt's ultimate return to a life of simplicity and art is not presented simplistically. That his masterpiece, "A Woman," combines "the light in Ruth Hailey's eyes, and that fire of love in Eleanor Wyndwood's" suggests something both more interesting and more mundane than peace in resignation. While Matt's mother repeats the querulous stereotype found too often in Zangwill's fiction, Ruth Hailey, the guardian angel, is a serious feminist, and Zangwill clearly endorses her position that "We do want the Franchise and the right to dress as we please, but these are only incidental aspects of the movement for the independence of women, though they lend themselves most readily to caricature. The woman of the future is today the working woman." Interestingly, none of the novel's original reviewers commented on this passage in the work. For today's reader, too, the lengthy debate on artistic value that makes up the chapter "The Symposium" is not necessarily tedious but rather a detailed look at a turn-of-the-century controversy. Zangwill, as might be expected, uses such debates to support his belief in realism as the highest form of truth. Matt early on wonders why he is drawn to the East End images of a London realist; in the end he is delineating the lives of the poor in his native town. As compellingly as Zangwill depicts the fin-de-siècle artistic life of London and Paris in this novel, his message is that art must have a message, or at least an ethical rather than a purely aesthetic foundation.

Sladen saw in Zangwill's moralism an affinity to the "seers of his race." Udelson has shown Zangwill's position as a Jew to have an even greater relevance in that Matt is "an individual ensnared in a tangle of contending identities." The down-to-earth "Peculiar" religion of his home—a sect Zangwill would treat further in *Jinny the Carrier* (1919)—may be seen as a displacement for the ghetto Judaism transcended but longed for by Esther Ansell and to some extent by Zangwill himself. Certainly the shaping power of youthful religion and the rebellion against it are once again explored in this work.

In 1895 Zangwill met the Zionist leader Theodor Herzl. Zangwill sponsored and introduced Herzl's first address on Zionism to an English-speaking audience at the Maccabeans Club on 24 November. Until late in his life Zangwill was the chief spokesman on Zionism for Anglo-Jewry and the chief representative of English Jews at international Zionist conferences, attending the first World Zionist Congress in Basel, Switzerland, in February 1897. Throughout most of 1897 he was also working on the fictionalized biographies of Jewish idealists, including controversial figures in Judaism, that would form *Dreamers of the Ghetto* (1898).

Zangwill's next novel, *The Mantle of Elijah,* was published in book form in 1900, after its serialization in *Harper's*. For the most part it escaped the accusations of longwindness aimed at *The Master;* in fact, its heavy reliance on dialogue and dramatic scenes suggests that Zangwill may have begun to tire of the novel form and was preparing for the career as a playwright and dramatic producer that would occupy him for the next twenty years. At the same time Zangwill's writing and his activities in general were becoming more political, and *The Mantle of Elijah* reflects that shift. Allegra Marshmont is the daughter of an idealistic cabinet minister who has rejected his aristocratic background to serve the cause of social justice. He is loudly acclaimed in the Radical district of Midstoke, where a young man named Broser gives an energetic speech in his support. When war is threatened to put down an insurrection in the fictional but presumably Asian or African country of Novabarba, Thomas Marshmont resigns his ministry rather than condone violence. Not long after, Allegra, who shares her father's high ideals, marries Broser and looks forward to a career as the wife of a Radical politician.

Once involved in party politics, however, Broser switches allegiances and follows the popular war crowd. Disillusioned, Allegra becomes attracted to the otherworldly Raphael Dominick, a man who is both Christian and Jew (Zangwill's desire for synthesis is much in evidence here) and who is reminiscent of one of the Norwegian playwright Henrik Ibsen's more depressed characters: at one point he refers to himself as a dead man. Raphael introduces Allegra to the saintly Margaret Engelborne, who is engaged in a race to see whether she or the invalid for whom she cares will die first. Allegra admires but will not emulate Margaret's self-abnegation, and she rejects Raphael's offer of love because she is married. At the end of the novel, however, it is clear that Allegra will leave Broser and go on to live an independent life. After following three male mentors in a search for meaningful action, she ultimately finds her greatest support in her father's sister, the duchess of Dalesbury.

Much is made in the novel of who will take on the "mantle of Elijah," Thomas Marshmont's legacy of pacifism and defense of the poor. At the end of the work Allegra considers accepting the mantle herself, but her plans remain vague. Both Wohlgelernter and Udelson have remarked on *The Mantle of Elijah* as a reflection of Zangwill's feminist convictions. But while it is true, as Wohlgelernter says, that Allegra's sister Joan is a dedicated worker for equality and the vote and that her encouragement is important in Allegra's decision to leave Broser, Allegra herself seems alternately dense and naive; she remains too long and too often in the position of disciple. The novel would, in general, have benefited from a more expansive development of characters and motives and more worthy

Frontispiece for The Mantle of Elijah, *from the 1925 edition of Zangwill's collected works*

objects of emulation than Raphael and the vaguely mystical Engelborne circle.

Still, *The Mantle of Elijah* remained a best-seller for months after its appearance, and its reviews, while mixed, were more consistently favorable than those of *The Master*. It is likely that the timeliness of its political theme—a critique of militarism directed against Britain's contemporary conduct of the war in South Africa—assisted the novel's popularity. Many critics, even some who lamented Zangwill's excessive self-consciousness of style, revealed their sympathy with his antimilitarist perspective. According to A. Macdonell in the December 1900 issue of *The Bookman* (London), for example, despite "an enormous amount of quite irrelevant matter about it . . . it is a very wise and wholesome and timely book. . . . A protest against the brutal ideals of the age!" The reviewer for *The Nation* (28 February 1901) remarked that "Mr. Zangwill's first intention was to speak his mind about the Victo-

rian English, and especially about Mr. Broser. This he has done very liberally, with the spirit of a pessimist, the judgment of an alien, and in a smashing, whacking style." (One wonders whether the London-born Zangwill was by that point accustomed to the "alien" designation.) Even the generally unfavorable review in *The Outlook* (1 December 1900) concluded by admitting that "the bite of the epigrams is so sharp, the side-views into English politics and society are so entertaining and suggestive, that one reads to the end with frequently renewed though not continuous pleasure."

In the decades following the publication of *The Mantle of Elijah* Zangwill turned increasingly to writing for the stage, with his play *The Moment of Death* (also called *The Moment Before*) produced in New York in 1900 and *The Revolted Daughter* produced in London the following year. In 1901 Zangwill again represented the English Zionist Federation at the Fifth World Zionist Congress. He would soon begin to criticize his fellow Zionists for delaying on resettlement efforts while Russian Jews faced violent persecution.

Zangwill married Edith Ayrton on 26 November 1903. A writer, pacifist, and feminist, she was not a Jew, but she and Zangwill had similar religious philosophies. (Her stepmother, Hertha Marks Ayrton, was Jewish by birth and was an important feminist and scientist.) In the same year he began serialization of *Italian Fantasies,* a collection of essays on social, religious, and artistic themes; it was published in book form in 1910. *Blind Children,* a collection of most of the serious poetry Zangwill had previously published in periodicals and in his books, appeared in 1903, as did *The Grey Wig: Stories and Novelettes.* Included in the latter volume is *The Serio-Comic Governess,* is the story of Eileen O'Keeffe/Nelly O'Neill, "respectable governess" by day, risqué comic singer at the music hall by night. Eileen is an intelligent and reflective protagonist, more reminiscent of the heroines of Zangwill's other novels than of some of the manipulative or victimized women who populate the short stories in *The Grey Wig*. She is assertive and armed with a ready wit, but, like Esther Ansell, she is frequently beset by doubts and melancholy. Eileen receives many marriage proposals, most of them unwelcome. She rejects all of her suitors and in the end returns to the French convent where she had received her early education. Her decision turns on the fact that neither of her most appealing suitors will accept Nelly and Eileen as equally important parts of her identity. She rejects the double standard that will allow an unsuspecting Colonel Doherty to dally with Nelly while wishing to marry the socially presentable Eileen and confronts his desire for the cleansing "white fire of your purity" with her reality: "London snow nicely trodden in." When the gentle and innocent Robert Maper claims that she has remained "unspotted" by the stage, simply repeating vulgarities written in a script, she insists "I'm a crow, not a parrot."

Adams finds this short novel's ending unsatisfactory and says that the "central character . . . does not engage one's sympathies." Udelson praises the story and sees in it, once again, a reflection of Zangwill's anxieties about being a Jew and an Englishman. But despite the heroine's moments of despair, *The Serio-Comic Governess* is not the anguished work Udelson describes. The music-hall material makes enlightening and entertaining use of Zangwill's love for the theater, and Eileen/Nelly has an energy and exuberance that make her a highly engaging protagonist. Eileen's decision to retreat from the world may be viewed as a sign of nineteenth-century "self-ownership," the idea that chastity or the denial of sex gave a woman independence and control over her destiny as well as her body. Thus, while neither Zangwill nor Eileen/Nelly resolves the dilemmas imposed by dual identity in *The Serio-Comic Governess,* Zangwill allows his protagonist her own solution—however imperfect—in an imperfect society unready to accept her complexity.

At the same time Zangwill was increasing his political activism. In 1905 Britain enacted antialien legislation that effectively ended Jewish immigration. After Herzl died and the Uganda Plan was rejected by the Seventh Zionist Congress, Zangwill founded the Jewish Territorial Organization (ITO) to promote the resettlement of persecuted Jews in whatever country would take them. In 1906 his organization accepted Jacob Schiff's Galveston Plan, which succeeded in repatriating many Russian Jews in the United States. Zangwill published his last collection of short fiction, *Ghetto Comedies,* in 1907. It may be said to close the circle of his ghetto writings at the same time as it reflects his increasing pessimism and the increasing urgency of the situation of European Jewry.

In the decade following *Ghetto Comedies* Zangwill's three children, Ayrton, Margaret, and Oliver, were born. Edith Zangwill published several short works in periodicals, with her six novels appearing between 1904 and 1928. Zangwill continued his work for the ITO and became active in the woman suffrage movement as a speaker and writer; many of his political writings were collected in *The War for the World* (1916). He continued to publish works, most of them polemical works on universalism and pacifism and most of them unsuccessful. The one great exception to Zangwill's dramatic failures in this period is *The Melting Pot* (1909), which attained great popularity in the United States. Its theme of the melding of the races in the American crucible won cheers from Theodore Roosevelt at its premiere though its promotion of intermarriage has continued to trouble Jews. The play's title gave a name to an American ideal.

In 1919 the novel *Jinny the Carrier* appeared. While Udelson calls the work "dense [and] overwritten," Adams writes that it "shows an ability to capture atmosphere and to create character that makes us regret the years that Zangwill wrote drama instead of novels." She adds, however, that it is "an anachronism, showing no evidence of having been written in the twentieth century." The novel is set in rural Essex at the time of the Great Exhibition (an event that is alluded to recurrently) and is dedicated affectionately to Edith Zangwill's aunt in Little Baddow, Essex, who had apparently been asking Zangwill for a "'bland' novel . . . one to be read when in bed with a sore throat." Indeed, it is remarkable how little actually happens in this novel of nearly six hundred pages, but by the end the reader has become involved in the fates of the few characters and the outcome—which is never really in doubt—of the central love story.

Jinny Boldero is brought up by her grandfather and eventually succeeds him as the town's "carrier." Providing messenger and parcel delivery service over a wide area in a cart drawn by a faithful and aging horse, Jinny has the respect and friendship of the local inhabitants and the independence that comes from successful entrepreneurship. Shortly after the novel begins, Jinny's childhood sweetheart, Will Flynt, returns to Essex from years in America. He will have none of Jinny's unconventional occupation, and although it is clear that the two are destined for each other, he does all he can to dissuade her from her work, including setting up a rival service that leaves Jinny and her grandfather near starvation. There is much debate about women's roles, in which Jinny always makes better sense, but it is not until Will's horses are destroyed in a flood, and Jinny saves him and his family using crafty stratagems, that Will recognizes that his efforts at subduing her have been pointless, and they agree to marry and live (in the novel's final words) "happy ever after." Subplots and subsidiary points of interest concern two theatrical families, a dressmaker inclined to mysticism, and religious rivalries in a community that supports a large sect of Peculiars and Christadelphians in addition to what seems to be an Anglican minority. Will Flynt's amusement at his parents' devout dissenting beliefs has its parallel in Matt Strang's rejection of his mother's faith in *The Master*. In addition, the chapelgoers practice forms of Christianity that Zangwill hints have affinities to Judaism. In *Jinny the Carrier,* as in many of Zangwill's "secular" works of fiction, positive representations of Jews and Jewishness appear prominently and unexpectedly. Will's need for a new suit of clothes takes him to the East End of London to be fitted "by the world-famous firm of 'Moses & Son.'" His experience with the firm leads him to reflect approvingly on the wisdom of refraining from work on the Sabbath.

According to Udelson, *Jinny the Carrier* was neither a critical nor a financial success, but the critical record is mixed. *The Dial* (23 August 1919) found "Jinny . . . a joy, but the novel as a whole . . . inordinately slow and long drawn out." Yet the enthusiastic reviewer for *The New York Times Review of Books* (10 August 1919) called the book "a leisurely, full-flavored narrative" whose method "gives time and scope for acquainting the reader with the ideas and beliefs of all the characters as well as with the small details of their daily lives." The critic for *The Athenaeum* (6 June 1919) was willing to excuse the novel's length for its "affectionate fullness" of development, and the writer for *The Saturday Review* (19 July 1919) called *Jinny the Carrier* a "long and interesting novel [in which] Mr. Zangwill breaks, for him, new ground, and does it on the whole with a success for which his previous have hardly prepared us." To be sure, both reviewers lamented what were seen as characteristic flaws in Zangwill's writing, his sometimes strained humor and elaborate diction, but, *The Saturday Review* concluded, "we readily forget his shortcomings when a book on the whole is as good as that now under review."

In 1920 Zangwill published *The Voice of Jerusalem,* a collection of essays on Judaism and the world situation of the Jews. His translation of *Selected Religious Poems of Solomon Ibn Gabirol* was published in 1923 by the Jewish Publication Society of America as the first volume in the Schiff Library of Jewish Classics. Zangwill became increasingly frustrated by how slowly organized Zionism was responding to the need to resettle persecuted Jews. In October 1923, in an address to the American Jewish Congress in Carnegie Hall, he declared political Zionism dead, severing his ties to the movement. The speech was published the same year as *Watchman, What of the Night?*

In 1923 Zangwill also began a novel, "The Baron of Offenbach," which he was never to finish; his typescript draft is in the British Library. As described by Udelson, "The Baron of Offenbach" purports to be the translation of a newly discovered manuscript by French and German followers of the eighteenth-century "heretical mystic and pseudomessiah" Jacob Frank. The novel is explicitly connected in Zangwill's preface to *Dreamers of the Ghetto,* which collected stories of Jewish idealists, many of them disillusioned, misled, or persecuted. Udelson sees autobiographical parallels between the French narrator in "The Baron of Offenbach" and Zangwill in his disillusionment with the Zionist movement. Zangwill's plays of this period (*Too Much Money* [1918], *The Cockpit* [1921], and *The Forcing House; or, The Cockpit Continued* [1926]) continued to fail, culminating in the disaster of his own production of *We Moderns* at the New Theatre in London in 1925. He resigned his leadership of the ITO, which was dissolved, and his health, emotional as well as physical, continued to deteriorate. Zangwill died in a nursing home at Midhurst, Sussex, on 1 August 1926. His 1923 address had hurt his reputation, but it did not destroy it. At his death he was eulogized, in speech and in print, by many of the leading Jewish figures of the day. In his writing he frequently made appeals on behalf of the oppressed, commenting on issues of identity, particularly in his works on Jewish subjects. Although for some decades his literary reputation was in eclipse, current scholarship suggests that the dilemmas Zangwill faced and described still strike a chord with readers. The continued publication of such works as *The Big Bow Mystery* and the republication of *Children of the Ghetto* indicate that Zangwill remains a figure to contend with in English and Jewish literary studies.

Interviews:

Raymond Blathwayt, "A Talk with Mr. Zangwill," *Great Thoughts,* 9 (1893): 302;

Isidore Harris, "Mr. Israel Zangwill Interviewed," *Bookman* (London), 13 (1898): 145–148;

Patricia Hoey, "Zangwill: An Aggressive, Vivid Factor Among Modern Intellectuals," *Nash's Magazine* (June 1912): 304–308;

Edward Price Bell, "Israel Zangwill on the Ku Klux Klan: A Reply to 'Imperial Wizard' Dr. H. W. Evans," *Landmark,* 4, no.6 (1924): 411–418.

Bibliographies:

Annamarie Peterson, "Israel Zangwill (1864–1926): A Selected Bibliography," *Bulletin of Bibliography,* 23, no. 6 (1961): 136–40;

Elsie Bonita Adams, "Israel Zangwill: An Annotated Bibliography of Writings About Him," *English Literature in Transition 1880–1920,* 13, no. 3 (1970): 209–244;

Bernard Winehouse, "The Literary Career of Israel Zangwill from its Beginning Until 1898," dissertation, University of London, 1970.

Biographies:

Joseph Leftwich, *Israel Zangwill* (London: James Clarke, 1957);

Joseph H. Udelson, *Dreamer of the Ghetto: The Life and Works of Israel Zangwill* (Tuscaloosa: University of Alabama Press, 1990).

References:

Elsie Bonita Adams, *Israel Zangwill* (New York: Twayne, 1971);

Jacques Ben Guigui, *Israel Zangwill, Penseur et Ecrivain (1864–1926)* (Toulouse: Imprimerie Toulousaine-R. Lion, 1975);

J. C. Benjamin, "Israel Zangwill (1864–1926): A Revaluation," *Jewish Quarterly,* 24, no. 3 (1976): 3–5;

E. F. Bleiler, Introduction to *Three Victorian Detective Novels:* The Unknown Weapon by Andrew Forrester, My Lady's Money by Wilkie Collins, The Big Bow Mystery by Israel Zangwill (New York: Dover, 1978);

Edward N. Calisch, *The Jew in English Literature, as Author and Subject* (Richmond, Va.: Bell Book & Stationery Co., 1909);

Bryan Cheyette, "The Other Self: Anglo-Jewish Fiction and the Representation of Jews in England, 1875–1905," in *The Making of Modern Anglo-Jewry,* edited by David Cesarani (London: Blackwell, 1990), pp. 97–111;

Frederick L. De Naples, "Unearthing Holmes: 1890s Interpretations of the Great Detective," in *Transforming Genres: New Approaches to British Fiction of the 1890s,* edited by Nikki Lee Manos and Meri-Jane Rochelson (New York: St. Martin's Press, 1994), pp. 215–235;

Lilian Falk, "A Nineteenth-Century Literary Representation of Nova Scotia Dialect," in *Papers from the Seventeenth Annual Meeting of the Atlantic Provinces Linguistic Association,* edited by Margaret Harry (Halifax, 1993), pp. 33–39.

Harold Fisch, "Israel Zangwill: Prophet of the Ghetto," *Judaism,* 13 (Fall 1964): 407–421;

Hamlin Garland, "Roadside Meetings of a Literary Nomad," *Bookman* (London), 71 (1930): 302–313;

John Gross, "Zangwill in Retrospect," *Commentary,* 38 (December 1964): 54–57;

Holbrook Jackson, "Israel Zangwill," *Bookman* (London), 46 (1914): 67–73;

Montagu Frank Modder, *The Jew in the Literature of England: To the End of the Nineteenth Century* (Philadelphia: Jewish Publication Society of America, 1939);

Meri-Jane Rochelson, "*The Big Bow Mystery:* Jewish Identity and the English Detective Novel," *Victorian Review,* 17 (Winter 1991): 11–20;

Rochelson, "Language, Gender, and Ethnic Anxiety in Zangwill's *Children of the Ghetto,*" *English Literature in Transition 1880–1920,* 31 (1988): 399–412;

Harold Williams, *Modern English Writers: Being a Study of Imaginative Literature 1890–1914* (London: Sidgwick & Jackson, 1918);

Bernard Winehouse, "Israel Zangwill's *Children of the Ghetto*: A Literary History of the First Anglo-Jewish Best-Seller," *English Literature in Transition 1880–1920,* 16 (1973): 93–117;

Maurice Wohlgelernter, *Israel Zangwill: A Study* (New York: Columbia University Press, 1964);

Linda Gertner Zatlin, *The Nineteenth-Century Anglo-Jewish Novel* (Boston: Twayne, 1981).

Papers:

The Central Zionist Archives in Jerusalem, Israel, file A120, holds by far the largest collection of Israel Zangwill's letters, diaries, photographs, clippings, manuscripts, and other papers; material on Zangwill also appears in the archives' files on Zionism and the Jewish Territorial Organization. Additional significant collections of letters and papers are at the British Library; the Cambridge University Library (in the collections of Dr. M. H. Salaman and R. A. Salaman); the Brotherton Collection, University of Leeds Library; the Jewish Theological Seminary of America; the Berg Collection of the New York Public Library; the American Jewish Archives, Cincinnati; the Philadelphia Jewish Archives at the Balch Institute; the University of California at Los Angeles; Columbia University; and the Yivo Institute for Jewish Research, New York. Manuscripts are in the Central Zionist Archives; the British Library; the Moccata Library of University College, London; the University of London Library; and the Klau Library, Hebrew Union College-Jewish Institute of Religion, New York and Cincinnati.

Checklist of Further Readings

Adcock, Arthur St. *The Glory That Was Grub Street.* London: Sampson Low, Marston, 1928; New York: Stokes, 1928.

Adcock. *The Gods of Modern Grub Street.* London: Sampson Low, Marston, 1923.

Allen, Walter. *The English Novel.* New York: Dutton, 1958.

Ardis, Ann. *New Woman, New Novels: Feminism and Early Modernism.* New Brunswick & London: Rutgers University Press, 1990.

Arata, Stephen. *Fictions of Loss in the Victorian Fin de Siècle.* Cambridge: Cambridge University Press, 1996.

Ashraf, P. M. *Introduction to Working-Class Literature in Great Britain. Part II: Prose.* Berlin: VEB Kongres-und Werbedruck Oberlungwitz, 1979.

Batchelor, John. *The Edwardian Novelists.* London: Duckworth, 1982.

Beauman, Nicola. *A Very Great Profession: The Women's Novel 1914-1939.* London: Virago, 1983.

Beckson, Karl. *London in the 1890s: A Cultural History.* New York: Norton, 1992.

Bennett, Tony. *Popular Fiction.* London: Routledge, 1990.

Bentley, Phyllis. *The English Regional Novel.* London: Allen & Unwin, 1941.

Bergonzi, Bernard. *Heroes' Twilight: A Study of the Literature of the Great War.* London: Constable, 1965.

Bergonzi. *The Turn of a Century: Essays on Victorian and Modern English Literature.* London: Macmillan, 1973.

Bjorhovde, Gerd. *Rebellious Structures. Women Writers and the Crisis of the Novel, 1880-1900.* Oxford: Norwegian University Press, 1987.

Blamires, Harry. *Twentieth Century English Literature.* London: Macmillan, 1982.

Bloom, Clive. *The "Occult" Experience and the New Criticism.* Sussex: Harvester, 1986.

Bradbury, Malcolm. *The Social Context of Modern English Literature.* Oxford: Blackwell, 1971.

Brandon, Ruth. *The New Women and the Old Men.* London: Secker & Warburg, 1990.

Breen, Jennifer. *In Her Own Write: Twentieth-Century Women's Fiction.* London: Macmillan, 1990.

Brewster, Dorothy, and Angus Burrell. *Dead Reckonings in Fiction.* New York: Longmans, Green, 1924.

Brewster and Burrell. *Modern Fiction.* New York: Columbia University Press, 1934.

Britain, Ian. *Fabianism and Culture: A Study in British Socialism and the Arts 1884-1918.* New York: Columbia University Press, 1982.

Brome, Vincent. *Four Realist Novelists: Arthur Morrison, Edwin Pugh, Richard Whiteing, William Pett Ridge.* London: Longmans, Green, 1965.

Bufkin, E. C. *The Twentieth-Century Novel in English.* Athens: University of Georgia Press, 1984.

Buitenhuis, Peter. *The Great War of Words: British, American, and Canadian Propaganda and Fiction, 1914–1933.* Vancouver: University of British Columbia Press, 1987.

Cadogan, Mary, and Wendy Craig. *Women and Children First: Aspects of War and Literature.* London: Gollancz, 1978.

Cavaliero, Glen. *The Rural Tradition in the English Novel 1900–1939.* London: Macmillan, 1977.

Chapple, J. A. V. *Documentary and Imaginative Literature, 1880–1920.* New York: Barnes & Noble, 1970.

Chevalley, Abel. *The Modern English Novel,* translated by Ben Ray Redman. New York: Haskell House, 1973.

Church, Richard. *British Authors: A Twentieth-Century Gallery.* London, New York & Toronto: Longmans, Green, 1948.

Church. *The Growth of the English Novel.* London: Methuen, 1951.

Clayton, John J. *Gestures of Healing: Anxiety and the Modern Novel.* Amherst: University of Massachusetts, 1991.

Cockburn, Claud. *Bestseller: The Books That Everyone Read 1900–1939.* London: Sidgwick & Jackson, 1972.

Colls, Robert, and Philip Dodd, eds. *Englishness: Politics and Culture 1880–1920.* London: Croom Helm, 1986.

Courtney, W. L. *The Feminine Note in Fiction.* London: Chapman & Hall, 1904.

Cox, C. B., and A. E. Dyson, eds. *The Twentieth-Century Mind—1900–1918.* London: Oxford University Press, 1972.

Crosland, Margaret. *Beyond the Lighthouse: English Women Novelists in the Twentieth Century.* London: Constable, 1981.

Cross, Nigel. *The Common Writer: Life in Nineteenth-Century Grub Street.* Cambridge: Cambridge University Press, 1985.

Cruse, Amy. *After the Victorians.* London: Allen & Unwin, 1938.

Cunningham, A. R. "The 'New Woman Fiction' of the 1890s," *Victorian Studies,* 17 (December 1973): 177–186.

Cunningham, Gail. *The New Woman and the Victorian Novel.* London: Macmillan, 1978.

Daims, Diva, and Janet Grimes. *Toward a Feminist Tradition: An Annotated Bibliography of Novels in English by Women 1891–1920.* New York: Garland, 1982.

Dangerfield, George. *The Strange Death of Liberal England.* New York: Capricorn Books/Putnam, 1961.

Davies, Tony. "Unfinished Business: Realism and Working-Class Writing," in *The British Working-Class Novel in the Twentieth Century,* edited by Jeremy Hawthorn. London: Arnold, 1984.

DeKoven, Marianne. *Rich and Strange: Gender, History, Modernism.* Princeton: Princeton University Press, 1991.

Dijkstra, Bram. *Idols of Perversity: Fantasies of Feminine Evil in Fin-de-Siècle Culture.* New York: Oxford University Press, 1986.

Dowling, Linda. "The Decadent and the New Woman in the 1890s," *Nineteenth-Century Fiction,* 334 (1979): 434–453.

Drew, Elizabeth A. *The Modern Novel. Some Aspects of Contemporary Fiction.* New York: Harcourt, Brace, 1926.

Ellmann, Richard, ed. *Edwardians and Late Victorians.* New York: Columbia University Press, 1959.

Elwin, Malcolm. *Old Gods Falling.* New York: Macmillan, 1939; reprinted, Freeport, N.Y.: Books for Libraries Press, 1971.

Ensor, R. C. K. *England 1870–1914.* Oxford: Clarendon Press, 1936.

Fernando, Lloyd. *"New Women" in the Late Victorian Novel.* University Park: Pennsylvania State University Press, 1977.

Fox, Pamela. *Class Fictions: Shame and Resistance in the British Working-Class Novel, 1890–1945.* Durham, N.C. & London: Duke University Press, 1994.

Fraser, G. S. *The Modern Writer and His World.* London: Deutsch, 1964.

Friedman, Alan. *The Turn of the Novel: The Transition to Modern Fiction.* New York & London: Oxford University Press, 1966.

Frierson, William C. *The English Novel in Transition 1885–1940.* Norman: University of Oklahoma Press / New York: Cooper Square, 1965.

Fussell, Paul. *The Great War and Modern Memory.* London: Oxford University Press, 1975.

Gawsworth, John. *Ten Contemporaries: Notes towards Their Definitive Bibliographies.* London: Joiner & Steele, 1933.

George, W. L. *A Novelist on Novels.* Port Washington, N.Y.: Kennikat Press, 1970.

Gerber, Richard. *Utopian Fantasy: A Study of English Utopian Fiction Since the End of the Nineteenth Century.* London: Routledge & Kegan Paul, 1955.

Gibbons, Tom. *Rooms in the Darwin Hotel: Studies in English Literary Criticism and Ideas 1880–1920.* Nedlands: University of Western Australia Press, 1973.

Gilbert, Sandra M., and Sandra Gubar. *The Madwoman in the Attic: The Woman Writer and the Nineteenth-Century Literary Imagination.* New Haven: Yale University Press, 1979.

Gill, Richard. *Happy Rural Seat: The English Country House and the Literary Imagination.* New Haven: Yale University Press, 1972.

Gillie, Christopher. *Movements in English Literature, 1900–1940.* Cambridge: Cambridge University Press, 1975.

Glicksberg, Charles I. *The Sexual Revolution in Modern English Literature.* The Hague: Nijhoff, 1973.

Gould, Gerald. *The English Novel of Today.* London: Castle, 1924.

Hager, Philip E., and Taylor Desmond. *The Novels of World War One: An Annotated Bibliography.* New York: Garland, 1981.

Harman, Barbara Leah, and Susan Meyer, eds. *The New Nineteenth Century: Feminist Readings of Underread Victorian Fiction.* New York & London: Garland, 1996.

Hamilton, Clayton. *A Manual of the Art of Fiction.* Garden City, N.Y.: Doubleday, Page, 1918.

Hawthorn, Jeremy, ed. *The British Working-Class Novel in the Twentieth Century.* London: Arnold, 1984.

Henkin, Leo J. *Darwinism in the English Novel: 1860–1910.* New York: Russell & Russell, 1963.

Hewitt, Douglas John. *English Fiction of the Early Modern Period 1890–1940.* London: Longman, 1988.

Hibberd, Dominic. *The First World War.* London: Macmillan, 1990.

Hicks, Granville. *Figures of Transition: A Study of British Literature at the End of the Nineteenth Century.* New York: Macmillan, 1939.

Hind, C. Lewis. *More Authors and I.* New York: Dodd, Mead, 1922.

Hochman, Baruch. *The Test of Character from the Victorian Novel to Modern.* Cranbury, N.J.: Fairleigh Dickinson, 1983.

Hoffman, Frederick J. *Freudianism and the Literary Mind.* Baton Rouge: Louisiana State University Press, 1957.

Hoffman. *The Mortal No: Death and The Modern Imagination.* Princeton: Princeton University Press, 1964.

Homberger, Eric. "Modernists and Edwardians," in *Ezra Pound: The London Years 1908–1920,* edited by Philip Grover (New York: AMS Press, 1977), pp. 1–14.

Hoops, R. *Der Einflus der Psychoanalyse auf die Englische Literatur.* Heidelburg: Winters, 1934.

Howarth, Patrick. *Play Up and Play the Game: The Heroes of Popular Fiction.* London: Eyre Methuen, 1973.

Hughes, H. Stewart. *Consciousness and Society: The Re-Orientation of European Social Thought 1890–1930.* London: MacGibbon & Kee, 1959.

Humm, Peter, Paul Stigant, and Peter Widdowson, eds. *Popular Fictions.* London: Methuen, 1986.

Hunter, Jefferson. *Edwardian Fiction.* Cambridge, Mass.: Harvard University Press, 1982.

Hynes, Samuel. *Edwardian Occasions: Essays on English Writing in the Early Twentieth Century.* London: Routledge, 1972.

Hynes. *The Edwardian Turn of Mind.* Princeton: Princeton University Press, 1968.

Hynes. *A War Imagined: The First World War and English Culture.* New York: Atheneum, 1991.

Ingle, Stephen. *Socialist Thought in Imaginative Literature.* London: Macmillan, 1979.

Ingram, Angela, and Daphne Patai. *Rediscovering Forgotten Radicals: British Women Writers 1889–1939.* Chapel Hill & London: University of North Carolina Press, 1993.

Jackson, Holbrook. *The Eighteen Nineties: A Review of Art and Ideas at the Close of the Nineteenth Century.* New York: Knopf, 1913.

Jameson, Storm. *The Georgian Novel and Mr. Robinson.* London: Heinemann, 1929.

Jeffreys, Sheila. *The Spinster and Her Enemies: Feminism and Sexuality 1880–1930*. London: Pandora, 1985.

Johnson, George M. "The Early Influence of Second Wave Psychology on British Prose Fiction," dissertation, McMaster University, 1990.

Johnson, R. Brimley. *Some Contemporary Novelists (Women)*. London: Parsons, 1920.

Karl, Frederick R. *Modern and Modernism: The Sovereignty of the Artist 1885–1925*. New York: Atheneum, 1988.

Keating, Peter J. *The Haunted Study: A Social History of the English Novel 1875–1914*. London: Secker & Warburg, 1989.

Keating. *Into Unknown England 1866–1913*. Manchester: Manchester University Press, 1976.

Keating. *The Working Classes in English Fiction*. London: Routledge & Kegan Paul, 1971.

Kennedy, J. M. *English Literature: 1880–1905*. London: Sampson Low, Marston, 1913.

Kenner, Hugh. *A Sinking Island*. London: Barrie & Jenkins, 1988.

Kermode, Frank. "The English Novel, circa 1907," in his *Essays on Fiction 1971–82*. London: Routledge & Kegan Paul, 1983.

Kern, Stephen. *The Culture of Time and Space 1880–1918*. London: Weidenfield & Nicolson, 1983.

Klaus, H. Gustav. *The Socialist Novel in Britain*. New York: St. Martin's Press, 1982.

Klaus, ed. *The Rise of Social Fiction 1880–1914*. Sussex: Harvester, 1987.

Klein, Holger, ed. *The First World War in Fiction*. London: Macmillan, 1976.

Kranidis, Rita S. *Subversive Discourses: The Cultural Production of Late Victorian Feminist Novels*. New York: St. Martin's Press, 1995.

Krishnamurti, G., comp. *Women Writers of the 1890s,* introduction by Margaret Drabble. London: Sotheran, 1991.

Kunitz, Stanley J., and Howard Haycraft, eds. *Twentieth Century Authors: A Biographical Dictionary of Modern Literature*. New York: Wilson, 1942.

Langbaum, Robert. *The Modern Spirit: Essays on the Continuity of Nineteenth and Twentieth-Century Literature*. New York & London: Oxford University Press, 1970.

Lauterbach, Edward S., and W. Eugene Davies. *The Transitional Age in British Literature, 1880–1920*. Troy, N.Y.: Whitson, 1973.

Lawrence, Margaret. *School of Femininity*. New York: Stokes, 1936; republished as *We Write as Women*. London: M. Joseph, 1936.

Leavis, Q. D. *Fiction and the Reading Public*. London: Chatto & Windus, 1932.

Ledger, Sally, and Scott McCracken, eds. *Cultural Politics at the Fin de Siecle*. Cambridge: Cambridge University Press, 1995.

Leed, Eric J. *No Man's Land: Combat and Identity in World War I*. Cambridge: Cambridge University Press, 1979.

Leslie, Anita. *Edwardians in Love*. London: Hutchinson, 1972.

Lester, John A. Jr. *Journey through Despair 1880–1914: Transformations in British Literary Culture*. Princeton: Princeton University Press, 1968.

Levine, George. *The Realistic Imagination: English Fiction from Frankenstein to Lady Chatterley*. Chicago: University of Chicago Press, 1981.

Lodge, David. *Modernism, Antimodernism and Postmodernism*. Birmingham, U.K.: University of Birmingham, 1977.

Mackenzie, Norman, and Jeanne Mackenzie. *The Fabians*. New York: Simon & Schuster, 1977.

Mais, S. P. B. *Some Modern Authors*. London: Richards, 1923.

Manos, Nikki Lee, and Meri-Jane Rochelson, eds. *Transforming Genres: New Approaches to British Fiction of the 1890s*. New York: St. Martin's Press, 1994.

Markovic, Vida E. *The Changing Face: Disintegration of Personality in the Twentieth-Century British Novel, 1900–1950*. Carbondale: Southern Illinois University Press, 1970.

Marwick, Arthur. *The Deluge: British Society and the First World War*. London: Bodley Head, 1965.

May, Keith. *Out of the Maelstrom: Psychology and the Novel in the Twentieth Century*. London: Elek, 1977.

McNichol, Stella. *The Early Twentieth Century British Novel: A Modern Introduction*. London: Arnold, 1992.

Meacham, Standish. *A Life Apart: The English Working Class, 1890–1914*. Cambridge, Mass.: Harvard University Press, 1977.

Meyers, Jeffrey. *Homosexuality and Literature: 1890–1930*. London: Athlone, 1977.

Miller, Jane Eldridge. *Rebel Women: Feminism, Modernism, and the Edwardian Novel*. London: Virago, 1994.

Mix, Katherine Lyon. *A Study in Yellow: The Yellow Book and Its Contributors*. Lawrence: University of Kansas Press, 1960.

Myers, W. L. *The Later Realism*. Chicago: University of Chicago Press, 1927.

Nelson, Carolyn Christensen. *British Women Fiction Writers of the 1890s*. New York: Twayne, 1996.

Neuberg, Victor E. *Popular Literature: A History and Guide*. Harmondsworth: Penguin, 1977.

Nowell-Smith, Simon, ed. *Edwardian England 1901–1914*. New York: Oxford University Press, 1964.

O'Day, Alan, ed. *The Edwardian Age: Conflict and Stability 1900–1914*. London: Macmillan, 1979.

Orel, Harold. *Popular Fiction in England, 1914–1918*. Lexington: University Press of Kentucky, 1992.

Overton, Grant Martin. *Authors of the Day*. New York: Doran, 1924.

Paterson, John. *Edwardians: London Life and Letters, 1901–1914*. Chicago: Ivan R. Dee, 1996.

Perl, Jeffrey M. *The Tradition of Return: The Implicit History of Modernism*. Princeton: Princeton University Press, 1984.

Priestley, J. B. *The Edwardians*. London: Sphere, 1972.

Pykett, Lyn. *The "Improper" Feminine: The Women's Sensation Novel and the New Woman Writing*. London & New York: Routledge, 1992.

Read, Donald, ed. *Edwardian England*. New Brunswick, N.J.: Rutgers University Press, 1982.

Rice, Thomas Jackson. *English Fiction, 1900–1950*, 2 volumes. Detroit: Gale Research, 1979, 1983.

Robbins, Bruce. *The Servant's Hand: English Fiction from Below*. New York: Columbia University Press, 1986.

Rose, Jonathan. *The Edwardian Temperament: 1895–1919*. Athens: Ohio University Press, 1986.

Rubenstein, David. *Before the Suffragettes: Women's Emancipation in the 1890s*. New York: St. Martin's Press, 1986.

Sandison, Alan. *The Wheel of Empire: A Study of the Imperial Idea in Some Late Nineteenth and Early Twentieth Century Fiction*. New York: St. Martin's Press, 1967.

Scanlon, Leone. "The New Woman in the Literature of 1883–1909," *University of Michigan Papers in Women's Studies*, 2, no. 2 (1976): 133–159.

Schwartz, Sanford. *The Matrix of Modernism: Pound, Eliot, and Early Twentieth-Century Thought*. Princeton: Princeton University Press, 1985.

Schwarz, Daniel R. *The Transformation of the English Novel 1890–1930*. London: Macmillan, 1989.

Scott-James, Rolfe A. *Fifty Years of English Literature, 1900–1950; with a Postscript, 1951–1955*. London: Longmans, Green, 1956.

Scott-James. *Modernism and Romance*. London: John Lane/Bodley Head, 1908.

Shaw, George Bernard. *The Sanity of Art: An Exposure of the Current Nonsense about Artists Being Degenerate*. London: New Age Press, 1908.

Showalter, Elaine. *A Literature of Their Own: British Women Novelists from Brontë to Lessing*. Princeton: Princeton University Press, 1977.

Showalter. *Sexual Anarchy: Gender and Culture at the Fin de Siecle*. New York: Viking Penguin, 1990.

Smith, David. *Socialist Propaganda in the Twentieth-Century British Novel*. London: Macmillan, 1978.

Sparrow, Gerald. *Vintage Edwardian Murder*. London: Barker, 1971.

Squillace, Robert. "Bennett, Wells, and the Persistence of Realism" in *The Columbia History of the British Novel*, edited by John Richetti. New York: Columbia University Press, 1994, pp. 658–684.

Stableford, Brian. *Scientific Romance in Britain 1890–1950*. London: Fourth Estate, 1985.

Staley, Thomas. *Twentieth Century Women Novelists*. London: Macmillan, 1982.

Stetz, Margaret Diane. "Life's 'Half-Profits': Writers and their Readers in Fiction of the 1890s," in *Nineteenth-Century Lives: Essays Presented to Jerome Hamilton Buckley*, edited by Laurence S. Lockbridge, John Maynard, and Donald D. Stone. Cambridge: Cambridge University Press, 1989.

Stevenson, Lionel. *The History of the English Novel*, volume 11: *Yesterday and After*. New York: Barnes & Noble, 1967.

Stokes, John. *In the Nineties*. Chicago: University of Chicago Press/Hemel Hempstead: Harvester Wheatsheaf, 1989.

Street, Brian V. *The Savage in Literature: Representations of "Primitive" Society in English Fiction 1858-1920*. London: Routledge, 1975.

Stubbs, Patricia. *Women and Fiction: Feminism and the Novel 1880-1920*. New York: Barnes & Noble, 1979.

Sturgis, Matthew. *Passionate Attitudes: The English Decadence of the 1890s*. London: Macmillan, 1995.

Sutherland, John. *The Stanford Companion to Victorian Fiction*. Stanford, Cal.: Stanford University Press, 1989.

Swinnerton, Frank. *The Georgian Literary Scene, 1910-1935*. London: Hutchinson, 1935.

Swinnerton. *A London Bookman*. London: Secker, 1928.

Thatcher, David S. *Nietzsche in England 1890-1914*. Toronto: University of Toronto Press, 1970.

Thompson, Paul. *The Edwardians: The Remaking of British Society*. London & New York: Routledge, 1992.

Tindall, William York. *Forces in Modern British Literature, 1885-1956*. New York: Vintage Books, 1956.

Trodd, Anthea. *A Reader's Guide to Edwardian Literature*. Calgary: University of Calgary Press, 1991.

Trotter, David. "Edwardian Sex Novels," *Critical Quarterly*, 31 (Spring 1989): 92-106.

Trotter. *The English Novel in History 1895-1920*. London & New York: Routledge, 1993.

Verschoyle, Derek, ed. *The English Novelists: A Survey of the Novel by Twenty Contemporary Novelists*. London: Chatto & Windus, 1936.

Ward, Alfred C. *Twentieth-Century English Literature, 1900-1960*. London: Methuen, 1964.

Waters, Chris. *British Socialists and the Politics of Popular Culture 1884-1914*. Manchester, U.K.: Manchester University Press, 1990.

Waugh, Arthur. *Tradition and Change*. London: Chapman & Hall, 1919; New York: Dutton, 1919.

West, George Cornwallis. *Edwardian Hey-Days*. London & New York: Putnam, 1930.

Williams, Harold. *Modern English Writers, 1890-1914*. London: Sidgwick & Jackson, 1919.

Williams, Ioan M. *The Realist Novel in England. A Study in Development*. London: Macmillan, 1974.

Williams, Raymond. *Culture and Society 1780-1950*. London: Chatto & Windus, 1958.

Williams. *The English Novel from Dickens to Lawrence*. London: Chatto & Windus, 1970.

Wiltsher, Anne. *Most Dangerous Women: Feminist Peace Campaigners of the Great War*. London & Boston: Pandora, 1985.

Wohl, Robert. *The Generation of 1914*. Cambridge, Mass.: Harvard University Press, 1979.

Contributors

Lynn M. Alexander	*University of Tennessee at Martin*
Leonard R. N. Ashley	*Brooklyn College of The City University of New York*
Katherine E. Ayer	*University of Southern California*
Richard Bleiler	*University of Connecticut*
Rebecca Brittenham	*Rutgers University*
Karen M. Carney	*John Carroll University*
George Allan Cate	*University of Maryland*
Laurie Clancy	*La Trobe University*
Diana Farr	*London, England*
Maria Aline Seabra Ferreira	*University of Aveiro (Portugal)*
Carol L. Hale	*University of Wisconsin–Eau Claire*
Colleen Hobbs	*Rutgers University*
Marilyn Hoder-Salmon	*Florida International University*
George J. Johnson	*Waterdown, Ontario, Canada*
George M. Johnson	*University College of the Cariboo*
Jill Tedford Jones	*Southwestern Oklahoma State University*
Shoshana Milgram Knapp	*Virginia Polytechnic Institute and State University*
Donald Mason	*McMaster University*
Carolyn Christensen Nelson	*West Virginia University*
Meri-Jane Rochelson	*Florida International University*
Jan Peter F. van Rosevelt	*University of South Carolina*
Paul W. Salmon	*University of Guelph*
David Smith	*University of Adelaide*
P. Joan Smith	*McMaster University*
Margaret Diane Stetz	*Georgetown University*
Eileen Sypher	*George Mason University*
Sue Thomas	*La Trobe University*
Eric Thompson	*Université du Québec à Chicoutimi*
Michele K. Troy	*Loyola University of Chicago*
Susan Winslow Waterman	*Rutgers University*
Kenneth Womack	*Pennsylvania State University at Altoona*

Cumulative Index

Dictionary of Literary Biography, Volumes 1-197
Dictionary of Literary Biography Yearbook, 1980-1997
Dictionary of Literary Biography Documentary Series, Volumes 1-17

Cumulative Index

DLB before number: *Dictionary of Literary Biography*, Volumes 1-197
Y before number: *Dictionary of Literary Biography Yearbook*, 1980-1997
DS before number: *Dictionary of Literary Biography Documentary Series*, Volumes 1-17

A

Abbey, Edwin Austin 1852–1911 .... DLB-188
Abbey Press DLB-49
The Abbey Theatre and Irish Drama, 1900-1945 .... DLB-10
Abbot, Willis J. 1863-1934 .... DLB-29
Abbott, Jacob 1803-1879 .... DLB-1
Abbott, Lee K. 1947- DLB-130
Abbott, Lyman 1835-1922 .... DLB-79
Abbott, Robert S. 1868-1940 .... DLB-29, 91
Abe, Kōbō 1924-1993 .... DLB-182
Abelard, Peter circa 1079-1142 .... DLB-115
Abelard-Schuman DLB-46
Abell, Arunah S. 1806-1888 ...... DLB-43
Abercrombie, Lascelles 1881-1938 .... DLB-19
Aberdeen University Press Limited DLB-106
Abish, Walter 1931- DLB-130
Ablesimov, Aleksandr Onisimovich 1742-1783 .... DLB-150
Abraham à Sancta Clara 1644-1709 .... DLB-168
Abrahams, Peter 1919- DLB-117
Abrams, M. H. 1912- DLB-67
Abrogans circa 790-800 .... DLB-148
Abschatz, Hans Aßmann von 1646-1699 .... DLB-168
Abse, Dannie 1923- DLB-27
Academy Chicago Publishers DLB-46
Accrocca, Elio Filippo 1923- DLB-128
Ace Books DLB-46
Achebe, Chinua 1930- DLB-117
Achtenberg, Herbert 1938- DLB-124
Ackerman, Diane 1948- DLB-120
Ackroyd, Peter 1949- DLB-155
Acorn, Milton 1923-1986 .... DLB-53
Acosta, Oscar Zeta 1935?- DLB-82
Actors Theatre of Louisville DLB-7
Adair, Gilbert 1944- DLB-194
Adair, James 1709?-1783? DLB-30
Adam, Graeme Mercer 1839-1912 .... DLB-99

Adam, Robert Borthwick II 1863-1940 .... DLB-187
Adame, Leonard 1947- DLB-82
Adamic, Louis 1898-1951 .... DLB-9
Adams, Alice 1926- Y-86
Adams, Brooks 1848-1927 .... DLB-47
Adams, Charles Francis, Jr. 1835-1915 .... DLB-47
Adams, Douglas 1952- Y-83
Adams, Franklin P. 1881-1960 ..... DLB-29
Adams, Henry 1838-1918 ... DLB-12, 47, 189
Adams, Herbert Baxter 1850-1901 .... DLB-47
Adams, J. S. and C. [publishing house] DLB-49
Adams, James Truslow 1878-1949 .... DLB-17; DS-17
Adams, John 1735-1826 ...... DLB-31, 183
Adams, John 1735-1826 and Adams, Abigail 1744-1818 ..... DLB-183
Adams, John Quincy 1767-1848 ..... DLB-37
Adams, Léonie 1899-1988 .... DLB-48
Adams, Levi 1802-1832 .... DLB-99
Adams, Samuel 1722-1803 ..... DLB-31, 43
Adams, Thomas 1582 or 1583-1652 .... DLB-151
Adams, William Taylor 1822-1897 .... DLB-42
Adamson, Sir John 1867-1950 ..... DLB-98
Adcock, Arthur St. John 1864-1930 .... DLB-135
Adcock, Betty 1938- DLB-105
Adcock, Fleur 1934- DLB-40
Addison, Joseph 1672-1719 ...... DLB-101
Ade, George 1866-1944 ...... DLB-11, 25
Adeler, Max (see Clark, Charles Heber)
Adonias Filho 1915-1990 .... DLB-145
Advance Publishing Company DLB-49
AE 1867-1935 .... DLB-19
Ælfric circa 955-circa 1010 ...... DLB-146
Aeschines circa 390 B.C.-circa 320 B.C. DLB-176
Aeschylus 525-524 B.C.-456-455 B.C. DLB-176
Aesthetic Poetry (1873), by Walter Pater DLB-35

After Dinner Opera Company Y-92
Afro-American Literary Critics: An Introduction DLB-33
Agassiz, Elizabeth Cary 1822-1907 ... DLB-189
Agassiz, Jean Louis Rodolphe 1807-1873 .... DLB-1
Agee, James 1909-1955 ..... DLB-2, 26, 152
The Agee Legacy: A Conference at the University of Tennessee at Knoxville Y-89
Aguilera Malta, Demetrio 1909-1981 .... DLB-145
Ai 1947- DLB-120
Aichinger, Ilse 1921- DLB-85
Aidoo, Ama Ata 1942- DLB-117
Aiken, Conrad 1889-1973 .... DLB-9, 45, 102
Aiken, Joan 1924- DLB-161
Aikin, Lucy 1781-1864 .... DLB-144, 163
Ainsworth, William Harrison 1805-1882 .... DLB-21
Aitken, George A. 1860-1917 ...... DLB-149
Aitken, Robert [publishing house] DLB-49
Akenside, Mark 1721-1770 .... DLB-109
Akins, Zoë 1886-1958 .... DLB-26
Akutagawa, Ryūnsuke 1892-1927 .... DLB-180
Alabaster, William 1568-1640 ..... DLB-132
Alain-Fournier 1886-1914 .... DLB-65
Alarcón, Francisco X. 1954- DLB-122
Alba, Nanina 1915-1968 .... DLB-41
Albee, Edward 1928- DLB-7
Albert the Great circa 1200-1280 .... DLB-115
Alberti, Rafael 1902- DLB-108
Albertinus, Aegidius circa 1560-1620 .... DLB-164
Alcaeus born circa 620 B.C. DLB-176
Alcott, Amos Bronson 1799-1888 ..... DLB-1
Alcott, Louisa May 1832-1888 .... DLB-1, 42, 79; DS-14
Alcott, William Andrus 1798-1859 .... DLB-1
Alcuin circa 732-804 .... DLB-148
Alden, Henry Mills 1836-1919 ..... DLB-79
Alden, Isabella 1841-1930 .... DLB-42

329

Cumulative Index

Alden, John B. [publishing house] DLB-49

Alden, Beardsley and Company DLB-49

Aldington, Richard
1892-1962 . . . . DLB-20, 36, 100, 149

Aldis, Dorothy 1896-1966 . . . . DLB-22

Aldis, H. G. 1863-1919 . . . . DLB-184

Aldiss, Brian W. 1925- DLB-14

Aldrich, Thomas Bailey
1836-1907 . . . . DLB-42, 71, 74, 79

Alegría, Ciro 1909-1967 . . . . DLB-113

Alegría, Claribel 1924- DLB-145

Aleixandre, Vicente 1898-1984 . . . . . DLB-108

Aleramo, Sibilla 1876-1960 . . . . DLB-114

Alexander, Charles 1868-1923 . . . . . . DLB-91

Alexander, Charles Wesley
[publishing house] DLB-49

Alexander, James 1691-1756 . . . . DLB-24

Alexander, Lloyd 1924- DLB-52

Alexander, Sir William, Earl of Stirling
1577?-1640 . . . . DLB-121

Alexie, Sherman 1966- DLB-175

Alexis, Willibald 1798-1871 . . . . DLB-133

Alfred, King 849-899 . . . . DLB-146

Alger, Horatio, Jr. 1832-1899 . . . . DLB-42

Algonquin Books of Chapel Hill DLB-46

Algren, Nelson 1909-1981 . . . . DLB-9; Y-81, Y-82

Allan, Andrew 1907-1974 . . . . DLB-88

Allan, Ted 1916- DLB-68

Allbeury, Ted 1917- DLB-87

Alldritt, Keith 1935- DLB-14

Allen, Ethan 1738-1789 . . . . DLB-31

Allen, Frederick Lewis 1890-1954 . . . . DLB-137

Allen, Gay Wilson
1903-1995 . . . . DLB-103; Y-95

Allen, George 1808-1876 . . . . DLB-59

Allen, George [publishing house] DLB-106

Allen, George, and Unwin
Limited DLB-112

Allen, Grant 1848-1899 . . . . DLB-70, 92, 178

Allen, Henry W. 1912- Y-85

Allen, Hervey 1889-1949 . . . . DLB-9, 45

Allen, James 1739-1808 . . . . DLB-31

Allen, James Lane 1849-1925 . . . . . . DLB-71

Allen, Jay Presson 1922- DLB-26

Allen, John, and Company DLB-49

Allen, Paula Gunn 1939- DLB-175

Allen, Samuel W. 1917- DLB-41

Allen, Woody 1935- DLB-44

Allende, Isabel 1942- DLB-145

Alline, Henry 1748-1784 . . . . DLB-99

Allingham, Margery 1904-1966 . . . . . DLB-77

Allingham, William 1824-1889 . . . . . . DLB-35

Allison, W. L.
[publishing house] DLB-49

The *Alliterative Morte Arthure* and
the *Stanzaic Morte Arthur*
circa 1350-1400 . . . . DLB-146

Allott, Kenneth 1912-1973 . . . . DLB-20

Allston, Washington 1779-1843 . . . . . . DLB-1

Almon, John [publishing house] DLB-154

Alonzo, Dámaso 1898-1990 . . . . DLB-108

Alsop, George 1636-post 1673 . . . . . . DLB-24

Alsop, Richard 1761-1815 . . . . DLB-37

Altemus, Henry, and Company DLB-49

Altenberg, Peter 1885-1919 . . . . DLB-81

Altolaguirre, Manuel 1905-1959 . . . . DLB-108

Aluko, T. M. 1918- DLB-117

Alurista 1947- DLB-82

Alvarez, A. 1929- DLB-14, 40

Amadi, Elechi 1934- DLB-117

Amado, Jorge 1912- DLB-113

Ambler, Eric 1909- DLB-77

*America: or, a Poem on the Settlement of the
British Colonies* (1780?), by Timothy
Dwight DLB-37

American Conservatory Theatre DLB-7

American Fiction and the 1930s DLB-9

American Humor: A Historical Survey
East and Northeast
South and Southwest
Midwest
West DLB-11

The American Library in Paris Y-93

American News Company DLB-49

The American Poets' Corner: The First
Three Years (1983-1986) Y-86

American Proletarian Culture:
The 1930s DS-11

American Publishing Company DLB-49

American Stationers' Company DLB-49

American Sunday-School Union DLB-49

American Temperance Union DLB-49

American Tract Society DLB-49

The American Trust for the
British Library Y-96

The American Writers Congress
(9-12 October 1981) Y-81

The American Writers Congress: A Report
on Continuing Business Y-81

Ames, Fisher 1758-1808 . . . . DLB-37

Ames, Mary Clemmer 1831-1884 . . . . DLB-23

Amini, Johari M. 1935- DLB-41

Amis, Kingsley
1922-1995 . . . . DLB-15, 27, 100, 139, Y-96

Amis, Martin 1949- DLB-194

Ammons, A. R. 1926- DLB-5, 165

Amory, Thomas 1691?-1788 . . . . DLB-39

Anania, Michael 1939- DLB-193

Anaya, Rudolfo A. 1937- DLB-82

Ancrene Riwle circa 1200-1225 . . . . . DLB-146

Andersch, Alfred 1914-1980 . . . . DLB-69

Anderson, Alexander 1775-1870 . . . . DLB-188

Anderson, Margaret 1886-1973 . . . . DLB-4, 91

Anderson, Maxwell 1888-1959 . . . . . . DLB-7

Anderson, Patrick 1915-1979 . . . . DLB-68

Anderson, Paul Y. 1893-1938 . . . . DLB-29

Anderson, Poul 1926- DLB-8

Anderson, Robert 1750-1830 . . . . . . DLB-142

Anderson, Robert 1917- DLB-7

Anderson, Sherwood
1876-1941 . . . . DLB-4, 9, 86; DS-1

Andreae, Johann Valentin
1586-1654 . . . . DLB-164

Andreas-Salomé, Lou 1861-1937 . . . . DLB-66

Andres, Stefan 1906-1970 . . . . DLB-69

Andreu, Blanca 1959- DLB-134

Andrewes, Lancelot
1555-1626 . . . . DLB-151, 172

Andrews, Charles M. 1863-1943 . . . . DLB-17

Andrews, Miles Peter ?-1814 . . . . DLB-89

Andrian, Leopold von 1875-1951 . . . . DLB-81

Andrić, Ivo 1892-1975 . . . . DLB-147

Andrieux, Louis (see Aragon, Louis)

Andrus, Silas, and Son DLB-49

Angell, James Burrill 1829-1916 . . . . . DLB-64

Angell, Roger 1920- DLB-171, 185

Angelou, Maya 1928- DLB-38

Anger, Jane flourished 1589 . . . . DLB-136

Angers, Félicité (see Conan, Laure)

Anglo-Norman Literature in the
Development of Middle English
Literature DLB-146

The Anglo-Saxon Chronicle
circa 890-1154 . . . . DLB-146

The "Angry Young Men" DLB-15

Angus and Robertson (UK)
Limited DLB-112

Anhalt, Edward 1914- DLB-26

Anners, Henry F.
[publishing house] DLB-49

Annolied between 1077
and 1081 . . . . DLB-148

Anselm of Canterbury
1033-1109 . . . . DLB-115

Anstey, F. 1856-1934 . . . . DLB-141, 178

Anthony, Michael 1932- DLB-125

Anthony, Piers 1934- DLB-8

Anthony Burgess's *99 Novels*:
An Opinion Poll Y-84

Antin, David 1932- DLB-169

Antin, Mary 1881-1949 . . . . Y-84

Anton Ulrich, Duke of Brunswick-Lüneburg
1633-1714 . . . . DLB-168

Antschel, Paul (see Celan, Paul)

Anyidoho, Kofi 1947- DLB-157

Anzaldúa, Gloria 1942- DLB-122

Anzengruber, Ludwig
1839-1889 . . . . DLB-129

Apess, William 1798-1839 . . . . DLB-175

Apodaca, Rudy S. 1939- DLB-82

Apollonius Rhodius third century B.C.
. . . . DLB-176

Apple, Max 1941- DLB-130

Appleton, D., and Company DLB-49

Appleton-Century-Crofts DLB-46

Applewhite, James 1935- DLB-105

Apple-wood Books DLB-46

Aquin, Hubert 1929-1977 . . . . DLB-53

Aquinas, Thomas 1224 or
1225-1274 . . . . DLB-115

Aragon, Louis 1897-1982 . . . . DLB-72

Aralica, Ivan 1930- DLB-181

Aratus of Soli circa 315 B.C.-circa 239 B.C.
. . . . DLB-176

Arbasino, Alberto 1930- DLB-196

Arbor House Publishing
Company DLB-46

Arbuthnot, John 1667-1735 . . . . . . DLB-101

Arcadia House DLB-46

Arce, Julio G. (see Ulica, Jorge)

Archer, William 1856-1924 . . . . DLB-10

Archilochhus mid seventh century B.C.E.
. . . . DLB-176

The Archpoet circa 1130?-? DLB-148

Archpriest Avvakum (Petrovich)
1620?-1682 . . . . DLB-150

Arden, John 1930- DLB-13

Arden of Faversham DLB-62

Ardis Publishers Y-89

Ardizzone, Edward 1900-1979 . . . . . DLB-160

Arellano, Juan Estevan 1947- DLB-122

The Arena Publishing Company DLB-49

Arena Stage DLB-7

Arenas, Reinaldo 1943-1990 . . . . . . DLB-145

Arensberg, Ann 1937- Y-82

Arguedas, José María 1911-1969 . . . DLB-113

Argueta, Manlio 1936- DLB-145

Arias, Ron 1941- DLB-82

Arishima, Takeo 1878-1923 . . . . . . DLB-180

Aristophanes
circa 446 B.C.-circa 386 B.C. . . . DLB-176

Aristotle 384 B.C.-322 B.C. DLB-176

Ariyoshi, Sawako 1931-1984 . . . . . . DLB-182

Arland, Marcel 1899-1986 . . . . DLB-72

Arlen, Michael
1895-1956 . . . . DLB-36, 77, 162

Armah, Ayi Kwei 1939- DLB-117

Armantrout, Rae 1947- DLB-193

Der arme Hartmann
?-after 1150 . . . . DLB-148

Armed Services Editions DLB-46

Armstrong, Martin Donisthorpe 1882-1974
. . . . DLB-197

Armstrong, Richard 1903- DLB-160

Arndt, Ernst Moritz 1769-1860 . . . . DLB-90

Arnim, Achim von 1781-1831 . . . . . DLB-90

Arnim, Bettina von 1785-1859 . . . . . DLB-90

Arnim, Elizabeth von (Countess Mary Annette
Beauchamp Russell) 1866-1941 . . . DLB-197

Arno Press DLB-46

Arnold, Edwin 1832-1904 . . . . DLB-35

Arnold, Edwin L. 1857-1935 . . . . . . DLB-178

Arnold, Matthew 1822-1888 . . . . . DLB-32, 57

Arnold, Thomas 1795-1842 . . . . . . DLB-55

Arnold, Edward
[publishing house] DLB-112

Arnow, Harriette Simpson
1908-1986 . . . . DLB-6

Arp, Bill (see Smith, Charles Henry)

Arpino, Giovanni 1927-1987 . . . . . . DLB-177

Arreola, Juan José 1918- DLB-113

Arrian circa 89-circa 155 . . . . DLB-176

Arrowsmith, J. W.
[publishing house] DLB-106

The Art and Mystery of Publishing:
Interviews Y-97

Arthur, Timothy Shay
1809-1885 . . . . DLB-3, 42, 79; DS-13

The Arthurian Tradition and Its European
Context DLB-138

Artmann, H. C. 1921- DLB-85

Arvin, Newton 1900-1963 . . . . DLB-103

As I See It, by
Carolyn Cassady DLB-16

Asch, Nathan 1902-1964 . . . . . . DLB-4, 28

Ash, John 1948- DLB-40

Ashbery, John 1927- DLB-5, 165; Y-81

Ashburnham, Bertram Lord
1797-1878 . . . . DLB-184

Ashendene Press DLB-112

Asher, Sandy 1942- Y-83

Ashton, Winifred (see Dane, Clemence)

Asimov, Isaac 1920-1992 . . . . . . DLB-8; Y-92

Askew, Anne circa 1521-1546 . . . . . DLB-136

Asselin, Olivar 1874-1937 . . . . DLB-92

Asturias, Miguel Angel
1899-1974 . . . . DLB-113

Atheneum Publishers DLB-46

Atherton, Gertrude 1857-1948 . . DLB-9, 78, 186

Athlone Press DLB-112

Atkins, Josiah circa 1755-1781 . . . . . DLB-31

Atkins, Russell 1926- DLB-41

The Atlantic Monthly Press DLB-46

Attaway, William 1911-1986 . . . . . . DLB-76

Atwood, Margaret 1939- DLB-53

Aubert, Alvin 1930- DLB-41

Aubert de Gaspé, Phillipe-Ignace-François
1814-1841 . . . . DLB-99

Aubert de Gaspé, Phillipe-Joseph
1786-1871 . . . . DLB-99

Aubin, Napoléon 1812-1890 . . . . . . DLB-99

Aubin, Penelope 1685-circa 1731 . . . DLB-39

Aubrey-Fletcher, Henry Lancelot
(see Wade, Henry)

Auchincloss, Louis 1917- DLB-2; Y-80

Auden, W. H. 1907-1973 . . . . . DLB-10, 20

Audio Art in America: A Personal
Memoir Y-85

Audubon, John Woodhouse
1812-1862 . . . . DLB-183

Auerbach, Berthold 1812-1882 . . . . DLB-133

Auernheimer, Raoul 1876-1948 . . . . DLB-81

Augier, Emile 1820-1889 . . . . DLB-192

Augustine 354-430 . . . . DLB-115

Austen, Jane 1775-1817 . . . . DLB-116

Austin, Alfred 1835-1913 . . . . DLB-35

Austin, Mary 1868-1934 . . . . DLB-9, 78

Austin, William 1778-1841 . . . . DLB-74

Author-Printers, 1476–1599 . . . . . . DLB-167

Author Websites Y-97

The Author's Apology for His Book
(1684), by John Bunyan DLB-39

An Author's Response, by
Ronald Sukenick Y-82

Authors and Newspapers
Association DLB-46

Authors' Publishing Company DLB-49

Avalon Books DLB-46

Avancini, Nicolaus 1611-1686 . . . . . DLB-164

Avendaño, Fausto 1941- DLB-82

Averroëö 1126-1198 . . . . DLB-115

Avery, Gillian 1926- DLB-161

Avicenna 980-1037 . . . . DLB-115

Avison, Margaret 1918- DLB-53

Avon Books DLB-46

Awdry, Wilbert Vere 1911- DLB-160

Awoonor, Kofi 1935- DLB-117

Ayckbourn, Alan 1939- DLB-13

Aymé, Marcel 1902-1967 . . . . DLB-72

Aytoun, Sir Robert 1570-1638 . . . . . DLB-121

Cumulative Index

Aytoun, William Edmondstoune 1813-1865 . . . . DLB-32, 159

B

B. V. (see Thomson, James)

Babbitt, Irving 1865-1933 . . . . DLB-63

Babbitt, Natalie 1932- DLB-52

Babcock, John [publishing house] DLB-49

Babrius circa 150-200 . . . . DLB-176

Baca, Jimmy Santiago 1952- DLB-122

Bache, Benjamin Franklin 1769-1798 . . . . DLB-43

Bachmann, Ingeborg 1926-1973 . . . . . DLB-85

Bacon, Delia 1811-1859 . . . . DLB-1

Bacon, Francis 1561-1626 . . . . DLB-151

Bacon, Roger circa 1214/1220-1292 . . . . DLB-115

Bacon, Sir Nicholas circa 1510-1579 . . . . DLB-132

Bacon, Thomas circa 1700-1768 . . . . . DLB-31

Badger, Richard G., and Company DLB-49

Bage, Robert 1728-1801 . . . . DLB-39

Bagehot, Walter 1826-1877 . . . . DLB-55

Bagley, Desmond 1923-1983 . . . . DLB-87

Bagnold, Enid 1889-1981 . . . DLB-13, 160, 191

Bagryana, Elisaveta 1893-1991 . . . . . DLB-147

Bahr, Hermann 1863-1934 . . . . . DLB-81, 118

Bailey, Alfred Goldsworthy 1905- DLB-68

Bailey, Francis [publishing house] DLB-49

Bailey, H. C. 1878-1961 . . . . DLB-77

Bailey, Jacob 1731-1808 . . . . DLB-99

Bailey, Paul 1937- DLB-14

Bailey, Philip James 1816-1902 . . . . . . DLB-32

Baillargeon, Pierre 1916-1967 . . . . . . DLB-88

Baillie, Hugh 1890-1966 . . . . DLB-29

Baillie, Joanna 1762-1851 . . . . DLB-93

Bailyn, Bernard 1922- DLB-17

Bainbridge, Beryl 1933- DLB-14

Baird, Irene 1901-1981 . . . . DLB-68

Baker, Augustine 1575-1641 . . . . DLB-151

Baker, Carlos 1909-1987 . . . . DLB-103

Baker, David 1954- DLB-120

Baker, Herschel C. 1914-1990 . . . . . . DLB-111

Baker, Houston A., Jr. 1943- DLB-67

Baker, Samuel White 1821-1893 . . . . DLB-166

Baker, Walter H., Company ("Baker's Plays") DLB-49

The Baker and Taylor Company DLB-49

Balaban, John 1943- DLB-120

Bald, Wambly 1902- DLB-4

Balde, Jacob 1604-1668 . . . . DLB-164

Balderston, John 1889-1954 . . . . DLB-26

Baldwin, James 1924-1987 . . . . . . DLB-2, 7, 33; Y-87

Baldwin, Joseph Glover 1815-1864 . . . . DLB-3, 11

Baldwin, Richard and Anne [publishing house] DLB-170

Baldwin, William circa 1515-1563 . . . . DLB-132

Bale, John 1495-1563 . . . . DLB-132

Balestrini, Nanni 1935- DLB-128, 196

Balfour, Arthur James 1848-1930 . . . . DLB-190

Ballantine Books DLB-46

Ballantyne, R. M. 1825-1894 . . . . . . DLB-163

Ballard, J. G. 1930- DLB-14

Ballerini, Luigi 1940- DLB-128

Ballou, Maturin Murray 1820-1895 . . . . DLB-79, 189

Ballou, Robert O. [publishing house] DLB-46

Balzac, Honoré de 1799-1855 . . . . . . DLB-119

Bambara, Toni Cade 1939- DLB-38

Bamford, Samuel 1788-1872 . . . . . . DLB-190

Bancroft, A. L., and Company DLB-49

Bancroft, George 1800-1891 . . . . DLB-1, 30, 59

Bancroft, Hubert Howe 1832-1918 . . . . DLB-47, 140

Bandelier, Adolph F. 1840-1914 . . . . DLB-186

Bangs, John Kendrick 1862-1922 . . . . DLB-11, 79

Banim, John 1798-1842 . . . . DLB-116, 158, 159

Banim, Michael 1796-1874 . . . . . DLB-158, 159

Banks, Iain 1954- DLB-194

Banks, John circa 1653-1706 . . . . DLB-80

Banks, Russell 1940- DLB-130

Bannerman, Helen 1862-1946 . . . . . DLB-141

Bantam Books DLB-46

Banti, Anna 1895-1985 . . . . DLB-177

Banville, John 1945- DLB-14

Baraka, Amiri 1934- DLB-5, 7, 16, 38; DS-8

Barbauld, Anna Laetitia 1743-1825 . . . . . . DLB-107, 109, 142, 158

Barbeau, Marius 1883-1969 . . . . DLB-92

Barber, John Warner 1798-1885 . . . . . DLB-30

Bàrberi Squarotti, Giorgio 1929- DLB-128

Barbey d'Aurevilly, Jules-Amédée 1808-1889 . . . . DLB-119

Barbour, John circa 1316-1395 . . . . . DLB-146

Barbour, Ralph Henry 1870-1944 . . . . DLB-22

Barbusse, Henri 1873-1935 . . . . DLB-65

Barclay, Alexander circa 1475-1552 . . . . DLB-132

Barclay, E. E., and Company DLB-49

Bardeen, C. W. [publishing house] DLB-49

Barham, Richard Harris 1788-1845 . . . . DLB-159

Barich, Bill 1943- DLB-185

Baring, Maurice 1874-1945 . . . . DLB-34

Baring-Gould, Sabine 1834-1924 . . . . DLB-156, 190

Barker, A. L. 1918- DLB-14, 139

Barker, George 1913-1991 . . . . DLB-20

Barker, Harley Granville 1877-1946 . . . . DLB-10

Barker, Howard 1946- DLB-13

Barker, James Nelson 1784-1858 . . . . . DLB-37

Barker, Jane 1652-1727 . . . . . DLB-39, 131

Barker, Lady Mary Anne 1831-1911 . . . . DLB-166

Barker, William circa 1520-after 1576 . . . . DLB-132

Barker, Arthur, Limited DLB-112

Barkov, Ivan Semenovich 1732-1768 . . . . DLB-150

Barks, Coleman 1937- DLB-5

Barlach, Ernst 1870-1938 . . . . . DLB-56, 118

Barlow, Joel 1754-1812 . . . . DLB-37

Barnard, John 1681-1770 . . . . DLB-24

Barne, Kitty (Mary Catherine Barne) 1883-1957 . . . . DLB-160

Barnes, Barnabe 1571-1609 . . . . . . DLB-132

Barnes, Djuna 1892-1982 . . . . . DLB-4, 9, 45

Barnes, Jim 1933- DLB-175

Barnes, Julian 1946- DLB-194; Y-93

Barnes, Margaret Ayer 1886-1967 . . . . . DLB-9

Barnes, Peter 1931- DLB-13

Barnes, William 1801-1886 . . . . DLB-32

Barnes, A. S., and Company DLB-49

Barnes and Noble Books DLB-46

Barnet, Miguel 1940- DLB-145

Barney, Natalie 1876-1972 . . . . DLB-4

Barnfield, Richard 1574-1627 . . . . . DLB-172

Baron, Richard W., Publishing Company DLB-46

Barr, Robert 1850-1912 . . . . DLB-70, 92

Barral, Carlos 1928-1989 . . . . DLB-134

Barrax, Gerald William 1933- DLB-41, 120

Barrès, Maurice 1862-1923 . . . . DLB-123

Barrett, Eaton Stannard
 1786-1820 . . . . DLB-116
Barrie, J. M. 1860-1937 . . . . DLB-10, 141, 156
Barrie and Jenkins DLB-112
Barrio, Raymond 1921- DLB-82
Barrios, Gregg 1945- DLB-122
Barry, Philip 1896-1949 . . . . DLB-7
Barry, Robertine (see Françoise)
Barse and Hopkins DLB-46
Barstow, Stan 1928- DLB-14, 139
Barth, John 1930- DLB-2
Barthelme, Donald
 1931-1989 . . . . DLB-2; Y-80, Y-89
Barthelme, Frederick 1943- Y-85
Bartholomew, Frank 1898-1985 . . . . . DLB-127
Bartlett, John 1820-1905 . . . . DLB-1
Bartol, Cyrus Augustus 1813-1900 . . . . DLB-1
Barton, Bernard 1784-1849 . . . . DLB-96
Barton, Thomas Pennant
 1803-1869 . . . . DLB-140
Bartram, John 1699-1777 . . . . DLB-31
Bartram, William 1739-1823 . . . . DLB-37
Basic Books DLB-46
Basille, Theodore (see Becon, Thomas)
Bass, T. J. 1932- Y-81
Bassani, Giorgio 1916- DLB-128, 177
Basse, William circa 1583-1653 . . . . . DLB-121
Bassett, John Spencer 1867-1928 . . . . . DLB-17
Bassler, Thomas Joseph (see Bass, T. J.)
Bate, Walter Jackson
 1918- DLB-67, 103
Bateman, Christopher
 [publishing house] DLB-170
Bateman, Stephen
 circa 1510-1584 . . . . DLB-136
Bates, H. E. 1905-1974 . . . . . DLB-162, 191
Bates, Katharine Lee 1859-1929 . . . . . DLB-71
Batsford, B. T.
 [publishing house] DLB-106
Battiscombe, Georgina 1905- DLB-155
The Battle of Maldon circa 1000 . . . . DLB-146
Bauer, Bruno 1809-1882 . . . . DLB-133
Bauer, Wolfgang 1941- DLB-124
Baum, L. Frank 1856-1919 . . . . DLB-22
Baum, Vicki 1888-1960 . . . . DLB-85
Baumbach, Jonathan 1933- Y-80
Bausch, Richard 1945- DLB-130
Bawden, Nina 1925- DLB-14, 161
Bax, Clifford 1886-1962 . . . . . . DLB-10, 100
Baxter, Charles 1947- DLB-130
Bayer, Eleanor (see Perry, Eleanor)
Bayer, Konrad 1932-1964 . . . . DLB-85
Baynes, Pauline 1922- DLB-160

Bazin, Hervé 1911- DLB-83
Beach, Sylvia 1887-1962 . . . . . DLB-4; DS-15
Beacon Press DLB-49
Beadle and Adams DLB-49
Beagle, Peter S. 1939- Y-80
Beal, M. F. 1937- Y-81
Beale, Howard K. 1899-1959 . . . . DLB-17
Beard, Charles A. 1874-1948 . . . . DLB-17
A Beat Chronology: The First Twenty-five
 Years, 1944-1969 . . . . DLB-16
Beattie, Ann 1947- Y-82
Beattie, James 1735-1803 . . . . DLB-109
Beauchemin, Nérée 1850-1931 . . . . . . DLB-92
Beauchemin, Yves 1941- DLB-60
Beaugrand, Honoré 1848-1906 . . . . . . DLB-99
Beaulieu, Victor-Lévy 1945- DLB-53
Beaumont, Francis circa 1584-1616
 and Fletcher, John 1579-1625 . . . . DLB-58
Beaumont, Sir John 1583?-1627 . . . . DLB-121
Beaumont, Joseph 1616–1699 . . . . . DLB-126
Beauvoir, Simone de
 1908-1986 . . . . DLB-72; Y-86
Becher, Ulrich 1910- DLB-69
Becker, Carl 1873-1945 . . . . DLB-17
Becker, Jurek 1937- DLB-75
Becker, Jurgen 1932- DLB-75
Beckett, Samuel
 1906-1989 . . . . DLB-13, 15; Y-90
Beckford, William 1760-1844 . . . . . . DLB-39
Beckham, Barry 1944- DLB-33
Becon, Thomas circa 1512-1567 . . . . DLB-136
Becque, Henry 1837-1899 . . . . DLB-192
Bećković, Matija 1939- DLB-181
Beddoes, Thomas 1760-1808 . . . . . . DLB-158
Beddoes, Thomas Lovell
 1803-1849 . . . . DLB-96
Bede circa 673-735 . . . . DLB-146
Beecher, Catharine Esther
 1800-1878 . . . . DLB-1
Beecher, Henry Ward
 1813-1887 . . . . DLB-3, 43
Beer, George L. 1872-1920 . . . . DLB-47
Beer, Johann 1655-1700 . . . . DLB-168
Beer, Patricia 1919- DLB-40
Beerbohm, Max 1872-1956 . . . . DLB-34, 100
Beer-Hofmann, Richard
 1866-1945 . . . . DLB-81
Beers, Henry A. 1847-1926 . . . . DLB-71
Beeton, S. O.
 [publishing house] DLB-106
Bégon, Elisabeth 1696-1755 . . . . DLB-99
Behan, Brendan 1923-1964 . . . . DLB-13

Behn, Aphra
 1640?-1689 . . . . DLB-39, 80, 131
Behn, Harry 1898-1973 . . . . DLB-61
Behrman, S. N. 1893-1973 . . . . . . DLB-7, 44
Belaney, Archibald Stansfeld (see Grey Owl)
Belasco, David 1853-1931 . . . . DLB-7
Belford, Clarke and Company DLB-49
Belitt, Ben 1911- DLB-5
Belknap, Jeremy 1744-1798 . . . . . DLB-30, 37
Bell, Adrian 1901-1980 . . . . DLB-191
Bell, Clive 1881-1964 . . . . DS-10
Bell, Gertrude Margaret Lowthian
 1868-1926 . . . . DLB-174
Bell, James Madison 1826-1902 . . . . . DLB-50
Bell, Marvin 1937- DLB-5
Bell, Millicent 1919- DLB-111
Bell, Quentin 1910- DLB-155
Bell, Vanessa 1879-1961 . . . . DS-10
Bell, George, and Sons DLB-106
Bell, Robert [publishing house] DLB-49
Bellamy, Edward 1850-1898 . . . . DLB-12
Bellamy, John [publishing house] DLB-170
Bellamy, Joseph 1719-1790 . . . . DLB-31
Bellezza, Dario 1944- DLB-128
La Belle Assemblée 1806-1837 . . . . . . DLB-110
Belloc, Hilaire
 1870-1953 . . . . . DLB-19, 100, 141, 174
Bellonci, Maria 1902-1986 . . . . DLB-196
Bellow, Saul
 1915- DLB-2, 28; Y-82; DS-3
Belmont Productions DLB-46
Bemelmans, Ludwig 1898-1962 . . . . . DLB-22
Bemis, Samuel Flagg 1891-1973 . . . . . DLB-17
Bemrose, William
 [publishing house] DLB-106
Benchley, Robert 1889-1945 . . . . DLB-11
Benedetti, Mario 1920- DLB-113
Benedictus, David 1938- DLB-14
Benedikt, Michael 1935- DLB-5
Benét, Stephen Vincent
 1898-1943 . . . . DLB-4, 48, 102
Benét, William Rose 1886-1950 . . . . . DLB-45
Benford, Gregory 1941- Y-82
Benjamin, Park 1809-1864 . . . . DLB-3, 59, 73
Benjamin, S. G. W. 1837-1914 . . . . . DLB-189
Benlowes, Edward 1602-1676 . . . . . DLB-126
Benn, Gottfried 1886-1956 . . . . DLB-56
Benn Brothers Limited DLB-106
Bennett, Arnold
 1867-1931 . . . . DLB-10, 34, 98, 135
Bennett, Charles 1899- DLB-44
Bennett, Gwendolyn 1902- DLB-51
Bennett, Hal 1930- DLB-33

Bennett, James Gordon 1795-1872 .... DLB-43
Bennett, James Gordon, Jr.
  1841-1918 .... DLB-23
Bennett, John 1865-1956 .... DLB-42
Bennett, Louise 1919- DLB-117
Benni, Stefano 1947- DLB-196
Benoit, Jacques 1941- DLB-60
Benson, A. C. 1862-1925 .... DLB-98
Benson, E. F. 1867-1940 ..... DLB-135, 153
Benson, Jackson J. 1930- DLB-111
Benson, Robert Hugh
  1871-1914 .... DLB-153
Benson, Stella 1892-1933 ...... DLB-36, 162
Bent, James Theodore 1852-1897 .... DLB-174
Bent, Mabel Virginia Anna ?-? DLB-174
Bentham, Jeremy
  1748-1832 .... DLB-107, 158
Bentley, E. C. 1875-1956 .... DLB-70
Bentley, Phyllis 1894-1977 .... DLB-191
Bentley, Richard
  [publishing house] DLB-106
Benton, Robert 1932- and Newman,
  David 1937- DLB-44
Benziger Brothers DLB-49
Beowulf circa 900-1000
  or 790-825 .... DLB-146
Beresford, Anne 1929- DLB-40
Beresford, John Davys
  1873-1947 .... DLB-162, 178, 197
Beresford-Howe, Constance
  1922- DLB-88
Berford, R. G., Company DLB-49
Berg, Stephen 1934- DLB-5
Bergengruen, Werner 1892-1964 ..... DLB-56
Berger, John 1926- DLB-14
Berger, Meyer 1898-1959 .... DLB-29
Berger, Thomas 1924- DLB-2; Y-80
Berkeley, Anthony 1893-1971 ..... DLB-77
Berkeley, George 1685-1753 .... DLB-31, 101
The Berkley Publishing
  Corporation DLB-46
Berlin, Lucia 1936- DLB-130
Bernal, Vicente J. 1888-1915 ...... DLB-82
Bernanos, Georges 1888-1948 ..... DLB-72
Bernard, Harry 1898-1979 .... DLB-92
Bernard, John 1756-1828 .... DLB-37
Bernard of Chartres
  circa 1060-1124? DLB-115
Bernari, Carlo 1909-1992 .... DLB-177
Bernhard, Thomas
  1931-1989 .... DLB-85, 124
Bernstein, Charles 1950- DLB-169
Berriault, Gina 1926- DLB-130
Berrigan, Daniel 1921- DLB-5

Berrigan, Ted 1934-1983 .... DLB-5, 169
Berry, Wendell 1934- DLB-5, 6
Berryman, John 1914-1972 ...... DLB-48
Bersianik, Louky 1930- DLB-60
Berthelet, Thomas
  [publishing house] DLB-170
Berto, Giuseppe 1914-1978 ...... DLB-177
Bertolucci, Attilio 1911- DLB-128
Berton, Pierre 1920- DLB-68
Besant, Sir Walter 1836-1901 ... DLB-135, 190
Bessette, Gerard 1920- DLB-53
Bessie, Alvah 1904-1985 .... DLB-26
Bester, Alfred 1913-1987 .... DLB-8
The Bestseller Lists: An Assessment Y-84
Betham-Edwards, Matilda Barbara (see Edwards,
  Matilda Barbara Betham-)
Betjeman, John 1906-1984 ..... DLB-20; Y-84
Betocchi, Carlo 1899-1986 ...... DLB-128
Bettarini, Mariella 1942- DLB-128
Betts, Doris 1932- Y-82
Beveridge, Albert J. 1862-1927 ..... DLB-17
Beverley, Robert
  circa 1673-1722 .... DLB-24, 30
Bevilacqua, Alberto 1934- DLB-196
Beyle, Marie-Henri (see Stendhal)
Bianco, Margery Williams
  1881-1944 .... DLB-160
Bibaud, Adèle 1854-1941 .... DLB-92
Bibaud, Michel 1782-1857 .... DLB-99
Bibliographical and Textual Scholarship
  Since World War II Y-89
The Bicentennial of James Fenimore
  Cooper: An International
  Celebration Y-89
Bichsel, Peter 1935- DLB-75
Bickerstaff, Isaac John
  1733-circa 1808 .... DLB-89
Biddle, Drexel [publishing house] DLB-49
Bidermann, Jacob
  1577 or 1578-1639 .... DLB-164
Bidwell, Walter Hilliard
  1798-1881 .... DLB-79
Bienek, Horst 1930- DLB-75
Bierbaum, Otto Julius 1865-1910 .... DLB-66
Bierce, Ambrose
  1842-1914? ... DLB-11, 12, 23, 71, 74, 186
Bigelow, William F. 1879-1966 ..... DLB-91
Biggle, Lloyd, Jr. 1923- DLB-8
Bigiaretti, Libero 1905-1993 ...... DLB-177
Bigland, Eileen 1898-1970 .... DLB-195
Biglow, Hosea (see Lowell, James Russell)
Bigongiari, Piero 1914- DLB-128
Billinger, Richard 1890-1965 ..... DLB-124
Billings, Hammatt 1818-1874 ..... DLB-188

Billings, John Shaw 1898-1975 ..... DLB-137
Billings, Josh (see Shaw, Henry Wheeler)
Binding, Rudolf G. 1867-1938 ..... DLB-66
Bingham, Caleb 1757-1817 .... DLB-42
Bingham, George Barry
  1906-1988 .... DLB-127
Bingley, William
  [publishing house] DLB-154
Binyon, Laurence 1869-1943 ...... DLB-19
Biographia Brittanica DLB-142
Biographical Documents I Y-84
Biographical Documents II Y-85
Bioren, John [publishing house] DLB-49
Bioy Casares, Adolfo 1914- DLB-113
Bird, Isabella Lucy 1831-1904 ..... DLB-166
Bird, William 1888-1963 .... DLB-4; DS-15
Birken, Sigmund von 1626-1681 .... DLB-164
Birney, Earle 1904- DLB-88
Birrell, Augustine 1850-1933 ...... DLB-98
Bisher, Furman 1918- DLB-171
Bishop, Elizabeth 1911-1979 ..... DLB-5, 169
Bishop, John Peale 1892-1944 ... DLB-4, 9, 45
Bismarck, Otto von 1815-1898 ..... DLB-129
Bisset, Robert 1759-1805 .... DLB-142
Bissett, Bill 1939- DLB-53
Bitzius, Albert (see Gotthelf, Jeremias)
Black, David (D. M.) 1941- DLB-40
Black, Winifred 1863-1936 .... DLB-25
Black, Walter J.
  [publishing house] DLB-46
The Black Aesthetic: Background DS-8
The Black Arts Movement, by
  Larry Neal DLB-38
Black Theaters and Theater Organizations in
  America, 1961-1982:
  A Research List DLB-38
Black Theatre: A Forum
  [excerpts] DLB-38
Blackamore, Arthur 1679-? DLB-24, 39
Blackburn, Alexander L. 1929- Y-85
Blackburn, Paul 1926-1971 .... DLB-16; Y-81
Blackburn, Thomas 1916-1977 ..... DLB-27
Blackmore, R. D. 1825-1900 ...... DLB-18
Blackmore, Sir Richard
  1654-1729 .... DLB-131
Blackmur, R. P. 1904-1965 .... DLB-63
Blackwell, Basil, Publisher DLB-106
Blackwood, Algernon Henry
  1869-1951 .... DLB-153, 156, 178
Blackwood, Caroline 1931- DLB-14
Blackwood, William, and
  Sons, Ltd. DLB-154
Blackwood's Edinburgh Magazine
  1817-1980 .... DLB-110

Blades, William 1824-1890 . . . . . . DLB-184

Blair, Eric Arthur (see Orwell, George)

Blair, Francis Preston 1791-1876 . . . . . DLB-43

Blair, James circa 1655-1743 . . . . DLB-24

Blair, John Durburrow 1759-1823 . . . . DLB-37

Blais, Marie-Claire 1939- DLB-53

Blaise, Clark 1940- DLB-53

Blake, George 1893-1961 . . . . DLB-191

Blake, Nicholas 1904-1972 . . . . DLB-77
(see Day Lewis, C.)

Blake, William
1757-1827 . . . . DLB-93, 154, 163

The Blakiston Company DLB-49

Blanchot, Maurice 1907- DLB-72

Blanckenburg, Christian Friedrich von
1744-1796 . . . . DLB-94

Blaser, Robin 1925- DLB-165

Bledsoe, Albert Taylor
1809-1877 . . . . DLB-3, 79

Blelock and Company DLB-49

Blennerhassett, Margaret Agnew
1773-1842 . . . . DLB-99

Bles, Geoffrey
[publishing house] DLB-112

Blessington, Marguerite, Countess of
1789-1849 . . . . DLB-166

The Blickling Homilies
circa 971 . . . . DLB-146

Blish, James 1921-1975 . . . . DLB-8

Bliss, E., and E. White
[publishing house] DLB-49

Bliven, Bruce 1889-1977 . . . . DLB-137

Bloch, Robert 1917-1994 . . . . DLB-44

Block, Rudolph (see Lessing, Bruno)

Blondal, Patricia 1926-1959 . . . . DLB-88

Bloom, Harold 1930- DLB-67

Bloomer, Amelia 1818-1894 . . . . DLB-79

Bloomfield, Robert 1766-1823 . . . . . . DLB-93

Bloomsbury Group DS-10

Blotner, Joseph 1923- DLB-111

Bloy, Léon 1846-1917 . . . . DLB-123

Blume, Judy 1938- DLB-52

Blunck, Hans Friedrich 1888-1961 . . . . DLB-66

Blunden, Edmund
1896-1974 . . . . DLB-20, 100, 155

Blunt, Lady Anne Isabella Noel
1837-1917 . . . . DLB-174

Blunt, Wilfrid Scawen
1840-1922 . . . . DLB-19, 174

Bly, Nellie (see Cochrane, Elizabeth)

Bly, Robert 1926- DLB-5

Blyton, Enid 1897-1968 . . . . DLB-160

Boaden, James 1762-1839 . . . . DLB-89

Boas, Frederick S. 1862-1957 . . . . . . DLB-149

The Bobbs-Merrill Archive at the
Lilly Library, Indiana University Y-90

The Bobbs-Merrill Company DLB-46

Bobrov, Semen Sergeevich
1763?-1810 . . . . DLB-150

Bobrowski, Johannes 1917-1965 . . . . . DLB-75

Bodenheim, Maxwell 1892-1954 . . . DLB-9, 45

Bodenstedt, Friedrich von
1819-1892 . . . . DLB-129

Bodini, Vittorio 1914-1970 . . . . DLB-128

Bodkin, M. McDonnell
1850-1933 . . . . DLB-70

Bodley Head DLB-112

Bodmer, Johann Jakob 1698-1783 . . . . DLB-97

Bodmershof, Imma von 1895-1982 . . . . DLB-85

Bodsworth, Fred 1918- DLB-68

Boehm, Sydney 1908- DLB-44

Boer, Charles 1939- DLB-5

Boethius circa 480-circa 524 . . . . DLB-115

Boethius of Dacia circa 1240-? DLB-115

Bogan, Louise 1897-1970 . . . . . . DLB-45, 169

Bogarde, Dirk 1921- DLB-14

Bogdanovich, Ippolit Fedorovich
circa 1743-1803 . . . . DLB-150

Bogue, David [publishing house] DLB-106

Böhme, Jakob 1575-1624 . . . . DLB-164

Bohn, H. G. [publishing house] DLB-106

Bohse, August 1661-1742 . . . . DLB-168

Boie, Heinrich Christian
1744-1806 . . . . DLB-94

Bok, Edward W. 1863-1930 . . . DLB-91; DS-16

Boland, Eavan 1944- DLB-40

Bolingbroke, Henry St. John, Viscount
1678-1751 . . . . DLB-101

Böll, Heinrich 1917-1985 . . . . . . DLB-69; Y-85

Bolling, Robert 1738-1775 . . . . DLB-31

Bolotov, Andrei Timofeevich
1738-1833 . . . . DLB-150

Bolt, Carol 1941- DLB-60

Bolt, Robert 1924- DLB-13

Bolton, Herbert E. 1870-1953 . . . . . . DLB-17

Bonaventura DLB-90

Bonaventure circa 1217-1274 . . . . . . DLB-115

Bonaviri, Giuseppe 1924- DLB-177

Bond, Edward 1934- DLB-13

Bond, Michael 1926- DLB-161

Boni, Albert and Charles
[publishing house] DLB-46

Boni and Liveright DLB-46

Bonner, Paul Hyde 1893-1968 . . . . . . DS-17

Robert Bonner's Sons DLB-49

Bonnin, Gertrude Simmons (see Zitkala-Ša)

Bonsanti, Alessandro 1904-1984 . . . . . DLB-177

Bontemps, Arna 1902-1973 . . . . . DLB-48, 51

The Book Arts Press at the University
of Virginia Y-96

The Book League of America DLB-46

Book Reviewing in America: I Y-87

Book Reviewing in America: II Y-88

Book Reviewing in America: III Y-89

Book Reviewing in America: IV Y-90

Book Reviewing in America: V Y-91

Book Reviewing in America: VI Y-92

Book Reviewing in America: VII Y-93

Book Reviewing in America: VIII Y-94

Book Reviewing in America and the
Literary Scene Y-95

Book Reviewing and the
Literary Scene Y-96, Y-97

Book Supply Company DLB-49

The Book Trade History Group Y-93

The Booker Prize Y-96

The Booker Prize
Address by Anthony Thwaite,
Chairman of the Booker Prize Judges
Comments from Former Booker
Prize Winners Y-86

Boorde, Andrew circa 1490-1549 . . . . DLB-136

Boorstin, Daniel J. 1914- DLB-17

Booth, Mary L. 1831-1889 . . . . DLB-79

Booth, Franklin 1874-1948 . . . . DLB-188

Booth, Philip 1925- Y-82

Booth, Wayne C. 1921- DLB-67

Booth, William 1829-1912 . . . . DLB-190

Borchardt, Rudolf 1877-1945 . . . . . . DLB-66

Borchert, Wolfgang
1921-1947 . . . . DLB-69, 124

Borel, Pétrus 1809-1859 . . . . DLB-119

Borges, Jorge Luis
1899-1986 . . . . DLB-113; Y-86

Börne, Ludwig 1786-1837 . . . . DLB-90

Borrow, George
1803-1881 . . . . DLB-21, 55, 166

Bosch, Juan 1909- DLB-145

Bosco, Henri 1888-1976 . . . . DLB-72

Bosco, Monique 1927- DLB-53

Boston, Lucy M. 1892-1990 . . . . DLB-161

Boswell, James 1740-1795 . . . . . DLB-104, 142

Botev, Khristo 1847-1876 . . . . DLB-147

Bote, Hermann
circa 1460-circa 1520 . . . . DLB-179

Botta, Anne C. Lynch 1815-1891 . . . . . DLB-3

Bottome, Phyllis 1882-1963 . . . . DLB-197

Bottomley, Gordon 1874-1948 . . . . . . DLB-10

Bottoms, David 1949- DLB-120; Y-83

Bottrall, Ronald 1906- DLB-20

Bouchardy, Joseph 1810-1870 . . . . . . DLB-192

Boucher, Anthony 1911-1968 . . . . DLB-8
Boucher, Jonathan 1738-1804. . . . . . DLB-31
Boucher de Boucherville, George
   1814-1894 . . . . DLB-99
Boudreau, Daniel (see Coste, Donat)
Bourassa, Napoléon 1827-1916. . . . . . DLB-99
Bourget, Paul 1852-1935. . . . . DLB-123
Bourinot, John George 1837-1902 . . . . DLB-99
Bourjaily, Vance 1922- DLB-2, 143
Bourne, Edward Gaylord
   1860-1908 . . . . DLB-47
Bourne, Randolph 1886-1918. . . . . . DLB-63
Bousoño, Carlos 1923- DLB-108
Bousquet, Joë 1897-1950 . . . . DLB-72
Bova, Ben 1932- Y-81
Bovard, Oliver K. 1872-1945. . . . . . DLB-25
Bove, Emmanuel 1898-1945 . . . . DLB-72
Bowen, Elizabeth 1899-1973 . . . DLB-15, 162
Bowen, Francis 1811-1890. . . . . . DLB-1, 59
Bowen, John 1924- DLB-13
Bowen, Marjorie 1886-1952 . . . . . . DLB-153
Bowen-Merrill Company DLB-49
Bowering, George 1935- DLB-53
Bowers, Claude G. 1878-1958 . . . . . DLB-17
Bowers, Edgar 1924- DLB-5
Bowers, Fredson Thayer
   1905-1991 . . . . DLB-140; Y-91
Bowles, Paul 1910- DLB-5, 6
Bowles, Samuel III 1826-1878 . . . . . DLB-43
Bowles, William Lisles 1762-1850 . . . . DLB-93
Bowman, Louise Morey
   1882-1944 . . . . DLB-68
Boyd, James 1888-1944 . . . . . . DLB-9; DS-16
Boyd, John 1919- DLB-8
Boyd, Thomas 1898-1935 . . . . . DLB-9; DS-16
Boyesen, Hjalmar Hjorth
   1848-1895. . . . . DLB-12, 71; DS-13
Boyle, Kay
   1902-1992 . . . . . DLB-4, 9, 48, 86; Y-93
Boyle, Roger, Earl of Orrery
   1621-1679 . . . . DLB-80
Boyle, T. Coraghessan 1948- Y-86
Božić, Mirko 1919- DLB-181
Brackenbury, Alison 1953- DLB-40
Brackenridge, Hugh Henry
   1748-1816. . . . . DLB-11, 37
Brackett, Charles 1892-1969 . . . . . . DLB-26
Brackett, Leigh 1915-1978 . . . . . . DLB-8, 26
Bradburn, John
   [publishing house]. DLB-49
Bradbury, Malcolm 1932- DLB-14
Bradbury, Ray 1920- DLB-2, 8
Bradbury and Evans. DLB-106

Braddon, Mary Elizabeth
   1835-1915 . . . . DLB-18, 70, 156
Bradford, Andrew 1686-1742 . . . . DLB-43, 73
Bradford, Gamaliel 1863-1932 . . . . . . DLB-17
Bradford, John 1749-1830. . . . . DLB-43
Bradford, Roark 1896-1948. . . . . . . DLB-86
Bradford, William 1590-1657 . . . . DLB-24, 30
Bradford, William III
   1719-1791. . . . . DLB-43, 73
Bradlaugh, Charles 1833-1891 . . . . . DLB-57
Bradley, David 1950- DLB-33
Bradley, Marion Zimmer 1930- DLB-8
Bradley, William Aspenwall
   1878-1939. . . . . DLB-4
Bradley, Ira, and Company DLB-49
Bradley, J. W., and Company. DLB-49
Bradshaw, Henry 1831-1886 . . . . . . DLB-184
Bradstreet, Anne
   1612 or 1613-1672 . . . . DLB-24
Bradwardine, Thomas circa
   1295-1349 . . . . DLB-115
Brady, Frank 1924-1986. . . . . DLB-111
Brady, Frederic A.
   [publishing house]. DLB-49
Bragg, Melvyn 1939- DLB-14
Brainard, Charles H.
   [publishing house]. DLB-49
Braine, John 1922-1986 . . . . . DLB-15; Y-86
Braithwait, Richard 1588-1673 . . . . . DLB-151
Braithwaite, William Stanley
   1878-1962. . . . . DLB-50, 54
Braker, Ulrich 1735-1798. . . . . DLB-94
Bramah, Ernest 1868-1942 . . . . DLB-70
Branagan, Thomas 1774-1843 . . . . . DLB-37
Branch, William Blackwell
   1927- DLB-76
Branden Press DLB-46
Brant, Sebastian 1457-1521 . . . . . . DLB-179
Brassey, Lady Annie (Allnutt)
   1839-1887 . . . . DLB-166
Brathwaite, Edward Kamau
   1930- DLB-125
Brault, Jacques 1933- DLB-53
Braun, Volker 1939- DLB-75
Brautigan, Richard
   1935-1984 . . . . . . DLB-2, 5; Y-80, Y-84
Braxton, Joanne M. 1950- DLB-41
Bray, Anne Eliza 1790-1883. . . . . . DLB-116
Bray, Thomas 1656-1730 . . . . DLB-24
Braziller, George
   [publishing house]. DLB-46
The Bread Loaf Writers'
   Conference 1983 . . . . Y-84
The Break-Up of the Novel (1922),
   by John Middleton Murry. DLB-36

Breasted, James Henry 1865-1935 . . . . DLB-47
Brecht, Bertolt 1898-1956 . . . . . . DLB-56, 124
Bredel, Willi 1901-1964. . . . . DLB-56
Breitinger, Johann Jakob
   1701-1776 . . . . DLB-97
Bremser, Bonnie 1939- DLB-16
Bremser, Ray 1934- DLB-16
Brentano, Bernard von
   1901-1964 . . . . DLB-56
Brentano, Clemens 1778-1842 . . . . . DLB-90
Brentano's DLB-49
Brenton, Howard 1942- DLB-13
Breslin, Jimmy 1929- DLB-185
Breton, André 1896-1966. . . . . DLB-65
Breton, Nicholas
   circa 1555-circa 1626 . . . . DLB-136
The Breton Lays
   1300-early fifteenth century DLB-146
Brewer, Luther A. 1858-1933 . . . . . DLB-187
Brewer, Warren and Putnam DLB-46
Brewster, Elizabeth 1922- DLB-60
Bridge, Ann (Lady Mary Dolling Sanders
   O'Malley) 1889-1974 . . . . DLB-191
Bridge, Horatio 1806-1893. . . . . . . DLB-183
Bridgers, Sue Ellen 1942- DLB-52
Bridges, Robert 1844-1930 . . . . . DLB-19, 98
Bridie, James 1888-1951. . . . . DLB-10
Brieux, Eugene 1858-1932 . . . . DLB-192
Bright, Mary Chavelita Dunne
   (see Egerton, George)
Brimmer, B. J., Company DLB-46
Brines, Francisco 1932- DLB-134
Brinley, George, Jr. 1817-1875 . . . . . DLB-140
Brinnin, John Malcolm 1916- DLB-48
Brisbane, Albert 1809-1890. . . . . DLB-3
Brisbane, Arthur 1864-1936. . . . . . . DLB-25
British Academy DLB-112
The British Library and the Regular
   Readers' Group Y-91
The British Critic 1793-1843. . . . . . . DLB-110
*The British Review and London
   Critical Journal* 1811-1825 . . . . . DLB-110
Brito, Aristeo 1942- DLB-122
Brittain, Vera 1893-1970. . . . . DLB-191
Broadway Publishing Company DLB-46
Broch, Hermann 1886-1951. . . . . DLB-85, 124
Brochu, André 1942- DLB-53
Brock, Edwin 1927- DLB-40
Brockes, Barthold Heinrich
   1680-1747 . . . . DLB-168
Brod, Max 1884-1968. . . . . DLB-81
Brodber, Erna 1940- DLB-157
Brodhead, John R. 1814-1873 . . . . . DLB-30

Brodkey, Harold 1930- DLB-130
Brodsky, Joseph 1940-1996. . . . . Y-87
Broeg, Bob 1918- DLB-171
Brome, Richard circa 1590-1652 . . . . . DLB-58
Brome, Vincent 1910- DLB-155
Bromfield, Louis 1896-1956 . . . . DLB-4, 9, 86
Bromige, David 1933- DLB-193
Broner, E. M. 1930- DLB-28
Bronk, William 1918- DLB-165
Bronnen, Arnolt 1895-1959 . . . . DLB-124
Brontë, Anne 1820-1849 . . . . DLB-21
Brontë, Charlotte 1816-1855 . . . . DLB-21, 159
Brontë, Emily 1818-1848 . . . . DLB-21, 32
Brooke, Frances 1724-1789 . . . . . . DLB-39, 99
Brooke, Henry 1703?-1783 . . . . DLB-39
Brooke, L. Leslie 1862-1940 . . . . DLB-141
Brooke, Margaret, Ranee of Sarawak
   1849-1936 . . . . DLB-174
Brooke, Rupert 1887-1915 . . . . DLB-19
Brooker, Bertram 1888-1955 . . . . . . DLB-88
Brooke-Rose, Christine 1926- DLB-14
Brookner, Anita 1928- DLB-194; Y-87
Brooks, Charles Timothy
   1813-1883. . . . . DLB-1
Brooks, Cleanth 1906-1994 . . . DLB-63; Y-94
Brooks, Gwendolyn
   1917- DLB-5, 76, 165
Brooks, Jeremy 1926- DLB-14
Brooks, Mel 1926- DLB-26
Brooks, Noah 1830-1903 . . . . . DLB-42; DS-13
Brooks, Richard 1912-1992 . . . . DLB-44
Brooks, Van Wyck
   1886-1963 . . . . DLB-45, 63, 103
Brophy, Brigid 1929- DLB-14
Brophy, John 1899-1965 . . . . DLB-191
Brossard, Chandler 1922-1993 . . . . . . DLB-16
Brossard, Nicole 1943- DLB-53
Broster, Dorothy Kathleen
   1877-1950 . . . . DLB-160
Brother Antoninus (see Everson, William)
Brotherton, Lord 1856-1930 . . . . . . DLB-184
Brougham and Vaux, Henry Peter
Brougham, Baron
   1778-1868. . . . . DLB-110, 158
Brougham, John 1810-1880 . . . . DLB-11
Broughton, James 1913- DLB-5
Broughton, Rhoda 1840-1920 . . . . . . DLB-18
Broun, Heywood 1888-1939 . . . . DLB-29, 171
Brown, Alice 1856-1948 . . . . DLB-78
Brown, Bob 1886-1959 . . . . DLB-4, 45
Brown, Cecil 1943- DLB-33
Brown, Charles Brockden
   1771-1810. . . . . DLB-37, 59, 73

Brown, Christy 1932-1981 . . . . DLB-14
Brown, Dee 1908- Y-80
Brown, Frank London 1927-1962 . . . . DLB-76
Brown, Fredric 1906-1972 . . . . DLB-8
Brown, George Mackay
   1921- DLB-14, 27, 139
Brown, Harry 1917-1986 . . . . DLB-26
Brown, Marcia 1918- DLB-61
Brown, Margaret Wise
   1910-1952 . . . . DLB-22
Brown, Morna Doris (see Ferrars, Elizabeth)
Brown, Oliver Madox
   1855-1874 . . . . DLB-21
Brown, Sterling
   1901-1989 . . . . DLB-48, 51, 63
Brown, T. E. 1830-1897 . . . . DLB-35
Brown, William Hill 1765-1793 . . . . . DLB-37
Brown, William Wells
   1814-1884 . . . . DLB-3, 50, 183
Browne, Charles Farrar
   1834-1867 . . . . DLB-11
Browne, Francis Fisher
   1843-1913 . . . . DLB-79
Browne, Michael Dennis
   1940- DLB-40
Browne, Sir Thomas 1605-1682 . . . . DLB-151
Browne, William, of Tavistock
   1590-1645 . . . . DLB-121
Browne, Wynyard 1911-1964 . . . . . . DLB-13
Browne and Nolan DLB-106
Brownell, W. C. 1851-1928 . . . . DLB-71
Browning, Elizabeth Barrett
   1806-1861 . . . . DLB-32
Browning, Robert
   1812-1889 . . . . DLB-32, 163
Brownjohn, Allan 1931- DLB-40
Brownson, Orestes Augustus
   1803-1876 . . . . DLB-1, 59, 73
Bruccoli, Matthew J. 1931- DLB-103
Bruce, Charles 1906-1971 . . . . DLB-68
Bruce, Leo 1903-1979 . . . . DLB-77
Bruce, Philip Alexander
   1856-1933 . . . . DLB-47
Bruce Humphries
   [publishing house] DLB-46
Bruce-Novoa, Juan 1944- DLB-82
Bruckman, Clyde 1894-1955 . . . . . . DLB-26
Bruckner, Ferdinand 1891-1958 . . . . DLB-118
Brundage, John Herbert (see Herbert, John)
Brutus, Dennis 1924- DLB-117
Bryan, C. D. B. 1936- DLB-185
Bryant, Arthur 1899-1985 . . . . DLB-149
Bryant, William Cullen
   1794-1878 . . . . DLB-3, 43, 59, 189

Bryce Echenique, Alfredo
   1939- DLB-145
Bryce, James 1838-1922 . . . . DLB-166, 190
Brydges, Sir Samuel Egerton
   1762-1837 . . . . DLB-107
Bryskett, Lodowick 1546?-1612 . . . . . DLB-167
Buchan, John 1875-1940 . . . DLB-34, 70, 156
Buchanan, George 1506-1582 . . . . . DLB-132
Buchanan, Robert 1841-1901 . . . . DLB-18, 35
Buchman, Sidney 1902-1975 . . . . . . DLB-26
Buchner, Augustus 1591-1661 . . . . . . DLB-164
Büchner, Georg 1813-1837 . . . . DLB-133
Bucholtz, Andreas Heinrich
   1607-1671 . . . . DLB-168
Buck, Pearl S. 1892-1973 . . . . . . DLB-9, 102
Bucke, Charles 1781-1846 . . . . DLB-110
Bucke, Richard Maurice
   1837-1902 . . . . DLB-99
Buckingham, Joseph Tinker 1779-1861 and
   Buckingham, Edwin
   1810-1833 . . . . DLB-73
Buckler, Ernest 1908-1984 . . . . DLB-68
Buckley, William F., Jr.
   1925- DLB-137; Y-80
Buckminster, Joseph Stevens
   1784-1812 . . . . DLB-37
Buckner, Robert 1906- DLB-26
Budd, Thomas ?-1698 . . . . DLB-24
Budrys, A. J. 1931- DLB-8
Buechner, Frederick 1926- Y-80
Buell, John 1927- DLB-53
Bufalino, Gesualdo 1920-1996 . . . . . DLB-196
Buffum, Job [publishing house] DLB-49
Bugnet, Georges 1879-1981 . . . . . . DLB-92
Buies, Arthur 1840-1901 . . . . DLB-99
Building the New British Library
   at St Pancras Y-94
Bukowski, Charles
   1920-1994 . . . . DLB-5, 130, 169
Bulatović, Miodrag 1930-1991 . . . . . DLB-181
Bulger, Bozeman 1877-1932 . . . . . . DLB-171
Bullein, William
   between 1520 and 1530-1576 . . . . DLB-167
Bullins, Ed 1935- DLB-7, 38
Bulwer-Lytton, Edward (also Edward Bulwer)
   1803-1873 . . . . DLB-21
Bumpus, Jerry 1937- Y-81
Bunce and Brother DLB-49
Bunner, H. C. 1855-1896 . . . . . . DLB-78, 79
Bunting, Basil 1900-1985 . . . . DLB-20
Buntline, Ned (Edward Zane Carroll Judson)
   1821-1886 . . . . DLB-186
Bunyan, John 1628-1688 . . . . DLB-39
Burch, Robert 1925- DLB-52

Burciaga, José Antonio 1940- DLB-82

Bürger, Gottfried August
1747-1794 . . . . DLB-94

Burgess, Anthony 1917-1993 . . . . DLB-14, 194

Burgess, Gelett 1866-1951 . . . . DLB-11

Burgess, John W. 1844-1931 . . . . DLB-47

Burgess, Thornton W.
1874-1965 . . . . DLB-22

Burgess, Stringer and Company DLB-49

Burick, Si 1909-1986 . . . . DLB-171

Burk, John Daly circa 1772-1808 . . . . DLB-37

Burke, Edmund 1729?-1797 . . . . DLB-104

Burke, Kenneth 1897-1993 . . . . . DLB-45, 63

Burke, Thomas 1886-1945 . . . . DLB-197

Burlingame, Edward Livermore
1848-1922 . . . . DLB-79

Burnet, Gilbert 1643-1715 . . . . DLB-101

Burnett, Frances Hodgson
1849-1924 . . . . . DLB-42, 141; DS-13, 14

Burnett, W. R. 1899-1982 . . . . DLB-9

Burnett, Whit 1899-1973 and
Martha Foley 1897-1977 . . . . . . DLB-137

Burney, Fanny 1752-1840 . . . . DLB-39

Burns, Alan 1929- DLB-14, 194

Burns, John Horne 1916-1953 . . . . Y-85

Burns, Robert 1759-1796 . . . . DLB-109

Burns and Oates DLB-106

Burnshaw, Stanley 1906- DLB-48

Burr, C. Chauncey 1815?-1883 . . . . . . DLB-79

Burroughs, Edgar Rice 1875-1950 . . . . . DLB-8

Burroughs, John 1837-1921 . . . . DLB-64

Burroughs, Margaret T. G.
1917- DLB-41

Burroughs, William S., Jr.
1947-1981 . . . . DLB-16

Burroughs, William Seward
1914- DLB-2, 8, 16, 152; Y-81, Y-97

Burroway, Janet 1936- DLB-6

Burt, Maxwell Struthers
1882-1954 . . . . DLB-86; DS-16

Burt, A. L., and Company DLB-49

Burton, Hester 1913- DLB-161

Burton, Isabel Arundell
1831-1896 . . . . DLB-166

Burton, Miles (see Rhode, John)

Burton, Richard Francis
1821-1890 . . . . DLB-55, 166, 184

Burton, Robert 1577-1640 . . . . DLB-151

Burton, Virginia Lee 1909-1968 . . . . . DLB-22

Burton, William Evans
1804-1860 . . . . DLB-73

Burwell, Adam Hood 1790-1849 . . . . . DLB-99

Bury, Lady Charlotte
1775-1861 . . . . DLB-116

Busch, Frederick 1941- DLB-6

Busch, Niven 1903-1991 . . . . DLB-44

Bushnell, Horace 1802-1876 . . . . DS-13

Bussieres, Arthur de 1877-1913 . . . . . DLB-92

Butler, Josephine Elizabeth
1828-1906 . . . . DLB-190

Butler, Juan 1942-1981 . . . . DLB-53

Butler, Octavia E. 1947- DLB-33

Butler, Pierce 1884-1953 . . . . DLB-187

Butler, Robert Olen 1945- DLB-173

Butler, Samuel 1613-1680 . . . . . DLB-101, 126

Butler, Samuel 1835-1902 . . . . DLB-18, 57, 174

Butler, William Francis
1838-1910 . . . . DLB-166

Butler, E. H., and Company DLB-49

Butor, Michel 1926- DLB-83

Butter, Nathaniel
[publishing house] DLB-170

Butterworth, Hezekiah 1839-1905 . . . . DLB-42

Buttitta, Ignazio 1899- DLB-114

Buzzati, Dino 1906-1972 . . . . DLB-177

Byars, Betsy 1928- DLB-52

Byatt, A. S. 1936- DLB-14, 194

Byles, Mather 1707-1788 . . . . DLB-24

Bynneman, Henry
[publishing house] DLB-170

Bynner, Witter 1881-1968 . . . . DLB-54

Byrd, William circa 1543-1623 . . . . . DLB-172

Byrd, William II 1674-1744 . . . . DLB-24, 140

Byrne, John Keyes (see Leonard, Hugh)

Byron, George Gordon, Lord
1788-1824 . . . . DLB-96, 110

Byron, Robert 1905-1941 . . . . DLB-195

C

Caballero Bonald, José Manuel
1926- DLB-108

Cabañero, Eladio 1930- DLB-134

Cabell, James Branch
1879-1958 . . . . DLB-9, 78

Cabeza de Baca, Manuel
1853-1915 . . . . DLB-122

Cabeza de Baca Gilbert, Fabiola
1898- DLB-122

Cable, George Washington
1844-1925 . . . . DLB-12, 74; DS-13

Cable, Mildred 1878-1952 . . . . DLB-195

Cabrera, Lydia 1900-1991 . . . . DLB-145

Cabrera Infante, Guillermo
1929- DLB-113

Cadell [publishing house] DLB-154

Cady, Edwin H. 1917- DLB-103

Caedmon flourished 658-680 . . . . . DLB-146

Caedmon School circa 660-899 . . . . DLB-146

Cafés, Brasseries, and Bistros DS-15

Cage, John 1912-1992 . . . . DLB-193

Cahan, Abraham
1860-1951 . . . . DLB-9, 25, 28

Cain, George 1943- DLB-33

Caird, Mona 1854-1932 . . . . DLB-197

Caldecott, Randolph 1846-1886 . . . . . DLB-163

Calder, John
(Publishers), Limited DLB-112

Calderón de la Barca, Fanny
1804-1882 . . . . DLB-183

Caldwell, Ben 1937- DLB-38

Caldwell, Erskine 1903-1987 . . . . DLB-9, 86

Caldwell, H. M., Company DLB-49

Caldwell, Taylor 1900-1985 . . . . DS-17

Calhoun, John C. 1782-1850 . . . . DLB-3

Calisher, Hortense 1911- DLB-2

A Call to Letters and an Invitation
to the Electric Chair,
by Siegfried Mandel DLB-75

Callaghan, Morley 1903-1990 . . . . . . DLB-68

Callahan, S. Alice 1868-1894 . . . . . . DLB-175

Callaloo Y-87

Callimachus circa 305 B.C.-240 B.C.
. . . . DLB-176

Calmer, Edgar 1907- DLB-4

Calverley, C. S. 1831-1884 . . . . DLB-35

Calvert, George Henry
1803-1889 . . . . DLB-1, 64

Calvino, Italo 1923-1985 . . . . DLB-196

Cambridge Press DLB-49

Cambridge Songs (Carmina Cantabrigensia)
circa 1050 . . . . DLB-148

Cambridge University Press DLB-170

Camden, William 1551-1623 . . . . . . DLB-172

Camden House: An Interview with
James Hardin Y-92

Cameron, Eleanor 1912- DLB-52

Cameron, George Frederick
1854-1885 . . . . DLB-99

Cameron, Lucy Lyttelton
1781-1858 . . . . DLB-163

Cameron, William Bleasdell
1862-1951 . . . . DLB-99

Camm, John 1718-1778 . . . . DLB-31

Camon, Ferdinando 1935- DLB-196

Campana, Dino 1885-1932 . . . . DLB-114

Campbell, Gabrielle Margaret Vere
(see Shearing, Joseph, and Bowen, Marjorie)

Campbell, James Dykes
1838-1895 . . . . DLB-144

Campbell, James Edwin
1867-1896 . . . . DLB-50

Campbell, John 1653-1728 . . . . DLB-43
Campbell, John W., Jr.
   1910-1971. . . . . DLB-8
Campbell, Roy 1901-1957 . . . . DLB-20
Campbell, Thomas
   1777-1844 . . . . DLB-93, 144
Campbell, William Wilfred
   1858-1918 . . . . DLB-92
Campion, Edmund 1539-1581 . . . . . DLB-167
Campion, Thomas
   1567-1620 . . . . DLB-58, 172
Camus, Albert 1913-1960. . . . . DLB-72
The Canadian Publishers' Records
   Database Y-96
Canby, Henry Seidel 1878-1961 . . . . . DLB-91
Candelaria, Cordelia 1943- DLB-82
Candelaria, Nash 1928- DLB-82
Candour in English Fiction (1890),
   by Thomas Hardy DLB-18
Canetti, Elias 1905-1994. . . . . . DLB-85, 124
Canham, Erwin Dain
   1904-1982 . . . . DLB-127
Canitz, Friedrich Rudolph Ludwig von
   1654-1699 . . . . DLB-168
Cankar, Ivan 1876-1918. . . . . DLB-147
Cannan, Gilbert 1884-1955 . . . . DLB-10, 197
Cannan, Joanna 1896-1961 . . . . DLB-191
Cannell, Kathleen 1891-1974. . . . . . . DLB-4
Cannell, Skipwith 1887-1957 . . . . . . DLB-45
Canning, George 1770-1827 . . . . . . DLB-158
Cannon, Jimmy 1910-1973 . . . . DLB-171
Cantwell, Robert 1908-1978 . . . . DLB-9
Cape, Jonathan, and Harrison Smith
   [publishing house]. DLB-46
Cape, Jonathan, Limited. DLB-112
Capen, Joseph 1658-1725. . . . . DLB-24
Capes, Bernard 1854-1918. . . . . DLB-156
Capote, Truman
   1924-1984 . . . . . . DLB-2, 185; Y-80, Y-84
Caproni, Giorgio 1912-1990. . . . . . . DLB-128
Cardarelli, Vincenzo 1887-1959 . . . . . DLB-114
Cárdenas, Reyes 1948- DLB-122
Cardinal, Marie 1929- DLB-83
Carew, Jan 1920- DLB-157
Carew, Thomas
   1594 or 1595-1640 . . . . DLB-126
Carey, Henry
   circa 1687-1689-1743 . . . . DLB-84
Carey, Mathew 1760-1839 . . . . . DLB-37, 73
Carey and Hart. DLB-49
Carey, M., and Company DLB-49
Carlell, Lodowick 1602-1675 . . . . . . DLB-58
Carleton, William 1794-1869 . . . . . . DLB-159

Carleton, G. W.
   [publishing house]. DLB-49
Carlile, Richard 1790-1843 . . . . DLB-110, 158
Carlyle, Jane Welsh 1801-1866. . . . . DLB-55
Carlyle, Thomas 1795-1881. . . . . DLB-55, 144
Carman, Bliss 1861-1929 . . . . DLB-92
Carmina Burana circa 1230 . . . . DLB-138
Carnero, Guillermo 1947- DLB-108
Carossa, Hans 1878-1956. . . . . DLB-66
Carpenter, Humphrey 1946- DLB-155
Carpenter, Stephen Cullen ?-1820? . . . DLB-73
Carpentier, Alejo 1904-1980. . . . . . . DLB-113
Carrier, Roch 1937- DLB-53
Carrillo, Adolfo 1855-1926 . . . . DLB-122
Carroll, Gladys Hasty 1904- DLB-9
Carroll, John 1735-1815 . . . . DLB-37
Carroll, John 1809-1884 . . . . DLB-99
Carroll, Lewis
   1832-1898 . . . . DLB-18, 163, 178
Carroll, Paul 1927- DLB-16
Carroll, Paul Vincent 1900-1968 . . . . DLB-10
Carroll and Graf Publishers DLB-46
Carruth, Hayden 1921- DLB-5, 165
Carryl, Charles E. 1841-1920 . . . . . . DLB-42
Carson, Anne 1950- DLB-193
Carswell, Catherine 1879-1946. . . . . DLB-36
Carter, Angela 1940-1992. . . . . DLB-14
Carter, Elizabeth 1717-1806. . . . . . . DLB-109
Carter, Henry (see Leslie, Frank)
Carter, Hodding, Jr. 1907-1972. . . . . DLB-127
Carter, Landon 1710-1778 . . . . DLB-31
Carter, Lin 1930- Y-81
Carter, Martin 1927- DLB-117
Carter and Hendee DLB-49
Carter, Robert, and Brothers. DLB-49
Cartwright, John 1740-1824 . . . . . . DLB-158
Cartwright, William circa
   1611-1643 . . . . DLB-126
Caruthers, William Alexander
   1802-1846. . . . . DLB-3
Carver, Jonathan 1710-1780 . . . . . . DLB-31
Carver, Raymond
   1938-1988. . . . . . . DLB-130; Y-84, Y-88
Cary, Joyce 1888-1957 . . . . . . DLB-15, 100
Cary, Patrick 1623?-1657 . . . . DLB-131
Casey, Juanita 1925- DLB-14
Casey, Michael 1947- DLB-5
Cassady, Carolyn 1923- DLB-16
Cassady, Neal 1926-1968 . . . . DLB-16
Cassell and Company. DLB-106
Cassell Publishing Company DLB-49
Cassill, R. V. 1919- DLB-6

Cassity, Turner 1929- DLB-105
Cassius Dio circa 155/164-post 229
   . . . . DLB-176
Cassola, Carlo 1917-1987 . . . . DLB-177
The Castle of Perseverance
   circa 1400-1425 . . . . DLB-146
Castellano, Olivia 1944- DLB-122
Castellanos, Rosario 1925-1974 . . . . . DLB-113
Castillo, Ana 1953- DLB-122
Castlemon, Harry (see Fosdick, Charles Austin)
Čašule, Kole 1921- DLB-181
Caswall, Edward 1814-1878 . . . . DLB-32
Catacalos, Rosemary 1944- DLB-122
Cather, Willa
   1873-1947. . . . . . . DLB-9, 54, 78; DS-1
Catherine II (Ekaterina Alekseevna), "The
   Great," Empress of Russia
   1729-1796 . . . . DLB-150
Catherwood, Mary Hartwell
   1847-1902 . . . . DLB-78
Catledge, Turner 1901-1983. . . . . . . DLB-127
Catlin, George 1796-1872 . . . . . DLB-186, 189
Cattafi, Bartolo 1922-1979 . . . . DLB-128
Catton, Bruce 1899-1978 . . . . DLB-17
Causley, Charles 1917- DLB-27
Caute, David 1936- DLB-14
Cavendish, Duchess of Newcastle,
   Margaret Lucas 1623-1673 . . . . DLB-131
Cawein, Madison 1865-1914 . . . . . . DLB-54
The Caxton Printers, Limited DLB-46
Caxton, William
   [publishing house]. DLB-170
Cayrol, Jean 1911- DLB-83
Cecil, Lord David 1902-1986 . . . . . . DLB-155
Cela, Camilo José 1916- Y-89
Celan, Paul 1920-1970 . . . . DLB-69
Celati, Gianni 1937- DLB-196
Celaya, Gabriel 1911-1991. . . . . DLB-108
Céline, Louis-Ferdinand
   1894-1961 . . . . DLB-72
The Celtic Background to Medieval English
   Literature. DLB-146
Celtis, Conrad 1459-1508 . . . . DLB-179
Center for Bibliographical Studies and
   Research at the University of
   California, Riverside Y-91
The Center for the Book in the Library
   of Congress. Y-93
Center for the Book Research. Y-84
Centlivre, Susanna 1669?-1723 . . . . . DLB-84
The Century Company. DLB-49
Cernuda, Luis 1902-1963 . . . . DLB-134
"Certain Gifts," by Betty Adcock. . . . DLB-105
Cervantes, Lorna Dee 1954- DLB-82

Cumulative Index

Chacel, Rosa 1898- DLB-134
Chacón, Eusebio 1869-1948 ...... DLB-82
Chacón, Felipe Maximiliano 1873-? DLB-82
Chadwyck-Healey's Full-Text Literary Data-bases: Editing Commercial Databases of Primary Literary Texts Y-95
Challans, Eileen Mary (see Renault, Mary)
Chalmers, George 1742-1825 ...... DLB-30
Chaloner, Sir Thomas 1520-1565 .... DLB-167
Chamberlain, Samuel S. 1851-1916 .... DLB-25
Chamberland, Paul 1939- DLB-60
Chamberlin, William Henry 1897-1969 .... DLB-29
Chambers, Charles Haddon 1860-1921 .... DLB-10
Chambers, W. and R. [publishing house] DLB-106
Chamisso, Albert von 1781-1838 .... DLB-90
Champfleury 1821-1889 .... DLB-119
Chandler, Harry 1864-1944 ...... DLB-29
Chandler, Norman 1899-1973 ...... DLB-127
Chandler, Otis 1927- DLB-127
Chandler, Raymond 1888-1959 ...... DS-6
Channing, Edward 1856-1931 ...... DLB-17
Channing, Edward Tyrrell 1790-1856 .... DLB-1, 59
Channing, William Ellery 1780-1842 .... DLB-1, 59
Channing, William Ellery, II 1817-1901 .... DLB-1
Channing, William Henry 1810-1884 .... DLB-1, 59
Chaplin, Charlie 1889-1977 ...... DLB-44
Chapman, George 1559 or 1560 - 1634 ...... DLB-62, 121
Chapman, John DLB-106
Chapman, Olive Murray 1892-1977 .... DLB-195
Chapman, William 1850-1917 ...... DLB-99
Chapman and Hall DLB-106
Chappell, Fred 1936- DLB-6, 105
Charbonneau, Jean 1875-1960 ...... DLB-92
Charbonneau, Robert 1911-1967 ...... DLB-68
Charles, Gerda 1914- DLB-14
Charles, William [publishing house] DLB-49
The Charles Wood Affair: A Playwright Revived Y-83
Charlotte Forten: Pages from her Diary DLB-50
Charteris, Leslie 1907-1993 ...... DLB-77
Charyn, Jerome 1937- Y-83

Chase, Borden 1900-1971 .... DLB-26
Chase, Edna Woolman 1877-1957 .... DLB-91
Chase-Riboud, Barbara 1936- DLB-33
Chateaubriand, François-René de 1768-1848 .... DLB-119
Chatterton, Thomas 1752-1770 ..... DLB-109
Chatto and Windus DLB-106
Chatwin, Bruce 1940-1989 ...... DLB-194
Chaucer, Geoffrey 1340?-1400 ..... DLB-146
Chauncy, Charles 1705-1787 ...... DLB-24
Chauveau, Pierre-Joseph-Olivier 1820-1890 .... DLB-99
Chávez, Denise 1948- DLB-122
Chávez, Fray Angélico 1910- DLB-82
Chayefsky, Paddy 1923-1981 .... DLB-7, 44; Y-81
Cheesman, Evelyn 1881-1969 ..... DLB-195
Cheever, Ezekiel 1615-1708 .... DLB-24
Cheever, George Barrell 1807-1890 .... DLB-59
Cheever, John 1912-1982 ...... DLB-2, 102; Y-80, Y-82
Cheever, Susan 1943- Y-82
Cheke, Sir John 1514-1557 ...... DLB-132
Chelsea House DLB-46
Cheney, Ednah Dow (Littlehale) 1824-1904 .... DLB-1
Cheney, Harriet Vaughn 1796-1889 .... DLB-99
Chénier, Marie-Joseph 1764-1811 .... DLB-192
Cherry, Kelly 1940 .... Y-83
Cherryh, C. J. 1942- Y-80
Chesnutt, Charles Waddell 1858-1932 .... DLB-12, 50, 78
Chesney, Sir George Tomkyns 1830-1895 .... DLB-190
Chester, Alfred 1928-1971 .... DLB-130
Chester, George Randolph 1869-1924 .... DLB-78
The Chester Plays circa 1505-1532; revisions until 1575 .... DLB-146
Chesterfield, Philip Dormer Stanhope, Fourth Earl of 1694-1773 ...... DLB-104
Chesterton, G. K. 1874-1936 .... DLB-10, 19, 34, 70, 98, 149, 178
Chettle, Henry circa 1560-circa 1607 .... DLB-136
Chew, Ada Nield 1870-1945 ...... DLB-135
Cheyney, Edward P. 1861-1947 ..... DLB-47
Chiara, Piero 1913-1986 .... DLB-177
Chicano History DLB-82
Chicano Language DLB-82
Child, Francis James 1825-1896 .... DLB-1, 64

Child, Lydia Maria 1802-1880 .... DLB-1, 74
Child, Philip 1898-1978 .... DLB-68
Childers, Erskine 1870-1922 ...... DLB-70
Children's Book Awards and Prizes DLB-61
Children's Illustrators, 1800-1880 .... DLB-163
Childress, Alice 1920-1994 ...... DLB-7, 38
Childs, George W. 1829-1894 ..... DLB-23
Chilton Book Company DLB-46
Chinweizu 1943- DLB-157
Chitham, Edward 1932- DLB-155
Chittenden, Hiram Martin 1858-1917 .... DLB-47
Chivers, Thomas Holley 1809-1858 .... DLB-3
Cholmondeley, Mary 1859-1925 .... DLB-197
Chopin, Kate 1850-1904 .... DLB-12, 78
Chopin, Rene 1885-1953 .... DLB-92
Choquette, Adrienne 1915-1973 ..... DLB-68
Choquette, Robert 1905- DLB-68
The Christian Publishing Company DLB-49
Christie, Agatha 1890-1976 ...... DLB-13, 77
Christus und die Samariterin circa 950 .... DLB-148
Christy, Howard Chandler 1873-1952 . DLB-188
Chulkov, Mikhail Dmitrievich 1743?-1792 .... DLB-150
Church, Benjamin 1734-1778 .... DLB-31
Church, Francis Pharcellus 1839-1906 .... DLB-79
Church, Richard 1893-1972 ...... DLB-191
Church, William Conant 1836-1917 .... DLB-79
Churchill, Caryl 1938- DLB-13
Churchill, Charles 1731-1764 .... DLB-109
Churchill, Sir Winston 1874-1965 .... DLB-100; DS-16
Churchyard, Thomas 1520?-1604 .... DLB-132
Churton, E., and Company DLB-106
Chute, Marchette 1909-1994 ...... DLB-103
Ciardi, John 1916-1986 .... DLB-5; Y-86
Cibber, Colley 1671-1757 .... DLB-84
Cima, Annalisa 1941- DLB-128
Čingo, Živko 1935-1987 .... DLB-181
Cirese, Eugenio 1884-1955 .... DLB-114
Cisneros, Sandra 1954- DLB-122, 152
City Lights Books DLB-46
Cixous, Hélène 1937- DLB-83
Clampitt, Amy 1920-1994 .... DLB-105

Clapper, Raymond 1892-1944 ...... DLB-29
Clare, John 1793-1864 .... DLB-55, 96
Clarendon, Edward Hyde, Earl of
 1609-1674 .... DLB-101
Clark, Alfred Alexander Gordon
 (see Hare, Cyril)
Clark, Ann Nolan 1896- DLB-52
Clark, C. E. Frazer Jr. 1925- DLB-187
Clark, C. M., Publishing
 Company DLB-46
Clark, Catherine Anthony
 1892-1977 .... DLB-68
Clark, Charles Heber
 1841-1915 .... DLB-11
Clark, Davis Wasgatt 1812-1871..... DLB-79
Clark, Eleanor 1913- DLB-6
Clark, J. P. 1935- DLB-117
Clark, Lewis Gaylord
 1808-1873 .... DLB-3, 64, 73
Clark, Walter Van Tilburg
 1909-1971 .... DLB-9
Clark, William (see Lewis, Meriwether)
Clark, William Andrews Jr.
 1877-1934 .... DLB-187
Clarke, Austin 1896-1974 ...... DLB-10, 20
Clarke, Austin C. 1934- DLB-53, 125
Clarke, Gillian 1937- DLB-40
Clarke, James Freeman
 1810-1888 .... DLB-1, 59
Clarke, Pauline 1921- DLB-161
Clarke, Rebecca Sophia
 1833-1906 .... DLB-42
Clarke, Robert, and Company..... DLB-49
Clarkson, Thomas 1760-1846...... DLB-158
Claudel, Paul 1868-1955......... DLB-192
Claudius, Matthias 1740-1815 ..... DLB-97
Clausen, Andy 1943- DLB-16
Clawson, John L. 1865-1933 ..... DLB-187
Claxton, Remsen and
 Haffelfinger DLB-49
Clay, Cassius Marcellus
 1810-1903 .... DLB-43
Cleary, Beverly 1916- DLB-52
Cleaver, Vera 1919- and
 Cleaver, Bill 1920-1981........ DLB-52
Cleland, John 1710-1789 .... DLB-39
Clemens, Samuel Langhorne (Mark Twain) 1835-1910
 ..... DLB-11, 12, 23, 64, 74, 186, 189
Clement, Hal 1922- DLB-8
Clemo, Jack 1916- DLB-27
Cleveland, John 1613-1658 ...... DLB-126
Cliff, Michelle 1946- DLB-157
Clifford, Lady Anne 1590-1676 .... DLB-151
Clifford, James L. 1901-1978 ..... DLB-103
Clifford, Lucy 1853?-1929 ... DLB-135, 141, 197

Clifton, Lucille 1936- DLB-5, 41
Clines, Francis X. 1938- DLB-185
Clode, Edward J.
 [publishing house].......... DLB-46
Clough, Arthur Hugh 1819-1861 .... DLB-32
Cloutier, Cécile 1930- DLB-60
Clutton-Brock, Arthur
 1868-1924 .... DLB-98
Coates, Robert M.
 1897-1973 .... DLB-4, 9, 102
Coatsworth, Elizabeth 1893- DLB-22
Cobb, Charles E., Jr. 1943- DLB-41
Cobb, Frank I. 1869-1923 .... DLB-25
Cobb, Irvin S.
 1876-1944......... DLB-11, 25, 86
Cobbe, Frances Power 1822-1904 ... DLB-190
Cobbett, William 1763-1835 .... DLB-43, 107
Cobbledick, Gordon 1898-1969 ..... DLB-171
Cochran, Thomas C. 1902- DLB-17
Cochrane, Elizabeth 1867-1922 ... DLB-25, 189
Cockerill, John A. 1845-1896..... DLB-23
Cocteau, Jean 1889-1963 .... DLB-65
Coderre, Emile (see Jean Narrache)
Coffee, Lenore J. 1900?-1984....... DLB-44
Coffin, Robert P. Tristram
 1892-1955 .... DLB-45
Cogswell, Fred 1917- DLB-60
Cogswell, Mason Fitch
 1761-1830 .... DLB-37
Cohen, Arthur A. 1928-1986...... DLB-28
Cohen, Leonard 1934- DLB-53
Cohen, Matt 1942- DLB-53
Colden, Cadwallader
 1688-1776 .... DLB-24, 30
Cole, Barry 1936- DLB-14
Cole, George Watson
 1850-1939 .... DLB-140
Colegate, Isabel 1931- DLB-14
Coleman, Emily Holmes
 1899-1974................ DLB-4
Coleman, Wanda 1946- DLB-130
Coleridge, Hartley 1796-1849....... DLB-96
Coleridge, Mary 1861-1907 ..... DLB-19, 98
Coleridge, Samuel Taylor
 1772-1834 .... DLB-93, 107
Colet, John 1467-1519 .... DLB-132
Colette 1873-1954 .... DLB-65
Colette, Sidonie Gabrielle (see Colette)
Colinas, Antonio 1946- DLB-134
Coll, Joseph Clement 1881-1921 ... DLB-188
Collier, John 1901-1980......... DLB-77
Collier, John Payne 1789-1883 ..... DLB-184
Collier, Mary 1690-1762 .... DLB-95

Collier, Robert J. 1876-1918 ...... DLB-91
Collier, P. F. [publishing house]..... DLB-49
Collin and Small DLB-49
Collingwood, W. G. 1854-1932..... DLB-149
Collins, An floruit circa 1653...... DLB-131
Collins, Merle 1950- DLB-157
Collins, Mortimer 1827-1876..... DLB-21, 35
Collins, Wilkie 1824-1889 ... DLB-18, 70, 159
Collins, William 1721-1759 ...... DLB-109
Collins, William, Sons and
 Company DLB-154
Collins, Isaac [publishing house]..... DLB-49
Collis, Maurice 1889-1973......... DLB-195
Collyer, Mary 1716?-1763?........ DLB-39
Colman, Benjamin 1673-1747 ..... DLB-24
Colman, George, the Elder
 1732-1794 .... DLB-89
Colman, George, the Younger
 1762-1836 .... DLB-89
Colman, S. [publishing house]...... DLB-49
Colombo, John Robert 1936- DLB-53
Colquhoun, Patrick 1745-1820 ..... DLB-158
Colter, Cyrus 1910- DLB-33
Colum, Padraic 1881-1972 .... DLB-19
Colvin, Sir Sidney 1845-1927...... DLB-149
Colwin, Laurie 1944-1992 .... Y-80
Comden, Betty 1919- and Green,
 Adolph 1918- DLB-44
Comi, Girolamo 1890-1968 .... DLB-114
The Comic Tradition Continued
 [in the British Novel]......... DLB-15
Commager, Henry Steele
 1902- DLB-17
The Commercialization of the Image of
 Revolt, by Kenneth Rexroth..... DLB-16
Community and Commentators: Black
 Theatre and Its Critics........ DLB-38
Compton-Burnett, Ivy
 1884?-1969 .... DLB-36
Conan, Laure 1845-1924......... DLB-99
Conde, Carmen 1901- DLB-108
Conference on Modern Biography Y-85
Congreve, William
 1670-1729.............. DLB-39, 84
Conkey, W. B., Company DLB-49
Connell, Evan S., Jr. 1924- DLB-2; Y-81
Connelly, Marc 1890-1980 ..... DLB-7; Y-80
Connolly, Cyril 1903-1974 .... DLB-98
Connolly, James B. 1868-1957 ..... DLB-78
Connor, Ralph 1860-1937 .... DLB-92
Connor, Tony 1930- DLB-40
Conquest, Robert 1917- DLB-27
Conrad, Joseph
 1857-1924........ DLB-10, 34, 98, 156

341

Conrad, John, and Company DLB-49

Conroy, Jack 1899-1990 .... Y-81

Conroy, Pat 1945- DLB-6

The Consolidation of Opinion: Critical
    Responses to the Modernists DLB-36

Consolo, Vincenzo 1933- DLB-196

Constable, Henry 1562-1613 ...... DLB-136

Constable and Company
    Limited............. DLB-112

Constable, Archibald, and
    Company DLB-154

Constant, Benjamin 1767-1830 ..... DLB-119

Constant de Rebecque, Henri-Benjamin de
    (see Constant, Benjamin)

Constantine, David 1944- DLB-40

Constantin-Weyer, Maurice
    1881-1964 .... DLB-92

Contempo Caravan: Kites in
    a Windstorm.............. Y-85

A Contemporary Flourescence of Chicano
    Literature Y-84

"Contemporary Verse Story-telling,"
    by Jonathan Holden......... DLB-105

The Continental Publishing
    Company DLB-49

A Conversation with Chaim Potok..... Y-84

Conversations with Editors.......... Y-95

Conversations with Publishers I: An Interview
    with Patrick O'Connor Y-84

Conversations with Publishers II: An Interview
    with Charles Scribner III Y-94

Conversations with Publishers III: An Interview
    with Donald Lamm Y-95

Conversations with Publishers IV: An Interview
    with James Laughlin.......... Y-96

Conversations with Rare Book Dealers I: An
    Interview with Glenn Horowitz..... Y-90

Conversations with Rare Book Dealers II: An
    Interview with Ralph Sipper Y-94

Conversations with Rare Book Dealers
    (Publishers) III: An Interview with
    Otto Penzler Y-96

The Conversion of an Unpolitical Man,
    by W. H. Bruford DLB-66

Conway, Moncure Daniel
    1832-1907................. DLB-1

Cook, Ebenezer
    circa 1667-circa 1732 .... DLB-24

Cook, Edward Tyas 1857-1919..... DLB-149

Cook, Michael 1933- DLB-53

Cook, David C., Publishing
    Company DLB-49

Cooke, George Willis 1848-1923..... DLB-71

Cooke, Increase, and Company DLB-49

Cooke, John Esten 1830-1886 ...... DLB-3

Cooke, Philip Pendleton
    1816-1850 .... DLB-3, 59

Cooke, Rose Terry
    1827-1892............. DLB-12, 74

Cook-Lynn, Elizabeth 1930- DLB-175

Coolbrith, Ina 1841-1928 ...... DLB-54, 186

Cooley, Peter 1940- DLB-105

Coolidge, Clark 1939- DLB-193

Coolidge, Susan (see Woolsey, Sarah Chauncy)

Coolidge, George
    [publishing house].......... DLB-49

Cooper, Giles 1918-1966 .... DLB-13

Cooper, James Fenimore
    1789-1851............. DLB-3, 183

Cooper, Kent 1880-1965 .... DLB-29

Cooper, Susan 1935- DLB-161

Cooper, William
    [publishing house].......... DLB-170

Coote, J. [publishing house]....... DLB-154

Coover, Robert 1932- DLB-2; Y-81

Copeland and Day DLB-49

Ćopić, Branko 1915-1984 .... DLB-181

Copland, Robert 1470?-1548 ..... DLB-136

Coppard, A. E. 1878-1957 ...... DLB-162

Coppel, Alfred 1921- Y-83

Coppola, Francis Ford 1939- DLB-44

Copway, George (Kah-ge-ga-gah-bowh)
    1818-1869............ DLB-175, 183

Corazzini, Sergio 1886-1907....... DLB-114

Corbett, Richard 1582-1635....... DLB-121

Corcoran, Barbara 1911- DLB-52

Cordelli, Franco 1943- DLB-196

Corelli, Marie 1855-1924 ..... DLB-34, 156

Corle, Edwin 1906-1956 .... Y-85

Corman, Cid 1924- DLB-5, 193

Cormier, Robert 1925- DLB-52

Corn, Alfred 1943- DLB-120; Y-80

Cornish, Sam 1935- DLB-41

Cornish, William
    circa 1465-circa 1524 .... DLB-132

Cornwall, Barry (see Procter, Bryan Waller)

Cornwallis, Sir William, the Younger
    circa 1579-1614 .... DLB-151

Cornwell, David John Moore
    (see le Carré, John)

Corpi, Lucha 1945- DLB-82

Corrington, John William 1932- DLB-6

Corrothers, James D. 1869-1917..... DLB-50

Corso, Gregory 1930- DLB-5, 16

Cortázar, Julio 1914-1984 .... DLB-113

Cortez, Jayne 1936- DLB-41

Corvinus, Gottlieb Siegmund
    1677-1746 .... DLB-168

Corvo, Baron (see Rolfe, Frederick William)

Cory, Annie Sophie (see Cross, Victoria)

Cory, William Johnson
    1823-1892 .... DLB-35

Coryate, Thomas
    1577?-1617 .... DLB-151, 172

Ćosić, Dobrica 1921- DLB-181

Cosin, John 1595-1672.......... DLB-151

Cosmopolitan Book Corporation..... DLB-46

Costain, Thomas B. 1885-1965 ...... DLB-9

Coste, Donat 1912-1957 .... DLB-88

Costello, Louisa Stuart 1799-1870 ... DLB-166

Cota-Cárdenas, Margarita
    1941- DLB-122

Cotten, Bruce 1873-1954 .... DLB-187

Cotter, Joseph Seamon, Sr.
    1861-1949 .... DLB-50

Cotter, Joseph Seamon, Jr.
    1895-1919 .... DLB-50

Cottle, Joseph [publishing house] DLB-154

Cotton, Charles 1630-1687 .... DLB-131

Cotton, John 1584-1652.......... DLB-24

Coulter, John 1888-1980 .... DLB-68

Cournos, John 1881-1966 .... DLB-54

Courteline, Georges 1858-1929 ..... DLB-192

Cousins, Margaret 1905- DLB-137

Cousins, Norman 1915-1990 ...... DLB-137

Coventry, Francis 1725-1754 ...... DLB-39

Coverdale, Miles
    1487 or 1488-1569 .... DLB-167

Coverly, N. [publishing house]...... DLB-49

Covici-Friede................ DLB-46

Coward, Noel 1899-1973 .... DLB-10

Coward, McCann and
    Geoghegan DLB-46

Cowles, Gardner 1861-1946 .... DLB-29

Cowles, Gardner ("Mike"), Jr.
    1903-1985............. DLB-127, 137

Cowley, Abraham
    1618-1667............. DLB-131, 151

Cowley, Hannah 1743-1809 .... DLB-89

Cowley, Malcolm
    1898-1989...... DLB-4, 48; Y-81, Y-89

Cowper, William
    1731-1800............ DLB-104, 109

Cox, A. B. (see Berkeley, Anthony)

Cox, James McMahon
    1903-1974 .... DLB-127

Cox, James Middleton
    1870-1957 .... DLB-127

Cox, Palmer 1840-1924.......... DLB-42

Coxe, Louis 1918-1993........... DLB-5

Coxe, Tench 1755-1824 .... DLB-37

Cozzens, James Gould
    1903-1978........ DLB-9; Y-84; DS-2

Cozzens's *Michael Scarlett* Y-97

Crabbe, George 1754-1832 .... DLB-93

Crackanthorpe, Hubert
1870-1896 . . . . DLB-135

Craddock, Charles Egbert
(see Murfree, Mary N.)

Cradock, Thomas 1718-1770 . . . . . . DLB-31

Craig, Daniel H. 1811-1895 . . . . . DLB-43

Craik, Dinah Maria
1826-1887 . . . . DLB-35, 136

Cramer, Richard Ben 1950- DLB-185

Cranch, Christopher Pearse
1813-1892 . . . . DLB-1, 42

Crane, Hart 1899-1932 . . . . DLB-4, 48

Crane, R. S. 1886-1967 . . . . DLB-63

Crane, Stephen 1871-1900 . . . . DLB-12, 54, 78

Crane, Walter 1845-1915 . . . . DLB-163

Cranmer, Thomas 1489-1556 . . . . . . DLB-132

Crapsey, Adelaide 1878-1914 . . . . DLB-54

Crashaw, Richard
1612 or 1613-1649 . . . . DLB-126

Craven, Avery 1885-1980 . . . . DLB-17

Crawford, Charles
1752-circa 1815 . . . . DLB-31

Crawford, F. Marion 1854-1909 . . . . . DLB-71

Crawford, Isabel Valancy
1850-1887 . . . . DLB-92

Crawley, Alan 1887-1975 . . . . DLB-68

Crayon, Geoffrey (see Irving, Washington)

Creamer, Robert W. 1922- DLB-171

Creasey, John 1908-1973 . . . . DLB-77

Creative Age Press DLB-46

Creech, William
[publishing house] DLB-154

Creede, Thomas
[publishing house] DLB-170

Creel, George 1876-1953 . . . . DLB-25

Creeley, Robert
1926- DLB-5, 16, 169; DS-17

Creelman, James 1859-1915 . . . . . . DLB-23

Cregan, David 1931- DLB-13

Creighton, Donald Grant
1902-1979 . . . . DLB-88

Cremazie, Octave 1827-1879 . . . . . . DLB-99

Crémer, Victoriano 1909?- DLB-108

Crescas, Hasdai
circa 1340-1412? DLB-115

Crespo, Angel 1926- DLB-134

Cresset Press DLB-112

Cresswell, Helen 1934- DLB-161

Crèvecoeur, Michel Guillaume Jean de
1735-1813 . . . . DLB-37

Crews, Harry 1935- DLB-6, 143, 185

Crichton, Michael 1942- Y-81

A Crisis of Culture: The Changing Role
of Religion in the New Republic
. . . . DLB-37

Crispin, Edmund 1921-1978 . . . . . . DLB-87

Cristofer, Michael 1946- DLB-7

"The Critic as Artist" (1891), by
Oscar Wilde DLB-57

"Criticism In Relation To Novels" (1863),
by G. H. Lewes DLB-21

Crnjanski, Miloš 1893-1977 . . . . . . DLB-147

Crockett, David (Davy)
1786-1836 . . . . DLB-3, 11, 183

Croft-Cooke, Rupert (see Bruce, Leo)

Crofts, Freeman Wills
1879-1957 . . . . DLB-77

Croker, John Wilson
1780-1857 . . . . DLB-110

Croly, George 1780-1860 . . . . DLB-159

Croly, Herbert 1869-1930 . . . . DLB-91

Croly, Jane Cunningham
1829-1901 . . . . DLB-23

Crompton, Richmal 1890-1969 . . . . . DLB-160

Cronin, A. J. 1896-1981 . . . . DLB-191

Crosby, Caresse 1892-1970 . . . . DLB-48

Crosby, Caresse 1892-1970 and Crosby,
Harry 1898-1929 . . . . DLB-4; DS-15

Crosby, Harry 1898-1929 . . . . DLB-48

Cross, Gillian 1945- DLB-161

Cross, Victoria 1868-1952 . . . . DLB-135, 197

Crossley-Holland, Kevin
1941- DLB-40, 161

Crothers, Rachel 1878-1958 . . . . DLB-7

Crowell, Thomas Y., Company DLB-49

Crowley, John 1942- Y-82

Crowley, Mart 1935- DLB-7

Crown Publishers DLB-46

Crowne, John 1641-1712 . . . . DLB-80

Crowninshield, Edward Augustus
1817-1859 . . . . DLB-140

Crowninshield, Frank 1872-1947 . . . . . DLB-91

Croy, Homer 1883-1965 . . . . DLB-4

Crumley, James 1939- Y-84

Cruz, Victor Hernández 1949- DLB-41

Csokor, Franz Theodor
1885-1969 . . . . DLB-81

Cuala Press DLB-112

Cullen, Countee
1903-1946 . . . . DLB-4, 48, 51

Culler, Jonathan D. 1944- DLB-67

The Cult of Biography
Excerpts from the Second Folio Debate:
"Biographies are generally a disease of
English Literature" — Germaine Greer,
Victoria Glendinning, Auberon Waugh,
and Richard Holmes Y-86

Cumberland, Richard 1732-1811 . . . . . DLB-89

Cummings, Constance Gordon
1837-1924 . . . . DLB-174

Cummings, E. E. 1894-1962 . . . . DLB-4, 48

Cummings, Ray 1887-1957 . . . . DLB-8

Cummings and Hilliard DLB-49

Cummins, Maria Susanna
1827-1866 . . . . DLB-42

Cundall, Joseph
[publishing house] DLB-106

Cuney, Waring 1906-1976 . . . . DLB-51

Cuney-Hare, Maude 1874-1936 . . . . . DLB-52

Cunningham, Allan 1784-1842 . . DLB-116, 144

Cunningham, J. V. 1911- DLB-5

Cunningham, Peter F.
[publishing house] DLB-49

Cunqueiro, Alvaro 1911-1981 . . . . . DLB-134

Cuomo, George 1929- Y-80

Cupples and Leon DLB-46

Cupples, Upham and Company DLB-49

Cuppy, Will 1884-1949 . . . . DLB-11

Curll, Edmund
[publishing house] DLB-154

Currie, James 1756-1805 . . . . DLB-142

Currie, Mary Montgomerie Lamb Singleton,
Lady Currie (see Fane, Violet)

Cursor Mundi circa 1300 . . . . DLB-146

Curti, Merle E. 1897- DLB-17

Curtis, Anthony 1926- DLB-155

Curtis, Cyrus H. K. 1850-1933 . . . . . DLB-91

Curtis, George William
1824-1892 . . . . DLB-1, 43

Curzon, Robert 1810-1873 . . . . DLB-166

Curzon, Sarah Anne
1833-1898 . . . . DLB-99

Cushing, Harvey 1869-1939 . . . . . . DLB-187

Cynewulf circa 770-840 . . . . DLB-146

Czepko, Daniel 1605-1660 . . . . DLB-164

D

D. M. Thomas: The Plagiarism
Controversy Y-82

Dabit, Eugène 1898-1936 . . . . DLB-65

Daborne, Robert circa 1580-1628 . . . . DLB-58

Dacey, Philip 1939- DLB-105

Dach, Simon 1605-1659 . . . . DLB-164

Daggett, Rollin M. 1831-1901 . . . . . . DLB-79

D'Aguiar, Fred 1960- DLB-157

Dahl, Roald 1916-1990 . . . . DLB-139

Dahlberg, Edward 1900-1977 . . . . . . DLB-48

Dahn, Felix 1834-1912 . . . . DLB-129

Dale, Peter 1938- DLB-40

Daley, Arthur 1904-1974 . . . . DLB-171

Dall, Caroline Wells (Healey)
1822-1912 . . . . DLB-1

Dallas, E. S. 1828-1879 . . . . DLB-55

Cumulative Index

The Dallas Theater Center DLB-7
D'Alton, Louis 1900-1951. . . . . DLB-10
Daly, T. A. 1871-1948 . . . . DLB-11
Damon, S. Foster 1893-1971 . . . . . . DLB-45
Damrell, William S.
 [publishing house]. DLB-49
Dana, Charles A. 1819-1897 . . . . . DLB-3, 23
Dana, Richard Henry, Jr.
 1815-1882. . . . . DLB-1, 183
Dandridge, Ray Garfield DLB-51
Dane, Clemence 1887-1965 . . . . . DLB-10, 197
Danforth, John 1660-1730 . . . . DLB-24
Danforth, Samuel, I 1626-1674. . . . . DLB-24
Danforth, Samuel, II 1666-1727 . . . . DLB-24
Dangerous Years: London Theater,
 1939-1945 . . . . DLB-10
Daniel, John M. 1825-1865. . . . . . . DLB-43
Daniel, Samuel
 1562 or 1563-1619. . . . . DLB-62
Daniel Press DLB-106
Daniells, Roy 1902-1979 . . . . DLB-68
Daniels, Jim 1956- DLB-120
Daniels, Jonathan 1902-1981 . . . . . DLB-127
Daniels, Josephus 1862-1948 . . . . . . DLB-29
Danis Rose and the Rendering
 of *Ulysses* Y-97
Dannay, Frederic 1905-1982 and
 Manfred B. Lee 1905-1971 . . . . . DLB-137
Danner, Margaret Esse 1915- DLB-41
Danter, John [publishing house]. . . . DLB-170
Dantin, Louis 1865-1945 . . . . DLB-92
Danzig, Allison 1898-1987. . . . . . . DLB-171
D'Arcy, Ella circa 1857-1937 . . . . . DLB-135
Darley, Felix Octavious Carr
 1822-1888 . . . . DLB-188
Darley, George 1795-1846 . . . . DLB-96
Darwin, Charles 1809-1882. . . . . DLB-57, 166
Darwin, Erasmus 1731-1802 . . . . . . DLB-93
Daryush, Elizabeth 1887-1977 . . . . . DLB-20
Dashkova, Ekaterina Romanovna
 (née Vorontsova) 1743-1810 . . . . DLB-150
Dashwood, Edmée Elizabeth Monica
 de la Pasture (see Delafield, E. M.)
Daudet, Alphonse 1840-1897 . . . . . DLB-123
d'Aulaire, Edgar Parin 1898- and
 d'Aulaire, Ingri 1904- DLB-22
Davenant, Sir William
 1606-1668 . . . . DLB-58, 126
Davenport, Guy 1927- DLB-130
Davenport, Marcia 1903-1996 . . . . . DS-17
Davenport, Robert ?-? DLB-58
Daves, Delmer 1904-1977 . . . . DLB-26
Davey, Frank 1940- DLB-53
Davidson, Avram 1923-1993. . . . . . . DLB-8

Davidson, Donald 1893-1968. . . . . . DLB-45
Davidson, John 1857-1909 . . . . DLB-19
Davidson, Lionel 1922- DLB-14
Davidson, Sara 1943- DLB-185
Davie, Donald 1922- DLB-27
Davie, Elspeth 1919- DLB-139
Davies, Sir John 1569-1626 . . . . . . DLB-172
Davies, John, of Hereford
 1565?-1618 . . . . DLB-121
Davies, Rhys 1901-1978 . . . . . DLB-139, 191
Davies, Robertson 1913- DLB-68
Davies, Samuel 1723-1761 . . . . DLB-31
Davies, Thomas 1712?-1785. . . . DLB-142, 154
Davies, W. H. 1871-1940. . . . . DLB-19, 174
Davies, Peter, Limited DLB-112
Daviot, Gordon 1896?-1952 . . . . . . DLB-10
 (see also Tey, Josephine)
Davis, Charles A. 1795-1867 . . . . . . DLB-11
Davis, Clyde Brion 1894-1962. . . . . . DLB-9
Davis, Dick 1945- DLB-40
Davis, Frank Marshall 1905-? DLB-51
Davis, H. L. 1894-1960 . . . . DLB-9
Davis, John 1774-1854 . . . . DLB-37
Davis, Lydia 1947- DLB-130
Davis, Margaret Thomson 1926- DLB-14
Davis, Ossie 1917- DLB-7, 38
Davis, Paxton 1925-1994. . . . . Y-94
Davis, Rebecca Harding
 1831-1910 . . . . DLB-74
Davis, Richard Harding 1864-1916
 . . . . DLB-12, 23, 78, 79, 189; DS-13
Davis, Samuel Cole 1764-1809. . . . . DLB-37
Davison, Peter 1928- DLB-5
Davys, Mary 1674-1732 . . . . DLB-39
DAW Books DLB-46
Dawn Powell, Where Have You Been All
 Our lives? Y-97
Dawson, Ernest 1882-1947 . . . . . . DLB-140
Dawson, Fielding 1930- DLB-130
Dawson, William 1704-1752 . . . . . . DLB-31
Day, Angel flourished 1586. . . . . . DLB-167
Day, Benjamin Henry 1810-1889 . . . . DLB-43
Day, Clarence 1874-1935. . . . . DLB-11
Day, Dorothy 1897-1980 . . . . DLB-29
Day, Frank Parker 1881-1950 . . . . . DLB-92
Day, John circa 1574-circa 1640 . . . . DLB-62
Day, John [publishing house] DLB-170
Day Lewis, C. 1904-1972 . . . . . DLB-15, 20
 (see also Blake, Nicholas)
Day, Thomas 1748-1789 . . . . DLB-39
Day, The John, Company DLB-46
Day, Mahlon [publishing house] DLB-49

Dazai, Osamu 1909-1948 . . . . DLB-182
Deacon, William Arthur
 1890-1977 . . . . DLB-68
Deal, Borden 1922-1985 . . . . DLB-6
de Angeli, Marguerite 1889-1987. . . . DLB-22
De Angelis, Milo 1951- DLB-128
De Bow, James Dunwoody Brownson
 1820-1867 . . . . DLB-3, 79
de Bruyn, Günter 1926- DLB-75
de Camp, L. Sprague 1907- DLB-8
De Carlo, Andrea 1952- DLB-196
The Decay of Lying (1889),
 by Oscar Wilde [excerpt] DLB-18
Dechert, Robert 1895-1975 . . . . . . DLB-187
Dedication, *Ferdinand Count Fathom* (1753),
 by Tobias Smollett DLB-39
Dedication, *The History of Pompey the Little*
 (1751), by Francis Coventry. . . . DLB-39
Dedication, *Lasselia* (1723), by Eliza
 Haywood [excerpt] DLB-39
Dedication, *The Wanderer* (1814),
 by Fanny Burney. DLB-39
Dee, John 1527-1609. . . . . DLB-136
Deeping, George Warwick
 1877-1950 . . . . DLB 153
Defense of *Amelia* (1752), by
 Henry Fielding DLB-39
Defoe, Daniel 1660-1731 . . . . DLB-39, 95, 101
de Fontaine, Felix Gregory
 1834-1896 . . . . DLB-43
De Forest, John William
 1826-1906 . . . . DLB-12, 189
DeFrees, Madeline 1919- DLB-105
DeGolyer, Everette Lee 1886-1956 . . . DLB-187
de Graff, Robert 1895-1981 . . . . Y-81
de Graft, Joe 1924-1978 . . . . DLB-117
De Heinrico circa 980? DLB-148
Deighton, Len 1929- DLB-87
DeJong, Meindert 1906-1991 . . . . . DLB-52
Dekker, Thomas
 circa 1572-1632 . . . . DLB-62, 172
Delacorte, Jr., George T.
 1894-1991 . . . . DLB-91
Delafield, E. M. 1890-1943 . . . . . . DLB-34
Delahaye, Guy 1888-1969 . . . . DLB-92
de la Mare, Walter
 1873-1956 . . . . DLB-19, 153, 162
Deland, Margaret 1857-1945 . . . . . . DLB-78
Delaney, Shelagh 1939- DLB-13
Delano, Amasa 1763-1823. . . . . . . DLB-183
Delany, Martin Robinson
 1812-1885 . . . . DLB-50
Delany, Samuel R. 1942- DLB-8, 33
de la Roche, Mazo 1879-1961 . . . . . DLB-68

344

Delavigne, Jean François Casimir 1793-1843 ... DLB-192
Delbanco, Nicholas 1942- ... DLB-6
De León, Nephtal 1945- ... DLB-82
Delgado, Abelardo Barrientos 1931- ... DLB-82
Del Giudice, Daniele 1949- ... DLB-196
De Libero, Libero 1906-1981 ... DLB-114
DeLillo, Don 1936- ... DLB-6, 173
de Lisser H. G. 1878-1944 ... DLB-117
Dell, Floyd 1887-1969 ... DLB-9
Dell Publishing Company ... DLB-46
delle Grazie, Marie Eugene 1864-1931 ... DLB-81
Deloney, Thomas died 1600 ... DLB-167
Deloria, Ella C. 1889-1971 ... DLB-175
Deloria, Vine, Jr. 1933- ... DLB-175
del Rey, Lester 1915-1993 ... DLB-8
Del Vecchio, John M. 1947- ... DS-9
de Man, Paul 1919-1983 ... DLB-67
Demby, William 1922- ... DLB-33
Deming, Philander 1829-1915 ... DLB-74
Demorest, William Jennings 1822-1895 ... DLB-79
De Morgan, William 1839-1917 ... DLB-153
Demosthenes 384 B.C.-322 B.C. ... DLB-176
Denham, Henry [publishing house] ... DLB-170
Denham, Sir John 1615-1669 ... DLB-58, 126
Denison, Merrill 1893-1975 ... DLB-92
Denison, T. S., and Company ... DLB-49
Dennery, Adolphe Philippe 1811-1899 ... DLB-192
Dennie, Joseph 1768-1812 ... DLB-37, 43, 59, 73
Dennis, John 1658-1734 ... DLB-101
Dennis, Nigel 1912-1989 ... DLB-13, 15
Denslow, W. W. 1856-1915 ... DLB-188
Dent, Tom 1932- ... DLB-38
Dent, J. M., and Sons ... DLB-112
Denton, Daniel circa 1626-1703 ... DLB-24
DePaola, Tomie 1934- ... DLB-61
Department of Library, Archives, and Institutional Research, American Bible Society ... Y-97
De Quille, Dan 1829-1898 ... DLB-186
De Quincey, Thomas 1785-1859 ... DLB-110, 144
Derby, George Horatio 1823-1861 ... DLB-11
Derby, J. C., and Company ... DLB-49
Derby and Miller ... DLB-49
Derleth, August 1909-1971 ... DLB-9; DS-17
The Derrydale Press ... DLB-46

Derzhavin, Gavriil Romanovich 1743-1816 ... DLB-150
Desaulniers, Gonsalve 1863-1934 ... DLB-92
Desbiens, Jean-Paul 1927- ... DLB-53
des Forêts, Louis-Rene 1918- ... DLB-83
Desiato, Luca 1941- ... DLB-196
Desnica, Vladan 1905-1967 ... DLB-181
DesRochers, Alfred 1901-1978 ... DLB-68
Desrosiers, Léo-Paul 1896-1967 ... DLB-68
Dessì, Giuseppe 1909-1977 ... DLB-177
Destouches, Louis-Ferdinand (see Céline, Louis-Ferdinand)
De Tabley, Lord 1835-1895 ... DLB-35
"A Detail in a Poem," by Fred Chappell ... DLB-105
Deutsch, Babette 1895-1982 ... DLB-45
Deutsch, Niklaus Manuel (see Manuel, Niklaus)
Deutsch, André, Limited ... DLB-112
Deveaux, Alexis 1948- ... DLB-38
The Development of the Author's Copyright in Britain ... DLB-154
The Development of Lighting in the Staging of Drama, 1900-1945 ... DLB-10
The Development of Meiji Japan ... DLB-180
De Vere, Aubrey 1814-1902 ... DLB-35
Devereux, second Earl of Essex, Robert 1565-1601 ... DLB-136
The Devin-Adair Company ... DLB-46
De Vinne, Theodore Low 1828-1914 ... DLB-187
De Voto, Bernard 1897-1955 ... DLB-9
De Vries, Peter 1910-1993 ... DLB-6; Y-82
Dewdney, Christopher 1951- ... DLB-60
Dewdney, Selwyn 1909-1979 ... DLB-68
DeWitt, Robert M., Publisher ... DLB-49
DeWolfe, Fiske and Company ... DLB-49
Dexter, Colin 1930- ... DLB-87
de Young, M. H. 1849-1925 ... DLB-25
Dhlomo, H. I. E. 1903-1956 ... DLB-157
Dhuoda circa 803-after 843 ... DLB-148
The Dial Press ... DLB-46
Diamond, I. A. L. 1920-1988 ... DLB-26
Dibdin, Thomas Frognall 1776-1847 ... DLB-184
Di Cicco, Pier Giorgio 1949- ... DLB-60
Dick, Philip K. 1928-1982 ... DLB-8
Dick and Fitzgerald ... DLB-49
Dickens, Charles 1812-1870 ... DLB-21, 55, 70, 159, 166
Dickinson, Peter 1927- ... DLB-161
Dickey, James 1923-1997 ... DLB-5, 193; Y-82, Y-93, Y-96; DS-7
Dickey, William 1928-1994 ... DLB-5

Dickinson, Emily 1830-1886 ... DLB-1
Dickinson, John 1732-1808 ... DLB-31
Dickinson, Jonathan 1688-1747 ... DLB-24
Dickinson, Patric 1914- ... DLB-27
Dickinson, Peter 1927- ... DLB-87
Dicks, John [publishing house] ... DLB-106
Dickson, Gordon R. 1923- ... DLB-8
Dictionary of Literary Biography Yearbook Awards ... Y-92, Y-93
The Dictionary of National Biography ... DLB-144
Didion, Joan 1934- ... DLB-2, 173, 185; Y-81, Y-86
Di Donato, Pietro 1911- ... DLB-9
Die Fürstliche Bibliothek Corvey ... Y-96
Diego, Gerardo 1896-1987 ... DLB-134
Digges, Thomas circa 1546-1595 ... DLB-136
Dillard, Annie 1945- ... Y-80
Dillard, R. H. W. 1937- ... DLB-5
Dillingham, Charles T., Company ... DLB-49
The Dillingham, G. W., Company ... DLB-49
Dilly, Edward and Charles [publishing house] ... DLB-154
Dilthey, Wilhelm 1833-1911 ... DLB-129
Dimitrova, Blaga 1922- ... DLB-181
Dimov, Dimitŭr 1909-1966 ... DLB-181
Dimsdale, Thomas J. 1831?-1866 ... DLB-186
Dingelstedt, Franz von 1814-1881 ... DLB-133
Dintenfass, Mark 1941- ... Y-84
Diogenes, Jr. (see Brougham, John)
Diogenes Laertius circa 200 ... DLB-176
DiPrima, Diane 1934- ... DLB-5, 16
Disch, Thomas M. 1940- ... DLB-8
Disney, Walt 1901-1966 ... DLB-22
Disraeli, Benjamin 1804-1881 ... DLB-21, 55
D'Israeli, Isaac 1766-1848 ... DLB-107
Ditzen, Rudolf (see Fallada, Hans)
Dix, Dorothea Lynde 1802-1887 ... DLB-1
Dix, Dorothy (see Gilmer, Elizabeth Meriwether)
Dix, Edwards and Company ... DLB-49
Dix, Gertrude circa 1874–? ... DLB-197
Dixie, Florence Douglas 1857-1905 ... DLB-174
Dixon, Ella Hepworth 1855 or 1857-1932 ... DLB-197
Dixon, Paige (see Corcoran, Barbara)
Dixon, Richard Watson 1833-1900 ... DLB-19
Dixon, Stephen 1936- ... DLB-130

Cumulative Index

Dmitriev, Ivan Ivanovich
  1760-1837 . . . . DLB-150

Dobell, Bertram 1842-1914 . . . . DLB-184

Dobell, Sydney 1824-1874 . . . . DLB-32

Döblin, Alfred 1878-1957. . . . . . . DLB-66

Dobson, Austin
  1840-1921 . . . . DLB-35, 144

Doctorow, E. L.
  1931- DLB-2, 28, 173; Y-80

Documents on Sixteenth-Century
  Literature. DLB-167, 172

Dodd, William E. 1869-1940. . . . . . DLB-17

Dodd, Anne [publishing house]. DLB-154

Dodd, Mead and Company DLB-49

Doderer, Heimito von 1896-1968 . . . . DLB-85

Dodge, Mary Mapes
  1831?-1905 . . . . DLB-42, 79; DS-13

Dodge, B. W., and Company DLB-46

Dodge Publishing Company DLB-49

Dodgson, Charles Lutwidge
  (see Carroll, Lewis)

Dodsley, Robert 1703-1764. . . . . . . DLB-95

Dodsley, R. [publishing house] DLB-154

Dodson, Owen 1914-1983 . . . . DLB-76

Doesticks, Q. K. Philander, P. B.
  (see Thomson, Mortimer)

Doheny, Carrie Estelle
  1875-1958 . . . . DLB-140

Doherty, John 1798?-1854. . . . . . . DLB-190

Domínguez, Sylvia Maida
  1935- DLB-122

Donahoe, Patrick
  [publishing house]. DLB-49

Donald, David H. 1920- DLB-17

Donaldson, Scott 1928- DLB-111

Doni, Rodolfo 1919- DLB-177

Donleavy, J. P. 1926- DLB-6, 173

Donnadieu, Marguerite (see Duras,
  Marguerite)

Donne, John 1572-1631 . . . . . . DLB-121, 151

Donnelley, R. R., and Sons
  Company DLB-49

Donnelly, Ignatius 1831-1901. . . . . . DLB-12

Donohue and Henneberry DLB-49

Donoso, José 1924- DLB-113

Doolady, M. [publishing house] DLB-49

Dooley, Ebon (see Ebon)

Doolittle, Hilda 1886-1961. . . . . . . DLB-4, 45

Doplicher, Fabio 1938- DLB-128

Dor, Milo 1923- DLB-85

Doran, George H., Company DLB-46

Dorgelès, Roland 1886-1973 . . . . . . DLB-65

Dorn, Edward 1929- DLB-5

Dorr, Rheta Childe 1866-1948 . . . . . DLB-25

Dorris, Michael 1945-1997 . . . . . . DLB-175

Dorset and Middlesex, Charles Sackville,
  Lord Buckhurst,
  Earl of 1643-1706 . . . . DLB-131

Dorst, Tankred 1925- DLB-75, 124

Dos Passos, John
  1896-1970 . . . . . DLB-4, 9; DS-1, DS-15

John Dos Passos: A Centennial
  Commemoration Y-96

Doubleday and Company DLB-49

Dougall, Lily 1858-1923 . . . . DLB-92

Doughty, Charles M.
  1843-1926. . . . . DLB-19, 57, 174

Douglas, Gavin 1476-1522 . . . . . . DLB-132

Douglas, Keith 1920-1944. . . . . . . DLB-27

Douglas, Norman 1868-1952 . . . . DLB-34, 195

Douglass, Frederick
  1817?-1895 . . . . DLB-1, 43, 50, 79

Douglass, William circa
  1691-1752 . . . . DLB-24

Dourado, Autran 1926- DLB-145

Dove, Arthur G. 1880-1946. . . . . . DLB-188

Dove, Rita 1952- DLB-120

Dover Publications DLB-46

Doves Press DLB-112

Dowden, Edward 1843-1913 . . . . DLB-35, 149

Dowell, Coleman 1925-1985 . . . . . DLB-130

Dowland, John 1563-1626. . . . . . . DLB-172

Downes, Gwladys 1915- DLB-88

Downing, J., Major (see Davis, Charles A.)

Downing, Major Jack (see Smith, Seba)

Dowriche, Anne
  before 1560-after 1613 . . . . DLB-172

Dowson, Ernest 1867-1900 . . . . DLB-19, 135

Doxey, William
  [publishing house]. DLB-49

Doyle, Sir Arthur Conan
  1859-1930 . . . . . . DLB-18, 70, 156, 178

Doyle, Kirby 1932- DLB-16

Doyle, Roddy 1958- DLB-194

Drabble, Margaret 1939- DLB-14, 155

Drach, Albert 1902- DLB-85

Dragojević, Danijel 1934- DLB-181

Drake, Samuel Gardner 1798-1875 . . . DLB-187

The Dramatic Publishing
  Company DLB-49

Dramatists Play Service DLB-46

Drant, Thomas
  early 1540s?-1578 . . . . DLB-167

Draper, John W. 1811-1882 . . . . . . DLB-30

Draper, Lyman C. 1815-1891 . . . . . DLB-30

Drayton, Michael 1563-1631 . . . . . DLB-121

Dreiser, Theodore
  1871-1945 . . . . DLB-9, 12, 102, 137; DS-1

Drewitz, Ingeborg 1923-1986 . . . . . . DLB-75

Drieu La Rochelle, Pierre
  1893-1945 . . . . DLB-72

Drinkwater, John 1882-1937
  . . . . DLB-10, 19, 149

Droste-Hülshoff, Annette von
  1797-1848 . . . . DLB-133

The Drue Heinz Literature Prize
  Excerpt from "Excerpts from a Report
  of the Commission," in David
  Bosworth's *The Death of Descartes*
  An Interview with David
  Bosworth Y-82

Drummond, William Henry
  1854-1907 . . . . DLB-92

Drummond, William, of Hawthornden
  1585-1649 . . . . DLB-121

Dryden, Charles 1860?-1931 . . . . . . DLB-171

Dryden, John 1631-1700 . . . DLB-80, 101, 131

Držić, Marin circa 1508-1567 . . . . . . DLB-147

Duane, William 1760-1835 . . . . DLB-43

Dubé, Marcel 1930- DLB-53

Dubé, Rodolphe (see Hertel, François)

Dubie, Norman 1945- DLB-120

Du Bois, W. E. B.
  1868-1963. . . . . DLB-47, 50, 91

Du Bois, William Pène 1916- DLB-61

Dubus, Andre 1936- DLB-130

Ducange, Victor 1783-1833 . . . . . . DLB-192

Du Chaillu, Paul Belloni
  1831?-1903 . . . . DLB-189

Ducharme, Réjean 1941- DLB-60

Dučić, Jovan 1871-1943 . . . . DLB-147

Duck, Stephen 1705?-1756 . . . . . . DLB-95

Duckworth, Gerald, and
  Company Limited. DLB-112

Dudek, Louis 1918- DLB-88

Duell, Sloan and Pearce DLB-46

Duerer, Albrecht 1471-1528 . . . . . . DLB-179

Dufief, Nicholas Gouin 1776-1834 . . . DLB-187

Duff Gordon, Lucie 1821-1869 . . . . . DLB-166

Duffield and Green DLB-46

Duffy, Maureen 1933- DLB-14

Dugan, Alan 1923- DLB-5

Dugard, William
  [publishing house] DLB-170

Dugas, Marcel 1883-1947 . . . . DLB-92

Dugdale, William
  [publishing house]. DLB-106

Duhamel, Georges 1884-1966 . . . . . DLB-65

Dujardin, Edouard 1861-1949 . . . . . DLB-123

Dukes, Ashley 1885-1959 . . . . DLB-10

du Maurier, Daphne 1907-1989 . . . . DLB-191

Du Maurier, George
  1834-1896 . . . . DLB-153, 178

Dumas, Alexandre *fils* 1824–1895.... DLB-192
Dumas, Alexandre *père* 1802-1870............DLB-119, 192
Dumas, Henry 1934-1968........DLB-41
Dunbar, Paul Laurence 1872-1906............DLB-50, 54, 78
Dunbar, William circa 1460-circa 1522.....DLB-132, 146
Duncan, Norman 1871-1916.......DLB-92
Duncan, Quince 1940-..........DLB-145
Duncan, Robert 1919-1988...DLB-5, 16, 193
Duncan, Ronald 1914-1982........DLB-13
Duncan, Sara Jeannette 1861-1922...............DLB-92
Dunigan, Edward, and Brother.....DLB-49
Dunlap, John 1747-1812.........DLB-43
Dunlap, William 1766-1839...........DLB-30, 37, 59
Dunn, Douglas 1942-..........DLB-40
Dunn, Harvey Thomas 1884-1952...DLB-188
Dunn, Stephen 1939-...........DLB-105
Dunne, Finley Peter 1867-1936...............DLB-11, 23
Dunne, John Gregory 1932-........Y-80
Dunne, Philip 1908-1992.........DLB-26
Dunning, Ralph Cheever 1878-1930...............DLB-4
Dunning, William A. 1857-1922...............DLB-17
Duns Scotus, John circa 1266-1308..........DLB-115
Dunsany, Lord (Edward John Moreton Drax Plunkett, Baron Dunsany) 1878-1957......DLB-10, 77, 153, 156
Dunton, John [publishing house]....DLB-170
Dunton, W. Herbert 1878-1936.....DLB-188
Dupin, Amantine-Aurore-Lucile (see Sand, George)
Durand, Lucile (see Bersianik, Louky)
Duranti, Francesca 1935-........DLB-196
Duranty, Walter 1884-1957........DLB-29
Duras, Marguerite 1914-.........DLB-83
Durfey, Thomas 1653-1723........DLB-80
Durrell, Lawrence 1912-1990.........DLB-15, 27; Y-90
Durrell, William [publishing house]...........DLB-49
Dürrenmatt, Friedrich 1921-1990.............DLB-69, 124
Dutton, E. P., and Company......DLB-49
Duvoisin, Roger 1904-1980........DLB-61
Duyckinck, Evert Augustus 1816-1878...............DLB-3, 64
Duyckinck, George L. 1823-1863.....DLB-3
Duyckinck and Company........DLB-49
Dwight, John Sullivan 1813-1893.....DLB-1

Dwight, Timothy 1752-1817........DLB-37
Dybek, Stuart 1942-..........DLB-130
Dyer, Charles 1928-...........DLB-13
Dyer, George 1755-1841.........DLB-93
Dyer, John 1699-1757..........DLB-95
Dyer, Sir Edward 1543-1607......DLB-136
Dylan, Bob 1941-............DLB-16

E

Eager, Edward 1911-1964........DLB-22
Eames, Wilberforce 1855-1937.....DLB-140
Earle, James H., and Company.....DLB-49
Earle, John 1600 or 1601-1665.....DLB-151
Early American Book Illustration, by Sinclair Hamilton.........DLB-49
Eastlake, William 1917-..........DLB-6
Eastman, Carol ?-............DLB-44
Eastman, Charles A. (Ohiyesa) 1858-1939...............DLB-175
Eastman, Max 1883-1969.........DLB-91
Eaton, Daniel Isaac 1753-1814.....DLB-158
Eberhart, Richard 1904-.........DLB-48
Ebner, Jeannie 1918-...........DLB-85
Ebner-Eschenbach, Marie von 1830-1916...............DLB-81
Ebon 1942-................DLB-41
Ecbasis Captivi circa 1045.........DLB-148
Ecco Press...............DLB-46
Eckhart, Meister circa 1260-circa 1328........DLB-115
The Eclectic Review 1805-1868......DLB-110
Eco, Umberto 1932-...........DLB-196
Edel, Leon 1907-............DLB-103
Edes, Benjamin 1732-1803........DLB-43
Edgar, David 1948-...........DLB-13
Edgeworth, Maria 1768-1849.........DLB-116, 159, 163
The Edinburgh Review 1802-1929.....DLB-110
Edinburgh University Press.......DLB-112
The Editor Publishing Company....DLB-49
Editorial Statements..........DLB-137
Edmonds, Randolph 1900-........DLB-51
Edmonds, Walter D. 1903-........DLB-9
Edschmid, Kasimir 1890-1966......DLB-56
Edwards, Amelia Anne Blandford 1831-1892...............DLB-174
Edwards, Edward 1812-1886......DLB-184
Edwards, Jonathan 1703-1758......DLB-24
Edwards, Jonathan, Jr. 1745-1801....DLB-37
Edwards, Junius 1929-..........DLB-33

Edwards, Matilda Barbara Betham- 1836-1919...............DLB-174
Edwards, Richard 1524-1566......DLB-62
Edwards, James [publishing house]...........DLB-154
Effinger, George Alec 1947-.......DLB-8
Egerton, George 1859-1945......DLB-135
Eggleston, Edward 1837-1902......DLB-12
Eggleston, Wilfred 1901-1986.......DLB-92
Ehrenstein, Albert 1886-1950......DLB-81
Ehrhart, W. D. 1948-............DS-9
Eich, Günter 1907-1972........DLB-69, 124
Eichendorff, Joseph Freiherr von 1788-1857...............DLB-90
1873 Publishers' Catalogues.......DLB-49
Eighteenth-Century Aesthetic Theories..............DLB-31
Eighteenth-Century Philosophical Background............DLB-31
Eigner, Larry 1926-1996........DLB-5, 193
Eikon Basilike 1649............DLB-151
Eilhart von Oberge circa 1140-circa 1195........DLB-148
Einhard circa 770-840..........DLB-148
Eiseley, Loren 1907-1977..........DS-17
Eisenreich, Herbert 1925-1986......DLB-85
Eisner, Kurt 1867-1919..........DLB-66
Eklund, Gordon 1945-...........Y-83
Ekwensi, Cyprian 1921-.........DLB-117
Eld, George [publishing house]...........DLB-170
Elder, Lonne III 1931-......DLB-7, 38, 44
Elder, Paul, and Company........DLB-49
Elements of Rhetoric (1828; revised, 1846), by Richard Whately [excerpt]....DLB-57
Elie, Robert 1915-1973..........DLB-88
Elin Pelin 1877-1949..........DLB-147
Eliot, George 1819-1880.....DLB-21, 35, 55
Eliot, John 1604-1690..........DLB-24
Eliot, T. S. 1888-1965....DLB-7, 10, 45, 63
Eliot's Court Press............DLB-170
Elizabeth I 1533-1603.........DLB-136
Elizabeth of Nassau-Saarbrücken after 1393-1456............DLB-179
Elizondo, Salvador 1932-........DLB-145
Elizondo, Sergio 1930-.........DLB-82
Elkin, Stanley 1930-......DLB-2, 28; Y-80
Elles, Dora Amy (see Wentworth, Patricia)
Ellet, Elizabeth F. 1818?-1877......DLB-30
Elliot, Ebenezer 1781-1849.....DLB-96, 190
Elliot, Frances Minto (Dickinson) 1820-1898...............DLB-166
Elliott, George 1923-...........DLB-68

Elliott, Janice 1931- DLB-14

Elliott, William 1788-1863 .... DLB-3

Elliott, Thomes and Talbot DLB-49

Ellis, Alice Thomas (Anna Margaret Haycraft) 1932- DLB-194

Ellis, Edward S. 1840-1916 .... DLB-42

Ellis, Frederick Staridge [publishing house] DLB-106

The George H. Ellis Company DLB-49

Ellis, Havelock 1859-1939 .... DLB-190

Ellison, Harlan 1934- DLB-8

Ellison, Ralph Waldo 1914-1994 .... DLB-2, 76; Y-94

Ellmann, Richard 1918-1987 .... DLB-103; Y-87

The Elmer Holmes Bobst Awards in Arts and Letters Y-87

Elyot, Thomas 1490?-1546 ...... DLB-136

Emanuel, James Andrew 1921- DLB-41

Emecheta, Buchi 1944- DLB-117

The Emergence of Black Women Writers DS-8

Emerson, Ralph Waldo 1803-1882 .... DLB-1, 59, 73, 183

Emerson, William 1769-1811 .... DLB-37

Emerson, William 1923-1997 .... Y-97

Emin, Fedor Aleksandrovich circa 1735-1770 .... DLB-150

Empedocles fifth century B.C. DLB-176

Empson, William 1906-1984 .... DLB-20

Enchi, Fumiko 1905-1986 .... DLB-182

Encounter with the West DLB-180

The End of English Stage Censorship, 1945-1968 .... DLB-13

Ende, Michael 1929- DLB-75

Endō, Shūsaku 1923-1996 .... DLB-182

Engel, Marian 1933-1985 .... DLB-53

Engels, Friedrich 1820-1895 .... DLB-129

Engle, Paul 1908- DLB-48

English Composition and Rhetoric (1866), by Alexander Bain [excerpt] DLB-57

The English Language: 410 to 1500 .... DLB-146

The English Renaissance of Art (1908), by Oscar Wilde DLB-35

Enright, D. J. 1920- DLB-27

Enright, Elizabeth 1909-1968 ...... DLB-22

L'Envoi (1882), by Oscar Wilde DLB-35

Epictetus circa 55-circa 125-130 ..... DLB-176

Epicurus 342/341 B.C.-271/270 B.C. DLB-176

Epps, Bernard 1936- DLB-53

Epstein, Julius 1909- and Epstein, Philip 1909-1952 ...... DLB-26

Equiano, Olaudah circa 1745-1797 .... DLB-37, 50

Eragny Press DLB-112

Erasmus, Desiderius 1467-1536 ..... DLB-136

Erba, Luciano 1922- DLB-128

Erdrich, Louise 1954- DLB-152, 178

Erichsen-Brown, Gwethalyn Graham (see Graham, Gwethalyn)

Eriugena, John Scottus circa 810-877 .... DLB-115

Ernest Hemingway's Toronto Journalism Revisited: With Three Previously Unrecorded Stories Y-92

Ernst, Paul 1866-1933 .... DLB-66, 118

Erskine, Albert 1911-1993 .... Y-93

Erskine, John 1879-1951 ...... DLB-9, 102

Erskine, Mrs. Steuart ?-1948 ...... DLB-195

Ervine, St. John Greer 1883-1971 .... DLB-10

Eschenburg, Johann Joachim 1743-c1820 ... DLB-97

Escoto, Julio 1944- DLB-145

Eshleman, Clayton 1935- DLB-5

Espriu, Salvador 1913-1985 .... DLB-134

Ess Ess Publishing Company DLB-49

Essay on Chatterton (1842), by Robert Browning DLB-32

Essex House Press DLB-112

Estes, Eleanor 1906-1988 .... DLB-22

Eszterhas, Joe 1944- DLB-185

Estes and Lauriat DLB-49

Etherege, George 1636-circa 1692 .... DLB-80

Ethridge, Mark, Sr. 1896-1981 ..... DLB-127

Ets, Marie Hall 1893- DLB-22

Etter, David 1928- DLB-105

Ettner, Johann Christoph 1654-1724 .... DLB-168

Eudora Welty: Eye of the Storyteller Y-87

Eugene O'Neill Memorial Theater Center DLB-7

Eugene O'Neill's Letters: A Review Y-88

Eupolemius flourished circa 1095 .... DLB-148

Euripides circa 484 B.C.-407/406 B.C. DLB-176

Evans, Caradoc 1878-1945 .... DLB-162

Evans, Charles 1850-1935 .... DLB-187

Evans, Donald 1884-1921 .... DLB-54

Evans, George Henry 1805-1856 ..... DLB-43

Evans, Hubert 1892-1986 .... DLB-92

Evans, Mari 1923- DLB-41

Evans, Mary Ann (see Eliot, George)

Evans, Nathaniel 1742-1767 .... DLB-31

Evans, Sebastian 1830-1909 .... DLB-35

Evans, M., and Company DLB-46

Everett, Alexander Hill 1790-1847 .... DLB-59

Everett, Edward 1794-1865 ...... DLB-1, 59

Everson, R. G. 1903- DLB-88

Everson, William 1912-1994 ...... DLB-5, 16

Every Man His Own Poet; or, The Inspired Singer's Recipe Book (1877), by W. H. Mallock DLB-35

Ewart, Gavin 1916- DLB-40

Ewing, Juliana Horatia 1841-1885 .... DLB-21, 163

The Examiner 1808-1881 .... DLB-110

Exley, Frederick 1929-1992 .... DLB-143; Y-81

Experiment in the Novel (1929), by John D. Beresford DLB-36

von Eyb, Albrecht 1420-1475 ...... DLB-179

"Eyes Across Centuries: Contemporary Poetry and 'That Vision Thing,'" by Philip Dacey DLB-105

Eyre and Spottiswoode DLB-106

Ezzo ?-after 1065 .... DLB-148

F

"F. Scott Fitzgerald: St. Paul's Native Son and Distinguished American Writer": University of Minnesota Conference, 29-31 October 1982 .... Y-82

Faber, Frederick William 1814-1863 .... DLB-32

Faber and Faber Limited DLB-112

Faccio, Rena (see Aleramo, Sibilla)

Fagundo, Ana María 1938- DLB-134

Fair, Ronald L. 1932- DLB-33

Fairfax, Beatrice (see Manning, Marie)

Fairlie, Gerard 1899-1983 .... DLB-77

Fallada, Hans 1893-1947 .... DLB-56

Falsifying Hemingway Y-96

Fancher, Betsy 1928- Y-83

Fane, Violet 1843-1905 .... DLB-35

Fanfrolico Press DLB-112

Fanning, Katherine 1927 .... DLB-127

Fanshawe, Sir Richard 1608-1666 .... DLB-126

Fantasy Press Publishers DLB-46

Fante, John 1909-1983 ...... DLB-130; Y-83

Al-Farabi circa 870-950 .... DLB-115

Farah, Nuruddin 1945- DLB-125

Farber, Norma 1909-1984 .... DLB-61

Farigoule, Louis (see Romains, Jules)

Farjeon, Eleanor 1881-1965 ...... DLB-160

Farley, Walter 1920-1989 .... DLB-22

Farmer, Penelope 1939- DLB-161

Farmer, Philip José 1918- DLB-8

Farquhar, George circa 1677-1707 .... DLB-84
Farquharson, Martha (see Finley, Martha)
Farrar, Frederic William
    1831-1903 .... DLB-163
Farrar and Rinehart............ DLB-46
Farrar, Straus and Giroux DLB-46
Farrell, James T.
    1904-1979 .... DLB-4, 9, 86; DS-2
Farrell, J. G. 1935-1979.......... DLB-14
Fast, Howard 1914- DLB-9
Faulkner and Yoknapatawpha Conference,
    Oxford, Mississippi............ Y-97
"Faulkner 100–Celebrating the Work," University
    of South Carolina, Columbia Y-97
Faulkner, William 1897-1962
    .... DLB-9, 11, 44, 102; DS-2; Y-86
Faulkner, George
    [publishing house].......... DLB-154
Fauset, Jessie Redmon 1882-1961 .... DLB-51
Faust, Irvin 1924- DLB-2, 28; Y-80
Fawcett Books................ DLB-46
Fawcett, Millicent Garrett 1847-1929 .. DLB-190
Fearing, Kenneth 1902-1961 .... DLB-9
Federal Writers' Project.......... DLB-46
Federman, Raymond 1928- Y-80
Feiffer, Jules 1929- DLB-7, 44
Feinberg, Charles E.
    1899-1988........... DLB-187; Y-88
Feind, Barthold 1678-1721........ DLB-168
Feinstein, Elaine 1930- DLB-14, 40
Feiss, Paul Louis 1875-1952....... DLB-187
Feldman, Irving 1928- DLB-169
Felipe, Léon 1884-1968 .... DLB-108
Fell, Frederick, Publishers........ DLB-46
Felltham, Owen 1602?-1668 .... DLB-126, 151
Fels, Ludwig 1946- DLB-75
Felton, Cornelius Conway
    1807-1862.................. DLB-1
Fenn, Harry 1837-1911 .... DLB-188
Fennario, David 1947- DLB-60
Fenno, John 1751-1798 .... DLB-43
Fenno, R. F., and Company....... DLB-49
Fenoglio, Beppe 1922-1963 .... DLB-177
Fenton, Geoffrey 1539?-1608 ..... DLB-136
Fenton, James 1949- DLB-40
Ferber, Edna 1885-1968...... DLB-9, 28, 86
Ferdinand, Vallery III (see Salaam, Kalamu ya)
Ferguson, Sir Samuel 1810-1886 ..... DLB-32
Ferguson, William Scott
    1875-1954................. DLB-47
Fergusson, Robert 1750-1774 ..... DLB-109
Ferland, Albert 1872-1943 .... DLB-92
Ferlinghetti, Lawrence 1919- DLB-5, 16

Fern, Fanny (see Parton, Sara Payson Willis)
Ferrars, Elizabeth 1907- DLB-87
Ferré, Rosario 1942- DLB-145
Ferret, E., and Company......... DLB-49
Ferrier, Susan 1782-1854 .... DLB-116
Ferrini, Vincent 1913- DLB-48
Ferron, Jacques 1921-1985 .... DLB-60
Ferron, Madeleine 1922- DLB-53
Ferrucci, Franco 1936- DLB-196
Fetridge and Company DLB-49
Feuchtersleben, Ernst Freiherr von
    1806-1849 .... DLB-133
Feuchtwanger, Lion 1884-1958...... DLB-66
Feuerbach, Ludwig 1804-1872...... DLB-133
Feuillet, Octave 1821-1890........ DLB-192
Feydeau, Georges 1862-1921 ...... DLB-192
Fichte, Johann Gottlieb
    1762-1814................. DLB-90
Ficke, Arthur Davison 1883-1945 .... DLB-54
Fiction Best-Sellers, 1910-1945....... DLB-9
Fiction into Film, 1928-1975: A List of Movies
    Based on the Works of Authors in
    British Novelists, 1930-1959 ...... DLB-15
Fiedler, Leslie A. 1917- DLB-28, 67
Field, Edward 1924- DLB-105
Field, Eugene
    1850-1895..... DLB-23, 42, 140; DS-13
Field, John 1545?-1588.......... DLB-167
Field, Marshall, III 1893-1956...... DLB-127
Field, Marshall, IV 1916-1965 ..... DLB-127
Field, Marshall, V 1941- DLB-127
Field, Nathan 1587-1619 or 1620 .... DLB-58
Field, Rachel 1894-1942 .... DLB-9, 22
A Field Guide to Recent Schools of American
    Poetry.................... Y-86
Fielding, Henry
    1707-1754......... DLB-39, 84, 101
Fielding, Sarah 1710-1768......... DLB-39
Fields, James Thomas 1817-1881 ..... DLB-1
Fields, Julia 1938- DLB-41
Fields, W. C. 1880-1946 .... DLB-44
Fields, Osgood and Company DLB-49
Fifty Penguin Years.............. Y-85
Figes, Eva 1932- DLB-14
Figuera, Angela 1902-1984 ...... DLB-108
Filmer, Sir Robert 1586-1653 ...... DLB-151
Filson, John circa 1753-1788 .... DLB-37
Finch, Anne, Countess of Winchilsea
    1661-1720................. DLB-95
Finch, Robert 1900- DLB-88
"Finding, Losing, Reclaiming: A Note on My
    Poems," by Robert Phillips..... DLB-105
Findley, Timothy 1930- DLB-53

Finlay, Ian Hamilton 1925- DLB-40
Finley, Martha 1828-1909......... DLB-42
Finn, Elizabeth Anne (McCaul)
    1825-1921 .... DLB-166
Finney, Jack 1911- DLB-8
Finney, Walter Braden (see Finney, Jack)
Firbank, Ronald 1886-1926........ DLB-36
Firmin, Giles 1615-1697.......... DLB-24
Fischart, Johann
    1546 or 1547-1590 or 1591 .... DLB-179
First Edition Library/Collectors'
    Reprints, Inc................. Y-91
First International F. Scott Fitzgerald
    Conference Y-92
First Strauss "Livings" Awarded to Cynthia
    Ozick and Raymond Carver
    An Interview with Cynthia Ozick
    An Interview with Raymond
    Carver Y-83
Fischer, Karoline Auguste Fernandine
    1764-1842 .... DLB-94
Fish, Stanley 1938- DLB-67
Fishacre, Richard 1205-1248....... DLB-115
Fisher, Clay (see Allen, Henry W.)
Fisher, Dorothy Canfield
    1879-1958................ DLB-9, 102
Fisher, Leonard Everett 1924- DLB-61
Fisher, Roy 1930- DLB-40
Fisher, Rudolph 1897-1934 ..... DLB-51, 102
Fisher, Sydney George 1856-1927 .... DLB-47
Fisher, Vardis 1895-1968.......... DLB-9
Fiske, John 1608-1677........... DLB-24
Fiske, John 1842-1901 .... DLB-47, 64
Fitch, Thomas circa 1700-1774...... DLB-31
Fitch, William Clyde 1865-1909...... DLB-7
FitzGerald, Edward 1809-1883 ..... DLB-32
Fitzgerald, F. Scott 1896-1940
    ..... DLB-4, 9, 86; Y-81; DS-1, 15, 16
F. Scott Fitzgerald Centenary
    Celebrations................. Y-96
Fitzgerald, Penelope 1916- DLB-14, 194
Fitzgerald, Robert 1910-1985....... Y-80
Fitzgerald, Thomas 1819-1891 ..... DLB-23
Fitzgerald, Zelda Sayre 1900-1948...... Y-84
Fitzhugh, Louise 1928-1974........ DLB-52
Fitzhugh, William
    circa 1651-1701............. DLB-24
Flagg, James Montgomery 1877-1960.. DLB-188
Flanagan, Thomas 1923- Y-80
Flanner, Hildegarde 1899-1987...... DLB-48
Flanner, Janet 1892-1978......... DLB-4
Flaubert, Gustave 1821-1880 ..... DLB-119
Flavin, Martin 1883-1967 .... DLB-9
Fleck, Konrad (flourished circa 1220)
    .... DLB-138

Flecker, James Elroy 1884-1915 . . . DLB-10, 19
Fleeson, Doris 1901-1970 . . . . DLB-29
Fleißer, Marieluise 1901-1974 . . . . DLB-56, 124
Fleming, Ian 1908-1964 . . . . DLB-87
Fleming, Paul 1609-1640 . . . . DLB-164
Fleming, Peter 1907-1971 . . . . DLB-195
The Fleshly School of Poetry and Other Phenomena of the Day (1872), by Robert Buchanan DLB-35
The Fleshly School of Poetry: Mr. D. G. Rossetti (1871), by Thomas Maitland (Robert Buchanan) DLB-35
Fletcher, Giles, the Elder 1546-1611 . . . . DLB-136
Fletcher, Giles, the Younger 1585 or 1586-1623 . . . . DLB-121
Fletcher, J. S. 1863-1935 . . . . DLB-70
Fletcher, John (see Beaumont, Francis)
Fletcher, John Gould 1886-1950 . . . DLB-4, 45
Fletcher, Phineas 1582-1650 . . . . . . DLB-121
Flieg, Helmut (see Heym, Stefan)
Flint, F. S. 1885-1960 . . . . DLB-19
Flint, Timothy 1780-1840 . . . . . DLB-73, 186
Florio, John 1553?-1625 . . . . DLB-172
Fo, Dario 1926- Y-97
Foix, J. V. 1893-1987 . . . . DLB-134
Foley, Martha (see Burnett, Whit, and Martha Foley)
Folger, Henry Clay 1857-1930 . . . . DLB-140
Folio Society DLB-112
Follen, Eliza Lee (Cabot) 1787-1860 . . . DLB-1
Follett, Ken 1949- DLB-87; Y-81
Follett Publishing Company DLB-46
Folsom, John West [publishing house] DLB-49
Folz, Hans between 1435 and 1440-1513 . . . . DLB-179
Fontane, Theodor 1819-1898 . . . . . DLB-129
Fonvisin, Denis Ivanovich 1744 or 1745-1792 . . . . DLB-150
Foote, Horton 1916- DLB-26
Foote, Mary Hallock 1847-1938 . . . DLB-186, 188
Foote, Samuel 1721-1777 . . . . DLB-89
Foote, Shelby 1916- DLB-2, 17
Forbes, Calvin 1945- DLB-41
Forbes, Ester 1891-1967 . . . . DLB-22
Forbes, Rosita 1893?-1967 . . . . DLB-195
Forbes and Company DLB-49
Force, Peter 1790-1868 . . . . DLB-30
Forché, Carolyn 1950- DLB-5, 193
Ford, Charles Henri 1913- DLB-4, 48
Ford, Corey 1902-1969 . . . . DLB-11
Ford, Ford Madox 1873-1939 . . . . DLB-34, 98, 162

Ford, Jesse Hill 1928- DLB-6
Ford, John 1586-? DLB-58
Ford, R. A. D. 1915- DLB-88
Ford, Worthington C. 1858-1941 . . . DLB-47
Ford, J. B., and Company DLB-49
Fords, Howard, and Hulbert DLB-49
Foreman, Carl 1914-1984 . . . . DLB-26
Forester, C. S. 1899-1966 . . . . DLB-191
Forester, Frank (see Herbert, Henry William)
"Foreword to Ludwig of Baviria," by Robert Peters DLB-105
Forman, Harry Buxton 1842-1917 . . . DLB-184
Fornés, María Irene 1930- DLB-7
Forrest, Leon 1937- DLB-33
Forster, E. M. 1879-1970 . . . . . DLB-34, 98, 162, 178, 195; DS-10
Forster, Georg 1754-1794 . . . . DLB-94
Forster, John 1812-1876 . . . . DLB-144
Forster, Margaret 1938- DLB-155
Forsyth, Frederick 1938- DLB-87
Forten, Charlotte L. 1837-1914 . . . . DLB-50
Fortini, Franco 1917- DLB-128
Fortune, T. Thomas 1856-1928 . . . . DLB-23
Fosdick, Charles Austin 1842-1915 . . . . DLB-42
Foster, Genevieve 1893-1979 . . . . . DLB-61
Foster, Hannah Webster 1758-1840 . . . . DLB-37
Foster, John 1648-1681 . . . . DLB-24
Foster, Michael 1904-1956 . . . . DLB-9
Foster, Myles Birket 1825-1899 . . . . DLB-184
Foulis, Robert and Andrew / R. and A. [publishing house] DLB-154
Fouqué, Caroline de la Motte 1774-1831 . . . . DLB-90
Fouqué, Friedrich de la Motte 1777-1843 . . . . DLB-90
Four Essays on the Beat Generation, by John Clellon Holmes DLB-16
Four Seas Company DLB-46
Four Winds Press DLB-46
Fournier, Henri Alban (see Alain-Fournier)
Fowler and Wells Company DLB-49
Fowles, John 1926- DLB-14, 139
Fox, John, Jr. 1862 or 1863-1919 . . DLB-9; DS-13
Fox, Paula 1923- DLB-52
Fox, Richard Kyle 1846-1922 . . . . . DLB-79
Fox, William Price 1926- DLB-2; Y-81
Fox, Richard K. [publishing house] DLB-49
Foxe, John 1517-1587 . . . . DLB-132
Fraenkel, Michael 1896-1957 . . . . . DLB-4
France, Anatole 1844-1924 . . . . . . DLB-123

France, Richard 1938- DLB-7
Francis, Convers 1795-1863 . . . . . . DLB-1
Francis, Dick 1920- DLB-87
Francis, Jeffrey, Lord 1773-1850 . . . DLB-107
Francis, C. S. [publishing house] . . . DLB-49
François 1863-1910 . . . . DLB-92
François, Louise von 1817-1893 . . . DLB-129
Franck, Sebastian 1499-1542 . . . . . DLB-179
Francke, Kuno 1855-1930 . . . . DLB-71
Frank, Bruno 1887-1945 . . . . DLB-118
Frank, Leonhard 1882-1961 . . . . DLB-56, 118
Frank, Melvin (see Panama, Norman)
Frank, Waldo 1889-1967 . . . . DLB-9, 63
Franken, Rose 1895?-1988 . . . . Y-84
Franklin, Benjamin 1706-1790 . . . . DLB-24, 43, 73, 183
Franklin, James 1697-1735 . . . . . . DLB-43
Franklin Library DLB-46
Frantz, Ralph Jules 1902-1979 . . . . DLB-4
Franzos, Karl Emil 1848-1904 . . . . DLB-129
Fraser, G. S. 1915-1980 . . . . DLB-27
Fraser, Kathleen 1935- DLB-169
Frattini, Alberto 1922- DLB-128
Frau Ava ?-1127 . . . . DLB-148
Frayn, Michael 1933- DLB-13, 14, 194
Frederic, Harold 1856-1898 . . . . DLB-12, 23; DS-13
Freeling, Nicolas 1927- DLB-87
Freeman, Douglas Southall 1886-1953 . . . . DLB-17; DS-17
Freeman, Legh Richmond 1842-1915 . . . . DLB-23
Freeman, Mary E. Wilkins 1852-1930 . . . . DLB-12, 78
Freeman, R. Austin 1862-1943 . . . . DLB-70
Freidank circa 117ć-circa 1233 . . . . DLB-138
Freiligrath, Ferdinand 1810-1876 . . . DLB-133
Frémont, John Charles 1813-1890 . . . DLB-186
Frémont, John Charles 1813-1890 and Frémont, Jessie Benton 1834-1902 . . . . DLB-183
French, Alice 1850-1934 . . . . . DLB-74; DS-13
French, David 1939- DLB-53
French, Evangeline 1869-1960 . . . . DLB-195
French, Francesca 1871-1960 . . . . . DLB-195
French, James [publishing house] . . . DLB-49
French, Samuel [publishing house] . . . DLB-49
Samuel French, Limited DLB-106
Freneau, Philip 1752-1832 . . . . . DLB-37, 43
Freni, Melo 1934- DLB-128
Freshfield, Douglas W. 1845-1934 . . . . DLB-174
Freytag, Gustav 1816-1895 . . . . . . DLB-129

Fried, Erich 1921-1988 . . . . DLB-85

Friedman, Bruce Jay 1930- DLB-2, 28

Friedrich von Hausen
 circa 1171-1190 . . . . DLB-138

Friel, Brian 1929- DLB-13

Friend, Krebs 1895?-1967? DLB-4

Fries, Fritz Rudolf 1935- DLB-75

Fringe and Alternative Theater
 in Great Britain DLB-13

Frisch, Max 1911-1991 . . . . . . DLB-69, 124

Frischlin, Nicodemus 1547-1590 . . . . DLB-179

Frischmuth, Barbara 1941- DLB-85

Fritz, Jean 1915- DLB-52

Fromentin, Eugene 1820-1876 . . . . . DLB-123

From *The Gay Science*, by
 E. S. Dallas DLB-21

Frost, A. B. 1851-1928 . . . . . DLB-188; DS-13

Frost, Robert 1874-1963 . . . . . . DLB-54; DS-7

Frothingham, Octavius Brooks
 1822-1895 . . . . DLB-1

Froude, James Anthony
 1818-1894 . . . . DLB-18, 57, 144

Fry, Christopher 1907- DLB-13

Fry, Roger 1866-1934 . . . . DS-10

Frye, Northrop 1912-1991 . . . . DLB-67, 68

Fuchs, Daniel
 1909-1993 . . . . DLB-9, 26, 28; Y-93

Fuentes, Carlos 1928- DLB-113

Fuertes, Gloria 1918- DLB-108

The Fugitives and the Agrarians:
 The First Exhibition Y-85

Fulbecke, William 1560-1603? DLB-172

Fuller, Charles H., Jr. 1939- DLB-38

Fuller, Henry Blake 1857-1929 . . . . . DLB-12

Fuller, John 1937- DLB-40

Fuller, Margaret (see Fuller, Sarah Margaret,
 Marchesa D'Ossoli)

Fuller, Roy 1912-1991 . . . . DLB-15, 20

Fuller, Samuel 1912- DLB-26

Fuller, Sarah Margaret, Marchesa
 D'Ossoli 1810-1850 . . . DLB-1, 59, 73, 183

Fuller, Thomas 1608-1661 . . . . DLB-151

Fullerton, Hugh 1873-1945 . . . . . . DLB-171

Fulton, Alice 1952- DLB-193

Fulton, Len 1934- Y-86

Fulton, Robin 1937- DLB-40

Furbank, P. N. 1920- DLB-155

Furman, Laura 1945- Y-86

Furness, Horace Howard
 1833-1912 . . . . DLB-64

Furness, William Henry 1802-1896 . . . . DLB-1

Furnivall, Frederick James
 1825-1910 . . . . DLB-184

Furthman, Jules 1888-1966 . . . . DLB-26

Furui, Yoshikichi 1937- DLB-182

Futabatei, Shimei (Hasegawa Tatsunosuke)
 1864-1909 . . . . DLB-180

The Future of the Novel (1899), by
 Henry James DLB-18

Fyleman, Rose 1877-1957 . . . . DLB-160

G

The G. Ross Roy Scottish Poetry
 Collection at the University of
 South Carolina Y-89

Gadda, Carlo Emilio 1893-1973 . . . . DLB-177

Gaddis, William 1922- DLB-2

Gág, Wanda 1893-1946 . . . . DLB-22

Gagnon, Madeleine 1938- DLB-60

Gaine, Hugh 1726-1807 . . . . DLB-43

Gaine, Hugh [publishing house] DLB-49

Gaines, Ernest J.
 1933- DLB-2, 33, 152; Y-80

Gaiser, Gerd 1908-1976 . . . . DLB-69

Galarza, Ernesto 1905-1984 . . . . . . DLB-122

Galaxy Science Fiction Novels DLB-46

Gale, Zona 1874-1938 . . . . DLB-9, 78

Galen of Pergamon 129-after 210 . . . DLB-176

Gall, Louise von 1815-1855 . . . . . . DLB-133

Gallagher, Tess 1943- DLB-120

Gallagher, Wes 1911- DLB-127

Gallagher, William Davis
 1808-1894 . . . . DLB-73

Gallant, Mavis 1922- DLB-53

Gallico, Paul 1897-1976 . . . . . . DLB-9, 171

Gallup, Donald 1913- DLB-187

Galsworthy, John
 1867-1933 . . . DLB-10, 34, 98, 162; DS-16

Galt, John 1779-1839 . . . . DLB-99, 116

Galton, Sir Francis 1822-1911 . . . . . DLB-166

Galvin, Brendan 1938- DLB-5

Gambit DLB-46

Gamboa, Reymundo 1948- DLB-122

Gammer Gurton's Needle DLB-62

Gannett, Frank E. 1876-1957 . . . . . . DLB-29

Gaos, Vicente 1919-1980 . . . . DLB-134

García, Lionel G. 1935- DLB-82

García Lorca, Federico
 1898-1936 . . . . DLB-108

García Márquez, Gabriel
 1928- DLB-113; Y-82

Gardam, Jane 1928- DLB-14, 161

Garden, Alexander
 circa 1685-1756 . . . . DLB-31

Gardiner, Margaret Power Farmer (see
 Blessington, Marguerite, Countess of)

Gardner, John 1933-1982 . . . . . DLB-2; Y-82

Garfield, Leon 1921- DLB-161

Garis, Howard R. 1873-1962 . . . . . . DLB-22

Garland, Hamlin
 1860-1940 . . . . DLB-12, 71, 78, 186

Garneau, Francis-Xavier
 1809-1866 . . . . DLB-99

Garneau, Hector de Saint-Denys
 1912-1943 . . . . DLB-88

Garneau, Michel 1939- DLB-53

Garner, Alan 1934- DLB-161

Garner, Hugh 1913-1979 . . . . DLB-68

Garnett, David 1892-1981 . . . . DLB-34

Garnett, Eve 1900-1991 . . . . DLB-160

Garnett, Richard 1835-1906 . . . . . . DLB-184

Garrard, Lewis H. 1829-1887 . . . . . . DLB-186

Garraty, John A. 1920- DLB-17

Garrett, George
 1929- DLB-2, 5, 130, 152; Y-83

Garrett, John Work 1872-1942 . . . . . DLB-187

Garrick, David 1717-1779 . . . . DLB-84

Garrison, William Lloyd
 1805-1879 . . . . DLB-1, 43

Garro, Elena 1920- DLB-145

Garth, Samuel 1661-1719 . . . . DLB-95

Garve, Andrew 1908- DLB-87

Gary, Romain 1914-1980 . . . . DLB-83

Gascoigne, George 1539?-1577 . . . . . DLB-136

Gascoyne, David 1916- DLB-20

Gaskell, Elizabeth Cleghorn
 1810-1865 . . . . DLB-21, 144, 159

Gaspey, Thomas 1788-1871 . . . . DLB-116

Gass, William Howard 1924- DLB-2

Gates, Doris 1901- DLB-22

Gates, Henry Louis, Jr. 1950- DLB-67

Gates, Lewis E. 1860-1924 . . . . DLB-71

Gatto, Alfonso 1909-1976 . . . . DLB-114

Gaunt, Mary 1861-1942 . . . . DLB-174

Gautier, Théophile 1811-1872 . . . . . DLB-119

Gauvreau, Claude 1925-1971 . . . . . . DLB-88

The *Gawain*-Poet
 flourished circa 1350-1400 . . . . . . DLB-146

Gay, Ebenezer 1696-1787 . . . . DLB-24

Gay, John 1685-1732 . . . . DLB-84, 95

The Gay Science (1866), by E. S. Dallas [excerpt]
 . . . . DLB-21

Gayarré, Charles E. A. 1805-1895 . . . . DLB-30

Gaylord, Edward King
 1873-1974 . . . . DLB-127

Gaylord, Edward Lewis 1919- DLB-127

Gaylord, Charles
 [publishing house] DLB-49

Geddes, Gary 1940- DLB-60

Geddes, Virgil 1897- DLB-4

Gedeon (Georgii Andreevich Krinovsky)
 circa 1730-1763 .... DLB-150

Geibel, Emanuel 1815-1884 .... DLB-129

Geiogamah, Hanay 1945- DLB-175

Geis, Bernard, Associates DLB-46

Geisel, Theodor Seuss
 1904-1991. .... DLB-61; Y-91

Gelb, Arthur 1924- DLB-103

Gelb, Barbara 1926- DLB-103

Gelber, Jack 1932- DLB-7

Gelinas, Gratien 1909- DLB-88

Gellert, Christian Füerchtegott
 1715-1769 .... DLB-97

Gellhorn, Martha 1908- Y-82

Gems, Pam 1925- DLB-13

A General Idea of the College of Mirania (1753),
 by William Smith [excerpts] DLB-31

Genet, Jean 1910-1986 .... DLB-72; Y-86

Genevoix, Maurice 1890-1980 ..... DLB-65

Genovese, Eugene D. 1930- DLB-17

Gent, Peter 1942- Y-82

Geoffrey of Monmouth
 circa 1100-1155 .... DLB-146

George, Henry 1839-1897 .... DLB-23

George, Jean Craighead 1919- DLB-52

George, W. L. 1882-1926 .... DLB-197

Georgslied 896? DLB-148

Gerhardie, William 1895-1977 ..... DLB-36

Gerhardt, Paul 1607-1676 .... DLB-164

Gérin, Winifred 1901-1981 .... DLB-155

Gérin-Lajoie, Antoine 1824-1882 .... DLB-99

German Drama 800-1280 .... DLB-138

German Drama from Naturalism
 to Fascism: 1889-1933. .... DLB-118

German Literature and Culture from
 Charlemagne to the Early Courtly
 Period DLB-148

German Radio Play, The DLB-124

German Transformation from the Baroque
 to the Enlightenment, The DLB-97

The Germanic Epic and Old English Heroic
 Poetry: *Widseth, Waldere,* and *The
 Fight at Finnsburg.* DLB-146

Germanophilism, by Hans Kohn DLB-66

Gernsback, Hugo 1884-1967 ..... DLB-8, 137

Gerould, Katharine Fullerton
 1879-1944 .... DLB-78

Gerrish, Samuel [publishing house] ... DLB-49

Gerrold, David 1944- DLB-8

The Ira Gershwin Centenary Y-96

Gersonides 1288-1344 .... DLB-115

Gerstäcker, Friedrich 1816-1872 .... DLB-129

Gerstenberg, Heinrich Wilhelm von
 1737-1823 .... DLB-97

Gervinus, Georg Gottfried
 1805-1871 .... DLB-133

Geßner, Salomon 1730-1788 .... DLB-97

Geston, Mark S. 1946- DLB-8

"Getting Started: Accepting the Regions You
 Own–or Which Own You," by Walter
 McDonald DLB-105

Al-Ghazali 1058-1111 .... DLB-115

Gibbings, Robert 1889-1958 ...... DLB-195

Gibbon, Edward 1737-1794 ...... DLB-104

Gibbon, John Murray 1875-1952 .... DLB-92

Gibbon, Lewis Grassic (see Mitchell,
 James Leslie)

Gibbons, Floyd 1887-1939 .... DLB-25

Gibbons, Reginald 1947- DLB-120

Gibbons, William ?-? DLB-73

Gibson, Charles Dana 1867-1944 .... DS-13

Gibson, Charles Dana
 1867-1944 .... DLB-188; DS-13

Gibson, Graeme 1934- DLB-53

Gibson, Margaret 1944- DLB-120

Gibson, Margaret Dunlop
 1843-1920 .... DLB-174

Gibson, Wilfrid 1878-1962 .... DLB-19

Gibson, William 1914- DLB-7

Gide, André 1869-1951 .... DLB-65

Giguère, Diane 1937- DLB-53

Giguère, Roland 1929- DLB-60

Gil de Biedma, Jaime 1929-1990 .... DLB-108

Gil-Albert, Juan 1906- DLB-134

Gilbert, Anthony 1899-1973 ...... DLB-77

Gilbert, Michael 1912- DLB-87

Gilbert, Sandra M. 1936- DLB-120

Gilbert, Sir Humphrey
 1537-1583 .... DLB-136

Gilchrist, Alexander
 1828-1861 .... DLB-144

Gilchrist, Ellen 1935- DLB-130

Gilder, Jeannette L. 1849-1916 ..... DLB-79

Gilder, Richard Watson
 1844-1909 .... DLB-64, 79

Gildersleeve, Basil 1831-1924 ...... DLB-71

Giles, Henry 1809-1882 .... DLB-64

Giles of Rome circa 1243-1316 ..... DLB-115

Gilfillan, George 1813-1878 ...... DLB-144

Gill, Eric 1882-1940 .... DLB-98

Gill, William F., Company DLB-49

Gillespie, A. Lincoln, Jr.
 1895-1950 .... DLB-4

Gilliam, Florence ?-? DLB-4

Gilliatt, Penelope 1932-1993 ...... DLB-14

Gillott, Jacky 1939-1980 .... DLB-14

Gilman, Caroline H. 1794-1888 .... DLB-3, 73

Gilman, W. and J.
 [publishing house] DLB-49

Gilmer, Elizabeth Meriwether
 1861-1951 .... DLB-29

Gilmer, Francis Walker
 1790-1826 .... DLB-37

Gilroy, Frank D. 1925- DLB-7

Gimferrer, Pere (Pedro) 1945- DLB-134

Gingrich, Arnold 1903-1976 ...... DLB-137

Ginsberg, Allen 1926- DLB-5, 16, 169

Ginzburg, Natalia 1916-1991 ..... DLB-177

Ginzkey, Franz Karl 1871-1963 .... DLB-81

Gioia, Dana 1950- DLB-120

Giono, Jean 1895-1970 .... DLB-72

Giotti, Virgilio 1885-1957 .... DLB-114

Giovanni, Nikki 1943- DLB-5, 41

Gipson, Lawrence Henry
 1880-1971 .... DLB-17

Girard, Rodolphe 1879-1956 ...... DLB-92

Giraudoux, Jean 1882-1944 .... DLB-65

Gissing, George 1857-1903 .. DLB-18, 135, 184

Giudici, Giovanni 1924- DLB-128

Giuliani, Alfredo 1924- DLB-128

Glackens, William J. 1870-1938 .... DLB-188

Gladstone, William Ewart
 1809-1898 .... DLB-57, 184

Glaeser, Ernst 1902-1963 .... DLB-69

Glancy, Diane 1941- DLB-175

Glanville, Brian 1931- DLB-15, 139

Glapthorne, Henry 1610-1643? DLB-58

Glasgow, Ellen 1873-1945 ...... DLB-9, 12

Glasier, Katharine Bruce 1867-1950 . DLB-190

Glaspell, Susan 1876-1948 ..... DLB-7, 9, 78

Glass, Montague 1877-1934 .... DLB-11

The Glass Key and Other Dashiell Hammett
 Mysteries Y-96

Glassco, John 1909-1981 .... DLB-68

Glauser, Friedrich 1896-1938 ..... DLB-56

F. Gleason's Publishing Hall DLB-49

Gleim, Johann Wilhelm Ludwig
 1719-1803 .... DLB-97

Glendinning, Victoria 1937- DLB-155

Glover, Richard 1712-1785 .... DLB-95

Glück, Louise 1943- DLB-5

Glyn, Elinor 1864-1943 .... DLB-153

Gobineau, Joseph-Arthur de
 1816-1882 .... DLB-123

Godbout, Jacques 1933- DLB-53

Goddard, Morrill 1865-1937 ...... DLB-25

Goddard, William 1740-1817 ...... DLB-43

Godden, Rumer 1907- DLB-161

Godey, Louis A. 1804-1878 .... DLB-73

Godey and McMichael DLB-49

Godfrey, Dave 1938- DLB-60

Godfrey, Thomas 1736-1763 . . . . . . DLB-31

Godine, David R., Publisher DLB-46

Godkin, E. L. 1831-1902 . . . . DLB-79

Godolphin, Sidney 1610-1643 . . . . . DLB-126

Godwin, Gail 1937- DLB-6

Godwin, Mary Jane Clairmont
  1766-1841 . . . . DLB-163

Godwin, Parke 1816-1904 . . . . . . DLB-3, 64

Godwin, William
  1756-1836 . . . . DLB-39, 104, 142, 158, 163

Godwin, M. J., and Company DLB-154

Goering, Reinhard 1887-1936 . . . . . DLB-118

Goes, Albrecht 1908- DLB-69

Goethe, Johann Wolfgang von
  1749-1832 . . . . DLB-94

Goetz, Curt 1888-1960 . . . . DLB-124

Goffe, Thomas circa 1592-1629 . . . . DLB-58

Goffstein, M. B. 1940- DLB-61

Gogarty, Oliver St. John
  1878-1957 . . . . DLB-15, 19

Goines, Donald 1937-1974 . . . . DLB-33

Gold, Herbert 1924- DLB-2; Y-81

Gold, Michael 1893-1967 . . . . . . DLB-9, 28

Goldbarth, Albert 1948- DLB-120

Goldberg, Dick 1947- DLB-7

Golden Cockerel Press DLB-112

Golding, Arthur 1536-1606 . . . . . . DLB-136

Golding, Louis 1895-1958 . . . . DLB-195

Golding, William 1911-1993 . DLB-15, 100; Y-83

Goldman, William 1931- DLB-44

Goldring, Douglas 1887-1960 . . . . . DLB-197

Goldsmith, Oliver
  1730?-1774 . . . . DLB-39, 89, 104, 109, 142

Goldsmith, Oliver 1794-1861 . . . . . DLB-99

Goldsmith Publishing Company DLB-46

Goldstein, Richard 1944- DLB-185

Gollancz, Victor, Limited DLB-112

Gómez-Quiñones, Juan 1942- DLB-122

Gomme, Laurence James
  [publishing house] DLB-46

Goncourt, Edmond de 1822-1896 . . . DLB-123

Goncourt, Jules de 1830-1870 . . . . . DLB-123

Gonzales, Rodolfo "Corky"
  1928- DLB-122

González, Angel 1925- DLB-108

Gonzalez, Genaro 1949- DLB-122

Gonzalez, Ray 1952- DLB-122

González de Mireles, Jovita
  1899-1983 . . . . DLB-122

González-T., César A. 1931- DLB-82

"The Good, The Not So Good," by
  Stephen Dunn DLB-105

Goodbye, Gutenberg? A Lecture at
  the New York Public Library,
  18 April 1995 . . . . Y-95

Goodison, Lorna 1947- DLB-157

Goodman, Paul 1911-1972 . . . . . . DLB-130

The Goodman Theatre DLB-7

Goodrich, Frances 1891-1984 and
  Hackett, Albert 1900- DLB-26

Goodrich, Samuel Griswold
  1793-1860 . . . . DLB-1, 42, 73

Goodrich, S. G. [publishing house] . . . DLB-49

Goodspeed, C. E., and Company . . . DLB-49

Goodwin, Stephen 1943- Y-82

Googe, Barnabe 1540-1594 . . . . . . DLB-132

Gookin, Daniel 1612-1687 . . . . . . DLB-24

Gordimer, Nadine 1923- Y-91

Gordon, Caroline
  1895-1981 . . . . DLB-4, 9, 102; DS-17; Y-81

Gordon, Giles 1940- DLB-14, 139

Gordon, Helen Cameron, Lady Russell
  1867-1949 . . . . DLB-195

Gordon, Lyndall 1941- DLB-155

Gordon, Mary 1949- DLB-6; Y-81

Gordone, Charles 1925- DLB-7

Gore, Catherine 1800-1861 . . . . . . DLB-116

Gorey, Edward 1925- DLB-61

Gorgias of Leontini circa 485 B.C.-376 B.C.
  . . . . DLB-176

Görres, Joseph 1776-1848 . . . . DLB-90

Gosse, Edmund 1849-1928 . . DLB-57, 144, 184

Gosson, Stephen 1554-1624 . . . . . . DLB-172

Gotlieb, Phyllis 1926- DLB-88

Gottfried von Straßburg
  died before 1230 . . . . DLB-138

Gotthelf, Jeremias 1797-1854 . . . . . DLB-133

Gottschalk circa 804/808-869 . . . . . DLB-148

Gottsched, Johann Christoph
  1700-1766 . . . . DLB-97

Götz, Johann Nikolaus
  1721-1781 . . . . DLB-97

Goudge, Elizabeth 1900-1984 . . . . . DLB-191

Gould, Wallace 1882-1940 . . . . . . DLB-54

Govoni, Corrado 1884-1965 . . . . . . DLB-114

Gower, John circa 1330-1408 . . . . . DLB-146

Goyen, William 1915-1983 . . . . DLB-2; Y-83

Goytisolo, José Agustín 1928- DLB-134

Gozzano, Guido 1883-1916 . . . . . . DLB-114

Grabbe, Christian Dietrich
  1801-1836 . . . . DLB-133

Gracq, Julien 1910- DLB-83

Grady, Henry W. 1850-1889 . . . . . . DLB-23

Graf, Oskar Maria 1894-1967 . . . . . DLB-56

Graf Rudolf between circa 1170
  and circa 1185 . . . . DLB-148

Grafton, Richard
  [publishing house] DLB-170

Graham, George Rex
  1813-1894 . . . . DLB-73

Graham, Gwethalyn 1913-1965 . . . . DLB-88

Graham, Jorie 1951- DLB-120

Graham, Katharine 1917- DLB-127

Graham, Lorenz 1902-1989 . . . . . . DLB-76

Graham, Philip 1915-1963 . . . . . . DLB-127

Graham, R. B. Cunninghame
  1852-1936 . . . . DLB-98, 135, 174

Graham, Shirley 1896-1977 . . . . . . DLB-76

Graham, Stephen 1884-1975 . . . . . DLB-195

Graham, W. S. 1918- DLB-20

Graham, William H.
  [publishing house] DLB-49

Graham, Winston 1910- DLB-77

Grahame, Kenneth
  1859-1932 . . . . DLB-34, 141, 178

Grainger, Martin Allerdale
  1874-1941 . . . . DLB-92

Gramatky, Hardie 1907-1979 . . . . . DLB-22

Grand, Sarah 1854-1943 . . . . DLB-135, 197

Grandbois, Alain 1900-1975 . . . . . . DLB-92

Grange, John circa 1556-? DLB-136

Granich, Irwin (see Gold, Michael)

Grant, Duncan 1885-1978 . . . . DS-10

Grant, George 1918-1988 . . . . DLB-88

Grant, George Monro 1835-1902 . . . DLB-99

Grant, Harry J. 1881-1963 . . . . . . DLB-29

Grant, James Edward 1905-1966 . . . DLB-26

Grass, Günter 1927- DLB-75, 124

Grasty, Charles H. 1863-1924 . . . . . DLB-25

Grau, Shirley Ann 1929- DLB-2

Graves, John 1920- Y-83

Graves, Richard 1715-1804 . . . . . . DLB-39

Graves, Robert
  1895-1985 . . . . . . DLB-20, 100, 191; Y-85

Gray, Alasdair 1934- DLB-194

Gray, Asa 1810-1888 . . . . DLB-1

Gray, David 1838-1861 . . . . DLB-32

Gray, Simon 1936- DLB-13

Gray, Thomas 1716-1771 . . . . DLB-109

Grayson, William J. 1788-1863 . . . DLB-3, 64

The Great Bibliographers Series Y-93

The Great War and the Theater, 1914-1918
  [Great Britain] DLB-10

The Great War Exhibition and Symposium at the
  University of South Carolina Y-97

Greeley, Horace 1811-1872 . . . DLB-3, 43, 189

Green, Adolph (see Comden, Betty)

Green, Duff 1791-1875 . . . . DLB-43

Green, Elizabeth Shippen 1871-1954 . . DLB-188

Green, Gerald 1922- DLB-28

Green, Henry 1905-1973 . . . . DLB-15

Green, Jonas 1712-1767. . . . . DLB-31

Green, Joseph 1706-1780 . . . . DLB-31

Green, Julien 1900- DLB-4, 72

Green, Paul 1894-1981. . . . . . DLB-7, 9; Y-81

Green, T. and S.
[publishing house]. DLB-49

Green, Thomas Hill 1836-1882. . . . . DLB-190

Green, Timothy
[publishing house]. DLB-49

Greenaway, Kate 1846-1901. . . . . . . DLB-141

Greenberg: Publisher DLB-46

Green Tiger Press. DLB-46

Greene, Asa 1789-1838 . . . . DLB-11

Greene, Belle da Costa 1883-1950 . . . DLB-187

Greene, Benjamin H.
[publishing house]. DLB-49

Greene, Graham 1904-1991
. . . DLB-13, 15, 77, 100, 162; Y-85, Y-91

Greene, Robert 1558-1592 . . . . . DLB-62, 167

Greene Jr., Robert Bernard (Bob)
1947- DLB-185

Greenhow, Robert 1800-1854 . . . . . . DLB-30

Greenlee, William B. 1872-1953 . . . . DLB-187

Greenough, Horatio 1805-1852 . . . . . . DLB-1

Greenwell, Dora 1821-1882. . . . . DLB-35

Greenwillow Books DLB-46

Greenwood, Grace (see Lippincott, Sara Jane Clarke)

Greenwood, Walter 1903-1974 . . . DLB-10, 191

Greer, Ben 1948- DLB-6

Greflinger, Georg 1620?-1677. . . . . . DLB-164

Gregg, W. R. 1809-1881. . . . . DLB-55

Gregg, Josiah 1806-1850 . . . . . DLB-183, 186

Gregg Press DLB-46

Gregory, Isabella Augusta
Persse, Lady 1852-1932 . . . . . . DLB-10

Gregory, Horace 1898-1982 . . . . DLB-48

Gregory of Rimini
circa 1300-1358 . . . . DLB-115

Gregynog Press DLB-112

Greiffenberg, Catharina Regina von
1633-1694 . . . . DLB-168

Grenfell, Wilfred Thomason
1865-1940 . . . . DLB-92

Greve, Felix Paul (see Grove, Frederick Philip)

Greville, Fulke, First Lord Brooke
1554-1628 . . . . DLB-62, 172

Grey, Sir George, K.C.B.
1812-1898 . . . . DLB-184

Grey, Lady Jane 1537-1554 . . . . DLB-132

Grey Owl 1888-1938. . . . . . DLB-92; DS-17

Grey, Zane 1872-1939 . . . . DLB-9

Grey Walls Press DLB-112

Grier, Eldon 1917- DLB-88

Grieve, C. M. (see MacDiarmid, Hugh)

Griffin, Bartholomew
flourished 1596 . . . . DLB-172

Griffin, Gerald 1803-1840 . . . . DLB-159

Griffith, Elizabeth 1727?-1793 . . . . DLB-39, 89

Griffith, George 1857-1906 . . . . DLB-178

Griffiths, Trevor 1935- DLB-13

Griffiths, Ralph
[publishing house] DLB-154

Griggs, S. C., and Company. DLB-49

Griggs, Sutton Elbert
1872-1930 . . . . DLB-50

Grignon, Claude-Henri 1894-1976 . . . . DLB-68

Grigson, Geoffrey 1905- DLB-27

Grillparzer, Franz 1791-1872 . . . . . . DLB-133

Grimald, Nicholas
circa 1519-circa 1562 . . . . DLB-136

Grimké, Angelina Weld
1880-1958. . . . . DLB-50, 54

Grimm, Hans 1875-1959 . . . . DLB-66

Grimm, Jacob 1785-1863 . . . . DLB-90

Grimm, Wilhelm 1786-1859 . . . . . . DLB-90

Grimmelshausen, Johann Jacob Christoffel von
1621 or 1622-1676 . . . . DLB-168

Grimshaw, Beatrice Ethel
1871-1953 . . . . DLB-174

Grindal, Edmund
1519 or 1520-1583 . . . . DLB-132

Griswold, Rufus Wilmot
1815-1857 . . . . DLB-3, 59

Grosart, Alexander Balloch
1827-1899 . . . . DLB-184

Gross, Milt 1895-1953 . . . . DLB-11

Grosset and Dunlap. DLB-49

Grossman, Allen 1932- DLB-193

Grossman Publishers DLB-46

Grosseteste, Robert
circa 1160-1253 . . . . DLB-115

Grosvenor, Gilbert H. 1875-1966 . . . . DLB-91

Groth, Klaus 1819-1899 . . . . DLB-129

Groulx, Lionel 1878-1967. . . . . DLB-68

Grove, Frederick Philip 1879-1949. . . . DLB-92

Grove Press DLB-46

Grubb, Davis 1919-1980 . . . . DLB-6

Gruelle, Johnny 1880-1938 . . . . DLB-22

von Grumbach, Argula
1492-after 1563? DLB-179

Grymeston, Elizabeth
before 1563-before 1604. . . . . . DLB-136

Gryphius, Andreas 1616-1664. . . . . . DLB-164

Gryphius, Christian 1649-1706 . . . . DLB-168

Guare, John 1938- DLB-7

Guerra, Tonino 1920-. DLB-128

Guest, Barbara 1920- DLB-5, 193

Guèvremont, Germaine
1893-1968 . . . . DLB-68

Guidacci, Margherita 1921-1992. . . . . DLB-128

Guide to the Archives of Publishers, Journals, and
Literary Agents in North American Libraries
. . . . Y-93

Guillén, Jorge 1893-1984. . . . . DLB-108

Guilloux, Louis 1899-1980 . . . . DLB-72

Guilpin, Everard
circa 1572-after 1608? DLB-136

Guiney, Louise Imogen 1861-1920. . . . DLB-54

Guiterman, Arthur 1871-1943 . . . . . . DLB-11

Günderrode, Caroline von
1780-1806. . . . . DLB-90

Gundulić, Ivan 1589-1638. . . . . DLB-147

Gunn, Bill 1934-1989 . . . . DLB-38

Gunn, James E. 1923- DLB-8

Gunn, Neil M. 1891-1973 . . . . DLB-15

Gunn, Thom 1929- DLB-27

Gunnars, Kristjana 1948- DLB-60

Günther, Johann Christian
1695-1723 . . . . DLB-168

Gurik, Robert 1932- DLB-60

Gustafson, Ralph 1909- DLB-88

Gütersloh, Albert Paris 1887-1973 . . . . DLB-81

Guthrie, A. B., Jr. 1901- DLB-6

Guthrie, Ramon 1896-1973 . . . . DLB-4

The Guthrie Theater DLB-7

Guthrie, Thomas Anstey (see Anstey, FC)

Gutzkow, Karl 1811-1878. . . . . DLB-133

Guy, Ray 1939- DLB-60

Guy, Rosa 1925- DLB-33

Guyot, Arnold 1807-1884. . . . . DS-13

Gwynne, Erskine 1898-1948. . . . . . . DLB-4

Gyles, John 1680-1755 . . . . DLB-99

Gysin, Brion 1916- DLB-16

H

H. D. (see Doolittle, Hilda)

Habington, William 1605-1654 . . . . . DLB-126

Hacker, Marilyn 1942- DLB-120

Hackett, Albert (see Goodrich, Frances)

Hacks, Peter 1928- DLB-124

Hadas, Rachel 1948- DLB-120

Hadden, Briton 1898-1929 . . . . DLB-91

Hagedorn, Friedrich von
1708-1754 . . . . DLB-168

Hagelstange, Rudolf 1912-1984 . . . . . . DLB-69
Haggard, H. Rider
   1856-1925 . . . . . . DLB-70, 156, 174, 178
Haggard, William 1907-1993 . . . . Y-93
Hahn-Hahn, Ida Gräfin von
   1805-1880 . . . . DLB-133
Haig-Brown, Roderick 1908-1976 . . . . DLB-88
Haight, Gordon S. 1901-1985 . . . . . . DLB-103
Hailey, Arthur 1920- DLB-88; Y-82
Haines, John 1924- DLB-5
Hake, Edward
   flourished 1566-1604 . . . . DLB-136
Hake, Thomas Gordon 1809-1895 . . . . DLB-32
Hakluyt, Richard 1552?-1616 . . . . . . DLB-136
Halbe, Max 1865-1944 . . . . DLB-118
Haldone, Charlotte 1894-1969 . . . . . . DLB-191
Haldane, J. B. S. 1892-1964 . . . . DLB-160
Haldeman, Joe 1943- DLB-8
Haldeman-Julius Company DLB-46
Hale, E. J., and Son DLB-49
Hale, Edward Everett
   1822-1909 . . . . DLB-1, 42, 74
Hale, Janet Campbell 1946- DLB-175
Hale, Kathleen 1898- DLB-160
Hale, Leo Thomas (see Ebon)
Hale, Lucretia Peabody
   1820-1900 . . . . DLB-42
Hale, Nancy
   1908-1988 . . . . DLB-86; DS-17; Y-80, Y-88
Hale, Sarah Josepha (Buell)
   1788-1879 . . . . DLB-1, 42, 73
Hales, John 1584-1656 . . . . DLB-151
Halévy, Ludovic 1834-1908 . . . . DLB-192
Haley, Alex 1921-1992 . . . . DLB-38
Haliburton, Thomas Chandler
   1796-1865 . . . . DLB-11, 99
Hall, Anna Maria 1800-1881 . . . . DLB-159
Hall, Donald 1928- DLB-5
Hall, Edward 1497-1547 . . . . DLB-132
Hall, James 1793-1868 . . . . DLB-73, 74
Hall, Joseph 1574-1656 . . . . DLB-121, 151
Hall, Radclyffe 1880-1943 . . . . DLB-191
Hall, Samuel [publishing house] DLB-49
Hallam, Arthur Henry 1811-1833 . . . . DLB-32
Halleck, Fitz-Greene 1790-1867 . . . . . DLB-3
Haller, Albrecht von 1708-1777 . . . . . DLB-168
Halliwell-Phillipps, James Orchard
   1820-1889 . . . . DLB-184
Hallmann, Johann Christian
   1640-1704 or 1716? DLB-168
Hallmark Editions DLB-46
Halper, Albert 1904-1984 . . . . DLB-9
Halperin, John William 1941- DLB-111

Halstead, Murat 1829-1908 . . . . DLB-23
Hamann, Johann Georg 1730-1788 . . . DLB-97
Hamburger, Michael 1924- DLB-27
Hamilton, Alexander 1712-1756 . . . . . DLB-31
Hamilton, Alexander 1755?-1804 . . . . DLB-37
Hamilton, Cicely 1872-1952 . . . . DLB-10, 197
Hamilton, Edmond 1904-1977 . . . . . . DLB-8
Hamilton, Elizabeth 1758-1816 . . . . DLB-116, 158
Hamilton, Gail (see Corcoran, Barbara)
Hamilton, Ian 1938- DLB-40, 155
Hamilton, Mary Agnes 1884-1962 . . . DLB-197
Hamilton, Patrick 1904-1962 . . . . DLB-10, 191
Hamilton, Virginia 1936- DLB-33, 52
Hamilton, Hamish, Limited DLB-112
Hammett, Dashiell 1894-1961 . . . . . . DS-6
Dashiell Hammett:
   An Appeal in TAC Y-91
Hammon, Jupiter 1711-died between
   1790 and 1806 . . . . DLB-31, 50
Hammond, John ?-1663 . . . . DLB-24
Hamner, Earl 1923- DLB-6
Hampson, John 1901-1955 . . . . DLB-191
Hampton, Christopher 1946- DLB-13
Handel-Mazzetti, Enrica von
   1871-1955 . . . . DLB-81
Handke, Peter 1942- DLB-85, 124
Handlin, Oscar 1915- DLB-17
Hankin, St. John 1869-1909 . . . . DLB-10
Hanley, Clifford 1922- DLB-14
Hanley, James 1901-1985 . . . . DLB-191
Hannah, Barry 1942- DLB-6
Hannay, James 1827-1873 . . . . DLB-21
Hansberry, Lorraine 1930-1965 . . . . DLB-7, 38
Hapgood, Norman 1868-1937 . . . . . . DLB-91
Happel, Eberhard Werner
   1647-1690 . . . . DLB-168
Harcourt Brace Jovanovich DLB-46
Hardenberg, Friedrich von (see Novalis)
Harding, Walter 1917- DLB-111
Hardwick, Elizabeth 1916- DLB-6
Hardy, Thomas 1840-1928 . . . . DLB-18, 19, 135
Hare, Cyril 1900-1958 . . . . DLB-77
Hare, David 1947- DLB-13
Hargrove, Marion 1919- DLB-11
Häring, Georg Wilhelm Heinrich (see Alexis,
   Willibald)
Harington, Donald 1935- DLB-152
Harington, Sir John 1560-1612 . . . . . DLB-136
Harjo, Joy 1951- DLB-120, 175
Harkness, Margaret (John Law)
   1854-1923 . . . . DLB-197
Harlow, Robert 1923- DLB-60

Harman, Thomas
   flourished 1566-1573 . . . . DLB-136
Harness, Charles L. 1915- DLB-8
Harnett, Cynthia 1893-1981 . . . . DLB-161
Harper, Fletcher 1806-1877 . . . . DLB-79
Harper, Frances Ellen Watkins
   1825-1911 . . . . DLB-50
Harper, Michael S. 1938- DLB-41
Harper and Brothers DLB-49
Harraden, Beatrice 1864-1943 . . . . . . DLB-153
Harrap, George G., and Company
   Limited DLB-112
Harriot, Thomas 1560-1621 . . . . DLB-136
Harris, Benjamin ?-circa 1720 . . . . DLB-42, 43
Harris, Christie 1907- DLB-88
Harris, Frank 1856-1931 . . . . . . DLB-156, 197
Harris, George Washington
   1814-1869 . . . . DLB-3, 11
Harris, Joel Chandler
   1848-1908 . . . . . . DLB-11, 23, 42, 78, 91
Harris, Mark 1922- DLB-2; Y-80
Harris, Wilson 1921- DLB-117
Harrison, Charles Yale
   1898-1954 . . . . DLB-68
Harrison, Frederic 1831-1923 . . . . DLB-57, 190
Harrison, Harry 1925- DLB-8
Harrison, Jim 1937- Y-82
Harrison, Mary St. Leger Kingsley
   (see Malet, Lucas)
Harrison, Paul Carter 1936- DLB-38
Harrison, Susan Frances
   1859-1935 . . . . DLB-99
Harrison, Tony 1937- DLB-40
Harrison, William 1535-1593 . . . . . . DLB-136
Harrison, James P., Company DLB-49
Harrisse, Henry 1829-1910 . . . . DLB-47
Harryman, Carla 1952- DLB-193
Harsdörffer, Georg Philipp
   1607-1658 . . . . DLB-164
Harsent, David 1942- DLB-40
Hart, Albert Bushnell 1854-1943 . . . . DLB-17
Hart, Julia Catherine 1796-1867 . . . . DLB-99
The Lorenz Hart Centenary Y-95
Hart, Moss 1904-1961 . . . . DLB-7
Hart, Oliver 1723-1795 . . . . DLB-31
Hart-Davis, Rupert, Limited DLB-112
Harte, Bret
   1836-1902 . . . . . DLB-12, 64, 74, 79, 186
Harte, Edward Holmead 1922- DLB-127
Harte, Houston Harriman 1927- DLB-127
Hartlaub, Felix 1913-1945 . . . . DLB-56
Hartleben, Otto Erich
   1864-1905 . . . . DLB-118
Hartley, L. P. 1895-1972 . . . . . . DLB-15, 139

Hartley, Marsden 1877-1943 . . . . DLB-54	Haywood, Eliza 1693?-1756 . . . . DLB-39	Heinz, W. C. 1915- DLB-171
Hartling, Peter 1933- DLB-75	Hazard, Willis P. [publishing house] DLB-49	Hejinian, Lyn 1941- DLB-165
Hartman, Geoffrey H. 1929- DLB-67	Hazlitt, William 1778-1830 . . . . DLB-110, 158	*Heliand* circa 850 . . . . DLB-148
Hartmann, Sadakichi 1867-1944 . . . . . DLB-54	Hazzard, Shirley 1931- Y-82	Heller, Joseph 1923- DLB-2, 28; Y-80
Hartmann von Aue circa 1160-circa 1205 . . . . DLB-138	Head, Bessie 1937-1986 . . . . DLB-117	Heller, Michael 1937- DLB-165
Harvey, Gabriel 1550?-1631 . . . . DLB-167	Headley, Joel T. 1813-1897 . . . . DLB-30, 183; DS-13	Hellman, Lillian 1906-1984 . . . . . DLB-7; Y-84
Harvey, Jean-Charles 1891-1967 . . . . . DLB-88	Heaney, Seamus 1939- DLB-40; Y-95	Hellwig, Johann 1609-1674 . . . . . . DLB-164
Harvill Press Limited DLB-112	Heard, Nathan C. 1936- DLB-33	Helprin, Mark 1947- Y-85
Harwood, Lee 1939- DLB-40	Hearn, Lafcadio 1850-1904 . . . DLB-12, 78, 189	Helwig, David 1938- DLB-60
Harwood, Ronald 1934- DLB-13	Hearne, John 1926- DLB-117	Hemans, Felicia 1793-1835 . . . . DLB-96
Haskins, Charles Homer 1870-1937 . . . . DLB-47	Hearne, Samuel 1745-1792 . . . . DLB-99	Hemingway, Ernest 1899-1961 . . DLB-4, 9, 102; Y-81, Y-87; DS-1, DS-15, DS-16
Hass, Robert 1941- DLB-105	Hearst, William Randolph 1863-1951 . . . . DLB-25	Hemingway: Twenty-Five Years Later Y-85
The Hatch-Billops Collection DLB-76	Hearst, William Randolph, Jr 1908-1993 . . . . DLB-127	Hémon, Louis 1880-1913 . . . . DLB-92
Hathaway, William 1944- DLB-120	Heartman, Charles Frederick 1883-1953 . . . . DLB-187	Hemphill, Paul 1936- Y-87
Hauff, Wilhelm 1802-1827 . . . . DLB-90	Heath, Catherine 1924- DLB-14	Hénault, Gilles 1920- DLB-88
A Haughty and Proud Generation (1922), by Ford Madox Hueffer DLB-36	Heath, Roy A. K. 1926- DLB-117	Henchman, Daniel 1689-1761 . . . . . . DLB-24
Haugwitz, August Adolph von 1647-1706 . . . . DLB-168	Heath-Stubbs, John 1918- DLB-27	Henderson, Alice Corbin 1881-1949 . . . . DLB-54
Hauptmann, Carl 1858-1921 . . . . DLB-66, 118	Heavysege, Charles 1816-1876 . . . . . . DLB-99	Henderson, Archibald 1877-1963 . . . . DLB-103
Hauptmann, Gerhart 1862-1946 . . . . DLB-66, 118	Hebbel, Friedrich 1813-1863 . . . . DLB-129	Henderson, David 1942- DLB-41
Hauser, Marianne 1910- Y-83	Hebel, Johann Peter 1760-1826 . . . . . . DLB-90	Henderson, George Wylie 1904- DLB-51
Hawes, Stephen 1475?-before 1529 . . . . DLB-132	Heber, Richard 1774-1833 . . . . DLB-184	Henderson, Zenna 1917-1983 . . . . DLB-8
Hawker, Robert Stephen 1803-1875 . . . . DLB-32	Hébert, Anne 1916- DLB-68	Henisch, Peter 1943- DLB-85
Hawkes, John 1925- DLB-2, 7; Y-80	Hébert, Jacques 1923- DLB-53	Henley, Beth 1952- Y-86
Hawkesworth, John 1720-1773 . . . . . DLB-142	Hecht, Anthony 1923- DLB-5, 169	Henley, William Ernest 1849-1903 . . . . DLB-19
Hawkins, Sir Anthony Hope (see Hope, Anthony)	Hecht, Ben 1894-1964 . . . . DLB-7, 9, 25, 26, 28, 86	Henniker, Florence 1855-1923 . . . . . . DLB-135
Hawkins, Sir John 1719-1789 . . . . DLB-104, 142	Hecker, Isaac Thomas 1819-1888 . . . . . DLB-1	Henry, Alexander 1739-1824 . . . . DLB-99
Hawkins, Walter Everette 1883-? DLB-50	Hedge, Frederic Henry 1805-1890 . . . . DLB-1, 59	Henry, Buck 1930- DLB-26
Hawthorne, Nathaniel 1804-1864 . . . . DLB-1, 74, 183	Hefner, Hugh M. 1926- DLB-137	Henry VIII of England 1491-1547 . . . . DLB-132
Hawthorne, Nathaniel 1804-1864 and Hawthorne, Sophia Peabody 1809-1871 . . . . DLB-183	Hegel, Georg Wilhelm Friedrich 1770-1831 . . . . DLB-90	Henry, Marguerite 1902- DLB-22
	Heidish, Marcy 1947- Y-82	Henry, O. (see Porter, William Sydney)
Hay, John 1835-1905 . . . . . DLB-12, 47, 189	Heißenbüttel 1921- DLB-75	Henry of Ghent circa 1217-1229 - 1293 . . . . DLB-115
Hayashi, Fumiko 1903-1951 . . . . DLB-180	Hein, Christoph 1944- DLB-124	Henry, Robert Selph 1889-1970 . . . . . DLB-17
Haycraft, Anna Margaret (see Ellis, Alice Thomas)	Heine, Heinrich 1797-1856 . . . . DLB-90	Henry, Will (see Allen, Henry W.)
Hayden, Robert 1913-1980 . . . . . . DLB-5, 76	Heinemann, Larry 1944- DS-9	Henryson, Robert 1420s or 1430s-circa 1505 . . . . . . DLB-146
Haydon, Benjamin Robert 1786-1846 . . . . DLB-110	Heinemann, William, Limited DLB-112	Henschke, Alfred (see Klabund)
Hayes, John Michael 1919- DLB-26	Heinlein, Robert A. 1907-1988 . . . . . . DLB-8	Hensley, Sophie Almon 1866-1946 . . . . DLB-99
Hayley, William 1745-1820 . . . . . DLB-93, 142	Heinrich Julius of Brunswick 1564-1613 . . . . DLB-164	Henson, Lance 1944- DLB-175
Haym, Rudolf 1821-1901 . . . . DLB-129	Heinrich von dem Türlîn flourished circa 1230 . . . . DLB-138	Henty, G. A. 1832?-1902 . . . . . . DLB-18, 141
Hayman, Robert 1575-1629 . . . . DLB-99	Heinrich von Melk flourished after 1160 . . . . DLB-148	Hentz, Caroline Lee 1800-1856 . . . . . . DLB-3
Hayman, Ronald 1932- DLB-155	Heinrich von Veldeke circa 1145-circa 1190 . . . . DLB-138	Heraclitus flourished circa 500 B.C. DLB-176
Hayne, Paul Hamilton 1830-1886 . . . . DLB-3, 64, 79	Heinrich, Willi 1920- DLB-75	Herbert, Agnes circa 1880-1960 . . . . . DLB-174
	Heiskell, John 1872-1972 . . . . DLB-127	Herbert, Alan Patrick 1890-1971 . . DLB-10, 191
Hays, Mary 1760-1843 . . . . . DLB-142, 158	Heinse, Wilhelm 1746-1803 . . . . DLB-94	Herbert, Edward, Lord, of Cherbury 1582-1648 . . . . DLB-121, 151

Herbert, Frank 1920-1986 . . . . DLB-8
Herbert, George 1593-1633 . . . . . . DLB-126
Herbert, Henry William
   1807-1858 . . . . DLB-3, 73
Herbert, John 1926- DLB-53
Herbert, Mary Sidney, Countess of Pembroke
   (see Sidney, Mary)
Herbst, Josephine 1892-1969 . . . . DLB-9
Herburger, Gunter 1932- DLB-75, 124
Èercules, Frank E. M. 1917- DLB-33
Herder, Johann Gottfried
   1744-1803 . . . . DLB-97
Herder, B., Book Company DLB-49
Herford, Charles Harold
   1853-1931 . . . . DLB-149
Hergesheimer, Joseph
   1880-1954 . . . . DLB-9, 102
Heritage Press DLB-46
Hermann the Lame 1013-1054 . . . . . DLB-148
Hermes, Johann Timotheus
   1738-1821 . . . . DLB-97
Hermlin, Stephan 1915- DLB-69
Hernández, Alfonso C. 1938- DLB-122
Hernández, Inés 1947- DLB-122
Hernández, Miguel 1910-1942. . . . . . DLB-134
Hernton, Calvin C. 1932- DLB-38
"The Hero as Man of Letters: Johnson,
   Rousseau, Burns" (1841), by Thomas
   Carlyle [excerpt] DLB-57
The Hero as Poet. Dante; Shakspeare (1841),
   by Thomas Carlyle. DLB-32
Herodotus circa 484 B.C.-circa 420 B.C.
   . . . . DLB-176
Heron, Robert 1764-1807 . . . . DLB-142
Herr, Michael 1940- DLB-185
Herrera, Juan Felipe 1948- DLB-122
Herrick, Robert 1591-1674 . . . . DLB-126
Herrick, Robert 1868-1938 . . . DLB-9, 12, 78
Herrick, William 1915- Y-83
Herrick, E. R., and Company DLB-49
Herrmann, John 1900-1959 . . . . DLB-4
Hersey, John 1914-1993 . . . . . . DLB-6, 185
Hertel, François 1905-1985 . . . . DLB-68
Hervé-Bazin, Jean Pierre Marie (see Bazin, Hervé)
Hervey, John, Lord 1696-1743 . . . . . DLB-101
Herwig, Georg 1817-1875 . . . . DLB-133
Herzog, Emile Salomon Wilhelm (see Maurois, André)
Hesiod eighth century B.C. DLB-176
Hesse, Hermann 1877-1962 . . . . DLB-66
Hessus, Helius Eobanus
   1488-1540 . . . . DLB-179
Hewat, Alexander
   circa 1743-circa 1824 . . . . DLB-30

Hewitt, John 1907- DLB-27
Hewlett, Maurice 1861-1923 . . . DLB-34, 156
Heyen, William 1940- DLB-5
Heyer, Georgette 1902-1974 . . . . DLB-77, 191
Heym, Stefan 1913- DLB-69
Heyse, Paul 1830-1914 . . . . DLB-129
Heytesbury, William
   circa 1310-1372 or 1373 . . . . . . DLB-115
Heyward, Dorothy 1890-1961 . . . . . . DLB-7
Heyward, DuBose
   1885-1940 . . . . DLB-7, 9, 45
Heywood, John 1497?-1580? DLB-136
Heywood, Thomas
   1573 or 1574-1641 . . . . DLB-62
Hibbs, Ben 1901-1975 . . . . DLB-137
Hichens, Robert S. 1864-1950. . . . . . DLB-153
Hickman, William Albert
   1877-1957 . . . . DLB-92
Hidalgo, José Luis 1919-1947 . . . . . . DLB-108
Hiebert, Paul 1892-1987 . . . . DLB-68
Hieng, Andrej 1925- DLB-181
Hierro, José 1922- DLB-108
Higgins, Aidan 1927- DLB-14
Higgins, Colin 1941-1988 . . . . DLB-26
Higgins, George V. 1939- DLB-2; Y-81
Higginson, Thomas Wentworth
   1823-1911 . . . . DLB-1, 64
Highwater, Jamake 1942?- DLB-52; Y-85
Hijuelos, Oscar 1951- DLB-145
Hildegard von Bingen
   1098-1179 . . . . DLB-148
Das Hildesbrandslied circa 820 . . . . DLB-148
Hildesheimer, Wolfgang
   1916-1991 . . . . DLB-69, 124
Hildreth, Richard
   1807-1865 . . . . DLB-1, 30, 59
Hill, Aaron 1685-1750 . . . . DLB-84
Hill, Geoffrey 1932- DLB-40
Hill, "Sir" John 1714?-1775 . . . . DLB-39
Hill, Leslie 1880-1960 . . . . DLB-51
Hill, Susan 1942- DLB-14, 139
Hill, Walter 1942- DLB-44
Hill and Wang DLB-46
Hill, George M., Company. DLB-49
Hill, Lawrence, and Company,
   Publishers DLB-46
Hillberry, Conrad 1928- DLB-120
Hilliard, Gray and Company DLB-49
Hills, Lee 1906- DLB-127
Hillyer, Robert 1895-1961 . . . . DLB-54
Hilton, James 1900-1954 . . . . . . DLB-34, 77
Hilton, Walter died 1396 . . . . DLB-146
Hilton and Company DLB-49

Himes, Chester
   1909-1984. . . . . DLB-2, 76, 143
Hindmarsh, Joseph
   [publishing house] DLB-170
Hine, Daryl 1936- DLB-60
Hingley, Ronald 1920- DLB-155
Hinojosa-Smith, Rolando
   1929- DLB-82
Hippel, Theodor Gottlieb von
   1741-1796 . . . . DLB-97
Hippocrates of Cos flourished circa 425 B.C.
   . . . . DLB-176
Hirabayashi, Taiko 1905-1972. . . . . . DLB-180
Hirsch, E. D., Jr. 1928- DLB-67
Hirsch, Edward 1950- DLB-120
The History of the
Adventures of Joseph Andrews
(1742), by Henry Fielding
   [excerpt] DLB-39
Hoagland, Edward 1932- DLB-6
Hoagland, Everett H., III 1942- DLB-41
Hoban, Russell 1925- DLB-52
Hobbes, Thomas 1588-1679. . . . . . . DLB-151
Hobby, Oveta 1905- DLB-127
Hobby, William 1878-1964 . . . . DLB-127
Hobsbaum, Philip 1932- DLB-40
Hobson, Laura Z. 1900- DLB-28
Hoby, Thomas 1530-1566. . . . . DLB-132
Hoccleve, Thomas
   circa 1368-circa 1437 . . . . DLB-146
Hochhuth, Rolf 1931- DLB-124
Hochman, Sandra 1936- DLB-5
Hocken, Thomas Morland
   1836-1910 . . . . DLB-184
Hodder and Stoughton, Limited DLB-106
Hodgins, Jack 1938- DLB-60
Hodgman, Helen 1945- DLB-14
Hodgskin, Thomas 1787-1869 . . . . . DLB-158
Hodgson, Ralph 1871-1962. . . . . . . DLB-19
Hodgson, William Hope
   1877-1918 . . . . . . DLB-70, 153, 156, 178
Hoe, Robert III 1839-1909 . . . . DLB-187
Hoffenstein, Samuel 1890-1947 . . . . . DLB-11
Hoffman, Charles Fenno
   1806-1884. . . . . DLB-3
Hoffman, Daniel 1923- DLB-5
Hoffmann, E. T. A. 1776-1822 . . . . . DLB-90
Hoffman, Frank B. 1888-1958 . . . . . DLB-188
Hoffmanswaldau, Christian Hoffman von
   1616-1679 . . . . DLB-168
Hofmann, Michael 1957- DLB-40
Hofmannsthal, Hugo von
   1874-1929 . . . . DLB-81, 118
Hofstadter, Richard 1916-1970 . . . . . DLB-17
Hogan, Desmond 1950- DLB-14
Hogan, Linda 1947- DLB-175

Hogan and Thompson DLB-49	Honan, Park 1928- DLB-111	Howe, E. W. 1853-1937 . . . . DLB-12, 25
Hogarth Press DLB-112	Hone, William 1780-1842 . . . . DLB-110, 158	Howe, Henry 1816-1893 . . . . DLB-30
Hogg, James 1770-1835 . . . . DLB-93, 116, 159	Hongo, Garrett Kaoru 1951- DLB-120	Howe, Irving 1920-1993 . . . . DLB-67
Hohberg, Wolfgang Helmhard Freiherr von 1612-1688 . . . . DLB-168	Honig, Edwin 1919- DLB-5	Howe, Joseph 1804-1873 . . . . DLB-99
	Hood, Hugh 1928- DLB-53	Howe, Julia Ward 1819-1910 . . . . DLB-1, 189
von Hohenheim, Philippus Aureolus Theophrastus Bombastus (see Paracelsus)	Hood, Thomas 1799-1845 . . . . DLB-96	Howe, Percival Presland 1886-1944 . . . . DLB-149
Hohl, Ludwig 1904-1980 . . . . DLB-56	Hook, Theodore 1788-1841 . . . . . . DLB-116	
Holbrook, David 1923- DLB-14, 40	Hooker, Jeremy 1941- DLB-40	Howe, Susan 1937- DLB-120
Holcroft, Thomas 1745-1809 . . . . DLB-39, 89, 158	Hooker, Richard 1554-1600 . . . . . . DLB-132	Howell, Clark, Sr. 1863-1936 . . . . . . DLB-25
	Hooker, Thomas 1586-1647 . . . . DLB-24	Howell, Evan P. 1839-1905 . . . . DLB-23
Holden, Jonathan 1941- DLB-105	Hooper, Johnson Jones 1815-1862 . . . . DLB-3, 11	Howell, James 1594?-1666 . . . . DLB-151
Holden, Molly 1927-1981 . . . . DLB-40		Howell, Warren Richardson 1912-1984 . . . . DLB-140
Hölderlin, Friedrich 1770-1843 . . . . . DLB-90	Hope, Anthony 1863-1933 . . . . DLB-153, 156	
Holiday House DLB-46	Hopkins, Ellice 1836-1904 . . . . DLB-190	Howell, Soskin and Company DLB-46
Holinshed, Raphael died 1580 . . . . DLB-167	Hopkins, Gerard Manley 1844-1889 . . . . DLB-35, 57	Howells, William Dean 1837-1920 . . . . . DLB-12, 64, 74, 79, 189
Holland, J. G. 1819-1881 . . . . DS-13		
Holland, Norman N. 1927- DLB-67	Hopkins, John (see Sternhold, Thomas)	Howitt, William 1792-1879 and Howitt, Mary 1799-1888 . . . . . . DLB-110
Hollander, John 1929- DLB-5	Hopkins, Lemuel 1750-1801 . . . . DLB-37	Hoyem, Andrew 1935- DLB-5
Holley, Marietta 1836-1926 . . . . DLB-11	Hopkins, Pauline Elizabeth 1859-1930 . . . . DLB-50	Hoyers, Anna Ovena 1584-1655 . . . . DLB-164
Hollingsworth, Margaret 1940- DLB-60		Hoyos, Angela de 1940- DLB-82
Hollo, Anselm 1934- DLB-40	Hopkins, Samuel 1721-1803 . . . . DLB-31	Hoyt, Palmer 1897-1979 . . . . DLB-127
Holloway, Emory 1885-1977 . . . . . . DLB-103	Hopkins, John H., and Son DLB-46	Hoyt, Henry [publishing house] DLB-49
Holloway, John 1920- DLB-27	Hopkinson, Francis 1737-1791 . . . . . DLB-31	Hrabanus Maurus 776?-856 . . . . . . DLB-148
Holloway House Publishing Company DLB-46	Hoppin, Augustus 1828-1896 . . . . . DLB-188	Hrotsvit of Gandersheim circa 935-circa 1000 . . . . DLB-148
	Horgan, Paul 1903- DLB-102; Y-85	
Holme, Constance 1880-1955 . . . . . . DLB-34	Horizon Press DLB-46	Hubbard, Elbert 1856-1915 . . . . DLB-91
Holmes, Abraham S. 1821?-1908 . . . . DLB-99	Horne, Frank 1899-1974 . . . . DLB-51	Hubbard, Kin 1868-1930 . . . . DLB-11
Holmes, John Clellon 1926-1988 . . . . . DLB-16	Horne, Richard Henry (Hengist) 1802 or 1803-1884 . . . . DLB-32	Hubbard, William circa 1621-1704 . . . DLB-24
Holmes, Oliver Wendell 1809-1894 . . . . DLB-1, 189		Huber, Therese 1764-1829 . . . . DLB-90
	Hornung, E. W. 1866-1921 . . . . DLB-70	Huch, Friedrich 1873-1913 . . . . DLB-66
Holmes, Richard 1945- DLB-155	Horovitz, Israel 1939- DLB-7	Huch, Ricarda 1864-1947 . . . . DLB-66
Holmes, Thomas James 1874-1959 . . . DLB-187	Horton, George Moses 1797?-1883? DLB-50	Huck at 100: How Old Is Huckleberry Finn? Y-85
Holroyd, Michael 1935- DLB-155		
Holst, Hermann E. von 1841-1904 . . . . DLB-47	Horváth, Ödön von 1901-1938 . . . . DLB-85, 124	Huddle, David 1942- DLB-130
		Hudgins, Andrew 1951- DLB-120
Holt, John 1721-1784 . . . . DLB-43	Horwood, Harold 1923- DLB-60	Hudson, Henry Norman 1814-1886 . . . . DLB-64
Holt, Henry, and Company DLB-49	Hosford, E. and E. [publishing house] DLB-49	
Holt, Rinehart and Winston DLB-46		Hudson, Stephen 1868?-1944 . . . . . DLB-197
Holtby, Winifred 1898-1935 . . . . . . DLB-191	Hoskyns, John 1566-1638 . . . . DLB-121	Hudson, W. H. 1841-1922 . . . . DLB-98, 153, 174
Holthusen, Hans Egon 1913- DLB-69	Hotchkiss and Company DLB-49	
Hölty, Ludwig Christoph Heinrich 1748-1776 . . . . DLB-94	Hough, Emerson 1857-1923 . . . . DLB-9	Hudson and Goodwin DLB-49
	Houghton Mifflin Company DLB-49	Huebsch, B. W. [publishing house] DLB-46
Holz, Arno 1863-1929 . . . . DLB-118	Houghton, Stanley 1881-1913 . . . . . . DLB-10	
Home, Henry, Lord Kames (see Kames, Henry Home, Lord)	Household, Geoffrey 1900-1988 . . . . . DLB-87	Hueffer, Oliver Madox 1876-1931 . . . DLB-197
	Housman, A. E. 1859-1936 . . . . DLB-19	Hughes, David 1930- DLB-14
Home, John 1722-1808 . . . . DLB-84	Housman, Laurence 1865-1959 . . . . . DLB-10	Hughes, John 1677-1720 . . . . DLB-84
Home, William Douglas 1912- DLB-13	Houwald, Ernst von 1778-1845 . . . . . DLB-90	Hughes, Langston 1902-1967 . . . . . . DLB-4, 7, 48, 51, 86
Home Publishing Company DLB-49	Hovey, Richard 1864-1900 . . . . DLB-54	
Homer circa eighth-seventh centuries B.C. DLB-176	Howard, Donald R. 1927-1987 . . . . DLB-111	Hughes, Richard 1900-1976 . . . . . DLB-15, 161
	Howard, Maureen 1930- Y-83	Hughes, Ted 1930- DLB-40, 161
Homer, Winslow 1836-1910 . . . . . . DLB-188	Howard, Richard 1929- DLB-5	Hughes, Thomas 1822-1896 . . . . . DLB-18, 163
Homes, Geoffrey (see Mainwaring, Daniel)	Howard, Roy W. 1883-1964 . . . . DLB-29	
	Howard, Sidney 1891-1939 . . . . . . DLB-7, 26	Hugo, Richard 1923-1982 . . . . DLB-5

Hugo, Victor 1802-1885 . . . . . . DLB-119, 192

Hugo Awards and Nebula Awards DLB-8

Hull, Richard 1896-1973 . . . . DLB-77

Hulme, T. E. 1883-1917 . . . . DLB-19

Humboldt, Alexander von
1769-1859 . . . . DLB-90

Humboldt, Wilhelm von
1767-1835 . . . . DLB-90

Hume, David 1711-1776 . . . . DLB-104

Hume, Fergus 1859-1932 . . . . DLB-70

Hummer, T. R. 1950- DLB-120

Humorous Book Illustration DLB-11

Humphrey, William 1924- DLB-6

Humphreys, David 1752-1818 . . . . . . DLB-37

Humphreys, Emyr 1919- DLB-15

Huncke, Herbert 1915- DLB-16

Huneker, James Gibbons
1857-1921 . . . . DLB-71

Hunold, Christian Friedrich
1681-1721 . . . . DLB-168

Hunt, Irene 1907- DLB-52

Hunt, Leigh 1784-1859 . . . . DLB-96, 110, 144

Hunt, Violet 1862-1942 . . . . . . DLB-162, 197

Hunt, William Gibbes 1791-1833 . . . . DLB-73

Hunter, Evan 1926- Y-82

Hunter, Jim 1939- DLB-14

Hunter, Kristin 1931- DLB-33

Hunter, Mollie 1922- DLB-161

Hunter, N. C. 1908-1971 . . . . DLB-10

Hunter-Duvar, John 1821-1899 . . . . . DLB-99

Huntington, Henry E.
1850-1927 . . . . DLB-140

Hurd and Houghton DLB-49

Hurst, Fannie 1889-1968 . . . . DLB-86

Hurst and Blackett DLB-106

Hurst and Company DLB-49

Hurston, Zora Neale
1901?-1960 . . . . DLB-51, 86

Husson, Jules-François-Félix (see Champfleury)

Huston, John 1906-1987 . . . . DLB-26

Hutcheson, Francis 1694-1746 . . . . . . DLB-31

Hutchinson, R. C. 1907-1975 . . . . . . DLB-191

Hutchinson, Thomas
1711-1780 . . . . DLB-30, 31

Hutchinson and Company
(Publishers) Limited DLB-112

von Hutton, Ulrich 1488-1523 . . . . . DLB-179

Hutton, Richard Holt 1826-1897 . . . . . DLB-57

Huxley, Aldous
1894-1963 . . . . . . DLB-36, 100, 162, 195

Huxley, Elspeth Josceline 1907- DLB-77

Huxley, T. H. 1825-1895 . . . . DLB-57

Huyghue, Douglas Smith
1816-1891 . . . . DLB-99

Huysmans, Joris-Karl 1848-1907 . . . . DLB-123

Hyde, Donald 1909-1966 and
Hyde, Mary 1912- DLB-187

Hyman, Trina Schart 1939- DLB-61

I

Iavorsky, Stefan 1658-1722 . . . . DLB-150

Ibn Bajja circa 1077-1138 . . . . DLB-115

Ibn Gabirol, Solomon
circa 1021-circa 1058 . . . . DLB-115

Ibuse, Masuji 1898-1993 . . . . DLB-180

The Iconography of Science-Fiction
Art DLB-8

Iffland, August Wilhelm
1759-1814 . . . . DLB-94

Ignatow, David 1914- DLB-5

Ike, Chukwuemeka 1931- DLB-157

Iles, Francis (see Berkeley, Anthony)

The Illustration of Early German
Literary Manuscripts,
circa 1150-circa 1300 . . . . DLB-148

"Images and 'Images,'" by
Charles Simic DLB-105

Imbs, Bravig 1904-1946 . . . . DLB-4

Imbuga, Francis D. 1947- DLB-157

Immermann, Karl 1796-1840 . . . . . . DLB-133

Impressions of William Faulkner Y-97

Inchbald, Elizabeth 1753-1821 . . . . DLB-39, 89

Inge, William 1913-1973 . . . . DLB-7

Ingelow, Jean 1820-1897 . . . . . . DLB-35, 163

Ingersoll, Ralph 1900-1985 . . . . DLB-127

The Ingersoll Prizes Y-84

Ingoldsby, Thomas (see Barham, Richard Harris)

Ingraham, Joseph Holt 1809-1860 . . . . DLB-3

Inman, John 1805-1850 . . . . DLB-73

Innerhofer, Franz 1944- DLB-85

Innis, Harold Adams 1894-1952 . . . . . DLB-88

Innis, Mary Quayle 1899-1972 . . . . . DLB-88

Inoue, Yasushi 1907-1991 . . . . DLB-181

International Publishers Company DLB-46

An Interview with David Rabe Y-91

An Interview with George Greenfield,
Literary Agent Y-91

An Interview with James Ellroy Y-91

Interview with Norman Mailer Y-97

An Interview with Peter S. Prescott Y-86

An Interview with Russell Hoban Y-90

Interview with Stanley Burnshaw Y-97

An Interview with Tom Jenks Y-86

"Into the Mirror," by
Peter Cooley DLB-105

Introduction to Paul Laurence Dunbar,
Lyrics of Lowly Life (1896),
by William Dean Howells DLB-50

Introductory Essay: Letters of Percy Bysshe
Shelley (1852), by Robert
Browning DLB-32

Introductory Letters from the Second Edition
of Pamela (1741), by Samuel
Richardson DLB-39

Irving, John 1942- DLB-6; Y-82

Irving, Washington 1783-1859
. . . . DLB-3, 11, 30, 59, 73, 74, 183, 186

Irwin, Grace 1907- DLB-68

Irwin, Will 1873-1948 . . . . DLB-25

Isherwood, Christopher
1904-1986 . . . . DLB-15, 195; Y-86

Ishiguro, Kazuo 1954- DLB-194

Ishikawa, Jun 1899-1987 . . . . DLB-182

The Island Trees Case: A Symposium on
School Library Censorship
An Interview with Judith Krug
An Interview with Phyllis Schlafly
An Interview with Edward B. Jenkinson
An Interview with Lamarr Mooneyham
An Interview with Harriet
Bernstein Y-82

Islas, Arturo 1938-1991 . . . . DLB-122

Ivanišević, Drago 1907-1981 . . . . . . DLB-181

Ivers, M. J., and Company DLB-49

Iwano, Hōmei 1873-1920 . . . . DLB-180

Iyayi, Festus 1947- DLB-157

Izumi, Kyōka 1873-1939 . . . . DLB-180

J

Jackmon, Marvin E. (see Marvin X)

Jacks, L. P. 1860-1955 . . . . DLB-135

Jackson, Angela 1951- DLB-41

Jackson, Helen Hunt
1830-1885 . . . . DLB-42, 47, 186, 189

Jackson, Holbrook 1874-1948 . . . . . . DLB-98

Jackson, Laura Riding 1901-1991 . . . . DLB-48

Jackson, Shirley 1919-1965 . . . . DLB-6

Jacob, Naomi 1884?-1964 . . . . DLB-191

Jacob, Piers Anthony Dillingham (see Anthony, Piers)

Jacobi, Friedrich Heinrich
1743-1819 . . . . DLB-94

Jacobi, Johann Georg 1740-1841 . . . . DLB-97

Jacobs, Joseph 1854-1916 . . . . DLB-141

Jacobs, W. W. 1863-1943 . . . . DLB-135

Jacobs, George W., and Company . . . DLB-49

Jacobson, Dan 1929- DLB-14

Jaggard, William
[publishing house] DLB-170

Jahier, Piero 1884-1966 . . . . DLB-114

Jahnn, Hans Henny
1894-1959 . . . . DLB-56, 124

Jakes, John 1932- Y-83

James, C. L. R. 1901-1989 . . . . DLB-125

James Dickey Tributes Y-97

James, George P. R. 1801-1860. . . . . DLB-116

James Gould Cozzens–A View from
Afar. Y-97

James Gould Cozzens Case Re-opened . . . Y-97

James Gould Cozzens: How to Read
Him. Y-97

James, Henry
1843-1916 . . . DLB-12, 71, 74, 189; DS-13

James, John circa 1633-1729 . . . . DLB-24

The James Jones Society Y-92

James Laughlin Tributes Y-97

James, M. R. 1862-1936. . . . . DLB-156

James, P. D. 1920- DLB-87; DS-17

James, Will 1892-1942 . . . . DS-16

James Joyce Centenary: Dublin, 1982. . . . Y-82

James Joyce Conference Y-85

James VI of Scotland, I of England
1566-1625. . . . . DLB-151, 172

James, U. P. [publishing house] DLB-49

Jameson, Anna 1794-1860. . . . . DLB-99, 166

Jameson, Fredric 1934- DLB-67

Jameson, J. Franklin 1859-1937. . . . . DLB-17

Jameson, Storm 1891-1986 . . . . DLB-36

Jančar, Drago 1948- DLB-181

Janés, Clara 1940- DLB-134

Janevski, Slavko 1920- DLB-181

Jaramillo, Cleofas M. 1878-1956 . . . . DLB-122

Jarman, Mark 1952- DLB-120

Jarrell, Randall 1914-1965 . . . . . . DLB-48, 52

Jarrold and Sons. DLB-106

Jarry, Alfred 1873-1907 . . . . DLB-192

Jarves, James Jackson 1818-1888 . . . . DLB-189

Jasmin, Claude 1930- DLB-60

Jay, John 1745-1829. . . . . DLB-31

Jefferies, Richard 1848-1887. . . . . DLB-98, 141

Jeffers, Lance 1919-1985 . . . . DLB-41

Jeffers, Robinson 1887-1962 . . . . DLB-45

Jefferson, Thomas 1743-1826 . . . . DLB-31, 183

Jelinek, Elfriede 1946- DLB-85

Jellicoe, Ann 1927- DLB-13

Jenkins, Elizabeth 1905- DLB-155

Jenkins, Robin 1912- DLB-14

Jenkins, William Fitzgerald (see Leinster,
Murray)

Jenkins, Herbert, Limited DLB-112

Jennings, Elizabeth 1926- DLB-27

Jens, Walter 1923- DLB-69

Jensen, Merrill 1905-1980. . . . . DLB-17

Jephson, Robert 1736-1803 . . . . DLB-89

Jerome, Jerome K.
1859-1927 . . . . DLB-10, 34, 135

Jerome, Judson 1927-1991. . . . . DLB-105

Jerrold, Douglas 1803-1857 . . . . DLB-158, 159

Jesse, F. Tennyson 1888-1958 . . . . . . DLB-77

Jewett, Sarah Orne 1849-1909 . . . . DLB-12, 74

Jewett, John P., and Company. DLB-49

The Jewish Publication Society. DLB-49

Jewitt, John Rodgers 1783-1821 . . . . . DLB-99

Jewsbury, Geraldine 1812-1880. . . . . . DLB-21

Jhabvala, Ruth Prawer 1927- . . DLB-139, 194

Jiménez, Juan Ramón 1881-1958 . . . . DLB-134

Joans, Ted 1928- DLB-16, 41

John, Eugenie (see Marlitt, E.)

John of Dumbleton
circa 1310-circa 1349 . . . . DLB-115

John Edward Bruce: Three
Documents DLB-50

John O'Hara's Pottsville Journalism Y-88

John Steinbeck Research Center. Y-85

John Updike on the Internet Y-97

John Webster: The Melbourne
Manuscript Y-86

Johns, Captain W. E. 1893-1968 . . . . DLB-160

Johnson, B. S. 1933-1973 . . . . . . DLB-14, 40

Johnson, Charles 1679-1748 . . . . DLB-84

Johnson, Charles R. 1948- DLB-33

Johnson, Charles S. 1893-1956. . . . DLB-51, 91

Johnson, Denis 1949- DLB-120

Johnson, Diane 1934- Y-80

Johnson, Edgar 1901- DLB-103

Johnson, Edward 1598-1672 . . . . DLB-24

Johnson E. Pauline (Tekahionwake)
1861-1913 . . . . DLB-175

Johnson, Fenton 1888-1958 . . . . . DLB-45, 50

Johnson, Georgia Douglas
1886-1966 . . . . DLB-51

Johnson, Gerald W. 1890-1980 . . . . . DLB-29

Johnson, Helene 1907- DLB-51

Johnson, James Weldon
1871-1938 . . . . DLB-51

Johnson, John H. 1918- DLB-137

Johnson, Linton Kwesi 1952- DLB-157

Johnson, Lionel 1867-1902 . . . . DLB-19

Johnson, Nunnally 1897-1977 . . . . . . DLB-26

Johnson, Owen 1878-1952 . . . . Y-87

Johnson, Pamela Hansford
1912- DLB-15

Johnson, Pauline 1861-1913. . . . . DLB-92

Johnson, Ronald 1935- DLB-169

Johnson, Samuel 1696-1772. . . . . DLB-24

Johnson, Samuel
1709-1784 . . . . . . DLB-39, 95, 104, 142

Johnson, Samuel 1822-1882 . . . . DLB-1

Johnson, Uwe 1934-1984 . . . . DLB-75

Johnson, Benjamin
[publishing house]. DLB-49

Johnson, Benjamin, Jacob, and
Robert [publishing house] DLB-49

Johnson, Jacob, and Company. DLB-49

Johnson, Joseph [publishing house] DLB-154

Johnston, Annie Fellows 1863-1931 . . . DLB-42

Johnston, David Claypole 1798?-1865 . DLB-188

Johnston, Basil H. 1929- DLB-60

Johnston, Denis 1901-1984 . . . . DLB-10

Johnston, George 1913- DLB-88

Johnston, Sir Harry 1858-1927 . . . . . DLB-174

Johnston, Jennifer 1930- DLB-14

Johnston, Mary 1870-1936 . . . . DLB-9

Johnston, Richard Malcolm
1822-1898 . . . . DLB-74

Johnstone, Charles 1719?-1800? DLB-39

Johst, Hanns 1890-1978 . . . . DLB-124

Jolas, Eugene 1894-1952 . . . . DLB-4, 45

Jones, Alice C. 1853-1933 . . . . DLB-92

Jones, Charles C., Jr. 1831-1893 . . . . . DLB-30

Jones, D. G. 1929- DLB-53

Jones, David 1895-1974 . . . . DLB-20, 100

Jones, Diana Wynne 1934- DLB-161

Jones, Ebenezer 1820-1860 . . . . DLB-32

Jones, Ernest 1819-1868 . . . . DLB-32

Jones, Gayl 1949- DLB-33

Jones, George 1800-1870 . . . . DLB-183

Jones, Glyn 1905- DLB-15

Jones, Gwyn 1907- DLB-15, 139

Jones, Henry Arthur 1851-1929 . . . . . DLB-10

Jones, Hugh circa 1692-1760. . . . . . . DLB-24

Jones, James 1921-1977 . . . DLB-2, 143; DS-17

Jones, Jenkin Lloyd 1911- DLB-127

Jones, LeRoi (see Baraka, Amiri)

Jones, Lewis 1897-1939 . . . . DLB-15

Jones, Madison 1925- DLB-152

Jones, Major Joseph (see Thompson, William
Tappan)

Jones, Preston 1936-1979. . . . . DLB-7

Jones, Rodney 1950- DLB-120

Jones, Sir William 1746-1794 . . . . . . DLB-109

Jones, William Alfred 1817-1900 . . . . . DLB-59

Jones's Publishing House DLB-49

Jong, Erica 1942- DLB-2, 5, 28, 152

Jonke, Gert F. 1946- DLB-85

Jonson, Ben 1572?-1637 . . . . . . DLB-62, 121

Jordan, June 1936- DLB-38

Joseph, Jenny 1932- DLB-40

Joseph, Michael, Limited DLB-112

Josephson, Matthew 1899-1978 . . . . . DLB-4

Josephus, Flavius 37-100 . . . . DLB-176

Josiah Allen's Wife (see Holley, Marietta)

Josipovici, Gabriel 1940- DLB-14

Josselyn, John ?-1675 . . . . DLB-24

Joudry, Patricia 1921- DLB-88

Jovine, Giuseppe 1922- DLB-128

Joyaux, Philippe (see Sollers, Philippe)

Joyce, Adrien (see Eastman, Carol)

A Joyce (Con)Text: Danis Rose and the Remaking of *Ulysses* Y-97

Joyce, James 1882-1941 . . . . DLB-10, 19, 36, 162

Judd, Sylvester 1813-1853 . . . . DLB-1

Judd, Orange, Publishing Company DLB-49

Judith circa 930 . . . . DLB-146

Julian of Norwich 1342-circa 1420 . . . . DLB-1146

Julian Symons at Eighty Y-92

June, Jennie (see Croly, Jane Cunningham)

Jung, Franz 1888-1963 . . . . DLB-118

Jünger, Ernst 1895- DLB-56

Der jüngere Titurel circa 1275 . . . . . . DLB-138

Jung-Stilling, Johann Heinrich 1740-1817 . . . . DLB-94

Justice, Donald 1925- Y-83

The Juvenile Library (see Godwin, M. J., and Company)

K

Kacew, Romain (see Gary, Romain)

Kafka, Franz 1883-1924 . . . . DLB-81

Kahn, Roger 1927 . . . . DLB-171

Kaikō, Takeshi 1939-1989 . . . . DLB-182

Kaiser, Georg 1878-1945 . . . . DLB-124

Kaiserchronik circca 1147 . . . . DLB-148

Kaleb, Vjekoslav 1905- DLB-181

Kalechofsky, Roberta 1931- DLB-28

Kaler, James Otis 1848-1912 . . . . DLB-12

Kames, Henry Home, Lord 1696-1782 . . . . DLB-31, 104

Kandel, Lenore 1932- DLB-16

Kanin, Garson 1912- DLB-7

Kant, Hermann 1926- DLB-75

Kant, Immanuel 1724-1804 . . . . DLB-94

Kantemir, Antiokh Dmitrievich 1708-1744 . . . . DLB-150

Kantor, Mackinlay 1904-1977 . . . . DLB-9, 102

Kaplan, Fred 1937- DLB-111

Kaplan, Johanna 1942- DLB-28

Kaplan, Justin 1925- DLB-111

Kapnist, Vasilii Vasilevich 1758?-1823 . . . . DLB-150

Karadžić, Vuk Stefanović 1787-1864 . . . . DLB-147

Karamzin, Nikolai Mikhailovich 1766-1826 . . . . DLB-150

Karsch, Anna Louisa 1722-1791 . . . . . DLB-97

Kasack, Hermann 1896-1966 . . . . . . DLB-69

Kasai, Zenzō 1887-1927 . . . . DLB-180

Kaschnitz, Marie Luise 1901-1974 . . . . DLB-69

Kaštelan, Jure 1919-1990 . . . . DLB-147

Kästner, Erich 1899-1974 . . . . DLB-56

Kattan, Naim 1928- DLB-53

Katz, Steve 1935- Y-83

Kauffman, Janet 1945- Y-86

Kauffmann, Samuel 1898-1971 . . . . . DLB-127

Kaufman, Bob 1925- DLB-16, 41

Kaufman, George S. 1889-1961 . . . . . . DLB-7

Kavanagh, P. J. 1931- DLB-40

Kavanagh, Patrick 1904-1967 . . . . DLB-15, 20

Kawabata, Yasunari 1899-1972 . . . . . DLB-180

Kaye-Smith, Sheila 1887-1956 . . . . . . DLB-36

Kazin, Alfred 1915- DLB-67

Keane, John B. 1928- DLB-13

Keary, Annie 1825-1879 . . . . DLB-163

Keating, H. R. F. 1926- DLB-87

Keats, Ezra Jack 1916-1983 . . . . DLB-61

Keats, John 1795-1821 . . . . . . DLB-96, 110

Keble, John 1792-1866 . . . . DLB-32, 55

Keeble, John 1944- Y-83

Keeffe, Barrie 1945- DLB-13

Keeley, James 1867-1934 . . . . DLB-25

W. B. Keen, Cooke and Company DLB-49

Keillor, Garrison 1942- Y-87

Keith, Marian 1874?-1961 . . . . DLB-92

Keller, Gary D. 1943- DLB-82

Keller, Gottfried 1819-1890 . . . . DLB-129

Kelley, Edith Summers 1884-1956 . . . . . DLB-9

Kelley, William Melvin 1937- DLB-33

Kellogg, Ansel Nash 1832-1886 . . . . . DLB-23

Kellogg, Steven 1941- DLB-61

Kelly, George 1887-1974 . . . . DLB-7

Kelly, Hugh 1739-1777 . . . . DLB-89

Kelly, Robert 1935- DLB-5, 130, 165

Kelly, Piet and Company DLB-49

Kelman, James 1946- DLB-194

Kelmscott Press DLB-112

Kemble, E. W. 1861-1933 . . . . DLB-188

Kemble, Fanny 1809-1893 . . . . DLB-32

Kemelman, Harry 1908- DLB-28

Kempe, Margery circa 1373-1438 . . . . DLB-146

Kempner, Friederike 1836-1904 . . . . . DLB-129

Kempowski, Walter 1929- DLB-75

Kendall, Claude [publishing company] . . DLB-46

Kendell, George 1809-1867 . . . . DLB-43

Kenedy, P. J., and Sons DLB-49

Kennan, George 1845-1924 . . . . DLB-189

Kennedy, Adrienne 1931- DLB-38

Kennedy, John Pendleton 1795-1870 . . . . DLB-3

Kennedy, Leo 1907- DLB-88

Kennedy, Margaret 1896-1967 . . . . . . DLB-36

Kennedy, Patrick 1801-1873 . . . . DLB-159

Kennedy, Richard S. 1920- DLB-111

Kennedy, William 1928- DLB-143; Y-85

Kennedy, X. J. 1929- DLB-5

Kennelly, Brendan 1936- DLB-40

Kenner, Hugh 1923- DLB-67

Kennerley, Mitchell [publishing house] DLB-46

Kenneth Dale McCormick Tributes Y-97

Kenny, Maurice 1929- DLB-175

Kent, Frank R. 1877-1958 . . . . DLB-29

Kenyon, Jane 1947- DLB-120

Keough, Hugh Edmund 1864-1912 . . . DLB-171

Keppler and Schwartzmann DLB-49

Kerlan, Irvin 1912-1963 . . . . DLB-187

Kern, Jerome 1885-1945 . . . . DLB-187

Kerner, Justinus 1776-1862 . . . . DLB-90

Kerouac, Jack 1922-1969 . . . . DLB-2, 16; DS-3

The Jack Kerouac Revival Y-95

Kerouac, Jan 1952- DLB-16

Kerr, Orpheus C. (see Newell, Robert Henry)

Kerr, Charles H., and Company DLB-49

Kesey, Ken 1935- DLB-2, 16

Kessel, Joseph 1898-1979 . . . . DLB-72

Kessel, Martin 1901- DLB-56

Kesten, Hermann 1900- DLB-56

Keun, Irmgard 1905-1982 . . . . DLB-69

Key and Biddle DLB-49

Keynes, John Maynard 1883-1946 . . . . DS-10

Keyserling, Eduard von 1855-1918 . . . DLB-66

Khan, Ismith 1925- DLB-125

Khaytov, Nikolay 1919- DLB-181

Khemnitser, Ivan Ivanovich 1745-1784 . . . . DLB-150

Kheraskov, Mikhail Matveevich
1733-1807 .... DLB-150

Khristov, Boris 1945- DLB-181

Khvostov, Dmitrii Ivanovich
1757-1835 .... DLB-150

Kidd, Adam 1802?-1831 .... DLB-99

Kidd, William
[publishing house] DLB-106

Kidder, Tracy 1945- DLB-185

Kiely, Benedict 1919- DLB-15

Kieran, John 1892-1981 .... DLB-171

Kiggins and Kellogg DLB-49

Kiley, Jed 1889-1962 .... DLB-4

Kilgore, Bernard 1908-1967 .... DLB-127

Killens, John Oliver 1916- DLB-33

Killigrew, Anne 1660-1685 .... DLB-131

Killigrew, Thomas 1612-1683 ...... DLB-58

Kilmer, Joyce 1886-1918 .... DLB-45

Kilwardby, Robert
circa 1215-1279 .... DLB-115

Kincaid, Jamaica 1949- DLB-157

King, Charles 1844-1933 .... DLB-186

King, Clarence 1842-1901 .... DLB-12

King, Florence 1936 .... Y-85

King, Francis 1923- DLB-15, 139

King, Grace 1852-1932 .... DLB-12, 78

King, Henry 1592-1669 .... DLB-126

King, Stephen 1947- DLB-143; Y-80

King, Thomas 1943- DLB-175

King, Woodie, Jr. 1937- DLB-38

King, Solomon [publishing house] DLB-49

Kinglake, Alexander William
1809-1891 .... DLB-55, 166

Kingsley, Charles
1819-1875 .... DLB-21, 32, 163, 178, 190

Kingsley, Mary Henrietta
1862-1900 .... DLB-174

Kingsley, Henry 1830-1876 .... DLB-21

Kingsley, Sidney 1906- DLB-7

Kingsmill, Hugh 1889-1949 .... DLB-149

Kingston, Maxine Hong
1940- DLB-173; Y-80

Kingston, William Henry Giles
1814-1880 .... DLB-163

Kinnell, Galway 1927- DLB-5; Y-87

Kinsella, Thomas 1928- DLB-27

Kipling, Rudyard
1865-1936 ...... DLB-19, 34, 141, 156

Kipphardt, Heinar 1922-1982 ..... DLB-124

Kirby, William 1817-1906 .... DLB-99

Kircher, Athanasius 1602-1680 .... DLB-164

Kirk, John Foster 1824-1904 ...... DLB-79

Kirkconnell, Watson 1895-1977 .... DLB-68

Kirkland, Caroline M.
1801-1864 .... DLB-3, 73, 74; DS-13

Kirkland, Joseph 1830-1893 .... DLB-12

Kirkman, Francis
[publishing house] DLB-170

Kirkpatrick, Clayton 1915- DLB-127

Kirkup, James 1918- DLB-27

Kirouac, Conrad (see Marie-Victorin, Frère)

Kirsch, Sarah 1935- DLB-75

Kirst, Hans Hellmut 1914-1989 .... DLB-69

Kiš, Danilo 1935-1989 .... DLB-181

Kita, Morio 1927- DLB-182

Kitcat, Mabel Greenhow
1859-1922 .... DLB-135

Kitchin, C. H. B. 1895-1967 .... DLB-77

Kizer, Carolyn 1925- DLB-5, 169

Klabund 1890-1928 .... DLB-66

Klaj, Johann 1616-1656 .... DLB-164

Klappert, Peter 1942- DLB-5

Klass, Philip (see Tenn, William)

Klein, A. M. 1909-1972 .... DLB-68

Kleist, Ewald von 1715-1759 ...... DLB-97

Kleist, Heinrich von 1777-1811 .... DLB-90

Klinger, Friedrich Maximilian
1752-1831 .... DLB-94

Klopstock, Friedrich Gottlieb
1724-1803 .... DLB-97

Klopstock, Meta 1728-1758 .... DLB-97

Kluge, Alexander 1932- DLB-75

Knapp, Joseph Palmer 1864-1951 .... DLB-91

Knapp, Samuel Lorenzo
1783-1838 .... DLB-59

Knapton, J. J. and P.
[publishing house] DLB-154

Kniazhnin, Iakov Borisovich
1740-1791 .... DLB-150

Knickerbocker, Diedrich (see Irving, Washington)

Knigge, Adolph Franz Friedrich Ludwig,
Freiherr von 1752-1796 ...... DLB-94

Knight, Damon 1922- DLB-8

Knight, Etheridge 1931-1992 ...... DLB-41

Knight, John S. 1894-1981 .... DLB-29

Knight, Sarah Kemble 1666-1727 .... DLB-24

Knight, Charles, and Company DLB-106

Knight-Bruce, G. W. H.
1852-1896 .... DLB-174

Knister, Raymond 1899-1932 ...... DLB-68

Knoblock, Edward 1874-1945 ..... DLB-10

Knopf, Alfred A. 1892-1984 .... Y-84

Knopf, Alfred A.
[publishing house] DLB-46

Knorr von Rosenroth, Christian
1636-1689 .... DLB-168

"Knots into Webs: Some Autobiographical
Sources," by Dabney Stuart DLB-105

Knowles, John 1926- DLB-6

Knox, Frank 1874-1944 .... DLB-29

Knox, John circa 1514-1572 ...... DLB-132

Knox, John Armoy 1850-1906 ..... DLB-23

Knox, Ronald Arbuthnott
1888-1957 .... DLB-77

Knox, Thomas Wallace 1835-1896 ... DLB-189

Kobayashi, Takiji 1903-1933 ..... DLB-180

Kober, Arthur 1900-1975 .... DLB-11

Kocbek, Edvard 1904-1981 ...... DLB-147

Koch, Howard 1902- DLB-26

Koch, Kenneth 1925- DLB-5

Kōda, Rohan 1867-1947 .... DLB-180

Koenigsberg, Moses 1879-1945 ..... DLB-25

Koeppen, Wolfgang 1906- DLB-69

Koertge, Ronald 1940- DLB-105

Koestler, Arthur 1905-1983 .... Y-83

Kohn, John S. Van E. 1906-1976 and
Papantonio, Michael 1907-1978 ... DLB-187

Kokoschka, Oskar 1886-1980 ..... DLB-124

Kolb, Annette 1870-1967 .... DLB-66

Kolbenheyer, Erwin Guido
1878-1962 .... DLB-66, 124

Kolleritsch, Alfred 1931- DLB-85

Kolodny, Annette 1941- DLB-67

Komarov, Matvei
circa 1730-1812 .... DLB-150

Komroff, Manuel 1890-1974 .... DLB-4

Komunyakaa, Yusef 1947- DLB-120

Koneski, Blaže 1921-1993 .... DLB-181

Konigsburg, E. L. 1930- DLB-52

Konrad von Würzburg
circa 1230-1287 .... DLB-138

Konstantinov, Aleko 1863-1897 ..... DLB-147

Kooser, Ted 1939- DLB-105

Kopit, Arthur 1937- DLB-7

Kops, Bernard 1926?- DLB-13

Kornbluth, C. M. 1923-1958 .... DLB-8

Körner, Theodor 1791-1813 ...... DLB-90

Kornfeld, Paul 1889-1942 .... DLB-118

Kosinski, Jerzy 1933-1991 ..... DLB-2; Y-82

Kosmač, Ciril 1910-1980 .... DLB-181

Kosovel, Srečko 1904-1926 ...... DLB-147

Kostrov, Ermil Ivanovich
1755-1796 .... DLB-150

Kotzebue, August von 1761-1819 .... DLB-94

Kotzwinkle, William 1938- DLB-173

Kovačić, Ante 1854-1889 .... DLB-147

Kovič, Kajetan 1931- DLB-181

Kraf, Elaine 1946- Y-81

Kramer, Jane 1938- DLB-185

Kramer, Mark 1944- DLB-185
Kranjčević, Silvije Strahimir
  1865-1908 .... DLB-147
Krasna, Norman 1909-1984 .... DLB-26
Kraus, Hans Peter 1907-1988 ...... DLB-187
Kraus, Karl 1874-1936 .... DLB-118
Krauss, Ruth 1911-1993 .... DLB-52
Kreisel, Henry 1922- DLB-88
Kreuder, Ernst 1903-1972 .... DLB-69
Kreymborg, Alfred 1883-1966 .... DLB-4, 54
Krieger, Murray 1923- DLB-67
Krim, Seymour 1922-1989 .... DLB-16
Krleža, Miroslav 1893-1981 ...... DLB-147
Krock, Arthur 1886-1974 .... DLB-29
Kroetsch, Robert 1927- .... ‰DLB-53
Krutch, Joseph Wood 1893-1970 .... DLB-63
Krylov, Ivan Andreevich
  1769-1844 .... DLB-150
Kubin, Alfred 1877-1959 .... DLB-81
Kubrick, Stanley 1928- DLB-26
Kudrun circa 1230-1240 .... DLB-138
Kuffstein, Hans Ludwig von
  1582-1656 .... DLB-164
Kuhlmann, Quirinus 1651-1689 .... DLB-168
Kuhnau, Johann 1660-1722 .... DLB-168
Kumin, Maxine 1925- DLB-5
Kunene, Mazisi 1930- DLB-117
Kunikida, Doppo 1869-1908 ...... DLB-180
Kunitz, Stanley 1905- DLB-48
Kunjufu, Johari M. (see Amini, Johari M.)
Kunnert, Gunter 1929- DLB-75
Kunze, Reiner 1933- DLB-75
Kupferberg, Tuli 1923- DLB-16
Kurahashi, Yumiko 1935- DLB-182
Kureishi, Hanif 1954- DLB-194
Kürnberger, Ferdinand
  1821-1879 .... DLB-129
Kurz, Isolde 1853-1944 .... DLB-66
Kusenberg, Kurt 1904-1983 ...... DLB-69
Kuttner, Henry 1915-1958 .... DLB-8
Kyd, Thomas 1558-1594 .... DLB-62
Kyffin, Maurice
  circa 1560?-1598 .... DLB-136
Kyger, Joanne 1934- DLB-16
Kyne, Peter B. 1880-1957 .... DLB-78

L

L. E. L. (see Landon, Letitia Elizabeth)
Laberge, Albert 1871-1960 .... DLB-68
Laberge, Marie 1950- DLB-60
Labiche, Eugène 1815-1888 ...... DLB-192

La Capria, Raffaele 1922- DLB-196
Lacombe, Patrice (see Trullier-Lacombe,
  Joseph Patrice)
Lacretelle, Jacques de 1888-1985 ..... DLB-65
Lacy, Sam 1903- DLB-171
Ladd, Joseph Brown 1764-1786 ..... DLB-37
La Farge, Oliver 1901-1963 .... DLB-9
Lafferty, R. A. 1914- DLB-8
La Flesche, Francis 1857-1932 .... DLB-175
Lagorio, Gina 1922- DLB-196
La Guma, Alex 1925-1985 .... DLB-117
Lahaise, Guillaume (see Delahaye, Guy)
Lahontan, Louis-Armand de Lom d'Arce,
  Baron de 1666-1715? DLB-99
Laing, Kojo 1946- DLB-157
Laird, Caroberth 1895- Y-82
Laird and Lee DLB-49
Lalić, Ivan V. 1931-1996 .... DLB-181
Lalić, Mihailo 1914-1992 .... DLB-181
Lalonde, Michèle 1937- DLB-60
Lamantia, Philip 1927- DLB-16
Lamb, Charles
  1775-1834 .... DLB-93, 107, 163
Lamb, Lady Caroline 1785-1828 .... DLB-116
Lamb, Mary 1764-1874 .... DLB-163
Lambert, Betty 1933-1983 .... DLB-60
Lamming, George 1927- DLB-125
L'Amour, Louis 1908?- Y-80
Lampman, Archibald 1861-1899 .... DLB-92
Lamson, Wolffe and Company DLB-49
Lancer Books DLB-46
Landesman, Jay 1919- and
  Landesman, Fran 1927- DLB-16
Landolfi, Tommaso 1908-1979 .... DLB-177
Landon, Letitia Elizabeth 1802-1838 ... DLB-96
Landor, Walter Savage
  1775-1864 .... DLB-93, 107
Landry, Napoléon-P. 1884-1956 .... DLB-92
Lane, Charles 1800-1870 .... DLB-1
Lane, Laurence W. 1890-1967 ..... DLB-91
Lane, M. Travis 1934- DLB-60
Lane, Patrick 1939- DLB-53
Lane, Pinkie Gordon 1923- DLB-41
Lane, John, Company DLB-49
Laney, Al 1896-1988 .... DLB-4, 171
Lang, Andrew 1844-1912 ... DLB-98, 141, 184
Langevin, André 1927- DLB-60
Langgässer, Elisabeth 1899-1950 .... DLB-69
Langhorne, John 1735-1779 ...... DLB-109
Langland, William
  circa 1330-circa 1400 .... DLB-146
Langton, Anna 1804-1893 .... DLB-99

Lanham, Edwin 1904-1979 .... DLB-4
Lanier, Sidney 1842-1881 .... DLB-64; DS-13
Lanyer, Aemilia 1569-1645 ...... DLB-121
Lapointe, Gatien 1931-1983 ...... DLB-88
Lapointe, Paul-Marie 1929- DLB-88
Lardner, John 1912-1960 .... DLB-171
Lardner, Ring
  1885-1933 ... DLB-11, 25, 86, 171; DS-16
Lardner, Ring, Jr. 1915- DLB-26
Lardner 100: Ring Lardner
  Centennial Symposium Y-85
Larkin, Philip 1922-1985 .... DLB-27
La Roche, Sophie von 1730-1807 .... DLB-94
La Rocque, Gilbert 1943-1984 ..... DLB-60
Laroque de Roquebrune, Robert (see Roquebrune,
  Robert de)
Larrick, Nancy 1910- DLB-61
Larsen, Nella 1893-1964 .... DLB-51
Lasker-Schüler, Else
  1869-1945 .... DLB-66, 124
Lasnier, Rina 1915- DLB-88
Lassalle, Ferdinand 1825-1864 .... DLB-129
Lathrop, Dorothy P. 1891-1980 .... DLB-22
Lathrop, George Parsons
  1851-1898 .... DLB-71
Lathrop, John, Jr. 1772-1820 ..... DLB-37
Latimer, Hugh 1492?-1555 ...... DLB-136
Latimore, Jewel Christine McLawler
  (see Amini, Johari M.)
Latymer, William 1498-1583 ..... DLB-132
Laube, Heinrich 1806-1884 ...... DLB-133
Laughlin, James 1914- DLB-48
Laumer, Keith 1925- DLB-8
Lauremberg, Johann 1590-1658 .... DLB-164
Laurence, Margaret 1926-1987 .... DLB-53
Laurentius von Schnüffis
  1633-1702 .... DLB-168
Laurents, Arthur 1918- DLB-26
Laurie, Annie (see Black, Winifred)
Laut, Agnes Christiana 1871-1936 .... DLB-92
Lauterbach, Ann 1942- DLB-193
Lavater, Johann Kaspar 1741-1801 ... DLB-97
Lavin, Mary 1912- DLB-15
Law, John (see Harkness, Margaret)
Lawes, Henry 1596-1662 .... DLB-126
Lawless, Anthony (see MacDonald, Philip)
Lawrence, D. H.
  1885-1930 ... DLB-10, 19, 36, 98, 162, 195
Lawrence, David 1888-1973 ...... DLB-29
Lawrence, Seymour 1926-1994 ..... Y-94
Lawrence, T. E. 1888-1935 ...... DLB-195
Lawson, John ?-1711 .... DLB-24
Lawson, Robert 1892-1957 ...... DLB-22

Lawson, Victor F. 1850-1925. . . . . . . DLB-25
Layard, Sir Austen Henry
  1817-1894 . . . . DLB-166
Layton, Irving 1912- DLB-88
LaZamon flourished circa 1200. . . . . DLB-146
Lazarević, Laza K. 1851-1890. . . . . . DLB-147
Lea, Henry Charles 1825-1909. . . . . . DLB-47
Lea, Sydney 1942- DLB-120
Lea, Tom 1907- DLB-6
Leacock, John 1729-1802 . . . . DLB-31
Leacock, Stephen 1869-1944 . . . . . . DLB-92
Lead, Jane Ward 1623-1704 . . . . . . DLB-131
Leadenhall Press DLB-106
Leapor, Mary 1722-1746 . . . . DLB-109
Lear, Edward 1812-1888 . . . DLB-32, 163, 166
Leary, Timothy 1920-1996 . . . . DLB-16
Leary, W. A., and Company DLB-49
Léautaud, Paul 1872-1956 . . . . DLB-65
Leavitt, David 1961- DLB-130
Leavitt and Allen DLB-49
Le Blond, Mrs. Aubrey
  1861-1934 . . . . DLB-174
le Carré, John 1931- DLB-87
Lécavelé, Roland (see Dorgeles, Roland)
Lechlitner, Ruth 1901- DLB-48
Leclerc, Félix 1914- DLB-60
Le Clézio, J. M. G. 1940- DLB-83
Lectures on Rhetoric and Belles Lettres (1783),
  by Hugh Blair [excerpts]. DLB-31
Leder, Rudolf (see Hermlin, Stephan)
Lederer, Charles 1910-1976. . . . . . . DLB-26
Ledwidge, Francis 1887-1917. . . . . . DLB-20
Lee, Dennis 1939- DLB-53
Lee, Don L. (see Madhubuti, Haki R.)
Lee, George W. 1894-1976. . . . . DLB-51
Lee, Harper 1926- DLB-6
Lee, Harriet (1757-1851) and
  Lee, Sophia (1750-1824) DLB-39
Lee, Laurie 1914- DLB-27
Lee, Li-Young 1957- DLB-165
Lee, Manfred B. (see Dannay, Frederic, and
  Manfred B. Lee)
Lee, Nathaniel circa 1645 - 1692 . . . . DLB-80
Lee, Sir Sidney 1859-1926. . . . . DLB-149, 184
Lee, Sir Sidney, "Principles of Biography," in
  Elizabethan and Other Essays. DLB-149
Lee, Vernon
  1856-1935. . . . DLB-57, 153, 156, 174, 178
Lee and Shepard DLB-49
Le Fanu, Joseph Sheridan
  1814-1873 . . . . . . DLB-21, 70, 159, 178
Leffland, Ella 1931- Y-84
le Fort, Gertrud von 1876-1971 . . . . DLB-66

Le Gallienne, Richard 1866-1947 . . . . . DLB-4
Legaré, Hugh Swinton
  1797-1843 . . . . DLB-3, 59, 73
Legaré, James M. 1823-1859. . . . . . . DLB-3
The Legends of the Saints and a Medieval
  Christian Worldview DLB-148
Léger, Antoine-J. 1880-1950. . . . . . . DLB-88
Le Guin, Ursula K. 1929- DLB-8, 52
Lehman, Ernest 1920- DLB-44
Lehmann, John 1907- DLB-27, 100
Lehmann, Rosamond 1901-1990 . . . . DLB-15
Lehmann, Wilhelm 1882-1968 . . . . . DLB-56
Lehmann, John, Limited. DLB-112
Leiber, Fritz 1910-1992. . . . . DLB-8
Leibniz, Gottfried Wilhelm
  1646-1716 . . . . DLB-168
Leicester University Press DLB-112
Leigh, W. R. 1866-1955. . . . . DLB-188
Leinster, Murray 1896-1975 . . . . DLB-8
Leisewitz, Johann Anton
  1752-1806. . . . . DLB-94
Leitch, Maurice 1933- DLB-14
Leithauser, Brad 1943- DLB-120
Leland, Charles G. 1824-1903 . . . . . DLB-11
Leland, John 1503?-1552 . . . . DLB-136
Lemay, Pamphile 1837-1918 . . . . . . DLB-99
Lemelin, Roger 1919- DLB-88
Lemercier, Louis-Jean-Népomucène
  1771-1840 . . . . DLB-192
Lemon, Mark 1809-1870 . . . . DLB-163
Le Moine, James MacPherson
  1825-1912 . . . . DLB-99
Le Moyne, Jean 1913- DLB-88
Lemperly, Paul 1858-1939. . . . . DLB-187
L'Engle, Madeleine 1918- DLB-52
Lennart, Isobel 1915-1971 . . . . DLB-44
Lennox, Charlotte
  1729 or 1730-1804 . . . . DLB-39
Lenox, James 1800-1880. . . . . DLB-140
Lenski, Lois 1893-1974 . . . . DLB-22
Lenz, Hermann 1913- DLB-69
Lenz, J. M. R. 1751-1792 . . . . DLB-94
Lenz, Siegfried 1926- DLB-75
Leonard, Elmore 1925- DLB-173
Leonard, Hugh 1926- DLB-13
Leonard, William Ellery
  1876-1944 . . . . DLB-54
Leonowens, Anna 1834-1914 . . . . DLB-99, 166
LePan, Douglas 1914- DLB-88
Leprohon, Rosanna Eleanor
  1829-1879 . . . . DLB-99
Le Queux, William 1864-1927 . . . . . DLB-70
Lerner, Max 1902-1992. . . . . DLB-29

Lernet-Holenia, Alexander
  1897-1976 . . . . DLB-85
Le Rossignol, James 1866-1969. . . . . DLB-92
Lescarbot, Marc circa 1570-1642. . . . DLB-99
LeSeur, William Dawson
  1840-1917 . . . . DLB-92
LeSieg, Theo. (see Geisel, Theodor Seuss)
Leslie, Doris before 1902-1982 . . . . . DLB-191
Leslie, Frank 1821-1880 . . . . . . DLB-43, 79
Leslie, Frank, Publishing House DLB-49
Lesperance, John 1835?-1891 . . . . . . DLB-99
Lessing, Bruno 1870-1940 . . . . DLB-28
Lessing, Doris 1919- DLB-15, 139; Y-85
Lessing, Gotthold Ephraim
  1729-1781 . . . . DLB-97
Lettau, Reinhard 1929- DLB-75
Letter from Japan. Y-94
Letter from London Y-96
Letter to [Samuel] Richardson on Clarissa
  (1748), by Henry Fielding DLB-39
A Letter to the Editor of The Irish
  Times Y-97
Lever, Charles 1806-1872. . . . . DLB-21
Leverson, Ada 1862-1933 . . . . DLB-153
Levertov, Denise 1923- DLB-5, 165
Levi, Peter 1931- DLB-40
Levi, Primo 1919-1987 . . . . DLB-177
Levien, Sonya 1888-1960 . . . . DLB-44
Levin, Meyer 1905-1981 . . . . DLB-9, 28; Y-81
Levine, Norman 1923- DLB-88
Levine, Philip 1928- DLB-5
Levis, Larry 1946- DLB-120
Levy, Amy 1861-1889 . . . . DLB-156
Levy, Benn Wolfe
  1900-1973 . . . . DLB-13; Y-81
Lewald, Fanny 1811-1889 . . . . DLB-129
Lewes, George Henry
  1817-1878 . . . . DLB-55, 144
Lewis, Agnes Smith 1843-1926 . . . . . DLB-174
Lewis, Alfred H. 1857-1914 . . . . DLB-25, 186
Lewis, Alun 1915-1944 . . . . DLB-20, 162
Lewis, C. Day (see Day Lewis, C.)
Lewis, C. S. 1898-1963 . . . . DLB-15, 100, 160
Lewis, Charles B. 1842-1924 . . . . . . DLB-11
Lewis, Henry Clay 1825-1850. . . . . . DLB-3
Lewis, Janet 1899- Y-87
Lewis, Matthew Gregory
  1775-1818 . . . . DLB-39, 158, 178
Lewis, Meriwether 1774-1809 and
  Clark, William 1770-1838 . . . DLB-183, 186
Lewis, R. W. B. 1917- DLB-111
Lewis, Richard circa 1700-1734 . . . . DLB-24

Lewis, Sinclair 1885-1951 . . . . DLB-9, 102; DS-1

Lewis, Wilmarth Sheldon 1895-1979 . . . . DLB-140

Lewis, Wyndham 1882-1957 . . . . . . DLB-15

Lewisohn, Ludwig 1882-1955 . . . . DLB-4, 9, 28, 102

Leyendecker, J. C. 1874-1951 . . . . . . DLB-188

Lezama Lima, José 1910-1976 . . . . . DLB-113

The Library of America DLB-46

The Licensing Act of 1737 . . . . DLB-84

Lichfield, Leonard I [publishing house] DLB-170

Lichtenberg, Georg Christoph 1742-1799 . . . . DLB-94

The Liddle Collection Y-97

Lieb, Fred 1888-1980 . . . . DLB-171

Liebling, A. J. 1904-1963 . . . . . . DLB-4, 171

Lieutenant Murray (see Ballou, Maturin Murray)

Lighthall, William Douw 1857-1954 . . . . DLB-92

Lilar, Françoise (see Mallet-Joris, Françoise)

Lillo, George 1691-1739 . . . . DLB-84

Lilly, J. K., Jr. 1893-1966 . . . . DLB-140

Lilly, Wait and Company DLB-49

Lily, William circa 1468-1522 . . . . . DLB-132

Limited Editions Club DLB-46

Lincoln and Edmands DLB-49

Lindesay, Ethel Forence (see Richardson, Henry Handel)

Lindsay, Alexander William, Twenty-fifth Earl of Crawford 1812-1880 . . . . DLB-184

Lindsay, Jack 1900- Y-84

Lindsay, Sir David circa 1485-1555 . . . . DLB-132

Lindsay, Vachel 1879-1931 . . . . DLB-54

Linebarger, Paul Myron Anthony (see Smith, Cordwainer)

Link, Arthur S. 1920- DLB-17

Linn, John Blair 1777-1804 . . . . DLB-37

Lins, Osman 1924-1978 . . . . DLB-145

Linton, Eliza Lynn 1822-1898 . . . . . DLB-18

Linton, William James 1812-1897 . . . . DLB-32

Lintot, Barnaby Bernard [publishing house] DLB-170

Lion Books DLB-46

Lionni, Leo 1910- DLB-61

Lippincott, Sara Jane Clarke 1823-1904 . . . . DLB-43

Lippincott, J. B., Company DLB-49

Lippmann, Walter 1889-1974 . . . . . DLB-29

Lipton, Lawrence 1898-1975 . . . . . DLB-16

Liscow, Christian Ludwig 1701-1760 . . . . DLB-97

Lish, Gordon 1934- DLB-130

Lispector, Clarice 1925-1977 . . . . . DLB-113

The Literary Chronicle and Weekly Review 1819-1828 . . . . DLB-110

Literary Documents: William Faulkner and the People-to-People Program Y-86

Literary Documents II: *Library Journal* Statements and Questionnaires from First Novelists Y-87

Literary Effects of World War II [British novel] DLB-15

Literary Prizes [British] DLB-15

Literary Research Archives: The Humanities Research Center, University of Texas Y-82

Literary Research Archives II: Berg Collection of English and American Literature of the New York Public Library Y-83

Literary Research Archives III: The Lilly Library Y-84

Literary Research Archives IV: The John Carter Brown Library Y-85

Literary Research Archives V: Kent State Special Collections Y-86

Literary Research Archives VI: The Modern Literary Manuscripts Collection in the Special Collections of the Washington University Libraries Y-87

Literary Research Archives VII: The University of Virginia Libraries Y-91

Literary Research Archives VIII: The Henry E. Huntington Library Y-92

"Literary Style" (1857), by William Forsyth [excerpt] DLB-57

Literatura Chicanesca: The View From Without DLB-82

Literature at Nurse, or Circulating Morals (1885), by George Moore DLB-18

Littell, Eliakim 1797-1870 . . . . DLB-79

Littell, Robert S. 1831-1896 . . . . . . DLB-79

Little, Brown and Company DLB-49

Little Magazines and Newspapers DS-15

The Little Review 1914-1929 . . . . DS-15

Littlewood, Joan 1914- DLB-13

Lively, Penelope 1933- DLB-14, 161

Liverpool University Press DLB-112

The Lives of the Poets DLB-142

Livesay, Dorothy 1909- DLB-68

Livesay, Florence Randal 1874-1953 . . . . DLB-92

"Living in Ruin," by Gerald Stern . . . DLB-105

Livings, Henry 1929- DLB-13

Livingston, Anne Howe 1763-1841 . . . . DLB-37

Livingston, Myra Cohn 1926- DLB-61

Livingston, William 1723-1790 . . . . . DLB-31

Livingstone, David 1813-1873 . . . . . DLB-166

Liyong, Taban lo (see Taban lo Liyong)

Lizárraga, Sylvia S. 1925- DLB-82

Llewellyn, Richard 1906-1983 . . . . . DLB-15

Lloyd, Edward [publishing house] DLB-106

Lobel, Arnold 1933- DLB-61

Lochridge, Betsy Hopkins (see Fancher, Betsy)

Locke, David Ross 1833-1888 . . . . DLB-11, 23

Locke, John 1632-1704 . . . . DLB-31, 101

Locke, Richard Adams 1800-1871 . . . . DLB-43

Locker-Lampson, Frederick 1821-1895 . . . . DLB-35, 184

Lockhart, John Gibson 1794-1854 . . . . DLB-110, 116 144

Lockridge, Ross, Jr. 1914-1948 . . . . DLB-143; Y-80

Locrine and Selimus DLB-62

Lodge, David 1935- DLB-14, 194

Lodge, George Cabot 1873-1909 . . . . DLB-54

Lodge, Henry Cabot 1850-1924 . . . . . DLB-47

Lodge, Thomas 1558-1625 . . . . DLB-172

Loeb, Harold 1891-1974 . . . . DLB-4

Loeb, William 1905-1981 . . . . DLB-127

Lofting, Hugh 1886-1947 . . . . DLB-160

Logan, James 1674-1751 . . . . . . DLB-24, 140

Logan, John 1923- DLB-5

Logan, William 1950- DLB-120

Logau, Friedrich von 1605-1655 . . . . DLB-164

Logue, Christopher 1926- DLB-27

Lohenstein, Daniel Casper von 1635-1683 . . . . DLB-168

Lomonosov, Mikhail Vasil'evich 1711-1765 . . . . DLB-150

London, Jack 1876-1916 . . . . . DLB-8, 12, 78

The London Magazine 1820-1829 . . . . . DLB-110

Long, Haniel 1888-1956 . . . . DLB-45

Long, Ray 1878-1935 . . . . DLB-137

Long, H., and Brother DLB-49

Longfellow, Henry Wadsworth 1807-1882 . . . . DLB-1, 59

Longfellow, Samuel 1819-1892 . . . . . . DLB-1

Longford, Elizabeth 1906- DLB-155

Longinus circa first century DLB-176

Longley, Michael 1939- DLB-40

Longman, T. [publishing house] DLB-154

Longmans, Green and Company DLB-49

Longmore, George 1793?-1867 . . . . . DLB-99

Longstreet, Augustus Baldwin 1790-1870 . . . . DLB-3, 11, 74

Longworth, D. [publishing house] DLB-49

Cumulative Index

Lonsdale, Frederick 1881-1954 . . . . . . DLB-10

A Look at the Contemporary Black Theatre Movement DLB-38

Loos, Anita 1893-1981 . . . . . DLB-11, 26; Y-81

Lopate, Phillip 1943- Y-80

López, Diana (see Isabella, Ríos)

Loranger, Jean-Aubert 1896-1942 . . . . . DLB-92

Lorca, Federico García 1898-1936 . . . DLB-108

Lord, John Keast 1818-1872 . . . . DLB-99

The Lord Chamberlain's Office and Stage Censorship in England DLB-10

Lorde, Audre 1934-1992 . . . . DLB-41

Lorimer, George Horace 1867-1939 . . . . DLB-91

Loring, A. K. [publishing house] DLB-49

Loring and Mussey DLB-46

Lossing, Benson J. 1813-1891 . . . . . . DLB-30

Lothar, Ernst 1890-1974 . . . . DLB-81

Lothrop, Harriet M. 1844-1924 . . . . . DLB-42

Lothrop, D., and Company DLB-49

Loti, Pierre 1850-1923 . . . . DLB-123

Lotichius Secundus, Petrus 1528-1560 . . . . DLB-179

Lott, Emeline ?-? DLB-166

The Lounger, no. 20 (1785), by Henry Mackenzie DLB-39

Louisiana State University Press Y-97

Lounsbury, Thomas R. 1838-1915 . . . . DLB-71

Louÿs, Pierre 1870-1925 . . . . DLB-123

Lovelace, Earl 1935- DLB-125

Lovelace, Richard 1618-1657 . . . . . . DLB-131

Lovell, Coryell and Company DLB-49

Lovell, John W., Company DLB-49

Lover, Samuel 1797-1868 . . . . . DLB-159, 190

Lovesey, Peter 1936- DLB-87

Lovingood, Sut (see Harris, George Washington)

Low, Samuel 1765-? DLB-37

Lowell, Amy 1874-1925 . . . . DLB-54, 140

Lowell, James Russell 1819-1891 . . . . . DLB-1, 11, 64, 79, 189

Lowell, Robert 1917-1977 . . . . DLB-5, 169

Lowenfels, Walter 1897-1976 . . . . DLB-4

Lowndes, Marie Belloc 1868-1947 . . . . DLB-70

Lowndes, William Thomas 1798-1843 . . . . DLB-184

Lownes, Humphrey [publishing house] DLB-170

Lowry, Lois 1937- DLB-52

Lowry, Malcolm 1909-1957 . . . . DLB-15

Lowther, Pat 1935-1975 . . . . DLB-53

Loy, Mina 1882-1966 . . . . DLB-4, 54

Lozeau, Albert 1878-1924 . . . . DLB-92

Lubbock, Percy 1879-1965 . . . . DLB-149

Lucas, E. V. 1868-1938 . . . . DLB-98, 149, 153

Lucas, Fielding, Jr. [publishing house] DLB-49

Luce, Henry R. 1898-1967 . . . . DLB-91

Luce, John W., and Company DLB-46

Lucian circa 120-180 . . . . DLB-176

Lucie-Smith, Edward 1933- DLB-40

Lucini, Gian Pietro 1867-1914 . . . . . DLB-114

Luder, Peter circa 1415-1472 . . . . . . DLB-179

Ludlum, Robert 1927- Y-82

Ludus de Antichristo circa 1160 . . . . . DLB-148

Ludvigson, Susan 1942- DLB-120

Ludwig, Jack 1922- DLB-60

Ludwig, Otto 1813-1865 . . . . DLB-129

Ludwigslied 881 or 882 . . . . DLB-148

Luera, Yolanda 1953- DLB-122

Luft, Lya 1938- DLB-145

Luke, Peter 1919- DLB-13

Lummis, Charles F. 1859-1928 . . . . . DLB-186

Lupton, F. M., Company DLB-49

Lupus of Ferrières circa 805-circa 862 . . . . DLB-148

Lurie, Alison 1926- DLB-2

Luther, Martin 1483-1546 . . . . DLB-179

Luzi, Mario 1914- DLB-128

L'vov, Nikolai Aleksandrovich 1751-1803 . . . . DLB-150

Lyall, Gavin 1932- DLB-87

Lydgate, John circa 1370-1450 . . . . . DLB-146

Lyly, John circa 1554-1606 . . . . . DLB-62, 167

Lynch, Patricia 1898-1972 . . . . DLB-160

Lynch, Richard flourished 1596-1601 . . . . DLB-172

Lynd, Robert 1879-1949 . . . . DLB-98

Lyon, Matthew 1749-1822 . . . . DLB-43

Lysias circa 459 B.C.-circa 380 B.C. DLB-176

Lytle, Andrew 1902-1995 . . . . . . DLB-6; Y-95

Lytton, Edward (see Bulwer-Lytton, Edward)

Lytton, Edward Robert Bulwer 1831-1891 . . . . DLB-32

M

Maass, Joachim 1901-1972 . . . . DLB-69

Mabie, Hamilton Wright 1845-1916 . . . . DLB-71

Mac A'Ghobhainn, Iain (see Smith, Iain Crichton)

MacArthur, Charles 1895-1956 . . . . DLB-7, 25, 44

Macaulay, Catherine 1731-1791 . . . . . DLB-104

Macaulay, David 1945- DLB-61

Macaulay, Rose 1881-1958 . . . . DLB-36

Macaulay, Thomas Babington 1800-1859 . . . . DLB-32, 55

Macaulay Company DLB-46

MacBeth, George 1932- DLB-40

Macbeth, Madge 1880-1965 . . . . DLB-92

MacCaig, Norman 1910- DLB-27

MacDiarmid, Hugh 1892-1978 . . . . . DLB-20

MacDonald, Cynthia 1928- DLB-105

MacDonald, George 1824-1905 . . . . DLB-18, 163, 178

MacDonald, John D. 1916-1986 . . . . DLB-8; Y-86

MacDonald, Philip 1899?-1980 . . . . . DLB-77

Macdonald, Ross (see Millar, Kenneth)

MacDonald, Wilson 1880-1967 . . . . . DLB-92

Macdonald and Company (Publishers) DLB-112

MacEwen, Gwendolyn 1941- DLB-53

Macfadden, Bernarr 1868-1955 . . . . DLB-25, 91

MacGregor, John 1825-1892 . . . . . . DLB-166

MacGregor, Mary Esther (see Keith, Marian)

Machado, Antonio 1875-1939 . . . . . DLB-108

Machado, Manuel 1874-1947 . . . . . DLB-108

Machar, Agnes Maule 1837-1927 . . . . DLB-92

Machen, Arthur Llewelyn Jones 1863-1947 . . . . DLB-36, 156, 178

MacInnes, Colin 1914-1976 . . . . DLB-14

MacInnes, Helen 1907-1985 . . . . DLB-87

Mack, Maynard 1909- DLB-111

Mackall, Leonard L. 1879-1937 . . . . . DLB-140

MacKaye, Percy 1875-1956 . . . . DLB-54

Macken, Walter 1915-1967 . . . . DLB-13

Mackenzie, Alexander 1763-1820 . . . . . DLB-99

Mackenzie, Alexander Slidell 1803-1848 . . . . DLB-183

Mackenzie, Compton 1883-1972 . . . . DLB-34, 100

Mackenzie, Henry 1745-1831 . . . . . . DLB-39

Mackenzie, William 1758-1828 . . . . . DLB-187

Mackey, Nathaniel 1947- DLB-169

Mackey, William Wellington 1937- DLB-38

Mackintosh, Elizabeth (see Tey, Josephine)

Mackintosh, Sir James 1765-1832 . . . . DLB-158

Maclaren, Ian (see Watson, John)

Macklin, Charles 1699-1797 . . . . DLB-89

MacLean, Katherine Anne 1925- DLB-8

MacLeish, Archibald 1892-1982 . . . . DLB-4, 7, 45; Y-82

MacLennan, Hugh 1907-1990 . . . . . DLB-68

Macleod, Fiona (see Sharp, William)
MacLeod, Alistair 1936- DLB-60
Macleod, Norman 1906-1985 .... DLB-4
Mac Low, Jackson 1922- DLB-193
Macmillan and Company DLB-106
The Macmillan Company DLB-49
Macmillan's English Men of Letters,
  First Series (1878-1892) DLB-144
MacNamara, Brinsley 1890-1963 .... DLB-10
MacNeice, Louis 1907-1963 ..... DLB-10, 20
MacPhail, Andrew 1864-1938 ...... DLB-92
Macpherson, James 1736-1796 ..... DLB-109
Macpherson, Jay 1931- DLB-53
Macpherson, Jeanie 1884-1946 ..... DLB-44
Macrae Smith Company DLB-46
Macrone, John
  [publishing house] DLB-106
MacShane, Frank 1927- DLB-111
Macy-Masius DLB-46
Madden, David 1933- DLB-6
Madden, Sir Frederic 1801-1873 .... DLB-184
Maddow, Ben 1909-1992 .... DLB-44
Maddux, Rachel 1912-1983 .... Y-93
Madgett, Naomi Long 1923- DLB-76
Madhubuti, Haki R.
  1942- DLB-5, 41; DS-8
Madison, James 1751-1836 .... DLB-37
Maeterlinck, Maurice 1862-1949 .... DLB-192
Magee, David 1905-1977 .... DLB-187
Maginn, William 1794-1842 .... DLB-110, 159
Mahan, Alfred Thayer 1840-1914 .... DLB-47
Maheux-Forcier, Louise 1929- DLB-60
Mafūz, Najīb 1911- Y-88
Mahin, John Lee 1902-1984 ...... DLB-44
Mahon, Derek 1941- DLB-40
Maikov, Vasilii Ivanovich
  1728-1778 .... DLB-150
Mailer, Norman 1923-
  DLB-2, 16, 28, 185; Y-80, Y-83; DS-3
Maillart, Ella 1903-1997 .... DLB-195
Maillet, Adrienne 1885-1963 ...... DLB-68
Maimonides, Moses 1138-1204 ..... DLB-115
Maillet, Antonine 1929- DLB-60
Maillu, David G. 1939- DLB-157
Main Selections of the Book-of-the-Month
  Club, 1926-1945 .... DLB-9
Main Trends in Twentieth-Century Book Clubs
  .... DLB-46
Mainwaring, Daniel 1902-1977 ..... DLB-44
Mair, Charles 1838-1927 .... DLB-99
Mais, Roger 1905-1955 .... DLB-125
Major, Andre 1942- DLB-60
Major, Clarence 1936- DLB-33

Major, Kevin 1949- DLB-60
Major Books DLB-46
Makemie, Francis circa 1658-1708 ... DLB-24
The Making of a People, by
  J. M. Ritchie DLB-66
Maksimović, Desanka 1898-1993 ... DLB-147
Malamud, Bernard
  1914-1986 .... DLB-2, 28, 152; Y-80, Y-86
Malerba, Luigi 1927- DLB-196
Malet, Lucas 1852-1931 .... DLB-153
Malleson, Lucy Beatrice (see Gilbert, Anthony)
Mallet-Joris, Françoise 1930- DLB-83
Mallock, W. H. 1849-1923 ..... DLB-18, 57
Malone, Dumas 1892-1986 .... DLB-17
Malone, Edmond 1741-1812 ...... DLB-142
Malory, Sir Thomas
  circa 1400-1410 - 1471 .... DLB-146
Malraux, André 1901-1976 .... DLB-72
Malthus, Thomas Robert
  1766-1834 .... DLB-107, 158
Maltz, Albert 1908-1985 .... DLB-102
Malzberg, Barry N. 1939- DLB-8
Mamet, David 1947- DLB-7
Manaka, Matsemela 1956- DLB-157
Manchester University Press DLB-112
Mandel, Eli 1922- DLB-53
Mandeville, Bernard 1670-1733 .... DLB-101
Mandeville, Sir John
  mid fourteenth century DLB-146
Mandiargues, André Pieyre de
  1909- DLB-83
Manfred, Frederick 1912-1994 ...... DLB-6
Manfredi, Gianfranco 1948- DLB-196
Mangan, Sherry 1904-1961 .... DLB-4
Manganelli, Giorgio 1922-1990 ..... DLB-196
Mankiewicz, Herman 1897-1953 .... DLB-26
Mankiewicz, Joseph L. 1909-1993 ... DLB-44
Mankowitz, Wolf 1924- DLB-15
Manley, Delarivière
  1672?-1724 .... DLB-39, 80
Mann, Abby 1927- DLB-44
Mann, Heinrich 1871-1950 ..... DLB-66, 118
Mann, Horace 1796-1859 .... DLB-1
Mann, Klaus 1906-1949 .... DLB-56
Mann, Thomas 1875-1955 .... DLB-66
Mann, William D'Alton
  1839-1920 .... DLB-137
Mannin, Ethel 1900-1984 ..... DLB-191, 195
Manning, Marie 1873?-1945 ...... DLB-29
Manning and Loring DLB-49
Mannyng, Robert
  flourished 1303-1338 .... DLB-146
Mano, D. Keith 1942- DLB-6

Manor Books DLB-46
Mansfield, Katherine 1888-1923 .... DLB-162
Manuel, Niklaus circa 1484-1530 ... DLB-179
Manzini, Gianna 1896-1974 ...... DLB-177
Mapanje, Jack 1944- DLB-157
Maraini, Dacia 1936- DLB-196
March, William 1893-1954 ..... DLB-9, 86
Marchand, Leslie A. 1900- DLB-103
Marchant, Bessie 1862-1941 ..... DLB-160
Marchessault, Jovette 1938- DLB-60
Marcus, Frank 1928- DLB-13
Marden, Orison Swett
  1850-1924 .... DLB-137
Marechera, Dambudzo
  1952-1987 .... DLB-157
Marek, Richard, Books DLB-46
Mares, E. A. 1938- DLB-122
Mariani, Paul 1940- DLB-111
Marie-Victorin, Frère 1885-1944 .... DLB-92
Marin, Biagio 1891-1985 .... DLB-128
Marinković, Ranko 1913- DLB-147
Marinetti, Filippo Tommaso
  1876-1944 .... DLB-114
Marion, Frances 1886-1973 .... DLB-44
Marius, Richard C. 1933- Y-85
The Mark Taper Forum DLB-7
Mark Twain on Perpetual Copyright Y-92
Markfield, Wallace 1926- DLB-2, 28
Markham, Edwin 1852-1940 ..... DLB-54, 186
Markle, Fletcher 1921-1991 .... DLB-68; Y-91
Marlatt, Daphne 1942- DLB-60
Marlitt, E. 1825-1887 .... DLB-129
Marlowe, Christopher 1564-1593 .... DLB-62
Marlyn, John 1912- DLB-88
Marmion, Shakerley 1603-1639 .... DLB-58
Der Marner
  before 1230-circa 1287 .... DLB-138
The *Marprelate* Tracts 1588-1589 ..... DLB-132
Marquand, John P. 1893-1960 .... DLB-9, 102
Marqués, René 1919-1979 .... DLB-113
Marquis, Don 1878-1937 .... DLB-11, 25
Marriott, Anne 1913- DLB-68
Marryat, Frederick 1792-1848 .... DLB-21, 163
Marsh, George Perkins
  1801-1882 .... DLB-1, 64
Marsh, James 1794-1842 .... DLB-1, 59
Marsh, Capen, Lyon and Webb DLB-49
Marsh, Ngaio 1899-1982 .... DLB-77
Marshall, Edison 1894-1967 ..... DLB-102
Marshall, Edward 1932- DLB-16
Marshall, Emma 1828-1899 ...... DLB-163
Marshall, James 1942-1992 ...... DLB-61

Cumulative Index

Marshall, Joyce 1913- DLB-88
Marshall, Paule 1929- DLB-33, 157
Marshall, Tom 1938- DLB-60
Marsilius of Padua
　circa 1275-circa 1342 . . . . DLB-115
Marson, Una 1905-1965. . . . . DLB-157
Marston, John 1576-1634 . . . . . DLB-58, 172
Marston, Philip Bourke 1850-1887. . . . DLB-35
Martens, Kurt 1870-1945 . . . . DLB-66
Martien, William S.
　[publishing house]. DLB-49
Martin, Abe (see Hubbard, Kin)
Martin, Charles 1942- DLB-120
Martin, Claire 1914- DLB-60
Martin, Jay 1935- DLB-111
Martin, Johann (see Laurentius von Schnüffis)
Martin, Violet Florence (see Ross, Martin)
Martin du Gard, Roger
　1881-1958 . . . . DLB-65
Martineau, Harriet 1802-1876
　. . . . . . DLB-21, 55, 159, 163, 166, 190
Martínez, Eliud 1935- DLB-122
Martínez, Max 1943- DLB-82
Martyn, Edward 1859-1923. . . . . DLB-10
Marvell, Andrew 1621-1678. . . . . . . DLB-131
Marvin X 1944- DLB-38
Marx, Karl 1818-1883 . . . . DLB-129
Marzials, Theo 1850-1920 . . . . DLB-35
Masefield, John
　1878-1967 . . . . DLB-10, 19, 153, 160
Mason, A. E. W. 1865-1948. . . . . DLB-70
Mason, Bobbie Ann
　1940- DLB-173; Y-87
Mason, William 1725-1797 . . . . DLB-142
Mason Brothers DLB-49
Massey, Gerald 1828-1907 . . . . DLB-32
Massey, Linton R. 1900-1974. . . . . . . DLB-187
Massinger, Philip 1583-1640 . . . . DLB-58
Masson, David 1822-1907. . . . . DLB-144
Masters, Edgar Lee 1868-1950 . . . . . . DLB-54
Mastronardi, Lucio 1930-1979. . . . . . DLB-177
Matevski, Mateja 1929- DLB-181
Mather, Cotton
　1663-1728. . . . . DLB-24, 30, 140
Mather, Increase 1639-1723. . . . . DLB-24
Mather, Richard 1596-1669. . . . . DLB-24
Matheson, Richard 1926- DLB-8, 44
Matheus, John F. 1887- DLB-51
Mathews, Cornelius
　1817?-1889. . . . . DLB-3, 64
Mathews, John Joseph
　1894-1979 . . . . DLB-175

Mathews, Elkin
　[publishing house] DLB-112
Mathias, Roland 1915- DLB-27
Mathis, June 1892-1927. . . . . DLB-44
Mathis, Sharon Bell 1937- DLB-33
Matković, Marijan 1915-1985 . . . . . . DLB-181
Matoš, Antun Gustav 1873-1914 . . . . DLB-147
Matsumoto, Seichō 1909-1992. . . . . . DLB-182
The Matter of England
　1240-1400 . . . . DLB-146
The Matter of Rome
　early twelfth to late fifteenth
　century. DLB-146
Matthews, Brander
　1852-1929. . . . . . . DLB-71, 78; DS-13
Matthews, Jack 1925- DLB-6
Matthews, William 1942- DLB-5
Matthiessen, F. O. 1902-1950 . . . . . . DLB-63
Maturin, Charles Robert
　1780-1824 . . . . DLB-178
Matthiessen, Peter 1927- DLB-6, 173
Maugham, W. Somerset
　1874-1965 . . DLB-10, 36, 77, 100, 162, 195
Maupassant, Guy de 1850-1893 . . . . DLB-123
Mauriac, Claude 1914- DLB-83
Mauriac, François 1885-1970 . . . . DLB-65
Maurice, Frederick Denison
　1805-1872 . . . . DLB-55
Maurois, André 1885-1967 . . . . DLB-65
Maury, James 1718-1769 . . . . DLB-31
Mavor, Elizabeth 1927- DLB-14
Mavor, Osborne Henry (see Bridie, James)
Maxwell, William 1908- Y-80
Maxwell, H. [publishing house] DLB-49
Maxwell, John [publishing house]. . . . DLB-106
May, Elaine 1932- DLB-44
May, Karl 1842-1912 . . . . DLB-129
May, Thomas 1595 or 1596-1650. . . . . DLB-58
Mayer, Bernadette 1945- DLB-165
Mayer, Mercer 1943- DLB-61
Mayer, O. B. 1818-1891. . . . . DLB-3
Mayes, Herbert R. 1900-1987. . . . . . DLB-137
Mayes, Wendell 1919-1992 . . . . DLB-26
Mayfield, Julian 1928-1984. . . . . DLB-33; Y-84
Mayhew, Henry 1812-1887 . . DLB-18, 55, 190
Mayhew, Jonathan 1720-1766 . . . . . . DLB-31
Mayne, Ethel Colburn 1865-1941 . . . DLB-197
Mayne, Jasper 1604-1672 . . . . DLB-126
Mayne, Seymour 1944- DLB-60
Mayor, Flora Macdonald
　1872-1932 . . . . DLB-36
Mayrocker, Friederike 1924- DLB-85
Mazrui, Ali A. 1933- DLB-125

Mažuranić, Ivan 1814-1890 . . . . . . DLB-147
Mazursky, Paul 1930- DLB-44
McAlmon, Robert
　1896-1956 . . . . DLB-4, 45; DS-15
McArthur, Peter 1866-1924. . . . . DLB-92
McBride, Robert M., and
　Company DLB-46
McCabe, Patrick 1955- DLB-194
McCaffrey, Anne 1926- DLB-8
McCarthy, Cormac 1933- DLB-6, 143
McCarthy, Mary 1912-1989 . . . . DLB-2; Y-81
McCay, Winsor 1871-1934. . . . . DLB-22
McClane, Albert Jules 1922-1991. . . . DLB-171
McClatchy, C. K. 1858-1936. . . . . . . DLB-25
McClellan, George Marion
　1860-1934 . . . . DLB-50
McCloskey, Robert 1914- DLB-22
McClung, Nellie Letitia 1873-1951. . . . DLB-92
McClure, Joanna 1930- DLB-16
McClure, Michael 1932- DLB-16
McClure, Phillips and Company DLB-46
McClure, S. S. 1857-1949 . . . . DLB-91
McClurg, A. C., and Company DLB-49
McCluskey, John A., Jr. 1944- DLB-33
McCollum, Michael A. 1946. . . . . Y-87
McConnell, William C. 1917- DLB-88
McCord, David 1897- DLB-61
McCorkle, Jill 1958- Y-87
McCorkle, Samuel Eusebius
　1746-1811. . . . . DLB-37
McCormick, Anne O'Hare
　1880-1954 . . . . DLB-29
McCormick, Robert R. 1880-1955. . . . DLB-29
McCourt, Edward 1907-1972. . . . . . . DLB-88
McCoy, Horace 1897-1955 . . . . DLB-9
McCrae, John 1872-1918. . . . . DLB-92
McCullagh, Joseph B. 1842-1896. . . . . DLB-23
McCullers, Carson
　1917-1967 . . . . DLB-2, 7, 173
McCulloch, Thomas 1776-1843 . . . . . DLB-99
McDonald, Forrest 1927- DLB-17
McDonald, Walter
　1934- DLB-105, DS-9
McDougall, Colin 1917-1984 . . . . . . DLB-68
McDowell, Obolensky DLB-46
McEwan, Ian 1948- DLB-14, 194
McFadden, David 1940- DLB-60
McFall, Frances Elizabeth Clarke
　(see Grand, Sarah)
McFarlane, Leslie 1902-1977 . . . . . . DLB-88
McFee, William 1881-1966 . . . . DLB-153
McGahern, John 1934- DLB-14

McGee, Thomas D'Arcy 1825-1868 . . . . DLB-99

McGeehan, W. O. 1879-1933 . . . DLB-25, 171

McGill, Ralph 1898-1969 . . . . DLB-29

McGinley, Phyllis 1905-1978 . . . . . DLB-11, 48

McGinniss, Joe 1942- DLB-185

McGirt, James E. 1874-1930 . . . . DLB-50

McGlashan and Gill DLB-106

McGough, Roger 1937- DLB-40

McGraw-Hill DLB-46

McGuane, Thomas 1939- DLB-2; Y-80

McGuckian, Medbh 1950- DLB-40

McGuffey, William Holmes 1800-1873 . . . . DLB-42

McIlvanney, William 1936- DLB-14

McIlwraith, Jean Newton 1859-1938 . . . . DLB-92

McIntyre, James 1827-1906 . . . . DLB-99

McIntyre, O. O. 1884-1938 . . . . DLB-25

McKay, Claude 1889-1948 . . . . DLB-4, 45, 51, 117

The David McKay Company DLB-49

McKean, William V. 1820-1903 . . . . . DLB-23

McKenna, Stephen 1888-1967 . . . . . DLB-197

The McKenzie Trust Y-96

McKinley, Robin 1952- DLB-52

McLachlan, Alexander 1818-1896 . . . . DLB-99

McLaren, Floris Clark 1904-1978 . . . . DLB-68

McLaverty, Michael 1907- DLB-15

McLean, John R. 1848-1916 . . . . DLB-23

McLean, William L. 1852-1931 . . . . . DLB-25

McLennan, William 1856-1904 . . . . . DLB-92

McLoughlin Brothers DLB-49

McLuhan, Marshall 1911-1980 . . . . . DLB-88

McMaster, John Bach 1852-1932 . . . . DLB-47

McMurtry, Larry 1936- DLB-2, 143; Y-80, Y-87

McNally, Terrence 1939- DLB-7

McNeil, Florence 1937- DLB-60

McNeile, Herman Cyril 1888-1937 . . . . DLB-77

McNickle, D'Arcy 1904-1977 . . . . . . DLB-175

McPhee, John 1931- DLB-185

McPherson, James Alan 1943- DLB-38

McPherson, Sandra 1943- Y-86

McWhirter, George 1939- DLB-60

McWilliams, Carey 1905-1980 . . . . . DLB-137

Mead, L. T. 1844-1914 . . . . DLB-141

Mead, Matthew 1924- DLB-40

Mead, Taylor ? DLB-16

Meany, Tom 1903-1964 . . . . DLB-171

Mechthild von Magdeburg circa 1207-circa 1282 . . . . DLB-138

Medill, Joseph 1823-1899 . . . . DLB-43

Medoff, Mark 1940- DLB-7

Meek, Alexander Beaufort 1814-1865 . . . . DLB-3

Meeke, Mary ?-1816? DLB-116

Meinke, Peter 1932- DLB-5

Mejia Vallejo, Manuel 1923- DLB-113

Melanchthon, Philipp 1497-1560 . . . . DLB-179

Melançon, Robert 1947- DLB-60

Mell, Max 1882-1971 . . . . DLB-81, 124

Mellow, James R. 1926- DLB-111

Meltzer, David 1937- DLB-16

Meltzer, Milton 1915- DLB-61

Melville, Elizabeth, Lady Culross circa 1585-1640 . . . . DLB-172

Melville, Herman 1819-1891 . . . . . DLB-3, 74

Memoirs of Life and Literature (1920), by W. H. Mallock [excerpt] DLB-57

Menander 342-341 B.C.-circa 292-291 B.C. DLB-176

Menantes (see Hunold, Christian Friedrich)

Mencke, Johann Burckhard 1674-1732 . . . . DLB-168

Mencken, H. L. 1880-1956 . . . . . . DLB-11, 29, 63, 137

Mencken and Nietzsche: An Unpublished Excerpt from H. L. Mencken's *My Life as Author and Editor* Y-93

Mendelssohn, Moses 1729-1786 . . . . . DLB-97

Méndez M., Miguel 1930- DLB-82

Mens Rea (or Something) Y-97

The Mercantile Library of New York Y-96

Mercer, Cecil William (see Yates, Dornford)

Mercer, David 1928-1980 . . . . DLB-13

Mercer, John 1704-1768 . . . . DLB-31

Meredith, George 1828-1909 . . . . DLB-18, 35, 57, 159

Meredith, Louisa Anne 1812-1895 . . . . DLB-166

Meredith, Owen (see Lytton, Edward Robert Bulwer)

Meredith, William 1919- DLB-5

Mergerle, Johann Ulrich (see Abraham ä Sancta Clara)

Mérimée, Prosper 1803-1870 . . . DLB-119, 192

Merivale, John Herman 1779-1844 . . . . DLB-96

Meriwether, Louise 1923- DLB-33

Merlin Press DLB-112

Merriam, Eve 1916-1992 . . . . DLB-61

The Merriam Company DLB-49

Merrill, James 1926-1995 . . . . DLB-5, 165; Y-85

Merrill and Baker DLB-49

The Mershon Company DLB-49

Merton, Thomas 1915-1968 . . . . DLB-48; Y-81

Merwin, W. S. 1927- DLB-5, 169

Messner, Julian [publishing house] DLB-46

Metcalf, J. [publishing house] DLB-49

Metcalf, John 1938- DLB-60

The Methodist Book Concern DLB-49

Methuen and Company DLB-112

Mew, Charlotte 1869-1928 . . . . . DLB-19, 135

Mewshaw, Michael 1943- Y-80

Meyer, Conrad Ferdinand 1825-1898 . . . DLB-129

Meyer, E. Y. 1946- DLB-75

Meyer, Eugene 1875-1959 . . . . DLB-29

Meyer, Michael 1921- DLB-155

Meyers, Jeffrey 1939- DLB-111

Meynell, Alice 1847-1922 . . . . . . DLB-19, 98

Meynell, Viola 1885-1956 . . . . DLB-153

Meyrink, Gustav 1868-1932 . . . . DLB-81

Michael M. Rea and the Rea Award for the Short Story Y-97

Michaels, Leonard 1933- DLB-130

Micheaux, Oscar 1884-1951 . . . . DLB-50

Michel of Northgate, Dan circa 1265-circa 1340 . . . . DLB-146

Micheline, Jack 1929- DLB-16

Michener, James A. 1907?- DLB-6

Micklejohn, George circa 1717-1818 . . . . DLB-31

Middle English Literature: An Introduction DLB-146

The Middle English Lyric DLB-146

Middle Hill Press DLB-106

Middleton, Christopher 1926- DLB-40

Middleton, Richard 1882-1911 . . . . . DLB-156

Middleton, Stanley 1919- DLB-14

Middleton, Thomas 1580-1627 . . . . . DLB-58

Miegel, Agnes 1879-1964 . . . . DLB-56

Mihailović, Dragoslav 1930- DLB-181

Mihalić, Slavko 1928- DLB-181

Miles, Josephine 1911-1985 . . . . DLB-48

Miliković, Branko 1934-1961 . . . . . . DLB-181

Milius, John 1944- DLB-44

Mill, James 1773-1836 . . . . DLB-107, 158

Mill, John Stuart 1806-1873 . . . . DLB-55, 190

Millar, Kenneth 1915-1983 . . . . DLB-2; Y-83; DS-6

Millar, Andrew [publishing house] DLB-154

Millay, Edna St. Vincent 1892-1950 . . . . DLB-45

Miller, Arthur 1915- DLB-7

Miller, Caroline 1903-1992 . . . . DLB-9

Miller, Eugene Ethelbert 1950- DLB-41

369

Miller, Heather Ross 1939- DLB-120	Mitchell, Loften 1919- DLB-38	Montgomery, Robert Bruce (see Crispin, Edmund)
Miller, Henry 1891-1980 ..... DLB-4, 9; Y-80	Mitchell, Margaret 1900-1949 ...... DLB-9	Montherlant, Henry de 1896-1972 .... DLB-72
Miller, Hugh 1802-1856 .... DLB-190	Mitchell, W. O. 1914- DLB-88	*The Monthly Review* 1749-1844 ...... DLB-110
Miller, J. Hillis 1928- DLB-67	Mitchison, Naomi Margaret (Haldane) 1897- DLB-160, 191	Montigny, Louvigny de 1876-1955 ... DLB-92
Miller, James [publishing house] DLB-49	Mitford, Mary Russell 1787-1855 .... DLB-110, 116	Montoya, José 1932- DLB-122
Miller, Jason 1939- DLB-7	Mitford, Nancy 1904-1973 .... DLB-191	Moodie, John Wedderburn Dunbar 1797-1869 .... DLB-99
Miller, Joaquin 1839-1913 .... DLB-186	Mittelholzer, Edgar 1909-1965 ...... DLB-117	Moodie, Susanna 1803-1885 .... DLB-99
Miller, May 1899- DLB-41	Mitterer, Erika 1906- DLB-85	Moody, Joshua circa 1633-1697 ..... DLB-24
Miller, Paul 1906-1991 .... DLB-127	Mitterer, Felix 1948- DLB-124	Moody, William Vaughn 1869-1910 .... DLB-7, 54
Miller, Perry 1905-1963 .... DLB-17, 63	Mitternacht, Johann Sebastian 1613-1679 .... DLB-168	Moorcock, Michael 1939- DLB-14
Miller, Sue 1943- DLB-143	Miyamoto, Yuriko 1899-1951 ...... DLB-180	Moore, Catherine L. 1911- DLB-8
Miller, Vassar 1924- DLB-105	Mizener, Arthur 1907-1988 ...... DLB-103	Moore, Clement Clarke 1779-1863 ... DLB-42
Miller, Walter M., Jr. 1923- DLB-8	Mo, Timothy 1950- DLB-194	Moore, Dora Mavor 1888-1979 ..... DLB-92
Miller, Webb 1892-1940 .... DLB-29	Modern Age Books DLB-46	Moore, George 1852-1933 .... DLB-10, 18, 57, 135
Millhauser, Steven 1943- DLB-2	"Modern English Prose" (1876), by George Saintsbury DLB-57	Moore, Marianne 1887-1972 .... DLB-45; DS-7
Millican, Arthenia J. Bates 1920- DLB-38	The Modern Language Association of America Celebrates Its Centennial Y-84	Moore, Mavor 1919- DLB-88
Mills and Boon DLB-112	The Modern Library DLB-46	Moore, Richard 1927- DLB-105
Milman, Henry Hart 1796-1868 ..... DLB-96	"Modern Novelists – Great and Small" (1855), by Margaret Oliphant DLB-21	Moore, T. Sturge 1870-1944 ...... DLB-19
Milne, A. A. 1882-1956 ...... DLB-10, 77, 100, 160	"Modern Style" (1857), by Cockburn Thomson [excerpt] DLB-57	Moore, Thomas 1779-1852 ..... DLB-96, 144
Milner, Ron 1938- DLB-38	The Modernists (1932), by Joseph Warren Beach DLB-36	Moore, Ward 1903-1978 .... DLB-8
Milner, William [publishing house] DLB-106	Modiano, Patrick 1945- DLB-83	Moore, Wilstach, Keys and Company DLB-49
Milnes, Richard Monckton (Lord Houghton) 1809-1885 .... DLB-32, 184	Moffat, Yard and Company DLB-46	The Moorland-Spingarn Research Center DLB-76
Milton, John 1608-1674 ...... DLB-131, 151	Moffet, Thomas 1553-1604 .... DLB-136	Moorman, Mary C. 1905-1994 .... DLB-155
Minakami, Tsutomu 1919- DLB-182	Mohr, Nicholasa 1938- DLB-145	Moraga, Cherríe 1952- DLB-82
The Minerva Press DLB-154	Moix, Ana María 1947- DLB-134	Morales, Alejandro 1944- DLB-82
Minnesang circa 1150-1280 .... DLB-138	Molesworth, Louisa 1839-1921 ..... DLB-135	Morales, Mario Roberto 1947- DLB-145
Minns, Susan 1839-1938 .... DLB-140	Möllhausen, Balduin 1825-1905 .... DLB-129	Morales, Rafael 1919- DLB-108
Minor Illustrators, 1880-1914 ..... DLB-141	Momaday, N. Scott 1934- DLB-143, 175	Morality Plays: *Mankind* circa 1450-1500 and *Everyman* circa 1500 .... DLB-146
Minor Poets of the Earlier Seventeenth Century DLB-121	Monkhouse, Allan 1858-1936 .... DLB-10	Morante, Elsa 1912-1985 .... DLB-177
Minton, Balch and Company DLB-46	Monro, Harold 1879-1932 .... DLB-19	Morata, Olympia Fulvia 1526-1555 .... DLB-179
Mirbeau, Octave 1848-1917 .... DLB-123, 192	Monroe, Harriet 1860-1936 .... DLB-54, 91	Moravia, Alberto 1907-1990 ...... DLB-177
Mirk, John died after 1414? DLB-146	Monsarrat, Nicholas 1910-1979 ...... DLB-15	Mordaunt, Elinor 1872-1942 ..... DLB-174
Miron, Gaston 1928- DLB-60	Montagu, Lady Mary Wortley 1689-1762 .... DLB-95, 101	More, Hannah 1745-1833 ...... DLB-107, 109, 116, 158
A Mirror for Magistrates DLB-167	Montague, C. E. 1867-1928 .... DLB-197	More, Henry 1614-1687 .... DLB-126
Mishima, Yukio 1925-1970 .... DLB-182	Montague, John 1929- DLB-40	More, Sir Thomas 1477 or 1478-1535 .... DLB-136
Mitchel, Jonathan 1624-1668 ...... DLB-24	Montale, Eugenio 1896-1981 ..... DLB-114	Moreno, Dorinda 1939- DLB-122
Mitchell, Adrian 1932- DLB-40	Monterroso, Augusto 1921- DLB-145	Morency, Pierre 1942- DLB-60
Mitchell, Donald Grant 1822-1908 .... DLB-1; DS-13	Montgomerie, Alexander circa 1550?-1598 .... DLB-167	Moretti, Marino 1885-1979 ...... DLB-114
Mitchell, Gladys 1901-1983 .... DLB-77	Montgomery, James 1771-1854 .... DLB-93, 158	Morgan, Berry 1919- DLB-6
Mitchell, James Leslie 1901-1935 ..... DLB-15	Montgomery, John 1919- DLB-16	Morgan, Charles 1894-1958 ..... DLB-34, 100
Mitchell, John (see Slater, Patrick)	Montgomery, Lucy Maud 1874-1942 .... DLB-92; DS-14	Morgan, Edmund S. 1916- DLB-17
Mitchell, John Ames 1845-1918 ..... DLB-79	Montgomery, Marion 1925- DLB-6	Morgan, Edwin 1920- DLB-27
Mitchell, Joseph 1908-1996 .... DLB-185; Y-96		Morgan, John Pierpont 1837-1913 .... DLB-140
Mitchell, Julian 1935- DLB-14		
Mitchell, Ken 1940- DLB-60		
Mitchell, Langdon 1862-1935 ...... DLB-7		

Morgan, John Pierpont, Jr.
1867-1943 . . . . DLB-140

Morgan, Robert 1944- DLB-120

Morgan, Sydney Owenson, Lady
1776?-1859 . . . . DLB-116, 158

Morgner, Irmtraud 1933- DLB-75

Morhof, Daniel Georg
1639-1691 . . . . DLB-164

Mori, Ōgai 1862-1922 . . . . DLB-180

Morier, James Justinian
1782 or 1783?-1849 . . . . DLB-116

Mörike, Eduard 1804-1875 . . . . . . DLB-133

Morin, Paul 1889-1963 . . . . DLB-92

Morison, Richard 1514?-1556 . . . . . DLB-136

Morison, Samuel Eliot 1887-1976 . . . . DLB-17

Moritz, Karl Philipp 1756-1793 . . . . . DLB-94

Moriz von Craûn
circa 1220-1230 . . . . DLB-138

Morley, Christopher 1890-1957 . . . . . DLB-9

Morley, John 1838-1923 . . . . DLB-57, 144, 190

Morris, George Pope 1802-1864 . . . . . DLB-73

Morris, Lewis 1833-1907 . . . . DLB-35

Morris, Richard B. 1904-1989 . . . . . . DLB-17

Morris, William
1834-1896 . . DLB-18, 35, 57, 156, 178, 184

Morris, Willie 1934- Y-80

Morris, Wright 1910- DLB-2; Y-81

Morrison, Arthur
1863-1945 . . . . DLB-70, 135, 197

Morrison, Charles Clayton
1874-1966 . . . . DLB-91

Morrison, Toni
1931- DLB-6, 33, 143; Y-81, Y-93

Morrow, William, and Company DLB-46

Morse, James Herbert 1841-1923 . . . . DLB-71

Morse, Jedidiah 1761-1826 . . . . DLB-37

Morse, John T., Jr. 1840-1937 . . . . . DLB-47

Morselli, Guido 1912-1973 . . . . . . DLB-177

Mortimer, Favell Lee 1802-1878 . . . . DLB-163

Mortimer, John 1923- DLB-13

Morton, Carlos 1942- DLB-122

Morton, H. V. 1892-1979 . . . . DLB-195

Morton, John P., and Company DLB-49

Morton, Nathaniel 1613-1685 . . . . . . DLB-24

Morton, Sarah Wentworth
1759-1846 . . . . DLB-37

Morton, Thomas
circa 1579-circa 1647 . . . . DLB-24

Moscherosch, Johann Michael
1601-1669 . . . . DLB-164

Moseley, Humphrey
[publishing house] DLB-170

Möser, Justus 1720-1794 . . . . DLB-97

Mosley, Nicholas 1923- DLB-14

Moss, Arthur 1889-1969 . . . . DLB-4

Moss, Howard 1922-1987 . . . . DLB-5

Moss, Thylias 1954- DLB-120

The Most Powerful Book Review in America
[*New York Times Book Review*] Y-82

Motion, Andrew 1952- DLB-40

Motley, John Lothrop
1814-1877 . . . . DLB-1, 30, 59

Motley, Willard 1909-1965 . . . . DLB-76, 143

Motte, Benjamin Jr.
[publishing house] DLB-154

Motteux, Peter Anthony
1663-1718 . . . . DLB-80

Mottram, R. H. 1883-1971 . . . . DLB-36

Mouré, Erin 1955- DLB-60

Mourning Dove (Humishuma)
between 1882 and 1888?-1936 . . . . DLB-175

Movies from Books, 1920-1974 . . . . . DLB-9

Mowat, Farley 1921- DLB-68

Mowbray, A. R., and Company,
Limited DLB-106

Mowrer, Edgar Ansel 1892-1977 . . . . DLB-29

Mowrer, Paul Scott 1887-1971 . . . . . DLB-29

Moxon, Edward
[publishing house] DLB-106

Moxon, Joseph
[publishing house] DLB-170

Mphahlele, Es'kia (Ezekiel)
1919- DLB-125

Mtshali, Oswald Mbuyiseni
1940- DLB-125

Mucedorus DLB-62

Mudford, William 1782-1848 . . . . . DLB-159

Mueller, Lisel 1924- DLB-105

Muhajir, El (see Marvin X)

Muhajir, Nazzam Al Fitnah (see Marvin X)

Mühlbach, Luise 1814-1873 . . . . . . DLB-133

Muir, Edwin 1887-1959 . . . . DLB-20, 100, 191

Muir, Helen 1937- DLB-14

Muir, John 1838-1914 . . . . DLB-186

Mukherjee, Bharati 1940- DLB-60

Mulcaster, Richard
1531 or 1532-1611 . . . . DLB-167

Muldoon, Paul 1951- DLB-40

Müller, Friedrich (see Müller, Maler)

Müller, Heiner 1929- DLB-124

Müller, Maler 1749-1825 . . . . DLB-94

Müller, Wilhelm 1794-1827 . . . . . . DLB-90

Mumford, Lewis 1895-1990 . . . . DLB-63

Munby, Arthur Joseph 1828-1910 . . . . DLB-35

Munday, Anthony 1560-1633 . . . DLB-62, 172

Mundt, Clara (see Mühlbach, Luise)

Mundt, Theodore 1808-1861 . . . . . . DLB-133

Munford, Robert circa 1737-1783 . . . . DLB-31

Mungoshi, Charles 1947- DLB-157

Munonye, John 1929- DLB-117

Munro, Alice 1931- DLB-53

Munro, H. H. 1870-1916 . . . . . DLB-34, 162

Munro, Neil 1864-1930 . . . . DLB-156

Munro, George
[publishing house] DLB-49

Munro, Norman L.
[publishing house] DLB-49

Munroe, James, and Company DLB-49

Munroe, Kirk 1850-1930 . . . . DLB-42

Munroe and Francis DLB-49

Munsell, Joel [publishing house] DLB-49

Munsey, Frank A. 1854-1925 . . . DLB-25, 91

Murakami, Haruki 1949- DLB-182

Munsey, Frank A., and
Company DLB-49

Murav'ev, Mikhail Nikitich
1757-1807 . . . . DLB-150

Murdoch, Iris 1919- DLB-14, 194

Murdoch, Rupert 1931- DLB-127

Murfree, Mary N. 1850-1922 . . . . DLB-12, 74

Murger, Henry 1822-1861 . . . . DLB-119

Murger, Louis-Henri (see Murger, Henry)

Murner, Thomas 1475-1537 . . . . . . DLB-179

Muro, Amado 1915-1971 . . . . DLB-82

Murphy, Arthur 1727-1805 . . . . . DLB-89, 142

Murphy, Beatrice M. 1908- DLB-76

Murphy, Emily 1868-1933 . . . . DLB-99

Murphy, John H., III 1916- DLB-127

Murphy, John, and Company DLB-49

Murphy, Richard 1927-1993 . . . . . . DLB-40

Murray, Albert L. 1916- DLB-38

Murray, Gilbert 1866-1957 . . . . DLB-10

Murray, Judith Sargent 1751-1820 . . . . DLB-37

Murray, Pauli 1910-1985 . . . . DLB-41

Murray, John [publishing house] DLB-154

Murry, John Middleton
1889-1957 . . . . DLB-149

Musäus, Johann Karl August
1735-1787 . . . . DLB-97

Muschg, Adolf 1934- DLB-75

The Music of *Minnesang* DLB-138

Musil, Robert 1880-1942 . . . . . DLB-81, 124

Muspilli circa 790-circa 850 . . . . . . DLB-148

Musset, Alfred de 1810-1857 . . . . . DLB-192

Mussey, Benjamin B., and
Company DLB-49

Mutafchieva, Vera 1929- DLB-181

Mwangi, Meja 1948- DLB-125

Myers, Frederic W. H. 1843-1901 . . . DLB-190

Myers, Gustavus 1872-1942 . . . . DLB-47

Myers, L. H. 1881-1944 . . . . DLB-15

Cumulative Index

Myers, Walter Dean 1937- DLB-33
Myles, Eileen 1949- DLB-193

N

Nabl, Franz 1883-1974 . . . . DLB-81
Nabokov, Vladimir
   1899-1977 . . . . . DLB-2; Y-80, Y-91; DS-3
Nabokov Festival at Cornell Y-83
The Vladimir Nabokov Archive
   in the Berg Collection Y-91
Nafis and Cornish DLB-49
Nagai, Kafū 1879-1959 . . . . DLB-180
Naipaul, Shiva 1945-1985 . . . . . DLB-157; Y-85
Naipaul, V. S. 1932- DLB-125; Y-85
Nakagami, Kenji 1946-1992 . . . . DLB-182
Nancrede, Joseph
   [publishing house] DLB-49
Naranjo, Carmen 1930- DLB-145
Narrache, Jean 1893-1970 . . . . DLB-92
Nasby, Petroleum Vesuvius (see Locke, David Ross)
Nash, Ogden 1902-1971 . . . . DLB-11
Nash, Eveleigh
   [publishing house] DLB-112
Nashe, Thomas 1567-1601? DLB-167
Nast, Conde 1873-1942 . . . . DLB-91
Nast, Thomas 1840-1902 . . . . DLB-188
Nastasijević, Momčilo 1894-1938 . . . . DLB-147
Nathan, George Jean 1882-1958 . . . . DLB-137
Nathan, Robert 1894-1985 . . . . DLB-9
The National Jewish Book Awards Y-85
The National Theatre and the Royal
   Shakespeare Company: The
   National Companies DLB-13
Natsume, Sōseki 1867-1916 . . . . DLB-180
Naughton, Bill 1910- DLB-13
Naylor, Gloria 1950- DLB-173
Nazor, Vladimir 1876-1949 . . . . DLB-147
Ndebele, Njabulo 1948- DLB-157
Neagoe, Peter 1881-1960 . . . . DLB-4
Neal, John 1793-1876 . . . . . . DLB-1, 59
Neal, Joseph C. 1807-1847 . . . . DLB-11
Neal, Larry 1937-1981 . . . . DLB-38
The Neale Publishing Company DLB-49
Neely, F. Tennyson
   [publishing house] DLB-49
Negri, Ada 1870-1945 . . . . DLB-114
"The Negro as a Writer," by
   G. M. McClellan DLB-50
"Negro Poets and Their Poetry," by
   Wallace Thurman DLB-50

Neidhart von Reuental
   circa 1185-circa 1240 . . . . DLB-138
Neihardt, John G. 1881-1973 . . . . . DLB-9, 54
Neledinsky-Meletsky, Iurii Aleksandrovich
   1752-1828 . . . . DLB-150
Nelligan, Emile 1879-1941 . . . . DLB-92
Nelson, Alice Moore Dunbar
   1875-1935 . . . . DLB-50
Nelson, Thomas, and Sons [U.S.] DLB-49
Nelson, Thomas, and Sons [U.K.] DLB-106
Nelson, William 1908-1978 . . . . DLB-103
Nelson, William Rockhill
   1841-1915 . . . . DLB-23
Nemerov, Howard 1920-1991 . . . DLB-5, 6; Y-83
Nesbit, E. 1858-1924 . . . . . DLB-141, 153, 178
Ness, Evaline 1911-1986 . . . . DLB-61
Nestroy, Johann 1801-1862 . . . . DLB-133
Neukirch, Benjamin 1655-1729 . . . . . DLB-168
Neugeboren, Jay 1938- DLB-28
Neumann, Alfred 1895-1952 . . . . . . DLB-56
Neumark, Georg 1621-1681 . . . . . . DLB-164
Neumeister, Erdmann 1671-1756 . . . . DLB-168
Nevins, Allan 1890-1971 . . . . . DLB-17; DS-17
Nevinson, Henry Woodd
   1856-1941 . . . . DLB-135
The New American Library DLB-46
New Approaches to Biography: Challenges
   from Critical Theory, USC Conference
   on Literary Studies, 1990 . . . . . . Y-90
New Directions Publishing
   Corporation DLB-46
A New Edition of *Huck Finn* Y-85
New Forces at Work in the American Theatre:
   1915-1925 . . . . DLB-7
New Literary Periodicals:
   A Report for 1987 . . . . Y-87
New Literary Periodicals:
   A Report for 1988 . . . . Y-88
New Literary Periodicals:
   A Report for 1989 . . . . Y-89
New Literary Periodicals:
   A Report for 1990 . . . . Y-90
New Literary Periodicals:
   A Report for 1991 . . . . Y-91
New Literary Periodicals:
   A Report for 1992 . . . . Y-92
New Literary Periodicals:
   A Report for 1993 . . . . Y-93
The New Monthly Magazine
   1814-1884 . . . . DLB-110
The New *Ulysses* Y-84
The New Variorum Shakespeare Y-85
A New Voice: The Center for the Book's First
   Five Years Y-83
The New Wave [Science Fiction] DLB-8

New York City Bookshops in the 1930s and
   1940s: The Recollections of Walter
   Goldwater Y-93
Newbery, John
   [publishing house] DLB-154
Newbolt, Henry 1862-1938 . . . . DLB-19
Newbound, Bernard Slade (see Slade, Bernard)
Newby, P. H. 1918- DLB-15
Newby, Thomas Cautley
   [publishing house] DLB-106
Newcomb, Charles King 1820-1894 . . . DLB-1
Newell, Peter 1862-1924 . . . . DLB-42
Newell, Robert Henry 1836-1901 . . . . DLB-11
Newhouse, Samuel I. 1895-1979 . . . . DLB-127
Newman, Cecil Earl 1903-1976 . . . . . DLB-127
Newman, David (see Benton, Robert)
Newman, Frances 1883-1928 . . . . . . Y-80
Newman, Francis William
   1805-1897 . . . . DLB-190
Newman, John Henry
   1801-1890 . . . . DLB-18, 32, 55
Newman, Mark [publishing house] DLB-49
Newnes, George, Limited DLB-112
Newsome, Effie Lee 1885-1979 . . . . . DLB-76
Newspaper Syndication of American
   Humor DLB-11
Newton, A. Edward 1864-1940 . . . . . DLB-140
Ngugi wa Thiong'o 1938- DLB-125
Niatum, Duane 1938- DLB-175
The *Nibelungenlied* and the *Klage*
   circa 1200 . . . . DLB-138
Nichol, B. P. 1944- DLB-53
Nicholas of Cusa 1401-1464 . . . . . . DLB-115
Nichols, Beverly 1898-1983 . . . . DLB-191
Nichols, Dudley 1895-1960 . . . . DLB-26
Nichols, Grace 1950- DLB-157
Nichols, John 1940- Y-82
Nichols, Mary Sargeant (Neal) Gove
   1810-1884 . . . . DLB-1
Nichols, Peter 1927- DLB-13
Nichols, Roy F. 1896-1973 . . . . DLB-17
Nichols, Ruth 1948- DLB-60
Nicholson, Edward Williams Byron
   1849-1912 . . . . DLB-184
Nicholson, Norman 1914- DLB-27
Nicholson, William 1872-1949 . . . . . DLB-141
Ní Chuilleanáin, Eiléan 1942- DLB-40
Nicol, Eric 1919- DLB-68
Nicolai, Friedrich 1733-1811 . . . . . . DLB-97
Nicolay, John G. 1832-1901 and
   Hay, John 1838-1905 . . . . DLB-47
Nicolson, Harold 1886-1968 . . . . DLB-100, 149
Nicolson, Nigel 1917- DLB-155
Niebuhr, Reinhold 1892-1971 . . DLB-17; DS-17

Niedecker, Lorine 1903-1970 . . . . DLB-48	The 1996 Nobel Prize in Literature: Wisława Szymborsha Y-96	"The Novel in [Robert Browning's] 'The Ring and the Book'" (1912), by Henry James DLB-32
Nieman, Lucius W. 1857-1935 . . . . . DLB-25	The 1997 Nobel Prize in Literature: Dario Fo Y-97	The Novel of Impressionism, by Jethro Bithell DLB-66
Nietzsche, Friedrich 1844-1900 . . . . . DLB-129	Nodier, Charles 1780-1844 . . . . DLB-119	Novel-Reading: *The Works of Charles Dickens, The Works of W. Makepeace Thackeray* (1879), by Anthony Trollope DLB-21
Nievo, Stanislao 1928- DLB-196	Noel, Roden 1834-1894 . . . . DLB-35	
Niggli, Josefina 1910- Y-80	Nogami, Yaeko 1885-1985 . . . . DLB-180	
Nightingale, Florence 1820-1910 . . . . DLB-166	Nogo, Rajko Petrov 1945- DLB-181	Novels for Grown-Ups Y-97
Nikolev, Nikolai Petrovich 1758-1815 . . . . DLB-150	Nolan, William F. 1928- DLB-8	The Novels of Dorothy Richardson (1918), by May Sinclair DLB-36
Niles, Hezekiah 1777-1839 . . . . DLB-43	Noland, C. F. M. 1810?-1858 . . . . . . DLB-11	Novels with a Purpose (1864), by Justin M'Carthy DLB-21
Nims, John Frederick 1913- DLB-5	Noma, Hiroshi 1915-1991 . . . . DLB-182	
Nin, Anaïs 1903-1977 . . . . . DLB-2, 4, 152	Nonesuch Press DLB-112	Noventa, Giacomo 1898-1960 . . . . . . DLB-114
1985: The Year of the Mystery: A Symposium Y-85	Noonan, Robert Phillipe (see Tressell, Robert)	Novikov, Nikolai Ivanovich 1744-1818 . . . . DLB-150
	Noonday Press DLB-46	
The 1997 Booker Prize Y-97	Noone, John 1936- DLB-14	Nowlan, Alden 1933-1983 . . . . DLB-53
Nissenson, Hugh 1933- DLB-28	Nora, Eugenio de 1923- DLB-134	Noyes, Alfred 1880-1958 . . . . DLB-20
Niven, Frederick John 1878-1944 . . . . DLB-92	Nordhoff, Charles 1887-1947 . . . . . . DLB-9	Noyes, Crosby S. 1825-1908 . . . . DLB-23
Niven, Larry 1938- DLB-8	Norman, Charles 1904- DLB-111	Noyes, Nicholas 1647-1717 . . . . DLB-24
Nizan, Paul 1905-1940 . . . . DLB-72	Norman, Marsha 1947- Y-84	Noyes, Theodore W. 1858-1946 . . . . . DLB-29
Njegoš, Petar II Petrović 1813-1851 . . . . DLB-147	Norris, Charles G. 1881-1945 . . . . . . DLB-9	N-Town Plays circa 1468 to early sixteenth century DLB-146
	Norris, Frank 1870-1902 . . . . DLB-12, 71, 186	Nugent, Frank 1908-1965 . . . . DLB-44
Nkosi, Lewis 1936- DLB-157	Norris, Leslie 1921- DLB-27	Nugent, Richard Bruce 1906- DLB-151
"The No Self, the Little Self, and the Poets," by Richard Moore DLB-105	Norse, Harold 1916- DLB-16	Nušić, Branislav 1864-1938 . . . . DLB-147
Nobel Peace Prize	North, Marianne 1830-1890 . . . . DLB-174	Nutt, David [publishing house] DLB-106
The 1986 Nobel Peace Prize: Elie Wiesel Y-86	North Point Press DLB-46	Nwapa, Flora 1931- DLB-125
	Nortje, Arthur 1942-1970 . . . . DLB-125	Nye, Bill 1850-1896 . . . . DLB-186
The Nobel Prize and Literary Politics . . . Y-86	Norton, Alice Mary (see Norton, Andre)	Nye, Edgar Wilson (Bill) 1850-1896 . . . . DLB-11, 23
Nobel Prize in Literature	Norton, Andre 1912- DLB-8, 52	
The 1982 Nobel Prize in Literature: Gabriel García Márquez Y-82	Norton, Andrews 1786-1853 . . . . DLB-1	Nye, Naomi Shihab 1952- DLB-120
The 1983 Nobel Prize in Literature: William Golding Y-83	Norton, Caroline 1808-1877 . . . . DLB-21, 159	Nye, Robert 1939- DLB-14
	Norton, Charles Eliot 1827-1908 . . . DLB-1, 64	
The 1984 Nobel Prize in Literature: Jaroslav Seifert Y-84	Norton, John 1606-1663 . . . . DLB-24	**O**
	Norton, Mary 1903-1992 . . . . DLB-160	
The 1985 Nobel Prize in Literature: Claude Simon Y-85	Norton, Thomas (see Sackville, Thomas)	Oakes, Urian circa 1631-1681 . . . . . . DLB-24
The 1986 Nobel Prize in Literature: Wole Soyinka Y-86	Norton, W. W., and Company DLB-46	Oakley, Violet 1874-1961 . . . . DLB-188
	Norwood, Robert 1874-1932 . . . . DLB-92	Oates, Joyce Carol 1938- DLB-2, 5, 130; Y-81
The 1987 Nobel Prize in Literature: Joseph Brodsky Y-87	Nosaka, Akiyuki 1930- DLB-182	
The 1988 Nobel Prize in Literature: Najīb Mahfūz Y-88	Nossack, Hans Erich 1901-1977 . . . . . DLB-69	Ōba, Minako 1930- DLB-182
	A Note on Technique (1926), by Elizabeth A. Drew [excerpts] DLB-36	Ober, Frederick Albion 1849-1913 . . . DLB-189
The 1989 Nobel Prize in Literature: Camilo José Cela Y-89	Notker Balbulus circa 840-912 . . . . . DLB-148	Ober, William 1920-1993 . . . . Y-93
The 1990 Nobel Prize in Literature: Octavio Paz Y-90	Notker III of Saint Gall circa 950-1022 . . . . DLB-148	Oberholtzer, Ellis Paxson 1868-1936 . . . . DLB-47
The 1991 Nobel Prize in Literature: Nadine Gordimer Y-91	Notker von Zweifalten ?-1095 . . . . . . DLB-148	Obradović, Dositej 1740?-1811 . . . . . DLB-147
The 1992 Nobel Prize in Literature: Derek Walcott Y-92	Nourse, Alan E. 1928- DLB-8	O'Brien, Edna 1932- DLB-14
	Novak, Slobodan 1924- DLB-181	O'Brien, Fitz-James 1828-1862 . . . . . DLB-74
The 1993 Nobel Prize in Literature: Toni Morrison Y-93	Novak, Vjenceslav 1859-1905 . . . . . . DLB-147	O'Brien, Kate 1897-1974 . . . . DLB-15
The 1994 Nobel Prize in Literature: Kenzaburō Ōe Y-94	Novalis 1772-1801 . . . . DLB-90	O'Brien, Tim 1946- DLB-152; Y-80; DS-9
	Novaro, Mario 1868-1944 . . . . DLB-114	O'Casey, Sean 1880-1964 . . . . DLB-10
The 1995 Nobel Prize in Literature: Seamus Heaney Y-95	Novás Calvo, Lino 1903-1983 . . . . . . DLB-145	Occom, Samson 1723-1792 . . . . DLB-175
		Ochs, Adolph S. 1858-1935 . . . . DLB-25

Cumulative Index

Ochs-Oakes, George Washington 1861-1931 . . . . DLB-137

O'Connor, Flannery 1925-1964 . . . . DLB-2, 152; Y-80; DS-12

O'Connor, Frank 1903-1966 . . . . . . DLB-162

Octopus Publishing Group DLB-112

Oda, Sakunosuke 1913-1947 . . . . . . DLB-182

Odell, Jonathan 1737-1818 . . . . . . DLB-31, 99

O'Dell, Scott 1903-1989 . . . . DLB-52

Odets, Clifford 1906-1963 . . . . . . DLB-7, 26

Odhams Press Limited DLB-112

O'Donnell, Peter 1920- DLB-87

O'Donovan, Michael (see O'Connor, Frank)

Ōe, Kenzaburō 1935- DLB-182; Y-94

O'Faolain, Julia 1932- DLB-14

O'Faolain, Sean 1900- DLB-15, 162

Off Broadway and Off-Off Broadway . . DLB-7

Off-Loop Theatres DLB-7

Offord, Carl Ruthven 1910- DLB-76

O'Flaherty, Liam 1896-1984 . . . . DLB-36, 162; Y-84

Ogilvie, J. S., and Company DLB-49

Ogot, Grace 1930- DLB-125

O'Grady, Desmond 1935- DLB-40

Ogunyemi, Wale 1939- DLB-157

O'Hagan, Howard 1902-1982 . . . . . DLB-68

O'Hara, Frank 1926-1966 . . . . DLB-5, 16, 193

O'Hara, John 1905-1970 . . . . DLB-9, 86; DS-2

Okara, Gabriel 1921- DLB-125

O'Keeffe, John 1747-1833 . . . . DLB-89

Okes, Nicholas [publishing house] DLB-170

Okigbo, Christopher 1930-1967 . . . . DLB-125

Okot p'Bitek 1931-1982 . . . . DLB-125

Okpewho, Isidore 1941- DLB-157

Okri, Ben 1959- DLB-157

Olaudah Equiano and Unfinished Journeys: The Slave-Narrative Tradition and Twentieth-Century Continuities, by Paul Edwards and Pauline T. Wangman DLB-117

Old English Literature: An Introduction DLB-146

Old English Riddles eighth to tenth centuries DLB-146

Old Franklin Publishing House DLB-49

Old German Genesis and *Old German Exodus* circa 1050-circa 1130 . . . . DLB-148

Old High German Charms and Blessings DLB-148

The *Old High German Isidor* circa 790-800 . . . . DLB-148

Older, Fremont 1856-1935 . . . . DLB-25

Oldham, John 1653-1683 . . . . DLB-131

Olds, Sharon 1942- DLB-120

Olearius, Adam 1599-1671 . . . . DLB-164

Oliphant, Laurence 1829?-1888 . . . . DLB-18, 166

Oliphant, Margaret 1828-1897 . . . DLB-18, 190

Oliver, Chad 1928- DLB-8

Oliver, Mary 1935- DLB-5, 193

Ollier, Claude 1922- DLB-83

Olsen, Tillie 1913?- DLB-28; Y-80

Olson, Charles 1910-1970 . . . . DLB-5, 16, 193

Olson, Elder 1909- DLB-48, 63

Omotoso, Kole 1943- DLB-125

"On Art in Fiction"(1838), by Edward Bulwer DLB-21

On Learning to Write Y-88

On Some of the Characteristics of Modern Poetry and On the Lyrical Poems of Alfred Tennyson (1831), by Arthur Henry Hallam DLB-32

"On Style in English Prose" (1898), by Frederic Harrison DLB-57

"On Style in Literature: Its Technical Elements" (1885), by Robert Louis Stevenson DLB-57

"On the Writing of Essays" (1862), by Alexander Smith DLB-57

Ondaatje, Michael 1943- DLB-60

O'Neill, Eugene 1888-1953 . . . . DLB-7

Onetti, Juan Carlos 1909-1994 . . . . . DLB-113

Onions, George Oliver 1872-1961 . . . . DLB-153

Onofri, Arturo 1885-1928 . . . . DLB-114

Opie, Amelia 1769-1853 . . . . . DLB-116, 159

Opitz, Martin 1597-1639 . . . . DLB-164

Oppen, George 1908-1984 . . . . DLB-5, 165

Oppenheim, E. Phillips 1866-1946 . . . . DLB-70

Oppenheim, James 1882-1932 . . . . . DLB-28

Oppenheimer, Joel 1930-1988 . . . DLB-5, 193

Optic, Oliver (see Adams, William Taylor)

Oral History Interview with Donald S. Klopfer Y-97

Orczy, Emma, Baroness 1865-1947 . . . . DLB-70

Origo, Iris 1902-1988 . . . . DLB-155

Orlovitz, Gil 1918-1973 . . . . DLB-2, 5

Orlovsky, Peter 1933- DLB-16

Ormond, John 1923- DLB-27

Ornitz, Samuel 1890-1957 . . . . . . DLB-28, 44

O'Rourke, P. J. 1947- DLB-185

Ortese, Anna Maria 1914- DLB-177

Ortiz, Simon J. 1941- DLB-120, 175

Ortnit and *Wolfdietrich* circa 1225-1250 . . . . DLB-138

Orton, Joe 1933-1967 . . . . DLB-13

Orwell, George 1903-1950 . . . DLB-15, 98, 195

The Orwell Year Y-84

Ory, Carlos Edmundo de 1923- . . . DLB-134

Osbey, Brenda Marie 1957- DLB-120

Osbon, B. S. 1827-1912 . . . . DLB-43

Osborne, John 1929-1994 . . . . DLB-13

Osgood, Herbert L. 1855-1918 . . . . . DLB-47

Osgood, James R., and Company DLB-49

Osgood, McIlvaine and Company DLB-112

O'Shaughnessy, Arthur 1844-1881 . . . . DLB-35

O'Shea, Patrick [publishing house] DLB-49

Osipov, Nikolai Petrovich 1751-1799 . . . . DLB-150

Oskison, John Milton 1879-1947 . . . . DLB-175

Osler, Sir William 1849-1919 . . . . . DLB-184

Osofisan, Femi 1946- DLB-125

Ostenso, Martha 1900-1963 . . . . DLB-92

Ostriker, Alicia 1937- DLB-120

Osundare, Niyi 1947- DLB-157

Oswald, Eleazer 1755-1795 . . . . DLB-43

Oswald von Wolkenstein 1376 or 1377-1445 . . . . DLB-179

Otero, Blas de 1916-1979 . . . . DLB-134

Otero, Miguel Antonio 1859-1944 . . . . DLB-82

Otero Silva, Miguel 1908-1985 . . . . . DLB-145

Otfried von Weißenburg circa 800-circa 875? DLB-148

Otis, James (see Kaler, James Otis)

Otis, James, Jr. 1725-1783 . . . . DLB-31

Otis, Broaders and Company DLB-49

Ottaway, James 1911- DLB-127

Ottendorfer, Oswald 1826-1900 . . . . DLB-23

Ottieri, Ottiero 1924- DLB-177

Otto-Peters, Louise 1819-1895 . . . . . DLB-129

Otway, Thomas 1652-1685 . . . . DLB-80

Ouellette, Fernand 1930- DLB-60

Ouida 1839-1908 . . . . DLB-18, 156

Outing Publishing Company DLB-46

Outlaw Days, by Joyce Johnson DLB-16

Overbury, Sir Thomas circa 1581-1613 . . . . DLB-151

The Overlook Press DLB-46

Overview of U.S. Book Publishing, 1910-1945 . . . . DLB-9

Owen, Guy 1925- DLB-5

Owen, John 1564-1622 . . . . DLB-121

Owen, John [publishing house] DLB-49

Owen, Robert 1771-1858 . . . . . DLB-107, 158

Owen, Wilfred 1893-1918 . . . . DLB-20	Panizzi, Sir Anthony 1797-1879. . . . . DLB-184	Pastorius, Francis Daniel 1651-circa 1720 . . . . DLB-24
Owen, Peter, Limited DLB-112	Panneton, Philippe (see Ringuet)	
The Owl and the Nightingale circa 1189-1199 . . . . DLB-146	Panshin, Alexei 1940- DLB-8	Patchen, Kenneth 1911-1972 . . . . . DLB-16, 48
	Pansy (see Alden, Isabella)	Pater, Walter 1839-1894 . . . . . . DLB-57, 156
Owsley, Frank L. 1890-1956 . . . . . . DLB-17	Pantheon Books DLB-46	Paterson, Katherine 1932- DLB-52
Oxford, Seventeenth Earl of, Edward de Vere 1550-1604 . . . . DLB-172	Papantonio, Michael (see Kohn, John S. Van E.)	Patmore, Coventry 1823-1896 . . . . DLB-35, 98
	Paperback Library DLB-46	Paton, Alan 1903-1988 . . . . DS-17
Ozerov, Vladislav Aleksandrovich 1769-1816 . . . . DLB-150	Paperback Science Fiction DLB-8	Paton, Joseph Noel 1821-1901 . . . . . . DLB-35
Ozick, Cynthia 1928- DLB-28, 152; Y-82	Paquet, Alfons 1881-1944 . . . . DLB-66	Paton Walsh, Jill 1937- DLB-161
	Paracelsus 1493-1541 . . . . DLB-179	Patrick, Edwin Hill ("Ted") 1901-1964 . . . . DLB-137
	Paradis, Suzanne 1936- DLB-53	
P	Pareja Diezcanseco, Alfredo 1908-1993 . . . . DLB-145	Patrick, John 1906- DLB-7
		Pattee, Fred Lewis 1863-1950 . . . . . . DLB-71
Pace, Richard 1482?-1536 . . . . DLB-167	Pardoe, Julia 1804-1862 . . . . DLB-166	Pattern and Paradigm: History as Design, by Judith Ryan DLB-75
Pacey, Desmond 1917-1975 . . . . DLB-88	Parents' Magazine Press DLB-46	
Pack, Robert 1929- DLB-5	Parise, Goffredo 1929-1986 . . . . . . DLB-177	Patterson, Alicia 1906-1963 . . . . . . DLB-127
Packaging Papa: *The Garden of Eden* Y-86	Parisian Theater, Fall 1984: Toward A New Baroque Y-85	Patterson, Eleanor Medill 1881-1948 . . . . DLB-29
Padell Publishing Company DLB-46		Patterson, Eugene 1923- DLB-127
Padgett, Ron 1942- DLB-5	Parizeau, Alice 1930- DLB-60	Patterson, Joseph Medill 1879-1946 . . . . DLB-29
Padilla, Ernesto Chávez 1944- DLB-122	Parke, John 1754-1789 . . . . DLB-31	
Page, L. C., and Company DLB-49	Parker, Dorothy 1893-1967 . . . . DLB-11, 45, 86	Pattillo, Henry 1726-1801 . . . . DLB-37
Page, P. K. 1916- DLB-68		Paul, Elliot 1891-1958 . . . . DLB-4
Page, Thomas Nelson 1853-1922 . . . . DLB-12, 78; DS-13	Parker, Gilbert 1860-1932 . . . . DLB-99	Paul, Jean (see Richter, Johann Paul Friedrich)
	Parker, James 1714-1770 . . . . DLB-43	Paul, Kegan, Trench, Trubner and Company Limited DLB-106
Page, Walter Hines 1855-1918 . . . . DLB-71, 91	Parker, Theodore 1810-1860 . . . . DLB-1	
Paget, Francis Edward 1806-1882 . . . . DLB-163	Parker, William Riley 1906-1968 . . . . DLB-103	Paul, Peter, Book Company DLB-49
	Parker, J. H. [publishing house] DLB-106	Paul, Stanley, and Company Limited DLB-112
Paget, Violet (see Lee, Vernon)	Parker, John [publishing house] DLB-106	
Pagliarani, Elio 1927- DLB-128	Parkman, Francis, Jr. 1823-1893 . . . . DLB-1, 30, 183, 186	Paulding, James Kirke 1778-1860 . . . . DLB-3, 59, 74
Pain, Barry 1864-1928 . . . . DLB-135, 197		
Pain, Philip ?-circa 1666 . . . . DLB-24	Parks, Gordon 1912- DLB-33	Paulin, Tom 1949- DLB-40
Paine, Robert Treat, Jr. 1773-1811 . . . DLB-37	Parks, William 1698-1750 . . . . DLB-43	Pauper, Peter, Press DLB-46
Paine, Thomas 1737-1809 . . . . DLB-31, 43, 73, 158	Parks, William [publishing house] DLB-49	Pavese, Cesare 1908-1950 . . . . . DLB-128, 177
	Parley, Peter (see Goodrich, Samuel Griswold)	Pavić, Milorad 1929- DLB-181
Painter, George D. 1914- DLB-155	Parmenides late sixth-fifth century B.C. DLB-176	Pavlov, Konstantin 1933- DLB-181
Painter, William 1540?-1594 . . . . . . DLB-136		Pavlović, Miodrag 1928- DLB-181
Palazzeschi, Aldo 1885-1974 . . . . . . DLB-114	Parnell, Thomas 1679-1718 . . . . DLB-95	Paxton, John 1911-1985 . . . . DLB-44
Paley, Grace 1922- DLB-28	Parr, Catherine 1513?-1548 . . . . . . DLB-136	Payn, James 1830-1898 . . . . DLB-18
Palfrey, John Gorham 1796-1881 . . . . DLB-1, 30	Parrington, Vernon L. 1871-1929 . . . . DLB-17, 63	Payne, John 1842-1916 . . . . DLB-35
		Payne, John Howard 1791-1852 . . . . . DLB-37
Palgrave, Francis Turner 1824-1897 . . . . DLB-35	Parrish, Maxfield 1870-1966 . . . . . . DLB-188	Payson and Clarke DLB-46
	Parronchi, Alessandro 1914- DLB-128	Paz, Octavio 1914-1998 . . . . Y-90
Palmer, Joe H. 1904-1952 . . . . DLB-171	Partridge, S. W., and Company DLB-106	Pazzi, Roberto 1946- DLB-196
Palmer, Michael 1943- DLB-169	Parton, James 1822-1891 . . . . DLB-30	
Paltock, Robert 1697-1767 . . . . DLB-39	Parton, Sara Payson Willis 1811-1872 . . . . DLB-43, 74	Peabody, Elizabeth Palmer 1804-1894 . . . . DLB-1
Pan Books Limited DLB-112		
Panama, Norman 1914- and Frank, Melvin 1913-1988 . . . . . DLB-26	Parun, Vesna 1922- DLB-181	Peabody, Elizabeth Palmer [publishing house] DLB-49
	Pasinetti, Pier Maria 1913- DLB-177	
Pancake, Breece D'J 1952-1979 . . . . . DLB-130	Pasolini, Pier Paolo 1922- DLB-128, 177	Peabody, Oliver William Bourn 1799-1848 . . . . DLB-59
Panero, Leopoldo 1909-1962 . . . . . . DLB-108	Pastan, Linda 1932- DLB-5	
Pangborn, Edgar 1909-1976 . . . . DLB-8	Paston, George (Emily Morse Symonds) 1860-1936 . . . . DLB-149, 197	Peace, Roger 1899-1968 . . . . DLB-127
"Panic Among the Philistines": A Postscript, An Interview with Bryan Griffin Y-81		Peacham, Henry 1578-1644? DLB-151
	The *Paston Letters* 1422-1509 . . . . . . DLB-146	Peacham, Henry, the Elder 1547-1634 . . . . DLB-172

Peachtree Publishers, Limited. DLB-46	"Personal Style" (1890), by John Addington Symonds. DLB-57	Phillips, Stephen 1864-1915. . . . . DLB-10
Peacock, Molly 1947- DLB-120	Perutz, Leo 1882-1957 . . . . DLB-81	Phillips, Ulrich B. 1877-1934. . . . . . . DLB-17
Peacock, Thomas Love 1785-1866 . . . . DLB-96, 116	Pesetsky, Bette 1932- DLB-130	Phillips, Willard 1784-1873. . . . . DLB-59
Pead, Deuel ?-1727 . . . . DLB-24	Pestalozzi, Johann Heinrich 1746-1827 . . . . DLB-94	Phillips, William 1907- DLB-137
Peake, Mervyn 1911-1968 . . . . DLB-15, 160	Peter, Laurence J. 1919-1990. . . . . . . DLB-53	Phillips, Sampson and Company. DLB-49
Peale, Rembrandt 1778-1860 . . . . . DLB-183	Peter of Spain circa 1205-1277 . . . . DLB-115	Phillpotts, Adelaide Eden (Adelaide Ross) 1896-1993 . . . . DLB-191
Pear Tree Press DLB-112	Peterkin, Julia 1880-1961. . . . . DLB-9	Phillpotts, Eden 1862-1960 . . . . . . DLB-10, 70, 135, 153
Pearce, Philippa 1920- DLB-161	Peters, Lenrie 1932- DLB-117	Philo circa 20-15 B.C.-circa A.D. 50 . . . . DLB-176
Pearson, H. B. [publishing house] DLB-49	Peters, Robert 1924- DLB-105	Philosophical Library DLB-46
Pearson, Hesketh 1887-1964. . . . . . DLB-149	Petersham, Maud 1889-1971 and Petersham, Miska 1888-1960. . . . . DLB-22	"The Philosophy of Style" (1852), by Herbert Spencer. DLB-57
Peck, George W. 1840-1916. . . . DLB-23, 42	Peterson, Charles Jacobs 1819-1887 . . . . DLB-79	Phinney, Elihu [publishing house] DLB-49
Peck, H. C., and Theo. Bliss [publishing house]. DLB-49	Peterson, Len 1917- DLB-88	Phoenix, John (see Derby, George Horatio)
Peck, Harry Thurston 1856-1914 . . . . DLB-71, 91	Peterson, Louis 1922- DLB-76	PHYLON (Fourth Quarter, 1950), The Negro in Literature: The Current Scene. DLB-76
Peele, George 1556-1596 . . . . . DLB-62, 167	Peterson, T. B., and Brothers DLB-49	*Physiologus* circa 1070-circa 1150 . . . . DLB-148
Pegler, Westbrook 1894-1969 . . . . . DLB-171	Petitclair, Pierre 1813-1860 . . . . DLB-99	Piccolo, Lucio 1903-1969 . . . . DLB-114
Pekić, Borislav 1930-1992 . . . . DLB-181	Petrov, Aleksandar 1938- DLB-181	Pickard, Tom 1946- DLB-40
Pellegrini and Cudahy DLB-46	Petrov, Gavriil 1730-1801 . . . . DLB-150	Pickering, William [publishing house] DLB-106
Pelletier, Aimé (see Vac, Bertrand)	Petrov, Vasilii Petrovich 1736-1799 . . . . DLB-150	Pickthall, Marjorie 1883-1922. . . . . . DLB-92
Pemberton, Sir Max 1863-1950 . . . . . DLB-70	Petrov, Valeri 1920- DLB-181	Pictorial Printing Company. DLB-49
Penfield, Edward 1866-1925. . . . . . DLB-188	Petrović, Rastko 1898-1949 . . . . . . DLB-147	Piercy, Marge 1936- DLB-120
Penguin Books [U.S.] DLB-46	*Petruslied* circa 854?. DLB-148	Pierro, Albino 1916- DLB-128
Penguin Books [U.K.] DLB-112	Petry, Ann 1908- DLB-76	Pignotti, Lamberto 1926- DLB-128
Penn Publishing Company DLB-49	Pettie, George circa 1548-1589 . . . . . DLB-136	Pike, Albert 1809-1891 . . . . DLB-74
Penn, William 1644-1718. . . . . DLB-24	Peyton, K. M. 1929- DLB-161	Pike, Zebulon Montgomery 1779-1813 . . DLB-183
Penna, Sandro 1906-1977 . . . . DLB-114	Pfaffe Konrad flourished circa 1172 . . . . DLB-148	Pilon, Jean-Guy 1930- DLB-60
Pennell, Joseph 1857-1926. . . . . . . DLB-188	Pfaffe Lamprecht flourished circa 1150 . . . . DLB-148	Pinckney, Josephine 1895-1957 . . . . . DLB-6
Penner, Jonathan 1940- Y-83	Pforzheimer, Carl H. 1879-1957 . . . . DLB-140	Pindar circa 518 B.C.-circa 438 B.C. DLB-176
Pennington, Lee 1939- Y-82	Phaer, Thomas 1510?-1560 . . . . DLB-167	Pindar, Peter (see Wolcot, John)
Pepys, Samuel 1633-1703 . . . . DLB-101	Phaidon Press Limited. DLB-112	Pinero, Arthur Wing 1855-1934 . . . . . DLB-10
Percy, Thomas 1729-1811. . . . . . . DLB-104	Pharr, Robert Deane 1916-1992 . . . . . DLB-33	Pinget, Robert 1919- DLB-83
Percy, Walker 1916-1990. . . DLB-2; Y-80, Y-90	Phelps, Elizabeth Stuart 1844-1911 . . . . DLB-74	Pinnacle Books DLB-46
Percy, William 1575-1648 . . . . DLB-172	Philander von der Linde (see Mencke, Johann Burckhard)	Piñon, Nélida 1935- DLB-145
Perec, Georges 1936-1982. . . . . DLB-83	Philby, H. St. John B. 1885-1960. . . . DLB-195	Pinsky, Robert 1940- Y-82
Perelman, Bob 1947- DLB-193	Philip, Marlene Nourbese 1947- DLB-157	Pinter, Harold 1930- DLB-13
Perelman, S. J. 1904-1979 . . . . . DLB-11, 44	Philippe, Charles-Louis 1874-1909 . . . . DLB-65	Piontek, Heinz 1925- DLB-75
Perez, Raymundo "Tigre" 1946- DLB-122	Phillipps, Sir Thomas 1792-1872 . . . . DLB-184	Piozzi, Hester Lynch [Thrale] 1741-1821. . . . . DLB-104, 142
Peri Rossi, Cristina 1941- DLB-145	Philips, John 1676-1708. . . . . DLB-95	Piper, H. Beam 1904-1964. . . . . DLB-8
Periodicals of the Beat Generation. . . . DLB-16	Philips, Katherine 1632-1664 . . . . . . DLB-131	Piper, Watty. DLB-22
Perkins, Eugene 1932- DLB-41	Phillips, Caryl 1958- DLB-157	Pirckheimer, Caritas 1467-1532 . . . . . DLB-179
Perkoff, Stuart Z. 1930-1974 . . . . . . DLB-16	Phillips, David Graham 1867-1911 . . . . DLB-9, 12	Pirckheimer, Willibald 1470-1530 . . . . DLB-179
Perley, Moses Henry 1804-1862 . . . . . DLB-99	Phillips, Jayne Anne 1952- Y-80	Pisar, Samuel 1929- Y-83
Permabooks DLB-46	Phillips, Robert 1938- DLB-105	Pitkin, Timothy 1766-1847 . . . . DLB-30
Perrin, Alice 1867-1934 . . . . DLB-156		
Perry, Bliss 1860-1954 . . . . DLB-71		
Perry, Eleanor 1915-1981. . . . . DLB-44		
Perry, Matthew 1794-1858 . . . . DLB-183		
Perry, Sampson 1747-1823 . . . . . . DLB-158		

The Pitt Poetry Series: Poetry Publishing Today Y-85

Pitter, Ruth 1897- DLB-20

Pix, Mary 1666-1709 . . . . DLB-80

Pixerécourt, René Charles Guilbert de 1773-1844 . . . . DLB-192

Plaatje, Sol T. 1876-1932 . . . . DLB-125

The Place of Realism in Fiction (1895), by George Gissing DLB-18

Plante, David 1940- Y-83

Platen, August von 1796-1835 . . . . . . DLB-90

Plath, Sylvia 1932-1963 . . . . . DLB-5, 6, 152

Plato circa 428 B.C.-348-347 B.C. DLB-176

Platon 1737-1812 . . . . DLB-150

Platt and Munk Company DLB-46

Playboy Press DLB-46

Playford, John [publishing house] DLB-170

Plays, Playwrights, and Playgoers DLB-84

Playwrights and Professors, by Tom Stoppard DLB-13

Playwrights on the Theater DLB-80

Der Pleier flourished circa 1250 . . . . DLB-138

Plenzdorf, Ulrich 1934- DLB-75

Plessen, Elizabeth 1944- DLB-75

Plievier, Theodor 1892-1955 . . . . DLB-69

Plimpton, George 1927- DLB-185

Plomer, William 1903-1973 . . DLB-20, 162, 191

Plotinus 204-270 . . . . DLB-176

Plumly, Stanley 1939- DLB-5, 193

Plumpp, Sterling D. 1940- DLB-41

Plunkett, James 1920- DLB-14

Plutarch circa 46-circa 120 . . . . DLB-176

Plymell, Charles 1935- DLB-16

Pocket Books DLB-46

Poe, Edgar Allan 1809-1849 . . . . DLB-3, 59, 73, 74

Poe, James 1921-1980 . . . . DLB-44

The Poet Laureate of the United States Statements from Former Consultants in Poetry Y-86

"The Poet's Kaleidoscope: The Element of Surprise in the Making of the Poem," by Madeline DeFrees DLB-105

"The Poetry File," by Edward Field DLB-105

Pohl, Frederik 1919- DLB-8

Poirier, Louis (see Gracq, Julien)

Polanyi, Michael 1891-1976 . . . . . . DLB-100

Pole, Reginald 1500-1558 . . . . DLB-132

Poliakoff, Stephen 1952- DLB-13

Polidori, John William 1795-1821 . . . . DLB-116

Polite, Carlene Hatcher 1932- DLB-33

Pollard, Edward A. 1832-1872 . . . . . DLB-30

Pollard, Percival 1869-1911 . . . . DLB-71

Pollard and Moss DLB-49

Pollock, Sharon 1936- DLB-60

Polonsky, Abraham 1910- DLB-26

Polotsky, Simeon 1629-1680 . . . . . . DLB-150

Polybius circa 200 B.C.-118 B.C. DLB-176

Pomilio, Mario 1921-1990 . . . . DLB-177

Ponce, Mary Helen 1938- DLB-122

Ponce-Montoya, Juanita 1949- DLB-122

Ponet, John 1516?-1556 . . . . DLB-132

Poniatowski, Elena 1933- DLB-113

Ponsard, François 1814-1867 . . . . . . DLB-192

Ponsonby, William [publishing house] DLB-170

Pontiggia, Giuseppe 1934- DLB-196

Pony Stories DLB-160

Poole, Ernest 1880-1950 . . . . DLB-9

Poole, Sophia 1804-1891 . . . . DLB-166

Poore, Benjamin Perley 1820-1887 . . . . DLB-23

Popa, Vasko 1922-1991 . . . . DLB-181

Pope, Abbie Hanscom 1858-1894 . . . . DLB-140

Pope, Alexander 1688-1744 . . . . DLB-95, 101

Popov, Mikhail Ivanovich 1742-circa 1790 . . . . DLB-150

Popović, Aleksandar 1929-1996 . . . . DLB-181

Popular Library DLB-46

Porlock, Martin (see MacDonald, Philip)

Porpoise Press DLB-112

Porta, Antonio 1935-1989 . . . . DLB-128

Porter, Anna Maria 1780-1832 . . . . DLB-116, 159

Porter, David 1780-1843 . . . . DLB-183

Porter, Eleanor H. 1868-1920 . . . . . . DLB-9

Porter, Gene Stratton (see Stratton-Porter, Gene)

Porter, Henry ?-? DLB-62

Porter, Jane 1776-1850 . . . . DLB-116, 159

Porter, Katherine Anne 1890-1980 . . . . DLB-4, 9, 102; Y-80; DS-12

Porter, Peter 1929- DLB-40

Porter, William Sydney 1862-1910 . . . . DLB-12, 78, 79

Porter, William T. 1809-1858 . . . . DLB-3, 43

Porter and Coates DLB-49

Portis, Charles 1933- DLB-6

Posey, Alexander 1873-1908 . . . . . . DLB-175

Postans, Marianne circa 1810-1865 . . . . DLB-166

Postl, Carl (see Sealsfield, Carl)

Poston, Ted 1906-1974 . . . . DLB-51

Postscript to [the Third Edition of] Clarissa (1751), by Samuel Richardson DLB-39

Potok, Chaim 1929- DLB-28, 152; Y-84

Potter, Beatrix 1866-1943 . . . . DLB-141

Potter, David M. 1910-1971 . . . . . . DLB-17

Potter, John E., and Company DLB-49

Pottle, Frederick A. 1897-1987 . . . . DLB-103; Y-87

Poulin, Jacques 1937- DLB-60

Pound, Ezra 1885-1972 . . DLB-4, 45, 63; DS-15

Povich, Shirley 1905- DLB-171

Powell, Anthony 1905- DLB-15

Powell, John Wesley 1834-1902 . . . . DLB-186

Powers, J. F. 1917- DLB-130

Pownall, David 1938- DLB-14

Powys, John Cowper 1872-1963 . . . . . DLB-15

Powys, Llewelyn 1884-1939 . . . . DLB-98

Powys, T. F. 1875-1953 . . . . . . DLB-36, 162

Poynter, Nelson 1903-1978 . . . . DLB-127

The Practice of Biography: An Interview with Stanley Weintraub Y-82

The Practice of Biography II: An Interview with B. L. Reid Y-83

The Practice of Biography III: An Interview with Humphrey Carpenter Y-84

The Practice of Biography IV: An Interview with William Manchester Y-85

The Practice of Biography V: An Interview with Justin Kaplan Y-86

The Practice of Biography VI: An Interview with David Herbert Donald Y-87

The Practice of Biography VII: An Interview with John Caldwell Guilds Y-92

The Practice of Biography VIII: An Interview with Joan Mellen Y-94

The Practice of Biography IX: An Interview with Michael Reynolds Y-95

Prados, Emilio 1899-1962 . . . . DLB-134

Praed, Winthrop Mackworth 1802-1839 . . . . DLB-96

Praeger Publishers DLB-46

Praetorius, Johannes 1630-1680 . . . . DLB-168

Pratolini, Vasco 1913—1991 . . . . . . DLB-177

Pratt, E. J. 1882-1964 . . . . DLB-92

Pratt, Samuel Jackson 1749-1814 . . . . DLB-39

Preface to Alwyn (1780), by Thomas Holcroft DLB-39

Preface to Colonel Jack (1722), by Daniel Defoe DLB-39

Preface to Evelina (1778), by Fanny Burney DLB-39

Preface to Ferdinand Count Fathom (1753), by Tobias Smollett DLB-39

Preface to Incognita (1692), by William Congreve DLB-39

Preface to *Joseph Andrews* (1742), by
 Henry Fielding DLB-39

Preface to *Moll Flanders* (1722), by
 Daniel Defoe DLB-39

Preface to *Poems* (1853), by
 Matthew Arnold DLB-32

Preface to *Robinson Crusoe* (1719), by
 Daniel Defoe DLB-39

Preface to *Roderick Random* (1748), by
 Tobias Smollett DLB-39

Preface to *Roxana* (1724), by
 Daniel Defoe DLB-39

Preface to *St. Leon* (1799), by
 William Godwin DLB-39

Preface to Sarah Fielding's *Familiar Letters*
 (1747), by Henry Fielding
 [excerpt] DLB-39

Preface to Sarah Fielding's *The Adventures of
 David Simple* (1744), by
 Henry Fielding DLB-39

Preface to *The Cry* (1754), by
 Sarah Fielding. DLB-39

Preface to *The Delicate Distress* (1769), by
 Elizabeth Griffin. DLB-39

Preface to *The Disguis'd Prince* (1733), by
 Eliza Haywood [excerpt] DLB-39

Preface to *The Farther Adventures of Robinson
 Crusoe* (1719), by Daniel Defoe . . . DLB-39

Preface to the First Edition of *Pamela* (1740), by
 Samuel Richardson DLB-39

Preface to the First Edition of *The Castle of
 Otranto* (1764), by
 Horace Walpole DLB-39

Preface to *The History of Romances* (1715), by
 Pierre Daniel Huet [excerpts] DLB-39

Preface to *The Life of Charlotta du Pont* (1723),
 by Penelope Aubin DLB-39

Preface to *The Old English Baron* (1778), by
 Clara Reeve. DLB-39

Preface to the Second Edition of *The Castle of
 Otranto* (1765), by Horace
 Walpole DLB-39

Preface to *The Secret History, of Queen Zarah,
 and the Zarazians* (1705), by Delariviere
 Manley DLB-39

Preface to the Third Edition of *Clarissa* (1751),
 by Samuel Richardson
 [excerpt] DLB-39

Preface to *The Works of Mrs. Davys* (1725), by
 Mary Davys DLB-39

Preface to Volume 1 of *Clarissa* (1747), by
 Samuel Richardson DLB-39

Preface to Volume 3 of *Clarissa* (1748), by
 Samuel Richardson DLB-39

Préfontaine, Yves 1937- DLB-53

Prelutsky, Jack 1940- DLB-61

Premisses, by Michael Hamburger. . . . DLB-66

Prentice, George D. 1802-1870. . . . . DLB-43

Prentice-Hall. DLB-46

Prescott, Orville 1906-1996. . . . . . . Y-96

Prescott, William Hickling
 1796-1859 . . . . DLB-1, 30, 59

The Present State of the English Novel (1892),
 by George Saintsbury DLB-18

Prešeren, Francè 1800-1849 . . . . . . DLB-147

Preston, May Wilson 1873-1949 . . . . DLB-188

Preston, Thomas 1537-1598 . . . . . . DLB-62

Price, Reynolds 1933- DLB-2

Price, Richard 1723-1791 . . . . DLB-158

Price, Richard 1949- Y-81

Priest, Christopher 1943- DLB-14

Priestley, J. B. 1894-1984
 . . . . DLB-10, 34, 77, 100, 139; Y-84

Primary Bibliography: A
 Retrospective Y-95

Prime, Benjamin Young 1733-1791 . . . DLB-31

Primrose, Diana
 floruit circa 1630 . . . . DLB-126

Prince, F. T. 1912- DLB-20

Prince, Thomas 1687-1758 . . . . . DLB-24, 140

The Principles of Success in Literature (1865), by
 George Henry Lewes [excerpt] . . . DLB-57

Printz, Wolfgang Casper
 1641-1717 . . . . DLB-168

Prior, Matthew 1664-1721 . . . . DLB-95

Prisco, Michele 1920- DLB-177

Pritchard, William H. 1932- DLB-111

Pritchett, V. S. 1900- DLB-15, 139

Procter, Adelaide Anne 1825-1864 . . . DLB-32

Procter, Bryan Waller
 1787-1874 . . . . DLB-96, 144

Proctor, Robert 1868-1903. . . . . . . DLB-184

Producing *Dear Bunny, Dear Volodya: The Friendship
 and the Feud*. Y-97

The Profession of Authorship:
 Scribblers for Bread Y-89

The Progress of Romance (1785), by Clara Reeve
 [excerpt] DLB-39

Prokopovich, Feofan 1681?-1736 . . . . DLB-150

Prokosch, Frederic 1906-1989 . . . . . DLB-48

The Proletarian Novel DLB-9

Propper, Dan 1937- DLB-16

The Prospect of Peace (1778), by
 Joel Barlow DLB-37

Protagoras circa 490 B.C.-420 B.C.
 . . . . DLB-176

Proud, Robert 1728-1813. . . . . DLB-30

Proust, Marcel 1871-1922. . . . . DLB-65

Prynne, J. H. 1936- DLB-40

Przybyszewski, Stanislaw
 1868-1927 . . . . DLB-66

Pseudo-Dionysius the Areopagite floruit
 circa 500 . . . . DLB-115

Public Domain and the Violation of
 Texts Y-97

The Public Lending Right in America
 Statement by Sen. Charles McC.
 Mathias, Jr. PLR and the Meaning
 of Literary Property Statements on
 PLR by American Writers Y-83

The Public Lending Right in the United Kingdom
 Public Lending Right: The First Year in the
 United Kingdom Y-83

The Publication of English
 Renaissance Plays. DLB-62

Publications and Social Movements
 [Transcendentalism] DLB-1

Publishers and Agents: The Columbia
 Connection Y-87

A Publisher's Archives: G. P. Putnam . . . Y-92

Publishing Fiction at LSU Press. Y-87

Pückler-Muskau, Hermann von
 1785-1871 . . . . DLB-133

Pufendorf, Samuel von
 1632-1694 . . . . DLB-168

Pugh, Edwin William 1874-1930 . . . . DLB-135

Pugin, A. Welby 1812-1852 . . . . . . DLB-55

Puig, Manuel 1932-1990. . . . . DLB-113

Pulitzer, Joseph 1847-1911 . . . . DLB-23

Pulitzer, Joseph, Jr. 1885-1955 . . . . . DLB-29

Pulitzer Prizes for the Novel,
 1917-1945. . . . . DLB-9

Pulliam, Eugene 1889-1975 . . . . . . DLB-127

Purchas, Samuel 1577?-1626 . . . . . . DLB-151

Purdy, Al 1918- DLB-88

Purdy, James 1923- DLB-2

Purdy, Ken W. 1913-1972 . . . . DLB-137

Pusey, Edward Bouverie
 1800-1882 . . . . DLB-55

Putnam, George Palmer
 1814-1872 . . . . DLB-3, 79

Putnam, Samuel 1892-1950 . . . . . . DLB-4

G. P. Putnam's Sons [U.S.] DLB-49

G. P. Putnam's Sons [U.K.] DLB-106

Puzo, Mario 1920- DLB-6

Pyle, Ernie 1900-1945. . . . . DLB-29

Pyle, Howard
 1853-1911 . . . . DLB-42, 188; DS-13

Pym, Barbara 1913-1980. . . . . . DLB-14; Y-87

Pynchon, Thomas 1937- DLB-2, 173

Pyramid Books DLB-46

Pyrnelle, Louise-Clarke 1850-1907 . . . DLB-42

Pythagoras circa 570 B.C.-? DLB-176

Q

Quad, M. (see Lewis, Charles B.)

Quaritch, Bernard 1819-1899 . . . . . . DLB-184

Quarles, Francis 1592-1644 . . . . . . DLB-126

The Quarterly Review
   1809-1967 . . . . DLB-110
Quasimodo, Salvatore 190č-1968 . . . . DLB-114
Queen, Ellery (see Dannay, Frederic, and Manfred B. Lee)
The Queen City Publishing House . . . DLB-49
Queneau, Raymond 1903-1976 . . . . . . DLB-72
Quennell, Sir Peter 1905-1993 . . . DLB-155, 195
Quesnel, Joseph 1746-1809 . . . . DLB-99
The Question of American Copyright
   in the Nineteenth Century
      Headnote
      Preface, by George Haven Putnam
      The Evolution of Copyright, by Brander Matthews
      Summary of Copyright Legislation in the United States, by R. R. Bowker
      Analysis oœ the Provisions of the Copyright Law of 1891, by George Haven Putnam
      The Contest for International Copyright, by George Haven Putnam
      Cheap Books and Good Books, by Brander Matthews DLB-49
Quiller-Couch, Sir Arthur Thomas
   1863-1944 . . . . DLB-135, 153, 190
Quin, Ann 1936-1973 . . . . DLB-14
Quincy, Samuel, of Georgia ?-? DLB-31
Quincy, Samuel, of Massachusetts
   1734-1789 . . . . DLB-31
Quinn, Anthony 1915- DLB-122
Quinn, John 1870-1924 . . . . DLB-187
Quintana, Leroy V. 1944- DLB-82
Quintana, Miguel de 1671-1748
   A Forerunner of Chicano
   Literature DLB-122
Quist, Harlin, Books DLB-46
Quoirez, Françoise (see Sagan, Françoise)

R

Raabe, Wilhelm 1831-1910 . . . . DLB-129
Rabe, David 1940- DLB-7
Raboni, Giovanni 1932- DLB-128
Rachilde 1860-1953 . . . . DLB-123, 192
Racin, Kočo 1908-1943 . . . . DLB-147
Rackham, Arthur 1867-1939 . . . . . . DLB-141
Radcliffe, Ann 1764-1823 . . . . . . DLB-39, 178
Raddall, Thomas 1903- DLB-68
Radichkov, Yordan 1929- DLB-181
Radiguet, Raymond 1903-1923 . . . . . DLB-65
Radishchev, Aleksandr Nikolaevich
   1749-1802 . . . . DLB-150
Radványi, Netty Reiling (see Seghers, Anna)
Rahv, Philip 1908-1973 . . . . DLB-137
Raičković, Stevan 1928- DLB-181

Raimund, Ferdinand Jakob
   1790-1836 . . . . DLB-90
Raine, Craig 1944- DLB-40
Raine, Kathleen 1908- DLB-20
Rainolde, Richard
   circa 1530-1606 . . . . DLB-136
Rakić, Milan 1876-1938 . . . . DLB-147
Rakosi, Carl 1903- DLB-193
Ralegh, Sir Walter 1554?-1618 . . . . . DLB-172
Ralin, Radoy 1923- DLB-181
Ralph, Julian 1853-1903 . . . . DLB-23
Ralph Waldo Emerson in 1982 . . . . . . Y-82
Ramat, Silvio 1939- DLB-128
Rambler, no. 4 (1750), by Samuel Johnson
   [excerpt] DLB-39
Ramée, Marie Louise de la (see Ouida)
Ramírez, Sergío 1942- DLB-145
Ramke, Bin 1947- DLB-120
Ramler, Karl Wilhelm 1725-1798 . . . . DLB-97
Ramon Ribeyro, Julio 1929- DLB-145
Ramous, Mario 1924- DLB-128
Rampersad, Arnold 1941- DLB-111
Ramsay, Allan 1684 or 1685-1758 . . . . DLB-95
Ramsay, David 1749-1815 . . . . DLB-30
Ranck, Katherine Quintana
   1942- DLB-122
Rand, Avery and Company DLB-49
Rand McNally and Company DLB-49
Randall, David Anton
   1905-1975 . . . . DLB-140
Randall, Dudley 1914- DLB-41
Randall, Henry S. 1811-1876 . . . . . . DLB-30
Randall, James G. 1881-1953 . . . . . . DLB-17
The Randall Jarrell Symposium: A Small
   Collection of Randall Jarrells
   Excerpts From Papers Delivered at
   the Randall Jarrel Symposium Y-86
Randolph, A. Philip 1889-1979 . . . . . DLB-91
Randolph, Anson D. F.
   [publishing house] DLB-49
Randolph, Thomas 1605-1635 . . . DLB-58, 126
Random House DLB-46
Ranlet, Henry [publishing house] DLB-49
Ransom, Harry 1908-1976 . . . . DLB-187
Ransom, John Crowe
   1888-1974 . . . . DLB-45, 63
Ransome, Arthur 1884-1967 . . . . . . DLB-160
Raphael, Frederic 1931- DLB-14
Raphaelson, Samson 1896-1983 . . . . . DLB-44
Raskin, Ellen 1928-1984 . . . . DLB-52
Rastell, John 1475?-1536 . . . . . DLB-136, 170
Rattigan, Terence 1911-1977 . . . . . . DLB-13
Rawlings, Marjorie Kinnan
   1896-1953 . . . . . DLB-9, 22, 102; DS-17

Raworth, Tom 1938- DLB-40
Ray, David 1932- DLB-5
Ray, Gordon Norton
   1915-1986 . . . . DLB-103, 140
Ray, Henrietta Cordelia
   1849-1916 . . . . DLB-50
Raymond, Ernest 1888-1974 . . . . . . DLB-191
Raymond, Henry J. 1820-1869 . . . DLB-43, 79
Raymond Chandler Centenary Tributes
   from Michael Avallone, James Elroy, Joe Gores,
   and William F. Nolan Y-88
Reach, Angus 1821-1856 . . . . DLB-70
Read, Herbert 1893-1968 . . . . . DLB-20, 149
Read, Herbert, "The Practice of Biography," in
   The English Sense of Humour and Other Essays DLB-149
Read, Opie 1852-1939 . . . . DLB-23
Read, Piers Paul 1941- DLB-14
Reade, Charles 1814-1884 . . . . DLB-21
Reader's Digest Condensed Books DLB-46
Readers Ulysses Symposium Y-97
Reading, Peter 1946- DLB-40
Reading Series in New York City Y-96
Reaney, James 1926- DLB-68
Rebhun, Paul 1500?-1546 . . . . DLB-179
Rèbora, Clemente 1885-1957 . . . . . . DLB-114
Rechy, John 1934- DLB-122; Y-82
The Recovery of Literature: Criticism in the
   1990s: A Symposium Y-91
Redding, J. Saunders
   1906-1988 . . . . DLB-63, 76
Redfield, J. S. [publishing house] DLB-49
Redgrove, Peter 1932- DLB-40
Redmon, Anne 1943- Y-86
Redmond, Eugene B. 1937- DLB-41
Redpath, James [publishing house] . . . DLB-49
Reed, Henry 1808-1854 . . . . DLB-59
Reed, Henry 1914- DLB-27
Reed, Ishmael
   1938- DLB-2, 5, 33, 169; DS-8
Reed, Rex 1938- DLB-185
Reed, Sampson 1800-1880 . . . . DLB-1
Reed, Talbot Baines 1852-1893 . . . . . DLB-141
Reedy, William Marion 1862-1920 . . . DLB-91
Reese, Lizette Woodworth
   1856-1935 . . . . DLB-54
Reese, Thomas 1742-1796 . . . . DLB-37
Reeve, Clara 1729-1807 . . . . DLB-39
Reeves, James 1909-1978 . . . . DLB-161
Reeves, John 1926- DLB-88
"Reflections: After a Tornado,"
   by Judson Jerome DLB-105

Cumulative Index

Regnery, Henry, Company. DLB-46
Rehberg, Hans 1901-1963. . . . . . . DLB-124
Rehfisch, Hans José 1891-1960 . . . . . DLB-124
Reid, Alastair 1926- DLB-27
Reid, B. L. 1918-1990. . . . . DLB-111
Reid, Christopher 1949- DLB-40
Reid, Forrest 1875-1947. . . . . DLB-153
Reid, Helen Rogers 1882-1970. . . . . DLB-29
Reid, James ?-? DLB-31
Reid, Mayne 1818-1883. . . . . . DLB-21, 163
Reid, Thomas 1710-1796. . . . . DLB-31
Reid, V. S. (Vic) 1913-1987 . . . . . DLB-125
Reid, Whitelaw 1837-1912 . . . . DLB-23
Reilly and Lee Publishing
 Company DLB-46
Reimann, Brigitte 1933-1973 . . . . . . DLB-75
Reinmar der Alte
 circa 1165-circa 1205 . . . . DLB-138
Reinmar von Zweter
 circa 1200-circa 1250 . . . . DLB-138
Reisch, Walter 1903-1983. . . . . DLB-44
Remarque, Erich Maria 1898-1970. . . . DLB-56
"Re-meeting of Old Friends": The Jack
 Kerouac Conference Y-82
Reminiscences, by Charles Scribner Jr. . . DS-17
Remington, Frederic
 1861-1909 . . . . DLB-12, 186, 188
Renaud, Jacques 1943- DLB-60
Renault, Mary 1905-1983 . . . . Y-83
Rendell, Ruth 1930- DLB-87
Representative Men and Women: A Historical
 Perspective on the British Novel,
 1930-1960 . . . . DLB-15
(Re-)Publishing Orwell Y-86
Research in the American Antiquarian Book
 Trade Y-97
Responses to Ken Auletta Y-97
Rettenbacher, Simon 1634-1706 . . . . DLB-168
Reuchlin, Johannes 1455-1522. . . . . DLB-179
Reuter, Christian 1665-after 1712. . . . DLB-168
Reuter, Fritz 1810-1874 . . . . DLB-129
Reuter, Gabriele 1859-1941 . . . . DLB-66
Revell, Fleming H., Company DLB-49
Reventlow, Franziska Gräfin zu
 1871-1918 . . . . DLB-66
Review of Reviews Office. DLB-112
Review of [Samuel Richardson's] Clarissa (1748),
 by Henry Fielding DLB-39
The Revolt (1937), by Mary Colum
 [excerpts] DLB-36
Rexroth, Kenneth
 1905-1982 . . . . . DLB-16, 48, 165; Y-82
Rey, H. A. 1898-1977 . . . . DLB-22
Reynal and Hitchcock DLB-46

Reynolds, G. W. M. 1814-1879 . . . . . DLB-21
Reynolds, John Hamilton
 1794-1852 . . . . DLB-96
Reynolds, Mack 1917- DLB-8
Reynolds, Sir Joshua 1723-1792 . . . . DLB-104
Reznikoff, Charles 1894-1976 . . . . DLB-28, 45
"Rhetoric" (1828; revised, 1859), by
 Thomas de Quincey [excerpt] DLB-57
Rhett, Robert Barnwell 1800-1876. . . . DLB-43
Rhode, John 1884-1964 . . . . DLB-77
Rhodes, James Ford 1848-1927 . . . . . DLB-47
Rhodes, Richard 1937- DLB-185
Rhys, Jean 1890-1979 . . . . . DLB-36, 117, 162
Ricardo, David 1772-1823 . . . . . DLB-107, 158
Ricardou, Jean 1932- DLB-83
Rice, Elmer 1892-1967 . . . . DLB-4, 7
Rice, Grantland 1880-1954 . . . . . DLB-29, 171
Rich, Adrienne 1929- DLB-5, 67
Richards, David Adams 1950- DLB-53
Richards, George circa 1760-1814 . . . . DLB-37
Richards, I. A. 1893-1979 . . . . DLB-27
Richards, Laura E. 1850-1943 . . . . . DLB-42
Richards, William Carey
 1818-1892 . . . . DLB-73
Richards, Grant
 [publishing house] DLB-112
Richardson, Charles F. 1851-1913 . . . . DLB-71
Richardson, Dorothy M.
 1873-1957 . . . . DLB-36
Richardson, Henry Handel (Ethel Florence
 Lindesay) 1870-1946 . . . . DLB-197
Richardson, Jack 1935- DLB-7
Richardson, John 1796-1852 . . . . . . DLB-99
Richardson, Samuel
 1689-1761 . . . . DLB-39, 154
Richardson, Willis 1889-1977 . . . . . . DLB-51
Riche, Barnabe 1542-1617 . . . . . . DLB-136
Richepin, Jean 1849-1926 . . . . DLB-192
Richler, Mordecai 1931- DLB-53
Richter, Conrad 1890-1968 . . . . DLB-9
Richter, Hans Werner 1908- DLB-69
Richter, Johann Paul Friedrich
 1763-1825 . . . . DLB-94
Rickerby, Joseph
 [publishing house] DLB-106
Rickword, Edgell 1898-1982 . . . . . . DLB-20
Riddell, Charlotte 1832-1906 . . . . . DLB-156
Riddell, John (see Ford, Corey)
Ridge, John Rollin 1827-1867 . . . . . DLB-175
Ridge, Lola 1873-1941 . . . . DLB-54
Ridge, William Pett 1859-1930 . . . . DLB-135
Riding, Laura (see Jackson, Laura Riding)
Ridler, Anne 1912- DLB-27

Ridruego, Dionisio 1912-1975 . . . . . DLB-108
Riel, Louis 1844-1885 . . . . DLB-99
Riemer, Johannes 1648-1714 . . . . . DLB-168
Riffaterre, Michael 1924- DLB-67
Riggs, Lynn 1899-1954 . . . . DLB-175
Riis, Jacob 1849-1914 . . . . DLB-23
Riker, John C. [publishing house] DLB-49
Riley, James 1777-1840 . . . . DLB-183
Riley, John 1938-1978. . . . . DLB-40
Rilke, Rainer Maria 1875-1926 . . . . . DLB-81
Rimanelli, Giose 1926- DLB-177
Rinehart and Company DLB-46
Ringuet 1895-1960 . . . . DLB-68
Ringwood, Gwen Pharis
 1910-1984 . . . . DLB-88
Rinser, Luise 1911- DLB-69
Ríos, Alberto 1952- DLB-122
Ríos, Isabella 1948- DLB-82
Ripley, Arthur 1895-1961 . . . . DLB-44
Ripley, George 1802-1880 . . . . DLB-1, 64, 73
The Rising Glory of America:
 Three Poems DLB-37
The Rising Glory of America: Written in 1771
 (1786), by Hugh Henry Brackenridge and
 Philip Freneau. DLB-37
Riskin, Robert 1897-1955 . . . . DLB-26
Risse, Heinz 1898- DLB-69
Rist, Johann 1607-1667 . . . . DLB-164
Ritchie, Anna Mowatt 1819-1870 . . . . DLB-3
Ritchie, Anne Thackeray
 1837-1919 . . . . DLB-18
Ritchie, Thomas 1778-1854 . . . . . . DLB-43
Rites of Passage
 [on William Saroyan] Y-83
The Ritz Paris Hemingway Award Y-85
Rivard, Adjutor 1868-1945 . . . . DLB-92
Rive, Richard 1931-1989 . . . . DLB-125
Rivera, Marina 1942- DLB-122
Rivera, Tomás 1935-1984 . . . . DLB-82
Rivers, Conrad Kent 1933-1968 . . . . . DLB-41
Riverside Press DLB-49
Rivington, James circa 1724-1802 . . . . DLB-43
Rivington, Charles
 [publishing house] DLB-154
Rivkin, Allen 1903-1990 . . . . DLB-26
Roa Bastos, Augusto 1917- DLB-113
Robbe-Grillet, Alain 1922- DLB-83
Robbins, Tom 1936- Y-80
Roberts, Charles G. D. 1860-1943 . . . . DLB-92
Roberts, Dorothy 1906-1993 . . . . . . DLB-88
Roberts, Elizabeth Madox
 1881-1941 . . . . DLB-9, 54, 102
Roberts, Kenneth 1885-1957 . . . . . . DLB-9

Roberts, William 1767-1849 . . . . DLB-142	Romero, Leo 1950- DLB-122	Routledge, George, and Sons DLB-106
Roberts Brothers DLB-49	Romero, Lin 1947- DLB-122	Roversi, Roberto 1923- DLB-128
Roberts, James [publishing house] . . . DLB-154	Romero, Orlando 1945- DLB-82	Rowe, Elizabeth Singer
Robertson, A. M., and Company DLB-49	Rook, Clarence 1863-1915 . . . . DLB-135	1674-1737 . . . . DLB-39, 95
Robertson, William 1721-1793 . . . . . DLB-104	Roosevelt, Theodore 1858-1919 . . DLB-47, 186	Rowe, Nicholas 1674-1718 . . . . DLB-84
Robins, Elizabeth 1862-1952 . . . . DLB-197	Root, Waverley 1903-1982 . . . . DLB-4	Rowlands, Samuel
Robinson, Casey 1903-1979 . . . . DLB-44	Root, William Pitt 1941- DLB-120	circa 1570-1630 . . . . DLB-121
Robinson, Edwin Arlington	Roquebrune, Robert de 1889-1978 . . . . DLB-68	Rowlandson, Mary
1869-1935 . . . . DLB-54	Rosa, João Guimarães	circa 1635-circa 1678 . . . . DLB-24
Robinson, Henry Crabb	1908-1967 . . . . DLB-113	Rowley, William circa 1585-1626 . . . . DLB-58
1775-1867 . . . . DLB-107	Rosales, Luis 1910-1992 . . . . DLB-134	Rowse, A. L. 1903- DLB-155
Robinson, James Harvey	Roscoe, William 1753-1831 . . . . DLB-163	Rowson, Susanna Haswell
1863-1936 . . . . DLB-47	Rose, Reginald 1920- DLB-26	circa 1762-1824 . . . . DLB-37
Robinson, Lennox 1886-1958 . . . . DLB-10	Rose, Wendy 1948- DLB-175	Roy, Camille 1870-1943 . . . . DLB-92
Robinson, Mabel Louise	Rosegger, Peter 1843-1918 . . . . DLB-129	Roy, Gabrielle 1909-1983 . . . . DLB-68
1874-1962 . . . . DLB-22	Rosei, Peter 1946- DLB-85	Roy, Jules 1907- DLB-83
Robinson, Mary 1758-1800 . . . . DLB-158	Rosen, Norma 1925- DLB-28	The Royal Court Theatre and the English
Robinson, Richard	Rosenbach, A. S. W. 1876-1952 . . . . DLB-140	Stage Company DLB-13
circa 1545-1607 . . . . DLB-167	Rosenbaum, Ron 1946- DLB-185	The Royal Court Theatre and the New Drama
Robinson, Therese	Rosenberg, Isaac 1890-1918 . . . . DLB-20	. . . . DLB-10
1797-1870 . . . . DLB-59, 133	Rosenfeld, Isaac 1918-1956 . . . . DLB-28	The Royal Shakespeare Company
Robison, Mary 1949- DLB-130	Rosenthal, M. L. 1917- DLB-5	at the Swan Y-88
Roblès, Emmanuel 1914- DLB-83	Rosenwald, Lessing J. 1891-1979 . . . . DLB-187	Royall, Anne 1769-1854 . . . . DLB-43
Roccatagliata Ceccardi, Ceccardo	Ross, Alexander 1591-1654 . . . . DLB-151	The Roycroft Printing Shop DLB-49
1871-1919 . . . . DLB-114	Ross, Harold 1892-1951 . . . . DLB-137	Royde-Smith, Naomi 1875-1964 . . . . . DLB-191
Rochester, John Wilmot, Earl of	Ross, Leonard Q. (see Rosten, Leo)	Royster, Vermont 1914- DLB-127
1647-1680 . . . . DLB-131	Ross, Lillian 1927- DLB-185	Royston, Richard
Rock, Howard 1911-1976 . . . . DLB-127	Ross, Martin 1862-1915 . . . . DLB-135	[publishing house] DLB-170
Rockwell, Norman Perceval	Ross, Sinclair 1908- DLB-88	Ruark, Gibbons 1941- DLB-120
1894-1978 . . . . DLB-188	Ross, W. W. E. 1894-1966 . . . . DLB-88	Ruban, Vasilii Grigorevich
Rodgers, Carolyn M. 1945- DLB-41	Rosselli, Amelia 1930- DLB-128	1742-1795 . . . . DLB-150
Rodgers, W. R. 1909-1969 . . . . DLB-20	Rossen, Robert 1908-1966 . . . . DLB-26	Rubens, Bernice 1928- DLB-14
Rodríguez, Claudio 1934- DLB-134	Rossetti, Christina Georgina	Rudd and Carleton DLB-49
Rodriguez, Richard 1944- DLB-82	1830-1894 . . . . DLB-35, 163	Rudkin, David 1936- DLB-13
Rodríguez Julia, Edgardo	Rossetti, Dante Gabriel 1828-1882 . . . . DLB-35	Rudolf von Ems
1946- DLB-145	Rossner, Judith 1935- DLB-6	circa 1200-circa 1254 . . . . DLB-138
Roethke, Theodore 1908-1963 . . . . DLB-5	Rostand, Edmond 1868-1918 . . . . . . DLB-192	Ruffin, Josephine St. Pierre
Rogers, Jane 1952- DLB-194	Rosten, Leo 1908- DLB-11	1842-1924 . . . . DLB-79
Rogers, Pattiann 1940- DLB-105	Rostenberg, Leona 1908- DLB-140	Ruganda, John 1941- DLB-157
Rogers, Samuel 1763-1855 . . . . DLB-93	Rostovsky, Dimitrii 1651-1709 . . . . . . DLB-150	Ruggles, Henry Joseph 1813-1906 . . . . DLB-64
Rogers, Will 1879-1935 . . . . DLB-11	Bertram Rota and His Bookshop Y-91	Rukeyser, Muriel 1913-1980 . . . . DLB-48
Rohmer, Sax 1883-1959 . . . . DLB-70	Roth, Gerhard 1942- DLB-85, 124	Rule, Jane 1931- DLB-60
Roiphe, Anne 1935- Y-80	Roth, Henry 1906?- DLB-28	Rulfo, Juan 1918-1986 . . . . DLB-113
Rojas, Arnold R. 1896-1988 . . . . DLB-82	Roth, Joseph 1894-1939 . . . . DLB-85	Rumaker, Michael 1932- DLB-16
Rolfe, Frederick William	Roth, Philip 1933- DLB-2, 28, 173; Y-82	Rumens, Carol 1944- DLB-40
1860-1913 . . . . DLB-34, 156	Rothenberg, Jerome 1931- DLB-5, 193	Runyon, Damon 1880-1946 . . DLB-11, 86, 171
Rolland, Romain 1866-1944 . . . . DLB-65	Rothschild Family DLB-184	*Ruodlieb* circa 1050-1075 . . . . DLB-148
Rolle, Richard	Rotimi, Ola 1938- DLB-125	Rush, Benjamin 1746-1813 . . . . DLB-37
circa 1290-1300 - 1340 . . . . DLB-146	Routhier, Adolphe-Basile	Rushdie, Salman 1947- DLB-194
Rölvaag, O. E. 1876-1931 . . . . DLB-9	1839-1920 . . . . DLB-99	Rusk, Ralph L. 1888-1962 . . . . DLB-103
Romains, Jules 1885-1972 . . . . DLB-65	Routier, Simone 1901-1987 . . . . DLB-88	Ruskin, John 1819-1900 . . . . DLB-55, 163, 190
Roman, A., and Company DLB-49		Russ, Joanna 1937- DLB-8
Romano, Lalla 1906- DLB-177		Russell, B. B., and Company DLB-49
Romano, Octavio 1923- DLB-122		Russell, Benjamin 1761-1845 . . . . DLB-43

Russell, Bertrand 1872-1970 . . . . . . DLB-100
Russell, Charles Edward 1860-1941 . . . . DLB-25
Russell, Charles M. 1864-1926 . . . . . DLB-188
Russell, Countess Mary Annette Beauchamp (see Arnim, Elizabeth von)
Russell, George William (see AE)
Russell, R. H., and Son DLB-49
Rutherford, Mark 1831-1913 . . . . . . DLB-18
Ruxton, George Frederick 1821-1848 . . . . DLB-186
Ryan, Michael 1946- Y-82
Ryan, Oscar 1904- DLB-68
Ryga, George 1932- DLB-60
Rylands, Enriqueta Augustina Tennant 1843-1908 . . . . DLB-184
Rylands, John 1801-1888 . . . . DLB-184
Rymer, Thomas 1643?-1713 . . . . . . DLB-101
Ryskind, Morrie 1895-1985 . . . . DLB-26
Rzhevsky, Aleksei Andreevich 1737-1804 . . . . DLB-150

S

The Saalfield Publishing Company DLB-46
Saba, Umberto 1883-1957 . . . . DLB-114
Sábato, Ernesto 1911- DLB-145
Saberhagen, Fred 1930- DLB-8
Sabin, Joseph 1821-1881 . . . . DLB-187
Sacer, Gottfried Wilhelm 1635-1699 . . . . DLB-168
Sachs, Hans 1494-1576 . . . . DLB-179
Sack, John 1930- DLB-185
Sackler, Howard 1929-1982 . . . . DLB-7
Sackville, Thomas 1536-1608 . . . . . . DLB-132
Sackville, Thomas 1536-1608 and Norton, Thomas 1532-1584 . . . . DLB-62
Sackville-West, Edward 1901-1965 . . . DLB-191
Sackville-West, V. 1892-1962 . . . . DLB-34, 195
Sadlier, D. and J., and Company DLB-49
Sadlier, Mary Anne 1820-1903 . . . . . DLB-99
Sadoff, Ira 1945- DLB-120
Saenz, Jaime 1921-1986 . . . . DLB-145
Saffin, John circa 1626-1710 . . . . . . DLB-24
Sagan, Françoise 1935- DLB-83
Sage, Robert 1899-1962 . . . . DLB-4
Sagel, Jim 1947- DLB-82
Sagendorph, Robb Hansell 1900-1970 . . . . DLB-137
Sahagún, Carlos 1938- DLB-108
Sahkomaapii, Piitai (see Highwater, Jamake)

Sahl, Hans 1902- DLB-69
Said, Edward W. 1935- DLB-67
Saiko, George 1892-1962 . . . . DLB-85
St. Dominic's Press DLB-112
Saint-Exupéry, Antoine de 1900-1944 . . . . DLB-72
St. John, J. Allen 1872-1957 . . . . . . DLB-188
St. Johns, Adela Rogers 1894-1988 . . . DLB-29
The St. John's College Robert Graves Trust Y-96
St. Martin's Press DLB-46
St. Omer, Garth 1931- DLB-117
Saint Pierre, Michel de 1916-1987 . . . DLB-83
Saintsbury, George 1845-1933 . . . . DLB-57, 149
Saki (see Munro, H. H.)
Salaam, Kalamu ya 1947- DLB-38
Šalamun, Tomaž 1941- DLB-181
Salas, Floyd 1931- DLB-82
Sálaz-Marquez, Rubén 1935- DLB-122
Salemson, Harold J. 1910-1988 . . . . . DLB-4
Salinas, Luis Omar 1937- DLB-82
Salinas, Pedro 1891-1951 . . . . DLB-134
Salinger, J. D. 1919- DLB-2, 102, 173
Salkey, Andrew 1928- DLB-125
Salt, Waldo 1914- DLB-44
Salter, James 1925- DLB-130
Salter, Mary Jo 1954- DLB-120
Salustri, Carlo Alberto (see Trilussa)
Salverson, Laura Goodman 1890-1970 . . . . DLB-92
Sampson, Richard Henry (see Hull, Richard)
Samuels, Ernest 1903- DLB-111
Sanborn, Franklin Benjamin 1831-1917 . . . . DLB-1
Sánchez, Luis Rafael 1936- DLB-145
Sánchez, Philomeno "Phil" 1917- DLB-122
Sánchez, Ricardo 1941- DLB-82
Sanchez, Sonia 1934- DLB-41; DS-8
Sand, George 1804-1876 . . . . . . DLB-119, 192
Sandburg, Carl 1878-1967 . . . . . DLB-17, 54
Sanders, Ed 1939- DLB-16
Sandoz, Mari 1896-1966 . . . . DLB-9
Sandwell, B. K. 1876-1954 . . . . DLB-92
Sandy, Stephen 1934- DLB-165
Sandys, George 1578-1644 . . . . . DLB-24, 121
Sangster, Charles 1822-1893 . . . . . . DLB-99
Sanguineti, Edoardo 1930- DLB-128
Sansom, William 1912-1976 . . . . . . DLB-139
Santayana, George 1863-1952 . . . . DLB-54, 71; DS-13
Santiago, Danny 1911-1988 . . . . . . DLB-122

Santmyer, Helen Hooven 1895-1986 . . . . Y-84
Sanvitale, Francesca 1928- DLB-196
Sapidus, Joannes 1490-1561 . . . . . . DLB-179
Sapir, Edward 1884-1939 . . . . DLB-92
Sapper (see McNeile, Herman Cyril)
Sappho circa 620 B.C.-circa 550 B.C. DLB-176
Sardou, Victorien 1831-1908 . . . . . . DLB-192
Sarduy, Severo 1937- DLB-113
Sargent, Pamela 1948- DLB-8
Saro-Wiwa, Ken 1941- DLB-157
Saroyan, William 1908-1981 . . . . DLB-7, 9, 86; Y-81
Sarraute, Nathalie 1900- DLB-83
Sarrazin, Albertine 1937-1967 . . . . . . DLB-83
Sarris, Greg 1952- DLB-175
Sarton, May 1912- DLB-48; Y-81
Sartre, Jean-Paul 1905-1980 . . . . DLB-72
Sassoon, Siegfried 1886-1967 . . . . DLB-20, 191
Sata, Ineko 1904- DLB-180
Saturday Review Press DLB-46
Saunders, James 1925- DLB-13
Saunders, John Monk 1897-1940 . . . . DLB-26
Saunders, Margaret Marshall 1861-1947 . . . . DLB-92
Saunders and Otley DLB-106
Savage, James 1784-1873 . . . . DLB-30
Savage, Marmion W. 1803?-1872 . . . . DLB-21
Savage, Richard 1697?-1743 . . . . . . DLB-95
Savard, Félix-Antoine 1896-1982 . . . . DLB-68
Saville, (Leonard) Malcolm 1901-1982 . . . . DLB-160
Sawyer, Ruth 1880-1970 . . . . DLB-22
Sayers, Dorothy L. 1893-1957 . . . . DLB-10, 36, 77, 100
Sayle, Charles Edward 1864-1924 . . . DLB-184
Sayles, John Thomas 1950- DLB-44
Sbarbaro, Camillo 1888-1967 . . . . . . DLB-114
Scalapino, Leslie 1947- DLB-193
Scannell, Vernon 1922- DLB-27
Scarry, Richard 1919-1994 . . . . DLB-61
Schaeffer, Albrecht 1885-1950 . . . . . DLB-66
Schaeffer, Susan Fromberg 1941- DLB-28
Schaff, Philip 1819-1893 . . . . DS-13
Schaper, Edzard 1908-1984 . . . . . . DLB-69
Scharf, J. Thomas 1843-1898 . . . . . . DLB-47
Schede, Paul Melissus 1539-1602 . . . . DLB-179
Scheffel, Joseph Viktor von 1826-1886 . . . . DLB-129
Scheffler, Johann 1624-1677 . . . . . . DLB-164
Schelling, Friedrich Wilhelm Joseph von 1775-1854 . . . . DLB-90
Scherer, Wilhelm 1841-1886 . . . . . . DLB-129

Schickele, René 1883-1940 . . . . DLB-66
Schiff, Dorothy 1903-1989 . . . . DLB-127
Schiller, Friedrich 1759-1805 . . . . . DLB-94
Schirmer, David 1623-1687 . . . . . . DLB-164
Schlaf, Johannes 1862-1941 . . . . . . DLB-118
Schlegel, August Wilhelm
　1767-1845 . . . . DLB-94
Schlegel, Dorothea 1763-1839 . . . . . DLB-90
Schlegel, Friedrich 1772-1829 . . . . . DLB-90
Schleiermacher, Friedrich
　1768-1834 . . . . DLB-90
Schlesinger, Arthur M., Jr. 1917- DLB-17
Schlumberger, Jean 1877-1968 . . . . . DLB-65
Schmid, Eduard Hermann Wilhelm (see Edschmid, Kasimir)
Schmidt, Arno 1914-1979 . . . . DLB-69
Schmidt, Johann Kaspar (see Stirner, Max)
Schmidt, Michael 1947- DLB-40
Schmidtbonn, Wilhelm August
　1876-1952 . . . . DLB-118
Schmitz, James H. 1911- DLB-8
Schnabel, Johann Gottfried
　1692-1760 . . . . DLB-168
Schnackenberg, Gjertrud 1953- DLB-120
Schnitzler, Arthur 1862-1931 . . . . DLB-81, 118
Schnurre, Wolfdietrich 1920- DLB-69
Schocken Books DLB-46
Scholartis Press DLB-112
The Schomburg Center for Research
　in Black Culture DLB-76
Schönbeck, Virgilio (see Giotti, Virgilio)
Schönherr, Karl 1867-1943 . . . . . . DLB-118
Schoolcraft, Jane Johnston
　1800-1841 . . . . DLB-175
School Stories, 1914-1960 . . . . DLB-160
Schopenhauer, Arthur 1788-1860 . . . . DLB-90
Schopenhauer, Johanna 1766-1838 . . . DLB-90
Schorer, Mark 1908-1977 . . . . DLB-103
Schottelius, Justus Georg
　1612-1676 . . . . DLB-164
Schouler, James 1839-1920 . . . . . . DLB-47
Schrader, Paul 1946- DLB-44
Schreiner, Olive 1855-1920 . . DLB-18, 156, 190
Schroeder, Andreas 1946- DLB-53
Schubart, Christian Friedrich Daniel
　1739-1791 . . . . DLB-97
Schubert, Gotthilf Heinrich
　1780-1860 . . . . DLB-90
Schücking, Levin 1814-1883 . . . . . . DLB-133
Schulberg, Budd 1914- . . DLB-6, 26, 28; Y-81
Schulte, F. J., and Company DLB-49
Schulze, Hans (see Praetorius, Johannes)
Schupp, Johann Balthasar
　1610-1661 . . . . DLB-164

Schurz, Carl 1829-1906 . . . . DLB-23
Schuyler, George S. 1895-1977 . . . DLB-29, 51
Schuyler, James 1923-1991 . . . . . . DLB-5, 169
Schwartz, Delmore 1913-1966 . . . . DLB-28, 48
Schwartz, Jonathan 1938- Y-82
Schwarz, Sibylle 1621-1638 . . . . . . DLB-164
Schwerner, Armand 1927- DLB-165
Schwob, Marcel 1867-1905 . . . . . . DLB-123
Sciascia, Leonardo 1921-1989 . . . . . DLB-177
Science Fantasy DLB-8
Science-Fiction Fandom and
　Conventions DLB-8
Science-Fiction Fanzines: The Time
　Binders DLB-8
Science-Fiction Films DLB-8
Science Fiction Writers of America and the
　Nebula Awards DLB-8
Scot, Reginald circa 1538-1599 . . . . DLB-136
Scotellaro, Rocco 1923-1953 . . . . . . DLB-128
Scott, Dennis 1939-1991 . . . . DLB-125
Scott, Dixon 1881-1915 . . . . DLB-98
Scott, Duncan Campbell 1862-1947 . . . DLB-92
Scott, Evelyn 1893-1963 . . . . DLB-9, 48
Scott, F. R. 1899-1985 . . . . DLB-88
Scott, Frederick George 1861-1944 . . . DLB-92
Scott, Geoffrey 1884-1929 . . . . DLB-149
Scott, Harvey W. 1838-1910 . . . . . . DLB-23
Scott, Paul 1920-1978 . . . . DLB-14
Scott, Sarah 1723-1795 . . . . DLB-39
Scott, Tom 1918- DLB-27
Scott, Sir Walter
　1771-1832 . . . . DLB-93, 107, 116, 144, 159
Scott, William Bell 1811-1890 . . . . . DLB-32
Scott, Walter, Publishing
　Company Limited DLB-112
Scott, William R.
　[publishing house] DLB-46
Scott-Heron, Gil 1949- DLB-41
Scribe, Eugene 1791-1861 . . . . DLB-192
Scribner, Arthur Hawley
　1859-1932 . . . . DS-13, 16
Scribner, Charles 1854-1930 . . . . . DS-13, 16
Scribner, Charles, Jr. 1921-1995 . . . . . Y-95
Charles Scribner's
　Sons DLB-49; DS-13, 16, 17
Scripps, E. W. 1854-1926 . . . . DLB-25
Scudder, Horace Elisha
　1838-1902 . . . . DLB-42, 71
Scudder, Vida Dutton 1861-1954 . . . DLB-71
Scupham, Peter 1933- DLB-40
Seabrook, William 1886-1945 . . . . . . DLB-4
Seabury, Samuel 1729-1796 . . . . . . DLB-31

Seacole, Mary Jane Grant
　1805-1881 . . . . DLB-166
The Seafarer circa 970 . . . . DLB-146
Sealsfield, Charles (Carl Postl)
　1793-1864 . . . . DLB-133, 186
Sears, Edward I. 1819?-1876 . . . . . . DLB-79
Sears Publishing Company DLB-46
Seaton, George 1911-1979 . . . . DLB-44
Seaton, William Winston
　1785-1866 . . . . DLB-43
Secker, Martin, and Warburg
　Limited DLB-112
Secker, Martin [publishing house] DLB-112
Second-Generation Minor Poets of the
　Seventeenth Century DLB-126
Sedgwick, Arthur George
　1844-1915 . . . . DLB-64
Sedgwick, Catharine Maria
　1789-1867 . . . . DLB-1, 74, 183
Sedgwick, Ellery 1872-1930 . . . . . . DLB-91
Sedley, Sir Charles 1639-1701 . . . . . DLB-131
Seeger, Alan 1888-1916 . . . . DLB-45
Seers, Eugene (see Dantin, Louis)
Segal, Erich 1937- Y-86
Šegedin, Petar 1909- DLB-181
Seghers, Anna 1900-1983 . . . . DLB-69
Seid, Ruth (see Sinclair, Jo)
Seidel, Frederick Lewis 1936- Y-84
Seidel, Ina 1885-1974 . . . . DLB-56
Seifert, Jaroslav 1901- Y-84
Seigenthaler, John 1927- DLB-127
Seizin Press DLB-112
Séjour, Victor 1817-1874 . . . . DLB-50
Séjour Marcou et Ferrand, Juan Victor (see Séjour, Victor)
Selby, Hubert, Jr. 1928- DLB-2
Selden, George 1929-1989 . . . . DLB-52
Selected English-Language Little Magazines
　and Newspapers [France,
　1920-1939] DLB-4
Selected Humorous Magazines
　(1820-1950) DLB-11
Selected Science-Fiction Magazines and
　Anthologies DLB-8
Selenić, Slobodan 1933-1995 . . . . . . DLB-181
Self, Edwin F. 1920- DLB-137
Seligman, Edwin R. A. 1861-1939 . . . DLB-47
Selimović, Meša 1910-1982 . . . . . . DLB-181
Selous, Frederick Courteney
　1851-1917 . . . . DLB-174
Seltzer, Chester E. (see Muro, Amado)
Seltzer, Thomas
　[publishing house] DLB-46
Selvon, Sam 1923-1994 . . . . DLB-125
Semmes, Raphael 1809-1877 . . . . . DLB-189

Senancour, Etienne de 1770-1846 . . . . DLB-119
Sendak, Maurice 1928- DLB-61
Senécal, Eva 1905- DLB-92
Sengstacke, John 1912- DLB-127
Senior, Olive 1941- DLB-157
Šenoa, August 1838-1881 . . . . DLB-147
"Sensation Novels" (1863), by
   H. L. Manse DLB-21
Sepamla, Sipho 1932- DLB-157
Seredy, Kate 1899-1975 . . . . DLB-22
Sereni, Vittorio 1913-1983 . . . . DLB-128
Seres, William
   [publishing house] DLB-170
Serling, Rod 1924-1975 . . . . DLB-26
Serote, Mongane Wally 1944- DLB-125
Serraillier, Ian 1912-1994 . . . . DLB-161
Serrano, Nina 1934- DLB-122
Service, Robert 1874-1958 . . . . DLB-92
Sessler, Charles 1854-1935 . . . . DLB-187
Seth, Vikram 1952- DLB-120
Seton, Ernest Thompson
   1860-1942 . . . . DLB-92; DS-13
Setouchi, Harumi 1922- DLB-182
Settle, Mary Lee 1918- DLB-6
Seume, Johann Gottfried
   1763-1810 . . . . DLB-94
Seuse, Heinrich 1295?-1366 . . . . DLB-179
Seuss, Dr. (see Geisel, Theodor Seuss)
The Seventy-fifth Anniversary of the Armistice:
   The Wilfred Owen Centenary and the Great
   War Exhibit at the University of
   Virginia Y-93
Sewall, Joseph 1688-1769 . . . . DLB-24
Sewall, Richard B. 1908- DLB-111
Sewell, Anna 1820-1878 . . . . DLB-163
Sewell, Samuel 1652-1730 . . . . DLB-24
Sex, Class, Politics, and Religion [in the
   British Novel, 1930-1959] DLB-15
Sexton, Anne 1928-1974 . . . . DLB-5, 169
Seymour-Smith, Martin 1928- DLB-155
Sgorlon, Carlo 1930- DLB-196
Shaara, Michael 1929-1988 . . . . Y-83
Shadwell, Thomas 1641?-1692 . . . . . DLB-80
Shaffer, Anthony 1926- DLB-13
Shaffer, Peter 1926- DLB-13
Shaftesbury, Anthony Ashley Cooper,
   Third Earl of 1671-1713 . . . . . . DLB-101
Shairp, Mordaunt 1887-1939 . . . . . . DLB-10
Shakespeare, William
   1564-1616 . . . . DLB-62, 172
The Shakespeare Globe Trust Y-93
Shakespeare Head Press DLB-112
Shakhovskoi, Aleksandr Aleksandrovich
   1777-1846 . . . . DLB-150

Shange, Ntozake 1948- DLB-38
Shapiro, Karl 1913- DLB-48
Sharon Publications DLB-46
Sharp, Margery 1905-1991 . . . . DLB-161
Sharp, William 1855-1905 . . . . DLB-156
Sharpe, Tom 1928- DLB-14
Shaw, Albert 1857-1947 . . . . DLB-91
Shaw, George Bernard
   1856-1950 . . . . DLB-10, 57, 190
Shaw, Henry Wheeler 1818-1885 . . . . DLB-11
Shaw, Joseph T. 1874-1952 . . . . DLB-137
Shaw, Irwin 1913-1984 . . . . DLB-6, 102; Y-84
Shaw, Robert 1927-1978 . . . . DLB-13, 14
Shaw, Robert B. 1947- DLB-120
Shawn, William 1907-1992 . . . . DLB-137
Shay, Frank [publishing house] DLB-46
Shea, John Gilmary 1824-1892 . . . . . DLB-30
Sheaffer, Louis 1912-1993 . . . . DLB-103
Shearing, Joseph 1886-1952 . . . . DLB-70
Shebbeare, John 1709-1788 . . . . DLB-39
Sheckley, Robert 1928- DLB-8
Shedd, William G. T. 1820-1894 . . . . DLB-64
Sheed, Wilfred 1930- DLB-6
Sheed and Ward [U.S.] DLB-46
Sheed and Ward Limited [U.K.] DLB-112
Sheldon, Alice B. (see Tiptree, James, Jr.)
Sheldon, Edward 1886-1946 . . . . DLB-7
Sheldon and Company DLB-49
Shelley, Mary Wollstonecraft
   1797-1851 . . . . . DLB-110, 116, 159, 178
Shelley, Percy Bysshe
   1792-1822 . . . . DLB-96, 110, 158
Shelnutt, Eve 1941- DLB-130
Shenstone, William 1714-1763 . . . . . DLB-95
Shepard, Ernest Howard
   1879-1976 . . . . DLB-160
Shepard, Sam 1943- DLB-7
Shepard, Thomas I,
   1604 or 1605-1649 . . . . DLB-24
Shepard, Thomas II, 1635-1677 . . . . . DLB-24
Shepard, Clark and Brown DLB-49
Shepherd, Luke
   flourished 1547-1554 . . . . DLB-136
Sherburne, Edward 1616-1702 . . . . . DLB-131
Sheridan, Frances 1724-1766 . . . . . DLB-39, 84
Sheridan, Richard Brinsley
   1751-1816 . . . . DLB-89
Sherman, Francis 1871-1926 . . . . DLB-92
Sherriff, R. C. 1896-1975 . . . . DLB-10, 191
Sherry, Norman 1935- DLB-155
Sherwood, Mary Martha
   1775-1851 . . . . DLB-163
Sherwood, Robert 1896-1955 . . . . . DLB-7, 26

Shiel, M. P. 1865-1947 . . . . DLB-153
Shiels, George 1886-1949 . . . . DLB-10
Shiga, Naoya 1883-1971 . . . . DLB-180
Shiina, Rinzō 1911-1973 . . . . DLB-182
Shillaber, B.[enjamin] P.[enhallow]
   1814-1890 . . . . DLB-1, 11
Shimao, Toshio 1917-1986 . . . . DLB-182
Shimazaki, Tōson 1872-1943 . . . . . . DLB-180
Shine, Ted 1931- DLB-38
Ship, Reuben 1915-1975 . . . . DLB-88
Shirer, William L. 1904-1993 . . . . DLB-4
Shirinsky-Shikhmatov, Sergii Aleksandrovich
   1783-1837 . . . . DLB-150
Shirley, James 1596-1666 . . . . DLB-58
Shishkov, Aleksandr Semenovich
   1753-1841 . . . . DLB-150
Shockley, Ann Allen 1927- DLB-33
Shōno, Junzō 1921- DLB-182
Short, Peter
   [publishing house] DLB-170
Shorthouse, Joseph Henry
   1834-1903 . . . . DLB-18
Showalter, Elaine 1941- DLB-67
Shulevitz, Uri 1935- DLB-61
Shulman, Max 1919-1988 . . . . DLB-11
Shute, Henry A. 1856-1943 . . . . DLB-9
Shuttle, Penelope 1947- DLB-14, 40
Sibbes, Richard 1577-1635 . . . . DLB-151
Sidgwick, Ethel 1877-1970 . . . . DLB-197
Sidgwick and Jackson Limited DLB-112
Sidney, Margaret (see Lothrop, Harriet M.)
Sidney, Mary 1561-1621 . . . . DLB-167
Sidney, Sir Philip 1554-1586 . . . . . . DLB-167
Sidney's Press DLB-49
Siegfried Loraine Sassoon: A Centenary Essay
   Tributes from Vivien F. Clarke and
   Michael Thorpe Y-86
Sierra, Rubén 1946- DLB-122
Sierra Club Books DLB-49
Siger of Brabant
   circa 1240-circa 1284 . . . . DLB-115
Sigourney, Lydia Howard (Huntley)
   1791-1865 . . . . DLB-1, 42, 73, 183
Silkin, Jon 1930- DLB-27
Silko, Leslie Marmon
   1948- DLB-143, 175
Silliman, Benjamin 1779-1864 . . . . . . DLB-183
Silliman, Ron 1946- DLB-169
Silliphant, Stirling 1918- DLB-26
Sillitoe, Alan 1928- DLB-14, 139
Silman, Roberta 1934- DLB-28
Silva, Beverly 1930- DLB-122
Silverberg, Robert 1935- DLB-8

Silverman, Kenneth 1936- DLB-111
Simak, Clifford D. 1904-1988 .... DLB-8
Simcoe, Elizabeth 1762-1850 .... DLB-99
Simcox, Edith Jemima 1844-1901.... DLB-190
Simcox, George Augustus
   1841-1905 .... DLB-35
Sime, Jessie Georgina 1868-1958 ..... DLB-92
Simenon, Georges
   1903-1989 .... DLB-72; Y-89
Simic, Charles 1938- DLB-105
Simmel, Johannes Mario 1924- DLB-69
Simmes, Valentine
   [publishing house] DLB-170
Simmons, Ernest J. 1903-1972 ..... DLB-103
Simmons, Herbert Alfred 1930- DLB-33
Simmons, James 1933- DLB-40
Simms, William Gilmore
   1806-1870 .... DLB-3, 30, 59, 73
Simms and M'Intyre DLB-106
Simon, Claude 1913- DLB-83; Y-85
Simon, Neil 1927- DLB-7
Simon and Schuster DLB-46
Simons, Katherine Drayton Mayrant
   1890-1969 .... Y-83
Simović, Ljubomir 1935- DLB-181
Simpkin and Marshall
   [publishing house] DLB-154
Simpson, Helen 1897-1940 .... DLB-77
Simpson, Louis 1923- DLB-5
Simpson, N. F. 1919- DLB-13
Sims, George 1923- DLB-87
Sims, George Robert
   1847-1922 .... DLB-35, 70, 135
Sinán, Rogelio 1904- DLB-145
Sinclair, Andrew 1935- DLB-14
Sinclair, Bertrand William
   1881-1972 .... DLB-92
Sinclair, Catherine
   1800-1864 .... DLB-163
Sinclair, Jo 1913- DLB-28
Sinclair Lewis Centennial
   Conference Y-85
Sinclair, Lister 1921- DLB-88
Sinclair, May 1863-1946 ...... DLB-36, 135
Sinclair, Upton 1878-1968 .... DLB-9
Sinclair, Upton [publishing house] DLB-46
Singer, Isaac Bashevis
   1904-1991 ...... DLB-6, 28, 52; Y-91
Singer, Mark 1950- DLB-185
Singmaster, Elsie 1879-1958 .... DLB-9
Sinisgalli, Leonardo 1908-1981 ..... DLB-114
Siodmak, Curt 1902- DLB-44
Siringo, Charles A. 1855-1928 ..... DLB-186
Sissman, L. E. 1928-1976 .... DLB-5

Sisson, C. H. 1914- DLB-27
Sitwell, Edith 1887-1964 .... DLB-20
Sitwell, Osbert 1892-1969 ..... DLB-100, 195
Skármeta, Antonio 1940- DLB-145
Skeat, Walter W. 1835-1912 .... DLB-184
Skeffington, William
   [publishing house] DLB-106
Skelton, John 1463-1529 .... DLB-136
Skelton, Robin 1925- DLB-27, 53
Skinner, Constance Lindsay
   1877-1939 .... DLB-92
Skinner, John Stuart 1788-1851 .... DLB-73
Skipsey, Joseph 1832-1903 .... DLB-35
Slade, Bernard 1930- DLB-53
Slamnig, Ivan 1930- DLB-181
Slater, Patrick 1880-1951 .... DLB-68
Slaveykov, Pencho 1866-1912 ..... DLB-147
Slaviček, Milivoj 1929- DLB-181
Slavitt, David 1935- DLB-5, 6
Sleigh, Burrows Willcocks Arthur
   1821-1869 .... DLB-99
A Slender Thread of Hope: The Kennedy
   Center Black Theatre Project DLB-38
Slesinger, Tess 1905-1945 .... DLB-102
Slick, Sam (see Haliburton, Thomas Chandler)
Sloan, John 1871-1951 .... DLB-188
Sloane, William, Associates DLB-46
Small, Maynard and Company DLB-49
Small Presses in Great Britain and Ireland,
   1960-1985 .... DLB-40
Small Presses I: Jargon Society Y-84
Small Presses II: The Spirit That Moves
   Us Press Y-85
Small Presses III: Pushcart Press Y-87
Smart, Christopher 1722-1771 ..... DLB-109
Smart, David A. 1892-1957 .... DLB-137
Smart, Elizabeth 1913-1986 .... DLB-88
Smellie, William
   [publishing house] DLB-154
Smiles, Samuel 1812-1904 .... DLB-55
Smith, A. J. M. 1902-1980 .... DLB-88
Smith, Adam 1723-1790 .... DLB-104
Smith, Adam (George Jerome Waldo Goodman)
   1930- DLB-185
Smith, Alexander 1829-1867 ..... DLB-32, 55
Smith, Betty 1896-1972 .... Y-82
Smith, Carol Sturm 1938- Y-81
Smith, Charles Henry 1826-1903 .... DLB-11
Smith, Charlotte 1749-1806 .... DLB-39, 109
Smith, Chet 1899-1973 .... DLB-171
Smith, Cordwainer 1913-1966 ...... DLB-8
Smith, Dave 1942- DLB-5
Smith, Dodie 1896- DLB-10

Smith, Doris Buchanan 1934- DLB-52
Smith, E. E. 1890-1965 .... DLB-8
Smith, Elihu Hubbard 1771-1798 ... DLB-37
Smith, Elizabeth Oakes (Prince)
   1806-1893 .... DLB-1
Smith, F. Hopkinson 1838-1915 ..... DS-13
Smith, George D. 1870-1920 ...... DLB-140
Smith, George O. 1911-1981 .... DLB-8
Smith, Goldwin 1823-1910 .... DLB-99
Smith, H. Allen 1907-1976 ..... DLB-11, 29
Smith, Harry B. 1860-1936 .... DLB-187
Smith, Hazel Brannon 1914- DLB-127
Smith, Henry
   circa 1560-circa 1591 .... DLB-136
Smith, Horatio (Horace)
   1779-1849 .... DLB-116
Smith, Horatio (Horace) 1779-1849 and
   James Smith 1775-1839 .... DLB-96
Smith, Iain Crichton
   1928- DLB-40, 139
Smith, J. Allen 1860-1924 .... DLB-47
Smith, Jessie Willcox 1863-1935 .... DLB-188
Smith, John 1580-1631 .... DLB-24, 30
Smith, Josiah 1704-1781 .... DLB-24
Smith, Ken 1938- DLB-40
Smith, Lee 1944- DLB-143; Y-83
Smith, Logan Pearsall 1865-1946 .... DLB-98
Smith, Mark 1935- Y-82
Smith, Michael 1698-circa 1771 .... DLB-31
Smith, Red 1905-1982 .... DLB-29, 171
Smith, Roswell 1829-1892 .... DLB-79
Smith, Samuel Harrison
   1772-1845 .... DLB-43
Smith, Samuel Stanhope
   1751-1819 .... DLB-37
Smith, Sarah (see Stretton, Hesba)
Smith, Seba 1792-1868 .... DLB-1, 11
Smith, Sir Thomas 1513-1577 ..... DLB-132
Smith, Stevie 1902-1971 .... DLB-20
Smith, Sydney 1771-1845 .... DLB-107
Smith, Sydney Goodsir 1915-1975 .... DLB-27
Smith, Wendell 1914-1972 .... DLB-171
Smith, William
   flourished 1595-1597 .... DLB-136
Smith, William 1727-1803 .... DLB-31
Smith, William 1728-1793 .... DLB-30
Smith, William Gardner
   1927-1974 .... DLB-76
Smith, William Henry
   1808-1872 .... DLB-159
Smith, William Jay 1918- DLB-5
Smith, Elder and Company DLB-154
Smith, Harrison, and Robert Haas
   [publishing house] DLB-46

Cumulative Index DLB 197

Smith, J. Stilman, and Company.....DLB-49

Smith, W. B., and Company......DLB-49

Smith, W. H., and Son.........DLB-106

Smithers, Leonard [publishing house]..........DLB-112

Smollett, Tobias 1721-1771.....DLB-39, 104

Smythe, Francis Sydney 1900-1949..............DLB-195

Snellings, Rolland (see Touré, Askia Muhammad)

Snodgrass, W. D. 1926-.........DLB-5

Snow, C. P. 1905-1980...DLB-15, 77; DS-17

Snyder, Gary 1930-.......DLB-5, 16, 165

Sobiloff, Hy 1912-1970..........DLB-48

The Society for Textual Scholarship and *TEXT*...................Y-87

The Society for the History of Authorship, Reading and Publishing............Y-92

Soffici, Ardengo 1879-1964.......DLB-114

Sofola, 'Zulu 1938-..........DLB-157

Solano, Solita 1888-1975..........DLB-4

Soldati, Mario 1906-.........DLB-177

Šoljan, Antun 1932-1993.........DLB-181

Sollers, Philippe 1936-.........DLB-83

Solmi, Sergio 1899-1981.........DLB-114

Solomon, Carl 1928-..........DLB-16

Solway, David 1941-..........DLB-53

Solzhenitsyn and America..........Y-85

Somerville, Edith Œnone 1858-1949..............DLB-135

Song, Cathy 1955-............DLB-169

Sono, Ayako 1931-............DLB-182

Sontag, Susan 1933-..........DLB-2, 67

Sophocles 497/496 B.C.-406/405 B.C. DLB-176

Šopov, Aco 1923-1982..........DLB-181

Sorge, Reinhard Johannes 1892-1916..............DLB-118

Sorrentino, Gilbert 1929-.............DLB-5, 173; Y-80

Sotheby, William 1757-1833.......DLB-93

Soto, Gary 1952-.............DLB-82

Sources for the Study of Tudor and Stuart Drama DLB-62

Souster, Raymond 1921-........DLB-88

The *South English Legendary* circa thirteenth-fifteenth centuries.............DLB-146

Southerland, Ellease 1943-.......DLB-33

Southern Illinois University Press......Y-95

Southern, Terry 1924-..........DLB-2

Southern Writers Between the Wars..................DLB-9

Southerne, Thomas 1659-1746.....DLB-80

Southey, Caroline Anne Bowles 1786-1854..............DLB-116

Southey, Robert 1774-1843.........DLB-93, 107, 142

Southwell, Robert 1561?-1595......DLB-167

Sowande, Bode 1948-.........DLB-157

Sowle, Tace [publishing house]..........DLB-170

Soyfer, Jura 1912-1939.........DLB-124

Soyinka, Wole 1934-...DLB-125; Y-86, Y-87

Spacks, Barry 1931-..........DLB-105

Spalding, Frances 1950-.........DLB-155

Spark, Muriel 1918-.......DLB-15, 139

Sparke, Michael [publishing house]..........DLB-170

Sparks, Jared 1789-1866........DLB-1, 30

Sparshott, Francis 1926-.........DLB-60

Späth, Gerold 1939-..........DLB-75

Spatola, Adriano 1941-1988......DLB-128

Spaziani, Maria Luisa 1924-......DLB-128

The Spectator 1828-............DLB-110

Spedding, James 1808-1881.......DLB-144

Spee von Langenfeld, Friedrich 1591-1635.............DLB-164

Speght, Rachel 1597-after 1630....DLB-126

Speke, John Hanning 1827-1864....DLB-166

Spellman, A. B. 1935-..........DLB-41

Spence, Thomas 1750-1814.......DLB-158

Spencer, Anne 1882-1975......DLB-51, 54

Spencer, Elizabeth 1921-.........DLB-6

Spencer, George John, Second Earl Spencer 1758-1834..............DLB-184

Spencer, Herbert 1820-1903.......DLB-57

Spencer, Scott 1945-............Y-86

Spender, J. A. 1862-1942........DLB-98

Spender, Stephen 1909-..........DLB-20

Spener, Philipp Jakob 1635-1705....DLB-164

Spenser, Edmund circa 1552-1599...DLB-167

Sperr, Martin 1944-...........DLB-124

Spicer, Jack 1925-1965......DLB-5, 16, 193

Spielberg, Peter 1929-............Y-81

Spielhagen, Friedrich 1829-1911.....DLB-129

"*Spielmannsepen*" (circa 1152-circa 1500).......DLB-148

Spier, Peter 1927-............DLB-61

Spinrad, Norman 1940-.........DLB-8

Spires, Elizabeth 1952-.........DLB-120

Spitteler, Carl 1845-1924.........DLB-129

Spivak, Lawrence E. 1900-......DLB-137

Spofford, Harriet Prescott 1835-1921...............DLB-74

Spring, Howard 1889-1965.......DLB-191

Squier, E. G. 1821-1888........DLB-189

Squibob (see Derby, George Horatio)

Stacpoole, H. de Vere 1863-1951..............DLB-153

Staël, Germaine de 1766-1817...DLB-119, 192

Staël-Holstein, Anne-Louise Germaine de (see Staël, Germaine de)

Stafford, Jean 1915-1979.......DLB-2, 173

Stafford, William 1914-..........DLB-5

Stage Censorship: "The Rejected Statement" (1911), by Bernard Shaw [excerpts]..............DLB-10

Stallings, Laurence 1894-1968.....DLB-7, 44

Stallworthy, Jon 1935-..........DLB-40

Stampp, Kenneth M. 1912-.......DLB-17

Stanev, Emiliyan 1907-1979......DLB-181

Stanford, Ann 1916-...........DLB-5

Stanković, Borisav ("Bora") 1876-1927..............DLB-147

Stanley, Henry M. 1841-1904..DLB-189; DS-13

Stanley, Thomas 1625-1678......DLB-131

Stannard, Martin 1947-........DLB-155

Stansby, William [publishing house]..........DLB-170

Stanton, Elizabeth Cady 1815-1902...DLB-79

Stanton, Frank L. 1857-1927......DLB-25

Stanton, Maura 1946-.........DLB-120

Stapledon, Olaf 1886-1950.......DLB-15

Star Spangled Banner Office.......DLB-49

Stark, Freya 1893-1993.........DLB-195

Starkey, Thomas circa 1499-1538....DLB-132

Starkie, Walter 1894-1976........DLB-195

Starkweather, David 1935-.........DLB-7

Starrett, Vincent 1886-1974.......DLB-187

Statements on the Art of Poetry.....DLB-54

The State of Publishing..........Y-97

Stationers' Company of London, The............DLB-170

Stead, Robert J. C. 1880-1959......DLB-92

Steadman, Mark 1930-..........DLB-6

The Stealthy School of Criticism (1871), by Dante Gabriel Rossetti.........DLB-35

Stearns, Harold E. 1891-1943.......DLB-4

Stedman, Edmund Clarence 1833-1908..............DLB-64

Steegmuller, Francis 1906-1994.....DLB-111

Steel, Flora Annie 1847-1929...DLB-153, 156

Steele, Max 1922-..............Y-80

Steele, Richard 1672-1729.....DLB-84, 101

Steele, Timothy 1948-..........DLB-120

Steele, Wilbur Daniel 1886-1970.....DLB-86

Steere, Richard circa 1643-1721.....DLB-24

Stefanovski, Goran 1952-.......DLB-181

Stegner, Wallace 1909-1993.....DLB-9; Y-93

Stehr, Hermann 1864-1940 . . . . DLB-66
Steig, William 1907- DLB-61
Stein, Gertrude
  1874-1946 . . . . . . DLB-4, 54, 86; DS-15
Stein, Leo 1872-1947 . . . . DLB-4
Stein and Day Publishers DLB-46
Steinbeck, John 1902-1968 . . . . DLB-7, 9; DS-2
Steiner, George 1929- DLB-67
Steinhoewel, Heinrich
  1411/1412-1479 . . . . DLB-179
Steloff, Ida Frances 1887-1989 . . . . . DLB-187
Stendhal 1783-1842 . . . . DLB-119
Stephen Crane: A Revaluation Virginia
  Tech Conference, 1989 . . . . Y-89
Stephen, Leslie 1832-1904 . . . DLB-57, 144, 190
Stephen Vincent Benét Centenary Y-97
Stephens, Alexander H. 1812-1883 . . . . DLB-47
Stephens, Alice Barber 1858-1932 . . . . DLB-188
Stephens, Ann 1810-1886 . . . . DLB-3, 73
Stephens, Charles Asbury
  1844?-1931 . . . . DLB-42
Stephens, James
  1882?-1950 . . . . DLB-19, 153, 162
Stephens, John Lloyd 1805-1852 . . . . DLB-183
Sterling, George 1869-1926 . . . . DLB-54
Sterling, James 1701-1763 . . . . DLB-24
Sterling, John 1806-1844 . . . . DLB-116
Stern, Gerald 1925- DLB-105
Stern, Gladys B. 1890-1973 . . . . . . DLB-197
Stern, Madeleine B. 1912- DLB-111, 140
Stern, Richard 1928- Y-87
Stern, Stewart 1922- DLB-26
Sterne, Laurence 1713-1768 . . . . DLB-39
Sternheim, Carl 1878-1942 . . . . DLB-56, 118
Sternhold, Thomas ?-1549 and
  John Hopkins ?-1570 . . . . DLB-132
Stevens, Henry 1819-1886 . . . . DLB-140
Stevens, Wallace 1879-1955 . . . . DLB-54
Stevenson, Anne 1933- DLB-40
Stevenson, D. E. 1892-1973 . . . . . . DLB-191
Stevenson, Lionel 1902-1973 . . . . . . DLB-155
Stevenson, Robert Louis 1850-1894
  . . . . DLB-18, 57, 141, 156, 174; DS-13
Stewart, Donald Ogden
  1894-1980 . . . . DLB-4, 11, 26
Stewart, Dugald 1753-1828 . . . . DLB-31
Stewart, George, Jr. 1848-1906 . . . . . DLB-99
Stewart, George R. 1895-1980 . . . . . . DLB-8
Stewart and Kidd Company DLB-46
Stewart, Randall 1896-1964 . . . . . . DLB-103
Stickney, Trumbull 1874-1904 . . . . . . DLB-54
Stieler, Caspar 1632-1707 . . . . DLB-164
Stifter, Adalbert 1805-1868 . . . . DLB-133

Stiles, Ezra 1727-1795 . . . . DLB-31
Still, James 1906- DLB-9
Stirner, Max 1806-1856 . . . . DLB-129
Stith, William 1707-1755 . . . . DLB-31
Stock, Elliot [publishing house] DLB-106
Stockton, Frank R.
  1834-1902 . . . . DLB-42, 74; DS-13
Stoddard, Ashbel
  [publishing house] DLB-49
Stoddard, Charles Warren
  1843-1909 . . . . DLB-186
Stoddard, Richard Henry
  1825-1903 . . . . DLB-3, 64; DS-13
Stoddard, Solomon 1643-1729 . . . . . . DLB-24
Stoker, Bram 1847-1912 . . . . DLB-36, 70, 178
Stokes, Frederick A., Company DLB-49
Stokes, Thomas L. 1898-1958 . . . . . . DLB-29
Stokesbury, Leon 1945- DLB-120
Stolberg, Christian Graf zu
  1748-1821 . . . . DLB-94
Stolberg, Friedrich Leopold Graf zu
  1750-1819 . . . . DLB-94
Stone, Herbert S., and Company DLB-49
Stone, Lucy 1818-1893 . . . . DLB-79
Stone, Melville 1848-1929 . . . . DLB-25
Stone, Robert 1937- DLB-152
Stone, Ruth 1915- DLB-105
Stone, Samuel 1602-1663 . . . . DLB-24
Stone and Kimball DLB-49
Stoppard, Tom 1937- DLB-13; Y-85
Storey, Anthony 1928- DLB-14
Storey, David 1933- DLB-13, 14
Storm, Theodor 1817-1888 . . . . DLB-129
Story, Thomas circa 1670-1742 . . . . . DLB-31
Story, William Wetmore 1819-1895 . . . . DLB-1
Storytelling: A Contemporary
  Renaissance Y-84
Stoughton, William 1631-1701 . . . . . . DLB-24
Stow, John 1525-1605 . . . . DLB-132
Stowe, Harriet Beecher
  1811-1896 . . . . . DLB-1, 12, 42, 74, 189
Stowe, Leland 1899- DLB-29
Stoyanov, Dimitŭr Ivanov (see Elin Pelin)
Strabo 64 or 63 B.C.-circa A.D. 25
  . . . . DLB-176
Strachey, Lytton
  1880-1932 . . . . DLB-149; DS-10
Strachey, Lytton, Preface to Eminent
  Victorians DLB-149
Strahan and Company DLB-106
Strahan, William
  [publishing house] DLB-154
Strand, Mark 1934- DLB-5
The Strasbourg Oaths 842 . . . . DLB-148

Stratemeyer, Edward 1862-1930 . . . . . DLB-42
Strati, Saverio 1924- DLB-177
Stratton and Barnard DLB-49
Stratton-Porter, Gene 1863-1924 . . . . . DS-14
Straub, Peter 1943- Y-84
Strauß, Botho 1944- DLB-124
Strauß, David Friedrich
  1808-1874 . . . . DLB-133
The Strawberry Hill Press DLB-154
Streatfeild, Noel 1895-1986 . . . . DLB-160
Street, Cecil John Charles (see Rhode, John)
Street, G. S. 1867-1936 . . . . DLB-135
Street and Smith DLB-49
Streeter, Edward 1891-1976 . . . . DLB-11
Streeter, Thomas Winthrop
  1883-1965 . . . . DLB-140
Stretton, Hesba 1832-1911 . . . . . DLB-163, 190
Stribling, T. S. 1881-1965 . . . . DLB-9
Der Stricker circa 1190-circa 1250 . . . DLB-138
Strickland, Samuel 1804-1867 . . . . . . DLB-99
Stringer and Townsend DLB-49
Stringer, Arthur 1874-1950 . . . . DLB-92
Strittmatter, Erwin 1912- DLB-69
Strniša, Gregor 1930-1987 . . . . DLB-181
Strode, William 1630-1645 . . . . DLB-126
Strong, L. A. G. 1896-1958 . . . . . . DLB-191
Strother, David Hunter 1816-1888 . . . . DLB-3
Strouse, Jean 1945- DLB-111
Stuart, Dabney 1937- DLB-105
Stuart, Jesse
  1906-1984 . . . . DLB-9, 48, 102; Y-84
Stuart, Lyle [publishing house] DLB-46
Stubbs, Harry Clement (see Clement, Hal)
Stubenberg, Johann Wilhelm von
  1619-1663 . . . . DLB-164
Studio DLB-112
The Study of Poetry (1880), by
  Matthew Arnold DLB-35
Sturgeon, Theodore
  1918-1985 . . . . DLB-8; Y-85
Sturges, Preston 1898-1959 . . . . DLB-26
"Style" (1840; revised, 1859), by
  Thomas de Quincey [excerpt] DLB-57
"Style" (1888), by Walter Pater DLB-57
Style (1897), by Walter Raleigh
  [excerpt] DLB-57
"Style" (1877), by T. H. Wright
  [excerpt] DLB-57
"Le Style c'est l'homme" (1892), by
  W. H. Mallock DLB-57
Styron, William 1925- DLB-2, 143; Y-80
Suárez, Mario 1925- DLB-82
Such, Peter 1939- DLB-60

Suckling, Sir John 1609-1641? ... DLB-58, 126
Suckow, Ruth 1892-1960 ...... DLB-9, 102
Sudermann, Hermann 1857-1928 .... DLB-118
Sue, Eugène 1804-1857 .... DLB-119
Sue, Marie-Joseph (see Sue, Eugène)
Suggs, Simon (see Hooper, Johnson Jones)
Sukenick, Ronald 1932- DLB-173; Y-81
Suknaski, Andrew 1942- DLB-53
Sullivan, Alan 1868-1947 .... DLB-92
Sullivan, C. Gardner 1886-1965 ..... DLB-26
Sullivan, Frank 1892-1976 .... DLB-11
Sulte, Benjamin 1841-1923 .... DLB-99
Sulzberger, Arthur Hays
 1891-1968 .... DLB-127
Sulzberger, Arthur Ochs 1926- DLB-127
Sulzer, Johann Georg 1720-1779 ..... DLB-97
Sumarokov, Aleksandr Petrovich
 1717-1777 .... DLB-150
Summers, Hollis 1916- DLB-6
Sumner, Henry A.
 [publishing house] DLB-49
Surtees, Robert Smith 1803-1864 ..... DLB-21
Surveys: Japanese Literature,
 1987-1995 .... DLB-182
A Survey of Poetry Anthologies,
 1879-1960 .... DLB-54
Surveys of the Year's Biographies
A Transit of Poets and Others: American
 Biography in 1982 .... Y-82
The Year in Literary Biography ... Y-83–Y-96
Survey of the Year's Book Publishing
The Year in Book Publishing Y-86
Survey of the Year's Children's Books
The Year in Children's Books
 .... Y-92–Y-96
Surveys of the Year's Drama
The Year in Drama
 .... Y-82–Y-85, Y-87–Y-96
The Year in London Theatre Y-92
Surveys of the Year's Fiction
The Year's Work in Fiction:
 A Survey Y-82
The Year in Fiction: A Biased View Y-83
The Year in
 Fiction Y-84–Y-86, Y-89, Y-94–Y-96
The Year in the
 Novel Y-87, Y-88, Y-90–Y-93
The Year in Short Stories Y-87
The Year in the
 Short Story Y-88, Y-90–Y-93
Survey of the Year's Literary Theory
The Year in Literary Theory Y-92–Y-93
Surveys of the Year's Poetry

The Year's Work in American
 Poetry Y-82
The Year in Poetry ... Y-83–Y-92, Y-94–Y-96
Sutherland, Efua Theodora
 1924- DLB-117
Sutherland, John 1919-1956 .... DLB-68
Sutro, Alfred 1863-1933 .... DLB-10
Swados, Harvey 1920-1972 .... DLB-2
Swain, Charles 1801-1874 .... DLB-32
Swallow Press DLB-46
Swan Sonnenschein Limited DLB-106
Swanberg, W. A. 1907- DLB-103
Swenson, May 1919-1989 .... DLB-5
Swerling, Jo 1897- DLB-44
Swift, Graham 1949- DLB-194
Swift, Jonathan 1667-1745 ... DLB-39, 95, 101
Swinburne, A. C. 1837-1909 ..... DLB-35, 57
Swineshead, Richard floruit
 circa 1350 .... DLB-115
Swinnerton, Frank 1884-1982 ...... DLB-34
Swisshelm, Jane Grey 1815-1884 ..... DLB-43
Swope, Herbert Bayard 1882-1958 .... DLB-25
Swords, T. and J., and Company DLB-49
Swords, Thomas 1763-1843 and
 Swords, James ?-1844 .... DLB-73
Sykes, Ella C. ?-1939 .... DLB-174
Sylvester, Josuah
 1562 or 1563 - 1618 .... DLB-121
Symonds, Emily Morse (see Paston, George)
Symonds, John Addington
 1840-1893 .... DLB-57, 144
Symons, A. J. A. 1900-1941 ...... DLB-149
Symons, Arthur 1865-1945 ... DLB-19, 57, 149
Symons, Julian 1912-1994 .. DLB-87, 155; Y-92
Symons, Scott 1933- DLB-53
A Symposium on *The Columbia History of
 the Novel* Y-92
Synge, John Millington
 1871-1909 .... DLB-10, 19
Synge Summer School: J. M. Synge and the Irish
 Theater, Rathdrum, County Wiclow, Ireland
 .... Y-93
Syrett, Netta 1865-1943 ...... DLB-135, 197
Szymborska, Wisława 1923- Y-96

T

Taban lo Liyong 1939?- DLB-125
Tabucchi, Antonio 1943- DLB-196
Taché, Joseph-Charles 1820-1894 .... DLB-99
Tachihara, Masaaki 1926-1980 ..... DLB-182
Tadijanović, Dragutin 1905- DLB-181
Tafolla, Carmen 1951- DLB-82

Taggard, Genevieve 1894-1948 ...... DLB-45
Taggart, John 1942- DLB-193
Tagger, Theodor (see Bruckner, Ferdinand)
Tait, J. Selwin, and Sons DLB-49
Tait's Edinburgh Magazine
 1832-1861 .... DLB-110
The Takarazaka Revue Company Y-91
Talander (see Bohse, August)
Talese, Gay 1932- DLB-185
Talev, Dimitŭr 1898-1966 .... DLB-181
Tallent, Elizabeth 1954- DLB-130
TallMountain, Mary 1918-1994 .... DLB-193
Talvj 1797-1870 .... DLB-59, 133
Tan, Amy 1952- DLB-173
Tanizaki, Jun'ichirō 1886-1965 ..... DLB-180
Tapahonso, Luci 1953- DLB-175
Taradash, Daniel 1913- DLB-44
Tarbell, Ida M. 1857-1944 .... DLB-47
Tardivel, Jules-Paul 1851-1905 ..... DLB-99
Targan, Barry 1932- DLB-130
Tarkington, Booth 1869-1946 .... DLB-9, 102
Tashlin, Frank 1913-1972 .... DLB-44
Tate, Allen 1899-1979 .. DLB-4, 45, 63; DS-17
Tate, James 1943- DLB-5, 169
Tate, Nahum circa 1652-1715 ...... DLB-80
Tatian circa 830 .... DLB-148
Taufer, Veno 1933- DLB-181
Tauler, Johannes circa 1300-1361 .... DLB-179
Tavčar, Ivan 1851-1923 .... DLB-147
Taylor, Ann 1782-1866 .... DLB-163
Taylor, Bayard 1825-1878 ..... DLB-3, 189
Taylor, Bert Leston 1866-1921 ...... DLB-25
Taylor, Charles H. 1846-1921 ...... DLB-25
Taylor, Edward circa 1642-1729 ..... DLB-24
Taylor, Elizabeth 1912-1975 .... DLB-139
Taylor, Henry 1942- DLB-5
Taylor, Sir Henry 1800-1886 ...... DLB-32
Taylor, Jane 1783-1824 .... DLB-163
Taylor, Jeremy circa 1613-1667 ..... DLB-151
Taylor, John 1577 or 1578 - 1653 ... DLB-121
Taylor, Mildred D. ?- DLB-52
Taylor, Peter 1917-1994 .... Y-81, Y-94
Taylor, William, and Company DLB-49
Taylor-Made Shakespeare? Or Is
 "Shall I Die?" the Long-Lost Text
 of Bottom's Dream? Y-85
Teasdale, Sara 1884-1933 .... DLB-45
The Tea-Table (1725), by Eliza Haywood [excerpt]
 DLB-39
Telles, Lygia Fagundes 1924- DLB-113
Temple, Sir William 1628-1699 ..... DLB-101
Tenn, William 1919- DLB-8

Tennant, Emma 1937- DLB-14
Tenney, Tabitha Gilman 1762-1837 ... DLB-37
Tennyson, Alfred 1809-1892 .... DLB-32
Tennyson, Frederick 1807-1898 ..... DLB-32
Terhune, Albert Payson 1872-1942 .... DLB-9
Terhune, Mary Virginia
  1830-1922 .... DS-13, DS-16
Terry, Megan 1932- DLB-7
Terson, Peter 1932- DLB-13
Tesich, Steve 1943- Y-83
Tessa, Delio 1886-1939 .... DLB-114
Testori, Giovanni 1923-1993 .... DLB-128, 177
Tey, Josephine 1896?-1952 .... DLB-77
Thacher, James 1754-1844 .... DLB-37
Thackeray, William Makepeace
  1811-1863 .... DLB-21, 55, 159, 163
Thames and Hudson Limited DLB-112
Thanet, Octave (see French, Alice)
Thatcher, John Boyd 1847-1909 .... DLB-187
The Theater in Shakespeare's Time ... DLB-62
The Theatre Guild DLB-7
Thegan and the Astronomer
  flourished circa 850 .... DLB-148
Thelwall, John 1764-1834 ...... DLB-93, 158
Theocritus circa 300 B.C.-260 B.C.
  .... DLB-176
Theodulf circa 760-circa 821 ..... DLB-148
Theophrastus circa 371 B.C.-287 B.C.
  .... DLB-176
Theriault, Yves 1915-1983 .... DLB-88
Thério, Adrien 1925- DLB-53
Theroux, Paul 1941- DLB-2
They All Came to Paris DS-16
Thibaudeau, Colleen 1925- DLB-88
Thielen, Benedict 1903-1965 ..... DLB-102
Thiong'o Ngugi wa (see Ngugi wa Thiong'o)
Third-Generation Minor Poets of the
  Seventeenth Century DLB-131
This Quarter 1925-1927, 1929-1932 ..... DS-15
Thoma, Ludwig 1867-1921 .... DLB-66
Thoma, Richard 1902- DLB-4
Thomas, Audrey 1935- DLB-60
Thomas, D. M. 1935- DLB-40
Thomas, Dylan
  1914-1953 .... DLB-13, 20, 139
Thomas, Edward
  1878-1917 .... DLB-19, 98, 156
Thomas, Gwyn 1913-1981 .... DLB-15
Thomas, Isaiah 1750-1831 ... DLB-43, 73, 187
Thomas, Isaiah [publishing house] DLB-49
Thomas, Johann 1624-1679 ...... DLB-168
Thomas, John 1900-1932 .... DLB-4
Thomas, Joyce Carol 1938- DLB-33

Thomas, Lorenzo 1944- DLB-41
Thomas, R. S. 1915- DLB-27
The Thomas Wolfe Collection at the University of
  North Carolina at Chapel Hill Y-97
The Thomas Wolfe Society Y-97
Thomasîn von Zerclære
  circa 1186-circa 1259 .... DLB-138
Thomasius, Christian 1655-1728 .... DLB-168
Thompson, David 1770-1857 .... DLB-99
Thompson, Dorothy 1893-1961 ..... DLB-29
Thompson, Francis 1859-1907 ..... DLB-19
Thompson, George Selden (see Selden, George)
Thompson, Henry Yates 1838-1928 .. DLB-184
Thompson, Hunter S. 1939- DLB-185
Thompson, John 1938-1976 .... DLB-60
Thompson, John R. 1823-1873 .... DLB-3, 73
Thompson, Lawrance 1906-1973 .... DLB-103
Thompson, Maurice 1844-1901 ... DLB-71, 74
Thompson, Ruth Plumly
  1891-1976 .... DLB-22
Thompson, Thomas Phillips
  1843-1933 .... DLB-99
Thompson, William 1775-1833 ..... DLB-158
Thompson, William Tappan
  1812-1882 .... DLB-3, 11
Thomson, Edward William
  1849-1924 .... DLB-92
Thomson, James 1700-1748 .... DLB-95
Thomson, James 1834-1882 .... DLB-35
Thomson, Joseph 1858-1895 ...... DLB-174
Thomson, Mortimer 1831-1875 ..... DLB-11
Thoreau, Henry David
  1817-1862 .... DLB-1, 183
Thornton Wilder Centenary at Yale Y-97
Thorpe, Thomas Bangs
  1815-1878 .... DLB-3, 11
Thoughts on Poetry and Its Varieties (1833),
  by John Stuart Mill DLB-32
Thrale, Hester Lynch (see Piozzi, Hester
  Lynch [Thrale])
Thucydides circa 455 B.C.-circa 395 B.C.
  .... DLB-176
Thulstrup, Thure de 1848-1930 .... DLB-188
Thümmel, Moritz August von
  1738-1817 .... DLB-97
Thurber, James
  1894-1961 .... DLB-4, 11, 22, 102
Thurman, Wallace 1902-1934 ..... DLB-51
Thwaite, Anthony 1930- DLB-40
Thwaites, Reuben Gold
  1853-1913 .... DLB-47
Ticknor, George
  1791-1871 .... DLB-1, 59, 140
Ticknor and Fields DLB-49
Ticknor and Fields (revived) DLB-46

Tieck, Ludwig 1773-1853 .... DLB-90
Tietjens, Eunice 1884-1944 ...... DLB-54
Tilney, Edmund circa 1536-1610 .... DLB-136
Tilt, Charles [publishing house] DLB-106
Tilton, J. E., and Company DLB-49
Time and Western Man (1927), by Wyndham
  Lewis [excerpts] DLB-36
Time-Life Books DLB-46
Times Books DLB-46
Timothy, Peter circa 1725-1782 ..... DLB-43
Timrod, Henry 1828-1867 .... DLB-3
Tinker, Chauncey Brewster
  1876-1963 .... DLB-140
Tinsley Brothers DLB-106
Tiptree, James, Jr. 1915-1987 .... DLB-8
Tišma, Aleksandar 1924- DLB-181
Titus, Edward William
  1870-1952 .... DLB-4; DS-15
Tlali, Miriam 1933- DLB-157
Todd, Barbara Euphan
  1890-1976 .... DLB-160
Tofte, Robert
  1561 or 1562-1619 or 1620 .... DLB-172
Toklas, Alice B. 1877-1967 .... DLB-4
Tokuda, Shūsei 1872-1943 .... DLB-180
Tolkien, J. R. R. 1892-1973 .... DLB-15, 160
Toller, Ernst 1893-1939 .... DLB-124
Tollet, Elizabeth 1694-1754 ...... DLB-95
Tolson, Melvin B. 1898-1966 .... DLB-48, 76
Tom Jones (1749), by Henry Fielding
  [excerpt] DLB-39
Tomalin, Claire 1933- DLB-155
Tomasi di Lampedusa,
  Giuseppe 1896-1957 .... DLB-177
Tomlinson, Charles 1927- DLB-40
Tomlinson, H. M. 1873-1958
  .... DLB-36, 100, 195
Tompkins, Abel [publishing house] ... DLB-49
Tompson, Benjamin 1642-1714 ..... DLB-24
Tondelli, Pier Vittorio 1955-1991 .... DLB-196
Tonks, Rosemary 1932- DLB-14
Tonna, Charlotte Elizabeth
  1790-1846 .... DLB-163
Tonson, Jacob the Elder
  [publishing house] DLB-170
Toole, John Kennedy 1937-1969 ...... Y-81
Toomer, Jean 1894-1967 ...... DLB-45, 51
Tor Books DLB-46
Torberg, Friedrich 1908-1979 ..... DLB-85
Torrence, Ridgely 1874-1950 ..... DLB-54
Torres-Metzger, Joseph V.
  1933- DLB-122
Toth, Susan Allen 1940- Y-86

Tottell, Richard [publishing house] DLB-170

Tough-Guy Literature DLB-9

Touré, Askia Muhammad 1938- DLB-41

Tourgée, Albion W. 1838-1905 . . . . . DLB-79

Tourneur, Cyril circa 1580-1626. . . . . DLB-58

Tournier, Michel 1924- DLB-83

Tousey, Frank [publishing house] DLB-49

Tower Publications DLB-46

Towne, Benjamin circa 1740-1793 . . . . DLB-43

Towne, Robert 1936- DLB-44

The Townely Plays fifteenth and sixteenth centuries DLB-146

Townshend, Aurelian by 1583 - circa 1651 . . . . DLB-121

Tracy, Honor 1913- DLB-15

Traherne, Thomas 1637?-1674 . . . . . DLB-131

Traill, Catharine Parr 1802-1899. . . . . DLB-99

Train, Arthur 1875-1945 . . . . . DLB-86; DS-16

The Transatlantic Publishing Company DLB-49

The Transatlantic Review 1924-1925 . . . . . DS-15

Transcendentalists, American. DS-5

transition 1927-1938. . . . . DS-15

Translators of the Twelfth Century: Literary Issues Raised and Impact Created. DLB-115

Travel Writing, 1837-1875 . . . . DLB-166

Travel Writing, 1876-1909 . . . . DLB-174

Traven, B. 1882? or 1890?-1969?. DLB-9, 56

Travers, Ben 1886-1980 . . . . DLB-10

Travers, P. L. (Pamela Lyndon) 1899- DLB-160

Trediakovsky, Vasilii Kirillovich 1703-1769 . . . . DLB-150

Treece, Henry 1911-1966 . . . . DLB-160

Trejo, Ernesto 1950- DLB-122

Trelawny, Edward John 1792-1881. . . . . DLB-110, 116, 144

Tremain, Rose 1943- DLB-14

Tremblay, Michel 1942- DLB-60

Trends in Twentieth-Century Mass Market Publishing DLB-46

Trent, William P. 1862-1939. . . . . . . DLB-47

Trescot, William Henry 1822-1898 . . . . DLB-30

Tressell, Robert (Robert Phillipe Noonan) 1870-1911 . . . . DLB-197

Trevelyan, Sir George Otto 1838-1928 . . . . DLB-144

Trevisa, John circa 1342-circa 1402 . . . . DLB-146

Trevor, William 1928- DLB-14, 139

Trierer Floyris circa 1170-1180 . . . . . . DLB-138

Trillin, Calvin 1935- DLB-185

Trilling, Lionel 1905-1975 . . . . . DLB-28, 63

Trilussa 1871-1950. . . . . DLB-114

Trimmer, Sarah 1741-1810 . . . . DLB-158

Triolet, Elsa 1896-1970 . . . . DLB-72

Tripp, John 1927- DLB-40

Trocchi, Alexander 1925- DLB-15

Troisi, Dante 1920-1989. . . . . DLB-196

Trollope, Anthony 1815-1882 . . . . DLB-21, 57, 159

Trollope, Frances 1779-1863 . . . . DLB-21, 166

Troop, Elizabeth 1931- DLB-14

Trotter, Catharine 1679-1749. . . . . . DLB-84

Trotti, Lamar 1898-1952 . . . . DLB-44

Trottier, Pierre 1925- DLB-60

Troupe, Quincy Thomas, Jr. 1943- . . DLB-41

Trow, John F., and Company DLB-49

Truillier-Lacombe, Joseph-Patrice 1807-1863 . . . . DLB-99

Trumbo, Dalton 1905-1976. . . . . . . DLB-26

Trumbull, Benjamin 1735-1820. . . . . DLB-30

Trumbull, John 1750-1831 . . . . DLB-31

Trumbull, John 1756-1843 . . . . DLB-183

Tscherning, Andreas 1611-1659. . . . . DLB-164

T. S. Eliot Centennial Y-88

Tsubouchi, Shōyō 1859-1935 . . . . . . DLB-180

Tucholsky, Kurt 1890-1935. . . . . . . DLB-56

Tucker, Charlotte Maria 1821-1893. . . . . DLB-163, 190

Tucker, George 1775-1861 . . . . . DLB-3, 30

Tucker, Nathaniel Beverley 1784-1851. . . . . DLB-3

Tucker, St. George 1752-1827 . . . . . DLB-37

Tuckerman, Henry Theodore 1813-1871 . . . . DLB-64

Tunis, John R. 1889-1975 . . . . . DLB-22, 171

Tunstall, Cuthbert 1474-1559 . . . . . . DLB-132

Tuohy, Frank 1925- DLB-14, 139

Tupper, Martin F. 1810-1889 . . . . . . DLB-32

Turbyfill, Mark 1896- DLB-45

Turco, Lewis 1934- Y-84

Turnball, Alexander H. 1868-1918 . . . DLB-184

Turnbull, Andrew 1921-1970 . . . . . . DLB-103

Turnbull, Gael 1928- DLB-40

Turner, Arlin 1909-1980. . . . . DLB-103

Turner, Charles (Tennyson) 1808-1879 . . . . DLB-32

Turner, Frederick 1943- DLB-40

Turner, Frederick Jackson 1861-1932 . . . . DLB-17, 186

Turner, Joseph Addison 1826-1868 . . . . DLB-79

Turpin, Waters Edward 1910-1968 . . . . DLB-51

Turrini, Peter 1944- DLB-124

Tutuola, Amos 1920- DLB-125

Twain, Mark (see Clemens, Samuel Langhorne)

Tweedie, Ethel Brilliana circa 1860-1940 . . . . DLB-174

The 'Twenties and Berlin, by Alex Natan DLB-66

Tyler, Anne 1941- DLB-6, 143; Y-82

Tyler, Moses Coit 1835-1900 . . . . DLB-47, 64

Tyler, Royall 1757-1826 . . . . DLB-37

Tylor, Edward Burnett 1832-1917 . . . . DLB-57

Tynan, Katharine 1861-1931 . . . . . . DLB-153

Tyndale, William circa 1494-1536 . . . . DLB-132

U

Udall, Nicholas 1504-1556 . . . . DLB-62

Ugrešić, Dubravka 1949- DLB-181

Uhland, Ludwig 1787-1862. . . . . . . DLB-90

Uhse, Bodo 1904-1963 . . . . DLB-69

Ujević, Augustin ("Tin") 1891-1955 . . . . DLB-147

Ulenhart, Niclas flourished circa 1600 . . . . DLB-164

Ulibarrí, Sabine R. 1919- DLB-82

Ulica, Jorge 1870-1926 . . . . DLB-82

Ulivi, Ferruccio 1912- DLB-196

Ulizio, B. George 1889-1969 . . . . . . DLB-140

Ulrich von Liechtenstein circa 1200-circa 1275 . . . . DLB-138

Ulrich von Zatzikhoven before 1194-after 1214 . . . . DLB-138

Ulysses, Reader's Edition Y-97

Unamuno, Miguel de 1864-1936 . . . . DLB-108

Under the Microscope (1872), by A. C. Swinburne DLB-35

Unger, Friederike Helene 1741-1813 . . . . DLB-94

Ungaretti, Giuseppe 1888-1970 . . . . . DLB-114

United States Book Company DLB-49

Universal Publishing and Distributing Corporation DLB-46

The University of Iowa Writers' Workshop Golden Jubilee Y-86

The University of South Carolina Press Y-94

University of Wales Press. DLB-112

"The Unknown Public" (1858), by Wilkie Collins [excerpt] DLB-57

Uno, Chiyo 1897-1996 . . . . DLB-180

Unruh, Fritz von 1885-1970 . . . . DLB-56, 118

Unspeakable Practices II: The Festival of
 Vanguard Narrative at Brown
 University. Y-93
Unsworth, Barry 1930- DLB-194
Unwin, T. Fisher
 [publishing house] DLB-106
Upchurch, Boyd B. (see Boyd, John)
Updike, John
 1932- . . . DLB-2, 5, 143; Y-80, Y-82; DS-3
Upton, Bertha 1849-1912 . . . . DLB-141
Upton, Charles 1948- DLB-16
Upton, Florence K. 1873-1922 . . . . . DLB-141
Upward, Allen 1863-1926. . . . . DLB-36
Urista, Alberto Baltazar (see Alurista)
Urzidil, Johannes 1896-1976 . . . . . . DLB-85
Urquhart, Fred 1912- DLB-139
The Uses of Facsimile Y-90
Usk, Thomas died 1388 . . . . DLB-146
Uslar Pietri, Arturo 1906- DLB-113
Ustinov, Peter 1921- DLB-13
Uttley, Alison 1884-1976 . . . . DLB-160
Uz, Johann Peter 1720-1796 . . . . . . DLB-97

V

Vac, Bertrand 1914- DLB-88
Vail, Laurence 1891-1968 . . . . DLB-4
Vailland, Roger 1907-1965 . . . . DLB-83
Vajda, Ernest 1887-1954 . . . . DLB-44
Valdés, Gina 1943- DLB-122
Valdez, Luis Miguel 1940- DLB-122
Valduga, Patrizia 1953- DLB-128
Valente, José Angel 1929- DLB-108
Valenzuela, Luisa 1938- DLB-113
Valeri, Diego 1887-1976. . . . . DLB-128
Valesio, Paolo 1939- DLB-196
Valgardson, W. D. 1939- DLB-60
Valle, Víctor Manuel 1950- DLB-122
Valle-Inclán, Ramón del
 1866-1936 . . . . DLB-134
Vallejo, Armando 1949- DLB-122
Vallès, Jules 1832-1885 . . . . DLB-123
Vallette, Marguerite Eymery (see Rachilde)
Valverde, José María 1926- DLB-108
Van Allsburg, Chris 1949- DLB-61
Van Anda, Carr 1864-1945 . . . . . . DLB-25
Van Dine, S. S. (see Wright, Williard Huntington)
Van Doren, Mark 1894-1972 . . . . . DLB-45
van Druten, John 1901-1957. . . . . . DLB-10
Van Duyn, Mona 1921- DLB-5
Van Dyke, Henry
 1852-1933. . . . . DLB-71; DS-13

Van Dyke, John C. 1856-1932 . . . . . DLB-186
Van Dyke, Henry 1928- DLB-33
van Gulik, Robert Hans 1910-1967 . . . DS-17
van Itallie, Jean-Claude 1936- DLB-7
Van Loan, Charles E. 1876-1919. . . . DLB-171
Van Rensselaer, Mariana Griswold
 1851-1934 . . . . DLB-47
Van Rensselaer, Mrs. Schuyler (see Van
 Rensselaer, Mariana Griswold)
Van Vechten, Carl 1880-1964 . . . . . DLB-4, 9
van Vogt, A. E. 1912- DLB-8
Vanbrugh, Sir John 1664-1726 . . . . . DLB-80
Vance, Jack 1916?- DLB-8
Vane, Sutton 1888-1963 . . . . DLB-10
Vanguard Press DLB-46
Vann, Robert L. 1879-1940 . . . . . . DLB-29
Vargas, Llosa, Mario 1936- DLB-145
Varley, John 1947- Y-81
Varnhagen von Ense, Karl August
 1785-1858 . . . . DLB-90
Varnhagen von Ense, Rahel
 1771-1833 . . . . DLB-90
Vásquez Montalbán, Manuel
 1939- DLB-134
Vassa, Gustavus (see Equiano, Olaudah)
Vassalli, Sebastiano 1941- DLB-128, 196
Vaughan, Henry 1621-1695. . . . . . . DLB-131
Vaughan, Thomas 1621-1666 . . . . . DLB-131
Vaux, Thomas, Lord 1509-1556 . . . . DLB-132
Vazov, Ivan 1850-1921 . . . . DLB-147
Vega, Janine Pommy 1942- DLB-16
Veiller, Anthony 1903-1965. . . . . . . DLB-44
Velásquez-Trevino, Gloria
 1949- DLB-122
Veloz Maggiolo, Marcio 1936- DLB-145
Venegas, Daniel ?-? DLB-82
Vergil, Polydore circa 1470-1555 . . . . DLB-132
Veríssimo, Erico 1905-1975 . . . . . . DLB-145
Verne, Jules 1828-1905 . . . . DLB-123
Verplanck, Gulian C. 1786-1870. . . . . DLB-59
Very, Jones 1813-1880. . . . . DLB-1
Vian, Boris 1920-1959 . . . . DLB-72
Vickers, Roy 1888?-1965 . . . . DLB-77
Victoria 1819-1901 . . . . DLB-55
Victoria Press DLB-106
Vidal, Gore 1925- DLB-6, 152
Viebig, Clara 1860-1952 . . . . DLB-66
Viereck, George Sylvester
 1884-1962 . . . . DLB-54
Viereck, Peter 1916- DLB-5
Viets, Roger 1738-1811. . . . . DLB-99
Viewpoint: Politics and Performance, by
 David Edgar DLB-13

Vigil-Piñon, Evangelina 1949- DLB-122
Vigneault, Gilles 1928- DLB-60
Vigny, Alfred de 1797-1863. . . . DLB-119, 192
Vigolo, Giorgio 1894-1983 . . . . DLB-114
The Viking Press DLB-46
Villanueva, Alma Luz 1944- DLB-122
Villanueva, Tino 1941- DLB-82
Villard, Henry 1835-1900. . . . . DLB-23
Villard, Oswald Garrison
 1872-1949. . . . . DLB-25, 91
Villarreal, José Antonio 1924- DLB-82
Villegas de Magnón, Leonor
 1876-1955 . . . . DLB-122
Villemaire, Yolande 1949- DLB-60
Villena, Luis Antonio de 1951- DLB-134
Villiers de l'Isle-Adam, Jean-Marie
 Mathias Philippe-Auguste, Comte de
 1838-1889. . . . . DLB-123, 192
Villiers, George, Second Duke
 of Buckingham 1628-1687 . . . . . . DLB-80
Vine Press DLB-112
Viorst, Judith ?- DLB-52
Vipont, Elfrida (Elfrida Vipont Foulds,
 Charles Vipont) 1902-1992 . . . . . DLB-160
Viramontes, Helena María
 1954- DLB-122
Vischer, Friedrich Theodor
 1807-1887 . . . . DLB-133
Vivanco, Luis Felipe 1907-1975. . . . . DLB-108
Viviani, Cesare 1947- DLB-128
Vizenor, Gerald 1934- DLB-175
Vizetelly and Company DLB-106
Voaden, Herman 1903- DLB-88
Voigt, Ellen Bryant 1943- DLB-120
Vojnović, Ivo 1857-1929. . . . . DLB-147
Volkoff, Vladimir 1932- DLB-83
Volland, P. F., Company. DLB-46
Vollbehr, Otto H. F. 1872?-
 1945 or 1946 . . . . DLB-187
Volponi, Paolo 1924- DLB-177
von der Grün, Max 1926- DLB-75
Vonnegut, Kurt
 1922- DLB-2, 8, 152; Y-80; DS-3
Voranc, Prežihov 1893-1950. . . . . . . DLB-147
Voß, Johann Heinrich 1751-1826 . . . . DLB-90
Voynich, E. L. 1864-1960. . . . . DLB-197
Vroman, Mary Elizabeth
 circa 1924-1967 . . . . DLB-33

W

Wace, Robert ("Maistre")
 circa 1100-circa 1175 . . . . DLB-146

Cumulative Index

Wackenroder, Wilhelm Heinrich
1773-1798 . . . . DLB-90

Wackernagel, Wilhelm
1806-1869 . . . . DLB-133

Waddington, Miriam 1917- DLB-68

Wade, Henry 1887-1969 . . . . DLB-77

Wagenknecht, Edward 1900- DLB-103

Wagner, Heinrich Leopold
1747-1779 . . . . DLB-94

Wagner, Henry R. 1862-1957 . . . . . DLB-140

Wagner, Richard 1813-1883 . . . . . . DLB-129

Wagoner, David 1926- DLB-5

Wah, Fred 1939- DLB-60

Waiblinger, Wilhelm 1804-1830 . . . . DLB-90

Wain, John
1925-1994 . . . . . . DLB-15, 27, 139, 155

Wainwright, Jeffrey 1944- DLB-40

Waite, Peirce and Company DLB-49

Wakeman, Stephen H. 1859-1924 . . . DLB-187

Wakoski, Diane 1937- DLB-5

Walahfrid Strabo circa 808-849 . . . . DLB-148

Walck, Henry Z. DLB-46

Walcott, Derek 1930- . . . DLB-117; Y-81, Y-92

Waldegrave, Robert
[publishing house] DLB-170

Waldman, Anne 1945- DLB-16

Waldrop, Rosmarie 1935- DLB-169

Walker, Alice 1944- DLB-6, 33, 143

Walker, George F. 1947- DLB-60

Walker, Joseph A. 1935- DLB-38

Walker, Margaret 1915- DLB-76, 152

Walker, Ted 1934- DLB-40

Walker and Company DLB-49

Walker, Evans and Cogswell
Company DLB-49

Walker, John Brisben 1847-1931 . . . . DLB-79

Wallace, Alfred Russel 1823-1913 . . . DLB-190

Wallace, Dewitt 1889-1981 and
Lila Acheson Wallace
1889-1984 . . . . DLB-137

Wallace, Edgar 1875-1932 . . . . DLB-70

Wallace, Lila Acheson (see Wallace, Dewitt,
and Lila Acheson Wallace)

Wallant, Edward Lewis
1926-1962 . . . . DLB-2, 28, 143

Waller, Edmund 1606-1687 . . . . . . DLB-126

Walpole, Horace 1717-1797 . . . . DLB-39, 104

Walpole, Hugh 1884-1941 . . . . DLB-34

Walrond, Eric 1898-1966 . . . . DLB-51

Walser, Martin 1927- DLB-75, 124

Walser, Robert 1878-1956 . . . . DLB-66

Walsh, Ernest 1895-1926 . . . . . . DLB-4, 45

Walsh, Robert 1784-1859 . . . . DLB-59

Waltharius circa 825 . . . . DLB-148

Walters, Henry 1848-1931 . . . . . . DLB-140

Walther von der Vogelweide
circa 1170-circa 1230 . . . . DLB-138

Walton, Izaak 1593-1683 . . . . DLB-151

Wambaugh, Joseph 1937- DLB-6; Y-83

Waniek, Marilyn Nelson 1946- DLB-120

Warburton, William 1698-1779 . . . . DLB-104

Ward, Aileen 1919- DLB-111

Ward, Artemus (see Browne, Charles Farrar)

Ward, Arthur Henry Sarsfield
(see Rohmer, Sax)

Ward, Douglas Turner 1930- DLB-7, 38

Ward, Lynd 1905-1985 . . . . DLB-22

Ward, Lock and Company DLB-106

Ward, Mrs. Humphry 1851-1920 . . . . DLB-18

Ward, Nathaniel circa 1578-1652 . . . . DLB-24

Ward, Theodore 1902-1983 . . . . . . DLB-76

Wardle, Ralph 1909-1988 . . . . DLB-103

Ware, William 1797-1852 . . . . DLB-1

Warne, Frederick, and
Company [U.S.] DLB-49

Warne, Frederick, and
Company [U.K.] DLB-106

Warner, Charles Dudley
1829-1900 . . . . DLB-64

Warner, Marina 1946- DLB-194

Warner, Rex 1905- DLB-15

Warner, Susan Bogert
1819-1885 . . . . DLB-3, 42

Warner, Sylvia Townsend
1893-1978 . . . . DLB-34, 139

Warner, William 1558-1609 . . . . . . DLB-172

Warner Books DLB-46

Warr, Bertram 1917-1943 . . . . DLB-88

Warren, John Byrne Leicester
(see De Tabley, Lord)

Warren, Lella 1899-1982 . . . . Y-83

Warren, Mercy Otis 1728-1814 . . . . . DLB-31

Warren, Robert Penn
1905-1989 . . . . DLB-2, 48, 152; Y-80, Y-89

Warren, Samuel 1807-1877 . . . . . . DLB-190

Die Wartburgkrieg
circa 1230-circa 1280 . . . . DLB-138

Warton, Joseph 1722-1800 . . . . DLB-104, 109

Warton, Thomas 1728-1790 . . . DLB-104, 109

Washington, George 1732-1799 . . . . DLB-31

Wassermann, Jakob 1873-1934 . . . . . DLB-66

Wasson, David Atwood 1823-1887 . . . . DLB-1

Waterhouse, Keith 1929- DLB-13, 15

Waterman, Andrew 1940- DLB-40

Waters, Frank 1902- Y-86

Waters, Michael 1949- DLB-120

Watkins, Tobias 1780-1855 . . . . DLB-73

Watkins, Vernon 1906-1967 . . . . . . DLB-20

Watmough, David 1926- DLB-53

Watson, James Wreford (see Wreford, James)

Watson, John 1850-1907 . . . . DLB-156

Watson, Sheila 1909- DLB-60

Watson, Thomas 1545?-1592 . . . . . . DLB-132

Watson, Wilfred 1911- DLB-60

Watt, W. J., and Company DLB-46

Watten, Barrett 1948- DLB-193

Watterson, Henry 1840-1921 . . . . . . DLB-25

Watts, Alan 1915-1973 . . . . DLB-16

Watts, Franklin [publishing house] . . . DLB-46

Watts, Isaac 1674-1748 . . . . DLB-95

Waud, Alfred Rudolph 1828-1891 . . . DLB-188

Waugh, Alec 1898-1981 . . . . DLB-191

Waugh, Auberon 1939- DLB-14, 194

Waugh, Evelyn 1903-1966 . . DLB-15, 162, 195

Way and Williams DLB-49

Wayman, Tom 1945- DLB-53

Weatherly, Tom 1942- DLB-41

Weaver, Gordon 1937- DLB-130

Weaver, Robert 1921- DLB-88

Webb, Beatrice 1858-1943 and
Webb, Sidney 1859-1947 . . . . . . DLB-190

Webb, Frank J. ?-? DLB-50

Webb, James Watson 1802-1884 . . . . DLB-43

Webb, Mary 1881-1927 . . . . DLB-34

Webb, Phyllis 1927- DLB-53

Webb, Walter Prescott 1888-1963 . . . DLB-17

Webbe, William ?-1591 . . . . DLB-132

Webster, Augusta 1837-1894 . . . . . . DLB-35

Webster, Charles L.,
and Company DLB-49

Webster, John
1579 or 1580-1634? DLB-58

Webster, Noah
1758-1843 . . . . . . DLB-1, 37, 42, 43, 73

Weckherlin, Georg Rodolf
1584-1653 . . . . DLB-164

Wedekind, Frank 1864-1918 . . . . . . DLB-118

Weeks, Edward Augustus, Jr.
1898-1989 . . . . DLB-137

Weeks, Stephen B. 1865-1918 . . . . . DLB-187

Weems, Mason Locke
1759-1825 . . . . DLB-30, 37, 42

Weerth, Georg 1822-1856 . . . . DLB-129

Weidenfeld and Nicolson DLB-112

Weidman, Jerome 1913- DLB-28

Weigl, Bruce 1949- DLB-120

Weinbaum, Stanley Grauman
1902-1935 . . . . DLB-8

Weintraub, Stanley 1929- DLB-111

Weise, Christian 1642-1708 . . . . DLB-168
Weisenborn, Gunther
   1902-1969 . . . . DLB-69, 124
Weiß, Ernst 1882-1940 . . . . DLB-81
Weiss, John 1818-1879 . . . . DLB-1
Weiss, Peter 1916-1982 . . . . DLB-69, 124
Weiss, Theodore 1916- DLB-5
Weisse, Christian Felix 1726-1804 . . . . DLB-97
Weitling, Wilhelm 1808-1871 . . . . . . DLB-129
Welch, James 1940- DLB-175
Welch, Lew 1926-1971? DLB-16
Weldon, Fay 1931- DLB-14, 194
Wellek, René 1903- DLB-63
Wells, Carolyn 1862-1942 . . . . DLB-11
Wells, Charles Jeremiah
   circa 1800-1879 . . . . DLB-32
Wells, Gabriel 1862-1946 . . . . DLB-140
Wells, H. G.
   1866-1946 . . . . DLB-34, 70, 156, 178
Wells, Robert 1947- DLB-40
Wells-Barnett, Ida B. 1862-1931 . . . . DLB-23
Welty, Eudora
   1909- DLB-2, 102, 143; Y-87; DS-12
Wendell, Barrett 1855-1921 . . . . DLB-71
Wentworth, Patricia 1878-1961 . . . . . DLB-77
Werder, Diederich von dem
   1584-1657 . . . . DLB-164
Werfel, Franz 1890-1945 . . . . . . DLB-81, 124
The Werner Company DLB-49
Werner, Zacharias 1768-1823 . . . . . . DLB-94
Wersba, Barbara 1932- DLB-52
Wescott, Glenway 1901- DLB-4, 9, 102
We See the Editor at Work Y-97
Wesker, Arnold 1932- DLB-13
Wesley, Charles 1707-1788 . . . . DLB-95
Wesley, John 1703-1791 . . . . DLB-104
Wesley, Richard 1945- DLB-38
Wessels, A., and Company DLB-46
Wessobrunner Gebet
   circa 787-815 . . . . DLB-148
West, Anthony 1914-1988 . . . . DLB-15
West, Dorothy 1907- DLB-76
West, Jessamyn 1902-1984 . . . . . DLB-6; Y-84
West, Mae 1892-1980 . . . . DLB-44
West, Nathanael 1903-1940 . . . . DLB-4, 9, 28
West, Paul 1930- DLB-14
West, Rebecca 1892-1983 . . . . . DLB-36; Y-83
West, Richard 1941- DLB-185
West and Johnson DLB-49
Western Publishing Company DLB-46
The Westminster Review 1824-1914 . . . . DLB-110
Weston, Elizabeth Jane
   circa 1582-1612 . . . . DLB-172

Wetherald, Agnes Ethelwyn
   1857-1940 . . . . DLB-99
Wetherell, Elizabeth (see Warner, Susan Bogert)
Wetzel, Friedrich Gottlob
   1779-1819 . . . . DLB-90
Weyman, Stanley J. 1855-1928 . . DLB-141, 156
Wezel, Johann Karl 1747-1819 . . . . . DLB-94
Whalen, Philip 1923- DLB-16
Whalley, George 1915-1983 . . . . DLB-88
Wharton, Edith
   1862-1937 . . . DLB-4, 9, 12, 78, 189; DS-13
Wharton, William 1920s?- Y-80
Whately, Mary Louisa
   1824-1889 . . . . DLB-166
Whately, Richard 1787-1863 . . . . . . DLB-190
What's Really Wrong With Bestseller
   Lists Y-84
Wheatley, Dennis Yates
   1897-1977 . . . . DLB-77
Wheatley, Phillis
   circa 1754-1784 . . . . DLB-31, 50
Wheeler, Anna Doyle
   1785-1848? DLB-158
Wheeler, Charles Stearns
   1816-1843 . . . . DLB-1
Wheeler, Monroe 1900-1988 . . . . DLB-4
Wheelock, John Hall 1886-1978 . . . . . DLB-45
Wheelwright, John
   circa 1592-1679 . . . . DLB-24
Wheelwright, J. B. 1897-1940 . . . . . . DLB-45
Whetstone, Colonel Pete (see Noland, C. F. M.)
Whetstone, George 1550-1587 . . . . . DLB-136
Whicher, Stephen E. 1915-1961 . . . . DLB-111
Whipple, Edwin Percy 1819-1886 . . DLB-1, 64
Whitaker, Alexander 1585-1617 . . . . . DLB-24
Whitaker, Daniel K. 1801-1881 . . . . . DLB-73
Whitcher, Frances Miriam
   1814-1852 . . . . DLB-11
White, Andrew 1579-1656 . . . . DLB-24
White, Andrew Dickson
   1832-1918 . . . . DLB-47
White, E. B. 1899-1985 . . . . . . DLB-11, 22
White, Edgar B. 1947- DLB-38
White, Ethel Lina 1887-1944 . . . . . . DLB-77
White, Henry Kirke 1785-1806 . . . . . DLB-96
White, Horace 1834-1916 . . . . DLB-23
White, Phyllis Dorothy James
   (see James, P. D.)
White, Richard Grant 1821-1885 . . . . DLB-64
White, T. H. 1906-1964 . . . . DLB-160
White, Walter 1893-1955 . . . . DLB-51
White, William, and Company DLB-49
White, William Allen 1868-1944 . . . DLB-9, 25
White, William Anthony Parker
   (see Boucher, Anthony)

White, William Hale (see Rutherford, Mark)
Whitechurch, Victor L. 1868-1933 . . . . DLB-70
Whitehead, Alfred North
   1861-1947 . . . . DLB-100
Whitehead, James 1936- Y-81
Whitehead, William 1715-1785 . . . DLB-84, 109
Whitfield, James Monroe 1822-1871 . . . DLB-50
Whitgift, John circa 1533-1604 . . . . . DLB-132
Whiting, John 1917-1963 . . . . DLB-13
Whiting, Samuel 1597-1679 . . . . DLB-24
Whitlock, Brand 1869-1934 . . . . DLB-12
Whitman, Albert, and Company DLB-46
Whitman, Albery Allson
   1851-1901 . . . . DLB-50
Whitman, Alden 1913-1990 . . . . Y-91
Whitman, Sarah Helen (Power)
   1803-1878 . . . . DLB-1
Whitman, Walt 1819-1892 . . . . . . DLB-3, 64
Whitman Publishing Company DLB-46
Whitney, Geoffrey
   1548 or 1552?-1601 . . . . DLB-136
Whitney, Isabella
   flourished 1566-1573 . . . . DLB-136
Whitney, John Hay 1904-1982 . . . . . DLB-127
Whittemore, Reed 1919- DLB-5
Whittier, John Greenleaf 1807-1892 . . . . DLB-1
Whittlesey House DLB-46
Who Runs American Literature? Y-94
Whose *Ulysses*? The Function of
   Editing Y-97
Wideman, John Edgar 1941- DLB-33, 143
Widener, Harry Elkins 1885-1912 . . . . DLB-140
Wiebe, Rudy 1934- DLB-60
Wiechert, Ernst 1887-1950 . . . . DLB-56
Wied, Martina 1882-1957 . . . . DLB-85
Wiehe, Evelyn May Clowes (see Mordaunt,
   Elinor)
Wieland, Christoph Martin
   1733-1813 . . . . DLB-97
Wienbarg, Ludolf 1802-1872 . . . . . . DLB-133
Wieners, John 1934- DLB-16
Wier, Ester 1910- DLB-52
Wiesel, Elie 1928- DLB-83; Y-86, Y-87
Wiggin, Kate Douglas 1856-1923 . . . . DLB-42
Wigglesworth, Michael 1631-1705 . . . . DLB-24
Wilberforce, William 1759-1833 . . . . . DLB-158
Wilbrandt, Adolf 1837-1911 . . . . . . DLB-129
Wilbur, Richard 1921- DLB-5, 169
Wild, Peter 1940- DLB-5
Wilde, Oscar 1854-1900
   . . . . . DLB-10, 19, 34, 57, 141, 156, 190
Wilde, Richard Henry
   1789-1847 . . . . DLB-3, 59

Wilde, W. A., Company	DLB-49
Wilder, Billy 1906-	DLB-26
Wilder, Laura Ingalls 1867-1957	DLB-22
Wilder, Thornton 1897-1975	DLB-4, 7, 9
Wildgans, Anton 1881-1932	DLB-118
Wiley, Bell Irvin 1906-1980	DLB-17
Wiley, John, and Sons	DLB-49
Wilhelm, Kate 1928-	DLB-8
Wilkes, Charles 1798-1877	DLB-183
Wilkes, George 1817-1885	DLB-79
Wilkinson, Anne 1910-1961	DLB-88
Wilkinson, Sylvia 1940-	Y-86
Wilkinson, William Cleaver 1833-1920	DLB-71
Willard, Barbara 1909-1994	DLB-161
Willard, L. [publishing house]	DLB-49
Willard, Nancy 1936-	DLB-5, 52
Willard, Samuel 1640-1707	DLB-24
William of Auvergne 1190-1249	DLB-115
William of Conches circa 1090-circa 1154	DLB-115
William of Ockham circa 1285-1347	DLB-115
William of Sherwood 1200/1205 - 1266/1271	DLB-115
The William Chavrat American Fiction Collection at the Ohio State University Libraries	Y-92
William Faulkner Centenary	Y-97
Williams, A., and Company	DLB-49
Williams, Ben Ames 1889-1953	DLB-102
Williams, C. K. 1936-	DLB-5
Williams, Chancellor 1905-	DLB-76
Williams, Charles 1886-1945	DLB-100, 153
Williams, Denis 1923-	DLB-117
Williams, Emlyn 1905-	DLB-10, 77
Williams, Garth 1912-	DLB-22
Williams, George Washington 1849-1891	DLB-47
Williams, Heathcote 1941-	DLB-13
Williams, Helen Maria 1761-1827	DLB-158
Williams, Hugo 1942-	DLB-40
Williams, Isaac 1802-1865	DLB-32
Williams, Joan 1928-	DLB-6
Williams, John A. 1925-	DLB-2, 33
Williams, John E. 1922-1994	DLB-6
Williams, Jonathan 1929-	DLB-5
Williams, Miller 1930-	DLB-105
Williams, Raymond 1921-	DLB-14
Williams, Roger circa 1603-1683	DLB-24
Williams, Rowland 1817-1870	DLB-184
Williams, Samm-Art 1946-	DLB-38
Williams, Sherley Anne 1944-	DLB-41
Williams, T. Harry 1909-1979	DLB-17
Williams, Tennessee 1911-1983	DLB-7; Y-83; DS-4
Williams, Ursula Moray 1911-	DLB-160
Williams, Valentine 1883-1946	DLB-77
Williams, William Appleman 1921-	DLB-17
Williams, William Carlos 1883-1963	DLB-4, 16, 54, 86
Williams, Wirt 1921-	DLB-6
Williams Brothers	DLB-49
Williamson, Henry 1895-1977	DLB-191
Williamson, Jack 1908-	DLB-8
Willingham, Calder Baynard, Jr. 1922-	DLB-2, 44
Williram of Ebersberg circa 1020-1085	DLB-148
Willis, Nathaniel Parker 1806-1867	DLB-3, 59, 73, 74, 183; DS-13
Willkomm, Ernst 1810-1886	DLB-133
Wilmer, Clive 1945-	DLB-40
Wilson, A. N. 1950-	DLB-14, 155, 194
Wilson, Angus 1913-1991	DLB-15, 139, 155
Wilson, Arthur 1595-1652	DLB-58
Wilson, Augusta Jane Evans 1835-1909	DLB-42
Wilson, Colin 1931-	DLB-14, 194
Wilson, Edmund 1895-1972	DLB-63
Wilson, Ethel 1888-1980	DLB-68
Wilson, Harriet E. Adams 1828?-1863?	DLB-50
Wilson, Harry Leon 1867-1939	DLB-9
Wilson, John 1588-1667	DLB-24
Wilson, John 1785-1854	DLB-110
Wilson, Lanford 1937-	DLB-7
Wilson, Margaret 1882-1973	DLB-9
Wilson, Michael 1914-1978	DLB-44
Wilson, Mona 1872-1954	DLB-149
Wilson, Romer 1891-1930	DLB-191
Wilson, Thomas 1523 or 1524-1581	DLB-132
Wilson, Woodrow 1856-1924	DLB-47
Wilson, Effingham [publishing house]	DLB-154
Wimsatt, William K., Jr. 1907-1975	DLB-63
Winchell, Walter 1897-1972	DLB-29
Winchester, J. [publishing house]	DLB-49
Winckelmann, Johann Joachim 1717-1768	DLB-97
Winckler, Paul 1630-1686	DLB-164
Wind, Herbert Warren 1916-	DLB-171
Windet, John [publishing house]	DLB-170
Windham, Donald 1920-	DLB-6
Wing, Donald Goddard 1904-1972	DLB-187
Wing, John M. 1844-1917	DLB-187
Wingate, Allan [publishing house]	DLB-112
Winnemucca, Sarah 1844-1921	DLB-175
Winnifrith, Tom 1938-	DLB-155
Winsloe, Christa 1888-1944	DLB-124
Winsor, Justin 1831-1897	DLB-47
John C. Winston Company	DLB-49
Winters, Yvor 1900-1968	DLB-48
Winthrop, John 1588-1649	DLB-24, 30
Winthrop, John, Jr. 1606-1676	DLB-24
Wirt, William 1772-1834	DLB-37
Wise, John 1652-1725	DLB-24
Wise, Thomas James 1859-1937	DLB-184
Wiseman, Adele 1928-	DLB-88
Wishart and Company	DLB-112
Wisner, George 1812-1849	DLB-43
Wister, Owen 1860-1938	DLB-9, 78, 186
Wither, George 1588-1667	DLB-121
Witherspoon, John 1723-1794	DLB-31
Withrow, William Henry 1839-1908	DLB-99
Wittig, Monique 1935-	DLB-83
Wodehouse, P. G. 1881-1975	DLB-34, 162
Wohmann, Gabriele 1932-	DLB-75
Woiwode, Larry 1941-	DLB-6
Wolcot, John 1738-1819	DLB-109
Wolcott, Roger 1679-1767	DLB-24
Wolf, Christa 1929-	DLB-75
Wolf, Friedrich 1888-1953	DLB-124
Wolfe, Gene 1931-	DLB-8
Wolfe, John [publishing house]	DLB-170
Wolfe, Reyner (Reginald) [publishing house]	DLB-170
Wolfe, Thomas 1900-1938	DLB-9, 102; Y-85; DS-2, DS-16
Wolfe, Tom 1931-	DLB-152, 185
Wolff, Helen 1906-1994	Y-94
Wolff, Tobias 1945-	DLB-130
Wolfram von Eschenbach circa 1170-after 1220	DLB-138
Wolfram von Eschenbach's *Parzival*: Prologue and Book 3	DLB-138
Wollstonecraft, Mary 1759-1797	DLB-39, 104, 158
Wondratschek, Wolf 1943-	DLB-75
Wood, Benjamin 1820-1900	DLB-23
Wood, Charles 1932-	DLB-13
Wood, Mrs. Henry 1814-1887	DLB-18

Wood, Joanna E. 1867-1927 . . . . DLB-92
Wood, Samuel [publishing house] DLB-49
Wood, William ?-? DLB-24
Woodberry, George Edward
   1855-1930 . . . . DLB-71, 103
Woodbridge, Benjamin 1622-1684 . . . . DLB-24
Woodcock, George 1912- DLB-88
Woodhull, Victoria C. 1838-1927 . . . . DLB-79
Woodmason, Charles circa 1720-? DLB-31
Woodress, Jr., James Leslie 1916- . . . DLB-111
Woodson, Carter G. 1875-1950 . . . . . DLB-17
Woodward, C. Vann 1908- DLB-17
Woodward, Stanley 1895-1965 . . . . . DLB-171
Wooler, Thomas
   1785 or 1786-1853 . . . . DLB-158
Woolf, David (see Maddow, Ben)
Woolf, Leonard 1880-1969 . . . . DLB-100; DS-10
Woolf, Virginia
   1882-1941 . . . . . DLB-36, 100, 162; DS-10
Woolf, Virginia, "The New Biography," *New York Herald Tribune*, 30 October 1927
   . . . . DLB-149
Woollcott, Alexander 1887-1943 . . . . . DLB-29
Woolman, John 1720-1772 . . . . DLB-31
Woolner, Thomas 1825-1892 . . . . DLB-35
Woolsey, Sarah Chauncy 1835-1905 . . . DLB-42
Woolson, Constance Fenimore
   1840-1894 . . . . DLB-12, 74, 189
Worcester, Joseph Emerson
   1784-1865 . . . . DLB-1
Worde, Wynkyn de
   [publishing house] DLB-170
Wordsworth, Christopher 1807-1885 . . DLB-166
Wordsworth, Dorothy 1771-1855 . . . . DLB-107
Wordsworth, Elizabeth 1840-1932 . . . . DLB-98
Wordsworth, William 1770-1850 . . DLB-93, 107
Workman, Fanny Bullock 1859-1925 . . DLB-189
The Works of the Rev. John Witherspoon
   (1800-1801) [excerpts] DLB-31
A World Chronology of Important Science
   Fiction Works (1818-1979) DLB-8
World Publishing Company DLB-46
World War II Writers Symposium at the
   University of South Carolina,
   12–14 April 1995 . . . . Y-95
Worthington, R., and Company DLB-49
Wotton, Sir Henry 1568-1639 . . . . . DLB-121
Wouk, Herman 1915- Y-82
Wreford, James 1915- DLB-88
Wren, Percival Christopher 1885-1941 . . DLB-153
Wrenn, John Henry 1841-1911 . . . . . DLB-140
Wright, C. D. 1949- DLB-120
Wright, Charles 1935- DLB-165; Y-82
Wright, Charles Stevenson 1932- DLB-33

Wright, Frances 1795-1852 . . . . DLB-73
Wright, Harold Bell 1872-1944 . . . . . DLB-9
Wright, James 1927-1980 . . . . DLB-5, 169
Wright, Jay 1935- DLB-41
Wright, Louis B. 1899-1984 . . . . DLB-17
Wright, Richard 1908-1960 . . DLB-76, 102; DS-2
Wright, Richard B. 1937- DLB-53
Wright, Sarah Elizabeth 1928- DLB-33
Wright, Willard Huntington ("S. S. Van Dine")
   1888-1939 . . . . DS-16
Writers and Politics: 1871-1918,
   by Ronald Gray DLB-66
Writers and their Copyright Holders:
   the WATCH Project Y-94
Writers' Forum Y-85
Writing for the Theatre, by
   Harold Pinter DLB-13
Wroth, Lady Mary 1587-1653 . . . . . DLB-121
Wroth, Lawrence C. 1884-1970 . . . . . DLB-187
Wurlitzer, Rudolph 1937- DLB-173
Wyatt, Sir Thomas
   circa 1503-1542 . . . . DLB-132
Wycherley, William 1641-1715 . . . . . DLB-80
Wyclif, John
   circa 1335-31 December 1384 . . . DLB-146
Wyeth, N. C.
   1882-1945 . . . . DLB-188; DS-16
Wylie, Elinor 1885-1928 . . . . DLB-9, 45
Wylie, Philip 1902-1971 . . . . DLB-9
Wyllie, John Cook
   1908-1968 . . . . DLB-140
Wynne-Tyson, Esmé 1898-1972 . . . . DLB-191

X

Xenophon circa 430 B.C.-circa 356 B.C.
   . . . . DLB-176

Y

Yasuoka, Shōtarō 1920- DLB-182
Yates, Dornford 1885-1960 . . . . DLB-77, 153
Yates, J. Michael 1938- DLB-60
Yates, Richard 1926-1992 . . DLB-2; Y-81, Y-92
Yavorov, Peyo 1878-1914 . . . . DLB-147
Yearsley, Ann 1753-1806 . . . . DLB-109
Yeats, William Butler
   1865-1939 . . . . . . DLB-10, 19, 98, 156
Yep, Laurence 1948- DLB-52
Yerby, Frank 1916-1991 . . . . DLB-76
Yezierska, Anzia 1885-1970 . . . . DLB-28
Yolen, Jane 1939- DLB-52

Yonge, Charlotte Mary
   1823-1901 . . . . DLB-18, 163
The York Cycle
   circa 1376-circa 1569 . . . . DLB-146
A Yorkshire Tragedy DLB-58
Yoseloff, Thomas
   [publishing house] DLB-46
Young, Al 1939- DLB-33
Young, Arthur 1741-1820 . . . . DLB-158
Young, Dick
   1917 or 1918 - 1987 . . . . DLB-171
Young, Edward 1683-1765 . . . . DLB-95
Young, Francis Brett 1884-1954 . . . . . DLB-191
Young, Stark 1881-1963 . . . DLB-9, 102; DS-16
Young, Waldeman 1880-1938 . . . . . . DLB-26
Young, William [publishing house] . . . DLB-49
Young Bear, Ray A. 1950- DLB-175
Yourcenar, Marguerite
   1903-1987 . . . . DLB-72; Y-88
"You've Never Had It So Good," Gusted by
   "Winds of Change": British Fiction in the
   1950s, 1960s, and After DLB-14
Yovkov, Yordan 1880-1937 . . . . DLB-147

Z

Zachariä, Friedrich Wilhelm
   1726-1777 . . . . DLB-97
Zajc, Dane 1929- DLB-181
Zamora, Bernice 1938- DLB-82
Zand, Herbert 1923-1970 . . . . DLB-85
Zangwill, Israel 1864-1926 . . . DLB-10, 135, 197
Zanzotto, Andrea 1921- DLB-128
Zapata Olivella, Manuel 1920- DLB-113
Zebra Books DLB-46
Zebrowski, George 1945- DLB-8
Zech, Paul 1881-1946 . . . . DLB-56
Zepheria DLB-172
Zeidner, Lisa 1955- DLB-120
Zelazny, Roger 1937-1995 . . . . DLB-8
Zenger, John Peter 1697-1746 . . . . DLB-24, 43
Zesen, Philipp von 1619-1689 . . . . . . DLB-164
Zieber, G. B., and Company DLB-49
Zieroth, Dale 1946- DLB-60
Zigler und Kliphausen, Heinrich Anshelm von
   1663-1697 . . . . DLB-168
Zimmer, Paul 1934- DLB-5
Zingref, Julius Wilhelm
   1591-1635 . . . . DLB-164
Zindel, Paul 1936- DLB-7, 52
Zinnes, Harriet 1919- DLB-193
Zinzendorf, Nikolaus Ludwig von
   1700-1760 . . . . DLB-168

Cumulative Index

Zitkala-Ša 1876-1938 . . . . DLB-175
Zola, Emile 1840-1902 . . . . DLB-123
Zolla, Elémire 1926- DLB-196
Zolotow, Charlotte 1915- DLB-52
Zschokke, Heinrich 1771-1848 . . . . . . DLB-94

Zubly, John Joachim 1724-1781 . . . . . DLB-31
Zu-Bolton II, Ahmos 1936- DLB-41
Zuckmayer, Carl 1896-1977 . . . . DLB-56, 124
Zukofsky, Louis 1904-1978 . . . . . DLB-5, 165
Zupan, Vitomil 1914-1987 . . . . DLB-181

Župančič, Oton 1878-1949 . . . . DLB-147
zur Mühlen, Hermynia 1883-1951 . . . . DLB-56
Zweig, Arnold 1887-1968 . . . . DLB-66
Zweig, Stefan 1881-1942 . . . . . . DLB-81, 118

ISBN 0-7876-1852-7

90000

PR
863
.L382

1999